THE INTERNATIONAL DIRECTORY OF COMPUTER AND INFORMATION SYSTEM SERVICES 1974

THE INTERNATIONAL DIRECTORY OF COMPUTER AND INFORMATION SYSTEM SERVICES 1974

Published for
The Intergovernmental Bureau for Informatics
Rome, Italy
by
EUROPA PUBLICATIONS LIMITED
18 BEDFORD SQUARE, LONDON, WC1B 3JN

First Edition 1969
Second Edition 1971
Third Edition 1974

© EUROPA PUBLICATIONS LIMITED 1974
ISBN 0 900 36267 7
Library of Congress Catalog Card Number 70–5680

AUSTRALIA AND NEW ZEALAND
James Bennett (Collaroy) Pty. Ltd., Collaroy, N.S.W., Australia
INDIA
UBS Publishers' Distributors Pvt. Ltd., P.O.B. 1882, 5 Ansari Road, Daryaganj, Delhi 6

PRINTED BY Unwin Brothers Limited
THE GRESHAM PRESS OLD WOKING SURREY ENGLAND

Produced by 'Uneoprint'
A member of the Staples Printing Group

(GO 401)

CONTENTS

	Page		Page
Foreword	vi	Libya	192
Explanatory Notes	vii	Malawi	192
		Malaysia	192
Algeria	1	Mauritius	193
Argentina	1	Mexico	194
Australia	6	Monaco	197
Austria	21	Morocco	197
Bahama Islands	24	Netherlands	198
Bangladesh	24	Netherlands Antilles	217
Belgium	24	New Zealand	217
Brazil	32	Nicaragua	221
Bulgaria	46	Nigeria	221
Cameroon	46	Norway	223
Canada	46	Pakistan	232
Chile	64	Panama	233
China, Republic of (Taiwan)	67	Paraguay	234
Colombia	68	Peru	234
Costa Rica	73	Philippines	235
Cyprus	74	Poland	236
Czechoslovakia	74	Portugal	240
Denmark	75	Puerto Rico	241
Ecuador	85	Rhodesia	242
Egypt	85	Romania	243
El Salvador	85	St. Vincent	244
Ethiopia	86	Singapore	244
Finland	86	South Africa	245
France	91	Spain	252
Gabon	116	Sri Lanka	258
German Democratic Republic	116	Sudan	258
Germany, Federal Republic of	117	Sweden	259
Ghana	142	Switzerland	281
Greece	143	Syria	294
Guatemala	144	Taiwan (*see* China)	
Honduras	145	Tanzania	295
Hong Kong	145	Thailand	295
Hungary	146	Trinidad and Tobago	296
Iceland	149	Tunisia	297
India	150	Turkey	297
Indonesia	159	Uganda	298
Iran	160	Union of Soviet Socialist Republics	299
Iraq	161	United Kingdom and Isle of Man	299
Ireland	162	United States of America	381
Israel	164	Uruguay	568
Italy	172	Venezuela	568
Ivory Coast	182	Viet-Nam, Republic of	569
Jamaica	182	Yugoslavia	569
Japan	183	Zaire	576
Jordan	189	Zambia	577
Kenya	189		
Korea, Republic of	190	Index of Institutions	579
Lebanon	190	Index of Installations	604

FOREWORD

This Directory, now in its third edition, is a result of the efforts made by the IBI-ICC towards achieving one of its main objectives: the dissemination of information relating to informatics.

The purpose of this book is to help users of informatics to locate computer and information services which are available in both the public and private sectors. This latest edition is a compilation of information contributed by nearly 3,000 institutions and firms from almost 100 countries. These contributors have been grouped in seven categories within each country (see Explanatory Notes, opposite). The Directory thus represents a unique reference book on the services maintained by governmental, educational and commercial organizations.

IBI-ICC's involvement in this activity began in 1969 with the publication of the first edition of the Directory. Since the acceptance of the Directory and its concept has exceeded anticipation, it is the hope and intention of the IBI-ICC to make a continuing effort to improve the work by extending the contents of future editions to new applications in areas of government, research, education and business, to the major benefit of the informatics community to which the book is dedicated.

January 1974

Fermin A. Bernasconi, Director
Intergovernmental Bureau for
Informatics–International
Computation Centre

EXPLANATORY NOTES

The information in this Directory is based on replies received in the form of a questionnaire and on information acquired by the Intergovernmental Bureau for Informatics. Entries which it has not been possible to verify have been marked with an asterisk.

We have endeavoured to cover as many countries as possible where data processing and consulting services are offered but it is inevitable that a number of institutions and firms may have been overlooked. If your organization is not included, we should appreciate your sending us your name and address so that we can send you a questionnaire at the time of publication of a fourth edition. Moreover, if any entries show incorrect addresses or if a listed firm is no longer in business, we should also appreciate being informed.

Entries have been placed in the following categories:

National Centres

Educational and Training Institutions

Universities and Colleges

Government Establishments or Agencies

Research Institutions

Consultants

Service Bureaux

In cases where companies act in a double capacity, it was necessary to select one category only. The Service Bureaux include commercial companies which also offer general computer services.

The information given under the different headings has been arranged as concisely as possible. The heading "Computer Installation" refers only to the computer (or computers) installed on the premises. In general, where no installation is shown it is to be assumed (except for partial entries) that these firms make use of external installations. The term *internal storage* refers to the *main* memory of the computer, and the capacity is given in bits of characters, where indicated, or otherwise in words or bytes.

Owing to the large number of entries in the Universities, Consultants and Service Bureaux sections of the United States, it was decided to divide these also by State. This criterion may be followed in future editions for other countries, where appropriate.

All correspondence on editorial matters should be addressed to: The Editor, International Directory of Computer and Information System Services, Intergovernmental Bureau for Informatics, 23 Viale Civiltà del Lavoro, 00144 Rome–EUR, Italy.

ALGERIA

GOVERNMENT ESTABLISHMENT

SONATRACH
Centre de Calcul
80 Avenue Ghermoul, Algiers
Telephone: 662707, extension 400

Officer
Mohamed Benyoucef, *Chef du Centre de Calcul*

Computer Installation
XDS Sigma 5 (2)–operating system: PASS; internal storage: 524,288 bits and 262,144 bits; magnetic tapes: 2; magnetic discs: 2 RAD 7204; 1 line printer.

XDS Sigma 7–operating system: BTM; internal storage: 3,148,728 bits; magnetic tapes: 6 9-track, 1 7-track; magnetic discs: 1 RAD 7232, 2 RAD 7204, 7 DP 7242; 1 line printer.

Coding Languages
COBOL, FORTRAN, SYMBOL, METASYMBOL, BASIC.

Contemplated Equipment
Remote processing.

Services Available
Advice, programming, education and training, operators, software packages, documentation, preparation of data, systems analysis. Operate on an open shop and time-sharing basis.

Fields of Application
Scientific, statistical, commercial, accounting, management, systems analysis, operational research.
Specialized areas: Sales analysis, linear programming, investment analysis, payroll, structural engineering, medical research.

Training
Courses in basic EDP, programming, analysis, exploitation, operating systems, operations (internal only), software (internal only).

RESEARCH INSTITUTION

INSTITUT D'ETUDES NUCLEAIRES*
Boulevard Frantz Fanon, B.P. 1147, Alger
Téléphone: 645009

Dirigeant
Daho Allab, *Directeur*

Equipment
IBM 1620–mémoire interne: 40K bits; disques magnétiques: 2 1311; 1 imprimante.

Langages de Programmation
FORTRAN, SPS.

Services Fournis
Enseignement et formation. Fonctionnement à porte ouverte.

Domaines d'Application
Scientifique, statistique.

Formation
Certificat d'Etudes Supérieures d'Informatique à la Faculté des Sciences d'Alger.
Stage de Programmation FORTRAN (15 jours–un ou deux par an).

SERVICE BUREAU

IBM WORLD TRADE CORPORATION*
Datacenter
Algiers

Computer Installation
IBM 360/40.

Services Available
Advice, operators, preparation of data, programming.

Fields of Application
Scientific, engineering, commercial.

ARGENTINA

EDUCATIONAL AND TRAINING INSTITUTION

CENTRO SUPERIOR DE PROCESAMIENTO DE LA INFORMACIÓN (CESPI)*
Calle 50 y 115, La Plata
Telephone: 43179

Officer
Dr. J. Gordon, *Director*

Computer Installation
IBM 360/50–operating systems: MFT II, DOS; internal storage: 257,536 bytes; magnetic tapes: 4 2415; magnetic discs: 5 2311; 1 line printer. *Remote processing features*: 6 1050 (APL, Rax, Coursewriter).
IBM 1620–internal storage: 60K positions; magnetic discs: 2 1311; 1 line printer.

Services Available
Consultation, programming, education and training, preparation of data, systems analysis. Operate on a closed shop basis. Available only to teachers, students and research organizations.

Fields of Application
Scientific, statistical, management, systems analysis, accounting.

Training
Three-year course in scientific calculation. Short courses in coding languages (APL, PL/1, FORTRAN IV) and systems operation.

UNIVERSITIES

UNIVERSIDAD CATÓLICA ARGENTINA "SANTA MARÍA DE LOS BUENOS AIRES"*
Faculty of Physical Sciences, Mathematics and Engineering
Carlos Pellegrini 1535, Buenos Aires
Telephone: 44–2479

Officers
Dr. Agustín Durañona y Vedia, *Dean of Faculty*
Ing. Jorge Cardenes, *Assistant*

Computer Installation
Internal storage: 40K bits; 1 line printer.

Services Available
Programming, education and training, operators, systems analysis.
Operate on a self-service basis.

Fields of Application
Scientific, statistical, systems analysis, operational research, educational.

Training
Engineering degree course in operational research.

UNIVERSIDAD CATÓLICA DE CÓRDOBA*
Obispo Trejo 323, Córdoba
Telephone: 23428

Officers
R. Barale, *Director*
Sr. Scandogliero, *Head of Equipment*

Computer Installation
BULL GENERAL ELECTRIC GE 115–operating system: TOS; internal storage: 8K bits; magnetic tapes: 4 MTH 163; 1 line printer.

Coding Languages
APS, TAB.

Services Available
Consultation, programming, education and training, operators, software packages, documentation, preparation of data, systems analysis. Operate on a self-service, open shop and block time basis.

Fields of Application
Education, scientific, commercial, management, systems analysis, accounting, statistical.
Specialized areas: Commercial and technical education.

Training
Courses in systems analysis and programming.

UNIVERSIDAD DE BUENOS AIRES
Centro de Cómputos
Facultad de Medicina, José Evaristo Uriburu 860, Buenos Aires

Officers
Dr. Tomás Angelillo Mackinlay, *Executive Director*
Jorge Osvaldo Victorero, *Administrative Secretary*
Carlos Oscar Poljak, *Technical Secretary*

Computer Installation
IBM 360/50–operating system: SOS; internal storage: 2,408K bits; magnetic tapes: 2; magnetic discs 9 2314; 2 line printers. *Remote processing features*: 10 IBM 1050 terminals.

Coding Languages
COBOL, FORTRAN, Assembler, PL/1.

Services Available
Advice, programming, education and training, operators, software packages, systems analysis. Operate on a block time basis. Priority is given to customers in the health field.

Fields of Application
Scientific, statistical, commercial, accounting, systems analysis, operational research.
Specialized areas: Medical research, health statistics.

UNIVERSIDAD DE BUENOS AIRES*
Instituto de Cálculo
Perú 222, Buenos Aires
Telephone: 34-8044

Dirigeants
Dr. Manuel Sadosky, Ing. Pedro Elias Zadunaisky, Dra. Rebeca Ch. de Guber, Ing. Jonas Paiuk, Prof. Wilfred Durán.

Equipement
ICL Mercury–1 imprimante.

Langages de Programmation
PIG 2, Autocode, COMIC.

Equipement Projeté
BULL GENERAL ELECTRIC GE 635 ou IBM 360/50 ou équivalent.

Services Fournis
L'Institut est un Service National de Calcul, et comme tel assiste les entreprises gouvernementales privées du pays et de l'étranger dans les problèmes de Calcul. Il loue temps de machine aux intéressés qui préparent leurs programmes et son personnel spécialisé étudie les divers aspects du calcul numérique et conseille sur les possibilités de résolution dans la machine.

Domaines d'Application
Applications a la statistique, à l'économie et aux calculs de la physique théorique.
Domaines spécialisés: Modèles mathématiques d'économie et hydraulique.

Formation
Cours de programmation pour Mercury et généraux.

UNIVERSIDAD DE LA PATAGONIA "SAN JUAN BOSCO"*
Barrio General Mosconi, Comodoro Rivadavia, Provincia del Chubut

Officer
M. Marolla, *Director of the Centre*

Computer Installation
IBM 1130–internal storage: 8,192 bits; magnetic discs: 1 2315; 1 line printer.

Coding Languages
FORTRAN IV, Assembler, RPG.

Services Available
Programming, education and training. Available only to the University.

Fields of Application
Scientific, commercial, educational.

UNIVERSIDAD DEL SALVADOR*
Tucumán 1859, Buenos Aires
Telephone: 46-1685

Officers
E. O. Tiscornia, *Director*
J. Fratini, *Head of Exploitation*

Argentina — Universities

Computer Installation
BULL GENERAL ELECTRIC GE 425 operating systems: MTPS/DPS/DAPS; internal storage: 32K words; magnetic tapes: 4 MTH 493, 1 MTH 492; magnetic discs: 3 DSU 160; 1 line printer.

Coding Languages
COBOL, FORTRAN, BAL, MAL, IDS.

Services Available
Consultation, programming, education and training, operators, software packages, documentation, preparation of data, systems analysis. Operate on a self-service and block time basis.

Fields of Application
Education, scientific investigation, commercial, management, systems analysis, accounting, statistical.
Specialized areas: Commercial and technical education.

Training
Courses in systems analysis and programming.

UNIVERSIDAD NACIONAL DE CÓRDOBA
Centro de Cálculo
Dirección de Planeamiento, Obispo Trejo 242, Córdoba
Telephone: 43494

Officer
Walter Monsberger, *Organizer*

Coding Languages
FORTRAN, COBOL.

Contemplated Equipment
Batch-processing equipment for the academic and administrative needs of the university, as a transition system towards a time-sharing system planned to be installed in 1976.

Fields of Application
Scientific, statistical, commercial, accounting, systems analysis, operational research.

UNIVERSIDAD NACIONAL DE CÓRDOBA
Centro de Computación y Procesamiento de Datos
Facultad de Ciencias Económicas, Ciudad Universitaria, Córdoba
Telephone: 24200

Computer Installation
IBM 1130—internal storage: 8K bits; magnetic discs: 1.

Coding Languages
FORTRAN IV, Assembler.

Services Available
Programming, education and training, systems analysis. Operate on a self-service basis.

Fields of Application
Scientific, statistical, operational research.
Specialized areas: Linear programming, investment.

Training
Courses in information systems and numerical calculation, and in FORTRAN IV programming.

UNIVERSIDAD NACIONAL DE TUCUMÁN*
Centro de Cómputos
Calle Ayacucho 482, San Miguel de Tucumán
Telephone: 22725

Dirigeant
Dr. R. E. Luccioni

Equipement
IBM 1620—mémoire interne: 60K bits; disques magnétiques: 1 1311.

Langages de Programmation
FORTRAN, SPS.

Equipement Projeté
Ordinateur de troisième génération.

Services Fournis
Programmation, enseignement et formation. Fonctionnement à porte fermée.

Domaine d'Application
Scientifique.

Formation
Cours en programmation.

UNIVERSIDAD NACIONAL DEL LITORAL*
Boulevard Pellegrini 2750, Santa Fé
Telephone: 25-995

Officer
A. A. Allassia, *Head of the Data Processing Service*

Computer Installation
NCR 400—operating system: magnetic cards; Internal storage: 80K words.

IBM 1407—operating system: punched cards; 1 line printer.

Coding Language
RPG.

Service Available
Documentation. Operate on a self-service basis.

Field of Application
Accounting.

UNIVERSIDAD TECNOLÓGICA NACIONAL
Centro de Cálculo
Medrano 971, Buenos Aires

Officers
Eitel H. Lauria, *Director*
Luis María Frediani, *Head of Computation Department*
Horacio V. Biscardi, *Head of Development Department*

Computer Installation
IBM 360/30—operating system: DOS; internal storage: 64K bytes; magnetic tapes: 4 2401, 2402, 2403; magnetic discs: 3 2311; 1 line printer. *Remote processing features*: 4 IBM 1050 terminals.

Coding Languages
Assembler, FORTRAN IV, COBOL, PL/1, RPG, oriented languages (STRESS, COGOL, etc.).

Services Available
Programming, education and training, operators, software packages, systems analysis. Operate on an off-line remote access, closed shop and block time basis. Priority is given to educational and research services and to state-owned enterprises.

Argentina — Universities

Fields of Application
Scientific, statistical, management, systems analysis.
Specialized areas: Analysis, structural engineering, applied mechanics.

Training
First degree course in systems analysis and post-graduate course in systems.

GOVERNMENT ESTABLISHMENT

SECRETARÍA DEL CONSEJO PROVINCIAL DE DESARROLLO*
San Juan 718, Corrientes
Telephone: 4858

Officers
C. E. Piattini, *Director of the Computer Centre*
J. J. de la Sota, *Manager of the Service Bureau*
L. E. Verga, *Foreign Relations*

Computer Installation
IBM 360/20—operating system: DPS; magnetic tapes: 4 2415; magnetic discs: 1 2311; 1 line printer.

Coding Languages
RPG, Assembler.

Contemplated Equipment
IBM 360/25—operating system; DOS; internal storage: 32K bits; magnetic tapes: 4 2415; magnetic discs: 3 2311; 2 line printers. *On-line satellite computer*: IBM 1130.

Services Available
Consultation, programming, education and training, operators, documentation, preparation of data, systems analysis. Operate on a self-service, block time, closed and open shop basis. Available to commercial and government organizations.

Fields of Application
Scientific, commercial, statistical, management, systems analysis, operational research, planning, tax processing, town and country planning, development planning.
Specialized areas: Linear programming, analysis of government administrative systems, taxation processes control, informatics for development.

Training
Courses in DOS, TOS, DPS, IOCS, RPG, Assembler, BASIC.

RESEARCH INSTITUTION

CENTRO DE INVESTIGACIÓN DE TÉCNICAS MATEMÁTICAS APLICADAS A LA DIRECCIÓN DE EMPRESAS (CITMADE)
Libertad 1235, Buenos Aires
Telephone: 44-0011, 42-6132

Officers
Ing. Julio C. Young Oliver, *Executive Assistant Director*
Lic. Carlos Salvador Rizzo, *Technical Secretary*
Lic. Edith R. Ortiz de Cuadra, *Chief of Computation Team*

Computer Installation
IBM 1130—operating system: DMS; internal storage: 256K bits; magnetic discs: 1 IBM 2315, 2 IBM 1316; 1 line printer.

Coding Languages
Assembler, RPG; FORTRAN, COBOL, PL/1.

Contemplated Equipment
IBM 1403 printer.

Services Available
Advice, programming, education and training, software packages, documentation, preparation of data, systems analysis. Operate on a self-service, block time and open shop basis. Services are restricted to the promotion of applications to management techniques.

Fields of Application
Statistical, commercial, production control, accounting, management, systems analysis, operational research.
Specialized area: Analysis

CONSULTANTS

COMPAÑÍA CUYANA DE CÓMPUTOS
9 de Julio 1836, Mendoza
Telephone: 56099, 54771

Officer
A. R. Amoretti, *Director*

Computer Installation
BULL GENERAL ELECTRIC GE 115—operating system: COS; internal storage: 8K bits; 1 line printer.

Coding Languages
TAB, APS.

Services Available
Consultation, programming, education and training, operators, software packages, documentation, preparation of data, systems analysis. Operate on a self-service, open shop and block time basis.

Fields of Application
Commercial, technical.

COMPTABLES ASESORES*
Sarmiento 2226, Buenos Aires
Telephone: 48-3480/6501/2648

Officers
L. Faerman, *Director*
Sra. M. de Rodriguez, *Head of Equipment*

Computer Installation
BULL GENERAL ELECTRIC GE 55—operating systems: EOS/BOS; internal storage: 5K bits.

Coding Languages
BASIC, GESAL.

Services Available
Consultation, programming, education and training, operators, software packages, documentation, preparation of data, systems analysis. Operate on a closed shop and block time basis.

Fields of Application
Commercial, technical.

CONSULTMAR S. A.*
Empresa de Estudios y Servicios
Lamadrid 2127, Mar del Plata
Telephone: 2-7082/83

Officers
J. E. Sanguinetti, *President*
H. J. Panzeri, *Director*

Argentina – Service Bureaux

Computer Installation
BULL GENERAL ELECTRIC GE 115–operating system: TOS; internal storage: 12K bytes; magnetic tapes: 4; 1 line printer.

Coding Languages
APS, TAB III, FORTRAN, COBOL.

Services Available
Consultation, programming, education and training, preparation of data, systems analysis. Operate on a self-service and time-sharing basis.

Fields of Application
Statistical, commercial, accounting, systems analysis, operational research.

Training
Courses in programming, systems analysis, management.

SERVICE BUREAUX

BAIRESCO*
Avenida Figueroa Alcorta 3259, Buenos Aires
Telephone: 85–1111

Officers
J. A. Seoane, *Director*
C. A. Etcheverry, *Head of Equipment*

Computer Installation
BULL GENERAL ELECTRIC GE 115–operating system: TOS; internal storage: 16K bits; magnetic tapes 4 MTH 9-track, 1 MTH 7-track, 1 line printer.

Services Available
Consultation, programming, education and training, operators, software packages, documentation, preparation of data, systems analysis. Operate on a self-service, open shop and block time basis.

Fields of Application
Commercial, technical.

BULL GENERAL ELECTRIC*
Sarmiento 1113, 6° piso, Buenos Aires
Telephone: 35-0022

Officer
J. C. Rossi, *Head of Equipment*

Computer Installation
BULL GENERAL ELECTRIC GE 55–operating systems: EOS/BOS; internal storage: 5K bits.

Services Available
Consultation, programming, education and training, operators, software packages, documentation, preparation of data, systems analysis. Operate on a self-service and block time basis.

Fields of Application
Commercial, scientific.

Training
Courses in systems analysis and programming.

INTERCONTINENTAL DATA SERVICES LTD.*
Buenos Aires

Computer Installation
ICL KDF8–magnetic tapes.

IBM WORLD TRADE CORPORATION
Datacenter
Avenida Pte. R.S. Peña 933, Buenos Aires
Telephone: 35-5011

Officers
N. Azpiazu, *Marketing Manager*
G. A. Pollitzer, *in charge of scientific problems*
J. Luchetti, *in charge of commercial problems*

Computer Installation
IBM 360/40–operating system: multiprogramming; internal storage: 64K bytes; magnetic tapes: 7 2400/II; magnetic discs: 5 2311/I; 2 line printers.

IBM 1401 (2)–internal storage: 8K bits; magnetic tapes: 4 729/II; 1 line printer each.

Services Available
Operators, preparation of data, programming, systems analysis. Operate on a closed shop and block time basis.

Fields of Application
Scientific, commercial.

Training
Programming courses.

KOLYNOS S.A.C.I.*
Avenida 12 de Octubre 2420, Quilmes
Telephone: 263-6011

Also at:
Pinzón 1445, piso 2, Buenos Aires

Officer
José Víctor Giacomino, *Director of Computer Centre*

Computer Installation
IBM 360/20–internal storage: 8K bits.

Coding Languages
Assembler, RPG, PCU.

Contemplated Equipment
IBM 360/25.

Services Available
Advice, programming, preparation of data, systems analysis. Operate on a self-service and closed shop basis. Available only to Kolynos S.A.C.I. and John Wyeth Labs. S.A.

Fields of Application
Statistical, commercial, accounting, management.

NCR ARGENTINA S.A.*
Corrientes 1615, Buenos Aires
Telephone: 49-6671

Officer
Ildefonso J. Rodríguez

Computer Installation
NCR 315 (2)–internal storage: 120K bits each; cram files: 6; magnetic tape: 1; 2 line printers.

Coding Languages
BEST, COBOL, FORTRAN, NEAT, PERT.

Services Available
Advice, operators, preparation of data, programming, software packages, systems analysis. Operate on a self-service, closed shop and block time basis.

Fields of Application
Commercial, production control, scientific, statistical, management, accounting, etc.
Specialized area: Management information.

PROCEDA S.R.L.*
Paseo Colón 746, Buenos Aires
Telephone: 30-8951/71

Officer
Eudaldo Feijoó, *Manager*

Computer Installation
IBM 1401 (2)—internal storage: 56K bits each; magnetic tapes: 4 7330 each; magnetic discs: 1 1405 each; 1 line printer each.

Coding Language
SDS.

Services Available
Programming, operators. Operate on a self-service and block time basis. Available to enterprises of the Bunge y Born group.

Fields of Application
Statistical, commercial, production control, accounting, management.

REFINERÍAS DE MAIZ S.A.I.C.*
Tucumán 117, Buenos Aires
Telephone: 32-2448

Officer
Carlos Kasis, *Director of Systems*

Computer Installation
IBM 360/30—operating system: DOS; internal storage: 32K bits; magnetic tapes: 2 2415/4; magnetic discs: 3 2311/1; 1 line printer.

Coding Languages
Assembler, COBOL.

Contemplated Equipment
Additional storage of 32K bits; four IBM 2314 disc units.

Services Available
Advice, programming, preparation of data, systems analysis. Operate on a closed shop and block time basis.

Field of Application
Commercial.

Computer Installation
IBM 360/50—operating system: MFT II; internal storage: 2,097,152 bits; magnetic tapes: 4 IBM 2415 (3 9-track, 1 7-track); magnetic discs: 7 IBM 2311; 1 line printer.
UNIVAC 1108—operating system: EXEC 8; internal storage: 7,077,888 bits; magnetic tapes: 2 16C, 2 12C; magnetic discs: 4 8414; 1 line printer. *On-line satellite computers*: PDP 11/45. *Remote processing features*: terminals.

Coding Languages
FORTRAN, Assembler, COBOL.

Contemplated Equipment
3 8440 disc drives, 1 1782 drum, 2 12C tape drives.

Services Available
Advice, programming, education and training, operators, software packages, documentation, systems analysis. Operate on a closed shop, open shop and time-sharing basis.

Fields of Application
Scientific, statistical, research, administration.
Specialized area: University research.

Training
Courses in elementary FORTRAN.

BALLARAT INSTITUTE OF ADVANCED EDUCATION
Lydiard Street South, Ballarat, Victoria 3350
Telephone: Buninyong 413500

Officers
E. J. Barker, *Principal*
R. T. Morrell, *Registrar and Business Manager*

Computer Installation
ICL 1901A—operating system: GEORGE 1S; internal storage: 393,216 bits; magnetic discs: 1 Twin Exchangeable Disc Store 2820/1; 1 line printer.

Coding Languages
FORTRAN, COBOL, ALGOL, PLAN, MINITRAN.

Services Available
Consultation, education and training, preparation of data. Operate on a block time basis.

Fields of Application
Scientific, commercial.
Specialized area: Education.

Training
Diploma of Business Studies (EDP).

AUSTRALIA

UNIVERSITIES AND COLLEGES

AUSTRALIAN NATIONAL UNIVERSITY
Computer Centre
P.O. Box 4, Canberra, A.C.T. 2600
Telephone: Canberra 49 3437

Officers
M. R. Osborne, *Director*
A. J. Harris, *Operations Manager*
Mrs. J. M. Bakalor, *Senior Programmer*

BENDIGO INSTITUTE OF TECHNOLOGY*
McCrae Street, Bendigo, Victoria 3550
Telephone: 30304

Officer
W. Williams, *Head of Business Studies Division*

Computer Installation
ICL 1900 series—operating system: George 1; internal storage: 394K bits; magnetic tapes: 14 7-track: 1 line printer.

Coding Languages
COBOL, FORTRAN, ALGOL, PLAN.

Australia — Universities and Colleges

Services Available
Advice, programming, systems analysis. Operate on a closed shop and block time basis. Available only to educational establishments.

Fields of Application
Scientific, statistical, commercial, production control, accounting, management, systems analysis, operational research.
Specialized area: Training in applied research at post-graduate level, including software development.

Training
Courses leading to post-graduate Diploma of Electronic Computing; Diploma of Information processing; Diploma of Business Studies—Data Processing. Short executive courses in EDP (3 days), management appreciation courses in EDP (12 weeks), and programming courses—COBOL and FORTRAN (1 week).

CANBERRA COLLEGE OF ADVANCED EDUCATION
P.O. Box 381, Canberra, A.C.T. 2601
Telephone: Canberra 512001

Officer
D. M. Millar, *Director of Computer Centre*

Computer Installation
BURROUGHS B6700—operating system: MCP; internal storage: 98,304 48-bit words; magnetic tapes: 2 B9391; magnetic discs: 1 B9487-1, 1 B9373-13; 1 line printer. *Remote processing features*: 35 TD700 display terminals, 11 ASR33 teletypes, 4 IE132A display terminals, 2 centronic printers.

Coding Languages
COBOL, FORTRAN, ALGOL, BASIC, PL/1, SNOBOL.

Contemplated Equipment
A mini-computer; additional disc capacity; a plotter; graphics.

Services Available
Consultation, programming, education and training, operators, software packages, documentation, preparation of data, systems analysis. Operate on a closed shop and block time basis. Services available to students and staff, and to outside users on a paying basis.

Fields of Application
Management, systems analysis, educational.

Training
A three-year course leading to a Bachelor of Arts in Computing studies; a one-year course leading to a Graduate Diploma in Computing Studies.

CAPRICORNIA INSTITUTE OF ADVANCED EDUCATION
Private Mail Bag 31, M.S. 76, Rockhampton, Queensland 4700

Officer
Ray W. Cheeseman, *Computer Manager*

Computer Installation
ICL 1901A—operating system: GEORGE 1S; internal storage: 16K 24-bit words; magnetic tapes: 2; magnetic discs: 1 Twin EDS; 1 line printer.

Coding Languages
FORTRAN, COBOL, PLAN.

Services Available
Advice, education and training, operators, software packages, preparation of data. Operate on a closed shop and block time basis.

Fields of Application
Scientific, statistical, commercial, operational research.

Training
Three-year course for Diploma in Science (Mathematics); courses in mathematics (three years offered), communication, physics, chemistry, biology (in first year), probability and statistics (in second year), and liberal studies (in third year).

CAULFIELD INSTITUTE OF TECHNOLOGY
900 Dandenong Road, Caulfield East, Victoria 3145
Telephone: 211-7722

Officers
J. Dann, *Manager, Computer Centre*
Dr. T. Pearcey, *Head, EDP Department*

Computer Installation
ICL 1904A—operating systems: GEORGE 3; internal storage: 2,359,296 bits; magnetic tapes: 6; magnetic discs: 4; 1 line printer. *Remote processing features*: Remote batch terminals, interactive teletypes.

Coding Languages
COBOL, FORTRAN, ALGOL, Assembly, BASIC, JEAN and own Elementary Compiler Language—'ECOLE'.

Services Available
Advice, education and training, preparation of data. Operate on a closed shop, time-sharing and remote access basis. Priority given to student exercises, then to administrative work.

Fields of Application
Scientific, statistical, commercial, management, operational research.
Specialized area: Linear programming.

Training
Courses leading to Bachelor of Applied Science (Electronic Data Processing), Diploma in Electronic Data Processing, Certificate of EDP (Operators and Coders), Diploma in Data Processing.

GORDON INSTITUTE OF TECHNOLOGY*
P.O. Box 122, Geelong, Victoria
Telephone: 95915

Also at:
Fenwick Street, Geelong, Victoria 3220

Officer
H. N. Trudgeon, *Head of Computer Department*

Computer Installation
ICL 1901A—operating system; GEORGE 1S; internal storage: 393,216 bits; magnetic discs: 1 Twin EDS; 1 line printer.

Coding Languages
PLAN, COBOL, FORTRAN, ALGOL.

Contemplated Equipment
Floating point hardware.

Services Available
Programming, education and training, preparation of data. Operate on a closed shop basis.

Australia — Universities and Colleges

Fields of Application
Scientific, commercial, packages.

Training
Courses leading to a Diploma of Information Processing; Diploma of Business Studies (Data Processing); Post-Graduate Diploma of Electronic Computation. COBOL and FORTRAN appreciation courses (2 hours a week for one year).

HOBART TECHNICAL COLLEGE*
26 Bathurst Street, Hobart, Tasmania 7002

Officer
J. E. Slevin, *Lecturer in Charge*

Computer Installation
ICL 1201—internal storage: 1,024 40-bit words; 1 line printer.

Contemplated Equipment
Additional core storage of 16K words, remote consoles, disc storage.

Services Available
Advice, preparation of data, systems analysis. Operate on an open shop basis.

Fields of Application
Scientific, commercial, accounting, management, systems analysis.

Training
Courses leading to a Certificate of Business Studies (Data Processing); also courses in Appreciation of Electronic Data Processing; Systems Analysis (Management and Accountancy Diplomas); Computer Utilization for Architects (Post-graduate). Programming Certificate in Systems Analysis.

HYDRO-UNIVERSITY COMPUTING CENTRE*
University of Tasmania, P.O. Box 252C, Hobart, Tasmania 7001

Officers
John Boothroyd, *Officer in Charge*

Computer Installation
ELLIOTT 503—operating system: ALGOL; internal storage: 319,488 plus 638,976 bits; 1 line printer.

PDP-8/L—internal storage: 49,152 bits; magnetic tapes: 4 DEC tapes; this will interface with the 503 so that each looks like a peripheral of the other.

Coding Languages
ALGOL, SAP.

Services Available
Consultation, programming, education and training, documentation. Operation on a closed shop basis, programming on an open shop basis.

Fields of Application
Mainly scientific and engineering numerical applications.
Specialized areas: Solution of eigenvalue problems, ALGOL teaching and application. FORTRAN is specifically excluded.

Training
Service courses are given to Hydro-Electric personnel and university staff in ALGOL programming and numerical methods (each of one term). Short courses are given as above and also for schools in Tasmania.

JAMES COOK UNIVERSITY OF NORTH QUEENSLAND
Townsville, Queensland 4811
Telephone: Townsville 79-3711

Officer
I. M. Hunter, *Computer Centre Manager*

Computer Installation
DECSYSTEM 10—operating system: TOPS-10 MONITOR; internal storage: 2,359,296 bits; magnetic tapes: 2 TU 10, 2 TU 50; magnetic discs: 2 DEC-RPO2; 1 line printer. *On-line satellite computer*: 1 PDP 8 at CSIRO. *Remote processing features*: 24 remote terminals.

Coding Languages
FORTRAN, COBOL, ALGOL, MACRO-10

Contemplated Equipment
Additional core.

Services Available
Advice, education and training, operators, software packages, preparation of data. Operate on a time-sharing basis. Outside customers limited to a proportion of total use.

Fields of Application
Scientific, statistical, commercial, accounting, operational research.
Specialized areas: Structural engineering, systems engineering.

Training
Programming courses in FORTRAN.

MACQUARIE UNIVERSITY*
North Ryde, New South Wales 2113

Officer
H. S. Hancock, *Senior Lecturer in Mathematics (in charge of Computing Laboratory)*

Computer Installation
IBM 1460—internal storage: 128K bits; magnetic tapes: 2 IBM 7330; magnetic discs: 1 IBM 1311; 1 line printer.

Contemplated Equipment
Univac 9200 as remote terminal to Univac 1108.

Coding Languages
FORTRAN, COBOL, Autocoder.

Fields of Application
Computer education (mainly), administration, scientific and economic research.

Training
Single semester courses (part of the B.A. degree) in general appreciation, FORTRAN programming, machine organization, linear programming and numerical analysis.

MONASH UNIVERSITY
Computer Centre
Wellington Road, Clayton, Victoria 3168
Telephone: 544-0811

Officer
Dr. C. J. Bellamy, *Director*

Australia — Universities and Colleges

Computer Installation
CDC 3200—operating system: MSOS (mass store operating system); internal storage: 768K bits, magnetic tapes: 4 7-track; magnetic discs: 2; 1 line printer. *On-line satellite computer*: PDP 8. *Remote processing features*: 20 teletype terminals connected to PDP 8 to enable background file processing on CDC 3200.

BURROUGHS B5500 (2)—operating system: MCP; internal storage: 32K 48-bit words; magnetic tapes: 10; magnetic discs: 2; 4 line printers. *Remote processing features*: terminal facilities via TTY.

Coding Languages
COBOL, FORTRAN, ALGOL.

Contemplated Equipment
BURROUGHS B6700 with core storage of 96K words.

Services Available
Advice, programming, education and training, operators, software packages, documentation, preparation of data, systems analysis. Operate on a closed shop, block time and remote access basis. Time-sharing terminals on premises.

Fields of Application
Scientific, statistical.
Specialized areas: Educational, medical applications.

Training
Introductory courses in FORTRAN and COBOL languages.

MOUNT LAWLEY TECHNICAL COLLEGE*
Harold Street, Perth, Western Australia 6000
Telephone: 28 6844

Officer
G. R. Gatti, *Senior Lecturer in Mathematics*

Coding Language
FORTRAN.

Contemplated Equipment
PDP 8, more teletypes.

Services Available
Education and training.

Fields of Application
Scientific, operational research, analysis.

NEW SOUTH WALES INSTITUTE OF TECHNOLOGY
Thomas Street, Broadway, New South Wales 2007
Telephone: 20922

Also at: North Sydney

Officers
Dr. S. Summersbee, *Head of the Department of Information Science*

Computer Installation
ICL 1904A—operating system: GEORGE 3; internal storage: 96K 24-bit words; magnetic tapes: 8; magnetic discs: 4 EDS: 2 line printers. *Remote processing features*: 1 RJE, 10 teletypewriters, 3 visual display units.
IBM 1401—internal storage: 16K 8-bit characters; magnetic tapes: 4 720; 1 line printer.
DATA GENERAL Nova—operating system: DOS; internal storage: 24K 16-bit words; magnetic discs: 1. *Remote processing features*: 3 Creed Envoy data-printers.
DATA GENERAL Nova—internal storage: 8K 16-bit words. *Remote processing features*: 2 teletypewriters.

Coding Languages
PLAN, COBOL, FORTRAN, ALGOL, EMMA, JEAN, BASIC, Nova Assembler, Autocoder.

Services Available
Consultation, programming, operators, software packages, preparation of data, systems analysis. Operate on a closed shop, remote access, open shop and time-sharing basis. Closed shop for ICL 1904A.

Fields of Application
Scientific, statistical, commercial, accounting, management, systems analysis, operational research.

Training
Information Processing diploma course (full or part time); extension courses in systems analysis, COBOL and FORTRAN programming.

PERTH TECHNICAL COLLEGE*
137 St. George's Terrace, Perth, Western Australia 6000
Telephone: 21-9623

Officers
G. E. Marshall, *Principal*
H. Wood, *Head of the Department of Accounting and Data Processing*

Training
Courses for Diploma in Computer Studies, Certificate in Data Processing.

PRESTON INSTITUTE OF TECHNOLOGY*
70 St. George's Road, Preston, Victoria 3072
Telephone: 478-1666

Officer
W. Martin, *Head of Computer Department*

Computer Installation
ICL 1901A—operating system: GEORGE 1S; internal storage: 393, 216 bits; magnetic discs: 1 Twin EDS; 1 line printer.

Coding Languages
FORTRAN, COBOL, ALGOL, PLAN.

Services Available
Consultation, programming, education and training. Operate on a block time basis. Available only to personnel and students of the Institute.

Fields of Application
All fields because of the educational nature of the establishment.
Specialized areas: Scientific and commercial programming.

Training
Diploma of Business Studies (Data Processing).
Short course in FORTRAN programming included in all engineering and chemistry diplomas.

SOUTH AUSTRALIAN INSTITUTE OF TECHNOLOGY
Box 1, Post Office, Ingle Farm, South Australia 5098
Telephone: 62-5313

Officer
D. B. Vigor, *Head of Data Processing*

Computer Installation
ICL 1903A–operating systems: GEORGE 2, MAXIMOP; internal storage: 1,600K bits; magnetic tapes: 4 7-track; magnetic discs: 3 EDS; 1 line printer. *On-line satellite computers*: PDP 8s. *Remote processing features*: 11 teletypewriters.

PDP-11/20–operating systems: Resource Time sharing, BASIC; internal storage: 448,752; magnetic tapes: 2 Dectapes; magnetic discs: 1. *On-line satellite computers*: PDP-8s. *Remote processing features*: 11 terminals.

Coding Languages
FORTRAN, COBOL, ALGOL, BASIC, PLAN.

Contemplated Equipment
Teletypewriters, data logging equipment.

Services Available
Advice, education and training, preparation of data. Operate on a remote access, closed shop and time-sharing basis. Available only to staff, students and consultancy clients.

Fields of Application
Scientific, statistical, commercial, accounting, systems analysis, operational research.
Specialized areas: Linear programming, analysis, structural engineering.

Training
Courses for Diploma in Technology in Data Processing, Bachelor of Applied Science in Data Processing, and a post-graduate Diploma.

SOUTH AUSTRALIAN INSTITUTE OF TECHNOLOGY
North Terrace, Adelaide, South Australia 5000
Telephone: 23-3866

Also at: The Levels, Pooraka, South Australia
Telephone: 62-5313.

Computer Installation
ICL 1903A–operating system GEORGE 2; internal storage: 64K 24-bit words; magnetic tapes: 4 7-track; magnetic discs: 3; 1 line printer.

Services Available
Consultation, education and training. Operate on a closed shop basis.

Fields of Application
Scientific, statistical, commercial, accounting, management, systems analysis, operational research.

Training
Courses for Diploma in Technology–Data Processing; B.App.Sc–Data Processing; Certificate in Business Studies–Data Processing. Extension studies in computing are available; programmes are announced each year.

SWINBURNE COLLEGE OF TECHNOLOGY
P.O. Box 218, Hawthorn, Victoria 3122
Telephone: 81-0301

Officer
G. A. K. Hunt, *Head of the Department of Computer Studies*

Computer Installation
ICL 1901A–operating system: GEORGE 1S; internal storage: 393,216 bits; magnetic discs: 1 Twin EDS; 1 line printer.

Coding Languages
COBOL, FORTRAN, ALGOL, CSL, PLAN, BASIC.

Contemplated Equipment
An Electronic Associates Inc. hybrid computer.

Services Available
Programming, education and training, software packages, preparation of data. Operate on a closed shop and time-sharing basis.

Fields of Application
Scientific, statistical, commercial, operational research, systems analysis.
Specialized areas: Linear programming, structural engineering, miscellaneous engineering.

Training
Degree courses in Business Studies, Applied Science, Mechanical Engineering, Production Engineering and Civil Engineering; diploma courses in Business Studies, Electrical Engineering and Chemical Engineering.

UNIVERSITY OF ADELAIDE
Computing Centre
Adelaide, South Australia 5001
Telephone: 23-4333

Officer
Dr. I. N. Capon, *Director*

Computer Installation
CDC 6400–operating system: SCOPE; internal storage: 3,930K bits; magnetic tapes: 6 607; magnetic disc: 6603; 2 line printers. *Remote processing features*: CDC 217-2, 713, 711, etc.

Coding Languages
FORTRAN (several versions), COMPASS, ALGOL, COBOL, SIMSCRIPT, SNOBOL, BASIC, MATRIX and Statistical Packages, etc.

Services Available
Advice, operators, preparation of data, programming, software packages, systems analysis. Operate on a remote access, closed shop and time-sharing basis. Limited availability to government, business and industry.

Fields of Application
All fields of University disciplines.
Specialized areas: Numerical analysis, theory of programming, linear programming, classification theory, simulation of physical systems, operations research, medical application of computer-based systems.

Training
Programming courses; undergraduate courses; postgraduate diploma.

UNIVERSITY OF MELBOURNE
Parkville, Melbourne, Victoria 3052
Telephone: 34-0484

Computer Installation
IBM 7044/1401–operating system: IBSYS; internal storage: 1,179,648 bits; magnetic tapes: 10 IBM 729; 2 line printers.

CDC Cyber 73–operating system: SCOPE; internal storage: 3,932,160 bits; magnetic tapes: 4 CDC 657; magnetic discs: 4 CDC 841; 1 line printer. *On-line satellite computer*: HEWLETT PACKARD 2100A.

Australia — Universities and Colleges

Coding Languages
FORTRAN, COBOL.

Services Available
Consultation, programming, education and training. Operate on a remote access, closed shop, block time and time-sharing basis.

Fields of Application
Scientific, accounting.

Training
B.Sc., M.Sc., Ph.D., D.Sc. degrees in Information Science; special subjects in other degree courses; short course for Commercial EDP Certificate (COBOL, Systems Analysis and Appreciation).

UNIVERSITY OF NEW ENGLAND
Armidale, New South Wales 2351
Telephone: Armidale 72-2911

Officers
Prof. E. J. Burr, *Director of Computer Centre*
R. G. Lyons, *Data Processing Manager*

Computer Installation
ICL 1904A—operating system: GEORGE 2; internal storage: 1,536K bits; magnetic tapes: 6 1972; magnetic discs: 3 EDS 30; 1 line printer. *Remote processing features*: teletype.

IBM 1620—operating system: Monitor; internal storage: 480K bits; magnetic discs: 1 1311; 1 line printer.

Coding Languages
PLAN, FORTRAN, ALGOL, COBOL, SPS.

Services Available
Advice, education and training, software packages, preparation of data. Operate on a remote access, open shop and time-sharing basis.

Fields of Application
Scientific, statistical, accounting.
Specialized areas: Linear programming, analysis, payroll.

Training
A one-year, full-time postgraduate course for a Diploma in Computing Science; service courses in computer programming.

UNIVERSITY OF NEW SOUTH WALES
Computing Services Unit
P.O. Box 1, Kensington, New South Wales 2028
Telephone: 662-2959

Officer
A. A. Thompson, *Manager*

Computer Installation
IBM 360/50—operating system: OS360; internal storage: 128K bytes; magnetic tapes: 2403, 2401; magnetic discs: 5 IBM 2311; 1 line printer.

Coding Languages
PL/1, FORTRAN, COBOL, Assembler, ALGOL, SNOBOL.

Contemplated Equipment
A new system incorporating a network of remote batch stations and interactive terminals.

Services Available
Advice, operators, software packages, preparation of data. Operate on a closed shop basis.

Fields of Application
Scientific, statistical, operational research.
Specialized areas: Linear programming, structural engineering, medical research.

Training
Non-credit courses in FORTRAN, SNOBOL and job control language.

UNIVERSITY OF NEW SOUTH WALES*
Wollongong University College
Wollongong, New South Wales 2500

Officer
K. P. Tognetti

Computer Installation
IBM 1620—internal storage: 60 x 4 x 1K bits; magnetic tapes: 3.

Coding Languages
FORTRAN, SPI.

Services Available
Consultation, programming, education and training. Operate on a self-service basis.

Fields of Application
Scientific, operational research.

Training
Computing subjects in mathematics, engineering and economics courses.

UNIVERSITY OF NEWCASTLE
Newcastle, New South Wales 2308
Telephone: 049-68 0401

Officer
Prof. J. J. Auchmuty, *Vice-Chancellor and Principal*

Computer Installation
ICL 1904A—operating system: GEORGE 2 and 3; internal storage: 64K 24-bit words; magnetic tapes: 2; magnetic discs: 3; 1 line printer. *Remote processing features*: 13 teletypewriters.

Coding Languages
FORTRAN, COBOL, ALGOL, PLAN.

Contemplated Equipment
A plotter.

Services Available
Advice, software packages. Operate on a closed shop and time-sharing basis.

Fields of Application
Scientific, commercial, management.

Training
A course leading to a Diploma in Computer Science.

UNIVERSITY OF QUEENSLAND
Computer Centre
St. Lucia, Brisbane, Queensland 4067
Telephone: 711377

Australia — Universities and Colleges

Computer Installation
BULL GENERAL ELECTRIC GE 225—magnetic tapes: 6; 1 line printer.

PDP-10—internal storage: 112K bits; magnetic tapes: 2; magnetic discs: 7; 1 line printer. *Remote processing features*: 40 remote teletypes.

Coding Languages
GAP, WIZ, FORTRAN, ALGOL, SNOBOL, GECOM, COBOL, MACRO, BASIC, AID, EDIT.

Services Available
Available for advice and operating services to outside customers for any purpose except regular time dependent work. Contract programming is not undertaken.

Fields of Application
General data processing, scientific computing, batch and via remote teletype terminals.
Specialized area: Operating systems.

Training
Short programming courses in specific service facilities offered.

UNIVERSITY OF SYDNEY
Basser Computing Centre
Sydney, New South Wales 2006
Telephone: 660-0522

Officers
R. B. Donnelly, *Manager*
B. G. Rowswell, *Systems Supervisor*
B. K. Haddon, *Applications Supervisor*

Computer Installation
IBM 7040—operating system: IBSYS; internal storage: 1,179,648 bits; magnetic tapes: 7 IBM 729; magnetic discs: 3 IBM 1311; 1 line printer. *On-line satellite computer*: IBM 1401.

ICL KDF9—operating system: Time-Sharing Director; internal storage: 1,572,864 bits; magnetic tapes: 4 ICL T1081, 1 TDR4; 1 line printer. *On-line satellite computers*: CDC 1700, IBM 1401.

Coding Languages
7040 Assembler (MAP), FORTRAN, COBOL, KDF9 Assembler (Usercode), ALGOL.

Contemplated Equipment
CDC Cyber 72-24 with remote consoles and remote batch.

Services Available
Advice, software packages, documentation, preparation of data. Operate on a closed shop basis.

Fields of Application
Scientific, statistical, accounting, management.
Specialized areas: Structural engineering, medical research, teaching.

Training
Courses provided by the Basser Department of Computer Science.

UNIVERSITY OF SYDNEY
School of Physics
The Basser Department of Computer Science
Sydney, New South Wales 2006
Telephone: 660-0522, extension 2541

Officers
Dr. J. M. Bennett, *Professor of Electronic Computing*
Dr. J. B. Hext, *Senior Lecturer*
Dr. A. H. J. Sale, *Senior Lecturer*

Computer Installation
CDC 1700—operating system: MSOS; internal storage: 16,384 x 16 bits; magnetic discs: 4. *Remote processing features*: PDP-8, KDF9 (remote character display).

PDP-8—internal storage: 8, 192 x 12 bits; 1 magnetic disc. *On-line satellite computers*: DEC 338, CRT display.

Contemplated Equipment
PDP-8/F.

Services Available
Education and training. Operate on a self-service and time-sharing basis. Available to all senior students, research students and staff.

Fields of Application
Scientific, statistical, teaching, research.
Specialized area: Computer architecture.

Training
Main Stream courses in Computer Science; Terminating courses in Automatic Computing, Computer Science Auxiliary, Diploma in Numerical Analysis and Automatic Computing; also non-credit courses in FORTRAN, COBOL and an assembly language.

UNIVERSITY OF WESTERN AUSTRALIA*
Nedlands, Western Australia 6009
Telephone: 86-3838

Officer
D. W. G. Moore, *Director*

Computer Installation
PDP-6—operating system: time-sharing; internal storage: 1,179,648 bits; magnetic tapes: 8; magnetic discs: 2 CDC 854 (Upgraded); 2 line printers. *On-line satellite computers*: PDP-8, 2 PDP-8/S. *Remote processing features*: 24 remote terminals over the campus.
IBM 1620—internal storage: 60K bits.

Coding Language
FORTRAN IV.

Contemplated Equipment
New computer installation.

Services Available
Advice, operators. Operate on a closed shop, open shop and time-sharing basis.

Fields of Application
Scientific, statistical.
Specialized areas: Research in interactive and real time computing.

Training
Diploma in computation. Also 3-day introductory programming courses.

WESTERN AUSTRALIAN INSTITUTE OF TECHNOLOGY*
Hayman Road, South Bentley, Western Australia 6102
Telephone: 68-1931

Officers
R. J. Hartley, *Head of Department*
D. Burn, *Computer Centre Manager*

Computer Installation
ICL 1902A—operating systems: GEORGE 1 and 2; internal storage: 32K 24-bit words; magnetic tapes: 2; magnetic discs: 2; 1 line printer. *Remote processing features*: 6 remote consoles—teletypes.

Coding Languages
FORTRAN IV, COBOL, ALGOL, PLAN.

Services Available
Consultation, programming, education and training, preparation of data. Operate on a closed shop basis.

Fields of Application
Research and planning, examination scheduling and results, routine administrative data processing, payroll.

Training
Associateship in Information Processing.

GOVERNMENT ESTABLISHMENTS

AUSTRALIAN ATOMIC ENERGY COMMISSION*
Applied Mathematics and Computing Section
Research Establishment
Private Mail Bag, Sutherland, New South Wales 2232
Telephone: 531-0111

Officers
D. J. Richardson, *Head*
N. W. Bennett, *Computer Research and Utilization*

Computer Installation
IBM 360/50—operating system: OS/360; internal storage: 2,097,152 bits; magnetic tapes: 2 9-track; magnetic discs: 4 2311; 1 line printer. *On-line satellite computer*: PDP-8.

Coding Languages
FORTRAN IV, COBOL, PL/1, Assembler.

Services Available
Advice, operators, preparation of data, software packages, systems analysis. Operate on a closed shop basis.

Field of Application
Atomic energy.
Specialized area: Nuclear codes.

BRISBANE CITY COUNCIL*
City Hall, Brisbane, Queensland
Telephone: 23020

Officer
John G. R. Morris, *Acting Chief Data Processing Officer*

Computer Installation
ICL 558 Punch Card Computer—internal storage: 25,860 bits.

Coding Language
Assembly.

Services Available
Programming, operators, preparation of data, systems analysis. Operate on a closed shop basis.

COMMONWEALTH SCIENTIFIC AND INDUSTRIAL RESEARCH ORGANIZATION (CSIRO)*
Division of Computing Research
P.O. Box 109, Canberra, A.C.T. 2601
Telephone: 48-7722

Also at: Adelaide, Brisbane, Griffith, Melbourne, Perth, Sydney and Townsville

Officer
Dr. P. J. Claringbold, *Acting Chief*

Computer Installation
Canberra:
CDC 3600—operating system: CSIRO DAD Monitor System; internal storage: 32K 48-bit words; magnetic tapes: 8 607; magnetic disc: 813; 3 line printers. *Remote processing features*: 6 DD 210 remote consoles, paper tape stations.

Melbourne, Sydney and Adelaide:
CDC 3200—operating system: CSIRO CSIDISC Monitor System: internal storage: 16K 24-bit words; magnetic tapes: 3 603; magnetic discs. 853, 854; 1 line printer.

Perth:
PDP-8/S—1 line printer. *Remote processing feature*: teletype console.

Griffith:
PDP-9—magnetic tape. *Remote processing feature*: teletype console.

Coding Languages
FORTRAN, COMPASS, ALGOL, SIMSCRIPT.

Contemplated Equipment
PDP-8, PDP-11.

Services Available
Advice, operators, preparation of data, software packages. Operate on a closed shop basis. Available only to CSIRO, universities and Commonwealth government departments.

Fields of Application
Application of computing techniques to physical, biological and agricultural sciences.
Specialized areas: Application of syntactic methods to computer generation of English descriptions of simple pictures; speech recognition; operating systems design; simulation languages; data-based management.

Training
Programming courses as required.

HOUSING COMMISSION, VICTORIA*
179 Queen Street, Melbourne, Victoria
Telephone: Melbourne 600511

Officers
L. Symes, *Chief Finance Officer*
W. Collins, *Data Processing Manager*

Computer Installation
ICL 1500—internal storage: 20K bits; magnetic tapes: 6; 1 line printer.

Fields of Application
Commercial, accounting, management.

LOCAL GOVERNMENT SUPERANNUATION BOARD*
235 Clarence Street, Sydney, New South Wales 2000

QUEENSLAND STATE TREASURY*
Electronic Data Processing Branch
P.O. Box 191, North Quay, Brisbane, Queensland
Telephone: Brisbane 32-0461

Australia – Government Establishments

Officers
N. J. Hall, *Computer Manager*
J. M. Watts, *Senior Systems Analyst*

Computer Installation
ICL 1904–operating system: EXEC.; internal storage: 786,432 bits; magnetic tapes: 6; 2 line printers.

Coding Languages
PLAN, FORTRAN, ALGOL, COBOL.

Contemplated Equipment
Duplicated or more powerful installation under consideration.

Services Available
Advice, preparation of data, programming, software packages, systems analysis. Operate on an open shop basis. Available only to governmental bodies, teaching institutions and research bodies.

Fields of Application
Non-technical applications include payroll, governmental accounting, electoral roll processing and examinations processing. Also statistical analysis of varying kinds. Technical work is conducted on an open shop basis and includes engineering design, survey calculations, forestry research and analysis, road alignment, etc.

SOUTH AUSTRALIAN PUBLIC SERVICE ADP CENTRE
12 Victoria Place, Adelaide, South Australia 5066
Telephone: 28-2627

Officer
P. C. Cornish, *Executive Officer*

Computer Installation
CDC Cyber 73–operating system: SCOPE; internal storage: 3,920,160 bits; magnetic tapes: 4; magnetic discs: 6 841, 3 844; 2 line printers. *Remote processing features*: 1 200-user batch terminals, 6 terminals (CRT and teletype).

CDC 3200–operating system: SCOPE; internal storage: 393,216 bits; magnetic tapes: 8; 1 line printer.

Coding Languages
COBOL, FORTRAN.

Contemplated Equipment
Core of 32K bits, 3 120Kc magnetic tapes, 2 841 disc drives, 1 700 computer and peripherals for Cyber 73.

Services Available
Advice, programming, education and training, operators, preparation of data, systems analysis. Operate on a remote access, closed shop and time sharing basis. Available to State Public Service Departments only.

Fields of Application
Scientific, commercial, accounting, management.

Training
Service courses only.

RESEARCH INSTITUTION

IBM SYSTEMS DEVELOPMENT INSTITUTE
80 Northbourne Ave., Canberra, A.C.T. 2601

Officers
Dr. G. H. Ford, *Director*
B. Scott, *Manager of the Computer Centre*

Computer Installation
IBM 360/67–operating system: CP/67, OS MVT HASP; internal storage: 768K bits; magnetic tapes: 4 2420, 2 2401; magnetic discs: 10 2314, 12 2311, 2 2301 drums; 2 line printers. *On-line satellite computer.* IBM 1130.
Remote processing features: 2741 Terminals APL, CMS, CRJE.

Coding Languages
PL/1, FORTRAN, Assembler, APL, COBOL.

Services Available
Advice, education and training, joint project work. Operate on a closed shop basis. Time-sharing terminals on premises.
Restrictions: Within the terms and conditions of the Systems Development Institute Charter.

Fields of Application
Scientific, statistical, commercial, management, systems analysis, operational research, data base.
Specialized area: Modelling, interactive systems.

CONSULTANTS

COMPUTER ENGINEERING APPLICATIONS PTY. LTD.*
Suite 711, 50 Miller Street, North Sydney, New South Wales 2060
Telephone: 92-5631

Officer
J. A. Deaker, *Manager*

Computer Installation
IBM 1130–operating system: MOD-1; internal storage: 8K bits; magnetic disc; 1 line printer.

Coding Language
FORTRAN.

Contemplated Equipment
Plotter.

Services Available
Consultation, preparation of data, programming. Operate on an open shop basis.

Fields of Application
Engineering calculations, payroll, costing.
Specialized areas: Structural, civil, mechanical, highways, traffic engineering.

E. H. COWLED PTY. LTD.
64 Seaforth Crescent, Seaforth, New South Wales 2092
Telephone: 945164

Officer
E. H. Cowled, *Managing Director*

Services Available
Advice, programming, education and training, documentation, systems analysis.

Fields of Application
Scientific, statistical, commercial, production control, accounting, management, systems analysis, operational research.
Specialized areas: Investment analysis, payroll, finance, membership systems, credit union.

Australia – Service Bureaux

McKINSEY & CO. INC.*
440 Collins Street, 8th Floor, Melbourne, Victoria

Services Available
Consultation, programming, systems analysis.

Fields of Application
Operations research, linear programming, simulation, statistical analysis.

P. A. MANAGEMENT CONSULTANTS PTY. LTD.*
150 Albert Road, South Melbourne, Victoria
Telephone: 699-1711

Also at:
221 Miller Street, North Sydney, New South Wales
Telephone: 929-7888

M.M.I. Building, 344 Queen Street, Brisbane, Queensland 4000
Telephone: 21-2999

Royal Exchange House, 38 Currie Street, Adelaide, South Australia
Telephone: 51-2649

Bank of N.S.W. Building, 110 William Street, Perth, Western Australia 6000
Telephone: 23-2679

Officers
K. J. Leadbeater, *Divisional Director, Computer Management Sciences Division*
M. J. Sloan, *Manager, Computer Services Division, Melbourne*
A. R. Barton, *Manager, Computer Services Division, Sydney*

Coding Languages
COBOL, RPG.

Services Available
Consultation, preparation of data, programming, systems analysis.

Fields of Application
Management information systems including normal accounting procedures, production and inventory control.

Training
Short courses in systems analysis (15 days) and EDP appreciation for management (3 days).

P. E. CONSULTING GROUP (AUST.) PTY. LTD.
13-15 O'Connell Street, Sydney, New South Wales
Telephone: 282861

Also at:
576 St. Kilda Road, Melbourne 3004
Telephone: 515318

Services Available
Consultation, systems analysis.

Fields of Application
General management consultancy in all fields, i.e. production, marketing, finance, personnel, etc. Development and application of advanced techniques, such as data processing and operational research. Consultancy at corporate level in organization studies, long-range planning, diversification and information systems.
Specialized areas: Technical consultancy in architectural, mechanical handling, project management and production engineering. Design and management of systems development projects, machine selection and installation management.

PEAT, MARWICK, MITCHELL & CO.
Tower Building, Australia Square, Sydney, New South Wales 2000
Telephone: 2-0538

Officer
N. H. McIntosh

Services Available
Consultation, systems analysis.

Fields of Application
Economic studies, general management, scientific management, operations research, project management, industrial engineering, marketing production and inventory control, information systems, general and cost accounting systems, equipment selection, data processing and transmission systems.
Specialized areas: Banking, transportation, insurance, retail, government and others.

URWICK INTERNATIONAL PTY. LIMITED
69 Macquarie Street, Sydney 2000, New South Wales
Telephone: 27-2905

Officer
R. C. Cullen, *Managing Director*

Services Available
Consultation, education and training, documentation, systems analysis.

Training
Courses in computer project management (1 week), computer systems analysis (3 weeks) and management of computer programming (1 week).

SERVICE BUREAUX

ACTA PTY. LTD.
P.O. Box 4006, Sydney, New South Wales 2001,
Telephone: 27-7911

Officer
F. A. Assenza, *Divisional Manager, Systems and Data Processing*

Computer Installation
HONEYWELL H2050–operating system: OS 2000; internal storage: 98,304 bits; magnetic tapes: 3 204B-4; magnetic discs: 2 277; 1 line printer.

Coding Languages
COBOL, Assembler, FORTRAN.

Services Available
Advice, programming, education and training, documentation, preparation of data, systems analysis. Operate on a closed and open shop, self-service and block time basis.

Fields of Application
Commercial, accounting, systems analysis, management.
Specialized areas: shipping and transport industries.

ADAPS LTD.*
P.O. Box 131, St. Kilda, Victoria 3182
Telephone: 940664

Australia – Service Bureaux

Officers
J. S. Thompson, *Managing Director*
J. M. H. Aikin, *Commercial Director*

Computer Installation
IBM 360/40–operating systems: Adaps DOSSIER, 360/OS, DOS rel. 18 and rel. 21; internal storage: 128K bytes; magnetic tapes: 4 2401, 2 2415; magnetic discs: 4 2311; 2 line printers.

Coding Languages
COBOL, FORTRAN, SCORE, Assembler, PL/1.

Contemplated Equipment
IBM 370/155.

Services Available
Advice, programming, education and training, software packages, preparation of data, systems analysis. Operate on a self-service, block time and open shop basis. Training in service bureau management offered only to overseas residents.

Fields of Application
Statistical, commercial, production control, accounting, management, systems analysis.
Specialized areas: Analysis, payroll, business model synthesis and simulation.

Training
Courses in management. Full-time training in facility operations and management provided for overseas participants.

ASSOCIATED COMPUTER SERVICES*
75 Flinders Lane, Melbourne, Victoria
Telephone: 654-4929, 654-4939

Officer
P. D. Fraser, *Manager*

Computer Installation
HONEYWELL H200–operating systems: BASIC or MOD. I; internal storage: 24K 9-bit characters; magnetic tapes: 5; 1 line printer.

Coding Languages
COBOL D, FORTRAN II, Easycoder, COBOL B.

Services Available
Advice, operators, preparation of data, programming, systems analysis. Operate on an open shop and block time basis.

Fields of Application
Scientific, commercial, production control, accounting, management operational research, etc.
Specialized areas: Commercial, accounting, statistical.

BURROUGHS LTD.*
8 Berry Street, North Sydney, New South Wales
Telephone: 92-0851

Also at: Melbourne, Victoria and Adelaide, South Australia.

Officer
W. L. Kerr, *General Manager*

Computer Installations
Sydney, Melbourne and Adelaide:
BURROUGHS B3500; internal storage: 1 million bits; magnetic tapes: 10; magnetic discs; 1 line printer. *On-line satellite computer*: TC 500.

Sydney and Melbourne:
BURROUGHS B500; internal storage: 115K bits; magnetic tapes: 4; magnetic discs; 1 line printer.

Coding Languages
COBOL, FORTRAN.

Contemplated Equipment
Burroughs B4500 and B6500.

Services Available
Advice, operators, preparation of data, programming.

Fields of Application
Scientific and commercial.

Training
Programming, operating and systems analysis.

CANBERRA COMPUTER CENTRE*
Flinders Way, Manuka, A.C.T.

Computer Installation
ICL 1901.
IBM 360/20.

COMMERCIAL COMPUTER CENTRE PTY. LTD.*
P.O. Box 301, 21 George Street, Parramatta, New South Wales 2150
Telephone: 635-4646, 637-6518, 631-9180

Officer
R. D. Rosengreen, *Managing Director*

Coding Languages
COBOL, FORTRAN, NEAT 3, PLAN, Easycoder.

Services Available
Advice, programming, education and training, software packages, preparation of data, systems analysis.

Fields of Application
Scientific, commercial, accounting, systems analysis.
Specialized areas: Sales analysis, medical research.

Training
Courses for punch card operators.

COMPUNET LTD.*
23 Cleg Street, Artarmon, New South Wales 2064
Telephone: 439-3155

Also at:
Phoenix House, 88 Northbourne Ave., Braddon, A.C.T. 2601
Telephone: 47-9111

74-76 Eastern Road, South Melbourne, Victoria 3205
Telephone: 69-6385

Officers
A. Smith, *Managing Director*
T. M. Boehm, *Director of Operations and Administration*

Computer Installation
UNIVAC 1108–operating system: EXEC II; internal storage: 234K bits; magnetic tapes: 4 7-track, 2 9-track; magnetic drums: 4 FH432, 1 Fastrand II. *On-line satellite computers*: 1 Univac 9300, 4 Univac 9200.

Australia — Service Bureaux

Services Available
Consultation, programming, education and training, operators, software packages, documentation, systems analysis. Operate on a remote access, block time and open shop basis.

Fields of Application
Scientific, statistical, commercial, accounting.

Training
General information on the use of packages provided and on the use of the system.

COMPUTER ACCOUNTING SERVICES PTY. LTD.*
64 Parramatta Road, Camperdown, New South Wales
Telephone: 519-3155

Officers
R. Berryman, *Managing Director*
P. Onley, *Operations Director*
T. van Schie, *Sales Director*

Computer Installation
HONEYWELL H2000 (2)—internal storage: 24K characters each; magnetic tapes: 5 each: 2 line printers.
HONEYWELL H2200—internal storage: 47K characters; magnetic tapes: 6; 1 line printer.

Coding Languages
Easycoder, COBOL.

Contemplated Equipment
Honeywell H115.

Services Available
Advice, preparation of data, programming, software packages, systems analysis. Operate on a closed shop and block time basis. Available for commercial data processing only.

Fields of Application
Commercial, accounting.
Specialized areas: Sales accounting/stock control.

COMPUTER SCIENCES OF AUSTRALIA PTY. LTD.*
8 Glen Street, Milsons Point, New South Wales 2061
Telephone: 92-90911

Officer
I. G. Esplin, *Managing Director*

Computer Installation
UNIVAC 1108—operating system: CSCX; magnetic tapes: 6 Uniservo VIIIC; magnetic discs: 2 Fastrand II, 2 FH 432, 2 FH 1782; 3 line printers. *Remote processing features*: Low-speed terminals, remote job entry.

Coding Languages
BASIC, FORTRAN, COBOL, Assembly.

Services Available
Advice, programming, education and training, operators, software packages, documentation, preparation of data, systems analysis. Operate on a remote access, closed shop, block time and time-sharing basis.

Fields of Application
Scientific, commercial, systems analysis.

Training
Courses in electronic data processing, including project management, systems analysis and high-level languages.

COMPUTER UTILITIES (BROOKVALE) PTY. LTD.
Marvic House, 658 Pittwater Road, Brookvale, New South Wales 2100
Telephone: 939-2782

Officers
E. H. Cowled, *Director*
M. A. Winny, *Director*

Computer Installation
The company operates a Terminet 300 terminal on Computer Sciences of Australia Pty. Ltd., INFONET Service and others.

Coding Languages
BASIC, FORTRAN, COBOL.

Services Available
Advice, programming, education and training, operators, documentation, preparation of data, systems analysis. Operate on a closed shop and time-sharing basis.

Fields of Application
Scientific, statistical, commercial, production control, accounting, management, systems analysis, operational research.
Specialized area: Inventory and production control.

COMPUTER UTILITIES (INDUSTRIAL) PTY. LTD.
377 Sussex Street, Sydney, New South Wales 2000
Telephone: 61-2522

Officers
E. H. Cowled, *Managing Director*
G. J. Docherty, *Manager*

Computer Installation
NCR Century 100—internal storage: 256K bits; magnetic tapes: 2; magnetic discs: 2 Twin Spindle; 1 line printer.

Coding Languages
COBOL, NEAT 3, FORTRAN.

Contemplated Equipment
Multiplexor connecting to remote terminal.

Services Available
Advice, programming, education and training, operators, preparation of data, systems analysis. Operate on a closed shop and block time basis.

Fields of Application
Scientific, statistical, commercial, production control, accounting, management, systems analysis, operational research.
Specialized areas: Investment, membership systems, credit unions, industrial associations.

CONTROL DATA AUSTRALIA PTY. LTD.*
221 Miller Street, North Sydney, New South Wales 2060
Telephone: 929-6522

Also at:
598 St. Kilda Road, Melbourne, Victoria 3004
Telephone: 51-0351

Officer
R. L. Ernst, *Director*

Australia – Service Bureaux

Computer Installation
Sydney:
CDC 6600–operating system: Scope 3.2; internal storage: 131K 60-bit words; magnetic tapes: 8 607 P; magnetic discs: 1 6638, 4 854; 3 line printers. *On-line satellite computer*: CDC 8090. *Remote processing features*: remote terminals (CDC 200) in N.S.W., Victoria and A.C.T.

Melbourne:
CDC 3300–operating system: Master 3.0; internal storage: 65K 24-bit words; magnetic tapes: 8 604; magnetic discs: 5 854; 1 line printer. *On line satellite computer*: CDC 160-A. *Remote processing features*: remote terminals (CDC 200) in Victoria.

Coding Languages
FORTRAN, COBOL, COMPASS (Assembly), ALGOL.

Contemplated Equipment
32K bits internal storage, 2 854 disc drives, remote terminals.

Services Available
Advice, preparation of data, software packages. Operate on a closed shop and block time basis.

Fields of Application
Scientific, statistical, commercial, production control, operations research, management.
Specialized areas: Linear programming, structural, civil and electrical engineering, transportation and urban planning.

Training
Short courses on applications software in all fields of specialization.

DATACARD COMPUTER SERVICES PTY. LTD.*
400 Sussex Street, Sydney, New South Wales 2000
Telephone: 211-2322

Officer
Bruce Gordon, *Managing Director*

Computer Installation
BULL GENERAL ELECTRIC GE 415–operating system: TOS; internal storage: 384K; magnetic tapes: 4 MTH300, 1 MTH403; 1 line printer.

Coding Languages
COBOL, Assembler.

Contemplated Equipment
IBM 360/30.

Services Available
Advice, operators, preparation of data, programming, systems analysis. Operate on a closed shop and block time basis.

Fields of Application
Commercial, production control, management.
Specialized areas: Advertising industry, hospital payrolls.

E.D.P. (AUST.) PTY. LTD.*
150 Albert Road, South Melbourne, Victoria 3205
Telephone: 699-1699

Also at:
64 Parramatta Road, Camperdown, N.S.W. 2050
Telephone: 660-5122

23 Leigh Street, Adelaide, S.A. 5000
Telephone: 51-6968

ELECTRONIC ASSOCIATES PTY. LTD.*
225 Park Street, South Melbourne, Victoria 3205

Officer
R. Cripps, *Southern Regional Manager*

Computer Installation
Analog and hybrid system.

Coding Languages
FORTRAN, HOI.

Service Available
Advice, preparation of data, programming, software packages, systems analysis, teaching. Operate on a self-service, open shop and block time basis.

Fields of Application
Scientific, statistical, production control, systems analysis, operational research.
Specialized areas: Linear programming, structural engineering, medical research, engineering research.

Training
Courses in hardware, software and analog and hybrid techniques.

EQUITABLE LIFE & GENERAL INSURANCE CO. LTD.*
80 Alfred Street, Milsons Point, Sydney, New South Wales
Telephone: 92-5821

Officer
Peter G. Avins

Computer Installation
HONEYWELL H120–internal storage: 16K bits; magnetic tapes: 4; 1 line printer.

Coding Languages
COBOL, Easycoder.

Contemplated Equipment
Honeywell 110 card system.

Services Available
Consultation, programming, operators, preparation of data, systems analysis. Operate on a self-service, open shop and block time basis.

Fields of Application
Statistical, management, systems analysis.

L. M. ERICSSON PTY. LTD.*
P.O. Box 41, Broadmeadows, Victoria 3046
Telephone: 309-2244

Computer Installation
ICL 1903A–operating system: GEORGE 2; internal storage: 65,536 24-bit words; magnetic tapes: 4; magnetic discs: 4; 2 line printers.

Coding Languages
PLAN 3, FORTRAN, COBOL, ALGOL.

Contemplated Equipment
Remote data collection and enquiry facilities.

Services Available
Advice, programming. Operate on a self-service basis.

Field of Application
Industrial management.
Specialized areas: Production control, inventory control.

Australia — Service Bureaux

HONEYWELL PTY. LTD.
203 New South Head Road, Edgecliff, New South Wales 2027
Telephone: 328-1911.

Also at: Canberra, Melbourne, Brisbane, Adelaide, Perth; and Wellington, New Zealand.

Computer Installation
Sydney:
BULL GENERAL ELECTRIC GE 265.
HONEYWELL H2200.
HONEYWELL H115.

Melbourne:
HONEYWELL H2200.
BULL GENERAL ELECTRIC GE 265.
HONEYWELL H1648.

Services Available
Advice, programming, preparation of data.

Fields of Application
Commercial, engineering.

IBM AUSTRALIA LIMITED
Data Processing Service
IBM Centre, Bradfield Highway and Kent Street, Sydney, New South Wales 2000
Telephone: 20531

Also at:
12-22 Rothschild Avenue, Rosebury, New South Wales 2081
Telephone: 663-0381

173 Fitzroy Street, St. Kilda, Victoria 3182
Telephone: 94-0501

95 North Terrace, Adelaide, South Australia 5000
Telephone: 51687

518 Brunswick Street, New Farm, Queensland 4005
Telephone: 58-2055

159 Adelaide Terrace, Perth, Western Australia 6000
Telephone: 25-8244

80 Northbourne Avenue, Canberra, A.C.T. 2601
Telephone: 48-8844

Enquiries about installations and services should be directed to the Head Office or relevant branch.

INDEPENDENT COMPUTING SERVICES PTY. LTD.*
424 St. Kilda Road, Melbourne, Victoria
Telephone: 267-2255

Officers
Colin Phillips, *Managing Director*
Noel Adams, *Technical Director*

Computer Installation
NCR Century 200 — operating system: B1; internal storage: 512K bits; magnetic tapes: 4 9-track, 1 7-track; magnetic discs: 6; 1 line printer.

ELLIOTT 4120 — internal storage: 24K 24-bit words; magnetic tapes: 5 7-track; 1 line printer.

Coding Languages
COBOL, ALGOL 60.

Services Available
Advice, programming, software packages, preparation of data, systems analysis. Operate on a closed shop and block time basis.

Fields of Application
Commercial, production control, accounting, management, systems analysis.
Specialized areas: Sales analysis, investment, structural engineering, bills of quantities, market research, stock control, management information systems.

INTERNATIONAL COMPUTERS (AUSTRALIA) PTY. LTD.
P.O. Box 300, North Sydney, New South Wales 2060

Also at:
568 St. Kilda Road, Melbourne, Victoria 3004
Telephone: 51-0241

316 Wakefield Street, Adelaide, South Australia 5000
Telephone: 233-022

8 Victoria Avenue, Perth, Western Australia 6000
Telephone: 219-481

33-46 Herschell Street, Brisbane, Queensland 4000
Telephone: 23-701

Newcastle Building, 120 Bunda Street, Civic Centre, Canberra, A.C.T. 2601
Telephone: 487-944

Kirksway House, Montpelier Retreat, Battery Point, Hobart, Tasmania 7000
Telephone: 34-2411

Enquiries about installations and services should be directed to the Head Office.

KEMPTHORNE INFORMATION SERVICES
142 Dorcas Street, South Melbourne, Victoria 3205

Officers
R. Leck, *General Manager*
F. Clough, *Operations Manager*
D. Clark, *Development Manager*

Computer Installation
NCR 315 100 — operating system: NEAT; internal storage: 120K; magnetic card handlers: 3 NCR 353-3; 1 line printer.

NCR Century 200 — internal storage: 32,768 bytes; 1 magnetic disc; 1 line printer.

Coding Languages
NEAT, BEST, COBOL, FORTRAN.

Services Available
Advice, programming, education and training, operators, software packages, documentation, preparation of data, systems analysis. Operate on a closed shop and block time basis.

Fields of Application
Statistical, commercial, production control, accounting, management.
Specialized area: Wholesaling inventory.

NATIONAL CASH REGISTER CO. LTD.*
14 York Street, Sydney, New South Wales

Also at: Melbourne, Victoria; Brisbane, Queensland; Adelaide, South Australia; Perth, Western Australia

Computer Installation
Sydney:
NCR 315.
NCR Century 200.

Australia – Service Bureaux

Melbourne:
NCR 315.

Brisbane:
NCR 315.

Adelaide:
NCR 315.

Perth:
NCR 315.

Services Available
Advice, operators, preparation of data, programming, software packages.

Fields of Application
Scientific, statistical and commercial.

SOUTHERN CROSS COMPUTER PTY. LTD.*
Ruthven Street, Toowoomba, Queensland 4350

Officers
W. Young, *Manager*
R. K. Smith, *Chief Programmer*

Computer Installation
ICL 1903–operating system: GEORGE 1S; internal storage: 16K words; magnetic tapes: 4 ICL; magnetic discs: 2 ICL; 1 line printer.

Coding Languages
COBOL, PLAN, FORTRAN.

Services Available
Advice, programming, software packages, preparation of data, systems analysis. Operate on a closed shop and block time basis.

Fields of Application
Statistical, commercial, production control, accounting, systems analysis.
Specialized area: Integrated book-keeping systems.

TECHNICOMPS PTY. LTD.*
P.O. Box 15, Chatswood, New South Wales 2067
Telephone: 41-5475, 41-3959

Officers
Robert Degotardi, *Managing Director*
John Hagan, *Director*

Computer Installation
IBM 1130–internal storage: 8K 16-bit words; magnetic disc.

Coding Language
FORTRAN IV.

Contemplated Equipment
1132 line printer.

Services Available
Advice, operators, preparation of data, programming, software packages, systems analysis. Operate on an open shop and block time basis.

Fields of Application
Scientific, technical.
Specialized areas: Road and highway design, surveying, land development.

THOMAS NATIONWIDE TRANSPORT COMPUTER CENTRE*
18 Burrows Road, St. Peters, New South Wales 2044
Telephone: 519-6741

Officers
Allan Redshaw, *Executive Director*
G. E. Wastle, *Manager*
R. Laurence, *Production Manager*

Computer Installation
NCR 315 100K (2)–internal storage: 130K bits each; CRAM units: 2 353/2; 2 line printers.

Coding Languages
NEAT, COBOL, BEST.

Contemplated Equipment
NCR Century 200 with satellite communications computer and CRT display terminals for on-line data preparation input and inquiry.

Services Available
Advice, operators, preparation of data, programming, systems analysis. Operate on a self-service, open shop and block time basis.

Fields of Application
Commercial, accounting, management.
Specialized areas: All of the above oriented to the transport industry.

UNITED DATA CENTRES PTY. LTD.*
A.D.C. Building, 189 Kent Street, Sydney, New South Wales
Telephone: 27-2005

Also at:
8 South Street, Rydalmere, New South Wales
Telephone: 638-5755

Officers
W. D. Sherington, *General Manager*
W. J. Regan, *Development Manager*
H. B. Fitz-Henry, *Customer Services Manager*
G. Firth, *Data Processing Manager*

Computer Installation
BURROUGHS B3500–operating system: MCP; internal storage: 50K bytes; magnetic tapes: 4; magnetic discs: 1; 1 line printer.

Coding Language
COBOL.

Contemplated Equipment
Additional core storage of 30K bytes; data bank of 100 million bytes; TC 500 terminal computers.

Services Available
Advice, programming, education and training, software packages, preparation of data, systems design, utility services. Operate on an open shop and utility usage basis.

Fields of Application
Commercial, accounting, inventory management, rural and industrial services.
Specialized areas: Payroll, debtors, wool accounting.

Training
Technical courses for utility users.

AUSTRIA

NATIONAL CENTRE

ÖSTERREICHISCHE STUDIENGESELLSCHAFT FÜR ATOMENERGIE GmbH
1082 Vienna, Lenaugasse 10
Telephone: 0222-427511 (Head Office);
0222-573649 (Research Centre)

Officers
Dr. Raphael Spann, *Commercial Director*
Prof. Dr. H. Grümm, *Scientific Director*
Dr. Bandion, *Co-ordinator*

Computer Installation
IBM 360/30 - operating system: DOS; internal storage: 512K bits; magnetic tapes: 4 IBM 2415/2; magnetic discs: 3 IBM 2311; 1 line printer. *On-line satellite computers:* PDP-8, PDP-11.

Coding Languages
FORTRAN IV, COBOL, PL/1, 360 Assembler.

Contemplated Equipment
IBM 1403 and control.

Services Available
Occasionally available on an open shop basis.

Field of Application
Scientific.
Specialized area: Process control computing.

EDUCATIONAL AND TRAINING INSTITUTION

DELTA-INSTITUT FÜR ARBEITSVEREINFACHUNG
1010 Vienna, Köllnerhofgasse 1
Telephone: 529388

Officer
Dr. Herbert Laszlo, *Director*

Services Available
Education and training.

Training
Public courses and special courses, held on the premises of firms, in electronic data processing and office organization.

UNIVERSITIES AND COLLEGES

HOCHSCHULE FÜR BODENKULTUR IN WIEN*
Rechenzentrum
1190 Vienna, Peter Jordan Strasse 82
Telephone: 34 25 00/307

Officers
Prof. Dr. Franz Ackerl
Frau Brigitte Weisser

Computer Installation
IBM 1130.

Services Available
Advice, operators, preparation of data. Operate on a self-service and closed shop basis. Available only for scientific research.

Fields of Application
Numerical calculations of scientific research of the University of Agriculture and Forestry.

HOCHSCHULE FÜR SOZIAL- UND WIRTSCHAFTSWISSENSCHAFTEN
Interfakultäres Rechenzentrum
4045 Linz, Auhof
Telephone: 31381, extension 429

Officers
Prof. Dr. Ing. Arno Schulz, *Director of Computing Centre*
Friedrich Roithmayr, *Manager*

Computer Installation
IBM 1130 – operating systems: Monitor, LEV; internal storage: 16,384 16-bit words; magnetic discs: 3 2310; 1 line printer.

Coding Languages
FORTRAN, PL/1, ALGOL, Assembler, RPG, APL, BASIC, GPSS.

Contemplated Equipment
Increased storage of 256K bytes, multiprogramming, time sharing, magnetic tapes and discs.

Service Available
Systems analysis. Operate on a closed shop and time-sharing basis.

Fields of Application
Scientific, statistical, systems analysis, operational research, administration.
Specialized areas: Sales analysis, linear programming.

Training
Studies in informatics.

LEOPOLD-FRANZENS UNIVERSITÄT INNSBRUCK*
Institut für Numerische Mathematik und Elektronische Informationsverarbeitung
6020 Innsbruck, Innrain 52
Telephone: 05222-22701

Officer
Prof. Dr. Rudolf Albrecht

Computer Installation
ZUSE Z 23 V – internal storage: 337,920 bits.

Coding Languages
Freiburger Code, Formelübersetzer, ALGOL.

Contemplated Equipment
Installation of a bigger computer.

Services Available
Advice, operators, preparation of data, programming, software packages. Operate on a self-service, closed shop and open shop basis.

Fields of Application
Mathematics, physics, engineering, statistics, games, etc.
Specialized area: Numerical analysis.

Austria – Universities and Colleges

TECHNISCHE HOCHSCHULE IN WIEN
Rechenzentrum
Abteilung Prozessrechenanlage
1040 Vienna, Gusshausstrasse 25
Telephone: 0222-657641/733

Officers
Prof. Dr. H. Stimmer, *Director*
Dr. M. Paul, *Manager*

Computer Installation
IBM 1800 – operating system: MPX; internal storage: 32K 16-bit words; magnetic discs: 3 2315; 1 line printer. *On-line satellite computers:* IBM System/7 and PDP-11/45. *Remote processing features:* 5 2740.

Coding Languages
FORTRAN, SAP (Assembler).

Contemplated Equipment
Core of 8K 16-bit words; IBM 1826 for TP with BSC.

Services Available
Advice, programming, education and training, operators, software packages, preparation of data, systems analysis. Operate on self-service, remote access and time-sharing basis. Available only to academic institutions.

Fields of Application
Scientific, production control, systems analysis.

Training
Programming languages and process computer utilization for students of electrical and mechanical engineering and computer science.

TECHNISCHE HOCHSCHULE IN WIEN
Rechenzentrum
Abteilung Digitalrechenanlage
1040 Vienna, Gusshausstrasse 25-29
Telephone: 0222-65 37 85

Officers
Dr. Hermann Bodenseher, *Hardware*
Dieter Schornböck, *Software*

Computer Installation
IBM 7040 – operating system: IBSYS (with integrated ALGOL 60 Compiler); internal storage: 32K 36-bit words; magnetic tapes: 5 IBM 729/5; magnetic disc: IBM 1301/1; 1 line printer.

Coding Languages
IBSYS – system including an ALGOL 60, FORTRAN IV, COBOL compiler.

Contemplated Equipment
CDC Cyber 74/16 – operating system: SCOPE; internal storage: 98K 60-bit words; 5 magnetic tapes; 4 magnetic discs; 2 line printers.

Services Available
Advice, education and training, operators, software packages. Operate on a closed shop basis. Priority given to academic and scientific institutions.

Fields of Application
Scientific, management, systems analysis.
Specialized areas: Structural engineering, computer science.

Training
Programming languages and computer utilization (digital and analog) for students of mathematics and other disciplines. Special two-year course in computer science.

GOVERNMENT ESTABLISHMENT

ÖSTERREICHISCHES STATISTISCHES ZENTRALAMT
1010 Vienna, Neue Burg
Telephone: 0222–524686

Officer
Prof. Dr. Lothar Bosse, *President*

Computer Installation
IBM 370/155 – operating systems: DOS,OS; internal storage: 768K bits; magnetic tapes: 6 3420; magnetic discs: 4 3330; 2 line printers.

Coding Languages
Assembler, PL/1, FORTRAN, COUNT, STAF.

Contemplated Equipment
Teleprocessing 3270, RJE (TSO,TCAM).

Services Available
Systems facilities, preparation of data. Available for selected governmental purposes.

Fields of Application
Statistical, management.

RESEARCH INSTITUTION

RECHENZENTRUM GRAZ*
8010 Graz, Steyrergasse 17
Telephone: 81-8-72, 87-0-98

Officers
Prof. Dr. Helmut Florian, *President*
Dr. Herbert Raimann, *Director*

Coding Languages
SPURT-Assembler, COBOL, FORTRAN, SORT/MERGE Generator, etc.

Services Available
For science, economy and public administration.

Fields of Application
Scientific and administrative, routine work, research work for departments at universities.
Specialized areas: Geodesy, numerical mathematics.

Training
Courses in COBOL and FORTRAN programming, UNIVAC 490 programming.

CONSULTANTS

KNIGHT WEGENSTEIN GmbH*
Vienna 1, Schottengasse 10
Telephone: 63 74 16

Services Available
Consultation, operators, preparation of data, programming, software packages, systems analysis.

Fields of Application
Real management information systems, all operating systems, process control.

UNTERNEHMENSBERATUNG DR. PARISINI
1010 Vienna, Christinengasse 4/15
Telephone: 0222-732151

Officer
Dr. Eberhard Parisini

Services Available
Advice, education and training, software packages, systems analysis.

Fields of Application
Commercial, accounting, systems analysis.
Specialized areas: Analysis, payroll.

Training
Austrian representative of the German "Akademie für Organization" providing basic and advanced courses in organization, and of the Swiss "IDV Institut für elektronische Datenverarbeitung" providing introductory courses in EDP and basic courses for EDP systems analysis. Also courses about standards of methods and techniques for developing application systems on EDP.

SERVICE BUREAUX

HONEYWELL BULL AG
Time-Sharing Service
1030 Vienna, Obere Donaustrasse 49-51

Officers
Dr. Peter Rihl, *Time-Sharing Manager*
Dr. Peter Kauer, *Time-Sharing Sales Manager*

Computer Installation
BULL GENERAL ELECTRIC GE 265 – operating system: MARK I; internal storage: 32K x 18 bits; magnetic tapes: 4; magnetic discs: 1; 1 line printer.

Coding Languages
FORTRAN, BASIC, ALGOL.

Services Available
Advice, programming, education and training, operators, software packages, documentation, systems analysis. Operate on a time-sharing basis.

Fields of Application
Scientific, statistical, management, operation research.
Specialized areas: Sales analysis, linear programming, investment analysis, structural engineering.

Training
Courses in the use of time-sharing system, all coding languages and special application packages.

INTERNATIONAL BÜROMASCHINEN GmbH*
Rechenzentrum
1080 Vienna, Plaristengasse 16

Also at:
8010 Graz, Lichtenfelsgasse 21
4010 Linz, Zollamtsstrasse 1
5024 Salzburg, Elisabethkai 58

Computer Installation
Vienna:
IBM 360/40 – operating systems: DOS, OS; internal storage: 128K bits; magnetic tapes: 4 2401; magnetic discs: 4 2311; 1 line printer.
IBM 360/40 – operating system: DOS; internal storage: 64K bits; magnetic tapes: 3 2401; magnetic discs: 2 2311; 1 line printer. *Remote processing features:* 2701-2780.

Graz:
IBM 360/20 – operating system: DPS; internal storage: 16K bytes; magnetic discs: 2 2311; 1 line printer.

Linz:
IBM 1401.

Coding Languages
COBOL, FORTRAN, PL/1, Assembler.

Services Available
Advice, operators, preparation of data, programming. Operate on a closed shop and block time basis.

Fields of Application
Commercial, accounting, technical, statistical.

SIEMENS GmbH*
Vertrieb Datentechnik-Rechenzentrum
1210 Vienna, Siemenstrasse 88
Telephone: 391531

Officers
Dipl. Ing. Leeb, *General Manager*
Herr Ritzinger, *Systems Manager*

Computer Installation
SIEMENS 4004/45 – operating systems: tape, tape-disc, disc; internal storage: 128K bits; magnetic tapes: 8; magnetic discs: 4; 2 line printers.

Coding Languages
Assembler, COBOL, LPG, FORTRAN, ALGOL.

Services Available
Advice, preparation of data, programming, systems analysis. Operate on a closed and open shop and block time basis.

Fields of Application
Commercial, statistical, scientific.

Training
Courses on system specification of the 4004, operating systems, Assembler, peripheral units and problem languages used at the centre.

SPERRY RAND UNIVAC*
1071 Vienna, Mariahilferstrasse 20
Telephone: 93 96 26

Officers
F.C. Grohs, *Director*
Miss Ute Fischer, *Director, Product Support*
W. Stert, *Director, Customer Engineering*

Computer Installation
UNIVAC 9400 – operating system: DOS; internal storage: 512K bits; magnetic tapes: 6 Uniservo VIC; magnetic discs: 4 8411; 1 line printer. *Remote processing features:* DCS.

UNIVAC 9300 – operating systems: TOS, DOS; internal storage: 256K bits; magnetic tapes: 6 Uniservo VIC; magnetic discs: 4 8411, 2 8410; 1 line printer. *Remote processing features:* DCS.

Coding Languages
Original machine languages.

Services Available
Advice, operators, preparation of data, programming, software packages, systems analysis. Operate on a closed shop basis.

Fields of Application
Scientific, commercial, accounting, management, systems analysis.

Training
Complete and extensive training for systems analysis, programmers and operators.

Austria — Service Bureaux

VEREINIGTE ÖSTERREICHISCHE EISEN- UND STAHLWERKE AG
4010 Linz/Donau, Postfach 2
Telephone: 07222-585

Officers
Otto Zich
Gernot Hillbrand

Computer Installation
IBM 370/145–operating systems: OS/MFT, HASP; internal storage: 512K bytes; magnetic tapes: 8 9-track; magnetic discs 6 3330, 3 2319; 2 line printers. *Remote processing features:* IBM 2780 and 2741 terminals, teletype.

Coding Languages
PL/1, FORTRAN, COBOL, RPG, Assembler, MARK IV.

Contemplated Equipment
A plotter.

Services Available
Advice, preparation of data, systems analysis. Operate on an open shop basis.

Fields of Application
Scientific, production control, operational research. *Specialized areas:* Linear programming, investment, structural engineering.

VORARLBERGER RECHENZENTRUM GmbH*
Klaudiastrasse 6, 6850 Dornbirn
Telephone: (05572) 4117

Officers
Engelbert Bader, *Director and Manager*
Dipl. Vw. Siegfried Gasser, *Director and Manager of sales and administration.*

Computer Installation
IBM 360/30–operating system: DOS; internal storage: 64K bits; magnetic discs: 2314; 1 line printer.

Coding Languages
PL/1, Assembler.

Contemplated Equipment
MDS Tape-unit.

Services Available
Advice, operators, programming, systems analysis. Operate on a block time, open and closed shop basis.

Field of Application
Commercial.
Specialized areas: Payroll, accounting.

Services Available
Advice, operators, preparation of data, programming, software packages, systems analysis.

Fields of Application
Scientific, commercial.

BANGLADESH

GOVERNMENT ESTABLISHMENT

ATOMIC ENERGY CENTRE
P.O. Box 164, Ramna, Dacca 2
Telephone: 283150–4

Officers
M. Haniffudin Miah, *Head of Computer Division*

Computer Installation
IBM 1620–operating system: Monitor I; internal storage: 60K digits; magnetic discs: 4 1311.

Coding Languages
FORTRAN II, SPS.

Contemplated Equipment
IBM 1627 plotter; IBM 1443 printer.

Services Available
Consultation, programming, education and training, systems analysis. Operate on a self-service basis. Normally available only to research and educational organizations; occasionally to commercial interests.

Fields of Application
Scientific, statistical, systems analysis, operational research.

Training
Three-four week course on FORTRAN programming and numerical analysis for scientific staff of Bangladesh Atomic Energy Commission.

BAHAMA ISLANDS

SERVICE BUREAU

IBM WORLD TRADE CORPORATION*
Nassau, New Providence Island

Computer Installation
IBM 1401.

BELGIUM

NATIONAL CENTRE

CENTRE DE TRAITEMENT AUTOMATIQUE DE L'INFORMATION
Dekenstraat 2, B-3000 Louvain

Officers
M. Verhelst, *President*
J. Van Hoorde, *Secretary*
J. H. Mutton, *Treasurer*

Services Available
Conferences, courses.

Field of Application
Management.

EDUCATIONAL AND TRAINING INSTITUTIONS

ÉCOLE ROYALE MILITAIRE
Centre d' Informatique
Avenue de la Renaissance 30, B-1040 Brussels

Officer
Gennart Govin, *Director*

Computer Installation
IBM 360/30–operating system: DOS; internal storage: 524,288 bits; magnetic tapes: 2 2475; magnetic discs: 3 2307; 1 line printer.

Coding Languages
PL/1, FORTRAN, Assembler.

Services Available
Advice, programming, education and training, computer time. Operate on a self-service and closed shop basis.

Fields of Application
Scientific, statistical, operation research.
Specialized area: Compiler writing.

MANAGEMENT CENTRE EUROPE–BRUSSELS*
Avenue des Arts 4, Brussels 4
Telephone: 19-03-96

Officers
Dr. W. O. Flechtner, *Managing Director*

Services Available
Education and training.

Training
Three-day courses in management information systems, introduction to EDP for managers, EDP for the smaller company, planning and designing computer based management information systems, application of quantitative techniques for management decision making, data communications, using data centres and service bureaux for business data processing, management of the data processing function.

UNIVERSITIES AND COLLEGES

FACULTÉ POLYTECHNIQUE DE MONS*
Centre d'Informatique
Rue de Houdain 9, Mons
Téléphone: Mons (65) 381 91

Dirigeant
D. Ribbens, *Docteur en sciences appliqu*ées

Equipement
IBM 1130–mémoire interne: 32K bits; disques magnétiques: 3 2310; 1 imprimante.

Langages de Programmation
ALGOL 60, FORTRAN II.

Services Fournis
Conseils, opérateurs, software packages, systems analysis. Fonctionnement en porte ouverte. Acceptent d'examiner tous les problèmes scientifiques et de gestion dans les limites de capacité de l'ordinateur.

Domaines d'Application
Tous les problèmes généralement confiés aux ordinateurs, et pour lesquels les programmes existent. Par ex.: méthodes de résolution des équations algébriques et différentielles; calcul matriciel; programmation linéaire; etc.
Domaines spécialisés: Mise au point de programmes spéciaux pour le synthèse des réseaux; compilation de LISP I-V; théorie des langages.

Formation
Programmation, langages algorithmiques divers.

KATHOLIEKE UNIVERSITEIT TE LEUVEN
Afdeling Toegepaste Wiskunde en Programmatie
Celestijnenlaan 200B, B-3030 Heverlee
Telephone: (016) 35821

Officers
L. Buyst, *Professor*
R. Piessens, *Assistant Professor*
Y. Willems, *Assistant Professor*

Computer Installations
The Applied Mathematics and Programming Division uses the University's IBM 370/155.

Coding Languages
FORTRAN, ALGOL, PL/1, FORMAC, LISP.

Services Available
Advice, education and training, software packages. Operate on remote access and open shop basis.

Fields of Application
Scientific, systems analysis.
Specialized area: Medical research.

Training
Engineer courses in computer science (3 years of specialization after 2 years of general courses in mathematics and physics) and applied mathematics (one post-graduate year); Doctor's course in applied sciences (including applied mathematics and computer science).

KATHOLIEKE UNIVERSITEIT TE LEUVEN*
Centre for Operations Research and Econometrics
De Croylaan 54, B-3030 Heverlee
Telephone: (016) 32601

Dirigeant
Dr. E. van Broekhoven

Equipement
Fait partie du Rekencentrum – Centre de Calcul de l'Université.

Langages de Programmation
ALGOL, FORTRAN.

Services Fournis
Conseils, programmation, software packages, documentation. Fonctionnement en self-service. Services fournis aux économistes de l'Université.

Domaines d'Application
Econométrie, économie mathématique, recherche opérationnelle.

KATHOLIEKE UNIVERSITEIT TE LEUVEN
Institute of Applied Economics
Dekenstraat 2, B-3000 Louvain
Telephone: (016) 28654

Field of Application
Management.

Training
Course leading to a Licenciate in Management Informatics.

KATHOLIEKE UNIVERSITEIT TE LEUVEN
Rekencentrum
De Croylaan 52, B-3030 Heverlee
Telephone: (016) 34931

Officers
Professor H. Florin, *President*
Professor H. Van de Vel, *Scientific Director*
R. Robeyns, *Administrative Director*

Computer Installation
IBM 370/155–operating system: OS/MVT; internal storage: 1,024K bytes; magnetic tapes: 8 3420; magnetic discs: 8 3330, 6 2314; 4 line printers.

IBM 360/40–operating system: DOS; internal storage: 24K bits; magnetic tapes: 5 2401; magnetic discs: 4 2314, 2 2311; 1 line printer.

Coding Languages
FORTRAN and WATFIV, COBOL, ALGOL, PL/1, Assembler, APL.

Contemplated Equipment
IBM 370/158.

Services Available
Advice, programming, education and training, software packages. Operate on a remote access, closed shop and time-sharing basis. In principle, service available only to university students and research workers (and university management).

Fields of Application
Scientific, statistical, accounting, management.

Training
Technical courses on programming and operating systems.

RIJKSUNIVERSITEIT TE GENT*
Rekenlaboratorium
Rozier 6, Gent

Dirigeant
Prof. Dr. C.C. Grosjean, *Director du Laboratoire de Calcul*

Equipement
IBM 360/30–système d'opération: DOS: mémoire interne: 65.536 bytes: disques magnétiques: 2 2311 amovibles; 1 imprimante.
IBM 1620–mémoire interne: 20.000 positions de mémoire décimales.

Langages de Programmation
FORTRAN IV, Assembler PL/1, SPS.

Equipement Projeté
Un printer rapide; six unités de bandes magnétiques.

Services Fournis
Conseils opérateurs, préparation des données, programmation. Fonctionnement en self-service et en porte fermée et en porte ouverte. Le centre effectue des calculs pour des institutions ou des chercheurs en dehors de l'Université, pour autant que les problèmes posés soient de nature scientifique.

Domaines d'Applications
Le laboratoire résout tous les problèmes qui lui sont présentés, pour autant que leur envergure ne dépasse pas la capacité de ses ordinateurs.

Formation
Enseignement d'un cours facultatif concernant l'emploi des machines du laboratoire ainsi que les méthodes principales du calcul numérique.

UNIVERSITÉ CATHOLIQUE DE LOUVAIN
Institut d'Astronomie et de Géophysique G. Lemaitre
Bâtiment Science 1, Chemin de Cyclotron 2,
1348 Louvain-la-Neuve

Dirigeant
Prof. O. Godart, *Directeur*

Equipement
PDP-8/E–mémoire interne: 8K mots de 12 bits; 1 imprimante par ligne. *Transmission des donn*ées *à distance:* ADC.

Langages de Programmation
FOCAL, BASIC, FORTRAN, PAL III, MACRO 8.

Services Fournis
Enseignement et formation, préparation des données, programmation. Fonctionnement en self-service et en porte ouverte. Fournis dans le domaine scientifique seulement.

Domaine d'Application
Scientifique.
Domaines spécialisés: Astronomie et astrophysique, géophysique interne et externe, météorologie, mécanique céleste et cosmologie.

VRIJ HOGER TECHNISCH INSTITUUT (VHTI)
Doorniksesteenweg 145, B-8500 Kortrijk
Telephone: (056) 17072

Officer
J. Vandenbulcke, *Director*

Computer Installations
PDP-8–operating system: OS; internal storage: 12K words; magnetic tapes: 2 DEC.

Coding Languages
FORTRAN, ALGOL, BASIC, PL/1, Assembler.

Fields of Application
Scientific, statistical, commercial, systems analysis.
Specialized areas: Sales analysis, linear programming, analysis, structural engineering, medical research, education.

Training
Diploma in informatics for programmers/analysts.

GOVERNMENT ESTABLISHMENTS

CAISSE GÉNÉRALE D'ÉPARGNE ET DE RETRAITE
Rue Fossé aux Loups 48, B-1000 Brussels

Officers
L. Aerts, *Vice-President*
J. Minet, *First Adviser*
J. D'Hooghe, *Chief of EDP Department*
M. Geerts, *Chief of Systems Concept Bureau*

Computer Installation
IBM 370/155(2)–operating system: OS; internal storage: 1,024K bytes each; magnetic tapes: 10 3420/7, 1 2415/4 each; magnetic discs: 3 3330; 2 line printers each.
Remote processing features: 1 card puncher, 2 card readers, Memorex 1603.

Coding Languages
COBOL, Assembler.

Contemplated Equipment
2 IBM 370/158; 50 intelligent, modular terminals (including 100 teller terminals).

Services Available
Programming, operators, preparation of data, systems analysis, execution. Operate on self-service, remote access and closed shop basis. Outside customers are limited to some governmental institutions.

Fields of Application
Accounting, management.
Specialized area: Payroll.

CENTRE D'ÉTUDE DE L'ÉNERGIE NUCLÉAIRE*
Administration Centrale
Avenue Eug. Plasky 144, B-1040 Bruxelles
Téléphone: (02) 35-61-25

Aussi:
2400 Mol
Téléphone: (014) 31801

Dirigeants
M.J. Goens, *Directeur Général*
M. S. Amelinckx, *Directeur Général Adjoint*

Equipement
IBM 360/44–système d'opération: DOS-RAX; mémoire interne: 1,024K bits; bandes magnétiques: 2 2401/1; disques magnétiques: 3 2311; 1 imprimante.

Langages de Programmation
FORTRAN IV, COBOL, Assembler.

Services Fournis
Etude, programmation, perforation, software.

Domaines d'Application
Calcul matriciel, solution numérique d'équations différentielles et aux dérivées partielles, calcul de fonctions de Bessel.
Domaines spécialisés: Etudes de réacteurs nucléaires.

INSTITUT NATIONAL DE STATISTIQUE
Rue de Louvain 44, B-1000 Bruxelles
Téléphone: 13.96.50

Dirigeants
A. Dillaerts, *Inspecteur Général*
R. van den Abeele, *Informaticien Directeur*

Equipement
BULL GENERAL ELECTRIC GE 425–système d'opération: DPS; mémoire interne: 32K mots (4 caractères); bandes magnétiques: 5 556 BPI; disques magnétiques: 4DSU 160; 1 imprimante.

BULL GENERAL ELECTRIC GE 425–système d'opération: DPS; mémoire interne: 32K mots (4 caractères); disques magnétiques: 4 DSU 160.
Calculateur satellite en ligne: DATANET 30.
Transmission des données à distance: 64 DATANETS on line (Liaison locale directe), mode conversationnelle.

BULL GENERAL ELECTRIC GE 415–système d'opération: DPS; mémoire interne: 32K mots; bandes magnétiques: 5 556 BPI; disques magnétiques: 4 DSU 160; 1 imprimante.

IBM 370/155–système d'opération: OS; mémoire interne: 1,024K bytes; bandes magnétiques: 8 (3420 and 2401); disques magnétiques: 4 2314, 8 3330; 1 imprimante.

IBM 360/20–système d'opération: IPS; mémoire interne: 16K bytes; bandes magnétiques: 5 2415; 1 imprimante.

Langages de Programmation
BAL, MAL, COBOL, RPG, FORTRAN, PL/1, Assembler.

Equipement Projeté
Philips P1400.

Services Fournis
Conseils, programmation, opérateurs, documentation, préparation des données. Fonctionnement à porte fermée. Services fournis seulement aux établissements ou agences gouvernementaux.

Domaine d'Application
Statistique.

INSTITUT ROYAL MÉTÉOROLOGIQUE DE BELGIQUE (I.R.M.)*
Avenue Circulaire 3, Uccle, B-1180 Bruxelles
Téléphone: 7409-41

Dirigeant
Prof. J. Van Isacker, *Directeur du Laboratoire de Calcul*

Equipement
IBM 7040–mémoire interne: 16K bits; bandes magnétiques: 4; 1 imprimante.

Langages de Programmation
FORTRAN IV, MAP.

Services Fournis
Accessible aux institutions scientifiques élaborant leur propres programmes.

Domaines d'Application
Météorologie–Prévisions numériques; recherches sur la dynamique et l'énergétique de l'atmosphère.

MINISTÈRE DES TRAVAUX PUBLICS*
Laboratoire de Recherches Hydrauliques
Berchemlei 115, B-2200 Borgerhout
Téléphone: 03/353820

Dirigeant
A. Sterling, *Directeur du Laboratoire*
E. Smets, *Chargé du centre de calcul*

Equipement
NCR Century 200–mémoire interne: 8K mots de 32 bits; bandes magnétiques; disques magnétiques: 6; 1 imprimante.

Langages de Programmation
FORTRAN, NEAT 3.

Equipement Projeté
Table traçante digitale.

Services Fournis
Programmation, préparation des données, systems analysis. Fonctionnement à porte fermée; services fournis au Ministère des Travaux Publics.

Domaines d'Application
Scientifique et technique. Calculs dans les domaines de l'hydrodynamique, de l'hydraulique, du génie civil concernant les ouvrages d'art hydrauliques projetés par le Ministére des Travaux Publics.
Domaines spécialisés: Les marées terrestres, maritimes et fluviales.

MINISTERIE VAN OPENBARE WERKEN
Dienst voor Programmatie, Informatie en Statistiek
Residence Palace, Wetstraat 155, B-1040 Brussels

Officer
G. Llaeys, *Director*

Computer Installation
SIEMENS 4004/45–operating system: DOS; internal storage: 128K bits; magnetic tapes: 9; magnetic discs: 9; 2 line printers. *Remote processing features:* 4 videos.

Coding Languages
Assembler, COBOL, FORTRAN (RPG).

Contemplated Equipment
Siemens 4004/155 with time-sharing expected for 1975.

Services Available
Advice, programming, education and training, software packages, documentation, preparation of data, systems analysis. Operate on open shop basis.

Fields of Application
Scientific, statistical, accounting, management, systems analysis, operational research.
Specialized areas: Linear programming, analysis, structural engineering, town and country planning.

Training
University diploma courses in Civil Engineering and Applied Mathematics, and in Business Administration; informatics courses through self study.

SOCIETÉ NATIONALE TERRIENNE
Avenue de la Toison d'Or 72, B-1060 Brussels

Officer
Dr. U.L.W. Van Twembeke, *Chief Engineer – Director*

Computer Installation
IBM 360/22–operating system: DOS; internal storage: 32K bits; magnetic tapes: 2 2415; magnetic discs: 2 2311; 1 line printers. *On-line satellite computer:* 1. *Remote processing feature:* 1.

Coding Languages
FORTRAN IV, RPG, Assembler.

Contemplated Equipment
IBM 370/125.

Services Available
Programming. Operate on self-service basis.

Fields of Application
Scientific, production control, operational research.
Specialized area: Cartographic research.

RESEARCH INSTITUTION

LITTON INDUSTRIES*
Mellonics Systems Development Division
Boulevard de Waterloo 39, Brussels 1
Telephone: 12-79-30

Officers
Bernard Jensen, *General Manager of European Operations*

Services Available
Consultation, systems analysis.

Fields of Application
Systems engineering, process control, information storage and retrieval, time-sharing and executive systems, etc.

CONSULTANTS

CABINET GILLES
Avenue Jupiter 131, B-1190 Brussels

Coding Language
COBOL

Services Available
Advice, programming, education and training, software packages, documentation, systems analysis.

Fields of Application
Commercial, accounting, management, systems analysis.
Specialized area: analysis.

Training
Courses in Basic Concepts and System Design.

CASE-CEGOS*
Boulevard St. Lazare 10, Bruxelles

Services Fournis
Conseils, programmation, software packages, analyse de systèmes.

Domaines d'Application
Tous domaines.

CENTRE D'ANALYSE ET DE PROGRAMMATION/ BELGIQUE S. A. (CAP)*
Rue Marc 16, Bruxelles 1
Téléphone: (02) 18-76-74

Dirigeants
Jacques Lescault
Philippe Sancke

Services Fournis
Conseils, programmation,software packages, systems analysis.

Domaines d'Application
Gestion, calcul scientifique, systèmes–temps réel, software, recherche et développement.

CENTRE POUR LE TRAITEMENT DE L'INFORMATION (CENTI BENELUX)*
Avenue des Arts 36, B-1040 Bruxelles
Téléphone: 13.20.52

Dirigeants
C. Boch, *Président*
J. C. Rougier, *Directeur*

Langages de Programmation
Tous les langages de troisième génération.

Services Fournis
Conseils, programmation, enseignement et formation, software packages, documentation, systems analysis. Fonctionnement à porte ouverte; services fournis à tous utilisateurs d'ensembles électroniques et tous candidats à la formation en informatique.

Domaines d'Application
Scientifique, statistique, contrôle des processus, comtabilité, gestion, systems analysis, recherche opérationnelle.
Domaines spécialisés: Assistance technique et formation, édition de manuels pédagogiques et de dossiers standards d'application et de programmation.

Formation
Initiation, Assembleur 360, COBOL, FORTRAN, PL/1, Analyse.

COMPUTER SCIENCES INTERNATIONAL S.A.*
Place du Champ de Mars 5, B-1050 Brussels
Telephone: (02) 136157

Officers
Dr. M. I. Montana, *President and General Manager*
M.L. Pulliam, *Vice-President, Operations Development*

Services Available
Consultation, programming, software packages, systems analysis, education and training, operators, preparation of data.

Fields of Application
Systems analysis, systems software, design and production, application systems, design and production, computer applications hardware and communications.
Specialized areas: Design of large-scale systems, project management, compiler writing, management information systems, real-time application.

Training
Standard courses in computer concepts, utilization of the computer, systems and programming project management and systems analysis and design. Also education system packages, requirements analysis, programme design, support services and specialized course development.

INSTITUT DE GESTION ET D'ORGANISATION S.A.
Avenue de Tervueren 194, Bruxelles 15
Téléphone: (02) 70-84-30

Services Fournis
Conseils et analyse de systèmes.

Domaines d'Application
Commercial, contrôle de production, comtabilité, gestion et analyse de systèmes.

Formation
Séminaires notamment sur la gestion intégrée (2 jours).

ARTHUR D. LITTLE S.A.*
Avenue des Arts 56, B-1040 Brussels
Telephone: 11-59-58

Officers
Basil Carmody
Joseph Leshick
Bret Tucker

Services Available
Diversified consulting in management and operational systems.

Fields of Application
Corporate information systems evaluation, planning and organization, computer system feasibility studies, computer equipment evaluations, EDP market research, systems analysis and design, inventory, production and distribution control, operational research and statistical analysis.

ORGANISATION SERVICE S.C.*
Avenue Kersbeek 331, Bruxelles 18
Téléphone: 76-64-39

Dirigeant
Henri Delvigne

Services Fournis
Conseils, analyse de systèmes.

Domaines d'Application
Analyse et aide du démarrage d'ordinateurs, expérience particulière série 360.

P.A. MANAGEMENT CONSULTANTS S.A.
Avenue Louise 386, Brussels 5
Telephone: 010-32-2, 48-65-55

Services Available
Consultation, programming, software packages, systems analysis.

Fields of Application
Comprehensive consultancy service to international management—from general investigations on an overall company or industry basis to specific tasks confined to one limited function.
Specialized areas: Management sciences (OR, EDP, and programming), company strategy, market research, personnel services, export marketing, finance and acquisition, etc.

URWICK INTERNATIONAL*
Rue de la Loi 64, B-1040 Brussels
Telephone: 12.59.02

Officer
D. F. Phillips, *Resident Partner*

Services Available
Consultation, education and training, software packages, systems analysis.

Fields of Application
Corporate planning, marketing, management information systems, environmental studies, technological forecasting, mergers and acquisitions, product development and diversification, planning programming and budgeting, financial planning and control, management training, operational research, data processing systems, computer simulation, computer equipment evaluation, project management, technology management, industrial engineering, control engineering, executive selection.

Training
Courses of one to six weeks in general management, management in research and development, management for the production executive, product planning and control, mathematics in management, computer project management, computer systems analysis, management of computer programming, site management in the construction industry.

WERNER ASSOCIATES INC.*
Avenue Louise 137, Brussels 5
Telephone: 37-71-75

Officer
Raoul Verret, *Executive Vice-President*

Services Available
Consultation.

Fields of Application
General management, manufacturing and technical, marketing services, administration, EDP feasibility studies, personnel.
Specialized area: Services to the textile industry.

CENTRE D'INFORMATIQUE GÉNÉRALE, S.A.
Rue des Colonies 35, 1000 Bruxelles
Téléphone: 02/13.61.95

Dirigeants
M. W. Kirkpatrick, *Administrateur délégué*
M. J. Francotte, *Directeur-Général*

Equipement
IBM 360/50 (2)—systèmes d'opération: OS, DOS, MFT II, MVT; mémoires internes: 512K bits; bandes magnétiques: 8 2401/5; disques magnétiques: 3 memorex 3660; 3 imprimantes. *Transmission des données à distance:* chaque 360/50 est équipé de 2702.

Langages de Programmation
COBOL, FORTRAN, PL/1, BAL.

Services Fournis
Conseils, programmation, enseignement et formation, opérateurs, software packages, documentation, préparation des données, analyse de systèmes et facilities management. Fonctionnement à porte ouverte et accès à distance. Time-sharing terminals sur les lieux.

Formation
Computer Concepts. Stages universitaires de courte durée.

CENTRUM VOOR INFORMATIE MANAGEMENT N.V.
Tavernierkaai 4, 2000 Antwerpen

Officers
K. Henneman, *Data Processing Manager*
G. van Belleghem, *Sales Manager*

Computer Installation
IBM 370/145—operating system: OS; internal storage: 256K bytes; magnetic tapes: 3 BASF 6340; magnetic discs: 4 IBM 3330; 1 line printer.

Coding Languages
Assembler, COBOL ANS, FORTRAN IV.

Services Available
Advice, programming, education and training, software packages, preparation of data, systems analysis. Operate on a closed shop basis.

Fields of Application
Commercial, accounting.
Specialized areas: Sales analysis, payroll.

DATACRAFT INTERNATIONAL
Boulevard du Souverain 209, B-1160 Brussels
Telephone: 730006

Officer
T. J. Lawrence, *Director of International Marketing*

Computer Installation
DATACRAFT DC6024/5—operating system: DOS; internal storage: 65K x 24 bits; magnetic disc: 1; 1 line printer. *Remote processing features:* interactive processing.

Services Available
Advice, programming, education and training, systems analysis. Operate on open shop and time-sharing basis.

Fields of Application
Scientific, production control.
Specialized areas: Medical research, engineering research.

ELECTRONIC ASSOCIATES INC.
European Continental Headquarters
Rue des Palais 116-120, B-1030 Brussels
Telephone: (02) 16.81.15

Officers
Dr. Ernst B. Naschke, *General Manager — European Operations*
W. Claes, *Director, European Computation Centre*
H. Courbon, *European Continental Sales Manager*

Computer Installation
PACER 100—operating systems: disc and magnetic tape; internal storage: 512K bits; magnetic tapes: AMPEX 9-track; magnetic discs: 1; 1 line printer. *Remote processing features:* Graphic terminals.

PACER 681 (analog)—parallel processor integrated with above to form a hybrid system PACER 600.

Coding Languages
Assembler (symbolic), FORTRAN IV, HOI.

Contemplated Equipment
Connection of equipment to terminals to promote remote access capabilities.

Services Available
Advice, programming, education and training, operators, software packages, documentation, systems analysis. Operate on open shop and time-sharing basis.

Fields of Application
Scientific, production control, systems analysis, simulation/design.
Specialized areas: Analysis, medical research, partial differential and/or differential equations.

Training
Training courses for hybrid application system analysts.

HONEYWELL BULL
Avenue Marnix 28, 1050 Bruxelles
Téléphone: 02/13.68.60

Belgium — Consultants

Dirigeants
Hugues E. Regout, *Directeur Général*
Philippe d'Ursel, *Secrétaire Général*
Jean Deschuyter, *Directeur Commercial*
Victor Vanhoof, *Directeur Service Entretien*
Christian Blondeau, *Directeur du Service Time-Sharing*
Alex Pousseur, *Directeur du Centre de Formation en Informatique.*

Equipement
BULL GENERAL ELECTRIC GE 265—système d'opération: Time-Sharing; mémoire interne: 16K + 16K bits; bandes magnétiques: 4 MTH 301; disques magnétiques: 1 DS 20; 1 imprimante. *Calculateurs satellites en ligne:* 1 unité arithmétique. *Transmission des données à distance:* en Time-Sharing.
BULL GENERAL ELECTRIC GE 120—mémoire interne: 16K bits; bandes magnétiques: 5 MTH 163; disques magnétiques: 2 DSU 130, 3 DSU 160; 1 imprimante.

Services Fournis
Enseignement et formation, software d'application. Fonctionnement à time-sharing.

Domaines d'Application
Tout l'éventail.

Formation
Formation des responsables de centres informatiques, des concepteurs, des analystes, des programmeurs et du personnel d'exploitation; formation des responsables de départements utilisateurs du service interne informatique et de leurs correspondants avec ce service; formation des professeurs enseignant l'informatique.

IBM OF BELGIUM S.A.
Rue Royale 67, B-1000 Brussels 1
Telephone: (02) 19.38.80

Also at: Antwerp, Charleroi, Hasselt, Courtrai, Ghent and Liège.

Computer Installation
Brussels:
IBM 370/155.
IBM 360/50.
IBM 360/40.
IBM 360/20 (2).
IBM 1130.

Antwerp
IBM 360/25.

Ghent
IBM 1401.

Liège:
IBM 360/20.

Services Available
Advice, operators, preparation of data, programming, software packages, systems analysis, time-sharing.

Fields of Application
Scientific and commercial.

NCR BELGIUM*
Place Surlet de Chokier 15, B-1000 Bruxelles
Téléphone: 19.04.68

Dirigeant
M. Lebrun, *Directeur du Centre*

Equipement
NCR 315—mémoire interne: 10.000 slabs; cartes magnétiques: 2 CRAM; 1 imprimante.

ORDA–B
Bierbeekstraat 84, B-3040 Korbeek 10

Officers
J. H. Mutton, *General Manager*
M. Flenneman, M. Vaw Belleghem, M. De Coster, *Managers*

Computer Installation
IBM 370/155—operating system: OS; internal storage: 1,024K bits; magnetic tapes: 8; magnetic discs: 8 3330; 4 line printers.
Remote processing features: RJE.

IBM 370/145—operating system: OS; internal storage: 248K bits; magnetic tapes: 2; magnetic discs: 4; 1 line printer.

Coding Languages
COBOL, Assembler, FORTRAN.

Contemplated Equipment
IBM 370/158.

Services Available
Advice, programming, education and training, preparation of data, systems analysis. Operate on open shop basis.

Fields of Application
Commercial, accounting, systems analysis.
Specialized area: Medical research.

REGIE T.T. INFORMATIQUE
Rue Carli 4, B-1140 Brussels
Telephone: (02) 15.88.70, extension 25341

Officers
M. Serrure, *Director General*
M. Brunin, *Chief Engineer – Director the Administration*
M. Hendrickx, *Chief Engineer – Director*
M. Vandecasteele, *Director*

Computer Installation
SIEMENS 4004/45 (10)—operating system: DOS; internal storage: 128K (8), 256K (2); magnetic tapes: 8 442; magnetic discs: 5-10 4579; 2 line printers. *Remote processing features:* CCM/Videos, T200 terminals.

SIEMENS 4004/46—operating system: TSOS; internal storage: 256K bits; magnetic tapes: 5 442; magnetic discs: 8 4579; 1 line printer. *Remote processing features:* CCM/Video, T200 terminals.

Coding Languages
Assembler, COBOL, FORTRAN, RPG, BASIC.

Service Available
Programming. Operate on remote access and open shop basis.

Fields of Application
Statistical, commercial, accounting, management.

S.A. SIEMENS N.V.
Centre de Calcul
Chaussée de Charleroi 116, Bruxelles 6

Equipement
SIEMENS 4004/45—mémoire interne: 196K bytes; bandes magnétiques: 9-pistes; disques magnétiques: 4 4004/564, 1 4580, 4 4581; 2 imprimantes.

Langages de Programmation
Assembler, COBOL, FORTRAN, ALGOL.

Services Fournis
Conseils, opérateurs, programmation, software packages, analyse de systèmes. Fonctionnement en self-service, en porte fermée, en porte ouverte et en abonnement machine.

Domaines d'Application
Scientifique, statistique, commercial.

UCC-AUTOMATION CENTER S.A.
Quai des Charbonnages, 60-62, B1080 Brussels
Telephone: (02) 28.31.57

Officers
D. Pauwels, *Center Manager*
F. Devriese, *Head of Special Projects*
F. Bernabe, *Head of Program-Analysis Service*
M. Schollaert, *Head of Production Service*

Computer Installation
BULL GENERAL ELECTRIC GE 415–internal storage: 64K bits; magnetic tapes: 5 MTH 7-track; 1 line printer.

IBM 1401–internal storage: 8K *ferrites;* magnetic tapes: 1 729/IV 7-track; 1 line printer. *Remote processing feature:* 1231 card reader.

IBM 370/135–operating system: DOS/VS; internal storage 192K bits; magnetic tapes: 5 3420/3 (4 9-track, 1 7-track); 1 line printer.

Coding Languages
COBOL, Autocoder.

Services Available
Advice, programming, preparation of data, systems analysis, production results. Operate on self-service and time-sharing basis.

Fields of Application
Statistical, commercial, production control, accounting, systems analysis, addressing, payroll.
Specialized area: Sales analysis.

BRAZIL

EDUCATIONAL AND TRAINING INSTITUTIONS

EMPRESA DE SISTEMAS DE COMPUTADORES LTDA. (ESC)
Rua Matias Aires 451, São Paulo 01309

Officers
Rudolf Möbus, *General Director*
Cesar Bruno Leyk, *Marketing Director*
Euclides Soares, *Technical Director*

Computer Installation
São Paulo:
SIEMENS 4004/45–operating system: PBS (DOS); internal storage: 128K bytes; magnetic tapes: 2 442-9, 1 442-2-7; magnetic discs: 3 4579, 4 564; 2 line printers.

Rio de Janeiro:
SIEMENS 4004/45–operating system: PBS (DOS); internal storage: 128K bytes; magnetic tapes: 4 4453; magnetic discs: 2 4579, 2 564; 1 line printer.

Coding Languages
COBOL, Assembler, RPG, FORTRAN.

Contemplated Equipment
São Paulo: SIEMENS 4004/45 II; internal storage: 256K bytes; magnetic tapes: 6 4453; magnetic discs: 3 4580.

Services Available
Advice, education and training, operators, software packages, documentation, systems analysis. Operate on a block time basis (pre-installation time).

Fields of Application
Scientific, statistical, commercial, production control, accounting, systems analysis.

Training
Courses in data processing, programming and operational systems.

UNID. PROCESSAMENTO DE DADOS (FEAUSP)
Caixa Postal 8030, São Paulo 02000

Officers
Prof. Flavio Fausto Manzoli, *Director*
Prof. Nicolau Reinhard, *Systems Analyst*

Computer Installation
IBM 1130–internal storage: 128K bits; magnetic discs: 1 1316; 1 line printer.

Coding Languages
Assembler, FORTRAN, RPG.

Contemplated Equipment
Expansions of memory; high-speed printer.

Services Available
Advice, programming, education and training, operators, preparation of data. Operate on a closed shop basis. Mainly providing EDP services to business and economics school faculty.

Fields of Application
Scientific, statistical, operational research.
Specialized areas: Linear programming, analysis, econometrics.

Training
Courses in introduction to computers, data processing, programming (FORTRAN and COBOL).

UNIVERSITIES AND COLLEGES

ESCOLA DE ENGENHARIA DE MARANHÃO
Campus Universitário, Caixa Postal 513, Bacanga, São Luís, Maranhão

Officers
Haroldo Lisboa Taveres, *General Director*
Francisco de Salles Batista Ferreira, *Teaching Director*
José Ribamar Araújo, *Administrative Director*

Computer Installation
IBM 1130–operating system: DOS; internal storage: 8K bits; magnetic discs: 1 2315; 1 line printer.

Coding Languages
FORTRAN IV, RPG, Assembler.

Services Available
Education and training. Operate on block time basis.

Fields of Application
Scientific, statistical.

ESCOLA DE ENGENHARIA MAUÁ
Instituto Mauá de Tecnologia (IMT)
Estrada das Lágrimas 2035, São Caetano do Sul, São Paulo

Officers
Prof. I. M. Rozemberg, *Director of School of Engineering*
Prof. Hazime Sato, *Co-ordinator of Informatics Centre*

Computer Installation
IBM 1130 – operating system: Monitor; internal storage: 16K 16-bit words; magnetic discs: 1 2315; 1 line printer; 1 plotter.

Coding Languages
FORTRAN IV, RPG, Basic, COBOL.

Contemplated Equipment
IBM 1403 printer, IBM 2310 disc.

Services Available
Advice, programming, education and training, software packages, systems analysis. Operate on a closed shop and block time basis.

Fields of Application
Scientific, statistical, systems analysis, operational research, general research.
Specialized areas: Linear programming, structural engineering, engineering research.

Training
Basic course in computer science, special courses in technical areas.

PONTIFÍCIA UNIVERSIDADE CATÓLICA DE CAMPINAS
Centro de Processamento de Dados
Praça Imaculada 105, Campinas 13100, Estado de São Paulo
Telephone: 9-3381

Officer
Antonio Carlos Lirani, *Director*

Computer Installation
IBM System/3/10 – operating system: DOS; internal storage: 24K bytes; magnetic discs: 4 IBM 5444; 1 line printer.

Coding Languages
RPG II, COBOL, FORTRAN, Assembler.

Contemplated Equipment
IBM 370/158 or equivalent.

Services Available
Programming, education and training, operators, preparation of data, systems analysis. Operate on a self-service basis.

Fields of Application
Scientific, statistical, commercial, accounting, management, systems analysis.
Specialized area: Academic control.

PONTIFÍCIA UNIVERSIDADE CATÓLICA DO RIO DE JANEIRO
Rio Datacentro
Rua Marqués de Sao Vicente 209, Gávea, Rio de Janeiro
Telephone: 227-1714

Officers
A. C. Olinto, *Director*
L. C. Martins, *Executive Director*

Computer Installation
IBM 370/165 – operating system: OS MVT-HASP; internal storage: 1,024K bytes; magnetic tapes: 2 3420; magnetic discs: 4 3330; 2 line printers. *On-line satellite computer*: IBM System/3. *Remote processing features*: 9 IBM 2741 terminals.

IBM 1130 – operating system: Monitor; internal storage: 8K bytes; 1 magnetic disc; 1 line printer.

IBM 7044/1401 – operating system: IBSYS; internal storage: 32K bytes; magnetic tapes: 8 729; 1 line printer.

Coding Languages
FORTRAN, COBOL, PL/1, Assembler, ALGOL, GPSS/360, WATFIV, SNOBOL, LISP.

Services Available
Advice, programming, education and training, operators, software packages, documentation, preparation of data, systems analysis. Operate on a self-service, remote access and open shop basis.

Field of Application
Scientific.
Specialized area: Academic research.

Training
Professional education on data processing; extension courses on specific areas of computer application.

UNIVERSIDADE DE SÃO PAULO
Centro de Computação Electrônica
Ed. J. O. Monteiro de Camargo, Cidade Universitária
"Armando de Salles Oliveira", Caixa Postal 8191, São Paulo

Officer
Paulo de Souza Moraes, *Executive Director*

Computer Installation
BURROUGHS B3500 – operating system: MCPV; internal storage: 1,040K bits; magnetic tapes: 5 800 BPI; magnetic discs: 2; 2 line printers.

Coding Languages
FORTRAN, COBOL, Assembler, BPL.

Services Available
Advice, programming, education and training, systems analysis. Operate on a self-service basis.

Fields of Application
Scientific, accounting, management.
Specialized areas: Analysis, payroll, structural engineering, medical research.

UNIVERSIDADE DE SÃO PAULO
Nuclear Physics Dept., Instituto de Física
Caixa Postal 20516, São Paulo
Telephone: 286-2742

Officer
Prof. Oscar Sala, *Head of Department*

Computer Installation
IBM 360/44 – operating system: Model 44 Programming System; internal storage: 1,572,864 bits; magnetic tapes: 5 2401; magnetic discs: 3 2314; 1 line printer. *On-line satellite computer*: 1 Honeywell DDP 516.

HONEYWELL DDP 516 – operating system: RTX-16; internal storage: 12K 16-bit words. *Remote processing features*: Linked to IBM 360/44.

Coding Languages
FORTRAN IV, Assembler.

Brazil – Universities and Colleges

Services Available
Advice, education and training, operators, software packages. Operate on a closed shop basis.

Field of Application
Scientific.

Training
Courses in programmed instruction: flowcharting and coding languages.

UNIVERSIDADE DE SÃO PAULO
Centro de Processamento de Dados, Escola de Engenharia de São Carlos
Avenida Dr. Carlos Botelho 1465, São Carlos 13560, Estado de São Paulo
Telephone: 4309, 4993

Officer
Dr. José Savério Lia, *Director*

Computer Installation
IBM 1130 – internal storage: 32K 16-bit words; magnetic discs: 3 2310; 2 line printers.

Coding Languages
Assembler, FORTRAN, RPG, COBOL, Basic, APL, ALGOL, SL/1.

Services Available
Programming, education and training, operators, documentation, preparation of data. Operate on a closed shop basis.

Fields of Application
Scientific, statistical, commercial, systems analysis, operational research.
Specialized areas: Payroll, structural engineering.

Training
Courses in introduction to computing, programming languages and information structures.

UNIVERSIDADE ESTADUAL DE CAMPINAS*
Centro de Computação
Caixa Postal 1170, Campinas, Estado de São Paulo
Téléphone: 25835, 25832, 25831 – ramal 17

Dirigeants
Dr. O. L. Liñhares, *Directeur du Centre de Calcul*

Equipement
IBM 1130 – mémoire interne: 8K mots; disques magnétiques: 1 2310; 1 imprimante.

Langages de Programmation
FORTRAN, Assembler, SL/1, ALGOL, BASIC, APL, COGO, STRESS.

Equipement Fournis
Conseils, programmation, enseignement et formation, préparation des données. Fonctionnement à porte fermée; services fournis à tous les instituts et facultés de l'Université de Campinas, et à d'autres instituts de recherche gouvernementale.

Domaines d'Application
Scientifique, statistique, enseignement et formation.
Domaines spécialisés: enseignement et formation.

Formation
Licence en Informatique.

UNIVERSIDADE FEDERAL DE MINAS GERAIS
Centro de Cálculo da Escola de Engenharia
Rua Espírito Santo 35, Belo Horizonte, Minas Gerais
Telephone: (0312) 224011

Officers
Harry Farrer, *Chief*

Computer Installation
IBM 1130 – operating system: DMS; internal storage: 16,384 x 16 bits; 1 magnetic disc; 1 line printer.

Coding Languages
FORTRAN, Assembler, RPG.

Services Available
Education and training, operators. Operate on a closed shop basis.

Fields of Application
Scientific, statistical, production control.
Specialized area: Structural engineering.

Training
Courses in FORTRAN, 1130-Assembler, RPG, 1130 operating system.

UNIVERSIDADE FEDERAL DE PARAÍBA
Instituto Central de Matemática
Departamento de Informática
Cidade Universitária, João Pessoa, Paraíba
Telephone: 2741, 2742

Officers
Prof. Hélio Ferreira da S. Guimarães, *Head of Department*
Prof. Kotaro Tanaka, *Head of Computer Centre*

Computer Installation
IBM 1130 – operating system: DMS; internal storage: 8,192 16-bit words; magnetic discs: 10; 1 line printer.

Coding Languages
FORTRAN IV, Assembler, RPG.

Services Available
Education and training. Operate on a self-service basis. Available only for purposes of university administration, education and training.

Fields of Application
Scientific, management.
Specialized areas: Payroll, structural engineering.

Training
Courses in FORTRAN language and introduction to computer science.

UNIVERSIDADE FEDERAL DE PERNAMBUCO
Centro de Processamento de Dados
Prédio dos Institutos Básicos, 1° andar, Cidade Universitária, Engenho do Meio, Recife, Pernambuco
Telephone: 273366

Officers
Rivaldo Alves Correia, *Executive Director*
Genilson Simões Cavalcante, *Chief of Analysis*

Computer Installation
IBM 1130 – operating system: Monitor; internal storage: 131,072 bits; magnetic discs: 1 disc cassette; 1 line printer.

BURROUGHS B500 – operating system: Model Control Program II; internal storage: 134,400 bits; magnetic tapes: 4 9384; magnetic discs: 4 9374; 1 line printer.

Coding Languages
Assembler, RPG, FORTRAN IV, APL, PMA, COBOL.

Contemplated Equipment
IBM 370 or Burroughs B6700.

Services Available
Programming, education and training. Operate on a self-service and block time basis.

Fields of Application
Scientific, statistical, commercial, accounting.
Specialized areas: Linear programming, payroll, structural engineering, medical research.

Training
Courses in programming, analysis and electronic computation.

UNIVERSIDADE FEDERAL DE SÃO CARLOS
Divisão de Computação
Via Washington Luiz, Km 235, Caixa Postal 384, São Carlos 13560
Telephone: 3632, 4951, 4952

Officers
Arthur João Catto, *Director*
Dioraci Garcia Pinatti, *Professor*
Euclides Robert Filho, *Professor*

Computer Installation
HEWLETT PACKARD 2100A—operating system: moving head disc; internal storage: 16K 16-bit words; 2 magnetic discs; 1 line printer.

Coding Languages
Assembler, FORTRAN, ALGOL, BASIC, SNOBOL.

Contemplated Equipment
Expansion of core memory to 32K words; another Hewlett Packard disc unit.

Services Available
Education and training. Operate on a self-service basis. Services restricted to meet the internal needs of the University and other educational institutions in related areas.

Fields of Application
Scientific, statistical, commercial.
Specialized areas: Analysis, payroll, structural engineering, control of students' activities.

Training
Courses in numerical applications, programming languages and programming techniques are provided for internal personnel.

UNIVERSIDADE FEDERAL DE SERGIPE
Centro de Processamento de Dados
Rue Vila Cristina 1051, Aracaju 49000, Sergipe
Telephone: 24-76

Officer
João Sampaio d'Avila, *Director*

Computer Installation
IBM 1130—operating system: Monitor; internal storage: 131,072 bits; magentic discs: 1 2315; 1 line printer.

Coding Languages
FORTRAN, RPG.

Services Available
Advice, programming, education and training, operators, systems analysis. Operate on a closed shop basis. The highest priority is given to education and research.

Fields of Application
Scientific, statistical, systems analysis, operational research.
Specialized area: Education.

Training
Courses in introduction to computer science and data processing.

UNIVERSIDADE FEDERAL DO PARANÁ
Centro de Computação Eletrônica
Centro Politécnico, Edifício de Administração, 3° andar, Curitiba
Telephone: 237614, ramal 84

Officers
Euro Brandão, *Director*
Jahyr Leal, *Assistant Professor*

Computer Installation
IBM 1130—operating system: Version 2, Monitor System; internal storage: 8K 16-bit words; magnetic disc: 1; 1 line printer.

Coding Languages
Assembler, FORTRAN, RPG, BASIC, APL.

Contemplated Equipment
IBM 370/135 with 6 remote terminals.

Services Available
Education and training. Operate on a closed shop basis.

Fields of Application
Scientific, statistical, systems analysis.
Specialized areas: Analysis, structural engineering, electrical engineering.

Training
Courses for operators and programmers; courses in systems analysis and introduction to computer science.

UNIVERSIDADE FEDERAL DO RIO DE JANEIRO
Núcleo de Computação Eletrônica
Caixa Postal 2324, Rio de Janeiro
Telephone: 230-0479

Officers
Denis França Leite, *Director*
Ysmar Vianna e Silva Filho, *Deputy Director*

Computer Installation
IBM 1130—operating system: DM2; internal storage: 512K bits; magnetic discs: 3 2310; 2 line printers.

IBM 360/40—operating system: OS-HASP; internal storage: 2,029K bits; magnetic tapes: 4 2401; magnetic discs: 8 2314; 1 line printer. *Remote processing features*: 10 2741 terminals.

IBM 370/145—operating system: OS-HASP; internal storage: 1,280K bits; magnetic tapes: 2 2420; magnetic discs: 6 2319; 1 line printer.

Coding Languages
FORTRAN, COBOL, PL/1, Assembler, BASIC.

Contemplated Equipment
IBM 360/65.

Brazil — Universities and Colleges

Services Available
Advice, programming, education and training, software packages, systems analysis. Operate on a closed shop basis. Services other than education, training and software packages are available primarily for university-related institutions.

Fields of Application
Scientific, systems analysis.

Training
Courses in programming, systems engineering and computer science.

UNIVERSIDADE FEDERAL DO RIO GRANDE DO SUL
Instituto de Física
Pôrto Alegre 90000, Rio Grande do Sul
Telephone: (0516) 24-5817

Officers
Werner A. Mundt, *Director*
Celso Müller, *Director of Research and Development*
John D. Rogers, *Co-ordinator of Graduate Programme*

Computer Installation
HEWLETT PACKARD 2100—operating system: disk; internal storage: 256K bits; magnetic tapes: 1 incremental; magnetic disc: 1; 1 line printer.

HEWLETT PACKARD 2114A—operating system: P.T.; internal storage: 128K bits.

Coding Languages
FORTRAN, ALGOL, Assembler, BASIC.

Contemplated Equipment
Satellite instrumentation computers.

Services Available
Advice, education and training, software packages. Operate on a self-service basis. In-house usage only.

Fields of Application
Scientific, hardware development.
Specialized area: Nuclear physics research.

Training
A course in applied physics, with specialization in digital electronics and instrumentation.

UNIVERSIDADE FEDERAL FLUMINENSE
Instituto de Matemática
Rua Miguel de Frias 9, Icarai, Niterói, Estado do Rio de Janeiro
Telephone: 722-7995, 722-7996, 722-5227

Officers
Jorge Emmanuel Barbosa, *Rector*
Joaquim Cardoso de Lemos, *Vice-Rector*

Computer Installation
IBM 1130—operating system: DMS; internal storage: 8K words; 1 magnetic disc; 1 line printer.

Coding Languages
FORTRAN, Assembler, RPG, BASIC, ALGOL, APL.

Contemplated Equipment
2 IBM 2311.

Services Available
Advice, programming, education and training, operators, systems analysis. Operate on a self-service basis.

Fields of Application
Scientific, statistical, commercial, management, systems analysis, operational research, education.
Specialized areas: Linear programming, analysis, payroll, structural engineering, medical research, general research.

Training
Courses in computer initiation, FORTRAN, application programmes.

UNIVERSIDADE FEDERAL RURAL DE PERNAMBUCO
Caixa Postal 2071, Recife 50000, Pernambuco
Telephone: 281347, 281357

Officers
Prof. Adierson Erasmo de Azevedo, *Rector*
Murilo Salgado Carneiro, *Vice-Rector*
Antônio Trigueiro Londres Barreto, *Director of Computer Centre*

Computer Installation
BURROUGHS B2000—internal storage: 28K bits.

Coding Language
Assembler.

Contemplated Equipment
Burroughs B1700.

Services Available
Education and training. Operate on a self-service basis only.

Fields of Application
Statistical, management.
Specialized areas: Payroll, academic control.

UNIVERSIDADE MACKENZIE
Centro de Processamento de Dados (CEPDAM)
Rue Itambé 135, São Paulo
Telephone: 256-6611

Officers
Rui José Arruda Campos, *Director*
Enrico Giulio Franco Polloni, *Planning Head*

Computer Installation
NCR Century 100—operating system: DOS; internal storage: 16K × 8 bits; 1 magnetic disc; 1 line printer.

Coding Languages
FORTRAN, COBOL, NEAT 3.

Services Available
Education and training. Operate on a remote access basis.

Fields of Application
Scientific, commercial, accounting, management.
Specialized areas: Payroll, students' scheduling, financial control.

GOVERNMENT ESTABLISHMENTS

CENTRAIS ELÉTRICAS DO SUL DO BRASIL S.A. (ELETROSUL)
Rua da Alfândega no. 90, Rio de Janeiro
Telephone: 224.65.77

Officers
Mario Lannes Cunha, *President of the Board*
Luiz Cals de Oliveira, *Administration*
Fernando Luiz Corrêa de Azevedo, *Engineering and Construction*
Agostinho Pereira Ferreira, *Operation and Planning*

Computer Installation
IBM 360/30–operating system: DOS; internal storage: 65K bytes; magnetic tapes: 4 2401; magnetic discs: 2 2314; 1 line printer.

Coding Languages
COBOL, FORTRAN, PL/1.

Contemplated Equipment
IBM 370/145.

Services Available
Operate on a block time basis.

Fields of Application
Scientific, statistical, commercial, production control, accounting, management, systems analysis, operational research.
Specialized area: Structural engineering.

CENTRO DE INFORMAÇÕES PARA O DESENVOLVIMENTO URBANO E LOCAL (CIDUL)
Rua Debret 23, 9° andar, Centro, Rio de Janeiro
Telephone: 221-5541

Computer Installation
IBM 360/50–operating system: OS-MFT; internal storage: 256K bytes; magnetic tapes: 8 2400; magnetic discs: 5 2314; 2 line printers.

Coding Languages
Assembler, FORTRAN IV, PL/1.

Contemplated Equipment
IBM 370/155.

Services Available
Advice, education and training, software packages, preparation of data, systems analysis. Operate on a block time basis.

Fields of Application
Scientific, statistical.
Specialized areas: Analysis, information retrieval in urban planning.

CENTRO DE PRESTAÇÃO DE SERVIÇOS TÉCNICOS DO ESTADO DE PERNAMBUCO (CETEPE)
Rua Dom Bosco 1329, Recife, Pernambuco
Telephone: 22.50.17, 22.11.11, 24.16.97

Officers
Pedro José Caminha Dueire, *President*
Laudo Bernardes, *Superintendent*
Marcio Lacerda, *Systems and Projects*
Jaime Pires Galvão (Filho), *Data Processing*
Jaime Pires d'Azevedo, *Administration*

Computer Installation
IBM 360/20–operating system: DPS or TPS; internal storage: 16K bytes; magnetic tapes: 4 2415; magnetic discs: 2 2311; 1 line printer.

Coding Languages
Assembler, RPG, FORTRAN, PL/1.

Services Available
Programming, education and training, systems analysis, operational research. Operate on a self-service and open shop basis.

Fields of Application
Statistical, commercial, systems analysis, operational research.
Specialized areas: Linear programming, analysis, payroll.

COMPANHIA DE PROCESSAMENTO DE DADOS DO ESTADO DO RIO GRANDE DO SUL (PROCERGS)
Caldas Junior 120, 12° andar, Pôrto Alegre, Rio Grande do Sul
Telephone: 24-5196

Officers
Flávio Sehn, *Managing Director*
Dionysio A. da Silva, *Technical Director*

Computer Installation
UNIVAC 1050–operating system: MIT-Rev. 19; internal storage: 192K bits; magnetic tapes: 5 Uniservo VIC; 1 line printer. *On-line satellite computers*: Univac 1004, Univac 1005.

BURROUGHS B6700–operating system: MCP; internal storage: 6,288K bits; magnetic tapes: 6 9495-6, 1 9391; magnetic discs: 1 9372-12, 2 9974-4; 2 line printers.
Remote processing features: 3 TC 500, 5 TD 700.

Coding Languages
Assembler, PAL, Burroughs, COBOL.

Services Available
Programming, education and training, operators, documentation, preparation of data, systems analysis. Operate on self-service and block time basis. Available only to government establishments.

Fields of Application
Commercial, accounting, management, systems analysis.
Specialized areas: Payroll, banks policy.

COMPANHIA DE PROCESSAMENTO DE DADOS DO MARANHÃO (PRODATA)
Rua Nina Rodrigues 43, 2° andar, São Luís, Maranhão
Telephone: 1650, 1755.

Also at:
Avenida Bacanga, s/n, São Luís, Maranhão
Telephone: 2952

Officers
Almir Aguiar Marques (Filho), *Executive Director*

Computer Installation
IBM 370/135–operating system: DOS; internal storage: 96K bytes; magnetic tapes: 4 3420; magnetic discs: 1 2319; 2 line printers.

IBM 1130–operating system: Monitor; internal storage: 8K bytes; magnetic discs: 1 11-31; 1 line printer.

Coding Languages
FORTRAN IV, COBOL, PL/1, Assembler.

Service Available
Operators. Operate on a self-service, closed shop and block time basis.

Fields of Application
Scientific, statistical, commercial, accounting.
Specialized areas: Analysis, payroll, structural engineering.

Training
Course for Bacharel em Direito.

COMPANHIA DO METROPOLITANO DE SÃO PAULO (METRÔ)
Rua Augusta 1626, São Paulo 01304
Telephone: 37-1571

Officer
Dr. Mário Sérgio Sabina Rossetto, *Manager*

Computer Installation
PHILIPS P250 (2)—operating system: Monitor; internal storage: 48K 16-bit words each; magnetic tapes: 2 XDS 7320 each; magnetic discs: 2 XDS 7201 each; 1 line printer.
PHILIPS P250—operating system: Monitor; internal storage: 32K 16-bit words; magnetic discs: 1 XDS 7201/02.

Coding Languages
FORTRAN, COBOL, PL/1, RPG, Assembler.

Contemplated Equipment
Management information services computer — main storage 256K bytes (minimum); 2 disc units; 2 tape units; 1 reader, printer, punch.

Services Available
Programming, education and training, software packages, documentation, preparation of data, systems analysis. Operate on block time basis.

Fields of Application
Scientific, statistical, commercial, accounting, management, systems analysis, operational research.
Specialized area: Analysis.

COMPANHIA ESTADUAL DE ÁGUAS DA GUANABARA (CEDAG)*
Rua do Riachuelo 287, Rio de Janeiro, Guanabara
Telephone: 2 32-1473

Officer
A. Turano, *Chief of Data Processing Division*

Computer Installation
BURROUGHS B3500—internal storage: 60K bytes; magnetic tapes: 3 B3390 7-track; 1 line printer.

Coding Languages
COBOL, FORTRAN.

Contemplated Equipment
2 disc file units of 10 million bytes each.

Services Available
Programming, preparation of data, systems analysis. Operate on a closed shop basis.

Fields of Application
Systems analysis in commercial management.

INSTITUTO BRASILEIRO DE INFORMÁTICA
Rua Visconde de Niterói 1246, Rio de Janeiro
Telephone: 264-0618

Officers
Prof. A. C. Olinto, *Managing Director*
Dr. Fernando Lacorte, *Production Director*
Dr. José Roberto R. dos Santos, *Systems Director*
Dr. Luiz Carlos Siqueira, *Projects Director*

Computer Installation
IBM 370/155—operating systems: OS, MVT/HASP; internal storage: 1 million bytes; magnetic tapes: 7 3420-7; magnetic discs: 8 (2319 and 3330); 2 line printers.

Coding Languages
COBOL, Assembler, PL/1, FORTRAN, CENTS, MARK IV.

Contemplated Equipment
Data Entry System: 12 3270 to be used in TSO.

Services Available
Programming, preparation of data. Operate on an open shop basis.

Fields of Application
Scientific, statistical, commercial, operational research.

INSTITUTO TECNOLÓGICO DE AERONÁUTICA*
São José dos Campos, Estado de São Paulo

Dirigeants
José Geraldo Vasconcellos
Geraldo da Silva Paranhos
Sebastião Cruz Silva

Equipement
IBM 1620—mémoire interne: 20K bits.
IBM 1130—mémoire interne: 16K bits.

Langages de Programmation
FORTRAN IV, Assembler, RPG, AFIT, SPS.

Services Fournis
Assistance technique, programmation et analyse statistique. Foncionnement en libre service.

Domaines d'Applications
Scientifique, statistique, analyse de systèmes, recherche opérationelle.

Formation
Langages, simulation, calcul numérique.

SERVIÇO FEDERAL DE PROCESSAMENTO DE DADOS (SERPRO)*
Central Office
Avenida Presidente Vargas 482, 18° andar, Rio de Janeiro

Also at: São Paulo, Pôrto Alegre, Recife and Curitiba

Officers
Dr. José Dion de Melo Telles, *Superintendent*
Dr. Mario Dias Ripper, *Training*

Computer Installation
Rio de Janeiro:
IBM 360/30—operating system: DOS; internal storage: 32K bytes, magnetic tapes: 4 2401; magnetic discs: 3 2311; 2 line printers.

São Paulo:
IBM 360/30—operating system: DOS; internal storage: 32K bytes; magnetic tapes: 4 2401; magnetic discs: 3 2311; 2 line printers.

Pôrto Alegre:
IBM 360/20—operating system: TOS; internal storage: 12K bytes; magnetic tapes: 4 2415; 1 line printer.

Recife:
IBM 360/20—internal storage: 8K; magnetic tapes: 4 2330; 1 line printer.

Curitiba:
UNIVAC 1004–internal storage: 924 words; 1 line printer.

Coding Languages
COBOL, RPG, Assembler.

Services Available
Advice, programming, systems analysis. Operate on a closed shop basis. Available only for federal, state and municipal use.

Fields of Application
Commercial, accounting.
Specialized area: Tax collection.

Training
Short courses for executives (20 hrs.) and for public servants (40 hrs.) about the general principles of computer utilization.

RESEARCH INSTITUTIONS

INSTITUTO DE PESQUISAS ESPACIAIS (INPE)
Avenida Astronautas s/n, Caixa Postal 515, São José dos Campos 12200, Estado de São Paulo
Telephone: 4866

Officers
Dr. Fernando de Mendonça, *General Director*
Dr. Luiz Gylvan Meira (Filho), *Scientific Director*
Eng. Gladiolo M. Fernandez, *Administrative Director*

Computer Installation
BURROUGHS B6700–operating system: MCP; internal storage: 3,145,728 bits; magnetic tapes: 4 B9392; 1 magnetic disc; 2 line printers.

BURROUGHS B3500–operating system: MCPV; internal storage: 1,120K bits; magnetic tapes: 4 B9381-4; 3 magnetic discs; 1 line printer.

Coding Languages
COBOL, ALGOL, FORTRAN, PL/1, BASIC.

Services Available
Programming, preparation of data, systems analysis. Operate on a closed shop basis.

Fields of Application
Scientific, systems analysis.

INSTITUTO DE PESQUISAS TECNOLÓGICAS
Cidade Universitária, Caixa Postal 7141, São Paulo 05508
Telephone: 260-2011

Officers
Prof. Alberto Pereira de Castro, *Director*
Lino Afonso de Lacerda Santos, *Deputy Director*
José Luiz de Almeida N. Junqueira (Filho), *Director of Information Centre*

Computer Installation
IBM 360/44–operating system: OS/360; internal storage: 128K bits; magnetic tapes: 4 2420; magnetic discs: 4 2311; 1 line printer.

Coding Languages
FORTRAN, PL/1, ALGOL, Assembler.

Contemplated Equipment
PDP-15.

Services Available
Programming, education and training, documentation, preparation of data, systems analysis, information systems development. Operate on a remote access, closed shop and block time basis.

Fields of Application
Scientific, accounting, management, systems analysis, operational research, information storage and retrieval.
Specialized areas: Analysis, structural engineering, naval engineering.

Training
Courses in computer expertise and programming languages.

INSTITUTO DE PESQUISAS TECNOLÓGICAS
Centro de Pesquisas Informaticas (CPI)
Cidade Universitária "Armando de Salles Oliveira", C.P. 7141, São Paulo 05508

Officer
José Luiz de Almeida N. Junqueira (Filho), *Director*

Coding Languages
COBOL, FORTRAN, PL/1.

Contemplated Equipment
IBM System/3 (to provide remote job entry) or BURROUGHS B1700.

Services Available
Documentation, preparation of data, systems analysis. Operate on a remote access basis.

Fields of Application
Scientific, statistical, systems analysis, operational research.
Specialized areas: Linear programming, analysis, structural engineering.

UNIVERSIDADE FEDERAL DO RIO DE JANEIRO
Instituto de Biofísica
Avenida Pasteur 458, Rio de Janeiro
Telephone: 246-4030, ramal 22

Officer
Dr. C. E. Rocha-Miranda, *Chief of Computer Unit*

Computer Installation
PDP-12–operating system: LAP 6; internal storage: 4K 12-bit words; magnetic tapes: 2 TU55.

Coding Language
Assembler.

Contemplated Equipment
An additional 4K words of core memory; 1 TU56 tape unit.

Services Available
Advice, programming, education and training. Operate on a self-service basis. Available only for on-line, real time use.

Field of Application
Scientific.
Specialized area: Medical research.

Training
Short courses on programming for students and Institute personnel.

CONSULTANTS

BURROUGHS ELECTRÔNICA LTDA.*
Rua Arauso Pôrto Alegre 36, 8° andar, Rio de Janeiro
Telephone: 52-2080

Officers
Georg Herz, *Electronic Data Processing Manager*

Computer Installation
BURROUGHS B3500—operating system: Burroughs MCP; internal storage: 60K bytes; magnetic tapes: 4; magnetic disc: Burroughs; 2 line printers. *On-line satellite computer*: B500.

Coding Languages
BASIC, Advanced Assembler, FORTRAN, COBOL.

Services Available
Rental of computer time, systems analysis. Operate on an open shop and block time basis.

Fields of Application
Varied fields.

Training
Regular programming courses.

COMPUTAÇÃO E PLANEJAMENTO S.A. (COMPLASA)
Rua Siqueira Campos 121, 10° andar, Copacabana, Rio de Janeiro
Telephone: 237-7931

Officers
João Rizzo, *Director*
Carlos E. M. Torres, *Director*
Paulo C. de Barros, *President*
Jean C. G. M. Schotte, *Production Manager*

Coding Languages
FORTRAN, ALGOL, COBOL, Assembler.

Services Available
Advice, programming, systems analysis. Operate on block time basis.

Fields of Application
Scientific, commercial.
Specialized area: Civil engineering.

PEAT, MARWICK, MITCHELL & CO.
Caixa Postal 949–ZC–00, Rio de Janeiro
Telephone: 224-6112

Officer
M. R. Cruz (Filho)

Services Available
Consultation, systems analysis.

Fields of Application
E nomic studies, general and scientific management, operations research, project management, industrial engineering, marketing, production and inventory control, information systems, general and cost accounting systems, data processing and transmission systems, etc.

PROCESSAMENTO DE DADOS S.A. (PRODASA)
Rua das Pernambucanas 339, Graças, Recife, Pernambuco
Telephone: 21-5707

Officers
Emir Glasner de Barros, *Managing Director*
José Britto Pinheiro Passos Jr., *Commercial Director*
Roberto Mário Gomes de Mattos Mafra, *Technical Director*
Claudio Gama Vieira, *Assistant Director*
Adson Silva de Carvalho, *Production Director*

Computer Installation
IBM 1130—internal storage: 262,144 bits; magnetic discs: 3 2315; 1 line printer.

Coding Languages
FORTRAN, RPG, Assembler.

Services Available
Programming, education and training, systems analysis, systems engineering management. Operate on a block time basis.

Fields of Application
Scientific, statistical, systems analysis, operational research, engineering.

SERETE S.A.
Rua Alta 355, São Paulo 05688
Telephone: 61-1181, 267-8022

Computer Installation
IBM 1130—operating system: DMS; internal storage: 256K bits; magnetic discs: 4 2310; 1 line printer.

Coding Languages
Assembler, FORTRAN, COBOL.

Contemplate 1 Equipment
IBM 370/125.

Services Available
Advice, programming, education and training, operators, software packages, documentation, preparation of data, systems analysis. Operate on a closed shop, block time and open shop basis.

Fields of Application
Scientific, statistical, accounting, management, systems analysis, operational research.
Specialized areas: Linear programming, analysis, structural engineering, engineering applications.

SERVICE BUREAUX

BARNESTADO S. A.
Processamento de Dados e Serviços
Avenida Visconde de Guarapuava 2295, Curitiba
Telephone: 23-6621

Officers
João Milczewski, *Administrative Director*
Bolívar José Wood, *Technical Director*
Claudio F. Gerhardt, *Chief Analyst*
Raul Orlandi, *Production Manager*

Computer Installation
IBM 360/25—operating system: DOS; internal storage: 48K bits; magnetic tapes: 4 2415; magnetic discs: 3 2314.

Coding Languages
Assembler, PL/1, COBOL, RPG.

Contemplated Equipment
IBM 370/135.

Services Available
Programming, education and training, operators, preparation of data, systems analysis. Operate on a self-service basis.

Field of Application
Commercial.
Specialized area: Payroll.

CENTRO ELECTRÔNICO WALMAP S.A.
Avenida Paulo de Frontin 670, Rio de Janeiro
Téléphone: 264-9632

Equipement
BURROUGHS B200—mémoire interne: 9,600 bits; bandes magnétiques: 4; 1 imprimante.
BURROUGHS B3500 (3)—mémoire interne: 90K bytes (chaque un); bandes magnétiques: 14; disques magnétiques: 3; 6 imprimantes.

Langage de Programmation
COBOL.

Services Fournis
Conseils, programmation, documentation, préparation des données, systems analysis, traitement. Fonctionnement en self-service. Services fournis pour la plupart à la Banco Nacional de Minas Gerais S.A. et plusieurs associées.

Domaines d'Application
Commercial, contrôle des processus, comptabilité, gestion, systems analysis.
Domaines spécialisés: Analyse des ventes, programmes linéaires, investissement, analyse, journal de paie.

COMPANHIA DE PROCESSAMENTO DO ESTADO DE SÃO PAULO (PRODESP)
Rua Pedro Vicente 205, São Paulo 01109
Telephone: 227-6100, 227-7173, 227-4433

Officers
Luiz de Freitas Bueno, *President*
Gustavo Damasio Monteiro, *Technical Director*
Mario Rosenthal, *Production Director*
Oswaldo Blum, *Financial and Administrative Director*

Computer Installation
IBM 360/65—operating system: OS-MVT-HASP; internal storage: 512K bytes; magnetic tapes: 10 2420, 2 2401; magnetic discs: 2 2314; 3 line printers.

Coding Languages
COBOL ANSI, FORTRAN IV, Assembler.

Contemplated Equipment
A similar installation.

Services Available
Advice, programming, education and training, operators, software packages, documentation, preparation of data, systems analysis. Operate on a closed shop and block time basis. Not available to private companies.

Fields of Application
Statistical, commercial, accounting, management, systems analysis, public administration.
Specialized areas: Analysis, payroll, tax administration, personnel administration.

Training
Basic training in electronic data processing for systems analysts, programmers and operators.

CONSTRUÇÕES E COMÉRCIO CAMARGO CORRÊA S.A.
Rua Funchal 220, Vila Olímpia

Officer
Jürgen Düssel, *Data Processing Manager*

Computer Installation
IBM 370/145—operating system: OS/VSI; internal storage: 262,144 bits; magnetic tapes: 3 3420; magnetic discs: 2 2319; 2 line printers. *Remote processing features:* 2701, 2740, 3272, 3277, 3286.

Coding Languages
COBOL, FORTRAN, Assembler, PL/1.

Services Available
Programming, operators, software packages, documentation, preparation of data, systems analysis. Operate on a closed shop, block time and open shop basis.

Fields of Application
Scientific, statistical, commercial, accounting, management, systems analysis, operational research.
Specialized areas: Sales analysis, linear programming, analysis, payroll, structural engineering.

CONSULTORIA E SERVIÇOS TÉCNICOS APLUB LTDA. (TÉCNICA APLUB)
Avenida Julio de Castilhos no. 10, Caixa Postal 2255, Pôrto Alegre 90000, Rio Grande do Sul

Officers
Amaury Soares Silveira
Marco Antônio Pereira Schneider

Computer Installation
IBM 360/40—operating systems: DOS, OS; internal storage: 64K bits; magnetic tapes: 6; magnetic discs: 3; 2 line printers.

Coding Languages
Assembler, PL/1.

Services Available
Education and training, software packages. Operate on a block time basis.

Fields of Application
Commercial, systems analysis.
Specialized area: Sales analysis.

COOPERATIVA AGRICOLA DE COTIA — COOPERATIVA CENTRAL
Centro de Processamento Eletrônico de Dados
Avenida Jaguaré 1487, São Paulo
Telephone: 260-1211

Officers
Leo Shiguemi Teshirogi, *EDP Manager*
Norio Nagase, *Systems Manager*
Hajime Kato, *Systems Engineer*

Computer Installation
IBM 360/25—operating system: DOS; internal storage: 49,152 bytes; magnetic tapes: 4 2401; magnetic discs: 3 2311; 1 line printer.

Coding Languages
COBOL, Assembler, FORTRAN.

Contemplated Equipment
IBM 370/135 (147,456 bytes).

Services Available
Advice, programming, operators, preparation of data, systems analysis. Operate on self-service basis.

Fields of Application
Commercial, accounting, management, operational research.
Specialized areas: Linear programming, analysis, payroll.

CREFIDATA S.A.
Processamento de Dados
Rua Sete de Setembro 666, Caixa Postal 1649,
Pôrto Alegre, Rio Grande do Sul

Dirigeant
Carlos Aurélio de M. Lima, *Directeur*

Equipement
BURROUGHS B3500–système d'opération: Multiprogramation; mémoire interne: 120K bytes; bandes magnétiques: 6 9-canaux; disque magnétique: type "read-per-track"; 1 imprimante.

Langages de Programmation
COBOL, FORTRAN, Assembler, BPL.

Services Fournis
Programmation, enseignement et formation, software packages, systems analysis. Fonctionnement à porte ouverte; services fournis à toutes les entreprises du groupe Crefisul.

Domaines d'Application
Commercial, calcul de coûts, comptabilité, systems analysis.
Domaines spécialisés: toutes les routines des institutions financières.

ENGENHARIA DE SEGUROS LTDA. (ENSEG)
Rua Barão de Itapeteninga 18, 14° andar, São Paulo 01042
Telephone: 35-6111

Officers
Luiz Campos Salles, *Director*
Antonio Paulo Noronha, *Methods and Procedures*
Tacito Pereira Nobre, *Systems Development*

Computer Installation
IBM 360/40–operating system: DOS-power; internal storage: 128K × 8 bits; magnetic tapes: 4 2401; magnetic discs: 2 2319; 2 line printers.

Coding Language
COBOL.

Services Available
Advice, programming, documentation, systems analysis. Operate on a self-service and block time basis. The main services are provided to one customer, an insurance company, but block time is available to others.

Fields of Application
Commercial, insurance administration.
Specialized area: Payroll.

ENGENHARIA PROCESSAMENTOS ELECTRÔNICOS LTDA. (ENGEPEL)
Rua Rio Grande do Norte 1164, Belo Horizonte, Minas Gerais
Telephone: 22-3561, 26-3085

Officers
Helio Mario Pimentel de Oliveira, *Co-Chairman*
Jean-Jacques Reuter, *Co-Chairman*

Computer Installation
IBM 1130–operating system: DMS; internal storage: 8K bits; magnetic discs: 3 2310; 1 line printer.

Coding Languages
FORTRAN, COBOL, Assembler, RPG.

Services Available
Programming, preparation of data, service bureau. Operate on a self-service, block time and open shop basis.

Fields of Application
Scientific, commercial.
Specialized areas: Sales analysis, payroll, structural engineering.

ESTUDOS E PROCESSAMENTOS LTDA. (DIGITAL)
Rua Miguel Pereira no. 34, Botafogo, Rio de Janeiro

Officers
Herval de Figueiredo Drummond, *Managing Director*
Sergio Augusto Araujo, *Commercial Director*
Márcia de Souza Drummond, *Technical Director*

Computer Installation
BURROUGHS B500; internal storage: 19,200 characters; magnetic tapes: 4; 1 line printer.

Coding Languages
Basic Assembler, Advanced Assembler, COBOL.

Contemplated Equipment
Burroughs B1726, Burroughs B3700.

Services Available
Advice, programming, operators, documentation, preparation of data, systems analysis. Operate on a closed shop and block time basis.

Fields of Application
Statistical, commercial, production control, accounting, management, systems analysis, operational research.
Specialized areas: Sales analysis, investment analysis, payroll.

GENERAL ELECTRIC DO BRASIL S.A.
Avenida Industrial 700, Santo André

Computer Installation
BULL GENERAL ELECTRIC GE 415–operating system: tape; internal storage: 393,216 bits; magnetic tapes: 6 9-track; 1 line printer.
BULL GENERAL ELECTRIC Gamma 10–operating system: card; internal storage: 24,576 bits; magnetic tapes: 2; 1 line printer.

Coding Languages
BAL, MAL, COBOL, FORTRAN, Assembler.

Contemplated Equipment
Another GE 415 system.

Services Available
Advice, programming, education and training, operators, documentation, preparation of data, systems analysis. Operate on a closed shop and block time basis.

Fields of Application
Scientific, commercial, production control, accounting, management.
Specialized areas: Sales analysis, investment, analysis, payroll.

Training
Courses in BAL, MAL, COBOL and FORTRAN.

HONEYWELL BULL DO BRASIL S.A.
Rua Antônio de Godoy 88, 4° andar, São Paulo
Telephone: 239-1938, 36-7097, 35-1482, 37-8943

Officers
Bernard Thouvenin, *Director General*
Yver Perrier, *Service Bureau Manager*

Computer Installation
BULL GENERAL ELECTRIC GE 120–operating system: Extended DOS; internal storage: 204,608 bits; magnetic tapes: 5 MTH; magnetic discs: 3 DSU; 1 line printer.
BULL GENERAL ELECTRIC GE 400–operating system: Magnetic tape OS; internal storage: 393,216 bits; magnetic tapes: 6 MTH; 1 line printer.
BULL GENERAL ELECTRIC GE 435–operating systems: MTPS, BOS/MT, EOS/MT; internal storage: 32K 24-bit words; magnetic tapes: 6 MTH 403; 1 line printer.
BULL GENERAL ELECTRIC GE 120–operating systems: ETOS, EDOS; internal storage: 24K 8-bit words; magnetic tapes: 4; magnetic discs: 3 DSU 160; 1 line printer.
BULL GENERAL ELECTRIC Gamma 10–operating system: MFTU; internal storage: 4,096 characters; 1 line printer.

Coding Languages
Assembler, COBOL, FORTRAN.

Services Available
Programming, education and training, software packages, documentation, preparation of data, systems analysis. Operate on a closed shop and block time basis.

Fields of Application
Scientific, statistical, commercial, accounting, management, operational research.
Specialized area: Payroll.

Training
Courses for personnel in operating, programming and systems analysis.

IBM DO BRASIL*
Centro de Serviços de Dados
Avenida Presidente Vargas 642, Loja, Rio de Janeiro
Telephone: 23-1951

Also at:
Avenida Alfonso Pena 1500, 10° andar, Belo Horizonte
Telephone: 24-8904
Rua Rosário 80, Curitiba, Paraná
Telephone: 4-5903
Rua Major Facundo 844, 6° andar, Fortaleza
Avenida Senador Salgado Filho 16, Pôrto Alegre
Telephone: 4-0788
Rua Siqueira Campos 45, 3° e 5° andares, Recife
Avenida Estados Unidos 27, 8° andar, Salvador–Bahia
Telephone: 2-3116
Rua Araujo 224, São Paulo
Telephone: 239-5884

Officers
Eduardo Frederico Saboga Weyll (Rio de Janeiro)
Pedro Alberto Pereira (Belo Horizonte)
Raul Alves (Curitiba)
Uirassú Borges (Fortaleza)
Wolfran Pinto Bittencourt (Pôrto Alegre)
Luiz Antonio Maia Chagas (Recife)
Nilson Lauria (Salvador)
Renato Classo (São Paulo)

Computer Installation
Rio de Janeiro:
IBM 360/40–operating system: DOS; internal storage: 65K bits; magnetic tapes: 6 2401; magnetic discs: 3 2311.
IBM 360/20 (2)–operating system: TPS; internal storage: 16K bits each; magnetic tapes: 4 2415.
IBM 1401–internal storage: 8K bits; magnetic tapes: 4 7330.

Belo Horizonte:
IBM 360/20–operating system: TPS; internal storage: 16K bits; magnetic tapes: 4 2415.
IBM 1401–internal storage: 8K bits; magnetic tapes: 4 7330; 1 line printer.

Curitiba, Recife:
IBM 360/20–internal storage: 16K bits; magnetic tapes: 4 2415.

Fortaleza:
IBM 1401–internal storage: 4K bits.

Pôrto Alegre:
IBM 1401–internal storage: 8K bits; magnetic tapes: 4 7330; 1 line printer.

Salvador:
IBM 1401 (2)–internal storage: 8K bits each; magnetic tapes: 4 7330; 1 line printer.

São Paulo:
IBM 360/40–operating system: DOS; internal storage: 64K bits; magnetic tapes: 5 2401; magnetic discs: 3 2311; 2 line printers.
IBM 360/20–operating system: TPS; internal storage: 16K bits; magnetic tapes: 4 2415; 1 line printer.
IBM 1130–operating system: DOS; internal storage: 131,072 bits; 1 line printer.
IBM 1401 (2)–operating system: TPS; internal storage: 12K bits each; magnetic tapes: 4 729 each; magnetic discs: 2 1311; 1 line printer.
IBM 1401–internal storage: 8K bits; magnetic tapes: 4 7330.

Coding Languages
COBOL, RPG, Autocoder, Assembler, FORTRAN.

Services Available
Advice, operators, preparation of data, programming, software packages, systems analysis. Operate on a self-service, closed shop, open shop and block time basis. (depending on the Centre).

Fields of Application
Statistics, payroll, accounting, stock control.
Specialized areas: Banking current account control (Rio de Janeiro, Belo Horizonte and Salvador); banking savings accounts (Curitiba and Recife); commercial and manufacturing (Pôrto Alegre).

INDUSTRIA ELETRICA BROWN BOVERI S.A.
Caixa Postal 5528, São Paulo
Telephone: 478-6200

Officers
Paulo M. Alqueres, *EDP Manager*
Paulo de Tarso S. Ribeiro, *Systems Engineer*
Aimone N. Meneguzzi, *Software Designer*

Computer Installation
IBM 360/30–operating system: DOS; internal storage: 256K bits; magnetic tapes: 2 2415; magnetic discs: 4 2311; 1 line printer.

Coding Languages
COBOL, Assembler, RPG, FORTRAN, PL/1.

Service Available
Hardware rental. Operate on a self-service basis.

Fields of Application
Scientific, statistical, commercial, production control, accounting.
Specialized areas: Linear programming, payroll.

Training
IBM courses for systems analysts, programmers and operators.

ITT DATA SERVICES
Avenida Presidente Vargas 962, 5° andar, Rio de Janeiro
Telephone: 243-8071, 243-4162

Officers
Herb Kolber and Mario Moraes, *Joint General Managers*

Computer Installation
IBM 360/50–operating system: OS/DOS; internal storage: 256K bits; magnetic tapes: 8 3420; magnetic discs: 5 2314; 2 line printers.

IBM 360/30–operating system: DOS; internal storage: 64K bits; magnetic tapes: 4 2401; magnetic discs: 3 2314; 1 line printer.

Coding Languages
COBOL, BAL, RPG, FORTRAN.

Contemplated Equipment
IBM 370/145 and IBM 370/135.

Services Available
Advice, programming, education and training, operators, software packages, documentation, preparation of data, systems analysis. Operate on a self-service, remote access and block time basis.

Fields of Application
Scientific, statistical, commercial, production control, accounting, management, systems analysis, facilities management.
Specialized areas: Linear programming, investment, analysis, payroll, structural engineering.

Training
Courses in key-punch operation and basic programming.

MONTEDATA S.A.
Processadora de Dados
Rua dos Andrados 1234, 21° andar, Pôrto Alegre, Rio Grande do Sul
Telephone: 25-6542

Officers
Oscar Bayard Salgado Miranda, *Director*
Aramis Camargo de Lemos, *Director*
Daniel Enk, *Chief Analyst*

Computer Installation
IBM 360/30–operating system: DOS; internal storage: 64K bytes; magnetic tapes: 6 2415; magnetic discs: 3 2319; 2 line printers.

IBM 370/145–operating system: DOS; internal storage: 256K bytes; magnetic tapes: 6 3420; magnetic discs: 3 2319; 2 line printers.

Coding Languages
COBOL, Assembler.

Services Available
Operate on self-service basis.

Fields of Application
Scientific, commercial, accounting.
Specialized area: Bank services.

PROCESSAMENTO ELETRÔNICO LTDA. (PROCEL)
Trav. Francisco Leonardo Truda 40, 25° andar, Pôrto Alegre 90000, Rio Grande do Sul
Telephone: (0512) 25-3166

Officers
Ervino Fritsch, *Director*
José B. Glass, *Director*
Luiz F. J. Maia, *Director*

Computer Installation
BURROUGHS B3500–operating system: MCP; internal storage: 720K bits; magnetic tapes: 4 9-track; magnetic disc: 1; 1 line printer.

Coding Languages
Assembler, FORTRAN, COBOL, BPL.

Contemplated Equipment
BURROUGHS B1700 (remote).

Services Available
Advice, software packages, systems analysis. Operate on closed shop and block time basis.

Fields of Application
Commercial, production control, management, systems analysis, operational research.
Specialized areas: Sales analysis, analysis, structural engineering.

PROGRESSO E DESENVOLVIMENTO DE SANTOS (PRODESAN)*
Pça. Expedicionários 10, Santos

Dirigeant
R. Rodrigues, *Chef*

Equipement
BURROUGHS B5000–mémoire interne: 19,200 positions; bandes magnétiques: 4; 1 imprimante.

Langage de Programmation
Assembler.

Service Fourni
Documentation. Fonctionnement à porte ouverte; services fournis à la Prefeitura Municipal de Santos et Banco do Estado de São Paulo S.A.

Domaines d'Application
Statistique, commercial, comptabilité, gestion.
Domaines spécialisés: Services publiques.

SCHEMA PROCESSAMENTO DE DADOS COMÉRCIO E IMPORTAÇAO LTDA.
Al. Barros 662, São Paulo
Telephone: 52-2345, 52-9015

Officers
Luigi Nese, *Director*
Gustavo José da Nova Lion, *Director*
Carlos Alberto Salvatore (Filho), *Director*
Henrique Zanetti, *Director*

Computer Installation
BURROUGHS B500–operating system: MCP-II; internal storage: 19,200 bits; magnetic tapes: 4; magnetic disc: 1; 1 line printer.

Coding Languages
Assembler, RPG, COBOL.

Contemplated Equipment
BURROUGHS B1700 or B3500.

Services Available
Education and training, preparation of data, systems analysis. Operate on a self-service and block time basis.

Fields of Application
Statistical, commercial, systems analysis.
Specialized areas: Sales analysis, analysis.

Training
Courses in coding languages (Assembler, COBOL, FORTRAN, RPG, MCP).

SERVIÇES ELETRÔNICOS DE CONTABILIDADE LTDA. (SEC)*
Avenida Angélica no. 1987, São Paulo
Téléphone: 256-7786, 256-3028

Dirigeants
G. R. Navas, *Directeur*
P. A. P. Roque, *Directeur*
C. Silveira, *Chef d'analyse de systèmes*

Equipement
BURROUGHS B200–mémoire interne: 9,600 bytes; bandes magnétiques: 4 B421; 1 imprimante.
BURROUGHS B3500–système d'opération: MCP (CP14S); mémoire interne: 60K bytes; bandes magnétiques: 5 9392; disques magnétiques: 2 9371; 2 imprimantes.

Langages de Programmation
Assembler, COBOL, langage machine.

Equipement Projeté
Un nouveau B3500 en remplacement du B200.

Services Fournis
Conseils, programmation, opérateurs, software packages, documentation, préparation des données, systems analysis. Fonctionnement à porte fermée. Services fournis au groupe de la banque Banco Português do Brasil S.A.

Domaines d'Application
Commercial, comptabilité, gestion, systems analysis.
Domaine spécialisé: Applications de banque.

SERVIMEC S.A.
Processamento de Dados
Rua Afonso Pena 332, São Paulo
Telephone: 227-1402, 227-2501, 227-2301

Computer Installation
BURROUGHS B500–operating system: TOS; internal storage: 115K bits; magnetic tapes: 4 7-track; 1 line printer.
SIEMENS 4004–operating system: DOS; internal storage: 1,028K bits; magnetic tapes: 4; magnetic discs: 2 4578; 2 line printers.

Coding Languages
COBOL, Assembler, PL/1.

Services Available
Programming, education and training, operators, software packages, documentation, preparation of data, systems analysis. Operate on a self-service and block time basis.

Fields of Application
Statistical, commercial, production control, accounting, management, systems analysis.
Specialized areas: Sales analysis, analysis, payroll.

Training
Courses for personnel in analysis, programming and operations.

SUPERDATA S.A.
Processamento de Dados
Rua São José 90, Grupos 1211/1403, Guanabara

Officers
Humberto Luiz Guariento, *Managing Director*
Márcio I. C. Costa, *Technical Director*

Computer Installation
IBM 370/135–operating system: DOS-power; internal storage: 144K bits; magnetic tapes: 4 3420; magnetic discs: 5 2319; 2 line printers.

Coding Languages
COBOL, Assembler, PL/1, RPG.

Contemplated Equipment
IBM 370/145 with storage of 256K bits.

Services Available
Programming, operators, software packages, preparation of data, systems analysis. Operate on a self-service, closed shop and block time basis.

Fields of Application
Commercial, production control, accounting, management, systems analysis.
Specialized areas: Sales analysis, investment analysis, payroll.

UNIVEST S.A. ADMINISTRAÇÃO E PARTICIPAÇÕES
Rua São Benedito 189, Santo Amaro, São Paulo
Telephone: 269-4233

Officers
Eng. Domingos Carelli Netto, *General Manager, Data Processing*
Eng. Peter Gerd Beversdorf, *Systems Development Manager*

Brazil – Service Bureaux

Computer Installation
IBM 370/145–operating system: DOS; internal storage: 160K bytes; magnetic tapes: 8 3420, 2 2401; magnetic discs: 2 2319; 3 line printers.

IBM 360/40 (2)–operating system: DOS, internal storage: 128K and 64K bytes; magnetic tapes: 8 2401; magnetic discs: 3 2318; 3 line printers.

Coding Languages
Assembler, COBOL, RPG.

Contemplated Equipment
IBM 370/158.

Services Available
Programming, preparation of data, systems analysis. Operate on a self-service basis.

Fields of Application
Commercial, accounting, management, systems analysis, operational research.
Specialized areas: Linear programming, investment analysis, payroll.

RESEARCH INSTITUTION

BULGARIAN ACADEMY OF SCIENCES*
Institute of Mathematics with Computing Centre
Sofia 26, Boul. A. Ivanov 1
Telephone: 62-11-61

Officers
Acad. Prof. Dr. L. Iliev, *Director*

Computer Installation
MINSK-22–operating system: MID-2; internal storage: 303, 104 bits; magnetic tapes: 4; 1 line printer.

Coding Languages
MID-2, ALGOL.

Services Available
Use of the computer is available to academic institutions in Bulgaria.

Fields of Application
Scientific, operational research.

BULGARIA

NATIONAL CENTRE

CENTRAL INSTITUTE FOR COMPUTING TECHNIQUES (CIIT)
Sofia, 55 Chapaev Street
Telephone: 73-51

Officer
Dr. Angel Angelov, *Director*

Computer Installation
IBM 360/25–operating system: DOS; internal storage: 64K bits; magnetic tapes: 2; magnetic discs: 4; 1 line printer.

ES-1012 (2)–operating system: DOS; internal storage: 128K bits; magnetic tapes: 4 ES-5012; magnetic discs: 4ES-5052; 2 line printers. *Remote processing features:* 2 ES-8501.

Coding Languages
Assembler, FORTRAN, PL/1, COBOL.

Contemplated Equipment
ISOT 0310 minicomputer.

Services Available
Advice, programming, software packages, documentation. Operate on a self-service basis.

Fields of Application
Scientific, production control, accounting, management.
Specialized area: Structural engineering.

Training
Courses in installation, maintenance and exploitation of ES-1020.

CAMEROON

UNIVERSITY

UNIVERSITY OF YAOUNDÉ
Faculty of Science
B.P. 812, Yaoundé

Officers
Prof. J. Kamsu Kom, *Dean of Faculty*
Prof. G. E. Tanyi, *Head of Mathematics Department*

Contemplated Equipment
A computer using FORTRAN in the new Computer Science Section of the Mathematics Department.

Training
Degree courses in Mathematics including Computer Sciences, and courses in Informatics.

CANADA

EDUCATIONAL AND TRAINING INSTITUTIONS

CONTROL DATA INSTITUTE
50 Hallcrown Place, Willowdale, Ontario
Telephone: 491-9191

Officer
M. Martyne, *Director*

Computer Installation
CDC 3150–operating system: MSOS; internal storage: 16K bits; magnetic tapes: 2; magnetic discs: 2; 1 line printer. *Remote processing features:* COMM Adaptor (8 terminals).

Coding Languages
FORTRAN, COBOL, COMPASS, Machine language, HASP, HALP, BASIC, Assembler, RPG (under language simulation).

Contemplated Equipment
CDC 713 terminals.

Services Available
Education and training. Operate on a remote access, closed and open shop basis. Available only to students who have High School graduation and have successfully passed aptitude tests.

Field of Application
Education.

Training
Courses in computer operations (diploma), computer programming (diploma), computer maintenance technology (diploma), and a selection of over 400 advanced technical and management science seminars and programmes.

ELECTRONIC COMPUTER PROGRAMMING INSTITUTE*
5th Floor, Terminal Towers, 105 Main Street East, Hamilton 20, Ontario

Officers
E. A. Garrett, *Administrator, Faculty and Placement Director*
Janet McLean, *Administrative Assistant*

Coding Languages
Assembler, RPG, COBOL.

Contemplated Equipment
UNIVAC 9200 with 16K - bit store and 4 tape drives.

Services Available
Programming, education and training.

Field of Application
Commercial.

Training
Courses in RPG, IBM 360 Assembly Language programming, COBOL and systems application programming.

ELECTRONIC COMPUTER PROGRAMMING INSTITUTE*
371 King Street, London, Ontario
Telephone: 434-2193

Officers
H. Herzing

Computer Installation
UNIVAC 9200—internal storage: 8K bits.

Contemplated Equipment
Disc and tape.

Services Available
Programming, education and training.

Field of Application
Educational.
Specialized areas: Programming, key punch operation.

Training
Courses on programming and key punch operation.

ELECTRONIC COMPUTER PROGRAMMING INSTITUTE OF MONTREAL*
1315 Boulevard de Maisonneuve West, Montreal 107, Quebec

Officers
H. Herzing, *President*
G. Klisivitch, *Director*

Coding Languages
COBOL, RPG, BAL.

Service Available
Programming.

HERZING INSTITUTES OF CANADA LTD.
185 Bay Street, Suite 306, Toronto, Ontario, M5J 1K6
Telephone: (416) 363-6187

Officers
J. B. Murchie, *Director*

Services Available
Advice, programming, education and training, operators, preparation of data, systems analysis. Operate on an open shop basis.

Field of Application
Commercial.

Training
Certificate and diploma courses in IBM 360 and 370 basic and advanced programming; other courses in BAL, RPG, FORTRAN, PL/1, COBOL, DASD, operating systems and systems analysis.

UNIVERSITIES AND COLLEGES

CARLETON UNIVERSITY
Computing Centre
Ottawa, Ontario K1S 5B6
Telephone: (613) 231-5555

Officers
Dr. W. Dietiker, *Director of Computing and Data Processing*
Dr. John Nielson, *Manager of Scientific Programming*
E. A. Seamen, *Manager of Systems and Operations*
D. J. Dunsmore, *Manager, Administrative Data Processing*

Computer Installation
XDS Sigma 9—operating system: Universal Timesharing System; internal storage: 6, 291, 456 bits; magnetic tapes: 6 9-track; magnetic discs: 8 removable, 4 fixed; 2 line printers. *On-line satellite computers: 2 PDP-11. Remote processing features:* 4 lines synchronous up to 9600 band, 80 lines asynchronous for timesharing.

Coding Languages
COBOL, FORTRAN, BASIC, APL, ALGOL.

Services Available
Very limited computing only. Operate on closed shop, remote access and time-sharing basis.

Fields of Application
Teaching, research, administration.

Canada – Universities and Colleges

Training
Courses in programming, numerical methods, computer science and computer applications in Engineering from 2nd year undergraduate to 1st year graduate level, by Engineering Faculty and Mathematics Department.
Short courses: Familiarization courses for High School students in computer programming and use: up-dating course in computer applications and programming for professional engineers.

DALHOUSIE UNIVERSITY
Computer Centre
Halifax, Nova Scotia
Telephone: (902) 424-3471

Officers
Intab Ali, *Acting Director*

Computer Installation
CDC 6400–operating system: SCOPE 3·3; internal storage: 3,900K bits; magnetic tapes: 2 7-track, 2 9-track; magnetic discs: 5 841; 1 line printer. *Remote processing features:* support interactive terminals.

Coding Languages
FORTRAN, COBOL, ALGOL, COMPASS, BASIC.

Services Available
Advice, education and training, software packages, preparation of data. Operate on a closed shop basis.

Fields of Application
Scientific, commercial, accounting, management.

Training
Short courses in FORTRAN, COBOL, job control language and BASIC.

DOCUMENTATIONS AUTOMATIQUE DES TEXTES JURIDIQUES DE L'UNIVERSITÉ DE MONTRÉAL
Service de Documentation Juridique (SEDOJ)
C.P. 6128, Montreal 101, Quebec
Telephone: (514) 343-7755

Officers
Prof. J. Boncher, *Director*
P. Stewart, *Head of Programming Division, Computing Centre*
Prof. E. MacKay, *Assistant Director*

Computer Installation
CDC Cyber 74–operating system: SCOPE; internal storage: 640K 6-bit characters; magnetic tapes: 14; magnetic discs: CDC 841 plus systems disc; 3 line printers. *On-line satellite computer:* PDP-11. *Remote processing features:* various speeds, character coder, several remote substational and simple terminals.

Coding Languages
Assembler, FORTRAN.

Contemplated Equipment
CDC 844 disc; medium-speed cathode ray tube and print terminals; 2 CDC 1700.

Service Available
Documentation. Operate on an open shop (via consultants) basis.

Field of Application
Case law documentation.

LAKEHEAD UNIVERSITY
Oliver Road, Thunder Bay 'P', Ontario

Officer
Alan T. McEwan, *Director of Computer Centre*

Computer Installation
IBM 360/50–operating system: MVT; internal storage: 1,280K bits; magnetic tapes: 3 2400; magnetic discs: 7 2314; 2 line printers. *Remote processing features:* 2922.

Coding Languages
PL/1, FORTRAN, COBOL, APL, Assembler.

Services Available
Advice, programming, education and training, operators, software packages, preparation of data, systems analysis. Operate on a remote access, closed shop, time sharing basis.

Fields of Application
Scientific, statistical, commercial, accounting, management.

Training
The B.Sc. Mathematics course has a computer science option, and the Diploma in Business Administration course has a computer systems option.

LOYOLA COLLEGE
7141 Sherbrooke Street West, Montreal 262, Quebec
Telephone: (514) 482-0320

Officer
Rev. P.G. Malone, *President*

Computer Installation
UNIVAC 9300–operating system: MOS; internal storage: 128K bits; magnetic tapes: 4; 1 line printer. *Remote processing features:* 2 line controllers.
PDP-11/45–operating system: DOS; internal storage: 256K bits; magnetic discs: 1 RKO5 cartridge; 1 line printer.

Coding Languages
FORTRAN, PL/1, RPG, COBOL, Assembler, BASIC.

Services Available
Operate on a remote access, closed shop and time-sharing basis.

Fields of Application
Scientific, statistical, accounting, instruction.

Training
Day and evening courses leading to Bachelor of Commerce (Major in Computer Science) and Bachelor of Science (Major in Computer Science).

McGILL UNIVERSITY*
Computing Centre
Montreal, Quebec
Telephone: 392-5974

Officers
Professor W. D. Thorpe, *Director*

Computer Installation
IBM 360/75–operating system: OS MVT, internal storage: 512K bits; magnetic tapes: 4. *Remote processing features:* 2780.

IBM 360/65–operating systems: RAX; internal storage: 256K bits; magnetic tapes: 2; magnetic discs: 2 2314; 1 line printer. *Remote processing features:* IBM 1050 tele-types, IBM 2741.

Coding Languages
FORTRAN, COBOL, SIMSCRIPT, GPSS, PL/I.

Services Available
Advice, operators, preparation of data. Operate on a closed shop, remote access and time-sharing basis. Primarily for university research but commercial customers may use the computers.

Fields of Application
General research problems.

Training
M.Sc. Programme in Computer Science.

McMASTER UNIVERSITY
Hamilton 16, Ontario
Telephone: (416) 522-4971

Officers
Dr. G. L. Keech, *Director of the Data Processing and Computing Centre.*

Computer Installation
IBM 370/155–operating system: OS MFT; internal storage: 512K bits; magnetic tapes: 5 3420; magnetic discs: 3 3330; 2 1403 line printers. *Remote processing features:* 2 2260 CRTS.

CDC 6400–operating system: SCOPE; internal storage: 65,536 60-bit words; magnetic tapes: 6 604; magnetic discs: 1 6603, 6 854; 2 line printers. *Remote processing features:* 4 CDC User 200, 5 teletypes.

Coding Languages
FORTRAN, COBOL, MAP, COMPASS, ALGOL, BASIC, RUN.

Services Available
Operate on a closed shop basis. Available to University mainly with some time available for outside users.

Fields of Application
Scientific, engineering, statistical, accounting, management.
Specialized areas: Social science, health science, business payroll.

Training
Outline programming courses, seminars.

MOHAWK COLLEGE OF APPLIED ARTS AND TECHNOLOGY
135 Fennell Avenue West, Hamilton 40, Ontario
Telephone: 389-4461

Officers
R. J. Dent, *Manager of the Computer Centre*

Computer Installation
IBM 360/25–operating systems: DOS; internal storage: 384K bits; magnetic discs: 3 2311; 1 line printer.
PDP-8/S–internal storage: 48K bits; magnetic discs: 1 DEC-DF32.
PDP-8/E–internal storage: 8K 12-bit words; magnetic tapes: 1 TU56; 1 line printer. *Remote processing feature:* 1 UT06.

DATA GENERAL Nova 1210–internal storage: 8K 16-bit words with HS reader punch.
PDP-12/A–internal storage: 8K bits; 1 line printer.
PDP-14.

Coding Languages
FORTRAN, COBOL, PL/1, 360 BAL, DEC PAL, FOCAL, BASIC.

Services Available
Consultation, programming, education and training, operators, documentation, preparation of data, systems analysis, minicomputer advice programming, interfacing. Operate on a closed shop and block time basis. Available to departments, staff and students of the College and by rental to outside industries.

Fields of Application
Scientific, statistical, commercial, production control, accounting, management, systems analysis, operational research, all for educational purposes.
Specialized areas: student records, process control, numerical control.

Training
Certificate courses in computer systems technology and data processing. A variety of short introductory data processing, computer fundamentals, programming systems, computer hardware, assembly language programming courses.

NOVA SCOTIA TECHNICAL COLLEGE *
1360 Barrington Street, Halifax, Nova Scotia
Telephone: (902) 429-8300

Officers
Dr. J. H. L. Ahrens, *Professor of Applied Mathematics*
Mrs. S. Sutherland

Computer Installation
IBM 1130–internal storage: 16K 16-bit words; magnetic disc: 1 2311; 1 line printer.

Coding Languages
Assembler, FORTRAN.

Services Available
Consultation, programming, education and training, operators. Operate on a self-service and open shop basis. Available to faculty, students and staff of the college. Commercial use also.

Fields of Application
Scientific, statistical, operational research.

Training
Short courses in FORTRAN, disc monitor system and general subjects.

ONTARIO INSTITUTE FOR STUDIES IN EDUCATION (OISE)
252 Bloor Street West, Toronto, Ontario, M5S 1V6

Officers
R. W. B. Jackson, *Director*
J. H. M. Andrews, *Assistant Director*

Computer Installation
PDP-9–operating system: time sharing developed locally; internal storage: 24K 18-bit words; magnetic tapes: 4; magnetic discs: 2 RBO9; 1 line printer.
TSS8–internal storage: 20K 12-bit words; magnetic tapes: 2 Electapes; magnetic discs: 2 RFO8. *On-line satellite computer:* PDP-10. *Remote processing features:* via 1200 bps lines.

Coding Languages
BASIC, FORTRAN, FOCAL, MACRO9, CAN (OISE-developed CAI author language).

Services Available
Education and Training, software packages, documentation. Operate on a remote access and time sharing basis. Available only to educational institutions or teachers and students.

Fields of Application
Scientific, statistical.
Specialized area: Education.

Training
University of Toronto M. Ed., M.A. and Ph.D. courses in Educational Theory (with specialization in computer applications to education).

QUEEN'S UNIVERSITY AT KINGSTON
Computing Centre
Kingston, Ontario
Telephone: 547-6250

Computer Installation
IBM 360/50–operating system: OS/360; internal storage: 4,096K bits; magnetic tapes: 3 2400/V; magnetic discs: 7 2314; 2 line printers. *Remote processing features:* 2 terminals.
BURROUGHS B6700–operating system: MCP; internal storage: 6,044K bits; magnetic tapes: 6; magnetic discs: 5 fixed head; 1 line printer. *Remote processing features:* 4 terminals.

Coding Languages
ALGOL, FORTRAN, PL/1, COBOL, APL, BASIC.

Services Available
Advice, programming, education and training, operators, software packages, documentation, preparation of data, systems analysis. Operate on a self-service, remote access, closed shop, block time and time-sharing basis.

Fields of Application
Scientific, statistical, management, operational research.
Specialized area: Education.

Training
Academic courses up to M.Sc. level.

ST. FRANCIS XAVIER UNIVERSITY*
Computer Centre
P.O. Box 67, Antigonish, Nova Scotia
Telephone: (902) 867-2230

Officers
Ronald MacKinnon, *Director*

Computer Installation
IBM 1620–internal storage: 40K bits; magnetic discs: 2 1311; 1 line printer.

Coding Languages
FORTRAN, SPS.

Contemplated Equipment
IBM 1130.

Services Available
Advice, operators, preparation of data, programming. Operate on a self-service and open shop basis.

Fields of Application
Scientific, statistical, operational research.

Training
Introductory course in computer science and short courses in FORTRAN and FORTRAN IID for IBM 1620 and an introduction to computer and general programming.

ST. MARY'S UNIVERSITY*
Computer Centre
Robie Street, Halifax, Nova Scotia
Telephone: 422-6421

Officers
A. M. Tangley, *Director*

Computer Installation
IBM 1130–internal storage: 8K 16-bit words; magnetic discs: 2; 1 line reader.

Coding Languages
FORTRAN IV, Assembler, SL/1, APL.

Services Available
Outside work for other educational institutions. Operate on a closed shop basis.

Fields of Application
Administration, scientific, educational.
Specialized areas: Payroll, accounting routines.

Training
Non-credit courses.

SIMON FRASER UNIVERSITY
Burnaby 2, British Columbia

Officers
Dr. T. Sterling, *Director – Computing Science*
R. Jewell, *Director – Computing Facility*

Computer Installation
IBM 370/155–operating system: MVT/HMP; internal storage: 1.5 million bytes; magnetic tapes: 4 IBM 3420/V; magnetic discs: 14 Memorex 3660; 2 line printers. *Remote processing features:* Low speed and RJE.

Coding Languages
FORTRAN, PL/1, BAL, COBOL, MARUN, MNERVA, APL, SNOBOL, ALGOL.

Services Available
Advice, education and training, software packages, preparation of data, systems analysis. Operate on a remote access, closed shop and time sharing basis. Available to commercial customers only for processing and data conversion services.

Fields of Application
Scientific, statistical, commercial, accounting, management, systems analysis.
Specialized areas: Payroll, university.

Training
Degree programme in Computer Science. Interdisciplinary support in Computer Science for a wide variety of programmes.

SIR GEORGE WILLIAMS UNIVERSITY
1455 de Maisonneuve Boulevard West, Montreal 107, Quebec
Telephone: 879-5925

Officers
Graham Martin, *Director, Computer Centre*

Computer Installation
CDC 6200—operating system: KRONOS; internal storage: 98K 60-bit words; magnetic tapes: 4 CDC 604 (60Kc tapes); magnetic discs: 10 CDC 841; 2 line printers. *Remote processing features:* 40 dial-in ports, 4 remote job entry card terminals.

Coding Languages
FORTRAN, COBOL, Assembler and special application languages.

Contemplated Equipment
Communication front-end, expansion of disc system and of communication.

Services Available
Advice, programming, education and training, software packages, computer time. Operate on a remote access, closed shop and time-sharing basis.

Fields of Application
Scientific, commercial, education.
Specialized areas: Analysis, payroll, software development.

Training
B.Sc. course in Computer Science, B.Comm. course in Quantitative Methods.

UNIVERSITÉ DE MONTRÉAL
Centre de Calcul
B.P. 6128, Montréal 101, Québec
Téléphone: 343-6011

Dirigeant
Jean A. Baudot, *Directeur du Centre*

Equipement
CDC Cyber 74—système d'opération: SCOPE; mémoire interne: 3,900K bits; bandes magnétiques: 8 604; disques magnétiques: 8 844; 3 imprimantes. *Calculateurs satellites en ligne:* PDP-11. *Transmission des données à distance:* terminaux CDC 200 et terminaux lents.
CDC 1700—système d'opération: MSOS; mémoire interne: 450K bits; bandes magnétiques 3 CDC 601; disques magnétiques: 3 854; 1 imprimante. *Transmission des données à distance:* terminal graphique interactif CDC 274 et terminaux lents.

Langages de Programmation
FORTRAN, COMPASS, LISP, SNOBOL, L6, SIMSCRIPT, BASIC, COBOL, ALGOL, BALM, MIMIC.

Services Fournis
Consultation, opérateurs, préparation des données programmation, software packaging, enseignement et formation, documentation. Fonctionnement en porte fermée et par accès à distance, contrat de service et time-sharing.

Domaines d'Application
Scientifique, recherches opérationelles.
Domaines spécialisés: informatique, documentation.

Formation
Informatique, B.Sc., M.Sc. et Ph.D. options: exploitation des ordinateurs, informatique théorie, recherche opérationelle et calcul scientifique.

UNIVERSITÉ DE SHERBROOKE
Service de l'Informatique
Sherbrooke, Québec

Dirigeant
G. Gosselin

Equipement
IBM 360/40—système d'opération: OS; mémoire interne: 256K octets; bandes magnétiques: 2415; disques magnétiques 2314/1; 1 imprimante.

Langages de Programmation
FORTRAN, COBOL, PL/1, Assembler, RPG, ALGOL.

Equipement Projeté
IBM 370/145.

Services Fournis
Conseils, programmation, opérateurs, analyse de programmerie. Fonctionnement à porte ouverte.

Domaines d'Application
Enseignement, administration, sciences.

Formation
Baccalauréat en sciences (informatique), Maîtrise en arts (analyse de systèmes).

UNIVERSITÉ LAVAL
Centre de traitement de l'information
Cité Universitaire, Sainte-Foy, Québec, G1H 7P4
Telephone: 656-3105

Officer
Louis P. A. Robichaud, *Director of the Centre*

Computer Installation
IBM 370/155—operating system: OS; internal storage: 1,024K bytes; magnetic tapes: 6 3420; magnetic discs: 8 3330; 3 line printers. *Remote processing features:* 2 medium speed, 32 low speed.
IBM 370/145—operating system: DOS; internal storage: 512K bytes; magnetic tapes: 6 3420; magnetic discs: 4 3330, 4 2314; 3 line printers. *Remote processing features:* 72 low speed.

Coding Languages
FORTRAN, Assembler, COBOL, PL/1, APL, etc.

Contemplated Equipment
IBM 370/158.

Services Available
Education and training, operators. Operate on a remote access, closed shop and time-sharing basis.

Fields of Application
Scientific, statistical, commercial, accounting, management, systems analysis, operational research, education.
Specialized areas: Payroll, structural engineering, medical research and non-numerical applications.

Training
Three B.Sc. courses.

UNIVERSITY OF ALBERTA
Department of Computing Science
615 General Services Bldg., Edmonton, Alberta T6G 2E1
Telephone: 432-5198

Officer
Dr. A. Wouk, *Chairman, Department of Computing Science*

Computer Installation
PDP-9—operating system: KM9-15; internal storage: 147,456 bits; magnetic discs: 1 RFO9.
PDP-8—internal storage: 49,152 bits.
PDP-8/L—internal storage: 49,152 bits.
INTERDATA 3—operating system: BOS5 4A; internal storage: 65,536 bits.
INTERDATA 4—operating system: BOS5 4A; internal storage: 65,536 bits.
MICRODATA 1606—internal storage: 65,536 bits.

Coding Languages
FORTRAN, FOCAL, ML1, Assembler.

Contemplated Equipment
PDP-11/45.

Services Available
Education and training. Operate on an open shop basis. Available only to staff and students of the University.

Fields of Application
Education.

Training
B.Sc., M.Sc. and Ph.D. degree courses.

UNIVERSITY OF BRITISH COLUMBIA
Computing Centre
Vancouver 8, British Columbia
Telephone: 736-6073

Officers
Dr. J. Kennedy, *Director*
A. G. Fowler, *Assistant Director*

Computer Installation
IBM 360/67—operating system: MTS; internal storage: 8 million bits; magnetic tapes: 5 9-track, 1 7-track; magnetic discs: 16 ITEL Double Density Drives; 3 line printers. *On-line satellite computers:* Adage Graphics Terminal and 2 PDP-8. *Remote processing features:* TTY 2741, CRT, IBM 2780, Minicomputers.

Coding Languages
FORTRAN, Assembler, PL/1, SNOBOL, COBOL, ALGOL, LISP.

Contemplated Equipment
IBM 370/168.

Services Available
Advice, operators, preparation of data, software packages, education and training, documentation. Operate on a remote access, closed shop and time-sharing basis. Available to staff and students of the University.

Fields of Application
Scientific, statistical.

Training
B.Sc., M.Sc. and Ph.D. courses in Computer Science.

UNIVERSITY OF CALGARY
Department of Computer Services
Calgary, Alberta, T2N 1N4
Telephone: (403) 284-6201

Officer
Dr. C. B. Marx, *Director*

Computer Installation
IBM 360/50—operating system: OS MFT/HASP; internal storage: 512K bits; magnetic tapes: 5 3420; magnetic discs: 10 CDC2312; 1 line printer. *Remote processing features:* Remote Data Entry — VIDEO/360.
CDC 6400—operating system: KRONOS.

Coding Languages
FORTRAN IV, Assembler, COBOL, COMPASS, RPG, PL/1, ALGOL.

Services Available
Advice, operators, preparation of data, programming, systems analysis, education and training. Operate on a closed shop, time-sharing and remote access basis. Available only to other educational institutions, government agencies, and non-profit organizations at commercial rates.

Fields of Application
Scientific and administrative systems development.
Specialized area: Information retrieval.

Training
Programming languages and applications packages.

UNIVERSITY OF MANITOBA
Computer Centre
Winnipeg, Manitoba
Telephone: (204) 474-9249

Officer
M. S. Doyle, *Director*

Computer Installation
IBM 360/65—operating system: OS-MVT; internal storage: 14,680,064 bits; magnetic tapes: 4 2400; magnetic discs: 4 2311, 1 2314; 3 line printers. *On-line satellite computers:* 2 1978, 1 PDP-9, 1 PDP-11. *Remote processing features:* 2260, 2741, 2780.

Coding Languages
FORTRAN IV, ALGOL, COBOL, Assembler, PL/1.

Services Available
Advice, operators, preparation of data, programming, software packages, systems analysis. Operate on a closed shop and remote access basis. Time-sharing terminals on premises.

Fields of Application
Scientific, statistical, systems analysis, operational research, teaching.

Training
Computer Science course at undergraduate and graduate level.

UNIVERSITY OF MANITOBA
Faculty of Medicine
Computer Department for Health Sciences
753 McDermot Ave., Winnipeg, Manitoba R3E 0W3

Officer
Dr. M. G. Saunders, *Director*

Computer Installation
CDC 1700—operating system: MSOS; internal storage: 512K bits; magnetic tapes: 1 609; magnetic discs: 2 854; 1 line printer. *On-line satellite computer:* connected to the CDC SC1700 (core to core). *Remote processing features:* 3 remote analog/digital systems.

Canada — Universities and Colleges

Coding Languages
FORTRAN IV (ASA), Assembler.

Contemplated Equipment
Floating point hardware, CDC 1733 disc controller.

Services Available
Consultation, programming, preparation of data. Operate on a closed shop and remote access basis; time-sharing terminals on the premises. Available to members of the Faculties of Medicine and Dentistry and restricted at the moment to research projects.

Fields of Application
All computer techniques used in medical research—statistics, mathematics, on-line I/0, real-time experiments in neurophysiology and respirology, etc.
Specialized areas: Medical research and research in optimal computer configuration for medical research.

UNIVERSITY OF MONTREAL
École polytechnique — Centre de Calcul
2500 ave Marie Guyard, Montreal 269, Quebec
Telephone: 344-4711

Officer
Prof. Bernard L. Lanctot, *Directeur du Centre de Calcul*

Computer Installation
IBM 360/50—operating system: OS/MFT; internal storage: 8 million bits; magnetic tapes: 2 2415; magnetic discs: 2 2319; 2 line printers. *Remote processing features:* low speed start-stop, BSYNC.

Coding Languages
FORTRAN IV, Assembler, COBOL, ALGOL.

Services Available
Advice, programming, education and training, operators, systems analysis. Operate on a remote access, closed shop and time-sharing basis.

Fields of Application
Scientific, commercial.

Training
Basic course in programming, advanced programming, numerical methods.

UNIVERSITY OF NEW BRUNSWICK*
Computing Centre
Fredericton, New Brunswick
Telephone: (506) 475-9471

Officer
W. D. Wasson, *Director of Computing Centre and Head of Computer Science Department*

Computer Installation
IBM 360/50—operating system: OS/MFT; internal storage: 384K bytes; magnetic tapes: 2 2401; magnetic discs: 9 2314; 2 line printers. *Remote processing features:* 2 2780 and 3 1130 RJE terminals.

Coding Languages
FORTRAN, SPS, COGO, PL/1, PACTOLUS, CSMP, MATLAND, ICES.

Services Available
Operators, programming, systems analysis. Operate on a closed shop basis.

Fields of Application
Statistics and mathematics, teaching and engineering applications.
Specialized areas: Electric power system computation, survey computations.

Training
M.Sc. programme in Computer science.

UNIVERSITY OF OTTAWA
Computing Centre
375 Nicholas Street, Ottawa, Ontario
Telephone: (613) 231-3203

Officers
William J. Lamb, *Director*
J. D. Massouras, *Manager, Operations*

Computer Installation
IBM 360/65—operating system: OS/MVT-HASP; internal storage: 768K bytes; magnetic tapes: 7 240; magnetic discs: 2 2314, 1 2303; 2 line printers. *Remote processing features:* 2 batch terminals.

Coding Languages
FORTRAN, COBOL, Assembler, PL/1, APL, SNOBOL, Coursewriter.

Contemplated Equipment
LCS

Services Available
Advice, programming, education and training, operators, software packages, preparation of data, systems analysis. Operate on a closed shop, remote access and block time basis.

Fields of Application
Scientific, statistical, accounting, management.
Specialized areas: Analysis, payroll.

Training
Programming service courses.

UNIVERSITY OF OTTAWA
Linguistics Documentation Centre
Ottawa, Ontario, K1N 6N5

Officer
Prof. B. Harris, *Director*

Computer Installation
IBM 360/65.

Coding Languages
FORTRAN, SNOBOL.

Services Available
Advice, software packages, documentation. Operate on a block time and time-sharing basis.

Field of Application
Scientific.
Specialized area: Linguistics research.

UNIVERSITY OF SASKATCHEWAN
Computer Centre
Regina, Saskatchewan, S45 3H6
Telephone: (306) 584-4633

Officer
Dr. L. R. Symes, *Director of Computer Centre*

Computer Installation
IBM 360/40—operating system: OS/MFT; internal storage: 2,048K bits; magnetic tapes: 2 2401; magnetic discs: 4 2314; 1 line printer. *On-line satellite computer:* PDP-11. *Remote processing features:* IBM 370/155.

Coding Languages
FORTRAN, Assembler, PL/1, COBOL, ALGOL, RPG.

Services Available
Advice, programming, software packages, systems analysis. Operate on a closed shop basis.

Fields of Application
Statistical, scientific, management, teaching.

Training
Computer science major leading to B.A., B.Sc. and B.Admin. degrees.

UNIVERSITY OF SASKATCHEWAN
Computation Centre
College Drive, Saskatoon, Saskatchewan
Telephone: (306) 343-2638

Officers
Dr. P. N. Nikiforuk, *Chairman, Computer Advisory Committee*
N. Glassel, *Manager, Computation Centre*

Computer Installation
IBM 370/155—operating system: OS-HASP/MVT/TSO; internal storage: 1,024K bytes; magnetic tapes: 5 3400; magnetic discs: 6 3330; 3 line printers. *On-line satellite computers:* HP2000A, PDP-11, PDP-8, Super Nova. *Remote processing features:* 3780 RJE Station.

Coding Languages
FORTRAN, PL/1, COBOL, ALGOL, WATFOR, Assembler, SNOBOL, WATFIV, SPITBOL, other student languages.

Services Available
Advice, operators, preparation of data, programming, software packages, systems analysis, education and training, documentation. Operate on a closed shop, remote access and time-sharing basis.

Fields of Application
Scientific, statistical, commercial, accounting, management, systems analysis.
Specialized areas: Analysis, payroll, medical research.

Training
Programming courses.

UNIVERSITY OF TORONTO
Computer Centre
Sandford Fleming Laboratories, 10 King's College Rd., Toronto, Ontario
Telephone: 928-4990

Officers
Dr. J. C. Wilson, *Director*
Prof. M. J. Dignam, *Chairman, UTCC Policy Committee*
Dr. T. E. Hull, *Chairman, Department of Computer Science*

Computer Installation
IBM 370/165—operating system: OS/MVT-HASP; internal storage: 16,384K bits; magnetic tapes: 6 2401; magnetic discs: 4 3330, 8 2314; 6 line printers. *On-line satellite computers:* IBM 360/20, IBM 1130, Data 100. *Remote processing features:* CRJE, HASP/RJE, HASP-to-HASP.

IBM 360/65—operating system: OS/MVT-HASP; internal storage: 12,288K bits; magnetic tapes: 2 2401; magnetic discs: 16 2314; 1 line printer. *Remote processing features:* ATS, APL, CPS, HASP/HASP.

IBM 7094—operating system: IBSYS; internal storage: 1,152K bits; magnetic tapes: 8 729; magnetic discs: 1 2302; 1 line printer.

Coding Languages
FORTRAN, ALGOL, COBOL, PL/1, Assembler, etc.

Contemplated Equipment
IBM 370/165 or 168.

Services Available
Advice, programming, education and training, operators, software packages, documentation, preparation of data. Operate on a self-service, remote access, closed shop, block time, open shop (7094) and time-sharing basis.

Fields of Application
Scientific, statistical, operational research.
Specialized areas: Analysis, structural engineering, medical research, education.

Training
The Computer Centre offers training only in local specific features. The Department of Computer Science offers: data processing and programming graduate and undergraduate; graduate programme in computer science leading to M.A. and Ph.D. degrees.

UNIVERSITY OF WATERLOO*
Waterloo, Ontario
Telephone: (519) 744-6111

Officer
J. Wesley Graham, *Professor of Applied Analysis and Computer Science.*

Computer Installation
IBM 360/75—operating systems: OS/MVT-HASP; internal storage: 16,770,216 bits; magnetic tapes: 4 2401; magnetic discs: 3 2314 disc drives; 6 line printers. *On-line satellite computers:* 2 IBM 20. *Remote processing features:* 75 2741 terminals, 8 2260 display units, 8 Datel 30 terminals.

IBM 360/44—operating system: DAMPS; internal storage: 1,048,576 bits; magnetic discs: 2 2311; 1 line printer.

IBM 360/40—internal storage: 2,097,152 bits; 1 line printer. *Remote processing features:* 25 2741 terminals.

Services Available
Consultation, programming, education and training, operators, software packages, documentation, systems analysis. Operate on a self-service, remote access and closed shop basis; time-sharing terminals on the premises. Available only to faculty, staff and students.

Fields of Application
Unlimited.

Training
Extensive graduate and undergraduate courses covering all aspects of computer studies; short courses in various programming languages.

UNIVERSITY OF WESTERN ONTARIO*
London, Ontario

Officer
G. T. Lake, *Director of Computer Science Department*

Computer Installation
PDP-10—operating system: MONITOR; internal storage: 6 million bits; magnetic tapes: 4 9-track; magnetic discs: 8 RPO2, 2 RD10; 1 line printer. *On-line satellite computers:* GE 115, Univac 9200. *Remote processing features:* 30 teletypes, 3 batch terminals.

IBM 7040—operating system: IBSYS; internal storage: 1,150K bits; magnetic tapes: 7 7-track; magnetic discs: 1 1301; 1 line printer. *On-line satellite computer:* Hardware interface to PDP-10. *Remote processing features:* remote access to IBM 360/85, IBM 360/65, Univac 1108, CDC 6680, etc.

Coding Languages
FORTRAN, COBOL, BASIC, AID, MAP, MACRO-10, ALGOL.

Services Available
Operators. Operate on a closed shop and remote access basis. Time-sharing terminals on the premises. Available only to educational institutions.

Fields of Application
Scientific.

Training
B.A., B.Sc. (Honours), B.Sc. (Pass) and M.S. courses in Computer Science.

UNIVERSITY OF WESTERN ONTARIO
Althouse College of Education
1137 Western Road, London, Ontario, N6G 1G7
Telephone: (519) 679-3824

Officers
Allan E. Lott, *Director*
John E. Walsh, *Associate Professor*

Computer Installation
IBM 1130—operating system: OS/V2; internal storage: 16K 16-bit words; magnetic tapes: 1 Infotec TS 1130 7-track; magnetic discs: 2 2310; 1 line printer.

Coding Languages
FORTRAN, COBOL, RPG, Assembler, SL/I, HYPO, BASIC, NDFOR.

Service Available
Student programme compilation. Operate on an open shop basis. Available only to educational institutions, government institutions e.g. libraries, hospitals. No commercial customers.

Field of Application
Education – teacher training.
Specialized areas: Optical mark reading on languages and applications.

Training
Post-graduate college, teacher training for Ontario secondary school system. Certificates are offered in the field of Computer Studies.

UNIVERSITY OF WINDSOR*
Windsor, Ontario
Telephone: (519) 253-4232

Officer
L. F. Miernicke, *Director, Computer Centre*

Computer Installation
IBM 1620—operating system: Monitor; internal storage: 40K bits; magnetic discs: 2; 1 line printer.

IBM 360/50—operating system: OS; internal storage: 256K; magnetic tapes: 2 2401; magnetic discs: 15 2314; 2 line printers.

Coding Languages
FORTRAN, SPS, PL/1, SNOBOL IV, COBOL, Assembler, ALGOL, WATFOR, RPG.

Contemplated Equipment
Increased storage of 256K bits for IBM 360/50.

Service Available
Operators. Operate on a closed and open shop basis. Availability limited by core size.

Fields of Application
General instruction, research and administrative data processing.

Training
Inter-faculty department of computer science.

YORK UNIVERSITY
4700 Keele Street, Downsview, Ontario
Telephone: 667-2317

Officers
F. D. Simpkin, *Director, Computer Services*

Computer Installation
IBM 370/155—operating system: HASP; internal storage: 1,024K bits; magnetic tapes: 5 3420; magnetic discs: 5 2314; 2 line printers.

Coding Languages
FORTRAN, COBOL, APL, Assembler, BASIC.

Services Available
Advice, operators, preparation of data, programming, software packages, systems analysis, education and training, documentation. Operate on a closed shop basis.

Fields of Application
Scientific, statistical, commercial, accounting, management, systems analysis, operational research.
Specialized area: Payroll.

GOVERNMENT ESTABLISHMENTS

BANK OF CANADA*
Research Department
234 Wellington Street, Ottawa, Ontario
Telephone: 232-6494

Coding Language
FORTRAN IV.

Services Available
Software packages and documentation. Programmes, test decks and manuals for the Databank-Massager System are available at nominal cost.

Fields of Application
Statistical, econometric.

Canada – Government Establishments

CORPORATION OF THE DISTRICT OF SURREY*
14245, 56th Avenue, Surrey, British Columbia
Telephone: 596-5111

Officer
R. W. Ruhwald, *Data Processing Co-ordinator*

Computer Installation
HONEYWELL H 200/120–operating system: OS MOD 1 (TR); internal storage: 16K bits; magnetic tapes: 5 204B 16; 1 line printer.

Coding Languages
COBOL, FORTRAN IV, Easycoder, RPG.

Services Available
Advice, programming, education and training, operators, software packages, documentation, preparation of data, systems analysis. Operate on a closed shop basis. Available only to municipal and provincial corporations in British Columbia.

Fields of Application
All governmental applications.
Specialized areas: Tax assessment and collection, social welfare, management cost control and information systems.

STATISTICS CANADA
Tunney's Pasture, Ottawa, Ontario, K1A 0T6
Telephone: (613) 996 7084

Officer
Dr. Sylvia Ostery, *Chief Statistician*

Computer Installation
IBM 370/165–operating system: MVT/HASP; internal storage: 12 million bits; magnetic tapes: 16 3420/7; magnetic discs: 12 3330; 5 line printers. *Remote processing features:* 4 remote batch terminals, 32 IBM 2741 terminals for RJE and ATS.

Coding Languages
COBOL, FORTRAN, PL/1, Assembler.

Contemplated Equipment
IBM 370/168; OCR system.

Services Available
Advice, software packages, documentation. Operate on a remote access, closed and open shop (research applications) and time sharing basis.

Field of Application
Statistical.
Specialized areas: Sociology, economics, mathematical statistics, data processing.

Training
Courses in COBOL, FORTRAN, Assembler, PL/1 and job control language; a variety of courses on how to use in-house developed utility programmes; computer operator training course; courses on computer concepts for subject matter staff.

RESEARCH INSTITUTIONS

BELL – NORTHERN RESEARCH
Box 3511, Station C, Ottawa, Ontario, K1Y 4H7

Officers
Dr. D. A. Chisolm, *President*
R. W. Quirk, *Vice-President, Administration*

H. L. Webster, *Executive Vice-President, Research and Development*
W. J. Inkster, *Vice-President, Systems Engineering*

Computer Installation
IBM 360/65–operating systems: CP/CMS, OS; internal storage: 1 million bytes; magnetic tapes: 6 Potter drives; magnetic discs: 24 2314; 2 line printers. *Remote processing features:* RJE, terminals.

Coding Languages
FORTRAN, COBOL, PL/1, APL, Assembler, MARK IV.

Contemplated Equipment
IBM 370/145 (backup for 360/65); IBM 370/168.

Services Available
Advice, programming, software packages, documentation, systems analysis. Operate on a self-service, remote access, block time, open shop and time-sharing basis. Available to batch users only on second and third shifts.

Fields of Application
Scientific, accounting, management, systems analysis, operational research.
Specialized areas: Analysis, payroll, switching system, digital simulation.

Training
CMS courses.

TELEDYNE EXPLORATION
221, 62nd Avenue S.W., Calgary, Alberta

Officer
L. C. Hughes, *Vice-President and Regional Manager*

Computer Installation
IBM 360/44–internal storage: 128K bits; magnetic discs: 4 3420; 1 line printer.

Coding Languages
FORTRAN, Assembly, COBOL.

Services Available
Preparation of data, programming, software packages. Operate on a self-service basis.

Fields of Application
Scientific, commercial.
Specialized area: Seismic operations.

CONSULTANTS

CENTI (CANADA) LTÉE*
Place du Canada no. 1365, Montréal 101, Québec
Téléphone: (514) 861-2035

Dirigeants
C. Boch, *Président*
J-C. Rougier, *Directeur*
P. Broutin, *Chef, Enseignement et Formation*

Services Fournis
Conseils, programmation, enseignement et formation, documentation, préparation des données, systems analysis.

Domaines d'Application
Gestion, organisation, scientifique, systèmes, recherche opérationnelle.

Formation
Formation de programmeurs et d'analystes.
Seminaires d'information de cadres et dirigeants à l'informatique et à l'analyse fonctionnelle.

COMPUTECH CONSULTING CANADA LTD.
1009, 1177 West Hastings Street, Vancouver, British Columbia
Telephone: 688-1371

Officers
G. R. Gisel, *President*
I. U. Reid, *Vice-President*

Coding Languages
Assembler, PL/1, FORTRAN, COBOL, BAL, RPG, NEAT/3, Easycoder.

Services Available
Advice, programming, education and training, documentation, systems analysis.

Fields of Application
Statistical, commercial, production control, accounting, management, systems analysis.
Specialized areas: Sales analysis, analysis, payroll.

Training
Short courses in general data processing, computers for management, computers for engineers, etc.

CYBERNETION CONSULTANTS LTD.*
2401 Oxford Tower, Edmonton, Alberta
Telephone: (403) 429-7271

Officers
W. B. McMinn, *President*
W. C. Stothers, *Vice-President*
A. B. Mitchell, *Secretary*

Computer Installation
IBM 1130—internal storage: 8K 16-bit words; magnetic discs: 1; 1 line printer.

Coding Languages
FORTRAN, IDEAL, COBOL, Assembler, APL.

Services Available
Advice, programming, systems and software design. Operate on a self-service and open shop basis.

Fields of Application
Scientific, statistical, commercial, production control, accounting, management, systems analysis, operational research.
Specialized areas: Linear programming, management information systems.

Training
Credit course in Computing Science from the Alberta Institute of Chartered Accountants.

DECCA RADAR CANADA (1967) LTD.*
23 Six Point Road, Toronto 570, Ontario
Telephone: (416) 239-1161, 4

Officer
T. Morrison

Computer Installation
BURROUGHS B4294 Accounting Calculator—internal storage: 9800 bits.

Coding Languages
Assembler, FORTRAN, ALGOL, COBOL.

Contemplated Equipment
HONEYWELL 16K bit computer complex, with data communications Rapid Access Mass Storage, and multi-terminal capabilities.

Services Available
Consultation, programming, education and training, software packages, documentation, preparation of data, systems analysis.

Fields of Application
Dynamic information systems design (traffic control systems), systems analysis, operational research, special hardware control equipment design, management information systems.

Training
Courses normally confined to the use of our specially designed equipment and systems.

INBUCON SERVICES LTD.*
Etobicoke Square, 4 Eva Road, Etobicoke, Ontario
Telephone: (416) 485-7689

Officer
H. W. Royl, *President*

Services Available
Consultation, preparation of data, programming, systems analysis.

Fields of Application
Manufacturing, accounting, management, operational research, marketing planning.
Specialized areas: Corporate planning, industrial and human relations.

KATES, PEAT, MARWICK AND CO.*
Prudential Building, 4 King Street West, Toronto 1, Ontario
Telephone: (416) 362-2371

Also at:
1155 Dorchester Boulevard West, Montreal 2, Quebec
Telephone: (514) 866-4961

900 West Hastings Street, Vancouver 1, British Columbia
Telephone: (604) 688-3661

309 Eight Avenue S.W., Calgary, Alberta
Telephone: (403) 266-6041

287 Broadway Avenue, Winnipeg 1, Manitoba
Telephone: (204) 942-3325

Officers
G. H. Cowperthwaite *(Toronto)*
R. D. Elhart *(Montreal)*
J. C. Witt *(Vancouver)*
A. Lennox *(Calgary)*
J. K. Stephenson *(Winnipeg)*

Services Available
Consultation, systems analysis, equipment feasibility studies, equipment selection, economic evaluations, conversion planning, organisation and management, software systems selection and modification, control systems.

Fields of Application
General and scientific management, operations research, project management, industrial engineering, marketing, production and inventory control, information systems, general and cost accounting systems, data processing and transmission systems and related areas.

KURTZ AND STEEL LTD.
2275 Speakman Drive, Sheridan Park, Ontario
Telephone: (416) 822-7710

Officers
B. Kurtz, *President*
K. A. Steel, *Vice-President*

Computer Installation
MOHAWK 7208 remote high speed terminal; 1 line printer.

Coding Languages
FORTRAN, COBOL.

Services Available
Programming, software packages, systems analysis. Operate on a remote access and open shop basis.

Fields of Application
Production control, management, systems analysis, operational research.
Specialized areas: Maintenance, production and construction scheduling.

L. & W. DATA SYSTEMS LTD.*
120 Eglinton Avenue East, Toronto 12, Ontario
Telephone: 481-7251

Officers
M. J. Lucas, *President*
D. P. Wray, *Vice-President*

Services Available
Consultation, programming, software packages, systems analysis.

Fields of Application
Scientific, accounting, management.
Specialized areas: On-line computer systems, simulation techniques.

ARTHUR D. LITTLE OF CANADA LTD.*
120 Eglinton Avenue East, Toronto 12, Ontario
Telephone: (416) 487-4114

Services Available
Consultation, systems analysis.

Fields of Application
Scientific, statistical, commercial, production control, operational research, management information systems, market research, inventory control, physical distribution.

P.S. ROSS & PARTNERS*
1 Place Ville Marie, Montreal 2, Quebec
Telephone: (514) 861-7481

Also at:
880 Chemin Ste-Foy, Quebec City, Quebec
Telephone: (418) 681-0081

3 Sir Winston Churchill Square, Edmonton, Alberta
Telephone: (403) 429-5102

20 Hughson Street South, Hamilton, Ontario
Telephone: (416) 525-5309

90 Sparks Street, Ottawa, Ontario
Telephone: (613) 236-9662

200 University Avenue, Toronto 1, Ontario
Telephone: (416) 383-8281

5161 George Street, Halifax, Nova Scotia
Telephone: (902) 422-5861

1177 West Hastings Street, Suite 1500, Vancouver 1, British Columbia
Telephone: (204) 942-3426

213 Notre-Dame Avenue, Winnipeg, Manitoba
Telephone: (204) 942-3426

Officers
A. R. Aird, *Chairman*
R. J. Rosen, *National Director, Computer Services*

Coding Languages
COBOL, FORTRAN, SIMSCRIPT.

Services Available
Consultation, programming, software packages, systems analysis.

Fields of Application
Implementation planning, systems design, feasibility studies, all functional areas.

Training
Management training programmes.

I. P. SHARP ASSOCIATES LTD.
P.O. Box 71, Toronto Dominion Centre, Toronto, Ontario

Also at:
Ottawa, Montreal, Kingston, Calgary, Vancouver, Rochester, Syracuse, New York, Philadelphia, Washington, Los Angeles, San Francisco.

Officer
I. P. Sharp, *President*

Computer Installation
IBM 370/145–operating system: DOS; internal storage: 512K bits; magnetic tapes: 4 2400; magnetic discs: 19 2314; 1 line printer. *On-line satellite computer:* IBM 370/145. *Remote processing feature:* APL time-sharing.

Coding Language
APL.

Contemplated Equipment
More IBM 370s.

Services Available
Consultation, programming, education and training, software packages, systems analysis. Operate on a remote access and time-sharing basis.

Fields of Application
Education, analysis, engineering, statistics, data processing.
Specialized areas: Accounting, simulation.

Training
Two-day APL programming course.

STEVENSON & KELLOGG LTD.
150 Eglinton Avenue East, Toronto 12, Ontario
Telephone: (416) 483-4313

Also at:
807 Sun Life Building, Montreal 2, Quebec
Telephone: (514) 866-1149

1112 West Pender Street, Vancouver 1,
British Columbia
Telephone: (604) 681-6167

407 Sovereign Building, Halifax, Nova Scotia
Telephone: (902) 422-5991

635 6th Avenue South West, Calgary, Alberta
Telephone: (403) 256-7278

Suite 1410, 130 Albert St., Ottawa, Ontario, K1P 5G4

Officers
E. C. Kehayas, *Director and Principal in charge of Computer Science Division*
V. W. Ruskin, *Principal, Systems Group*

Coding Languages
FORTRAN, COBOL, SIMSCRIPT, GASP.

Services Available
Advice, programming, education and training, software packages, documentation, systems analysis, feasibility studies.

Fields of Application
Scientific, statistical, commercial, production control, accounting, management, systems analysis, operational research.
Specialized areas: Sales analysis, linear programming, investment, analysis, payroll, structural engineering, financial planning.

Training
Short courses in systems design and analysis.

URWICK, CURRIE & PARTNERS LTD.*
120 Adelaide Street West, Toronto 1, Ontario
Telephone: (416) 366-1921

Also at:
630 Dorchester Boulevard West, Montreal, Quebec
Telephone: (514) 866-3721

130 Albert Street, Ottawa 4, Ontario
Telephone: (613) 237 5632

1111 West Hastings Street, Vancouver 1, British Columbia
Telephone: (604) 685-1732

1700 One Lombard Place, Winnipeg, Manitoba
Telephone: (204) 943-8896

Officer
G. A. Brown *(Toronto)*

Computer Installation
Terminal to a Bull General Electric GE 265.

Coding Languages
FORTRAN IV, BASIC.

Services Available
Consultation, programming, software packages, systems analysis.

Fields of Application
Scientific, statistical, commercial, production control, accounting, management, operational research, etc.

Training
Two-week courses in management science and electronic data processing.

WOODS, GORDON & CO.*
409 Granville Street, Vancouver 2, British Columbia
Telephone: (604) 682-1931

Also at:
500 St. James Street West, Montreal 126, Quebec
Telephone: (514) 288-8281

15 Wellington Street West, Toronto, Ontario
Telephone: (416) 368-4761

291 Dundas Street, London, Ontario
Telephone: (519) 433-3901

286 Smith Street, Winnipeg, Manitoba
Telephone: (204) 942-6351

850 Elveden House, Calgary, Alberta
Telephone: (403) 269-7391

600 Toronto-Dominion Bank Building, Edmonton, Alberta
Telephone: (403) 422-5181

Officers
W. H. Penhorwood
L. G. Delicaet

Computer Installations
Montreal:
IBM 360/25–operating system: DOS; internal storage: 96K bits; magnetic discs: 3 2311; 1 line printer.

IBM 1130–internal storage: 32K bits; magnetic discs: 2 2311; 1 line printer.

Coding Languages
COBOL, Assembler, FORTRAN.

Services Available
Consultation, systems analysis, programming, accounting packages. Operate on an open shop basis.

Fields of Application
Statistical, commercial, production control, operational research.
Specialized areas: Accounting, management, systems analysis, linear programming, cash flow analysis.

Training
Introduction to the computer–1 week (run in conjunction with local service bureaux computer audit courses), introduction to electronic data processing.

CANADIAN GENERAL ELECTRIC CO. LTD.*
214 King Street West, Toronto 1, Ontario
Telephone: (416) 366-7311

Also at:
Suite 305, 1177 West Hastings Street, Vancouver 1, British Columbia
Telephone: (604) 681-8136

1155 Dorchester Boulevard West, Suite 3604, Montreal 102, Quebec
Telephone: (514) 866-4448

District Offices at Calgary, Edmonton, Burlington, Ottawa, Montreal

Officers
J. G. P. King, *Manager, Information Services Business Section*
D. J. L. Hughes, *Manager, Western Region*
E. Kofoed, *Manager, Central and Eastern Regions*

Computer Installation
BULL GENERAL ELECTRIC GE 115–operating systems: TOS and DOS; internal storage: 12K bits; magnetic tapes: 1 7-track, 4 9-track. *Remote processing features:* remote batch capability to BULL GENERAL ELECTRIC GE 625.

BULL GENERAL ELECTRIC GE 265–operating system: DOS; internal storage: 16K bits; magnetic tapes: 4 7-track; magnetic disc: 1; 1 line printer. *Remote processing features:* Approximately 150 remote teletypes.

BULL GENERAL ELECTRIC GE 425–operating system: TOS; internal storage: 16K bits; magnetic tapes: 8 7-track; 1 line printer.

BULL GENERAL ELECTRIC GE 625–operating system: DOS; internal storage: 64K bits; magnetic tapes: 8 7-track; magnetic discs: 6; 2 line printers. *On-line satellite computers:* immediate call back or delayed call back.

Coding Languages
GE 115: APS, EAPS, LOGEL, FORTRAN IV, COBOL '65, SORT/MERGE, GERTS.
GE 265: BASIC, ALGOL, FORTRAN.
GE 425: MAP, BAP, COBOL, FORTRAN, SORT, MERGE, RPG, IDS, CPM, DAPS.
GE 625: GMAP, COBOL, FORTRAN, ALGOL, JOVIAL, SYMSCRIPT, PERT TIME, PERT COST, CPM, BMD, SORT, MERGE, RPG, GEFRC.

Services Available
Batch service: advice, operators, preparation of data, programming, software packages, systems analysis. Operate on a self-service closed shop, open shop, remote access and block time basis.
Time-sharing: advice, software packages, conversational problem solving. Operate on a remote access and time-sharing basis.

Fields of Application
All fields.

Training
Introduction to time-sharing; BASIC, FORTRAN and ALGOL courses.

CANADIAN GENERAL ELECTRIC CO. LTD.
Suite 305, 1177 West Hastings Street, Vancouver 1, British Columbia.
Telephone: (604) 681-8136

Officer
D. J. L. Hughes, *Regional Manager*

Computer Installation
Terminals only.

Coding Languages
BASIC, FORTRAN, ALGOL, COBOL.

Services Available
Operate on a time-sharing basis.

Fields of Application
Scientific, statistical, commercial, production control, accounting, management, operational research.
Specialized areas: Sales analysis, investment, payroll, structural engineering, operational research.

COMPUTEL SYSTEMS LTD.
1200 St. Laurent Blvd., Ottawa, K1K 38B
Telephone: (613) 746-4353

Officers
R. T. Horwood
R. T. Lane
A. M. Wyszkowski
R. A. Skene

Computer Installation
UNIVAC 1108–operating systems: EXEC II, EXEC VIII; internal storage: 131K 36-bit words; magnetic tapes: 8 VIII C; 3 line printers.

IBM 360/65–operating system: OS/MVT; internal storage: 1 million bits; magnetic tapes: Shares 18 3420s and 2401s with the IBM 370/165; magnetic discs: Shares 23 2314s and 6 3330s with the IBM 370/165; 4 line printers.

IBM 370/165–operating system: OS/MVT; internal storage: 1·5 million bits; magnetic tapes, magnetic discs and line printers: *see above.*

The three computers share the following:
On-line satellite computers: IBM 360/20, UNIVAC 9200, UNIVAC 9300, MDS 2400. *Remote processing features:* BSC, 48005, 20005, 12006, 3006, 13453.

Coding Languages
All Assembler and High Level.

Contemplated Equipment
An IBM 370/168, more 3420 tapes, more 3330 discs, more internal storage, drums and tapes for the UNIVAC 1108.

Services Available
Programming, operators, software packages, computation. Operate on a remote access, closed shop and time-sharing basis.

Fields of Application
Scientific, statistical, commercial, accounting, management, operational research.
Specialized areas: Econometrics, MARK IV, AUTOFLOW.

Training
Short course on all aspects of the use of UNIVAC and IBM equipment, JCL, languages, data management, debugging, MARK IV, statistical methods and econometric packages.

COMPUTER SCIENCES CANADA LTD.*
1470 Don Mills Road, Don Mills, Ontario
Telephone: 444-2511

Officer
W. M. Richburg, *President*

Computer Installation
UNIVAC 1108–operating system: CSCX; internal storage: 7,077,888 bits; magnetic tapes: 6 Uniservo VIII C; magnetic drums: 2 Fastrand II; 2 FH432, 2 FH1782; 3 line printers. *Remote processing features:* Conversational CSC Infonet Basic Compiler and Applications Library, RJE, Conversational RJE.

Coding Languages
BASIC, FORTRAN, COBOL, Assembly.

Services Available
Advice, programming, education and training, operators, software packages, documentation, preparation of data, systems analysis. Operate on a remote access, closed shop, block time and time-sharing basis.

Fields of Application
All areas of commercial and scientific data processing applications, systems programming, systems engineering and education.

Training
Courses in EDP concepts and application, project management, systems analysis and high-level languages. Also systems development support training and EDP educational systems for clients.

CONSOLIDATED COMPUTER SERVICES LTD.*
48 Yonge Street, Toronto, Ontario

Also at:
Northdale House, North Circular Road, London, N.W.10 (United Kingdom)

Officers
W. G. Hutchison, *Group Vice-President, Marketing*
A. Baldry, *Marketing Director, United Kingdom*
R. P. Wickes, *Vice-President, Europe*

Computer Installation
HEWLETT PACKARD 2116 B—operating system: in-house modified; internal storage: 32K words; magnetic tapes: 2; magnetic discs: 4; 1 line printer. *Remote processing features:* Interactive conversational time-sharing.

CCS 2100—operating system: time-sharing; internal storage: 16K plus 32K bits; magnetic tapes: 1; magnetic discs: Rotating Memory Devices. *Remote processing features:* interactive time-sharing—Teletype 35, 33 ASR KSR, Terminals—Datapoint 3200 CRT Terminals.

Coding Languages
Assembler, BASIC.

Services Available
Programming, preparation of data. Operate on a remote access and time-sharing basis.

Fields of Application
Commercial, scientific, mathematical.
Specialized area: Business application packages.

Training
Short courses in BASIC (2 days), Advanced BASIC (1 day), BASIC Conversion (1 day), and a one-day Executive Seminar.

CONTROL DATA CANADA LTD.*
151 Slater Street, Ottawa 4, Ontario
Telephone: (613) 237-3700

Officer
H. H. McNeilly

Computer Installation
CDC 3600—operating system: SCOPE; internal storage: 3,145,728 bits; magnetic tapes: 12 607; 1 line printer. *On-line satellite computer:* CDC 160-A.

CDC 6600—operating system: SCOPE; internal storage: 7,864,320 bits; magnetic tapes: 8 607; magnetic discs: 1 6638; 1 line printer. *On-line satellite computer:* CDC 160-A.

Coding Languages
FORTRAN, COBOL.

Services Available
Advice, operators, preparation of data, programming, software packages, systems analysis. Operate on a block time basis.

Fields of Application
Scientific, statistical, management, operational research.

COVER-ALL COMPUTER SERVICES LTD.*
1468 Victoria Park Ave., Toronto 16, Ontario

Officer
T. A. Hurl, *Vice-President*

Coding Languages
COBOL, PL/1, RPG, Autocoder, 360 Assembler.

Services Available
Consultation, programming, education and training, operators, software packages, documentation, preparation of data, systems analysis. Operate on an open shop and block time basis.
Brokers of computer time (IBM 360/20, 25, 30, 40, 50 and 65, UNIVAC 9200 and 9300, HONEYWELL H 120, H 200 and H 1200).

Fields of Application
General EDP consulting, systems analysis, contract programming, installation management, development implementation, processing of proprietory systems, educational and training programmes.
Specialized area: Brokerage of computer time.

Training
Five-day course in 360 DOS Systems Generation.

EDP INDUSTRIES LTD.*
2256 West 12th Avenue, Vancouver, British Columbia
Telephone: 736-7725

Also at:
40 Wynford Drive, Don Mills, Ontario
Telephone: 449-4040

525 — One Westmount Square, Montreal, Quebec
Telephone: 937-5326

Officers
W. R. Wood, *President*
D. H. McVeigh, *Director of Marketing*

Computer Installation
HONEYWELL H200(2)—operating system: MOD I; internal storage: 32K bits each; magnetic tapes: 5 each; 1 line printer.

HONEYWELL H125—operating system: MOD I; internal storage: 32K bits; magnetic tapes: 6; 1 line printer.

HONEYWELL H1250—operating system: MOD I ext.; internal storage: 49K bits; magnetic tapes: 6; 1 line printer.

Coding Language
COBOL.

Contemplated Equipment
Time-sharing terminals.

Services Available
Advice, programming, software packages, preparation of data, systems analysis. Operate on a closed shop, block time and time-sharing basis.

Fields of Application
Commercial, accounting, management, systems analysis.
Specialized areas: Data products (packages), general accounting packages, software products, data management, languages and conversion.

EMPIRE DATA CENTRES LTD.*
180 Montee de Liesse Road, St-Laurent, Quebec
Telephone: 636-0330

Officer
K. N. Bennett, *General Manager*

Computer Installation
HONEYWELL H120—internal storage: 12K bits; magnetic tapes: 3; 1 line printer.

Services Available
Preparation of data, programming, systems analysis. Operate on a closed shop and block time basis.

Fields of Application
Statistical, commercial, accounting, management, invoicing, inventory control.
Specialized areas: Accounts receivable, payroll.

ÉTUDES ET TRAITEMENT DES DONNÉES (MONTREAL) INC.*
Suite 3150, Place Victoria, Montreal 3, Quebec
Telephone: 861-8391

Officer
Bernard Lachapelle

Computer Installation
NCR 315/100 (2)—internal storage: 120K bits each; magnetic tapes: 5 each; 1 line printer each.

Coding Language
COBOL.

Contemplated Equipment
2 NCR 615 Century 200, each with 64K bytes storage; 8 magnetic tapes; 8 discs; 2 line printers.

Services Available
Programming, systems analysis. Operate on a closed shop basis.

Field of Application
Commercial.
Specialized areas: Payroll applications, accounts receivable.

IBM CO. LTD.*
Datacentres
36 King Street East, Toronto, Ontario
Telephone: (416) 362-6051

Also at:
P.O. Box 55, 636 Main Street East, Hamilton, Ontario
Telephone: (416) 527-4594

P.O. Box 820, 259 King Street West, Kitchener, Ontario
Telephone: (519) 745-6193-4

Terminal A, P.O. Box 3592, 781 Richmond Street, London, Ontario
Telephone: (519) 433-1701

150 Laurier Avenue West, Ottawa, Ontario
Telephone: (613) 236-0271

670 Ouellette Avenue, Windsor, Ontario
Telephone: (519) 256-7844

477 Princess Street, Kingston, Ontario
Telephone: (613) 546-2209

P.O. Box 41, 15 King Street, St. Catharine's, Ontario
Telephone: (416) 682-6641

528 9th Avenue S.W., Calgary, Alberta
Telephone: (403) 266-6241

10012 107th Street, Edmonton, Alberta
Telephone: (403) 429-5271

1445 West Georgia Street, Vancouver, British Columbia
Telephone: (604) 682-5515

695 Fort Street, Victoria, British Columbia
Telephone: (604) 385-3444

373 Broadway Avenue, Winnipeg, Manitoba
Telephone: (204) 942-2181

44 Prince William Street, Saint John, New Brunswick
Telephone: (506) 657-3344

Centennial Building, P.O. Box 517, 1645 Granville Street, Halifax, Nova Scotia
Telephone: (902) 429-2810

5 Place Ville Marie, Montreal, Quebec
Telephone: (514) 874-6080

1305 St. Foy Road, Quebec
Telephone: (418) 681-4171

2255 Albert Street, Regina, Saskatchewan
Telephone: (306) 527-0674

322 22nd Street West, Saskatoon, Saskatchewan
Telephone: (306) 653-4151

Officers
A. W. Lemke, *Manager (Toronto)*
R. K. Crosby, *Manager (Calgary)*
J. R. Wickware, *Manager (Vancouver)*
G. Whitton, *Manager (Winnipeg)*
A. B. Schneiderman, *Manager (Saint John)*
T. C. Rogers, *Manager (Halifax)*
W. F. Steele, *Manager (Montreal)*
B. C. Smith, *Manager (Regina)*

Computer Installation
A variety of systems: IBM 360s, ranging from the smallest model to some of the largest; IBM 1401s, IBM 1460s and IBM 7090 computers.

Coding Languages
RPG, Autocoder, COBOL, FORTRAN, AL, etc.

Services Available
Advice, operators, preparation of data, programming, software packages, systems analysis.

Fields of Application
All fields.

JOHNSTON TERMINALS LTD.
2020 Yukon Street, Vancouver, British Columbia

Officer
R. Severson, *EDP Supervisor*

Computer Installation
BURROUGHS B2500—internal storage: 40K bits; magnetic tapes: 4; magnetic discs: 1; 1 line printer.

Coding Language
COBOL.

Services Available
Programming, operators, software packages, preparation of data, systems analysis. Operate on a self-service and block time basis. Available for accounting and commercial applications.

Fields of Application
Commercial, accounting.

NATIONAL DATACENTRE CORPORATION LTD.
181 West Pender Street, Vancouver 3, British Columbia
Telephone: (604) 682-4262

Also at:
44 King Street West, Toronto, Ontario

Officers
J. G. Bartlett, *Executive Vice-President*
P. D. Thomas, *Director of Systems and Planning*
W. A. Brealey, *Director of Marketing*

Computer Installation
UNIVAC 9400—operating system: OS, DOS, TOS; internal storage: 131K bits; magnetic tapes: 4; magnetic discs: 3; 1 line printer.

UNIVAC 9300—operating system: TOS; internal storage: 32K bits; magnetic tapes: 6; 1 line printer.

UNIVAC 1050—internal storage: 20K bits; 1 line printer.

Coding Languages
COBOL, Assembler, RPG, FORTRAN IV, PAL, REGENT, PL/1.

Contemplated Equipment
UNIVAC 9700 tape/disc system.

Services Available
Advice, operators, preparation of data, programming, software packages, systems analysis, documentation. Operate on a self-service, remote access, block time and open shop basis. Engineering and scientific applications are limited.

Fields of Application
Statistical, commercial, accounting, management, systems analysis.
Specialized areas: Sales analysis, payroll, insurance accounting, financial statements.

RAPID DATA COMPUTER SERVICES (HAMILTON) LTD.
795 King Street East, Hamilton, Ontario
Telephone: (416) 545-0292

Officers
Philip G. Bartley, *Manager*
Diane Mendell, *Operations Supervisor*

Computer Installation
HONEYWELL H200/120—operating system: MOD 1 (MSR); internal storage: 32K bits; magnetic tapes: 5; magnetic discs: 2; 1 line printer.

Coding Languages
COBOL, Easycoder.

Contemplated Equipment
An off-line communications network using a HONEYWELL G58 mini-computer or keytape communicators.

Services Available
Advice, programming, education and training, operators, software packages, documentation, preparation of data, systems analysis, Operate on a self-service, block time and open shop basis.

Fields of Application
Statistical, commercial, production control, accounting, management, systems analysis.
Specialized area: Insurance company processing.

REAL TIME CORPORATION LTD.
797 Don Mills Road, Don Mills, Ontario M3C IV1
Telephone: (416) 429 0440

Officers
G. E. Meinzer, *President*
N. E. Anderson, *Vice-President*

Computer Installation
UNIVAC 9400—operating system: DOS; internal storage: 131K bits; magnetic tapes: 5 Uniservo; magnetic discs: 4 8414; 1 line printer. *On-line satellite computer:* UNIVAC 1005.

UNIVAC 1004—internal storage: 2K bits; magnetic tapes: 2; 1 line printer. *Remote processing features:* DLT 1.

Coding Languages
Assembler, COBOL, RPG.

Services Available
Programming, operators, documentation, preparation of data, systems analysis. Operate on an open shop basis.

Fields of Application
Statistical, commercial, accounting, management, systems analysis.
Specialized areas: Sales analysis, analysis, general insurance.

SETAK COMPUTING SERVICES CORPORATION LTD.*
20 Spadina Road, Toronto 4, Ontario
Telephone: 927-1633

Officers
Dr. J. Kates, *President*
D. M. Kaplan, *Executive Vice-President*

Computer Installation
BURROUGHS B 5500—internal storage: 24K bits; magnetic tapes: 6; magnetic discs: 1; *Remote processing features:* Data communications hardware for remote TWX stations.

BURROUGHS B 500—internal storage: 19.2K characters; magnetic tapes: 2; magnetic discs: 1; *Remote processing features:* Data communications hardware for remote stations.

Coding Languages
COBOL, ALGOL, FORTRAN II, FORTRAN IV.

Services Available
Rental of computer time for programme development and production, programming and other EDP services; scientific and commercial time-sharing.

Fields of Application
Scientific and commercial data processing.
Specialized areas: Statistical packages, critical path method, on-line order entry systems.

Canada – Consultants

STATISTICAL REPORTING AND TABULATING LTD.*
3425 Dundas Street West, Toronto, Ontario
Telephone: (416) 766-8191

Officers
C. G. Green, *President*
George McDonald, *Vice-President*

Computer Installation
BURROUGHS B263—internal storage: 10K bits.

SYMBIONICS SYSTEMS LTD.*
550 Berry Street, Winnipeg 21, Manitoba
Telephone: (204) 772-9491

Also at:
No. 104, 600-6th Avenue SW, Calgary, Alberta
Telephone: (403) 263-4960

and at:
Edmonton, Alberta

Officers
B. A. Hodson, *President*
D. R. Sprague, *Vice-President, Operations*

Computer Installation
CDC 6500—internal storage: 3,900K bits; magnetic tapes: 4 7-track, 1 9-track; magnetic discs: 1; 1 line printer.
Remote processing features: 2 RJE, teletypewriters.

Coding Languages
COBOL, FORTRAN, Assembler, ALGOL, SIMSCRIPT, SOLIS.

Services Available
Consultation, programming, software packages, systems analysis. Operate on an open shop and remote access basis.

Fields of Application
Scientific, statistical, commercial, accounting, management, systems analysis, operational research.

SYSTEMS DIMENSIONS LTD.
770 Brookfield Road, Ottawa, Ontario, KIV 6J5
Telephone: (613) 731-6910

Officer
G. A. Fierheller, *President*

Computer Installation
IBM 360/85—operating system: OS/MVT; internal storage: 2 million bytes; magnetic tapes: 1 2385, 16 2420; magnetic discs: 4 2314; 4 line printers.
Remote processing features: 2 Model 20.

Coding Languages
COBOL, FORTRAN, PL/1, WATFOR, Assembler, ALGOL, RPG.

Contemplated Equipment
Additional high-speed terminals.

Services Available
Advice, education and training, software packages. Operate on a remote access basis.

Fields of Application
Scientific, statistical, commercial, accounting, management.
Specialized area: Analysis.

Training
Short course in Job Control Language (3 days).

UNIVAC CANADA LTD.*
984 Bay Street, Toronto, Ontario
Telephone: WA4-0651

Services Available
Advice, operators, preparation of data, programming, software packages, systems analysis.

Fields of Application
Scientific, commercial, accounting.
Specialized areas: Numerical control, payroll and inventory applications.

WELBY COMPUTER SERVICES LIMITED
306 Metcalf Street, Ottawa, Ontario
Telephone: (613) 237-0882

Also at:
4333 St. Catherine Street West, Montreal, Quebec
Telephone: (514) 932-7156

Officers
G. Malcolm Welch
D. D. Duncan
H. Stimmer

Computer Installation
UNIVAC 1050—internal storage: 24K bits; magnetic tapes: 6; 1 line printer.

UNIVAC 1050—internal storage: 28K bits; magnetic tapes: 7; 1 line printer.

BURROUGHS B5500—internal storage: 194K characters; magnetic tapes: 4; magnetic discs: 1; 1 line printer.

Coding Languages
PAL, FORTRAN, COBOL.

Services Available
Operators, preparation of data, programming, software packages, systems analysis.

Fields of Application
Statistical, commercial, accounting, management.
Specialized area: Municipal.

CHILE

UNIVERSITIES

UNIVERSIDAD CATÓLICA DE CHILE*
Computing Center
Faculty of Mathematics and Physical Sciences
Casilla 114 D, Santiago
Telephone: 569912, 567611

Officer
Eng. José Dekovié T., *Head of Computing Centre*

Computer Installation
IBM 1620—internal storage: 20K bits; 1 line printer.

Coding Languages
FORTRAN, SPS.

Services Available
Advice, programming, systems analysis. Operate on a self-service and open shop basis.

Field of Application
Compiler development.

Training
Programming courses at different levels.

UNIVERSIDAD DE CHILE
Centro de Computación
Beauchef 993, Santiago
Telephone: 92226

Officers
Fernando Silva Alvear, *Director*
Juan Ricardo Giadach Giadach, *Co-ordinator of Operations*
Carlos Pérez García, *Chief of Extension*

Computer Installation
IBM 360/40—operating system: OS-DOS; internal storage: 128K bytes; magnetic tapes: 4 2400; magnetic discs: 2 2311; 1 line printer.

Coding Languages
FORTRAN, COBOL, ALGOL, Assembler, PL/1.

Contemplated Equipment
IBM 370/145 with internal storage of 512K bytes.

Services Available
Programming, education and training, operators, software packages, preparation of data, systems analysis.

Fields of Application
Scientific, statistical, commercial, accounting, management, systems analysis.

Training
Language and application courses.

UNIVERSIDAD DE CONCEPCIÓN
Centro de Ciencias de Computación e Información
Casilla 1186, Concepción
Telephone: 24985/82

Officers
José Duran Reyes, *Director*
Marcelo Pardo Brown, *Academic Secretary*

Computer Installation
IBM 1620—operating system: Monitor; internal storage: 160K bits; magnetic discs: 2 1311; 1 line printer.

Coding Languages
FORTRAN, SNOBOL, LISP 1.5, SPS.

Services Available
Advice, programming, education and training, software packages, preparation of data, systems analysis. Operate on a closed shop basis. Normally available only to university members.

Fields of Application
Scientific, accounting, management, systems analysis operational research.
Specialized area: Education.

Training
Courses in computer programming, and systems analysis for engineers.

UNIVERSIDAD DEL NORTE
Centro de Computación
Angamos 0610, Casilla 1280, Antofagasta
Telephone: 21697

Officer
Jorge Gana Leay, *Director*

Computer Installation
IBM 1130—operating system: DMS 2; internal storage: 108K bits; 1 line printer. *On-line satellite computer:* Plotter IBM 1627.

Coding Languages
Assembler, FORTRAN, APL.

Contemplated Equipment
IBM 370/145.

Services Available
Advice, programming, education and training, operators, preparation of data, systems analysis. Operate on a closed shop and block time basis.

Fields of Application
Scientific, statistical, accounting, systems analysis, operational research.
Specialized area: Simulation.

Training
Courses in programming languages; graduate courses in systems analysis, simulation, numerical analysis.

UNIVERSIDAD TÉCNICA DEL ESTADO*
Centro de Computación
Avenida Ecuador 3469, Casilla 4637, Santiago
Telephone: 97401-08

Officers
Prof. Mario Meza F.
Dr. Jaime Michelow V.

Coding Languages
Machine Language (B-204, B-205) VAMP, SAC.

Services Available
Advice operators, preparation of data, programming, software packages, systems analysis. Operate on a closed shop basis. Available for scientific programming only.

Contemplated Equipment
Installation of magnetic tapes.

UNIVERSIDAD TÉCNICA "FEDERICO SANTA MARÍA"
Departamento de Computación
Casilla 110-V, Valparaíso
Telephone: 61498

Officer
Dr. Reinaldo E. Giudici, *Director of the Computing Department and Professor of Computation.*

Computer Installation
IBM 1620—internal storage: 20K bits.
Note: The University also has an IBM 360/40 in Santiago.

Coding Languages
PDQ–FORTRAN (extension of '1620 FORTRAN with Format'); Symbolic Programming Language.

Contemplated Equipment
IBM 370/145.

Services Available
Advice, programming, education and training, software packages, systems analysis. Operate on a self-service, remote access and block time basis. Available for research and education in other institutions; limited availability to industry in case of special problems.

Fields of Application
Scientific, systems analysis, operational research.
Specialized area: Numerical problems of engineering science.

Training
Degree course in Computer Science; basic instruction in computing for engineers.

BURROUGHS B3500 (B3012)–operating system: MCP; internal storage: 120K bytes; magnetic tapes: 4 B9392; magnetic discs: 1 B9370; 1 line printer.

Coding Languages
ANS, COBOL, FORTRAN.

Contemplated Equipment
Bi-processor IRIS-80 and IRIS-60 ordered from CII, to be installed in October 1973.

Services Available
Advice, programming, education and training, software packages, documentation, preparation of data, systems analysis, research and development. Operate on an open shop and block time basis.

Fields of Application
Statistical, commercial, accounting, management, systems analysis, operational research.
Specialized areas: Linear programming, analysis, payroll.

Training
Courses in systems analysis, on COBOL for programmers, on IBM equipment for programme operators; courses for operator managers; counterpart.

RESEARCH INSTITUTION

UNIVERSIDAD CATÓLICA DE CHILE
Programa Interdisciplinario de Investigaciones en Educación (PIIE)
Bustos 2431, Santiago
Telephone: 743126

Officers
Dr. Ernesto Schiefelbein, *Director*
Dr. Beatrice Avalos, *Acting Director*

Services Available
Software packages, systems analysis.

Field of Application
Systems analysis.
Specialized areas: Linear programming, educational research.

IBM CHILE S.A.C. LTDA*
Agustinas 1235–1ro piso, Santiago

Computer Installation
IBM 1401 tape.

Services Available
Advice, operators, preparation of data, programming.

Fields of Application
Statistical and commercial.

PROCESAMIENTOS ELECTRÓNICOS S.A.C. (PROCESAC)
Moneda 1123, 5º piso, Santiago
Telephone: 722004-86629

Officers
Gastón Bobillier Camus, *General Manager*
Alejandro Castro Ugarte, *Administrative Manager*
Luis Medel Corral, *Sales Manager*

Computer Installation
IBM 360/40–operating system: DOS; internal storage: 64K bits; magnetic tapes: 4; magnetic discs: 4; 1 line printer.

Coding Languages
Assembler, PL/1, FORTRAN, COBOL, RPG.

Contemplated Equipment
Additional storage of 64K bits; 1 line printer.

SERVICE BUREAUX

EMPRESA NACIONAL DE COMPUTACIÓN E INFORMATICA LTDA
Huérfanos 1376, Casilla 14796, Santiago

Officers
Raimundo Beca I., *President*
Hugo Segovia V., *Planning Vice-President*
Gonzalo Vargas, *Operation's Vice-President*
Romulo Tromben, *Administrative Vice-President*
Bolívar Quiroga, *Engineering Vice-President*

Computer Installation
IBM 360/50–operating system: OS MFT-II; internal storage: 512K bytes; magnetic tapes: 8 2400; magnetic discs: 2 2314, 6 2311; 2 line printers.

IBM 360/40(2)–operating system: OS MFT-II; internal storage: 512K bytes; magnetic tapes: 6 2400; magnetic discs: 4 2311, 1 2314; 2 line printers.

Services Available
Advice, programming, operators, documentation, preparation of data, systems analysis. Operate on a self-service and block time basis.

Fields of Application
Commercial, production control, accounting, management, systems analysis.
Specialized areas: Sales analysis, linear programming, analysis, payroll, structural engineering.

REPUBLIC OF CHINA (TAIWAN)

UNIVERSITIES

NATIONAL CHIAO TUNG UNIVERSITY*
College of Engineering
45 Po-Ai Street, Hsinchu, Taiwan

Officers
C. C. Lee, *Director of the Computer Centre*

Computer Installation
IBM 1620 – internal storage: 20K decimal digits.

Coding Languages
FORTRAN I and II-M, SPS, Machine Language.

Services Available
Programming, education and training, operators. Operate on a closed shop basis.

Fields of Application
Scientific, statistical.

Training
M.S. and Ph.D. degree courses in Information Theory, Theory of Computation, Digital Computation, Switching Theory, Combinatorial Mathematics, Logical Design of Digital Computers, Numerical Analysis, Automata Theory, Computer Languages, Data Processing, Coding Theory, etc. Eight-week training course in Computer Application.

NATIONAL TAIWAN UNIVERSITY*
Computer Centre
1 Roosevelt Road, Section 1, Taipei, Taiwan

Officers
Prof. Chu Yao-I, *Director*
Assoc. Prof. Chien-ping Wu, *Officer*

Computer Installation
CDC 3150 – operating systems: Real Time System (tape), Mass Storage Operating System (disc); internal storage: 393,216 bits; magnetic tapes: 4 601; magnetic discs: 2 854; 1 line printer.

Coding Languages
FORTRAN, COBOL, ALGOL.

Services Available
Programming, education and training, operators, preparation of data, systems analysis. Operate on a closed shop basis.

Fields of Application
Scientific, statistical, commercial, systems analysis, production control.

Training
Courses in Computer Programming, Numerical Method, Programming Languages. Also an eight-week Computer Programming course including FORTRAN, COBOL, ALGOL, Numerical Methods and Linear Programming.

RESEARCH INSTITUTION

CHUNG SHAN INSTITUTE OF SCIENCE AND TECHNOLOGY
Computer Centre
P.O. Box 1-6, Lungtan, Taiwan 325

Officer
Liu Hsin-pi, *Director*

Computer Installation
CDC Cyber 72/14 – operating system: SCOPE 3.4; internal storage: 3,932K bits; magnetic tapes: 4 CDC 604; magnetic discs: 4 CDC 841; 2 line printers. *Remote processing features:* 2 CDC 731, CDC 711, 713.
HEWLETT PACKARD 2116B – operating system: MTBCS; internal storage: 8K bits; magnetic tapes: 0735; 1 line printer.

Coding Languages
CDC FORTRAN Extended, COBOL, BASIC, ALGOL, MIMIC, CSSL.

Services Available
Advice, programming, education and training, systems analysis. Operate on a remote access and block time basis. Available only to government establishments.

Fields of Application
Scientific, statistical, commercial, production control, accounting, management, systems analysis, operational research.

Training
Courses in programming languages.

SERVICE BUREAUX

CHINA DATA PROCESSING CENTER
1 Roosevelt Road, Section 1, Taipei, Taiwan
Telephone: 345201–345203, 324601–324605

Officers
F. C. Wang, *Chairman*
Howell S. C. Chou, *President*
C. K. Shih, *Vice-President*
C. H. Hu, *Vice-President*

Computer Installation
UNIVAC 9400 – internal storage: 131K bytes; magnetic tapes: 6 UNISERVO 12; magnetic discs: 4 UNIVAC 8414-92; 2 line printers. *Remote processing features:* 2 UNIVAC DCT 1000.

Coding Languages
RPG, Assembler, FORTRAN IV, COBOL.

Services Available
Advice, preparation of data, programming, software packages, systems analysis, card punching and verifying. Operate on a remote access, closed shop, block time and open shop basis.

Fields of Application
Statistical, commercial, scientific, production control, accounting, systems analysis, etc.
Specialized areas: Inventory control, payroll, billing.

Training
Courses in basic concept of computer and languages.

IBM TAIWAN CORPORATION
3rd floor, International Building, 6 Tung Hua North Road, Taipei 104, Taiwan
Telephone: 724121-724129

Officer
W. M. Whitmyre, *General Manager*

Computer Installation
IBM 360/40–operating system: OS/DOS; internal storage: 2,048K bits; magnetic tapes: 6 2401; magnetic discs: 6 2319; 2 line printers.

Coding Languages
PL/1, COBOL, RPG II, FORTRAN, Assembler.

Services Available
Advice, programming, education and training, operators, software packages, documentation, preparation of data, systems analysis. Operate on a self-service, closed shop, block time and open shop basis.

Fields of Application
Scientific, statistical, commercial, production control, accounting, management, systems analysis, operational research.
Specialized areas: Sales analysis, linear programming, analysis, payroll, structural engineering.

Training
Standard IBM education courses.

COLOMBIA

UNIVERSITIES

PONTIFICIA UNIVERSIDAD JAVERIANA
Faculty of Electronic Engineering
Carrera 7a, No. 40-62, Apartado Aéreo 5315, Bogotá 1, D.E.
Telephone: 459105

Officers
Luis Guillermo Uribe
Francisco Viveros

Computer Installation
CODIDAC (designed and constructed in the faculty) – internal storage: 80K bits; magnetic tape; 1 line printer.

Coding Languages
Proper language without compiler.

Contemplated Equipment
Line printer.

Services Available
Education and training. Operated on a self-service basis. Available only to students.

Field of Application
Scientific.

UNIVERSIDAD DE ANTIOQUÍA*
Calle 67, Carrera 53A, Apartado Aéreo 1226, Medellín

Dirigeant
S. R. Pérez

Equipement
IBM 1130–mémoire interne: 8K bits; disques magnétiques: 1; 1 imprimante.

IBM 360/30–mémoire interne: 32K bytes; bandes magnétiques: 2; disques magnétiques: 4 2311: 1 imprimante.

Langages de Programmation
RPG, FORTRAN, Assembler, COBOL.

Services Fournis
Programmation, enseignement et formation, opérateurs, systems analysis. Fonctionnement à porte ouverte. Services fournis aux universités.

Domaines d'Application
Scientifique, statistique, commercial, systems analysis, recherche opérationnelle.

UNIVERSIDAD DE LOS ANDES
Biblioteca General
Calle 18A, Carrera 1E, Apartado Aéreo 4976, Bogotá, D.E.

Officer
María Victoria Franco de Jaramillo, *Director*

Computer Installation
IBM 360/44–operating systems: OS and PS; internal storage: 100K bits; magnetic tapes: 2 9-track; magnetic discs: 3 2311; 1 line printer.

Coding Languages
Assembler, COBOL, ALGOL, SIMSCRIPT, FORTRAN, PL/1, LISP.

Contemplated Equipment
Increased storage.

Services Available
Advice, programming, education and training, operators, software packages, documentation, preparation of data, systems analysis.

Fields of Application
Scientific, statistical, commercial, accounting, systems analysis, operational research.
Specialized areas: Linear programming, structural engineering, medical research.

Training
Diploma course for Systems and Computer Engineering.

UNIVERSIDAD DE LOS ANDES
Centro de Cómputo
Apartado Aéreo 4976, Bogotá, D.E.
Telephone: 824066

Dirigeants
Heberto Pachón, *Directeur du Centre de Computation*
Carlos J. Amaya, *Doyen de la Faculté d'Ingénieurs*

Equipment
IBM 360/44–système d'opération; OS 360; mémoire interne: 131,072 bytes (8 bits); bandes magnétiques: 2 2401-2; disques magnétiques: 3 2311; 1 imprimante.

Langages de Programmation
FORTRAN, COBOL, ALGOL, PL/1, LISP, BAL.

Services Fournis
Conseils, programmation, enseignement et formation, software packages, systems analysis. Fonctionnement à porte fermée et en abonnement machine.

Colombia – Universities

Domaines d'Application
Scientifique, statistique, commercial, systems analysis, recherche opérationnelle, enseignement.
Domaines spécialisés: Analyse, génie de structure.

Formation
Systèmes et Computation (diplôme).

UNIVERSIDAD DEL CAUCA
Facultad de Ingeniería Electrónica y Telecomunicaciones
Calle 5, No. 4-70, Popayán, Cauca
Telephone: 3020

Officers
Dr. Pablo Grech Mayor, *Dean of Faculty*
Dr. Ovidio Sarrio González, *Director of Computing Centre*

Computer Installation
IBM 1130–operating system: DMS V2; internal storage: 131K bits; magnetic discs: 10 2315; 1 line printer.

Coding Languages
FORTRAN, Assembler, RPG, APL.

Contemplated Equipment
IBM 2310 disc store; additional storage of 16K 16-bit words; IBM plotter model 1.

Services Available
Advice, programming, education. Operate on an open shop basis. Available only to university students, staff and administrators.

Fields of Application
Scientific, statistical, accounting, systems analysis, operational research.
Specialized areas: Analysis, structural engineering, electronic engineering.

Training
Non-diploma courses in programming (FORTRAN), applied numerical methods, Assembler.

UNIVERSIDAD DEL VALLE
División de Ingeniería
Centro de Cálculo Electrónico
Apartado Aéreo 2188, Cali

Computer Installation
IBM 1130–operating system: DOS; internal storage: 256K bits; magnetic discs: 2 2310; 1 line printer.

Coding Languages
FORTRAN, RPG, APL, COBOL, Assembler, ALGOL.

Services Available
Advice, programming, education and training, software packages, preparation of data, systems analysis. Operate on a closed shop basis.

Fields of Application
Scientific, statistical, systems analysis, operational research.
Specialized areas: Linear programming, structural engineering.

UNIVERSIDAD INDUSTRIAL DE SANTANDER
Apartado Aéreo 678, Bucaramanga, Santander
Telephone: 56 141

Officers
Ing. Daniel Casas O., *Manager of Computing Centre*
Alvaro Navas C., *Educational Systems Supervisor*
Sta. Elsa Méndez, *Administrative Systems Supervisor*

Computer Installation
IBM 1620–internal storage: 20K bits; 1 line printer.

Coding Languages
FORTRAN II, SPS-LAG.

Contemplated Equipment
BURROUGHS B1726 with a central memory of 57K bytes; a 750 printer; 2 magnetic tapes; 2 magnetic discs.

Services Available
Programming, education and training, software packages. Operate on an open shop basis. Available for educational uses and internal administrative systems.

Fields of Application
Scientific, statistical, operational research.
Specialized areas: Payroll, structural engineering.

UNIVERSIDAD PONTIFICIA BOLIVARIANA
P.O. Box 1178, Medellín
Telephone: 48-93-87

Officer
Mons. Félix Henao Botero, *Rector Magnífico*

Computer Installation
IBM 1130–internal storage: 16K bits; magnetic discs: 1; 1 line printer.

Coding Languages
FORTRAN, RPG, Assembler.

Contemplated Equipment
5 magnetic tapes, 5 magnetic discs, 1 line printer.

Services Available
Education and training. Operate on an open shop basis. Available only to university members.

Fields of Application
Scientific, operational research.
Specialized areas: Linear programming, payroll.

Training
Elementary courses in programming.

UNIVERSIDAD TECNOLÓGICA DE PEREIRA
Computer Centre
Apartado Aéreo 97, Pereira, Risaralda
Telephone: 32781

Officer
José J. Mora T., *Director*

Computer Installation
IBM 1130; operating system: DMS 2; internal storage: 8K bits; magnetic discs: 1 2315; 1 line printer.

Coding Languages
Assembler, FORTRAN.

Services Available
Advice, programming, education and training, software packages, preparation of data, systems analysis. Operate on a closed shop basis. Available for education and research purposes only.

Fields of Application
Scientific, statistical, management, systems analysis, operational research.
Specialized areas: Linear programming, investment analysis.

Training
Courses in computer programming, data processing, numerical analysis within electrical, industrial and mechanical engineering.

GOVERNMENT ESTABLISHMENTS

BANCO CAFETERO
Avenida Jiménez 7-65, Apartado Aéreo 6824, Bogotá, D.E.

Officers
Rodrigo Munera Z., *General Manager*
Dr. Esteban Uribe Angel, *Systems Manager*

Computer Installation
BURROUGHS B3500—operating system: MCP 5.1—S; internal storage: 80K bits; magnetic tapes: 4; magnetic discs: 1; 1 line printer.

Coding Languages
COBOL, FORTRAN.

Contemplated Equipment
Additional memory of 40K bits; 1 line printer.

Services Available
Advice, programming, operators, software packages, preparation of data, systems analysis. Operate on a block time basis.

Field of Application
Commercial.

CENTRO DISTRITAL DE SISTEMATIZACIÓN Y SERVICIOS TÉCNICOS
Carrera 30 No. 24-90, 2° piso, Bogotá, D. E.
Telephone: 449202, 449204

Officers
Mario Castellanos Beltrán, *Manager*
Luis Francisco Vargas C., *Technical Assistant Manager*
Ernesto Alvarez Pinzón, *Operational Assistant Manager*

Computer Installation
IBM 360/30—operating system: DOS; internal storage: 64K bits; magnetic tapes: 4 2401; magnetic discs: 3 2311; 2 line printers.

Coding Languages
COBOL, FORTRAN, Assembler.

Services Available
Programming, operators, documentation, preparation of data, systems analysis. Operate on a block time basis.

Fields of Application
Statistical, commercial, accounting, management, systems analysis.
Specialized areas: Analysis, payroll.

DEPARTAMENTO NACIONAL DE ESTADÍSTICA
Centro Administrativo Nacional, Vía El Dorado, Bogotá, D.E.
Telephone: 449201

Officers
Alvaro Velásquez Cock, *Head of the Department*
Nicolas Dib David, *Director of Processing*
Enrique Sin Clavijo, *Director of Technical Information*
Alfredo Sarmiento, *Director of Socio-Economic Analysis*

Computer Installation
IBM 370/145—operating system: MFT-II; internal storage: 512K bits; magnetic tapes: 6 2401-V; magnetic discs: 8 3330; 2 line printers. *Remote processing features:* 6 2780 terminals, 1 1130.

Coding Languages
COBOL, FORTRAN, Assembler.

Contemplated Equipment
8 3420-7; 6 3780 terminals.

Services Available
Advice, programming, education and training, operators, software packages, documentation, preparation of data, systems analysis. Operate on a remote access and closed shop basis. Priority given to government bodies.

Field of Application
Statistical.

DEPARTAMENTO NACIONAL DE PLANEACIÓN
Carrera 10 No. 27-27, piso 11, Bogotá, D.E.
Telephone: 824055

Officers
Dr. Luis Eduardo Rosas Peña, *Head of Department*
Dr. Eduardo Sarmiento Palacio, *Secretary-General*

Computer Installation
IBM 1130—operating system: MONITOR 2; internal storage: 128K bits; magnetic disc: 2315; 1 line printer. *Remote processing features:* 2780 terminal connected with IBM 360/50 at Dane, connexion with IBM 370/145 at Dane.

Coding Languages
FORTRAN IV, Assembler, RPG, APL.

Services Available
Programming, systems analysis, production of information. Operate on a closed shop basis.

Fields of Application
Scientific, statistical, accounting, systems analysis, operational research, model implementation.
Specialized areas: Linear programming, investment, payroll.

EMPRESA COLOMBIANA DE PETRÓLEOS (ECOPETROL)*
Apartado Aéreo 5938, Bogotá, D.E.
Téléphone: 451101

Dirigeants
C. Amaya

Equipement
IBM 1410—mémoire interne: 40K bits; bandes magnétiques: 6 729-02; 1 imprimante.

Langages de Programmation
Autocoder, COBOL, FORTRAN.

Equipement Projeté
IBM 360/40—mémoire interne: 64K bits.

Services Fournis
Programmation, opérateurs, documentation, préparation des données, systems analysis. Services fournis à Policolsa et Banco Popular, seulement avec nos opérateurs.

Domaines d'Application
Comptabilité, commercial, statistique.

MINISTERIO DE HACIENDA Y CREDITO PÚBLICO*
División de P.A.D.
Oficina 529, Bogotá, D.E.
Téléphone: 342301

Dirigeants
G. Herrán G.
G. Angel

Equipement
IBM 360/40–système d'opération: DOS; mémoire interne: 128K bits; bandes magnétiques: 6 2401; disques magnétiques: 9 2314; 2 imprimantes.

Langages de Programmation
COBOL, Assembler 360, FORTRAN.

Equipement Projeté
Tele-processing. Un deuxième ordinateur de la capacité d'un IBM 360/50 ou 360/65.

Services Fournis
Programmation, opérateurs, systems analysis. Fonctionnement à porte fermée; fournis a toute le ministère.

Domaines d'Application
Commercial (impôts), comptabilité.
Domaines spécialisés: Statistique des impôts; modèles mathématiques des impôts en étude.

Formation
Opération de l'Ordinateur (3–4 semaines), Programmation (Assembler, BTAM, QTAM–1–2 mois pous nos techniciens), Système colombien d'impôts (2–3 semaines).

MUNICIPIO DE MEDELLÍN
Palacio Municipal, Oficina 138, Medellín

Officer
German Tovar Q., *Director of Organization and Systemization*

Computer Installation
IBM 360/30–internal storage: 32K bits; magnetic tapes: 2 2401; magnetic discs: 4 2311; 1 line printer.
IBM 370/135–internal storage: 98K bytes; magnetic tapes: 2 2401; magnetic discs: 3 2319; 1 line printer.

Coding Languages
COBOL, PL/1, RPG II, FORTRAN IV.

Services Available
Advice, programming, operators, software packages, systems analysis. Operate on a self-service basis. Available only to government agencies.

Fields of Application
Scientific, statistical, commercial, accounting, management, systems analysis.
Specialized areas: Linear programming, payroll, structural engineering.

CONSULTANTS

COMPAÑIA COLOMBIANA DE SISTEMAS (COLSISTEMAS)
Carrera 7 No. 17-01, Bogotá, D.E.
Telephone: 429127

Officers
Fabio Roberto González, *General Manager*
Xavier Caro, *Director*
German Herran, *Director*
Eduardo Ospina, *Director*

Computer Installation
IBM 360/50–operating system: MFT-2; magnetic tapes: 6 2400; magnetic discs: 1 2314; 2 line printers.
Remote processing feature: 2770 running under HASP.

Coding Languages
PL/1, COBOL F, Assembler F, COBOL USA, FORTRAN G.

Contemplated Equipment
Additional tape units.

Services Available
Advice, programming, operators, software packages, preparation of data, systems analysis. Operate on a remote access and closed shop basis.

Fields of Application
Scientific, statistical, commercial, accounting, management, systems analysis.
Specialized areas: Sales analysis, payroll, inventory.

INTERCONSULT SA*
Carrera 13 No. 27-75, 7º piso, Apartado Aéreo 14909, Bogotá, D.E.
Telephone: 410-560, 410-361

Officer
C. N. García-Reyes

Services Available
Consultation, systems analysis.

Fields of Application
Economic studies, general and scientific management, operations research, project management, industrial engineering, marketing, production and inventory control, information systems, general and cost accounting systems, data processing and transmission systems, etc.

INTERNATIONAL COMPUTER SERVICES S.A.
Carrera 10 No. 16-39, piso 8, Bogotá, D.E.
Telephone: 346702

Officers
Enrique González Moreno, *General Manager*
Hugo Fernández P., *Technical Manager*
Alfonso Angel R., *Services Manager*

Computer Installation
BURROUGHS B3500–operating system: MCP; internal storage: 60K bytes; magnetic tapes: 4; magnetic discs: 1; 1 line printer. *Remote processing feature:* off-line printers.

Coding Languages
COBOL, FORTRAN, Assembler.

Contemplated Equipment
Key to tape peripherals, increased storage (60K bytes) and disc (10 million bytes).

Services Available
Advice, programming, education and training, software packages, documentation, preparation of data, systems analysis. Operate on a self-service, block time and open shop basis.

Fields of Application
Statistical, commercial, accounting, management, systems analysis.
Specialized areas: Sales analysis, analysis, payroll.

Training
Seminars at executive level on systems and computers.

PROCOMPUTOS LTDA.
Carrera 52 No. 72-132, P.O. Box 15408, Barranquilla

Officers
José A. Paternostro, *General Manager*
José M. Voros, *Operations Director*
Ricardo Cabas, *Programming Director*

Computer Installation
BURROUGHS B500—operating system: MCP II; internal storage: 192K bits; magnetic tapes; magnetic discs: 1; 1 line printer.

Coding Languages
COBOL, Assembler.

Contemplated Equipment
BURROUGHS B1726.

Services Available
Programming, education and training, preparation of data, systems analysis. Operate on a block time basis.

Fields of Application
Statistical, commercial, accounting.
Specialized areas: Sales, analysis, analysis, payroll.

Training
Courses in COBOL programming and systems analysis.

SERVICE BUREAUX

ANÁLISIS Y SISTEMATIZACIÓN ELECTRÓNICA LTDA. (ANALICE)
Carrera 3A No. 18-24, piso 7, Bogotá, D.E.
Telephone: 417191, 423867

Officers
Jaime Parra Martínez, *General Manager*
Saady Parra Martínez, *Systems Manager*
Alfonso Parra Martínez, *Administrative Manager*

Computer Installation
BURROUGHS B500—operating system: MCP-2SSR; internal storage: 19K bits; magnetic tapes: 4; magnetic discs: 2; 1 line printer.

Coding Languages
COBOL, Assembler.

Services Available
Advice, programming, education and training, operators, software packages, documentation, preparation of data, systems analysis. Operate on a self-service basis.

Fields of Application
Statistical, commercial, accounting, systems analysis.
Specialized areas: Sales analysis, analysis, payroll, general and cost accounting.

CENTRO DE INFORMACIÓN Y CÓMPUTO S.A. (CICSA)
Edificio Belmonte, 6º piso, Carrera 1a No. 24-56, P.O.B. 7641, Cali
Telephone: 791835, 791962, 791951

Officers
Alejandro Agodelo G., *Manager*
Rafael Restrepo R., *Head of Systems and Programming Department*

Computer Installation
BURROUGHS B3500—operating system: MCP 5.2; internal storage: 64K bytes; magnetic tapes: 4; magnetic discs: 1; 1 line printer.

Coding Languages
COBOL, FORTRAN, Assembler, Program Generators.

Contemplated Equipment
BURROUGHS B3500 for in-house back-up.

Services Available
Advice, programming, education and training, operators, software packages, documentation, preparation of data, systems analysis, K.P.B. verifying.

Fields of Application
Statistical, commercial, production control, accounting, management, systems analysis, operational research, technical.
Specialized areas: Sales analysis, investment analysis, payroll.

Training
Certificate courses in Introduction to Computers and Diagramming Techniques, COBOL, FORTRAN and Assembler.

FABRICATO S.A.*
Apartado Aéreo 698, Medellín

Officers
Dr. A. González, *Director, Systems Division*
Dr. J. M. Román, *Director, Operations Research Division*

Computer Installation
IBM 1401—internal storage: 16K bits; magnetic tapes: 4; 1 line printer.

IBM 360/40—operating system: DOS; internal storage: 64K bits; magnetic tapes: 4; magnetic discs: 2 2314; 1 line printer.

Coding Languages
Autocoder, FORTRAN II and IV, COBOL, PL/1, Assembly Language, RPG.

Services Available
Programming, systems analysis. Operate on a self-service basis. Available to Fabricato S.A. and other industries.

Fields of Application
Commercial, management, operational research.

IBM COLOMBIA LTDA*
Carrera 10a., 19-64, Bogotá, D.E.
Telephone: 420168

Also at:
Barranquilla, Cali and Medellín

Principal Officers
Arturo González Gascón, *General Manager*
Alvaro Aguirre, *Secretary General*

Computer Installation
Bogotá:
IBM 1410 (2)–internal storage: 20K bits; magnetic tapes: 4 729-4; 1 line printer.
IBM 1460 (2)–internal storage: 16K bits; magnetic tapes: 4 726-6; 1 line printer.
Barranquilla:
IBM 1410.
Cali:
IBM 360/25–internal storage: 32K bytes; magnetic tapes: 4 2401; magnetic discs.
IBM 2318; 1 line printer.
Medellín:
IBM 360/20.

Coding Languages
Autocoder, IOCS.

Contemplated Equipment
IBM 360/50.

Services Available
Advice, operators, preparation of data, programming, etc.

SEGUROS BOLÍVAR*
Carrera 10 no. 16-39, Bogotá, D.E.
Téléphone: 43-71-20

Dirigeants
H. Perea, *Chef*
C. López, *Adjoint*

Equipment
IBM 1401–mémoire interne: 16K bits; bandes magnétiques: 4 729-II; 1 imprimante.

Langages de Programmation
Autocoder, FORTRAN II and IV.

Services Fournis
Conseils, programmation, enseignement et formation, préparation des données. Fonctionnement en self-service.

Domaines D'Application
Statistique, comptabilité, systems analysis, gestion.
Domaines spécialisés: Calcul de mathématique, actuarielles.

COSTA RICA

UNIVERSITY

UNIVERSIDAD DE COSTA RICA
Centro de Cálculo Electrónico
Ciudad Universitaria Rodrigo Facio, San José
Telephone: 25-55-55

Officer
Mario A. Feoli, *Director*

Computer Installation
IBM 1620–operating system: Monitor; internal storage: 240K bits; magnetic discs: 1 1311; 1 line printer.

Coding Languages
FORTRAN II-D, ALGOL, SPS II-D.

Contemplated Equipment
IBM 360/40 with standard peripheral equipment.

Services Available
Advice, programming, education and training, operators, software packages. Operate on a closed shop basis. Available to members of the University of Costa Rica, and to outside customers only when time allows.

Fields of Application
Scientific, statistical, accounting, management, systems analysis, operational research.
Specialized areas: Analysis, structural engineering, teaching, research.

Training
Courses in engineering, statistics, sociology, psychology and numerical methods for students of FORTRAN II.

SERVICE BUREAUX

IBM WORLD TRADE CORPORATION*
San José

Computer Installation
IBM 1401 card.

Services Available
Advice, operators, preparation of data, programming.

Fields of Application
Statistical, commercial.

SISTEMAS ANALITICOS S.A. (ASC)
Apartado 6244, San José
Telephone: 22-81-56

Officers
Carlos Saborio, *President*
Lance T. Parker, *Vice-President*

Computer Installation
DATA GENERAL Nova–operating system: RTOS; internal storage: 128K bits; magnetic tapes: 1 9-track; 1 line printer.
DATA GENERAL Nova–operating system: RTDOS; internal storage: 256K bits; magnetic discs; 1 line printer.
DATA GENERAL Nova 800–operating system: special; internal storage: 512K bits; magnetic discs; 2 line printers. *Remote processing features:* 40 terminals.

Coding Languages
FORTRAN IV, FORTRAN V, ALGOL 60, Nova Assembler, BASIC, RPG.

Contemplated Equipment
Nova 800 (4,096K bits) with teleprocessing.

Services Available
Advice, programming, software packages, systems analysis, turn key systems. Operate on a remote access and time-sharing basis.

Fields of Application
Scientific, statistical, commercial, accounting, management information systems.

CYPRUS

GOVERNMENT ESTABLISHMENT

MINISTRY OF FINANCE
Treasury Department
Nicosia

Officers
S. Z. Nathanael, *Accountant-General*
L. I. Martides, *Data Processing Manager*

Computer Installation
NCR Century 100–internal storage: 32K bits; magnetic tapes: 2 633-119; magnetic discs: 1 655-101; 1 line printer.

Coding Languages
FORTRAN, COBOL, NEAT 3.

Services Available
Advice, programming, preparation of data, systems analysis. Operate on a closed shop basis. Available to government and semi-government departments.

Fields of Application
Scientific, statistical, commercial, accounting.
Specialized areas: Payroll, government accounting.

Services Available
Advice, programming, systems analysis. Operate on a closed shop basis.

Field of Application
Education.
Specialized area: On-line process control.

VYSOKÁ ŠKOLA EKONOMICKÁ*
Institute of Computing Science (INCOS)
Prague 3, Nám. G. Klimenta 4
Telephone: 220-401

Officers
Doc. Ing. J. Zelinka, *Director of INCOS*
Ing. I. Palla, *Deputy Director*

Computer Installation
ELLIOTT 4120–internal storage: 589,824 bits; magnetic tapes: 6 4100; 1 line printer.

Coding Languages
NEAT, ALGOL 4100, FORTRAN, COBOL, Language H.

Services Available
Consultation, programming, education and training, preparation of data, systems analysis. Operate on a self-service, open shop and time-sharing basis. Available for University research.

Fields of Application
Scientific, statistical, commercial, accounting, systems analysis, operational research.

Training
Courses in NEAT, ALGOL, COBOL, FORTRAN.

CZECHOSLOVAKIA

UNIVERSITIES AND COLLEGES

TECHNICAL UNIVERSITY OF OSTRAVA*
Computer Centre
Ostrava 1, Osvoboditelu 33
Telephone: 261-91

Officers
Dipl. Ing. Antonin V. Motyčka, *Head of Computer Centre*
Dipl. math. Jindřich Cernorsky, *Research Analyst*
Dipl. math. Eva Hrabcová, *Research Analyst*
Dipl. Phys. Jarmila Kobertová, *Research Analyst*
Dipl. math. Jaroslav Libicher, *Research Analyst*
Dipl. Ing. Jan Stefan, *Research Analyst*

Computer Installation
ODRA 1003–internal storage: 327,680 bits.

Coding Languages
Autocode Most 1.

Contemplated Equipment
Time-sharing computer.

GOVERNMENT ESTABLISHMENTS

KANCELARSKE STROJE*
(Czechoslovak State Computing Centre)
Prague

Computer Installation
ELLIOTT 503.
MINSK 22.

Service Available
Advice, programming.

Field of Application
Industrial.

UNITED NATIONS DEVELOPMENT PROGRAMME
Computing Research Centre
Bratislava, Dúbravská 7
Telephone: 46531-6

Officers
Prof. Anton Klas, *Director*
Ing. Jozef Linkeš, *Deputy Director*

Computer Installation
CDC 3300–operating systems: MASTER 3.2; internal storage: 2,752,512 bits; magnetic tapes: 4 604; magnetic discs: 8 854; 2 line printers. *Remote processing features:* 2 USER 200 terminals, 3 teletypes.

Coding Languages
ANSI FORTRAN, ANSI COBOL, ALGOL, SIMULA, SNOBOL, PASCAL, META, COMPASS.

Contemplated Equipment
2 604 magnetic tapes; 1 NORD mini-computer; 2 Vasta Teletype compatible remote displays.

Services Available
Advice, education and training, operators, software packages, documentation, preparation of data. Operate on a remote access, closed shop and time-sharing basis. Priority given to internal users.

Fields of Application
Scientific, statistical, management, systems analysis.
Specialized areas: Investment, analysis, information systems.

Training
Short-term courses for specialized staff from statistical offices: information systems, programming systems, systems analysis, mathematics.

RESEARCH INSTITUTIONS

INSTITUTE OF SOLID STATE PHYSICS
162 53 Prague 6, Cukrovarnická 10
Telephone: 355500

Officer
Dr. Jaroslav Nadrchal, *Head of Department of Information Processing*

Computer Installation
TESLA 200–operating system: tape oriented; internal storage: 512K bits; magnetic tapes: 6 9-track; 1 line printer.

Coding Languages
FORTRAN, Assembly, ML/1, ALGOL 60 and 68.

Contemplated Equipment
Disc units, new magnetic tapes.

Services Available
Advice, operators, software packages, documentation, preparation of data. Operate on a closed shop basis. Available only for scientific computation.

Field of Application
Scientific.

VYZKUMNÝ ÚSTAV MATEMATICKÝCH STROJU*
Prague 1, Loretanské nám. 3

Officer
Ing. Vratislav Gregor, *Director*

Computer Installation
EPOS 1/2–internal storage: 4K bits; magnetic tapes: 4; 2 line printers.

Coding Languages
EPOS, ALGOL, MPS ALGOL, Autocode EPOS, Autocode MSP.

Services Available
Preparation of data, programming. Operate on an open shop basis.

Field of Application
Development of new mathematical machines.
Specialized area: Time-sharing.

SERVICE BUREAU

INSTITUTE FOR RATIONALIZATION OF PRODUCTION AND MANAGEMENT IN THE ENGINEERING INDUSTRY (ORGAPROJEKT)
112 39 Prague 1, Dlouhá 39
Telephone: 610 43/7, 628 53/5, 668 41/5

Officers
Oldřich Honc, *General Manager*
Václav Landfeld, *Technical Director*
Jiří Fafek, *Economic Director*

Services Available
Advice, programming, education and training, documentation, preparation of data, systems analysis. Available mainly to the engineering industry.

Fields of Application
Commercial, production control, accounting, management, systems analysis, operational research.
Specialized areas: Sales analysis, linear programming, investment, analysis, payroll, structural engineering.

Training
Courses in management and organization for technical and administrative staff in industry, and specialized courses on the introduction of subsystems in management.

DENMARK

EDUCATIONAL AND TRAINING INSTITUTION

DANISH EDP COUNCIL
58 Bredgade, 1260 Copenhagen K

Officer
Mogens Boman, *Manager*

Services Available
Advice, education and training.

Training
Courses in programming, systems description, management and operating.

UNIVERSITIES AND COLLEGES

ÅRHUS UNIVERSITET*
Regionale EDP-Center
Ny Munkegade, 8000 Århus
Telephone: 128355

Officers
Board of Directors:
Professor Sven Bundgaard
Professor Svend Fredens
Professor Jens Holt
Professor Gunnar Bonde
Professor Svend E. Rasmussen

Computer Installation
CDC 6400–operating system: SCOPE; internal storage: 2 million plus 7.7 million bits; magnetic tapes: 2 657, 7 659; magnetic discs: 5 841; 1 line printer.
Remote processing features: Approx. 50 small terminals, 3 CDC 200 User terminals, 1 IBM 1130.

Coding Languages
ALGOL, FORTRAN, SIMULA, COMPASS.

Services Available
Advice, operators, preparation of data, programming. Operate on a closed shop, remote access and time-sharing basis. Available only for scientific and research work.

Field of Application
Scientific research.

DANMARKS TEKNISKE HØJSKOLE
Institute of Computing Sciences
Building 344, 2800 Lyngby, Copenhagen

Officers
Prof. Per Gert Jensen
Prof. Christian Gram

Computer Installation
IBM 370/165—operating systems: OS360, Monitor; internal storage: 32 million bits; 2 line printers. *Remote processing features:* 2 Fast Remote Batch Terminals; teletypes.

RC4000—operating system: BOSS; internal storage: 896K bits; magnetic tapes: 3 Ampex 9-track; magnetic discs: 1 CDC; 1 line printer. *Remote processing features:* teletype, RJE.

Coding Languages
ALGOL, ALGOL W, FORTRAN, Assembler.

Services Available
Operators, programming. Operate on an open shop basis. Available only to institutes of the Technical University.

Fields of Application
Scientific, management.
Specialized area: Systems programming.

Training
Elementary courses in computer science; advanced courses in hardware and software.

HANDELSHØJSKOLEN I ÅRHUS
Computer Centre
Fuglesangsalle 4, 8210 Århus V
Telephone: (06)154166

Officer
J. Olsen, *Manager*

Computer Installation
RC4000—operating system: BOSS 2; internal storage: 6,528K bits; magnetic tapes: 2 RC749; magnetic discs: 2 RC433, RC4818; 1 line printer. *On-line satellite computer:* RECAU.

Coding Languages
ALGOL 6, FORTRAN IV, SLANG, PASCAL.

Contemplated Equipment
Internal storage module, 3,256K bits.

Services Available
Programming, education and training, documentation, preparation of data, systems analysis. Operate on a self-service, remote access and time-sharing basis. Available for institutional research and education.

Fields of Application
Scientific, statistical, commercial, management, systems analysis, operational research.
Specialized areas: Sales analysis, linear programming, investment, analysis, medical research.

Training
Basic training in systems analysis and programming. Advanced training in database management, investment simulation, operations research and simulation.

KØBENHAVNS UNIVERSITET
Regional EDP—Centre
Blegdamsuej 19, Copenhagen

Officer
Dr. J. H. Gunn, *Director*

Computer Installation
UNIVAC 1108—operating system: EXEC 8; internal storage: 192K x 36 bits; magnetic tapes: 6; magnetic discs: 4 8414 2 FIII; 3 line printers. *On-line satellite computers:* 2 9300. *Remote processing features:* batch, demand terminals.

Coding Languages
FORTRAN, ALGOL, COBOL, etc.

Contemplated Equipment
Univac 1110 to replace 1108.

Services Available
Advice, education and training, software packages, documentation. Operate on a self-service, remote access, closed shop and time-sharing basis. Available for research and higher education.

Fields of Application
Scientific, statistical.

NORTHERN EUROPE UNIVERSITY COMPUTING CENTRE (NEUCC)
Regional Computing Centre
Building 305, Danmarks Tekniske
Højskole, 2800 Lyngby, Copenhagen
Telephone: (01) 881-277

Officer
Hans Jørgen Helms, *Director*

Computer Installation
IBM 370/165—operating system: OS/MVT HASP; internal storage: 16 million bits; magnetic tapes: 5; magnetic discs: 10 spindles; 3 line printers.

Coding Languages
ALGOL, COBOL, FORTRAN, PL/1.

Services Available
Advice, education and training, software packages, documentation. Operate on a remote access, closed shop and time-sharing basis. Services restricted to education and research.

Field of Application
Scientific.

Training
Non-credit courses for users.

GOVERNMENT ESTABLISHMENTS

DANMARKS STATISTIK
Frederiksholms Kanal 27, Copenhagen K
Telephone: (01) 12-16-75

Officers
N. V. Skak-Nielsen, *Statistician*
Arne Bunckenburg, *Head of EDP Department*

Computer Installation
IBM 360/40–operating system: DOS; internal storage: 128K bytes; magnetic tapes: 5 IBM 3420; magnetic discs: 6 IBM 2319; 1 line printer.

Contemplated Equipment
IBM 370/145 with storage of 512K bytes.

Services Available
Advice, programming, preparation of data. Operate on a closed shop basis.

Field of Application
Statistical.

I/S DATACENTRALEN AF 1959
Ved Stadsgraven 15, 2300 Copenhagen
Telephone: ASTA 1022

Officer
Willy Olsen, *General Manager*

Computer Installation
IBM 370/155 (5)–operating system: OS/MFT; internal storage: 8,192K bits each (2) or 12,288K bits each (3); magnetic tapes: 62 IBM 3420/7; magnetic discs: 26 IBM 3330/1, 4 IBM 2319; 10 line printers.

Coding Languages
FANS COBOL, Assembler, FORTRAN, PL/1, RPG.

Contemplated Equipment
3 IBM 370/158.

Services Available
Advice, programming, education and training, operators, software packages, documentation, preparation of data, systems analysis. Operate on a remote access and closed shop basis.

Field of Application
Commercial.
Specialized area: Payroll.

RESEARCH INSTITUTION

ATOMENERGIKOMMISSIONENS FORSØGSANLAEG RISØ
Risø, 4000 Roskilde
Telephone: (03) 35 51 01

Officer
Leif Hansson, *Head of Computer Group*

Computer Installation
BURROUGHS B6700–operating system: MCP; internal storage: 48K x 52 bits; 1 line printer.

Coding Languages
ALGOL, FORTRAN, COBOL.

Services Available
Advice, operators, software packages, documentation, preparation of data. Operate on a closed shop basis. Available only to customers who have some connection with the establishment.

Field of Application
Scientific.
Specialized area: Nuclear engineering.

CONSULTANTS

A–DATA*
Vesterbrogade 43, 1620 Copenhagen V
Telephone: (01) 21 49 42

T. BAK-JENSEN A/S*
Finsensvej 15, 2000 Copenhagen F
Telephone: (01) 108211

Officer
Helge Milo, *Assistant Director*

Services Available
Advice, programming, systems analysis.

Fields of Application
Management consulting services within every field of work apart from scientific, but mainly within economical (banking and insurance), commercial and industrial business activities.
Specialized areas: Feasibility studies, informational analyses, advice on choice of computer and configuration, assistance on systems analysis and programming. EDP-organizational problems and follow-up on economics.

Training
Users' courses with a duration of 1 week and a few courses in COBOL programming with duration of 4 weeks (160 hours).

CAPITAL COMPUTER APPLICATIONS*
B.P. House, Århus Viby–5

Officer
D. B. Wilkinson, *Director in charge of overseas operations*

Services Available
Consultation, programming, software packages, systems analysis.

Fields of Application
Design and implementation of computer-based data processing systems.
Specialized areas: Accounting and management information for retail organizations.

IMAR CONSULT NR.NORDISK RATIONALISERING A/S*
Roholmsvej 17, 2620 Albertslund

Services Available
Consultation, systems analysis.

Fields of Application
General management, e.g. long range planning, organization planning, information systems; finance/accounting; manufacturing, e.g. production scheduling, inventory control; engineering; marketing.

PARSONS & WILLIAMS INC.*
Nyropsgade 43, 1602 Copenhagen V
Telephone: 11-20-00

Services Available
Consultation, software packages, systems analysis.

Fields of Application
Production control, management system design, operations research, and programming.

Training
Short courses in management science.

STEVENSON, JORDAN AND HARRISON A/S*
Norrevoldgade 11, Copenhagen K

Services Available
Consultation, systems analysis.

Fields of Application
Statistical, commercial, production control, management, operational research.

SERVICE BUREAUX

ADB CENTRALEN AB*
Fredericiagade 16, Copenhagen
Telephone: (01) 112-301

Services Available
Programming, systems analysis.

Fields of Application
Commercial, production control, accounting, management.

ALFA NUMMERISK DATA BUREAU*
Puggaardsgade 2, 1573 Copenhagen V
Telephone: 11-19-62

Officers
Eli Skjold, *President*
Per Illum, *Data Manager*

Services Available
Advice, preparation of data, programming, systems analysis. Operate on an open shop and block time basis.

Fields of Application
Statistical, commercial, management.

BOGFØRINGSFORENINGEN AUTOMATIONSCENTRALEN*
Farimagsvej 53, Naestved
Telephone: (03) 726044

Computer Installation
IBM 1440—internal storage: 16K bits; magnetic discs: 3 1311; 1 line printer.

IBM 360/30—operating system: DOS; internal storage: 32K bits; magnetic discs: 3 2311; 1 line printer.

Coding Languages
Autocoder.

Services Available
Advice, operators, preparation of data, programming, systems analysis. Operate on a self-service, open shop and block time basis.

Field of Application
Commercial.
Specialized area: Banking.

BULL GENERAL ELECTRIC*
Østergade 3, 1100 Copenhagen K
Telephone: 15-15-07

Officers
Léon Philips, *General Manager*
P. Reinseth, *Manager*
J. Massiak, *School Manager*

Services Available
Advice, preparation of data, programming, systems analysis and any other service connected with data processing equipment sales activities.

Fields of Application
All fields.

Training
About 50 courses a year, comprising general items like COBOL, FORTRAN, etc. and special items connected to the machine park.

CARD PUNCHING SERVICE*
16 Gyldenloevesgade, 369 Copenhagen K
Telephone: (01) Palae 9262

Officer
Mrs. Erna Larsen, *Manager*

Service Available
Preparation of data (card punching).

Fields of Application
Mostly commercial.

CBC BYGGEADMINISTRATION A/S
Kokkedal Industripark 28, 2980 Kokkedal

Computer Installation
BURROUGHS B3500—operating system: MCP-V; internal storage: 80K bytes; magnetic tapes: 4 B9381; magnetic discs: 1 B9373; 1 line printer.

Coding Language
COBOL.

Services Available
Advice, programming, education and training, operators, software packages, documentation, preparation of data, systems analysis. Operate on a self-service, closed-shop, block time and open shop basis.

Fields of Application
Statistical, commercial, accounting, management, systems analysis.
Specialized areas: Investment, analysis, building project management.

Training
Courses in project planning, project control, project analyses, accounting systems.

COMPETANCE EDB-SERVICE A/S
Frederiksberggade 19, 1459 Copenhagen K
Telephone: 11-70-70

Officer
Ulf Thomsen, *General Manager*

Coding Languages
COBOL, PL/1, FORTRAN, Assembler.

Services Available
Programming, systems analysis, computer time bank.

DANSK SIEMENS A/S*
EDB Afdelingen, Nikolaigade 26, Copenhagen

Computer Installation
SIEMENS 3003–internal storage: 16K bits; magnetic tapes.

Services Available
Advice, operators, programming, software packages, systems analysis.

Fields of Application
Scientific, statistical, commercial.

DATA-INFORM A/S
Nordlandsvej 82, 8240 Risskov
Telephone: (06) 17 55 00

Also at:
Kirkevej 1-3, 2630 Tåstrup, Copenhagen
Telephone: (01) 99 55 77

Toldbodgade 9, 5000 Odense
Telephone: (09) 14 22 44

Lyngvej 3, 9000 Aalborg
Telephone: (08) 18 25 00

Officers
O. Wennemoes, *Director*
F. S. Jensen, *Director*

Computer Installation
ICL 1903T–operating system: GEORGE 2; internal storage: 64K 24-bit words; magnetic tapes: 9; magnetic discs: 3 EDS 60; 2 line printers. *On-line satellite computer:* 7020.

RC 3600–internal storage: 16K 8-bit bytes; 1 magnetic tape; 1 line printer.

Coding Languages
COBOL, PLAN, FORTRAN.

Contemplated Equipment
ICL 1902A off-line satellite computer.

Services Available
Programming, education and training, documentation, preparation of data, systems analysis. Operate on a closed shop, remote access and block time basis.

Fields of Application
Commercial, accounting, management.
Specialized areas: Standard systems for accounting, budget control, payroll, sales analysis, stock control; special systems for accountants and advertising agencies.

DATAMATIC A/S*
Datagaarden, Tagensvej 86, 2200 Copenhagen N

Also at:
Grenåvej 315, Århus.

Vesterbros Torv, Odense.

Officers
Poul Wendelboe, *Sales Director*
J. Schlosser, *Business Manager*

Computer Installations
ICL 1902A–internal storage: 128K characters; magnetic tapes: 4; magnetic discs: 2; 1 line printer.

UNIVAC 1004 (2)–internal storage: 1K characters; 1 line printer each.

FRIDEN 10–internal storage: 60K characters; magnetic tapes: 1; magnetic discs: 1; 1 line printer.

Fields of Application
Commercial, accounting.
Specialized areas: Sales analysis, payroll.

DATASKOLEN*
Købmagergade 41, 1150 Copenhagen K
Telephone: (01) 116864

Officer
Jørgen Hansen

Coding Languages
Assembler, COBOL.

Services Available
Advice, programming, systems analysis.

Contemplated Equipment
SIEMENS 4004/35.

Fields of Application
Accounting, marketing research.
Specialized area: Inventory control.

Training
Courses in programming and systems analysis; short courses in the principles of data processing (30 hours), computer techniques and input-output techniques.

ELEKTRONISK BOGFØRING FOR REVISORER (EBR)*
Dag Hammerskjoelds Alle 5, 2100 Copenhagen Ø

Field of Application
Accounting.

EDB-CENTRALEN*
Bredgade 2, 7400 Herning
Telephone: (07) 122022

Officer
Bent Hansen, *General Manager*

Computer Installation
IBM 360/30–operating system: DOS; internal storage: 64K bits; magnetic tapes: 2 2401/5; magnetic discs: 3 IBM 1311; 1 line printer.

Coding Languages
COBOL, FORTRAN, Assembler.

Contemplated Equipment
IBM 360/40.

Services Available
Advice, operators, preparation of data, programming, systems analysis. Operate on an open shop basis.

Fields of Application
Commercial, statistical, production control, accounting.
Specialized area: Banking.

FORSIKRINGSSELSKABERNES DATA CENTRAL
Lindevangs Alle 11, Copenhagen F
Telephone: FA 2235

Officers
Henrik Svensson, *Director*
Elo Hansen, *Foreign Relations*

Computer Installation
IBM 360/40–operating system: DOS; internal storage: 128K bits; magnetic tapes: 4 3420/3; magnetic discs: 2 Memorex 660B; 1 line printer.

Coding Languages
COBOL, Assembler, RPG.

Services Available
Operators, preparation of data, programming, software packages, systems analysis, documentation. Operate on a self-service, closed shop, open shop and block time basis. Jobs at present primarily for insurance companies.

Field of Application
Commercial.
Specialized area: Insurance business.

FORSTAEDERNES BANK AKTS.*
Hovedvejen 110, 2600 Glostrup

A/S FYNS DATA SERVICE
Rugårdsvej 101, 5000 Odense

Officer
Bent Larsen

Computer Installation
ICL 1902A–internal storage: 24K bits; magnetic tapes: 4; magnetic discs: 3; 1 line printer.

Coding Languages
COBOL, PLAN.

Services Available
Programming, education and training, operators, preparation of data, systems analysis.

Fields of Application
Statistical, commercial, accounting, management.

GEODATA A/S*
Dagmarhus, H.C. Andersens Boulevard 12, 1553 Copenhagen V
Telephone: (01) 14 14 90

Officer
Bent Erik Hansen, *Data Processing Manager*

Computer Installation
IBM 360–operating system: DOS; magnetic tapes: 2 2415; magnetic discs: 2 2311; 1 line printer. *Remote processing features:* MDS 6403.

Coding Languages
PL/1, FORTRAN, Assembler, RPG, COBOL.

Services Available
Programming, preparation of data, systems analysis. Operate on a self-service, closed shop, block time and open shop basis.

Fields of Application
Commercial, accounting, management, engineering.
Specialized areas: Structural engineering, surveying.

Training
Introductory courses in electronic data processing and PL/1 language.

HORSENS DATACENTRAL
Fabrikvej 7, 8700 Horsens
Telephone: (05) 627711

Officer
John Morling, Engtoften 8, 8700 Horsens

Computer Installation
UNIVAC 1004/3 (2)–operating system: ICL; internal storage: 4K bits each; 2 line printers.

ICL 1902A–internal storage: 32K words.

Coding Languages
XS-3, COBOL.

Services Available
Advice, preparation of data, programming, systems analysis. Operate on a closed shop basis.

Fields of Application
Statistical, commercial, production control, accounting.

IBM A/S*
Ved Vesterport 6, 1646 Copenhagen
Telephone: (01) 15-11-55

Also at:
Nytorv 5, 9000 Ålborg
Telephone: 12-30-22

Banegardsvej. 34, 8000 Århus C
Telephone: (06) 13-31-77

Vestergåde 11, 5000 Odense
Telephone: (09) 11-04-88

Computer Installation
Copenhagen:
IBM 360/40 (2)–operating system: DOS; internal storage: 128K bits each; magnetic tapes: 2 2402/2, 2 2403/3, 6 2401/6; magnetic discs: 4 2311/1 each.
Århus, Ålborg, Odense:
IBM 360/20–magnetic tape: 2415/2.

Services Available
Advice, operators, programming, systems analysis. Operate on a self-service and closed shop basis.

Fields of Application
Scientific, commercial, statistical, accounting, production control, operational research, etc.

Training
All educational activity is performed by the IBM Denmark Education Center.

INTERNATIONAL COMPUTERS AND TABULATORS A/S*
Bredgade 23, Copenhagen K
Telephone: Minerva 5588

Computer Installation
ICL 1500–internal storage: 140K bits; magnetic tapes: 7; 1 line printer.

ICL 1903–operating system: GEORGE 1; internal storage: 393,216 bits; magnetic tapes: 6; magnetic discs: 1; 1 line printer.

Coding Languages
PLAN, COBOL, ALGOL, FORTRAN.

Contemplated Equipment
Exchangeable discs; cassette tape stations.

Services Available
Advice, preparation of data, programming, software packages, systems analysis. Operate on a self-service and open shop basis.

Fields of Application
Scientific, mathematical and commercial data processing.
Specialized areas: PERT—Auto-dealers' package (invoicing, accounting, spares, statistics).

Training
Courses in all aspects of the use of computers.

A/S JYDSK DATA CENTER*
Dianavej 2, 7100 Vejle
Telephone: (05) 82-67-00

Also at:
Kuldyssen 13, 2630 Tåstrup
Telephone: (01) 99-76-00

Officer
Knud Frederiksen, *General Manager*

Computer Installation
NCR 315—internal storage: 10K bits; magnetic tapes: 1 334/131; magnetic discs: 4 353/1; 1 line printer.

NCR 615/200—operating system: B1; internal storage: 64K bits; magnetic tapes: 2 633/117; magnetic discs: 4 655/201; 1 line printer.

Coding Languages
NEAT, BEST, COBOL, FORTRAN.

Services Available
Preparation of data, programming, software packages, systems analysis. Operate on a closed shop and block time basis.

Fields of Application
General accounting, payroll, stock control (lumber and iron dealers, automobile dealers).

Training
Courses in installation of business-orientated systems.

I/S KOMMUNERNES EDB-CENTRAL*
Brøndbyøster Boulevard 22, Brøndbyøster,
2650 Copenhagen HV.
Telephone: (01) 75-45-11

Computer Installation
IBM 360/30—operating system: DOS; internal storage: 64K bits; magnetic tapes: 4 2401/5; magnetic discs: 2 2311; 1 line printer.

IBM 1401—internal storage: 16K bits; magnetic tapes: 4 7330; 1 line printer.

IBM 360/40—operating system: DOS; internal storage: 256K bytes; magnetic tapes: 8 2401; magnetic discs: 3 2311; 2 line printers.

IBM 360/50—operating system: DOS; internal storage: 256K bytes; magnetic tapes: 8 2420; magnetic discs: 4 2311; 2 line printers.

Coding Languages
PL/1 (360), Autocoder (1401).

Services Available
Advice, preparation of data, programming, systems analysis. Operate on a closed shop basis. Priority given to the 300 member-municipalities.

Fields of Application
Commercial and technical.

LANDBRUGETS EDB-CENTRALER (LEC)*
Bytoften, 8240 Risskov

Officers
O. Kjaerup, *Director*
A. Egholm, *Deputy Director*
R. Klausen, *Deputy Director*
J. Krabbe, *General Manager*

Computer Installation
IBM 360/50—operating system: DOS; internal storage: 256K 8-bit bytes; magnetic tapes: 8 IBM 2401/5, 2 IBM 2415/1; magnetic discs: 8 IBM 2314; 2 line printers.
Remote processing features: IBM 2701 (terminals IBM 1050 and IBM 2260).

IBM 360/30—operating system: DOS; internal storage: 64K 8-bit bytes; magnetic tapes: 6 IBM 2401/2; magnetic discs: 3 IBM 2311; 1 line printer.

IBM 360/20—internal storage: 8K bytes; magnetic tapes: 2 IBM 2415/1; 1 line printer.

Coding Languages
COBOL, FORTRAN, Assembler.

Contemplated Equipment
IBM 360/40; tele-processing equipment.

Services Available
Advice, programming, software packages, preparation of data, systems analysis. Operate on a remote access and closed shop basis. Priority given to agricultural applications.

Fields of Application
Scientific, statistical, commercial, production control, accounting, management, operational research.
Specialized areas: Linear programming, agricultural models.

Training
Courses in applications; computer education for agriculture; specialized training to suit customers' requirements.

NATIONAL CASH REGISTER CO.
NCR Data Center
Teglvaerksgade 31, 2100 Copenhagen Ø.
Telephone: (01) 29-15-55

Officer
A. Kidal, *Manager*

Computer Installation
NCR 315/RMC—operating systems: CRAM/TAPE EXEC.; internal storage: 240K bits; magnetic tapes: 2 NCR 7-track, 5 NCR CRAM-1 (Card Random Access Memory); 1 line printer.

NCR Century 200—internal storage: 512K bits; magnetic tapes: 5; magnetic discs: 2 NCR dual spindle; 1 line printer.

Coding Languages
NEAT 3, COBOL, BEST.

Contemplated Equipment
NCR 315/100.

Denmark – Service Bureaux

Services Available
Advice, operators, preparation of data, programming, systems analysis. Operate on a closed shop and block time basis.

Fields of Application
Commercial, statistical, accounting.

NORD DATA A/S*
Møllevej, 2990 Nivå

OK DATA*
Vesterbrogade 1, 1620 Copenhagen V
Telephone: (01) 12 32 00

Officer
O. Stangegård, *Director of the Computer Centre*

Computer Installation
IBM 360/40 – operating system: OS; internal storage: 256K bits; magnetic tapes: 5 2400/II; magnetic discs: 8 2314; 1 line printer. *Remote processing features:* 2 2780 terminals.
BULL GENERAL ELECTRIC GE 235/245 – internal storage: 32K 20-bit words; magnetic tapes: 2 Ampex; magnetic discs: 1; 1 line printer. *Remote processing features:* TTY type 33.

Coding Languages
COBOL, ALGOL, FORTRAN, BASIC.

Services Available
Consultation, programming, education and training, software packages, systems analysis. Operate on a closed shop, remote access, block time and time-sharing basis.

Fields of Application
All.

Training
Courses in Management and EDP (3½ days), EDP for Project Personnel (3 weeks), Introduction to EDP (1 or 5 days), seminars etc.

H. H. OSTERBYE
Bredgade 20, 1260 Copenhagen K

Officers
K. Jørgensen, *Managing Director*
P. Thyghøj, *Managing Director*

Computer Installations
SIEMENS 4004 Model 45 – operating system: TOS-DOS; internal storage: 128K bytes; magnetic tapes: 8; magnetic discs: 3 564; 2 line printers.

Coding Languages
COBOL, Assembler, FORTRAN, BASIC.

Services Available
Advice, preparation of data, programming, systems analysis.

Fields of Application
Commercial, production control, accounting, management, systems analysis.

PABST HULKORTSERVICE*
Vesterbrogade 43, 1620 Copenhagen V
Telephone: (01) 21-49-42

RATIONEL DATABEHANDLING A/S (RDB)
Søndre Ringvej 41-45, 2600 Glostrup
Telephone: (01) 964004

Officer
Christian Sørensen, *Director*

Computer Installation
SIEMENS 4004/55 – operating system: DOS; internal storage: 4,192K bits; magnetic tapes: 7; magnetic discs: 1 IBM 2314; 2 line printers.

Coding Languages
FORTRAN, COBOL, ALGOL, Autocoder.

Contemplated Equipment
3 9-track tapes, 2 4570.

Services Available
Advice, preparation of data, programming, systems analysis. Operate on an open shop, remote access and time-sharing basis.

Fields of Application
Scientific, statistical, commercial, accounting, management.
Specialized areas: Medical research, management in education.

A/S REGNECENTRALEN*
Headquarters and Service Centre
Falkoneralle 1, 2000 Copenhagen F
Telephone: (01) 10-53-66

Other Centres:
Vestergade 37, 5000 Odense
Telephone: (09) 12-53-66

Guldsmedgade 3-9, 8000 Århus C
Telephone: (06) 12-53-66

Kastetvej 4, 9000 Ålborg
Telephone: (08) 12-53-66

Officers
Niels Ivar Bech, *Director*
Paul Dahlgaard, *Director*

Computer Installation
CDC 1604 A and CDC 1604 B – internal storage: 1,572,864 bits each; magnetic tapes: 16 CDC 606; 1 line printer.

GIER (4) – internal storage: 43,008 bits plus 537,600 bits on drum each; magnetic tapes: 4 Ampex TM-7 each; 1 line printer each.

Coding Languages
ALGOL 60, FORTRAN.

Contemplated Equipment
RC 4000, a third generation computer, is under development.

Services Available
Advice, operators, preparation of data, programming, software packages, systems analysis. Operate on a closed shop basis.

Fields of Application
Design and development of hardware and software systems.
Specialized areas: Compiler techniques, real-time processing, and administrative data processing.

Denmark – Service Bureaux

Training
Courses are arranged as required, covering the following subjects: programming (ALGOL), mathematical and statistical problems, and administrative and technical applications.

CHRISTIAN ROVSING A/S
Marielundvej 46B, 2730 Herlev
Telephone: (01) 918833

Officer
Chr. F. Rovsing

Computer Installation
BURROUGHS B5700.
IBM 370/145.

Coding Languages
ALGOL, COBOL, FORTRAN IV, BASIC, PL/1.

Contemplated Equipment
IBM 370/155.

Services Available
Advice, programming, education and training, operators, software packages, systems analysis. Operate on a remote access, closed shop and block time basis.

Fields of Application
Scientific, statistical, commercial, production control, management, systems analysis, operational research.
Specialized areas: Sales analysis, linear programming, analysis, structural engineering, medical research and statistics.

Training
Courses are tailored to specific needs of students.

SPS A/S*
Rolighedsvej 11, 392255 Copenhagen
Telephone: 11-23-22

Officer
M. Pust, *Director*

Computer Installation
GIER–internal storage: 680K bits; magnetic tapes: 4; 1 line printer.
DATASAAB D22: internal storage: 1,200K bits; magnetic tapes: 6; magnetic discs: 2; 1 line printer.

Coding Languages
COBOL, DAC 3, ALGOL.

Services Available
Software packages, systems analysis. Operate on an open shop and block time basis.

Fields of Application
Commercial, statistical, production control.
Specialized area: Payroll.

SCAN DATA*
Vesterbrogade 35, 1620 Copenhagen V

Officer
John Helge Jensen, *Director*

Services Available
Advice, programming, systems analysis.

Fields of Application
Statistical, commercial, accounting.

SILKEBORG DATACENTRAL A/S*
Lillehøjvej 29, 8600 Silkeborg
Telephone: (06) 824300

Officer
J. Bech Christensen, *General Manager*

Computer Installation
IBM 360/30–operating system: DOS; internal storage: 64K bits; magnetic tapes: 2 2401/5; magnetic discs: 2 2311; 1 line printer.

Coding Language
COBOL.

Contemplated Equipment
IBM 360/25–internal storage: 32K bits; magnetic tapes: 1 2415/4; magnetic discs: 2 2311; 1 line printer.

Services Available
Advice, operators, programming, systems analysis. Operate on an open shop basis.

Fields of Application
Scientific, commercial, production control, accounting, management.
Specialized areas: Production planning and inventory management.

Training
Short courses in General EDP (3 days), Orientation (1 day), Analysing and Documentation Techniques (5 days).

K. LUND SIMONSEN A/S
Bymidten 22-30, 3500 Værløse
Telephone: (01) 48 33 65

Officers
K. Lund Simonsen, *Managing Director*
Bjørn Brostad, *Manager of Consultancy Division*
Henning Kjær, *Manager of Research Division*
John Pedersen, *Manager of Service Bureau Division*

Computer Installation
BURROUGHS B4700–operating system: MCPV; internal storage: 120K bits; magnetic tapes: 9; magnetic discs: 1; 2 line printers.

Coding Languages
Assembler, COBOL, RPG.

Services Available
Advice, programming, education and training, software packages, documentation, systems analysis, SB-functions. Operate on a block time basis.

Fields of Application
Statistical, commercial, accounting, management, systems analysis.
Specialized areas: Sales analysis, investment, analysis, payroll, medical research, banking.

Training
Specialized courses in systems engineering.

SLAGELSE DATA SERVICE A/S
Bjergbygade 1, 4200 Slagelse
Telephone: (03) 52-54-22

Officer
Tom Mastrup

Computer Installation
UNIVAC 9400—internal storage: 65K bits; 2 magnetic tapes; 2 magnetic discs; 1 line printer.

Coding Languages
COBOL, FORTRAN, RPG, Assembler.

Services Available
Advice, preparation of data, programming, software packages, systems analysis, documentation. Operate on a remote access, closed shop and block time basis.

Fields of Application
Statistical, commercial, production control, accounting, management, systems analysis, operational research.
Specialized areas: Sales analysis, investment, analysis, payroll.

SPAREKASSERNES DATACENTRALER
Meldahlsgade 1, 1613 Copenhagen V
Telephone: (01) 11-45-55

Also at:
St. Glasvej 55, 5000 Odense
Telephone: (09) 13-32-22

Frederiksgade 72, 8000 Århus C
Telephone: (06) 13-00-66

Officers
Niels-Aage Nielsen, *General Manager*
Aage Melbye, *Deputy General Manager*

Computer Equipment
BULL GENERAL ELECTRIC GAMMA 30 (5)—internal storage: 10K words each (4), 20K words (1); 5 magnetic tapes; 5 line printers.
IBM 370/155—internal storage: 1,024K bits; magnetic tapes: 12 3420/5; magnetic discs: 6 3330; 4 line printers.

Coding Languages
PL/1, Assembler.

Services Available
Operate on a remote access, closed shop and time-sharing basis. Available for members of the Danish Savings Bank Association only.

Field of Application
Accounting.
Specialized area: Banking.

SYDFYNS DATACENTRAL*
Mølmarksvej 198, 5700 Svendborg
Telephone: (09) 215353

Officer
Jørn Thygesen, *Director*

Computer Installation
IBM 360/20—operating system: DPS; internal storage: 16K bytes; magnetic discs: 2 2311; 1 line printer.

Coding Languages
RPG, Assembler.

Services Available
Advice, operators, preparation of data, programming, systems analysis. Operate on a self-service and open shop basis.

Fields of Application
Scientific, statistical, commercial, production control, accounting, general ledger, government, operational research.

Training
Courses in general information of electronic processing systems; system analysis; programming.

SYSTEMS ANALYSIS CORP. A/S
Kronprinsessegade 14, 1306 Copenhagen K
Telephone: 11 85 01

Officers
F. Danielsen, *Manager*
C. Toftgaard, *Chief Adviser*
N. Clausen, *Chief Programmer*

Coding Languages
All.

Services Available
Consultation, programming, education and training, software packages, documentation, systems analysis.

Fields of Application
Scientific, statistical, commercial, production control, accounting, management, systems analysis, operational research.
Specialized area: Advanced information systems.

Training
Courses in advanced applications.

VESTJYDSK DATA BUREAU (VDB)*
Randersvej 32, 6700 Esbjerg
Telephone: (05) 122699

Officer
O. Olsen, *Director*

Computer Installation
UNIVAC 9300—internal storage: 24K bytes; magnetic tapes: 4; 2 line printers.

Coding Languages
COBOL, Assembler, FORTRAN, RPG.

Field of Application
Accounting.
Specialized area: Payroll.

VESTJYDSK EDB-CENTER
77 Tarphagevej, 6700 Sædding pr. Esbjerg
Telephone: (05) 30600

Officers
Bent Laursen, *Manager*
Richard Nielsen, *Assistant Manager*

Computer Installation
NCR Century 200—operating system: B1; internal storage: 64K bits; magnetic tapes: 3; magnetic discs: 2; 1 line printer.

Coding Languages
COBOL, NEAT 3.

Contemplated Equipment
Multiprogramming.

Services Available
Advice, programming, education and training, operators, software packages, documentation, preparation of data, systems analysis. Operate on a self-service and open shop basis.

Field of Application
Commercial.
Specialized area: Payroll.

ECUADOR

SERVICE BUREAU

IBM DEL ECUADOR, C.A.
Avenida 12 de Octubre 1281, Casilla 642, Quito
Telephone: 524700

Also at:
9 de Octubre 1505, P.O. Box 3686, Guayaquil
Telephone: 513437

Officers
Galo Eguez Balseca, *General Manager*
Alfonso Falcony, *DP Marketing Manager*
Gustavo Heinert, *Branch Manager (Guayaquil)*

Computer Installation
Quito:
IBM 360/30 – magnetic discs: 4 2230.

Guayaquil:
IBM 360/20 – operating system: DPS; internal storage: 16K bytes; magnetic tapes: 4; 1 line printer.

Coding Languages
RPG, Assembler, PL/1.

Services Available
Advice, operators, programming, software packages. Operate on a self-service and block time basis.

Fields of Application
Statistical, commercial, scientific.

Training
A two-month course in COBOL language.

EGYPT

EDUCATIONAL AND TRAINING INSTITUTION

SCIENTIFIC COMPUTATION CENTRE
Sarwat Street, Dokky, Cairo

Officer
Prof. Dr. A.E. Sarhan, *Head of Board of Directors*

Computer Installation
ICL 1905E–internal storage: 64K 24-bit words; magnetic tapes: 6 7-track; magnetic discs: 5; 2 line printers.

Coding Languages
PLAN, FORTRAN, ALGOL, COBOL.

Services Available
Advice, education and training.

Training
Post-graduate courses leading to a Diploma or Master's degree in Computer Science.

SERVICE BUREAU

IBM WORLD TRADE CORPORATION*
3 Kasr Elnil Street, Cairo

Officers
I. A. Soliman, *General Manager*
A. Loutfi, *Service Bureau Manager*

Computer Installation
IBM 1401 – operating system: Tape.

Coding Languages
Autocoder, FORTRAN.

Contemplated Equipment
IBM 360/30.

Services Available
Preparation of data, programming. Operate on an open shop, block time and self-service basis.

Fields of Application
Scientific, statistical, commercial, production control, accounting.
Specialized areas: Sales analysis, linear programming, payroll, structural engineering.

Training
Courses in 1401 Autocoder, 360 orientation and 360 Assembler, RPG and PL/1.

EL SALVADOR

SERVICE BUREAU

IBM WORLD TRADE CORPORATION*
San Salvador

Computer Installation
IBM 360/30.

Services Available
Advice, preparation of data, programming.

Fields of Application
Statistical, commercial.

ETHIOPIA

UNIVERSITY

HAILE SELLASSIE I UNIVERSITY
P.O. Box 1176, Addis Ababa
Telephone: 01-110-844

Officers
Dr. Aklilu Habte, *President*
Dr. Mulugeta Wodajo, *Academic Vice-President*
Dr. Fassil G. Kiros, *Business Vice-President*

Computer Installation
IBM 360/20 – operating system: TOS; internal storage: 128K bits; magnetic tapes: 4 2415; 2 line printers.

IBM 1130 – operating system: DOS; internal storage: 64K bits; magnetic discs: 2; 2 line printers.

Coding Languages
RPG, FORTRAN.

Services Available
Advice, programming, operators, preparation of data, systems analysis. Operate on a closed shop basis. Available to University students and staff only.

Fields of Application
Scientific, accounting, management.
Specialized areas: Payroll, research.

FINLAND

NATIONAL CENTRE

TILASTOLLINEN PÄÄTOIMISTO
(Central Statistical Office)
Annankatu 44, 00100 Helsinki 10
Telephone: 645121

Computer Installation
IBM 360/25 – operating system: DOS; internal storage: 48K bits; magnetic tapes: 4 2415; magnetic discs: 2 2311; 1 line printer.

Coding Languages
PL/1, Assembler, RPG, FORTRAN.

Contemplated Equipment
IBM 370/125.

Services Available
Programming, systems analysis. Operate on a closed shop basis.

Field of Application
Statistical.

UNIVERSITIES AND COLLEGES

ÅBO AKADEMI
Domkyrkotorget 3, 20500 Åbo (Turku) 50

Officers
Dr. Karl-Gustav Fogel, *Vice-Chancellor*
Carl-Erik Sundman, *Administrative Manager*

Computer Installation
IBM 1130 – operating system: DMS – V2; internal storage: 16K 16-bit words; magnetic discs: 1 2310, 1 1131; 1 line printer. *Remote processing feature:* terminal to UNIVAC 1108 used by all Finnish universities.

HONEYWELL H316 – internal storage: 16K bits; magnetic discs: 2.

Coding Languages
FORTRAN, ALGOL, SIMULA, LISP, Assembler, MIMIC.

Contemplated Equipment
IBM 1130 to be replaced.

Services Available
Advice, education and training, systems analysis, computer time. Operate on an open shop basis. Available to students only.

Fields of Application
Scientific, statistical, commercial, systems analysis, operational research. *Specialized areas:* Linear programming analysis, structural engineering.

Training
University courses and diploma.

ÅBO AKADEMI
School of Economics
Institute of Microeconomics and Management Science
Henriksgatan 7, 20500 Åbo (Turku) 50
Telephone: 921-335133

Officer
Prof. Caj-Gunnar Lindström, *Head of the Institute*

Computer Installation
UNIVAC DCT 2000 connected to a UNIVAC 1108 central computer used by all Finnish universities.

Coding Languages
FORTRAN, COBOL, ALGOL, BASIC.

Services Available
Advice, systems analysis. Operate on a self-service and time-sharing basis. Available for education and research purposes only.

Fields of Application
Scientific, systems analysis.
Specialized areas: Linear programming, investment, analysis.

HELSINGIN YLIOPISTO
Computing Centre
Töölönkatu 11, 00100 Helsinki 10
Telephone: 440703

Officer
Lars Backström, *Director of Computing Centre*

Computer Installation
BURROUGHS B6700 – operating system: MCP; internal storage: 3,145K bits; magnetic tapes: 4 9-track, 1 7-track; magnetic discs: 2.

Coding Languages
ALGOL, FORTRAN, COBOL, HYLPS, BASIC.

Contemplated Equipment
Dual disc drive.

Services Available
Advice, programming, education and training, operators, software packages, preparation of data. Operate on a remote access, closed shop and time-sharing basis. Available mainly for university research work.

Fields of Application
Scientific, statistical, operational research.
Specialized areas: Linear programming, medical research, statistical analysis, university administration.

Training
Short programming courses in HYLPS, FORTRAN and BASIC; short courses in statistical data processing, linear programming, multivariate methods in research.

HELSINGIN YLIOPISTO*
Department of Nuclear Physics
Computation Bureau
Siltavuorenpenger 20, Helsinki 17
Telephone: 61477

Officers
Professor K.V. Laurikainen, *Director of the Computation Bureau*
Tuomas Hirvonen, *Systems Supervisor*

Computer Installation
PDP-15/30 — operating system: background/foreground Monitor; internal storage: 16K x 18 bits; magnetic tapes: 2 TU56 Dual DEC tape; 1 line printer.
EA1 TR-48 analogue.

Coding Languages
Macro Assembler, FORTRAN IV.

Services Available
Advice, programming. Operate on self-service, open shop and block time basis.

Fields of Application
Scientific, statistical.
Specialized areas: Research connected with nuclear physics, analysis of bubble chamber pictures, statistical analysis.

Training
A course in programming at least once a year.

JYVÄSKYLÄN YLIOPISTO*
Seminaarinkatu 15, 40100 Jyväskylä 10
Telephone: 941-10920

Officer
H. Laitinen, *Director*

Computer Installation
IBM 1130/2C — operating system: DMS; internal storage: 256K bits; magnetic discs: 1 2314; 1 line printer.

Coding Languages
Assembler, BASIC, FORTRAN IV.

Services Available
Consultation, programming, education and training, operators, software packages, documentation, preparation of data. Operate on a closed shop basis. Available to students and personnel of the University.

Fields of Application
Scientific, statistical.

KAUPPAKORKEAKOULU
(Helsinki School of Economics)
Runeberginkatu 14-16, 00100 Helsinki 10
Telephone: 440211

Officer
Veikko Jääskeläinen, *Professor of Quantitative Methods*

Computer Installation
IBM 1131/3C — internal storage: 16,384 16-bit words; magnetic discs: 2 2315; 1 line printer. *Remote processing feature:* linked to Univac 1108.

Coding Languages
FORTRAN IV, BASIC, COBOL, APL, Assembler.

Services Available
Programming, operators, preparation of data. Operate on a time-sharing basis. Only overtime is available to outside customers.

Fields of Application
Statistical, production control, accounting, management, systems analysis, operational research.
Specialized area: Education.

Training
Courses in programming and computer science.

LAPPEENRANNAN TEKNILLINEN KORKEAKOULU
Tullitie 6, 53100 Lappeenranta 10

Services Available
Available only to the University's students and teachers.

Fields of Application
Scientific, statistical, operational research.

OULUN YLIOPISTO
Institute of Electronic Data Processing
Kauppurienkatu 33, 90100 Oulu 10
Telephone: 981-14863

Officer
Pentti Korhonen, *Machines Manager*

Computer Installation
HONEYWELL H1642 — internal storage: 16K bits; magnetic tapes: 1 4150; magnetic discs: 2 173; 1 line printer. *Remote processing features:* terminal to Univac 1108. PDP—8/E — internal storage: 16K 12-bit words.

Coding Languages
FORTRAN, DAP, EDIT, SOLUE, BASIC, TEACH.

Contemplated Equipment
Magnetic disc, Honeywell H1644 (extension).

Services Available
Advice, programming, operators, software packages, documentation, preparation of data. Operate on a time-sharing basis.

Fields of Application
Scientific, statistical, systems analysis.

Training
University courses.

Finland – Universities and Colleges

TAMPEREEN TEKNILLINEN KORKEAKOULU
Laskentakeskus
Satamakatu 17B, 33200 Tampere 20
Telephone: 931-32941

Officer
Prof. Topi Urponen, *Director of Computing Centre*

Computer Installation
HONEYWELL DDP 516 – operating system: BOS III; internal storage: 256K bits; magnetic discs: 1 CDC 9433; 1 line printer.
The University also has access to the Univac 1108 of the Ministry of Education, and to the Honeywell H1642 of Tampere University.

Coding Languages
FORTRAN IV, DAP-Assembler, FORTRAN V, ALGOL, BASIC, SIMULA I, GPSS.

Contemplated Equipment
Telephone link from DDP 516 to Univac 1108.

Services Available
Advice, education and training. Operate on a self-service and block time basis. Available only to the University's students, personnel and research workers.

Field of Application
Scientific.
Specialized area: Structural engineering.

Training
Data processing courses and practical training courses.

TAMPEREEN YLIOPISTO*
Tietokonekeskus (Computer Centre)
Kalevantie 4, Tampere
Telephone: 21040

Officers
Pertti Järvinen, *Director*
Reino Kurki-Suonio, *Professor*

Computer Installation
UNIVAC 1108.

Coding Languages
Autocode, ALGOL, SURVO 66 (statistical programming language).

Contemplated Equipment
Paper-tape station and on-line teleprinter.

Services Available
Advice, operators, programming, software packages. Operate on a self-service and open shop basis. Available only for research institutes.

Fields of Application
Statistical, scientific.

Training
Software package course (1 month).

TEKNILLINEN KORKEAKOULU*
(Helsinki University of Technology)
02150 Otaniemi, Helsinki
Telephone: 460144

Officer
J. Virkkanen

Computer Installation
HEWLETT PACKARD 2116B – operating systems: HP 2000A, DOS; internal storage: 16K x 16-bits; magnetic tapes: 1 7970A; magnetic discs: 1 2774A; 1 line printer.
Remote processing features: 16-terminal local TS network.

ELLIOTT 803B – internal storage: 8K x 39 bits.

Coding Languages
BASIC, ALGOL, FORTRAN.

Services Available
Consultation, programming, education and training, operators, software packages, documentation, preparation of data. Operate on a remote access and time-sharing basis. Available to students, research workers and teachers.

Fields of Application
Scientific, statistical, operational research.

GOVERNMENT ESTABLISHMENTS

FINNISH STATE COMPUTER CENTRE
Vattuniemenkatu 8A, 00210 Helsinki 21
Telephone: 90/670151

Officers
Otto Karttunen, *Director-in-Chief*
Arvo E. Pöntinen, *Administration Manager*
Juhani Ryhänen, *Production Manager*

Computer Installation
IBM 370/145 – operating system: OS/MFT; internal storage: 4,194,304 bits; magnetic tapes: 10 3420/5; magnetic discs: 4 3330, 2 2319; 3 line printers. *Remote processing features:* 2 DATA 100.

IBM 360/50 – operating system: OS/MFT; internal storage: 2,097,152 bits; magnetic tapes: 8 3420; magnetic discs: 8 2314; 3 line printers.

IBM 360/22 (4) – operating system: DOS; internal storage: 262,144 bits each; magnetic tapes: 4 2415 each; magnetic discs: 2 2311 each; 1 line printer each.

UNIVAC 1108 – operating system: EXEC 8; internal storage: 7,056K bits; magnetic tapes: 8 Uniservo VIIIC; magnetic discs: 4 8414, 2 Fastrand III, 3 FH 432, 1 FH 1782; 2 line printers. *On-line satellite computer:* Univac 9300. *Remote processing features:* 25 DCT 2000, 2 Univac 9200 34 tty lines, 150 tty, 8 Uniscope 100.
Note: The Univac 1108 is administered by the Ministry of Education and runs under Computer Centre management.

Coding Languages
Assembler, FAS, FORTRAN IV.

Contemplated Equipment
IBM 370/145; PDP-11/40.

Services Available
Consultation, programming, education and training, operators, software packages, preparation of data, systems analysis. Operate on a remote access, closed shop, block time and time-sharing basis. Priority given to data processing activities required by Government administration.

Fields of Application
Scientific, statistical, commercial, accounting, management, systems analysis, operational research.

ILMATIETEEN IAITOS
(Finnish Meteorological Institute)
P.O. Box 503, 00101 Helsinki 10
Telephone: 11-922

Officers
Prof. Lauri A. Vuorela, *Director*
Dr. Daniel Söderman, *Data Processing Manager*

Computer Installation
DATASAAB D22 – operating system: DIR, GPR; internal storage: 32K 24-bit words; magnetic tapes: 5 Hewlett-Packard 2131-1; 1 line printer.

Coding Languages
MAC, ALGOL-Genius.

Contemplated Equipment
Tektronix display unit.

Services Available
Advice, operators, preparation of data. Operate on a closed shop basis. Available to the Institute's members and to the Institute of Marine Research.

Fields of Application
Scientific, meteorology.
Specialized areas: Weather-forecasting, meteorological statistics.

NATIONAL BOARD OF SURVEY
Organization Division
Hämeentie 31A, Helsinki 50
Telephone: 711855

Officer
Kalevi Rossi

Computer Installation
UNIVAC 9200 – operating system: REM, MOS; internal storage: 8,192 8-bit bytes; 1 line printer. *Remote processing features:* Linked to a Univac 1108.

Coding Languages
FORTRAN, Assembler.

Contemplated Equipment
A mini-computer with storage of about 64K 8-bit bytes.

Services Available
Advice, programming, operators, software packages, preparation of data. Operate on a closed shop basis. Priority given to Government requirements.

Field of Application
Statistical.
Specialized area: Survey.

OPETUSMINISTERIO
(Ministry of Education)
Computer Team
Rauhankatu 4, 00170 Helsinki 17
Telephone: 11636

Officer
Auvo Sarmanto, *Head of Computer Team*

Computer Installation
DCT 500 – linked to UNIVAC 1108.

Coding Languages
BASIC, Conversational FORTRAN, Assembler, FORTRAN V, COBOL, ALGOL.

Contemplated Equipment
Enlarging of Univac 1108 as well as some universities' computers.

Services Available
Advice, education and training, software packages, documentation. Operate on remote access, open shop and time-sharing basis. Services are available to universities in Finland, and the main computer is also available to the Ministry of Education, the Bank of Finland, the State Computer Centre and, for basic research projects, to State Research Institutes.

Fields of Application
Scientific, academic, administrative.
Specialized areas: Medical research, research in natural sciences and technology.

CONSULTANTS

EF MANAGEMENT CONSULTANTS OY
Lilla Robertsgaten 13B, Helsingfors
Telephone: 648 108

Officer
R. Itäinen, *Director*

Services Available
Consultation, systems analysis.

Fields of Application
Production control, accounting, management.
Specialized area: Management systems.

PRODUKTIONSTEKNIK AB*
Centralgatan 1, Helsinki 10

Services Available
Consultation, systems analysis.

Fields of Application
General management, e.g. long range planning, organization planning, information systems, objectives, policies. Finance/accounting, e.g. financial analysis and planning, budgetary programs, general accounting. Manufacturing. e.g. production scheduling, inventory control, facilities. Engineering, e.g. production engineering, value engineering. Marketing, e.g. marketing strategy, marketing planning, market surveys, sales management.
Specialized areas: MTM-based industrial engineering and maintenance control (UMS), project planning and Pert applications, systems analysis and systems planning with EDB, operations research, value analysis, training programs.

SERVICE BUREAUX

IBM FINLAND*
Helsinki

Also at:
Tampere and Turku

Computer Installation
Helsinki:
IBM 360/40.
IBM System/3 (3).
IBM 1401.

Tampere:
IBM 360/20.

Turku:
IBM 360/20.

Services Available
Advice, operators, preparation of data, programming, software packages, systems analysis.

Fields of Application
Scientific, statistical, commercial.

KALLE ANTTILA OY
EDP Department
Lönnrotinkatu 18, 00120 Helsinki 12
Telephone: 602211

Officers
Yrjö Akiola, *EDP Manager*
Jorma Lilja, *Systems Manager*

Computer Installation
IBM 370/135 – operating system: OS/VS1; internal storage: 192K bits; magnetic tapes: 4 3420/003; magnetic discs: 3 3330; 1 line printer.

RC 2000 – internal storage: 1K bits; magnetic tapes 1 709; 1 line printer.

RC 3000 – internal storage: 1K bits; magnetic tapes: 1 709; 1 line printer.

Services Available
Programming, operators, software packages, preparation of data. Operate on a closed shop basis.

Fields of Application
Production control, accounting, retail.
Specialized areas: Sales analysis, investment, payroll.

LASKENTAKESKUS OY*
Lotsgatan 4, Helsinki 16
Telephone: 135 77

Officer
Jaakko Salojoki, *Manager*

Computer Installation
IBM 360 – internal storage: 32K bits; magnetic tapes: 4; magnetic discs: 2 2311; 1 line printer.

Services Available
Advice, operators, preparation of data, programming.

Fields of Application
Commercial, accounting.

OY NOKIA AB*
Electronics Division
P.O. Box 10780, Tallbergink, 1 C, Helsinki 10
Telephone: 61991

Also at:
Hatanpäänvaltat, 34, Tampere

Officers
K. Wikstedt, *General Manager*
R. Suoniemi, *Manager, Computer Operations*

Computer Installation
BULL GENERAL ELECTRIC GE 615 – operating system: GECOS III; internal storage: 128K 36-bit words; magnetic tapes: 8 MTH 405, 1 MTH 301; magnetic disc: 1 DSU 167; 2 line printers.

BULL GENERAL ELECTRIC GE 425 – internal storage: 800K bits; magnetic tapes: 6 MTH 200; magnetic discs: shared with GE 415 below; 1 line printer.

SIEMENS 2002 – internal storage: 350K bits; magnetic tapes: 6 Ampex TM-4; magnetic drum; 1 line printer.

BULL GENERAL ELECTRIC GE 415 – operating system: DPS; internal storage; 400K bits; magnetic tapes: 6 MTH 200; magnetic discs: 3 DSU 160.

BULL GENERAL ELECTRIC GE 115 – operating system: TOS; internal storage: 130K bits; magnetic tapes: 4 MTH 107; 1 line printer.

Coding Languages
Symbolic Assembly Language, COBOL, FORTRAN, ALGOL.

Contemplated Equipment
Remote processing facilities from GE 115 to GE 615.

Services Available
Advice, operators, preparation of data, programming, software packages, systems analysis. Operate on a self-service and closed shop basis.

Fields of Application
Commercial, accounting, production control, scientific, statistical etc.; all aspects of data processing service.
Specialized areas: Payroll packages, invoicing packages, statistical applications, production scheduling.

Training
Courses in programming and system analysis (1-3 weeks); application oriented seminars (1-3 days).

OPERAATIOTUTKIMUSTOIMISTO SEPPÄLÄ KY
Jääkärinkatu 13 A 19, 00150 Helsinki 15
Telephone: Helsinki 665866

Officers
Yrjö Seppälä, *Manager*
Hilkka Seppälä, *Systems Analyst*

Coding Language
FORTRAN.

Services Available
Advice, programming, software packages. Operate on a time-sharing basis.

Field of Application
Operational research.
Specialized areas: Linear programming, investment, urban planning.

OY PARAGON AB
Mannerheimintie 40, Helsinki 10
Telephone: 44 04 51

Officer
C. Bounatirou

Computer Installation
BURROUGHS B3700 – operating system: MCP; internal storage: 720K bits; magnetic tapes: 4; magnetic discs: 1; 1 line printer. *On-line satellite computer:* TC 500.

BURROUGHS B6700 – operating system: MCP; magnetic tapes: 5; magnetic discs: 1; 1 line printer. *On-line satellite computer:* TC 500.

Coding Languages
COBOL, ALGOL, FORTRAN.

Service Available
Software packages. Operate on a self-service, closed shop, remote access, block time basis and time-sharing basis.

Fields of Application
Scientific, statistical, commercial, production control, accounting, management.

SUOMEN SEDAB OY*
Töölöntullinkatu 8, Helsinki 25

Officer
Rolf Backlund

Computer Installation
IBM 360/30—operating system: DOS; internal storage: 64K bits; magnetic tapes: 2 PCS 2415; magnetic discs: 4 PCS 2311; 1 line printer.

Coding Languages
Assembler, COBOL, FORTRAN.

Contemplated Equipment
IBM 2314 disc drives.

Services Available
Programming, preparation of data, data processing. Operate on a closed shop basis.

Fields of Application
Commercial, production control, accounting.
Specialized area: Cost accounting.

TIETOTEHDAS OY
02610 Kilo
Telephone: 90-52521

Officers
Juhani Salonoja, *Managing Director*
Seppo Hamilo, *Operations Manager*
Risto Kari, *Systems Manager*
Kalevi Kontinen, *Products Manager*

Computer Installation
IBM 370/155—operating system: OS/MFT; internal storage: 6,200K bits; magnetic tapes: 15 3420; magnetic discs: 18 2319; 3 line printers. *On-line satellite computer:* IBM 360/20. *Remote processing features:* display terminals, batch terminals.

IBM 360/40—operating system: OS/MFT; internal storage: 1,600K bits; magnetic tapes: 5 2401; magnetic discs: 5 2314; 1 line printer.

Coding Languages
COBOL, FORTRAN, Assembler.

Contemplated Equipment
Honeywell H6080.

Services Available
Advice, programming, education and training, software packages, preparation of data, systems analysis. Operate on a remote access and closed shop basis.

Fields of Application
Commercial, accounting, management, operational research.

Training
Basic courses in automatic data processing; basic courses and advanced courses for systems analysts.

FRANCE

EDUCATIONAL AND TRAINING INSTITUTIONS

ASSOCIATION POUR LE DÉVELOPPEMENT DE L'INFORMATIQUE DE GESTION (ADIGE)*
6 rue des Fabres, 13 Marseille 1er
Téléphone: 21.07.78

Dirigeants
M. Palidoni

Langages de Programmation
FORTRAN, COBOL, Autocoder.

Services Fournis
Enseignement et formation. Fournis aux administrations, entreprises et sociétés.

Formation
Certificat en COBOL, FORTRAN et Analyse.
Stages de courte durée: Initiation à l'Ordinateur (1, 2 ou 3 jours), Méthode PERT (2 ou 3 jours), Jeu d'Entreprise (2 jours).

ASSOCIATION POUR LE DÉVELOPPEMENT DE L'INFORMATIQUE DANS LA RÉGION RHÔNE-ALPES (ADIRA)*
2 rue Ml Dode, 38 Grenoble

Dirigeants
B. Delapalme, *Président du Conseil d'Administration*

Langages de Programmation
Assembleur, COBOL, FORTRAN, PL/1.

Service Fournis
Enseignement et formation, documentation. Fournis à toutes les entreprises publiques ou privées de la région Rhône-Alpes.

Formation
Stages d'une semaine: Introduction à l'utilisation des ordinateurs et à la programmation; Méthodes numériques élémentaires et langage FORTRAN; Le langage COBOL et ses applications élémentaires en gestion; Gestion automatisée; Méthodes élémentaires; Méthodes élémentaires en recherche opérationnelle; Exemples simples d'applications de la programmation en se servant du PL/1.

CENTRE ACADÉMIQUE DE TRAITEMENT DE L'INFORMATION*
1 rue Victor Cousin, 75005 Paris
Téléphone: 325 24-13, postes 721 et 720

Dirigeants
J. Lemasson, *Chef de Centre*

Equipement
IBM 360/40—systèmes d'opération: OS, MFT 2; mémoire interne: 256K octets; disques magnétiques: 1 2314; 2 imprimantes.

Langages de Programmation
COBOL, Assembleur.

Service Fourni
Programmation. Fonctionnement à porte fermée. Fourni à autres services académiques.

Domaines d'Application
Gestion, statistique.

CENTRE D'ÉTUDES PRATIQUES D'INFORMATIQUE ET D'AUTOMATIQUE (CEPIA)
Domaine de Voluceau, Rocquencourt, 78150 Le Chesnay
Telephone: 954.90.20, 954.56.00

Officers
André Danzin, *President*
René Malgoire, *Vice-President and Director*

Computer Installation
CII Iris 50 – operating system: SIRIS 2; internal storage: 1,150K bits; magnetic tapes: 4; magnetic discs: 4 DIMAS; 2 line printers.

CII 10070 – operating system: SIRIS 7; internal storage: 4,000K bits; magnetic tapes: 6; magnetic discs: 4 DIMAS, 3 RAD; 2 line printers.

CII 9080 – operating system: BPM; internal storage: 1,000K bits; magnetic tapes: 4; magnetic discs: 1; 1 line printer.

Coding Languages
FTN, COBOL, Assembler.

Services Available
Education and training, documentation, systems analysis.

Fields of Application
Scientific, statistical, commercial, production control, accounting, management, systems analysis, operational research.

Training
Courses on information processing.

CENTRE UNIVERSITAIRE DE FORMATION ET D'ÉDUCATION PERMANENTE (CUFEP)*
10 rue de l'Université, 86 Poitiers
Téléphone: (49) 41.02.06

Dirigeants
M. Taboury, *Directeur*
M. Siredey, *Responsable des cours*

Langages de Programmation
Assembleur IBM 1620, FORTRAN, GAP, (RPG de chez IBM).

Services Fournis
Enseignement et formation. Services fournis aux auditeurs de cours du soir.

Domaines d'Application
Commercial, gestion.

Formation
Informatique Générale, Informatique de Gestion (2 ans).

CHAMBRE DE COMMERCE ET D'INDUSTRIE*
27 avenue de Friedland, 75008 Paris
Téléphone: ELY 66-93

Dirigeants
J. L. Groboillot

Equipement
IBM 360/40 – systèmes d'opération: OS, RAX.

Langages de Programmation
FORTRAN, BASIC.

Services Fournis
Conseils, enseignement et formation, software packages. Fonctionnement accès à distance. Fournis aux établissements d'enseignement et de formation.

Domaine d'Application
Formation.
Domaine spécialisé: Informatique de gestion.

Formation
Tous cours dans le domaine de l'informatique de gestion (Diplômes HEC et ISA).

COMPAGNIE IBM FRANCE
Centre National d'Éducation
75 Edouard Vaillant, 92100 Boulogne/Billancourt
Telephone: 604-42-10

Officers
Jacques de Combret, *Director*
Christian Enlart, *Marketing Manager*

Computer Installation
IBM 360/50 – operating systems: OS, US, DOS; magnetic tapes; magnetic discs: 2311, 2314, 3330; 5 line printers.
Remote processing features: IBM 370/145 – features: as above. IBM 360/40 – features: as above. IBM System/3 – features: as above.

Services Available
Education and training, software packages, documentation. Operate on a remote access, closed shop, block time, open shop and time-sharing basis. Available only to IBM customers.

Fields of Application
Commercial, production control, accounting, management, systems analysis.

Training
Information sessions for managers; introductory courses in equipment and methods; practical courses at various levels for managers and personnel in information processing and use of equipment.

ÉCOLE PROFESSIONELLE SUPÉRIEURE DE L'INFORMATIQUE*
26 Cité Trévise, 75009 Paris
Téléphone: TAI.66.50 et 51

Dirigeants
J. Brettes, *Directeur*

Services Fournis
Enseignement et formation.

Domaine d'Application
Gestion.

Formation
Programmeur IBM 360/30 Assembleur, DOS, Job Control, Programmeur IBM 360/20 GAP, Analystes, Opérateurs, Perforeuses.

France – Educational and Training Institutions

INSTITUT D'INFORMATIQUE ET DE GESTION*
5 rue Quentin Bauchart, 75008 Paris
Téléphone: 256-22-45

Dirigeants
P. de Cassini, *Directeur*
J. P. Brichant, *Secrétaire général*

Langages de Programmation
COBOL, Assembleur.

Services Fournis
Enseignement et formation. Fonctionnement par time-sharing.

Domaines d'Application
Scientifique, commercial, contrôle des processus, gestion bancaire et administrative.

Formation
Formation de base, Applications (6 mois à temps partiel-Diplôme de l'INSIG).
Stages d'un mois à temps partiel: Gestion Administrative, Bancaire, Comptable, Commerciale, de Production.

INSTITUT FRANÇAIS DE GESTION (IFG)
Institut National d'Informatique de Gestion (INIG);
Institut National de Gestion Prévisionelle et de Contrôle de Gestion (ICG)
22 avenue de la Grande Armée, 75017 Paris
Téléphone: 754.29.82, 380.79.41

Dirigeants
Roger Labourier, *Directeur Général*
Mme. Lalanne, *Secrétaire Générale*
Jacques Thierry, *Directeur des Etudes*

Langages de Programmation
COBOL, FORTRAN.

Services Fournis
Enseignement et formation, software packages.

Domaines d'Application
Statistique, commercial, contrôle de production, comptabilité, gestion, systems analysis.
Domaines spécialisés: Analyse des ventes, investissement, analyse.

Formation
Cours de traitement de l'information pour étudiants et exécutifs.

INSTITUT FRANÇAIS DES EXPERTS COMPTABLES*
Commission de l'Informatique
139 rue du Faubourg Saint-Honoré, 75008 Paris
Téléphone: BALZAC 69-65

Dirigeants
M. Braudo, *Président de la Commission*

Services Fournis
Organisation de conférences, création de commissions pour l'étude de tous les problèmes qui concernent les experts comptables, création de centres d'audition de cours d'informatique etc.

Domaines d'Application
Comptabilité, gestion, recherche opérationnelle.

Formation
La formation est confiée au Centre de Formation Professionnelle Supérieure de Comptabilité et de Gestion, 41 rue de Bellechasse, Paris.

INSTITUT INTERNATIONAL D'INFORMATIQUE (III)
B.P. 276, Centre de Tri, 38044 Grenoble
Téléphone: (76) 87.52.11

Aussi:
86 avenue Émile Zola, 75015 Paris
Téléphone: 577 16.58

5 rue Loxum, Bruxelles (Belgique)

Dirigeant
J.-C. Viallet, *Directeur Général*

Equipement
Grenoble:
IBM 360/65 et 360/40 couplés – système d'opération: ASP; mémoire interne: 256K + 256K octets; bandes magnétiques: 11 2401 et 2403; disques magnétiques: 15 2311 et 2314; 5 imprimantes. *Calculateurs satellites en ligne:* 2 IBM 360/20. *Transmission des données à distance:* 3 1050.

Paris:
IBM 360/20–mémoire interne: 16K octets; bandes magnétiques: 2 2415; 1 imprimante. *Transmission des données à distance:* relié au centre de Grenoble par ligne haute performance.

Chambéry:
IBM 360/20–mémoire interne: 16K octets. *Transmission des données à distance:* relié au centre de Grenoble par ligne haute performance.

Langages de Programmation
Assembleur, GAP, PL/1, COBOL, FORTRAN, ALGOL, NLG, PVS, NLT.

Equipement Projeté
IBM 360/50–mémoire interne: 512K bits.

Services Fournis
Conseils, programmation, enseignement et formation, software packages, documentation, préparation des données, systems analysis, travaux à façon, vente d'heures libre service. Fonctionnement à porte fermée, en abonnement machine, accès à distance et en self-service.

Domaines d'Application
Scientifique, gestion, comptabilité, systems analysis, recherche opérationnelle, ordonnancement, planification, traitement de fichiers, typologie, segmentation, fusion d'eaquêtes, évaluation et optimisation de plans médias, techniques graphiques, développement de software et exploitation, télétraitement.
Domaines spécialisés: gestion, ordonnancement, marketing, techniques, graphiques, téléutilisation, recherche langages spécialisés.

Formation
Formation secondaire informatique – Diplôme bacalauréat H (1 an).
Stages de courte durée: Initiation à l'informatique; formation aux languages de programmation et aux techniques d'analyse.

INSTITUT NATIONAL DES SCIENCES APPLIQUÉES (INSA)*
Centre d'Actualisation Scientifique et Technique (CAST)
20 avenue Albert Einstein, 69 Villeurbanne
Téléphone: (78) 84 56 49

Dirigeants
Prof. J. Robin, *Directeur Général de l'INSA*
Prof. R. Arnal, *Directeur du Département Informatique*
J. P. Paris, *Directeur de CAST*

Equipement
IBM 1130 (3)–mémoire interne: 8K mots de 16 bits;
disques magnétiques: 512K mots de 16 bits; 1 imprimante.

TÉLÉMÉCANIQUE T 2000–système d'opération: DOS;
mémoire interne: 32K mots de 19 bits; disques magnétiques: 256K; 1 imprimante. *Transmission des données à distance:* time-sharing basic et divers équipements spécialisés PDP 8/S.

Langages de Programmation
FORTRAN, ALGOL, Assembleur, APT, IFAPT.

Equipement Projeté
Iris 50.

Services Fournis
Enseignement et formation. Fonctionnement en self-service.

Domaines d'Application
Scientifique, contrôle des processus, commande numérique de machines-outils.

Formation
Formation en cinq ans d'ingénieurs option informatique spécialistes systèmes et temps réel, contrôle de processus. *Stages de courte durée (cours de perfectionnement destinés aux ingénieurs en exercice):* Programmation FORTRAN, utilisation des ordinateurs dans le domaine des travaux pratiques, utilisation des ordinateurs pour le contrôle de processus, commande numérique des machines-outils (programmation manuelle et automatique, langage IFAPT, contournage).

INSTITUT UNIVERSITAIRE DE TECHNOLOGIE(IUT)
Département Informatique
43 boulevard du 11 Novembre, 69621 Villeurbanne
Téléphone: (78) 68 03 27

Dirigeant
Richard Bouché, *Directeur du Département*

Equipement
ICL 1901A–système d'opération: GEORGE 1S; mémoire interne: 16K mots de 24 bits; bandes magnétiques: 2; disques magnétiques: 1; 1 imprimante.

CII Iris 10–système d'opération: IUT Lyon; mémoire interne: 32K octets; bandes magnétiques: 1 Ampex; disques magnétiques: 1 SAGEM. *Transmission des données à distance:* 8 terminaux Teletypes.

Langages de Programmation
FORTRAN, COBOL, Assembler.

Services Fournis
Enseignement et formation. Fonctionnement en self-service, à porte fermée et en time-sharing. Fournis principalement à l'IUT et l'Université de Lyon.

Domaines d'Application
Scientifique, commercial, gestion, enseignement.

Formation
Cours en Informatique: Diplôme Universitaire de Technologie et Diplôme d'Etude Approfondie.

UNIVERSITIES AND COLLEGES

CENTRE INTERUNIVERSITAIRE DE CALCUL DE GRENOBLE
B.P. 53, 38041 Grenoble
Telephone: (76) 87.45.61

Officers
Prof. N. Gastinel, *Director*
M. du Masle, *Engineer*
M. Bellot, *Engineer*

Computer Installation
IBM 360/67–operating systems: CP/CMS, ASP/MVT; internal storage: 1 million x 8 bits; magnetic tapes: 4; magnetic discs: 3 2314; 2 line printers. *On-line satellite computers:* PDP-8, IBM 360/20, IBM 1130. *Remote processing features:* 60 consoles.

CII 10070–operating system: SIRIS 7; internal storage: 256K x 8 bits; magnetic tapes: 3; magnetic discs: 4. *Remote processing features:* 12 consoles.

Coding Languages
All languages.

Services Available
Programming, education and training, software packages, systems analysis, research. Operate on a self-service, remote access and time-sharing basis.

Fields of Application
Scientific, statistical, systems analysis, operational research.

Training
Diploma courses in connexion with Université Scientifique et Médicale de Grenoble: Maîtrise d'Informatique, Maîtrise d'Informatique appliquée à la Gestion, and with the university's Institut de Programmation: Programmeur d'Etudes, Programmeur Expert en Systèmes Informatiques; and in connexion with Institut National Polytechnique – Ecole d'Ingénieurs Mathématiciens et Informaticiens.

CENTRE INTERUNIVERSITAIRE DE TRAITEMENT DE L'INFORMATION 2
91 boulevard de l'Hôpital, 75634 Paris
Telephone: 587-18-52

Officer
J. C. Hirel, *Director*

Computer Installation
PDP-10–operating system: TOPS; internal storage: 1,300K bits; magnetic tapes: 3; magnetic discs: 3; 1 line printer. *On-line satellite computers:* 2 CII 10010, 2 TMF 600. *Remote processing features:* 54 teletypewriters.

Coding Languages
FORTRAN, ALGOL, COBOL, BASIC, SNOBOL.

Contemplated Equipment
Increased storage of 600K bits; magnetic discs; magnetic tapes.

Services Available
Advice, programming, education and training, operators, software packages. Operates on a self-service, remote access and time-sharing basis.

Fields of Application
Scientific, statistical, hospital management.
Specialized area: Medical research.

CENTRE NATIONAL DE LA RECHERCHE SCIENTIFIQUE (CNRS)*
Centre de Calcul
Faculté des Sciences, Université d'Aix-Marseille
70 route Léon Lachamp, 13009 Marseille
Téléphone: 41.16.49 et 41.16.50

Dirigeants
H. Morel, *Directeur*
J. P. Decamps, *Ingénieur, chef du département Etudes*
A. Gosset, *Ingénieur, chef du département Exploitation*

Equipement
IBM 360/44—systèmes d'opération: PS44, OS; mémoire interne: 64K bits; bandes magnétiques: 3 2401/5, 2 2401/4; disques magnétiques: 2 2311, 2 2315; 1 imprimante.

Equipement Projeté
Extension mémoire 128K bits; 2 2314 disques.

Services Fournis
Conseils, programmation, enseignement et formation, opérateurs, software packages, documentation, préparation des données, systems analysis. Fonctionnement à porte ouverte et en self-service. Fournis à CNRS, Enseignement Supérieur.

Domaines d'Application
Scientifique, gestion, recherche opérationnelle.

Formation
Stages de courte durée pour les opérateurs, programmeurs et analystes.

COLLÈGE DE FRANCE*
Laboratoire de Physique Atomique et Moléculaire
11 place Marcelin-Berthelot, 75005 Paris
Téléphone: 033-81-60

Equipement
CII 90/80—système d'opération: Train; mémoire interne: 32K bits; bandes magnétiques: 7 Ampex; 1 imprimante.
CII 90/10—mémoire interne: 16K bits; bandes magnétiques: 3 Ampex.

Langages de Programmation
FORTRAN.

Service Fourni
Programmation. Fonctionnement à porte fermée et par time-sharing. Fourni aux chercheurs scientifiques.

Domaine d'Application
Scientifique.

ÉCOLE CENTRALE DES ARTS ET MANUFACTURES*
1 rue Montgolfier, 75003 Paris
Téléphone: TUR 53-46

Dirigeants
P. Bastien, *Membre de l'Académie des Sciences, Directeur de la Recherche Scientifique*
P. Azou, *Chef du Département de Physique*
H. Veysseyre, *Chef de la Section de Mathématiques Appliquées.*

Equipement
SETI-PALLAS—mémoire interne: 32K caractères de 7 bits; bandes magnétiques: 1; 1 imprimante.

Langages de Programmation
FORTRAN IV, ALGOL 60, MAGE II, LOUP.

Equipement Projeté
Quatre bandes magnétiques rapides (34,000 caractères/seconde).

Services Fournis
Conseils, opérateurs, préparation des données, programmation, software packages, analyse de systèmes. Fonctionnement en self-service et en porte ouverte. Les services sont fournis après passation d'un contrat agréé par la Direction scientifique en fonction de l'intérêt du sujet étudié.

Domaine d'Application
Calcul scientifique.

Formation
Cours en langages de programmation.

ÉCOLE NATIONALE D'INGÉNIEURS
Centre de Perfectionnement en Sciences Appliquées
Ile du Saulcy, Metz 57
Téléphone: (87) 68-06.35

Dirigeant
M. Maurice, *Directeur de l'Ecole*

Equipement
IBM 1130—système d'opération: Monitor 2; mémoire interne: 8K mots; disques magnétiques: 2 2315; 1 imprimante. *Transmission des données à distance:* 1130 connecté à un IBM 360/40 de Nancy par lignes 4 fils—2400 Bauds.

Langages de Programmation
Assembleur, FORTRAN, GAP, en connexion: COBOL, PL/1, FORTRAN, Assembleur.

Equipement Projeté
1130 avec table traçante, bandes perforées.

Services Fournis
Enseignement et formation. Fonctionnement à porte fermée.

Domaines d'Application
Gestion, scientifique.

Formation
Cours d'Initiation, de Base de logique 360, de Pupitreurs, et cours Langages (COBOL, FORTRAN, PL/1, Assembleur).

ÉCOLE NATIONALE SUPÉRIEURE DE LA MÉTALLURGIE ET DE L'INDUSTRIE DES MINES
54042 Nancy
Telephone: (28) 53.72.32

Officers
C. Chambon, *Director of School*
G. Chandler, *Head of Informatics Laboratory*

Computer Installation
TELEMECANIQUE T1600—operating system: BOS; internal storage: 262,144 bits; magnetic discs: 1 fixed head. *On-line satellite computers:* 3 teletype-like terminals. CDC 200—1 line printer.

Coding Languages
FORTRAN, PL/1600, PASCAL, Assembly.

Contemplated Equipment
Additional terminals, line printer, card reader for T1600.

Services Available
Advice, education and training, preparation of data. Operate on a remote access and time-sharing basis.

Fields of Application
Scientific, statistical, commercial, accounting.

Training
Courses in programming languages; informal training given to those with a knowledge of a programming language who wish to use time-sharing or batch service.

ÉCOLE SUPÉRIEURE D'ÉLECTRICITÉ
10 avenue Pierre Larousse, 92240 Malakoff
Téléphone: 655-92-22

Dirigeants
Prof. J. Hebenstreit, *Chef de la section Informatique et du Centre de Calcul*

Equipement
CII 10070–système d'opération: SIRIS 7; mémoire interne: 1,500K bits; bandes magnétiques: 2; disques magnétiques: 4; 1 imprimante. *Calculateurs satellites en ligne:* 1 HEWLETT PACKARD 2100, 1 CII IRIS 50.
IBM 1130–mémoire interne: 128K bits; disques magnétiques: 1 monodisc: 1 imprimante. *Calculateurs satellites en ligne:* 1 HEWLETT PACKARD 2116.
PHILIPS P880–mémoire interne: 128K bits; disque magnétiques: 1 monodisc.

Langages de Programmation
Assembly, FORTRAN, COBOL, BASIC, LSE.

Services Fournis
Conseils, programmation, enseignement et formation. Fonctionnement à porte fermée et par accès à distance; time-sharing terminals sur les lieux.

Domaine d'Application
Scientifique.

Formation
Diplôme de spécialité: Informatique.
Stages d'Initiation aux ordinateurs (15 jours) et stages FORTRAN (8 jours).

FACULTÉ DES SCIENCES DE ST. JÉRÔME*
Centre de Calcul
Marseille 13ème
Téléphone: 50-31-61

Dirigeants
R. Phan-Tan-Luu, *Responsable*
R. Romanetti
L. Bouscasse

Equipement
IBM 1130–système d'opération: batch processing; mémoire interne: 16K mots; disques magnétiques: 2310.

Langages de Programmation
FORTRAN IV, ALGOL, Assembleur.

Equipement Projeté
Terminal sur un ordinateur puissant ou acquisition d'un ordinateur de moyenne puissance.

Services Fournis
Conseils, programmation, enseignement et formation, software packages, documentation. Fonctionnement à porte ouverte et par time-sharing. Fournis à tous laboratoires universitaires et administrations.

Domaines d'Application
Scientifique, statistique, comptabilité, gestion, recherche opérationnelle, simulation de calcul analogique.

Formation
Cours d'Initiation à l'informatique: utilisation d'un langage scientifique–le FORTRAN IV, de moniteur, et de simulation.

INSTITUT UNIVERSITAIRE DE TECHNOLOGIE
Département Informatique
143 avenue de Versailles, 75016 Paris
Telephone: 224.61.50

Officer
R. Sabatier, *Director of Department*

Computer Installation
ICL 1901A–operating system: GEORGE; internal storage: 384K bits; magnetic tapes: 4; 1 tandem magnetic disc; 1 line printer.

Coding Languages
PLAN, FORTRAN, COBOL.

Training
Two-year course leading to Diplôme Universitaire de Technologie.

INSTITUT UNIVERSITAIRE DE TECHNOLOGIE-INFORMATIQUE
Boulevard Charlemagne, 64000 Nancy
Telephone: 27.09.41

Officer
G. Tissier, *Head of Department*

Computer Installation
ICL 1901A–operating system: GEORGE 1S; internal storage: 16K x 24 bits; magnetic discs: 2 TEDS; 1 line printer.

Coding Languages
FORTRAN, COBOL, ALGOL, Assembler PLAN.

Services Available
Programming, education and training. Operate on a closed shop basis. Priority given to students at the Institute.

Field of Application
Education.

Training
Diploma courses for Diplôme Universitaire de Technologie-Informatique.

UNIVERSITÉ DE BESANÇON*
Faculté des Sciences
Laboratoire d'Informatique de l'Académie
La Bouloie, Besancon (Doubs)
Téléphone: (81) 83-73-36

Dirigeant
M. Iellou

Equipement
CAB 500–mémoire interne: 200K bits.

Langages de Programmation
Lang. machine, PAF, ALGOL.

Equipement Projeté
Remplacement imminent par une ordinateur à bandes et disques.

Services Fournis
Conseils, programmation. Fonctionnement en self-service et en porte ouverte.

Domaines d'Application
Domaines spécialisés: Calcul matriciel: comparaison des méthodes.

UNIVERSITÉ DE BORDEAUX I*
Faculté des Sciences
Laboratoire de Calcul Numérique
351 cours de la Libération, 33400 Talence
Téléphone: 992 92 81, poste 573

Dirigeants
M. Blondel, *Professeur*
M. Haugazeau, *Professeur*

Equipement
IBM 360/44–mémoire interne: 128K bits; bandes magnétiques: 1 2415; disques magnétiques: 3 2311; 1 imprimante.

Equipement Projeté
IBM 360/65.

Services Fournis
Programmation, enseignement et formation. Fonctionnement à porte fermée. Fournis aux laboratoires de recherche de l'Université de Bordeaux et au service de scolarité.

Domaines d'Application
Scientifique, statistique, gestion.

Formation
Cours en analyse numérique et informatique.

UNIVERSITÉ DE CAEN*
Centre de Calcul Statistique et Econométrie
Laboratoire de Mathématiques Appliquées
Faculté des Sciences
Esplanade de la Paix, 14000 Caen (Calvados)
Téléphone: 81-62-53

Dirigeant
Professeur D. Pham

Langages de Programmation
FORTRAN I, PASO II, ALGOL, FORTRAN IV, Autocode.

Equipement Projeté
PALLAS F32: 1 imprimante, 4 dérouleurs bandes magnétiques.

Services Fournis
Conseils, programmation, software packages, analyse de systèmes. Fonctionnement en self-service et en porte fermée.

Domaines d'Application
Analyse des programmes scientifiques (enseignement et recherche).
Domaines spécialisés: Programmes linéaires.

Formation
Cours en langages de programmation.

UNIVERSITÉ DE GRENOBLE*
Service de Mathématiques Appliquées et Laboratoire de Calcul
38 Grenoble Gare
Téléphone: (76) 87.45.61, 87.75.71, 87.93.71.

Dirigeants
Professeur J. Kuntzmann, *Directeur du Service de Mathématiques Appliquées*
Professeur B. Vauquois, *Directeur du Centre d'Etudes de la Traduction Automatique (CNRS)*
Professeur N. Gastinel, *Directeur du Laboratoire, Directeur de l'Institut de Programmation.*

Equipement
IBM 360/40–système d'opération: OS/PCP/ASP; mémoire interne: 128K bits; bandes magnétiques: 4 2400; disques magnétiques: 5 2311; 1 imprimante.

IBM 360/67–mémoire interne: 512K bits; disques magnétiques: 8 2314; 1 imprimante. *Calculateurs satellites en ligne:* IBM 360/40, PDP-8. *Transmission des données à distance:* 1130, 2250, 2 2260, 62 2741.
IBM 1401.

Langages de Programmation
FAP, FORTRAN, ALGOL, COBOL.

Services Fournis
Conseils, opérateurs, préparation des données, programmation, software packages, analyse de systèmes. Fonctionnement en self-service, en porte ouverte et par accès à distance. Exécute des travaux de recherche sur contrats pour des organismes publics ou privés.

Domaines d'Application
Exécution de calculs. Recherche dans le domaine des méthodes de calcul, de la programmation, de la logique appliquée, de la construction des machines, de la recherche opérationnelle. Enseignement: analyse numérique, langages de programmation, recherche opérationnelle, algèbre appliquée.
Domaines spécialisés: Problèmes différentiels et aux dérivées partielles, construction de compilateurs, traduction automatique.

Formation
Diplôme d'études supérieures techniques de programmation; Institut universitaire de technologie (Programmation): forme des programmeurs de gestion en deux ans; Maîtrise d'informatique, Institut de programmation (forme en 9 mois des programmeurs scientifiques).

UNIVERSITÉ DE NANCY I ET DE NANCY II
Case officielle 140, 54000 Nancy
Téléphone: (28) 27.38.99 (Nancy I),
(28) 27.30.85 (Nancy II)

Equipement
CII 10070–système d'opération: BPM-BTM-SIRIS 7; mémoire interne: 128K bytes de 8 bits; bandes magnétiques: 8 9-pistes; disques magnétiques: 2 RAD; 1 imprimante. *Calculateurs satellites en ligne:* 2 CII 10010 et consoles.

ICL 1901A–système d'opération: GEORGE 1S et 1A; mémoire interne: 16K mots de 24 bits; disques magnétiques: 2; 1 imprimante.

Langages de Programmation
FORTRAN, COBOL, ALGOL 60, METASYMBOL.

Services Fournis
Enseignement et formation. Fonctionnement par accès à distance et partage de temps.

Domaines d'Application
Scientifique, statistique, commercial, gestion, analyse de systèmes, recherche.
Domaines spécialisés: Analyse, recherche médicale.

Formation
Maîtrise d'Informatique; DEA d'Informatique; Diplôme Universitaire de Technologie.

UNIVERSITÉ DE NICE
Institut Universitaire de Technologie
Département Informatique
95 chemin de Fabron, 06200 Nice
Telephone: 86.71.85

Officers
J. Moussiegt, *Director of the Institute*
M. Cornillon, *Head of Informatics Department*

Computer Installation
IBM 360/25 – operating system: DOS; internal storage: 192K bits; magnetic discs: 2 2311; 1 line printer.

Coding Languages
Assembler 360, COBOL, FORTRAN, PL/1, RPG.

Contemplated Equipment
TÉLÉMÉCANIQUE T1600.

Service Available
Operate on a closed shop basis. Available only within the national education system.

Fields of Application
Commercial, educational.

Training
Two-year courses for undergraduates.

UNIVERSITÉ D'ORLÉANS
Unité d'Education et de Recherche (UER) de Sciences Fondamentales et Appliquées
Campus Universitaire, 45045 Orléans

Officer
Prof. C. Fric, *Director*

Computer Installation
PDP-8/E – internal storage: 8K 12-bit words; 1 line printer.

Coding Languages
FOCAL 8, BASIC, Assembler.

Contemplated Equipment
Increased storage of 24K words, 2 magnetic tapes, 1 magnetic disc, BENSON.

Services Available
Education and training. Operate on a self-service, closed shop and time-sharing basis.

Field of Application
Scientific.

Training
Courses in numerical analysis for first-year students; algorithm; language.

UNIVERSITÉ DE PARIS IX (PARIS-DAUPHINE)
Centre de Calcul
Place du Maréchal de Lattre de Tassigny, 75016 Paris
Telephone: 553.50.20

Officer
Prof. Charles Berthet, *Head of the Computing Centre*

Computer Installation
IBM 1130 – internal storage: 128K bits; 1 magnetic disc; 1 line printer. *Remote processing feature:* connected to a UNIVAC 1110.

PDP-8E – internal storage: 192K bits; magnetic tapes: 2; 9 line printers.

Coding Languages
FORTRAN, BASIC, PL/1.

Services Available
Advice, education and training. Operate on a self-service, open shop and time-sharing basis. Available to students of the university.

Fields of Application
Scientific, statistical, commercial, management, operational research, administrative.

Training
Courses in initiation to Computers and Computing for all students at the university, specialized courses in Management, Economy, and Administration.

UNIVERSITÉ DE PARIS VI
Institut de Programmation de Paris
4 place Jussieu, 75005 Paris
Telephone: 336.2525

Officers
Prof. de Possel, *Honorary Director*
Prof. J. Azsac, *Director*
Prof. Vignes, *Assistant Director*

Computer Installation
CDC 2600 – operating system: Drumscope; internal storage: 3,072K bits; magnetic tapes: 3; magnetic drum; 1 line printer.

ELLIOTT 4130 – operating system: home-made; internal storage: 768K bits; fixed head disc; 1 line printer. *On-line satellite computers:* ELBIT 100 x 8TTY. *Remote processing features:* 8 TTY with multiplexor.

Coding Languages
ALGOL, FORTRAN, COBOL, PL/1, APL, ATF (home definition language), SIMULA, SUMSCRIPT, GPSS, etc.

Services Available
Education and training, systems analysis, hardware prototype. Operate on a closed shop and time-sharing basis. Available only in connexion with public research and education.

Fields of Application
Scientific, systems analysis, operational research, machine architecture.
Specialized areas: Structural engineering, education.

Training
Diploma courses in programming and informatics; Doctorate courses (engineering).

UNIVERSITÉ DE POITIERS
Centre d'Informatique et de Calcul
40 avenue du Recteur Pineau, 86022 Poitiers
Téléphone: (49) 46-25-62

Dirigeant
T. Alziary de Roquefort, *Directeur*

Equipement
IBM 1620—système d'opération: Moniteur; mémoire interne: 40K mots de 6 bits (DCB); disques magnétiques: 1311 pour dispack 1316.

IBM 1130—système d'opération: Moniteur II; mémoire interne: 8192 mots de 16 bits (binaire); disques magnétiques: dispack 2315; 1 imprimante.

Langages de Programmation
FORTRAN II-D et IV, COBOL, RPG, ASM.

Equipement Projeté
CII IRIS 45.

Services Fournis
Programmation, enseignement et formation. Fonctionnement à porte fermée. Fournis principalement aux laboratoires de recherche de l'Université et au service de scolarité.

Domaine d'Application
Scientifique.

Formation
Cours en analyse numérique; programmation; informatique pour Maîtrise Science et Techniques; recyclage FORTRAN; informatique pour la quatrième année de Sciences Economiques.

UNIVERSITÉ DE RENNES I*
Faculté des Sciences
Centre de Calcul
B.P. 25A, 35042 Rennes
Téléphone: 36-48-15

Dirigeant
J. Cea, *Directeur du Centre de Calcul*

Equipement
CII 10070—système d'opération: BPM; mémoire interne: 64K bits; bandes magnétiques: 4 9-pistes; disques magnétiques: 1 RAD, 2 DIAM; 1 imprimante.

IBM 1620—système d'opération: BCM; mémoire interne: 40K caractères; disques magnétiques: 1 DAM.

Langages de Programmation
SYMBOL, METASYMBOL, FORTRAN IV, COBOL 65.

Services Fournis
Conseils, programmation, enseignement et formation, opérateurs. Fonctionnement à porte fermée. Fournis aux universités, organismes d'Etat, et éventuellement au privé.

Domaines d'Application
Scientifique, statistique, comptabilité, gestion, recherche opérationnelle.

Formation
Maîtrise d'Informatique.

UNIVERSITÉ DE STRASBOURG II*
Faculté des Sciences
Centre de Calcul
7 rue René Descartes, 57000 Strasbourg
Téléphone: 35.34-02

Dirigeant
A. Mignot, *Directeur*

Equipement
IBM 360/44—mémoire interne: 64K octets; disques magnétiques: 1 2311; 1 imprimante.

Langages de Programmation
FORTRAN II, Assembleur 360.

Equipement Projeté
Extensions terminaux—enseignement.
Machine type IBM 360/67 ou BULL GENERAL ELECTRIC GE 635 avec terminaux lourds ou légers.

Services Fournis
Programmation, enseignement et formation, software packages. Fonctionnement à porte fermée. Fournis à l'ensemble des laboratoires de recherche et aux enseignants de l'Université de Strasbourg.

Domaines d'Application
Scientifique, statistique, gestion, systèmes, etc.
Domaines spécialisés: Informatique numérique et mathématique appliquée, informatique non numérique: théorie des systèmes et langages, recherches en software.

Formation
Initiation à l'Informatique pour les étudiants de 1er cycle—Mathématique, Physique; Algorithmique et programmation en maîtrise d'Enseignement de Mathématique; *Maîtrise d'Informatique:* formation théorique et pratique à l'Informatique numérique et non numérique. Stages de programmation FORTRAN ou Assembleur et algorithmique (15 jours), et d'initiation à l'Analyse Numérique (15 jours).

UNIVERSITÉ DE TOULOUSE III*
Faculté des Sciences
Institut de Calcul Numérique
118 route de Narbonne, 31400 Toulouse
Telephone: 52-12-12.

Dirigeant
Professeur E. Durand, *Directeur*

Equipement
IBM 7044—système d'opération: IBSYS; mémoire interne: 32K x 36 bits: bandes magnétiques: 10 729-V; disques magnétiques: 1 1301; 1 imprimante.

Langages de Programmation
MAP, FORTRAN, ALGOL, COBOL.

Equipement Projeté
CII 10070.

Services Fournis
Conseils, opérateurs, programmation, software packages. Fonctionnement à porte ouverte.

Domaines d'Application
Tout ce qui concerne l'Informatique.

Formation
Cours de programmation—Maîtrise d'Informatique, certificats d'Analyse Numérique.

UNIVERSITÉ DE TOURS
Unité d'Education et de Recherche (UER)
Aménagement-Géographie-Informatique
Laboratoire d'Informatique
Parc de Grandmont, 37 Tours
Telephone: (47) 28-02.35

Dirigeant
R. Benoit, *Maître de Conférences*

Equipement
Il n'y a pas d'installations propres à l'UER. L'Unité emploi un IBM 370/155 au Centre Calcul de CEA (Limeil) et un IBM 370/165 au Centre de Calcul du CNRS (Orsay).

Langages de Programmation
FORTRAN, COBOL.

Services Fournis
Programmation, enseignement et formation.

Domaines d'Application
Scientifique, statistique, recherche opérationnelle.
Domaines spécialisés: Statistiques appliquées (sciences humaines, biologie, etc), sémiologie graphique.

Formation
Certificat Universitaire d'Informatique; Maîtrise des Sciences et Techniques de l'Aménagement.

GOVERNMENT ESTABLISHMENTS

CENTRE D'ÉTUDES TECHNIQUES DE L'ÉQUIPEMENT
Zone Industrielle des Milles, 13 Aix-en-Provence

Officers
D. Robequain, *Chief of ADP Division*
J. Lillo, *Head of Management Department*
M. Gambach, *Head of Information Systems Department*
M. Gouvant, *Head of Training and Methodology Department*

Computer Installation
IBM 370/155–operating system: OS/MFT; internal storage: 768K bits; magnetic tapes: 8 3420; magnetic discs: 8 3330; 2 line printers. *On-line satellite computers:* IBM 4130, IBM System/3. *Remote processing features:* IBM 2780, IBM 2740, MDS 7500.

Coding Languages
COBOL, FORTRAN, PL/1, Assembler.

Contemplated Equipment
Increased storage of 1,024K bits; 1 line printer.

Services Available
Advice, programming, education and training, operators, software packages, documentation, preparation of data, systems analysis. Operate on a self-service, remote access, closed shop and time-sharing basis. Available to local governmental agencies.

Fields of Application
Scientific, statistical, accounting, management, systems analysis.
Specialized areas: Linear programming, payroll, payroll data bank.

Training
Courses for agents of the Ministry of Planning, Equipment, Housing and Tourism.

CONSERVATOIRE NATIONAL DES ARTS ET MÉTIERS*
292 rue St.-Martin, 75003 Paris
Téléphone: TURbigo 64-40

Dirigeants
Paul Guérin, *Directeur*
A. Hocquenghem, *Professeur responsable du fonctionnement du Centre de Calcul*
P. Namian, *Professeur*
M. Solin, *Chef de travaux*

Equipement
IBM 360/30–mémoire interne: 64K caractères; bandes magnétiques: 4 (9 pistes); disques magnétiques: 2; 1 imprimante.

CAB 500–mémoire interne: 16K bits.

Equipement Projeté
IBM 360/40.

Services Fournis
Conseils, opérateurs, préparation des données, programation. Fonctionnement en self-service, en porte ouverte, en abonnement machine et par time-sharing.

Domaines d'Application
Analyse numérique, informatique d'entreprise.
Domaines spécialisés: Calculs d'optique.

Formation
Formation de programmeurs-analystes et diplômés de l'enseignement supérieur technique; informatique et mathématiques appliquées (cours du soir).

INSTITUT GÉOGRAPHIQUE NATIONAL*
Direction: 136 bis, rue de Grenelle, 75007 Paris
Centre de Traitement de l'Information:
2 avenue Pasteur, 94 St. Mandé (Seine)
Téléphone: DAU 66-80

Dirigeants
Ingénieur Général Laclavère, *Directeur*
M. Créhange, Ing. *(Photogrammétrie)*
M. H. Bizouard, Ing. *(Géodésie)*
M. Vidal, Ing. *(Gestion)*

Equipement
IBM 360/25–système d'operation: DOS; mémoire interne: 48K bits; bandes magnétiques: 2; disques magnétiques: 3 2311; 1 imprimante. *Traitement des données à distance:* 360/50 en téléprocessing.

Langages de Programmation
PL/1, FORTRAN, GAP, Assembleur.

Services Fournis
Programmation, analyse de systèmes. Fonctionnement en porte fermée.

Domaines d'Application
Scientifiques, calculs géodésiques et aéro-triangulation analytique, application de gestion.
Domaines spécialisés: Recherches en cartographie automatique.

Formation
Travaux pratiques des élèves de l'école des sciences géographiques.

MAISON DES SCIENCES DE L'HOMME*
Centre de Calcul
13 Cité de Pusy, 75017 Paris
Téléphone: 924-93-24

Dirigeants
B. Jaulin, *Directeur (S-directeur d'études à l'école pratique des hautes études)*
S. Regnier, *S. Directeur*

Langages de Programmation
FORTRAN, ALGOL, PL/1.

Equipement Projeté
IBM 360/50.

Services Fournis
Conseils, programmation, analyse de systèmes.

Domaines d'Application
Problèmes de mathématiques appliquées, programme de calcul adapté aux diverses sciences humaines, programme de simulation.

UNITED NATIONS EDUCATIONAL, SCIENTIFIC AND CULTURAL ORGANIZATION (UNESCO)*
7 et 9 place de Fontenoy, 75700 Paris
Téléphone: 566 57-57

Dirigeants
M. Chase, *Directeur, Office de l'Informatique de gestion*
Mme. G. Balesko

Equipement
ICL 1902A—mémoire interne: 32K mots de 24 bits; bandes magnétiques: 4; disques magnétiques: 4; 1 imprimante.

Langages de Programmation
COBOL, FORTRAN, PLAN.

Services Fournis
Fournis à l'UNESCO et aux états membres de l'UNESCO.

Domaines d'Application
Scientifique, statistique, comptabilité, gestion, systems analysis.

CENTRE EXPÉRIMENTAL EUROCONTROL*
B.P. 15, Aérodrome de Brétigny-sur-Orge, 91 Brétigny

Dirigeants
D. D. Lipman, *Directeur*
M. G. Maignan, *Chef de la Division Informatique*

Equipement
TELEFUNKEN TR 4—système d'opération: BS; mémoire interne: 32K bits; bandes magnétiques: 3 MDS 251, 2 MDS 252; 1 imprimante. *Calculateurs satellites en ligne:* CII 10020 (voir ci-dessous). *Transmission des données à distance:* Ligne téléphonique Modem 1200 bauds; liaison avec un calculateur à la S.N.I.A.S., Toulouse.

CII 10020—système d'opération: RBM; mémoire interne: 64K bits; bandes magnétiques: 2; disques magnétiques: 1 RAD, 3 10^6 octets: 1 imprimante. *Calculateurs satellites en ligne:* Interconnecté avec le TR 4, un autre 10020 et un Myriad 2. *Transmission des données à distance:* 2.

CII 10020—système d'opération RBM; mémoire interne: 16K bits; disques magnétiques: 1 RAD, 3 10^6 octets. *Calculateurs satellites en ligne:* Interconnecté avec le TR 4, un autre 10020 et un Myriad 2.

MARCONI MYRIAD 2—système d'opération: MILOS; mémoire interne: 32K bits; disques magnétiques: 1 CDC. *Calculateurs satellites en ligne:* Interconnecté avec les deux 10020.

Langages de Programmation
SUSA, TEXAS, SYMBOL, User's Code, ALGOL, FORTRAN IV, EUROCORAL.

Equipement Projeté
1 Myriad 2 supplémentaire.

Services Fournis
Conseils, programmation, documentation, systems analysis. Fonctionnement à porte fermée et en self-service. Fournis à l'Agence Eurocontrol.

Domaines d'Application
Scientifique, systems analysis, recherche opérationnelle.
Domaine spécialisé: Simulation dynamique.

CENTRE EXPÉRIMENTAL DE RECHERCHES ET D'ETUDES DU BATIMENT ET DES TRAVAUX PUBLICS (CEBTP)*
12 rue Brancion, 75015 Paris
Téléphone: LEC 21-69 et VAU 95-49

Dirigeants
F. Le Bourre, *Directeur Général du CEBTP*
E. Absi, *Ingénieur en Chef attaché à la Direction du CEBTP*

Equipement
IBM 1130—système d'opération: DISC MONITOR; mémoire interne: 16K bits; 1 imprimante.

Langages de Programmation
FORTRAN, RPG, COBOL.

Services Fournis
Conseils, préparation des données, programmation, software d'application. Fonctionnement en self-service et en porte ouverte.

Domaines d'Application
Scientifique, statistique, recherche opérationelle.
Domaines spécialisés: Analyse de vente, programmation, journal de paie, génie de structure, mécanique des sols.

Formation
Cours en FORTRAN.

CENTRE NATIONAL DE LA RECHERCHE SCIENTIFIQUE (CNRS)
Groupe des Laboratoires de Bellevue
1 place Aristide Briand, 92 Bellevue-Meudon
Téléphone: 626-07-50

Dirigeants
Dr. Hubert Curien, *Directeur Général*
A. G. Isnard, *Administrateur des Laboratoires de Bellevue*
M. Chanoine, *responsable scientifique du Bureau de Calcul*

Equipement
SETI-PALLAS—mémoire interne: 32K caractères de 7 bits; bandes magnétiques: 1; 1 imprimante.

Langages de Programmation
MAGE (scientifique), LOUP (langage machine), FORTRAN.

Services Fournis
Conseils, programmation. Fonctionnement en self-service.

Domaines d'Application
Propre à chaque laboratoire.

CENTRE NATIONAL DE LA RECHERCHE SCIENTIFIQUE (CNRS)
Laboratoires de Marseille
Centre de Physique Théorique
31 chemin Joseph Aiguier, 13279 Marseille
Téléphone: 75-42-42

Dirigeant
Prof. A. Visconti, *Directeur*

Equipement
UNIVAC 1004 relié par liaison téléphonique spécialisée 2400bds à l'UNIVAC 1110 d'Orsay.

Langages de Programmation
FORTRAN, SNOBOL, LISP.

Services Fournis
Conseils. Fonctionnement en self-service; services fournis aux laboratoires du CNRS et des universités.

Domaine d'Application
Scientifique.

COMPAGNIE INTERNATIONALE POUR L'INFORMATIQUE (CII)
Centre Scientifique
IMAG, B.P. 53, 38041 Grenoble
Telephone: (76) 87-45-61

Officer
Louis Bolliet, *Director*

Computer Installation
CII 10070/Iris 80–operating systems: SIRIS 7, SIRIS 8; internal storage: 96K bits; magnetic tapes: 2 9-track; magnetic discs: 3 RAD, 3 DIAM; 1 line printer. *On-line satellite computer:* CII Iris 45. *Remote processing features:* 9 teletypes (outside).

Coding Languages
FORTRAN, SIMULA, COBOL, LP/70, BASIC.

Contemplated Equipment
CII Iris 80 (two-processor system with partitioning and reconfiguration), MITRA 15 (telecommunications processor for network applications).

Services Available
Advice, programming, education and training. Operate on a remote access and time-sharing basis.

Fields of Application
Data base and operating systems, programming methodology.
Specialized area: Computer systems architecture.

INSTITUT BLAISE PASCAL*
23 rue du Maroc, 75019 Paris
Téléphone: 205-9921

Dirigeants
R. de Possel
B. Damgé
M. Gross
Cl. Picard
M. P. Schützenberger
J. Paoli
P. Février

Equipement
IBM 360/50–système d'opération: OS/360; mémoire interne: 128K mots de 4 octets; bandes magnétiques: 4 2400; disque magnétique: 2314; 3 imprimantes.

CDC 3600–système d'opération: Tape Scope; mémoire interne: 9K mots; bandes magnétiques: 8 607; 1 imprimante.

IBM 1401 (2)–mémoire interne: 16K bits chacune; bandes magnétiques: 4 729 IV; 1 imprimante.

ELLIOTT 803–mémoire interne: 8K bits; bandes magnétiques: 2; 1 téletype.
CAB 500.

Langages de Programmation
ALGOL, FORTRAN, PAF, divers autres langages spéciaux et langages-machine.

Services Fournis
Conseils, opérateurs, préparation des données, software packages. Fonctionnement à porte ouverte, par accès à distance et par time-sharing. Fournis à l'education nationale et autres administrations de l'Etat.

Domaines d'Application
Travaux de nature variée dans le domaine du traitement de l'information numérique et non numérique.
Domaines spécialisés: Etudes originales en algèbre matricielle et théorie des nombres; grammaires formelles; langages de programmation; compilation d'ALGOL; documentation automatique; équations intégro-différentielles; équations aux dérivées partielles; théories de l'information, des graphes, des questionnaires.
Etude et réalisation d'un matériel pédagogique pour l'enseignement de l'électronique.
Réalisation d'un lecteur automatique lisant tous les caractères d'imprimerie usuels.

Formation
L'Institut de Programmation de la Faculté des Sciences de Paris assure la formation des opérateurs-programmeurs, des programmeurs d'études et des experts en traitement de l'information; il constitue aussi des équipes pour le traitement des problèmes d'intérêt général.

INSTITUT DE RECHERCHE D'INFORMATIQUE ET D'AUTOMATIQUE (IRIA)
Domaine de Voluceau, Rocquencourt, B.P.5, 78150 Le Chesnay

Officers
André Danzin, *Director*
Monpetit, *Deputy Director*
Laguionie, *Secretary General*

Computer Installation
CII Iris 50–operating system: SIRIS 2; internal storage: 1,150K bits; magnetic tapes: 4; magnetic discs: 4 DIMAS, 5 DIAM; 1 line printer.

CII 10070–operating system: SIRIS 7; internal storage: 1 million bits; magnetic tapes: 6; magnetic discs: 4 DIMAS, 3 RAD; 2 line printers.

CII 9080–operating system: BPM; internal storage: 1 million bits; magnetic tapes: 4; magnetic discs: 1; 1 line printer.

Coding Languages
FTN, COBOL, Assembler.

Services Available
Advice, documentation. Operate on a block time, open shop and time-sharing basis.

Field of Application
Scientific.
Specialized areas: Analysis, medical research, information retrieval.

OBSERVATOIRE DE MARSEILLE
2 place Le Verrier, Marseille 4ème
Téléphone: 50.05.29

Dirigeants
G. Monnet, *Directeur*
A. Pourcelot, *Chef de Service Calcul*

Equipement
IBM 1130–système d'opération: prégroupement; mémoire interne: 8K mots de 16 bits; disques magnétiques: 1 2315; 1 imprimante.

Langage de Programmation
FORTRAN IV.

Equipement Projeté
Télémécanique T 1600.

Services Fournis
Fonctionnement en self-service et par accès à distance.
Fournis seulement à l'université.

Domaine d'Application
Scientifique.

SOCIÉTÉ NATIONALE D'ÉTUDES DE CONSTRUCTION DE MOTEURS D'AVION (SNECMA)*
22 Quai Galliéni, Suresnes (Seine)
Téléphone: LONgchamp 28-70

Dirigeants
P. Margouty, Ingénieur Civil des Mines, *Chef du Service de Calcul Electronique*
C. Bismuth, Ingénieur E.N.S.A.M., *Chef du Service de Programmation Technique*

Equipement
IBM 360/44–système d'opération: OS/360/44; mémoire interne: 32K bits; bandes magnétiques: 2 2401 (7 pistes), 2 2401 (9 pistes); disques magnétiques: 2 2315 ramkit; 1 imprimante. *Transmission des données à distance*: Telex.

Langage de Programmation
FORTRAN IV.

Services Fournis
Conseils, opérateurs, préparation des données, programmation, software packages. Fonctionnement en self-service.

Domaines d'Application
Domaines spécialisés: Simulation de réacteurs d'avion sur calculatrice digitale.

CIE FSE THOMSON HOUSTON-HOTCHKISS BRANDT*
9 avenue Réaumur, 92 Le Plessis Robinson
Téléphone: 736-43-21, 642-59-09

Dirigeants
Edmond G. Doppler, *Directeur*
Charles Letellier
Bertrand Herz

Equipement
BULL GENERAL ELECTRIC GE 225–mémoire interne: 8K bits; bandes magnétiques: 6 7-canaux; 1 imprimante.

Langages de Programmation
GAP, GECOM, COBOL, FORTRAN, WIZ, en particulier un compilateur FORTRAN IV à un passage.

Equipement Projeté
Bull General Electric GE 265 avec time-sharing.

Services Fournis
Conseils, programmation, software packages. Fonctionnement en self-service, en porte ouverte et par time-sharing.

Domaines d'Application
Gestion, recherche opérationnelle, calcul scientifique.

CONSULTANTS

CABINET P. DE LOS RIOS*
13 Domaine de Maurin, 34 Montpellier–Lattes
Téléphone: 67-29-70-13

Dirigeant
P. de Los Rios, *Conseiller de Gestion*

Services Fournis
Conseils, préparation des données, analyse de systèmes.

Domaines d'Application
Comptabilité, gestion, analyse des processus.
Domaines spécialisés: Relations activité–coûts, PERT.

Formation
Cours en Système PERT.

GEORGES ET GILBERT CASTELLANET*
7 square Henri Delormel, 75014 Paris
Téléphone: 702-37-64, 825-54-62

Dirigeants
Georges Castellanet
Jean Henneguy

Services Fournis
Conseils, programmation.

Domaines d'Application
Statistique, commercial, gestion.
Domaines spécialisés: Programmes géneraux professionels dans le transport public routier.

Formation
Stages d'initiation de chefs d'entreprise: initiation économique, gestion industrielle, gestion commerciale, informatique.

CEGOS–INFORMATIQUE*
Institut pour le Développement Economique et Technique (IDET)
107 Bureaux de la Colline, 92 St. Cloud
Téléphone: 602 11 22

Bureaux européens: Bruxelles (Belgique)

Dirigeants
M. Gelinier, *Président Directeur Général de l'IDET*
M. Bauvin, *Directeur Général de CEGOS-Informatique (Division de l'IDET)*
M. Arnaud
M. du Chaxel
M. Paya

Equipement
IBM 360/30 (2)–système d'opération: DOS; mémoire interne: 64K octets; bandes magnétiques: 8 729 II; disques magnétiques: 2 2311; 2 imprimantes. *Transmission des données à distance*: MDS 1103.

IBM 360/65–système d'opération: OS; mémoire interne: 512K bits; bandes magnétiques: 11; disques magnétiques: 2314; 2 imprimantes.

Langages de Programmation
Assembleur, COBOL, FORTRAN.

Equipement Projeté
IBM 360/65.

Services Fournis
Conseils, opérateurs, préparation des données, programmation, software packages, analyse de systèmes. Fonctionnement en self-service et en abonnement machine.

Domaines d'Application
Tous les domaines.

Formation
25 stages de courte durée.

CENTRE DES TECHNIQUES D'ORGANISATION ET DE DIRECTION (CETOD)*
7 rue Godot de Mauroy, 75009 Paris
Téléphone: 073-39-50

Dirigeants
J. Petithory, *Directeur-Gérant*
G. Lebegue, *Ingénieur en Chef*
M. Curdel, *Ingénieur en Chef*

Services Fournis
Conseils, préparation des données, programmation. Fournis au clientèle industrielle, administrative et commerciale (secteur privé et public).

Domaines d'Application
Commercial, comptabilité, gestion, recherche opérationnelle.

Formation
Stages de courte durée: Initiation technologique et méthodologique à l'utilisation des ordinateurs (3 à 8 jours); analyse et simplification du travail administratif (12 à 20 jours).

CENTRE POUR LE TRAITEMENT DE L'INFORMATION (CENTI)
128 rue de Rennes, 75006 Paris
Téléphone: 222-25-31

Dirigeants
Charles Boch, *Président Directeur Général*
Joseph Barbou des Courières, *Directeur Général Adjoint*
Jean Capdeville, *Secrétaire Général*

Services Fournis
Conseils, programmation, enseignement et formation, opérateurs, packages, documentation, analyse de systèmes.

Domaines d'Application
Scientifique, statistique, commercial, contrôle de production, comptabilité, gestion, analyse de systèmes, recherche opérationnelle.

Formation
Cours pour tous les spécialistes; conférences générales sur le traitement de données; livres techniques.

COMI*
92 rue du Docteur-Vaillant, 78 Saint-Cyr-l'Ecole
Téléphone: 951-31-35

Dirigent
B. Alpern

Langages de Programmation
FORTRAN IV et V, BASIC, COBOL, ALGOL, PL/1, Assembleur.

Equipement Projeté
IBM 360/30.

Services Fournis
Conseils, programmation, software packages.

Domaines d'Application
Scientifique, gestion, recherche opérationnelle.
Domaine specialisé: Traitement graphique d'informations.

COMPAGNIE FRANÇAISE D'ORGANISATION (COFROR)*
10 rue Louis Vicat, 75015 Paris
Téléphone: VAU 41-69

Dirigeant
E. Aubert, *Gérant*

Services Fournis
Conseils, analyse de systèmes.

Domaines d'Application
Travaux d'étude et d'analyse de systèmes dans l'informatique, gestion, contrôle de production.

Formation
Stages de formation à différents niveaux, adaptés aux problèmes informatiques de l'entreprise.

COMPAGNIE GÉNÉRALE D'INFORMATIQUE (CGI)
84 rue de Grenelle, 75007 Paris
Téléphone: 707-67-43

Dirigeants
Robert A. Mallet, *Président*
Jacques Debuisson, *Directeur Général*

Equipement
IBM 360/50—système d'opération: OS MVT; mémoire interne: 512K bits; bandes magnétiques: 8; disques magnétiques: 4 2314; 2 imprimantes.

Langages de Programmation
COBOL, PL/1, Assembler.

Services Fournis
Conseils, programmation, enseignement et formation, software packages, analyse de systèmes.

Domaines d'Application
Commercial, contrôle de production, comptabilité, gestion, analyse de systèmes.
Domaines spécialisés: Analyse, journal de paie.

Formation
La CGI a inventé et encouragé la méthode CORIG pour le dessin et l'exécution des systèmes pour le traitement de données.

COMPAGNIE PARISIENNE D'INGÉNIEURS-CONSEILS (COPIC)*
40 avenue du Président-Wilson, 75016 Paris
Téléphone: 553-21-02, 553-94-39, 553-42-95

Dirigeants
G. Gourod
S. Briès

Service Fourni
Conseils.

Domaines d'Application
Gestion prévisionnelle, comptabilité, gestion des stocks, statistiques de toute sorte, prévisions de vente, recherche opérationnelle.
Domaines spécialisés: Spécification, classification, codification, normalisation d'entreprise; approvisionnement; fabrication en séries additives; marketing industriel.

France – Consultants

COMPAGNIE DES SYSTÈMES ET SERVICES D'INFORMATIONS (ISS)*
6/8 rue Firmın Gillot, 75015 Paris
Téléphone: VAU 50.40

Dirigeants
G. Hureau, *Président Directeur Général*
P. Chougnet, *Directeur Général Adjoint*
A. de Turckheim, *Secrétaire Général*
F. Loiseau, *Att. aux R. E.*

Langages de Programmation
PL/1, Assembleur, COBOL, FORTRAN.

Equipement Projeté
Matériel temps réel non défini.

Services Fournis
Conseils, programmation, software packages, systems analysis, conception et organisation de systèmes de formations. Fournis aux entreprises et institutions publiques et privées.

Domaines d'Application
Etudes de systèmes, software, informatique de gestion et de comptabilité (packages), recherche opérationnelle, formation/information.
Domaines spécialisés: Conception assistée par ordinateur, informatique médicale, simulation.

COMPUTER SCIENCES INTERNATIONAL FRANCE S.A. (CSIF)*
13 rue de la Baume, 75008 Paris

Officers
Dr. M. I. Montana, *President and General Manager*
M. L. Pulliam, *Operations Director*
B. Lorimy, *Manager of Programme Development*

Services Available
Advice, programming, education and training, operators, software packages, preparation of data, systems analysis.

Fields of Application
Management, systems analysis.
Specialized areas: Compiler writing, management information systems.

Training
Standard courses: Computer Concepts for Management; Management Utilization of the Computer; Systems and Programming Project Management; Systems Analysis and Design.

DIEBOLD FRANCE S.A.
63 rue la Boétie, 75008 Paris
Téléphone: 256-04-66

Dirigeants
Philippe Leboucq, *Président Directeur Général*
Hugues Desazars de Montgailhard, *Directeur Général Adjoint*
Jacques Lobet, *Directeur*

Services Fournis
Conseils, enseignement et formation, conception de systèmes, audit informatique, étude des marchés et produits d'information.

Domaine d'Application
Gestion d'entreprises.

Formation
Cours d'initiation à l'informatique pour cadres et dirigeants; séminaires de mise à jour et de perfectionnement.

GROUPE OPÉRA*
Département Informatique
37 avenue de l'Opéra, 75002 Paris
Téléphone: 073-51-33

Dirigeants
Michel Vielajus
Jean-Paul Menard

Langages de Programmation
COBOL, FORTRAN, Assembleur.

Services Fournis
Conseils, préparation des données, programmation, software packages, analyse de systèmes.

Domaine d'Application
Informatique de gestion.
Domaines spécialisés: Distribution et commercialisation bâtiment, construction métallique, génie civil et chimie quantique.

Formation
Cours d'Analyse fonctionnelle, cours d'Analyse organique.
Stages de courte durée: L'ordinateur et la moyenne entreprise (2 jours); l'ordinateur et les entreprises de distribution (5 jours); l'ordinateur dans les laboratoires pharmaceutiques (5 jours); les cadres devant l'ordinateur (5 jours); application de l'ordinateur dans le domaine bancaire (5 jours).

BERNARD HAUS
55 rue des Grands Champs, 75020 Paris
Telephone: 628-75-82

Officer
B. Haus, *President*

Services Available
Advice, programming, education and training, systems analysis. Operate on a self-service and remote access basis; time-sharing terminals on the premises. Available to time-sharing prospects, service bureaux and all institutions.

Fields of Application
Scientific, statistical, commercial, production control, accounting, management, systems analysis, operational research.
Specialized areas: Sales analysis, analysis, medical research.

LES INGÉNIEURS ASSOCIÉS
44 rue la Boétie, 75008 Paris
Téléphone: 359-59-92

Dirigeants
Georges Lapoirie, *Gérant*
René Minghetti, *Gérant*

Services Fournis
Conseils, préparation des données.

Domaines d'Application
Statistique commerciale, comptabilité, gestion, recherche opérationnelle.

France – Consultants

McKINSEY & CO. INC.*
40 avenue Georges V, 75008 Paris

Services Available
Advice, systems analysis.

Fields of Application
Commercial, management.

PAUL MARTHOURET S.A.*
4 rue Marcelin Blanc, 69 Sainte Foy Les Lyon
Téléphone: 51-23-15

Dirigeant
Paul Marthouret

Equipement
HONEYWELL H125–mémoire interne: 20,480 positions; bandes magnétiques: 5; 1 imprimante. *Transmission des données à distance*: Prévue sur réseau TELEX et sur liaisons spécialisées.

Langage de Programmation
COBOL.

Services Fournis
Conseils, préparation des données, programmation, analyse de systèmes. Fonctionnement en porte fermée et accès à distance. Fournis plus spécialement aux maisons de transport.

Domaines d'Application
Facturation, taxation automatique des ports, comptabilité, gestion, comptabilité analytique, statistique.
Domaines spécialisés: Tous traitements des données, transports.

Formation
Stages de courte durée: La technologie administrative du transport (2 jours); la perspective des télécommunications; la pratique des télécommunications.

ORDINA*
10 rue Auber, 75009 Paris

Dirigeants
P. Bocquel, *Directeur Général*
J. Lafargue, *Directeur Technique*

Services Fournis
Personnel pour conseils, programmation et opérateurs. Fournis aux entreprises possédant un service informatique.

Domaine d'Application
Gestion.

Formation
Réservée à notre personnel.

ORGANISATION YVES BOSSARD ET PIERRE MICHEL (OBM)*
85 avenue Emile Zola, 75015 Paris
Téléphone: VAU 89-89

Dirigeants
P. Michel, *Président*
Y. Bossard

Services Fournis
Conseils, préparation des données, programmation, software packages, analyse de systèmes.

Formation
Méthode correcte d'analyse et de programmation et nombreux cours sur ordinateurs.

ORGANISATION MAURICE BRESSY (OMB)*
3 avenue Jules Ferry, Cauzon, Rhône 69 (près Lyon)
Téléphone: 42-0098

Dirigeants
Maurice Bressy, *Conseil gestion*
Alain Bourbon, *Ingénieur en chef Informatique*

Equipement
IBM 360/20 (3).
BULL GENERAL ELECTRIC Gamma 10.

Services Fournis
Conseils, préparation des données, programmation, analyse de systèmes. Fonctionnement en self-service et par time-sharing.

Domaines d'Application
Gestion intégrée, comptabilité, controle des processus, recherche opérationnelle.
Domaines spécialisés: Gestion dans l'industrie textile et l'industrie alimentaire.

Formation
Les stages sont organisés uniquement pour et dans les entreprises clientes de notre Société de conseil.

P.A. MANAGEMENT CONSULTANTS S.A.*
16 avenue Hoche, 75008 Paris
Telephone: 010-33-1, 267-22-50

Services Available
Consultation, programming, software packages, systems analysis.

Fields of Application
Comprehensive consultancy service to international management–from general investigations on an overall company or industry basis to specific tasks confined to one limited function.
Specialized areas: Management sciences (OR, EDP and Programming), company strategy, market research, personnel services, export marketing, finance and acquisition, etc.

OFFICE OF GRAHAM PARKER*
17 avenue Matignon, 75008 Paris
Telephone: Elysées 67-15

Services Available
Consultation, systems analysis.

Fields of Application
Consulting services in commercial, production control, management and systems analysis.

PEAT, MARWICK, MITCHELL & CO.*
20 rue Louis-le-Grand, 75002 Paris
Telephone: 073-5494

Officer
J. C. Booth, Jr.

Services Available
Consultation, systems analysis, implementation studies.

Fields of Application
Economic studies, general and scientific management, operations research, project management, industrial engineering, marketing, production and inventory control, information systems, general and cost accounting systems, data processing and teleprocessing systems, etc.

PERROT–DESNOIX ET CIE S.A.*
217 rue Saint Honoré, 75001 Paris
Téléphone: 265-87-41

Dirigeant
Philippe Perrot-Desnoix, *Président Directeur Général, Ingénieur ECP*

Service Fourni
Conseils.

Domaines d'Application
Commercial, préparation à l'usage de l'ordinateur.
Domaine spécialisé: Marketing.

Formation
Stages de courte durée: Session de 2 jours sur l'application de l'informatique aux problèmes suivants: Étude de Marché, Analyse des Ventes, Gestion des Stocks des produits finis, tableau de Bord.

SOCIÉTÉ D'ENGINEERING APPLIQUÉ AU TRAITEMENT DE L'INFORMATION (SEAT)*
126 rue Réaumur, 75002 Paris
Téléphone: 231-10-95, 231-14-46

Dirigeants
J. Mayer, *Directeur Général*
S. P. de Picciotto, *Directeur Marketing et Développement*
G. d'Aubert, *Directeur Technique*
J. C. Debord, *Directeur Technique*

Services Fournis
Conseils, programmation, software packages, systems analysis.

Domaines d'Application
Tous les domaines.
Domaines spécialisés: Calculs scientifiques, commande numérique.

SOCIÉTÉ D'ÉTUDES DES SYSTÈMES D'AUTOMATION (SESA)
23 avenue de Neuilly, 75016 Paris
Telephone: 722-10-00

Officers
Christian Rheims, *President Director General*
Jacques Stern, *Director General*
Jacques Arnould, *Deputy Director General*

Services Available
Advice, programming, education and training, operators, software packages, systems analysis, systems engineering.

Fields of Application
Scientific, commercial, production control, accounting, management, systems analysis, operational research, computer-aided design.
Specialized areas: Analysis, structural engineering, medical research, reliability and maintenance.

Training
Courses in process control, industrial applications, computer-aided design, teleprocessing and terminals, methodology and techniques of software construction.

SOCIÉTÉ D'INGÉNIEURS CONSEILS EN ORGANISATION (SICOR)*
23 avenue du Général Leclerc, 75014 Paris
Téléphone: 535 16-79

Dirigeant
Gilbert Bloch, *Ingénieur des Mines, Conseil Direction*

Services Fournis
Conseils, études d'opportunité, analyse conceptuelle.

Domaines d'Application
Statistique commercial, contrôle de production, comptabilité, gestion.

SOCIÉTÉ GÉNÉRALE DE RECHERCHE ET PROGRAMMATION (SOGREP)*
10 rue Girardin, 13 Marseilles 7e
Téléphone: (91) 52. 63. 27

Langage de Programmation
COBOL.

Services Fournis
Conseil en organisation et informatique, formation.

Domaines d'Application
Comptabilité, gestion, modèle et simulation.

Formation
Stages de courte durée: 3 semaines de recherche opérationnelle et initiation à l'informatique.

SOCIÉTÉ INFOR*
92 Chemin de Saint-Priest, 69 Chassieu
Téléphone: 26. 63. 60, poste 270

Aussi:
Siège Social: 45 rue de la Bourse, Lyon II-69
Téléphone: 42. 59. 01

Dirigeants
J. C. Schalburg, *Président Directeur Général*
J. M. Frely, *Directeur Administratif et Commercial*
G. Gaillard, *Directeur Technique*
L. Squizzato, *Chef de Service Exploitation*

Equipement
SIEMENS 4004/45 – mémoire interne: 128K bits; bandes magnétiques: 4; disques magnétiques: 4; 2 imprimantes.
Transmission des données à distance: Lignes téléphoniques avec utilisation d'un contrôleur de communication.

Langages de Programmation
COBOL, FORTRAN, Assembleur, RPG.

Services Fournis
Conseils, programmation, enseignement et formation, opérateurs, software packages, documentation, préparation des données, systems analysis. Fonctionnement à porte fermée, en abonnement machine, par accès à distance et par time-sharing.

Domaines d'Application
Scientifique, statistique, commercial, contrôle des processus, comptabilité, gestion, systems analysis, recherche opérationnelle, documentation automatique.

France — Consultants

Formation
Cours de formation interne permanente.
Stages de courte durée: Simulation de gestion sur ordinateur, Initiation des Ingénieurs et Cadres à l'Informatique, Initiation aux systèmes informatiques, La documentation automatique, Comment passer à l'ordinateur, Les petits ordinateurs de bureau, Les problèmes de saisie et leurs solutions, L'ordinateur et l'agent de maîtrise, L'entreprise à l'heure de l'informatique, Organisation et gestion d'un service de l'informatique.

SORPRA*
84 ter, avenue de Brogny, 74 Annecy
Téléphone: 57.00.61 et 57.06.38

Aussi:
9 rue Roquépine, 75008 Paris
Téléphone: 265. 68. 15

171 Cours Lafayette, 69 Lyon 6e
Téléphone: 52.35.14

37 rue Gal Ferrié, 38 Grenoble
Téléphone: 87.40.18

Dirigeant
F. Odin, *Directeur Général*

Langages de Programmation
Tous les langages spécifiques de constructeurs ainsi que les langages universels: COBOL, PL/1, FORTRAN, ALGOL.

Services Fournis
Conseils, programmation, enseignement et formation, software packages.

Domaines d'Application
Conseil et assistance en informatique de gestion et en calcul scientifique et technique.
Domaine spécialisé: Recherche documentaire.

Formation
Cycles organisés sur demande des utilisateurs en langages de programmation et méthodes d'analyse.

SPENCER STUART AND ASSOCIÉS S.A.*
39 avenue Franklin D. Roosevelt, 75008 Paris
Telephone: 225-07-40, 225-30-43

SYNTHÈSE DES TECHNIQUES DE L'ORGANISATION (SYTORGA)*
7 square de l'Alboni, Parly 2, 78 Le Chesnay
Téléphone: 954.04.41 et 954.56.67

Services Fournis
Conseils, enseignement et formation, software packages, documentation, préparation des données, systems analysis.

Domaines d'Application
Tous domaines de gestion.

Formation
Stages pour directeurs, cadres responsables et analystes.

TECHNIQUES ET SYSTÈMES INFORMATIQUE (TECSI)
46 rue la Boétie, 75008 Paris

Officer
J. Bentz, *General Manager*

ANDRÉ VIDAL & ASSOCIÉS*
15 rue Henri Heine, 75016 Paris
Téléphone: 224-90.91–90.92–90.93

Dirigeants
André Vidal, *Président Directeur Général*
Philippe Avenati, *Relations extérieures*
François Morin, *Formation et Informatique*

Langages de Programmation
FORTRAN, COBOL.

Services Fournis
Conseils, préparation des données, programmation, software packages, analyse de systèmes.

Domaines d'Application
Gestion, comptabilité, statistique, commercial, recherche operationnelle.
Domaine spécialisé: Simulation de gestion.

Formation
Stages organisés à la demande: *Informatique*: Généralités sur les matériels, analyse, programmation FORTRAN, COBOL (1 à 2 semaines par langage avec exercices); *Gestion*: Tous sujets.

WESTINGHOUSE MANAGEMENT SYSTEMS S.A.
41 avenue George V, 75008 Paris
Telephone: 225.02.37

Officers
Michel Judet, *President*
Eric Lutaud, *Commerical Director*

SERVICE BUREAUX

CAISSE RÉGIONALE DE CRÉDIT AGRICOLE MUTUEL D'AVIGNON ET DE VAUCLUSE*
77 à 81 bis, rue Joseph-Vernet, Avignon
Téléphone: 81-69-30

Equipement
ICL 1903A—système d'operation: Exécutif; mémoire interne: 324 mots; bandes magnétiques: 1 1972; disques magnétiques: 1 2802; 1 imprimante. *Calculateurs satellites en ligne*: DS 4 C.G.C.T. *Transmission des données à distance*: Ligne téléphonique 1200 bauds.

Langages de Programmation
PLAN, COBOL.

Services Fournis
Enseignement et formation, software packages, documentation. Fonctionnement à porte fermée.

Domaines d'Application
Statistique, commercial, comptabilité, gestion.

Formation
Cours constructeur et séminaires d'information.

CATI—COFIGAT
Avenue du Marché Commun, 44000 Nantes

Officer
M. Putero, *General Manager*

Computer Installation
IBM 360/25—internal storage: 48K bytes; magnetic tapes: 2 2415; magnetic discs: 4 Memorex 630; 1 line printer.

Coding Languages
BAL, PL/1, COBOL.

CATI–MÉCANORGA–ERGEM
32 rue des Jeûneurs, 75002 Paris

Officer
V. Guermont, *General Manager*

Computer Installation
IBM 360/30–operating system: DOS; internal storage: 64K bytes; magnetic tapes: 4 Promodata 2450; magnetic discs: 5 Memorex 660; 1 line printer.

IBM 370/145–operating system: DOS; internal storage: 256K bytes; magnetic tapes: 7 Promodata 3450; magnetic discs: 11 Memorex 660; 1 line printer. *Remote processing features*: IBM 2701 (4 lines), IBM 2740, 1050.

Coding Languages
BAL, PL/1, COBOL.

CEDIS
8 rue des Docks, B.P. 1169, 25003 Besançon
Téléphone: (81) 80-08-43

Dirigeants
J. Mathey, *Directeur administratif*
J.-C. Bouret, *Chef de Service*
J.-C. Vallet, *Chef du Service Etudes*
H. Vacaire, *Chef du Service Exploitation*

Equipement
HONEYWELL–BULL 2060–système d'opération: OS 2000; mémoire interne: 131K bits; bandes magnétiques: 10; disques magnétiques: 2; 1 imprimante.

Langage de Programmation
COBOL.

Domaines d'Application
Statistique, commercial, gestion.

CENTRE D'ANALYSE ET DE PROGRAMMATION (CAP EUROPE)
21 rue Leriche, 75015 Paris
Téléphone: 533-57-20

Dirigeants
Philippe Dreyfus, *Président de CAP Europe*
Jacques Lescault, *Président de CAP France*

Langages de Programmation
COBOL, 360 Assembler, PL/1.

Services Fournis
Conseils, programmation, enseignement et formation, opérateurs, software packages, analyse de systèmes.

Domaines d'Application
Commercial, gestion, analyse de systèmes.

Formation
Cours de programmation.

CENTRE D'ÉTUDES ET DE TRAITEMENT SUR ORDINATEUR (CETOR)*
10 boulevard de Verdun, 92 Courbevoie

Dirigeant
J. M. Vigneron

Equipement
IBM 360/30–système d'opération: DOS; mémoire interne: 64K bits; bandes magnétiques: 4 2442; disques magnétiques; 3 2311; 1 imprimante.

Langages de Programmation
Assembleur, FORTRAN, COBOL.

Equipement Projeté
IBM 360/50.

Services Fournis
Conseils, programmation, préparation des données. Fonctionnement à porte fermée.

Domaines d'Application
Scientifique, statistique, gestion, recherche opérationnelle.

CENTRE DE TRAITEMENT DE L'INFORMATION (CTI)*
25 rue Henri Moreau, 92 Asnières
Telephone: 793 00 67

Officer
Marc Meslay, *Executive Manager*

Computer Installation
IBM 360/30–operating systems: DOS; internal storage: 256K bits; magnetic tapes: 4 2400/2; magnetic discs: 3 2311; 1 line printer

Coding Languages
COBOL, RPG, Assembler, PL/1, FORTRAN.

Contemplated Equipment
IBM 360/30 with storage of 64K bytes.

Services Available
Advice, programming, software packages, systems analysis. Operate on a closed shop and block time basis.

Fields of Application
Commercial, production control, accounting.

CENTRE DE TRAITEMENT DES INFORMATIONS*
Chemin de Beauregard, B.P. 444, 13 Aix-en-Provence
Téléphone: 27-83-18

Dirigeant
M. Jacques Roos, *Président Directeur Général*

Equipement
ICL 1902–mémoire interne: 16K bits; bandes magnétiques: 4; 1 imprimante.

Langages de Programmation
PLAN, FORTRAN, COBOL.

Equipement Projeté
4 dérouleurs à 20Kc, 2 files de disques (6000 mots supplémentaires).

Service Fournis
Software packages, principalement tout ce qui concerne le bâtiment et les travaux publics.

Domaines d'Application
Scientifique, statistique, recherche opérationelle, comptabilité, gestion.
Domaine spécialisé: Uniquement de la vente de services, l'ordinateur étant notre outil.

CENTRE ÉLECTRONIQUE DE GESTION (CEG)
2 rue René Fonck, 41000 Blois

Also at:
26 rue Vincent Chevard, 28007 Chartres

Officer
J. F. Mayet, *General Manager*

Computer Installation
IBM 360/22—operating system: DOS; internal storage: 32K bytes; magnetic tapes: 2 2415; magnetic discs: 2 2311; 1 line printer.

IBM 360/20—operating system: BPS; internal storage: 16K bytes; 1 line printer.

Coding Languages
BAL, COBOL, RPG.

CENTRE FRANÇAIS DE RECHERCHE OPÉRATIONNELLE (CFRO)
50 rue de Petites-Ecuries, 75010 Paris

Officer
G. Raffoul, *General Manager*

Computer Installation
IBM 360/40—operating system: OS MFT; internal storage: 256K bytes; magnetic tapes: 8 Promodata 3450; magnetic discs: 10 Memorex 660; 1 line printer. *Remote processing features*: IBM 2702 and IBM 2740.

Coding Languages
BAL, COBOL, FORTRAN.

Services Available
Analytical and consulting services, computing facilities, and the use of special and proprietary programmes available to clients.

Fields of Application
Business data processing (service bureau); teleprocessing; real time.

CENTRES INFORMATIQUE PHILIPS
4–6 avenue du Général Leclerc, 9220 Fontenay-aux-Roses
Telephone: 702.29.91, 702.63.20

Officers
Ph. Marescaux, *Director*
P. Braudel, *Assistant*

Computer Installation
PHILIPS P1100—internal storage: 512K bits; magnetic tapes: 7 P1061; magnetic discs: 5 P1041; 1 line printer.

PHILIPS P9200 TS—internal storage: 512K bits; magnetic netic discs: 2 P1041; 1 line printer. *On-line satellite computer*: P9201 (64K bits). *Remote processing features*: modem cabinet, multiplexor.

Coding Languages
Extended BASIC, ALGOL 60, FORTRAN IV, COBOL.

Contemplated Equipment
Data communication; remote processing, Philips P1175 (768K bits fast core, 4 million bits mass core).

Services Available
Advice, programming, operators, software packages, preparation of data, systems analysis. Operate on a remote access, closed shop and time-sharing basis.

Fields of Application
Scientific, statistical, commercial, production control, accounting, management, system analysis.
Specialized areas: Sales analysis, investment analysis, payroll, structural engineering, medical research.

COMPAGNIE AMIENOISE DE MÉCANOGRAPHIE*
70 rue des Jacobins, 80 Amiens
Téléphone: 91-76-66

Dirigeants
Maurice Donda, *Directeur Général*
José Barbry

Equipement
BULL GENERAL ELECTRIC GAMMA 10.

Services Fournis
Conseils. Fonctionnement en self-service et en abonnement machine.

Domaines d'Application
Statistique, commercial, comptabilité, gestion.

COMPAGNIE INTERNATIONALE POUR L'INFORMATIQUE (CII)*
Centre de Calcul
68 route de Versailles, 78 Louveciennes
Téléphone: 951-86-00

Dirigeants
MM. Dorleac, *Directeur Général*
Auricoste, *Directeur Général Adjoint*
Kallmann, *Directeur Commercial*
Quarez, *Directeur du Sce Assistance Clients*
Couriet-Bossan, *Directeur du Centre de Calcul*

Equipement
CAE 510—mémoire interne: 16K mots de 18 bits; bandes magnétiques: 2 URM COOK; 1 imprimante.

CAE 90/10—mémoire interne: 16K mots de 12 bits; bandes magnétiques: 2 URM; disques magnétiques: 6; 1 imprimante.

CAE 90/40—système d'opérations: Autonome et Moniteur d'enchaînement; mémoire interne: 24K mots de 24 bits; bandes magnétiques: 3 URM Ampex; disques magnétiques: Rad ou Dispac; 1 imprimante.

SEA 4000—mémoire interne: 16K caractères de 6 bits; bandes magnétiques: 8 URM PEN 5 B; 1 imprimante.

SEA 3900—mémoire interne: 16K caractères de 6 bits; bandes magnétiques: 9 URM PEN 3; 1 imprimante.

CII 10020—système d'opérations: Moniteur de base et Moniteur disque; mémoire interne: 8K mots de 16 bits (extension prévue 24K); bandes magnétiques: 2 URM; disques magnétiques: 1 RAD; 1 imprimante. *Transmission des données à distance*: Liaison Télégraphique, Liaison téléphonique 1200 à 4800 bauds, Visualisation.

CII 10070—mémoire interne: 32K mots de 32 bits (extension prévue 64K mots; bandes magnétiques: 4 URM 9 pistes, 2 URM 7 pistes; disques magnétiques: 1 RAD; 1 imprimante. *Calculateur satellite en ligne*:

CII 10020. *Transmission des données à distance*: Télégraphie, 64 lignes entrée/sortie, Téléphonique, 1200 à 4800 bauds, Visualisation.

Langages de Programmation
Assembler, ALGOL, FORTRAN II et IV, COBOL.

France – Service Bureaux

Services Fournis
Conseils, préparation des données, programmation, software packages, analyse de systèmes. Fonctionnement en porte fermée et porte ouverte.

Domaines d'Application
Tous les domaines.

COMPTABILITÉ STATISTIQUE INFORMATIC (CSI)
14 rue Forest, 75018 Paris

Officer
M. Pol de la Bourdonnaye, *General Manager*

Computer Installation
IBM 370/155–operating system: DOS, OS/MFT; internal storage: 512K bytes; magnetic tapes: 8 Promodata 3450; magnetic discs: 16 Memorex 660; 2 line printers.
BULL GENERAL ELECTRIC Gamma 30–internal storage: 20K characters; magnetic tapes: 8; 1 line printer.

Coding Languages
BAL, PL/1, COBOL.

CORANORD*
40 rue Haxo, 75020 Paris
Téléphone: 797-46-70

Aussi:
84 rue de Trévise, Lille (Nord)
Téléphone: 53-20-23

Dirigeants
Maurice Donda, *Directeur Général*
Jacques Donda (*Paris*)
Gérard Lemesre (*Lille*)

Equipement
Paris:
BULL GENERAL ELECTRIC Gamma 10.
BULL GENERAL ELECTRIC GE 120

Lille:
BULL GENERAL ELECTRIC Gamma 30–bandes magnétiques; 1 imprimante.
BULL GENERAL ELECTRIC GE 427–mémoire interne: 48K bits; bandes magnétiques; disques magnétiques; 1 imprimante.
BULL GENERAL ELECTRIC Gamma 10.

Langages de Programmation
Autocoder, COBOL.

Services Fournis
Conseils, opérateurs, programmation. Fonctionnement en self-service et abonnement machine.

Domaines d'Application
Statistique, commercial, contrôle des processus, comptabilité, gestion.

EUROPE INFORMATIQUE
10 rue Victor Masse, 75009 Paris
Telephone: 285.07.13

Officer
J. F. Jacq, *Director*

Services Available
Advice, programming, education and training, preparation of data, systems analysis.

Fields of Application
Scientific, statistical, commercial, production control, accounting, management, systems analysis.

FRANLAB INFORMATIQUE
4 avenue de Bois Préau, 92500 Rueil Malmaison
Telephone: 967.11.10, 967.17.66

Officers
Pierre Jacquard, *President and Director General*
Jean-Marie Lasvergeres, *Director General*
Michel Lanchon, *Deputy Director*

Computer Installation
CDC Cyber 76–operating system: SCOPE V2; internal storage: 3,840K bits plus 15,360K bits; magnetic tapes: 6 607, 1 659, 1 60036; magnetic discs: 4 844, 1 817; 4 line printers. *Remote processing features*: 8 UT200, 4 LSBT, 2 TTY.
CDC Cyber 72–operating system: SCOPE 3.4; other features: as above.

Coding Languages
FORTRAN RUN, FORTRAN FTN, COBOL, COMPASS.

Services Available
Advice, programming, education and training, operators, software packages, documentation, preparation of data, systems analysis. Operate on a self-service, remote access and block time basis.

Fields of Application
Scientific, statistical, commercial, production control, accounting, management, systems analysis, operational research.
Specialized areas: Linear programming, investment analysis, payroll, structural engineering, medical research.

GÉNÉRAL DE SERVICE INFORMATIQUE (GSI)
46 rue de la Boétie, 75008 Paris
Telephone: LAB 17.09

Officers
G. Besse, *Chairman*
J. Raiman, *President*

Services Available
Advice, programming, education and training, software packages, documentation, preparation of data, systems analysis, facilities management. Operate on a remote access basis.

Fields of Application
Scientific, statistical, commercial, production control, accounting, management, systems analysis, operational research.
Specialized areas: Sales analysis, linear programming, investment, analysis, payroll, structural engineering, medical research.

GÉNÉRAL DE SERVICE INFORMATIQUE
GSI–Distribution
1 rue Ampère, 91300 Massy

Officer
J. C. Letuve, *General Manager*

France — Service Bureaux

Computer Installation
IBM 370/145—operating system: DOS; internal storage: 256K bytes; magnetic tapes: 6 Telex 6420; magnetic discs: 11 Telex 5312; 2 line printers. *Remote processing features*: IBM 2848, 7 IBM 2260.

Coding Languages
BAL, PL/1.

GÉNÉRAL DE SERVICE INFORMATIQUE
GSI—Entreprises
69 rue Legendre, 75015 Paris

Officer
A. Cicurel, *General Manager*

Computer Installation
IBM 370/145—operating system: OS/MFT; internal storage: 384K bytes; magnetic tapes: 6 3420/5; magnetic discs: 11 Memorex 660; 2 line printers.

IBM 360/40—operating system: DOS; internal storage: 256K bytes; magnetic tapes: 6 Promodata 2450; magnetic discs: 8 Memorex 660; 1 line printer.

Coding Languages
BAL, PL/1, FORTRAN, NLG, PVS, NLT.

GESTELEC*
20 boulevard Saint Denis, 75010 Paris
Téléphone: 770-38-00, 770-38-01

Dirigeants
Gérard Guez, *Gérant*
Armand Benaim, *Directeur*
M. Fatry, *Secrétaire Général*

Equipement
UNIVAC 9300 et UNIVAC 1004—mémoire interne: 32K et 2K bits; bandes magnétiques: 6; disques magnétiques: 4 pistes; 2 imprimantes. *Transmission des données à distance*: 9300-1108.

Langages de Programmation
Assembler, RPG, COBOL, FORTRAN.

Equipement Projeté
IBM 360/40.

Services Fournis
Conseils, opérateurs, préparation des données, programmation, analyse de systèmes. Fonctionnement en abonnement machine et en travail sous contrat.

Domaines d'Application
Scientifique, statistique, commercial, comptabilité, gestion, recherche opérationnelle.
Domaines spécialisés: Gestion, comptabilité, mise en forme des données.

HEWLETT-PACKARD FRANCE
Quartier de Courtaboeuf, B.P. no. 6, 91401 Orsay
Telephone: 907-78-25

Officers
Didier Guerin, *Manager of Data Centre*
Rodolphe Weber, *Computer Sales Manager*

Computer Installation
HEWLETT PACKARD 2100 (4)—operating systems: DOS, DOS-M, RTE, Time-sharing; internal storage: 8K bits, 16K bits, 24K bits, 32K bits; magnetic tapes: 2 HP 7970; magnetic discs: 2 HP 7900; 2 line printers.

Coding Languages
Assembler, FORTRAN, BASIC, ALGOL, SNOBOL.

Contemplated Equipment
HEWLETT PACKARD 3000.

Services Available
Advice, programming, education and training, operators, software packages, documentation, preparation of data, systems analysis. Operate on an open shop and time-sharing basis.

Fields of Application
Scientific, commercial, production control, management, systems analysis.

Training
Two-week course in Basic Control System; one-week course in Disc Operating System; one-week course in Real Time Executive System.

IBM FRANCE*
116 avenue de Neuilly, 92 Neuilly-sur-Seine
Téléphone: MER 62-00

Dirigeants
G. Auer, *Directeur du Service Bureau*
J. C. Laloi, *Directeur Commercial du Service Bureau*

Equipement
IBM 360/75–360/65 connectés; systèmes d'opération: OS/360, ASP; mémoire interne: 1024K bits; bandes magnétiques: 20 2400; disques magnétiques: 3 2311, 3 2314 à 8 modules, 4 2301; 8 imprimantes. *Calculateurs satellites en ligne*: 2780, 1130. *Transmission des données à distance*: HS/RJE.

IBM 360/50 (2)—système d'opération: RAX; mémoire interne: 512K bits; bandes magnétiques: 2 2400; disques magnétiques: 12 2311; 1 imprimante.
Autres systèmes (360/40 et 360/50) en Province.

Services Fournis
Programmation, software packages, documentation, préparation des données. Fonctionnement à porte fermée et ouverte, en abonnement machine, en self-service, par access à distance et par time-sharing.

Domaines d'Application
Tous calculs à façon.

Formation
Formation interne du personnel, Langages (FORTRAN, COBOL, PL/1), Systèmes (DOS, OS), Télétraitement (RAX, RJE, CRBE), Méthodologie du Traitement de l'Information. Stages de courte durée réservés aux élèves de grandes écoles et d'écoles assurant une formation de programmeurs.

LEBON INFORMATIQUE
44 avenue de Chatou, 92 Rueil
Telephone: 977.02.33

Officers
Gerard Laurent, *Manager*
Henri Apter, *Development Division Manager*
Michel Guittard, *Sales Division Manager*

Services Available
Advice, programming, education and training, software packages, systems analysis, computer engineering.

Fields of Application
Production control, management, systems analysis, operational research, process control.
Specialized areas: Linear programming, structural engineering.

MÉCANORGA*
19 rue Godillot, St. Ouen
Téléphone: 606.1808

Dirigeants
M. Bouiges, *Président Directeur Général*
M. Larroque, *Directeur Commercial*

Equipement
IBM 360/25 – système d'opération: DOS; mémoire interne: 48K bits; bandes magnétiques: 4 2415; disques magnétiques: 4 2311; 1 imprimante.

Langages de Programmation
Assembleur, COBOL, FORTRAN, GAP.

Services Fournis
Conseils, programmation, préparation des données. Fonctionnement en abonnement machine et en self-service.

Domaines d'Application
Statistique, commercial, comptabilité, gestion.
Domaines spécialisés: Paie, facturation, gestion du stock.

N.C.R. FRANCE*
191 rue de Vaugirard, 75015 Paris
Téléphone: 566.53.77

Dirigeants
M. Striblen, *Presse-Documentation*
M. Bittar, *Education*

Langages de Programmation
NEAT/3, COBOL, FORTRAN.

Services Fournis
Conseils, programmation, enseignement et formation, opérateurs, software packages, documentation, préparation des données, systems analysis.

Domaine d'Application
Gestion.

Formation
Cours d'information et d'initiation et formation.

QUATERNAIRE INFORMATIQUE S.A.*
105 rue des Moines, 75017 Paris

Dirigeant
J. P. Carlier, *Directeur Général*

Equipement
IBM 360/30 – système d'opération: DOS; mémoire interne: 64K bits; bandes magnétiques: 4 2415; disques magnétiques: 3 2311; 1 imprimante.

Langages de Programmation
Assembleur, GAP, COBOL, FORTRAN.

Equipement Projeté
IBM 360/40 ou second système 360/30.

Services Fournis
Conseils, programmation, software packages, préparation des données. Fonctionnement à porte ouverte.

Domaines d'Application
Scientifique, statistique, commercial, comptabilité, gestion, recherche opérationnelle.

Formation
Stages d'analyse et de programmation par l'intermédiaire de la société filiale 'Quaternaire Education'.

SERVICE INFORMATIQUE HONEYWELL BULL
179-181 avenue Charles de Gaulle, 92 Neuilly-sur-Seine
Telephone: 747 70 42

Also at:
11 rue Godefroy Cavaignac, 75011 Paris
Telephone: 805 06 30

15 rue de l'Atlas, 75019 Paris
Telephone: 206 15 34

57 avenue d'Iéna, 75016 Paris
Telephone: 553 69 19

17 rue Montolieu, 13 Marseille 2e
Telephone: 90 64 21

25 boulevard Notre Dame, 13 Marseille 6e
Telephone: 53 40 40

43 boulevard Notre Dame, 13 Marseille 6e
Telephone: 37 29 09

Centre Blaise Pascal, 2 boulevard d'Orléans, 76 Rouen
Telephone: 70 01 05

Centre Gustave Flaubert, 76 Petit Couronne
Telephone: 72 30 06

12 rue de la Donelière, 35 Rennes
Telephone: 59 26 63

70 rue des Jacobins, 80 Amiens
Telephone: 91 76 66

5 rue Ampère, 38 Grenoble
Telephone: 96 12 18

Centre du Mans, rue de Belle Ile, 72 Coulaines
Telephone: 28 96 49

Centre de Nantes, 9 rue des Compagnons, 44 Saint-Herblain
Telephone: 73 39 20

84 rue de Trévise, 59 Lille
Telephone: 52 03 46

11 quai André Lassagne, 69 Lyon
Telephone: 27 15 11

6 rue Buisson, 42 Saint-Etienne
Telephone: 33 20 59

17 rue Fevret, 21 Dijon
Telephone: 30 21 01

16 rue Gutenberg Prolongée, 06 Nice
Telephone: 87 24 28

24 rue Valentin Magnan, 66 Perpignan
Telephone: 50 30 62

4 rue Scatisse, 30 Nîmes
Telephone: 67 58 98

4 rue Damette, 84 Avignon
Telephone: 81 38 75

Officers
Marc Dubruel, *President Director General*
Primus Berger, *Director General*
Albert Boyer, *Secretary General*

Computer Installation
40 computers: BULL GENERAL ELECTRIC Gamma 10, Gamma 30, GE 100, GE 400, GE 6000.

Coding Language
COBOL.

Services Available
Advice, programming, education and training, operators, software packages, preparation of data, systems analysis. Operate on a self-service, remote access, closed shop, block time and open shop basis.

Fields of Application
Commercial, production control, accounting, management, systems analysis.
Specialized areas: Sales analysis, payroll.

Training
Courses in introduction to computers, COBOL and FORTRAN programming, remote access.

S.E.T.M.*
76 avenue de Champs Elysées, 75008 Paris
Téléphone: ELY.68.04 et 05

Dirigeants
M. Poulet, *Directeur Général Adjoint*
M. l'Huillier, *Directeur Technique*
M. Lente, *Relations Extérieures*

Equipement
IBM 360/40 (2)–système d'opération: DOS; mémoire interne: 128K et 256K bits; bandes magnétiques: 1 2400; disques magnétiques: 1 2314; 2 imprimantes.

Langages de Programmation
Assembleur, COBOL, PL/1, FORTRAN, GAP.

Equipement Projeté
Lecture optique, teleprocessing.

Services Fournis
Conseils, programmation, enseignement et formation, opérateurs, software packages, préparation des données. Fonctionnement en abonnement machine et à porte ouverte.

Domaines d'Application
Gestion administrative (comptabilité, paie), financière, commerciale et gestion de production.

SIA INTERNATIONAL*
35 boulevard Brune, 75014 Paris
Téléphone: 842-60-00

Officers
Jacques Lesourne, *Chairman of the Board*
Robert Lattes, *President*
Jean Céron, *Financial and Administrative Director*
Pierre Mathelot, *Director of Development*
Gérard Letellier, *Technical Director*
Jaques Weber, *Vice Technical Director, Manager of Systems Department*
Jeanne Poyen, *Consultant*

Computer Installation
CDC 6600–operating system: SCOPE; internal storage: 128K bits; magnetic tapes: 8 CDC 607, 2 CDC 609; magnetic discs: 1 CDC 6638; 3 line printers. *Remote processing features*: Remote batch processing with either CDC or non-CDC terminals with card reader, line printer and (or) card punch.

CDC 3600–operating system: SCOPE 5.2; internal storage 65,536 48-bit words; magnetic tapes: 12 CDC 607.

Coding Languages
FORTRAN 6600 (and FORTRAN IV), FORTRAN extended (VASI compatible), COMPASS, ALGOL, COBOL, MICMAC (macrogenerator), SIMSCRIPT, DAPHNE, BUDGET.

Services Available
Advice, operators, preparation of data, programming, software packages, systems analysis. Operate on a self-service, open shop, closed shop, block time, remote access and time-sharing basis.

Fields of Application
Scientific applications, data processing, basic and applied software.
Specialized areas: Advanced programming, partial differential equations, scheduling problems, survey analysis, linear programming.

Training
Programming courses (FORTRAN, COBOL, DAPHNE, etc.); summer schools in Information Processing; short seminars on various subjects.

SIEMENS S.A.F.*
39 boulevard Ornano, 93 Saint-Denis
Téléphone: 243.30.20

Officers
Jürgen Schwab, *Director, Informatics Division*
André Delalaing, *Deputy Director*
André Vincent, *Sales Director*

Computer Installation
SIEMENS 4004/45–operating systems: TOS/TDOS/DOS; internal storage: 128K bits; magnetic tapes: 6; magnetic discs: 4; 1 line printer. *Remote processing features*: Processing controller, screens.

SIEMENS 4004/35–operating system: TOS/TDOS/DOS; internal storage: 64K bits; magnetic tapes: 8; magnetic discs: 4; 1 line printer.

Coding Languages
Assembler, COBOL, FORTRAN, ALGOL, RPG.

Services Available
All services. Operate on an open shop basis.

Fields of Application
Scientific, statistical, commercial, production control, accounting, management, systems analysis, operational research, etc.
Specialized areas: Sales analysis, linear programming, investment analysis, payroll, structural engineering, medical research, etc.

Training
Courses for client personnel in coding languages and in the use of the Siemens range of computers.

SOCIÉTÉ D'APPLICATIONS ET DE MÉTHODES MÉCANOGRAPHIQUES (SAMM)
101 boulevard Murat, 75016 Paris
Telephone: 525.75.75

Officers
Bernard Dorléac, *Chairman*
Gaston Bichet, *General Manager*
Jean-Paul Devai, *Sales Manager*

Computer Installation
IBM 360/40 and IBM 370/135 (5 altogether)—operating system: DOS and OS; internal storage: 64K bits, 128K bits, 140K bits, 240K bits; magnetic tapes: 30 3420 III and V; magnetic discs: 13 2319; 5 line printers. *Remote processing features*: IBM 2780 terminal and Olivetti DE520.

CII Iris 50—operating system: SIRIS 2; internal storage: 128K bits; magnetic tapes: 6 7237; magnetic discs: 6 MD 25; 2 line printers.

Coding Languages
COBOL, Assembler, FORTRAN, BASIC, APL.

Contemplated Equipment
IBM 370/125.

Services Available
Advice, programming, software packages, preparation of data, systems analysis. Operate on a self-service, remote access, closed shop, block time, open shop and time-sharing basis.

Fields of Application
Scientific, statistical, commercial, production control, accounting, management, systems analysis, operational research, computer-aided design.
Specialized areas: Investment, analysis, electronic circuits.

SOCIÉTÉ D'ÉTUDES DES SYSTÈMES D'AUTOMATION (SESA)*
23 avenue de Neuilly, 75016 Paris
Téléphone: 722-10-00

Aussi:
SESA Toulon, 'La Marseillaise', avenue Franklin Roosevelt, 83 Toulon.
SESA Deutschland GmbH, Frankfurt-am-Main, Bockenheimer Landstrasse 51–53, République fédérale d'Allemagne.

Dirigeants
C. Rheims, *Président Directeur Général*
Mme. M. Gazale, *Chargée des Relations Extérieures*

Equipement
IBM 1130—mémoire interne: 16K mots; disques magnétiques: 1. *Transmission des données à distance*: 1 IBM 1130 est relié à un 360/50.

Langages de Programmation
FORTRAN, COBOL, ALGOL, PL/1, Assembleur.

Services Fournis
Conseils, programmation, enseignement et formation, software packages, préparation des données, systems analysis. Fournis aux entreprises privées et aux administrations.

Domaines d'Application
Software, systèmes de gestion automatisée, contrôle des processus, temps réel.
Domaines spécialisés: Commande numérique de machine-outil, fiabilité, automatisme, software de base, software d'applications.

Formation
Sessions d'information pour cadres dirigeants (générales) et pour ingénieurs utilisateurs (spécialisés) (1 à 3 jours). Sessions générales en tous aspects d'informatique.

SOCIÉTÉ DE GESTION ÉLECTRONIQUE (SOGELEC)*
34 avenue du Roule, 92 Neuilly-sur-Seine

Dirigeants
M. Bois, *Directeur Général*
M. Nolasco, *Directeur Technique*
M. Eschbach, *Attaché de Direction*

Equipement
ICL 1902A—mémoire interne: 32K mots; bandes magnétiques: 4 9-pistes, 2 7-pistes; disques magnétiques: 2; 2 imprimantes.
UNIVAC 9300—mémoire interne: 12K bits; 1 imprimante.

Langages de Programmation
PLAN, COBOL, FORTRAN, RPG, Assembleur.

Services Fournis
Conseils, programmation, opérateurs, préparation des données. Fournis à toutes sociétés ou organismes.

Domaines d'Application
Scientifique, statistique, commercial, comptabilité, gestion.

SOCIÉTÉ INDUSTRIELLE DE TRAVAUX DE BUREAUX (SITB-ORDINAC)*
38 rue des Jeûneurs, 75002 Paris
Téléphone: CEN 12-34, 37-42, 38-21

Dirigeants
A. Arthaud, *Président et Directeur Général*
C. Lamouche, *Directeur Général Adjoint*
Ph. Arthaud, *Directeur Technique*
F. Lorin, *Directeur Commercial*

Equipement
IBM 360/30—système d'opération: DOS; mémoire interne: 64K bits; bandes magnétiques: 4 2401/2; disques magnétiques: 3 2311; 1 imprimante.

IBM 360/30—système d'operation: DOS; mémoire interne: 32K bits; bandes magnétiques: 5 2401/2; disques magnétiques: 3 2311; 1 imprimante.

IBM 360/25 (2)—système d'opération: BPS; mémoire interne: 16K bits; bandes magnétiques: 4 2401/2; 1 imprimante.

IBM 360/20—système d'operation: CPS; mémoire interne: 12K bits; 1 imprimante.

Langages de Programmation
Assembler 360, RPG, COBOL.

Services Fournis
Préparation des données, programmation, packages. Fonctionnement en self-service et par accès à distance.

Domaines d'Application
Comptabilité, gestion, statistique.
Domaines spécialisés: Comptabilité des opérations de Bourse, gestion immobilière, gestion de Crédits, comptabilité bancaire.

Formation
Programmeurs Assembleur 360.

France – Service Bureaux

SOCIÉTÉ PERFORAS*
20 rue Dussault, 94 Saint Maur
Téléphone: 283.48.73

Dirigeant
M. Goldmann

Services Fournis
Préparation des données, perforation, vérification.
Fonctionnement à porte ouverte.

SOGECIM*
7 place d'Iéna, 75016 Paris
Téléphone: 256-66-00

Dirigeants
R. Maviel
A. Vidal

Equipement
IBM 360/40—système d'opération: DOS; mémoire interne: 128K bits; bandes magnétiques: 7 2400; disques magnétiques: 4 2311; 1 imprimante.

HONEYWELL H1200—mémoire interne: 48K bits; bandes magnétiques: 5.

Langages de Programmation
COBOL, FORTRAN, Assembler.

Services Fournis
Opérateurs, programmation. Fonctionnement en self-service, en porte fermée et en porte ouverte.

Domaines d'Application
Gestion administrative, commercial, statistique.
Domaines spécialisés: Gestion de stock (système intégré), dépouillement d'enquête.

ZÉRO UN INFORMATIQUE
41 rue de la Grauge-aux-Belles, 75010 Paris
Téléphone: 202 29 10

Dirigeants
Maurice Réfrégier, *Président*
Clément Pillerault, *Directeur General*
Gilbert Cristini, *Directeur de la Rédaction*

Services Fournis
Documentation, informations d'actualité, études de fond.

Domaines d'Application
Tous.

GABON

GOVERNMENT ESTABLISHMENT

MINISTÈRE DE L'ÉCONOMIE ET DES FINANCES
Direction de L'Informatique
B.P. 2156, Libreville
Telephone: 225-38

Officers
Jean-Felix Mbah, *Director*
Michel Mofouma-Modoumet, *Deputy Director*
Jacques Césaré, *Systems Engineer*
Jean-Claude Mailhé, *Technical Consultant*

Computer Installation
CII Iris 50—operating system: SIRIS 2; internal storage: 80K bits; magnetic tapes: 2 72327; magnetic discs: 4 DIMAS; 1 line printer.

Coding Languages
COBOL, ASSIRIS, FORTRAN.

Contemplated Equipment
2 DIMAS.

Services Available
Advice, programming, operators, preparation of data, systems analysis. Operate on a self-service and closed shop basis.

Fields of Application
Scientific, statistical, accounting, management, operational research.
Specialized area: Payroll.

GERMAN DEMOCRATIC REPUBLIC

UNIVERSITY

UNIVERSITÄT ROSTOCK*
Rechenzentrum
Universitätsplatz, 25 Rostock
Telephone: 69332

Officers
Dr. Immo O. Kerner, *Director*
Herr Teubner, *Officer for Foreign Relations*

Computer Installation
ZRA 1–1 line printer.

Coding Languages
ALGOL compiler with minor restrictions.

Services Available
Available for outside customers without any restriction.

Fields of Application
Numerical analysis, education and training of students.
Specialized area: Algorithmic languages.

Training
Programming in machine language, programming in ALGOL.

FEDERAL REPUBLIC OF GERMANY

NATIONAL CENTRE

DEUTSCHES RECHENZENTRUM*
61 Darmstadt, Rheinstrasse 75
Telephone: 06151/86321

Officer
Dr. E. Glowatzki, *Director*

Computer Installation
IBM 7094/I–operating system: IBSYS; internal storage: 1,179,648 bits; magnetic tapes: 13 729/IV; magnetic discs: 1 1301 (1 module); 1 line printer.
TELEFUNKEN TR 440–operating system: BS3/1; internal storage: 6,553,600 bits; magnetic tapes: 12 MDS 252; magnetic discs: 1 SSP 500; 2 line printers.

Coding Languages
FORTRAN, ALGOL, COBOL, DL-EDC, FAP, MAP, TAS, LP90, PERT, GPSS III, SIMSCRIPT, FORMAC, LISP, MIDAS, MIMIC, DSL.

Contemplated Equipment
Replacement of the IBM 7094; final version of the TR 440.

Services Available
Consultation, education and training, software packages. Operate on a closed shop basis. Available to universities and other non-profit-making research institutions.

Field of Application
Scientific.

Training
Two-year course for Mathematical-Technical Assistants; special programming courses on programming languages and applications not covered by university courses (10 days).

UNIVERSITIES AND COLLEGES

ALBERT-LUDWIGS-UNIVERSITÄT FREIBURG
Projekt CUU
7800 Freiburg-im-Breisgau, Schänzlestrasse 9-11
Telephone: 0761-2032717.

Officer
Prof. Dr. Klaus Haefner

Computer Installation
SIEMENS 4004/45–operating system: PBS 14/ICU/PLANIT; internal storage: 196K bytes; magnetic tapes: 2; magnetic discs: 2; 1 line printer. *Remote processing features*: about 20 terminals.

Coding Languages
ICU/PLANIT, FORTRAN, ALGOL, Assembler.

Contemplated Equipment
Siemens 4004/150.

Services Available
Advice, education and training. Operate on a time-sharing basis.

Fields of Application
Scientific, computer-based learning.

Training
Introduction to design of course work for computer-based learning systems.

BAYERISCHE AKADEMIE DER WISSENSCHAFTEN
Leibnitz-Rechenzentrum
8000 Munich 2, Barrerstrasse 21
Telephone: 0811-2105393

Officers
Prof. Dr. G. Seegmüller, *Director*
F. Peischl, *Manager*

Computer Installation
TELEFUNKEN TR 440-Twin–operating system: BS3; internal storage: 13,107,200 bits; magnetic tapes: 8 MDS 252; magnetic discs: 16 PSP; 4 line printers. *On-line satellite computers*: 2 Telefunken TR80.

Coding Languages
ALGOL 60, FORTRAN IV, COBOL, PS440, TASS.

Services Available
Advice, software packages, systems analysis. Operate on a remote access, closed shop and time-sharing basis. Available to both Munich universities.

Field of Application
Scientific
Specialized area: Compilers and operating systems.

Training
Lectures on system programming.

BAYERISCHE JULIUS-MAXIMILIANS-UNIVERSITÄT WÜRZBURG*
Institut für Angewandte Mathematik
87 Würzburg, Kaiserstrasse 27
Telephone: 31591

Also:
Rechenzentrum
Röntgenring 8
Telephone: 31593

Officers
Prof. Dr. W. Velte, *Director*
Prof. Dr. J. Stoer

Computer Installation
ELECTROLOGICA X8–internal storage: 48K 28-bit words; 1 line printer
ZUSE Z22R.

Coding Languages
ALGOL 60, ELAN, FORTRAN IV.

Services Available
Operate on a self-service and closed shop basis. Only limited time available.

CHRISTIAN-ALBRECHTS-UNIVERSITÄT KIEL
Institut für Informatik und praktische Mathematik
2300 Kiel 1, Neue Universität, Olshausenstrasse 40-60

Officers
Prof. Dr. Bodo Schlender, *Director*
Prof. Dr. Karl Heinrich Weise, *Director*
Dipl.-Math. Peter Grosse, *Computer Centre Manager*

Federal Republic of Germany – Universities and Colleges

Computer Installation
ELECTROLOGICA X8 – operating system: Batch-Monitor; internal storage: 27K × 64 bits; magnetic tapes: 4 1530; magnetic discs: 2 1430; 1 line printer. *On-line satellite computer*: Electrologica X1.

PDP-10 – operating system: Time-Sharing Monitor; internal storage: 36K × 64 bits; magnetic tapes: 8 TU 55; magnetic discs: 4 RPO2; 1 line printer. *On-line satellite computer*: PDP-8.

Coding Languages
ALGOL, FORTRAN, LISP.

Services Available
Education and training, operators, software packages, documentation. Operate on a closed shop and time-sharing basis.

Field of Application
Scientific.

EBERHARD-KARLS-UNIVERSITÄT TÜBINGEN
Interfakultäres Zentrum für Datenverarbeitung
7400 Tübingen, Köllestrasse 1
Telephone: (07122) 712901

Officer
Dr. Martin Graef, *Director*

Computer Installation
CDC 3300 – operating system: MASTER; internal storage: 2,752,512 bits; magnetic tapes: 4 CD 604, 1 CD 609; magnetic discs: 5 CD 854; 1 line printer. *On-line satellite computer*: 1 PDP 15. *Remote processing features*: 1 CD 200 user terminal.

Coding Languages
ALGOL, FORTRAN, COMPASS, COBOL, META, LISP, SIMULA.

Services Available
Advice, operators, preparation of data, programming, software packages, systems analysis. Operate on a closed shop basis.

Fields of Application
Specialized areas: Non-numerical applications of computers such as theorem proving, research in linguistics, textual editing, computer typesetting.

Training
Introduction to programming (ALGOL, COBOL, COMPASS, FORTRAN, LISP).

EBERHARD-KARLS-UNIVERSITÄT TÜBINGEN
Zentrum für neue Lernverfahren
7400 Tübingen, Münzgasse 11
Telephone: 07122-712075

Officers
Prof. Dr. Zifreund, *Director*
Hartmut Simon, *Principal Investigator*

Computer Installation
The Centre is linked to a Siemens 4004/45 at the University of Freiburg by means of 2 Siemens FS 200.

Coding Language
ICU-PLANIT.

Contemplated Equipment
A large time-sharing system.

Services Available
Education and training. Operate on a time-sharing basis. Restricted to members and institutions of the University.

Field of Application
Scientific.
Specialized area: Computer-based learning systems.

Training
Regular courses as introduction to the development and instructional use of computer-based learning systems.

FACHHOCHSCHULE ULM
79 Ulm, Prittwitzstrasse, Postfach 33
Telephone: 0731-61301

Officers
Prof. Dr. R. Herschel, *Head of Informatics Department*
Dipl.-Ing. F. Krien, *Head of Computer Centre*

Computer Installation
SIEMENS 305 – operating system: ORG I/MZS 300; internal storage: 16,348 24-bit words; magnetic discs: 1 PSK2; 1 line printer.

Coding Languages
ALGOL 60, FORTRAN IV, PROSA 300 (Assembler).

Contemplated Equipment
Data transmission equipment, EKG-processing equipment.

Services Available
Operate on an open shop and time-sharing basis.

Fields of Application
Scientific, production control.

Training
Four-year course leading to Dipl.-Ing. in Informatics. Course leading to Dipl.-Inf. is planned.

FRIEDRICH-ALEXANDER UNIVERSITÄT ERLANGEN-NÜRNBERG
Rechenzentrum
8520 Erlangen, Martenstrasse 1

Officer
Dr. R. Wolf, *Academic Director*

Computer Installation
CDC 3300 – operating system: Master; internal storage: 3,145,728 bits; magnetic tapes: 2 601, 2 604; magnetic discs: 4 854, 5 841; 2 line printers. *Remote processing features*: 12 teletypewriters, 12 display units.

Coding Languages
FORTRAN, ALGOL, COBOL, COMPASS.

Service Available
Operate on a self-service and block time basis. Restricted to University Institutes.

Field of Application
Scientific.

Training
Programming courses are run by the Department of Computer Science.

Federal Republic of Germany — Universities and Colleges

INSTITUT FÜR INFORMATIK
Computer-Aided Instruction Group
7000 Stuttgart 1, Herdweg 51
Telephone: 0711-784-2513

Officers
Dr. Joachim Laubsch, Dr. Ing. Kenji Hanakata, *Research Associates*

Computer Installation
TELEFUNKEN TR 440–operating system: BS 3.

Coding Languages
ALGOL, PLANIT, FORTRAN.

Services Available
Operate on a time-sharing basis.

Field of Application
Scientific.
Specialized area: Computer-aided instruction.

JOHANNES GUTENBERG-UNIVERSITÄT MAINZ
Rechenzentrum
65 Mainz, Jakob-Welder-Weg 7
Telephone: 172656

Officer
Dr. H. Wacker, *Director of Computing Center*

Computer Installation
CDC 3300–operating system: MASTER; internal storage: 112K bits; magnetic tapes: 4 CD 604; magnetic discs: 7 CD 854; 1 line printer.

SIEMENS 2002–internal storage: 12K bits.

TELEFUNKEN RA 463/2–Electronic Analog Computer.

Coding Languages
ALGOL 60 (ALCOR), PROSA, FORTRAN II, IV, COMPASS, COBOL, SIMULA.

Service Available
Operators. Customers programme by themselves (open shop in the old sense), no direct access to the computer (closed shop in the new sense). Available to scientific institutions only.

Fields of Application
Numerical analysis, especially error analysis and application of functional analysis.

Training
Principles of numerical analysis and of computer programming.

RHEINISCHE FRIEDRICH-WILHELMS-UNIVERSITÄT BONN
Rechenzentrum
5300 Bonn, Liebfrauenweg 3
Telephone: 731-4294

Computer Installation
IBM 370/165–operating system: OS-MVT-HASP; internal storage: 2,048K bytes; magnetic tapes: 6 2420, 2 2401; magnetic discs: 4 3330; 3 line printers. *Remote processing features*: 6 remote batch stations, 4 2741.

Coding Languages
Assembler, FORTRAN IV, COBOL ANS, ALGOL 60, PL/1, RPG.

Contemplated Equipment
IBM 370/168.

Services Available
Advice. Operate on a remote access, closed shop and time-sharing basis.

Fields of Application
Scientific, statistical.

RHEINISCH-WESTFÄLISCHE TECHNISCHE HOCHSCHULE AACHEN
51 Aachen, Seffenter Weg 23
Telephone: 4221

Officers
Prof. Dr. F. Reutter, *Director of the Computer Centre*
Prof. Dr. D. Haupt, *Deputy Director*

Computer Installation
CDC 6400–operating system: SCOPE 3.3; internal storage: 96K 60-bit words; magnetic tapes: 7 CD 604; magnetic disc: CD 6638; 3 line printers. *Remote processing features*: CDC INTERCOM Terminals (SIE T 100 Teletypewriters).

SIEMENS 2002–internal storage: 12K 48-bit words; magnetic tapes: 3 TM2; 1 line printer.

CDC 1700–operating system: MSOS 2.0; internal storage: 32K 16-bit words; magnetic tapes: 1 CD 608; magnetic discs: 1 CD 854.

Coding Languages
SYMBOL (Assembler), ALGOL 60-ALCOR Mainz, FORTRAN, COMPASS.

Services Available
Advice, operators, preparation of data, programming, software packages, systems analysis. Operate on a closed shop, remote access and time-sharing basis. Limited availability to customers outside University.

Fields of Application
All fields of scientific research.
Specialized area: Traffic problems.

Training
Programming courses.

RUHR-UNIVERSITÄT BOCHUM
Rechenzentrum
4630 Bochum, Universitätsstrasse 150 NA

Officer
Prof. Dr. H. Ehlich, *Director*

Computer Installation
TELEFUNKEN TR 440–operating system: TNS 440; internal storage: 12,582,912 bits; magnetic tapes: 5 MDS 252; magnetic discs: 1 TSP 500, 2 WSP 414-8; 2 line printers. *On-line satellite computer*: Telefunken TR 86. *Remote processing features*: 46 FSR 105, 2 SIG 100.

TELEFUNKEN TR 86–internal storage: 393,216 bits; magnetic tapes: 1 MDS 252, 1 MAS 55.

Coding Languages
ALGOL, COBOL, FORTRAN, BASIC, RPG, TAS, AIDA, BCPL.

Contemplated Equipment
RK 443-1 with MSP 482-2.

Services Available
Advice, education and training, software packages, systems analysis. Operate on a closed shop and time-sharing basis. No financial profit allowed to users.

Fields of Application
Scientific, statistical, management, systems analysis.

Training
Long and short courses in ALGOL, FORTRAN, COBOL, AIDA, TAS; long courses in Construction of Compilers and Computer Graphics.

TECHNISCHE HOCHSCHULE DARMSTADT
Rechenzentrum
6100 Darmstadt, Hochschulstrasse 1
Telephone: 162054

Officer
Dr. J. G. Lührs

Computer Installation
IBM 7040 – operating system: IBSYS; internal storage: 32,768 36-bit words; magnetic tapes: 8 729/IV; 1 line printer. *On-line satellite computer*: IBM 1401.

IBM 1401 – internal storage: 4K bits; magnetic tapes: 2 729/IV.

Coding Languages
ALGOL 60, FORTRAN IV, COBOL, Assembler, MAP.

Services Available
Consultation, education and training, operators, software packages. Operate on an open shop basis. Available only to University institutes for problems of courses and research.

Fields of Application
Scientific, educational.

Training
Two courses in programming for the training of students.

TECHNISCHE UNIVERSITÄT BERLIN
Abteilung Angewandte Elektronische Datenverarbeitung
1000 Berlin 12, Strasse des 17. Juni 135
Telephone: (0311) 343-3760

Officers
Prof. Dr. Uwe Pape
Dr. Herbert Weber

Computer Installation
IBM 360/67.
CDC 6500.

Coding Languages
ALGOL 60, PL/1, FORTRAN VI, LISP.

Services Available
Education and training, software packages.

Fields of Application
Scientific, production control, management, systems analysis, operational research, information systems.
Specialized areas: Medical research, administration, graphs and networks, data structures.

TECHNISCHE UNIVERSITÄT BERLIN
Institut für Informationsverarbeitung
1000 Berlin 10, Einsteinufer 37
Telephone: (0311) 314-3222

Officer
Dr.-Ing. Peter Rechenberg, *Professor of Computer Science*

Computer Installation
IBM 360/67 – internal storage 768K bytes; magnetic tapes: 5; magnetic discs: 8; 2 line printers. *Remote processing features*: over 20 terminals.

CII 9040 – operating system: Monarch; internal storage: 384K bits; magnetic tapes: 2; magnetic discs: 1; 1 line printer.

Coding Languages
FORTRAN, PL/1, ALGOL, etc.

Services Available
Operate on a closed shop and time-sharing basis.

Field of Application
Scientific.

Training
Courses leading to a Diplom-Informatiker degree.

TECHNISCHE UNIVERSITÄT BERLIN*
Rechen institut
1000 Berlin 12, Strasse des 17. Juni 135
Telephone: (0311) 314-2703.

Officer
Prof. Dr. K. Jaeckel, *Director of the Institute*

Computer Installation
ICL 1909 – operating system: GEORGE; internal storage: 786,432 bits; magnetic tapes: 4 ICL 1973; magnetic discs: 2 ICL 2802; 1 line printer.

CDC 6400 – operating system: SCOPE; internal storage: 3,932,160 bits; magnetic tapes: 4 CDC 604; magnetic discs: 2 CDC 6603, 2 10098/10124; 2 line printers.

Coding Languages
ALGOL, COBOL, COMPASS, FORTRAN, PLAN.

Contemplated Equipment
Terminals for CDC 6400.

Services Available
Advice, operating, programming, software packages. Operate on a closed shop basis.

Fields of Application
All fields of interest to University.
Specialized area: Numerical mathematics.

Training
Courses in programming, special software and operating.

TECHNISCHE UNIVERSITÄT CAROLO-WILHELMINA ZU BRAUNSCHWEIG
Institut für Datenverarbeitungsanlagen
3300 Braunschweig, Schleinitzstrasse 23
Telephone: (0531) 391-2727

Officer
Prof. Dr.-Ing. Hans-Otto Leilich

Computer Installation
HEWLETT PACKARD 2116 B – operating system: DOS; internal storage: 16K 16-bit words; magnetic discs: 1 HP 2770/A; 1 line printer.

Coding Languages
Assembler, BASIC, FORTRAN IV, ALGOL.

Services Available
Operate on a self-service basis. Restricted to members and students of the Institute.

Fields of Application
Scientific, systems analysis.
Specialized area: Structural engineering.

TECHNISCHE UNIVERSITÄT CAROLO-WILHELMINA ZU BRAUNSCHWEIG
3300 Braunschweig, Pockelstrasse 14, Postfach 3329
Telephone: (0531) 391-2277

Officer
Dr. Georg Bayer, *Head of Computing Centre*

Computer Installation
ICL 1907 and ICL 1906S—operating systems: GEORGE 3 and 4; internal storage: 5,376K bits; magnetic tapes: 8; magnetic discs: 7; 3 line printers.
ELECTROLOGICA XI (2)—internal storage: 648K bits; 1 line printer.

Coding Languages
ALGOL 60, FORTRAN, COBOL, ALGOL 68.

Services Available
Advice, education and training. Operate on a self-service, remote access, closed shop, block time, open shop and time-sharing basis.

Fields of Application
Scientific, commercial.

TECHNISCHE UNIVERSITÄT CLAUSTHAL
Rechenzentrum
3392 Clausthal-Zellerfeld, Adolf-Römer-Strasse 2A, Postfach 230
Telephone: 05323-72352

Officer
Prof. Dr. J. Albrecht, *Director*

Computer Installation
TELEFUNKEN TR 4—internal storage: 3,145,728 bits; magnetic tapes: 3 MDS 251, 1 MDS 252; magnetic discs: 1 SSP; 1 line printer.

Coding Languages
ALGOL 60, FORTRAN IV, COBOL, TEXAS.

Services Available
Special arrangements made for outside customers. Operate on a self-service and closed shop basis. Available only to members of universities in Federal Germany.

Fields of Application
Numerical analysis, programming languages.
Specialized area: Operating systems for remote job processing.

Training
Lectures on system programming.

TECHNISCHE UNIVERSITÄT HANNOVER*
Institut für Massivbau
Hannover, Brühlstrasse 27
Telephone: 7622176

Officers
Dr. Ing. K. Dierks
Dipl. Ing. J. Lierse

Computer Installation
ZUSE Z22R—internal storage: 312,512 bits.
HEWLETT PACKARD 2116B—internal storage: 131,072 bits.

Coding Languages
Freiburger Code, ALGOL 60, FORTRAN IV, BASIC.

Service Available
Advice. Operate on an open shop basis. Restricted to fundamental research projects.

Fields of Application
Application of the computer to structural mechanics.
Specialized area: Development of so-called digital computer methods for problems in mechanics, e.g. structures like frames, plates, shells and reinforced and prestressed concrete structures.

Training
Application of ALGOL in structural mechanics.

TECHNISCHE UNIVERSITÄT MÜNCHEN
8002 Munich, Arcisstrasse 21
Telephone: 2105-394

Officer
Dr. F. L. Bauer, *Professor of Higher Mathematics*

Computer Installation
TELEFUNKEN TR 440—operating system: BS 3; internal storage: 13,107,200 bits; magnetic tapes: 2 MDS 252; magnetic discs: 1 SSP 500, 2 WSP 414/8; 3 line printers.
On-line satellite computer: TR 86 S. *Remote processing features*: 48 visual display units.

Coding Languages
ALGOL, FORTRAN, TAS.

Services Available
Advice, software packages. Operate on a self-service, open shop and time-sharing basis. Available only for scientific and educational use.

Fields of Application
Scientific, systems analysis.
Specialized areas: Analysis, system development, programming languages.

Training
Diploma in Informatics and courses in numerical analysis and programming.

TECHNISCHE UNIVERSITÄT MUNCHEN*
Geodätisches Institut
8002 Munich, Arcisstrasse 21
Telephone: 2105-401

Computer Installation
ZUSE Z23—internal storage: 337,920 bits; 1 line printer.

Coding Languages
Freiburger Code, ALGOL 60.

Services Available
Operate on a self-service and closed shop basis.

Field of Application
Geodesy.
Specialized area: Engineering measurements.

Federal Republic of Germany – Universities and Colleges

TECHNISCHE UNIVERSITÄT MÜNCHEN*
Institut für Angewandte Mathematik
8002 Munich, Arcisstrasse 21
Telephone: 2105 304

Officer
Dr. J. Heinhold, *Professor of Applied Mathematics and Mathematical Statistics*

Computer Installation
CII 9010–internal storage: 8K 12-bit words; magnetic tapes: DIMAG.

Coding Languages
FORTRAN, SYMBOL.

Services Available
Operate on a closed shop basis.

Fields of Application
Mathematics, operational research, optimization techniques.

Training
University courses in analogue computation; FORTRAN courses.

UNIVERSITÄT FRIDERICIANA KARLSRUHE*
Rechenzentrum
7500 Karlsruhe 1, Kaiserstrasse 12, Postfach 6380
Telephone: (0721) 608 3158

Officers
M. Berger, *Manager*
Prof. Dr. U. Kulisch, *Director*

Computer Installation
ELECTROLOGICA X8–operating system: HYDRA; internal storage: 64K 27-bit words; magnetic discs: 2; 1 line printer. *On-line satellite computer*: RDP-8/I. *Remote processing features*: 32 Teletype-Terminals.

Coding Languages
ALGOL, KARLA (internal code, self-made Assembler).

Services Available
Consultation, education and training, operators. Operate on a closed shop and time-sharing basis. Available to members of the University.

Field of Application
Scientific.

Training
Dipl.-Inf. in Informatics; lectures on programming and ALGOL 60.

UNIVERSITÄT HAMBURG
Institut für Informatik
2000 Hamburg 13, Schlueterstrasse 66/72

Officers
Prof. Dr. H. H. Nagel, Prof. Dr. W. Brauer, Prof. Dr. E. Jessen, Prof. Dr. Wendt

Computer Installation
DIGITAL EQUIPMENT System 1050–internal storage: 2.3 million bits; magnetic tapes: 3 9-track, 1 7-track, 8 DEC tapes; magnetic discs: 4; magnetic drums: 2; 2 line printers.
PDP-8.
PDP-11.
MINCAL.
DATA GENERAL Nova.

Coding Languages
ALGOL, FORTRAN, LISP, GASP, SIMI, BCPL, SNOBOL BUSS, etc.

Contemplated Equipment
Additional core storage, terminals and disc packs.

Services Available
Operate on an open shop basis for Institute members and on a time-sharing basis for students.

Fields of Application
Scientific, accounting, system simulation, computer networks.
Specialized areas: Medical research, computers in education, pattern recognition.

Training
Two-year course for Informatik-Vordiplom, four-year course for Informatik-Diplom.

UNIVERSITÄT HAMBURG*
Rechenzentrum
2000 Hamburg 13, Rothenbaumchaussee 81
Telephone: 441972651

Officers
Prof. Dr. h. c. Lothar Collatz
Prof. Dr. R. Ansorge
Dr. Harry Feldmann

Computer Installation
TELEFUNKEN TR 4 (2)–internal storage: 32K 48-bit words; magnetic tapes: 6 Telefunken MDS 251, 4 MDS 252; magnetic discs: 1 Telefunken-Burroughs SSP 500-4 each; 1 line printer each.

Coding Languages
ALGOL, FORTRAN, COBOL, TEXAS (Telefunken-Externkode-Assembler).

Comptemplated Equipment
TELEFUNKEN TR 440, TELEFUNKEN TR 865.

Services Available
Advice, software packages, systems analysis. Operate on a closed shop basis. Available only for scientific purposes.

Fields of Application
Scientific, statistical, management, systems analysis, operational research.
Specialized areas: Numerical methods, automata theory, programming languages.

Training
Courses on numerical methods, programming, computer science.

UNIVERSITÄT ZU KÖLN
Betriebswirtschaftliches Institut für Organisation und Automation (BIFOA)
5000 Cologne 41, Universitätsstrasse 45
Telephone: (0221) 44-60-81

Officers
Prof. Dr. Erwin Grochla, *Managing Director*
Prof. Dr. Norbert Szyperski, *Director*

Services Available
Education and training, documentation, systems analysis, research. Special conditions for members of the Society for the promotion of BIFOA.

Fields of Application
Commercial, management.

Training
Specialized seminars, conferences, symposia, forums.

UNIVERSITÄT ZU KÖLN
Rechenzentrum
5000 Cologne 41 (Lindenthal)
Telephone: 470 2603

Officers
Prof. Dr. P. Schmitz, *Director*
G. Schwichtenberg, *Operating and Planning*
Dr. W. Trier, *Systems Software*
Dr. A. Sattler, *Applications Software*
K. Peschlow, *Advisory Services and Training*

Computer Installation
SIEMENS 4004/55G–operating system: PBS; internal storage: 256K 8-bit bytes; magnetic tapes: 1 Siemens 4443; magnetic discs: 1 Siemens 4580, 1 Siemens 564, 7 Memorex; 2 line printers.

Coding Languages
ALGOL, COBOL, FORTRAN IV, PL/1, RPG, Assembler.

Contemplated Equipment
CDC Cyber 72/76.

Services Available
Advice, education and training, operators, software packages, documentation. Operate on a closed shop and block time basis. Interests of commercial installations must not be touched.

Fields of Application
Scientific, statistical, analysis and programming in all fields relevant to university purposes.
Specialized areas: Numerical analysis, statistical data analysis.

Training
Courses on introduction to data processing, programming languages, operating system and job control language, application of software packages.

UNIVERSITÄT KONSTANZ
Rechenzentrum
7750 Konstanz, Werner-Sombart-Strasse 30, Postfach 733
Telephone: 07531/88-1

Officer
Josef Jaschke, *Director of the Computer Centre*

Computer Installation
TELEFUNKEN TR 86–operating system: BESY 70; internal storage: 786,432 bits; magnetic tapes: 3 MDS 205-86; magnetic discs: 1 SSP 300-86; 1 line printer.

TELEFUNKEN TR 4–operating system: Platten-Betriebssystem, newest MV; internal storage: 1,703,936 bits; magnetic tapes: 1 MDS 252, 7 MDS 251 A; magnetic discs: 1 Burroughs; 1 line printer.

Coding Languages
TAS 86, ALGOL, FORTRAN, COBOL, TEXAS.

Contemplated Equipment
Terminal to the Computer Centre of the University of Freiburg, simulating a UNIVAC 1004.

Services Available
Consultation, programming, education and training, operators, software packages. Operate on a self-service basis.

Fields of Application
Scientific, statistical, commercial.
Specialized area: Library catalogues.

Training
Short courses in ALGOL, FORTRAN, COBOL, introduction to electronic data processing.

UNIVERSITÄT DES SAARLANDES*
Rechenzentrum
6600 Saarbrücken, Im Stadtwald

Officers
H. Frick, *Manager*
H. Martin, *Technical Manager*

Computer Installation
CDC 3300–operating system: MASTER; internal storage: 64K 24-bit words; magnetic tapes: 4 CD608; magnetic discs: 4 CD854; 1 line printer.

ELECTROLOGICA X1–internal storage: 20K bits; magnetic tapes: 3; 1 line printer.

Coding Languages
ALGOL 60, Usasi FORTRAN, Usasi COBOL, COMPASS.

Services Available
Operators, software packages. Operate on a closed shop basis. Available to scientific institutions only.

Fields of Application
Scientific, management.

UNIVERSITÄT STUTTGART
Rechenzentrum
Abteilung A: 7 Stuttgart 1, Herdweg 51
   Telephone: (0711) 2078-279
Abteilung B: 7 Stuttgart 80, Pfaffenwaldring 27
   Telephone: (0711) 7843633

Officers
Dr. K.-U. Dobler, *Director of Division A*
Dr. James C. Almond, *Director of Division B*
W. D. Schubring, *Manager of Software Development*

Computer Installation
CDC 6600–operating system: SCOPE 3.3; internal storage: 7,864,320 bits; magnetic tapes: 4 CDC 604; magnetic discs: 1 CDC 6638; 3 line printers. *On-line satellite computer*: 1 CDC 8231.

‡TELEFUNKEN TR 440–operating system: BS 3; internal storage: 6,291,456 bits; magnetic tapes: 3 MDS 252; magnetic discs: 8 WSP 414; 2 line printers. *On-line satellite computer*: 1 Telefunken TR 86. *Remote processing features*: 20 terminals.

TELEFUNKEN TR 4–operating system: Betriebssystem TR 4; internal storage: 1,572,864 bits; 1 line printer.

PDP 15/20–operating system: DOS; internal storage: 294,912 bits; magnetic tapes: 4; magnetic discs: 1; 1 line printer.

†HRS 860–operating system: BESY 70; internal storage: 786,432 bits; magnetic discs: 1.

Coding Languages
Assembler, COMPASS, FORTRAN, ALGOL 60, SIMULA, SIMSCRIPT, COBOL, MIMIC, APT, BASIC, SORT/MERGE, SNOBOL, TASS, AIDA, BCPL, GPSS, LISP, PLANIT, PS 40, TEXAS, EULER, SUSA, PASCAL, Macro Assembler, FOCAL.

Contemplated Equipment
CDC 7600.

Services Available
Software packages, documentation. Operate on a closed shop, open shop and time-sharing basis. Partially available for outside customers.

Fields of Application
Scientific, statistical, general university service.

Training
Courses in operating, FORTRAN and ALGOL 60.

†Shared with the Institut für Informatik.

UNIVERSITÄT ULM
Rechenzentrum
7900 Ulm-Wiblingen, Schlossbau 38
Telephone: 0731-177-280

Officer
Dipl.-Math. Th. Hansen, *Computer Centre Director*

Computer Installation
TELEFUNKEN TR 4–operating system: PBS; internal storage: 1.6 million bits; magnetic tapes: 4 MDS 252; magnetic discs: 1PS; 1 line printer.

CDC 1700–operating system: Tape Scope; internal storage: 256K bits; magnetic tapes: 2 MT 609.

Coding Languages
ALGOL, COBOL, FORTRAN, Assembler.

Services Available
Programming, education and training, preparation of data, systems analysis. Operate on a self-service and closed shop basis.

Fields of Application
Scientific, statistical, commercial.

Training
Courses in programming for members of the University.

WESTFÄLISCHE WILHELMS-UNIVERSITÄT MÜNSTER*
Rechenzentrum
44 Münster, Roxeler Strasse 60
Telephone: 490-3182

Officer
Prof. Dr. Helmut Werner, *Director of the Computing Centre*

Computer Installation
IBM 360/50G–operating system: OS/360; internal storage: 512K bytes; magnetic tapes: 4 IBM 2415/5; magnetic discs: 4 IBM 2311 and IBM 2314; 3 line printers.

Coding Languages
ALGOL, FORTRAN IV, PL/1, Assembler, COBOL, RPG.

Service Available
Advice. Operate on a closed shop basis.

Fields of Application
Specialized areas: Linear and non-linear Tschebyscheff-approximation.

Training
Programming courses.

GOVERNMENT ESTABLISHMENTS

BAYERISCHES STAATSMINISTERIUM FÜR ERNÄHRUNG, LANDWIRTSCHAFT UND FORSTEN
8000 Munich 22, Ludwigstrasse 2
Telephone: 0811-21821

Computer Installation
IBM 370/155–operating system: OS/MVT; internal storage: 1,024K bytes; magnetic tapes: 6 3420; magnetic discs: 8 3330; 4 line printers. *Remote processing features*: 1 2780, 2 2770, 1 5985, 6 3270.

Coding Languages
PL/1, COBOL, FORTRAN IV, ASS.

Contemplated Equipment
IBM 370/158, VS/2.

Services Available
Education and training, preparation of data. Operate on a remote access and closed shop basis. Available only to government departments.

Fields of Application
Scientific, commercial, management.
Specialized areas: Linear programming, IMS and STAIRS application.

BUNDESANSTALT FÜR STRASSENWESSEN (BAST)
Rechenzentrum des Bundesministers für Verkehr (BMV) und der BAST
5000 Cologne 51, Bruehler Strasse 1
Telephone: 0221-37021

Officer
Dipl.-Ing. Peter P. Canisius, *Head of Centre*

Computer Installations
SIEMENS 4004/46–operating systems: time-sharing BSV, PBS; internal storage: 1 million bits; magnetic tapes: 6; magnetic discs: 5; 1 line printer. *On-line satellite computer*: Siemens 301. *Remote processing features*: 12 terminals with hard copy.

SIEMENS 301–operating system: OTG; internal storage: 16K 24-bit words; magnetic tapes: 1; magnetic discs: 1.
Remote processing features: Analog-Input.

Coding Languages
FORTRAN, ALGOL, COBOL, PL/1, Assembler, PROSA.

Services Available
Advice, programming, education and training, documentation, preparation of data, systems analysis. Operate on a closed shop and time-sharing basis. Restricted to government users only.

Fields of Application
Scientific, statistical, operational research.

Training
Special training for civil servants.

BUNDESMINISTERIUM DER JUSTIZ
Juristisches Informationssystem
53 Bonn

Officer
Dr. Josef Fabry, *Director*

Coding Languages
COBOL, Assembler, PL/1.

Service Available
Advice. Operate on a self-service and time-sharing basis.

Field of Application
Scientific.
Specialized area: Law, juridical decisions and literature.

BUNDESMINISTERIUM FÜR ARBEIT UND SOZIALORDNUNG
5300 Bonn-Duisdorf, Bonnerstrasse 85
Telephone: 02221-741

Officer
Dipl.-Math. Paul Winkler, *Deputy Chief of the Department*.

Computer Installation
SIEMENS 4004/45 – operating system: PBS; internal storage: 384K bits; magnetic tapes: 6 Siemens 405; magnetic discs: 6 Siemens 4581; 1 line printer. *Remote processing features*: 6 terminals.

Coding Languages
Assembler, COBOL, FORTRAN, RPG.

Contemplated equipment
Change to Siemens 4004/150.

Services Available
Advice, documentation, preparation of data, systems analysis. Operate on a self-service, remote access and closed shop basis.

Fields of Application
Scientific, statistical, accounting, management, systems analysis, judicial information systems.
Specialized areas: Linear programming, analysis, model constructions for social applications.

DATENZENTRALE SCHLEWSIG-HOLSTEIN
2300 Kiel, Sophienblatt 82-86, Postfach 536
Telephone: 0431-6071

Officers
Herr Gebhardt, *Managing Director*
Herr Steinbrinck, *Director*
Herr Marwedel, *Director*

Computer Installation
IBM 370/145 – operating systems: DOS, OS MFT; internal storage: 256K bits; magnetic tapes: 8 2401; magnetic discs: 2 2319; 2 line printers.

IBM 370/145 – operating systems: DOS, OS MFT; internal storage: 256K bits; magnetic tapes: 6 2401; magnetic discs: 2 2319; 1 line printer.

IBM 360/40 – operating system: DOS; internal storage: 256K bits; magnetic tapes: 5 2401, 1 2415; magnetic discs: 9 2319; 1 line printer. *Remote processing features*: 16 teleprinters, 3 screens.

IBM 360/40 – operating system: DOS; internal storage: 256K bits; magnetic tapes: 2 2401, magnetic discs: 6 2319; 1 line printer.

SIEMENS 4004/150 – operating system: PBS 15; internal storage: 256K bits; magnetic tapes: 6 4453; magnetic discs: 1 4579; 2 line printers.

Coding Languages
COBOL, Assembler, FORTRAN, PL/1.

Contemplated Equipment
IBM 370/145 with 512K bits internal storage; 3 IBM 370/135 with 240K bits internal storage.

Services Available
Advice, programming, education and training, operators, software packages, documentation, preparation of data, systems analysis. Operate on a remote access, closed shop and block time basis. Normally available only for public administration.

Fields of Application
Statistical, commercial, accounting, systems analysis.
Specialized area: Data bases for public purposes.

Training
Basic training in electronic data processing for customers.

GESELLSCHAFT FÜR MARKTFORSCHUNG mbH (GFM)
2000 Hamburg 53, Langelohstrasse 134
Telephone: 0411-80-20-11

Officer
Prof. Dr. J. E. Schwenzer, *Director General*

Computer Installation
IBM 1130 – operating system: OS-005; internal storage: 262,144 bits; magnetic tapes: 4 2415; 1 line printer.

Coding Languages
Assembler, FORTRAN.

Services Available
Programming, operators, software packages. Operate on a closed shop basis.

Fields of Application
Scientific, statistical.
Specialized area: Market research.

INNENMINISTERIUM DES LANDES NORDRHEIN-WESTFALEN
Landesdatenbank Nordrhein-Westfalen (Datenbank für statistische Informationen)
4000 Düsseldorf, Elisabethstrasse 5
Telephone: 0211-871-464

Officers
Dr. Herbert Hosse, *Director for Ministry*
Dr. Vorschulte, *Director for Statistical Office*

Computer Installation
IBM 370/155 – operating system: OS-MVT; internal storage: 12,288K bits; magnetic tapes: 12 3420; magnetic discs: 2 3330, 1 2314; 6 line printers. *Remote processing feature*: TSO.

Coding Languages
Assembler, COBOL, FORTRAN.

Contemplated Equipment
IBM 370/165.

Services Available
Advice, programming. Operate on a remote access and time-sharing basis.

Fields of Application
Statistical, management.

RESEARCH INSTITUTIONS

DEUTSCHE FORSCHUNGS- UND VERSUCHSANSTALT FÜR LUFT- UND RAUMFAHRT E.V. (DFVLR)
Rechenzentrum Braunschweig
3300 Braunschweig, Postfach 3267
Telephone: (0531) 3951

Officer
Dr. A. Wallenhauer, *Head of the Computing Centre*

Computer Installation
SIEMENS 4004/60–operating system: PBS; internal storage: 3,145,728 bits; magnetic tapes: 4 442-2-9, 2 432-2-9; magnetic discs: 4 4579; 1 line printer. *Remote processing feature:* 1 DUST 4666.

EAI Pacer 600 Hybrid–internal storage: 262,144 bits; magnetic tapes: 4 EAI 1700.

Coding Languages
Assembler, ALGOL, FORTRAN.

Services Available
Consultation, programming, education and training, operators, software packages, documentation, systems analysis. Operate on a remote access and closed shop basis. Available only to DFVLR institutes.

Field of Application
Scientific.
Specialized area: Aeronautical research.

Training
Courses for mathematical-technical assistants.

DEUTSCHE FORSCHUNGS- UND VERSUCHSANSTALT FÜR LUFT- UND RAUMFAHRT E.V. (DFVLR)
Rechenzentrum Oberpfaffenhofen (RZO)
8031 Oberpfaffenhofen
Telephone: 08153/8625

Officer
R. Dierstein, *Director*

Computer Installation
TELEFUNKEN TR 440–operating system: BS3 (drum-disc oriented); internal storage: 6,291,456 bits; magnetic tapes: 5 MDS 252; magnetic discs: 7 WSP 414; 2 line printers. *On-line satellite computer*: 1 Telefunken TR 86. *Remote processing features*: Batch and Dialog time-sharing (visual display).

Coding Languages
ALGOL 60, FORTRAN IV, FORTRAN ASA, COBOL, BASIC, Assembler (TASS).

Contemplated Equipment
WSP 430 magnetic discs.

Services Available
Consultation, software packages. Operate on a closed shop and remote access basis.

Field of Application
Scientific research.
Specialized areas: Space research, data bank systems.

Training
Short courses in programming and topics of data processing, in connection with Carl-Cranz-Gesellschaft, Heidelberg (15 courses, each 2 weeks).

GESELLSCHAFT FÜR MATHEMATIK UND DATENVERARBEITUNG mbH (GMD)*
5201 St. Augustin-Birlinghoven, Schloss
Telephone: Siegburg 23041-5

Officers
Dr. R. Ebert, *Head of Computing Department*
Dr. P. Heyderhoff, *Head of Professional Training Programmes*
C. R. Rudolph, *Foreign Relations*

Computer Installation
IBM 7090–operating systems: FMS, IBSYS; internal storage: 1,179,648 bits; magnetic tapes: 15 729; 1 line printer. *On-line satellite computer*: IBM 1410.

SIEMENS 4004/46–operating system: TSOS; internal storage: 2,097,120 bits; magnetic tapes: 4 4004/442; magnetic discs: 8 4004/564C; 1 line printer. *Remote processing features*: 15 Siemens 8150 terminals.

IBM 360/50–*Remote processing features:* 34 CRT terminals (32 IBM 2260. 1 IBM 2265, 1 IBM 2250) and 15 IBM 2741 communication terminals.

Coding Languages
FORTRAN II and IV, Interactive FORTRAN, FAP, Assembler, COBOL, PL/1, LISP, BASIC.

Contemplated Equipment
Powerful computer to replace the IBM 7090/1410 at the Computing Centre for Bonn University.

Services Available
Consultation, education and training, operators, software packages, documentation. Operational basis: IBM 7090/1410–closed shop; Siemens 4004/46–time-sharing terminals on the premises, closed shop batch processing. Restrictions: IBM 7090/1410–universities and research establishments only; Siemens 4004/46–German ministries and government agencies only; IBM 360/50–for research purposes only.

Fields of Application
Scientific (numerical analysis, functional analysis, etc.), statistical, systems analysis, operational research.
Specialized area: Information system R&D, specifically for public administration.

Training
Complete half-year courses in theoretical and applied informatics on two levels: Programmers and Systems Analysts; Professional Training of Programming Assistants (2 half-years); 1-3 week courses: Introduction to EDP, FORTRAN, COBOL, PL/1, Operating Systems.

INSTITUT FÜR DEUTSCHE SPRACHE
LDV Division
68 Mannheim, L 11, 10
Telephone: (0621) 101302

Officers
Prof. Dr. Hugo Moser, *President of the Institute*
Prof. G. Ungeheuer, *Computational Linguistics*
P. J. Wolfangel, *Head of Data Processing*

Computer Installation
SIEMENS 4004/35–operating system: PBS DOS; internal storage: 524,288 bits; magnetic tapes: 4 9-track; magnetic discs: 2; 1 line printer.

Coding Languages
Assembler, FORTRAN IV, ALGOL.

Federal Republic of Germany – Consultants

Contemplated Equipment
IBM 370/145 with storage of 512K bytes.

Services Available
Advice, software packages, documentation, preparation of data. Operate on a closed shop and block time basis. Available for scientific (non-profit) applications.

Fields of Application
Scientific, statistical, information systems.
Specialized areas: Code conversion routines, text search routines, non-numerical data processing, manipulation and analysis of natural languages texts.

Training
Courses in linguistic data processing.

INSTITUT FÜR MEDIZINISCHE DATENVERARBEITUNG DER GESELLSCHAFT FÜR STRAHLEN- UND UMWELTFORSCHUNG mbH
8000 München 81, Arabellastrasse 4/I
Telephone: (0811) 91 60 11

Officers
Prof. Dr. H. J. Lange, *Head of the Research Group for Medical Data Processing*
D. Jurksch, *Head of the Computer Centre*
W. Gothier, *Head of Data Programming*
R. Reitner, *Head of Patient File Programming*
Dr. R. Blomer, *Head of the Software Group*
Dr. R. Thurmayr, *Co-ordinator of the Clinical Research Group*
S. J. Pöppl, *Head of the Biosignal Processing Group*

Computer Installation
SIEMENS 4004/46–operating system: TSOS; internal storage: 256K bytes; magnetic tapes: 6 4446-2-9 and 4446-2-7; 2 line printers. *Remote processing features*: Teletypes, videodisplays.

IBM 1800–operating system: MPX; internal storage: 393,216 bits; magnetic tapes: 1 2401/2; magnetic discs: 2 1810/B02; 1 line printer. *Remote processing features*: 1 analog/digital converter.

Coding Languages
COBOL, BASIC, DIALOG-FORTRAN, FORTRAN IV, Assembler

Contemplated Equipment
CDC 1700 with storage of 8K bits; CDC 915.

Services Available
Consultation, preparation of data, systems analysis. Operate on a closed shop, remote access and time-sharing basis.

Fields of Application
Scientific, statistical.
Specialized areas: Computer-aided decisions in medical diagnoses (patient files, algorithms of decision aid).

INTERNATIONALE ATOMREAKTORBAU GmbH (INTERATOM)*
Postfach 506, Bensberg/Köln
Telephone: Bensberg 51

Officers
Dr. Berke, *Director*
Dr. Harde, *Director*
Dr. G. Memmert, *Research Department*

Computer Installation
CDC 6400–operating system: SCOPE 3.2; internal storage: 48K 60-bit words; magnetic tapes: 4 CDC 606; magnetic discs: 4 854; 1 line printer.

Coding Languages
FORTRAN extended, COBOL.

Contemplated Equipment
3 841 disc drives.

Services Available
Operators, software packages. Operate on a closed shop basis.

Fields of Application
Scientific, Commercial.

VEREIN DEUTSCHER EISENHÜTTENLEUTE/ BETRIEBSFORSCHUNGSINSTITUT*
4000 Düsseldorf, Breitstrasse 27

Officers
Dr. K. H. Mommertz, *Director of the Institute*
Dr. J. Radestock, *Director of the Computer Centre*

Computer Installation
IBM 1130–Internal storage: 8K 16-bit words; magnetic discs: 5 2310.

Coding Languages
FORTRAN, ALGOL, RPG, Assembler

Services Available
Consultation, programming, systems analysis. Operate on a closed shop basis. Available to the iron and steel industry.

Fields of Application
Scientific, research evaluation, applied statistics, operational research, systems analysis, software evaluation.
Specialized area: Information centre (data-bank) for material properties.

CONSULTANTS

AIV–INSTITUT*
61 Darmstadt, Schöfferstrasse 2

Officers
P. K. Kreis, *Proprietor*
K. F. Erbach, *Training of Personnel*

Computer Installation
SIEMENS 4004/45–internal storage: 128K bytes; magnetic tapes: 4; magnetic discs: 4 2311.

Coding Languages
Assembler, COBOL, FORTRAN IV, ALGOL.

Services Available
Consultation, programming, education and training, software packages, documentation, systems analysis. Operate on a closed shop and block time basis.

Fields of Application
All fields.
Specialized areas: Commercial data processing, basic software.

Training
Courses for systems analysts and computer management assistants; short courses in Systems Analysis, Introduction to EDP, Programming Languages (COBOL, FORTRAN, PL/1, RPG, Assembler) and specialized fields.

AUTINFORM GmbH & CO.*
62 Wiesbaden, Uhlandstr. 3
Telephone: 06121-373904

Officers
Johannes Michalowsky
Karl-Heinz Gucella

Services Available
Consultation, preparation of data, programming, software packages, systems analysis.

Fields of Application
Scientific, commercial, accounting, software, compiler implementation
Specialized areas: Real time and teleprocessing.

Training
Courses given on a customer request basis; Assembler of third generation computers; high-level languages (COBOL, FORTRAN, ALGOL, PL/1). Short EDP appreciation courses for management and/or students.

DIPL.–KFM. HELMUT BLAU*
8035 Gauting b. München, Dianastrasse 2 1/2
Telephone: 0811/862674

Services Available
Consultation, programming, education and training, systems analysis.

Fields of Application
Commercial, production control, accounting, management, systems analysis.

AXEL BOJE UNTERNEHMENSBERATUNG
4000 Düsseldorf, Sternstrasse 70
Telephone: 48 52 35

Officers
H. J. Klatt, *Chief Consultant*
C. G. Lauter, *Chief Consultant*

Coding Languages
Assembler, COBOL, FORTRAN, PL/1, ALGOL, etc.

Services Available
Consultation, programming, education and training, software packages, documentation, systems analysis.

Fields of Application
Statistical, commercial, production control, accounting, management, systems analysis, operational research.
Specialized area: Office organization.

Training
Organization and Methods in Selling, Purchasing and Accounting (all with EDP), Methods and Techniques of Office Machines and EDP, Planning of Office Buildings, Sociometric Research in Offices.

BOOZ, ALLEN & HAMILTON INTERNATIONAL B.V.
4 Düsseldorf, Steinstrasse 2,
Telephone: (0211) 32 04 81

Officers
Jürgen G. Peddinghaus, *Vice-President and Managing Director (Northern Europe)*
Edward J. Gulas, *Vice-President and Manager of Computer Systems (Northern Europe)*

Services Available
Advice, programming, education and training, systems analysis.

Fields of Application
Scientific, statistical, commercial, production control, accounting, management, systems analysis, operational research, engineering, research and development.
Specialized areas: Sales analysis, linear programming, investment, analysis, payroll, equipment evaluation, information retrieval, data communication.

BOSBOOM–C.O.P.I.C. GmbH*
4 Düsseldorf, Mintrop Strasse 20/IV, Postfach 6713

Services Available
Consultation, systems analysis.

Fields of Application
General management consultancy (management development, training, group dynamics, work study, maintenance, etc.). Computer-oriented consultancy (systems analysis, production control, treatment of data, etc.).
Specialized areas: Assisting management with the organizational changes in view of the introduction of the computer. Determining the required data and improving their quality. Classification and coding of these data and of the firm's assets in general.

DIPL. KFM WOLFGANG BREZINA, EDP–CONSULTING*
8000 München 13, 131 Schellingstrasse
Telephone: 525847

Services Available
Consultation, programming, education and training, systems analysis.

Fields of Application
Commercial, production control, accounting, management, systems analysis, operational research applications within industry and commerce.

DR. K. BROKATE
1 Berlin 37, Schuetzallee 2

Services Available
Advice, programming, education and training.

Fields of Application
Scientific, commercial, management.
Specialized area: Data bases.

BUNKER RAMO ELECTRONIC DATA SYSTEMS GmbH
8000 Munich 81, Arabellastrasse 5/108

Officers
W. Gilbert, *General Manager*
M. Sthultz, *Technical Director*
W. Schneider, *EDP Centre Manager*

Computer Installations
HONEYWELL–BULL 2050–operating system: OS–2000; internal storage: 128K bytes; magnetic tapes: 3; magnetic discs: 3; 1 line printer.

Federal Republic of Germany – Consultants

Coding Languages
Assembly, COBOL, FORTRAN, DL/1, etc.

Contemplated Equipment
Honeywell–Bull 2040 with 96K bytes internal storage, 3 magnetic tapes, 2 magnetic discs, 1 line printer and on-line VDU terminals.

Services Available
Advice, programming, software packages, documentation, systems analysis, system design. Operate on a closed shop basis.

Fields of Application
Commercial, accounting, systems analysis, operational research, on-line systems for data base management systems.
Specialized area: Data base management systems.

CEGOS INSTITUT FÜR DATENVERARBEITUNG
8000 Munich 2, Brienner Strasse 5
Telephone: 0811-22-23-24

Officer
Marc de Trentinian, *Managing Director*

Services Available
Advice, programming, education and training, software packages, systems analysis.

Fields of Application
Scientific, statistical, commercial, production control, accounting, management, systems analysis, operational research.
Specialized areas: Sales analysis, linear programming, investment, analysis, payroll, structural engineering, medical research.

COMPUTER SCIENCES INTERNATIONAL DEUTSCHLAND GmbH (CSID)*
6000 Frankfurt am Main, Schwindstrasse 3
Telephone: 0611-77 00 37

Officers
Dr. M. I. Montana, *President and General Manager*
H. W. Seppi, *Director of Operations*
H. K. Weiler, *Manager of Programme Development*

Services Available
Advice, programming, education and training, operators, software packages, preparation of data, systems analysis.

Fields of Application
Management, systems analysis.
Specialized areas: Compiler writing, management information systems.

Training
Standard courses: Computer Concepts for Management; Management Utilization of the Computer; Systems and Programming Project Management; System Analysis and Design.

DBO-SYSTEME FÜR DATENVERARBEITUNG UND BETRIEBSWIRTSCHAFTLICHE ORGANISATION GmbH
4000 Düsseldorf, Kaiser-Friedrich-Ring 57
Telephone: 0211-56363

Officer
H. Becker

Coding Language
COBOL.

Services Available
Consultation, programming, education and training, software packages, systems analysis.

Fields of Application
Modular information systems in the fields of sales, stockkeeping, planning, cost control, cost accounting and bookkeeping.

DEUTSCHE BEDAUX GmbH
6000 Frankfurt am Main, Rossertstrasse 2

Officers
Dr. Dietrich Legat, *General Manager*
Dr. Robert B. Weinstein, *General Manager*

Services Available
Advice, education and training, systems analysis.

Fields of Application
Production control, management, systems analysis, operational research.

DIEBOLD DEUTSCHLAND GmbH*
6000 Frankfurt am Main, Wiesenhüttenstrasse 18
Telephone: (0611) 23 54 54

Officers
Günther Leue, *General Manager*
Franz-Erich Hänsel, *Director of Management Consulting*
Peter Feuser, *Director of Market Research*
Hans-Jürgen Schwab, *Director of Special Services*

Services Available
Advice, programming, systems analysis.

Fields of Application
Commercial, management, systems analysis, operational research.
Specialized area: Management information systems.

DOBIESS*
Unternehmensberatung für Datenverarbeitung
3 Hannover 1, Heinrichstrasse 37
Telephone: 2 85 88

Also at:
2 Hamburg 70, Litzowstrasse 39
Telephone: 680391

Officer
E. Dobiess

Coding Languages
Assembler, RPG, COBOL.

Services Available
Consultation, programming, education and training, software packages, systems analysis.

Fields of Application
Commercial, scientific, management, accounting.

Training
Short courses in Standard Data Processing in Industry and Commerce, EDP for the Retail Trade, External Data Processing and a general introduction to computers, their cost and function.

DIPL.-ING. WOLFRAM ERDLEN
8031 Seefeld/Obb., Münchenerstrasse 6
Telephone: 7630

Officer
Dipl.-Ing. W. Erdlen

Services Available
Advice, documentation, systems analysis.

Fields of Application
Statistical, commercial, production control, management, systems analysis, operational research.
Specialized areas: Linear programming, investment analysis, structural engineering.

HANS FREIBICHLER AUSBILDUNGSPLANUNG UND DIDAKTISCHE PROGRAMMIERUNG
6900 Heidelberg 1, Ziegelhaeuser Landstrasse 45
Telephone: 06221-46956

Officer
Dipl.-Psych. Hans Freibichler

Coding Languages
Coursewriter, LIDIA, PLANIT, UIL, TUTOR, BASIC, APL, Assembler

Services Available
Advice, programming, education and training. Available to schools, universities, industrial training and education.

Field of Application
Training.
Specialized area: CAI system development and application.

GESELLSCHAFT FÜR ORGANISATIONS- UND PROGRAMMIERUNGSSYSTEME mbH (GOP)*
6200 Wiesbaden, Galileistrasse 10a
Telephone: 06121/52 20 40

Officers
H. Lamberth
L. Beeser

Coding Languages
Assembler, COBOL, PL/1, FORTRAN.

Services Available
Consultation, programming, education and training, operators.

Fields of Application
Cost accounting, commercial, statistical, management information, systems analysis.

Training
Programming courses.

GESELLSCHAFT FÜR PROZESSSTEUERUNGS- UND INFORMATIONSSYSTEME mbH (PSI)
1000 Berlin 31, Katharinenstrasse 19/20
Telephone: 0311-886-80-21

Also at:
7852 Aschaffenburg-Goldbach, Dammer Weg 37
Telephone: 06021-51061

Officers
Dietrich Jaeschke, *General Manager*
Wolfgang Dedner, Hans Rueff, *Managers*

Coding Languages
Assembler, FORTRAN.

Services Available
Advice, programming, education and training, documentation, systems analysis, consulting and engineering.

Fields of Application
Scientific, production control, systems analysis, process control.
Specialized areas: Structural engineering, medical research, real time, process control.

Training
Courses in process control, production control and management.

GUTACKER EDV BERATUNG GmbH
7 Stuttgart 1, Sophienstrasse 19
Telephone: (0711) 642097

Officer
G. Gutacker

Coding Languages
COBOL, PL/1, Assembler, FORTRAN, ALGOL, PROSA, Easycoder, Autocoder, SPS, RPG II.

Services Available
Consultation, programming, education and training, software packages, documentation, systems analysis.

Fields of Application
Commercial, statistical, accounting, management information systems.

Training
Courses in COBOL (14 days), IBM OS (28 days), MIS (30 days).

IKO SOFTWARE SERVICE GmbH
7000 Stuttgart 80, Vaihinger Strasse 49
Telephone: 0711-71-40-06

Officer
Dr.-Ing. Michael Sörensen, *General Manager*

Computer Installation
UNIVAC 1108–operating system: EXEC 8; internal storage: 4,752K bits; magnetic tapes: 2 Uniservo VI/C magnetic discs: 3 FH 432, 1 FH 880, 1 Fastrand III; 2 line printers. *On-line satellite computers*: 1 Univac 9300, 1 Univac 9200, 2 DCT2000.

Coding Languages
FORTRAN, COBOL, ALGOL, Assembler, RPG.

Contemplated Equipment
Increased care storage of 65K words; 8440 disc unit; 2 Uniservo VI/C.

Services Available
Programming, operators, software packages, documentation, systems analysis, engineering. Operate on a remote access and closed shop basis.

Fields of Application
Scientific, systems analysis, engineering.
Specialized area: Structural engineering.

Training
Yearly courses in structural engineering and application software.

Federal Republic of Germany – Consultants

INTEGRATA GmbH
74 Tübingen, Biesingerstrasse 10

Officer
Dr. Heilmann, *Manager*
Dr. Reblin, *Manager*

Services Available
Consultation, operators, preparation of data, programming, software packages, systems analysis, education and training, documentation.

Fields of Application
Statistical, commercial, production control, accounting, management, systems analysis.
Specialized areas: Sales analysis, analysis, payroll, medical research.

Training
Seminars and workshops.

KIENBAUM UNTERNEHMENSBERATUNG GmbH
5270 Gummersbach 1, Postfach 1509, Ahlefelder Strasse 47
Telephone: 02261 77 0 98

Coding Languages
ALGOL, COBOL, FORTRAN, PL/1, Assembler, PROSA, RPG.

Services Available
Advice, preparation of data, programming, software packages, systems analysis, translation of EDP literature.

Fields of Application
Management information systems, operations research, systems planning, etc.

KNIGHT WEGENSTEIN GmbH*
6 Frankfurt am Main, Grueneburgweg 115

Also at:
Düsseldorf, Berliner Allee 47
Telephone: 12257

Services Available
Consultation, operators, preparation of data, programming, software packages, systems analysis.

Fields of Application
Real management information systems, all operating systems, process control.

KÖNIG-UNTERNEHMENSBERATUNG*
7026 Bonlanden/Stuttgart, Postfach 1180
Telephone: 0711/796666

Services Available
Consultation, programming, preparation of data, systems analysis.

Fields of Application
Commercial, production control, accounting, systems analysis.

McKINSEY & CO. INC.
4 Düsseldorf, 12 Jägerhofstrasse
Telephone: (0211) 48 45 61

Coding Languages
FORTRAN, PL/1, COBOL, BASIC.

Services Available
Consultation, programming, software packages, systems analysis, systems design. Operate on a time-sharing basis.

Fields of Application
Commercial, production control, accounting, management, systems analysis, operational research.
Specialized areas: Sales analysis, linear programming, investment, information systems, financial models.

P.A. MANAGEMENT CONSULTANTS GmbH*
6000 Frankfurt am Main, Westendstrasse 18a
Telephone: 72-81-41

Officers
John Wholey, *Director for Germany*
Alan Beaton, *Manager*

Services Available
Consultation, programming, software packages, systems analysis, feasibility studies.

Fields of Application
Commercial, production control, accounting, management, operational research, etc.
Specialized areas: Computer feasibility studies; installation, planning and control.

PEAT, MARWICK, MITCHELL & CO.*
6 Frankfurt am Main, Sandgasse 6
Telephone: 28-56-41

Officer
H. Funnen

Services Available
Consultation, systems analysis.

Fields of Application
Economic studies, general management, scientific management, operations research, industrial engineering, marketing, production and inventory control, information systems, general and cost accounting, data processing and transmission systems, etc.
Specialized areas: Banking, transportation, insurance, government and others.

H.S. PÜHLHORN*
865 Kulmbach, Dr. Martin-Luther-Strasse 17
Telephone: 09221-2522

Also at:
8500 Nürnberg, Schwanenweg 3
Telephone: 0911-590050

Coding Languages
RPG, Assembler, COBOL.

Services Available
Advice, programming, education and training, software packages, documentation, systems analysis.

Fields of Application
Statistical, commercial, production control, accounting, management, systems analysis, operational research.
Specialized area: Management systems.

Federal Republic of Germany – Consultants

KURT SALMON ASSOCIATES GmbH
61 Darmstadt, Wilhelmineplatz 8
Telephone: 21810, 24305

Officer
E. J. Chipps, *Vice-President*

Services Available
Consultation, programming, software packages, systems analysis.

Fields of Application
Management information systems, production control and planning, overall systems analysis, incentives and payroll, forecasting, industrial engineering, advanced analytical methods training, quality control, material utilization, marketing, etc.
Specialized areas: Clothing, textiles and retail industries exclusively.

SYSTEMBERATUNG GmbH
7500 Karlsruhe 41, Brändströmstrasse 13
Telephone: 0721-472278

Officer
Hans-Hermann Böhm, *Manager*

Services Available
Advice, programming, education and training, software packages, systems analysis.

Fields of Application
Production control, accounting, management, systems analysis, operational research.
Specialized areas: Sales analysis, linear programming, investment.

Training
Courses in systems analysis, operations research, accounting and management.

SERVICE BUREAUX

AC-SERVICE GmbH*
605 Offenbach, Strahlenberger Strasse 105-107
Telephone: 0611-886081/85

Computer Installation
BULL GENERAL ELECTRIC GE 415–operating system: MTPS; internal storage: 16K bits; magnetic tapes: 5 MT 21; 1 line printer.

COPE 45–operating system: EXEC 2; internal storage: 8K bits; magnetic tapes: 1 Ampex; 1 line printer. *Remote processing features*: Terminal for remote batch processing.

Coding Languages
Assembler (MAP), COBOL, FORTRAN.

Services Available
Consultation, programming, operators, software packages, documentation, systems analysis. Operate on a closed shop basis.

Fields of Application
Scientific, statistical, commercial, accounting.

AC-SERVICE GESELLSCHAFT FÜR AUTOMATISCHE DATENVERARBEITUNG mbH*
4000 Düsseldorf 1, Marienstrasse 14
Telephone: 353443

Also at:
6000 Frankfurt am Main, Hochstrasse 29
Telephone: 287116

2000 Hamburg 13, Rothenbaumchaussee 58
Telephone: 418004

8000 München 2, Blumenstrasse 48
Telephone: 241654

7000 Stuttgart-Vaihingen, Industriestrasse 15
Telephone: 78-59-51

Officers
Hans Werner Kerscht, *Manager (Düsseldorf)*
Walter Büttner, *Manager (Frankfurt)*
Klaus Kaiser, *Manager (Hamburg)*
Lothar Bergmann, *Manager (Munich)*
Gunter Ziesing, *Manager (Stuttgart)*

Computer Installation
Düsseldorf:
IBM 1410–internal storage: 40K bits; magnetic tape: IBM 7330/01.

Frankfurt:
BULL GENERAL ELECTRIC GE 415-internal storage: 16K bits; magnetic tapes: 5 MTH 201.

Hamburg:
IBM 1401–internal storage: 8K bits; magnetic tapes: 4 IBM 7330/01.

Munich:
BULL GENERAL ELECTRIC GE 415–internal storage: 16K bits; magnetic tapes: 5 MTH 200-01.

Stuttgart:
IBM 1401 (2)–internal storage: 16K bits each; magnetic tapes: 6 IBM 729-02.

Coding Languages
COBOL, FORTRAN, MAKRO (GE), Autocoder:

Services Available
Advice, operators, preparation of data, programming, systems analysis. Operate on a closed shop basis.

Fields of Application
Statistical, commercial, production control, accounting, management.

ADV/ORGA UNTERNEHMENSBERATUNG*
(ADV/ORGA Informationszentrum, ADV-Rechenzentrum)
294 Wilhelmshaven, Virchowstrasse 21
Telephone: 04421-26222

Also at:
29 Oldenburg, Elsässer Strasse 66
Telephone: 0441-25884/5

Computer Installation
IBM 360/25–operating system: DOS; internal storage: 48K bits; magnetic tapes: 4 2401; magnetic discs: 2 2311; 1 line printer.

Coding Languages
Assembler, RPG.

Contemplated Equipment
Same model, including teleprocessing.

Services Available
Programming, software packages, preparation of data, systems analysis. Operate on a self-service, closed and open shop and block time basis.

Fields of Application
Commercial, accounting.
Specialized area: Standard programmes for personal payment and book-keeping.

Training
Full courses for organization and programming; short courses in data organization, programme languages, cost accounting, etc.

ALLGEMEINE ELEKTRICITÄTS-GESELLSCHAFT (AEG-TELEFUNKEN)*
7750 Konstanz, Bücklestrasse 1-5
Telephone: Nr. Durchwahl (07531) 601416, Vermittlung (07531) 601

Also at:
5100 Aachen 1, Lagerhaustrasse 23-27

1000 Berlin 10, Ernst-Reuter-Platz 7

4600 Dortmund, Ernst-Mehlich-Str. 6

6000 Frankfurt am Main 1, Mainzer Landstr. 349

2000 Hamburg-Altona, Paulinenallee 55

3000 Hannover-Linden, Göttinger Chaussee 76

2300 Kiel-Ellerbek, Werfstr. 90

7750 Konstanz, Obere Laube 65

6800 Mannheim, Postfach 2408

8000 München 5, Klenzestr. 57

8500 Nürnberg 2, Gleissbühlstr. 11

7000 Stuttgart-Vaihingen, Industriestr. 62

7900 Ulm, Neue Strasse 113-115

Officers
Ing. A. Friedenstab (Konstanz)

Computer Installation
Konstanz:
TELEFUNKEN TR4 (2)–operating system: MONITOR; internal storage: 32K 48-bit words each; magnetic tapes: 14 Telefunken MDS 257 A3 on-line, 1 Telefunken MDS 252 off-line; magnetic disc: Burroughs; 3 line printers.
TELEFUNKEN TR 440
TELEFUNKEN Analog.

Coding Languages
SUSA, TEXAS, ALGOL, FORTRAN, COBOL.

Services Available
Advice, operators, preparation of data, programming, software packages, systems analysis. Operate on a closed shop basis.

Fields of Application
General programming in all fields of interest for a computer manufacturer.
Specialized area: System programming.

Training
Programming courses for TR4, TR440 and Analog Computer.

AVINER, WEISENER U. GALLER KG*
Elektronische Datenverarbeitung
2 Hamburg 50, Bahrenfelder Steindamm 110
Telephone: 89-81-06

Officers
A. Aviner, *Administration and Sales*
P. Galler, *Software and Programming*
P. Weisener, *EDP Department*

Computer Installation
HONEYWELL H200–internal storage: 16K bits.
HONEYWELL H125–internal storage: 28K bits; magnetic tapes: 4.

Coding Language
Easycoder.

Services Available
Consultation, programming, systems analysis. Operate on an open shop basis.

Fields of Application
Commercial, accounting, management, systems analysis.

DATEN-SERVICE BECK GmbH*
Unterläpder Rechenzentrum
7107 Neckarsulm, Friedrich Ebert Str. 9
Telephone: 6888

Officer
Helmut Beck

Computer Installation
IBM 360/25(2)–internal storage: 49,152 bytes each; magnetic tapes: 1 2415 each; magnetic discs: 3 2311 each; 1 line printer each.

Coding Languages
RPG, Assembler, DOS.

Contemplated Equipment
On-line satellite computers, remote processing features.

Services Available
Advice, operators, preparation of data, programming, systems analysis. Operate on a self-service and time-sharing basis.

Fields of Application
Statistical, commercial, accounting, management, operational research.
Specialized areas: Sales analysis, linear programming, payroll, book-keeping

B-O-G*
6 Frankfurt am Main, Kurfürstenstr. 95

Also at:
28 Bremen, Breitenweg 25

Computer Installation
Frankfurt:
HONEYWELL H200.

Federal Republic of Germany – Service Bureaux

KG KARL-HEINZ BOTH GmbH & CO.*
Gesellschaft für Büroorganisation
4 Düsseldorf, Lindemannstr. 5
Telephone: 67-36-38, 67-26-22, 67-15-79, 67-18-06

Officers
Karl-Heinz Both, *Director*
Günter Edeler
Erich Müller

Services Available
Preparation of data, programming,

Fields of Application
Commercial and industrial.

BÜRO FÜR DATENVERARBEITUNG GmbH*
2000 Hamburg 13, Postfach 1307
Telephone: 5602041

Officers
Peter Horst Schenck, *Director*
Klaus Enxing, *Officer for Organization and Programming*.

Computer Installation
HONEYWELL H2200–internal storage: 131 K bits: magnetic tapes: 8 Honeywell 204 B4; magnetic discs: 2 253B; 2 line printers.

Coding Languages
Easycoder, COBOL.

Contemplated Equipment
HONEYWELL H3200

Services Available
Advice, preparation of data, programming. Operate on a closed shop and block time basis.

Fields of Application
Commercial, accounting.

CAE DATENVERARBEITUNGSSYSTEME FÜR WISSENSCHAFT UND WIRTSCHAFT GmbH*
6 Frankfurt am Main-Niederrad 1,
Lyoner Strasse, C11 Haus
Telephone: (0611) 66051

Officer
Gabriel Warocquier, *Business Manager*

CENTURY COMPUTER DEUTSCHLAND GmbH*
605 Offenbach, Marktplatz 6-8
Telephone: 883985

Also at:
Cologne, Munich, Berlin, Hamburg and Milan (Italy).

Officers
A. E. Baron, *President*
Dr. H. Lob, *General Director*

Computer Installation
HONEYWELL H1250 (3)–operating systems: MOS, DOS; internal storage: 131K bits; magnetic tapes: 8; magnetic discs: 4; 1 line printer.

HONEYWELL H200–operating systems: MOS, DOS; internal storage: 65K bits; magnetic tapes: 8; magnetic discs: 4; 1 line printer.

Coding Languages
COBOL H, F, I.

Services Available
Consultation, programming, operators, software packages, documentation, preparation of data, systems analysis. Operate on a self-service, open shop and block time basis.

Fields of Application
Statistical, commercial, accounting, management, systems.

COMBYTE SOFTWARE GmbH
645 Hanau, Postfach 171
Telephone: 06181-251663

Officers
Axel Schwab, *President*
H.-P. Jost, *Vice-President*

Services Available
Advice, programming, software packages, systems analysis. Operate on a block time basis.

Fields of Application
Statistical, commercial, accounting, management, systems analysis, operational research.

CONTROL DATA GmbH*
6 Frankfurt am Main, Niddastrasse 40
Telephone: 71231

Officer
Fred W. Zeitler, *Director*

Computer Installation
CDC 6600–operating system: SCOPE; internal storage: 131K 60-bit words; magnetic tapes: 4 CD 604; magnetic discs: 1 CD 6638; 2 line printers. *Remote processing features*: Terminals.

CDC 3300–operating system: MASTER; internal storage: 65K 24-bit words; magnetic tapes: 7 CD 604; magnetic discs: 6 CD 854; 1 line printer.

CDC 8092–operating system: TAS, BALD, NIMP; internal storage: 4K 8-bit words; magnetic tapes; 1 CD 604 (shared with CDC 3300).

Coding Languages
COMPASS, FORTRAN, COBOL, ALGOL, SORT/MERGE, SIMSCRIPT.

Services Available
Advice, programming, software packages, preparation of data, systems analysis. Operate on a remote access and closed shop basis.

Fields of Application
Scientific, commercial, accounting, operational research, market research.
Specialized areas: Linear programming, payroll, structural engineering, questionnaire analysis.

DEMAG EDV-SERVICE GmbH
4100 Duisburg, Wolfgang-Reuter-Platz
Telephone: 02131-605-2339

Officers
Dr. Wolfgang Fassbender, *General Manager*
Günter Neugebauer, *Sales Manager*
Dr. Roland Schneider, *Systems Manager*

Computer Installation
UNIVAC 1108–operating system: EXEC 8; internal storage: 196K bits; magnetic tapes: 12; magnetic discs: 1 Fastrand; 2 line printers. *On-line satellite computer*: 9003. *Remote processing features*: 1 9002, 3 DCT 2000.

Federal Republic of Germany – Service Bureaux

Coding Languages
COBOL, FORTRAN, DPS.

Services Available
Programming, education and training, software packages, systems analysis, facilities management. Operate on a remote access, closed shop, block time and time-sharing basis.

Fields of Application
Scientific, commercial, production control, accounting, management, systems analysis, operational research.
Specialized area: Software development for systems design and realization.

Training
Courses in COBOL, FORTRAN, DPS, decision tables, EDP project management and methods for analysing and realizing by DPS.

DEUTSCHE BAU- UND BODENBANK AG
Rechenzentrum
6500 Mainz, Im Münchfel 1-5
Telephone: 06131-30-11

Computer Installation
IBM 360/40 – operating system: DOS; internal storage: 1,048,576 bits; magnetic tapes: 12 2401, 3420; magnetic discs: 2 2319; 1 line printer.

IBM 370/145 – operating system: DOS; internal storage: 3,145,728 bits; magnetic tapes and discs: as above; 2 line printers.

Coding Language
Assembler

Contemplated Equipment
4 IBM 3333.

Services Available
Software packages, preparation of data, systems analysis. Operate on a closed shop basis.

Fields of Application
Commercial, accounting.
Specialized area: Payroll.

DEUTSCHE BAUGRUPPE GmbH & CO.
8000 Munich 21, Westendstrasse 170
Telephone: 571073

Officers
Gerhard Schwab, *Data Processing Manager*
Josef Moissl, *Sales Manager*

Computer Installation
UNIVAC 1106 – operating system: EXEC 8; internal storage: 131K 36-bit words; magnetic tapes: 4 Univac 16, 4 Univac 12; magnetic discs: 6 8414; 2 line printers. *On-line satellite computer*: Univac 9300.

Coding Languages
FORTRAN, COBOL, RPG.

Contemplated Equipment
Remote processing features.

Services Available
Advice, programming, education and training, documentation, systems analysis. Operate on a closed shop and time-sharing basis.

Fields of Application
Scientific, commercial, accounting, management, systems analysis.
Specialized areas: Analysis, payroll, structural engineering.

Training
Users' training only.

DEUTSCHE UTIMACO GmbH*
6 Frankfurt am Main, Hanauer Land Str. 423a
Telephone: 0611-411004

Officer
Garben, *Manager of the Service Bureau*

Computer Installation
BULL GENERAL ELECTRIC GAMMA 10 – internal storage: 4K bits; 1 line printer.

HONEYWELL H125 – operating system: MOD 1; internal storage: 20K bits; magnetic tapes: 4 204B; 1 line printer.

Coding Language
COBOL D.

Services Available
Preparation of data, programming. Operate on an open shop basis.

Fields of Application
Commercial, statistical.

EDP RESOURCES DEUTSCHLAND AG*
638 Bad Homburg v.d.H., Louisenstrasse 98
Telephone: (06172) 2 10 43

Also at:
2 Hamburg 1, Schauenburger Strasse 55-57
Telephone: (0411) 366617

4 Düsseldorf, Kosterstrasse 45
Telephone: (0211) 358830

Officer
K. W. Hackel, *President*

Computer Installation
Several IBM 360 model 25, 30, 40 and 50 are available through the operational leasing business.

Services Available
Consultation, programming, education and training, software packages, systems analysis.

Fields of Application
Systems analysis and development, scientific, statistical, operational research, commercial, accounting, production control.

ELEKTRONISCHE DATENVERARBEITUNGS-GESELLSCHAFT mbH (EDV)*
Wuppertalbarmen, Erichstr. 4

Computer Installation
NCR 315.

Federal Republic of Germany – Service Bureaux

ELEKTRONISCHES RECHENZENTRUM*
850 Bayreuth, Krenz 25
Telephone: 0921-5793

Officers
Herr Zink
Frau Albrecht
Frau Potzel

Computer Installation
IBM 1130–internal storage: 131,072 bits; magnetic discs: 1 IBM 1131; 1 line printer.

Coding Languages
FORTRAN, SAP.

Contemplated Equipment
Second disc unit, IBM 1403 printer.

Services Available
Advice, operators, preparation of data, programming, software packages, systems analysis. Operate on a self-service and open shop basis.

Fields of Application
Commercial, production control, accounting, scientific.

ELEKTRONISCHES RECHENZENTRUM GmbH*
48 Bielefeld, Detmolder Str. 108
Telephone: 42704

Officers
Udo Bussemas, *Director*
Hans Bussemas, *Director*
Udo Landwehr

Computer Installation
SIEMENS 4004/25–internal storage: 16K bits; magnetic tapes: 4.

Coding Languages
Assembler, LPG.

Services Available
Advice, operators, programming. Operate on an open shop basis.

Fields of Application
Commercial, accounting.

EX DATA GmbH*
8500 Nürnberg, Marienstrasse 6
Telephone: 57 32 79

Officers
H. B., *Managing Director*
P. F., *Director of the Computer Centre*

Computer Installation
ICL 1903–operating system: EXEC; internal storage: 768K bits; magnetic tapes: 6; 1 line printer.

ICL 1904–operating system: EXEC; internal storage: 768K bits; magnetic tapes: 6; 1 line printer.

Coding Language
COBOL.

Contemplated Equipment
ICL–MEDS 240 million characters; IBM 360/20 for computer letters.

Service Available
Operators. Operate on a closed shop basis. Available for standard programmes to all customers without own EDP.

Fields of Application
Statistical, commercial, accounting, management, systems analysis.
Specialized area: External data processing.

FACIT GmbH*
EDB-Rechenzentrale
C Düsseldorf-Holthausen, Bonner Strasse 117
Telephone: 79-11-01

Officer
Lars Rosberg, *Managing Director*

Coding Language
ALGOL 60.

Services Available
Operators, preparation of data, programming, systems analysis. Operate on a closed shop basis.

Fields of Application
Applied mathematics, technology, commercial data processing.

GEMINI COMPUTER SYSTEMS DEUTSCHLAND GmbH*
6000 Frankfurt am Main, Meisengasse 8
Telephone: 0611/285497

Also at:
4000 Düsseldorf, Grafenbergallee 57
8000 München, Dachauer Strasse 50
2200 Elmshorn, Klostersande 50

Officers
S. Hoppe, *General Manager*
H. G. Martin, *Marketing Manager*

Services Available
Consultation, programming, education and training, operators, software packages, documentation, systems analysis.

Fields of Application
Basic software (languages development, compiler development, operating systems development etc.), software application for scientific, statistical, commercial, production control, accounting, process control purposes, operational research on respective systems analysis.

Training
Courses in PL/1.

HENKEL & CIE. AG
4133 Pratteln, Hardmatt 55
Téléphone: 061/81 63 31

Dirigeant
Dr. H. J. Gadient, *Directeur*

Equipement
HONEYWELL H120–système d'opération: MOD 1; mémoire interne: 20,479 mots; bandes magnétiques: 4 204B16; 1 imprimante.

Langages de Programmation
Easycoder, COBOL.

Services Fournis
Programmation, opérateurs, documentation, systems analysis. Fonctionnement en self-service et à porte fermée.

Federal Republic of Germany – Service Bureaux

Domaines d'Application
Statistique, commercial, contrôle de production, comptabilité, systems analysis, recherche operationnelle.

HEWLETT-PACKARD VERTRIEBSGESELLSCHAFT mbH
6000 Frankfurt am Main 56, Berliner Strasse 117
Telephone: 0611-50041

Officers
Karl Döring, *Country Manager*
Wilhelm Graffmann, *Government and Public Relations Manager*

Computer Installation
HEWLETT PACKARD 3000–operating systems: Time-sharing, Batch, RTE; internal storage: 128K bytes; magnetic tapes: HP7970; magnetic discs: 8 HP7900, ISS; 2 line printers. *On-line satellite computer*: HP2000. *Remote processing features*: RJE.
HEWLETT PACKARD 2000–operating systems: Time-sharing, Batch, RTE; internal storage: 64K bytes; magnetic tapes: HP7970; magnetic discs: HP7900; 3 line printers. *Remote processing features*: RJE.

Coding Languages
Assembler, FORTRAN II and IV, ALGOL 60, SNOBOL, BASIC, SPL, BASIC 3000.

Services Available
Advice, programming, education and training, software packages, preparation of data, systems analysis. Operate on a self-service and time-sharing basis.

Fields of Application
Scientific, statistical, production control, management, systems analysis, operational research.
Specialized areas: Structural engineering, medical research, automatic test systems.

Training
Courses for customers in system programming (usually two weeks).

HONEYWELL BULL GmbH*
5 Köln 1, Hohenstaufenring 62
Telephone: 0221-20371

IBAT–BÜRO FÜR ELEKTRONISCHE DATENVERARBEITUNG–A. TRIESTRAM*
43 Essen, Alfredstrasse 64
Telephone: 77 84 41/42

Officer
A. Triestram

Coding Languages
COBOL, FORTRAN, PL/1, machine languages.

Services Available
Consultation, programming, software packages, documentation, preparation of data, systems analysis.

Fields of Application
Commercial (wages and earnings systems, book-keeping, invoicing, statistics, budget control), technical (manufacturing control, process control, optimization problems, quality control).
Specialized areas: IDS-COBOL (Integrated Data Store), process control (mainly Siemens computers).

ID ANWENDUNGS–SOFTWARE FORSCHUNGS–ZENTRUM GmbH
3353 Bad Gandersheim/Harz
Telephone: 05382-2060

Also at:
1 Berlin 15, Bundesallee 22

Officers
Dr. K. Börning
J. P. Gutsch

Coding Languages
COBOL, FORTRAN, Assembler, RPG, PL/1.

Services Available
Consultation, programming, education and training, software packages, documentation, systems analysis. Operate on a block time and time-sharing basis.

Fields of Application
Statistical, commercial, production control, accounting, management, systems analysis, operational research.
Specialized areas: Building industry and housing.

IFU*
Hamburg

Officers
Dr. R. Vieweg
P. Sass

Computer Installation
UNIVAC 9300–operating system: DOS; internal storage: 32K bits; magnetic tapes: 5 UNIVAC IV; 1 line printer.

Coding Languages
Assembler, COBOL, RPG.

Services Available
Consultation, programming, education and training, operators, software packages, documentation, preparation of data, systems analysis. Operate on a self-service, closed shop and block time basis.

Fields of Application
Statistical, commercial, production control, accounting, management, systems analysis, operational research.
Specialized area: Programme packages for shipping agency.

INTERLOGIC GESELLSCHAFT FÜR COMPUTER-UND PROGRAMM-SERVICE mbH & CO. KG
4816 Sennestadt, Bielefelder Strasse 14.
Telephone: 05205-6897.

Officers
Karl Friedrich Flockenhaus, Andreas Ketels, *Partners*

Coding Languages
FORTRAN, COBOL, PL/1, Assembler.

Services Available
Programming, software packages, preparation of data, systems analysis.

Fields of Application
Scientific, statistical, management, systems analysis, operational research.
Specialized areas: Sales analysis, analysis.

Federal Republic of Germany – Service Bureaux

**INTERNATIONALE BÜRO MASCHINEN GmbH
(IBM DEUTSCHLAND)***
IBM Data Processing Centres
Sindelfingen-Wuertt, Tuebinger Allee No. 49-51
Telephone: Boblingen 6611

Also:
IBM Rechenzentrum
8900 Augsburg, Ulrichsplatz 4
Telephone: (0821) 2-30-71

IBM Rechenzentrum
1000 Berlin 10, Ernst-Reuter-Platz 2
Telephone: (0311) 310331

IBM Rechenzentrum
4800 Bielefeld, Friedrich-Ebert-Strasse 14
Telephone: (0521) 3-36-61

IBM Rechenzentrum
5300 Bonn, Maargasse 15
Telephone: (02221) 5-69-41

IBM Rechenzentrum
2800 Bremen, Faulenstrasse 2-12
Telephone: (0421) 31-49-91

IBM Distrikt Rechenzentrum
4600 Dortmund, Südwall 37-39
Telephone: (0231) 52-01-01

IBM Distrikt Rechenzentrum
4000 Düsseldorf, Berliner Allee 52, Postfach 4420
Telephone: (0211) 87731

IBM Rechenzentrum
4300 Essen, Huyssenallee 86
Telephone: (02141) 2-08-31

IBM Distrikt Rechenzentrum
6000 Frankfurt am Main, Wilhelm-Leuschnerstrasse 32, Postfach 16 464
Telephone: (0611) 26-051

IBM Rechenzentrum
7800 Freiburg, Grünwälderstrasse 10-14
Telephone: (0761) 3-61-44

IBM Distrikt Rechenzentrum
2000 Hamburg 11, Ost-West-Strasse 23
Telephone: (0411) 3-01-11

IBM Rechenzentrum
3000 Hannover, Goseriede 12
Telephone: (0511) 1-84-71

IBM Rechenzentrum
7500 Karlsruhe, Karlstrasse 45
Telephone: (0721) 2-79-51

IBM Rechenzentrum
3500 Kassel, Kurt-Schumacher-Strasse 31
Telephone: (0561) 1-95-51

IBM Rechenzentrum
2300 Kiel, Andreas-Gayk-Strasse 13
Telephone: (0431) 5-15-51

IBM Rechenzentrum
5000 Köln, Gürzenichstrasse 27
Telephone: (0221) 23-35-46

IBM Rechenzentrum
6800 Mannheim, L 15, 15-16
Telephone: (0621) 29-91

IBM Distrikt Rechenzentrum
8000 München, Arnulfstrasse 101
Telephone: (0811) 5-16-10-04

IBM Rechenzentrum
8500 Nürnberg, Bayreuther Strasse 6a
Telephone: (0911) 53-32-33

IBM Rechenzentrum
6600 Saarbrücken, Am Neumarkt 15
Telephone: (0681) 2-45-61

IBM Distrikt Rechenzentrum
7000 Stuttgart, Ossietzkystrasse 7-9
Telephone: (0711) 22-12-61

IBM Rechenzentrum
79 Ulm, Glöcklerstrasse 1
Telephone: (0731) 6-15-51

IBM Rechenzentrum
5600 Wuppertal, Wall 29
Telephone: (02121) 45-04-71

Officer
K. Horbelt, *Manager*

Computer Installation
Augsburg, Bonn, Bremen, Essen, Freiburg, Karlsruhe, Kassel, Kiel, Mannheim, Nürnberg, Saarbrücken, Ulm and Wuppertal:
IBM 360/20 (13)–internal storage: 16K bits each; 1 line printer each.

Berlin:
IBM 360/40–operating system: DOS; internal storage: 128K bits; magnetic tapes: 8 IBM 2401/2; magnetic discs: 5 IBM 2311/1; 2 line printers.

Bielefeld:
IBM 360/40–operating system: DOS; internal storage: 128K bits; magnetic tapes: 5 IBM 2401/2; magnetic discs: 3 IBM 2311/1; 2 line printers.

Dortmund and Stuttgart:
IBM 360/40 (2)–operating system: DOS; internal storage: 128K bits each; magnetic tapes: 8 IBM 2401/2 each; magnetic discs: 5 IBM 2311/1 each; 2 line printers each.

IBM 360/50 (2)–operating system: DOS; internal storage: 256K bits each; magnetic tapes: 8 IBM 2401/5 each; magnetic discs: IBM 2314/1 each; 2 line printers each.

Düsseldorf:
IBM 360/65–operating system: ASP; internal storage: 512K bits; magnetic tapes: 12 IBM 2401 3; magnetic discs: 2 IBM 2301/1, 8 IBM 2311/1; 3 line printers. *On-line satellite computer*: IBM 360/50. *Remote processing features*: 2 IBM 2701/1.

IBM 360/40–operating systems: DOS, RAX; internal storage: 128K bits; magnetic tapes: 5 IBM 2401/2; magnetic discs: 3 IBM 2311/1; 1 line printer.

Frankfurt, München:
IBM 360/40 (2)–operating system: DOS; internal storage: 128K bits each; magnetic tapes: 8 IBM 2401/2 each; magnetic discs: 5 IBM 2311/1 each; 2 line printers each.

IBM 360/50 (2)–operating system: DOS; internal storage: 256K bits each; magnetic tapes: 8 IBM 2401/5 each; magnetic discs: 6 IBM 2311/1 each; 2 line printers each.

Hamburg:
IBM 360/40–operating system: DOS; internal storage: 128K bits; magnetic tapes: 5 IBM 2401/2; magnetic discs: 4 IBM 2311/1; 2 line printers.

IBM 360/50–operating system: DOS; internal storage: 256K bits; magnetic tapes: 8 IBM 2401/5; magnetic discs: 6 IBM 2311/1; 2 line printers.

Hannover:
IBM 360/40–operating system: DOS; internal storage: 128K bits; magnetic tapes: 8 IBM 2401/2; magnetic discs: 4 IBM 2311/1; 2 line printers.

Köln:
IBM 360/40–operating system: DOS; internal storage: 128K bits; magnetic tapes: 5 IBM 2401/2; magnetic discs: 5 IBM 2311/1; 2 line printers.

Coding Languages
COBOL, FORTRAN, ALGOL, PL/1, SPS, Assembler, FARGO, RPG, STAR, IOCS, Matrix Interpretation System, etc.

Services Available
Advice, operators, preparation of data, programming, software packages, systems analysis. Operate on a self-service, closed shop, remote access, and time-sharing basis.

Fields of Application
Scientific, commercial, accounting, statistical, production control, operational research.

Training
DP school for customers and prospects.

INSTITUT FÜR DATENSYSTEM-ENTWICKLUNG EDV-BERATUNG
2800 Bremen 44, Zum Panrepel 10
Telephone: 42 10 39

Officers
J. P. Schoon
H. Stodte
H. Reul

Computer Installation
SIEMENS 4004–135/2–operating system: PBS; internal storage: 192K bytes; magnetic tapes; magnetic discs.

Coding Languages
Assembler, COBOL, PL/1, FORTRAN.

Services Available
Consultation, programming, education and training, software packages, documentation, systems analysis. Operate on a self-service, closed shop and block time basis.

Fields of Application
Systems analysis, accounting, production control, statistical, commercial.
Specialized areas: Systems engineering and methods, computer efficiency, standard programming logic (SPL)

ITT DATENSERVICE
Geschäftsbereich der Deutsche ITT Industries GmbH
7000 Stuttgart 30, Kurze Strasse 8
Telephone: 0711-89161

Also at:
Berlin, Frankfurt

Officers
C. Müller, *General Manager*
E. Erlen, *Controller*

Computer Installation
IBM 370/145 and IBM 370/155–operating systems: OS/MFT, OS/MVT, HASP; internal storage: 384K bytes (IBM 370/145), 1,024K bytes (IBM 370/155); magnetic tapes: 8 3420-005, 4 3420-007; magnetic discs: 22 3330; 4 line printers.

IBM 360/40–operating system: OS, DOS; internal storage: 256K bytes; magnetic tapes: 4 2401-005; magnetic discs: 8 2314; 1 line printer.

Coding Languages
COBOL, Assembler.

Contemplated Equipment
IBM 370/158.

Services Available
Programming, education and training, software packages, documentation, preparation of data, systems analysis. Operate on a remote access, closed shop and block time basis.

Fields of Application
Statistical, commercial, accounting, management, systems analysis, real time systems.
Specialized areas: Sales analysis, analysis, payroll, data base retrieval systems, development of standard packages.

Training
Courses of commercial applications: accounting, production, stock control, management, scientific.

RECHENZENTRUM KOCH*
69 Heidelberg, Berliner Str. 14

MATHEMATISCHER BERATUNGS- UND PROGRAMMIERUNGSDIENST GmbH (MBP)
4600 Dortmund, Kleppingstrasse 26
Telephone: 0231/528697-99

Officers
Dr. Hans Pärli, *Manager*
Dr. Christoph Heinrich, *Manager*

Coding Languages
ALGOL, COBOL, FORTRAN, PL/1, Assembler.

Services Available
Consultation, programming, education and training, software packages, systems analysis. Operate on a closed shop basis.

Fields of Application
Scientific, statistical, commercial, production control, accounting, management, systems analysis, operational research.
Specialized areas: Sales analysis, linear programming, investment, analysis, payroll, structural engineering, medical research, civil engineering, process control.

Training
A multi-media course for EDP programmers and system analyst beginners; other EDP courses to suit customers' requirements.

Federal Republic of Germany – Service Bureaux

MESSERSCHMITT-BOELKOW-BLOHM GmbH
Dynamics Division, Cybernetics, EDV-Service Software
8000 Munich 80, Postfach 80 11 49
Telephone: 0811-6000-2403

Officers
L. Boelkow, *President*
G. Kuhlo, *Head of Dynamics Division*
W. Hagenbucher, *Head of Subdivision Cybernetics*

Computer Installation
IBM 370/165—operating system: OS-MVT; internal storage: 1,536K bits; magnetic tapes: 15 3420; magnetic discs: 16 3330; 6 line printers. *Remote processing features*: 1 2780, 1 2916.

IBM 370/145—operating systems: DOS, OS-MFT; internal storage: 384K bits.
IBM 360/40.
IBM 360/25.

Coding Languages
FORTRAN, PL/1, COBOL, etc.

Services Available
Advice, programming, software packages, systems analysis, computing, drafting and plotting service. Operate on a closed shop and time-sharing basis.

Fields of Application
Scientific, production control, systems analysis, operational research, graphical data processing.
Specialized areas: Linear programming, structural engineering, computer aided design, architecture.

METRA DIVO*
Informatics Division
6 Frankfurt am Main, Am Eisernen Schlag 31
Telephone: 520061

Officers
Hr. Dr. Dippel, Hr. Reul, *Directors of Informatics Division*
Hr. Exner, *Director of Computer Centre*

Computer Installation
SIEMENS 4004/45-F—operating system: PBS; internal storage: 131,072 bytes; magnetic tapes: 1 442-2-9; magnetic discs: 4 564; 1 line printer.

Services Available
Consultation, programming, education and training, operators, software packages, documentation, preparation of data, systems analysis. Operate on a closed shop basis.

Fields of Application
Development of business applications of software and basic software, including systems analysis, and operations research; development of generalized data bank systems.
Specialized areas: Production control, programme generators.

NATIONAL REGISTRIER KASSEN GmbH*
Rechenzentrum
6 Frankfurt am Main, Baseler Str. 35-37
Telephone: 230304

Also at:
85 Augsburg, Ulmer Str. 160
Telephone: 40851

1 Berlin 44, Thiemannstr. 1-11
Telephone: 68781

2 Hamburg 22, Winterhude Weg 72
Telephone: 2201146

Officers
J. Krieter, *Division Manager*
B. Raffel, *Assistant Division Manager*
S. Hayder, *Manager (Administration)*
H. Jarisch, *Manager (Hamburg)*
G. Lorch, *Manager (DC Berlin)*
D. Schädlich, *Manager (DC Frankfurt)*
J. Scheiwe, *Manager (DC Augsburg)*

Computer Installation
Hamburg:
NCR 315—internal storage: 240K bits; magnetic tapes: 7; 1 line printer.

Berlin:
NCR 315—internal storage: 240K bits; magnetic tapes: 6; 1 line printer.

Frankfurt:
NCR 315—internal storage: 240K bits; magnetic tapes: 7; 1 line printer.

Augsburg:
NCR 315—internal storage: 240K bits; magnetic tapes: 6; 1 line printer.

NCR 315—internal storage: 240K bits; magnetic tapes: 6; 1 line printer.

Coding Languages
NEAT, preferably BEST.

Services Available
Advice, operators, preparation of data, programming, systems analysis. Operate on a self-service and closed shop basis.

Fields of Application
Commercial, financial, stock control, sales statistics, invoicing, accounting.
Specialized area: Optical reading of journal tapes.

JOSEF NIEDERMAIR MÜNCHEN (NM-IDV)
Organisationsberatung für Integrierte Datenverarbeitung
8000 Munich 71, Becker-Gundahl-Strasse 3
Telephone: 089-78-12-62

Officer
Josef Niedermair

Computer Installation
PDP-11—internal storage: 23,632 bits; magnetic tapes: 25; magnetic discs: 20; 8 line printers.
UNIVAC 1108—details included above.
UNIVAC 1106—details included above.
IBM 370/155—details included above.
IBM 370/135—details included above.
SINGER 10—details included above.

Coding Languages
Assembler, COBOL, BASIC, FORTRAN, ALGOL, DPS.

Services Available
Advice, programming, education and training, operators, software packages, documentation, preparation of data, systems analysis, hardware interfaces. Operate on a self-service, remote access, closed shop, block time, open shop and time-sharing basis.

Fields of Application
Scientific, statistical, commercial, production control, accounting, management, systems analysis, operational research, facilities management.
Specialized areas: Sales analysis, linear programming, investment analysis, payroll, structural engineering, medical research, automatic processing.

Federal Republic of Germany — Service Bureaux

Training
Special courses in organization, systems analysis and programming.

PRAKLA GmbH*
3 Hannover, Haarstr. 5
Telephone: 0511-80721

Computer Installation
CDC 3300—internal storage: 786,432 bits; magnetic tapes: 4 9-track, 1 7-track, 1 21-track; magnetic discs: 1 CDC 841/3; 1 line printer.

CDC 3300—internal storage: 393,216 bits; magnetic tapes: 4 9-track; magnetic discs: 2 CD 854.

CDC 3200—internal storage: 393,216 bits; magnetic tapes: 4 9-track, 1 7-track; magnetic discs: 2 CD 854.

CDC 3200—internal storage: 393,216 bits; magnetic tapes: 4 9-track, 1 21-track; magnetic discs: 2 CD 854.

TIAC APC 980 C—internal storage: 131,072 bits; magnetic tapes: 2 9-track, 2 7-track, 1 21-track.

ELLIOTT 803B—internal storage: 319,488 bits.

Coding Languages
COMPASS, COBOL, FORTRAN, Machine Code, Autocode.

Services Available
Consultation, preparation of data. Operate on a self-service and closed shop basis.

Fields of Application
Scientific, commercial.
Specialized area: Applied geophysics.

Training
Introduction to digital seismic processing (30-40 hours).

PRODATA—INTERNATIONAL DATENVERARBEITUNG GmbH*
6 Frankfurt am Main, Eschersheimer Landstrasse 60/62
Telephone: 55 03 55

Officer
A. W. Kölb, *Executive Manager*

Computer Installation
SIEMENS 4004/35—operating systems: DOS, TDOS; internal storage: 64K bits; magnetic tapes: 4; magnetic discs: 3; 1 line printer.

Coding Languages
EBCDIC, PL/1, RPG, COBOL, FORTRAN, Assembler.

Services Available
Consultation, programming, education and training, operators, software packages, documentation, preparation of data, systems analysis. Operate on a self-service closed and open shop, remote access, block time and time-sharing basis.

Fields of Application
Production, commercial, service, scientific.

Training
Seminars for operators, programmers and systems analysts.

RECHEN- UND ENTWICKLUNGSINSTITUT FÜR EDV IM BAUWESEN
7000 Stuttgart 80 (Vaihingen), Schulze-Delitzsch-Strasse 28
Telephone: 0711-73 30 67

Officers
Dr. Klein
Dr. Schade
Herr Thomas

Computer Installation
SIEMENS 4004/55G—operating system: TDOS/PBS; internal storage: 2,096K bits; magnetic tapes: 2 4004/432, 4 4004/4443; magnetic discs 5 4004/5645, 5 4004/4581; 2 line printers.

Coding Languages
FORTRAN IV, COBOL, Assembler, FORTRAN II, SPS, ALGOL.

Services Available
Advice, operators, preparation of data, programming, systems analysis. Operate on a closed shop and remote access basis.

Fields of Application
Commercial, operational research, civil engineering.

RECHENZENTRALE FÜR WIRTSCHAFT UND VERWALTUNG (RWV)*
43 Essen-Stoppenberg, Ernestinenstrasse 60

Computer Installation
HONEYWELL H200.

SIEMENS AG*
Wernerwerk für Telegrafen- und Signaltechnik,
Werk für Datenverarbeitung, DV-Rechenzentrum
8000 München 25, Hofmannstr. 51
Telephone: 722-2486

European subsidiaries: Vienna (Austria); Brussels (Belgium); Copenhagen (Denmark); Paris (France); Milan (Italy); The Hague (Netherlands); Madrid (Spain); Fahrweid (Switzerland);

Computer Installation
Rechenzentrum II:
SIEMENS 2002—internal storage: 15K bits; magnetic tapes: 3; 1 line printer.

Rechenzentrum III and V:
SIEMENS 3003 (2)—internal storage: 16K bits each; magnetic tapes; 1 line printer each.

Rechenzentrum VII:
SIEMENS 4004/45—internal storage: 262K bits; magnetic tapes: 5; 1 line printer.

Coding Languages
Assembler, COBOL, FORTRAN, ALGOL.

Services Available
Advice, operators, programming, software packages, systems analysis. Operate on a self-service, open shop and block time basis.

Fields of Application
Scientific, statistical, commercial.

SPERRY RAND GmbH*
Geschäftsbereich Univac
6 Frankfurt am Main, Neue Mainzer Strasse 57
Telephone: 21961

Rechenzentrum Wuppertal
56 Wuppertal-E, Herzogstrasse 32
Telephone: 44 50 27

Rechenzentrum Stuttgart
7 Stuttgart-Vaihingen, Pfaffenwaldring 27
Telephone: 68 10 39

Computer Installation
Frankfurt:
UNIVAC 9400.
Wuppertal:
UNIVAC 1108.
Stuttgart
UNIVAC 1107.

DR. SUCHAN RATIO-DATA GmbH
694 Weinheim, Konrad-Adenauer-Strasse 1
Telephone: (06201) 2022

Officers
Dr. Hans Suchan, *Managing Director*
W. Pfeifer, *Systems Engineer*
N. J. Modi, *Consultant*

Computer Installation
IBM SYSTEM/3, MODEL 10—internal storage: 16K bits; magnetic discs: 1; 1 line printer.

Coding Language
RPG II.

Contemplated Equipment
Teleprocessing equipment; magnetic discs.

Services Available
Advice, programming, software packages, preparation of data. Operate on a closed shop basis.

Fields of Application
Commercial, accounting, management.
Specialized area: Analysis.

TREUGA DATENSERVICE NEUY KG*
62 Wiesbaden, Webergasse 12
Telephone: 780-90

Also at:
2 Hamburg 26, Normannenweg 12

Officers
Edith Neuy, *President*
Günter Boes, *General Manager*

Computer Installation
UNIVAC 9200—internal storage: 16K bits; magnetic discs: 4; 1 line printer.

Coding Languages
RPG, Assembler.

Contemplated Equipment
Magnetic tapes.

Services Available
Advice, programming. Operate on an open shop basis.

Fields of Application
Commercial, accounting.

GHANA

UNIVERSITIES

UNIVERSITY OF GHANA
Computer Science Unit
P.O. Box 65, Legon, Accra
Telephone: 75381

Officer
Prof. John R. Koster, *Acting Head of Computer Science Unit*

Computer Installation
IBM 1620—internal storage: 360K bits.
IBM 360/20—1 line printer.

Coding Languages
FORTRAN II, SPS, RPG.

Contemplated Equipment
IBM 1130 with 512K bits, 3 disc drives, 1 line printer.

Services Available
Advice, programming, education and training, preparation of data. Operate on a self-service and closed shop basis.

Fields of Application
Scientific, statistical, accounting.

Training
Courses in operating and programming; diploma in computer science.

UNIVERSITY OF SCIENCE AND TECHNOLOGY*
University Post Office, Kumasi, Ashanti
Telephone: 3201-3210

Officer
Prof. N. R. Smith, *Head of the Department of Mechanical Engineering*

Computer Installation
IBM 1620—internal storage: Binary Coded Decimal 60K, approximately equivalent to 200K bits.

Coding Languages
FORTRAN, FORTRAN II, SPS.

Contemplated Equipment
ICL 1902A.

Services Available
Consultation, programming, education and training. Operate on a self-service basis. Available to staff, students and Government research institutions; not available for commercial work.

Fields of Application
Scientific, technical, statistical.

Training
Student training in computation. Short courses, usually on FORTRAN, for staff and scientific workers.

Greece — Universities

GOVERNMENT ESTABLISHMENTS

OFFICE OF THE NATIONAL REDEMPTION COUNCIL (N.R.C.)
Management Services Division
P.O. Box 1627, Accra
Telephone: Accra 65461

Officers
F. W. Beecham, *Deputy Secretary to N. R. C.*
E. K. Katakity, *Principal Secretary*

Services Available
Advice. Available to public organizations only.

WEST AFRICAN EXAMINATIONS COUNCIL
P.O. Box 917, Accra

Also at:
Private Mail Bag 1022, Yaba, Lagos, Nigeria

Officer
J. Nettey, *Computer Operations Manager*

Computer Installation
IBM 360/20–operating system: TPS; internal storage: 16K bits; magnetic tapes: 4 2415; 1 line printer. *Remote processing features.*

Coding Languages
RPG, BAL, PCU.

Services Available
Advice, programming, operators. Operate on a self-service basis. Available only to educational establishments.

Field of Application
Systems analysis.
Specialized area: Processing and analysis of examination results.

SERVICE BUREAU

IBM WORLD TRADE CORPORATION
Dakmak House, Kojo Thompson Road, P.O. Box 1507, Accra
Telephone: 66201

Officer
J. D. Fummey, *Branch Manager*

Computer Installation
IBM 360/30–operating system: DOS; internal storage: 64K bits; magnetic tapes: 4 2401; magnetic discs: 4 2311; 1 line printer.

Coding Languages
RPG, Assembler, COBOL, FORTRAN.

Services Available
Advice, operators, preparation of data, programming, education and training, software packages, documentation, systems analysis. Operate on a self-service, block time, closed and open shop basis.

Fields of Application
Scientific, statistical, commercial, accounting, systems analysis.
Specialized areas: Sales analysis, analysis, payroll.

Training
Courses in DP concepts, RPG II, RPG, COBOL, flow-charting, Assembler, PL/1, FORTRAN and systems analysis.

GREECE

UNIVERSITIES

ARISTOTELEION PANEPISTIMION THESSALONIKIS
Department of Mathematics
Odos Panepistimiou, Thessaloniki
Telephone: 2392414 or 238780

Officers
Prof. N. Stephanidis, *Head of Department*
Dr. C. Dokoutsi-Akritidou, Mrs. E. Bora-Senta, *Programmers and analysts*

Computer Installation
IBM 1620/II–internal storage: 360K bits; magnetic discs: 2 1311/2, 2 1311/3; 1 line printer.

Coding Languages
GOTRAN, FORTRAN without FORMAT, FORTRAN I, FORTRAN II, FORTRAN II-D, SPS, SPS II-D.

Contemplated Equipment
UNIVAC 1106.

Services Available
Programming, education and training, documentation, preparation of data. Operate on a closed shop basis. Available primarily to members of the University.

Fields of Application
Scientific, statistical, accounting.
Specialized areas: Linear programming, analysis, payroll, structural engineering.

Training
Undergraduate courses: Introduction to Computer Programming, Coding Languages (FORTRAN II) and applications (Practice).

ETHNIKON KAI KAPODISTRIAKON PANEPISTIMION ATHINON
Unit of Applied Mathematics
Panepistemiopolis, Athens 621
Telephone: 743213

Officer
Prof. Dr. Nikolaos Apostolatos, *Chairman*

Computer Installation
CDC 3300–operating system: Master 3.2; internal storage: 3,145,728 bits; magnetic tapes: 5 CDC 604; magnetic discs: 4 CDC 841; 2 line printers. *On-line satellite computer*: CDC 1700. *Remote processing features*: 200 UT.

Coding Languages
FORTRAN, COBOL, ALGOL.

Contemplated Equipment
New computer system for the University.

Services Available
Education and training. Operate on a remote access basis.

Fields of Application
Scientific, statistical, applied mathematics.
Specialized area: Numerical analysis.

Training
Courses introducing computer science, numerical methods and programming of digital computers.

ETHNIKON METSOVION POLYTECHNEION ATHINAI
Odos Patission 42, Athens 147
Telephone: 61921-357

Officers
K. Theophilopoulos, *Professor of Electrical Engineering*
Dr. G. Papakonstantinou, *Lecturer*

Computer Installations
IBM 1620–operating system: Monitor I; internal storage: 24K bits; magnetic discs: 2 1311/3; 1 line printer.

CDC 200 UT terminal connected on a CDC 3300; 1 line printer.

Coding Languages
FORTRAN II, SPS, FORTRAN, COBOL, ALGOL, COMPASS, META.

Services Available
Advice, programming, education and training, operators, preparation of data. Operate on a closed shop basis.

Fields of Application
Scientific, statistical.
Specialized area: Structural engineering.

Training
Courses in Computer Science and FORTRAN programming.

CONSULTANTS

ARTHUR D. LITTLE–HELLAS S.A.
6 Sophocleous Street, Box 512, Athens 121
Telephone: 3240-375

Services Available
Consultation, systems analysis.

Fields of Application
Scientific, statistical, commercial, production control, operational research, management information systems, market research, inventory control, physical distribution.

P.A. MANAGEMENT CONSULTANTS S.A.*
12 Pindarou Street, Athens B4
Telephone: 610-835

Officer
G. E. Duane, *Manager*

Services Available
Advice, programming, systems analysis.

Fields of Application
Finance: Policy, profit planning, budgetary control, costing and accounting. Marketing: Policy, distribution, planning and control of sales force, exports. Production: Layout and methods, time standards and incentives, plant maintenance, factory and office planning, production control, stores and purchasing, quality and material control. Administration: Clerical methods, office machinery, computers, operational research. Personnel: Management organization, recruitment, remuneration, personnel management, operative training.

Training
In all fields courses of training of the clients' staff are arranged to meet the particular requirements of the assignment. Seminars on all aspects of our consulting services.

DOXIADIS ASSOCIATES COMPUTER CENTER LTD. (DACC)
24 Stratiotikou Syndesmou Str., Athens 136
Telephone: 639-112

Officers
Demetrios D. Vingileos, *General Manager*
Denis N. Sarientis, *Systems Division Manager*
Andrew N. Copelis, *Manager of Administration and Finance*
George Pelekuouvi, *Manager Field of Engineering*
Stylianos Markakis, *Manager Service Bureau*

Computer Installation
UNIVAC 1107–operating system: EXEC 2; internal storage: 65K 36-bit words; magnetic tapes; 6 IIIC; magnetic discs: 2 FH 880 drums. *On-line satellite computers*: 2 UNIVAC. 1004.

Coding Languages
FORTRAN, COBOL.

Services Available
Advice, programming, software packages, systems analysis, education and training, operators and preparation of data. Operate on a self-service basis.

Fields of Application
Scientific, statistical, commercial, accounting, operational research.
Specialized areas: Sales analysis, linear programming, payroll, structural engineering and analysis.

IBM WORLD TRADE CORPORATION*
Mitropoleos 1, Athens 118
Telephone: 221-976

Computer Installation
IBM 1401 (2).

Services Available
Advice, operators, preparation of data, programming.

Fields of Application
Statistical and commercial.

GUATEMALA

SERVICE BUREAU

IBM DE GUATEMALA S.A.
7a Avenida 12-32, Zona 1, Guatemala City
Telephone: 85721

Officers
Carlos Osorio A., *General Manager*
Jorge A. Ramirez, *Data Processing Manager*

Computer Installation
IBM 360/25–operating system: DOS; internal storage: 48K bytes; magnetic tapes: 4 2401; magnetic discs: 3 2311; 2 line printers.

Coding Languages
PL/1, RPG II, Assembler.

Services Available
Operators, preparation of data, programming and system analysis. Operate on a closed shop and block time basis.

Fields of Application
Accounting and commercial.
Specialized areas: Sales analysis, payroll.

Computer Installation
ICL 1904A–operating system: GEORGE 3; internal storage: 96K 24-bit words; magnetic tapes: 4 7-track; magnetic discs: 5; 1 line printer. *Remote processing features*: 2 Batch terminals, 4 teletypewriters, 1 visual display unit.

Coding Languages
FORTRAN, ALGOL, COBOL, MOP, MINIMOP, JEAN, BASIC.

Contemplated Equipment
Communications processor.

Services Available
Advice, programming, education and training, operators, software packages, documentation, preparation of data, systems analysis. Operate on a remote access, closed shop and time-sharing basis. Restricted to academic usage except by special arrangement.

Fields of Application
Scientific, statistical, commercial, accounting, management, systems analysis, operational research, teaching.
Specialized areas: Structural engineering, medical research, language translation, university applications.

Training
Diploma course in systems analysis; short courses in languages and applications packages.

HONDURAS

SERVICE BUREAU

IBM WORLD TRADE CORPORATION*
Tegucigalpa

Computer Installation
IBM 1401.

Service Available
Advice, operators, preparation of data, programming.

Fields of Application
Statistical, commercial.

SERVICE BUREAUX

IBM WORLD TRADE CORPORATION*
Hong Kong

Computer Installation
IBM 360/30.

Services Available
Advice, operators, preparation of data, programming, software packages, systems analysis.

Fields of Application
Scientific, statistical, commercial.

TAIKOO DOCKYARD AND ENGINEERING COMPANY OF HONG KONG LTD.*
Quarry Bay, P.O.B.N. 1, Hong Kong
Telephone: 602211

Computer Installation
ICL 1901–internal storage: 192K bits; magnetic tapes; 1 line printer.

Coding Languages
PLAN, COBOL, FORTRAN, NICOL.

HONG KONG

UNIVERSITY

UNIVERSITY OF HONG KONG AND THE CHINESE UNIVERSITY OF HONG KONG
Joint Universities Computer Centre Ltd.
Tung Ying Building (16th floor), 100 Nathan Road, Kowloon
Telephone: 3-68-7211

Officer
T. P. Goldingham, *Director*

Services Available
Programming, education and training, operators, software packages, documentation, preparation of data, systems analysis. Operate on a self-service basis.

Fields of Application
Scientific, commercial, accounting, management, analysis.
Specialized area: Job costing.

HUNGARY

EDUCATIONAL AND TRAINING INSTITUTIONS

HUNGARIAN COMPUTER EDUCATION CENTRE*
Budapest XIV, Törökőr u. 18
Telephone: 832-761

Officers
Sándor Faragó, *Director*
Mrs. Marta Jäger, *Officer in charge of Foreign Relations*

Contemplated Equipment
CII 10010; IBM 360/35.

Services Available
Education and training.

Field of Application
Training purposes.

Training
Many courses on Data Processing, Computer Programming and Computer Operation.
Short Courses: courses on micro-film techniques. Decision tables. Operation Research and the practical application of mathematics in business.
Special: File organization. Operational systems. Microfilm techniques. Linear programming.

MANAGEMENT TRAINING CENTRE*
Budapest VIII, Könyves Kálmán Krt. 48-52.
Telephone: 344-500

Computer Installation
ICL 1905E—internal storage: 768K bits; magnetic tapes: 4 DRICO Type 6, ICL 1972; magnetic discs: 2 CDC, ICL 2802; 1 line printer.

Coding Languages
PLAN, COBOL, FORTRAN, ALGOL.

Services Available
Consultation, programming, education and training, operators, software packages, documentation, preparation of data, systems analysis.

Fields of Application
Production control, accounting, management, systems analysis, operational research.

Training
Specialized courses for top management.

UNIVERSITY

NEHÉZIPARI MŰSZAKI EGYETEM*
(Technical University of Heavy Industry)
Computation Laboratory
Miskolc, Egyetemváros
Telephone: 13-691

Officers
Dr. Gyula Gáspár, *Professor, Head of Department*
Dr. J. Gyuula Obádovics, *University Lecturer, Leader of the Computation Laboratory*
Dr. Antal Nikodémusz, *University Lecturer*

Computer Installation
ODRA 1013—internal storage: 8K bits.

Coding Languages
MOST 1, ALGOL, machine code.

Contemplated Equipment
MINSK 22.

Services Available
Advice, operators, programming. Operate on a self-service basis.

Fields of Application
Scientific and technical calculations, education tasks.
Specialized area: Numerical analysis.

Training
Programming courses.

GOVERNMENT ESTABLISHMENTS

BUREAU FOR COMPUTATION AND FOR MECHANIZATION OF BUILDING ADMINISTRATION*
Budapest XIII, Váci-ut 4.

Officers
Iván Kádar Kádár, *Director*
Loránt Németh, *Head of Department of Scientific Research and Programming*
Vilmos Nemény, *Foreign Relations*

Computer Installation
URAL 2—1 line printer.

Coding Language
Machine code.

Services Available
Available to other firms and institutions related to the building industry.

Field of Application
Building industry.

DATORG
(Foreign Trade Company for Data Processing and Organization)
Budapest V, Dorottya u. 6
Telephone: 180-814

Officers
Dr. Iván Kádár, *Deputy Director*
Dr. Péter Kovács, *Head of the Department for Macro-organization*

Computer Installation
SIEMENS 4004—operating system: DOS; internal storage: 64K bytes; magnetic tapes: 4 9-track, 2 7-track; magnetic discs: 4 564; 1 line printer.

Coding Language
Assembler.

Contemplated Equipment
One more line printer.

Services Available
Advice, programming, operators, software packages, documentation, preparation of data, systems analysis. Operate on a closed shop basis.

Fields of Application
Statistical, commercial, accounting, management, systems analysis, operational research.
Specialized areas: Sales analysis, linear programming, analysis, payroll.

INFELOR RENDSZERTECHNIKAI VALLALAT*
(Infelor Systems Engineering Co.)
Budapest XII, Szilágyi fasor 20/A
Telephone: 364-144

Also at: Budapest II, Frankel Leó ut 106-108
Telephone: 163-241

Officers
F. Rabár, *Director*
B. Dömölki, *Deputy Director*
T. Lampl, *in charge of Operations Research*
I. Siklaky, *in charge of Organization*
G. Pádár, *in charge of Systems Analysis*
G. Szakolczay, *in charge of Econometrics*
T. Szentiványi, *in charge of Computer Engineering*

Computer Installation
MINSK 22–internal storage: 12K 37-bit words; magnetic tapes; 1 line printer.

MINSK 2–internal storage: 8K 37-bit words; magnetic tapes.

Coding Languages
MITRA, automode-type language with macro instruction facilities, ALGOL 60.

Services Available
Consultation, programming, operators, software packages, preparation of data, systems analysis. Operate on self-service, closed and open shop basis. Service available mainly to staff, remaining time being sold on time-sharing basis.

Fields of Application
Specialized area: Software development.

IPARGAZDASZGI, SZERVEZESI ES SZÁMITASTECHNIKAI INTEZET*
(Institute for Industrial Economy, Organization and Computation)
Budapest, Krisztina Krt. 55
Telephone: 359-150. 359-760

Officer
Josef Fekete, *Director*

Computer Installation
BULL GENERAL ELECTRIC GE 115.
IBM 1440.

Services Available
Consultation, preparation of data, programming. Operate on a contractual basis.

Fields of Application
Metallurgy, engineering and chemical industry, commercial, operations research.
Specialized areas: Management problems, industrial economics and organization, mechanical data logging.

Training
Courses for managers, data logging machine experts, operators and programmers.

KÖZPONTI STATISZTIKAI HIVATAL SZAMITOKÖZPONT*
(Central Statistical Office Directorate for Computing Techniques)
Budapest II, Buday László u. 1-3,
Telephone: 358-743

Officers
Dr. László Ormai, *Director of Directorate for Computer Techniques*
Zoltan Kalan, *Assistant Director*
Ferenc Haraszti, *Supervisor Statistical Computing*
G. I. Tarjan, *Head of Programme Library and Documentation*

Computer Installation
ICL 1904F–internal storage: 64K 24-bit words; magnetic tapes: 6 1973; magnetic discs: 3 2802; 1 line-printer.

ICL 1904/1–internal storage: 32K 24-bit words; magnetic tapes: 6 1973; 2 line printers. IBM 360/20.

Coding Languages
PLAN, COBOL, ALGOL, FORTRAN, NICOL.

Services Available
Advice, preparation of data, programming, software packages. Operate on a closed shop and open shop basis. The main customer is the Statistical Office. The remaining machine-time and programming capacity (if any) are divided among other customers, according to the importance of the problems.

Field of Application
Statistics.
Specialized areas: Mathematical programming and software development.

VOLÁN TRÖSZT ELEKTRONIKA
1502 Budapest XI, Karolina u. 65
Telephone: 667-644, 668-998

Officers
Dr. Tamás Tápay, *Director*
Dr. János Östör, *Deputy Director*
Jánosné Kenyeres, *Head of Systems Analysis Division*

Computer Installation
UNIVAC 9400–operating system: DOS; internal storage: 1 million bits; magnetic tapes: 6 Uniservo VIC; magnetic discs: 4 Univac 8411; 1 line printer. *On-line satellite computer*: 1 Univac 1005. *Remote processing features*: Uniscope 100.

UNIVAC 1050–operating system: OPR; internal storage: 168K bits; magnetic tapes: 6 Uniservo VIC; 1 line printer.

Coding Languages
Assembler, COBOL, FORTRAN.

Services Available
Operate on a closed shop basis.

Fields of Application
Statistical, commercial, accounting, management.
Specialized areas: Analysis, motor transport problems.

RESEARCH INSTITUTIONS

MAGYAR TUDOMÁNYOS AKADÉMIA
(Hungarian Academy of Sciences)
Központi Fizikai Kutató Intézete
(Central Research Institute for Physics)
1525 Budapest 114, P.O. Box 49
Telephone: 166-440, 166-547

Officers
Dr. Lénárd Pál, *Director*
M. Sándory, *Deputy Director*

Computer Installation
ICL 1905–operating system: Executive; internal storage: 786,432 bits; magnetic tapes: 6 7-track; 1 line printer.
On-line satellite computer: TPA 1001.

Coding Languages
PLAN, FORTRAN IV, ALGOL 60.

Services Available
Advice, operators, software packages, documentation, preparation of data, bibliographical references and abstracts. Operate on a closed shop and block time basis. Available primarily to the scientists of the Institute and to outside customers by special arrangement.

Field of Application
Scientific.
Specialized areas: Physical and chemical research electronics.

MAGYAR TUDOMÁNYOS AKADÉMIA*
(Hungarian Academy of Sciences)
Számitástechnikai és Automatizálási Intézete
(Institute for Computation and Automation)
Budapest XI, Kende u. 13-17
Telephone: 466-997

Officers
A. Kóvacs, *Head of the Computing Centre*
L. Rittgasser, *Manager of the Service Bureau*
Dr. B. Sebestyén, *Head of Satellite Computers Department*

Computer Installation
MINSK 22–internal storage: 8K 37-bit words; magnetic tapes: 4 + 3 (Russian + Ampex TM7); 1 line printer.
CII 10010–internal storage: 16K bits.

Coding Languages
MITRA, Elliott A103, INZENYER, ALGOL, Assembler, FORTRAN.

Services Available
Advice, operators, preparation of data, programming, software packages, systems analysis. Operate on a self-service and block time basis. Available only for customers working in the field of scientific research.

Fields of Application
Scientific, process control.

NIM IGÜSZI*
Budapest V, Markó-u. 16

Officers
P. Póka, *Director of Computer Centre*
J. Vajda, *in charge of Foreign Relations*
J. Urik, *in charge of Personnel*

Computer Installation
ICL 1903A–operating system: GEORGE 2; internal storage: 768K bits; magnetic tapes: 4 1972/2; magnetic discs: 3 2802/2.

ELLIOTT 803B–internal storage: 320K bits; magnetic tapes: 2.

Coding Languages
ICL 1903A: PLAN, COBOL, ALGOL, FORTRAN, EMA.
Elliott 803B: Autocode, ALGOL, GRAPHOCODE (own), TREMP (own).

Contemplated Equipment
ICL system 4/70 or 1904A.

Services Available
Consultation, programming, software packages, preparation of data, systems analysis. Operate on closed shop and block time basis.

Fields of Application
Scientific, commercial, systems analysis, operational research, software developing.
Specialized areas: Drawing, compiler developing.

SERVICE BUREAUX

BELKERESKEDELMI ÜGYVITELSZERVEZÉSI ÉS INFORMÁCIÓFELDOLGOZÁSI INTEZET, KERINFORG*
Budapest V, Dorottya u. 4,
Telephone: 188-235

Officers
Dr. Hegedüs Andrásné, *Director*

Computer Installation
HONEYWELL H2200–operating system: MOD 1; internal storage: 64K x 6 bits; magnetic tapes: 5 204B; magnetic discs: 2 259; 1 line printer.

Coding Languages
Easycoder, Assembler, COBOL, FORTRAN, Extended CSL.

Contemplated Equipment
One line printer, three tapes, one disc, one main memory of 32K bits.

Services Available
Consultation, programming, education and training, operators, documentation, preparation, systems analysis. Operate on an open shop basis. Available to wholesale trading companies and home trade.

Field of Application
Commercial.

Training
A one-week course in data processing for management.

ÉLGAVE
(EDP Service Bureau of the Food Industry)
1111 Budapest XI, Budafoki u. 59
Telephone: 666-031

Officers
Dezső Lakatos, *Director*
Tibor Hunfalvy, *Deputy Director*
János Kozma, *Systems Manager*

Computer Installation
BULL GENERAL ELECTRIC GE 115 (3)–operating system: DOS; internal storage: 96K bits each (2), 64K bits; magnetic discs: 3 DSU 130 each (2), 2 DSU 130; 1 line printer each.

Coding Languages
Autocoder, TAB, RPG, COBOL.

Services Available
Consultation, programming, operators, software packages, documentation, preparation of data, systems analysis. Operate on a closed shop basis. Service restricted to the food industry.

Fields of Application
Statistical, commercial, accounting, management, systems analysis.
Specialized areas: Sales analysis; stock control.

FŐVÁROSI ÉPITŐIPARI ÜZEMGAZDASÁGI ÉS ÜGYVITELTECHNIKAI IRODA*
(Operative Economical and Administrative Office of the Municipal Building Industry)
Budapest XI, Ballagi Mor u. 14
Telephone: 250-090

Officers
József Siványi, *Manager*
Dr. György Lombos, *Leader of consultation and systems analysis*
Istvan Lukács, *Leader of data processing and programming*

Computer Installation
UNIVAC 1004–internal storage: 12K bits.
UNIVAC 1005–internal storage: 24K bits.

Coding Languages
ORELL 3, ORELL 5, MODUL, PÁL.

Services Available
Consultation, programming, operators, software packages, preparation of data, systems analysis. Operate on a closed shop basis.

Fields of Application
Statistical, commercial, management, systems analysis, operational research.
Specialized areas: Research and solution of administrative problems in the building industry.

IRODAGÉPTECHNIKA VÁLLALAT*
Budapest, Bécsi u. 8-10
Telephone: 182980

Officers
János Hováth, *Director*
Ing. Ede Lindmeyer, *Deputy Director*

Services Available
Consultation, programming, education and training, operators. Operate on a self-service basis.

Fields of Application
Scientific, statistical, commercial, production control, accounting, management, systems analysis, operational research.

MAGYAR VEGYIPARI EGYESÜLÉS*
(United Hungarian Chemical Works)
Engineering and Computing Centre
Budapest, Hungária Körut 178
Telephone: 213-380

Officers
Sandor Gór-Nagy, *President*
Miklós Preisich, *Vice-President*

Computer Installation
GIER–internal storage: 43K bits; magnetic tapes: 1 Ampex TM7; magnetic discs: 1 CDC 9433; 1 line printer.

Coding Language
ALGOL.

Services Available
Operators, preparation of data, programming, software packages. Operate on a closed shop basis.

Fields of Application
Production control, management, operational analysis, scientific.

SZÁMITÁSTECHNIKAI ÉS UGYVITELSZERVEZŐ VÁLLALAT (SZUV)*
(Enterprise for Computing Services and Management Organization)
Budapest VIII, Kun Béla-tér 2
Telephone: 331-960

Officers
István Öry, *Director of the Enterprise*
László Pinter, *Deputy Director*

Computer Installation
ICL 1904 (2)–internal storage: 780,432 bits each; magnetic tapes: 6 1972 each; 1 line printer each.

GIER–internal storage: 43,008 bits; magnetic tapes: 3 Ampex TM-7; magnetic drum: Lorenz; 1 line printer.

UNIVAC 1004–internal storage: 16,384 bits.
BULL GENERAL ELECTRIC 115 (5)–internal storage: 98,304 bits each; 1 line printer each.

Coding Languages
ALGOL, COBOL, NICOL, OREL, TAB, APS.

Services Available
Advice, operators, preparation of data, programming, systems analysis. Operate on an open shop basis.

Fields of Application
Scientific, statistical, commercial, production control, accounting, management, operational research, etc.

ICELAND

NATIONAL CENTRE

SKÝRSLUVÉLAR RÍKISINS OG REYKJAVÍKUR-BORGAR
Háaleitisbraut 9, Reykjavík
Telephone: 86144

Officer
Bjarni P. Jónasson, *Manager*

Computer Installation
IBM 360/30–operating system: DOS; internal storage: 262,144 bits: magnetic tapes: 2 2415; magnetic discs: 2 2311; 1 line printer.

IBM 370/135–operating system: DOS; internal storage: 1,180K bits; magnetic tapes: 4 2415; magnetic discs: 6 2314; 2 line printers.

Coding Languages
RPG, AL, PL/1, FORTRAN.

Services Available
Programming, operators, preparation of data, systems analysis. Operate on a closed shop basis.

Fields of Application
Statistical, commercial, accounting.

INDIA

EDUCATIONAL AND TRAINING INSTITUTIONS

INDIAN INSTITUTE OF MANAGEMENT
Ahmedabad 15, Gujarat State
Telephone: 83411

Officers
Dr. S. Paul, *Director*
Prof. J. G. Krishnayya, *Chairman of the Computer Committee*

Computer Installation
HEWLETT PACKARD 2116B—operating systems: Time Share BASIC and DOS; internal storage: 16K x 16 bits; magnetic tapes: 2 HP7970; magnetic drums: 2 VR 1016. *Remote processing features*: 16 teletypewriters, 2 Infoton Alphameric CRT and 10″ x 10″ CRT.

Coding Languages
BASIC, FORTRAN VI, ALGOL.

Contemplated Equipment
Line printer, plotter, graf/pen input device.

Services Available
Advice, education and training, software packages, systems analysis. Operate on a block time and time-sharing basis.

Fields of Application
Statistical, management, operational research.
Specialized areas: Investment, structural engineering.

Training
Courses in workshop on simulation and real time (1 week) and EDP and Management Applications (2 weeks); postgraduate course in Business Management (2 weeks); Informatics diploma course (9 months).

INDIAN INSTITUTE OF SCIENCE
Bangalore 560012
Telephone: 3191

Officers
Prof. S. Dhawan, *Director*
Dr. A. A. Shamim, *Resident-in-charge of the Computer Centre*

Computer Installation
IBM 360/44—operating system: 44-PS; internal storage: 65,536 bytes; magnetic tapes: 2 2401/01; magnetic discs: 2 2315 DASD; 1 line printer.

Coding Languages
FORTRAN IV, COBOL, PL/1.

Contemplated Equipment
Additional internal storage of 65,536 bytes; two IBM 2314; IBM 1627 plotter; data acquisition system (real time).

Services Available
Advice, programming, education and training. Operate on a closed shop basis.

Fields of Application
Scientific, statistical, systems analysis, operational research.
Specialized areas: Analysis, structural engineering, research.

Training
Courses for M.E. and Ph.D.—School of Automation (Computer Science).

UNIVERSITIES AND COLLEGES

INDIAN INSTITUTE OF TECHNOLOGY, BOMBAY*
Powai, Bombay 76
Telephone: 581421

Officers
J. R. Isaac, *Director*
R. D. Kumas
S. S. S. P. Rao

Computer Installation
MINSK 2—internal storage: 4,096 37-bit words; magnetic tapes: 4; 1 line printer.

Coding Languages
ACE, ALGOL.

Contemplated Equipment
Expansion into MINSK 22.

Services Available
Consultation, programming, education and training, operators, software packages, preparation of data. Operate on an open shop basis. Service available to students, staff and research workers of the Institute.

Fields of Application
Scientific, engineering design and research problems of the Institute.
Specialized areas: Hardware and software oriented projects of students of computer technology.

Training
Undergraduate and postgraduate courses in computer technology; B. Tech., M. Tech. and Ph.D. degrees; short courses in programming and numerical analysis.

INDIAN INSTITUTE OF TECHNOLOGY, DELHI*
Hauz Khas, New Delhi 29
Telephone: 79163

Officers
Prof. J. C. Shouri, *Acting Head, Computer Centre*
Dr. K. D. Sharma
Dr. P. C. P. Bhatt

Computer Installation
ICL 1909—internal storage: 384K bits; magnetic tapes: 2 1971/1; magnetic discs: 2 2801/1; 1 line printer.

Coding Languages
FORTRAN, ALGOL, PLAN, EMA, COBOL.

Contemplated Equipment
Extension of core store to 32K bits; addition of magnetic tapes; second line printer.

Services Available
Education and training, operators, preparation of data. Operate on a closed shop basis. Restricted to IIT users and applicants approved by Head of Computer Centre.

Fields of Application
Scientific, statistical, operational research.
Specialized area: Numerical analysis.

Training
Diploma course in numerical analysis and automatic computation (under Maths. dept.). Short courses in FORTRAN programming and system programming.

INDIAN INSTITUTE OF TECHNOLOGY, KANPUR
Computer Centre
Kanpur 16, Uttar Pradesh
Telephone: 37121

Officers
Dr. H. K. Kesavan, *Head, and Professor of Electrical Engineering*
Dr. V. Rajaraman, *Associate Professor, Electrical Engineering*
Dr. H. N. Mahabala, *Assistant Professor, Electrical Engineering*
Dr. V. K. Stokes, *Assistant Professor, Mechanical Engineering*

Computer Installation
IBM 1620–operating system: 1620 magnetic tape operating system developed at the Institute; internal storage: 40K x 6 bits; magnetic tapes: 3 IBM 7330.

IBM 7044–operating system: IBSYS; internal storage: 32,768 x 36 bits; magnetic tapes: 8 729VI; 1 line printer. *On-line satellite computer*: IBM 1401. *Remote processing features*: 6 1014.

IBM 1401–operating system: IIT; internal storage: 1600 x 6 bits; magnetic tapes: 4 729V; magnetic discs: 5 1311; 1 line printer.

IBM 1800–operating systems: TSX, MPX; internal storage: 16,384 x 16 bits; magnetic tapes: 1 2401; magnetic discs: 2 1810.

IBM 1620–operating system: IIT; internal storage: 40K x 6 bits; magnetic tapes: 3 7330.

Coding Languages
FORTRAN IV, COBOL, ALGOL, SNOBOL, DYNAMO, LISP.

Services Available
Advice, education and training, operators, software packages, documentation. Operate on a closed shop basis. Not available for routine or commercial data processing.

Field of Application
Scientific.
Specialized areas: Linear programming, structural engineering.

Training
Compulsory and optional undergraduate courses; specialization courses in M.Tech. Electrical Engineering. Courses leading to M. Tech and Ph.D. in Computer Science.

INDIAN INSTITUTE OF TECHNOLOGY, MADRAS
Madras 600036
Telephone: 802740

Officers
Dr. A. Ramachandran, *Director*
Prof. S. Sampath, *Deputy Director*

Computer Installation
IBM 370/155–operating systems: Various; internal storage: 512K bytes; magnetic tapes: 3 drives; magnetic discs: 4 drives; 2 line printers. *Remote processing features*: 3 teletype terminals with R.I. features.

Coding Languages
FORTRAN G and H. BASIC, ALGOL, COBOL E and F, PL/1, GPSS, RPG.

Services Available
Advice, programming, education and training, operators, software packages, documentation, preparation of data, systems analysis. Operate on a time-sharing basis.

Fields of Application
Scientific, statistical, commercial, systems analysis, operational research.
Specialized areas: Linear programming, analysis, structural engineering, scientific research.

Training
M. Tech. course in Computer Science.

JADAVPUR UNIVERSITY*
Calcutta 32
Telephone: 46-4771

Computer Installation
ISIJU-1–internal storage: 16K characters; magnetic drum: Hokusin.

Coding Languages
SPS, FORTRAN.

Contemplated Equipment
Magnetic tape units, line printer.

Services Available
Advice, programming. Operate on a self-service and open shop basis.

Fields of Application
Scientific, statistical, production control, accounting, management, operational research, etc.

Training
One year post-graduate Computer Science Diploma Course. Short courses in programming.

PANJAB UNIVERSITY
Centre for Advanced Study in Mathematics
Chandigarh 14
Telephone: 25142

Officer
S. C. Mathur, *Head of Computer Centre and Reader in Computation*

Computer Installation
IBM 1620/I–internal storage: 20K core locations; 1 line printer.

Coding Languages
FORTRAN, Machine, Assembly.

Contemplated Equipment
One TDC 12 or TDC 16.

Services Available
Consultation, programming, education and training, software packages, operators, programming, systems analysis. Operate on a self-service and closed shop basis.

Fields of Application
Scientific, statistical, systems analysis, operational research.

Training
Courses twice a year in FORTRAN, Machine and Assembly programming and numerical methods.

UNIVERSITY OF CALCUTTA
Computer Centre
Institute of Radio Physics and Electronics,
92 Acharya Prafulla Chandra Road, Calcutta–700009
Telephone: 35-9115/9116

Officer
Dr. A. K. Choudhury, *Professor of Radio Physics and Chemistry*

Computer Installations
IBM 1130; internal storage: 261,144 bits; magnetic discs: 25 2315; 1 line printer.

Coding Languages
FORTRAN IV, Assembler.

Contemplated Equipment
IBM 360 and ancillary equipment, together with remote processing features.

Services Available
Advice, programming, education and training, software packages, preparation of data. Operate on an open shop basis. Available to educational, research and training institutions, universities and colleges only.

Fields of Application
Scientific, statistical, operational research.
Specialized area: Linear programming.

Training
Training on programming and operation is provided to research workers, teachers and students of different universities and research institutions.

UNIVERSITY OF DELHI*
Physics Department
Delhi 1
Telephone: 228993

Officer
Dr. P. S. Grover

Computer Installation
IBM 1620/1–internal storage: 40K bits.

Coding Languages
GOTRAN, FORGO, FORTRAN, SPS.

Contemplated Equipment
IBM 360/44.

Services Available
Programming, education and training. Operate on a self-service and open shop basis. Available to all engaged in active research, though users must be familiar with the operation of the machine.

Field of Application
Scientific research

Training
Short courses in programming and computer operating.

UNIVERSITY OF KURUKSHETRA
Department of Mathematics
Kurukshetra, Haryana

Officer
Dr. S. D. Chopra, *Senior Professor and Head of Department of Mathematics.*

Computer Installation
TDC 12–internal storage: 4K bits.

Coding Language
FORTRAN.

Contemplated Equipment
TDC 16 Processor with 16K bit storage; card reader, magnetic tapes, magnetic discs, line printer.

Services Available
Advice, education and training and software packages. Operate on a self-service and open shop basis.

Field of Application
Scientific.
Specialized areas: Numerical analysis, seismology.

Training
Courses in Numerical Analysis and Automatic Computing (one year–diploma), and short courses in programming.

GOVERNMENT ESTABLISHMENTS

DEFENCE RESEARCH AND DEVELOPMENT LABORATORY*
Chandryangutta Linea, Hyderabad–5 (A.P.)
Telephone: 40105

Officers
Air Cdre V. Ganesan, *Director*
Lt.-Col. A. Balasubramanian, *Principal Scientific Officer-in-Charge, Computer Section*
J. C. Bhattacharyya, *Senior Scientific Officer, Grade I*
G. Sankaran, *Senior Scientific Officer, Grade II*

Computer Installation
IBM 1620–internal storage: 20K bits.
PACE 231R.

Coding Languages
FORTRAN I, FORTRAN II, SPS, AFIT, PDQ.

Contemplated Equipment
Additional 20K bits memory, ADDA link unit.

Services Available
Available to outside customers depending on the workload on the machine.

Fields of Application
Problem formulation and applications in numerical analysis, systems programming.
Specialized areas: Problems pertaining to defence research and development such as trajectory evaluations, optimization studies, simulation techniques etc.

EASTERN RAILWAY*
Data Processing Centre
Mughalsarai
Telephone: 59

Also at:
D.P.M.'s Residence P. and T. No. 98

Officer
Data Processing Manager

India – Government Establishments

Computer Installation
IBM 1401 – operating system card orientated; internal storage: 4K bits; 1 line printer.

Coding Language
Autocoder.

Services Available
Consultation, programming, operators, documentation, preparation of data, systems analysis. Operate on a self-service basis. Service available to Eastern Railway and Railway Board.

Fields of Application
Statistical, management, operational research.
Specialized area: Transportation (railway traffic).

INDIAN STATISTICAL INSTITUTE
Electronic Computer Division
203 Barrackpore Trunk Road, Calcutta 35
Telephone: 56-3222

Officers
Prof. J. Roy, *Head, Computer Science Unit*
Dr. D. Dutta Majumder, *Professor of Electronics and Communication Sciences Laboratory*.

Computer Installation
HONEYWELL H400 – internal storage: 2,048K 48-bit words, magnetic tapes: 4 404; 1 line printer.

Coding Languages
COBOL, EASY, FORTRAN II.

Services Available
Advice, programming, education and training, software packages, systems analysis. Operate on an open shop basis. Available mainly for research and training purposes.

Fields of Application
Scientific, statistical, management, systems analysis, operational research.
Specialized areas: Linear programming, analysis, structural engineering.

Training
One-year, postgraduate diploma course; specialisation in computer science in M. Stat. degree course; three-month intensive course on programming.

INTEGRAL COACH FACTORY*
Madras-38
Telephone: 61091

Officers
Sundar Raj, *Financial Advisor and Chief Accounts Officer*
S. Ananthanarayanan, *Data Processing Manager*

Computer Installation
IBM 1401 – internal storage: 8K bits; magnetic tapes: 1 7330; magnetic discs: 3 1311; 1 line printer.

Coding Languages
Autocoder, FORTRAN.

Contemplated Equipment
Plans to increase core storage to 12,000 positions.

Service Available
Time on computer system. Operate on a block time basis.

Fields of Application
Production control, accounting and inventory management; personnel data including preparation of pay bills and maintenance of leave accounts.

JOINT PLANT COMMITTEE*
18 Rabindra Sarani, Calcutta-1
Telephone: 34-8621

Officers
R. P. Sharma, *Executive Secretary*
N. D. Deo, *Programmer-in-Charge*

Computer Installation
IBM 1401 – internal storage: 12K bits; magnetic tapes: 4 7330; magnetic discs: 2 1311; 1 line printer.

Coding Languages
Autocoder, FORTRAN, COBOL.

Service Available
Operators, preparation of data. Operate on a closed and open shop basis. Service available to outside organizations by prior arrangement.

Field of Application
Statistical.
Specialized area: Order statistics.

NATIONAL AERONAUTICAL LABORATORY
Kodihalli, Post Bag No. 1779, Bangalore 17
Telephone: 52251, 52252, 52254

Officers
Dr. S. R. Valluri, *Director*
Shri L. Ramanathan, *Administrative Officer*
Dr. S. Khrishnan, *Head, Electronics Division*
Dr. R. Sankar, *Head, Computer Section*

Computer Installation
ICL Sirius – internal storage: 4K 40-bit words.

Coding Languages
Autocode, Assembler, Machine Code (Sirius).

Contemplated Equipment
An additional core-memory of 1,000 words for the Sirius computer is contemplated. This will be built in NAL itself.

Services Available
Advice, operators, preparation of data, software packages for Sirius, hardware packages for ICL 1004. Operate on an open shop basis. Available only to scientific and educational institutions.

Fields of Application
Scientific, statistical accounting, systems analysis, operational research, documentation and inventory control.
Specialized areas: Numerical method, development of software and hardware packages, payroll, structural engineering.

Training
Courses are held periodically in programming. Training in numerical analysis and programming given to trainees from educational institutions.

PROGRAMME EVALUATION ORGANISATION*
(Planning Commission)
Yojana Bhaven, Parliament Street, New Delhi 1
Telephone: 381240

Officers
Dr. P. K. Mukherjee, *Chief*
Shri T. R. Puri, *Joint Director*
Shri R. C. Chanda, *Deputy Director*

Computer Installation
IBM 1620/II—internal storage: 40K characters; magnetic discs: 3 1311; 1 line printer.

Coding Languages
FORTRAN II-D, SPS II-D.

Contemplated Equipment
Magnetic tape units.

Services Available
Consultation, operators, preparation of data, programming, software packages, systems analysis. Operate on an open shop basis. Available mainly for government departments and research institutions.

Fields of Application
Scientific, statistical, operational research.

SOUTH CENTRAL RAILWAY*
Secunderabad-25
Telephone: 77411

Officers
K. A. Chandrasekharan, *Electronic Data Processing Manager*

Computer Installation
IBM 1401—internal storage: 12K bits; magnetic tapes: 4 7330; 1 line printer.

Coding Languages
Autocoder, FORTRAN II, FORTRAN IV.

Contemplated Equipment
729 magnetic tapes; third generation computer.

Services Available
Programming, operators, preparation of data, systems analysis. Operate on a self-service basis. Service available to railways only.

Fields of Application
Statistical, commercial, accounting, management, operations research.
Specialized areas: Railway operations.

SOUTHERN RAILWAY*
Madras
Telephone: 39101

Computer Installation
IBM 1401—internal storage: 12K bits; magnetic tapes: 4 7330; 1 line printer.

Coding Language
Autocode.

Contemplated Equipment
Faster tape drives.

Services Available
Operate on a closed shop basis. Marginal time sold to others, depending on availability of time.

Fields of Application
Statistical, accounting, management.
Specialized area: Railway transportation.

STATE BANK OF INDIA*
Central Office, Bombay 1

Computer Installation
IBM 1401—internal storage: 12K bits; magnetic tapes; magnetic disc.

Service Available
Computer time.

WESTERN RAILWAY*
Data Processing Centre
First Floor, New Churchgate Building, Bombay-1
Telephone: 297706

Officer
H. Krishnamurthy, *E. D. P. Manager*

Computer Installation
IBM 1401—internal storage: 12K 8-bit characters; magnetic tapes: 4 729/II; 1 line printer.

Coding Languages
Autocoder, FORTRAN.

Services Available
Programming, operators, documentation, preparation of data, systems analysis. Operate on a self-service basis.

Fields of Application
Accounting, statistical, commercial, management.

Training
Courses run by IBM.

RESEARCH INSTITUTIONS

AHMEDABAD TEXTILE INDUSTRY'S RESEARCH ASSOCIATION (ATIRA)*
Navrangpura, Ahmedabad-9
Telephone: 77651/2

Officer
B. S. Chandramurty, *Assistant Director and Head of Group for Operational Studies*

Computer Installation
IBM 1620—internal storage: 360K bits; 1 line printer.

Coding Languages
SPS III, FORTRAN II.

Contemplated Equipment
ICL 1901A with 16K disc storage and Twin Exchangeable Disc Units.

Services Available
Consultation, programming, education and training, operators, preparation of data, systems analysis. Operate on a block time and open shop basis. Available only to members of ATIRA and educational institutions.

Fields of Application
Scientific, statistical, commercial, production control, accounting, management, systems analysis, operational research.
Specialized areas: management decisions and controls; production planning, cost analysis, cost and budgetary controls, sales analysis, inventory control, cotton blending, information for operational control etc. Data processing: pay-rolls, accounting, production statistics, invoicing, dividend warrants, share certificates etc.

Training
Short courses for staff in computer programming and topics to develop systems and procedures.

BHABHA ATOMIC RESEARCH CENTRE*
Computer Facility
Trombay, Bombay-85
Telephone: 523321

Officers
P. K. Patwardhan, *Officer-in-Charge*

Computer Installation
HONEYWELL H400 – internal storage: 4K 48-bit words; magnetic tapes: 5 404-3; 1 line printer.

Coding Languages
Automath, FORTRAN II, COBOL, EASY.

Contemplated Equipment
Paper tape reader, cathode ray tube display output device.

Services Available
Consultation, preparation of data, programming, education and training, systems analysis. Operate on a closed shop basis.

Fields of Application
Scientific, statistical, accounting, management, systems analysis, engineering design.
Specialized areas: Nuclear data processing, feasibility studies on engineering design.

Training
Short courses in users' programming in COBOL, Automath, EASY.

CENTRAL MECHANICAL ENGINEERING RESEARCH INSTITUTE*
Computer Centre
Durgapur, West Bengal
Telephone: 2261-2-3

Officer
Dr. A. C. Shamihoke, *Head*

Computer Installation
IBM 1620/I – internal storage: 60K bits; magnetic discs: 3 1311; 1 line printer.

Coding Languages
FORTRAN II, SPS III, FORGO

Services Available
Advice, operators, programming, software packages. Operate on an open shop basis.

Fields of Application
Mechanical engineering problems.
Specialized areas: Numerical analysis and statistical analysis of data.

Training
Courses in FORTRAN and SPS.

COUNCIL OF SCIENTIFIC AND INDUSTRIAL RESEARCH*
Regional Research Laboratory
Hyderabad-9
Telephone: 71351

Officers
Dr. Asghar Husain, *Head*
P. J. Reddy, *Officer-in-Charge*

Computer Installation
IBM 1620 – operating system: FORTRAN II; internal storage: 40K bits; 1 line printer.

Coding Languages
FORTRAN II, SPS.

Contemplated Equipment
Magnetic disc drive, graphical plot, increased storage.

Services Available
Programming, education and training, software packages, systems analysis. Operate on a closed shop basis. Service available to engineering, scientific and university staff.

Fields of Application
Scientific, accounting, operational research, systems analysis.
Specialized areas: Chemical engineering, simulation, design, optimization.

Training
Short courses in FORTRAN, numerical analysis.

COUNCIL OF SCIENTIFIC AND INDUSTRIAL RESEARCH*
Structural Engineering Research Centre
Roorkee, Uttar Pradesh
Telephone: 480,235

Officers
Prof. G. S. Ramaswamy, *Director*
N. V. Raman, *Scientist-in-Charge Computer Center*

Computer Installation
IBM 1620/I – internal storage: 60K bits; 1 line printer.

Coding Languages
FORTRAN II, FORGO.

Contemplated Equipment
Magnetic tape and disc storage unit.

Services Available
Advice, operators, preparation of data, programming, software packages. Operate on a closed shop basis. Free services allowed for research and academic purposes, but computer time and programming services are chargeable for business concerns.

Field of Application
Computer analysis of structures.
Specialized areas: Numerical analysis, applied mathematics and computer analysis of structures with matrix methods.

Training
Intensive course on computer programming, special course on 'Mechanical Design of Transmission Lines & Towers', advanced course on digital computation applied to structural analysis.

HINDUSTAN AERONAUTICS LTD.*
Bangalore–17
Telephone: 53201, extension 348

Officer
Dr. R. Sankaranarayanan, *Manager*

Computer Installation
HONEYWELL H400–internal storage: 96K bits; magnetic tapes: 4 404-3; 1 line printer.
ELLIOTT 803B–internal storage: 156K bits.

Coding Languages
HONEYWELL H400–COBOL, FORTRAN II.
ELLIOTT 803B–Autocode Mark II.

Services Available
Consultation, programming, operators, preparation of data. Operate on an open shop basis.

Fields of Application
Scientific, production control, accounting.
Specialized area: Application of computers to aircraft design and production.

INDIAN COUNCIL OF AGRICULTURAL RESEARCH (ICAR)*
Institute of Agricultural Research Statistics
Library Avenue, New Delhi-12
Telephone: 587121

Officers
D. L. Ralhan, *Director*
D. K. Bahl, *Programmer*
K. V. Sathe, *Programmer*

Computer Installation
IBM 1620/II–operating system: Monitor II; internal storage: 40K digits; magnetic discs: 3 1311; 1 line printer.

Coding Languages
FORTRAN II-D, SPS II-D.

Contemplated Equipment
Third generation computer with remote processing features.

Services Available
Consultation, programming, educational and training, operators, software packages, preparation of data, systems analysis. Operate on an open shop basis. Service available to agricultural research institutes and universities, agricultural research workers, Ministry of Food and Agriculture, India, and international agencies engaged in agricultural research and development. Not available for commercial work.

Fields of Application
Scientific, statistical, operational research.
Specialized areas: Agriculture, including fishery, forestry, statistics, and animal husbandry.

Training
Short courses in computer programming and data processing for agricultural workers.

INDIAN POSTS AND TELEGRAPHS DEPARTMENT*
Telecommunications Research Centre
Khurshid Lal Bhavan, Janpath, New Delhi
Telephone: Delhi 46861, extension 340

Computer Installation
ELLIOTT 803B–internal storage: 8,192 40-bit words; magnetic tapes.

Coding Languages
Machine Code, Autocode, ALGOL.

Services Available
Consultation, programming. Operate on an open shop basis. Services available to Indian Posts and Telegraphs Department, and to universities and other Government agencies on request.

Fields of Application
Scientific, statistical.
Specialized areas: Computer-aided design and development of passive and active electrical networks; telephone traffic applications; development of software for stored programme Controlled Electronic Exchange Project.

Training
Short courses in ALGOL programming and methods of numerical analysis for officers of Indian Posts and Telegraphs Department.

INDIAN SPACE RESEARCH ORGANIZATION (ISRO)*
Thumba Equatorial Rocket Launching Station (TERLS)
Telephone: 8351/7

Officer
J. T. George

Computer Installation
MINSK 2–internal storage: 151,552 bits; magnetic tapes: 4 random access; 1 line printer.

Coding Languages
Autocode, Machine.

Contemplated Equipment
Card reader, doubling memory, 144-character printer.

Services Available
Consultation, programming, education and training, software packages. Operate on an open shop basis. Available only to members of ISRO.

Field of Application
Scientific.
Specialized area: Space research.

Training
Computer training for staff members only.

INSTITUTE OF TROPICAL METEOROLOGY*
University Road, Poona–5
Telephone: 55221/271

Officers
Dr. R. Ananthakrishnan, *Director*
R. Suryanarayana, *Head of Computer Section*

Computer Installations
IBM 1620–internal storage: 60K bits; 1 line printer.

Coding Languages
FORTRAN II, SPS.

Contemplated Equipment
IBM 360.

Services Available
Education and training. Operate on a block time basis.

Fields of Application
Scientific research and statistical analysis.
Specialized areas: Weather prediction, climatological research, cloud physics, etc.

Training
Short courses in FORTRAN programming with applications to meteorology.

PHYSICAL RESEARCH LABORATORY
Navrangpura, Ahmedabad-380009, Gujarat
Telephone: 76242

Officer
S. R. Thakore, *Assistant Director*

Computer Installation
IBM 360/44—operating system: PS, OS and DOS; internal storage: 256K bits; magnetic tapes: 2, magnetic discs: 2 2311; 1 line printer.

Coding Languages
FORTRAN, Assembler, COBOL, PL/1.

Contemplated Equipment
Three IBM 2319 disc units, 3 IBM 3420 magnetic tapes, IBM 2671 paper tape, IBM 1627 plotter, 2 IBM 2740 terminals.

Services Available
Consultation, programming, education and training, operators, software packages, preparation of data, systems analysis. Operate on a closed shop basis.

Fields of Application
Scientific, statistical, commercial, accounting, systems analysis, operational research.

TATA INSTITUTE OF FUNDAMENTAL RESEARCH*
Computer Group
Colaba, Bombay 5
Telephone: 213650/213664

Officer
R. Narasimhan, *Head of Computer Group*

Computer Installation
CDC 3600—operating system: SCOPE; internal storage: 1,572,864 bits; magnetic tapes: 10 CDC 607; 1 line printer.

CDC 160A—internal storage: 98,304 bits; magnetic tapes: 2 CDC 607; 1 line printer.

Coding Languages
Assembly, FORTRAN IV, ALGOL, COBOL.

Contemplated Equipment
On-line data processor OLDAP in advanced state of completion, time-sharing system.

Services Available
Advice, operators, preparation of data, software packages. Operate on a closed shop basis. In general available for all research oriented work.

Fields of Application
Scientific, engineering, system programming.
Specialized areas: Thin film memory fabrication, integrated circuit design and fabrication, microsystem assemblies; analysis and synthesis of speech; analysis and synthesis of pictorial data; metatheory of programming languages.

Training
Programming courses.

CONSULTANTS

ASSOCIATED BUSINESS CONSULTANTS
6A Middleton Street, Calcutta-16
Telephone: 44-7071

Officers
B. P. Agrawal, *Managing Director*
J. V. R. Rao, *Director, Computer Service Bureau*

Computer Installation
IBM 1401—internal storage: 8K bits; magnetic tapes: 4 7330; magnetic discs: 3 1311; 1 line printer.

Coding Languages
Autocoder, FORTRAN, SPS.

Contemplated Equipment
IBM 360/25.

Services Available
Consultation, programming, education and training, operators, documentation, preparation of data, systems analysis. Operate on a self-service, open shop and block time basis.

Fields of Application
Scientific, statistical, commercial, production, accounting, operational research, etc.
Specialized areas: PERT, materials management.

TATA CONSULTANCY SERVICES
Air India Building, Nariman Point, Bombay-1
Telephone: 298022

Officers
N. A. Palkhivala, *Chairman, Executive Committee*
P. M. Agerwala, *Director-in-Charge*
F. C. Kohli, *General Manager*

Computer Installation
IBM 1401—internal storage: 16K bits; magnetic tapes: 6 729V; 1 line printer.

IBM 1401—internal storage: 16K bits; magnetic tapes: 4 729V, 1 line printer.

ICL 1903—internal storage: 16K bits; magnetic tapes: 8; 2 line printers.

Coding Languages
Autocoder, FORTRAN II, FORTRAN IV, COBOL, PLAN.

Contemplated Equipment
Two ICL 1901A systems; two Burroughs B1726 systems.

Services Available
Consultation, programming, education and training, operators, software packages, documentation, preparation of data systems analysis. Operate on closed and open shop and block time basis. Service available to business and industry in general.

Fields of Application
Consultancy services to scientific management, including operations research, management information systems, industrial engineering, EDP systems configuration design, computer systems, etc.
Specialized areas: Computer systems, software development, operations research, inventory control, management information systems.

Training
No formal training programmes but courses available to clients to enable them to make effective use of computer services.

SERVICE BUREAUX

AHMEDABAD ELECTRICITY CO. LTD.
Electricity House, Laldarwaja, Ahmedabad-1
Telephone: 24261

Also at:
Jubilee House, Shahpur Road, Ahmedabad
Telephone: 24764

Officers
K. N. Rad, *Chief Executive*
S. Datta, *Deputy Chief Executive*

Computer Installation
IBM 1401—internal storage: 8K 7-bit characters: magnetic tapes: 4 7330; 1 line printer.

Coding Languages
Autocoder, FORTRAN.

Services Available
Programming, education and training, operators, software packages, preparation of data, systems analysis. Operate on a self-service basis.

Fields of Application
Statistical, commercial, accounting, management.
Specialized areas: Sales analysis, payroll.

Training
One-year course in systems analysis and programming for selected applicants.

ALEMBIC CHEMICAL WORKS COMPANY LTD.*
Alembic Road, Baroda-3, Gujarat
Telephone: 8235

Officer
N. B. Vaze, *Director of Finance*

Computer Installation
ICL 1300—internal storage: 614,400 bits; magnetic tapes: 4.

Coding Languages
MPL-2, MAC.

Contemplated Equipment
ICL 1901A with T.E.D.S. and magnetic tapes.

Services Available
Consultation, programming, education and training, systems analysis. Operate on a block time basis. Service available to other industrial and research organizations.

Fields of Application
Sales statistics, payroll accounting, share accounting, inventory control, branch accounting, cost accounting.

BOMBAY SUBURBAN ELECTRIC SUPPLY LTD.
Electricity House, P.B. 6808. Santacruz (East), Bombay-55 AS
Telephone: 532211

Officer
Sarwottam S. Thakur, *E.D.P. Officer*

Computer Installation
IBM 1401—internal storage: 8K bits; magnetic tapes: 4 7330; 1 line printer.

IBM 1401—internal storage: 16K bits; magnetic tapes: 4 729V; magnetic discs: 2 1311; 1 line printer.

Coding Languages
SPS, Autocoder, FORTRAN, COBOL.

Contemplated Equipment
Third generation multiprocessing computer.

Services Available
Consultation, programming, operators, documentation, preparation of data, systems analysis. Operate on a closed and open shop and block time basis.

Fields of Application
Statistical, commercial, production control, accounting, management, systems analysis.
Specialized area: Utility billing.

COMPUTER SERVICES INTERNATIONAL*
'Sunder Mahal', Marine Drive/Veer Nariman Road junction, Churchgate, Bombay 20.
Telephone: 29-2846

Also at:
518 Churchgate Chambers, 5 New Marine Lines, Bombay 20

Officer
Q. F. X. Gomes, *Director, Systems*

Computer Installation
IBM 1401, IBM 1460, IBM 1620.

Coding Languages
Autocoder, FORTRAN IV, COBOL.

Contemplated Equipment
IBM 024 punching machines.

Services Available
Consultation, programming, education and training, operators, documentation, preparation of data, systems analysis. Service available to all approved candidates.

Fields of Application
Statistical, commercial, production control, accounting, management, systems analysis, operational research, etc.

Training
Courses in computer programming and systems analysis, Autocoder, FORTRAN, COBOL, computer concepts for management personnel, operations research. Computer operator's course. Numerous short courses.

HINDUSTAN MOTORS LTD.*
P.O. Hindmotor, Hooghly, West Bengal
Telephone: 63-1374

Officer
R. K. Dokeniya, *Systems Manager*

Computer Installation
IBM 1401—internal storage: 12K bits; magnetic tapes: 4 7330; magnetic discs: 2 1311; 1 line printer.

Coding Languages
Autocoder, FORTRAN.

Services Available
Consultation, programming, operators, preparation of data, systems analysis. Operate on closed and open shop and on a self-service basis. Service available to all industries.

Fields of Application
Commercial, production control, accounting, statistical.
Specialized areas: Production control, inventory control.

IBM WORLD TRADE CORPORATION*
Bombay

Also at:
16 Strand Road, Calcutta 1
and New Delhi

Computer Installation
Bombay:
IBM 1410.
IBM 1620.
IBM 1401 tape.

Calcutta:
IBM 1401 (2).

New Delhi:
IBM 7044.
IBM 1620.

Services Available
Advice, operators, preparation of data, programming.

Fields of Application
Statistical, commercial.

KIRLOSKAR OIL ENGINES LTD.
Lakshmanrao Kirloskar Road, Kirkee, Poona 411003
Computer at: Kothrud, Poona 411029
Telephone: 55346-47-48; (Computer) 53211/55604

Officers
V. Y. Gaitonde, *Executive, Finance and Credit*
V. Desikan, *Manager, Computer Division*

Computer Installation
ICL 1902—internal storage: 196,608 bits; magnetic tapes: 4.

Coding Languages
PLAN, COBOL, FORTRAN.

Contemplated Equipment
Additional storage of 196,608 bits.

Services Available
Programming, operators, systems analysis. Operate on a closed and open shop basis. Services available to all if sufficient time available.

Fields of Application
Commercial, production control, accounting, management.
Specialized areas: Inventory control, engine design problems.

UNIVERSAL DESIGN SYSTEMS (INDIA) PRIVATE LTD.*
G 16 N.D.S.E., New Delhi 49
Telephone: 62-6492

Officers
Mr. A. K. Bahn, *Director, also in charge of Foreign Relations*
Dr. R. K. Bhan, *Manager, Service Bureau*

Coding Languages
FORTRAN, COBOL, SPS, GPSS, Autocoder.

Services Available
Consultation, programming, software packages, documentation, preparation of data, systems analysis.

Fields of Application
Scientific, statistical, commercial, accounting, management systems.
Specialized areas: Engineering, applied mathematics.

INDONESIA

COLLEGE

INSTITUT TEKNOLOGI BANDUNG
Jalan Ganeca 10, Bandung

Officers
Dr. Ir. Kudrat Soemintapoera, *Director*
Dr. Ir. Harjono Djojodihardjo, *Director of Research and Development*
Ir. Harsono, *Director of EDP Systems*

Computer Installation
IBM 1401—internal storage 16K x 8 bits; magnetic tapes: 4 7330; 1 line printer.

Coding Languages
Autocoder, FORTRAN IV, FORTRAN II.

Contemplated Equipment
Disc unit.

Services Available
Advice, programming, education and training and systems analysis. Operate on a closed shop basis.

Fields of Application
Scientific, statistical, commercial.
Specialized areas: Linear programming, analysis, structural engineering, other engineering.

Training
Courses in Autocoder and FORTRAN programming.

GOVERNMENT ESTABLISHMENTS

CENTRAL BUREAU OF STATISTICS
Data Processing Centre
Jalan Dr. Sutomo No. 8, Djakarta
Telephone: 46289

Officer
Dr. Sam Suharto, *Director*

Computer Installation
ICL 1903A—magnetic tapes 6; magnetic discs: 2.
UNIVAC 1050—1 line printer.

Coding Languages
PLAN, FORTRAN, COBOL.

Services Available
Advice, programming, operators, software packages, documentation, preparation of data and systems analysis. Operate on a closed shop and block time basis. Available mainly to government agencies.

Fields of Application
Scientific, statistical and management.
Specialized area: Statistical data processing.

Training
Courses for programmers and system analysts, for internal needs only.

DEPARTMENT OF PUBLIC WORKS
Computer Centre
Djl. Pattimura, 7 Kebajoran Baru, Djakarta
Telephone: 71910

Officer
Soenarjono Danoedjo, *Director*

Computer Installation
IBM 1130—operating system: DMS; internal storage: 16K 16-bit binary words; magnetic discs: 1 2310 B2; 1 line printer.

Coding Languages
FORTRAN IV, IBM 1130 RPG, Assembler.

Services Available
Advice, programming, education and training, operators, preparation of data, systems analysis. Operate on self-service basis. Service available to the Government and to private enterprise.

Fields of Application
Scientific, statistical, project control/management, systems analysis, operational research.
Specialized areas: Linear programming, analysis, payroll, structural engineering, public works engineering.

Training
Courses in FORTRAN, 1130 RPG, network-planning method, systems analysis; introduction to the computer system; IBM STRESS, IBM PCS and IBM SSP packages.

CONSULTANT

POPE, EVANS & ROBBINS INTERNATIONAL LTD.
P.O. Box 2487, Djakarta
Telephone: 40909

Officers
K. Dreher, *Vice President and Resident Managing Director*
B. Pantell, *Computer Systems Manager*

Coding Languages
COBOL, FORTRAN, BAL, PL/1.

Services Available
Advice, programming, education and training, software packages, documentation, systems analysis. No hardware services available.

Fields of Application
Statistical, commercial, management.

Training
Programmer courses (certificates of completion provided).

IRAN

UNIVERSITIES

DÂNESHGÂHÉ ISFAHAN
Computer Centre
Isfahan
Telephone: (031) 29011, extension 263

Officer
Firouz Parvaz, *Director of Computer Centre*

Computer Installation
IBM System 3—operating system: DOS; internal storage: 192K bits; magnetic discs: 9 5444; 2 line printers.

Coding Languages
FORTRAN, COBOL, RPG, Assembler.

Contemplated Equipment
Time-sharing terminals, dual programming feature.

Services Available
Advice, programming, education and training, and systems analysis. Operate on a self-service basis. Available to anyone on the approval of the Chancellor.

Fields of Application
Scientific, statistical, commercial, accounting, systems analysis.
Specialized areas: Analysis, payroll, statistics and scientific research.

Training
Courses for university students in basic and advanced Computer Programming and Analysis.

DÂNESHGÂHÉ PAHLAVI
Computer Centre
Shiraz
Telephone: 6104, extensions 570 and 27895

Officer
Dr. Iradj Tadjbakhsh, *Director*

Computer Installation
IBM 1130—operating system: DOS; internal storage: 32K bits; 1 line printer.

Coding Languages
FORTRAN IV, RPG, Assembler, COBOL.

Contemplated Equipment
IBM 370/135 with storage of 98K bytes; 4 2741 terminals.

Services Available
Consultation, programming, education and training, preparation of data, systems analysis. Operate on a closed shop basis.

Fields of Application
Scientific, statistical, commercial.
Specialized areas: Analysis, structural engineering.

Training
Courses on numerical analysis and computer programming as mathematics option.

DÂNESHGÂHÉ SANATI ARYA-MEHR
Eisenhower Blvd., P.O. Box 3406, Teheran
Telephone: 97-5052

Officer
Dr. Mehdi B. Kermani, *Director of Computer Centre and Professor of Computer Sciences*

Computer Installation
CDC 6400—operating system: SCOPE 3.3; internal storage: 3,932,160 bits; magnetic tapes: 3 7-track, 2 9-track; magnetic discs: 3 841; 1 line printer. *Remote processing features*: batch and time-sharing.

Coding Languages
FORTRAN, COBOL, BASIC, ALGOL 60, SIMSCRIPT, OPTIMA, Intercom, SORT/MERGE, MIMIC, etc.

Services Available
Programming, education and training, software packages and systems analysis. Operate on a closed shop and time-sharing basis.

Fields of Application
Scientific, statistical, commercial, accounting, management, systems analysis, operational research.
Specialized areas: Linear programming, analysis, payroll, structural engineering.

Training
Courses for B.S. and M.S. in computer sciences; other courses include: basic computer programming, Assembler and machine code, numerical analysis I and II, comparative study of programming languages, compiler writing and design of assemblers, business data processing, operational research, etc.

CONSULTANT

MINISTRY OF FINANCE
Data Processing Centre
Nasser Khosrow Ave., Teheran
Telephone: 315 218

Officer
Ali Nowtash, *General Director*

Computer Installations
IBM 360/40 (2)—operating system: DOS; internal storage: 128K bits each; magnetic tapes: 3 2420 and 1 2401 each; magnetic discs: 3 2314 each; 2 line printers each.

Coding Languages
COBOL, PL/1, FORTRAN.

Services Available
Advice, programming, education and training, operators, software packages, documentation, preparation of data, systems analysis. Operate on a self-service, block time and open shop basis.

Fields of Application
Statistical, commercial, accounting, management, systems analysis.
Specialized area: Payroll.

SERVICE BUREAU

IBM WORLD TRADE CORPORATION*
Teheran

Computer Installation
IBM 1460.

Services Available
Advice, operators, preparation of data, programming.

Fields of Application
Statistical, commercial.

IRAQ

NATIONAL CENTRE

NATIONAL COMPUTER CENTRE
P.O. Box 3261, Al-Nafoora Square, Baghdad
Telephone: 86151/2/3

Officer
Naim Hassan al-Adhadh, *Director General*

Services Available
Advice, programming, education and training, systems analysis.

Fields of Application
Commercial, management and systems analysis.
Specialized area: Analysis.

Training
Courses in programming (COBOL and FORTRAN) and systems analysis.

UNIVERSITY

UNIVERSITY OF BAGHDAD
College of Engineering
Bab Al-Maodham, Baghdad

Officer
Dr. T. T. Niami, *Head of Department*

Computer Installation
IBM 1130—operating system: Batch; internal storage: 256K bits; magnetic discs: 3 2315; 1 line printer.

Coding Languages
FORTRAN, Assembler, ALGOL, RPG, DPS, etc.

Contemplated Equipment
Link with IBM 370.

Services Available
Advice, programming, education and training. Available to students and for research only.

Fields of Application
Scientific, statistical.

Training
Courses in programming, computer applications and computer science and numerical techniques.

GOVERNMENT ESTABLISHMENTS

IRAQI REPUBLIC RAILWAYS
Computer Department
Baghdad Central Station
Telephone: 30011

Officers
A. J. Sa'adi, *Director General*
M. Haba, *General Technical Inspector*
M. A. L. Mahmoud, *Computer Manager*

Computer Installation
ICL 1902–operating system: executive; internal storage: 196K bits; magnetic tapes 4 1971; 2 line printers.

Coding Languages
PLAN, COBOL, FORTRAN

Services Available
Programming, preparation of data, systems analysis. Operate on a self-service basis.

Fields of Application
Commercial, statistical.
Specialized areas: Payroll, inventory.

Training
Courses in programming, systems analysis and design, engineering maintenance, operation, control.

NATIONAL ELECTRICITY ADMINISTRATION
Jumhuriya Street, Baghdad
Telephone: 68551/5 (Exchange), 65029 (Director)

Officers
A. I. Dewachi, *Director*
Mrs. R. Al-Saadi, *Head of Systems*

Computer Installation
NCR 315/100–operating system: CRM/IIB; internal storage: 240K bits; magnetic cards: 4 CRAM; 2 line printers.

Coding Languages
NEAT 315, BEST, COBOL, FORTRAN IV.

Services Available
Advice, programming, education and training, software packages, documentation, preparation of data, systems analysis. Operate on a closed shop basis.

Fields of Application
Scientific, statistical, commercial, accounting, management, systems analysis.
Specialized areas: Payroll, power systems analysis and billing.

IRELAND

UNIVERSITIES AND COLLEGES

AN FORAS TALÚNTAIS*
(Agricultural Institute)
33 Merrion Road, Ballsbridge, Dublin 4
Telephone: 693222

Officers
Dr. T. Walsh, *Director*
J. Kilroy, *Head of Scientific Liaison Office*
Dermot Harrington, *Acting Head, Statistics and Biometrics Department*

Computer Installation
ELLIOTT 803–internal storage: 4K 39-digit words

Coding Languages
Elliott Autocode, Machine code, ALGOL, FORTRAN.

Services Available
Advice, operators, preparation of data, programming. Operate on a closed shop basis. Available to outside users for research purposes as time allows and at the discretion of the Director.

Fields of Application
All aspects of processing for agricultural research.
Specialized area: Statistical analysis.

NATIONAL UNIVERSITY OF IRELAND*
University College
Cork
Telephone: (021) 26871

Officers
C. T. G. Dillon
P. G. O'Regan

Computer Installation
IBM 1130–internal storage: 512K bits; magnetic discs: 3; 1 line printer.

IBM 1620–operating system: MONITOR 1; internal storage: 240K bits; magnetic disc: 1311.

Coding Language
FORTRAN.

Contemplated Equipment
Link between 1130 and IBM 360

Services Available
Advice, preparation of data, programming, statistical analysis. Operate on an open shop basis.

Fields of Application
Scientific, statistical, operational research.

NATIONAL UNIVERSITY OF IRELAND*
University College
Stillorgan Road, Dublin 4
Telephone: 69-32-44

Officer
Dr. F. Anderson, *Director*

Computer Installation
IBM 360/50–internal storage: 2,097,152 bits; magnetic tapes: 2 2415; magnetic discs: 4 2311; 2 line printers.

IBM 1620/I–internal storage: 240K bits.

Coding Languages
FORTRAN, COBOL, PL/1, Assembler.

Contemplated Equipment
2 2741; 2314 disc drives.

Services Available
Advice, operators, preparation of data. Operate on a closed shop and remote access basis.

Fields of Application
Scientific, engineering and statistical calculations for interested University Depts. Records, accounting, payroll for University administration.

Ireland – Service Bureaux

Training
Regular courses in programming. Computer science as part of engineering courses. B.Sc. General includes Computer Science.

NATIONAL UNIVERSITY OF IRELAND
University College
Galway
Telephone: Galway 7611

Officer
Prof. O'Keefe, *Engineering School*

Computer Installation
IBM 1800–operating system: TSX time shares executive (card based); internal storage: 16,250K x 16 bits; magnetic tapes: 1; magnetic discs: 3; *Remote processing features*: Electrical input/output to laboratories, both digital and analog. 1 line printer.

Contemplated Equipment
Terminal to large system.

Services Available
Education and training. Operate on a self-service, closed and open shop and time-sharing basis. Available for education, academic research and educational administration. Other usage by President's consent.

Fields of Application
Education, academic research, educational administration. *Specialized areas*: University interests.

Training
Courses in computation are incorporated into academic curricula. Tutorials are also available.

UNIVERSITY OF DUBLIN, TRINITY COLLEGE
Computer Laboratory
Dublin 2
Telephone: 772941

Officers
J. J. Moriarty, *Director, Computer Laboratory*
Dr. J. G. Byrne, *Head, Department of Computer Science*

Computer Installation
IBM 360/44–operating system: O.S.; internal storage: 2,097,152 bits; magnetic tapes: 1 2415; magnetic discs: 4 2311; 1 line printer. *Remote processing features*: 8 2260, 6 2741, 1 ASR 33.

Coding Languages
FORTRAN, PL/1, COBOL, Assembler, BASIC.

Services Available
Advice, education and training, operators, preparation of data. Operate on a remote access, closed shop and time-sharing basis.

Fields of Application
Scientific, statistical, commercial, accounting, operational research.
Specialized areas: Payroll, structural engineering, bibliographic data processing.

Training
Diploma courses in Computing for Engineers and in Systems Analysis. Degree courses leading to B.A.I. in Engineering/Computer Science, B.Sc. in Computer Science, M.Sc. in Computer Applications and in Information Science.

GOVERNMENT ESTABLISHMENT

DUBLIN HEALTH AUTHORITY*
1 James Street, Dublin 8
Telephone: 754264

Computer Installation
ICL 1901A–operating system: automatic operator; internal storage: 16K bits core; magnetic tapes: 4; 1 line printer.

Coding Languages
COBOL, FORTRAN.

Services Available
Limited service available to allied hospitals and medical boards (payroll applications and social surveys).

Fields of Application
Statistical, accounting, research (surveys).

CONSULTANTS

P.A. MANAGEMENT CONSULTANTS LTD.*
Hume House, Ballsbridge, Dublin 4
Telephone: 684346

Also at:
1A South Mall, Cork.

(*See* under United Kingdom)

P.-E. CONSULTING GROUP LTD.*
24 Fitzwilliam Place, Dublin 2

(*See* under United Kingdom)

SYSTEM DYNAMICS LTD.
72 Merrion Square, Dublin 2
Telephone: (01) 64701

Officers
F. J. Kennedy
T. E. McGovern

Services Available
Advice, programming, education and training, software packages, systems analysis.

Fields of Application
Scientific, commercial, production control, accounting, operational research, telecommunications.
Specialized areas: Transport, real time applications.

Training
Courses developed to meet clients' training requirements.

SERVICE BUREAUX

BARIC COMPUTING SERVICES LTD.*
ICL House, Adelaide Road, Dublin 2
Telephone: 56761

(*See* under United Kingdom)

COMPUTER SERVICES LTD.
Swords Road, Santry, Dublin 9
Telephone: 375181

Ireland – Service Bureaux

Officers
J. M. Doherty, *Managing Director*
J. B. O'Sullivan, *Technical Director*

Computer Installation
ICL 1902A–operating system: GEORGE 1S; internal storage: 393,216 bits; magnetic tapes: 4; magnetic discs: 2; 1 line printer.

Coding Languages
PLAN, COBOL.

Services Available
Programming, software packages, documentation, preparation of data, systems analysis. Operate on a self-service and closed shop basis.

Fields of Application
Scientific, statistical, commercial, accounting, management.
Specialized areas: Sales analysis, payroll, typesetting.

IBM IRELAND LTD.*
2 Burlington Road, Dublin 4
Telephone: 60151

Officers
John O'Leary, *Manager of Data Centre Services*

Computer Installation
IBM 360/40–internal storage: 128K bits; magnetic tapes: 4 2311; magnetic discs: 5 2401 II; 1 line printer.
IBM 1401–internal storage: 16K bits; 1 line printer.
IBM 1401–internal storage: 16K bits; magnetic tapes: 5 7330; 1 line printer.

Coding Languages
SPS, COBOL, Assembler.

Services Available
Advice, operators, preparation of data, programming, software packages, systems analysis. Operate on a self-service and block time basis.

Fields of Application
Commercial, accounting, systems analysis, management, statistical. Limited scientific applications.

MAY ROBERTS LTD.
Grand Canal Quay, Dublin 2

Officer
P. J. Little, *Data Processing Manager*

Computer Installation
ICL 1901–internal storage: 1,573,864 bits; magnetic tapes: 4; 1 line printer.

Coding Languages
COBOL, FORTRAN, ALGOL.

Contemplated Equipment
ICL 1903.

Services Available
Consultation, programming, education and training, software packages, systems analysis. Operate on a self-service basis.

Fields of Application
Commercial, accounting.

PUNCH CARD SERVICE CENTRE*
Data Preparation and Training Division
179 Pearse Street, Dublin 2
Telephone: 778678

Officer
Gabriel M. Murphy

Services Available
Education and training, operators, documentation, preparation of data. Operate on a self-service basis.

Training
Key-punch operators' course.

ISRAEL

EDUCATIONAL AND TRAINING INSTITUTION

CENTRE FOR EDUCATIONAL TECHNOLOGY
8 Shederot Jacob, P.O. Box 93, Herzlia
Telephone: (03) 938813, (03) 938619

Officers
Dr. Yona Peless, *General Director*
Ing. Amnon Oren, *Head of Computer Centre*

Computer Installations
PDP-11/20–operating system: RSTS-11 time-sharing; internal storage: 28K x 16 bits; magnetic tapes: dual DEC tapes; magnetic discs: 1 RF11; 1 line printer.
Remote processing features: 16 terminals.

Contemplated Equipment
RK05 Cartridge (1.2 million words).

Services Available
Advice, education and training, documentation and preparation of data. Operate on an open shop and time-sharing basis.

Fields of Application
Scientific, educational.

Training
Courses in Computer Literacy for 10th grade classes, Computer Problem Solving and Simulation for 11th and 12th grade classes, and Computer Assisted Instruction programmes.

UNIVERSITIES AND COLLEGES

HA-TECHNION
(Israel Institute of Technology)
Computer Centre
Technion City, Haifa
Telephone: (04) 225-111

Officer
Dr. Doron Cohen

Computer Installation
IBM 370/165–operating system: MVT; internal storage: 2,000K bytes; magnetic tapes: 5 3420; magnetic discs: 8 3330; 1 line printer. *On-line satellite computers*: 3. *Remote processing features*: 2.

Coding Languages
ALGOL, FORTRAN, PL/1, COBOL, RPG, Assembler 360.

Services Available
Advice, education and training, operators, software packages. Operate on a remote access, closed shop and time sharing basis.

Fields of Application
Scientific, statistical, commercial, production control, accounting, management, operational research.

HA-UNIVERSITA HA-IVRIT BI-YERUSHALAYIM
(The Hebrew University of Jerusalem)
Givat-Ram, Jerusalem
Telephone: 30211, extension 218

Officers
M. Leev, *Director of the Computation Centre*

Computer Installation
CDC 6600–operating system: SCOPE 3.4; internal storage: 65K bit words; magnetic tapes: 4 604; magnetic discs: 1 6638, 8 844; 3 line printers. *Remote processing features*: 1 200 terminal, 1 UNITECH terminal.

CDC 6400– operating system: SCOPE 3.4; internal storage: 65K words; linked to peripherals of CDC 6600.

Coding Languages
FORTRAN, COBOL, SIMSCRIPT, SNOBOL.

Services Available
Consultation, systems analysis. Operate on a closed shop basis. Available only to staff, students and administrators of the university.

Fields of Application
Scientific, statistical, systems analysis.

UNIVERSITA BAR-ILAN
Ramat-Gan
Telephone: 03-752114

Officer
E. Ben-Kohan, *Director of Computing Centre*

Computer Installation
IBM 360/50–operating system: OS, HASP; internal storage: 152K plus 1 million bits; magnetic tapes: 3 2401; magnetic discs: 1 2314; 1 line printer. *Remote processing features*: 14 2741, 3 2260, 3 1050.

Coding Languages
FORTRAN IV, APL, COBOL, PL/1, Assembler, SNOBOL.

Services Available
Consultation, programming, education and training, operators, software packages, documentation, preparation of data, systems analysis. Operate on a self-service, closed shop, remote access and block time basis. Available to both academic and administrative sides of the University.

Fields of Application
Scientific, statistical, commercial, production control, accounting, management, systems analysis, operational research.
Specialized area: Information retrieval of legal material, applied to Rabbinical responsa.

Training
Undergraduate course in Computer Science leading to B.A. and B.Sc. Short courses in FORTRAN, use of statistical packages, and courses for high school teachers.

UNIVERSITAT HANEGEV
(University of the Negev)
Beer-Sheva
Telephone: 057-2209

Officers
J. Regev, *Head of Computer Services Unit*
Dr. M. Hanani, *Head of Computer Science Department*

Computer Installation
IBM 1130–operating system: DM2; internal storage: 256K bits; magnetic discs: 3; 1 line printer.

Coding Languages
FORTRAN, Assembler, COBOL, APL, SC/1.

Services Available
Advice, programming. Operate on a closed shop basis.

Fields of Application
Scientific, statistical, commercial.

Training
Course in Computer Science leading to B.A.; Introduction to Programming courses for most students in engineering and natural sciences faculties.

UNIVERSITAT TEL-AVIV
Louis Calder Jr. Computation Center
Ramat-Aviv, Tel-Aviv
Telephone: 416 111

Officers
Prof. Shalom Abarbanel, *Chairman of Computer Committee*
Tom Meyer, *Director of Computation Center*

Computer Installation
CDC 6600–operating system: SCOPE 3.3; internal storage: 98K × 60 bits; magnetic tapes: 8 841, 1 808; 4 line printers. *Remote processing features*: 4 200-user terminals, 6 TTY.

Coding Languages
FORTRAN, COBOL, ALGOL, COMPASS, BASIC, SIMSCRIPT, SIMULA.

Contemplated Equipment
CDC 6400 with storage of 32K bits.

Services Available
Programming, operators, software packages, documentation. Operate on a remote access, block time and time-sharing basis.

Fields of Application
Scientific, statistical, commercial.
Specialized areas: Linear programming, medical research.

GOVERNMENT ESTABLISHMENTS

INSTITUTE FOR PETROLEUM RESEARCH AND GEOPHYSICS*
P.O.B. 269, Holon

Officers
Dr. A. Ginzburg, *Director of the Institute*
A. Ashkenazi, *Head of the Computer Centre*

Computer Installation
IBM 360/44—operating systems: 44 PS, DOS; internal storage: 1,024K bits; magnetic tapes: 2 2400; magnetic discs: 2 2311; 1 line printer.

Coding Languages
Assembler, FORTRAN, COBOL, PL/1, RPG, ALGOL.

Services Available
Programming, operators, software packages, preparation of data, systems analysis. Operate on a closed shop basis.

Field of Application
Scientific.
Specialized area: Seismic data processing.

MINISTRY OF FINANCE*
Accountant General
Ropin Street 2, Jerusalem
Telephone: 63111

Officer
R. Silver, *Director of the Computer Centre*

Computer Installation
NCR Century 100—internal storage: 32K bits; magnetic tapes: 3 633-119; magnetic discs: 1 655-101; 1 line printer.

Coding Languages
NEAT-3, COBOL.

Contemplated Equipment
Changeover to an NCR Century 200.

Services Available
Programming, operators. Operate on a self-service basis. Available only to government departments.

Fields of Application
Accounting and budgetary reporting.

NATIONAL INSURANCE INSTITUTE*
13 Weizman Ave., Jerusalem
Telephone: 02-51211

Officers
A. Palmon, *Director of the Computer Service*
E. Gafni, *Director of Public Relations*
Y. Levanon, *Director of Training*

Computer Installation
NCR Century 200— internal storage: 64K bytes; magnetic tapes: 4; magnetic discs: 1; 1 line printer.

Services Available
Programming, operators, preparation of data, systems analysis. Operate on a self-service basis.

Fields of Application
Accounting, management.

OFFICE MECHANIZATION CENTRE
P.O.B. 13016, Jerusalem
Telephone: 02-55111

Also at:
Tel Aviv
Telephone: 03-828181

Officers
D. Chevion, *Director*
H. Dudai, *Deputy Director*
A. Shatz, *Deputy Director*

Computer Installation
IBM 370/165—operating system: OS, MVT; internal storage: 1.5 million bytes; magnetic tapes: 12 3420/5; magnetic discs: 10 3330, 8 2314; 5 line printers. *On-line satellite computer*: IBM 360/30. *Remote processing features*: 2703 to 2780, 2770, 360/20, 3780, 2740.

Coding Languages
COBOL, FORTRAN, MARK IV, BAL.

Contemplated Equipment
IBM 370/168 with storage of 2 million bytes and 12 3330 disc drives; 3705, communication control; Extensions of interactive communications facilities.

Services Available
Programming, operators, planning, systems design. Operate on a closed shop basis. Government centre available to the public sector but not to private firms.

Fields of Application
Government information systems and information centres regarding population register, medical records and hospitals, inventory control, foreign trade, payroll, cultural planning, statistical tabulations in various fields of administration, RJE and telecommunication set-up with a number of customers.

Training
One-year systems analysts courses, and refresher courses of 1-4 weeks for systems analysts and programmers.

'TEFAHOT' ISRAEL MORTGAGE BANK LTD.
9 Heleni Hamalka Street, Jerusalem
Telephone: 227331

Officer
M. Lahav

Computer Installation
IBM 360/25—operating systems: BPS, DOS; internal storage: 384K bits; magnetic tapes: 4 2401; magnetic discs: 2 2311; 1 line printer. *On-line satellite computer*: 1.

Coding Languages
RPG, Assembler, COBOL.

Contemplated Equipment
3 Punches, 2 verifiers.

Services Available
Consultation, programming, operators, preparation of data, systems analysis. Operate on a self-service basis.

Fields of Application
Mainly accounting.

RESEARCH INSTITUTIONS

DATA PROCESSING RESEARCH DEMONSTRATION CENTRE FOR THE BLIND AND OTHERWISE HANDICAPPED*
1 Maimon Street, Jerusalem

Officer
E. Shapir

Computer Installation
IBM 360/20—internal storage: 8K bits.

Services Available
Consultation, education and training. Operate on a self-service basis.

Field of Application
Management.

Training
Courses for Unit Record Operators, 360/20 Operators and 360/20 Programmers. Short course for Key Punchers.

ILTAM CORPORATION FOR PLANNING AND RESEARCH LTD.
18 Keren Hayesod, P.O. Box 7170, Jerusalem
Telephone: 28377

Officers
A. Gertz, *Director-General*
E. Wardi, *Chief Assistant*
E. Wagner, *Chief Assistant*

Services Available
Advice, education and training.

Training
International seminars on informatics.

ISRAEL INSTITUTE OF PRODUCTIVITY*
4 Henrietta Szold Street, Tel Aviv
Telephone: 25 31 31

Officers
A. Ronell, *Director of Systems and ADP Department*
T. Siegel, *Chief Systems Analyst*
N. Levy, *Chief Programmer*

Services Available
Consultation, programming, education and training, systems analysis. Operate on a block time basis.

Training
3-6 month courses in Basic and Advanced Systems Analysis. 5-day Appreciation courses for Managers.

WEIZMANN INSTITUTE OF SCIENCE
Rehovot
Telephone: Rehovot 951721

Officer
Smil Ruhman, *Professor of Computer Sciences*

Computer Installation
GOLEM B—internal storage: 8.4 million bits; magnetic tapes: 5 CDC 9580, 3 CDC 607; magnetic discs: 4 IBM 2314; 2 line printers.

Coding Language
FORTRAN IV.

Contemplated Equipment
4 IBM 3330, time-sharing, graphic terminal.

Services Available
Operate on a self-service basis.

Field of Application
Scientific.
Specialized areas: Matrix inversion, design automation.

Training
Courses related to applied mathematics, geophysics and seismology, and in computer engineering and science, design automation, programming.

CONSULTANTS

ADVANCED TECHNOLOGY LTD.
8 Smuts Street, Tel Aviv
Telephone: 442697

Officers
Prof. D. Shimshoni, *Chairman*
M. Bunstin, *Managing Director*

Services Available
Consultation, programming, systems analysis.

Fields of Application
Scientific, management, systems analysis, operational research.

ALEF RESEARCH AND DEVELOPMENT LTD.
Julius Simon Street, Haifa Bay 26110, P.O. Box 10069
Telephone: 04-729188/9

Officer
A. Shani

Services Available
Consultation, programming, systems analysis.

Fields of Application
Scientific, systems analysis.
Specialized areas: Programming and system design for numerical control systems.

COMBIT (ISRAEL) LTD.
26 Herut Street, Ramat-Gan
Telephone: (03) 795538

Officers
Z. Ettinger, N. Gertner, *Joint Managing Directors*

Services Available
Advice, programming, software packages, documentation, systems analysis.

Fields of Application
Commercial, production control, accounting, management, systems analysis, operational research.
Specialized areas: Payroll, production control, inventory control.

COMPUTERS AND ORGANIZATION LTD.*
12 Shlomo Hamelech Street, Tel Aviv
Telephone: 220959

Also at:
8 Samuel Hanagid Street, Jerusalem
Telephone: 23924

Officers
Y. Neeman, *Co-manager*
M. Livnat, *Co-manager*
Z. Spillman, *Senior Executive*

Services Available
Advice, programming, systems analysis, software packages.

Fields of Application
Commercial, organization, systems analysis.
Specialized areas: Production and inventory control, data banks, management information systems.

CONTAHAL LTD.
54 Ibn Gvirol Street, Tel Aviv
Telephone: 263263

Officers
Dr. M. Gutterman, *General Manager*
Y. Milman, *Assistant to the General Manager*
E. Atar, *Manager ADP*

Coding Languages
All languages.

Services Available
Consultation, programming, education and training, software packages, documentation, preparation of data, systems analysis, operations research.

Fields of Application
Scientific, statistical, commercial, production control, accounting, management, systems design and analysis, operational research, operating systems, formation and management of computer centres.

ELECTRO-MISRAD*
9 Carlibach Street, Tel-Aviv

Services Available
Consultation, systems analysis.

Fields of Application
Management, tax and revenue collection integrated systems, retail distribution systems.

ELNIV SOFTWARE*
86/88 Hagiborim Street, Haifa
Telephone: 04-42411

Also at:
85 Ha'Universita Street, Ramat-Aviv
Telephone: 03-414050

Officer
H. P. Rogoway, *Manager*

Computer Installation
ELBIT 100—operating system: BASIC; internal storage: 48,152 bits; magnetic tapes: 2; magnetic discs: 1; 1 line printer.

Time also rented in larger computers.

Coding Languages
Assembler, COBOL, FORTRAN, PL/1.

Contemplated Equipment
Time-sharing terminals on the premises.

Services Available
Consultation, programming, software packages, systems analysis. Available to end users, manufacturers and software houses, but not to service bureaux.

Fields of Application
Software design and development, contract programming, remote processing, information systems, software package development, operations research. Many of these activities are directed towards export.
Specialized areas: Real-time systems, programming languages and processors, information systems.

GERTZBERG OREN & CO. LTD.*
49 La-Guardia Street, Tel-Aviv
Telephone: 32923, 35594

Officers
M. Getzberg, *President, in charge of Management Controls and Industrial Engineering sections*
A. Oren, *Vice President, in charge of Computer Applications section*

Coding Languages
Assembly languages for: IBM 360, CDC 3300, NCR 315, NCR 500, Philco 2000, Philco 1000; COBOL, FORTRAN, NCR BEST.

Services Available
Advice, preparation of data, programming, software packages, systems analysis.

Fields of Application
Statistical, commercial, production control, accounting, management, operational research, etc.

Training
Short courses in programming, systems analysis, hardware selection and installation planning.

INDUSTRIES DEVELOPMENT CORPORATION*
4 Chopin Street, Jerusalem

Also at:
58 Moriah Street, Haifa

Officers
M. Rosner
I. Hoffman

Services Available
Consultation, programming, software packages, documentation, preparation of data, systems analysis.

Fields of Application
Statistical, commercial, accounting, management, systems analysis, operational research.

MANAGEMENT ACCOUNTING AND EDP CONSULTANTS LTD. (MANHIM)
79a University Street, Ramat-Aviv, Tel-Aviv 69201
Telephone: 414481

Officer
M. Pnini, *Director*

Service Available
Advice.

Fields of Application
Commercial, accounting and management.

NATAM—SYSTEMS ANALYSIS & OPERATIONS RESEARCH LTD.
9 Washington Street, P.O.B. 3521, Jerusalem
Telephone: 02-227055, 225796

Also at:
9 Lincoln Street, Tel-Aviv
Telephone: 03-284268/9

2 Ayalon Street, Haifa
Telephone: 04-244425

Officers
Dr. F. Moser, *Managing Director, Jerusalem*
Dr. I. Amit, *Managing Director, Tel-Aviv*

Coding Languages
IBM 360—Assembler, COBOL, FORTRAN, RPG.
CDC 3000 and 6000 series—Assembler, COBOL, FORTRAN.
NCR 315—NEAT.

Services Available
Consultation, programming, education and training, software packages, documentation, systems analysis.

Fields of Application
Systems analysis for large-scale commercial systems, operations research and development of mathematical models, feasibility studies, general consultancy.

SHEKEM LTD.*
Jerusalem Bvd. 8, Jaffa
Telephone: 825231 and 829700

Officer
A. Lachover

Computer Installation
IBM 360/20—operating systems: BPS, TPS, internal storage: 12K bits; magnetic tapes: 4 2415; 1 line printer.

Coding Languages
RPG, Assembler, Utility.

Services Available
Programming, operators, preparation of data. Operate on a self-service basis.

Fields of Application
Commercial, production control, accounting, management.

SYSTEMS TECHNOLOGY CORP. LTD. (S.T.C.)*
34 Yitzhak Street, Tel Aviv
Telephone: 39037

Officers
D. Taiber
Z. Neuman

Services Available
Consultation, programming, software packages, systems analysis. Operate on a block time basis.

Fields of Application
Scientific, statistical, commercial, production control, accounting, management, systems analysis, operational research.
Specialized areas: Management science, operational research, data processing systems.

TAHAL CONSULTING ENGINEERS LTD.*
54 Ibn Gevirol Street, Tel Aviv
Telephone: 263263

Officers
A. Wiener, *President*
D. Quastler, *Vice-President*

Computer Installation
IBM 1130/3C—operating system: Disc Monitor; internal storage: 256K bits; magnetic discs: 3 IBM 2315; 1 line printer.

Coding Language
FORTRAN IV.

Contemplated Equipment
IBM 1130/2B.

Services Available
Advice, preparation of data, programming, systems analysis, software packages, operational research.

Fields of Application
Engineering (civil, hydraulic, structural), water resources, operational research, statistical, management science, project control.

SERVICE BUREAUX

"BADAL" COMPUTER & MANAGEMENT SERVICES LTD.
3 Karlibach Street, Tel Aviv 67 132
Telephone: 285223

Officer
Y. Ben-Shachar, *Manager*

Computer Installation
NCR 315—internal storage: 20K slabs; magnetic tapes: 3 332; magnetic discs: 3 CRAM 353.

BURROUGHS B4704—operating system: MCP; internal storage: 150K bytes; magnetic tapes: 6 B9393, 2 B9391; magnetic discs: B9375; 1 line printer.

Coding Languages
NEAT (NCR 315), COBOL (B4704).

Contemplated Equipment
Additional disc of 60 million bytes.

Services Available
Advice, operators. Operate on a block time and open shop basis. Available mostly on a block time basis.

Field of Application
Banking services.

DATA AUTOMATION LTD.*
10 Karlibach Street, Tel Aviv
Telephone: 265455

Officer
E. E. Efrat, *Manager of the Service Bureau*

Coding Languages
COBOL, PL/1, Assembler, FORTRAN, COMPASS.

Services Available
Programming, education and training, preparation of data, systems analysis. Operate on a block time basis.

Fields of Application
Statistical, commercial, systems analysis.
Specialized areas: Insurance, accounting.

Training
First degree course in Planning and Programming. Short courses (7-8 months) in Computers—usage and ways of operation, Report programme generator (IBM 360/20), Assembler (IBM 360/50), COBOL (IBM 360/50, CDC 6600).

HAMASHBIR HAMERKAZI ISRAEL CO-OPERATIVE WHOLESALE SOCIETY LTD.*
P.O.B. 130, 56 Giborej Israel, Tel Aviv
Telephone: 39955

Israel – Service Bureaux

Officers
E. Friedman
E. Matz

Computer Installation
IBM 360/30–operating systems: BPS, TOS, Compatibility; internal storage: 32K bits; magnetic tapes: 4 2401/001; 1 line printer.

Coding Languages
Assembler, RPG, COBOL.

Contemplated Equipment
Exchange of tapes to 2401/002, addition of 32K bits internal storage, addition of 4 2314/AO1 disc drives.

Services Available
Consultation, programming, education and training, operators, documentation, preparation of data, systems analysis. Operate on an open shop basis.

Fields of Application
Commercial, accounting, statistical, management, systems analysis.

IDAN COMPUTERS LTD.
34 Ytzhak Saden Street, Tel Aviv
Telephone: 03-39821

Officers
A. S. Morag
A. Sonnenfeld
Y. Rosner

Computer Installation
IBM 1130–internal storage: 8K words; magnetic discs: 1; 1 line printer. *Remote processing features*: 1 Calcomp plotter.

IBM 1130–internal storage: 8K 16-bit words; magnetic discs: 1. *Remote processing features*: 1 220 Benson flatbed plotter.

Coding Languages
Assembler, RPG, FORTRAN IV.

Services Available
Consultation, programming, software packages, systems analysis. Operate on a self-service and open shop basis.

Fields of Application
Scientific, statistical, production control, management, systems analysis, operational research, engineering.
Specialized areas: Road design, maps, special monitoring software.

IBM ISRAEL DATA CENTRE SERVICES*
15 Lincoln Street, Tel Aviv
Telephone: 266111

Officer
M. Eshkol

Computer Installation
IBM 360/40 (2)–operating systems: DOS, OS; internal storage: 1,048,576 bits; magnetic tapes: 6 2400; magnetic discs: 5 2314, 3 2311; 1 line printer.

IBM 360/30–operating system: DOS; internal storage: 524,288 bits; magnetic tapes: 4 2400; magnetic discs: 3 2311; 1 line printer.

IBM 360/20–internal storage: 131,072 bits; magnetic tapes: 4 2400; 1 line printer.

IBM 360/25–operating system: BPS; internal storage: 262,144 bits; magnetic tapes: 4 2400; 1 line printer.

Services Available
Programming, operators, systems analysis. Operate on a block time basis.

Fields of Application
Commercial, scientific, production control, accounting, billing, education.

KEZEV STATISTICAL CONSULTANCY AND DATA PROCESSING LTD.*
28 Hillel Street, Jerusalem

Services Available
Consultation, programming.

Fields of Application
Statistics, production control, surveys, payroll, inventory control.

LOCAL AUTHORITIES DATA PROCESSING CENTRE
29 Carlibach Street, Tel Aviv
Telephone: 281257, 283020

Officers
S. Rothem, *Chairman of the Board*
D. Galinka, *Managing Director*

Computer Installation
IBM 370/145–operating system: DOS; internal storage: 256K bits; magnetic tapes: 4 3420; magnetic discs: 7 2319; 1 line printer. *Remote processing features*: 2740 terminals.

IBM 370/135–operating system: DOS; internal storage: 144K bits; magnetic tapes: 4 3420; magnetic discs: 3 2319; 1 line printer.

Coding Languages
COBOL, Assembler, RPG.

Services Available
Advice, programming, systems analysis, data processing. Operate on a closed shop and block time basis. Available only to local authorities.

Fields of Application
Statistical, accounting, management, systems analysis.
Specialized area: Local authorities.

MEM ALEF ELECTRONIC COMPUTERS LTD.
75 Herzl Street, P.O.B. 2300, Ramat Gan
Telephone: 723272

Officer
J. Rosenne

Coding Languages
COBOL, Assembler, RPG.

Services Available
Consultation, programming, software packages, systems analysis.

Fields of Application
Commercial, accounting, statistical, scientific.
Specialized areas: Requisitions, payroll, linear programming.

MHD COMPUTERS*
Systems Analysing and Support Groups
El-Al Building, 32 Ben-Yehuda Street, P.O.B. 26068, Tel Aviv
Telephone: 54987

Officer
B. J. Johananoff, *Managing Director*

Services Available
Consultation, programming, education and training, software packages, systems analysis. Operate on a self-service basis. Available to all EDP users.

Fields of Application
Statistical, production control, commercial, accounting, management, systems analysis, operational research.
Specialized areas: Data collection and teleprocessing systems.

Training
EDP—Introduction and General Information; Programming—360 Assembler, COBOL, RPG, PL/1, FORTRAN and PERT; Systems Analysis. Short introductory and general information course in EDP.

I. E. MITTWOCH AND SONS LTD.
5 Druyanov Street, Tel Aviv
Telephone: 281151

Officers
J. D. Mittwoch, L. E. Mittwoch, *General Managers*
Y. Alster, *Data Processing Centre Manager*

Computer Installations
NCR 315—operating systems: CRAM, tape; internal storage: 40K slabs; magnetic tapes: 5; 1 line printer.

NCR Century 200— operating system: B1; internal storage: 64K bits; magnetic tapes: 5 9-track, 1 7-track; magnetic discs: 4; 1 line printer.

Coding Languages
NEAT, BEST, COBOL, FORTRAN.

Contemplated Equipment
Expansion of Century 200.

Services Available
Advice, programming, education and training, preparation of data, systems analysis and processing. Operate on a closed shop and block time basis.

Fields of Application
Scientific, statistical, commercial, production, accounting, management, systems analysis, operational research.
Specialized area: Sales analysis.

MLL STATISTICS INSTITUTE AND OFFICE EFFICIENCY LTD.
12 Karlibach Street, Tel Aviv
Telephone: 30914/5

Also at:
Jerusalem, Haifa, Ashdod

Officers
Arie Shemesh, *Director*
Shor Amiram, *Director*

Computer Installation
Tel Aviv:
IBM 360/20—internal storage: 16K bits; 2 line printers.

IBM 360/30—internal storage: 64K bits; magnetic tapes: 4; magnetic discs: 4; 1 line printer.

IBM 370/135—internal storage: 144K bits.

Haifa and Ashdod:
IBM 360/20—internal storage: 16K bits; 1 line printer.

Coding Languages
SPS, RPG, Assembler, COBOL (using other computers).

Contemplated Equipment
IBM 360/25.

Services Available
Advice, operators, preparation of data, programming, software packages, systems analysis. Operate on a self-service and block time basis.

Fields of Application
Production control, statistics, accounting, etc.
Specialized areas: Insurance business, marketing, supermarket and stocks, payroll, public opinion researches, accounting, stock control.

MUNICIPALITY OF TEL AVIV
EDP Centre
Kikar Malchei Israel, Tel Aviv

Officer
R. Elgad, *Director of the Computer Centre*

Computer Installation
IBM 360/30—operating system: DOS, R-26; internal storage: 96K bits; magnetic tapes: 4 2400; magnetic discs: 3 2314; 1 line printer.

Coding Languages
COBOL, RPG, Assembler.

Service Available
Preparation of data. Operate on a block time basis.

Fields of Application
Statistical, commercial, accounting, management.
Specialized areas: Tax collection; wages and salaries.

Training
Training, given by IBM, includes basic courses in coding languages. Advanced training depends upon requirements.

POLGAT WOOLLEN INDUSTRIES LTD.*
P.O.B. 15, Kiriat-Gat
Telephone: 051-91121

Also at:
75 Nahalat Benyamin Street, Tel Aviv
Telephone: 03-622931

Officer
I. Rosner

Computer Installation
IBM 360/20—operating system: CARDS; internal storage: 8K bytes; 1 line printer.

Coding Languages
RPG, BASIC, Assembler.

Services Available
Programming, operators, preparation of data, systems analysis. Operate on a self-service and block time basis.

Field of Application
Commercial.
Specialized area: Production control—textiles.

'YAEL' MANAGEMENT AUTOMATION CO. LTD.
2 Hakhaluzim Street, Tel Aviv
Telephone: 828166 and 823991

Computer Installation
NCR Century 200—operating system: DOS; internal storage: 64K bits; magnetic tapes: 5; magnetic discs: 2; 1 line printer.

Coding Languages
COBOL, FORTRAN, RPG, Assembler, PL/1, NEAT, BEST.

Contemplated Equipment
Telecommunication consoles, random mass-storage, Mohawk data recorders.

Services Available
Consultation, programming, education and training, software packages, documentation, preparation of data, systems analysis. Operate on a self-service, closed and open shop and block time basis. Available to governmental, public and private enterprises and health institutions.

Fields of Application
Scientific, statistical, accounting, management, systems analysis, commercial, personnel management, inventory control, economic analysis, budget control, public utilities.
Specialized areas: Medical information and health data banks, population registries and record linkage, administrative and statistical systems, especially population and housing census and linkage with population registries.

Training
Courses in Systems Analysis and Programming, and in Keyboard Punching.

ITALY

NATIONAL CENTRE

CENTRO NAZIONALE UNIVERSITARIO DI CALCOLO ELETTRONICO
Via Santa Maria 36, 56100 Pisa
Telephone: 45245

Officers
Prof. Alessandro Faedo, *Director*
Prof. Guido Torrigiani, *Secretary of Management Committee*

Computer Installation
IBM 360/67—operating systems: CP/CMS, APL/CMS, OS; internal storage: 1,024K bytes; magnetic tapes: 4 2400; magnetic discs: 2 2314; 2 line printers. *On-line satellite computers*: IBM 2780, IBM 2770, IBM 1130. *Remote processing features*: IBM 2703 line adaptor, IBM 2701.

IBM 370/155—operating system: OS/MVT; internal storage: 768K bytes; magnetic tapes: 6 2400; magnetic discs: 6 3330; 2 line printers. *On-line satellite computers*: IBM 260/20, IBM 1130. *Remote processing feature*: IBM 2701.

IBM 7090—operating system: TSX; internal storage: 32K words; magnetic tapes: 12 729VI, 3 729IV; 1 line printer.

IBM 1800—operating system: TSX; internal storage: 32K words; magnetic tapes: 2 2401/2; magnetic discs: 1 2310; 1 line printer.

Coding Languages
Assembler-F, ALGOL-F, ALGOL-W, COBOL-U, FORTRAN-G, Language-H, WATFIV, PL/360, APL, BRUIN, SNOBOL, FORMAC, FORDECAL, LISP, GPSS, GAMING DYNAMO, CSMP, MAP 7090.

Contemplated Equipment
Additional storage of 256K bytes for the 370/155; IBM 2701.

Services Available
Advice, education and training. Operate on a remote access, closed shop and time-sharing basis. Available only to universities and scientific institutions.

Fields of Application
Scientific, systems analysis, operational research.
Specialized areas: Linear programming, analysis, structural engineering, medical research, computer sciences, computational linguistics.

Training
Three-month courses for operators and programmers; one to three week courses on computer languages, programming, internals, and specialized subjects such as statistical applications, computer music, etc.

UNIVERSITIES AND COLLEGES

ISTITUTO UNIVERSITARIO DI VENEZIA*
Centro Calcolo Elettronico
Calle Foscari, Venezia
Telephone: 29823

Officer
Prof. Mario Volpato, *Director*

Computer Installation
OLIVETTI ELEA 6001—internal storage: 20K bits; magnetic tapes: 4; 1 line printer.

Coding Languages
BASIC, FORTRAN I and II, PSYCO.

Contemplated Equipment
BULL GENERAL ELECTRIC GE 415.

Services Available
Advice, programmers, operators. Available to customers in scientific management.

Fields of Application
Statistics, operational research.
Specialized areas: Linear programming, dynamic programming.

POLITECNICO DI MILANO*
Centro di Calcolo
Piazza Leonardo da Vinci 32, 20100 Milano
Telephone: 2361550

Officers
Dr. Ing. G. Kacin

Italy – Universities and Colleges

Computer Installation
UNIVAC 1108–operational system: EXEC 8; internal storage: 131,072 plus 196,608 bits; magnetic tapes: 4 VI C; magnetic discs: 4 FH 432, 2 Fastrand II; 1 line printer. *On-line satellite computer*: UNIVAC 1004. *Remote processing features*: 15 terminals.

IBM 7040–operating systems: IBSYS 9.3; internal storage: 32,768 bits; magnetic tapes: 7 729/V; 1 line printer.

Services Available
Consultation, operators, software packages, documentation. Operate on a closed shop, remote access and time-sharing basis. Available to universities and industry.

Field of Application
Scientific.

POLITECNICO DI TORINO*
Centro di Calcolo
Corso Duca degli Abruzzi 24, 10124 Torino
Téléphone: 551616

Dirigeant
Prof. Pietro Bujano

Equipement
OLIVETTI ELEA 6001/S–mémoire interne: 20K bits; bandes magnétiques: 3; 1 imprimante.

Langage de Programmation
Assembler.

Equipement Projeté
IBM 1800.

Service Fourni
Programmation. Fonctionnement à porte fermée.

UNIVERSITÀ DEGLI STUDI DI BARI*
Centro Elettronico di Calcolo
presso Istituto di Chimica Generale
Via Amendola 173, Bari
Telephone: 41034

Officers
Prof. Vladimiro Scatturini
Archille Petriganni
Alfredo Panerai
Michele Salvati
Tommaso Salvemini
Alberto Bonetti

Computer Installation
IBM 360/40–internal storage: 8,348K bits; magnetic tapes: 7 9-tracks; magnetic discs: 3 IBM 2311; 1 line printer.

IBM 1620–internal storage: 60K bits.

Coding Languages
FORTRAN, SPS.

Services Available
Operators, preparation of data, programming, systems analysis. Operate on a closed shop basis.

Fields of Application
Analysis and programming for research in university.

Training
Programming, elements of computer science; numerical methods for digital computers.

UNIVERSITÀ DEGLI STUDI DI MILANO
Centro di Calcolo
Via Mangiagalli 14, 20133 Milano
Telephone: 2361060

Officers
Ing. Sergio Bedini, *Director*
Dr. Carlo Rusconi, *Deputy Director*

Computer Installation
CII 10020–operating system: RBM; internal storage: 256K bits; magnetic tape: 1 7372; magnetic disc: 1 DIAD; 1 line printer.

UNIVAC 1106–operating system: EXEC 8; internal storage: 262K 36-bit words; magnetic tapes: 4 UNISERVO VI C 7-track, 2 9-track; magnetic discs: 6 8414; 3 line printers. *On-line satellite computers*: 7 batch terminals.

Coding Languages
MAP, FORTRAN, COBOL (ANSI), COMIT, ALGOL, SNOBOL, SLIP, PREFOR, SIMBOL.

Services Available
Advice, programming, education and training, operators, software packages. Operate on a self-service, remote access and open shop basis.

Fields of Application
Scientific, statistical, accounting, management.
Specialized area: Numerical methods.

UNIVERSITÀ DEGLI STUDI DI TRIESTE
Centro di Calcolo
Via Diaz 21, 34124 Trieste
Téléphone: 38776, 37308

Dirigeants
Antonia Marussi, *Président du Comité Directif*
Claudio de Ferra, *Directeur*

Equipement
CDC 6200– système d'opération: SCOPE 3.3; mémoire interne: 32K mots de 60 bits; bandes magnétiques: 4 604, 1 609; disques magnétiques: 1 813; 2 imprimantes. *Transmission des données à distance*: 1 6673 contrôleur.

Langages de Programmation
FORTRAN, COBOL, COMPASS, ALGOL, SIMSCRIPT.

Equipement Projeté
1 863 bobine.

Services Fournis
Programmation, enseignement et formation, préparation des données, analyse de systèmes.

Domaines d'Application
Scientifique, gestion.

UNIVERSITÀ DI NAPOLI*
Centro di Calcolo Elettronico
Piazzalo Tecchio, 80125 Napoli
Telephone: 61-65-33

Officers
Prof. Ing. Luigi Tocchetti, *President*
Prof. Ing. Giorgio Savastano, *Director*
Ing. B. Fadini, *Assistant Professor of Electronic Computers*

Computer Installation
CDC G-20–internal storage: 32K 32-bit words; magnetic tapes: 4 CDC MT10C; 2 line printers.

HP 2115A–internal storage: 8K 16-bit words.

HITACHI 505.

Coding Languages
SNAP, FORTRAN, Assembler, ALGOL, BASIC.

Services Available
Limited availability to business outside the University.

Fields of Application
All fields of University disciplines.
Specialized area: Engineering problems.

Training
'Electronic Computer' courses for students of engineering (5th year), sub-section electronic. Specialization courses in 'The theory and the techniques of using electronic computers' for the graduates of the technical scientific faculties.

UNIVERSITÀ DI PADOVA
Centro di Calcolo
Sezione Gestione-Administrazione
Via San Francesco 11, 35100 Padova
Telephone: 45394

Sezione Scientifico-Didattica
Via Belzoni 3, 35100 Padova
Telephone: 650641, 651195

Officers
Prof. C. Panattoni, *Director of the Management and Administrative Section*
Dr. M. E. Crescenti, *Director of the Scientific and Educational Section*

Computer Installations
IBM 370/145–operating system: OS; internal storage: 512K bytes; magnetic tapes: 4 IBM 3420; magnetic discs: 4 IBM 3336, 3 IBM 2319; 2 line printers.

IBM S7–internal storage: 16K bytes; magnetic discs: 1 IBM 5026.

CDC 1700–operating system: MSOS 3.0; internal storage: 24K 18-bit words; magnetic tapes: 2 CDC 601; magnetic discs: 1 CDC 854; 1 line printer. The CDC 1700 is linked with a CDC 6600 of the Centro di Calcolo di Casalecchio di Reno (Bologna).

Coding Languages
PL/1, FORTRAN IV, BASIC, ALGOL, Assembler, COBOL.

Services Available
Consultation, programming, education and training, operators, systems analysis. Operate on a remote access, closed shop and block-time basis.

Fields of Application
Scientific, statistical, commercial, systems analysis.

UNIVERSITÀ DI ROMA*
Centro di Calcolo Interfacolta
Piazzale delle Scienze 5, 00100 Roma

Officer
Franco de Santis, *Director*

Computer Installation
UNIVAC 1108–operating systems: EXEC 111, EXEC 8; internal storage: 36K bits; magnetic tapes: 4 V111C, 2 VIC; magnetic drums: 4 FH432, 1 Fastrand; 3 line printers.

Coding Languages
FORTRAN, ALGOL, COBOL, Assembler, etc.

Services Available
Consultation, education and training, operators, software packages, documentation, systems analysis. Operate on a self-service, remote access, closed and open shop and time-sharing basis.

Fields of Application
Scientific, statistical, commercial, systems analysis, operational research.

Training
3-week courses in FORTRAN and LISP.

UNIVERSITÀ DI ROMA
Facoltà di Ingegneria
Servizio di Calcolo
Via Eudossiana 18, 00184 Rome
Telephone: 465235

Officer
G. di Pillo, *Head of the Service*

Computer Installation
UNIVAC 5200–operating system: MOS; internal storage: 65,536 bits.

HEWLETT PACKARD 2100– operating system: paper tape; internal storage: 65,536 bits; magnetic tape: 1.

Coding Languages
Assembler, FORTRAN.

Services Available
Advice, documentation. Available only to researchers and students of the Faculty of Engineering.

Field of Application
Scientific.

GOVERNMENT ESTABLISHMENT

EUROPEAN SPACE RESEARCH INSTITUTE (ESRIN)
Casella Postale n. 64, 00044 Frascati

Officers
N. Isotta, *Director*
P. Senni, *Administration*
R. Russel, *Marketing*

Computer Installation
IBM 360/50–operating system: HASP; internal storage: 4,096K bits; magnetic tapes: 3 2401; magnetic disc: 1403. *On-line satellite computer*: PDP 11. *Remote processing features*: IBM 370/155, 8 IBM 2321 Data Cell Storages.

Coding Languages
FORTRAN, Assembler, PL/1.

Service Available
Documentation. Operate on a remote access and closed shop basis. No commercial use.

Fields of Application
Scientific.
Specialized areas: Documentation, retrieval, databank.

RESEARCH INSTITUTIONS

CENTRO INFORMAZIONI STUDI ESPERIENZE (CISE)
Servizio di Calcolo
Via Redecesio 12, 20090 Segrate, Milan
Telephone: 2133251

Officer
A. Ghirardi, *Head*

Computer Installations
IBM 1800–operating system: MPX; internal storage: 512K bits; magnetic discs: 3 1810; 1 line printer. *On-line satellite computer*: Varian 620/i.

VARIAN 620–operating system: GOS (Graphic Operating System CISE); internal storage: 256K bits; magnetic tapes: 1 7-track, 1 9-track; 1 line printer: 1100† 245 lpm; *Remote processing feature*: Teletype (0.5km)

Coding Languages
Assembler, FORTRAN

Services Available
Advice, programming, operators, software packages, systems analysis. Operate on a closed shop basis.

Field of Application
Scientific.

CENTRO ITALIANO STUDI E RICHERCHE S.p.A. (CISER)*
Via N. Paganini 7, 00198 Roma
Telephone: 850-606, 868-047, 860-554.

Officers
Sergio Firrao
Sergio Lieto

Coding Languages
Assembler (IBM), Easycoder (Honeywell), FORTRAN.

Services Available
Consultation, software packages.

Fields of Application
Statistical applications for social, economic, psychological and market research.

CENTRO STUDI E APPLICAZIONI IN TECNOLOGIE AVANZATE (CSATA)
Via Amendola 173, 70126 Bari
Telephone: 33.10.44

Officers
Prof. A. Romano, *President*
Prof. F. Ferrero, *Director*
Dr. G. Piscitelli, *Head of Computing Centre*

Computer Installations
IBM 360/65–operating system: MVT; internal storage 6,144K bits; magnetic tapes: 4 2403, 2402, 2401; magnetic disc: 1 2314; 3 line printers. *On-line satellite computer*: IBM 1800. *Remote processing features*: CRJE, HASP.

Coding Languages
Assembler, FORTRAN G and H, PI/1, COBOL, ALGOL.

Contemplated Equipment
1 Selector Channel, 1 IBM 2319 with 3 magnetic discs.

Services Available
Advice, programming, education and training, software packages, systems analysis, social services. Operate on a remote access, open shop and time-sharing basis.

Fields of Application
Scientific, statistical, commercial, accounting, management, systems analysis, educational, social services.
Specialized areas: Analysis, structural engineering, medical research.

Training
Systems analyst and systems programmer courses.

COMITATO NAZIONALE PER L'ENERGIA NUCLEARE (CNEN)*
Centro di Calcolo
Via Mazzini 2, 40138 Bologna
Téléphone: 307562-3-4-5, 307572-3-4-5

Dirigeants
Prof. Ezio Clementel, *Directeur*
V. Benzi, *Directeur Adjoint*
R. Manzini, *Chef de Service de Direction*

Equipement
IBM 360/75–système d'opération: OS-MVT-HASP; mémoire interne: 1.024K bytes; bandes magnétiques: 2 2401/III, 2 2401/VI; disques magnétiques: 1 2314/AD; 2 imprimantes. *Transmission des données à distance*: 2 IBM 360/44, 1 IBM 1130.

IBM 7094/7040–système d'opération: Fortran Monitor System, IBSYS-IBJOB sur 7094, sous le contrôle du 'Direct Couple Operating System' placé sur 7040; mémoire interne: 32K bits; bandes magnétiques: 16 IBM 729-VI; disques magnétiques: IBM 1301 couplée au calculateur IBM 7040; 3 imprimantes. *Transmission des données à distance*: Transmission et réception des données et des programmes par voie; terminales à bande magnétique 7702 installées au 'Centro di Calcolo del CNEN–Bologna et au C.S.N.– Casaccia (Roma)', éloignées entre eux environ 400 Km. et raccordées au moyen d'un pont radio. Un 'software' spécial a été produit pour la manipulation à distance d'archives des données au 1401. Ce moyen permet la transmission de données à la velocité de 2400 baudes.
IBM 1401–mémoire interne: 16K bits; bandes magnétiques: 2 IBM 729-II; disques magnétique: 1 IBM 1311; 1 imprimante.

Langages de Programmation
ALGOL, Assembler, COBOL, FORTRAN, PL/1, RPG.

Services Fournis
Conseils, programmation, software packages, préparation des données, analyse de systèmes. Fonctionnement en self-service, par accès à distance, à porte fermée et en time-sharing. Fournis seulement aux instituts de recherche.

Domaine d'Application
Scientifique.
Domaine spécialisé: Recherche.

Formation
Cours en langages de programmation et systèmes d'opération.

Italy — Research Institutions

COMITATO NAZIONALE PER L'ENERGIA NUCLEARE (CNEN)
Centre de Calcul Analogique et Hybride
Laboratoire de Génie Nucléaire
Centro Casaccia, Strada Anguillarese, Roma
Téléphone: 4698

Dirigeants
A. Mathis
M. di Bartolomeo

Equipement
EAI 640—mémoire interne: 32K bits; bandes magnétiques: 2; disques magnétiques: 1; 1 imprimante. *Calculateur satellite en ligne*: EAI 8800 analogue. *Transmission des données à distance*: Interface analogique-numérique EAI 8831.
Calculateur analogique CNEN. Simulateurs spéciaux CNEN. 2 Calculateurs analogiques EAI-PACE 231-R.

Services Fournis
Conseils, opérateurs. Fonctionnement en porte ouverte. Fournis aux utilisateurs de l'extérieur, avec conditions fixées pour chacun des cas.

Equipement Projeté
Logique de contrôle et mémoires de fonctions pour l'emploi itératif des calculateurs analogiques.

Domaines d'Application
Calcul analogique et hybride.
Domaines spécialisés: Simulation des réacteurs nucléaires et des plantes associées, en vue de l'Analyse des accidents et du projet des systèmes de régulation et de sécurité.

COMITATO NAZIONALE PER L'ENERGIA NUCLEARE (CNEN)
Gruppo Calcoli Numerici dei Laboratori Nazionali di Frascati
Casella Postale n. 70, Frascati (Roma)
Telephone: 941041, 941191, 941401

Officer
Prof. A. Turrin, *Head of Computer Section*

Computer Installation
IBM 360/44—operating system: DOS; internal storage: 128K 8-bit bytes; magnetic tapes: 1 7-track, 1 9-track; magnetic discs: 2 2311; 1 line printer. *On-line satellite computer*: 1 IBM S/7.

Coding Languages
FORTRAN, PL/1, Assembler, COBOL, RPG.

Contemplated Equipment
IBM 370/135.

Fields of Application
Scientific, systems analysis.
Specialized areas: High-energy nuclear physics, plasma physics, beam dynamics, Monte Carlo methods.

CONSIGLIO NAZIONALE DELLE RICERCHE (CNR)*
Istituto di Elaborazione della Informazione (IEI)
Via Santa Maria 46, Pisa
Telephone: 46323, 49391

Officer
Prof. G. Capriz, *Director of the Institute*

Computer Installation
HEWLETT PACKARD 2116B—operating system: Time-sharing; internal storage: 762K bits; magnetic tapes: 2 HP 7970; magnetic discs: 1 HP 2771A. *Remote processing features*: 8 teleprinters.

PDP-8/I—internal storage: 98K bits; magnetic tapes: 1 Ampex; magnetic discs: 1 DF 32.

ELDA—internal storage: 18K bits; magnetic tapes: 1 Ampex, 1 Honeywell.

Coding Languages
BASIC, FORTRAN, ALGOL.

Contemplated Equipment
Data plotter, CRT display.

Services Available
Programming, scientific co-operating. Operate on a time-sharing and open shop basis. Restricted to customers with scientific problems.

Fields of Application
Scientific, statistical, systems analysis, operational research.
Specialized areas: Medical research, numerical analysis, non-linear systems, image analysis, linguistics.

Training
Postgraduate course in Information Science.

CONSIGLIO NAZIONALE DELLE RICERCHE (CNR)*
Istituto Nazionale per le
Applicazioni del Calcolo (INAC)
Piazzale delle Scienze 7, Roma
Téléphone: 49-94, 49-18-50

Dirigeants
Prof. A. Ghizzetti, *Directeur*
Conseil de Direction: Prof. G. Scorza (*Président*), Prof. E. De Giorgi, Prof. G. Evangelisti, Prof. A. Ghizzetti, Prof. G. Grioli, Prof. D. Dainelli, Prof. Ing. P. Ercoli, *Sous-directeurs*

Equipement
FERRANTI 1 (avec plusieurs modifications)—disques magnétiques.

Services Fournis
Services de consultation mathématique et de calcul.

Domaines d'Application
Analyse mathématique et numérique; programmation; électronique et théorie des ordinateurs.

CONSIGLIO NAZIONALE DELLE RICERCHE (CNR)
Laboratorio di Cibernetica
Via Toiano 2, 80072 Arco Felice, Napoli
Telephone: 8671255

Officer
Prof. E. Caianiello, *Director*

Computer Installation
HEWLETT PACKARD 2116 B—operating system: DOS; internal storage: 16K x 16 bits; magnetic discs: 2 monodiscs.

Coding Languages
Assembler, FORTRAN II and IV, ALGOL.

Contemplated Equipment
Plotter.

Italy – Consultants

Service Available
Advice. Operate on a self-service basis.

Field of Application
Scientific.
Specialized area: EEG Siprol analysis

Training
EEG Siprol analysis, pattern negotiation and Neuron network simulation courses.

ISTITUTO CENTRALE DI STATISTICA (ISTAT)*
Via Cesare Balbo 16, Roma
Telephone: 4673

Officers
Dr. Gastone Barsanti
Dr. Amleto di Torrice

Computer Installations
IBM 360/40 (2)–operating system: DOS; internal storage: 131K bits; magnetic tapes: 6 IBM 2401/V; magnetic discs: IBM 2314; 2 line printers. *Remote processing facilities*: IBM 2780/II terminals.

IBM 360/25–operating system: BPS; internal storage: 32K bits; 1 line printer.

Coding Languages
COBOL, FORTRAN IV, Assembler.

Contemplated Equipment
An expansion of the centre is foreseen.

Services Available
ISTAT provides data-processed official statistics.

Field of Application
Statistical.

SNAM PROGETTI S.p.A.*
Gruppo Matematica Applicata
Laboratori Riuniti Studi e Ricerche (LRSR)
20097 San Donato Milanese
Téléphone: 5353

Dirigeants
Prof. Marcello De Maldé, *Directeur des LRSR*
Prof. Antonio Lovati, *Directeur du Département d'Analyse et de Méthodes de Recherches*
Ing. Giorgio Spallanzani, *Responsable du Groupe matematica Applicata*

Equipement
PACE 231R analogique.
SNAM LRSR analogique à resaux passifs.
HITACHI 505 et PDP 8/I hybride.

Service Fournis
Analyse de systèmes. Fonctionnement en porte ouverte. Disponibles normalement pour les travaux demandés par les Sociétés du Groupe ENI, mais avec possibilité d'effectuer aussi des travaux pour l'extérieur.

Domaines d'Application
Résolution des problèmes relatifs à l'activité de recherche scientifique de la SNAM Progetti Laboratori Riuniti Studi e Ricerche.
Domaines spécialisés: Simulation des conduits pétrolifères et du gaz; simulation pour la régulation et système d'analyse des installations chimique-pétrolifères; simulation des réacteurs nucléaires; approche statistique des problèmes scientifiques techniques.

SOCIETÀ SISPRE*
Centro di Calcolo
Via Salaria 913, Roma
Téléphone: 835994, 836590, 836265

Dirigeants
Ing. R. Corbò, *Directeur*
Ing. M. Passerini, *Chef du Centre de Calcul*

Equipement
OLIVETTI ELEA 6001–mémoire interne: 20K bits; bandes magnétiques: 2; 1 imprimante.
PACE 231/R analogue.

Langage de Programmation
FORTRAN.

Services Fournis
Heures de calcul scientifique avec programmation et consultations.

Domaines d'Application
Intégration numérique des équations différentielles ordinaires ou dérivées partielles, résolutions de systèmes d'équations algébriques, etc.
Domaines spécialisés: Aérodynamique, propulsion, système d'analyse, etc.

CONSULTANTS

BEDAUX CONSULTANTS S.p.A.*
Via Fatebenefratelli 15, 20121 Milano
Telephone: 650-755, 650-766

Officer
Roberto Amadi

Computer Installation
Remote processing features: GE time-sharing terminal.

Coding Language
BASIC GE.

Services Available
Consultation, preparation of data.

Field of Application
Accounting.
Specialized area: Work time computation.

COMPUTER SCIENCES INTERNATIONAL ITALIA S.p.A. (CSIT)*
Appt. 7, Building A, Viale Liegi 33, 00198 Rome
Telephone: 6-855784

Also at:
Corsa Europa 10, Milan
Telephone: 2-791915, 2-780187

Officers
Dr. M. I. Montana, *President and General Manager*
M. Pulliam, *Director of Operations*
E. Randazzo, *Manager of Government Systems*
C. Borroni, *Manager of Industrial Systems*

Services Available
Advice, programming, education and training, operators, software packages, preparation of data, systems analysis.

Fields of Application
Management, systems analysis.
Specialized areas: Compiler writing, management information systems.

Italy — Consultants

Training
Standard courses: Computer Concepts for Management; Management Utilization of the Computer; Systems and Programming Project Management; System Analysis and Design.

EUROPEAN COMPUTER SERVICES S.p.A. (ECS)
Viale Liegi 41, 00198 Roma
Telephone: 859588, 866479

Officer
Dr. Alvise di Robilant, *Managing Director*

Services Available
Advice, programming, software packages, preparation of data, systems analysis.

Fields of Application
Scientific, statistical, commercial, accounting, management, systems analysis, operational research.
Specialized areas: Analysis, structural engineering.

KNIGHT WEGENSTEIN SRL.*
Via De' Bardi 33, Florence
Telephone: 261-260

Services Available
Consultation, operators, preparation of data, programming, software packages, systems analysis.

Fields of Application
Real management information systems, all operating systems, process control.

OFFICE OF GRAHAM PARKER*
Via Verdi 2, 20121 Milan
Telephone: 872-354

Officer
Dr. Ing. A. G. Rosania, *Manager, Italian Operating*

Services Available
Consultation, systems analysis.

Fields of Application
Consulting services in commercial, production control, management and systems analysis.

P.A. CONSULENZA DIREZIONALE*
Via Turati 40, 20121 Milano
Telephone: 66-75-67

Officers
J. Wholey
N. Redaelli

Services Available
Consultation, systems analysis.

Field of Application
Consultancy service to international management.
Specialized areas: Management sciences (or EDP and programming), company strategy, market research, personnel services, finance and acquisition, etc.

P.E. ITALIA S.p.A.*
Via Sant' Orsola 8, Milan
Telephone: 86-90-560

Services Available
Consultation, software packages, systems analysis.

Fields of Application
General management consultancy in all fields, i.e. production, marketing, finance, personnel, etc.; development and application of advanced techniques, such as data processing and operational research; consultancy at corporate level in organization studies, long-range planning, diversification and information systems.
Specialized area: HOCUS (Hand or Computer Universal Simulator), a special simulation system and programme.

Training
Courses on HOCUS (3 days).

PEAT, MARWICK, MITCHELL & CO.
Piazza F. Meda 3, 20121 Milan
Telephone: 78-22-41

Officer
W. L. Ghirardelli

Services Available
Consultation, systems analysis.

Fields of Application
Economic studies, general and scientific management, operations research, project management, industrial engineering, marketing production and inventory control, information systems, general and cost accounting systems, data processing and transmission systems, etc.

PRAXIS CALCOLO S.p.A.
Via Visconti di Modrone 32, Milan
Telephone: 799601, 782691, 705037

Also at:
Via Firenze 43, Rome

Officers
Enrico Albani, *General Manager*
Massimo Merlino, *Operations Research Manager*
Giovanni Medusei, *Commercial Systems Manager*

Services Available
Advice, software packages, systems analysis.

Fields of Application
Scientific, statistical, management, systems analysis, operational research.
Specialized areas: Sales analysis, linear programming, investment analysis, payroll.

SERVICE BUREAUX

A.T.M.*
Foro Buonoparte, 61-Milano
Telephone: 895841

Officer
Gianmaria Airaghi

Computer Installation
HONEYWELL H200—operating systems: Mode 1, Mode 2; internal storage: 32K bits; magnetic tapes: 5; 1 line printer.

Coding Languages
Easycoder, COBOL, FORTRAN.

Contemplated Equipment
Card-reader, card-punch, printer, tape-units.

Service Available
Preparation of data. Operate on a closed shop basis.

Italy – Service Bureaux

Fields of Application
Statistical, commercial, accounting, management research.

Training
Up-dating courses on new programming techniques and procedure analysis for staff, usually held at equipment supplier's premises. Short courses in PERT, BUDGET, operational research.

AUTOMATION CENTER S.p.A.*
Via T. Calco 2, Milan
Telephone: 433-881

Officer
Dario de Benedetti, *Manager*

Computer Installation
BULL GENERAL ELECTRIC GE 415–internal storage: 16K bits; magnetic tapes: 5 MTH 200-01.

Coding Languages
COBOL, FORTRAN, MAKRO (GE).

Services Available
Advice, operators, preparation of data, programming, systems analysis. Operate on a closed shop basis.

Fields of Application
Statistical, commercial, production control, accounting, management.

CENTRO S.p.A.*
Viale del Lavoro 33, 37100 Verona
Telephone: 500769

Computer Installation
BULL GENERAL ELECTRIC GE 415–operating system: TOS; internal storage: 8K bits; magnetic tapes: 3; 1 line printer. *Remote processing features*: GE time-sharing terminal (connected with Milan).

Coding Languages
APS, TAB II.

Services Available
Consultation, operators, preparation of data, programming, systems analysis. Operate on a self-service and block time basis.

Fields of Application
Statistical, commercial, production control, accounting (scientific–GE time-sharing service).

CONTROL DATA ITALIA S.p.A.*
Via C. Colombo 418-420, 00145 Roma
Telephone: 5137741

Also at:
Corso Europa 2, 20122 Milano
Telephone: 799733, 792770, 790426

Pizza Rossetti 1, 16129 Genova
Telephone: 592251

Officers
D. G. Familiant, *Regional Manager, Rome*
G. Samarughi, *Operation (Rome)*

Computer Installation
Rome, Milan and Genoa:
CDC 3300–internal storage: 16K bits; magnetic tapes: 6; 1 line printer. *On-line satellite computer*: 200 U/T connected to CDC 6600.

Coding Languages
Assembly, COBOL, FORTRAN.

Services Available
Advice, operators, preparation of data, programming.

Fields of Application
All fields of data processing.

ELABORAZIONE AUTOMATICA DATI S.R.L. (EAD)
Via Carlo Roma 47, 20129 Milano
Telephone: 733013, 733378

Officer
Ing. Vittorio Cionini, *General Manager*

Computer Installation
SIEMENS 4004/45–operating system: DOS; internal storage: 128K bytes; magnetic tapes: 2; magnetic discs: 6; 1 line printer.

Coding Languages
COBOL, Assembler.

Services Available
Consultation, operators, programming, software packages, systems analysis. Operate on a block time basis.

Fields of Application
Commercial, statistical, production control, management, scientific.
Specialized areas: Calculation of structures in the engineering field, management of big files of addresses, payroll accounting.

HONEYWELL INFORMATION SYSTEMS ITALIA*
Time-Sharing Service
Via G. Fara 20, 20124 Milano
Telephone: 667741

Officers
Luciano Marradi, *Manager of Time-Sharing Service*
Carlo E. Sironi, *Customer Application Support Manager*
Carlo A. Valente, *Sales Manager*
Gianfranco Conti, *I.P.C. Manager*

Computer Installation
GE 265 (2)–operating system: MARK I; internal storage: 32K words each: magnetic discs: 4 each. *On-line satellite computers*: Remote Multiplexers.

Coding Languages
BASIC, ALGOL, FORTRAN, EDITOR.

Services Available
Programming, software packages, systems analysis. Operate on a time-sharing basis.

Fields of Application
Scientific, statistical, management, operational research.
Specialized areas: Investment analysis, numerical control, engineering.

Training
Courses in coding languages (BASIC and FORTRAN) and numerical control.

IANUS S.p.A.*
Via Flaminia 330, 00196 Roma
Telephone: 391255-300703-399500

Officers
Dr. Salvatore Ceglia
Dr. Adelmo Castellani

Computer Installation
HONEYWELL H110–magnetic tapes: 4; 1 line printer.

Coding Languages
COBOL, Easycoder.

Services Available
Consultation, programming, operators, software packages, preparation, systems analysis. Operate on a self-service basis.

Fields of Application
Statistical, commercial, accounting, management, systems analysis, operational research.

IBM ITALIA S.p.A.*
Direzione DCS (Data Center Services)
Via Pirelli 18, Milano
Telephone: 6338

Also at:
Corso Unione Sovietica 169, Torino

Via S. Sebastiano 11, Genova

Via Galatti 1/1, Trieste

Via Marsala 73, Verona

Via Boldrini 12, Bologna

Via Gramsci 39, Firenze

Via L. Rizzo 20, Roma

Corso Vittorio Emanuele 698, Napoli

Via G. Bonomo 4, Palermo

Via Lanusei 24, Cagliari

Officer
Guido De Giuli, *Manager of DCS*

Computer Installation
Milan:
IBM 1401 (3)–internal storage: 1 of 98,304 bits and 2 of 131,072 bits each; magnetic tapes: 8 IBM 729/5; magnetic discs: 2 IBM 1311/1; 1 line printer each.

IBM 360/20 (3)–operating systems: DPS and TPS; internal storage: 131,072 bits each; magnetic tapes: IBM 2415/2; magnetic discs: 2 IBM 2311/11; 1 line printer each.

IBM 360/40 (2)–operating systems: DOS and OS; internal storage: 1,048,576 bits each; magnetic tapes: 14 IBM 2401/2, 2 IBM 2401/5; magnetic discs: 10 IBM 2311/1; 3 line printers.

IBM 360/50–operating systems: OS and DOS; internal storage: 4,194,304 bits; magnetic tapes: 8 IBM 2401/3; magnetic discs: 3 IBM 2311/1, 1 IBM 2314/1; 2 line printers.

IBM 1130/20B–internal storage: 65,536 bits; magnetic discs: 1 IBM 2315.

Turin:
IBM 1401 (2)–internal storage: 131,072 bits each; magnetic tapes: 4 IBM 729/2; 1 line printer each.

IBM 360/20–internal storage: 131,072 bits; 1 line printer.

IBM 360/40–operating systems: DOS and OS; internal storage: 1,048,576 bits; magnetic tapes: 6 IBM 2401/2; magnetic discs: 3 IBM 2311/1; 1 line printer.

Genoa:
IBM 1401–internal storage: 98,304 bits; magnetic discs: 1 IBM 1311/2, 1 IBM 1311/4; 1 line printer.

Trieste:
IBM 1401–internal storage: 98,304 bits; 1 line printer.

Verona:
IBM 1401 (2)–internal storage: 98,304 and 32,768 bits; magnetic tapes: 4 IBM 729/5; magnetic discs: IBM 1311/4; 1 line printer each.

IBM 360/20–internal storage: 131,072 bits; magnetic discs: 2 IBM 1311/11; 1 line printer.

Bologna:
IBM 1401–internal storage: 98,304 bits; magnetic tapes: 4 IBM 729; 1 line printer.

IBM 360/20 (2)–internal storage: 131,072 bits each; magnetic tapes: 1 IBM 2415/2; magnetic discs: 2 IBM 2311/11; 2 line printers.

IBM 360/40–internal storage: 524,288 bits; magnetic tapes: 6 IBM 2401/2; magnetic discs: 3 IBM 2311/1; 1 line printer.

Florence:
IBM 1401–internal storage: 131,072 bits; magnetic tapes: 6 IBM 729/5; magnetic discs: 2 IBM 1311/1; 1 line printer.

IBM 360/20–internal storage: 131,072 bits; 1 line printer.

Rome:
IBM 1460–internal storage: 131,072 bits; magnetic tapes: 4 IBM 729/5; 1 line printer.

IBM 360/20 (2)–internal storage: 131,072 bits each; magnetic tapes: 1 IBM 2415/2; 2 line printers.

IBM 360/40 (2)–internal storage: 1,048,576 bits each; magnetic tapes: 2 IBM 2401/5, 12 IBM 2401/2; magnetic discs: 8 IBM 2311/1; 3 line printers each.

IBM 1130/20B–internal storage: 65,536 bits; magnetic discs: 1 IBM 2315.

Naples, Palermo and Cagliari:
IBM 1401 (3)–internal storage: 98,304 bits each; magnetic tapes: 4 IBM 729/5 (Naples), 4 IBM 729/2 (Palermo); magnetic discs: 1 1311/2, IBM 1311/4 (Cagliari); 1 line printer each.

Coding Languages
SPS, Autocoder, RPG, COBOL, Assembler, PL/1, FORTRAN.

Services Available
Advice, operators, preparation of data, programming, software packages, systems analysis. Operate on a self-service, closed shop and block time basis.

Fields of Application
Commercial, scientific.

Training
Short courses in Sistema a schede perforate: corsi informativi, generali, di specializzazione (3-10 days); sistemi elettronici: 1401, 1440, 360, 360/20, 1130 e 1800– corsi di introduzione di programmazione, di organizzazione, di operatori, ecc. (2-15 days); tecniche di gestione aziendale (2-7 days).

Italy – Service Bureaux

ISTITUTO E. MESCHINI*
Via Polleri 3, Genova
Telephone: 290-684

Also at:
Via Piave 7, Roma
Telephone: 483497

Officers
Prof. A. Meschini (*Rome*)
Prof. Dr. E. Barbera (*Genoa*)

Computer Installation
IBM 360–internal storage: 16K bytes; magnetic discs:
2 IBM 2311; 1 line printer.

Coding Languages
COBOL, FORTRAN, RPG, Assembler, PL/1, RPG II.

Contemplated Equipment
IBM 360/25.

Services Available
Advice, preparation of data, programming, systems analysis. Operate on a closed shop and block time basis.

Fields of Application
Statistical, commercial, production control, accounting.
Specialized areas: Invoicing, sales analysis, sales statistics, commercial calculations.

Training
Courses in introduction to data processing, basic programming, flowcharting techniques, languages, operating systems.

SERVIZIO INTERNAZIONALE ELABORAZIONE DATI, S.p.A. (SIED)*
Viale della Civilta del Lavoro 38, 00144 Roma
Telephones: 593 661; 593 655; 593 556

Officer
Dr. F. F. Selig, *General Manager*

Computer Installation
IBM 360/40–operating systems: IBM OS, IBM DOS; internal storage: 1,649,248 bits; magnetic tapes: 5 IBM 2401/2; magnetic discs: IBM 2314A1, 2 IBM 2311; 1 line printer.

Coding Languages
COBOL, FORTRAN, Assembler, PL/1, MARK IV.

Contemplated Equipment
IBM 360/50.

Services Available
Consultation, programming, preparation of data, systems analysis. Operate on a block time and closed shop basis, with remote access to any Mohawk Data Systems transmission unit in Europe.

Fields of Application
Scientific, statistical, commercial, production control, accounting, management, systems analysis, operational research.
Specialized areas: Petroleum exploration and production, data processing employee relations, marketing.

SINGER FRIDEN DIVISION*
Via Giorgio Jan 5/A, 20129 Milano

Officer
Giuseppe Confalonieri

Computer Installation
FRIDEN 10–operating system: FOS; internal storage 150K bits; magnetic discs: 2; 1 line printer.

Coding Languages
Assembler, RPG.

Services Available
Consultation, programming, education and training, operators, software packages, documentation, systems analysis. Operate on a block time basis.

Fields of Application
Statistical, commercial, production control, accounting, management, systems analysis.
Specialized area: Multiprogramming.

Training
Courses in programming languages, data management, system analysis and design; short courses covering FRIDEN 10 equipment.

SYSTEM PRINTING ITALIANA, S.p.A.
Via Matteo Bartoli 248, 00143 Roma
Telephone: 5000 853/5

Officers
Pericle Staderini, *President*
Renato de Mattia, *Vice-President*

Computer Installation
IBM 370/145–operating system: DOS 3; internal storage: 256K bits; magnetic tapes: 4 2321; magnetic discs: 4 2314; 2 line printers. *On-line satellite computer*: Olivetti TC 380.

Coding Languages
COBOL ANSI, FORTRAN, Assembler 360-370, RPG/2.

Contemplated Equipment
IBM 370/135 with 256K bits; IBM system/3/10 with 64K bits.

Services Available
Advice, programming, education, software packages, preparation of data, system analysis. Operate on a self-service, block time, closed and open shop basis.

Fields of Application
Statistical, commercial, accounting, management, systems analysis.
Specialized areas: Sales analysis, payroll, structural engineering, banking.

Training
Courses for programmers, operators and analysts, all on an individual basis.

SYNTAX S.p.A.
Via Gaetano Negri 8, Milano
Telephone: 860807, 860281, 866901

Also at:
Via G. Cassiodoro 9, Roma
Telephone: 311965, 316671

Officers
G. Baldovini, *Managing Director*
M. Italiani, *Technical Manager*

Coding Languages
Assembler, COBOL, FORTRAN, PL/1.

Services Available
Advice, programming, education and training, software packages, documentation, systems analysis, basic software development.

Fields of Application
Scientific, commercial, production control, accounting, management, system analysis.
Specialized areas: Payroll, medical research, message switching, operating systems and compilers.

IVORY COAST

NATIONAL CENTRE

OFFICE CENTRAL DE LA MÉCANOGRAPHIE
B.P. 937, Abidjan
Telephone: 22-89-62

Officers
Raphaël Kouakou, *Director of the National Centre for Accounting and Informatics*
Mme. Eliane Ekra, *Head of the Informatics Training Bureau*

Computer Installation
IBM 360/40 (2)–operating system: OS/MFT; internal storage: 2,097,152 bits each; magnetic tapes: 3 2400 each; 8 magnetic discs each; 2 (and 1) line printers.
BULL GENERAL ELECTRIC Gamma 30–internal storage: 320K bits; magnetic tapes: 6; 1 line printer.

Coding Languages
COBOL, FORTRAN, Assembler.

Contemplated Equipment
Bull General Electric GE 400; IBM 360/70.

Services Available
Programming, education and training. Operate on a self-service basis.

Fields of Application
Scientific, statistical, commercial, accounting.
Specialized areas: Analysis, payroll.

Training
Courses in programming languages and analysis.

SERVICE BUREAU

IBM SERVICE BUREAU
B.P. 964, Abidjan
Telephone: 22.25.24

Officers
M. Lassus-Débat, *General Manager for West Africa*
M. Steip, *Office Manager of Service Bureau*

Computer Installation
IBM 360/40–operating system: DOS; internal storage: 128K bits; magnetic tapes: 4 2401; magnetic discs: 3 2311; 1 line printer.

IBM System/3–operating system: DSM; internal storage: 16K bits; magnetic discs: 1 5444/2; 1 line printer.

Coding Languages
Assembler, COBOL, PL/1, GAP, GAP II.

Contemplated Equipment
A 1403 printer; a 2314 disc unit.

Services Available
Advice, programming, education and training, software packages, documentation, preparation of data, systems analysis. Operate on a self-service, block time and open shop basis. Available only for private firms.

Fields of Application
Statistical, commercial, accounting, systems analysis.
Specialized areas: Sales analysis, analysis, payroll, structural engineering.

Training
Courses in programming, logic and introduction to computers.

JAMAICA

UNIVERSITY

UNIVERSITY OF THE WEST INDIES*
Department of Mathematics
Computing Centre
Mona, Kingston 7
Telephone: 76661

Officer
Dr. Ronald C. Read

Computer Installation
IBM 1620–internal storage: 20K bits; magnetic discs: 1 IBM 1311.

Coding Languages
1620 SPS, FORTRAN.

Services Available
Advice, operators, preparation of data, programming, software packages. Operate on an open shop basis.

Fields of Application
Programming in all fields of interest to the University.
Specialized areas: X-ray crystallography, ionospheric research, seismology, medical and other statistics; non-numerical applications; applications to graph-theory and combinatorial problems; computer marking of examinations.

Training
Courses in SPS or FORTRAN held about three times per year.

GOVERNMENT ESTABLISHMENT

MUNICIPAL AND WATER COMPUTER SERVICES
21 Church Street, Kingston

Officer
Brian Wood, *Data Processing Manager/Consultant*

Computer Installation
ICL 1902A—operating system: GEORGE 1; internal storage: 16,384 24-bit words; magnetic tapes: 4 1971; magnetic discs: 2 2802/3; 1 line printer.

Coding Language
COBOL.

Services Available
Advice, programming, operators, documentation, systems analysis. Operate on a closed shop basis.

Fields of Application
Commercial, accounting, management, systems analysis.
Specialized areas: Payroll, billing.

CONSULTANT

PEAT, MARWICK, MITCHELL & CO.
The Victoria Mutual Building, 6 Duke Street, P.O. Box 76, Kingston
Telephone: 2-6646

Officer
Christopher A. Green, *Principal*

Services Available
Advice, programming, education and training, documentation, systems analysis, facility management.

Fields of Application
Statistical, commercial, accounting, management, systems analysis, operational research.
Specialized areas: Sales analysis, linear programming, analysis, payroll.

SERVICE BUREAU

IBM WORLD TRADE CORPORATION
52-56 Knutsford Boulevard, New Kingston, Kingston 5
Telephone: 69315/7, 69324/7

Officers
E. D. Poodts, *General Manager*
C. G. Symon, *Marketing Manager*
D. J. Duff, *Manager of Service Centre*

Computer Installation
IBM 360/30—operating system: DOS; internal storage: 64K bytes; magnetic tapes: 4 2401; magnetic discs: 4 2314; 1 line printer.

Coding Languages
RPG I, RPG II, COBOL, PL/1, Assembler, FORTRAN IV.

Contemplated Equipment
IBM 370/135.

Services Available
Advice, operators, preparation of data, programming, software packages, systems analysis, education and training, documentation. Operate on a self-service, closed shop and block time basis.

Fields of Application
Scientific, statistical, commercial, production control, accounting, management, systems analysis, operational research.
Specialized areas: Sales analysis, analysis, payroll.

Training
Basic IBM courses in fundamentals, programming and systems design.

JAPAN

NATIONAL CENTRE

JAPAN INFORMATION PROCESSING DEVELOPMENT CENTER (JIPDEC)
Kikai Shinko Kaikan, 5-8 Shibakoen, 3-chome, Minato-ku, Tokyo 105

Officers
Shogo Namba, *President*
Tamotsu Saito, *Vice-President*
Tsuyoshi Yoshida, *Executive Director*

Computer Installation
FACOM 230/60—operating system: MONITOR V; internal storage: 6,912K bits; magnetic tapes: 6 9-track, 1 7-track; magnetic discs: 2; 2 line printers. *On-line satellite computers*: 11 terminals. *Remote processing features*: Real time, remote batch.

NIPPON ELECTRIC NEAC 2200/500—operating system: MOD IV; internal storage: 3,144K bits; magnetic tapes: 6 7-track; magnetic discs: 5; 2 line printers.

HITAC 8450—operating system: Extended DOS Multi-staged; internal storage: 3,144K bits; magnetic tapes: 6 9-track; magnetic discs: 1; 2 line printers.

Coding Languages
Assembler, FORTRAN, COBOL, ALGOL, PL/1.

Services Available
Advice, programming, education and training, software packages, systems analysis.

Fields of Application
Scientific, statistical, commercial, production control, accounting, management, systems analysis.
Specialized areas: Sales analysis, linear programming, analysis, payroll.

Training
Courses for the staff of government departments or enterprises.

UNIVERSITIES AND COLLEGES

GUNMA UNIVERSITY
Computer Centre
1-5-1 Tenjincho Kiryusi, Gunma
Telephone: 0277 (22) 3181

Officer
Prof. Tosifumi Morita

Computer Installation
OKITAC 5090C—internal storage: 200K bits; magnetic tapes: 2 OKITAC 5099; 1 line printer.

Coding Languages
OKIPAL, OKISAP, OKISIP, ALGOLIP, FORTRAN.

Services Available
Advice, programming. Operate on a closed shop basis.

Field of Application
Scientific.

KYOTO UNIVERSITY
Data Processing Centre
Yoshida Honmachi, Sakyo-ku, Kyoto
Telephone: 075-751-2111

Officer
Dr. Hiroshi Nishihara, *Director*

Computer Installation
FACOM 230/60 (System I)–operating system: MONITOR V; internal storage: 7 million bits. magnetic tapes: 3 F603F; magnetic discs: 5 F461K; 3 line printers.
FACOM 230/60 (System II)–operating system: MONITOR V; internal storage: 11 million bits; magnetic tapes: 1 F603D, 7 F603F; magnetic discs: 1 F471K, 1 F461K; 3 line printers. *On-line satellite computers*: 6 FACOM-R. Remote-batch/conversational processing.

FACOM 270/30 (System III)–operating system: MONITOR III; internal storage: 1 million bits; magnetic tapes: 2 F603F; 1 line printer.

Coding Languages
Assembler (FASP), FORTRAN, ALGOL, COBOL, PL/1, BACCUS.

Contemplated Equipment
FACOM 230-75.

Services Available
Advice, operators. Operate on a remote access, closed shop and open shop basis. Available to staff and graduate students in Japanese universities for academic research work.

Fields of Application
Scientific, statistical, systems analysis, operational research. *Specialized areas*: Linear programming, analysis, structural engineering, medical research.

OSAKA INSTITUTE OF TECHNOLOGY*
Electronic Computing Laboratory
158, 1-chome, Omiya Kitano-cho, Asahi-ku, Osaka
Telephone: (06)-952-3131

Officers
Dr. Torahiko Sugiura, *Professor of Electronics and Director of Electronic Computing Laboratory*
Michizo Kimura

Computer Installation
FACOM 231–internal storage: 32K characters; magnetic tapes: 2; 1 line printer.

Coding Languages
ALGOL, S 2(FACOM), FASP (FACOM).

Services Available
Available for research, business, etc.

Field of Application
Numerical analysis.

OSAKA UNIVERSITY*
Computation Center
1-1 Machikaneyama-cho, Toyonaka City, Osaka

Officer
Prof. Shuji Takagi, *Director*

Computer Installation
NIPPON ELECTRIC NEAC 2200/500–operating systems: NEAC 2200 MOD III and NEAC Time Sharing System; internal storage: 3,145,728 bits; magnetic tapes: 6 N204B-5, 2 N204B-2; magnetic discs: 4 N259; 2 line printers. *On-line satellite computer*: NEAC 2200/500.

NIPPON ELECTRIC NEAC 2200/500–operating system: NEAC 2200 MOD III; internal storage: 2,359,296 bits; magnetic tapes: 5 N204B-5; magnetic discs: 3 N259; 1 line printer.

Coding Languages
FORTRAN IV, ALGOL 60, COBOL, NEAC 2200 Easycoder Assembly System.

Services Available
Consultation, education and training, operators. Operate on a closed shop basis with time sharing terminals on premises. Available to instructors of universities or colleges and investigators of the educational authorities in Japan.

Fields of Application
Scientific research and development, mainly numerical analysis, statistical processing, operations research, software development, etc.

Training
Short courses in FORTRAN IV programming.

TOHOKU UNIVERSITY*
Computer Centre
1-1 2 Chome Katahira, Sendai
Telephone: 0222-27-6200

Also at:
Data Station, Aramaki Aza Aoba, Sendai
Telephone: 0222-22-1800

Officers
Dr. Juro Oizumi, *Director*
Tadashi Takahashi, *Assistant Director*

Computer Installations
NIPPON ELECTRIC NEAC 2230–operating system: NARC 3; internal storage: 122,500 bits; magnetic tapes: 4 N543A; 1 line printer.

NIPPON ELECTRIC NEAC 2200/500(4)–operating systems: MOD 3, MOD 4; internal storage: 1,572,864 bits (2 units), 3,145,728 bits (2 units); magnetic tapes: N543A, 2 N204C-15, 14 N204B-9; magnetic discs: N 261, 9 N259; 5 line printers. *Remote processing features:* NEAC-TSS.

Coding Languages
Assembler-L, FORTRAN-L, ALGOL-L, COBOL-L, BPL.

Contemplated Equipment
NIPPON ELECTRIC NEAC 2200/700; curve plotter.

Services Available
Consultation, education and training, preparation of data, systems analysis; operate on a closed shop basis with remote access and time-sharing terminals on premises. Service available to universities and colleges in the northeastern district of Japan.

Fields of Application
Natural and human sciences; technical, educational.
Specialized areas: Numerical analysis, remote data processing.

Training
Short introductory and advanced courses in FORTRAN and ALGOL; TSS course.

UNIVERSITY OF TOKYO*
Computer Centre
2-11-16 Yayoi, Bunkyoko, Tokyo
Telephone: 03 (812) 2111

Officers
Prof. Hidetosi Takahasi

Computer Installations
HITAC 5020E—internal storage: 65K x 32 bits; magnetic tapes: 11 H-3485; magnetic discs: 6 HITAC 5050; 2 line printers.

HITAC 5020—internal storage: 32K x 32 bits; 1 line printer.

Coding Language
FORTRAN.

Service Available
Operators. Operate on a closed shop basis.

WASEDA UNIVERSITY*
Electronic Computation Centre
Nishiokubo 4-170, Shijuku-ku, Tokyo

Officers
Prof. Michio Soshiroda
Prof. Yasuo Tamura

Computer Installations
IBM 7040—operating systems: DOS and TOS; internal storage: 1,179,648 bits; magnetic tapes: 10 729-V; 1 line printer.

IBM 360/20—operating systems: DOS and TOS; magnetic tapes: 2; magnetic discs: 2 2311; 1 line printer.

Services Available
Advice, programming, education and training, operators, software packages, systems analysis. Operate on a closed shop basis.

Fields of Application
Scientific, statistical, accounting, management, systems analysis, operational research.

Training
Short courses of instruction in the use of a programming language.

GOVERNMENT ESTABLISHMENTS

BUREAU OF STATISTICS
Office of the Prime Minister, 95 Wakamatsucho, Shinjuku, Tokyo 162
Telephone: (03) 202-1111

Officer
Yasumori Kato, *Director*

Computer Installation
IBM 370/155—operating system: OS; internal storage: 4,194K bits; magnetic tapes: 8 IBM 3420/005; magnetic discs: 8 IBM 3330/001; 2 line printers.

NIPPON ELECTRIC NEAC 2200/500—operating system: IOCS; internal storage: 1,572K bits; magnetic tapes: 7 N204B-9; magnetic discs: 2 N259; 2 line printers.

NIPPON ELECTRIC NEAC 2200/400—operating system: IOCS; internal storage: 786K bits; magnetic tapes: 7 N204B-9; 1 line printer.

Coding Languages
PL/1, Assembler.

Services Available
Advice, preparation of data, data processing. Operate on a closed shop basis. Processing services are available only to government organizations.

Field of Application
Statistical
Specialized area: Linear programming.

Training
The Statistical Training Institute of the Prime Minister's Office provides courses in computer programming and systems analysis, mainly for statistical personnel in central and local government.

ELECTRICAL COMMUNICATION LABORATORY*
Musasino-si Midorityo 3-535, Tokyo
Telephone: 0422-51-7151

Officers
Masayosi Miyazaki, *Director*
Masumi Sindo, *Chief of Computational Section*

Computer Installation
NIPPON ELECTRIC NEAC 2200/400—operating system: MODE 1; internal storage: 1,179,648 bits; magnetic tapes: 5 N204B; magnetic disc: N259; 2 line printers.

Coding Languages
Assembler, FORTRAN, COBOL.

Services Available
Advice, operators, programming, systems analysis. Operate on a self-service and closed shop basis. Available only for research and engineering.

Fields of Application
Analysis and programming in all fields of interest to the Laboratory.
Specialized areas: Solution of numerical calculations, data processing and simulations encountered in scientific and business problems.

Training
Courses in programming languages.

ELECTROTECHNICAL LABORATORY*
(Denki Shinkenjo)
2-chome, Nagatacho, Chiyoda-ku, Tokyo
Telephone: 581-0441

Officers
T. Momota, *Director of Electrotechnical Laboratory*
K. Noda, *Chief of Electronic Computer Division, and Chief of Data Processing Section*
M. Jotaki, *Chief of Automatic Control Division*

Computer Installation
FACOM 230/50—operating system: MONITOR 0, 1, 2; internal storage: 32K 42-bit words; magnetic tapes: FACOM 603 B; 1 line printer.

ETL MK II—1 line printer.

ETL MK IV A—internal storage: 1K words.

ETL MK IV B—internal storage: 1K words; magnetic tapes: 4.

ETL MK VI—internal storage: 12K 4-bit words; 1 line printer.
Precision and magnetic analogue computers.

Services Available
Advice, operators, programming, FACOM 230/50, ETL MK II and ETL MK IVA available to outside customers for research.

Field of Application
Scientific research.
Specialized areas: Study of logical mathematics, especially its applications to relay networks; computer construction and design; study of ultra high speed computer using Esaki diodes (Dynamic Asynchronous Logic Circuit System, DALC System); investigation into number codes; experimental pilot model based on zero-sum cyclic 3-adic numbers (error detecting codes). Study of spatial circuit, especially its applications to pattern recognition.

Training
Logical mathematical ultra high speed computer; computers for automatic control; mechanical translation.

KANAWAGA PREFECTURAL GOVERNMENT*
Commerce and Industry Department
No. 1, Nihon-Odori, Naka-ku, Yokohama
Telephone: 045-201-1111

Officer
Toshio Irie, *Director*

Computer Installation
TOSBAC 4200.

RESEARCH INSTITUTIONS

INSTITUTE OF INFORMATION TECHNOLOGY (IIT)
World Trade Center Building, 7th Floor,
2-4-1 Hamamatsucho, Minato-ku, Tokyo 105
Telephone: Tokyo (03)-435-6511

Officers
Dr. Z. Yamauti, *President*
Dr. S. Imamura, *Executive Director*

Computer Installations
FACOM 6—operating systems: BOS, OS, ROS; internal storage: 78K bits; magnetic tapes: 2F603F; magnetic discs: 3 F462K-1; 1 line printer.

HITAC 10—internal storage: 131K bits.

Coding Languages
FORTRAN, ALGOL, COBOL, PL/1, Assembler.

Contemplated Equipment
Additional TSS terminals.

Services Available
Advice, education and training, systems analysis. Operate on a self-service and open shop basis.

Fields of Application
Scientific, statistical, commercial, production control, accounting, management, systems analysis, operational research.

Training
Courses for Systems Engineers, Senior Programmers, Data Processing Instructors, Data Processing Management and Management Research.

JAPAN COMPUTER USAGE DEVELOPMENT INSTITUTE*
3-2-5 Kasumigaseki, Chiyoda-Ku, Tokyo
Telephone: (03)-581-6401

Officers
Kogoro Uemura, *Chairman*
Keiichiro Hirata, *Vice-Chairman*
Hidezo Inaba, *President*
Toshio Kitagawa, *Vice-President*
Sakae Furukawa, *Managing Director*

Services Available
Education and training. Primarily for the members of the Institute.

JAPAN INFORMATION PROCESSING DEVELOPMENT CENTRE*
15 Shibakoen 21, Minato-ku, Tokyo

Officers
T. Yoshida, *Executive Director*
Syoiti Miki, *Manager of Electronic Computer Department*

Computer Installation
NEAC 2206—internal storage: 490K bits; magnetic tapes: 6 543, 1 542; 2 line printers.

TOSBAC 5100/20—operating system: COS; internal storage: 131,072 bits; magnetic tapes: 6 MTH 0074; 1 line printer.

HITAC 5020—operating systems: MONITOR; internal storage: 2,097,152 bits; magnetic tapes: 6 H3485; 1 line printer.

OKIMINITAC 5000—operating system: MOS; internal storage: 131,072 bits; magnetic bits; magnetic tapes: 2 T II; 1 line printer.

FACOM 230/50—operating system: MONITOR; internal storage: 2,621,440 bits; magnetic tapes: 9 F-603E; magnetic disc: F631B; 1 line printer.

Coding Languages
SIP 100 (Symbolic Input Program), SIP 101, NEC Compiler, NERC (Neac Arithmetic Compiler), OKISIP.

Services Available
Advice, operators, preparation of data, programming, software packages, systems analysis. Operate on a closed shop and open shop basis.

Fields of Application
Inversion of matrix of order 50-60 airborne survey triangulation scientific engineering computation.

Training
Programmer training courses for beginners are held six times a year.

CONSULTANT

PEAT, MARWICK, MITCHELL & CO.
3-M Building 1-21, 7-chome, Akasaka, Minato-ku, Tokyo
Telephone: 402-1470

Officer
Kyo Hata

Services Available
Advice, systems analysis.

Fields of Application
Economic studies, general and scientific management, operations research, project management, industrial engineering, marketing, production and inventory control, information systems, general and cost accounting systems, data processing and transmission systems, etc.

SERVICE BUREAUX

HOKUSHIN ELECTRIC WORKS LTD.*
Digital Engineering Division
312 Shimomaruko, Ota-ku, Tokyo
Telephone: 732-4141

Officer
Tetsuya Miyauchi, *Director*

Computer Installation
HOC 510–internal storage: 208K bits.

Coding Languages
FORTRAN, Assembler.

Services Available
Advice, operators, preparation of data, programming, systems analysis.

Field of Application
Engineering.
Specialized areas: Computer control systems for such customers as iron and steel, petroleum and chemical works, etc.

Training
Training of engineers for customers.

IBM JAPAN LTD.*
Scientific Data Centre
Wakamatso Building, No. 3-5 Nihonbashi Honcho, Chou-ku, Tokyo
Telephone: 279-0611

Also at:
Tokyo Data Centre No. 1
No. 2-5, Nibancho, Kojimachi, Chiyoda-ku, Tokyo
Telephone: 262-6111

Tokyo Data Centre No. 2
Sotetsu Building, No. 1-3-23, Kitasaiwaicho, Nishi-ku, Yokohama
Telephone: 311-1561

Nagoya Data Centre
Hirokoji Building, No. 1-9-32, Nishiki, Naka-ku, Nagoya
Telephone: 211-4111

Osaka Data Centre
No. 2-45, Junkeidori, Minami-ku, Osaka
Telephone: 271-2712

Officers
Takeji Tanaka, *Branch Manager (Scientific Data Centre)*
Hideo Ohata, *Branch Manager (Tokyo Data Centre No. 1)*
Shigeru Nozue, *Branch Manager (Yokohama)*
Shiichi Inui, *Branch Manager (Nagoya)*
Itaro Yokoi, *Branch Manager (Osaka)*

Computer Installation
Tokyo (Scientific Data Centre):
IBM 360/75–operating system: OS/360; internal storage: 512K bytes; magnetic tapes: 3 2401; magnetic discs: 1 2314, 2 2311; 3 line printers.

IBM 7090–operating system: IBSYS; internal storage: 32K 36-bit words; magnetic tapes: 12 729; 1 line printer.

Tokyo (Data Centre No. 1)
IBM 360/40–operating system: DOS/360; internal storage: 128K bytes; magnetic tapes: 6 2401; magnetic discs: 4 type 2311; 2 line printers.

IBM 360/20–internal storage: 16K bytes; magnetic tapes: 2 2415; 1 line printer.

Yokohama:
IBM 1401–internal storage: 12K characters; magnetic tapes: 4 729; 1 line printer.

Nagoya:
IBM 360/40–operating system: DOS/360; internal storage: 128K bytes; magnetic tapes: 6 2401; magnetic discs: 4 2311; 2 line printers.

IBM 1401–internal storage: 12K characters; magnetic tapes: 4 729; 1 line printer.

Osaka:
IBM 360/50–operating system: OS/360; internal storage: 256K bytes; magnetic tapes: 1 2401, 1 2402; magnetic discs: 4 2311; 2 line printers.

IBM 1401–internal storage: 12K characters; magnetic tapes: 4 729; magnetic disc: 1311; 1 line printer.

Coding Languages
FORTRAN, COBOL, RPG, Autocoder.

Contemplated Equipment
IBM 360/40–256K bytes (Scientific Data Centre);
IBM 360/40–64K bytes (Yokohama and Osaka);
IBM 360/20–16K bytes (Nagoya).

Services Available
Advice, operators, preparation of data, programming, software packages. Operate on a self-service, closed shop, open shop and block time basis.

Fields of Application
Scientific, statistical, commercial, production control, accounting, management, operational research, etc.
Specialized areas: Nuclear calculation, civil engineering, ship building, linear programming, simulation (Scientific Data Centre).

Training
Application and Programming Language courses.

MITSUBISHI OFFICE MACHINERY COMPANY, LTD.*
6-1 Hatchobori 2-chome, Chuo-ku, Tokyo
Telephone: 03-552-4501

Also at:
Osaka, Nagoya, Fukuoka, Hiroshima, Shizuoka, Sendai, Kobe.

Officer
Rokiya Ono

Computer Installations
BULL GENERAL ELECTRIC GE 115 (4)–operating systems: TOS and DOS; internal storage: 16K bits; magnetic tapes: 5 MTH 103; magnetic discs: 4 DSU-130; 1 line printer.

BULL GENERAL ELECTRIC GE 130–operating systems: ETOS and EDOS; internal storage: 32K bits; magnetic tapes: 4 MTH 166; magnetic discs: 3 DSU-160; 2 line printers.

BULL GENERAL ELECTRIC GE 55 (2)–internal storage: 5K bytes; 1 serial printer.

BULL GENERAL ELECTRIC Gamma 10 (4)–internal storage: 4 K characters; 1 line printer.

Coding Languages
Assembler, COBOL, FORTRAN, RPG, TAB.

Services Available
Advice, programming, education and training, operators, software packages, documentation, preparation of data, systems analysis. Operate on an open shop basis.

Fields of Application
Scientific, statistical, commercial, production control, accounting, management, systems analysis, operational research.

Training
Programming courses in the following languages: COBOL, FORTRAN, RPG, TAB, GE 50 series Assembler language, GE 100 series Assembler language, GAMMA 10 series Assembler language; Application courses in GEIMS (General Electric Inventory Management System) and TIPP (Typical Industrial Production Planning). Short course: Introduction to EDP in 2 days.

NIPPON ELECTRIC COMPANY, LTD.*
7-15, Shiba Gochome, Minato-ku, Tokyo 108
Telephone: Tokyo (03) 452-1111

Officer
Koji Kobayashi, *President*

Computer Installations
NIPPON ELECTRIC NEAC 2200/500(9)–operating systems: OS MOD 1, OS MOD III, OS MOD IV; internal storage: 5144K bits; magnetic tapes: 12; magnetic discs: 6; 2 line printers.

NIPPON ELECTRIC NEAC 2200/400(4)–operating systems: OS MOD I, OS MOD III, OS MOD IV; internal storage: 1572K bits; magnetic tapes: 10; magnetic discs: 4; 2 line printers.

NIPPON ELECTRIC NEAC 2200/250–operating systems: OS MOD I, OS MOD III, OS MOD IV; internal storage: 576K bits; magnetic tapes: 8; magnetic discs: 2; 2 line printers.

NIPPON ELECTRIC NEAC 2200/200 (28)–operating systems: OS MOD I, OS MOD III, OS MOD IV; internal storage: 390K bits; magnetic tapes: 6; magnetic discs: 2; 2 line printers.

NIPPON ELECTRIC NEAC 2200/100(2)–operating systems: OS MOD I, OS MOD III, OS MOD IV; internal storage: 192K bits; magnetic tapes: 4; 1 line printer.

NIPPON ELECTRIC NEAC 2200/50(3)–operating systems: OS MOD I, OS MOD III, OS MOD IV; internal storage: 96K bits; magnetic tapes: 4; magnetic discs: 1; 1 line printer.

Coding Languages
Assembler, COBOL, FORTRAN.

Services Available
Advice, programming, education and training, software packages, systems analysis. Operate on a closed shop basis.

Fields of Application
Scientific, statistical, commercial, accounting, production control, management, systems analysis, operational research, etc.

Training
Basic course for Junior Programmers; programming course for Senior Programmers; operating system course and management science course for System Engineers. Short courses of 5 days' duration for Top and Middle Management.

NIPPON SOFTWARE COMPANY LTD.*
19-Mori Building, 20-Shiba Akefune-cho, Minato-ku, Tokyo
Telephone: (03) 591-8241

Officers
Atsushi Fujii, *Managing Director of Computer Centre*
Tadao Sato, *Manager of Computer Centre*

Computer Installation
FACOM 230/60–operating system: OS with TSS (M-V); internal storage: 524K bytes (2620A); magnetic tapes: 3 F603F; magnetic discs: 2 F461L, 9 F472K; 1 line printer.

NIPPON ELECTRIC NEAC 2200/400–operating system: Monitor System (Mode IV); internal storage: 262K bytes (N400); magnetic tapes: 6 N2048B-5; magnetic discs: 2 N259; 1 line printer.

IBM 360/50–operating system: MFT; internal storage: 524K bytes (2050 I); magnetic tapes: 2 2401-006; magnetic discs: 9 2314, 2 2311; 2 line printers. *On-line satellite computers:* 2 2741-001, 2 2260-001.

Services Available
Advice, programming, education and training, operators, software packages, documentation, preparation of data, systems analysis. Operate on a self-service, remote access, block time, closed shop and open shop basis; time-sharing terminals on premises.

Fields of Application
Scientific, statistical, commercial, production control, accounting, management, systems analysis, operational research.
Specialized areas: Systems software, management science.

Training
Introductory, middle and advanced computer languages courses; course for management; systems engineering course.

TOKYO SHIBAURA ELECTRIC CO. LTD.*
1, 1-Chome, Uchisaiwai-cho, Chiyoda-ku, Tokyo
Telephone: (501) 5411

Computer Installation
TOSBAC 3400.
TOSBAC 5100.

JORDAN

NATIONAL CENTRE

ROYAL SCIENTIFIC SOCIETY
P.O. Box 6945, Amman

Officer
Dr. Elie J. Baghdady, *President*

Computer Installation
IBM 360/20—internal storage: 12K bytes; magnetic discs: 2 2311; 1 line printer.
IBM 1130—internal storage: 16K words; magnetic tapes: 4 drives; magnetic discs: 3 drives (2310); 1 line printer.

Coding Languages
Assembler, RPG, COBOL, FORTRAN.

Contemplated Equipment
A computer with remote processing features.

Services Available
Advice, programming, education and training, operators, software packages, documentation, preparation of data, systems analysis. Operate on a self-service, time-sharing, closed and open shop basis.

Fields of Application
Scientific, statistical, commercial, production control, accounting, management, systems analysis, operational research.
Specialized areas: Sales analysis, linear programming, analysis, payroll, structural engineering, medical research, management systems.

Training
On-the-job training.

KENYA

UNIVERSITY

UNIVERSITY OF NAIROBI*
Computing Centre
P.O. Box 30197, Nairobi
Telephone: 27441, extensions 451/4

Officer
R. J. P. Scott

Computer Installation
ICL 1902A—operating systems: GEORGE 1S; internal storage: 384K bits; magnetic tapes: 4; 1 line printer.

Coding Languages
PLAN, FORTRAN IV, COBOL, ALGOL, CSL.

Contemplated Equipment
2 disc drives, increase in internal storage of 384K bits, graph plotter, remote terminals.

Services Available
Advice, programming, education and training, operators, software packages, preparation of data. Operate on a closed and open shop basis. Available to the University and to Government research establishments.

Fields of Application
Engineering, statistical analysis, university administration.

Training
Programming courses as part of degree programmes. Short courses in Basic FORTRAN IV (15 hours), Further FORTRAN IV (9 hours) and Appreciation of Computing (10 hours).

GOVERNMENT ESTABLISHMENT

KENYA COMMERCIAL BANK
Computer Centre
P.O. Box 18051, Nairobi

Officers
A. R. Hendry, *Computer Manager*
G. L. Spencer, *Training Officer*

Computer Installation
ICL 1901—operating system: GEORGE 1; internal storage: 16 million bits; magnetic tapes: 4 ICL 1971; 1 line printer.
ICL 1902A—operating system: GEORGE 1 and 2; internal storage: 16 million bits; magnetic tapes: 4 ICL 1973; 1 line printer.

Coding Languages
ICL PLAN, COBOL.

Contemplated Equipment
Data communications equipment.

Services Available
Advice, preparation of data. Operate on a block time basis.

Fields of Application
Statistical, commercial, accounting, management.
Specialized areas: Investment, payroll.

Training
No training provided for outside users.

SERVICE BUREAU

INTERNATIONAL COMPUTERS (EAST AFRICA) LTD.
P.O. Box 30293, Nairobi
Telephone: 21811

Officers
J. E. A. Robertson, *Managing Director*
J. T. Dunwoody, *Sales Manager*
M. J. Okech, *Bureau Manager*

Computer Installation
ICL 1902—operating system: GEORGE 2; internal storage: 32K 24-bit words; magnetic tapes: 6; magnetic discs: 2; 1 line printer.

Coding Languages
COBOL, PLAN, FORTRAN.

Contemplated Equipment
ICL 1902A.

Services Available
Advice, programming, education and training, operators, software packages, documentation, preparation of data, systems analysis. Operate on a closed shop basis.

Fields of Application
Scientific, statistical, commercial, accounting, management, systems analysis.
Specialized areas: Sales analysis, investment, payroll.

Training
Courses in systems analysis and design, programming, operating and data preparation (for ICL customers' staff only).

REPUBLIC OF KOREA

EDUCATIONAL AND TRAINING INSTITUTION

KOREA COMPUTER CENTER
10, 2-KA Pil-Dong, Chung-ku, Seoul
Telephone: 26-4724-6

Officer
Chu Yong Lee, *President*

Computer Installation
FACOM 230/25–operating system: BOS II and ROS; internal storage: 96K bytes; magnetic tapes: 4 603F; magnetic discs: 3 F427; 1 line printer.

CDC 3200–operating system: MSOS; internal storage: 32K words; magnetic tapes: 6; magnetic discs: 4 804; 1 line printer.

Coding Languages
Assembler, COBOL, FORTRAN.

Contemplated Equipment
IBM 370/135.

Services Available
Advice, programming, education and training, operators, software packages, documentation, preparation of data, systems analysis. Operate on a closed shop, block time and open shop basis.

Fields of Application
Scientific, statistical, commercial, production control, accounting, management, systems analysis.
Specialized areas: Sales analysis, payroll, banking.

Training
Courses in processing and coding languages.

RESEARCH INSTITUTION

KOREA INSTITUTE OF SCIENCE AND TECHNOLOGY
39-1, Hawolgok-Dong, Seoul
Telephone: 94-0140

Officer
Dr. Sang Joon Hahn, *President*

Computer Installation
CDC Cyber 72–operating system: SCOPE; internal storage: 4,380K bits; magnetic tapes: 10 604; magnetic discs: 8 841; 2 line printers. *Remote processing features:* 2 sets of 200-UT and interactive terminals.

CDC 1700–operating system: Tape SCOPE; internal storage: 192K bits; magnetic tapes: 2 608.

Coding Languages
FORTRAN, COBOL, ALGOL, Basic, Compass, Draft.

Services Available
Advice, programming, education and training, preparation of data, systems analysis. Operate on a remote access, closed shop and time-sharing basis.

Fields of Application
Scientific, statistical, commercial, accounting, management, systems analysis, operational research, message switching.

Training
Courses in language training, systems analysis and case studies.

LEBANON

NATIONAL CENTRE

CONSEIL NATIONAL DE LA RECHERCHE SCIENTIFIQUE*
Centre de Calcul Scientifique
Boulevard de la Cité Sportive, Imm. Dagher, Beirut
Téléphone: 302287

Dirigeant
M. R. Mansour

Equipement
IBM 1130–système d'opération: DM.V2; mémoire interne: 16K mots; disques magnétiques: 1 2315; 2 imprimantes.

Langages de Programmation
FORTRAN, Assembleur-GAP.

Services Fournis
Conseils, programmation, systems analysis. Fonctionnement en abonnement machine.

Domaines d'Application
Recherche scientifique, statistique, systems analysis, calcul technique, recherche opérationnelle, contrôle de projets, administration publique.

Formation
Initiation à l'Informatique.

UNIVERSITIES AND COLLEGES

AMERICAN UNIVERSITY OF BEIRUT*
Computer Center
Beirut
Telephone: 292860

Officers
Cecil Kirkis, *Director*
Dicran Keosheyan, *Assistant Director*

Computer Installation
IBM 1401 – internal storage: 12K bits.

IBM 1620 – internal storage: 60K bits; magnetic disc: 1; 1 line printer.

IBM 1130 – internal storage: 8K bits; magnetic discs: 2;

Coding Languages
FORTRAN II, Autocoder, SPS, FORTRAN IV, Assembler.

Services Available
Available on excess time basis to outside customers.

Fields of Application
Academic, research, applied mathematics, data processing.
Specialized areas: Petroleum industry data processing, hospital data processing.

Training
Basic FORTRAN, Advanced FORTRAN, Business Data Processing.

ÉCOLE SUPÉRIEURE D'INGÉNIEURS DE BEYROUTH
Mar Roukoz, B.P. 1514, Beirut
Telephone: 268550, 263297, 263299

Officers
Rev. Père Alban de Jerphanion, *Chancellor*
Prof. Pierre Lalangue, *Director of Studies*
Georges Malkoun, *Systems Engineer*

Computer Installation
IBM 1130 – operating system: OS 1130, level II; internal storage: 8K bits; magnetic discs: 1 2315; 1 line printer. *Remote processing features:* 1142-6 reader and punch, 1017 paper tape punch, 1018 paper tape reader.

Coding Languages
Assembler, FORTRAN IV, RPG, COBOL.

Contemplated Equipment
A plotter; additional internal storage of 16K bits; 2 satellite discs.

Services Available
Advice, programming, education and training, software packages, preparation of data, systems analysis. Operate on a self-service and open shop basis.

Fields of Application
Scientific, statistical, commercial, management.
Specialized areas: Linear programming, structural engineering.

Training
Courses in hardware, software, programming, operational research and numerical calculations.

INSTITUT DE STATISTIQUE DE BEYROUTH
Rue de Damas, B.P. 3855, Beirut
Telephone: 220825

Officer
Michel Pietri, *Director*

Fields of Application
Scientific, statistical, operational research.

Training
Courses in statistics, informatics and coding languages (FORTRAN and COBOL). Students may work for a "certificat d'aptitude" in the use of statistical methods from the Institut de Statistique at the University of Paris, France.

GOVERNMENT ESTABLISHMENT

DIRECTION CENTRALE DE LA STATISTIQUE
Ministère du Plan, Beirut
Telephone: 270092

Officers
Ibrahim Trabulsi, *Director*
Hazem Nahas, *Service Chief*

Computer Installation
BULL GENERAL ELECTRIC GE 120 – operating system: EDOS; internal storage: 32K bits; magnetic tapes: 3 MTH 101; magnetic discs: 2 DSU 160; 1 line printer.

Coding Languages
APS II, COBOL.

Services Available
Advice, statistics.

Field of Application
Statistical.

CONSULTANT

ASSOCIATED BUSINESS CONSULTANTS LTD.
Gefinor Building, P.O. Box 5736, Beirut
Telephone: 342860

Officers
Walid Kudsi, *Manager of Commercial Systems*
Emile Khouri, *Manager of Scientific Systems*

Computer Installation
UNIVAC 9400 – operating system: DOS/TOS; internal storage: 520K bits; magnetic tapes: 4 Uniservo VI C; magnetic discs: 3 8414; 2 line printers. *On-line satellite computers:* UNIVAC 9300 with storage of 32K bytes. *Remote processing features:* On-line Slave Local System.

IBM 1130 – operating system: Monitor; internal storage: 65,600 bits; magnetic discs: 1 2314; 1 line printer.

Coding Languages
COBOL, FORTRAN, RPG, Assembler.

Contemplated Equipment
Additional core storage.

Services Available
Advice, programming, education and training, software packages, documentation, systems analysis. Operate on a closed shop, block time and time-sharing basis.

Fields of Application
Scientific, statistical, commercial, accounting, management, systems analysis, operational research.
Specialized areas: Sales analysis, analysis, market research, industrial management.

Training
Three-stage diploma course in Business Automation.

LIBYA

UNIVERSITY

UNIVERSITY OF LIBYA*
Faculty of Science
Tripoli

Officer
Dr. Saad Ben Hemid.

Computer Installation
FORTREND 1620—magnetic discs: 1 line printer.

Services Available
Education and training. Operate on a self-service basis.

Fields of Application
Educational and scientific research.

GOVERNMENT ESTABLISHMENT

MINISTRY OF PLANNING
Census and Statistical Department
Demask Street, Tripoli
Telephone: 34091, extension 231

Officer
L. Z. Carmous, *Head of the Computer Centre*

Computer Installation
ICL 1902—internal storage: 16K 24-bit words; magnetic tapes: 4; 2 line printers.

Coding Languages
COBOL, FORTRAN, PLAN.

Contemplated Equipment
A larger system with four tapes and three discs.

Services Available
Advice, programming, education and training, preparation of data, systems analysis. Operate on a block time basis. Available to government agents only.

Fields of Application
Statistical, commercial, accounting, systems analysis.

Training
Short courses in COBOL and FORTRAN.

MALAWI

GOVERNMENT ESTABLISHMENT

MALAWI RAILWAYS LTD.
P.O. Box 5492, Limbe

Officer
G. R. F. Arnold, *Data Processing Manager*

Computer Installation
ICL 1901A—internal storage: 16K bits; magnetic tapes: 4 1971/2; magnetic discs: 2 2801/2; 1 line printer.

Coding Languages
COBOL, PLAN, FORTRAN.

Services Available
Operators, preparation of data.

Fields of Application
All fields will eventually be covered.

Training
Five-week course in COBOL programming.

MALAYSIA

UNIVERSITY

UNIVERSITI MALAYA
Computer Centre
Lembah Pantai, Kuala Lumpur

Officers
Prof. Ong Yeen Fook, *Director*
Mrs. Lee Sau Lan, *Lecturer*

Computer Installation
IBM 1130—operating system: DOS; internal storage: 16K 16-bit words; magnetic discs: 3; 1 line printer.

Coding Languages
FORTRAN IV, RPG, COBOL, SL/1, Assembler.

Services Available
Advice, programming, education and training, software packages, documentation, preparation of data, systems analysis. Operate on a self-service basis. Available to University staff and students and to limited Government personnel.

Fields of Application
Scientific, statistical, accounting.

Training
Short courses in Elementary Computer Science (30 hours), Elementary FORTRAN (8 hours), Advanced FORTRAN (8 hours), COBOL Programming, Systems Analysis.

GOVERNMENT ESTABLISHMENTS

DEPARTMENT OF STATISTICS
Young Road, Kuala Lumpur
Telephone: Kuala Lumpur 88922/4

Officer
Ong Seng Wah, *Computer Manager*

Computer Installation
ICL 1904A—operating systems: Executive and GEORGE; internal storage: 1,536K bits; magnetic tapes: 10 ICL 1973/1 and 1973/2; magnetic discs: 2 ICL 2802/2; 2 line printers.

Coding Languages
Assembly, COBOL, FORTRAN.

Contemplated Equipment
2 EDS 60.

Services Available
Programming, education and training, preparation of data, systems analysis. Operate on a closed shop basis. Available to Government departments that do not possess data processing facilities.

Field of Application
Statistical.

Training
Short courses in Programming and Systems Analysis in conjunction with the manufacturer.

SURVEY DEPARTMENT
Jalan Gurney, Kuala Lumpur
Telephone: 03-21311

Officer
Director-General of Survey

Computer Installation
IBM 1130—operating system: disk; internal storage: 131,072 bits; magnetic discs: 1 IBM 1131; 1 line printer.
PACER 100—operating system: tape; internal storage: 259,072 bits; magnetic tape: 1.

Coding Languages
FORTRAN, RPG, Assembler.

Services Available
Advice, programming, education and training, operators, systems analysis. Operate on a self-service basis.

Fields of Application
Scientific, statistical, management, systems analysis, operational research.

SERVICE BUREAU

IBM WORLD TRADE CORPORATION
Kuala Lumpur

Also at:
Singapore City, Singapore

Computer Installation
IBM 360/25.

Services Available
Advice, operators, preparation of data, programming, software packages.

Fields of Application
Scientific, statistical, commercial.

MAURITIUS

UNIVERSITY

UNIVERSITY OF MAURITIUS
Réduit
Telephone: 4-1041 to 4-1049

Officer
C. K. S. Chong Hok Yuen, *Data Processing Instructor*

Computer Installation
ICL 1004—internal storage: 5,766 bits; 1 line printer.

Coding Language
Self Machine Code.

Contemplated Equipment
Magnetic tape unit.

Services Available
Operate on a self-service and block time basis. Available for University use only.

Fields of Application
Scientific, statistical, accounting, management, systems analysis.
Specialized area: Payroll.

Training
Courses in Computer Appreciation, Computer Programming, Systems Analysis and Design.

GOVERNMENT ESTABLISHMENT

MINISTRY OF FINANCE
Data Processing Division
Port Louis
Telephone: 2-3767

Officer
T. Elsdon, *Head of Division*

Computer Installation
ICL 1902A—operating system: GEORGE 1 and 2; internal storage: 32K bits; magnetic tapes: 4; magnetic discs: 3; 2 line printers.

Services Available
Advice, programming, education and training, operators, software packages, documentation, preparation of data, systems analysis. Operate on a closed shop basis. Services not available to the private sector.

Fields of Application
Statistical, production control, accounting, management, systems analysis.
Specialized areas: Analysis, payroll, population statistics, trade figures, prices.

Training
Courses in programming languages (PLAN, COBOL, FORTRAN), systems analysis, design and operating.

CONSULTANT

INTERNATIONAL COMPUTERS LTD.
Anglo Mauritius House, Port Louis

Officer
W. T. Harniman, *Director of Island Operations*

Computer Installation
ICL operates 1901A computers for the Government, the Central Electricity Board and Mauritius Computing Services.

Coding Languages
COBOL, ALGOL, FORTRAN, PLAN.

Contemplated Equipment
Universal document readers, larger core store, paper tape equipment, data communication.

Services Available
Advice, programming, education and training, software packages, systems analysis. All services available on request.

Fields of Application
Statistical, commercial, accounting, management, government, meteorological, hydrological, educational.
Specialized area: Sugar estate work.

Training
Courses in Programming PLAN, Systems Analysis, School Teaching and University Lecturing.
Short course in Management Education.

SERVICE BUREAUX

CENTRAL ELECTRICITY BOARD*
Royal Road, Curepipe
Telephone: Curepipe 1500

Computer Installation
ICL 1901A–operating system: PATSY; internal storage: 32K characters; magnetic tapes: 4; 1 line printer.

Coding Languages
COMPACT, ALGOL, FORTRAN, PLAN, COBOL.

Contemplated Equipment
Universal document reader.

Services Available
Operate on a closed shop basis.

Fields of Application
Accounting, statistical, management.

MAURITIUS COMPUTING SERVICES LTD.
18 Edith Cavell Street, Port Louis
Telephone: 2-3737

Officer
Bernard Koenig, *Manager*

Computer Installation
ICL 1901A–internal storage: 196,608 bits; magnetic tapes: 4; 1 line printer.

Coding Languages
PLAN, COBOL, FORTRAN.

Services Available
Advice, programming, education and training, operators, software packages, documentation, preparation of data, systems analysis. Operate on a closed shop and block time basis.

Fields of Application
Statistical, commercial, accounting, systems analysis.
Specialized area: Sugar industries.

Training
Short course for punch operators.

MEXICO

NATIONAL CENTRE

CENTRO NACIONAL DE CÁLCULO*
I.P.N. Zacatenco, México 14, D.F.
Telephone: 5-86-47-11

Officers
Enrique Melrose A., *Director*
Mario Baez Camargo, *Assistant Director*

Computer Installation
CDC 3150–operating system: MSOS; internal storage: 32K bits; magnetic tapes: 4; magnetic discs: 2; 1 line printer.

IBM 1130–internal storage: 8K bits; magnetic discs: 1; 1 line printer.

PDP-8/I–internal storage: 8K bits; magnetic discs: 1, *On-line satellite computers:* 2 teletypes.

UNIVAC 8055–internal storage: 96K characters; magnetic tapes: 6; 1 line printer.

Coding Languages
FORTRAN, COBOL, REC, ALGOL, Assembler, COMPASS.

Contemplated Equipment
Time-sharing and multiprogramming equipment.

Services Available
Advice, programming, software packages, systems analysis. Operate on a closed shop and open shop basis. Available for research and education only.

Fields of Application
Scientific, management, operational research.

Training
Courses leading to M.Sc. in Computing Sciences.

UNIVERSITIES AND COLLEGES

INSTITUTO TECNOLÓGICO Y DE ESTUDIOS SUPERIORES DE MONTERREY
Sucursal de Correos "J", Monterrey, Nuevo León
Telephone: 58-20-00, extension 131

Officers
Ing. Fernando García Roel, *President*
Dr. Fernando J. Jaimes, *Director of the Computer Centre*

Computer Installation
CDC 3300–operating system: Master; internal storage: 1,560 million bits; magnetic tapes: 2 601; magnetic discs: 4 841; 1 line printer.

IBM S/7–internal storage: 192K bits. *Remote processing features:* Analog to digital and digital to analog conversion, digital inputs and outputs.

Coding Languages
FORTRAN, COBOL, ALGOL, Compass, Assembler, MSP.

Contemplated Equipment
HEWLETT PACKARD 2126B Minicomputer with internal storage of 128K bits.

Mexico – Universities and Colleges

Services Available
Advice, programming, education and training, software packages, preparation of data, systems analysis. Operate on a closed shop and block time basis. Priority given to educational, research, administrative and extension services.

Fields of Application
Scientific, statistical, commercial, production control, accounting, management, systems analysis, operational research.
Specialized areas: Linear programming, analysis, payroll, structural engineering.

Training
The School of Science and Humanities offers a Bachelor degree in computer science.

UNIVERSIDAD AUTÓNOMA DE GUADALAJARA
Paseo de las Águilas 7000, Lomas del Valle, Tercera Sección, Guadalajara, Jalisco

Officers
Dr. Luis Garibay Gutiérrez, *Rector*
Lic. Antonio Leaño, *Vice-Rector*
Lic. Carlos Pérez Vizcaíno, *Secretary General*

Computer Installation
NCR Century 200 – operating system: B1 disc; internal storage: 262,144 bits; magnetic tapes: 2 NCR 633; magnetic discs: 2 NCR 655; 1 line printer.

Coding Languages
FORTRAN, COBOL, NEAT/3.

Services Available
Advice, programming, education and training, operators, software packages, documentation, preparation of data, systems analysis. Operate on a closed shop basis.

Fields of Application
Scientific, management, systems analysis, operational research.
Specialized areas: Analysis, payroll, structural engineering, medical research.

Training
Courses in coding languages (FORTRAN and COBOL).

UNIVERSIDAD IBEROAMERICANA*
Avenida Cerro de las Torres 395, México 21, D.F.
Téléphone: 5-49-35-00, extension 125

Dirigeant
Prof. Andrés Lasaga Gómez, *Directeur*

Equipement
IBM 1130 – mémoire interne: 8K mots; disques magnétiques.

Langages de Programmation
FORTRAN, RPS, Assembleur.

Services Fournis
Programmation, enseignement et formation, software packages, documentation, systems analysis. Fonctionnement en abonnement machine.

Formation
Maîtrise en Systèmes.

UNIVERSIDAD LA SALLE DE MÉXICO
Avenida Benjamin Franklin 47, Col. Escandon Z.P.18, México 18, D.F.
Telephone: 516-25-48/157

Officers
Dr. Guillermo Alba López, *Rector*
Ing. Bernardo Ardavín Migoni, *Secretary General*
Ing. Jaime Palacios Castañon, *Director of Computing Centre*

Computer Installation
IBM 360/30 – operating system: DOS; internal storage: 64K bits; magnetic tapes 2 2400; magnetic discs: 4 2314; 1 line printer.

The University also has access to a SEPAC-DELTA I on a time-sharing basis.

Coding Languages
COBOL, ALGOL, FORTRAN, BASIC, PL/1, Assembler.

Contemplated Equipment
IBM 1130 with APL terminal and disc devices.

Services Available
Advice, programming, education and training, software packages, systems analysis. Operate on a self-service and time-sharing basis. Available to students, teachers and research services.

Fields of Application
Scientific, statistical, commercial, production control, accounting, management, operational research.
Specialized areas: Linear programming, investment analysis, structural engineering.

UNIVERSIDAD NACIONAL AUTÓNOMA DE MÉXICO
Centro de Investigación en Matemáticas Aplicadas, Sistemas y Servicios (CIMASS)
Apartado Postal 20-726, México 20, D.F.
Telephone: 548-54-65

Officers
Dr. Renato Iturriaga, *Director*
Dr. Tomás Garza, *Associate Director*

Computer Installation
BURROUGHS B6700 – operating system: MCP; internal storage: 144K 48-bit words; magnetic tapes: 4; magnetic discs: 10; 2 line printers. *Remote processing features:* 32 remote terminals.

Coding Languages
ALGOL, FORTRAN, COBOL, BASIC.

Contemplated Equipment
DC 1100 remote job entry; 64K word mass memory.

Services Available
Advice, education and training, operators, software packages, documentation, systems analysis. Operate on a remote access, closed shop and time-sharing basis. Services available only to the university faculty and students.

Fields of Application
Scientific, statistical, systems analysis, operational research.

Training
Courses in programming.

GOVERNMENT ESTABLISHMENTS

INSTITUTO MEXICANO DEL SEGURO SOCIAL
Informática
Tokio 80, 6° piso, México 6, D.F.
Telephone: 511-9241, 533-2858

Officers
Sergio F. Beltran, *Director*
Rafael Olivera P., *Deputy Director*

Computer Installation
CDC 6400–operating system: SCOPE 3.4; internal storage: 800K bits; magnetic tapes: 10 607; magnetic discs: 8 841, 2 821; 3 line printers. *On-line satellite computers:* CDC 1700. *Remote processing features:* Video terminals.

IBM 370/155–operating system: OS; internal storage: 1 million bits; magnetic tapes: 10; magnetic discs: 16 3330; 2 line printers. *On-line satellite computer:* CDC 1700. *Remote processing features:* RJE and video terminals.

Coding Languages
COBOL, FORTRAN, BASIC, ALGOL.

Contemplated Equipment
CDC 6400 with internal storage of 65K 60-bit words.

Services Available
Advice, programming, education and training, software packages, systems analysis, data base implementation. Operate on a remote access, open shop and time-sharing basis. Primarily for the Social Security Institute.

Fields of Application
Scientific, statistical, management, systems analysis, operational research.
Specialized areas: Analysis, payroll, medical research and administration, data base operation.

Training
Courses in informatics and systems.

SECRETARÍA DE RECURSOS HIDRÁULICOS
Dirección de Procesamiento Electrónico
Paseo de la Reforma 69, 1er piso, México 1, D.F.
Telephone: 535-12-51

Officers
Leobardo Palomino Benson, *General Manager of Methods and Organization*
Javier Belaunzarán García, *EDP Manager*

Computer Installation
CDC 3300–operating system: MASTER; internal storage: 1,966,080 bits; magnetic tapes: 4 604; magnetic discs: 3 841; 2 line printers. *Remote processing features:* 2 MDS-1103 off-line.

Coding Languages
FORTRAN, COBOL.

Contemplated Equipment
More powerful communications equipment.

Services Available
Advice, programming, systems analysis and development. Operate on an open shop basis. Available only for use by the institution.

Fields of Application
Scientific, statistical, commercial, management, systems analysis.
Specialized areas: Analysis, payroll, hydraulic engineering.

CONSULTANTS

ARTHUR D. LITTLE DE MEXICO, S.A.*
Avenida Paseo de la Reforma 116, México 6, D.F.
Telephone: 535-49-20

Services Available
Advice, systems analysis.

Fields of Application
Scientific, statistical, commercial, production control, operational research, management information systems, market research, inventory control, physical distribution.

MORRIS & ELLIOTT, S.A. DE C.V.*
463-502 Melchor Ocampo, México 5, D.F.
Telephone: 11-09-62, 11-09-45

Also at:
1060 Ninos Héroes, Guadalajara, Jalisco
Telephone: 5-48-13

505 Edif. Alanis Tamez, Monterrey, Nuevo León

Officers
Agustín Pesqueira R., *Vice-President and General Manager*
Roger T. White, *Vice-President–Northern Division*
Germán Castaneda A., *Supervisor*
Reynelle G. Cornish, *Supervisor*

Service Available
Advice.

Fields of Application
General management, marketing, industrial engineering, manufacturing, office and clerical.

PEAT, MARWICK, LIVINGSTONE DE MÉXICO*
Edificio Anahuac, No. 51 Paseo de la Reforma, México 1, D.F.
Telephone: 46-00-58

Officer
J. I. Bustamante

Services Available
Advice, systems analysis.

Fields of Application
Economic studies, general and scientific management, operations research, project management, industrial engineering, marketing, production and inventory control, information systems, general and cost accounting systems, data processing and transmission systems, etc.

SERVICE BUREAUX

IBM DE MEXICO, S.A.*
Data Centers
No. 132, Benjamin Franklin, Condesa, México 18, D.F.
Telephone: 516-30-00

Also at:
No. 665, Avenida Juárez, Guadalajara, Jalisco
Telephone: 14-70-96

212 Padre Mier, Poniente
Telephone: 43-21-15

Officers
Jorge Saldaña Tapia *(Mexico City)*
Nicanor Infiesta *(Guadalajara)*
Aurelio Balli *(Monterrey)*

Computer Installation
Mexico City:
IBM 360/40(2)–operating system: DOS; internal storage: 65K and 256K bytes; magnetic tapes: 6 2401/2; magnetic discs: 4 2311; 1 line printer.

Guadalajara and Monterrey:
IBM 360/20–internal storage: 16K bytes; magnetic discs: 2; 1 line printer.

IBM 360/30–magnetic tapes: 4; magnetic discs: 3.

Coding Languages
RPG, COBOL, FORTRAN, PL/1, Assembler.

Services Available
Preparation of data, programming. Operate on a self-service, block time and systems usage basis.

Fields of Application
Statistics, production control, accounting, payroll.

SERVICIOS INFORMÁTICA DE HONEYWELL BULL
Avenida Nuevo León 250, Col.Hipodromo Condesa,
México 11, D.F.

Computer Installation
HONEYWELL H1200–operating system: OS-200; internal storage: 131K bytes; magnetic tapes: 5 204B; magnetic discs: 4 273, 2 172; 1 line printer.

BULL GENERAL ELECTRIC Gamma 10; operating system: BASIC; internal storage: 4,096 bytes.

Coding Languages
Easycoder, COBOL, FORTRAN, BASIC.

Services Available
Advice, programming, education and training, operators, software packages, documentation, preparation of data, systems analysis. Operate on a self-service, closed shop, block time and open shop basis.

Fields of Application
Statistical, commercial, accounting, management, systems analysis.
Specialized areas: Sales analysis, linear programming, analysis, payroll, medical research.

Training
Courses in data processing, systems analysis and programming languages.

MONACO

CONSULTANT

CONSEILS ET ENGINEERING D'AFFAIRES (C.E.A.)
Monaco-Ville
Telephone: 30.08.43, 30.07.00

Officers
Jean Vallée, *Director of Studies*
Guy Lévy-Soussan, *Director of Studies*

Service Available
Advice.

Fields of Application
Commercial, management, operational research.
Specialized areas: Sales analysis, investment.

SERVICE BUREAU

MONACO INTERNATIONAL MANAGEMENT SERVICES (M.I.M.S.)
"La Ruche" 6, Rue de l'industrie
Telephone: 30.35.09

Officer
Gérard J. Barlet, *President and Delegate Administrator*

Computer Installation
IBM 310–internal storage: 8K bits.

Coding Language
GAP II.

Services Available
Programming, operators, software packages, preparation of data. Operate on an open shop basis.

Fields of Application
Statistical, commercial, accounting.
Specialized areas: Sales analysis, payroll.

MOROCCO

SERVICE BUREAU

COMPAGNIE IBM FRANCE*
15 Rue Idriss Lahrizi, Casablanca

Computer Installation
IBM 360/40–internal storage: 128K bytes; magnetic tapes: 5 2401/002; magnetic discs: 4 2311; 1 line printer.

Coding Languages
COBOL, Assembler.

Services Available
Advice, operators, preparation of data, programming. Operate on a self-service and block time basis.

Fields of Application
Scientific, statistical, commercial.
Specialized areas: Sales analysis, linear programming, payroll.

Training
Courses in COBOL, Assembler and teleprocessing.

NETHERLANDS

NATIONAL CENTRE

STUDIECENTRUM NOVI
Stadhouderskade 6, Amsterdam
Telephone: 165666

Officers
A. C. Groothoff, J. D. Roosingh, *Managing Directors*

Computer Installation
The Centre is connected to a UNIVAC 1108 by means of a DCT 2000 terminal and also has 3 teletype terminals connected to Honeywell-Bull time-sharing.

Coding Languages
COBOL, FORTRAN, BASIC.

Services Available
Advice, education and training, documentation.

Fields of Application
Commercial, management, systems analysis.

Training
Various programming and systems analysis courses.

EDUCATIONAL AND TRAINING INSTITUTIONS

NATIONAAL INSTITUUT VOOR DE ONTWIKKELING VAN WISKUNDIGE OPVOEDING (IOWO)
Tiberdreef 4, Utrecht
Telephone: 030 - 611611

Officers
Prof. Dr. H. Freudenthal, *Director*
Drs. E. J. Wijdenveld, *General Director*
G. A. Vonk, *Director of Informatics and Applied Mathematics*

Computer Installation
PDP-8/I–internal storage: 8K 12-bit words; magnetic discs: 1 DF32. *Remote processing features:* used as a remote station of a CDC Cyber 73/26.

Coding Languages
FORTRAN, BASIC, ALGOL, ECOL, FOCAL.

Services Available
Education and training, processing. Operate on a remote access basis. Available to representatives of secondary education and vocational training institutions.

Fields of Application
Scientific, statistical, commercial.
Specialized area: Education.

Training
In-service training for teachers in secondary education.

SINGER BUSINESS MACHINES
International Marketing Services
Oude Kleefsebaan 103, Berg en Dal

Officer
K. F. Schmiedeke, *Director*

Computer Installation
SINGER System 10–internal storage: 70K bits; magnetic tapes: 4; magnetic discs: 6; 3 line printers. *Remote processing features:* MDTS, MDRS.

Coding Languages
Assembler, RPG.

Services Available
Advice, programming, education and training, software packages, documentation, systems analysis. Operate on a closed shop and block time basis.

Fields of Application
Commercial, accounting, management, systems analysis.

Training
Diploma for basic and updating courses on Singer equipment.

UNIVERSITIES AND COLLEGES

HUYGENS LYCEUM VOORBURG
Carel Vosmaerstraat 1, Voorburg
Telephone: 070-872222

Officers
Drs. G. H. A. Engberts, *Director*
G. A. Wouters, *Assistant Director*
Ir. H. J. A. M. Bodelier, *Teacher and Computer Department Manager*

Computer Installation
PDP-8/E–operating systems: OS/8, EDUSYSTEM 30; internal storage: 8K bits; magnetic tapes: 2 DEC tape.

Coding Languages
BASIC, FORTRAN IV, PAL-D (Assembler).

Contemplated Equipment
Disc unit.

Services Available
Education and training, running programmes. Operate on a limited closed shop basis. Available to educational institutions.

Fields of Application
Management, education.

KATHOLIEKE UNIVERSITEIT TE NIJMEGEN
Universitair Rekencentrum
Tournooiveld, Driehuizerweg 200, Nijmegen
Telephone: 080-558833

Officer
Drs. Th. W. A. Eppink, *Information Officer*

Computer Installation
IBM 370/155–operating system: OS-MVT-HASP; internal storage: 8 million bits; magnetic tapes: 5 2400; magnetic discs: 3330; 2 line printers. *On-line satellite computers:* PDP-7, PDP-9, PDP-11. *Remote processing features:* 4 displays 2260, 2 typeterminals 2741.

Coding Languages
FORTRAN, COBOL, PL/1, ALGOL, RPG, PLANIT.

Contemplated Equipment
IBM 370/158 with internal storage of 12 million bits.

Netherlands – Universities and Colleges

Services Available
Advice, programming (limited), education and training, operators, software packages. Operate on a closed shop and time-sharing basis. Available to educational institutions.

Fields of Application
Scientific, statistical, accounting.
Specialized area: Payroll.

Training
Two-year evening course in applied computer science; short FORTRAN courses.

LANDBOUWHOGESCHOOL TE WAGENINGEN
Rekencentrum
De Dreyen 11, Wageningen 6140
Telephone: 08370-83775

Officers
Ir. M. S. Elzas, *Director of the Computer Centre*
Drs. H. Legrand, *Assistant Director*

Computer Installation
CDC 3200–operating system: MSOS-MP. 4.2; internal storage: 32K 24-bit words; magnetic tapes: 2 CD 601; magnetic discs: 2 CD 854; 1 line printer. *Remote processing features:* 4 Teletypes, 1 Tektr 4002A, link to CDC 6500.

PDP-8/E–operating system: LAB 8-E/BASIC; internal storage: 8K 12-bit words; magnetic tapes: 1 cassette PI70. *Remote processing features:* data acquisition equipment.

Coding Languages
FORTRAN, ALGOL, COBOL, BASIC, COMPASS, MACRO 8.

Contemplated Equipment
CDC 3300 or PDP-10/40.

Services Available
Advice, programming, education and training, software packages, documentation, preparation of data. Operate on a remote access, closed shop, open shop and time-sharing basis.

Fields of Application
Scientific, statistical, accounting, management, systems analysis, operational research.
Specialized area: Simulation.

Training
Courses in programming languages and computer science.

RIJKSUNIVERSITEIT TE GRONINGEN
Rekencentrum
Universiteit scomplex Paddepoel,
Postbus 800, Groningen
Telephone: 050-116938

Officers
Dr. D. W. Smits, *Director*
Dr. H. J. van Linde

Computer Installation
CDC Cyber 74/16–operating system: SCOPE 3.4; internal storage: 98K 60-bit words; magnetic tapes: 4 659-2; 1 657-1; magnetic discs: 6 844-2; 2 line printers. *Remote processing features:* 2 200 UT (batch terminals), 6 teletypewriters.

TELEFUNKEN TR 4–operating system: Band Betriebssystem; internal storage: 32,768 48-bit words; magnetic tapes: 7 Telefunken MDS-251A; 1 line printer.

PDP 9–internal storage: 24K 18-bit words; magnetic tapes: 1 Tu 10, 1 Datamec TU 20A, 1 Honeywell 7600, 3 TU 55; magnetic discs: 1 Burroughs RB 09; 1 line printer.

Coding Languages
ALGOL, FORTRAN, COBOL, COMPASS, TEXAS, MACRO.

Contemplated Equipment
A front-end satellite computer and display terminals.

Services Available
Advice, machine time. Operate on a remote access, closed shop and block time basis.

Fields of Application
Scientific, university administration.

Training
Programming courses.

RIJKSUNIVERSITEIT TE LEIDEN*
Centraal Reken-Instituut
Stationsplein 20, Leiden

Officer
Prof. Dr. G. Zoutendijk

Computer Installation
IBM 360/50–operating system: OS/MFT; internal storage: 4,194,304 bits; magnetic tapes: 4 2401/2, 1 2401/1; magnetic discs: 1 2314; 2 line printers. *On-line satellite computer:* IBM 1800. *Remote processing features:* Home-made terminal system–CRILAN.

Coding Languages
PL/1, FORTRAN, ALGOL, RPG, Assembler.

Contemplated Equipment
IBM 360/65.

Services Available
Advice, programming, education and training, software packages, documentation, preparation of data. Operate on a self-service, open shop, remote access and time-sharing basis. Available to the University and peripheral institutions.

Fields of Application
Mainly scientific.
Specialized areas: Radio-astronomy, conversational terminal system–CRILAN.

Training
Courses in programming languages for members of the University.

RIJKSUNIVERSITEIT TE UTRECHT*
Kromme Nieuwe Gracht 29, Utrecht
Telephone: 030-29441

Officer
L. P. van der Wal, *Data Processing Manager*

Computer Installation
IBM 1401–internal storage: 16K bits; magnetic tapes: 4 729 II; 1 line printer.

Netherlands — Universities and Colleges

Contemplated Equipment
Sorter, interpreter, burster, decollator, key-punches.

Services Available
Advice, programming, operators, software packages, documentation, preparation of data, systems analysis. Operate on a self-service and closed shop basis. Available to the University administration and for some scientific applications.

Fields of Application
Scientific, accounting, systems analysis.
Specialized area: Linguistic research.

RIJKSUNIVERSITEIT TE UTRECHT*
Department of Medical and Physiological Physics
Eisenhowerlaan 4, Utrecht
Telephone: 030-938848

Officers
W. A. van de Grind
W. A. Aarnink

Computer Installation
CDC 1700—operating system: MSOS: internal storage: 20K 18-bit words; magnetic discs: 2.

Coding Languages
FORTRAN IV, Assembler.

Services Available
Advice, operators, preparation of data. Operate on an open shop basis. Available to research workers and students of the Department and to others as far as time allows.

Fields of Application
Scientific, systems analysis, statistical analysis.
Specialized area: Simulation of nerve cells and neuron networks.

RIJKSUNIVERSITEIT TE UTRECHT*
Department of Physiology
Vondellaan 24, Utrecht
Telephone: (030)-882221

Officer
Dr. E. D. Gerlings

Computer Installation
PDP-8/L—operating system: DISK/DEC-tape monitor system; internal storage: 4K 12-bit words; magnetic tapes: 1 TCO1/TU55; magnetic discs: 1 DF32.

Coding Languages
PALD and subsets of ALGOL and FORTRAN II.

Contemplated Equipment
Additional storage, visual display.

Services Available
Programming, software packages, documentation. Operate on an open shop basis. Available to research staff of the Department.

Field of Application
Scientific.
Specialized area: On-line real time analysis of vector cardiograms during physical exercise.

Training
A short course for medical students covering memory organization, principles of mass storage devices, some aspects of high level languages and principles of assembly codes.

RIJKSUNIVERSITEIT TE UTRECHT*
Elektronisch Rekencentrum
Budapestlaan 6, 'de Uitof', Utrecht
Telephone: 030-539111

Officer
Prof. Dr. A. van der Sluis

Computer Installation
ELECTROLOGICA X8—internal storage: 1·3 million bits; magnetic tapes: 2; magnetic discs: 2; 1 line printer.
On-line satellite computer: PDP-8/I.

Services Available
Advice, education and training, operators, software packages, documentation, systems analysis. Operate on an open shop basis. Available to members of the University.

Fields of Application
Scientific, statistical.

Training
Courses in Numerical Analysis (1 year), ALGOL (4 weeks).

ROBERT J. VAN DER GRAAFF LABORATORIUM*
Universiteitscentrum 'de Uitof', Utrecht
Telephone: 030-539111

Officer
R. Engmann, *Research Associate*

Computer Installation
CDC 1700—operating system: MSOS; internal storage: 16K 16-bit words; magnetic tapes: 1 CDC 601; magnetic discs: 1 CDC 853.

Contemplated Equipment
X-Y plotter, point plotter.

Services Available
Advice, programming, education and training, documentation, preparation of data. Operate on a self-service basis. Available to staff members and students of the nuclear physics group.

Fields of Application
On-line data processing and data reduction in scientific experiments (nuclear physics).

STICHTING ACADEMISCH REKENCENTRUM AMSTERDAM (SARA)
De Boelelaan 1105, Amsterdam
Telephone: 023-485430

Officers
T. Schipper, *Director*
R. Brinkhuijsen, *Assistant Director*

Computer Installation
CDC Cyber 73/26—operating system: SCOPE 3·4; internal storage: 98K 60-bit words; magnetic tapes: 4 659 2, 2 657 2; magnetic discs: 5 844 2; 2 line printers. *On-line satellite computers:* 2 732, 2 PDP-11. *Remote processing features:* CRT, TTY, batch stations.

Coding Languages
ALGOL, BASIC, COBOL, FORTRAN, COMPASS.

Contemplated Equipment
PDP-11 data communications front-end computer.

Service Available
Advice. Operate on a remote access, closed shop, block time and time-sharing basis.

Field of Application
Scientific.

TECHNISCHE HOGESCHOOL EINDHOVEN
Computing Centre
Insulindelaan 2, Postbus 513, Eindhoven
Telephone: 040-474553

Officers
Dr. B. J. M. Morselt, *Director*
R. J. M. van Eyndhoven, *in charge of operations*
Miss M. J. F. M. Fransen, *Secretary*

Computer Installation
BURROUGHS B6700—internal storage: 160K x 48 bits; magnetic tapes: 6; magnetic discs: 2; 3 line printers.

ELECTROLOGICA X8—internal storage: 48K 27-bit words; magnetic tapes: 3; 1 line printer.

PHILIPS 9200—internal storage: 36,864 16-bit words; magnetic discs: 2; 1 line printer.

PACE 231R.

EAI 680.

Coding Languages
ALGOL 60, FORTRAN, PL/1, COBOL, ELAN, LISP, ALGOL, BASIC.

Services Available
Advice, programming, education and training, operators, documentation, preparation of data, systems analysis. Operate on a closed and open shop basis. Available to staff and students of the University and high schools in the area.

Fields of Application
Scientific, commercial.

Training
University courses in Operating Systems; The Art of Programming and Computer Science Topics; training for programmers by Computing Centre; four-day courses in ALGOL and other programming languages.

TECHNISCHE HOGESCHOOL TE DELFT
Computing Centre
Michiel de Ruyterweg 10-12, Delft
Telephone: 015-133222, extension 5020

Officers
G. Akos, *Director*
R. Scherpenzeel, *Director*

Computer Installation
IBM 360/65—operating system: OS-MVT-HASP; internal storage: 768K bytes plus 1,024K bytes; magnetic tapes: 5 2401 2; magnetic discs: 6 2319; 3 line printers. *On-line satellite computers:* 1 PDP-7, 1 PDP-11/45, 1 Hewlett Packard 2100. *Remote processing features:* Fast remote terminals (2780, 3780), 56 remote terminals (2741, 1050, 2260).

AD-4/IBM 1800 hybrid system.

AD-4/PDP-11/45 hybrid system.

PDP-11/45.

Coding Languages
Assembler, ALGOL, FORTRAN, PL/1, COBOL.

Contemplated Equipment
IBM 370/168.

Services Available
Advice, education and training, software packages, systems analysis. Operate on a remote access, closed shop and time-sharing basis.

Fields of Application
Scientific, statistical, operational research.

Training
"Non-credit" courses are run by the Computing Centre, others by the Department of Mathematics.

TECHNISCHE HOGESCHOOL TE DELFT
Department of Mathematics
132 Julianalaan, Delft

Officers
Prof. Dr. W. L. van der Poel
H. E. Barreveld

Computer Installation
PDP-8—operating system: OS8; internal storage: 8K bits; magnetic tapes: 2 DEC; magnetic discs: 1 DF32.

PDP-9—operating system: DOS; internal storage: 16K bits; magnetic tapes: 4 DEC; magnetic discs: 4 RF9; 1 line printer. *Remote processing features:* 4 remote teletypewriters.

Coding Languages
ALGOL, FORTRAN, LISP, SNOBOL, TRAC, EULER, etc.

Contemplated Equipment
PDP-11/45.

Services Available
Education and training, software packages. Operate on a self-service and open shop basis. Available only to students.

Fields of Application
System programming, education.

Training
Ph.D. in Computer Science.

TECHNISCHE HOGESCHOOL TWENTE*
Computing Centre
Postbus 217, Enschede
Telephone: 05420-44644

Officers
Drs. H. G. van Kooten, *President*
D. J. J. Vinke, *Manager of Production*
P. Eilers, *Manager System Programming*
Ir. H. Q. J. Meershoek, *Numerical Mathematical Service*

Computer Installation
IBM 360/50—operating system: OS/360; internal storage: 256K plus 1,024K bytes; magnetic tapes: 1 2415; magnetic discs: 8 2311; 1 line printer. *Remote processing features:* direct data transmission.

Coding Languages
Assembler, FORTRAN IV, PL/1, ALGOL.

Service Available
Advice. Operate on a closed shop, time-sharing and remote access basis. Available only for scientific establishments.

Fields of Application
All research and educational programmes of the Institute.
Specialized areas: Numerical analysis, software design, compiler building.

Training
ALGOL lectures and training, compiler software.

TILBURG SCHOOL OF ECONOMICS, SOCIAL SCIENCES AND LAW
Computing Centre
Hogeschoollaan 225, Tilburg
Telephone: 013-669111

Officers
Drs. A. J. van Reeken, *Director (in charge of research and development)*
J. van Gessel, *in charge of production*
C. F. M. Verkoulen, *in charge of training*

Computer Installation
ICL 1903A–operating system: GEORGE 2; internal storage: 1,572,864 bits; magnetic tapes: 4 1971/2; magnetic discs: 3 2815; 1 line printer.

Coding Languages
PLAN, FORTRAN, COBOL, ALGOL, CSL, SOSIOL.

Services Available
Advice, programming, education and training, operators, software packages, documentation, preparation of data, systems analysis. Operate on a closed shop basis. Available for scientific use only.

Fields of Application
Scientific, statistical, management, systems analysis, operational research.
Specialized areas: Mathematics, economics.

Training
Automatic Information Processing (Introduction–Bachelor's course, Advanced–Master's course), Systems Analysis, Accountancy. Short courses on Introduction to Programming (100 hours), FORTRAN (40 hours), COBOL (50 hours), ALGOL (30 hours).

UNIVERSITEIT VAN AMSTERDAM
Faculty of Economics
Jodenbreestraat 23, Amsterdam
Telephone: 020-5254181

Officers
F. J. Meijer, *Head of Department*

Computer Installation
PDP-8/I–operating systems: OS8, COS 300; internal storage: 98,304 bits; magnetic tapes: 4 DEC; 1 line printer.

Coding Languages
PAL, BASIC, DIBOL, FORTRAN, SERA.

Contemplated Equipment
PDP-11/10 as a concentrator for CDC Cyber 73.

Services Available
Operate on a self-service and open shop basis. Available only to students and scientific personnel.

Fields of Application
Accounting, education.

Training
Course in computer science forming part of the master's degree course in the Faculty of Economics.

UNIVERSITY HOSPITAL, UTRECHT*
Department of Cardiology
101 Catharijnesingel, Utrecht
Telephone: 030-28234

Officer
A. J. Hoelen

Computer Installation
PDP-15/40–operating system: DEC-DISK; internal storage: 442,368 bits; magnetic tapes: 3 DEC-tapes; magnetic discs: 1 RP09. *On-line satellite computer:* PDP-8/L. *Remote processing features:* data acquisition.

Coding Languages
FORTRAN IV, MACRO 9, FOCAL.

Contemplated Equipment
Line printer, videodisc.

Services Available
Advice, programming, preparation of data. Available to members of the University. Priority to members of the Department of Cardiology.

Fields of Application
Biomedical and physiological research.
Specialized area: Cardiovascular research.

VRIJE UNIVERSITEIT TE AMSTERDAM
Department of Informatics
De Boelelaan 1105, Amsterdam
Telephone: 020-485472

Officer
Dr. R. P. van de Riet, *Professor of Informatics*

Computer Installation
The University uses the facilities of the Mathematical Centre, Amsterdam, and of the SARA Computing Centre, Amsterdam.

Contemplated Equipment
PDP-11/45.

Service Available
Education and training. Operate on a remote access basis. Available only to students and university staff.

Field of Application
Scientific.
Specialized area: Formula manipulation.

Training
Courses in informatics, data structures and programming, computer organization, compiler construction.

GOVERNMENT ESTABLISHMENTS

CENTRUM VOOR AUTOMATISERING BREDA-TILBURG (CBT)
Stadhuisplein 130, Tilburg
Telephone: 013-328405

Officer
H. F. M. Stokman, *Director*

Netherlands – Government Establishments

Computer Installation
IBM 360/40–operating system: DOS; internal storage: 128K bytes; magnetic tapes: 2 2415; magnetic discs: 6 2314; 1 line printer.

IBM 360/20–operating system: DPS; internal storage: 32K bytes; magnetic tapes: 2 2415; magnetic discs: 2 2311; 1 line printer.

Coding Languages
PL/1, RPG, Assembler.

Services Available
Preparation of data, systems analysis. Operate on a closed shop basis. Available only for municipalities and other governmental agencies.

Fields of Application
Accounting, management.
Specialized area: Public administration.

CENTRUM VOOR AUTOMATISERING NOORD-HOLLAND
3 Nassauplein, Haarlem

Officers
A. Sandtke, *Director*
P. Flapper, *Systems Manager*

Computer Installation
IBM 360/20–internal storage: 131K bits; 1 line printer.

PHILIPS 1175–operating system: ES; internal storage: 1,048,576 bits; magnetic tapes: 5 1061 002; magnetic discs: 1 1045 001; 1 line printer.

Coding Languages
RPG, COBOL.

Contemplated Equipment
One 2415/1 magnetic tape.

Service Available
Preparation of data. Operates on a closed shop basis. Available mainly to the local governments of the county of Noord-Holland.

Fields of Application
Statistical, accounting, management.
Specialized area: Payroll.

GEMEENTELIJK CENTRUM VOOR ELEKTRONISCHE INFORMATIEVERWERKING*
Buitenveldertselaan 106, Amsterdam
Telephone: 020-441776

Officers
P. A. Tas, *Director*
H. Breederveld, *Deputy Director*
P. T. J. Ploeger, *Head of Personnel Training*

Computer Installation
ICL 1904A–operating systems: GEORGE 2 and 3; internal storage: 1,572,864 bits; magnetic tapes: 4 2504/1, 4 2504/3; magnetic discs: 4 2802/3 EDS; 1 line printer. *Remote processing features:* 2 teletypewriters.

Coding Languages
COBOL, FORTRAN.

Services Available
Advice, programming, education and training, operators, documentation, preparation of data, systems analysis. Operate on a closed shop and time-sharing basis.

Fields of Application
Scientific, statistical, accounting, management, systems analysis, technical.

Training
Four-month course for Systems Analysts; short courses in FORTRAN and introductory and specific topics.

INSTITUTE TNO FOR MATHEMATICS, INFORMATION PROCESSING AND STATISTICS
Koningin Marialaan 21, P.O. Box 297, The Hague
Telephone: 070-824161

Also at:
Staringgebouw, Prinses Marijkeweg 11, P.O. Box 100, Wageningen
Telephone: 08370-19100

Officers
Dr. J. P. M. de Kroon, *Director*
Drs. H. Loeven, *Deputy Director*
J. C. A. Zaat, *Deputy Director (Wageningen)*
A. A. Koene, *Head of Computing Centre*

Computer Installation
CDC Cyber 72–operating system: SCOPE 3.4; internal storage: 48K 60-bit words; magnetic tapes: 2 659, 1 657; magnetic discs: 6 841; 1 line printer. *Remote processing feature:* 1 200 user terminal.

IBM 1130–operating system: Monitor; internal storage: 139,264 bits; magnetic discs: 2; 1 line printer.

UNIVAC 10/04–internal storage: 5,766 bits; 1 line printer.

Coding Languages
COMPASS (Cyber Assembler); FORTRAN IV, ALGOL, COBOL.

Contemplated Equipment
PDP-11/40.

Services Available
Advice, preparation of data, programming, software packages, systems analysis. Operate on a closed shop basis.

Fields of Application
All kinds of scientific and technical computations.
Specialized areas: Statistical computations, matrix calculations, differential equations, linear programming, cost accounting, design of experiments, mathematical traffic models.

NEDERLANDS ORGAAN VOOR DE BEVORDERING VAN DE INFORMATIEVERZORGING (NOBIN)
Burgemeester van Karnebeeklaan 19, The Hague
Telephone: 070-607833

Officers
A. van der Laan, Dr. A. van Loen, *Managers*

Services Available
Advice, sponsoring of research and development projects.

Field of Application
Databank systems.
Specialized area: Information storage and retrieval.

Netherlands – Government Establishments

RIJKS COMPUTERCENTRUM (RCC)
(Netherlands Government Computer Centre)
Fauststraat 1, Apeldoorn
Telephone: 05760-10441

Officers
W. J. Muhring, *Director*
P. J. Peters
J. Roos

Computer Installation
IBM 360/50—operating system: OS-MFT; internal storage: 256K bits; magnetic tapes: 8 2403-5, 1 2415-1; magnetic discs: 1 2314, 5 2311; 2 line printers.

IBM 360/50—operating system: OS-MFT; internal storage: 256K bits; magnetic tapes: 2 2401-4, 8 2401-5; magnetic discs: 2314; 2 line printers. *Remote processing features:* terminals 2260, 3735.

Coding Languages
ANS COBOL, Assembler 360, FORTRAN.

Services Available
Advice, preparation of data, programming, systems analysis. Operate on a closed shop and open shop basis. Available only to official agencies and institutions.

Fields of Application
Statistical, commercial, accounting, management, law-enforcement, information retrieval.
Specialized area: Mass payroll.

RESEARCH INSTITUTIONS

INTERNATIONAL INSTITUTE FOR AERIAL SURVEY AND EARTH SCIENCES
Computer Department
144 boulevard 1945, P.O. Box 6, Enschede

Officers
A. van den Boogart, *Head of Department*
B. Kunji

Computer Installation
PDP-11/45—operating systems: DOS, RSTS; internal storage: 704K bits; magnetic tapes; magnetic discs: 2 RK05, 1 RS64; 1 line printer.

Coding Languages
Assembler, BASIC, FORTRAN.

Services Available
Consultation, programming, education and training, systems analysis. Operate on a self-service, closed shop and time-sharing basis. Available primarily to organizations in developing countries, dealing with the survey of natural resources and mapping.

Fields of Application
Scientific, statistical, management, systems analysis, operational research, information processing for aerial survey and earth sciences.
Specialized areas: Digital mapping, geodesy.

Training
Courses in programming and data processing as part of the courses in aerial survey and earth sciences.

NEDERLANDS INSTITUUT VOOR PRAEVENTIEVE GENEESKUNDE TNO
Wassenaarse Weg 56, P.O. Box 124, Leiden
Telephone: 01710-50940

Officer
J. W. van Wingen, *Co-ordinator of Computing Activities*

Computer Installation
The Institute has access to the IBM 360/65 installation of Leiden University Computing Centre.

Coding Languages
ALGOL 60, FORTRAN, PL/I, CSMP.

Service Available
Advice. Operate on a closed shop basis. Occasional service provided to outside customers.

Fields of Application
Scientific, statistical.
Specialized areas: Medical research, survey data processing.

NEDERLANDS SCHEEPSBOUWKUNDIG PROEFSTATION*
(Netherlands Ship Model Basin – NSMB)
Haagsteeg 2, Box 28, Wageningen
Telephone: 08370-4481

Officers
Prof. Dr. Ir. W. P. A. van Lammeren, *General Director*
Prof. Dr. Ir. J. D. van Manen, *Managing Director*
Drs. H. le Grand, *Head (Programming) of Computer Centre*
Ir. A. W. Ruys, *Head (Production) of Computer Centre*

Computer Installation
ELECTROLOGICA X1—internal storage: 8K 28-bit words.

CDC 3300—operating system: MSOS; internal storage: 16K 24-bit words; magnetic discs: 2 853.

EAI 693 Hybrid (EAI 690 analog, EAI 640 digital)—internal storage: 8K 16-bit words; linked to mock-up of ship's bridge and used for research on and simulation of manoeuvring of ships, and for training ships' pilots and captains.

Coding Languages
COMPASS, ALGOL, FORTRAN.

Contemplated Equipment
Additional care of 16K bits for CDC 3300.

Services Available
Advice, preparation of data. Operate on an open shop basis.

Fields of Application
Scientific, production control, operational research.
Specialized areas: Data reduction, structural engineering, ship hydrodynamics, numerical control of flame cutting machines.

Training
Data preparation for NSMB ship programmes; use of NALS (Numerical Control Adapted Language for Shipbuilding).

Netherlands – Consultants

STICHTING BEVORDERING COMPUTERTOEPASSING BOUWWEZEN (BCB)
Weena 720, Rotterdam
Telephone: 010-147177

Officers
S. A. Jonker, A. Ram, *General Managers*

Computer Installation
IBM 370/135 – operating system: OS VS1; internal storage: 847,872 bits; magnetic discs: 6 2119; 1 line printer.

Coding Languages
Assembler-F, COBOL-F, ANSCOBOL.

Contemplated Equipment
Teletype compatible terminals.

Services Available
Advice, programming, education and training, preparation of data, systems analysis. Operate on a closed shop and block time basis. Closed shop available only to customers dealing with the building industry.

Fields of Application
Scientific, commercial, production control, accounting, management.
Specialized area: Payroll.

STICHTING MATHEMATISCH CENTRUM*
2e Boerhaavestraat 49, Amsterdam-O
Telephone: 947272

Officer
Prof. Dr. Ir. A van Wijngaarden, *Director and Head of the Computation Department*

Computer Installation
ELECTROLOGICA X8 – internal storage: 49,152 27-bit words; magnetic tapes; magnetic discs; 1 line printer.
On-line satellite computer: Internal satellite device CHARON to be implemented.

Coding Languages
ALGOL 60, FORTRAN, ALGOL 68 in development.

Contemplated Equipment
Extensions of X8: increase of memory by 16,384 words, disc files, magnetic tapes.

Services Available
Advice, operators, preparation of data, programming, software packages. Operate on a closed shop basis.

Fields of Application
Pure and applied mathematics, mathematical statistics, operations research, computation.
Specialized areas: Research on automatic programming languages, construction of compilers for ALGOL 60, research on processes of numerical analysis.

CONSULTANTS

APPLIED DYNAMICS EUROPE
Sluisjeskijk 155, Rotterdam
Telephone: 010-298811

Officers
A. A. S. Verwey, *Manager*
D. Beekman, *Systems Engineer, in charge of Training*
P. Adriaanse, *Systems Engineer, in charge of Training*

Computer Installation
IBM 1130 – operating system: 1130–OS; internal storage: 8,192 16-bit words; magnetic discs: 1 2315. *On-line satellite computer:* Applied Dynamics AD4 with amplifiers, integrators, multipliers and coefficient units; interface to IBM 1130 for full hybrid operation.

Contemplated Equipment
Line printer, disc unit.

Services Available
Consultation, programming, education and training, operators, software packages, documentation, preparation of data, systems analysis. Operate on a self-service, closed and open shop basis.

Fields of Application
Scientific, statistical and technical systems analysis, hybrid computation.
Specialized areas: Partial differential equations, simulation of industrial processes and control systems, hybrid software and hardware development.

Training
Analog Programming and Maintenance, Hybrid Programming and Maintenance. Five-day courses in Analog and Hybrid Computation.

ADVIESBUREAU R. ARONSON N.V.*
Baronielaan 152, Breda
Telephone: 01600-43652

Officers
R. Aronson
Dr. Ir. F. Dijkman

Services Available
Consultation, programming. Available only to hospitals and other health services, hotels, recreation centres, penitentiary institutions.

Fields of Application
Management, operational research, analyses of function.
Specialized areas: Project engineering, supply surveying, planning of equipment, turn-key projects.

BEDAUX NEDERLAND N.V.*
Vondelstraat 87, Amsterdam

Services Available
Consultation, programming, software packages.

Fields of Application
Management, software, data processing system consulting.

BERENSCHOT-DIEBOLD B.V.
Churchill laan 11, Utrecht

Also at:
International Rogier Centre, 19th floor,
Brussels, Belgium

Officers
Dr. Th. J. Steenbergen, *Director*
Jan G. Tromp, *Manager*
André S. A. Verschraege, *Manager (Brussels)*

Services Available
Advice, education and training, systems analysis, information systems, appraisal, long term planning, data processing.

Fields of Application
Scientific, statistical, commercial, production control, accounting, management, systems analysis, operational research, on-line real time.
Specialized areas: Sales analysis, linear programming, investment, analysis.

Training
Short courses for management on how to manage the data processing function.

COMPUMAR
Division of Trost Marketing and Research
14 Ereprijsstraat, Soest
Telephone: 02155-14403

Officer
R. L. A. Trost, *Managing Director*

Services Available
Consultation, education and training, documentation, preparation of data. Operate through batch processing of survey data via own 'Compumar' marketing analysis programmes on an IBM 360/40 system.

Field of Application
Commercial: the use of computer systems in marketing.
Specialized area: Consumer marketing.

Training
Data Processing for Executives (course devised by the Management Education Institute of Renton, Washington, U.S.A.).

COMPUTER ANALYSE EN PROGRAMMERING N.V. (CAP NEDERLAND)
Emmastraat 30, Amsterdam
Telephone: 020-763898

Officers
Dr. A. M. C. Helmer, *Director*
A. Edelman, *Administration Manager*

Services Available
Consultation, programming, education and training, software packages, documentation, systems analysis.

Fields of Application
Scientific, statistical, commercial, production control, accounting, management, systems analysis, operational research.
Specialized areas: Sales analysis, linear programming, analysis, payroll, real-time system.

CONSULTDATA NEDERLAND B.V.
Emmaplein 5, Amsterdam
Telephone: 020-763976

Officer
Drs. M. de Vries, *General Manager*

Computer Installation
BULL GENERAL ELECTRIC GE58–operating system: DOS; internal storage: 10K bits; magnetic discs: 2 DSU 162; 1 line printer. *Remote processing features.*

HONEYWELL H6000–operating system: GECOS; internal storage: 36K bits; 1 line printer. *On-line satellite computer:* Mark II system. *Remote processing features.*

Coding Languages
GESAL, M-COBOL, ANS-COBOL (GE58); BASIC, FORTRAN IV (H6000).

Contemplated Equipment
Integration of the two computers.

Services Available
Advice, programming, education and training, documentation, systems analysis. Operate on a self-service, remote access, block time, open shop and time-sharing basis.

Fields of Application
Scientific, statistical, commercial, production control, accounting, management, systems analysis, operational research.
Specialized areas: Sales analysis, linear programming, analysis, payroll, medical research.

CONSULTING ENGINEERS
Koekoeklaan 5, Leidschendam 21310
Telephone: 01761-6429

Officer
Ir. H. A. Nossbaum, *Engineer*

Fields of Application
Data communication, computer evaluation, computer networks.

INGENIEURSBUREAU SANDWIJK N.V.*
Wilson-plein 19, Haarlem
Telephone: 023-312680

Officers
Ing. J. M. Sandwijk, *Director*
Ir. E. R. Godding, *Chief Consultant*

Coding Languages
ALGOL, FORTRAN, APT.

Services Available
Consultation, preparation of data.

Fields of Application
Production control, management, operational research.
Specialized area: Industrial.

INPUT B.V.
Advies- en servicebureau voor administratieve autom.
Zaalbergstraat 14, Alphen aan den Rijn
Telephone: 01720-74688

Officer
H. L. Bruning

Coding Languages
COBOL, PL/1, Assembler.

Services Available
Consultation, programming, operators, preparation of data, systems analysis.

Fields of Application
Commercial, accounting, statistical, systems analysis.

INTERNATIONAL SYSTEMS RESEARCH N.V.*
Westermarkt 2, Amsterdam
Telephone: Amsterdam 227844

Also at:
Griffiths House, 2 Kingston Road, New Malden, Surrey (U.K.)
Telephone: 01-942 1101

Netherlands — Consultants

Officer
A. H. Lines, *Managing Director*

Services Available
Consultation, programming, education and training, software packages, systems analysis.

Fields of Application
Consultants in business planning (long-term plans and strategy) and business information and control systems.

Training
Special short courses arranged on a wide range of subjects, including Distribution, Corporate Planning, Stock Control, Computer Selection, Use of Operational Research.

IVA SOFTWARE N.V.*
Horvathweg 1, Schiedam
Telephone: 010-375134

Also at:
William Boothlaan 15a, Rotterdam
Telephone: 010-124150

Officer
J. Rolloos

Computer Installation
On-line satellite computer: Univac DCT 2000; 1 line printer. *Remote processing features:* Univac 1108 at Heerlen.

Coding Languages
FORTRAN, COBOL, PL/1, ALGOL, Assembler.

Services Available
Consultation, programming, education and training, software packages, systems analysis. Operate on a remote access and time-sharing basis.

Fields of Application
Scientific, statistical, commercial, accounting, management, systems analysis.
Specialized areas: Civil engineering, traffic analysis, data base management.

Training
FORTRAN, PLOTTER-Programming, Management Information.

KLYNVELD KRAAYENHOF & CO.
139 De Lairessestraat, Amsterdam
Telephone: 020-719071

Officers
H. Bakker, B. Drent, G. Eveleens, E. Joëls, P. Koelmans, P. Schmidt, J. H. Urbanus, J. Verheul, *Partners*

Computer Installation
PHILIPS P1100.

Services Available
Advice, education and training, documentation, systems analysis. The computer is available for internal use only.

Fields of Application
Statistical, accounting, management, systems analysis, operational research.
Specialized areas: Analysis, payroll, information systems.

McKINSEY & CO.*
Paulus Potterstraat 8, Amsterdam-Z
Telephone: 020-761555

Officers
J. B. van den Berg, *Managing Director*
H. H. Williams, *Principal*
J. W. van Dijk, *Principal*

Services Available
Consultation, programming, software packages, systems analysis.

Fields of Application
Operational research, management problems including marketing, financial management, facility planning, production, transportation, manpower planning, distribution, compensation.
Specialized areas: Linear programming, risk analysis, simulation, other OR techniques.

RAADGEVEND BUREAU DRS. D. VAN DER LELIE N.V.*
Herman Colleniusstraat 23, Groningen
Telephone: 050-20050/20055

Services Available
Consultation, systems analysis.

Fields of Application
Statistical, production control, management, operational research, etc.

RAADGEVEND EFFICIENCY BUREAU BOSBOOM EN HEGENER N.V.*
De Lairessestraat 111-115, 1007 Amsterdam
Telephone: 020-736666

Also:
Branch offices and daughter firms in Amsterdam, Utrecht, Tilburg and Düsseldorf

Officers
J. B. M. Edelman Bos and J. Ijkel, *Managing Directors*

Coding Languages
COBOL, FORTRAN, Basic Assembler.

Contemplated Equipment
Philips/Electrologica P9205; P880.

Services Available
Consultancy on innovation, structural and operational problems; data collection; data flow and processing; classification and coding; systems analysis; project management; operational research and traffic flow calculations; operate on a closed shop basis.

Fields of Application
Management information systems; production control; network analysis (on the arrow, on the node); information retrieval.
Specialized areas: Traffic studies, urban and rural planning; work preparation and scheduling procedures for drawing offices; management information systems for the building industry.

Training
General courses: management training, systems analysis and design, classification and coding; programming (FORTRAN). Also courses for industry, public administration, hospitals and other public service institutions.

Netherlands – Consultants

SYSTEMS AND RESEARCH (NEDERLAND) N.V.*
Diergaardesingel 68-70, Rotterdam
Telephone: (010)-147133

Also at:
New York (U.S.A.), London (U.K.), Brussels (Belgium), Stockholm (Sweden), (LEASCO affiliates).

Coding Languages
COBOL, PL/1, FORTRAN, ALGOL, Assembler.

Services Available
Consultation, programming, software packages, systems analysis. Available to selected industries, e.g. banking, finance, shipping, distribution.

Fields of Application
Scientific, statistical, commercial, accounting, management, systems analysis, operational research, linear programming, computer audits, hardware selection.
Specialized areas: Banking, finance, transportation, distribution.

WERKWINKEL
Voorstraat 148, Lekkerkerk
Telephone: 01805-1240

Officers
Simon A. Jonker, *Manager*
Cora Jonker - van Spronsen, *Managing Clerk*

Services Available
Advice, programming, documentation, systems analysis, facilities management.

Fields of Application
Commercial, management, systems analysis, marketing.
Specialized area: Sales analysis.

SERVICE BUREAUX

ALGEMEEN REKEN CENTRUM N.V.*
Singel 323-347, Amsterdam
Telephone: 020-249542

Computer Installation
ELECTROLOGICA X1–internal storage: 8K bits.
IBM 360/20–internal storage: 8K bits.

APPLIED DYNAMICS' EUROPEAN COMPUTATION CENTRE
c/o Van Rietschoten & Houwens' E.M.N.V.
Sluisjesdyk 155, P.O. Box 5054, Rotterdam 22
Telephone: 290011

Officer
M. S. Elzas, *Manager of Service Bureau*

Computer Installation
IBM 1130–operating system: Disc Monitor 1130-II; internal storage: 131,072 bits; magnetic discs: 2311-2315. *On-line satellite computer:* Applied dynamics AD4 analog/hybrid computer. *Remote processing features:* ASR 33.

APS COMPUTER CENTRUM N.V.*
Kastenjelaan 53, Arnhem
Telephone: (08300) 3-39-39

Computer Installation
UNIVAC 1004–internal storage: 1K bits. *Remote processing features:* Data line to Univac 1107 in Zürich.

Services Available
Advice, preparation of data, programming, systems analysis.

N.V. AUTOMATISERINGSMAATSCHAPPIJ YSELBREIN*
Bursesteeg, Deventer
Telephone: 74411

Officers
Drs. D. J. Henstra, *Director*
D. Brouwer, *Assistant Director*

Computer Installation
HONEYWELL H1200–operating system: MOD. 1; internal storage: 32K bits; magnetic tapes: 4 204B-7; 1 line printer.
PHILIPS 8000–internal storage: 196,600 bits.

Coding Language
COBOL.

Services Available
Advice, operators, preparation of data, programming, systems analysis. Operate on a closed shop basis.

Fields of Application
Commercial, production control (e.g. typesetting), accounting, management information, legal documentation, teletype, punched tape input/output to 1130, connected by storage access channel to AD4 computer.

Coding Languages
FORTRAN, Assembler.

Contemplated Equipment
For analog AD4: Interface (high speed); for digital: line printer (high speed).

Services Available
Advice, preparation of data, programming (if necessary), software packages, systems analysis. Operate on a self-service, open shop and block time basis.

Fields of Application
Scientific, systems analysis (technical), statistical.
Specialized areas: Hybrid computation, especially with respect to partial differential equations.

Training
Operators' and maintenance courses in hybrid computation (1 week).

BERTELS N.V. MAIL ORDER*
Binnenrotte 118, Rotterdam
Telephone: 132660

Officer
A. Boomenkamp, *EDP Manager*

Computer Installation
NCR Century 200–operating system: Monitor; internal storage: 32K bits; magnetic tapes: 2; magnetic discs: 4; 1 line printer.

Coding Language
NEAT 3.

Services Available
Programming, operators, systems analysis. Operate on a self-service basis. Available primarily for the company's own use.

Netherlands – Service Bureaux

BULL GENERAL ELECTRIC (NEDERLAND) N.V.†
Service Bureau
Vliegtuigstraat 26, Amsterdam-W
Telephone: 020-158955

Also at:
Brouwersstraat 4, Amersfoort
Telephone: 03490-11545

Kwinkemplein 49, Groningen
Telephone: 050-21044

Fruitweg 9, The Hague
Telephone: 070-650950

Standhuisplein 18, Tilburg
Telephone: 04250-36050

Officers
J. B. de Römph, *General Manager*
H. J. Beekmann, *Manager (Amsterdam)*
F. van Schooten, *Manager (Amersfoort)*
P. B. van Werkhoven, *Manager (Groningen)*
Ph. Deijs, *Manager (The Hague)*
W. F. E. Snapper, *Manager (Tilburg)*

Computer Installation
Amsterdam:
BULL GENERAL ELECTRIC Gamma 30–operating system: TOS; internal storage: 20K 7-bit words; magnetic tapes: 8; 1 line printer.

Amersfoort:
BULL GENERAL ELECTRIC GE120–operating systems: ETOS and EDOS; internal storage: 24K x 8 bits; magnetic tapes: 1 7-track, 5 9-track; 1 line printer.

Amersfoort, Groningen, The Hague and Tilburg:
BULL GENERAL ELECTRIC GAMMA 10–internal storage: 4,096 characters.

The Hague:
BULL GENERAL ELECTRIC GE120–operating systems: ETOS and EDOS; internal storage: 24K x 8 bits; magnetic tapes: 1 7-track, 5 9-track; 1 line printer.

Coding Languages
COBOL, Code Gamma 10.

Contemplated Equipment
BULL GENERAL ELECTRIC GE120 for Amsterdam/Groningen and Tilburg.

Services Available
Advice, operators, preparation of data, programming, software packages, systems analysis. Operate on a closed shop basis. Time sharing is a self-contained division separate from the Service Bureaux.

Fields of Application
Scientific, statistical, commercial, accounting, management.
Specialized areas: Standard programmes for wages, invoicing, book-keeping, etc.

Training
Various courses connected with information processing.

BUREAU DR. B. J. M. VAN SPAENDONCK
Reitseplein 1, Tilburg
Telephone: 013-678000

Officer
P. van Dongen, *Manager*

Computer Installation
PHILIPS P1075–operating system: BASIC; internal storage: 64K bits; magnetic tapes: 2; magnetic discs: 2; 1 line printer.

Coding Language
COBOL.

Services Available
Advice, programming, software packages, preparation of data, systems analysis. Operate on a self-service and block time basis.

Fields of Application
Commercial, accounting, management, system analysis.
Specialized areas: Sales analysis, payroll.

CENTRUM VOOR INFORMATIEVERWERKING N.V.
Croeselaan 22, P.O. Box 2233, Utrecht

Officers
C. van Uitert, *Joint Managing Director*
Dr. Ir. P. van Bommel, *Joint Managing Director*

Computer Installation
IBM 360/25–operating system: DOS; internal storage: 48K bits; magnetic tapes: 2 2415; magnetic discs: 4 2311; 1 line printer. *Remote processing feature:* 1052 console.

SIEMENS 4004/45(2)–operating system: DOS; internal storage: 262K bits; magnetic tapes: 16 4443-2-9; magnetic discs: 2 564, 9 4579; 2 line printers. *Remote processing features:* 2 97 consoles.

SIEMENS 4004/150–operating system: DOS; internal storage: 512K bits; magnetic tapes: 8 4453; magnetic discs: 8 4581, 6 4579; 2 line printers. *Remote processing feature:* 4217 console.

SIEMENS 404/6(2)–operating system: COS I; internal storage: 65K bits; magnetic discs: 2 564. *Remote processing features:* 2 2121 consoles.

SIEMENS 4004/16–operating system: TOS; internal storage: 16K bits; magnetic tapes: 4 432-2-9; magnetic discs: 2 564; 1 line printer.

IBM 1130–operating system: DMS VII; internal storage: 16K bits; magnetic discs: 2310; 1 line printer.

IBM 360/20–operating system: TOS; internal storage: 16K bits; magnetic tapes: 4 2415; 1 line printer.

Services Available
Advice, programming, education and training, operators, software packages, preparation of data, systems analysis, turn-key agreements. Operate on a self-service, remote access, closed shop and open shop (IBM 1130 only) basis.

Fields of Application
Scientific, statistical, commercial, production control, accounting, management, systems analysis, operational research.
Specialized areas: Linear programming, investment analysis, payroll, rail traffic control, seat reservation.

Training
Courses in management, systems development, systems analysis, programming, operating and processing.

CMG (EUROPE) N.V.*
Van Heenvlietlaan 142-144, Amsterdam Buitenveldert
Telephone: 020-429978

Officers
D. J. Gorman, B.E. Mills, R. R. Fawcett, C. L. Paul, N. J. Scholfield, *Joint Directors*

Netherlands – Service Bureaux

Coding Languages
COBOL, FORTRAN, ALGOL, Assembler, PLAN.

Services Available
Consultation, operators, software packages, systems analysis. Operate on a self-service, closed and open shop, remote access and block time basis.

Fields of Application
Commercial, production control, accounting, management, systems analysis.
Specialized area: Financial professional systems.

COBOEKING N.V.*
Minervalaan 63, Amsterdam

Also at:
Wibautstraat 18, Amsterdam-O.

Officer
A. G. Minoli, *Manager*

Computer Installation
IBM 360/20–internal storage: 32K bits; magnetic tapes: 2 2415; magnetic discs: 2 2311; 1 line printer.

Coding Languages
RPG, Assembler.

Services Available
Consultation, programming, operators, preparation of data, systems analysis. Operate on an open shop basis.

Fields of Application
Statistical, commercial, accounting, systems analysis.
Specialized area: Distribution and subscriptions of books and magazines.

N.V. COMMERCIEEL COMPUTER CENTRUM*
3 Lange Voorhout, The Hague
Telephone: 070-614711

Officer
P. A. Stolk, *Manager*

Computer Installation
NCR 315–internal storage: 30K bits; 3 CRAM units; 1 line printer.

Coding Languages
COBOL, NEAT.

Contemplated Equipment
NCR Century 200.

Services Available
Advice, operators, programming, software packages, systems analysis. Operate on a closed shop basis.

Field of Application
Commercial.
Specialized area: Insurance.

COMPUTER CENTRUM "EUROPOORT" N.V.*
Wijnbrugstraat 22, Postbus 1097, Rotterdam 1
Telephone: (010) 14-42-60

Officer
R. G. J. van Mil, *Managing Director*

Computer Installation
UNIVAC 1005-III–internal storage: 4K bits; magnetic tapes: 2; Uniservo VI C; 1 line printer. *Remote processing features:* Dial-line with Univac 1007 in Zürich and with Univac 1007 in Birmingham.

Coding Language
Assembler.

Contemplated Equipment
9300 with memory of 16K bits, 4 tape units.

Services Available
Advice, operators, preparation of data, programming, systems analysis. Operate on a self-service, closed shop and open shop basis.

Fields of Application
Commercial and statistical work, scientific work (via dial-lines on Univac 1007).
Specialized areas: Hospital administration (full programme package), manufacturing and inventory, shipping administration (full programme package).

COMPUTER SERVICE HOLLAND B.V.
Wijnhaven 22, Rotterdam
Telephone: 010-114420

Officer
K. W. A. Englebrecht, *Managing Director*

Computer Installation
SIEMENS 4004/45–internal storage: 128K bits; magnetic tapes: 6; magnetic discs: 4; 1 line printer.

Services Available
Advice, systems analysis, programming, data processing.

Fields of Application
Statistical, commercial, accounting.

COMPUTER SCIENCES INTERNATIONAL NEDERLAND NV (CSIN)
Professor Bavincklaan 3, Amstelveen

Also at:
Postbus 161, Apeldoorn
Telephone: 5760-35050

Officers
Dr. M. I. Montana, *President and General Manager*
R. E. Trainer, *Managing Director*
W. Raaijmakers, *Manager of Programme Development*
P. S. Kraabel, *Director of Data Centre*

Computer Installation
IBM 360/65–operating system: OS/MVT; internal storage: 512K plus 1,024K bytes; magnetic tapes: 6 2401, 2 2415; magnetic discs: 2 2314, 2 2311; 2 line printers. *Remote processing features:* remote batch or conversational working.

Services Available
Advice, programming, education and training, software packages, systems analysis. Operate on a remote access and block time basis.

Fields of Application
Systems analysis, design and production of systems, software and application systems, all areas of computer applications.
Specialized areas: Design of large-scale systems, project management, compiler writing.

Netherlands – Service Bureaux

Training
Courses in Computer Concepts for Management, Management Utilization of the Computer, Systems and Programming Project Management, and Systems Analysis and Design. Complete education system package; multimedia classroom facilities; education/training requirements analysis; education programme design and development; user training support services; specialized course development.

CONTROL DATA HOLLAND N.V.
CDC Data Services – Nederland
J. C. van Markenlaan 5, Rijswijk (ZH)

Also at:
Stockholm (Sweden), Stuttgart, Frankfurt, Düsseldorf (Federal Germany), Milan, Rome (Italy), Oslo (Norway), Brussels (Belgium), Copenhagen (Denmark), Paris (France), London (U.K.).

Officer
M. J. van Gennip, *Manager*

Computer Installation
CDC 6600–operating system: SCOPE; internal storage: 7,864,320 bits; magnetic tapes: 8 607, 2 609; magnetic discs: 4 854, 1 6671; 2 line printers; *On-line satellite computers:* 2 8090. *Remote processing features:* CDC MARC-II, MARC-III and MARC-IV terminals.

Coding Languages
FORTRAN, COBOL, ALGOL, COMPASS, SIMSCRIPT, SIMULA.

Services Available
Programming, software packages. Operate on a self-service, closed shop, remote access, block time and time-sharing basis.

Fields of Application
Scientific, statistical, commercial, accounting, management, operational research, civil engineering, optics, simulation, market research.

N.V. DIENSTVERLENING OVERHEIDS ADMINISTRATIVE (DOA) EN AUTOMATISERINGS SERVICE CENTRUM (ASC) VAN N. SAMSOM N.V.
Wilhelminalaan 1, Alphen a/d Rijin
Telephone: (01720) 96633

Computer Installation
IBM 360/40–internal storage: 256K bits; magnetic tapes: 4; magnetic disc: 2314.

IBM 360/25–internal storage: 16K bits; magnetic tapes 4 MFCM.

IBM 370/145–internal storage: 512K bits; magnetic tapes: 3 3330, 3 2319.

Services Available
Advice, preparation of data, programming, software packages, systems analysis. Operate on an open shop and remote access basis.

N. V. ELECTROLOGICA*
Bordewijkstraat 4, Rijswijk (Z. H.)
Telephone: 907620

Officers
Dr. E. Hort
Drs. B. J. Loopstra
Drs. C. S. Scholten
Ir. D. J. B. Aris
J. van Eybergen
Ir. H. W. Schneider

Computer Installation
ELECTROLOGICA X8–operating system: multiprogramming; internal storage: 884,736 bits; magnetic tapes: 6; magnetic discs: 1; 1 line printer.

Coding Languages
ALGOL 60, ZEBRA, FORTRAN.

Services Available
Advice, operators, programming, software packages, systems analysis. Operate on a closed shop and time-sharing basis.

Field of Application
Administrative automation.

Training
Courses in programming and operating.

ELECTRONISCH COMMUNICATIE CENTRUM*
Laan van Meerdervoort 1, The Hague
Telephone: (070) 11-21-74

Computer Installation
MINSK 2–internal storage: 40K bits; magnetic tapes: 4.

MINSK 23–internal storage: 40K bits; magnetic tapes: 4.

NAIRI–internal storage: 18K bits; magnetic tape: 1.

Services Available
Advice, programming, systems analysis.

ELECTRONISCH REKEN EN ADMINISTRATIE-CENTRUM (ERAC)*
Gasthuisstraat 7, 's-Hertogenbosch
Telephone: (04100) 3-63-42

Computer Installation
UNIVAC 1005 (2)–internal storage: 4K bits each.

FACTA N.V.
Stadhoudersplantsoen 214, The Hague
Telephone: 070-624811

Officers
J. Pennock, *Director*
J. van Vliet, *Production Manager*

Computer Installation
ICL 1903A–operating systems: GEORGE 2 and 3; internal storage: 1,536K bits; magnetic tapes: 4 9-track PE, 2 7-track NRZI; magnetic discs: 6; 1 line printer.

Coding Languages
COBOL, ALGOL, FORTRAN, PLAN.

Services Available
Advice, programming, operators, software packages, preparation of data, systems analysis. Operate on a self-service, closed and open shop and block time basis.

Fields of Application
Commercial, network planning.

Netherlands – Service Bureaux

GRAFICOM B.V.
Wibautstraat 148-150, Amsterdam
Telephone: 020-914400

Officers
J. J. van Capelle, *Director*
F. B. Vriesema, *Head of Software Department*
J. Roodhorst, *Head of Hardware Department*

Computer Installation
See under Perscombinatic, Computer Centre.

Coding Languages
RPG, PL/1, Assembler.

Contemplated Equipment
IBM 370/135.

Services Available
Programming, preparation of data, systems analysis. Operate on a closed shop basis.

Fields of Application
Administration, text processing.
Specialized area: Text processing.

Training
Various IBM courses.

GRAFISCH ADMINISTRATIE CENTRUM (GRAFAC)*
Willemsparkweg 37, Amsterdam
Telephone: (020) 73-88-20

Computer Installation
IBM 360/20 – internal storage: 16K bits; magnetic tapes: 4.

HAAGS COMPUTER SERVICE CENTRUM N.V.*
Noordeinde 143, The Hague
Telephone: (070) 11-72-42

Computer Installation
NCR 500 – internal storage: 400 words.

Services Available
Advice, preparation of data, programming, systems analysis.

IBM NEDERLAND NV*
Head Office: Johan Huizingalaan 257, Amsterdam
Telephone: 020-786622

Also at:
Ir. J. P. van Muylwijkstraat 2, Arnhem
Telephone: 085-452190

Oude Stadsgracht 1, Gebouw DELA, Eindhoven
Telephone: 040-68010

Haaksbergenstraat 111, Enschede
Telephone: 05420-10435

Westerhaven 13, Groningen
Telephone: 050-81345

Markt 501-512, Hengelo
Telephone: 05400-18361

In de Boogaard C56, Rijswijk
Telephone: 070-905150

Coolsingel 49, Rotterdam
Telephone: 010-144377

Jaarbeursplein 22, Utrecht
Telephone: 030-15944

Computer Installation
Amsterdam:
IBM 360/40(2) – internal storage: 131K bits each; magnetic tapes: 5 each; magnetic discs: 5 each.

IBM 360/20(3) – internal storage: 16K bits each; magnetic tapes: 4, 4 and 2. *Remote processing features:* input and output via data communication lines.

Arnhem:
IBM 360/20 – internal storage: 16K bits. *Remote processing feature:* direct data transmission connection with SB-Rijswijk.

Eindhoven:
IBM 360/20 – internal storage: 16K bits. *Remote processing feature:* as Arnhem.

Groningen:
IBM 360/20 – internal storage: 16K bits.

Rijswijk:
IBM 360/65 – internal storage: 1,024K bits; magnetic tapes: 10; magnetic discs: 8.

IBM 360/20 – internal storage: 16K bits; magnetic tapes: 2.

IBM 1401C (2) – internal storage: 16K bits each; magnetic tapes: 2 and 4.

IBM 1130 – internal storage: 16K bits; magnetic tapes: 8. *Remote processing features:* as Amsterdam.

Rotterdam:
IBM 360/40(2) – internal storage: 256K bits each; magnetic tapes: 5 and 4; magnetic discs: 6 and 5.

IBM 360/20 – internal storage: 16K bits; magnetic tapes: 2. *Remote processing feature:* as Arnhem.

Utrecht:
IBM 360/20 – internal storage: 16K bits. *Remote processing feature:* as Arnhem.

INFONET B.V.
Nieuwe Prinsengracht 75, Amsterdam
Telephone: 020-62495

Officers
L. J. van Geest, *Administrative Director*
P. J. Vinken, *Commercial Director*
E. A. Koldenhof, *Technical Director*

Computer Installation
NCR 315-501 RMC – internal storage: 40K bits; magnetic tapes: 4 NCR 334/131; magnetic cards: 4 NCR 353 CRAM-5; 1 line printer. *Remote processing features:* terminal service.

ELLIOTT 503 – internal storage: 8K bits; external memory via link with NCR CRAM-5 units.

Coding Languages
NEAT for NCR purposes; PL/1 and Assembler for IBM programming.

Services Available
Advice, preparation of data, programming, software, systems analysis. Operate on a self-service, remote access, open shop and time-sharing basis.

Fields of Application
All fields of information systems and databank systems.
Specialized areas: Information network systems, library systems, databank systems, hospital systems, graphic systems.

INGENIEURSBUREAU RESCONA*
Populierenlaan 333, Amstelveen
Telephone: (02964) 4-00-00

Computer Installation
ELLIOTT 503—internal storage: 8K bits.
NCR 315—internal storage: 20K bits; magnetic tapes: 2.

Services Available
Advice, preparation of data, programming, systems analysis.

N.V. INSTITUT VOOR ELECTRONISCHE ADMINISTRATIE
Diergaardesingel 68-70, Rotterdam
Telephone: 132320

Officers
C. Timmer, *Managing Director*
D. van der Net, *Controller*
B. R. Lawrence, *Data-Processing Manager*

Computer Installation
IBM 360/50—operating systems: OS, DOS; internal storage: 384K bits; magnetic tapes: 10 2401; magnetic discs: 8 2314, 4 2311; 3 line printers.
IBM 360/20—operating system: TPS; internal storage: 12K bits; magnetic tapes: 4 2415/II; 1 line printer.

Coding Languages
SPS, Autocoder, Assembler, RPG, COBOL, PL/1.

Services Available
Advice, preparation of data, programming, software packages, systems analysis. Operate on a self-service, open shop and block time basis.

Fields of Application
Production control, commercial, accounting, management, systems analysis.
Specialized areas: Standard programmes for monthly and weekly payroll, membership and subscription administration, insurance, finance administration, optical reading.

INTOMART*
(Institute for Applied Market Research)
Steynlaan 13, Hilversum
Telephone: 02950-40251

Officers
F. A. Becht, *Director*
F. A. Nauta, *Director*
M. Hartsuiker, *Foreign relations, scientific studies*
A. J. Duetz, *Programming, training scientific personnel*

Computer Installation
ELECTROLOGICA X2—internal storage: 20K bits; magnetic tapes: 2; 1 line printer.

Coding Languages
ELAN (Electrologica Language), ALGOL 60.

Services Available
Advice, preparation of data, programming.

Fields of Application
Scientific research, accounting.
Specialized areas: Radio and television audits and rating service, ad hoc market research surveys and continuous market research operations.

LARC*
Computercentrum
Postbus 159, Ijsselkade 10, Zutphen
Telephone: (05750) 5145

Officer
J. Vledder, *Manager*

Computer Installation
BULL GENERAL ELECTRIC Gamma 30—internal storage: 140K bits; magnetic tapes: 8; 1 line printer.

Coding Languages
COBOL, Autocoder.

Services Available
Advice, preparation of data, programming, systems analysis. Operate on a closed shop and open shop basis.

Fields of Application
Statistical, commercial, accounting, management.
Specialized areas: Commercial statistics, stock control, wages.

LOGISTERION
Centrum voor Elektronicsch Rekenen
H.A. Kramers en Zoon's Handelmaatschappij N.V.
Groothandelsgebouw A4, Rotterdam-4
Telephone: (010) 11-96-48

Officer
F. H. Bouws

Computer Installation
IBM 1130—internal storage: 8K bits; magnetic disc.

Coding Languages
PAF, ALGOL, PAF-FORTRAN, FORTRAN.

Services Available
Advice, preparation of data, programming, systems analysis.

Fields of Application
Scientific, statistical, commercial, operational research.
Specialized areas: Civil engineering, planning chemistry, mechanics.

Training
Programming courses.

NCR REKENCENTRUM
Laan van Meerdervoort 92, Gravenhage
Telephone: 070-321682

Officer
Th. C. van der Plaats, *Data Processing Manager*

Computer Installation
NCR 315—internal storage: 60K bits; magnetic tapes: 2; 1 line printer.

Coding Languages
NEAT, BEST.

Contemplated Equipment
Off-line equipment.

Services Available
Consultation, programming, education and training, operators, software packages, documentation, preparation of data, systems analysis. Operate on a self-service, open shop and block time basis.

Fields of Application
Statistical, commercial, accounting.
Specialized area: Retail business applications.

Training
Various courses given by the Head Office: NCR Netherlands, Buitenveldertselaan 3, Amsterdam. Short courses in Programming, Systems Analysis and General Introductory courses.

NEDERLANDSE ACCOUNTANTS-MAATSCHAP*
Rekencentrum
Industrieweg 130, Rotterdam 8
Telephone: 010-151800-151007

Officer
T. Okker

Computer Installation
BULL GENERAL ELECTRIC Gamma 10 (3)—internal storage: 24,576 bits each.
BULL GENERAL ELECTRIC GE 415—operating systems: BOS, TOS, extended operating system; internal storage: 393,216 bits; magnetic tapes: 8 MT-17; 1 line printer.

Coding Languages
Basic Assembly, COBOL, Macro Assembly, FORTRAN.

Services Available
Advice, operators, preparation of data, programming, systems analysis. Operate on a closed shop basis.

Fields of Application
Statistical, commercial, production control, accounting, operational research.

NORDINED N.V.*
Gebouw "Van Sijpesteyn", Jaarbeursplein 22, Utrecht
Telephone: (030) 938545

PERSCOMBINATIE
Computer Centre
Wibautstraat 148-150, Amsterdam-0
Telephone: 020-914400

Officers
J. J. van Capelle, *Head of Computer Centre*
F. B. Vriesema, *Head of Software Department*
J. Roodhorst, *Head of Hardware Department*

Computer Installation
IBM 360/30—operating system: DOS; internal storage: 64K bits; magnetic tapes: 2 2415; magnetic discs: 4 2311; 2 line printers. *Remote processing features:* 2540, 1017, 1018.

IBM 360/20—operating system: DPS; internal storage: 32K bits; magnetic tapes: 2 2415; magnetic discs: 2 2311; 1 line printer. *Remote processing features:* 2560, 2501.

Coding Languages
Assembler, RPG, PL/1.

Contemplated Equipment
IBM 370/135.

Services Available
Programming, software packages, systems analysis. Operate on a self-service basis.

Fields of Application
Text processing, special administration for newspapers.

Training
Various IBM courses.

PROGRAMMA NEDERLAND N.V.*
Data Processing Service and Consultants
Jan van Nassaustraat 15, The Hague
Telephone: 070-245143

Coding Languages
Assembler, COBOL, PL/1, FORTRAN, ALGOL, BEST, NEAT, etc.

Services Available
Consultation, programming, education and training, operators, software packages, documentation, preparation of data, systems analysis. Operate on a self-service and closed and open shop basis.

Fields of Application
Scientific, statistical, commercial, production control, accounting, management, systems analysis, operational research, office applications.
Specialized area: Office computers.

Training
Practice Analysis and Programming courses.

RAET AUTOMATION CONSULTANCY AND SERVICE BUREAU
1 Sickeszplein, Arnhem
Telephone: 085-452022

Officers
Drs. J. M. Albers
Ir. H. Matthes

Computer Installation
IBM 370/145—operating system: OS; internal storage: 512K bits; magnetic tapes: 8; magnetic discs: 11; 2 line printers.

IBM 370/135—operating system: OS; magnetic tapes: 3; magnetic discs: 3; 1 line printer.

PHILIPS P1075—internal storage: 48K bits; magnetic tapes: 1; magnetic discs: 1; 1 line printer.

Coding Languages
PL/1, COBOL, FORTRAN.

Services Available
Advice, programming, education and training, operators, software packages, documentation, preparation of data, systems analysis. Operate on a remote access, closed shop, block-time and time-sharing basis.

Fields of Application
Statistical, commercial, production control, accounting, management, systems analysis, operational research.
Specialized areas: Linear programming, investment, analysis, payroll, structural engineering.

Training
Courses in modular programming, management games, advanced PL/1.

REKENCENTRUM C. VAN DE VELDEN N.V.*
Gildemeestersplein 298, Arnhem
Telephone: 085-434168/629062

Officers
C. van de Velden
G. Dorenbos

Computer Installation
IBM 360/20–operating system: DPS; internal storage: 16K bits; magnetic discs: 2 2311; 1 line printer.

Coding Languages
Assembler, RPG.

Contemplated Equipment
Switching of IBM papertape reader to RC 2000.

Services Available
Consultation, programming, operators, preparation of data, systems analysis. Operate on a self-service, closed and open shop and block time basis.

Fields of Application
Statistical, commercial, production control, accounting, management, systems analysis.
Specialized areas: Systems for programmed balance, business analysis for management.

REKENCENTRUM 'INFORMATRON' N.V.*
Johan Jongkindstraat 61, Amsterdam
Telephone: 020-155876

Officer
J. van Alten

Computer Installation
BULL GENERAL ELECTRIC GE55–internal storage: 5K bits; 1 line printer.

Coding Languages
BASIC, GESAL.

Services Available
Programming, operators, software packages. Operate on an open shop basis.

Fields of Application
Statistical, commercial, production control, accounting, management.
Specialized areas: Payroll, insurance.

B. V. REKENCENTRUM OGEM
Coolsingel 49, Rotterdam
Telephone: 010-132740

Officers
E. O. J. Jans, *Managing Director*
Ir. L. Hoogerwerf, *Assistant to the Managing Director*

Computer Installation
IBM 370/145–operating system: OS/MFT - OS VS1; internal storage: 384K bits; magnetic tapes: 2 3420/003, 2 3420/007; magnetic discs: 2 2319, 1 2318; 1 line printer. *Remote processing features:* RC 7000, 2770, 3270.

Coding Languages
Assembler, COBOL F (ANS-COBOL), FORTRAN IV.

Services Available
Advice, programming, operators, systems analysis. Operate on a remote access and closed shop basis.

Fields of Application
Scientific, commercial, production control, accounting, systems analysis.
Specialized areas: Sales analysis, linear programming, payroll, structural engineering, heating (climate control).

REKENCENTRUM VOOR ADMINISTRATIE, EFFICIENCY EN TECHNIEK (RAET)*
Sickesplein 1, Arnhem
Telephone: 085-420542

Computer Installation
IBM 360/40–operating system: DOS; internal storage: 128K bits; magnetic tapes: 4 2401; magnetic discs: 4 2314; 1 line printer.

IBM 360/40–operating system: OS; internal storage: 192K bits; magnetic tapes: 2 2401; magnetic discs: 6 2314; 1 line printer.

Coding Languages
FORTRAN, COBOL, PL/1, Assembler.

Services Available
Advice, preparation of data, programming, systems analysis, software packages. Operate on a closed shop basis.

Training
Training in network planning.

N.V. REKENCENTRUM VOOR HANDEL EN INDUSTRIE (RHI)*
Delftsestraat 5, Rotterdam
Telephone: (010) 130955

Officers
N. H. van der Ent, *Production Manager*
R. P. W. M. Pas, *Programming Manager*
A. Sluiter, *General Manager*

Computer Installation
Rotterdam:
UNIVAC 1050–internal storage: 20,000 characters; magnetic tapes: 4 VI C; 1 line printer.

UNIVAC 9200–internal storage: 8K bytes; 1 line printer.

UNIVAC 1005–internal storage: 4K characters; magnetic tapes: 2 VI C; 1 line printer.

Coding Languages
RPG, Assembler.

Services Available
Advice, operators, preparation of data, programming, systems analysis. Operate on a self-service, open shop and block time basis.

Fields of Application
Scientific, statistical, commercial, production control, accounting, operational research, etc.

SAMSOM AUTOMATISERINGS SERVICE CENTRUM NV
Margrietlaan 1a, P.O. Box 4, Alphen aan de Rijn
Telephone: 01720-96633

Officers
E. Boer, *Managing Director*
W. Donker, *Manager for Consulting and System Development*
J. J. Kroese, *Manager for Information Storage and Retrieval Systems*
A. W. Kars, *Manager of Computer Department*

Computer Installation
IBM 370/145–operating system: OS; internal storage: 512K bytes; magnetic tapes: 6 3420; magnetic discs: 1 2319, 3 3330; 2 line printers. *Remote processing features:* CICS control programme, RJE.

Coding Languages
COBOL, PL/1, Assembler.

Services Available
Advice, programming, software packages, documentation, systems analysis, management. Operate on a remote access, closed and open shop and block-time basis.

Fields of Application
Statistical, commercial, accounting, management, systems analysis, information storage and retrieval.
Specialized areas: Analysis, payroll, health insurance, libraries and catalogues, trade information systems.

SIEMENS NEDERLAND N.V.
Computing Centre
Prinses Beatrixlaan 26, P.O. Box 1068, The Hague
Telephone: 070-782782

Officers
A. Roza, *Sales Manager*
K. W. Wiessing, *Automation Manager*

Computer Installation
SIEMENS 4004/151G—operating systems: VMOS, DOS, TDOS; internal storage: 256K bytes; magnetic tapes: 2 432-2-9, 6 4453; magnetic discs: 4 564, 3 4580/81; 2 line printers. *Remote processing features:* control unit datatransmission 4666.

Coding Languages
Assembler, COBOL, ALGOL, FORTRAN, RPG.

Contemplated Equipment
Time-sharing and remote processing facilities.

Services Available
Advice, programming, education and training, operators, software packages, documentation, preparation of data, systems analysis. Operate on a self-service, remote access, closed shop, block time, open shop and time-sharing basis.

Fields of Application
Scientific, statistical, commercial, production control, accounting, management, systems analysis, operational research, data retrieval.
Specialized areas: Sales analysis, linear programming, analysis, payroll, structural engineering, medical research.

Training
Various courses.

SPAARBANK VOOR DE STAD AMSTERDAM
Singel 548, Box 1036, Amsterdam
Telephone: 22-90-22

Officer
N. M. A. ter Wolbeek

Computer Installation
NCR 315—internal storage: 390K bits; magnetic discs: 4 CRAM-5; 1 line printer. *On-line satellite computer:* NCR 321. *Remote processing features:* 99 NCR line adaptors, 140 SIEMENS 8220 terminals, 50 SIEMENS ERG concentrators.

NCR 315—internal storage: 390K bits; magnetic tapes: 2. *On-line satellite computers:* NCR 321. (All peripheral units are interchangeable except the 321.)

Services Available
Consultation, programming, systems analysis. Operate on a closed shop basis. Available mainly to savings banks.

Field of Application
Banking.
Specialized areas: On-line banking accounts, on-line change.

STICHTING HET R.K. GASTHUIS
Dienst Informatie Verwerking
Jan van Beverwijckstraat 2a, Tilburg
Telephone: 013-438333

Officer
Drs. H. J. Rots, *Director*

Computer Installation
IBM 1800—operating system: MPX; internal storage: 512K bits; magnetic discs: 3 1810; 1 line printer.

Coding Languages
Assembler, FORTRAN.

Contemplated Equipment
Two IBM 2311 magnetic disc units.

Services Available
Operate on a self-service basis.

Fields of Application
Production control, management.
Specialized area: Medical research.

S. V. Z. COMPUTER CENTRE*
Westzeedyk 399-401, Rotterdam 6
Telephone: 256820

Officer
W. F. Posthumus, *Managing Director*

Computer Installation
IBM 360/30—operating system: BOS; internal storage: 16K bits; magnetic discs: 2 2311; 2 line printers.

Coding Language
Assembler.

Contemplated Equipment
Additional storage of 16K bits and 2311 disc drive; DOS operating system.

Services Available
Consultation, programming, software packages, systems analysis. Operate on a closed shop basis. Available to the members of the Port of Rotterdam Employers' Association.

Fields of Application
Statistical, commercial, production control, accounting, management, systems analysis.
Specialized areas: Payroll processing, passenger and vehicle reservations on the North Sea ferry service.

UNIVERSITY COMPUTING COMPANY (NEDERLAND) N.V.
Gedempte Gracht 40, The Hague
Telephone: 070-659856

Officer
D. M. Muir, *Managing Director*

Computer Installation
Linked to dual Univac 1108 system in London via 960c baud modem.

Coding Languages
ALGOL, FORTRAN, COBOL, Assembler.

Services Available
Programming, software packages, preparation of data, systems analysis. Operate on a remote access, open shop and time-sharing basis.

Fields of Application
Scientific, statistical, commercial, production control, accounting, management, systems analysis, operational research.
Specialized areas: Linear programming, structural engineering, APT.

VERENIGING VOOR CENTRALE ELEKTRONISCHE ADMINISTRATIE (CEA)
Prins Willem Alexanderlaan 651, Apeldoorn
Telephone: 05760-99111

Officers
Drs. J. G. Gerritsen, *Production Director*
G. F. Boreel, *Sales and Marketing Director*
A. R. Cramer, *Manager*

Computer Installation
IBM 370/145 – operating system: OS/MVT; internal storage: 512K bytes; magnetic tapes: 12 3420/5, 2 3420/7; magnetic discs: 4 3330; 2 line printers.
SIEMENS 4004/35 – operating system: DOS; internal storage: 64K bytes; magnetic tapes: 6 432; magnetic discs: 2 564; 2 line printers.

Coding Languages
ANS-COBOL, Assembler.

Services Available
Advice, programming, education and training, operators, documentation, preparation of data, leasing. Operate on a closed and open shop basis. Not available for scientific applications.

Fields of Application
Statistical, commercial, production control, accounting, management.
Specialized areas: Payroll, financial administration.

VIERHAND RECLAMEDIENSTEN N.V.*
Spaarne 51-55-59, Haarlem
Telephone: (023) 1-84-80

Computer Installation
HONEYWELL H200 – internal storage: 12K bits; magnetic tapes: 4.

'VOLMAC' AUTOMATION CENTRE B.V.
Coolsingel 75, Rotterdam
Telephone: 010-132830

Also at:
Amsterdam, Arnhem, Eindhoven, Düsseldorf, Antwerp, Brussels.

Officers
J. C. L. Mol, *Director*
J. J. van Oosterom, *Director*

Coding Languages
COBOL, PL/1, Assembler.

Services Available
Consultation, programming, education and training, software packages, documentation, systems analysis.

Fields of Application
Commercial, accounting, management, systems analysis.
Specialized areas: Analysis, efficiency in computer usage.

Training
Short courses in efficient programming, COBOL, PL/1, Assembler, data management.

NETHERLANDS ANTILLES

SERVICE BUREAU

IBM WORLD TRADE CORPORATION*
Willemstad, Curaçao

Computer Installation
IBM 1401.

Services Available
Advice, operators, preparation of data, programming.

Fields of Application
Statistical, commercial.

NEW ZEALAND

UNIVERSITIES

UNIVERSITY OF AUCKLAND
Computer Centre
Private Bag, Auckland
Telephone: 74-740

Officer
Dr. J. C. B. White, *Director of Computer Centre*

Computer Installation
BURROUGHS B6700 – operating system: MCP; internal storage: 4 million bits; magnetic tapes: 4 PE, 1 NRZI; magnetic discs: 3; 2 line printers. *On-line satellite computers:* 1 DC1200. *Remote processing features:* communications processor.
Also about 7 small computers for process control and data-logging.

Coding Languages
FORTRAN, ALGOL, COBOL, BASIC, PL/I and others.

Services Available
Operate on a remote access and closed shop basis.

Fields of Application
Scientific, statistical, commercial, accounting, operational research.

Training
Courses in programming, statistical computation, numerical analysis and others.

New Zealand – Universities

UNIVERSITY OF CANTERBURY
Computer Centre
Private Bag, Christchurch 1
Telephone: 71-649

Officers
N. C. Phillips, *Vice-Chancellor and Rector*
B. A. M. Moon, *Director of Computer Centre*

Computer Installation
BURROUGHS B6718–operating system: MCP II; internal storage: 262,144 15-bit words; magnetic tapes: 5; magnetic discs: 2; 1 line printer. *On-line satellite computers:* 1 DC1200, 1 TC500, 1 PDP 11.

Coding Languages
FORTRAN, ALGOL 60, COBOL, PL/1.

Contemplated Equipment
Interactive graphics unit, electrostatic printer/plotter, disc packs, additional satellite computers.

Services Available
Advice, operators, software packages, documentation, preparation of data. Operate on a remote access and closed shop basis. Available outside the University on a limited basis for research and educational use.

Fields of Application
Scientific, statistical.
Specialized area: Student programming systems.

Training
Occasional extension courses; undergraduate programming courses using Cantran system; courses in Computer Science Department of University.

UNIVERSITY OF OTAGO
Computing Centre
P.O.Box 56, Dunedin
Telephone: 40-109

Officer
Dr. B. G. Cox, *Director*

Computer Installation
BURROUGHS B6700–operating system: MCP; internal storage: 3,072K bits; magnetic tapes: 5; magnetic discs: 2; 1 line printer. *On-line satellite computers:* 2. *Remote processing features:* VDU terminals and teletype terminals.

PDP-11/10–internal storage: 128K bits; magnetic tapes: 1.

Coding Languages
ALGOL, PL/1, FORTRAN, COBOL, BASIS, SNOBOL, LISP.

Services Available
Advice, programming (limited), education and training, operators, software packages, preparation of data, systems analysis. Operate on a remote access, closed shop and time-sharing basis. Available to all students and staff for course work, research and development work.

Fields of Application
Scientific, statistical, commercial, all areas of university work including administration.
Specialized areas: Payroll, medical research.

Training
Academic courses in computing (Science and Commerce); programming courses.

VICTORIA UNIVERSITY OF WELLINGTON*
P.O. Box 196, Wellington C.1
Telephone: 46040

Officer
R. B. Payne, *Reader in Computer Science*

Computer Installation
IBM 1130–operating system: DOS; internal storage: 131,072 bits; magnetic discs: 1; 1 line printer.

Coding Languages
ALGOL, FORTRAN, APL.

Services Available
Advice, preparation of data, software packages. Operate on an open shop basis.

Fields of Application
Scientific, statistical, operational research, etc.

Training
One-week course in ALGOL.

GOVERNMENT ESTABLISHMENTS

DEPARTMENT OF SCIENTIFIC AND INDUSTRIAL RESEARCH (DSIR)
Applied Mathematics Division
P.O. Box 196, Wellington
Telephone: 58-769

Officer
Dr. H. R. Thompson, *Director*

Computer Installation
ELLIOTT 503–operating system: DOS; internal storage: 1,597,440 bits; magnetic tapes: 6 NCR 315; 2 line printers.

HEWLETT PACKARD 2100A–operating system: DOS-M; internal storage: 384K bits; magnetic discs: 1 7900, 1 7901. *Remote processing features:* 5 ASR33 teletypes.

Coding Languages
Symbolic Assembler, SAC (Elliott), ALGOL (Elliott).

Services Available
Advice, programming, software packages, documentation, systems analysis. Operate on a remote access and closed shop basis.

Fields of Application
Scientific, statistical, operational research.
Specialized areas: Linear programming, scientific information retrieval.

NEW ZEALAND POST OFFICE
Electronic Data Processing Division
Post Office Headquarters, Wellington
Telephone: 29976

Officers
F. B. Leighton, *Director of Management Services*
R. C. Williams, *Principal, Electronic Data Processing Division*

Computer Installation
ICL 4/50–operating system: DOS; internal storage: 131,072 bits; magnetic tapes: 8; magnetic discs: 3 RDS8; 2 line printers.

Coding Languages
System 4, Usercode, COBOL, FORTRAN.

Services Available
Advice, programming, operators, documentation, preparation of data, systems analysis. Operate on a closed shop basis. For Government service only.

Fields of Application
Scientific, statistical, commercial, accounting, systems analysis.

CONSULTANT

P.A. MANAGEMENT CONSULTANTS LTD.
Legal House, Kitchener Street, Auckland 1
Telephone: 32-743

Also at:
8 Moturoa Street, Wellington
Telephone: 40-082

Officer
V. A. Huddleston *(Auckland)*

Services Available
Consultation, programming, systems analysis.

Fields of Application
Management information systems including normal accounting procedures, production and inventory control.

SERVICE BUREAUX

CHALLENGE CORPORATION LTD.
P.O. Box 1895, Wellington Ci.
Telephone: 49670

Also at:
London (U.K. Head Office) and Melbourne (Australia Head Office)

Officer
I. R. Small, *EDP Manager*

Computer Installation
ICL 4/30 (2)–operating systems: DOS, TOS (back-up); internal storage: 65K bytes each; magnetic tapes: 8 4454; magnetic discs: 4 4452; 3 line printers.

Coding Languages
COBOL, Assembler, FORTRAN, RPG.

Services Available
Consultation, programming, software packages, preparation of data. Operate on a self-service basis.

Fields of Application
Commercial, production control, accounting, management, operational research.

COMPUTER BUREAU LTD.*
76 Chester Street, Christchurch
Telephone: 65145

Officer
Dr. G. B. Battersby, *Chief Executive*

Computer Installation
ICL 1902A–operating system: GEORGE 1; internal storage: 770K bits; magnetic tapes: 4; magnetic discs: 2; 2 line printers.

Coding Languages
PLAN, COBOL, FORTRAN.

Services Available
Preparation of data, programming, systems analysis. Operate on a closed shop basis.

Fields of Application
Commercial, accounting, systems analysis.
Specialized areas: Retail accounting, insurance, local government.

Training
Courses in systems analysis (6 weeks), programming (3 weeks).

COMPUTER BUREAU (WAIKATO) LTD.*
P.O. Box 9144, Hamilton North
Telephone: Hamilton 84319

Officer
G. E. Dickinson, *Manager*

Computer Installation
ICL 1902–operating system: EXEC; internal storage: 16K 24-bit words; magnetic tapes: 4 ICL 1971/2; 1 line printer.

Coding Languages
COBOL, PLAN, ALGOL, FORTRAN.

Services Available
Programming, education and training, operators, software packages, documentation, preparation of data, systems analysis. Operate on a closed shop basis.

Fields of Application
Scientific, statistical, commercial, production control, accounting, management systems, systems analysis, operational research, market research.

Training
Four-week course in systems analysis.

CONSOLIDATED BRICK AND PIPE INVESTMENTS LTD.*
P.O. Box 15004, New Lynn, Auckland 7

Computer Installation
ICL 1901–internal storage: 384K bits; magnetic tapes: 4; magnetic discs: 2; 1 line printer.

Coding Languages
PLAN, COBOL, FORTRAN, ALGOL.

Contemplated Equipment
Document reader, magnetic tape encoders, remote input terminals (off-line).

Services Available
Consultation, programming, operators, software packages, preparation of data. Operate on a closed shop and block time basis. Available mainly to subsidiaries, others if time permits.

Fields of Application
Scientific, statistical, commercial, production control, accounting, management, systems analysis, operational research.
Specialized areas: Commercial accounting, accounts payable and sales statistics, raw material control, invoicing and debtor control.

ELECTRONIC DATA SYSTEMS LTD.
P.O. Box 2633, Auckland
Telephone: 31-932

Also at:
P.O. Box 3667, Wellington.

Officers
A. M. G. Vial, *Bureau Manager*
S. Curran, *Operations Manager*

Computer Installation
Auckland:
BURROUGHS B2500–operating system: MCP; internal storage: 50K bytes; magnetic tapes: 4 9-track; magnetic discs: 1; 1 line printer.

Wellington:
BURROUGHS B2500–operating system: MCP; internal storage: 80K bytes; magnetic tapes: 4 9-track; magnetic discs: 1; 2 line printers. *Remote processing feature:* off-line terminal link to Christchurch over leased line.

Coding Language
COBOL.

Services Available
Programming, education and training, operators, software packages, documentation, preparation of data, systems analysis. Operate on a closed shop basis.

Fields of Application
Commercial, accounting, management.
Specialized area: Package developments for chartered accountants.

Training
Short courses in systems and programming and in customer appreciation.

IBM NEW ZEALAND LTD.
155 The Terrace, Wellington
Telephone: 49200

Also at:
11 Turner Street, Auckland
Telephone: 73619

P.O. Box 9225, Hamilton North
Telephone: 81785

271 Madras Street, Christchurch
Telephone: 50178

Officers
T. McCrorie, *New Zealand Data Centre Manager*
P. Norris, *Wellington Data Centre Manager*
D. Hutley, *Auckland Data Centre Manager*
J. Greenlees, *Hamilton Data Centre Manager*
P. van Oorschot, *Christchurch Data Centre Manager*

Computer Installation
Wellington:
IBM 360/50–operating systems: OS, MFT II, HASP; internal storage: 4,096K bits; magnetic tapes: 8 2401V; magnetic discs: 8 2311, 14 2314; 3 line printers.
On-line satellite computers: 2 IBM 360/20 (one each in Hamilton and Christchurch). *Remote processing features:* batch RJE.

Auckland:
IBM 360/40–operating systems: DOS, POWER; internal storage: 2,048K bits; magnetic tapes: 8 2401II; magnetic discs: 5 2311, 5 2314; 2 line printers.

Coding Languages
COBOL, PL/1, Assembler.

Contemplated Equipment
Additional IBM 360/40 for Wellington; IBM 370/145 with internal storage of 1 million bytes planned for third quarter of 1974.

Services Available
Advice, programming, education and training, operators, software packages, documentation, preparation of data, systems analysis. Operate on a self-service, remote access, closed shop and block time basis.

Fields of Application
Scientific, statistical, commercial, production control, accounting, management, systems analysis.
Specialized areas: Insurance, OCR.

INTERNATIONAL COMPUTERS (NEW ZEALAND) LTD.
Wellington Computer Center
Shell House, 96-102 The Terrace, P.O. Box 394, Wellington
Telephone: 57784

Also at:
P.O. Box 2121, Auckland
Telephone: 31385

Officers
G. A. Hyam, *General Manager*
W. Marriott, *Wellington Services Manager*
G. E. Duhs, *Auckland Services Manager*

Computer Installation
Wellington:
ICL 1903A–operating systems: GEORGE and MOP; internal storage: 1,572,864 bits; magnetic tapes: 4; magnetic discs: 4; 2 line printers; communications equipment allowing up to 8 on-line teletypewriters.

Auckland:
ICL 1903A–operating system: GEORGE; internal storage: 1,179,648 bits; magnetic tapes: 4; magnetic discs: 3; 1 line printer.

Coding Languages
COBOL, PLAN, FORTRAN, ALGOL, JEAN.

Services Available
Advice, preparation of data, programming, software packages, systems analysis. Operate on a self-service, open shop, block time, time-sharing and remote access basis.

Fields of Application
Scientific, statistical, commercial, production control, accounting, management, systems analysis, operational research.

Training
Courses in all aspects of the use of computers.

NATIONAL CASH REGISTER CO. LTD.
Data Centre
125 Albert Street, Auckland 1
Telephone: 33-893

Also at:
P.O. Box 6359, Wellesley Street, Auckland 1

Officer
R. C. McLeod

Computer Installation
NCR 315/100—internal storage: 240K bits; magnetic tapes: 5 7-track; 1 line printer.

Coding Languages
COBOL, BEST, NEAT, FORTRAN II.

Services Available
Consultation, programming, software packages, preparation of data, systems analysis. Operate on a remote access and block time basis.

Fields of Application
Scientific, statistical, commercial, production control, accounting, management.
Specialized areas: Retail automation, optical reading.

Training
Restricted to customer training only.

WINSTONE LTD.
P.O. Box 395, Auckland

Officers
E. Gallimore, *Director*
M. T. Still, *Data Processing Manager*

Computer Installation
ICL 1902S—operating system: GEORGE 2; internal storage: 32K 24-bit words; magnetic tapes: 4 1971/2; magnetic discs: 3 EMD; 2 line printers.

Coding Languages
PLAN, COBOL.

Contemplated Equipment
Visual display unit; communications processor.

Services Available
Advice, preparation of data, machine time. Operate on a closed shop basis.

Fields of Application
Commercial, accounting, management.

WRIGHT, STEPHENSON & CO. LTD.
P.O. Box 1845, Wellington C
Telephone: 49670

Also at:
London, U.K. (head office); Melbourne, Australia

Officer
I. R. Small, *EDP Manager*

Computer Installation
ICL 4/30—operating systems: DOS, TOS (back-up); internal storage: 65K bits; magnetic tapes: 6 4454; magnetic discs: 2 4425; 2 line printers.

Coding Languages
COBOL, Assembler, FORTRAN, RPG.

Services Available
Advice, programming, software packages, systems analysis. Operate on a self-service basis.

Fields of Application
Commercial, production control, accounting, management, operational research.

NICARAGUA

UNIVERSITY

UNIVERSIDAD NACIONAL AUTÓNOMA DE NICARAGUA
Centro Electronico de Computación
Recinto Universitario "Ruben Dario", Apartado Postal 663, Managua
Telephone: 80619

Officers
René Gutiérrez, *Director*
José B. Lau, *Deputy Director*

Computer Installation
IBM System/3/10—operating system: DOS; magnetic discs: 1 5444; 1 line printer.

Coding Languages
RPG II, FORTRAN IV.

Contemplated Equipment
Another IBM 5444 disc unit; one IBM 5471 printer-keyboard; a computer with storage capacity up to 16K bits.

Services Available
Programming, education and training, systems analysis. Operate on a closed shop and block time basis. Closed shop available only to faculty members, students and administrators, block time to commercial and industrial institutions.

Fields of Application
Commercial, accounting, systems analysis, education.
Specialized areas: Payroll, academic registration.

NIGERIA

UNIVERSITIES

AHMADU BELLO UNIVERSITY
Department of Mathematics and Computer Sciences
Zaria
Telephone: Zaria 2581, extension 45

Officers
Prof. I. Abubakar, *Head of Department*
A. H. Hartley, *Computer Supervisor*

Computer Installation
ICL 1901—operating system: EXECUTIVE CONTROL; internal storage: 393,216K bits; magnetic tapes: 4 1971, 4 2501; 1 line printer.

Coding Languages
PLAN, FORTRAN, ALGOL, COBOL, LISP.

Services Available
Advice, programming, education and training, documentation, preparation of data, systems analysis. Operate on a closed shop basis.

Fields of Application
Scientific, statistical, systems analysis.
Specialized area: Payroll.

Training
Computer science courses as part of undergraduate programme in mathematics.

IBADAN UNIVERSITY
Computing Centre
Ibadan
Telephone: Ibadan 21051/502

Officer
Olu Longe, *Director*

Computer Installation
IBM 1620—operating system: MONITOR I Disk, card operating system also available; internal storage: 240K bits; magnetic discs: 1 1311; 1 line printer.

IBM 370/135—operating system: DOS; internal storage: 144K bytes; magnetic tapes: 2 2415; magnetic discs: 3 2319; 1 line printer.

Coding Languages
FORTRAN II, 1620 SPS, FORTRAN IV, COBOL, RPG, PL/1, Assembler.

Services Available
Consultation, programming, education and training, operators, software packages, documentation, preparation of data. Operate on an open shop basis. Service available to university staff and students; service given to outsiders only when time available.

Fields of Application
Scientific, statistical, administration.

Training
Courses in numerical analysis as option for B.Sc. Hons. Mathematics. Graduate specialization in computer science. Short courses in FORTRAN and Assembler programming, RPG, and library courses.

UNIVERSITY OF IFE
Department of Computer Science
Ile-Ife

Officer
Dr. L. E. Rosenthal, *Acting Head of Department*

Computer Installation
IBM 360/25—operating system: DOS; internal storage: 384K bits; magnetic discs: 2 2311; 1 line printer.

Coding Languages
FORTRAN, COBOL, PL/1, Assembly, RPG.

Contemplated Equipment
IBM 370/135 with tapes, discs, remote printer and reader, video terminals and plotter.

Services Available
Consultation, programming, education and training, operators, software packages, preparation of data, systems analysis. Operate on a self-service and closed and open shop basis.

Fields of Application
Scientific, statistical, accounting, management, systems analysis.
Specialized areas: Analysis, payroll, medical research, student records.

Training
Courses leading to a B. Sc. degree in Computer Science, with either Mathematics or Economics; also courses in user training.

UNIVERSITY OF LAGOS*
Institute of Computer Sciences
Akoka, Lagos
Telephone: Lagos 41361—9/412

Officer
Dr. O. J. Fagbemi

Computer Installation
IBM 1620—operating system: Monitor 1; internal storage: 60K bits; magnetic discs: 2 1311; 1 line printer.

Coding Languages
FORTRAN IID, NCE, SPS.

Contemplated Equipment
IBM 360/40.

Services Available
Consultation, programming, education and training, operators, preparation of data, systems analysis. Operate on a self-service, open and closed shop basis.

Fields of Application
Scientific, statistical, commercial, systems analysis, operational research.
Specialized areas: Optimization, stochastic processes, generalized data processing, linear programming, systems control, partial differential equations, economic models, hydrological research, meteorology.

Training
Contributions to B.Sc. Mathematics and Engineering. Postgraduate courses for diploma master's and doctoral degrees in Computer Science. Short courses in basic computer programming; (planned) intermediate course in computer programming; introductory course in systems analysis.

GOVERNMENT ESTABLISHMENTS

NIGERIAN PORTS AUTHORITY*
Accounts Department
26/28 Marina, Lagos
Telephone: 55020, extension 240

Officer
Principal Accountant, Mechanization

Contemplated Equipment
ICL 1900 series computer.

Services Available
Operate on a self-service basis.

Fields of Application
Statistical, accounting, management, systems analysis.

Training
COBOL programming course; systems analysis course; design course.

WEST AFRICAN EXAMINATIONS COUNCIL
Private Mail Bag 1022, Yaba, Lagos

Also at:
P.O. Box 917, Accra, Ghana

Officers
M. J. Quirk, *Systems Development Manager*
J. A. Gbago, *Data Processing Manager*
Z. A. Olonisakin, *Computer Operations Manager*

Computer Installation
IBM 360/20–operating system: TPS; internal storage: 16K bits; magnetic tapes: 4 2415; 1 line printer. *Remote processing features.*

Coding Languages
RPG, BAL, PCU.

Contemplated Equipment
IBM 370/125 with DOS operating system.

Services Available
Advice, programming, operators. Operate on a self-service basis. Available only to educational establishments.

Field of Application
Systems analysis.
Specialized area: Processing and analysis of examination results.

CONSULTANT

P.E. CONSULTING GROUP (WEST AFRICA) LTD.*
19 Oba Akran Avenue, P.O. Box 6, Ikeja, Lagos State
Telephone: 33763

Service Available
Consultation.

Fields of Application
General management consultancy in all fields. Using consultant personnel from our parent company in U.K., we give advice to clients thinking of making computer applications.

SERVICE BUREAUX

COMPUTER SERVICES LTD.
P.O. Box 1024, Lagos
Telephone: Lagos 56020

Officers
Mrs. J. L. Underwood
A. O. Alcande

Computer Installation
IBM 370/135–operating system: DOS; internal storage: 96K bits; magnetic tapes: 2 2400; magnetic discs: 4 2319; 1 line printer.

Coding Languages
RPG, COBOL, Assembler, FORTRAN.

Contemplated Equipment
Data terminals.

Services Available
Consultation, programming, operators, documentation, preparation of data, systems analysis. Operate on a self-service, closed and open shop and block time basis.

Fields of Application
Statistical, commercial, production control, accounting, systems analysis, operational research, inventory control, financial control, market research.

Training
One-day courses in general or specific computer subjects.

IBM NIGERIA LTD.
8-10 Yakubu Gowon Street, Lagos
Telephone: 55830

Officer
R. G. Niedermayr, *Managing Director*

Computer Installation
IBM 360/40–operating system: DOS; internal storage: 196K bytes; magnetic tapes: 4; magnetic discs: 4; 1 line printer.

Coding Languages
COBOL, RPG, FORTRAN IV.

Services Available
Programming, education and training, software packages, preparation of data, systems analysis. Operate on a self-service, closed shop, block time and open shop basis.

Fields of Application
Statistical, commercial, accounting.
Specialized areas: Sales, analysis, payroll.

Training
Courses mainly in programming.

STANDARD BANK NIGERIA LIMITED
Computer Operations Centre
208/212 Yakubu Gowon Street, P.O. Box 2334, Lagos
Telephone: 24538

Officer
N. P. Southey, *Computer Development Manager*

Computer Installation
ICL 1902A–internal storage: 384K bits; magnetic tapes: 4 1971; magnetic discs: 2 2302; 1 line printer.

Coding Languages
PLAN, COBOL.

Services Available
Advice, programming, operators. Operate on a self-service basis.

Fields of Application
Statistical, commercial, accounting, management, systems analysis.
Specialized areas: Banking.

NORWAY

EDUCATIONAL AND TRAINING INSTITUTION

MØRE OG ROMSDAL DISTRIKTSHØGSKOLE
6400 Molde
Telephone: (072) 51077

Officer
Arne Aurdal, *Instructor*

Computer Installation
PDP-11/45–operating systems: RSTS 1145, BATCH; internal storage: 32K x 16 bits; magnetic tapes: 1 dectape unit; magnetic discs: 2 RK-05 cartridge discs: 1 line printer. *Remote processing features.*

Norway – Educational and Training Institution

Coding Languages
BASIC-PLUS, FORTRAN, MACRO II, FOCAL.

Services Available
Advice, programming, education and training, systems analysis. Operate on a remote access, open shop and time-sharing basis. Available only to schools and public institutions.

Fields of Application
Scientific, statistical, commercial, systems analysis, operational research.
Specialized areas: Linear programming, analysis.

Training
Courses for systems analysis and EDP consultant.

UNIVERSITIES AND COLLEGES

AGDER DISTRIKTSHØGSKOLE
Department of Computer Science and Informatics
4600 Kristiansand
Telephone: (042) 17380

Officers
Tor Brattvaag
Harek Tøfte

Computer Installation
NORD 1–operating systems: TSS 2·5 NORDOPS; internal storage: 512K bits; magnetic tapes: 1; magnetic discs: 1 line printer. *Remote processing feature:* via TS-terminals.

Coding Languages
FORTRAN, MAC.

Contemplated Equipment
More teletypewriters and 1 disc drive.

Services Available
Advice, education and training. Operate on a closed shop and time-sharing basis.

Fields of Application
Scientific, statistical, accounting, management, systems analysis.

Training
Courses in computer science and informatics.

ROGALAND COLLEGE
Eiganesveien 32, 4000 Stavanger
Telephone: 26560

Officers
Kjølv Egeland, *Director*
Tor-Ivar W. Pedersen, *EDB Manager*

Computer Installations
IBM 370/145–operating system: OS-MFT (OS/VS1); internal storage: 256K bytes; magnetic tapes: 4 IBM 3420/7; magnetic discs: 8 IBM 2314 spindles; 2 line printers. *Remote processing features.*

NORD 1–operating system: NORDOPS; internal storage: 24K 16-bit words; magnetic discs: 1. *Remote processing features:* time-sharing.

Coding Languages
FORTRAN IV, COBOL, PL/1, RPG, BASIC, Assembly, MARK IV.

Contemplated Equipment
2 IBM 3330, storage module of 256K bytes.

Services Available
Advice, education and training, systems analysis. Operate on a closed shop and time-sharing basis.

Fields of Application
Scientific, commercial, accounting, management, systems analysis.

Training
Courses specializing in computer and information systems.

UNIVERSITETET I BERGEN*
Avdeling for Elektronisk Databehandling
Lars Hillesgate 19, 5000 Bergen
Telephone: 12040

Officer
Kåre FlØisand, *Head of Department*

Computer Installation
IBM 360/50–operating system: MFT II; internal storage: 3,072K bits; magnetic tapes: 2 2415; magnetic discs: 1 2314; 1 line printer. *On-line satellite computer:* IBM 1130 at Norges Handelshøyskole (Norwegian School of Economics and Business Administration). *Remote processing features.*

SAM II–operating system: own Monitor; internal storage: 256K bits. Linked to multiplexor channel IBM 360/50.

NORD 1.

Coding Languages
FORTRAN II, III and IV, PL/1, COBOL, ALGOL, Assembly.

Contemplated Equipment
New installation.

Services Available
Development work, real time systems. Operate on a closed shop, remote access and time-sharing basis.

Fields of Application
Scientific, data management.
Specialized area: Common university applications.

UNIVERSITETET I OSLO
Blindern, Oslo 3
Telephone: 46 68 00

Officers
Rolf Nordhagen, *Managing Director*
Dag Belsnes, *Research and Development Manager*
Odd Aurmo, *Operations Manager*

Computer Installation
CDC 3300–operating system: Master; internal storage: 2·4 million bits; magnetic tapes: 2 601, 3 659, 3 854, 4 841; 2 line printers. *On-line satellite computers:* 2 NORD 1. *Remote processing features:* CDC Cyber 74 is available via batch terminals.

Coding Languages
FORTRAN, COBOL, SIMULA, ALGOL, COMPASS, META.

Services Available
Education and training. Operate on a closed shop and time-sharing basis.

Field of Application
Scientific.

Training
Courses in computer science and numerical analysis for both higher and lower degrees.

UNIVERSITETET I OSLO
Student Administration
P.O. Box 294, Blindern, Oslo 3
Telephone: (02) 466880

Officers
A. Beisland, *Administration Manager*
K. Smoerdal, *Operations Manager*

Computer Installation
CDC 3170–operating system: Master; internal storage: 1,554,432 bits; magnetic tapes: 2 CDC 604; magnetic discs: 1 CDC 841-4; 1 line printer.

Coding Languages
SIMULA, COBOL, FORTRAN, COMPASS.

Services Available
Advice, programming, software packages. Operate on a closed shop basis.

Fields of Application
Scientific, statistical, commercial, production control, accounting, operational research.
Specialized areas: Sales analysis, analysis, payroll.

UNIVERSITETET I TROMSØ
Nordlysobservatorief
P.O. Box 953, 9000 Tromsø
Telephone: 083-86060

Officers
Torstein Gabrielsen
Peter Kraft
Willy Jensen
Jo Piene

Computer Installation
NORD 1–operating system: NORDOPS; internal storage: 64K x 16 bits; magnetic tapes: 2; magnetic discs: 4; 1 line printer. *On-line satellite computers:* NORD 20, NORDCOM. *Remote processing features.*

Coding Languages
FORTRAN IV.

Services Available
Operate on a closed shop and time-sharing basis.

Field of Application
Scientific.
Specialized area: Medical research.

Training
B.A. and M.Sc. programme from 1974.

UNIVERSITETET I TRONDHEIM
Norges Tekniske Høgskole (NTH)
Regnesentret (RUNIT)
7034 Trondheim
Telephone: (075) 35555

Officer
Karl G. Schjetne, *Director*

Computer Installation
UNIVAC 1108–operating system: EXECUTIVE 8; internal storage: 7,077,888 bits; magnetic tapes: 6 Uniservo VIII C; magnetic drums: 2 FH880, 3 FH432, 1 Fastrand III; 1 line printer. *On-line satellite computers:* 3 Univac 1004. *Remote processing features:* 3 terminals, 1 IDIOM interactive graphic display, 1 PDP-11 frontend processor, 25 teletypewriters and alphanumeric displays.

Coding Languages
ALGOL, FORTRAN V, COBOL, SLEUTH (Assembler).

Services Available
Advice, preparation of data, programming, software packages, systems analysis. Operate on a closed shop and open shop basis.

Fields of Application
Technical, scientific and administrative computer applications.
Specialized areas: Software development, numerous engineering and scientific applications.

Training
Courses in ALGOL, FORTRAN, SLEUTH (Assembly language), SIMULA; logical design of computers; specialized application of computers; compiler techniques; operating systems; file structures.

GOVERNMENT ESTABLISHMENTS

NORSK REGNESENTRAL*
Forskningsveien 1b, Oslo 3
Telephone: 466930

Officers
Drude Berntsen, *Director*
Knut Elgsaas, *Project Director*
Kristen Nygaard, *Research Director*

Computer Installation
UNIVAC 1004 (2)–linked to Univac 1108 at COMPUTAS in Oslo.
The Centre is also linked to a CDC 6600 in Stockholm (Sweden) by means of a CEC II terminal.

Coding Languages
ALGOL, COBOL, FORTRAN, SLEUTH, SIMULA.

Services Available
Advice, programming, software packages, systems analysis, research.

Fields of Application
Scientific, statistical, commercial, systems analysis, operational research, simulation.
Specialized areas: Linear programming, simulation, database structure, compiler techniques.

Training
Courses in SIMULA, simulation methods, numerical analysis.

NORWEGIAN WATER RESOURCES AND ELECTRICITY BOARD
Hydrological Division
Middelthuns GT 29, Postboks 5091, Majorstua, Oslo 3

Officer
J. Otnes, *Chief Hydrologist*

Norway – Government Establishments

Computer Installation
CDC 3200–operating system: MSOS; internal storage: 32K words; magnetic tapes: 3; magnetic discs: 4; 1 line printer.

Coding Languages
FORTRAN, COBOL.

Services Available
Preparation of data, hydrological analysis. Operate on a closed shop basis.

Fields of Application
Hydrological data processing.

STATENS DRIFTSSENTRAL FOR ADMINISTRATIV DATABEHHANDLING
(Norwegian State Computer Centre)
Dronningens gate 14, Oslo 1
Telephone: Oslo 421990

Officers
Rudolf Jacobsen, *Managing Director*
Åge Borg Andersen, Roar Gulbrandsen, Bjørn Jh. Nilsen, *Directors General*

Computer Installation
HONEYWELL H6060 Dual–operating system: GCOS; internal storage: 4 million characters; magnetic tapes: 4 MTH 505; magnetic discs: 8 DSU 180. *Remote processing features:* RJE, TSS.

Coding Languages
Primary COBOL.

Contemplated Equipment
8 MTH 505, 1 MTS Controller, 1 MTH 501, 1 IOM, 1 DSS 190.

Services Available
Advice, education and training. Operate on a closed shop basis. Available to government service only.

Field of Application
Commercial.

STATISTISK SENTRALBYRÅ
(Central Bureau of Statistics)
Dronningensgt. 16, Oslo-Dep., Oslo 1
Telephone: 413660

Officers
Petter Jakob, *Director*
E. Aurbahhen, *Assistant Director*

Computer Installation
IBM 360/40–operating system: DOS; internal storage: 128K bits; magnetic tapes: 1 2401/5, 1 2401/2, 2 2402/5; magnetic disos: 5 2311/1; 1 line printer.

IBM 1401–internal storage: 4K bits; magnetic tape: 1; 1 line printer.

Coding Languages
Autocoder, FORTRAN IV, Assembler, COBOL.

Services Available
Programming, data processing, preparation of data. Operate on a closed shop basis. Available only to government agencies.

Fields of Application
Data processing in the production of statistics.
Specialized areas: Statistical computations, econometric computations.

RESEARCH INSTITUTIONS

INSTITUTT FOR ATOMENERGI
OECD Halden Reactor Project
Box 173, 1751 Halden
Telephone: 82760

Officers
J. E. Lunde, *Project Manager*
M. Øvreeide, *Section Leader, Control Engineering and Systems Development*

Computer Installation
IBM 1800–operating system: TSX; internal storage: 32K x 18 bits; magnetic tapes: 2 2401; magnetic discs: 3 1810, 1 2515; 1 line printer.

NORD 1–operating system: SINTRAN; internal storage: 24K x 16 bits; magnetic discs: 2; 1 line printer.

GIER–internal storage: 42,100 bits; magnetic tapes: Ampex.

NORD 20–operating system: MON; internal storage: 8K x 16 bits.

NORD 10–operating system: TSS; internal storage: 24K x 16 bits; magnetic discs: 2; 1 line printer.

NORD 5–operating system: TSS; internal storage: 32K x 32 bits.

Coding Languages
FORTRAN, ALGOL, BASIC, Assembler.

Contemplated Equipment
Terminal to CDC Cyber 74.

Services Available
Software packages, systems analysis. Operate on a closed shop and block time basis. Essentially restricted to organizations in countries which are signatories to the Project.

Fields of Application
Scientific, computer process control research and development, datalogging, experimental analysis.
Specialized areas: Process control, computer control methods and associated software for dynamic control, process supervision, man-machine communication.

CHR. MICHELSENS INSTITUTT FOR VIDENSKAP OG AANDSFRIHET*
Physical Science Section
Nygaardsgt. 114, 5000 Bergen
Telephone: 17633

Officer
Dr. Jan A. Anderson, *Director of Research*

Computer Installation
PDP-8–internal storage: 4K bits.

NORD 1–internal storage: 16K bits; magnetic discs: NCR EM-31; 1 line printer.

Coding Languages
Assembly, FORTRAN (basic).

Services Available
Software services, programming, software packages, systems analysis. Operate on an open shop basis.

Fields of Application
Process control, production control, operational research, computer aided design.
Specialized areas: Mathematical models of physical systems.

A/S NORSK DATA–ELEKTRONIKK
Økernveien 145, Oslo 5
Telephone: (472) 217371

Officers
K. R. Johansen, *Director*
P. Bjørge, *Technical Director*
Otto Stabenfeldt, *Marketing Director*

Computer Installation
NORD 1–internal storage: 512K bits; magnetic discs: DUAL NDR 416; 1 line printer. *Remote processing features:* MODEM displays, teletypewriters.

NORD 1–internal storage: 256K bits; magnetic drum: Vermont.

NORD 1–internal storage: 32K words.

Coding Languages
FORTRAN IV, BASIC, Assembler.

Contemplated Equipment
NORD 10, time-sharing system, 4-colour display graphic/alphanumeric.

Services Available
Advice, programming, education and training, operators, software packages, documentation, preparation of data, systems analysis. Operate on a self-service, open shop and time-sharing basis.

Fields of Application
Scientific, systems analysis, software development.

Training
Courses in Assembler, FORTRAN and BASIC languages, operating systems, hardware service of NORD 1, NORD 10, NORD 20 and peripherals.

REGNEANLEGGET BLINDERN-KJELLER
Box 70, 2007 Kjeller
Telephone: (02) 71-45-70

Officers
S. A. Øvergaard, *Director*
A. Torkildsen, *Systems Manager*

Computer Installation
CDC Cyber 74/18–operating system: SCOPE 3·4; internal storage: 7,864,320 bits; magnetic tapes: 2 659/1, 8 606; magnetic discs: 4 844, 5 841, 2 863; 1 line printer. *Remote processing features:* 32 lines, 75/50,000 baud.

Coding Languages
FORTRAN, COBOL, COMPASS, SIMULA, ALGOL 60, SYMPL.

Services Available
Advice, operators, software packages, preparation of data. Operate on a remote access, closed shop and time-sharing basis. Preference given to own needs.

Fields of Application
Scientific, statistical, management, numerical analysis.
Specialized areas: Reactor calculations, inventory control, compiler construction.

Training
Frequent programming courses.

CONSULTANTS

DATA RÅD A/S*
Lilletorget 1, Oslo 1
Telephone: (02) 411100, 415163, 415179

Officer
N. V. Nilsson, *General Manager*

Services Available
Advice, programming, systems analysis, software packages.

Fields of Application
Accounting, statistical, commercial, operational research, production control, marketing.
Specialized areas: Data processing for the certified public accountant and EDP education for the users.

Training
Three-day courses in EDP–general principles, programming, systems design; organization of EDP process.

TOM GILB
Iver Holstersvei 2, 1410 Kolbotn
Telephone: (472) 801697

Officer
Tom Gilb, *President*

Services Available
Advice, education and training, systems analysis, course development and teacher training.

Fields of Application
Commercial, accounting, management, systems analysis.
Specialized fields: Computer selection, building up EDP organizations and EDP system design.

Training
Courses in many aspects of computer use.

IKO SOFTWEAR SERVICE A/S
Nils Hansenvei 2, Oslo 6
Telephone: (02)204230

Officers
Kolbjørn Braa, *Managing Director*
Odd de Presno, *Marketing Manager*

Coding Languages
All ordinary languages.

Contemplated Equipment
Univac 1106.

Services Available
Advice, programming, education and training, operators, software packages, documentation, preparation of data, systems analysis.

Fields of Application
Scientific, statistical, commercial, production control, accounting, management, systems analysis, operational research.
Specialized areas: Sales analysis, analysis, payroll, structural engineering, network planning.

SIVILINGENIÖR ROLF HÖYER A/S*
Majorstuveien 21, Oslo 3
Telephone: 69-52-89

Officer
Sivilingeniör Rolf Höyer, *Director*

Coding Languages
Assembler, ALGOL, COBOL, FORTRAN.

Services Available
Consultation, preparation of data, programming, systems analysis.

Fields of Application
Systems analysis, operational research, commercial systems, management information systems.
Specialized areas: Design of management information systems; operational research related to planning and operation of large hydro-electric power systems.

Training
One-two week courses in programming.

SERVICE BUREAUX

A/S ADMINISTRATIV DATA BEHANDLING*
Akersgaten 47, Oslo 1
Telephone: 337058

Officer
Per Stampe, *Manager*

Computer Installation
IBM 360/20–operating system: DO4; internal storage: 16K bits; magnetic discs: 2 IBM 2311/12; 1 line printer. *Remote processing features:* 1 Gier RC2000 paper tape reader.

Coding Languages
RPG, Assembler.

Services Available
Programming, preparation of data, systems analysis. Operate on a block time and open shop basis.

Fields of Application
Statistical, commercial, accounting, systems analysis.

A/S BERGEN DATASENTER
Comprising:
A/S EMMA
HOLKORTSENTRALEN FOR VESTLANDET A/L
INTEGRERT DATABEHANDLING A/S (IDA)
Lars Hillesgt. 19, 5000 Bergen
Telephone: (475) 323020

Officers
B. Larsen, *Director of the Computer Centre*
T. Hermanrud, *Manager, A/S EMMA*
H. W. Gullestad, *Manager, Holkortsentralen*
Ø. Tvedt, *Manager, IDA*

Computer Installation
IBM 370/155–operating systems: OS, MFT/HASP; internal storage: 4,096K bits; magnetic tapes: 4 3420/VII; magnetic discs: 5 3330; 3 line printers. *Remote processing features:* 3 PDP-11 RJE terminals, 1 IBM 370/135 FJE.

Coding Languages
Assembly, ANS-COBOL, PL/1.

Services Available
Advice, programming, education and training, software packages, preparation of data, systems analysis. Operate on a self-service basis.

Fields of Application
Statistical, commercial, production control, accounting, management, systems analysis, operational research.
Specialized areas: Sales analysis, payroll.

JOHAN F. BÖHMER
Vennersborgveien 9, Oslo 2
Telephone: 02-558630

Also at:
Teloygt 4, 1500 Moss
Telephone: 032-53516

Officer
Johan F. Böhmer

Coding Languages
ALGOL, ALGOL/GENIUS, COBOL, FORTRAN.

Services Available
Advice, programming, education and training, documentation, preparation of data, systems analysis.

Fields of Application
Scientific, statistical, commercial, accounting, systems analysis, operational research.
Specialized areas: Linear programming, analysis, structural engineering.

Training
Courses on ALGOL programming (48 hours) and Survey on EDP Applications (24 hours).

A.S. COMPUTAS
Økernveien 145, Oslo 5
Telephone: (02) 220155

Officers
Trond Vahl, *General Manager*
Per Boman, *Sales Manager*

Computer Installation
UNIVAC 1108–operating system: EXEC 8; internal storage: 192K 36-bit words; magnetic tapes: 2 9-track, 8 7-track; magnetic discs: 2 Fastrand III and 6 drums; 3 line printers. *Remote processing features:* CTMC 32 lines.

IBM 370/155–operating system: OS HASP; internal storage: 1024K bytes; magnetic tapes: 6 3420; magnetic discs: 10 3330; 1 line printer. *Remote processing feature:* Memorex 1270.

Coding Languages
COBOL, FORTRAN, ALGOL, SIMULA, GPSS 1100, SIMSCRIPT 1·5, ANSICOBOL, NUALGOL, CFOR, BASIC, Assembler, PDP, IM–0.

Contemplated Equipment
1 CTMC, 2 UNIVAC 8440 discs, IBM 370/158.

Services Available
Advice, programming, education and training, operators, software packages, documentation, preparation of data, systems analysis, special softwear, programme pool, programme library. Operate on a remote access, block time, open shop and time-sharing basis.

Fields of Application
Scientific, statistical, commercial, production control, accounting, management, systems analysis, operational research, seismic data processing.
Specialized fields: Sales analysis, linear programming, investment, analysis, payroll, structural engineering, computer science.

Training
Courses in many aspects of computer use.

DATA LOGIC A/S
Karl Johansgt. 13, Oslo 1
Telephone: 330256

Officers
K. Marthinsen, *Managing Director*
K. Grude, *Chief Consultant*

Coding Languages
COBOL, Assembler, RPG II in common use; knowledge of other languages.

Services Available
Advice, programming, education and training, documentation, systems analysis.

Fields of Application
Specialized areas: Sales analysis, linear programming, investment, analysis, payroll, production and stock control, data base design.

Training
Individually designed courses for management. General course in project management based on ARDI.

A/S DATA-AUTOMASION
Økernun 145, Økern, Oslo 5
Telephone: 217351

Officer
Hans Hovland, *Director*

Computer Installation
DATASAAB D22—operating system: OS; internal storage: 960K bits; magnetic tapes: 4 9-track; magnetic discs: 2; 1 line printer.

Coding Languages
ALGOL/GENIUS, COBOL, DAC, ALGOL.

Services Available
Advice, programming, education and training, software packages, preparation of data, systems analysis. Operate on a self-service, closed shop and block time basis.

Fields of Application
Statistical, commercial, accounting, management, systems analysis.
Specialized areas: Sales analysis, payroll.

DATASENTRALEN A/S
Nils Hansensvei 2, Oslo 6
Telephone: (02) 204230

Officers
Kolbjørn Braa, *Managing Director*
Odd de Presno, *Marketing Manager*

Computer Installation
UNIVAC 9400—operating system: DOS; internal storage: 855K bits; magnetic tapes: 4 UNISERVO 12; magnetic discs: 2 8414; 1 line printer.

Coding Languages
COBOL, RPG, FORTRAN, Assembler.

Services Available
Advice, programming, education and training, operators, software packages, documentation, preparation of data, systems analysis. Operate on a closed shop and block time basis.

Fields of Application
Scientific, statistical, commercial, production control, accounting, management, systems analysis, operational research.
Specialized areas: Sales analysis, analysis, payroll, structural engineering (ASKA), network planning (OPTIMA).

DATA-TJENESTE A/S*
St. Halvardsgt. 77, Oslo 6
Telephone: 67-64-21

Officer
Birger Nes

Computer Installation
BULL GENERAL ELECTRIC GE 415—internal storage: 16K bits; magnetic tapes: 6; magnetic discs: 2; 1 line printer.

Coding Languages
COBOL, MAP.

Contemplated Equipment
Off-line data transmission equipment.

Services Available
Programming, systems analysis. Operate on an open shop and block time basis.

Field of Application
Commercial.
Specialized area: Bank applications.

Training
One-week course in bank system.

DRAMMENSVASSDRAGETS DATASENTRAL*
Storgaten 11, Hønefoss
Telephone: 067-22388

Officer
K. E. Sjørbotten, *Manager*

Computer Installation
BULL GENERAL ELECTRIC Gamma 10.

EDB-SERVICE A/S*
Postboks 368, Sentrum, Oslo 1

Officer
T. Thorsen, *General Manager*

Computer Installation
IBM 360/20—internal storage: 16K bits; magnetic tapes: 4 2415/05; 1 line printer.

Coding Language
RPG.

Services Available
Operate on a self-service, block time and open shop basis.

Field of Application
Commercial.
Specialized areas: Direct marketing, computer letters.

FELLESDATA/SIS
Marstrandgt. 6, Oslo 5
Telephone: 155750

Officer
L. K. Olaussen, *Managing Director*

Computer Installation
IBM 370/155–operating system: OS, MVT; internal storage: 512K bits; magnetic tapes: 6 3420; magnetic discs: 4 3330; 4 line printers.
BULL GENERAL ELECTRIC GE 425–operating system: BOS/MT; internal storage: 16K 24-bit words; magnetic tapes: 6; 1 line printer.

Coding Languages
Assembler, ANS COBOL (IBM); MACRO, Assembly (GE).

Contemplated Equipment
Two IBM 3330 disc units.

Services Available
Programming, operators, preparation of data, systems analysis. Operate on a closed shop basis. Mainly functions as a service centre for the Norwegian Savings Banks.

Field of Application
Accounting.
Specialized area: Banking.

INTEGRERT DATABEHANDLING A/S*
Thv. Meyers gate 11, Oslo 5
Telephone: 3777080

IBM A/S.*
Datasenter
Dronn Mauds Gate 10, Oslo
Telephone: 20-54-50

Computer Installation
IBM 360/40.
IBM 1410.
IBM 1620.
IBM 1401.

Services Available
Advice, operators, preparation of data, programming, software packages, systems analysis.

Fields of Application
Scientific, statistical, commercial.

NATIONAL KASSA REGISTER A/S
NCR Datasentral
Fossveien 24, Oslo 5
Telephone: 371960

Officers
R. Berge, *Manager*
R. Bredeg, *DPC Manager*
C. Edvardsen, *Account Representative*

Computer Installation
NCR 315/100–internal storage: 240K bits; magnetic tapes: 6; 1 line printer.

Coding Languages
NEAT, BASIC.

Services Available
Advice, operators, preparation of data, programming, software packages, systems analysis. Operate on a closed shop basis.

Fields of Application
Business applications.
Specialized areas: Banking and retail.

A/S NOR-DATA
Sluppenveien 12, 7000 Trondheim
Telephone: 35480

Officers
Ralph Høibakk, *President*
Tore Rønning, *Director*
Odd Jørgensen, *Director*

Computer Installation
IBM 370/145–operating systems: OS, HASP; internal storage: 384K bits; magnetic tapes: 4 3420; magnetic discs: 8 2319; 2 line printers. *Remote processing features:* 3 2701.

Coding Languages
COBOL, FORTRAN, PL/1, Assembler, RPG.

Services Available
Advice, programming, education and training, software packages, documentation, preparation of data, systems analysis. Operate on a remote access, closed shop and time-sharing basis.

Fields of Application
Commercial, accounting, systems analysis, newspapers.
Specialized areas: Analysis, payroll, order entry, school scheduling.

Training
Courses in execution and control; short courses in BASIC, management and project planning in EDP; users' instruction courses in the school scheduling system.

A/L NORD-NORGES HULLKORTSENTRAL*
Box 25, Grønnegt. 27/29, 9001 Tromsø
Telephone: 083-85566

Officer
Terje Walnum

Computer Installation
IBM 360/30–operating system: DOS; internal storage: 64K bits; magnetic tapes: 4 IBM 2415; magnetic discs: 2 IBM 2311; 1 line printer.

Coding Languages
Assembler, COBOL, FORTRAN, RPG.

Contemplated Equipment
On-line terminal.

Services Available
Advice, preparation of data, programming, software packages, systems analysis. Operate on a closed shop basis.

Fields of Application
Commercial, accounting, management, systems analysis.
Specialized area: Medical research.

Training
Courses in Introduction to EDP, programming and users' education.

Norway – Service Bureaux

A/S NORSK HULLKORT–SERVICE*
Mariboes Gate 16, Oslo 1
Telephone: 20-44-58

Computer Installation
BULL GENEREL ELECTRIC GE 415.
BULL GENERAL ELECTRIC Gamma 10.

OSLO DATASENTER A/S*
P.O. Box 61, Lilleaker, Oslo 2
Telephone: 559497

Officers
Ivar Jacobsen, *General Manager*
Miklos Tangstrøm, *Assistant Manager*

Computer Installation
BULL GENERAL ELECTRIC GE 115–operating system: DOS; internal storage: 128K bits; magnetic tapes: 3; magnetic discs: 2 05130; 1 line printer.

Coding Languages
APS (Assembler), COBOL, FORTRAN, TAB, RPG.

Contemplated Equipment
BULL GENERAL ELECTRIC GE 120; DSU 160 disc units.

Services Available
Systems development, programming, punching production. Operate on a closed shop (open on block time) basis.

Field of Application
Commercial.

SKOGBRUKETS DATASENTRAL A/S*
Ryensvingen 15, Oslo 6
Telephone: 67-51-80

Officer
Bertil Akselsen, *Manager of the Service Bureau*

Computer Installation
IBM 360/20–internal storage: 16K bits; 1 line printer.

Coding Languages
RPG, PCU, Assembler.

Services Available
Administrative routines in connection with forestry and forest industries.

Fields of Application
Statistical, commercial, accounting.

TIME-SHARING A/S
Staalfjaera 9, Oslo 9
Telephone: 257750

Officer
Leif Jarodd

Computer Installation
BULL GENERAL ELECTRIC GE 265–operating system: MARK I Version 7; internal storage: 672K bits; magnetic tapes: 4 MTH 690; magnetic discs: 4 DSF 204; 1 line printer. *Remote processing features:* time-sharing 40 lines.

HONEYWELL H6030–operating system: GECOS III, SRD; magnetic tapes: 8; magnetic discs: 12 DSU 180; 2 line printers. *On-line satellite computer. Remote processing features:* TS 10/15/30 ch and RJE up to 4800 baud.

Contemplated Equipment
Machine at price level of 25,000,000 Norwegian kroner.

Services Available
Consultation, programming, education and training, operators, software packages, documentation, preparation of data, systems analysis. Operate on a self-service, open shop, remote access and time-sharing basis.

Fields of Application
Scientific, statistical, commercial, production control, accounting, management, systems analysis, operational research.

Training
Short courses on programming in BASIC, advanced BASIC, ALGOL, FORTRAN, etc.; simulation; application courses in various fields.

A/S TRØNDER-DATA*
Postboks 654, 7001 Trondheim
Telephone: 075/18075

Officer
D. Langsøe, *Manager*

Computer Installation
BULL GENERAL ELECTRIC GE 415–operating system: MTPS; internal storage: 16K bits; magnetic tapes: 6; 1 line printer.

Coding Languages
MAP, COBOL.

Contemplated Equipment
Additional storage of 32K bits; 6 DSU 167; DATANET 20.

Services Available
Preparation of data, programming, systems analysis. Operate on a closed shop basis.

Fields of Application
Commercial, accounting, management.
Specialized area: Banking.

VESTDATA A/S*
P.O. Box 1210, 5001 Bergen
Telephone: 91307, 91308

Computer Installation
BULL GENERAL ELECTRIC GE 415–operating systems: BOS/MT (basic), EOS/MT (extended), AIOS/MT (abbreviated); internal storage: 200K bits; magnetic tapes: 6; 1 line printer.

Coding Languages
MACRO Assembly Language, Basic Assembly Language, COBOL, FORTRAN, RPG.

Services Available
Advice, preparation of data, programming, systems analysis. Operate on a closed shop basis.

Fields of Application
Commercial, production control, accounting, management, operational research.

PAKISTAN

UNIVERSITIES

UNIVERSITY OF THE PANJAB*
Department of Administrative Science
New Campus, Lahore
Telephone: 81194/28

Officer
Dr. M. Afzal, *Head of the Department*

Computer Installation
The University uses computer time of the Water and Power Development Authority.

Coding Languages
FORTRAN, COBOL.

Contemplated Equipment
IBM 360/40.

Services Available
Education and training.

Fields of Application
Accounting, management, systems analysis.

Training
Short courses in systems analysis, programming, languages, etc.

WEST PAKISTAN UNIVERSITY OF ENGINEERING AND TECHNOLOGY
Data Processing Centre of the Mathematics Department
Grand Trunk Road, Lahore 31

Officers
Prof. Asghar Hameed, *Chairman, Mathematics Department*
Ghulam M. Malik, *Data Processing Manager*

Computer Installation
IBM 1130–operating system: DMS; internal storage: 256K bits; magnetic discs: 1 2315 cartridge; 1 line printer.

Coding Languages
FORTRAN IV, PLAN, Assembler.

Contemplated Equipment
IBM 2310, IBM 1627, IBM 1055, IBM 407.

Services Available
Advice, programming, education and training, software packages, systems analysis. Operate on a closed shop basis.

Fields of Application
Scientific, statistical, systems analysis.
Specialized areas: Analysis, structural engineering.

Training
Courses in Computer Science, Numerical and Computer Methods, and Computer Science and Numerical Analysis. Short course in programming.

GOVERNMENT ESTABLISHMENTS

PAKISTAN COMPUTER BUREAU
26-A Satellite Town, Rawalpindi
Telephone: 41351-3

Officer
Ijax H. Khawaja, *Systems Analyst*

Computer Installation
IBM 360/40–operating system: DOS; internal storage: 128K bits; magnetic tapes: 4 2401; magnetic discs: 4 2311; 1 line printer.

Coding Languages
COBOL, FORTRAN, Assembler.

Services Available
Advice, programming, education and training, systems analysis. Available to government departments and semi-state bodies.

Fields of Application
Accounting, systems analysis.

Training
Courses in EDP orientation (1 week); technical courses in Programming, File Organization, Card Design, etc.; user training course in Basic EDP and Data Control.

STATE BANK OF PAKISTAN
Computer Unit
Statistics Department, Central Directorate, Karachi
Telephone: 234141

Officer
Director, Statistics Unit, State Bank

Computer Installation
ICL 1901–internal storage: 8K 24-bit words; magnetic tapes: 1 1971/2; 1 line printer.

Coding Languages
PLAN, FORTRAN.

Contemplated Equipment
An increase in core store capacity to 16K words and to add paper tape reader punch.

Services Available
Consultation, programming, education and training, preparation of data. Service available to government departments and other semi-autonomous bodies.

Fields of Application
Monetary, banking, financial statistics.
Specialized areas: Balance of payments, banking statistics, financial analysis.

Training
6-8 week training courses in computer programming for staff when necessary.

SERVICE BUREAUX

EWP COMPUTER SERVICES LTD.*
8 Bangalore Town, Main Drigh Road, Karachi
Telephone: 47-10-19

Officer
Sikander Latif, *Executive Director*

Computer Installation
ICL 1902/1—operating system: EXECUTIVE; internal storage: 196,608 bits; magnetic tapes: 4; 1 line printer.

Coding Languages
PLAN, FORTRAN, COBOL.

Services Available
Consultation, preparation of data, programming, systems analysis. Operate on a self-service and open shop basis.

Fields of Application
All types of commercial applications; solution of engineering problems; consultants to government and industry on setting up computer network in Pakistan. *Specialized areas:* Adaptation of modern techniques to conditions prevailing in underdeveloped countries.

Training
Computer training centre, providing 3-4 week courses in systems analysis and design and 4-week training course for programmers.

IBM WORLD TRADE CORPORATION*
Karachi

Computer Installation
IBM 1401.

Services Available
Advice, operators, preparation of data, programming.

Fields of Application
Statistical, commercial.

UNITED BANK LTD.
Computer Division
1st Floor, State Life Building, I. I. Chundrigar Road, Karachi 2

Also at:
54 Haider Road, Rawalpindi Cantt.

Officers
Allauddin Shaik, *Senior Vice-President*
Khalid A. Sherwan, *Data Processing Manager*
Saeed Anwar, *Customer Services Manager*

Computer Installation
IBM 360/40—operating system: DOS; internal storage: 1,170K bits; magnetic tapes: 5 2400, 3 2314; magnetic discs: 1 2311; 1 line printer. *Remote processing features:* 3 IBM 2740 terminals.

IBM 1401—internal storage: 112K bits; magnetic tapes: 4 729; 1 line printer.

Contemplated Equipment
IBM 370/135.

Services Available
Consultation, programming, operators, documentation, preparation of data, systems analysis. Operate on a block time and open shop basis. Available to industrial, commercial and government organizations.

Fields of Application
Statistical, commercial, production control, accounting, management, information systems, systems analysis. *Specialized areas:* Inventory management, PERT.

Training
Courses in computer programming and short courses in computer orientation; programming and principles of computer operations (2-6 weeks).

PANAMA

UNIVERSITY

UNIVERSIDAD DE PANAMÁ*
Centro de Cómputo Electrónico, 3368, Panamá 4
Téléphone: 230965

Dirigeant
Dr. Eduardo A. Briceño, *Directeur*

Equipement
NCR 315—système d'opération: centrale; mémoire interne: 10K slabs; bandes magnétiques: 1 334-101; cram magnétiques: 3 353; 1 imprimante.

Langages de Programmation
NEAT, FORTRAN, COBOL.

Equipement Projeté
NCR Century 615/200 avec mémoire de 64K bytes.

Services Fournis
Programmation, enseignement et formation, software packages, documentation, systems analysis. Fonctionnement en self-service. Services fournis à l'université et aux agences gouvernementales.

Domaines d'Application
Scientifique, statistique, commercial, systems analysis, recherche opérationelle.

Formation
Cours de programmation en FORTRAN et COBOL.

SERVICE BUREAU

IBM DE PANAMÁ, S.A.
P.O. Box 851, Panama 1
Telephone: 25-0250

Officer
F. Garcia, *General Manager*

Computer Installation
IBM 360/30—operating system: DOS; internal storage: 64K bytes; magnetic tapes: 4 2415/5; magnetic discs: 2 2311; 1 line printer.

Coding Languages
PL/1, COBOL, RPG, Assembler.

Services Available
Advice, preparation of data, programming, systems analysis; operate on a block time, closed shop and open shop basis.

Fields of Application
Scientific, commercial, accounting, etc.

PARAGUAY

UNIVERSITY

UNIVERSIDAD NACIONAL DE ASUNCIÓN
Instituto de Ciencias Básicas
Centro Nacional de Computación
Avenida España 1098, Casilla de Correo 1439, Asunción
Telephone: 24-106

Officers
Dr. Antonio Masulli Fuster, *Director*
Lic. José Luis Benza, *Deputy Director*

Computer Installation
IBM 1130–operating system: DOS; internal storage: 16K 16-bit words; magnetic discs: 1 2315; 1 line printer.

Coding Languages
FORTRAN IV, BASIC, RPG, APL, Assembler.

Contemplated Equipment
IBM 2310 disc.

Services Available
Advice, programming, education and training, systems analysis. Operate on a self-service, closed shop and block time basis.

Fields of Application
Scientific, statistical, commercial, accounting, systems analysis, operational research.
Specialized areas: Analysis, payroll, structural engineering, mathematical calculations.

Training
Certificate courses in FORTRAN IV and Introduction to Data Processing. Diploma courses for students at the Instituto only in RPG, FORTRAN, Assembler and BASIC languages; language, automata and switching theories; mathematical logic; Boolean algebra.

GOVERNMENT ESTABLISHMENT

CORPORACIÓN DE OBRAS SANITARIAS (CORPOSANA)
José Berges 516, Asunción
Telephone: 25001/3, 24030, 25527, 24040

Computer Installation
NCR Century 100–operating system: B1; internal storage: 16K bits; magnetic tapes: 1 736/101; magnetic discs: 2 655; 1 line printer.

Coding Languages
NEAT 3, COBOL, FORTRAN, RPG.

Contemplated Equipment
Increase of 16K bits in storage, 2 633 magnetic tape units, 1 655 magnetic disc unit.

Services Available
Programming, operators, documentation, preparation of data, systems analysis. Operate on a self-service and block time basis.

Fields of Application
Scientific, statistical, commercial, accounting, management, systems analysis.
Specialized areas: Investment analysis, payroll.

Training
NCR courses in coding languages and systems analysis.

CONSULTANT

CONSULTEC S.R.L.
Coronel Bogado 892, Asunción
Telephone: 43-371, 46-392

Officers
Nestor M. Britez Airaldi, *Director General*
Luis F. Meyer, *Director*

Coding Languages
FORTRAN IV, NEAT 3, RPG.

Services Available
Programming, documentation, preparation of data, systems analysis.

Fields of Application
Commercial, accounting, management, systems analysis, operational research.
Specialized areas: Sales analysis, linear programming, investment, analysis.

PERU

UNIVERSITIES

PONTIFICIA UNIVERSIDAD CATÓLICA DEL PERU
Centro de Computación
Apartado 5289, Lima 7
Telephone: 612900

Officers
Jorge Solis Tovar, *Director*
Carlos Joo Leey, *Production Manager*
Jesus Moreno Mirando, *Systems Manager*

Computer Installation
IBM 1130–operating system: DMS VZ/8; internal storage: 8K 16-bit words; magnetic discs: 1 2315; 1 line printer.

Coding Languages
FORTRAN IV, COBOL, RPG, Assembler.

Contemplated Equipment
Additional storage of 8K bits, IBM 2311 disc pack, IBM 1403 printer, IBM 1133 multiplier channel.

Services Available
Advice, programming, education and training, operators, software packages, documentation, preparation of data, systems analysis, structural analysis. Operate on a block time basis. Available to the University only.

Fields of Application
Scientific, statistical, production control, management, systems analysis, operational research, structural analysis.
Specialized areas: Linear programming, analysis, payroll, structural engineering, medical research.

Training
Courses in FORTRAN IV with engineering and social science applications.

UNIVERSIDAD NACIONAL DE INGENIERÍA
Centro de Computo
Avenida Tupac Amaru s/n., Casilla Postal No. 1301, Lima
Telephone: 81-1070

Officers
Victor Yockteng Martinez, *Manager of the Data Processing Division*
Roger Sulem Hauyon, *Manager of the Production Department*

Computer Installation
IBM 360/40—operating system: OS-DOS; internal storage: 1,024K bits; magnetic tapes: 3 2401/5; magnetic discs: 3 2311 and 3 2319; 1 line printer.

Coding Languages
Fortran IV, COBOL, PL/1, Assembler, RPG.

Contemplated Equipment
IBM 370/135 with 192K bytes storage.

Services Available
Advice, programming, operators, software packages, documentation, preparation of data, systems analysis. Operate on a self-service basis.

Fields of Application
Scientific, statistical, commercial, accounting, management, systems analysis, operational research.
Specialized areas: Linear programming, analysis.

SERVICE BUREAU

IBM WORLD TRADE CORPORATION*
Lima

Computer Installation
IBM 360/30.
IBM 1401.

Services Available
Advice, operators, preparation of data, programming.

Fields of Application
Statistical, commercial.

Coding Languages
Assembler, FORTRAN IV, RPG.

Services Available
Programming, education and training, documentation, preparation of data, systems analysis. Operate on an open shop basis. Service available to university, commercial, industrial and government institutions in Baguio City area.

Fields of Application
Electronic data processing, commercial data processing, accounting, research involving statistical and linear processing and programming, project studies using PERT-CPM.

Training
B.Sc. Commerce, Major in EDP; B.Sc. Applied Mathematics, Major in Computer Numerical methods.
Short courses in basic computer science, FORTRAN programming, keypunching.

UNIVERSITY OF SANTO TOMAS*
España Street, Manila, D-403
Telephone: 47231 local 227

Officer
Carlitos Algarme, *Co-ordinator*

Computer Installation
IBM 1620/1— internal storage: 20K bits.

Coding Languages
Machine Language, FORTRAN (with FORMAT), SPS III.

Contemplated Equipment
IBM 360/40.

Services Available
Education and training. Operate on a self-service basis. Service available to students and faculty members, also to other selected applicants.

Fields of Application
Engineering, scientific.

Training
Courses forming part of curriculum for engineering students; digital computer fundamentals, machine language and FORTRAN programming, numerical analysis with advanced FORTRAN programme.

PHILIPPINES

UNIVERSITIES

SAINT LOUIS UNIVERSITY*
P.O. Box 71, Baguio City B-202
Telephone: Baguio City 3043, 2793

Officers
José B. Abinoja, *Systems Analyst for Applications Development*
Paul E. Fronda, *Supervisor of EDP operations*

Computer Installation
IBM 1130—operating system: DISK MONITOR; internal storage: 128K bits; magnetic discs: 2; 1 line printer.

SERVICE BUREAU

IBM PHILIPPINES, INC.
Data Centre Services
IBM Building, 8757 Paseo de Roxas, Makati, Rizal
Telephone: 886571

Officers
R. O. Reyes, *General Manager*
E. H. Sarte, *DCS Manager*
R. M. Manato, *Computing Centre and Plans and Control Manager*

Computer Installation
IBM 360/50—operating systems: OS, MFT II; internal storage: 512K bytes; magnetic tapes: 6 2401 II; magnetic discs: 8 2314; 1 line printer.

Coding Languages
COBOL, FORTRAN, Assembler, RPG, PL/1.

Services Available
Advice, preparation of data, programming, software packages, systems analysis; provide repetitive and non-repetitive services. Operate on a block time basis.

Fields of Application
Scientific, statistical, commercial.
Specialized areas: Stock brokerage, demand deposit, sales analysis, linear programming, engineering.

POLAND

EDUCATIONAL AND TRAINING INSTITUTIONS

ZAKŁAD ELEKTRONICZNEJ TECHNIKI OBLICZENIOWEJ
Ul. Heyki 14, 70631 Szczecin
Telephone: 374-65

Officer
Zdzisław Bogdanowicz, *Director*

Computer Installation
ODRA 1304—operating system: GEORGE 2; internal storage: 819,200 bits; magnetic tapes: 6 PT-2; 1 line printer.
MINSK 22—internal storage: 303,104 bits; magnetic tapes: 16 LPM; 2 line printers.

Coding Languages
PLAN, COBOL, ALGOL, FORTRAN, MAT-4.

Contemplated Equipment
ODRA 1305 with remote processing features; IBM 2772 terminal for IBM 360/50.

Services Available
Advice, programming, education and training, software packages, documentation, preparation of data, systems analysis, data processing. Operate on a self-service, block time and open shop basis.

Fields of Application
Scientific, statistical, commercial, accounting, management, systems analysis.
Specialized areas: Investment, analysis, payroll, structural engineering.

Training
Diploma courses in systems analysis and programming.

UNIVERSITIES AND COLLEGES

POLITECHNIKA GDAŃSKA*
Instytut Cybernetyki Technicznej, Gdańsk-Wrzeszcz, ul. Majakowskiego 11/12
Telephone: 471317

Officers
Prof. Jerzy Seidler
Dr. Tadeusz Bartkowski

Computer Installation
ZAM 41 Alfor—operating system: SUPERVISOR; internal storage: 12K 24-bit words; magnetic tapes: 1; 1 line printer.

Coding Languages
ALGOL, ZAM 41, PJP (Assembler).

Contemplated Equipment
Off-line input of analog computer; physical random number generator.

Services Available
Consultation, programming, education and training. Operate on a self-service and open shop basis.

Fields of Application
Educational, scientific, statistical.
Specialized area: Stochastic simulation.

POLITECHNIKA WROCŁAWSKA
Wybrzeże Stanisława Wyspiańskiego 27, Wrocław 2
Telephone: 270-51

Officers
Dr. Mieczysław Bazewicz, *Director of the Informatics Department*
Dr. Jerzy Battek, *Director of the Computing Centre*

Computer Installation
ODRA 1304—operating system: GEORGE 2; internal storage: 868K bits; magnetic tapes: 6 PT-2; magnetic discs: 4 ICL 2802; 1 line printer.

ODRA 1305—operating systems: MINIMOP, GEORGE 3; internal storage: 3,072K bits; magnetic tapes: 6 PT-3; magnetic discs: 8 ICL 2802; 1 line printer.

Coding Languages
PLAN, ALGOL-60, FORTRAN, COBOL, JEAN, BASIC.

Contemplated Equipment
Another ODRA 1305 computer and an ODRA 1325 on-line satellite computer.

Services Available
Advice, programming, education and training, software packages, preparation of data, systems analysis. Operate on a remote access, closed shop, block time and time-sharing basis.

Fields of Application
Scientific, statistical, accounting, management, systems analysis, operational research, teaching by computer.
Specialized areas: Linear programming, analysis, payroll, structural engineering, medical research, sampling and processing measurements data.

Training
Programming courses in the languages ALGOL, FORTRAN and JEAN.

POLSKA AKADEMIA NAUK*
(Polish Academy of Sciences)
Computation Centre
Room 1050, Palac Kultury i Nauki, Warsaw
Telephone: 20-28-73

Officers
Prof. Dr. W. Prosnak, *Director of the Computation Centre*
Prof. Dr. M. Warmus, *Head of Mathematical Laboratory*
Dr. E. Łuczywek, *Head of Service Bureau*
Dr. hab. T. Pietrzkiewicz, *Head of Operations Research Laboratory*

Computer Installation
ODRA 1204—operating systems: SOW, SODA; internal storage: 393,216 bits; magnetic drums: 2; 1 line printer.

Coding Languages
ALGOL 60, MOST, LYAPAS, JAS, URODA.

Contemplated Equipment
ODRA 1204; ODRA 1304.

Services Available
Programming, software packages, preparation of data, consultation. Operate on a closed and open shop basis. Priority given to the institutions of the Polish Academy of Sciences.

Fields of Application
Scientific, statistical, systems analysis, operational research, software development.
Specialized areas: Linear programming, data reduction, discreet models, econometrics, computer systems structure, programming languages, operating systems, theory of motion of celestial bodies, computation of flow fields.

Training
Courses and regular seminars on programming techniques and computer application.

UNIWERSYTET IM. ADAMA MICKIEWICZA W POZNANIU
Computing Laboratory
60769 Poznań, Matejki 48/49
Telephone: 624-92

Officer
Dr. Mirosław Krzyśko, *Head of the Laboratory*

Computer Installation
ODRA 1204—operating systems: MASON, BOSS; internal storage: 393,216 bits; 1 line printer.

Coding Languages
ALGOL-1204, MOST 2B, JAS B.

Contemplated Equipment
ODRA 1305.

Services Available
Advice, programming, education and training, software packages. Operate on a self-service and block time basis.

Fields of Application
Scientific, statistical, pattern recognition.
Specialized areas: Structural engineering, medical research.

UNIWERSYTET MARII CURIE-SKŁODOWSKIEJ
Numerical Methods Department
Nowotki 10, 20-031 Lublin
Telephone: 33-669

Officer
Dr. Światomir Ząbek, *Director of Department*

Computer Installation
ODRA 1013—operating system: PROM 013; internal storage: 319,488 bits.

ODRA 1204—operating system: SOW, BOSS, MASON; internal storage: 393,216 bits.

Coding Languages
Basic, JAS, ALGOL-1204.

Services Available
Advice, programming, education and training, operators, preparation of data. Operate on a closed shop basis. Available to state and co-operative institutions only.

Fields of Application
Scientific, operational research.
Specialized area: Linear programming.

UNIWERSYTET ŚLĄSKI
Computation Centre
40-007 Katowice, ul. Uniwersyteska 4
Telephone: 368-47

Officer
Dr. Józef Kuzminski, *Head of Centre*

Computer Installation
ODRA 1204—operating system: MASON; internal storage: 16K 24-bit words; 1 line printer.

ODRA 1003—operating system: MOST I; internal storage: 8K 39-bit words. *Remote processing features:* 1 teletyper.

Coding Languages
ALGOL, Machine Language.

Contemplated Equipment
Magnetic drums.

Services Available
Programming, education and training. Operate on a self-service basis.

Field of Application
Scientific.
Specialized areas: Physics, chemistry, mathematics.

UNIWERSYTET WARSZAWSKI*
Zakład Obliczen Numerycznych
Palac Kultury i Nauki, VIII pietro, Warszawa
Telephone: 200211, extension 2512

Officers
Professor Dr. Stanislaw Turski, *Director*
Mgr. inz. Leon Swiderski, *Vice-Director*
Mgr. Jan Madey, *Officer in charge of training of Scientific Personnel and Programming.*

Computer Installation
GIER—operating system: HELP 3; internal storage: 5,120 42-bit words; FACIT ECM 64A Carousel; 1 line printer.

Coding Languages
SLIP, ALGOL 60, (Gier ALGOL compiler).

Contemplated Equipment
Third generation computer with multiprogramming and multiaccess.

Services Available
Advice, operators, preparation of data, programming, software packages, systems analysis. Operate on an open shop basis.

Fields of Application
Numerical methods, programming languages, education.
Specialized areas: Linear algebra, differential equations, operational research, ALGOL.

Training
Yearly 2 ALGOL and Gier ALGOL courses for outside customers, regular programming courses and seminars at the University. Short 4-6 weeks fellowships.

UNIWERSYTET WROCŁAWSKI*
Institute of Mathematics
Computational Centre
pl. Nankiera 15, Wrocław
Telephone: 30516

Officer
Mgr. Ryszard Wrona, *Head*

Computer Installation
ELLIOTT 803 B–internal storage: 320K bits; magnetic tapes: 4.

ODRA 1204–operating system: SOW; internal storage: 393K bits.

Coding Languages
Mark III, ALGOL 60, JAS, MOST 2.

Contemplated Equipment
For ODRA 1204; 2 magnetic drums, 2 magnetic tapes, 1 line printer.

Services Available
Preparation of data, programming, software packages, numerical methods. Operate on an open shop basis.

Fields of Application
Scientific, statistical.
Specialized areas: Linear programming, minimizing of functions, approximation theory, automatic programming.

Training
Courses in programming for students of mathematics, engineers, etc.

WYŻSZA SZKOŁA EKONOMICZNA
(Graduate School of Economics)
ul. Komandorska 118/120, 53-345 Wrocław
Telephone: 710-21

Officers
Zdzisław Hellwig, *Director and Professor of Statistics*
Henryk Sobis, *Chief of Institute of Computer Science*

Computer Installation
ODRA 1003–internal storage: 8,192 39-bit words.

ODRA 1204–internal storage: 16K 24-bit words; magnetic drums; 1 line printer.

Coding Languages
MOST (ALGOL and MARK in combination), ALGOL, JAS.

Contemplated Equipment
ODRA 1305 with internal storage of 64,128K 24-bit words, 4 magnetic discs, magnetic drum, line printer.

Services Available
Limited availability to outside users for research only.

Fields of Application
Statistical and numerical analysis.
Specialized areas: Regression analysis and approximation, linear programming.

Training
Courses in programming and data processing.

GOVERNMENT ESTABLISHMENTS

BIURO PROJEKTÓW I REALIZACJI INWESTYCJI PRZEMYSŁU SYNTEZY CHEMICZNEJ (PROSYNCHEM)
Computer Centre
ul. Strzody 11, 44-101 Gliwice
Telephone: 91-10-81

Officers
Kazimierz Torbicz, *Bureau Director*
Krzysztof Novak, *Centre Manager*
Kazimierz Feliszerski, *Deputy Manager*

Computer Installation
ZAM 41–operating system: SO 141; internal storage: 491,152 bits; magnetic tapes: 7 PT2 RAWAR; magnetic drums: 2 PBS IMM; 2 line printers.

Coding Languages
PJEG, MAKRO-SAS (Assemblers); ALGOL, COBOL, SAKO.

Contemplated Equipment
Third generation computer.

Services Available
Advice, programming, operators, preparation of data. Operate on a closed shop and block time basis. Preference given to chemical engineering bureaux.

Fields of Application
Scientific, systems analysis.
Specialized area: Chemical engineering.

Training
Courses for programmers and seminars for users.

CENTRAL STATISTICAL OFFICE*
Warszawa 58, ul. Wawelska 1/3

Officer
Dr. Tadeusz Walczak

Computer Installation
ICL 1905–operating system: EXECUTIVE, GEORGE; internal storage: 786,432 bits; magnetic tapes: 10 1973; magnetic discs: 4 2801; 2 line printers.

Coding Languages
PLAN, COBOL, ALGOL, FORTRAN, EMA, NICOL.

Services Available
Operate on a closed shop basis.

Field of Application
Statistical.

Training
Programming courses for staff. Short courses in PLAN and COBOL.

CENTRALNY OŚRODEK DOSKONALENIA KADR KIEROWNICZYCH*
(Management Development Centre)
Warsaw 22, ul. Wawelska 56
Telephone: 25-12-81

Officers
Zbigniew Prochot, *Director of the Centre*
Dr. Janusz Gościński, *Deputy Director*
Zbigniew Drabek, *Computer Manager*

Computer Installation
ICL 1300–internal storage: 51,600 bits; magnetic tapes: 4; 1 line printer.

Coding Languages
MPL II, MAC, COMPACT-COBOL.

Services Available
Advice, programming, systems analysis and design. Operate on a closed shop basis.

Fields of Application
Production control with EDP, management, systems analysis, educational.

Training
Four-month course for systems analysts; four-week course for project leaders; one-week appreciation course for managers.

DOLNOŚLĄKIE BIURO PROJEKTÓW GÓRNICZYCH*
(Lower Silesian Mine Planning Office)
ul. Rosenbergów 25, Wroclaw
Telephone: 810-81

Officers
Lucjan Schmidt, *General Manager of the Office*
Jerzy Bednarczyk, *Chief Engineer*
Tadeusz Maslowski, *Superintendent of the Laboratory*

Computer Installation
ODRA 1003A–internal storage: 8,192 40-bit words; 1 teletype.

Coding Languages
Machine Language Code, Autocode MOST-1.

Contemplated Equipment
Analogue computer ELWAT-1.

Services Available
The laboratory works principally for its parent organization but also for other organizations in the field of engineering computations.

Fields of Application
Programming and computing for opencast mine planning and designing.

INSTYTUT ENERGETYKI
Zakład Techniki Cyfrowej
(Institute of Power, Computer Division)
ul. Mysia 2, 00950 Warsaw
Telephone: 21-07, extension 859

Officers
M. Jaczewski, *Director*
A. Kuczyński, *Head of Computer Division*
Prof. J. Wojciechowski, *Research Manager*
J. Gniewiewski, *Head of Foreign Relations Section*

Computer Installation
ODRA 1204–operating systems: SOW, BOSS, MASON; internal storage: 16,384 24-bit words; 1 line printer.

ODRA 1204–operating systems: SOW, MASON; internal storage: 16,384 24-bit words.

Coding Languages
JAS 2, MOST 2, ALGOL.

Contemplated Equipment
ODRA 1305 with EXECUTIVE operating system, storage of 128K 24-bit words, 6 magnetic tapes PT3, 6 magnetic discs EDS 2802, 2 line printers, remote processing.

Services Available
Advice, programming, education and training, operators, software packages, preparation of data, systems analysis. Operate on a self-service, block time and open shop basis.

Fields of Application
Scientific, systems analysis, operational research.
Specialized areas: Linear programming, payroll, structural engineering, electric power.

Training
Courses in computer languages.

KOMISJA PLANOWANIA PRZY RADZIE MINISTROW
Plac 3 Krzyzy 3/5, Warsaw
Telephone: 282280

Officers
Andrzej Dąbkowski, *Principal Adviser to the Chairman of the Planning Commission*

Coding Languages
FORTRAN, COBOL.

Contemplated Equipment
A computer with a minimum core store of 500K bits.

Services Available
Education and training, software packages, documentation, systems analysis. Operate on a closed shop and time-sharing basis.

Fields of Application
Scientific, statistical, management, systems analysis, operational research.
Specialized areas: Linear programming, investment, analysis, state planning systems and sub-systems.

Training
Courses in systems design and computer languages.

RESEARCH INSTITUTIONS

INSTITUTE OF FUNDAMENTAL TECHNICAL RESEARCH (IFTR)
Computing Laboratory
Warsaw, ulica Świętokrzyska 21
Telephone: 264396

Officer
Dr. Jacek Maczyński, *Head of Laboratory*

Computer Installation
ODRA 1204–internal storage: 400K bits.

Contemplated Equipment
Line printer, drum storage and visual display output.

Services Available
Consultation, education and training, operators, documentation. Operate on a self-service basis. Service available to members of IFTR staff.

Field of Application
Scientific.
Specialized areas: Fluid and solid mechanics.

Training
Postgraduate course in computer utilization.

INSTYTUT ELEKTROTECHNIKI-ZAKŁAD TECHNIKI OBLICZENIDWEJ*
Warszawa–Miedzylesie, ulica Pozaryskiego 28
Telephone: 123350

Officer
Stanisław Ostrowski

Computer Installation
ELLIOTT 803B–internal storage: 159,744 bits; magnetic tapes: 3; 1 line printer.

Coding Languages
MARK, Language H.

Services Available
Consultation, programming, operators, software packages, documentation, preparation of data. Operate on an open shop basis.

Fields of Application
Scientific (management).
Specialized area: Electronics.

SERVICE BUREAU

CENTRALNY OŚRODEK INFORMATYKI GÓRNICTWA I ENERGETYKI
Katowice, ulica Kościuszki 30
Telephone: 511441

Officer
Dr. Aleksander Golinowski, *Director of the Computer Centre*

Computer Installation
ICL 1904E–operating system: GEORGE 2; internal storage: 1,550K bits; magnetic tapes: 6 1973; magnetic discs: 2 EDS 2802; 2 line printers.

Coding Languages
PLAN, COBOL, FORTRAN, ALGOL.

Contemplated Equipment
ICL 1904S with remote processing features.

Services Available
Advice, programming, education and training, documentation, preparation of data, systems analysis. Operate on a closed shop basis. Mainly for the coal mining industry.

Fields of Application
Statistical, commercial, accounting, management, systems analysis.

Training
Courses in programming, operating and systems design.

PORTUGAL

UNIVERSITY

UNIVERSIDADE DO PORTO
Laboratório de Cálculo Automático
Faculdade de Ciências
Porto
Telephone: 25498

Officers
R. S. Nunes, *Director*
F. A. Machado, *Systems Analyst*
M. J. Barros, *Administration Chief*

Computer Installation
ELLIOTT 4100–internal storage: 16K 24-bit words; magnetic tapes: 4; 1 line printer.

ELLIOTT 4130–operating system: Batch; internal storage: 64K x 24 bits; magnetic tapes: 4; magnetic discs: 2; 1 line printer.

Coding Languages
FORTRAN IV, ALGOL, NEAT, BASIC.

Services Available
Advice, education and training, operators, software packages, documentation, systems analysis. Operate on a block time and open shop basis.

Fields of Application
Scientific, accounting.

Training
One-month post-graduate courses in programming.

GOVERNMENT ESTABLISHMENT

LABORATORIO NACIONAL DE ENGENHARIA CIVIL
Avenida do Brasil, Lisboa 5
Telephone: 722131

Officers
M. Rocha, *Laboratory Director*
F. Borges, *Administrative Head*
A. Ravara, *Head of Division*

Computer Installation
ELLIOTT 4130–internal storage: 32K 24-bit words; magnetic tapes: 3; 1 line printer.

Coding Languages
NEAT, FORTRAN IV, ALGOL 60.

Services Available
Advice, programming, operators, preparation of data. Operate on an open shop basis.

Field of Application
Civil engineering.
Specialized areas: Elasticity, linear algebra, non-linear structural analysis, suspension bridges, equations, architecture, hydraulics.

Training
Courses in ALGOL 60.

RESEARCH INSTITUTION

CENTRO DE CÁLCULO CIENTÍFICO*
Rua D. Joao V. 30, Lisboa
Téléphone: 680121

Dirigeant
Egídio Namorado, *Sous-Directeur*

Equipement
ELLIOTT 4130–système d'operation: T30C; mémoire interne: 64K bits; bandes magnétiques: 4; 1 imprimante.

IBM 1620–mémoire interne: 40K bits.

Langages de Programmation
FORTRAN, ALGOL, COBOL, NEAT H.

Equipement Projeté
Disques magnétiques, terminals, graphical display.

Services Fournis
Programmation, enseignement et formation, opérateurs, software packages, documentation, préparation des données. Fonctionnement en self-service. Services fournis aux institutions culturelles.

Domaine d'Application
Scientifique.
Domaines spécialisés: Physique, mathématique et photogrammétrie.

CONSULTANT

CETEL
Rua Ponta Delgada 80, 1° andar, Lisboa
Telephone: 538006

Officers
Dr. Esteves Belo, *Director*
Dr. Manzanares Abecassis, *Director*
Dr. B. de Araujo, *Director*
Dr. Casquilho, *Director*

Services Available
Advice, education and training, systems analysis.

Fields of Application
Statistical, commercial, production control, accounting, management, systems analysis, operational research.
Specialized areas: Sales analysis, investment, analysis, payroll.

Training
Courses in programming, COBOL, IBM Assembler, NCR NEAT-Century, multi-programming, teleprocessing, internal storage potential, systems analysis; introduction course to computers; general sessions on methodology.

SERVICE BUREAUX

IBM PORTUGUESA SARL*
Rua Duque de Palmela 25, Lisboa
Telephone: 53-89-43

Also at:
R. Sá da Bandeira 720, Porto
Telephone: 24271

Officers
G. Tortel, *General Manager (Lisbon)*
J. Pena Ribeiro, *S.B. Manager (Lisbon)*
R. Vasconcelos, *S.B. Operations Manager (Lisbon)*
A. Azevedo, *IBM Representative (Porto)*
A. Grilo, *DCS Operations Manager (Porto)*

Computer Installation
Lisbon:
IBM 360/30 E–operating system: DOS2; internal storage: 32K bytes; magnetic tapes: 3 2401; magnetic discs: 3 2311; 1 line printer.

IBM 1401–internal storage: 12K bits; magnetic tapes; 5 729 IV; 1 line printer.

IBM 1620–internal storage: 20K bits.

Porto:
IBM 1401–internal storage: 12K bits.

Coding Languages
SPS, Autocoder.

Services Available
Operators, preparation of data, programming, software packages, systems analysis. Operate on a self-service, open shop and block time basis.

Field of Application
Commercial.

Training
Programming courses.

SOCIEDADE LUSITANA DE ORGANIZACÕES LDA. (SOLOR)*
56a Avenida República, Lisboa
Telephone: 767058

Officer
M. A. Fernandes Costa, *General Manager*

Computer Installation
UNIVAC 1005–internal storage: 4K 6-bit words; 1 line printer.

UNIVAC 9300–internal storage: 32K bits; magnetic tapes: 6.

Coding Languages
Assembler, RPG, FORTRAN, COBOL.

Services Available
Advice, preparation of data, programming, systems analysis. Operate on a closed shop and block time basis.

Fields of Application
Scientific, statistical, commercial, accounting.

Training
Six to eight programming courses per year; general introductory course.

PUERTO RICO

UNIVERSITY

UNIVERSITY OF PUERTO RICO*
P.O. Box 21869, U.P.R. Station
Telephone: 764-0000, extensions 631, 474

Officer
Osvaldo Ferrer, *Manager of Computer Center*

Computer Installation
IBM 360/30–operating system: DOS; internal storage: 64K bits; magnetic tapes: 5 2401; magnetic discs: 2 2311; 1 line printer.

IBM 1130–internal storage: 8K bits; 1 line printer.

Coding Languages
COBOL, FORTRAN, Assembler.

Contemplated Equipment
IBM 360/40–internal storage: 196K bits.

Services Available
Programming, education and training, documentation and systems analysis. Operate on a closed shop basis. Available to University students, professors, researchers and administrators.

Fields of Application
Scientific, statistical, accounting, equipment inventory, planning, systems analysis.
Specialized areas: Registration, student scheduling.

Training
Short courses: Introduction to Punched Card Methods, Data Processing Using Electronic Computers, Computer Programming, Advanced Data Processing.

SERVICE BUREAU

SERVICE BUREAU CORPORATION*
117 Eleanor Roosevelt, Hato Rey, 99018
(*see* under New York, U.S.A.)

RHODESIA

UNIVERSITY

UNIVERSITY OF RHODESIA
P.O. Box MP167, Mount Pleasant, Salisbury
Telephone: 36635

Officers
Dr. E. R. Swart
P. F. Ridler

Computer Installation
ICL 1901A—operation system: GEORGE; internal storage: 16K 24-bit words; magnetic discs: 2; 1 line printer.

Coding Languages
FORTRAN, ALGOL, COBOL, PLAN.

Services Available
Advice, programming, operators, preparation of data, systems analysis. Operate on a self-service, closed shop and open shop basis. Available only to a small number of customers on a self-service and open shop basis.

Fields of Application
Scientific, statistical.

Training
Courses in FORTRAN programming and elementary numerical analysis.

CONSULTANT

P.E. CONSULTING GROUP (RHODESIA) (PVT.) LTD.*
Barclay House, Stanley Avenue, Salisbury

Services Available
Consultation, systems analysis.

Fields of Application
General management consultancy in all fields, i.e. production, marketing, finance, personnel, etc. Development and application of advanced techniques, such as data processing and operational research. Consultancy at corporate level in organization studies, long-range planning, diversification and information systems.
Specialized areas: Technical consultancy in mechanical handling, project management and production engineering. Design and management of systems development projects, machine selection and installation management.

SERVICE BUREAUX

IBM WORLD TRADE CORPORATION*
P.O. Box 3891, Salisbury
Telephone: 20356

Computer Installation
IBM 1401—internal storage: 32K bits; 1 line printer.

Coding Languages
SPS, Basic Autocoder.

Services Available
Programming, systems analysis. Operate on a self-service and block time basis.

Field of Application
Commercial.

INTERNATIONAL COMPUTERS (CENTRAL AFRICA) (PRIVATE) LTD.
Robinson House, Union Avenue, P.O. Box 2196, Salisbury
Telephone: 61341

Officers
J. L. Jeffreys, *Managing Director*
A. F. T. Shibler, *Bureau Manager*
D. N. Graham, *Sales Manager*
R. K. Olivier, *Operations Manager*

Computer Installation
ICL 1500—internal storage: 20K characters; magnetic tapes: 6; 1 line printer.
ICL 1510—internal storage: 20K characters; magnetic tapes: 6; 1 line printer.

Coding Language
FAS FORTRAN.

Services Available
Advice, programming, education and training, operators, software packages, preparation of data, systems analysis. Operate on a closed shop and block time basis.

Fields of Application
Commercial, accounting.

Training
Three-year computer cadetship.

NCR CENTRAL AFRICA (PVT) LTD.*
Corner of Fourth Street and Speke Avenue, Salisbury
Telephone: 60811

Officer
B. H. Ageson, *Managing Director*

Computer Installation
NCR 315—internal storage: 10K bits; magnetic discs: 2 353 CRAM; 1 line printer.

Coding Languages
NEAT, BEST.

Contemplated Equipment
353 CRAM, 2 tape handlers.

Services Available
Advice, operators, preparation of data, programming, software packages, systems analysis. Operate on a block time basis.

Fields of Application
Commercial, systems analysis, management.

Training
Short courses in NEAT programming (10 days) and BEST programming (3 days).

ROMANIA

NATIONAL CENTRE

NATIONAL INSTITUTE FOR SCIENTIFIC AND TECHNICAL INFORMATION AND DOCUMENTATION
Bucharest, Str. Cosmonauților 27-29
Telephone: 13.40.10

Officer
Vasile Tărăboi, *Director*

Computer Installation
CII Iris 50—operating system: SIRIS II; internal storage: 128K bits; magnetic tapes: 4; magnetic discs: 4 CDC; 1 line printer.

Coding Languages
COBOL, FORTRAN, ASSIRIS, MAGIRIS.

Service Available
Documentation.

Fields of Application
Scientific, statistical, commercial, management, operational research.

COLLEGES

LICEUL DE INFORMATICĂ
Str. 23 August No. 22, Cluj
Telephone: 26277

Officer
Prof. Aurel Clamba, *Director*

Coding Languages
FORTRAN, COBOL, ASSIRIS.

Contemplated Equipment
FELIX.

Services Available
Education and training. Operate on a self-service basis.

Fields of Application
Production control, management.
Specialized area: Analysis.

"STEFAN GHEORGHIU" ACADEMY
EDP and Consultancy Centre
Sos. Odaii 20, P.O. Box 282, Bucharest—Otopeni
Telephone: 335250, 335259

Officer
V. Marinescu, *Director*

Computer Installation
IBM 360/40—operating system: DOS 25 and DOS 26; internal storage: 128K bytes; magnetic tapes: 4 24/5/2; magnetic discs: 4 2311/1; 1 line printer. *Remote processing features:* 2 IBM 1050 systems.

Coding Languages
COBOL, FORTRAN, Assembler, PL/1.

Services Available
Advice, programming, education and training, software packages, preparation of data, systems analysis. Operate on a self-service, remote access, block time and open shop basis.

Fields of Application
Scientific, commercial, production control, accounting, management, systems analysis, operational research, management consultancy.
Specialized areas: Sales analysis, linear programming, analysis, payroll, structural engineering.

Training
Certificate courses in systems analysis, mathematical modelling, management and organization consultancy.

GOVERNMENT ESTABLISHMENT

COMPUTER AND MECHANOGRAPHIC CENTRE FOR DATA PROCESSING*
Bucharest, Drumul Taberei
Telephone: 317261

Officer
N. Costake, *Director Eng.*

Computer Installation
ICL 1905—operating system: GEORGE; internal storage: 32K x 24 bits; magnetic tapes: 10; 2 line printers.

Coding Languages
PLAN, FORTRAN, COBOL, ALGOL.

Contemplated Equipment
Punched card input-output 2-unit extendible discs.

Services Available
Consultation, programming, education and training, operators, software packages. Services available to Central Statistical Board and outside customers.

Fields of Application
Production control, accounting, management, systems analysis, operational research.

Training
No official programme; courses organized as necessary.

RESEARCH INSTITUTIONS

ACADÉMIA REPUBLICII SOCIALISTE ROMÂNIA*
Institutul de Calcul
Cluj, Bul. Republicii 37
Telephone: 129-08

Dirigeant
T. Popoviciu, *Directeur*

Equipement
DACICC-1—mémoire interne: 36,864 bits.

Langage de Programmation
DACICC Code.

Services Fournis
Conseils, opérateurs, préparation des données, programmation, software packages. Fonctionnement en self-service.

Domaines d'Application
Théorie de l'approximation de fonction avec applications aux calculs numériques.
Domaines spécialisés: Analyse numérique, interpolation, nomographie, recherche opérationnelle, programmation aux calculateurs.

CENTRE OF ECONOMIC COMPUTATION AND ECONOMIC CYBERNETICS
Bucharest, M. Eminescu 5-7
Telephone: 129115

Officers
Prof. Manea Manescu, *President of the Scientific Council*
Eng. Valeriu Pescaru, *Scientific Deputy Director*
Eng. Constantin Bilciu, *Technical Director*

Computer Installation
IBM 360/40—operating system: DOS; internal storage: 524,288 bits; magnetic tapes: 4 2415/2; magnetic discs: 2 2311/1; 1 line printer. *Remote processing features:* NEAC 1240.

Coding Languages
FORTRAN IV, COBOL, PL/1, Assembler, RPG, NEAC COPCODER.

Services Available
Consultation, programming, education and training, software packages, preparation of data, systems analysis. Operate on a block time basis. Services available for macro-economic and micro-economic applications, training, scientific research and to workers and students.

Fields of Application
Scientific, statistical, production control, management, systems analysis, operational research.
Specialized areas: Mathematical models, operational research, programming, languages for economic data processing.

Training
Courses for students of economic sciences; postgraduate courses; participation in educational programme of Faculty of Economic Computation and Economic Cybernetics, Academy of Economic Studies. Short courses in mathematical models, including macro-economic applications; systems analysis and applied operational research methods; programming languages.

ST. VINCENT

GOVERNMENT ESTABLISHMENT

MINISTRY OF FINANCE
Data Processing Division
Kingstown
Telephone: 2111, extension 59

Computer Installation
ICL 1901A—internal storage: 8K bits; magnetic discs: 1 exchangeable twin disc transport; 1 line printer.

Coding Languages
COBOL, FORTRAN.

Service Available
Preparation of data. Operate on a self-service basis. Available only to the governments of St. Vincent and other islands of the West Indies.

Fields of Application
Accounting, statistical, commercial.

SINGAPORE

CONSULTANT

COMPUTER SYSTEMS ADVISERS (PTE) LTD.
Room 512, 5th floor, Shaw House, Orchard Road,
Singapore 9
Telephone: 378775

Officers
Johnny Moo, *Managing Director*
K. S. Choy, *Manager*

Coding Languages
PLAN, COBOL, FORTRAN, Assembler, PAL, DIBOL, Macro Assembler, BASIC-PLUS.

Contemplated Equipment
Systems based on the PDP-8 and PDP-11.

Services Available
Advice, programming, education and training, software packages, documentation, systems analysis. Operate on a block time basis.

Fields of Application
Statistical, commercial, accounting, management, systems analysis.
Specialized areas: Sales analysis, analysis, payroll.

SERVICE BUREAUX

IBM WORLD TRADE CORPORATION
Singapore City

Also at:
Kuala Lumpur (Malaysia).

Computer Installation
IBM 360/30.

Services Available
Advice, operators, preparation of data, programming, software packages.

Fields of Application
Scientific, statistical, commercial.

INTERNATIONAL COMPUTERS LTD.
Uniteers Building, River Valley Road, P.O. Box 356, Singapore 9

Officer
John K. C. Pang, *Manager*

Computer Installation
ICL 1900 series—operating system: MINIMOP, GEORGE; internal storage: 768K bits; magnetic tapes: 4 9-track, 2 7-track; magnetic discs: 2 EDS. *Remote processing features:* teletype terminals.

Coding Languages
1900 PLAN Assembler, COBOL, FORTRAN.

Contemplated Equipment
Document reader; additional peripheral equipment; dual central processor.

Services Available
Consultation, programming, education and training, software packages, documentation, preparation of data, systems analysis. Operate on a remote access and block time basis.

Fields of Application
Scientific, statistical, commercial, accounting, management, systems analysis.

Training
Programming, systems analysis, management appreciation course. Short appreciation courses, e.g. critical path, engineering programmes.

Fields of Application
Scientific, statistical, commercial, accounting, systems analysis, operational research.
Specialized areas: Linear programming, payroll, nuclear physics.

RHODES UNIVERSITY*
P.O. Box 94, Grahamstown
Telephone: Grahamstown 2023

Officer
Prof. R. Braae, *Director*

Computer Installation
ICL 1901A—operating system: EXECUTIVE; internal storage: 16K 24-bit words; magnetic discs: 1 TEDS; 1 line printer.

Coding Languages
EMA, FORTRAN, PLAN.

Contemplated Equipment
ICL 1902A; tape; graph plotter.

Services Available
Programming, education and training. Operate on a self-service basis. Service available to all staff and students of Rhodes University.

Fields of Application
Scientific, statistical.

Training
Computer Science I and II leading to B.Sc.; short service courses in EMA.

SOUTH AFRICA

UNIVERSITIES AND COLLEGES

POTCHEFSTROOM UNIVERSITY FOR CHRISTIAN HIGHER EDUCATION*
Potchefstroom, Transvaal
Telephone: Potchefstroom 3361

Officers
W. P. Robbertse
J. F. de Beer

Computer Installation
IBM 1130—operating system: Monitor; internal storage: 128K bits; magnetic discs: 3 IBM 2315; 1 line printer.

Coding Languages
FORTRAN IV, 1130 Assembler, APL, RPG.

Contemplated Equipment
Graph plotter, extended internal storage.

UNIVERSITY OF CAPE TOWN*
Computer Centre
P.O. Box 594, Cape Town
Telephone: 698531

Officers
Prof. D. G. Parkyn, *Director*
G. Craye, *Senior Systems Analyst*
W. B. de V. Smit, *Supervisor*

Computer Installation
IBM 1130—operating system: Batch mode; internal storage: 256K bits; magnetic tapes: 2; magnetic discs: 3; 1 line printer.

Coding Languages
FORTRAN, 1130 Assembler.

Contemplated Equipment
Medium range system.

Services Available
Only to research institutes.

Fields of Application
Scientific, statistical, commercial, accounting.
Specialized areas: Numerical and statistical analysis.

Training
Programming, computer science, numerical analysis, computation.

South Africa – Universities and Colleges

UNIVERSITY OF DURBAN–WESTVILLE
Private Bag X4001, Durban, Natal
Telephone: 821211

Officers
Prof. R. P. S. Horn, *Head, Department of Engineering*
Prof. F. Calitz, *Head, Department of Statistics*

Coding Languages
FORTRAN, COBOL, ALGOL

Contemplated Equipment
Computer in 1975 or 1976.

Fields of Application
Scientific, statistical, commercial, engineering.

Training
Three-year course in computer science.

UNIVERSITY OF NATAL
King George V Avenue, Durban
Telephone: 352461

Officer
G. L. Webb, *Director of the Computer Centre*

Computer Installation
BURROUGHS B5700–operating system: MCP; internal storage: 1,436K bits; magnetic tapes: 3 9311; magnetic discs: 4 9374; 2 line printers. *On-line satellite computer*: HEWLETT PACKARD 2100. *Remote processing features*: 6 teletypewriters.

IBM 1130–operating system: DISC MONITOR II; internal storage: 256K bits; magnetic discs: 1 2315; 1 line printer.

Coding Languages
ALGOL, FORTRAN, COBOL, BASIC, SNOBOL (B5700); FORTRAN (IBM 1130).

Services Available
Advice, education and training, operators. Operate on a self-service, remote access and closed shop basis.

Fields of Application
Scientific, statistical.

Training
Four-year B.Sc. honours course in Computer Science; service courses to other faculties; non-degree programming courses.

UNIVERSITY OF PORT ELIZABETH
P.O. Box 1600, Port Elizabeth
Telephone: 2-7961

Officers
G. J. Mulder, *Director of Computer Centre*
R. McD. Dodds, *Professor of Computer Science*

Computer Installation
ICL 1901A–operating system: GEORGE 1S; internal storage: 16K x 24 bits; magnetic tapes: 4 1971; magnetic discs: 1 2821; 1 line printer.

Coding Languages
PLAN, FORTRAN, COBOL, ALGOL.

Services Available
Advice, programming, education and training, operators, preparation of data, systems analysis. Operate on a closed and open shop basis. Available only to University users.

Fields of Application
Scientific, statistical, accounting, management.

Training
Degree courses leading to B.Sc., B.Com., B.A., B.Sc. (Hons.) and M.Sc. in Computer Science; service courses in scientific programming, linear programming, operations research, survey analysis, and for commercial students.

UNIVERSITY OF PRETORIA
Brooklyn, Pretoria
Telephone: 746071

Officers
F. G. Heymann, *Head of Electrical Engineering Department*
J. P. Le Roux, *Officer in charge of Computing Centre*

Computer Installation
IBM 360/50–operating system: OS; internal storage: 8,212,896 bits; magnetic tapes: 2 2415; magnetic discs: 6 2314; 1 line printer. *Remote processing features*: 5 2741.

Coding Languages
PL/1, FORTRAN, COBOL, ALGOL, RPG, Assembler.

Contemplated Equipment
Line printer, card reader, terminals, discs and tapes.

Service Available
Computer time. Operate on a closed shop and time-sharing basis. Available only to students, staff and administration of the University.

Fields of Application
Scientific, statistical, commercial, operational research.
Specialized areas: Payroll, student record system.

Training
Programming courses in PL/1 and FORTRAN.

UNIVERSITY OF SOUTH AFRICA*
P.O. Box 392, Pretoria
Telephone: Pretoria 33621

Officer
Dr. R. H. Venter, *Professor of Computer Science*

Computer Installation
ICL 1902A–operating system: GEORGE 2; internal storage: 768K bits; magnetic tapes: 6 1971/3; magnetic discs: 2 2801/2; 2 line printers.

Coding Languages
PLAN, COBOL, FORTRAN, ALGOL.

Services Available
Education and training. Operate on a closed shop basis. Service available to university and outside users.

Fields of Application
Scientific, statistical, commercial, accounting, management, systems analysis, operations research.

Training
Computing Science I, II, III as possible courses leading to B.Sc. and B.Comm.; Computing Science IV leading to B.Sc. (Hons.); Computing Science V leading to M.Sc.; D. Phil. in Computing Science.

UNIVERSITY OF STELLENBOSCH*
Computing Centre
Stellenbosch
Telephone: 6073

Officers
Dr. G. L. Murray, *Professor of Computer Science*
Dr. S. R. Göldner, *Chairman of Control Committee*

Computer Installation
IBM 360/50–operating system: OS; internal storage: 1,024K bits; magnetic tapes: 2 2415; magnetic discs: 4 2311; 1 line printer.

Coding Languages
FORTRAN, ALGOL, PL/1, COBOL, RPG, Assembler, LISP, SNOBOL.

Services Available
Operate on a closed shop basis. Limited availability to business outside the University.

Fields of Application
All fields of University disciplines.
Specialized area: Numerical analysis.

Training
Programming courses.

UNIVERSITY OF THE ORANGE FREE STATE
Computer Centre
P.O. Box 339, Bloemfontein
Telephone: 89881

Officer
J. S. du Plessis, *Director*

Computer Installation
ICL 1902A–operating system: GEORGE 1S and 2; internal storage: 32K words; magnetic tapes: 2; magnetic discs: 2; 1 line printer.

Coding Languages
PLAN, COBOL, FORTRAN.

Contemplated Equipment
CALCOMP 563 drum graph plotter with off-line tape deck model 763.

Services Available
Advice, preparation of data. Operate on a closed shop basis. Top priority is given to university applications.

Fields of Application
Scientific, statistical, management, systems analysis.
Specialized areas: Linear programming, analysis, payroll, medical research.

Training
Courses in FORTRAN programming for staff and students; courses in data processing (e.g. for commercial degrees) and computer science (for science degrees).

UNIVERSITY OF THE WITWATERSRAND
Computing Centre
1 Jan Smuts Avenue, Johannesburg, Transvaal
Telephone: 724-1311

Officers
J. T. Steele, *Manager*
J. F. A. Wiederhold, *Operations Supervisor*
K. May, *Senior Systems Programmer*

Computer Equipment
IBM 360/50–operating system: OS, MVT; internal storage: 10,027K bits; magnetic tapes: 4 3420; magnetic discs: 12 2319; 3 line printers.

IBM 370/145–operating system US I; internal storage: 2,359K bits; magnetic tapes, discs and line printer shared.

Coding Languages
FORTRAN, COBOL, PL/1, Assembler.

Services Available
Advice, education and training, operators, software packages. Operate on a self-service and closed shop basis.

Fields of Application
Scientific, statistical, commercial, systems analysis, operational research.
Specialized areas: Engineering education, programming systems.

GOVERNMENT ESTABLISHMENTS

CITY TREASURER'S DEPARTMENT
P.O. Box 834, Port Elizabeth

Officer
S. E. Boult, *Principal Accountant–Data Processing*

Computer Installation
ICL 1901A–operating system: GEORGE 1S; internal storage: 384K bits; magnetic tapes: 4 1971/2; magnetic discs: 1 2821/1; 1 line printer.

Coding Languages
COBOL, PLAN, FORTRAN.

Services Available
Consultation, software packages. Operate on a closed shop basis. Service available to local government.

Fields of Application
Accounting, statistical, management, scientific.
Specialized area: Utility billing.

DEPARTMENT OF STATISTICS*
Schoemanstreet, Pretoria
Telephone: 28151

Officer
Secretary

Computer Installation
ICL 4/50–operating system: 5J; internal storage: 131K bits; magnetic tapes: 8; magnetic discs: 4; 2 line printers.

Coding Languages
Usercode, COBOL, RPG, FORTRAN.

Services Available
Operate on a closed shop basis. Service available to government departments only.

Fields of Application
Statistical, accounting.

South Africa – Government Establishments

HUMAN SCIENCES RESEARCH COUNCIL
Private Bag X 41, Pretoria
Telephone: 483944

Officers
P. M. Robbertse, *Director*
A. J. van Rooy, *Educational, Statistical and Psychological Research*
J. D. Venter, *Sociological and Manpower Research, Information, Research Publications and the Evaluation of Certificates*

Services Available
Advice, operators, preparation of data, programming, software packages. Operate on a closed shop basis. Available only to customers doing research in Human Sciences.

Field of Application
Research.
Specialized areas: Test development, statistical analysis.

SOUTH AFRICAN RAILWAYS*
Data Processing Department
Durban
c/o South African Railways, Johannesburg

Officer
G. van der Veer, *Manager of Data Processing Headquarters*

Computer Installation
ICL 4/50 – operating system: tape; internal storage: 131K bytes; magnetic tapes: 10 4452/1, 1 4456; 2 line printers.

Coding Languages
COBOL, FORTRAN, RPG, Assembler.

Services Available
Consultation, programming, operators, software packages, documentation, preparation of data, systems analysis. Operate on a self-service basis.

Fields of Application
Statistical, commercial, production control, accounting, operational research.

SOUTH AFRICAN RAILWAYS*
Data Processing Department
Johannesburg

Officer
G. van der Veer, *Manager of Data Processing Headquarters*

Computer Installation
IBM 360/40 – operating system: DOS; internal storage: 128K bytes; magnetic tapes: 6 2420, 1 2401; magnetic discs: 1 2314; 1 line printer.
ICL 4/50 – operating system: tape/disc; magnetic tapes: 8 4452/1, 2 4452; magnetic discs: 2 4425; 2 line printers.

Coding Languages
FORTRAN, COBOL, RPG, Assembler.

Services Available
Consultation, programming, operators, software packages, documentation, preparation of data, systems analysis. Operate on a self-service basis.

Fields of Application
Statistical, commercial, production control, accounting, systems analysis, operational research.

RESEARCH INSTITUTIONS

ATOMIC ENERGY BOARD*
Computer Centre
Private Bag 256, Pretoria
Telephone: 79-4441

Officer
O. G. P. Grosskopf, *Head of Computing Services*

Computer Installation
IBM 360/40H – operating systems: OS; internal storage: 256K bytes; magnetic discs: 2 2311; 1 line printer.

Coding Languages
Assembler, FORTRAN IV, ASA, COBOL.

Contemplated Equipment
IBM 2415 magnetic tape.

Services Available
Advice, preparation of data. Operate on a closed shop basis

Fields of Application
Reactor kinetics, heat transfer, chemical engineering problems.

SOUTH AFRICAN COUNCIL FOR SCIENTIFIC AND INDUSTRIAL RESEARCH (CSIR)
National Research Institute for Mathematical Sciences
Division of Computer Science
P.O. Box 395, Pretoria
Telephone: 74-6011

Officers
Prof. C. Jacobsz, *Head of Division*
Dr. E. N. van Deventer, *Installation Supervisor*

Computer Installation
IBM 360/65 – operating systems: HASP, OS/MVT; internal storage: 768K bytes fast core, 1,000K bytes LCS; magnetic tapes: 1 7-track, 2 9-track; magnetic discs: 2 2314; 2 line printers. *On-line satellite computers*: 2 IBM 1130. *Remote processing features*: 2 RJE terminals.

Coding Languages
Assembler, FORTRAN, PL/1, ALGOL, COBOL, RPG, etc.

Contemplated Equipment
Increased internal storage, upgrading to 1,048K bytes fast core.

Services Available
Advice, programming, education and training, software packages, documentation, preparation of data. Operate on a remote access, closed and open shop and time-sharing basis.

Fields of Application
Scientific, statistical, operational research.
Specialized area: Numerical analysis.

CONSULTANTS

AUTOMATED BUSINESS SYSTEMS (PTY.) LTD.
P.O. Box 61609, Marshalltown, Transvaal
Telephone: 834-1052

Officers
Mervyn Gerald Smythe, *Director*
Raymond John Pople, *Director*

Coding Languages
COBOL, RPG 11.

Services Available
Advice, programming, education and training, documentation, systems analysis.

Fields of Application
Commercial, accounting, systems analysis.
Specialized area: H.P. leasing.

P. E. CONSULTING GROUP S.A. (PTY.) LTD.*
P.O. Box 1145, Cape Town

Also at:
Johannesburg (Head Office), Durban, Salisbury (Rhodesia)

Officers
J. A. D. Bell, *Director, Technical Division*
P. J. Burman, *Specialist Consultant*
D. A. Woodland, *Specialist Consultant*
M. P. N. Brereton, *Specialist Consultant*

Services Available
Consultation, education and training, systems analysis.

Fields of Application
Production control, accounting, management, systems analysis, operational research.
Specialized area: Operational simulation.

Training
Short Courses: 'Choosing a Computer'; 'Projects Planning and Control'; 'HOCUS Simulation'.

PEAT, MARWICK, MITCHELL & CO.*
5th Floor, Amcor House, P.O. Box 7400, Johannesburg
Telephone: 834-4651

Officer
D. L. de Beer

Services Available
Consultation, systems analysis.

Fields of Application
Economic studies, general and scientific management, operations research, project management, industrial engineering, marketing, production and inventory control, information systems, general and cost accounting systems, data processing and transmission systems, etc.

SCHWARTZ, FINE, KANE & CO.*
15th floor, National Board House, 94 Pritchard Street, Johannesburg
Telephone: 28-2373

Officer
L. H. Fine, *Head of Management Services Department*

Service Available
Advice.

Fields of Application
Commercial, accounting, management, operational research.
Specialized areas: Management reporting, feasibility studies.

Training
Short courses in supervision and computer applications.

THE SOFTWARE HOUSE (PTY.) LTD.
P.O. Box 3669, Pretoria
Telephone: 76-6591

Officers
P. W. Barth, *Managing Director*
H. Livingstone, *Director*

Computer Installation
CDC 3500—operating system: MASTER; internal storage: 6 million bits; magnetic tapes: 8 607; magnetic discs: 20 841, 1 821; 4 line printers. *Remote processing features*: 1 200 UT, 2 731; via RESPOND.

CDC 3500—operating system: MASTER; internal storage: 4 million bits; magnetic tapes: 6 607; magnetic discs: 10 841; line printers shared with system above. (*Note*: This installation is owned by the South African Iron and Steel Corporation).

Coding Languages
ANSI COBOL, ANSI FORTRAN, Compass, ALGOL.

Services Available
Programming, education and training, software packages, documentation, systems analysis, equipment selection. Operate on a remote access and time-sharing basis.

Fields of Application
Statistical, commercial, production control, management, systems analysis.
Specialized areas: Medical research, public health, data base management.

SYSTEMS ADVISERS (PTY.) LTD.
823/830 Stock Exchange Building, corner of Fox and Saver Streets, Johannesburg
Telephone: 834-2137

Officers
H. J. Raine, *Director*
R. F. Trinkl, *Director*

Coding Language
IBM Assembler.

Services Available
Advice, programming, software packages, systems analysis. Specializing in financial and investment applications.

Fields of Application
Commercial, accounting, management.
Specialized areas: Investment, stock broking.

URWICK INTERNATIONAL (PTY.) LTD.*
18th Floor, Glencairn, 73 Market Street, P.O. Box 8730, Johannesburg
Telephone: Johannesburg 22-9026

Officers
R. J. M. Shelton, *Managing Director*
C. H. Devenport, *Director*

Services Available
Consultation, programming, education and training, documentation, systems analysis.

Fields of Application
Management of the computer; all types of feasibility studies; applications of the computer; project control; systems analysis and programming.
Specialized areas: Management information systems, project management.

Training
Short courses in computer project management, systems analysis, modular programming.

SERVICE BUREAUX

ALCAN ALUMINIUM OF SOUTH AFRICA LTD.*
P.O. Box 74, Pietermaritzburg

Officer
Data Processing Manager

Computer Installation
ICL 1901—internal storage: 384K bits; magnetic tapes: 4; 1 line printer.

Coding Languages
PLAN, COBOL, FORTRAN.

Contemplated Equipment
ICL 1903; E/discs and tape or Burroughs B3500 fixed disc and magnetic tape.

Services Available
Operate on an open shop basis. Service available to City Computer Bureau.

Fields of Application
Accounting, payroll systems, statistical, development work on production control.

ALPHA COMPUTER CENTRE (CAPE) (PTY.) LTD.*
P.O. Box 1100, Parow East, Cape Province
Telephone: 98-1492

Also at:
P.O. Box 4470, Durban

Officer
L. T. Horne, *Managing Director*

Computer Installation
ICL 1902A—operating system: Auto Operator; internal storage: 393,216 bits; magnetic discs: 3 2802/3; 1 line printer.

Coding Languages
PLAN 3, COBOL, FORTRAN.

Contemplated Equipment
ICL 1903A.

Services Available
Programming, operators, preparation of data, systems analysis. Operate on a closed shop and block time basis.

Fields of Application
Commercial, accounting, production control, management.

ALPHA COMPUTER CENTRE (PTY.) LTD.*
100 Pendlebury Road, Mobeni, Natal
Telephone: 822061

Officers
J. C. Daley, *Managing Director*
T. W. Metelerkamp, *Director*
G. F. Hollis, *Director*
J. S. Rosmarin, *Director*

Computer Installation
ICL 1902A—operating system: GEORGE 1; internal storage: 786,432 bits; magnetic discs: 4 2802; 2 line printers.

Coding Languages
COBOL, PLAN, FORTRAN.

Services Available
Consultation, programming, documentation, preparation of data, systems analysis. Operate on a remote access open shop and block time basis.

Fields of Application
Scientific, statistical, commercial, production control, accounting, management.

COMMERCIAL AND INDUSTRIAL COMPUTER SERVICES (PTY.) LTD.*
3rd Floor, Heerengracht, Cor. De Korte and Streets, Braamfontein, P.O. Box 11281, Johannesburg
Telephone: 724-9527

Also at:
Durban and Cape Town

Computer Installation
NCR Century 200—operating systems: Disc, NCR B2 Executive (or NCR 200 systems disc based); internal storage: 64K bits; magnetic tapes: 4; magnetic discs: 6; 1 line printer.

NCR 315—operating system: tape; internal storage: 10K 12-bit words; magnetic tapes: 5; 1 line printer.

NCR 315—operating system: tape; internal storage: 10K 12-bit words; magnetic tapes: 2; 1 line printer.

Coding Languages
COBOL, FORTRAN, NEAT.

Contemplated Equipment
2 NCR CRAM units of 145 million characters each; 2 discs of 4 million characters each; 1 paper tape punch; 1 Multiplexor; 1 64K byte memory.

Services Available
Consultation, programming, operators, software packages, documentation, systems analysis. Operate on an open shop basis.

Fields of Application
Scientific, statistical, commercial, production control, accounting, management systems, systems analysis.
Specialized areas: Commercial and industrial accounting procedures.

COMPUTER SCIENCES S.A. LTD.*
Computer Sciences Centre, Juta and Station Streets, Braamfontein, Johannesburg
Telephone: 724-9301

Officer
C. J. Beyleveld, *President*

South Africa – Service Bureaux

Computer Installation
UNIVAC 1108–operating system: CSCX; internal storage: 7,077,888 bits; magnetic tapes: 6 Uniservo VIII C; magnetic discs: 2 Fastrand II, 2FH 432, 2 FH 1782; 3 line printers. *Remote processing features*: Conversational and Remote job Entry.

Coding Languages
BASIC, FORTRAN, COBOL, Assembly.

Services Available
Advice, programming, education and training, operators, software packages, documentation, preparation of data, systems analysis. Operate on a remote access, closed shop, block time and time-sharing basis.

Fields of Application
Scientific, commercial.

Training
Courses in EDP concepts and applications, project management, systems analysis, high-level languages; also training for customers' staff.

IBM SOUTH AFRICA (PTY.) LTD.*
18 Rissik Street, P.O. Box 1419, Johannesburg
Telephone: 836-1101

Also at: Cape Town and Durban

Officers
V. G. Bray, *Country DC Manager*
J. J. Meyer, *Manager of Operations*

Computer Installation
IBM 360/40–operating systems: DOS, OS; internal storage: 128K bytes; magnetic tapes: 8 IBM 2401/5; magnetic discs: 4 IBM 2311; 1 line printer.

IBM 360/30–operating systems: DOS, OS; internal storage: 64K bytes; magnetic tapes: 5 IBM 2402/1; magnetic discs: 3 IBM 2311; 1 line printer. *Remote processing features*: 2 IBM 2260 Display Stations.

IBM 1401–internal storage: 16K 6-bit characters: magnetic tapes: 4 IBM 729/5; magnetic discs: 2 IBM 1311; 1 line printer.

IBM 1401–internal storage: 16K 6-bit characters; magnetic tapes: 4 IBM 729/5; 1 line printer.

IBM 360/20–internal storage: 16K bytes; 1 line printer.

IBM 1440–internal storage: 16K 6-bit characters; magnetic discs: 4 IBM 1311; 1 line printer.

Coding Languages
COBOL, FORTRAN, Assembler, PL/1, RPG, Autocoder.

Contemplated Equipment
A further IBM 360/40, compatible with the present system and featuring RCA 301 (ICL 1500) compatibility, which will replace the currently installed 360/30; IBM 2250 display consoles; expansion of 360 systems to 512K bytes or greater.

Services Available
Advice, programming, operators, software packages, data preparation, systems analysis. Operate on a self-service, closed shop, open shop and block time basis.

Fields of Application
Commercial, accounting.

Training
All IBM courses are for IBM employees, customers and prospects. All subjects from unit record machines, through programming to operating systems, are taught. Course duration varies from 2 days to 6 weeks.

INTERNATIONAL COMPUTERS S.A. (PTY.) LTD.*
P.O. Box 7018, Johannesburg
Telephone: 836-2031

Officer
E. S. Russell, *Management Services Manager*

Computer Installation
ICL 1902–internal storage: 394K bits; magnetic tapes: 4; magnetic discs: 2; 1 line printer. *Remote processing features*: Interrogating Typewriter.

Coding Languages
COBOL, PLAN 3, NICOL.

Services Available
Advice, preparation of data, programming, software packages, systems analysis. Operate on an open shop, remote access and block time basis.

Fields of Application
Accounting, statistical, production control, PERT, scientific, systems analysis, management information, salaries and wages, stock control, etc.

Training
Courses in systems, programming, operating and DP engineering; also Computer Appreciation courses (1 to 2 weeks).

LEO COMPUTER BUREAUX (PTY.) LTD.*
P.O. Box 4164, Johannesburg
Telephone: 838-7545

Also at:
Durban, Port Elizabeth, Cape Town, Pretoria

Computer Installation
ICL Leo III–operating system: Leo III Master Routine; internal storage: 768K bits; magnetic tapes: 8; 1 line printer.

ICL 4/50–operating systems: ICL Multi-Job and ICL 5J; internal storage: 1,048K bits; magnetic tapes: 6; magnetic discs: 3 ICL 711; 3 line printers. *Remote processing features:* Programme development under Multi-Job.

IBM 1130–internal storage: 64K bits; magnetic discs: 1; 1 line printer.

BURROUGHS B283 (5)–operating system: MCP; internal storage: 115,200 bits; magnetic tapes: 3; magnetic discs: 1; 1 line printer.

Coding Languages
CLEO (on Leo III), COBOL, FORTRAN.

Services Available
Consultation, programming, education and training, operators, software packages, documentation, preparation of data, systems analysis. Operate on a self-service, remote access, closed shop, block time and time-sharing terminals basis. Available within a price limitation (minimum of 50 rand per month).

Fields of Application
Management information systems, general commercial accounting systems, accounting packages, scientific packages.
Specialized areas: Mining payrolls and stock control.

Training
Internal training and customer staff training only.

MANAGEMENT COMPUTER SERVICES SOUTH AFRICA (PTY.) LTD.
P.O. Box 61498, Marshalltown, Transvaal, South Africa 220932;
P.O. Box 2252, Cape Town, South Africa 411062

Officer
P. C. Swallow, *Managing Director*

Computer Installation
BURROUGHS B3500 (2)—internal storage: 90K bytes each; magnetic tapes: 5 each, magnetic discs: 1 each; 1 line printer each.

Coding Languages
COBOL, FORTRAN.

Services Available
Advice, programming, education and training, software packages, documentation, preparation of data, systems analysis. Operate on a self-service, block time and open shop basis.

Fields of Application
Commercial, accounting, management, systems analysis.
Specialized areas: Sales analysis, analysis, payroll.

NATAL OIL AND SOAP INDUSTRIES (PTY.) LTD.*
P.O. Box 8, Jacobs, Natal
Telephone: 876931

Officer
D. C. William, *EDP Manager*

Computer Installation
ICL 1901A—operating systems: Executive Programme and Auto-Operator; internal storage: 16,380 24-bit words; magnetic discs: 2 ICL 2802; 1 line printer.

Contemplated Equipment
ICL 1902A processor with 2 magnetic tape drives and Mohawk data transmission with off-line printer to associated company.

Services Available
Programming, operators, documentation, systems analysis. Operate on a block time basis. Service available to any firm with own EDP personnel and data preparation facilities. Minimum contract of one year, with 6 months' notice.

Fields of Application
Statistical, commercial, production control, accounting, systems analysis.
Specialized area: Costing control.

NATIONAL CASH REGISTER COMPANY*
P.O. Box 3591, Johannesburg

Officer
O. B. Loetzee, *Manager*

Computer Installation
NCR 315—internal storage: 40K bits; magnetic tapes: 5 33 VIC; 3 CRAM units.

Coding Languages
NCR, NEAT, BEST, FORTRAN II.

Services Available
Advice, preparation of data, programming, systems analysis.

Field of Application
General commercial.

Training
Courses in systems, programming and operating.

OLIVETTI AFRICA (PTY.) LTD.*
15 Stiemens Street, Braamfontein, Johannesburg
Telephone: 724-1181

Also at:
P.O. Box 4158, Johannesburg

Officer
P. de Walder

Computer Installation
ICL 1901A—operating system: Executive; internal storage: 16K 24-bit words; magnetic tapes: 4; 1 line printer.

Coding Languages
COBOL, PLAN.

Contemplated Equipment
TEDS, off-line conversion of paper tape to magnetic tape.

Services Available
Programming, systems analysis. Operate on a closed shop and block time basis. Service available to Olivetti equipment users only for closed shop, to all for block time.

Field of Application
Commercial.

Training
Appreciation courses for own staff only.

SPAIN

UNIVERSITIES AND COLLEGES

ESCUELA DE ARQUITECTURA*
Laboratorio de Cálculo Electrónico
Avenida Generalísimo 1001, Barcelona
Telephone: 2051805

Dirigeant
Juan Margarit Consarnau, *Directeur*

Équipement
IBM 1620—mémoire interne: 20K bits.

Langages de Programmation
FORTRAN FORMAT, FORTRAN PDQ.

Équipement Projeté
Installation d'une machine plus puissante.

Spain – Universities and Colleges

Services Fournis
Conseils, opérateurs, préparation des données.
Fonctionnement en porte fermée. Pour les architectes essentiellement.

Domaines d'Applications
Problèmes d'organisation (PERT) et statistiques.
Domaine spécialisé: Calcul des structures.

ESCUELA TÉCNICA SUPERIOR DE INGENIEROS DE MINAS
Centro de Informática aplicada – Fundación Gómez-Pardo, Calle Ríos Rosas 21, Madrid 3
Telephone: 2549449

Officer
S. Minguet Melian, *Director*

Computer Installation
IBM 1620–operating system: DMS; internal storage: 60K bits; 2 magnetic discs; 1 line printer.
IBM 1130–operating system: MONITOR; internal storage: 32K bits; 5 magnetic discs; 1 line printer.

Coding Languages
FORTRAN, SPS, RPG, Assembler.

Contemplated Equipment
IBM System/3.

Services Available
Programming, education and training, operators, software packages, documentation. Operate on a self-service basis.

Fields of Application
Scientific, statistical, operational research.
Specialized areas: Linear programming, structural engineering, geological research, mineral research.

UNIVERSIDAD DE BARCELONA
Facultad de Ciencias
Laboratorio de Cálculo
Avenda José Antonio 585, Barcelona 7
Telephone: 2219772

Officer
Lorenzo Guilera

Computer Installation
IBM 360/30–operating system: DOS; internal storage: 96K bits; magnetic tapes: 4 2311; 1 line printer.

Coding Languages
PL/1, FORTRAN IV, Assembler, COBOL.

Contemplated Equipment
Large scale system with time-sharing and on-line satellite computers.

Services Available
Education and training, software packages, documentation, preparation of data. Operate on a closed shop basis.

Fields of Application
Scientific, statistical, operational research.

Training
Diploma course for Programmer of Applied Science; 15-day course in information handling, 15-day course in methods of calculation, 5-day course in simulation.

UNIVERSIDAD DE MADRID
Centro de Cálculo
Avenida Complutense, Madrid 3
Telephone: 4493606.

Officers
Dr. Florentino Briones, *Director*
Ernesto García-Camerero, *Deputy Director*

Computer Installation
IBM 7090/1401–operating system: IBSYS; internal storage: 1,152K bits; magnetic tapes: 12 IBM 72911; 1 line printer.

Coding Languages
FORTRAN IV, MAP, COBOL, ALGOL, GPSS, LISP.

Contemplated Equipment
A computer with a storage of 8,000K bits and more than 25 terminals.

Services Available
Advice, education and training. Operate on a closed shop and open shop basis. Only for teaching and research purposes within the university.

Field of Application
Scientific.

Training
Courses in programming languages, mainly FORTRAN IV.

UNIVERSIDAD DE NAVARRA*
Escuela Técnica Superior de Ingenieros Industriales
Centro de Cálculo
Urdaneta 7, San Sebastián
Telephone: 23880

Officers
F. Pena Möller, *Director*
Carlos Jordana
José Miro
Manuel Bueno

Computer Installation
IBM 1620/I–internal storage: 20K bits; magnetic discs: 1 1311/3.

Coding Languages
FORTRAN, SPS.

Contemplated Equipement
Additional memory of 20K bits, disc storage, graphic display units.

Services Available
Programming, systems analysis. Operate on a closed shop basis.

Fields of Application
Electrical, mechanical and civil engineering, studies of numerical analysis and topics in operational research.

Training
Introduction to automatic computing (1 semester).

GOVERNMENT ESTABLISHMENTS

MINISTERIO DE EDUCACIÓN Y CIENCIA
Centro de Proceso de Datos
Vitruvio 4, Madrid 6
Telephone: 2629610

Officers
Fernando Rodríguez Garrido, *Deputy Director General for Organization and Automation*
Fernando Piera Gómez, *Executive Director of the Data Processing Centre*

Computer Installation
UNIVAC 1108 II–operating system: EXEC 8; internal storage: 5 million bits; magnetic tapes: 7 Uniservo VIC; magnetic discs: 6 8414; 3 line printers. *On-line satellite computers*: Univac 9300 and 2 Univac 1004 II. *Remote processing features*: 8 DCT 2000, 8 DCT 500, 13 U 300.

Coding Languages
COBOL, FORTRAN V, NU-ALGOL, GPSS, Assembler, LISP I.S., SNOBOL, ALGOL/SIMULA.

Contemplated Equipment
New terminals and enhancement of the present configuration.

Service Available
Advice. Operate on a remote access, closed shop and time-sharing basis. Available only to centres depending on the Ministry or other public institutions.

Fields of Application
Scientific, statistical, management, systems analysis, operational research.

MINISTERIO DE JUSTICIA
Oficina de Mecanización
San Bernardo 45, Madrid 8
Telephone: 2218928

Officers
Marcelino R. Cabanas, *Director General*
Gabriel Covarrubias, *Chief of the Programming Department*
Benito Roldán, *Chief of the Mechanization Office*

Computer Installation
NCR Century 200–operating system: BASIC-1; internal storage: 32K bytes; magnetic tapes: 4 633-119; magnetic discs: 2 655-201; 1 line printer.

Coding Languages
NEAT-3, COBOL.

Contemplated Equipment
A computer with storage of 256K bytes, 6 tapes, 4 discs, 1 printer.

Services Available
Documentation, information storage and retrieval. Operate on a self-service basis.

Fields of Application
Statistical, management, information storage and retrieval.

RESEARCH INSTITUTIONS

CENTRO DE LA INFORMÁTICA, TÉCNICA Y MATERIAL ADMINISTRATIVOS (CITEMA)
Plaza de Conde de Valle de Suchil 8, Madrid 15
Telephone: 2235532

Officers
Luis Alberto Petit, *Chairman*
Francisco Lacalle, *Assistant*
Carlos Guzman, *Assistant*

Services Available
Advice, education and training, documentation.

Fields of Application
Scientific, statistical, commercial, production control, accounting, management, systems analysis, operational research.
Specialized areas: Sales analysis, linear programming, investment, analysis, payroll, structural engineering, medical research.

IBÉRICA DE RACIONALIZACIÓN, AUTOMACIÓN Y CÁLCULO (IRAC)*
Calle General Martínez Campos 42, Madrid 10
Téléphone: 223-52-84

Dirigeant
Dr. Ing. R. Boulet, *Directeur*

Équipement
ICL Sirius–mémoire interne: 4K bits.

Langages de Programmation
Autocode, Langage matriciel, Langage machine.

Services Fournis
Pour problèmes de recherche et d'affaires. Des conditions spéciales sont faites pour l'utilisation périodique de Sirius. Travaux à forfait programmés par IRAC.

Domaines d'Applications
Systèmes de vérification de programmes, calcul de matrices, structures moléculaires, barrages voute, mécanique des sols, equations différentielles, programmation symbolique, traitement des données, stabilité de taluds (Bishop) routes, canaux, nivellements.

Formation
Cours en Autocode et traitement de l'information.

CONSULTANTS

B.I.T., S.A.*
Manila 49, Barcelona 17
Telephone: 203.68.50

Also at:
Avenida Generalísimo 132, Madrid 16
Telephone: 215.68.40

Officers
Martín Rodríguez Peraire, *General Manager*
Salvador Alemany Mas, *Barcelona Centre Manager*
Carlos Niño Mayer, *Madrid Centre Manager*

Coding Languages
COBOL, FORTRAN, PL/1 and basic languages.

Services Available
Advice, systems analysis, programming, training, software packages.

Fields of Application
Production control, management.

Training
Courses for programmers, systems analysts, management; course in data processing applications to the different enterprise areas.

P.A. CONSULTORES DE DIRECCIÓN*
Avenida José Antonio 59, Madrid 2
Téléphone: 248-27-41

Dirigeants
A. Beaton, *Directeur Général*

Services Fournis
Conseils, analyse de systèmes.

Domaines d'Applications
Gestion financière et commerciale, production, administration de l'entreprise, mécanographie, études de rentabilité et choix d'ensembles électroniques, recherche opérationnelle.

SOFEMASA
Torre de Madrid (Pl. 10), Calle Princesa 1, Madrid 13
Telephone: 248.96.08

Officers
Paul Ducholet, *Director General*
Bernard d'Arexy, *Assistant Director General*

Service Available
Advice.

Fields of Application
Scientific, statistical, commercial, production control, accounting, management, systems analysis, operational research.
Specialized areas: Sales analysis, linear programming, analysis, medical research.

TEA-INFORMÁTICA
Fray Bernardino de Sahagún s/n, Madrid 16
Telephone: 458-83-11

Muntaner 462, Barcelona 6
Telephone: 247-26-88

Hurtado de Amézaga 3, Bilbao 8
Telephone: 32-86-07

Services Available
Advice, programming, education and training, software packages, documentation, preparation of data, systems analysis.

Fields of Application
Statistical, commercial, production control, accounting, management, systems analysis, operational research.
Specialized areas: Sales analysis, analysis, payroll.

Training
Courses in systems analysis and computer operation.

SERVICE BUREAUX

BULL-GENERAL ELECTRIC S.A.*
Avenida Generalísimo 80, Madrid 16
Téléphone: 2597800

Dirigeants
M. Santero, *Chef du Bureau T F.*
M. Rincon, *Directeur, Relations Extérieures*
M. Saez Vacas, *Chef, Formation du Personnel*

Équipement
BULL GENERAL ELECTRIC Gamma 10 – mémoire interne: 4.096 caractères; 1 imprimante.

Langage de Programmation
Langage machine.

Équipement Projeté
BULL GENERAL ELECTRIC GE 120.

Services Fournis
Programmation, enseignement et formation, opérateurs, préparation des données, systems analysis. Fonctionnement en abonnement machine. Services fournis à Bull-General Electric.

Domaines d'Application
Comptabilité, gestion, systems analysis, statistiques.

Formation
Programmeur Gamma 10.

CAJA DE AHORROS Y MONTE DE PIEDAD DE CÁDIZ,*
Plaza de San Agustín no 3, Cádiz
Téléphone: 212210

Dirigeants
Carlos Pajares López, *Directeur*

Équipement
Système d'opération: NEAT; mémoire interne: 10K mots; bandes magnétiques: 5; 1 imprimante.

Service Fourni
Programmation. Fonctionnement en self-service.

Domaines d'Application
Statistique, commercial, contrôle des processus, compatabilité.

CAJA DE AHORROS DE GRANADA*
Plaza Villamena 1, Granada

Dirigeants
Antonio Lames Orihuela
José Martín González
Rafael Martín Amador
Juan Martín Rojas
José Luis López García

Equipement
NCR 315 – système d'opération: on-off-line; mémoire interne: 10K bits; 1 imprimante. *Transmission des données à distance*: 7 bureaux on-line.

Langages de Programmation
NEAT, BEST, MOST.

Services Fournis
Conseils, programmation, opérateurs, documentation, préparation des données, systems analysis. Fonctionnement en self-service.

Domaines d'Application
Commercial, statistique, scientifique, comptabilité.

CAJA PROVINCIAL DE AHORROS*
Centro de Cálculo Electrónico
Calle Sevilla 1, Córdoba
Telephone: 224750

Officers
Professor Dr. D. Jordano, *Scientific Director*
Dr. A. Ramírez-Medina, *Programmer (Scientific)*
R. García, *Director of Bank Branch*

Computer Installation
IBM 1620/1 – internal storage: 20K bits; magnetic discs: 1 1311; 1 line printer.

Coding Languages
SPS II-D, FORTRAN II-D.

Services Available
Advice, operators, preparation of data, programming, software packages. Operate on a self-service basis. Available only for animal production and biological research, namely animal breeding.

Fields of Application
Experimental biology and animal production.
Specialized area: Animal genetics.

Training
Courses in programming the IBM 1620 computer; FORTRAN II-D; electronic computers applied to improving animal production.

CÁLCULO S.A.
Calle Marqués de Cubas 18, Madrid 14
Telephone: 221.17.58 and 232.40.90

Officers
José María Sunyer Aldomá, *Delegate Adviser*
Mariano Hernández Molina, *General Director*
Enrique Sanchis Moll, *Technical Director*

Computer Installation
IBM 360/30 – operating system: DOS and BPS; internal storage: 32,768 bits; magnetic tapes: 4 2401; magnetic discs: 1 2319; 1 line printer.

Coding Languages
Assembler, COBOL.

Contemplated Equipment
IBM 370/125.

Services Available
Advice, programming, software packages, systems analysis. Operate on a block time and open shop basis.

Field of Application
Commercial.
Specialized areas: Sales analysis, payroll, insurance companies.

CÁLCULO Y TRATAMIENTO DE LA INFORMACIÓN SA (CTI)
Guzmán el Bueno 133, Madrid
Telephone: 253-03-00

Also at:
Provenza 216, Barcelona
Telephone: 254-43-29

Eduardo Dato 22, Seville
Telephone: 63-41-50

Príncipe 5, Bilbao
Telephone: 21-46-21

Officer
Jean Louis Deguill Cottrelle, *Director General*

Computer Installation
UNIVAC 1106 – operating system: EXECUTIVE 8; internal storage: 4,500K bits; magnetic tapes: 8 Uniservo 12; magnetic discs: 6 8414. *On-line satellite computer*: 1 Univac 9200. *Remote processing features*: linked with 3 Univac 9200.

IBM 360/40 – operating system: DOS; internal storage: 1,000K bits; magnetic tapes: 6 2400/2; magnetic discs: 2 2314; 2 line printers.

Coding Languages
COBOL, FORTRAN, Assembler.

Contemplated Equipment
Two IBM 370/125.

Services Available
Advice, programming, education and training, operators, software packages, documentation, preparation of data, systems analysis. Operate on a self-service, remote access, closed shop, block time, open shop and time-sharing basis.

Fields of Application
Production control, accounting, management, systems analysis.
Specialized areas: Sales analysis, analysis, payroll, survey analysis, production planning.

Training
Courses for customers on COBOL and modular programming.

CENTRO TÉCNICO DE PROCESO DE DATOS S.A. (CETECSA)
Orense 1, Plaza Galicia, Alicante
Telephone: 22.97.47

Officers
J. L. Dura, *Managing Director*
T. Noland, *Systems Manager*

Computer Installation
IBM 370/145 – operating system: DOS + POWER; internal storage: 1,179,648 bits; magnetic tapes: 2 3420; magnetic discs: 6 2319; 1 line printer. *Remote processing features*: IBM 2780 terminal in Bilbao.

Coding Languages
PL/1, COBOL, FORTRAN IV.

Services Available
Advice, programming, operators, software packages, preparation of data, systems analysis. Operate on a closed shop and block time basis.

Fields of Application
Commercial, production control, accounting, operational research.
Specialized areas: Local government administration, pharmaceutical industry, boot and shoe industry, college reports, stock control, payrolls, accounts.

DELTA INFORMÁTICA S.A.
Castellana 86, Madrid 6
Telephone: 2628884

Officers
José M. Pérez de Acha, *Operating Manager*
Manuel Costa Romero, *Technical Manager*

Computer Installation
UNIVAC 9300 – operating system: TOS; internal storage: 32K bytes; magnetic tapes: 4 U-12; 1 line printer.

UNIVAC 9700 – operating system: OS; internal storage: 196K bytes; magnetic tapes: 4 U-12; magnetic discs: 3 8414, 1 8411; 1 line printer. *Remote processing features*: Uniscope 100 (4 units).

Coding Languages
COBOL, FORTRAN, RPG, Assembler.

Services Available
Advice, programming, software packages, preparation of data, systems analysis, mathematical models. Operate on a remote access and closed shop basis.

Fields of Application
Scientific, statistical, commercial, production control, accounting, management, systems analysis, operational research.
Specialized areas: Sales analysis, linear programming, payroll, mathematical models.

INSTITUTO DEUSTO S.A.*
Universidad Comercial de Deusto
Apartado 869, Bilbao
Téléphone: 217068

Dirigeants
José Miguel Rincon, *Directeur*

Équipement
NCR 315/100 – mémoire interne: 10K bits; bandes magnétiques: 5; 1 imprimante.

Langages de Programmation
Z-Assembler, COBOL, FORTRAN (UNIVAC); BEST, NEAT, COBOL, FORTRAN (NCR).

Services Fournis
Conseils, préparation des données, programmation, analyse de systèmes. Fonctionnement en porte ouverte et en abonnement machine.

Domaines d'Applications
Gestion, comptabilité, commercial, statistique, recherche opérationnelle. Tous travaux de type économique d'entreprises.

Formation
Stages de courte durée: Notions sur Cybernétique, descriptions de machines, notions de programmation (FORTRAN et COBOL), analyses et problèmes (2 mois).

IBM*
Serrano 5, Madrid
Telephone: 2/25-93-02

Also at:
Plaza Urquinaona 14, Barcelona
Telephone: 2/22-65-73

Officers
A. Serrano *(Madrid)*
A. Garcés *(Barcelona)*

Computer Installation
IBM 360/40 – operating system: DOS; internal storage: 64K bits; magnetic tapes: 6; magnetic discs: 4; 1 line printer.
IBM 1401 – internal storage: 16K bits; magnetic tapes: 4; magnetic discs: 2; 1 line printer.

Coding Languages
COBOL, FORTRAN, Assembler, IOCS, Autocoder.

Contemplated Equipment
IBM 360/40 with storage of 128K bits, 6 tapes, 4 discs (Madrid); IBM 360/20 with storage of 16K bits (Madrid and Barcelona).

Services Available
Advice, operators, preparation of data, programming. Operate on a self-service, closed shop and block time basis.

Fields of Application
Commercial, government, accounting, banking, insurance, production control, statistical, scientific, operational research.

Training
IBM courses.

SERESCO S.A.
Ronda San Pedro 33, Barcelona 10
Telephone: 232-60-27

Officer
Pedro Raventos Curcurull, *General Manager*

Computer Installation
IBM 370/145 – operating system: OS; internal storage: 512K x 8 bits; magnetic tapes: 7 3420; magnetic discs: 6 2314; 2 line printers. *Remote processing features*: 3 2701.

IBM 370/135 – operating system: DOS; internal storage: 96K bits; magnetic tapes: 4 2415; magnetic discs: 3 2314.

BULL GENERAL ELECTRIC GE 415 (3) – operating system: MTPS; internal storage: 16K x 24 bits each; magnetic tapes: 5 each; 1 line printer each.

Coding Language
COBOL.

Services Available
Programming, systems analysis. Operate on a remote access, closed shop and block time basis.

Field of Application
Commercial.
Specialized areas: Sales analysis, payroll.

SERESCODATA S.A.*
Progreso 39, Sevilla
Telephone: 23.23.40

Dirigeant
Antonio Villa, *Directeur Général*

Équipement
BULL GENERAL ELECTRIC GE 415 – système d'opération: TOS; mémoire interne: 16K mots de 24 bits; bandes magnétiques: 5; 1 imprimante.

Langages de Programmation
COBOL, Assembler.

Services Fournis
Conseils, opérateurs, programmation, software packages, préparation des données, analyse des systèmes. Fonctionnement en self-service et service complet, time-sharing et remote batch.

Domaines d'Application
Facturation, statistique, paye, contrôle de stocks, applications de calcul scientifique et technique, PERT, etc.
Domaines specialisés: Programme modulaire paye; programme modulaire pour des compagnies d'assurances.

Formation
Cours d'introduction a la mécanisation (40 heures); séminaire d'analyse de systèmes (60 heures); COBOL (72 heures); IBM 360 Assembler (70 heures); FORTRAN (40 Heures).

SIEMENS S.A.
Joaquín García Morato 10, Madrid 10
Telephone: 410-13-62

Officer
Dr. Francisco Cobian García

Computer Installation
SIEMENS 4004/35—operating system: DOS; internal storage: 528,288 bits; magnetic tapes: 6; magnetic discs: 2; 2 line printers.

Coding Languages
COBOL, FORTRAN, Assembler.

Services Available
Advice, programming, education and training, operators, software packages, documentation, preparation of data, systems analysis. Operate on a self-service, block time and open shop basis.

Fields of Application
Most general and specialized fields.

Training
Introductory, programming and analysis courses for customers.

Computer Installation
ICL 1901/35—operating system: ICL 1900 executive control; internal storage: 384K bits; magnetic tapes: 4 7-track; 1 line printer.

Contemplated Equipment
1350 LPM printer.

Services Available
Consultation, programming, education and training, operators, software packages, documentation, preparation of data, systems analysis. Operate on an open shop basis. Available to State Engineering Corp., other Government corporations and departments, and to the private sector. Priority given to Government institutions.

Fields of Application
Scientific, statistical, commercial, production control, accounting, management, systems analysis, operational research, mathematical economics, simulation.

Training
3-year course for Trainee Programmers—equivalent to degree, for Government employment; 6-week courses in FORTRAN and Systems Analysis; one-week course in PERT.

SRI LANKA

UNIVERSITY

UNIVERSITY OF SRI LANKA*
P.O. Box 1490, Colombo

Coding Language
FORTRAN.

Contemplated Equipment
Computer and accessories.

Service Available
Programming.

Fields of Application
Scientific, statistical.

Training
One-term course in Computer Programming in FORTRAN.

GOVERNMENT ESTABLISHMENT

STATE ENGINEERING CORPORATION*
Computer Division
P.O. Box 194, Colombo 2

Officer
S. N. Amerasinghe, *Manager*

SUDAN

UNIVERSITY

UNIVERSITY OF KHARTOUM*
Computer Centre
P.O. Box 321, Khartoum
Telephone: 71779, 77941

Officer
Julian Rees, *Director*

Computer Installation
ELLIOTT 803B—internal storage: 319,488 bits; magnetic tapes: 5 Elliott magnetic film handlers.

Coding Languages
ALGOL, Autocoder, NCR Language H, Machine Code.

Services Available
Consultation, programming, education and training, operators, software packages, documentation, preparation of data, systems analysis. Operate on an open shop basis. Service available to commercial interests but university users have priority.

Fields of Application
General scientific, administrative and commercial computing.

Training
Short courses in ALGOL.

SWEDEN

NATIONAL CENTRES

NATIONAL DATA CENTRE FOR ADMINISTRATIVE DATA PROCESSING (DAFA)
Voltavägen 17, S-16113 Bromma 13
Telephone: 08 252765

Officers
Hans Rällfors, *General Manager*
Gert Persson, *Planning Director and Deputy General Manager*
Arne Magnussen, *ADP Director, Chief of Customers' Services Division*
Per Hasselskog, *ADP Director, Chief of Technical Division*
Gunnar Wingstedt, *ADP Director, Chief of Operations Division*

Computer Installation
IBM 370/158 and IBM 370/145 (coupled)—operating system: MVT-HASP; internal storage: 18,000K bits; magnetic tapes: 16 3420 VII; magnetic discs: 22 3330; 4 line printers. *On-line satellite computer*: IBM 3705. *Remote processing features*: 70 remote terminals (IBM 2780, 2771, 2770, 2260).

IBM 370/155—operating system MVT-HASP; internal storage: 8,000K bits; magnetic tapes: 6 3420; magnetic discs: 5 3330; 2 line printers. *On-line satellite computer*: IBM 3705. *Remote processing features*: IBM 2780 and IBM 2260 terminals.

Coding Languages
COBOL, FORTRAN.

Contemplated Equipment
More terminals.

Services Available
Advice, programming, preparation of data, systems analysis. Operate on a remote access, closed shop, block time and time-sharing basis.

Fields of Application
Commercial, accounting, management, systems analysis. *Specialized area*: Payroll.

Training
Courses in systems technique II (IBM OS internal functions), DATA registration (Key-700 disc). Various individually designed courses.

STATENS VÄGVERK*
Fack 102, 20 Stockholm 12
Telephone: 229660

Officer
Herbert Nordin

Computer Installation
DATASAAB D22—operating system: OS 22; internal storage: 64K bits; magnetic tapes: 6 Uniservo III A, 5 magnetic discs: 2 Datasaab 2123-2; 1 line printer.

Coding Languages
ALGOL, ALGOL-GENIUS, FORTRAN, DAC 3.

Contemplated Equipment
2 magnetic discs.

Service Available
Consultation. Operate on a closed shop basis.

Fields of Application
Scientific, statistical, production control, accounting, operational research, technical.

STOCKHOLMS DATAMASKINCENTRAL*
(Stockholm Data Centre)
Fack 10450, Stockholm 80

Officer
Civ. Ing. Björn Kleist, *Director*

Computer Installation
IBM 360/75 I—operating system: MVT/HASP; internal storage: 4,194,304 bits plus 8,388,608 bits; magnetic tapes: 4 IBM 2401/2; magnetic discs: 1 IBM 2314; 2 line printers. *Remote processing features*: 2 IBM 360/20, 2 IBM 2780 terminals, 20 IBM 1050.

Coding Languages
FORTRAN, ALGOL, PL/1, COBOL, SORT.

Contemplated Equipment
IBM 2314 disc storage.

Services Available
Advice, programming, software packages. Operate on a remote access, block time, closed shop and time-sharing basis.

Fields of Application
Scientific, statistical, commercial, operational research.

STATISTISKA CENTRALBYRÅNS
(National Central Bureau of Statistics)
Computer Centre
Fack, S-102 50 Stockholm
Telephone: 08-140560

Officers
Ingvar Ohlsson, *Director General*
Stig Brolenius, *Director of Computer Centre*
Christer Arvas, *Director, ECP Methods*

Computer Installation
IBM 360/50—operating system: OS, MVT; internal storage: 1,000K bytes; magnetic tapes: 10 2400; magnetic discs: 2 2314, 1 BASF 6114; 2 line printers. *Remote processing features*: EAI DCT terminal.

Coding Languages
COBOL, Assembler, FORTRAN, etc.

Services Available
Programming, preparation. Operate on a remote access and closed shop basis.

Field of Application
Statistical.

SVENSKA STADSFÖRDBUNDET*
Hornsgatan 15, Stockholm, SÖ
Telephone: 22-29-60

Officer
R. Skarström

Sweden – National Centres

Computer Installation
UNIVAC 1107–operate system: EXEC 2; internal storage: 65,536 36-bit words; magnetic tapes: 6 Uniservo III A, 5 Uniservo VI C; 3 line printers. *On-line satellite computer*: Univac 1004. *Remote processing features*: Communication terminal.

ICL 1901–internal storage: 8,192 24-bit words; magnetic tapes: 4 1971/2; 1 line printer.

Coding Languages
COBOL, ALGOL, FORTRAN, SIMULA.

Service Available
Advice. Operate on a closed shop basis. Limited availability to outside customers.

Fields of Application
Ready-made systems for users with similar problems. Data processing in form of 'standard routine packages' for communities throughout Sweden.

UNIVERSITIES AND COLLEGES

CHALMERS TEKNISKA HÖGSKOLA
Department of Computer Sciences
Fack, S-402 20 Göteborg 5
Telephone: 031 810100

Officer
Mats-Ake Hugoson, *Head of Department*

Coding Languages
ALGOL, PL/1, COBOL, FORTRAN, Assembly, APL, LISP, SNOBOL, PL/360, ALGOL W, SIMULA 67, GPSS, etc.

Contemplated Equipment
Minicomputer system, to be used both as a stand-alone system and for data communication purposes.

Service Available
Education and training. Operate on a remote access, closed shop and time-sharing basis.

Training
University courses in Numerical Analysis, ADP and Datalogy (Computer Science) at undergraduate and graduate level.

GÖTEBORGS DATACENTRAL
(Göteborg Universities' Data Centre)
Data Centre
Kapellgangen 5, Box 1970, S-400 12 Göteborg 19
Telephone: 31-81720

Officers
Asst. Prof. Göran Pettersson, *Director*
Lars-Alle Furingsten, *Systems Manager*

Computer Installation
IBM 360/65–operating system: MFT II, HASP; internal storage: 512K plus 1,024K bits; magnetic tapes: 4 2400; magnetic discs: 2 BASF 6014, 1 2311; 3 line printers. *Remote processing feature*: GUTS (Göteborg Universities' Terminal System).

Coding Languages
ALGOL, Assembler, COBOL, BASIC, FORTRAN, PL/1, SIMULA 67, PL/360.

Services Available
Advice, programming, education and training, software packages, documentation, preparation of data, systems analysis. Operate on a self-service, remote access, closed and open shop, block time and time-sharing basis.

Fields of Application
Scientific, statistical, commercial, production control, accounting, management, systems analysis, operational research.
Specialized areas: Linear programming, analysis, payroll, structural engineering, medical research.

Training
User-orientated courses on job control languages and application packages; courses on programming in co-operation with the Department of Computer Science.

KUNGLIGA TEKNISKA HÖGSKOLAN
(Royal Institute of Technology)
Department of Speech Communication
100 44 Stockholm 70

Officer
J. C. Liljncrants

Computer Installation
CDC 1700–internal storage: 16K bits; magnetic tapes: Ampex TM4111; magnetic discs: 2 CDC 853.

Coding Languages
Machine code, FOCAL.

Services Available
Operate on a self-service basis. Services available to scientists studying speech.

Field of Application
Scientific.
Specialized areas: Speech signals; generation of synthetic speech.

KUNGLIGA TEKNISKA HÖGSKOLAN
(Royal Institute of Technology)
Library-Documentation Centre
Valhallavägen 81, S-100 44 Stockholm
Telephone: 08 236520

Officers
Björn V. Tell, *Head Librarian*
Zofia Gluchowicz, *Head of Documentation Department*

Computer Installations
IBM 360/30F–operating system: DOS; internal storage: 64K bits; magnetic tapes: 1 2401, 1 2403; magnetic discs: 3 2311; 1 line printer.

IBM 360/75–operating systems: OS, MVT, HASP; internal storage: 1 million plus 1 million bits; magnetic tapes: 4 2401, 2; magnetic discs: 16 2314, 8 BASF 6214; 2 line printers. *On-line satellite computers*: Hewlett Packard 2000; *Remote processing features*: RJE (Remote Batch).

Coding Languages
Assembler, COBOL.

Services Available
Advice, education and training, software packages and computer information retrieval in current awareness–SDI service – and retrospective literature searches. Operate on a closed shop and time-sharing basis.

Fields of Application
Scientific, research and development of computerized information retrieval techniques.
Specialized areas: Implementation of computerized information retrieval techniques in the literature of all fields of science and technology.

Training
Short courses and seminars for the users of the SDI service.

LINKÖPINGS HÖGSKOLA
Department of Mathematics
S-581 83 Linköping
Telephone: 013 11 17 00

Officers
Ake Björck, *Professor of Numerical Analysis*
Bo Flyme

Computer Installation
Terminal to Univac 1108 in Lund.

Coding Languages
COBOL, ALGOL, FORTRAN.

Services Available
Education and training. Operate on a self-service and remote access basis.

Fields of Application
Scientific and education.

LUNDS UNIVERSITET
Computing Centre
Sölvegatan 18, S-223 62 Lund
Telephone: 046-1246 20

Officer
I. Dahlstrand, *Manager*

Computer Installation
UNIVAC 1108–operating system: EXEC 8; internal storage: 4,700K bits; magnetic tapes: 6; magnetic discs: Fastrand III; 4 line printers.

Coding Languages
FORTRAN, ALGOL, COBOL.

Contemplated Equipment
8 8414 discs to replace Fastrand III.

Services Available
Programming, operators, preparation of data, systems analysis. Operate on a self-service, remote access, closed and open shop, block time and time-sharing basis.

Fields of Application
Scientific, statistical.
Specialized area: Payroll.

LUNDS UNIVERSITET
Universitetsfilialen Växjö
Department of Computer Sciences
Fack, S-351 01 Växjö
Telephone: 04 70/23120

Officers
Dr. Mats Apelkrans, *Head of Department*
C. Ulf Cederling, *Lecturer*

Computer Installation
UNIVAC 1108/128K–operating system: EXEC 8; internal storage: 4,718,592 bits; magnetic tapes: 8; magnetic drums: Fastrand; 4 line printers.

Coding Languages
ALGOL, FORTRAN V, COBOL, Assembler, LISP, SIMULA.

Services Available
Advice, programming and education and training. Operate on a self-service and closed shop basis.

Fields of Application
Scientific and statistical.
Specialized area: Technical problems.

STOCKHOLMS UNIVERSITET
Department of Administration Information Processing
Fack, S-104 05 Stockholm
Telephone: 08 150160

Officers
Börje Langefors, *University Professor*
Janis Bubenko, *Associate Professor*
Mats Lundeberg, *Head Lecturer*

Computer Installations
HEWLETT PACKARD 2000A–operating systems: Time-sharing BASIC, DOS; internal storage: 262,144 bits; magnetic discs: 1.

Coding Languages
TSB-BASIC ALGOL, FORTRAN, Assembler, COBOL, SIMULA 67, FORTRAN IV.

Contemplated Equipment
Minicomputer as a remote-batch-terminal to an IBM 360/75, IBM 370/155, CDC 3600 and CDC 6000.

Services Available
Programming and education and training. Operate on a block time basis. Available only to schools and research institutions.

Fields of Application
Scientific, management, systems analysis.

Training
Various courses for universities and technical colleges.

STOCKHOLMS UNIVERSITET
Department of Information Processing
Fack, S-104 05 Stockholm
Telephone: 08-150160

Officers
Börje Langefors, *University Professor*
Janis Bubenko, *Associate Professor*

Computer Installation
HEWLETT PACKARD 2116B–operating systems: TSB, DOS; internal storage: 16,384 16-bit words; magnetic discs: 2773-01. *Remote processing features:* 14 teletypewriters, 1 cathode ray tube.

Coding Languages
BASIC, ALGOL, FORTRAN II and IV, Assembler, SNOBOL.

Services Available
Education and training, systems analysis. Operate on a time-sharing basis. Available only to members of the University.

Fields of Application
Scientific, systems analysis.
Specialized areas: Educational uses.

UNIVERSITETET I UMEÅ*
Computing Center
Lasarettet, Umeå
Telephone: (090) 18050-678

Officers
O. Arvedson, *Director*

Computer Installation
IBM 1620–internal storage: 60K bits; magnetic disc; 1 line printer.

Coding Languages
FORTRAN II-D, SPS.

Services Available
This computation centre is designed only for scientific works. Standard programmes are available without restrictions. Operating time, advice, programming, and punching offered at fixed hourly rate.

Fields of Application
Scientific and technical computations.

UNIVERSITET I UPPSALA
Data Centre
Box 2103, S-750 02 Uppsala 2
Telephone: 018-111330

Officers
Dr. Werner Schneider, *Director*
Dr. Bengt Olsen, *Director, Applications Programming*
Klaus Appel, *Director, Systems Programming*

Computer Installation
IBM 370/155–operating systems: OS/360, HASP, TSO; internal storage: 6,000K bits; magnetic tapes: 2 3420, 2 2415; magnetic discs: 6 3330; 3 line printers. *Remote processing features*: 1 2701, 1 2702, 7 lines.

CDC 3600–operating system: DRUM SCOPE; internal storage: 1,500K bits; magnetic tapes: 4 604; magnetic drums: 2 863; 2 line printers. *On-line satellite computer*: CDC 8090.

Coding Languages
FORTRAN, ALGOL, COBOL, PL/1, SIMULA/67.

Contemplated Equipment
A further 2,000K bits internal storage for IBM 370/155.

Services Available
Advice, programming, software, packages, documentation, preparation of data, systems analysis. Operate on a remote access, closed shop, block time and time-sharing basis.

Fields of Application
Scientific, statistical, commercial, accounting, management, systems analysis, medical information systems.
Specialized areas: Payroll, medical research.

Training
Courses provided by the Department of Computer Science.

GOVERNMENT ESTABLISHMENTS

AB ATOMENERGI
Fack, 611 01 Nyköping

Officer
Bengt Tollander

Computer Installation
IBM 360/30F–operating system: DOS; internal storage: 512K bits; magnetic tapes: 2; magnetic discs: 3; 1 line printer.

Services Available
Consultation, programming. Operate on a partly open, partly closed shop basis.

Fields of Application
Scientific (nuclear).
Specialized area: Information retrieval.

CENTRALA FOLKBOKFÖRINGS-OCH UPPBÖRDSNÄMNDEN (CFU)*
Fack, 102 70 Stockholm 9
Telephone: 08-180100

Computer Installations
DATASAAB D22–operating system: OS21; internal storage: 393,216 bits; magnetic tapes: 5 9-track; 1 line printer.

DATASAAB D220 (6)–operating system: OS21; internal storage: 393,216 bits each; magnetic tapes: 10 9-track; 1 line printer each.

DATASAAB D21 (8)–operating system: OS21; internal storage: 393,216 bits; magnetic tapes: 5 9-track; 1 line printer. *On-line satellite computer*: 1.

Coding Languages
DAC (D21 assembly code).

Services Available
Consultation, programming, operators, software packages, documentation, preparation of data, systems analysis. Operate on a self-service basis.

Fields of Application
CFU-systemet and service.
Specialized areas: Population registration, tax collection.

Training
Courses in EDP (14 days); administrative rationalization (14 days); management training (14 days).

FÖRSVARETS CIVILFÖRVALTNING*
Fack, 104 50 Stockholm 80
Telephone: 08-630060

Officer
Ad C-A Lundström

Computer Installation
IBM 360/30–operating system: TOS; internal storage: 32K bits; magnetic tapes: 6 2401; 1 line printer.

Coding Languages
COBOL, Autocoder.

Services Available
Consultation, programming, operators, preparation of data. Operate on an open shop basis. Available for State applications.

Fields of Application
Statistical, accounting, management.
Specialized area: Payroll.

Sweden – Government Establishments

LANDMÄTERISTYRELSEN, TEKNISKA BYRÅN
Förmansvägen 2, Box 43070, 100 72 Stockholm 43

Officers
Axel Jorbeck, *Head*
C. U. Thorsell, *Manager of Data Processing*

Computer Installation
GIER–operating system: HELP 3; internal storage: 42K plus 168K bits; magnetic tapes: 4 Ampex TM7; 1 line printer.

Coding Language
ALGOL 60.

Contemplated Equipment
2 Kingmatic Plotters Mark II.

Services Available
Consultation, programming, education and training, operators, software packages, documentation, preparation of data, systems analysis. Operate on a self-service and open shop basis. Provide a geodetic data processing service, with priority given to the needs of the National Land Survey Organization.

Fields of Application
Scientific, statistical, accounting.
Specialized areas: Geodesy, photogrammetry, forest evaluation, regression analysis.

POSTBANKEN*
(Postal Savings and Giro Service)
105 05 Stockholm
Telephone: 08-236500, 236520

Officers
Tord Wetterberg (*Service Bureau*)
Sven Eklund (*Service Bureau*)
Bertil Eklund (*Foreign Relations*)

Computer Installations
IBM 360/50 (3)–operating system: DOS; internal storage: 256K bits each; magnetic tapes: 10 2401; magnetic discs: 3 2314; 12 line printers.

IBM 1410 (2)–internal storage: 40K bits each; magnetic tapes: 13 729; 1 line printer.

Services Available
In co-operation with SEDAB (Swedish Electronic Data Processing Company): Consultation, programming, preparation of data, systems analysis. Operate on a closed shop basis. Services available only to account holders in the postal giro service.

Fields of Application
Accounting, statistics, production of payment forms, etc.

STATENS JÄRNVÄGAR*
(Swedish State Railways)
105 50 Stockholm
Telephone: 08-226420

Officer
Sven Bernegård, *Development and Research Department*

Computer Installation
IBM 360/40, IBM 360/50, IBM 3968 (communication computer used as a batch computer)–operating systems: 360/40/50, MFT II; 3968, BPS; internal storage: 256K bits (3968: 128K bits); magnetic tapes: 2 2401, 3 2402; magnetic discs: 2314-001, 2314-A01, 2314-A02; 3 line printers.

IBM 360/30–operating system: DOS; internal storage: 32K bits; magnetic tapes: 1 2415; magnetic discs: 3 2311; 1 line printer.

Coding Languages
PL/1, Assembler, FORTRAN.

Services Available
Services available only to Swedish State Railways and subsidiary companies.

Fields of Application
Scientific, statistical, commercial, accounting, management, systems analysis, operational research.

SWEDISH PLANNING AND RATIONALIZATION INSTITUTE OF THE HEALTH AND SOCIAL SERVICES (SPRI)
Box 1109, S-111 81 Stockholm
Telephone: 08 141720, 08 235760

Officers
Olle Nelander, *President*
Robert Nilsson, *Director*
Sven Wendel, *Assistant Director*

Computer Installations
DATASAAB D22–operating system: MK–dirigent; internal storage: 64K words; magnetic tapes: 5; magnetic discs: 4; 1 line printer.

Coding Languages
COBOL, FORTRAN.

Services Available
Advice, programming, operators, software packages, documentation, preparation of data and systems analysis. Operate on a closed shop basis. Available only to organizations within the Health and Social Services.

Fields of Application
Statistical, production control, accounting and systems analysis.
Specialized areas: Analysis, payroll, medical research and EDP systems for Health care.

VÄRNPLIKTSVERKET
(Enrolment Board of the Armed Forces)
Fack, S-171 20 Solna 1
Telephone: 08-830960

Officer
Olle Bran, *EDP Manager*

Computer Installation
BURROUGHS B3500–operating system: MCPV; internal storage: 960K bits; magnetic tapes: 2 9381-4; magnetic discs: 2 9372-1, 3 9375-3; 1 line printer. *Remote processing feature*: TC 500.

BURROUGHS B2500–operating system: MCPV; internal storage: 960K bits; magnetic tapes: 1 9381-4; magnetic discs: 2 9372-1, 2 9375-3; 1 line printer. *Remote Processing feature*: TC 500.

BURROUGHS B2500–operating system: MCP, internal storage: 720K bits; magnetic tapes: 1 9381-4; magnetic discs: 1 9372-1, 1 9375-3; 1 line printer. *Remote processing feature*: TC 500.

Coding Language
COBOL.

Service Available
Computer time. Operate on a closed shop basis.

Fields of Application
Management, personnel handling.

VARVSINDUSTRINS DATACENTRAL AB
(The Swedish Shipbuilders' Computing Centre Ltd.)
Lindholmen, Fack, 402 70 Göteborg 8
Telephone: (031) 513780

Officer
Åke Jacobsson, *Managing Director*

Computer Installation
IBM 370/145–operating systems: OS, MFTII; internal storage: 512K bytes; magnetic tapes: 6 3420; magnetic discs: 14 2319; 2 line printers. *On-line satellite computers*: MDS 2400 (2405, 2435, 2445, 2454).

UNIVAC III–internal storage: 16K bits; magnetic tapes: 8; 2 line printers. *On-line satellite computer*: Univac 1004.

Coding Languages
FORTRAN, ALGOL, COBOL.

Services Available
Advice, programming, education and training, software packages, documentation, preparation of data, systems analysis. Operate on a batch-service, remote access, closed shop and block time basis.

Fields of Application
Scientific, statistical, commercial, production control, accounting, management, systems analysis, operational research, technical calculations, numerical control.
Specialized area: Shipbuilding.

Training
Short courses in numerical control (VIKING system).

RESEARCH INSTITUTIONS

APOTEKSBOLAGET AB
Humlegårdsgatan 17, 105 14 Stockholm

Officers
Åke Nohrlander, *President*
Ian Nordenstam, *Director*
Ian Palm, *EDP Manager*

Computer Installation
IBM 370/135–operating system: DOS POWER; internal storage: 240K bytes; magnetic tapes: 4 3420-3; magnetic discs: 6 3330; 1 line printer. *Remote processing feature*: 3270.

Coding Languages
ANS, COBOL.

Service Available
Computer time. Operate on a closed shop basis.

Fields of Application
Statistical, commercial, accounting, management.
Specialized area: Payroll.

FLYGTEKNISKA FÖRSÖKSANSTALTEN–FFA*
(Aeronautical Research Institute)
Ranhammarsvägen 12-14 161 11 Bromma 11

Officer
G. I. Johnson

Computer Installation
ICL 1901A–operating system: Executive; internal storage: 16K bits; magnetic tapes: 4 1971/2; 1 line printer.

Coding Languages
FORTRAN, PLAN.

Services Available
Consultation, programming, operators, documentation, preparation of data, systems analysis. Operate on a closed shop basis. Services available to FFA and some outside customers.

Field of Application
Scientific.
Specialized area: Evaluation of wind-tunnel data.

Training
IBM and ICL courses used for training.

FORSKNINGSINSTITUTET FÖR ATOMFYSIK
(Research Institute for Physics)
Roslagsvägen 100, S-104 05 Stockholm 50
Telephone: 08 150360

Officer
Prof. Sölve Hultberg

Computer Installations
TRASK–operating system: ECM; internal storage: 32K x 40 bits; magnetic tapes: FACIT carousel ECM 64; 1 line printer.

Coding Languages
ALGOL, Assembly.

Services Available
Programming and preparation of data. Operate on a self-service and open shop basis.

Field of Application
Scientific.
Specialized area: Nuclear research.

RESEARCH INSTITUTE OF NATIONAL DEFENCE (1)
104 50 Stockholm 80
Telephone: 631500

Officers
Elsa-Karin Boestad-Nilsson
Lena Jönsson
Arne Bergström

Computer Installation
Various small computers. Customer of Stockholm Data Centre, using IBM 360/75 and PDP 10/70 governmental computers.

Coding Language
FORTRAN.

Contemplated Equipment
SIMULA compiler for DEC 10.

Services Available
Programming, software packages, documentation. Operate on a closed shop basis. Priority given to needs of the Institute.

Fields of Application
Scientific, statistical, numerical analysis.
Specialized areas: Image processing, artificial intelligence, information retrieval, Monte Carlo and other simulations, differential equations.

RESEARCH INSTITUTE OF NATIONAL DEFENCE (2)

Officer
P. O. Lundbom

Computer Installation
EMR Advance 6130—internal storage: 256K bits; magnetic tapes: 61P/MD-05; magnetic discs: 61P/DD-60.

Coding Languages
ASIST, BASIC FORTRAN, FORTRAN IV.

Contemplated Equipment
Tape unit, line printer.

Services Available
Consultation, preparation of data, programming, systems analysis. Operate on an open shop basis. Priority given to the needs of the Institute.

Fields of Application
Scientific, statistical.
Specialized areas: Conversion and processing of analogue data, time series analysis.

RESEARCH INSTITUTE OF NATIONAL DEFENCE (3)

Officer
Jonas Agerberg

Computer Installation
EAI 8945 Hybrid—operating systems: OS, DOS; internal storage: 512K bits; magnetic tapes: 2 Ampex TM; magnetic disc: Data Disk 7200; 1 line printer.

Coding Languages
FORTRAN IV, EAI 640 Assembler, HOI.

Services Available
Programming, software packages, systems analysis. Operate on a self-service basis. Priority given to the needs of the Institute.

Fields of Application
Scientific, statistical.
Specialized areas: Simulation, automatic control.

RESEARCH INSTITUTE OF NATIONAL DEFENCE (4)
Section FOA Index
Fack, S-104 50 Stockholm 80

Officer
Wolfram E. M. Uhlmann, *Head of Section*

Computer Installation
IBM 360/75—operating systems: OS, MVT, HASP, GUTS; internal storage: 1 million bytes; magnetic tapes: 4 2401-2; magnetic discs: 16 2314, 1 2301, 8 BASF 6214; 2 line printers. *On-line satellite computers*: 2 IBM 360/20. *Remote processing features*: 1 2780 terminal, 1 1130, 26 1050, 1 2471, 1 Marconi.

PDP-10—internal storage: 96K words; magnetic tapes: 4 DEC, 2 TU; magnetic discs: 3 RPO3, 1 RM10-B; 1 line printer. *Remote processing features*: 20 Dataprinters 300 KSR, 2 Graphic terminals 4012.

Coding Languages
FORTRAN, COBOL, ALGOL, PL/1, Assembler.

Services Available
Advice, programming, software packages, documentation. Operate on a self-service, remote access, open shop and time-sharing basis.

Fields of Application
Information retrieval, documentation.

SWEDISH METEOROLOGICAL AND HYDROLOGICAL INSTITUTE
P.O. Box 12108, 102 23 Stockholm 12
Telephone: 08-520000

Officer
Dr. Lennart Bengtsson, *Head of Numerical Division*

Computer Installation
DATASAAB D22—operating system: MAC (own system), OS; internal storage: 1,081,344 bits; magnetic tapes: 4 2131-22; magnetic discs: 2 2187; 1 line printer. *On-line satellite computer*: Datasaab D5/20.

Coding Languages
ALGOL, FORTRAN, Assembler (Both D22 and own).

Services Available
Operate on a closed shop and self-service basis, depending on user. Available to the Institute and other users of meteorological programmes.

Field of Application
Scientific.
Specialized area: Meteorological applications, including weather analyses and forecasts.

CONSULTANTS

ADB KONSULT AB*
Box 7020, 12704 Skärholmen
Telephone: (08) 7100430

Officer
L. Strandberg

Services Available
Consultation, programming, software packages, systems analysis.

Field of Application
General commercial.

ADMINISTRATIV RATIONALISERING AB*
Mäster Samuelsgatan 49, Box 40076, 103 42 Stockholm 40
Telephone: (08) 224730

Fields of Application
Accounting, management, systems analysis, operational research.

AKTUELLDATA AB*
Skolvägen 8 G, Mölnlycke
Telephone: (031) 735840, 730029

Officer
Ing. Sven Lindh

Computer Installation
Time hired on an IBM 360/30 computer owned by an industrial concern.

Coding Languages
COBOL, PL/1, RPG, IBM Autocoder.

Services Available
Consultation, programming, systems analysis.

Sweden – Consultants

Fields of Application
Commercial, accounting, systems analysis.
Specialized area: Stock control.

ALLMÄNNA INGENJÖRSBYRÅN AB*
Artillerigatan 42, Stockholm Ö
Telephone: (08) 63-55-40

Officer
Rune Algesten, *Manager*

BROR ANDERSSON AB (BRA)
Bredängstorget 1, 127 32 Skärholmen
Telephone: (08) 880125

Officers
Bo Sigfried Söderberg, *Managing Director*
Bror Tingsnäs, *Software Manager*
Olof Risberg, *Development Manager*

Services Available
Programming, software packages, systems analysis, and development efficiency. Operate on a time-sharing basis.

Fields of Application
Commercial, management and systems analysis.
Specialized area: Analysis.

ÅNGPANNEFÖRENINGEN
Box 783, S-101 31 Stockholm 1
Telephone: (08) 234600

Also at:
Falun, Gävle, Göteborg, Halmstad, Jönköping, Karlstad, Kristianstad, Luleå, Malmö, Norrköping, Skellefteå, Sundsvall, Umeå and Växjö.

Officers
Kurt Molker, *Director of Computer Centre*
Bo Friberg, *Foreign Relations*

Computer Installation
ICL 1901A–operating system: GEORGE 1S; internal storage: 393K bits; magnetic tapes: 4 1971/2; magnetic discs: 1 twin EDS 2821/1; 1 line printer.

The centre also has data terminals in Stockholm, Göteborg, Malmö and Sundsvall, connected on a time-sharing basis to the IBM 370/145 of Datema AB, the Bull General Electric GE 235 of Honeywell-Bull AB and the GE 635 of Industridata AB.

Coding Languages
FORTRAN, COBOL, PLAN, BASIC, ALGOL.

Contemplated Equipment
Magnetic discs: 1 control unit 2802/0, 2 driver units 2802/2.

Services Available
Advice, programming and systems analysis. Operate on a remote access, closed shop and time-sharing basis.

Fields of Application
Scientific, process control, structural analysis, systems analysis, electrical engineering and network planning.
Specialized areas: Process control in chemical industries, pulp and paper mills, power and heating plants, network planning, structural engineering problems in these areas and electrical engineering.

ASBJÖRN HABBERSTAD AB*
Box 13058, Göteborg C
Telephone: (031) 26-22-40

Also at:
Kungsgatan 60, Stockholm C

Officer
Reidar Varmo, *Manager*

Services Available
Advice, systems analysis, operations analysis, evaluation of computer-purchase.

Fields of Application
Statistical, commercial, production control, management, systems analysis, operational research.
Specialized area: Management consultancy.

BRANSCH–KONSULT AKTIEBOLAG*
Brunkebergstorg 15, Stockholm C
Telephone: (08) 20-90-95

Also at:
Baltzarsgatan 25, Malmö
Telephone: (040) 11-77-10

Arlagatan 12, Borås
Telephone: (033) 13-49-31

Storgatan 4, Värnamo
Telephone: (0370) 164-30

Officers
Reino Lindgren, *Director*
Lars Nilsson *(Malmö)*
Karl-Erik Friman *(Borås-Värnamo)*

TEKN.LIC JOHAN F. BÖHMER KONSULTERANDE INGENJÖRSBYRÅ AB*
Katarina Bangata 15, 116 25 Stockholm SO
Telephone: 41-01-08

European Offices: Oslo (Norway)

Officer
Johan F. Böhmer

Computer Installation
Use a DATASAAB D21 installed at Industridata AB.

Coding Languages
ALGOL, ALGOL-GENIUS, FORTRAN, COBOL, etc.

Services Available
Consultation, preparation of data, programming, software packages, systems analysis.

Fields of Application
The usual applications of ADP in science, engineering and commerce.
Specialized areas: Technical problems, engineering design/computation.

CERTA AB*
Barnhusgatan 20, Stockholm C
Telephone: (08) 10-71-81

Officer
Ethel Johansson, *Manager*

Services Available
Consultation, programming, systems analysis.

Sweden – Consultants

COMPUTER SYSTEMS INTERNATIONAL AB (CSI)*
Box 472, S-171 04 Solna 4
Telephone: Stockholm 27-28-65

Officers
Sven Davidson, *Managing Director*
Sven Söderström, *Production Planning*

Coding Languages
COBOL for IBM 360.

Services Available
Consultation, programming, systems analysis.

Field of Application
Administrative data processing.

CONSULTA AB*
Fregattvägen 12, Lidingö 1
Telephone: (08) 775-02-20

Officer
G. Markström, *Manager*

CYBERNETICS INTERNATIONAL AB
P.O. Box 48, 182 11 Danderyd 1
Telephone: Stockholm 7530300

Officer
Lennart H. Schwieler, *Managing Director*

Services Available
Consultation, programming, education and training, software packages, documentation, systems analysis.

Fields of Application
Scientific, statistical, commercial, production control, accounting, management, systems analysis.

DATA LJUNGGREN*
Transtigen 4, 216 18 Malmö
Telephone: (040) 15-12-80

Officer
Åke Ljunggren, *Manager*

Coding Languages
ALGOL-GENIUS, COBOL, FORTRAN.

Services Available
Systems analysis, programming.

Field of Application
Systems analysis.
Specialized area: Information systems for constructors.

DATAANALYS AB
Shepsbron 18, S-111 30 Stockholm
Telephone: (08) 218410

Officer
Ulf Buxrud, *President*

Coding Languages
COBOL, Assembly, PL/1.

Services Available
Advice, programming, software packages, systems analysis, planning technique.

Fields of Application
Commercial, systems analysis, software development.

AB DATABYRÅN CASSEMAR & HALLMAN*
Rottnerosbacken 253, Farsta
Telephone: (08) 942781

Officers
B. Cassemar, *Manager*
T. Magnusson

Coding Languages
IBM Assembly Language, COBOL, PL/1, FORTRAN, ALGOL.

Services Available
Consultation, preparation of data, programming, systems analysis.

Fields of Application
Hospital information systems, statistical systems, commercial routines in general.
Specialized areas: Hospital, laboratory and administrative routines.

EKONOMISK FÖRETAGSLEDNING (EF) AB
Member of the PA Management Consultants Group
Fack, S-171 20 Solna
Telephone: (08) 981880

Also at:
Göteborg, Malmö, Copenhagen (Denmark), Århus (Denmark), Helsinki (Finland).

Officers
Eric R. Wilkinson, *Managing Director*
Gunnar Rylander, *Director, Solna office*
Erik Hermelin, *Chief, EDP group*

Services Available
Advice, software packages, systems analysis, feasibility studies, EDP development and installation, EDP organization, EDP audit.

Fields of Application
Commercial, production control, accounting, management, systems analysis, operational research.
Specialized area: Investment.

ESSELTE AR-KONSULT AB
Vasagatan 16, Fack 101 10 Stockholm 1
Telephone: (08) 22-95-00

Officer
Gert Bråberg, *Director*

Computer Installation
IBM 370/135–operating system: DOS; internal storage: 196K bits; magnetic tapes: 8 3420; magnetic discs: 6 2319; 1 line printer. *Remote processing feature*: DIGISET typesetter.

Coding Languages
PL/1, Assembler.

Services Available
Programming, operators, systems analysis. Operate on a closed shop basis.

Fields of Application
Graphic application, typesetting.

Sweden – Consultants

HIFAB AKTIEBOLOG*
Administrativ Rationalisering AB
Box 40076, 103 42 Stockholm 4
Telephone: (08) 22-47-20

Officers
Lars Brundin
Björn-Ake Krantz
Ulf Lindén, *General Manager*

IMARconsultRN*
Box 1129, S-111 81 Stockholm
Telephone: 24-13-80

European Offices: Produktionsteknik AB, Helsinki (Finland); Nordisk Rationalisering A/S, Copenhagen (Denmark); Rasjonelt Noeringsliv A/S, Oslo (Norway); Imarco AG, Zürich (Switzerland)

Officers
Rune Mattsson, *Managing Director*
Thure Lagerström, *Chief Officer for Training of Personnel*
Gunnar Bark, *Chief Officer for Management Information Systems*
Prof. Börje Langefors, *Scientific Adviser*
Prof. Hans T. Thorelli, *Scientific Adviser*

Coding Languages
FORTRAN, COBOL, Assembler, ALGOL

Services Available
Consultation, systems analysis.

Fields of Application
General management, e.g. long range planning, organization planning, information systems, objectives, policies; Finance accounting, e.g. financial analysis and planning, budgetary programs, general accounting; Manufacturing, e.g. production scheduling, inventory control facilities; Engineering, e.g. production engineering, value engineering; marketing, e.g. marketing strategy, marketing planning, market surveys, sales management.
Specialized areas: MTM-based industrial engineering and maintenance control (UMS), project planning and PERT applications, systems analysis and systems planning with EDB, operations research, value analysis, training programs.

Training
Short courses in network planning and management information systems.

INDUSTRI-MATEMATIK AB*
Box 20025, 161 20 Bromma 20
Telephone: (08) 981560

Officers
Martin Leimdörfer, *President*
Hans Ebenfelt, *Vice-President*
Bo Eriksson, *Head, Mathematical analysis*
Bo Arvén, *Head, Information Retrieval, and Commercial Applications*
Claes Johansson, *Head, Systems Development*

Coding Languages
FORTRAN, ALGOL, COBOL, BAL, COMPASS, etc.

Services Available
Consultation in system engineering, operations research, data processing. Operation of direct access and other information retrieval services.

Fields of Application
Scientific, statistical, commercial, production and distribution control, accounting, management, medical and industrial data, collection and processing, process computer applications, industrial automation, inventory control. Program conversion between different computers. Program optimation for maximum economy.
Specialized areas: Reliability and maintenance technology. Data bank development and maintenance for banks and insurance companies. Cost effectiveness of models, applied to industrial and government activities. Transport optimization. Simulation and Monte Carlo Studies.

Training
Short courses (1-5 days). Operations research, reliability and maintenance techniques, operation of computer installations, interactive information retrieval systems, computerized documentation.

INFORMATION SYSTEM AB*
Box 1013, S-171 21 Solna 1
Telephone: 83-44-60

Also at:
Industrigaten 13, Malmö Ö
Telephone: (040) 18-03-45

Officers
Bengt Öhrn, *Managing Director*
Olle Dopping, *Foreign Relations and Training*
Karl-Gustav Ahlgren, *Manager (Malmö)*

Coding Languages
COBOL, ALGOL-GENIUS, RPG, FORTRAN.

Services Available
Consultation, operators, preparation of data, programming, software packages, systems analysis. Operate a 'facility management' service, whereby we contract to staff and operate data processing centres owned by individual firms or groups of firms.

Fields of Application
Management, production control, systems analysis, commercial, accounting, computer selection.
Specialized areas: Management information systems, production control and simulation systems, computer type setting, facility management.

Training
Courses in systems analysis methodology (2-3 days); data base management (1-5 days); management standards for data processing (2 days).

INFORSYSTEM AB*
Ferievägen 8, Bromma
Telephone: (08) 87-80-50

Officer
Lennart Lindberg, *Director*

Services Available
Advice, systems analysis.

Fields of Application
Management, data processing methods.

INGENJÖRSFIRMA NORDISK ADB AB*
Fack, S-171 20 Solna
Telephone: (08) 82-02-70

Sweden – Consultants

Officers
Göran Waernér, *General Manager and Foreign Relations*
Bo Hallmén, *Manager for Production*
H.-G. Ricknell, *Manager for Training Courses for Clients*
Bo Segnestam, *Manager for Research and Programming Services*
Ake Bengtsson, *Manager for Consulting for Structural Computations*

Computer Installation
Purchase block time on BULL GENERAL ELECTRIC GE 625 and UNIVAC 1107 computers.

Coding Languages
FORTRAN IV, ALGOL.

Services Available
Programming, software packages in structural engineering, consulting for structural calculations.

Fields of Application
Scientific, engineering.
Specialized area: Structural engineering.

AB KNIGHT*
Östra Torggatan 6, 652 24 Karlstad
Telephone: (054) 15 67 50

Also at: Stockholm, Göteborg, Malmö, Västerås

Services Available
Consultation, operators, preparation of data, programming, software packages, systems analysis.

Fields of Application
Real management information systems, all operating systems, process control.

KONSULTERANDE BYRÅN I ÖREBRO AB*
Ringgatan 19, Box 352, Örebro 1
Telephone: (019) 12-43-55

Officer
Lars-Ake Larsson, *Director*

B. LUDVIGSON INGENJÖRSBYRÅ AB*
Kungsportsavenyen 31-35, S-411 36 Göteborg
Telephone: (031) 81-02-20

Officer
Birger Ludvigson

Coding Language
ALGOL.

Contemplated Equipment
On-line terminal.

Services Available
Consultation, operators, preparation of data, programming, systems analysis.

Fields of Application
Structural design and soil mechanics.

NORDISK ADB AB*
Box 40198, 103 44 Stockholm
Telephone: (08) 246335

Officer
Ake Bengtsson

Computer Installation
UNIVAC 1104.

Coding Languages
FORTRAN, ALGOL, BASIC.

Services Available
Advice, programming, education and training, software packages, documentation, preparation of data, systems analysis.

Fields of Application
Scientific, systems analysis.
Specialized area: Structural engineering.

PARSONS & WILLIAMS INC.*
Box 43007, Stockholm 43
Telephone: (08) 19-19-80

Officers
Robert F. Williams, *President*
Ole C. Nord, *Secretary*

Services Available
Consultation, software packages, systems analysis.

Fields of Application
Production control, management system design, operations research, and programming.

Training
Short courses in management science.

AB PROGRAMATOR*
Östhammarsgatan 75, Stockholm Ö
Telephone: (08) 63-07-15

Officers
Civ.ing. Lars Irstad, *Managing Director*
Karl-Adam Bonnier, *Head of the Board*

Coding Languages
COBOL, Assembler.

Services Available
Consultation, programming, systems analysis.

Fields of Application
Scientific, statistical, commercial, production control, accounting, management, systems analysis, operational research.
Specialized areas: Hardware and software evaluation.

RATIONELL PLANERING AB*
Hagavägen 85, Solna
Telephone: (08) 27-15-25

Officer
Kaj Sifvert, *Managing Director*

Services Available
Consultation, preparation of data, systems analysis.

Fields of Application
Project planning, scheduling and control mainly using network planning; total project management.
Specialized areas: Project planning in technical as well as administrative fields.

Training
Courses in network planning (2–3 days).

Sweden – Consultants

SEMKA AB*
Prästgårdsgatan 30, Sundbyberg
Telephone: (08) 281700

Officer
Gunnar Ekman, *President*

Coding Languages
FORTRAN, COBOL, PL/1.

Services Available
Advice, preparation of data, programming, software packages.

Fields of Application
Operations research, media and marketing planning, design of experiments, production control.

AB SAM SJÖBERG*
Blodboksgatan 35, V. Fröllinda
Telephone: (031) 290244

Officer
Sam Sjöberg

Coding Languages
Assembly-Level, PL/1, FORTRAN IV.

Services Available
Consultation, programming, systems analysis.

Fields of Application
Production control, management, operational research.
Specialized areas: Self-adaptive systems for production control.

Training
Three-week courses in systems analysis.

SD STOCKHOLMS DATATJÄNST AB
Rindögatan 40, Fack, S-100 52 Stockholm 29
Telephone: (08) 670745

Officers
Björn Sundström, *General Manager*
Olle Källhammar, *Technical Manager*

Computer Installation
BURROUGHS B3500–internal storage: 60K bytes; magnetic tapes: 4 9-track; 1 line printer. *On-line satellite computers*: multiline controls, 4 on-line adaptable.

Coding Languages
COBOL, RPG, FORTRAN.

Services Available
Advice, programming, software packages, documentation, preparation of data, systems analysis. Operate on a self-service, block time, open shop and time-sharing basis.

Fields of Application
Commercial, accounting, systems analysis.
Specialized areas: Sales analysis, analysis.

Training
Courses for staff degreed from Royal Institute of Technology, electronic division (doctor), aeronautical division.

SYSTEMS PROGRAMMING LTD. SVENSKA AB (SPL INTERNATIONAL)*
Birger Jarlsgatan 7, 111 45 Stockholm
Telephone: 08-232090

Officer
Marketing Director: Sture Karlsson

Coding Languages
ALGOL, COBOL, DAC-SAAB, FORTRAN, 301 and 1301 Machine Code, PLAN-ICL, RPG, 360 and Spectra Assembler.

Services Available
Consultation, programming, education and training, operators, software packages, documentation, systems analysis.

Fields of Application
All.
Specialized areas: Banking systems, communication systems, MIS.

Training
Real-time courses (10–14 days).

SYSTEMKONSULT AKTIEBOLAG*
Stortorget 9, 252 20 Hälsingborg
Telephone: (042) 13-06-00

Officer
Sven G. Dahlbo, *Manager*

Service Available
Consultation.

Fields of Application
Administrative data processing, office organization.

AB TELEPLAN
Fack, S-171 20 Solna
Telephone: 0046 08 981000

Officers
G. Stein, *Managing Director*
T. Wikland, *Technical Manager*

Computer Installation
ICL 1902A–operating system: Executive/GEORGE; internal storage: 384K bits; magnetic tapes: 4 9-track; magnetic discs: 1 EDS; 1 line printer.

Coding Languages
COBOL, FORTRAN, Assembler.

Services Available
Advice, programming, software packages, documentation, systems analysis, offer valuation. Operate on a closed shop basis.

Fields of Application
Scientific, statistical, management, systems analysis, operational research.
Specialized areas: Linear programming, analysis, planning.

SERVICE BUREAUX

ADB PRODUKTION AB
Strandbergsgatan 49 S-112 51 Stockholm
Telephone: (08) 13 13 90

Officer
Jan Nordlund, *Director*

Computer Installation
IBM 370/135–internal storage: 144K bits; magnetic tapes: 4 3420; magnetic discs: 5 660; 1 line printer.

Coding Language
COBOL.

Services Available
Advice, preparation of data, programming, system analysis, computer time. Operate on a closed shop and block time basis.

Fields of Application
Commercial, accounting.

ADB–SYSTEM AB
Viktoragatan 39, Box 19049, 40012 Göteborg 19
Telephone: (031) 813410

Also at:
Bryggargatan 14, Box 354, Borås
Telephone: (033) 1384-88

Officer
Bertil Skoog, *Director (Göteborg)*

Computer Installation
UNIVAC 1050–operating system: OPR; internal storage: 32,768 6-bit positions; magnetic tapes: 4 Uniservo IIIA, 4 Uniservo VI C; 1 line printer.

ICL 1902A–internal storage: 16K 24-bit words; magnetic tapes: 4; 1 line printer.

Coding Languages
PAL (Univac 1050); COBOL, PLAN (ICL 1902A).

Services Available
Advice, operators, programming, systems analysis. Operate on a closed shop basis.

Field of Application
Commercial.
Specialized areas: Standardized commercial programmes.

AR SERVICE I SUNDSVALL AB*
Rådhusgatan 18 A, Sundsvall
Telephone: (060) 11-90-90

Officer
Arne Wiklund, *Manager*

Services Available
Advice, preparation of data, programming.

Fields of Application
Commercial, accounting.

AB AURIGA*
Surbrunnsgatan 10, 114 21 Stockholm
Telephone: 150620

Officer
Elbe Kruse

Services Available
Consultation, programming, operators, software packages, documentation, preparation of data, systems analysis, Operate on a block time open shop basis.

Field of Application
Commercial.
Specialized area: Optical reading.

AUTOCODE AB*
Ankdammsgatan 40, 17143 Solna
Telephone: (08) 83-43-95

Officer
Lennart von Sydow, *Director*

Computer Installation
PDP-8–internal storage: 8K bits; magnetic tapes: 4; high speed paper tape line printers.

Coding Languages
PAL, ALFACODE, FORTRAN.

Services Available
Electronics design and interfacing with esp. PDP-8. Operate on a closed shop basis.

Fields of Application
Application of special computers in a real time environment of process control.
Specialized area: Computer-aided typesetting of directories.

AUTOMATION CENTER AB*
Slaklhusgatan 39-41, Box 51, Johanneshov 1
Telephone: (08) 39-04-00

Also at:
Göteborgsvägen 97, Mölndal 2
Telephone: (031) 87-00-50

Hamnvägen 7, Kristinehamn 3
Telephone: (0550) 188-88

Drottninggatan 12, Karlstad 1
Telephone: (054) 113-32

Hindbyvägen 4, Malmö 15
Telephone: (040) 94-70-30

Officers
Karl-Erik Kärlin, *Director (Johanneshov)*
Gunnar Anderson, *Manager (Mölndal)*
Roger Lindbland, *Manager (Kristinehamn)*
Jimmy Cederman, *Manager (Karlstad)*
Rune Drakenborg, *Manager (Malmö)*

Computer Installation
Johanneshov, Mölndal and Karlstad:
IBM 360/30–internal storage: 64K bits each; magnetic tapes: 5, 4 and 6 respectively; magnetic discs: 3 2311, 2 2311 and 2 2311 respectively; 1 line printer each.

Services Available
Advice, operators, preparation of data, programming, systems analysis.

Fields of Application
Commercial, industrial.

BONNIERDATA AB
Fack, 100 31 Stockholm 21
Telephone: 246200

Officers
Bo Falk, *President*
Boo Marions, *Vice-President*

Sweden – Service Bureaux

Computer Installations
UNIVAC 1106–operating system: EXEC 8; internal storage: 262K 36-bit words; magnetic tapes: 10 Uniservo VIII C 8 Uniservo XII; magnetic drums: 4 Fastrand III; 2 line printers. *Remote processing features*: 11 cathode ray tubes, 19 teletypewriters, 7 remote batch terminals

Coding Languages
COBOL, FORTRAN, Assembler.

Contemplated Equipment
Univac 1106.

Services Available
Advice, programming, education and training, operators, software packages, documentation, preparation of data and systems analysis. Operate on a remote access, closed shop and time-sharing basis.

Fields of Application
Statistical, commercial, production control, accounting and operational research.
Specialized areas: Linear programming, analysis, payroll and structural engineering.

BROSTROM SHIPPING COMPANY
Data Processing Department
Box 2521, S-403 17 Göteborg

Computer Installations
MOHAWK PPS 2400–internal storage: 32K bytes; magnetic tapes: 1 MDS 2433; magnetic discs: 2 MDS; 1 line printer.

IBM 370/145–operating system: OS; internal storage: 512K bytes; magnetic tapes: 4 3420; magnetic discs: 12 2319; 2 line printers.

Coding Languages
RPG, COBOL, Assembler.

Services Available
Advice, programming, education and training, operators, software packages, documentation, registration data and systems analysis. Operate on a closed shop basis. Available only to companies within the shipping group.

Fields of Application
Statistical, accounting, tracking and documentation.

Training
Courses for people within the company's group: EDP Introduction course (500 people), Basic Course EDP (80 people), Project Administration (45 people).

BURROUGHS AB*
Banérgatan 10, S-115 22 Stockholm NÖ
Telephone: (08) 635880

Also at:
Berzeliigatan 12-14, Göteborg
Rönneholmsvägen 26, Malmö

Officer
Thorbjörn Nilsson, *Director*

Computer Installation
Stockholm:
BURROUGHS B3500–operating system: MCP; internal storage: 1 million bits; magnetic tapes: 8 9-track, 1 7-track; 1 line printer.

Coding Languages
COBOL, FORTRAN, Burroughs Advanced Assembler.

Services Available
Advice, software packages, systems analysis. Operate on a block time basis. Available only to Burroughs computer customers and block time customers.

Fields of Application
Scientific, statistical, commercial, production control, accounting, management, operational research.

Training
Courses for customers.

AB BYGG-ADB*
Vretenvägen 8, Solna
Telephone: (08) 29-02-70

Officer
Christer Ugander, *Managing Director*

Computer Installation
IBM 360/30–operating system: BPS; internal storage: 16K bits; magnetic tapes: 4 2401; 1 line printer.

IBM 360/30–operating system: DOS; internal storage: 64K 8-bit bytes; magnetic tapes: 5 2401; magnetic discs: 5 2311; 2 line printers.

Coding Languages
Assembler, RPG, COBOL, FORTRAN, PL/1.

Services Available
Advice, preparation of data, programming, software packages, systems analysis. Operate on closed shop basis.

Fields of Application
Accounting, payrolls, invoicing, systems analysis, punching, OCR.
Specialized areas: Automatic data processing for the building industry, e.g. estimating, planning, cost control and machine costs.

Training
Network planning courses for the standard package.

CONTROL DATA SWEDEN AB
CDC Data Services (Scandinavia)
Box 42107, S-0126 12 Stockholm 42

Officers
M. J. Elton, *Managing Director*
C. Enquist, *Sales Manager*
G. Carlsson, *Analytical Services Manager*
J. Hedman, *Operations Manager*

Computer Installation
CDC 6600–operating system: SCOPE; internal storage: 131,072 60-bit words; magnetic tapes: 8 607, 2 609; magnetic discs: 1 6638, 8 841; 2 line printers. *Remote processing features*: remote on-line batch terminals serving Denmark, Finland, Norway and Sweden.

Coding Languages
FORTRAN, COBOL, ALGOL, COMPASS, SIMULA.

Contemplated Equipment
CDC 1700 remote batch synchronous terminal service; CDC Cyber 70 interactive asynchronous terminal service.

Services Available
Advice, programming, education and training, software packages, preparation of data, systems analysis. Operate on a remote access, closed shop and block time basis.

Sweden – Service Bureaux

Fields of Application
Scientific, statistical, management, systems analysis, operational research.
Specialized areas: Linear programming, investment, structural engineering, simulation.

Training
Courses in advanced programming, circuit analysis, corporate modelling, data management, linear programming, simulation methods and structural analysis.

COUNTER DATA AB*
Box 30012, 104 25 Stockholm 30
Telephone: (08) 54-12-15

Officer
Wilford Lindgren, *Director*

Computer Installation
ICL 1901–internal storage: 16K bits.

Coding Languages
PLAN, COBOL, FORTRAN.

Services Available
Advice, preparation of data, programming, systems analysis. Operate on an open shop basis.

Fields of Applications
Statistical, commercial, production control, accounting, management, systems analysis.

DATA LOGIC AB
Ankdammsgayan 25, 171 43 Solna

Also at:
Kungsgatan 10, 632 21 Eskilstuna
Klangfårgsgatan 11, 421 52 Västra Frölunda
Malmborgsgatan 4 III, 211 38 Malmö

Officer
Sune Eliasson, *Managing Director*

Services Available
Advice, programming, education and training, software packages, documentation, systems analysis.

Fields of Application
Scientific, statistical, commercial, production control, accounting, management, systems analysis.

AB DATAORGANISATION*
Tauastgatan 26B, 117 24 Stockholm
Telephone: 438393, 438313

Officers
Lars Brikell
Nils Persson

Computer Installation
SIEMENS 4004/35–internal storage: 524,284 bits; magnetic tapes: 4; magnetic discs: 3 IBM 2311; 1 line printer.

Coding Languages
COBOL, Assembler.

Services Available
Consultation, programming, operators, preparation of data, systems analysis. Operate on a block time basis.

Fields of Application
Statistical, commercial, accounting, production control.

DATAPROJEKT AB*
Nordmarksvägen 6, S-123 51 FARSTA-Stockholm
Telephone: (08) 64-19-20

Officer
Ing. E. Arkedal

Coding Languages
ALGOL, ALGOL-GENIUS, FORTRAN, machine-oriented programming languages.

Services Available
Programming, software packages, systems analysis.

Fields of Application
Administrative routines, technical/scientific problems.
Specialized areas: Production control of hydro-thermal electric systems (dynamic progr.).

DATARUTIN AB
Segelbätsu 9, 112 64 Stockholm

Officer
Gunnar Gerggren, *Manager*

Computer Installation
IBM 360/25–operating system: DOS; internal storage: 32K bits; magnetic tapes: 4 2415; magnetic discs: 3 2311; 1 line printer.

Coding Languages
Assembler, COBOL.

Contemplated Equipment
IBM 370/125.

Services Available
Advice, programming, operators, software packages, documentation, preparation of data, systems analysis. Operate on a block time and open shop basis.

Fields of Application
Statistical, commercial, accounting, management.
Specialized areas: Sales analysis, payroll.

AB DATA-SERVICE*
Box 93, Danderyd 1
Telephone: (08) 755-27-20

Also at:
Andra Långgatan 44, Göteborg 7
Telephone: (031) 42-03-00

Hermansgatan 5, Malmö
Telephone: (040) 93-55-30

Officers
Baltzar Grill, *Director*
Gunnar Hedelin, *Manager (Göteborg)*
Paul-Erik Jensen, *Manager (Malmö)*

Computer Installation
Danderyd:
IBM 360/40–internal storage: 128K bits; magnetic tapes: 7; magnetic discs: 3; 1 line printer.

BULL GENERAL ELECTRIC Gamma 10–internal storage: 4K bits; 1 line printer.

SIEMENS 4004/45–internal storage: 131K bits; magnetic tapes: 6; magnetic discs: 2; 1 line printer.

Göteborg:
BULL GENERAL ELECTRIC GE 425–internal storage: 32K bits; magnetic tapes: 6; magnetic discs: 3; 1 line printer.

Malmö
SIEMENS 4004/45–internal storage: 131K bits; magnetic tapes: 6; magnetic discs: 3; 1 line printer.

Services Available
Advice, operators, preparation of data, programming, systems analysis.

Field of Application
Commercial.

AB DATA-SERVICE
Box 20 106, 161 20 Bromma, Stockholm
Telephone: 08 730 05 60

Also at:
Box 12 049, 200 23 Malmö 12
Telephone: 040 18 00 30

Box 31 098, 400 32 Göteborg 31
Telephone: 031 42 03 00

Box 2073, 600 02 Norrköping
Telephone: 011 12 98 90

Officers
Stockholm:
Anders Rönn, *President*
Rolf Levin, *Sales Manager*
Bengt Glantzberg, *Technical Director*
Lars Jernberg, *Branch Office Manager*

Malmö and Göteborg:
Roland Lindqvist, *Branch Office Manager*

Norrköping:
Lars-Olaf Löfström, *Branch Office Manager*

Computer Installations
Stockholm:
BURROUGHS B4700–operating system: MCPV; internal storage: 3,200K bits; magnetic tapes: 12; magnetic discs; 4 line printers. *Remote processing features*.

Göteborg:
BURROUGHS B3700–operating system: MCPV; internal storage: 1,200K bits; magnetic tapes: 7; magnetic discs; 1 line printer.

Malmö
BURROUGHS B4700–operating system: MCPV; internal storage: 1,200K bits; magnetic tapes: 7; magnetic discs; 1 line printer.

Norrköping:
BURROUGHS B3700–operating system: MCPV; internal storage: 1,200K bits; magnetic tapes: 7; magnetic discs; 1 line printer.

Coding Language
COBOL.

Contemplated Equipment
EVL Remote Batch Terminals.

Services Available
Advice, programming, education and training, software packages, preparation of data, systems analysis. Operate on a closed shop and block time basis.

Fields of Application
Statistical, commercial, production control, accounting, management.
Specialized areas: Sales analysis, payroll, invoicing, stock control and bookkeeping accounts receivable.

Training
Only courses for customer personnel using standard packages.

DATEMA AB*
Huvudstagatan 1, Solna
Telephone: (08) 834020

Officer
Kjell Hellberg, *Managing Director*

Computer Installation
IBM 360/25–operating system: DOS; internal storage: 30K bytes; magnetic tapes: 4; magnetic discs: 3; 1 line printer. *Remote processing features*: IBM 2780 and IBM 2770 terminals.

IBM 360/50–operating system: Time-sharing; internal storage: 512K bits; magnetic discs: 6 2311. *Remote processing features*: IBM 1050, 2740, TTY, CRT.

Coding Languages
COBOL, FORTRAN, BASIC, Assembler.

Services Available
Advice, programming, software packages, systems analysis. Operate on a closed shop and time-sharing basis.

Fields of Application
Business administration, mathematical programming.

EKONOMISK DATA BEHANDLING AB
Fack, 161 Bromma 20
Telephone: (08) 730 05 75

Officer
Lars Berglöf, *Director*

Services Available
Education and training.

Field of Application
Accounting.
Specialized areas: Analysis, payroll.

ELEKTRO DATA BOLAGET (EDB)*
Eriksgatan 48, Stockholm K
Telephone: (08) 24-72-40

Also at:
Petersgatan 105, Norrköping
Telephone: (011) 12-98-90

Ånstagatan 6-8, 7106 Örebro
Telephone: (019) 14 04 50.

Gustav Adolfstorg 49, 20312 Malmö
Telephone: (040) 11 77 10.

Officers
C. Olivijn, *President*
R. Lindqvist, *Vice-President*
J. Levander (*Stockholm*)
Gunnar Nyström (*Norrköping*)
B. Wärmé (*Örebro*)
C. Birgersson (*Malmö*)

Computer Installation
Stockholm:
IBM 360/40–operating system: DOS; internal storage: 192K bits; magnetic tapes: 8; magnetic discs: 1 2314; 2 line printers.

Norrköping:
IBM 360/30–operating system: DOS; internal storage: 64K bits; magnetic tapes: 5; magnetic discs: 4 2311; 1 line printer.

Örebro:
IBM 360/20–internal storage: 16K bits.

Coding Languages
Assembler, COBOL.

Services Available
Advice, operators, preparation of data, programming, systems analysis. Operate on a closed shop basis.

Field of Application
Commercial.
Specialized areas: Accounting: general ledger, cost accounting, accounts receivable, payroll-billing, sales statistics, inventory control, organization systems.

HALMSTAD DATASERVICE AB*
Svetsaregatan, Box 16, Halmstad 1
Telephone: 035-101133

Officer
Sigvard Hultman

Computer Installation
BULL GENERAL ELECTRIC Gamma 30–internal storage: 20K bits; magnetic tapes: 6; 1 line printer.

Coding Languages
Assembly, COBOL.

Services Available
Advice, operators, preparation of data, programming, software packages, systems analysis. Operate on a self-service, open shop and block time basis.

Fields of Application
Statistical, commercial, accounting, salary, etc.

HONEYWELL BULL AB
Sveavägen 163, Stockholm 23
Telephone: (08) 24-66-20

Officer
Sture Genberg, *Manager*

Computer Installation
BULL GENERAL ELECTRIC Gamma 30–internal storage: 20K bits; magnetic tapes: 8; 1 line printer.

RCA 501–internal storage: 65K bits; magnetic tapes: 7; 1 line printer.

Services Available
Advice, operators, preparation of data, programming, software packages, systems analysis.

Fields of Application
Scientific, commercial.

ICL DATA AB
Industrivägen 10, 171 88 Solna
Telephone: 830700

Officer
Björn Winckler

Computer Installation
ICL 1903A–operating system: GEORGE 2 and 3; internal storage: 1,572,864 bits; magnetic tapes: 5 9-track, 4 7-track, 5 2802; 2 line printers. *Remote processing features.*

Coding Languages
PLAN, COBOL, ALGOL, FORTRAN.

Services Available
Consultation, programming, education and training, operators, software packages, documentation, preparation of data, systems analysis. Operate on a block time, closed shop, remote access and time-sharing basis.

Fields of Application
Scientific, statistical, commercial, production control, accounting, management.
Specialized areas: PERT, inventory control.

Training
Programming and software courses.

IBM SVENSKA AB
IBM Data Center Stockholm
Sandhamnsgatan 71, Stockholm
Telephone: (08) 63 10 60

Also:
IBM Data Center Göteborg
Box 195, Göteborg
Telephone: (031) 420880

IBM Data Center Malmö
Box 4104, Malmö 4
Telephone: (040) 7 37 50

IBM Data Centre Västerås
Stora Torget 2, Västerås
Telephone: (021) 11-02-80

Officers
Per Stölfors, *Manager for Sweden*
Christen Odén *(Stockholm)*
Ove Orsvärn *(Göteborg)*
Bengt Cederwald *(Malmö)*
Willie Andersson (*Västerås*)

Computer Installation
Stockholm:
IBM 360/65 (2)–internal storage: 1,028K bits each.

Göteborg:
IBM 360/50–internal storage: 512K bits.

Malmö:
IBM 360/50–internal storage: 512K bits.

Västerås:
IBM 360/40–internal storage: 256K bits.

Coding Languages
FORTRAN, COBOL, PL/1, RPG.

Services Available
Operators, preparation of data, programming, systems analysis. Operate on a self-service, closed shop, open shop, remote access and block time basis.

Fields of Application
Scientific and commercial, both pre-planned and individually designed.

INDUSTRIDATA AB
Albygatan 102, Fack, S-171 20 Solna 1
Telephone: (08) 98-03-50

Offices at:
Stockholm, Göteborg, Linköping, Malmö and Västerås

Officers
Bertil Brynander, *Managing Director*
Rune Algesten, *Assistant Director*
Per-Axel Liljequist, *Technical Director*

Computer Installation
DATASAAB D22 (5)—internal storage: 1,500K bits; magnetic tapes: 6; magnetic discs: 6; 1 line printer.

BULL GENERAL ELECTRIC GE 635—operating system GECOS III; internal storage: 160K bits; magnetic tapes: 8; magnetic discs: 5; 3 line printers. *On-line satellite computer*: DN 355. *Remote processing features*: TTY, GE 115.

Coding Languages
ALGOL, ALGOL-GENIUS, FORTRAN, COBOL, DAC, GEMAP, BASIC, SIMSCRIPT.

Services Available
Advice, operators, preparation of data, programming, software packages, systems analysis. Operate on a closed shop, remote access, block time and time-sharing basis.

Fields of Application
Scientific, commercial, statistical, production control, accounting, management, systems analysis.
Specialized areas: Sales analysis, linear programming, investment analysis, payroll, structural engineering.

Training
Courses in application of computers to commercial, technical and statistical problems; courses in coding languages (1-5 days).

KOMMERSIELL DATABEHANDLING AB
Lergöksgatan 1, 421 22 Västra Frölunda

Officers
Sven-Göran Ehrnlund, *Managing Director*
Agneta Magnusson, *Manager*
Jerry Johansson, *Manager*

Computer Installation
ICL 1902S (2)—operating system: GEORGE 2; internal storage: 24K bits each; magnetic tapes: 4 1971 each; magnetic discs: 2 EDS 8 each; 1 line printer each.

Coding Languages
PLAN, COBOL, ALGOL, FORTRAN.

Contemplated Equipment
Off-line terminal equipment.

Services Available
Advice, programming, education and training, software packages, documentation, preparation of data, systems analysis. Operate on a closed shop basis.

Fields of Application
Statistical, commercial, production control, accounting, management.
Specialized areas: Sales analysis, payroll, book-keeping, sales ledger.

Training
Courses in book-keeping, stock control and payroll applications, provided on special request.

KOMMUN-DATA AB
Fack, S-126 12 Stockholm 42

Officers
Rune Skarström, *General Manager*
Gunnar Karlström, *Deputy Manager*

Computer Installation
UNIVAC 1106—operating system: EXEC 8; internal storage: 6,900K bits; magnetic tapes: 2 Uniservo 12, 8 Uniservo VI C; 2 line printers.

UNIVAC 1107—operating system: EXEC 2; internal storage: 2,300K bits; magnetic tapes: 8 Uniservo VI C, 9 Uniservo 16; 8 line printers. *On-line satellite computer*: 1.

Coding Languages
COBOL, ANSI-COBOL, FORTRAN, Assembler.

Services Available
Advice, programming, education and training, preparation of data, systems analysis. Operate on a closed shop and time-sharing basis.

Field of Application
Accounting.

LANTBRUKSDATA
63184 Eskilstuna
Telephone: 016 21170

Officers
Lennart Nagrell, *Managing Director*
Bertil Holmer, *Research and Development Manager*
Goran Ledell, *Operations Manager*
Orvar Larsson, *Projects Manager*

Computer Installations
IBM 370/145—operating systems: OS, MFT, HASP; internal storage: 512K bits; magnetic tapes: 15 3420-5; magnetic discs: 13 2319, 12 3330; 3 line printers. *Remote processing features*: 3780 plus Data 100.

IBM 370/135—operating system: DOS; internal storage: 144K bits, magnetic tapes: 3 3420-3; magnetic discs: 6 2319; 1 line printer. *On-line satellite computers*: System 7.

BULL GENERAL ELECTRIC GE 425—operating system: DAPS; internal storage: 128K bits; magnetic tapes: 5 MTH 405, 4 MTH 403; magnetic discs: 3 DSU 160; 2 line printers.

RCA 301; internal storage: 40K bits, magnetic tapes: 12; 1 line printer.

Coding Language
COBOL.

Contemplated Equipment
PERTEC 3700 computer.

Sweden – Service Bureaux

Services Available
Advice, programming, education and training, operators, software packages, documentation and preparation of data. Operate on a remote access, closed shop and block time basis.

Fields of Application
Scientific (biology), commercial, accounting and banking.
Specialized areas: Sales analysis, payroll.

LITTON BUSINESS SYSTEMS AB DATASERVICE*
Vretenvägen 2, Solna
Telephone: (08) 98 11 00

Officer
Gérard Kauffmann, *Manager*

NATIONAL CASH REGISTER CO. OF SWEDEN AB (NCR)*
Kungsgaten 70, Stockholm C
Telephone: (08) 22-83-20

Officer
B. Wagner, *Manager*

Computer Installation
NCR 315/100 – internal storage: 30K bits; 1 line printer.

Services Available
Advice, operators, preparation of data, programming.

NORRDATA AB
Bankgatan 10, 852 33 Sundsvall
Telephone: 0600 150710

Also at:
Kanalgatan 71, 931 00 Skellefteå
Telephone: 0910-77430

Kvartermästargatan 10, 951 00 Luleå
Telephone: 0920-20520

Regeringsgatan 42, 111 53 Stockholm
Telephone: 08-200202

Officer
Börje Carlsson, *Managing Director*

Computer Installation
ICL 1903A – operating system: GEORGE 2; internal storage: 1,228,800 bits; magnetic tapes: 2 1971, 4 2504; magnetic discs: 3 2802; 1 line printer. *Remote processing features*: ICL 7920 scanner, IBM 370/145.

Coding Language
COBOL.

Services Available
Advice, programming, education and training, preparation of data, systems analysis. Operate on a closed shop and time-sharing basis.

Fields of Application
Statistical, commercial, production control, accounting.
Specialized area: Medical research.

ÖREBRO DATA AB (ÖDAB)*
Klostergatan 11-13, Örebro
Telephone: (019) 12-48-80

Officer
Ake Frodin, *Manager*

Computer Installation
IBM 360/20 – internal storage: 16K bits; magnetic tapes: 4.

Services Available
Advice, preparation of data, programming.

Field of Application
Administrative data processing.

PN-DATA AB & ACO. DATA-BOLAGEN*
Huvudstagatan 12, Solna
Telephone: (08) 83-65-20, 83-65-85

Officer
Per Norell, *Managing Director*

Computer Installation
UNIVAC 9300 – internal storage: 16K bits; magnetic tapes: 4 Uniservo VI; 1 line printer.

Coding Languages
RPG, Assembly, COBOL.

Contemplated Equipment
Univac 9400.

Services Available
Advice, operators, preparation of data, programming, software packages, systems analysis. Operate on a closed shop and block time basis.

Fields of Application
Commercial, systems analysis.
Specialized areas: Hotels and restaurants.

Training
Training courses for own customers on own systems during one or two days.

PROGRESS RATIONALISERINGS AB
Abygatan 109, S-171 54 Solna
Telephone: (08) 289450

Officer
Ing. Hans Wenger, *Manager*

Coding Languages
COBOL, Assembler.

Services Available
Advice, programming, software packages, systems analysis.

Fields of Application
Commercial, production control.
Specialized areas: Warehouse stock control, purchasing routines.

RATIONELLA DATA AB*
Kvartermästaregatan 10, Box 238, Luleå
Telephone: (0920) 20520

Officer
Roland Carlsson, *Manager*

Computer Installation
IBM 360/20 – internal storage: 8K bits; 1 line printer.

Coding Languages
COBOL, RPG.

Services Available
Advice, operators, preparation of data, programming, software packages, systems analysis.

Fields of Application
Commercial, accounting, production control.

RDB DATABYRÅ AB*
Instrumentvägen 10, 126 53 Hägersten-Stockholm
Telephone: (08) 180290

Officer
Sune Liljenstam, *Managing Director*

Computer Installation
DATASAAB D220M–internal storage: 144K bits; magnetic tapes: 4; magnetic discs: 2; 1 line printer.

Coding Language
COBOL.

Services Available
Advice, preparation of data, programming, software packages, systems analysis. Operate on an open shop and time-sharing basis.

Fields of Application
Statistical, commercial, accounting, management.

REELLTIDS-DATA AB*
Nytorgsg 29, Stockholm 11622
Telephone: (08) 23 18 70

Services Available
Advice, programming, systems analysis.

SAAB-SCANIA AB
Data Service Section
S-581 88 Linköping
Telephone: 013 11 15 00

Officers
Sven Yngvell, *General Manager*
Gunnar Hallin, *Manager, EDP Techniques and Methodology*
Lars Gunnarsson, *Manager, Systems Development and Programming*
Sven Sandin, *Manager, Scientific Programming*
Gunnar Hermanson, *Manager, Sales*
Stig Jonsson, *Manager, Data Processing Services*

Computer Installation
DATASAAB D22–operating system: OS22M; internal storage: 3,145,728 bits; magnetic tapes: 12 9-track, 1 7-track; magnetic discs: 24; 2 line printers. *On-line satellite computer*: DATASAAB D5/30 (Communications Processor). *Remote processing features*: Typewriters, CRT terminals and satellite computers.

DATASAAB D22–operating system: OS22M; internal storage: 2,359,296 bits; magnetic tapes: 7 9-track, 1 7-track; magnetic discs: as above; 1 line printer. *On-line computer satellite computer*: as above.

DATASAAB D22–operating system: OS22M; internal storage: 2,359,296 bits; magnetic tapes: 8 9-track; magnetic discs: 12; 2 line printers. *On-line satellite computers*: DATASAAB D5/20 (Communications Processor). *Remote processing features*: Typewriters, CRT terminals and satellite computers.

DATASAAB D22–operating system: OS22M; internal storage: 2,359,296 bits; magnetic tapes: 4 9-track; magnetic discs: 6; 1 line printer.

DATASAAB D21–operating system: OS21; internal storage: 786,432 bits; magnetic tapes: 7 9-track, 1 7-track, 2 14-track; 1 line printer.

DATASAAB D21–operating system: OS21; internal storage: 786,432 bits; magnetic tapes: 8 14-track, 1 7-track; 1 line printer.

IBM 7070–internal storage: 500K bits; magnetic tapes: 11 729/II.

IBM 1401–internal storage: 24K bits; magnetic tapes: 2 729/II.

PDP-11/20–operating system: DOS; internal storage: 262,144 bits. *On-line satellite computer*: attached to PDP-11/45 below.

PDP-11/45–operating system: DOS; internal storage: 393,216 bits; magnetic tapes: 2 9-track; magnetic disc: 1. *On-line satellite computer*: attached to PDP-11/20 above.

HEWLETT PACKARD 2000F–operating system: Time-sharing BASIC; internal storage: 524,288 bits; magnetic tape: 1 9-track; magnetic disc: 1, and 1 drum; *On-line satellite computer*: 1 Communications Processor of 8K 16-bit words. *Remote processing features*: Typewriter terminals.

Coding Languages
ALGOL, ALGOL-GENIUS, COBOL, FORTRAN, BASIS.

Contemplated Equipment
IBM 360/20, DATASAAB D23.

Services Available
Advice, programming, operators and systems analysis. Operate on a remote access and closed shop basis.

Fields of Application
Scientific, commercial, production control, accounting, management, systems analysis and operational research.

SAMKONTOR AB*
Studentgatan 1, Malmö 4
Telephone: (040) 747-20

Officer
Lennart Bengtson, *Director*

Computer Installation
BULL GENERAL ELECTRIC Gamma 10–internal storage: 4K bits; 1 line printer.

Services Available
Advice, preparation of data, programming.

SIFFER-SERVICE DATACENTRAL AB
Kungsgatan 74, Box 430, S-101 25 Stockholm
Telephone: 08 233800

Officers
Rein Puusepp, *General Manager*
Sven-Olof Södervall, *Production Manager*
Göran Larsson, *Systems Manager*

Computer Installation
UNIVAC 9400–operating system: OS/4; internal storage: 65K bits; magnetic tapes: 6 Uniservo VIC; magnetic discs: 2 8414; 1 line printer.

UNIVAC 1050 (2)–operating system: TOS; internal storage: 20K bits each; magnetic tapes: 3 Uniservo VIC each; 1 line printer each.

Coding Languages
Assembler, RPG, FORTRAN, COBOL (9400); Assembler, COBOL (1050).

Contemplated Equipment
Univac 9700.

Services Available
Advice, programming, operators, software packages, documentation, preparation of data, systems analysis, COM-service. Operate on a closed shop and block time basis.

Fields of Application
Statistical, commercial, accounting, management.
Specialized areas: Market research, banking.

SKOGSBRUKETS DATACENTRAL (SDC)*
Björneborgsgatan 37, Fack, 851 01 Sundsvall 1
Telephone: (060) 154150

Also at:
Klövergatan 2, Fack, 56101 Huskvarna 1
Telephone: (036) 132620

Officers
Olof Lindbäck, *Manager*
Per-Erik Persson, *Training, Foreign Relations*

Computer Installation
IBM 360/50—operating system: OS-MFT; internal storage: 384K bits; magnetic tapes: 3 2401/3, 8 2401/2 (Pool); magnetic discs: 3 2311, 1 2314; 3 line printers.
IBM 360/40—operating system: OS-MFT; internal storage: 128K bits; magnetic tapes: 8 2401/2, 8 2401/2 (Pool); magnetic discs: 4 2311; 1 line printer.
IBM 360/40—operating system: OS-MFT; internal storage: 128K bits; magnetic tapes: 5 2401/1; magnetic discs: 1 2314; 2 line printers.

Coding Languages
COBOL, PL/1.

Services Available
Advice, preparation of data, programming, systems analysis. Operate on a closed shop and block time basis. Priority given to Swedish forestry.

Fields of Application
Commercial, accounting, management.
Specialized areas: Data processing for forest companies.

Training
Courses on introduction to EDP (5 days); Introduction to IBM 360 (5 days); COBOL Programming (10 days); Systems Analysis (5 days).

CARL SODERBERG AB
Data Department
Strandbergsgatan 57 III, S-112 51 Stockholm
Telephone: (08) 540100

Officers
Göran Kjellberg, *Data Manager*
Bo Strömbäck, *Systems Manager*
Lennart Rundqvist, *Operations Manager*

Computer Installation
ICL 1902A—internal storage: 393,216 bits; magnetic tapes: 2; 1 line printer 1933/2.

Coding Languages
PLAN, COBOL.

Services Available
Advice, operators, preparation of data. Operate on a self-service, closed shop and open shop basis.

Field of Application
Commercial.
Specialized areas: Stock book-keeping and control, salaries, for food store chain, use of barmarked documents.

SÖDERTALJE DATA AB
Oxelvagen 42, Nacka
Telephone: (08) 773-05-00

Officer
Charlie Lundström, *Director*

Computer Installation
BURROUGHS B500—magnetic tapes: 4; 1 line printer.

Services Available
Advice, preparation of data, programming.

SPARBANKERNAS DATACENTRALER AB*
Fack, 103 20, Stockholm 16
Telephone: (08) 14 10 20

Also at:
Göteborg, Linköping and Malmö

Stockholm:
IBM 370/155—operating system: OS/DOS; internal storage: 1,024K bits; magnetic tapes: 12 2401/6; magnetic discs: 1 2314, 1 Memorex 660; 3 line printers. *On-line satellite computer*: IBM 3967.

IBM 360/40—operating system: OS/DOS; internal storage: 256K bits; magnetic tapes: 5 2401, 1 2402, 1 2403; magnetic discs: 1 2314, 2 2311; 1 line printer. *Remote processing features*: 2701, 2702, 7772.

Göteborg:
IBM 370/155—operating system: OS; internal storage: 384K bits; magnetic tapes: 6 2401/5; magnetic discs: 1 2314, 2 2311; 2 line printers.

Linköping:
BULL GENERAL ELECTRIC Gamma 30 (2)—internal storage: 20K bits; magnetic tapes: 8 each; 2 line printers.

IBM 360/40—operating system: OS; internal storage: 256K bits; magnetic tapes: 6 2401/5; magnetic discs: 1 2314, 2 2311; 1 line printer.

Malmö:
IBM 360/50—operating system: 384K bits; magnetic tapes: 6 2401/5; magnetic discs: 2 2311, 1 Memorex 660; 2 line printers. *Remote processing features*: 2701, 7772.

Services Available
Advice, operators, preparation of data, programming, software packages, systems analysis. Operate on a closed shop and remote access basis. Available only to savings banks.

Fields of Application
Basic banking applications and bank customers' applications.
Specialized areas: Banking, real-time.

STANSRUTIN AB
Grondalsv, 110, Box 44011, 100 73 Stockholm 44
Telephone: (08) 774 2640

Officers
Tryggve Norin, *Director*
Svante Norin, *Director*

Sweden – Service Bureaux

Services Available
Preparation of data, programming.

Fields of Application
Specialized area: Selling of accessories.

STOCKHOLMS DATATJÄNST AB*
Kampementsgatan 28, Stockholm NO
Telephone: (08) 60-91-44

Officer
Björn Sundström, *Manager*

Services Available
Advice, preparation of data, programming, systems analysis.

Fields of Application
Commercial, scientific.

STROEDE AB
Fack, 423, 03 Torslanda
Telephone: Göteborg 513030

Officer
Åke Stroede, *Manager*

Computer Installation
ICL 1901A–internal storage: 16K bits; magnetic tapes: 4; 1 line printer.

Coding Languages
COBOL, PLAN.

Services Available
Consultation, programming, operators, preparation of data. Operate on a closed shop basis.

Fields of Application
Commercial, management.

SVENSKA ELEKTRONISKA DATA AB (SEDAB)*
Importörvägen 23, 121 73 Johanneshov
Telephone: (08) 91-01-70

Also at:
Sedab Stockholm AB
Brunnbyvägen 11,
121 73 Johanneshov
Telephone: 08/91 01 70

Sedab Servicebyrå AB
Storgatan 1, 851 06 Sundsvall
Telephone: 060/12 17 00

Sedab Databehandling AB
S. Kaserngatan 9, 291 00 Kristianstad
Telephone: 044/12 09 81

Sedab Malmö AB
Södergatan 12, 211 34 Malmö
Telephone: 040/742 45

Sedab Göteborg AB
Lilla Nygatan 2, 411 09 Göteborg
Telephone: 031/11 53 80

European centre: Lucerne (Switzerland)

Officers
Bengt Warden, *General Manager* (*Johanneshov*)
Lennart Henriksson, *General Manager* (*Johanneshov*)
Bo Karlsson, *General Manager* (*Sundsvall*)
Karl Olsson, *General Manager* (*Kristianstad*)
Sune Davidson, *General Manager* (*Malmö, Göteborg*)

Computer Installation
Johanneshov and Malmö:
IBM 360/40–operating systems: DOS; internal storage: 128K bits each; magnetic tapes: 7 2400 each; magnetic discs: 1 2314 each; 1 line printer.

Johanneshov:
IBM 360/20–internal storage: 8K bits; 1 line printer.

Kristianstad:
IBM 360/20–internal storage: 16K bits; magnetic tapes: 4; 1 line printer.

Sundsvall:
BULL GENERAL ELECTRIC Gamma 10–1 line printer.
BULL GENERAL ELECTRIC GE 120–internal storage: 24K bits; magnetic tapes: 5; 1 line printer.

Coding Languages
COBOL, Assembler, RPG.

Services Available
Consultation, operators, preparation of data, programming, software packages, systems analysis. Operate on a closed shop and block time basis.

Fields of Application
Statistical, commercial, accounting, management.

SIEMENS DATA SKANDINAVIEN
Norra Stationsgatan 63-65, S-109 35 Stockholm
Telephone: (08) 229640

Officer
B. Aslund, *Manager*

Computer Installation
SIEMENS 4064/45–operating system: PBS; internal storage: 2,048K bits; magnetic tapes: 10; magnetic tapes: 7; 2 line printers. *Remote processing features*.

Coding Languages
COBOL, FORTRAN, Assembler, ALGOL, ANSI-COBOL, PL/1, RPG.

Services Available
Advice, programming, education and training, operators, software packages, documentation, preparation of data, systems analysis. Operate on a self-service, remote access, closed shop, block time and open shop basis.

Fields of Application
Commercial, production control, accounting, management.
Specialized areas: Investment, analysis, payroll.

SVERIGES KREDITBANK ADB SERVICE*
Box 7042, 103 81 Stockholm 7
Telephone: 249000

Officer
Hans Larsson, *Manager*

Computer Installation
IBM 360/40–operating system: DOS; internal storage: 192K bits; magnetic tapes: 4 2401/004; magnetic discs: 1 2314; 1 line printer. *Remote processing features*: 2701.

Coding Languages
COBOL, A/L.

Services Available
Consultation, programming, systems analysis. Operate on a block time and closed shop basis. Service available to the Kreditbank's customers.

Fields of Application
Statistical, commercial, accounting.
Specialized area: Standard application packages.

TELEVERKETS INDUSTRIAVDELNING (TELI)*
Fack 14901 Nynäshamm
Telephone: 0752-12120

Computer Installation
ICL 1903/1–magnetic tapes: 8 ICL 1972/2; 1 line printer.
Remote processing features: telephone terminal ICL 7020.

Coding Languages
PLAN, COBOL, FORTRAN.

Fields of Application
Statistical, commercial, accounting.

TRASK DATASYSTEM AB
Stockholmsvägen 34, 182 74 Stocksund

Officers
G. Hellström, *Director*
Z. Horvath, *Director*
A. Bring, *Director*

Computer Installation
TRASK 2–internal storage: 1,280K bits; magnetic tapes: 2 Kennedy 8108; magnetic discs: 2 CDC 9425; 1 line printer. *On-line satellite computers*: 3 TRASK P200.

Coding Languages
ALGOL, Assembler.

Services Available
Programming, education and training, software packages, preparation of data, systems analysis. Operate on a self-service and open shop basis.

Fields of Application
Scientific, production control, accounting.

TRETORN DATACENTER*
Rönnåsgatan 10, Hälsingborg
Telephone: (042) 12-61-00

Officer
Bo Lindberg, *Director*

Computer Installation
IBM 360/30–internal storage: 64K bits; magnetic tapes: 2; magnetic discs: 4 2311; 1 line printer.
IBM 1130.

Services Available
Advice, operators, preparation of data, programming.

Fields of Application
Commercial, production control.

TRYGG-HANSA
Data Centre
Fack, 102 40 Stockholm 5
Telephone: (08) 248000

Officer
Bertil Eklund, *Data Centre Manager*

Computer Installation
IBM 370/145–operating system: OS, MFT; internal storage: 512K bits; magnetic tapes: 12 3420/5; magnetic discs: 1 3330; 4 line printers.

Coding Languages
COBOL, PL/1, Assembler, FORTRAN, RPG, Autocoder, ICL PLAN.

Contemplated Equipment
RJE terminal 5985, 6 3270 displays, 3704.

Services Available
Advice, operators, software packages, preparation of data. Operate on a closed shop and block time basis.

Field of Application
Commercial.
Specialized area: Insurance.

VIVE-STANS AB*
Drottningholmsvägen 24, Stockholm K
Telephone: (08) 54-59-50

Officer
Margareta Håkansson, *Manager*

W. DATA AB*
Fack, Huskvarna 1
Telephone: (036) 13-28-60

Officer
Agne Näslund, *Director*

Computer Installation
IBM 360/40–internal storage: 131K bits; magnetic tapes: 4; magnetic discs: 1 2314: 2 line printers.

Services Available
Advice, preparation of data, programming.

Fields of Application
Commercial, industrial.

SWITZERLAND

UNIVERSITIES AND COLLEGES

ÉCOLE POLYTECHNIQUE FÉDÉRALE DE LAUSANNE
Computing Centre
Avenue de Cour 33, 1007 Lausanne
Telephone: (021) 26-46-21

Officers
Prof. Ch. Blanc, *Director*
Pierre Santschi, *Head of Computing Centre*

Computer Installation
CDC Cyber 7326–operating system: SCOPE 3.4; internal storage: 6 million bits; magnetic tapes: 4 9-track, 2 7-track; magnetic discs: 1 6638, 1 841-6; 2 line printers.
Remote processing features: UT 200, TTY, CRT.

Coding Languages
FORTRAN, COBOL, ALGOL, COMPASS, etc.

Contemplated Equipment
Extension of memory.

Services Available
Advice, programming, education and training. Operate on a remote access, closed shop, block time and time-sharing basis.

Fields of Application
Scientific, statistical, commercial, accounting, management, operational research.
Specialized area: University environment.

Training
Courses in computing science provided by the Polytechnic.

EIDGENÖSSISCHE TECHNISCHE HOCHSCHULE ZÜRICH
Computer Centre
Clausiusstrasse 55, 8006 Zürich
Telephone: 01-326211

Officers
Dipl. Ing. Alfred Schai, *Director*
Dr. Carl August Zehnder, *Head of Co-ordination and Information*

Computer Installation
CDC 6500 and CDC 6400—operating system: SCOPE 3.2 (ETHOS); internal memory: 131K and 65K (plus 500K) 60-bit words; magnetic tapes: 6 604; magnetic discs: 821, 2 6638; 6 line printers. *On-line satellite computers*: 4 CDC 1700. *Remote processing features*: 40,800 baud, 64 Olivetti TTY, 15 displays.

CDC 1604A and CDC 160A—operating system: COOP; internal memory: 32K 48-bit works; magnetic tapes: 8 CDC 606; magnetic discs: 1 CDC 852; 1 line printer.
IBM 1620.
PDP-9 Hybrid (PACE).

Coding Languages
ALGOL, FORTRAN, COBOL, SCALLOP, SYMBAL, PASCAL, COMPASS (Assembler), CODAP (Assembler).

Contemplated Equipment
On-line consoles.

Services Available
Advice, operators, education and training. Operate on a remote access, time-sharing and closed shop basis (6500 + 6400); on a self-service and open shop basis (1604 + 160A). Available to members of the institute, to members of linked institutes and occasionally to paying clients.

Fields of Application
Scientific, statistical, commercial, production control, management, systems analysis, operational research.
Specialized areas: Numerical and systems problems, information languages.

Training
23-day course in informatics.

TECHNIKUM WINTERTHUR (INGENIEURSCHULE)
Technikumstrasse 9, 8400 Winterthur
Telephone: 052 235431

Officer
B. Widmer, *Director*

Computer Installation
IBM 1620—internal storage: 40K decimals; magnetic discs: 1 IBM 1311; 1 line printer.

Coding Languages
SPS, FORTRAN IID.

Services Available
Education and training. Operate on an open shop basis.

Fields of Application
Scientific, educational.

Training
Courses in programming FORTRAN IID.

UNIVERSITÄT BASEL*
Rechenzentrum
Leohardsgraben 3, Basel
Telephone: (061) 24-62-45

Officer
Prof. Dr. P. Leepin, *Director*

Computer Installation
IBM 1620—internal storage: 60K bits; magnetic discs: 1.

Coding Languages
FORTRAN, some SPS.

Field of Application
Scientific.

UNIVERSITÄT ZÜRICH
Institut für elektronische Datenverarbeitung
Sumatrastrasse 30, 8006 Zürich
Telephone: 01 321872

Officer
Dr. K. Bauknecht, *Professor*

Computer Installation
IBM 370/155—operating system: OS MVT; internal storage: 1,500K bits; magnetic tapes: 4 3420; magnetic discs: 4 3330, 8 2319; 1 line printer. *On-line satellite computers*: PDP-11/45, BURROUGHS B1700.
Remote processing features: 30 IBM 2741, TTY, Olivetti, IBM 3780.

Coding Languages
FORTRAN, PL/1, ASS, COBOL, ALGOL.

Services Available
Advice, programming, education and training. Operate on a remote access, closed shop and time-sharing basis. Available to the University and high schools.

Fields of Application
Scientific, statistical, management, systems analysis, operational research.
Specialized areas: Linear programming, medical research.

Training
Courses as part of the University curriculum.

UNIVERSITÉ DE FRIBOURG
Institut pour l'Automation et la Recherche Opérationnelle
1 route du Jura, 1700 Fribourg
Telephone: (037) 22-89-88

Officer
Prof. Dr. E. Billeter, *Director*

Computer Installation
PDP-11/20–operating system: DOS; internal storage: 384K bits; magnetic tapes: 1 9-track; magnetic discs: 1; 1 line printer.

Coding Languages
Assembler, FORTRAN, FOCAL, RPG (in preparation).

Contemplated Equipment
IBM 370/145.

Services Available
Advice, education and training, software packages, documentation, preparation of data, systems analysis. Operate on a closed shop basis.

Fields of Application
Scientific, statistical, commercial, management, systems analysis, operational research.
Specialized areas: Sales analysis, linear programming, analysis, payroll.

Training
Two-year post-graduate course in Informatics; Informatics Diploma course; several special courses for working people

UNIVERSITÉ DE LAUSANNE
Service de Calcul de la Faculté des Sciences
Place du Château 6, 1005 Lausanne
Telephone: (021) 21 63 45

Officer
A. Merbach, *Professor*

Computer Installation
CDC Cyber 7326–operating system: SCOPE 33; internal storage: 100K bits; 2 line printers. *On-line satellite computers*: CDC 200-UT and teletypes. (*Note*: This computer is owned by the University of Lausanne and the Swiss Federal Institute of Technology, Lausanne).

Contemplated Equipment
CDC 1700.

Services Available
Operate on a self-service, remote access and time-sharing basis.

Fields of Application
Scientific.
Specialized area: Research.

UNIVERSITÉ DE NEUCHÂTEL
Centre de Calcul Electronique
Chantemerle 20, 200 Neuchâtel
Telephone: (038) 24-50-24

Officers
P. Banderet, *Professor*
F. Martin, *Assistant Professor*

Computer Installation
IBM 1130–operating system: DMS V2; internal storage: 256K bits; magnetic discs 3 2315; 1 line printer. *Remote processing features*: used as satellite for Univac 1108 or CDC 5600 (CDC Cyber 73/26).

Coding Languages
FORTRAN, ALGOL 60, Assembler, APL.

Services Available
Advice, programming. Operate on a closed shop basis.

Field of Application
Scientific.

Training
University courses in computer science; degree courses in Mathematics, including computer science.

GOVERNMENT ESTABLISHMENTS

DATENVERARBEITUNGSDIENST DER STADT BERN
Postfach 2648, 3001 Berne
Telephone: (031) 25-02-21

Officer
E. Ehrismann, *Chief*

Computer Installation
IBM 360/30–operating system: DOS; internal storage: 96K bytes; magnetic tapes: 2 2415/1; magnetic discs: 1 2314/1; 1 line printer. *Remote processing features*: 8 IBM 2260 local.

Coding Languages
Assembler, PL/1.

Contemplated Equipment
IBM 370/145 with storage of 256K bytes; magnetic discs 3330 and 2314; 2 3420 tape units; 1 1403 N-1 printer.

Services Available
Advice, operators, preparation of data. Operate on an open shop basis.

Fields of Application
Statistical, commercial, accounting.
Specialized areas: Payroll, public utilities' consumption (electricity, gas, water).

EIDGENOSSISCHES STATISTISCHES AMT*
Elektronisches Rechenzentrum der Bundesverwaltung
Hallwylstrasse 15, Bern
Telephone: (031) 61-78-34

Officers
Dr. A. Meli, *Director of the Eidg. Stat. Amt*
Dr. K. Steiner, *Head of the Rechenzentrum*

Computer Installation
IBM 7074–operating system: FOS; internal storage: 530K bits; magnetic tapes: 8 729 II.

Coding Languages
IBM 1401: SPS-II; IBM 7074: Full Autocoder, COBOL, FOS-FORTRAN; IBM 360: COBOL, FORTRAN.

Service Available
Machine time. Operate on a self-service basis.

Fields of Application
Statistics, accounting, engineering, management.

NORDOSTSCHWEIZ. KRAFTWERKE A.G.
Parkstrasse 23, 5401 Baden

Computer Installation
CDC 3100–operating system: MSOS; internal storage: 768K bits; magnetic tapes: 4 601; magnetic discs: 3 854; 1 line printer.

CDC 1700–operating system: MSOS; internal storage: 256K bits; magnetic discs: 1 854; 2 line printers. *Remote processing features*: 2 typewriters, data acquisition system.

Coding Languages
FORTRAN, COBOL, Assembler.

Service Available
Advice. Operate on an open shop basis.

Fields of Application
Scientific, commercial, production control (power).

SWISS FEDERAL RAILWAYS
Division for Organization and Informatics
Bollwerk 10, Bern
Telephone: (031) 60 11 11

Officer
Hans Walter, *Manager, Data Systems Division*

Computer Installation
IBM 360/65–operating system: MFT II; internal storage: 768K bits; magnetic tapes: 9 2405/5, 1 2401/2, 4 2420/5, 1 2415; magnetic discs: 2 2314, 3 2311; 4 line printers.

IBM 360/40–operating system: MFT II; internal storage: 256K bits; tapes, discs and line printers shared with 360/65 above.

IBM 360/30–operating system: MFT II; internal storage: 16K bits; tapes, discs and line printers shared with 360/65 above.

IBM 1401.

Coding Languages
COBOL, FORTRAN.

Services Available
Software packages, preparation of data. Operate on a remote access and closed shop basis.

Fields of Application
Scientific, statistical, commercial, accounting, management, operational research.
Specialized areas: Linear programming, investment, payroll.

RESEARCH INSTITUTIONS

CERN
(European Organization for Nuclear Research)
Data Handling Division
1211 Genève 23
Telephone: (022) 41-98-11

Officers
G. R. Macleod, *Division Leader*
T. Block, *Head, Central Computer Services*
D. Ball, *Head, Computer Centre Group*

Computer Installation
CDC 6600–operating system: CERN SCOPE; internal storage: 7,200K bits; magnetic tapes: 8 607, 4 626, 2 609; magnetic discs: 1 6638, 1 6603; 3 line printers. *On-line satellite computers*: CDC 3100, ICL Argus 500, 2 IBM 1130. *Remote processing features*: 3 RIOS, 20 terminals.

CDC 6500–operating system: CERN SCOPE; internal storage: 7,900K bits; magnetic tapes: 8 607, 2 609; magnetic discs: 1 6638, 1 6603; 2 line printers. *On-line satellite computers*: shares those of CDC 6600. *Remote processing features*: shares those of CDC 6600.

CDC 7600–operating system: SCOPE 2.0; internal storage: 3,900K bits plus 30,700K bits; magnetic discs: 2 7638. *On-line satellite computer*: front-ended by CDC 6400.

CDC 6400–operating system: SCOPE 3.3; internal storage: 3,900K plus 30,200K (ECS) bits; magnetic tapes: 12 659, 6 607; magnetic discs: 16 841; 3 line printers. *On-line satellite computers*: 5 CTL Modular 1. *Remote processing features*: RIOS, terminals.

Coding Languages
ASA FORTRAN, Assembler

Contemplated Equipment
2 CDC 844 discs systems, 3 more RIOS on 7600/6400 system.

Services Available
Operate on a remote access, closed shop and time-sharing basis. Free service to scientists participating in work done at CERN. Available to other customers only on very exceptional grounds.

Field of Application
Scientific.
Specialized area: High energy physics.

INSTITUT DE RECHERCHES TECHNICO-ECONOMIQUES*
2 cours de Rive, 1204 Genève
Telephone: 022-242365

Dirigeants
A. Karamaounas, *Administrateur-Directeur*

Equipement
HONEYWELL H200–mémoire interne: 20K mots; bandes magnétiques: 4; 1 imprimante. *Transmission des données à distance.*

Equipement Projeté
2 disques.

Services Fournis
Programmation, enseignement et formation, préparation des données. Fonctionnement en abonnement machine et à porte ouverte.

Domaines d'Application
Scientifique, statistique, commercial, comptabilité, gestion, recherche opérationnelle, PERT.

Formation
Cours en perforation, programmation COBOL, programmation Assembler.

MONSANTO RESEARCH S.A.
Eggbühlstrasse 36, 8050 Zürich
Telephone: (051) 486776

Officers
Dr. H. H. Zeiss, *Director*
Dr. J. J. Daly, *Systems*

Computer Installation
ELLIOTT 803B.

Coding Language
Autocode.

Services Available
By arrangement.

Field of Application
Chemistry.
Specialized areas: Crystallography and molecular structure.

CONSULTANTS

KARL E. ANDERMATT MANAGEMENT CONSULTANTS*
Feldstrasse 45, 8800 Thalwil-Zürich
Telephone: 051-925305

Officer
K. E. Andermatt

Services Available
Advice, education and training, systems analysis.

Fields of Application
Management, marketing, information systems, inventory management.

Training
One-day courses in Marketing and EDP, Information Systems, Inventory Management.

COMPUTER ENTERPRISES AG*
Neugasse 29, Postfach 123, 6301 Zug
Telephone: 042-21 21 44

Officers
A. Wiget, *Administrator*
F. Legroux, *Director*
E. Wintzen, *Controller for Western Europe*

Coding Languages
COBOL, FORTRAN, ALGOL, PL/1.

Services Available
Advice, programming, systems analysis.

Fields of Application
Scientific, commercial, management.
Specialized area: Feasibility studies.

DATRON AG FÜR DATENVERARBEITUNG UND ORGANISATION
Burgstrasse 47/49, 9000 St Gallen
Telephone: 071-233485

Also at:
Zürich

Officer
Walter Rupp, *Director*

Computer Installation
UNIVAC 1050—internal storage: 32K bits; magnetic tapes: 6; 2 line printers.

IBM 360/40—internal storage: 128K bits; magnetic tapes: 2 2400; magnetic discs: 9 2314; 1 line printer.

IBM 360/30—internal storage: 64K bits; magnetic tapes: 2 2400; magnetic discs: 5 2311; 1 line printer.

BURROUGHS B3500—operating system: MCP; internal storage: 120K bits; magnetic tapes: 3 B9381; magnetic discs: 4 B9372; 1 line printer. *Remote processing features*: Datacom handler for real time and remote batch.

Coding Languages
COBOL, FORTRAN, PL/1, RPG.

Contemplated Equipment
CDC 200 to CDC 6500; MDS 1115 off-line system.

Services Available
Consultation, programming, operators, software packages, documentation, preparation of data, systems analysis. Operate on a remote access, closed shop, block time, open shop and time-sharing basis.

Fields of Application
Commercial, statistical, accounting, systems analysis, management, scientific.
Specialized areas: Sales analysis, analysis, medical research, standard routines for industry and trade.

DIGITRON AG
Weyermattstrasse 4, 2560 Nidau
Telephone: 032-6 04 41

Also at:
2555 Brügg-Biel

Officer
H. R. Müller

Computer Installation
PDP-8 (3)—internal storage: 4K x 12 bits.
PDP-8L—internal storage: 8K x 12 bits; magnetic tapes: 2 TU-28; magnetic discs: 2 RS-08.
IBM System/7—operating system: Disc. *Remote processing features*: 35 terminals.
PDP-11/40 (2)—operating system: Disc/Tape. *Remote processing features*: 40 terminals.

EDP ASSISTANCE LTD.*
Schützengraben 21, 4001 Basel

Also at:
Zürich and Lausanne

Officers
M. Schultheiss, *General Manager*
J. Brühwiler, *Managing Director*

Services Available
Consultation, programming, education and training, software packages, documentation, preparation of data, systems analysis. Operate on a time-sharing basis.

Field of Application
Statistical, commercial, production control, accounting, management, systems analysis.

ARMIN E. FEHR
Alte Landstrasse 190, 8800 Thalwil

Services Available
Consultation, education and training, systems analysis.

Fields of Application
Statistical, commercial, production control, accounting, management, systems analysis.

INFORAMA S.A.
8 rue Charles-Humbert, 1205 Geneva
Telephone: 022-20 93 06

Officers
Alexandre Tic, *President*
Fabio Ferrari, *Delegate Administrator*
Victor Kunzle, *Director*

Coding Languages
COBOL, PL/1, RPG II.

Services Available
Advice, programming, education and training, software packages, preparation of data, systems analysis.

Fields of Application
Statistical, commercial, accounting, management, systems analysis, operational research.
Specialized areas: Sales analysis, analysis, payroll.

Training
Courses in COBOL to COBOL-ANS conversion and DOS to OS conversion.

INSTITUT BEDAUX INTERNATIONAL S.A.*
5 place St. François, Lausanne

Also at: Paris, France; Frankfurt am Main, Federal Republic of Germany; Milan, Italy; Amsterdam, Netherlands; Madrid, Spain.

Services Available
Consultation, programming, software packages.

Fields of Application
Management, software, data processing system consulting.

AG INSTITUT FÜR AUTOMATION*
Ceresstrasse 27, 8008 Zürich
Telephone: 322582

Also at:
Graf Adolf-Strasse 23, Düsseldorf, Federal Republic of Germany
Schottengasse 10, Vienna, Austria

Officers
G. E. Burgmeister, *President*
W. Schneiter and D. Mathieu, *Vice-Presidents*
H. Lindenmann, *Software Services*

Computer Installation
SIEMENS 4004/45 (RCA Spectra 70).

Coding Languages
COBOL, FORTRAN, PL/1, Assembler.

Services Available
Consultation, programming, education and training, software packages, documentation, preparation of data, systems analysis.

Fields of Application
Computer evaluation, efficiency analysis, system design, organization and training of EDP divisions, design and implementation of Integrated Management Information Services.

KNIGHT WEGENSTEIN AG*
Förrlibuckstrasse 66, 8005 Zürich
Telephone: 051-442922.

Also at:
17 Gubelstrasse, Zug
London and Manchester, United Kingdom, Düsseldorf and Frankfurt am Main, Federal Republic of Germany, Brussels, Belgium, Milan, Italy, Vienna, Austria.

Officers
Willy O. Wegenstein, *Executive President*
Paul E. Martin, *Group Co-ordinator, Computer Projects*

Coding Languages
CAPS IBM 360 Assembler, PL/1, FORTRAN, COBOL, RPG.

Services Available
Consultation, operators, preparation of data, programming, software packages, systems analysis.

Fields of Application
Real management information systems, all operating systems, process control.

ARTHUR D. LITTLE S.A./AG*
Seefeldstrasse 224, 8008 Zürich
Telephone: 051-47-42-42

Services Available
Consultation, systems analysis.

Fields of Application
Scientific, statistical, commercial, production control, operational research, management information systems, market research, inventory control, physical distribution.

McKINSEY & CO.*
Zollikerstrasse 225, 8008 Zürich

Services Available
Consultation, programming, software packages, systems analysis.

Fields of Application
Operations research, linear programming, simulation, statistical analysis.

METRON DATENVERARBEITUNG AG*
Froehlichstrasse 33, 5200 Brugg
Telephone: (056) 41-41-04

Officers
Dr. Wilhelm Vogt, *Director*
Christian Lerch
Theo Vogel

Computer Installation
CDC 3100—internal storage: 400K bits; 1 line printer

Coding Languages
FORTRAN, ALGOL, COBOL.

Services Available
Consultation, programming, software packages, systems analysis. Operate on a closed shop basis.

Fields of Application
Information systems for public administration, operational research, mathematical planning models.
Specialized areas: Problems of public administration, data banks for urban planning and research, application of EDP on planning problems.

SYSTEMS PROGRAMMING. S.A.*
40 rue des Vollandes, 1207 Geneva

Also at: Milan, Italy, Stockholm, Sweden.

Services Available
Consultation, programming, software packages, systems analysis.

Switzerland – Service Bureaux

Fields of Application
Feasibility studies, systems design, software and development, management, training.

UNIDATA A.G.
8623 Wetzikon 3
Telephone: 01-77 54 44

Officer
Bernhard Vischer, *President*

Coding Language
FORTRAN IV.

Services Available
Programming, software packages.

Fields of Application
Scientific, commercial, management.
Specialized area: Information storage and retrieval.

SERVICE BUREAUX

AKTIENGESELLSCHAFT FÜR DATENVER-ARBEITUNG UND BETRIEBSWIRTSCHAFTLICHE ORGANISATION (DBO)*
Gottfried-Keller-Strasse 7, 8001 Zürich
Telephone: (051) 35-24-10

Officer
Dr. Eric Funk

Services Available
Advice, programming, software packages, systems analysis.

Fields of Application
Management, operational research, etc.
Specialized areas: Sales analysis, accounting.

Training
Courses in sales analysis and control by region (MEREG), by type of article (MESORT) and by class of customer (MEGROS); two-day course on introduction to the DBO System.

ARBEITSSTELLE FÜR WIRTSCHAFTLICHE DATENVERARBEITUNG AG (A WIDA)*
Pfingstweidstrasse 31, 8005 Zürich
Telephone: (051) 42-86-86

Officers
H. P. Hunkeler
M. Renggli, *General Manager*

Contemplated Equipment
IBM 1130.

Services Available
Preparation of data, software packages. Operate on an open shop basis. Available only for engineers, architects and contractors.

Fields of Application
Commercial, technical, management.
Specialized areas: Commercial applications for construction.

ARITHMA AG*
Konradstrasse 58, 8005 Zürich
Telephone: 44-55-60

Officer
E. J. Meier, *Managing Director*

Computer Installation
UNIVAC 1107—operating system: Exec II; internal storage: 65K bits; magnetic tapes: 7 IIIC; 2 line printers. *On-line satellite computers*: 2 Univac 1004. *Remote processing features*: 4 telephone lines to computer.

Coding Languages
FORTRAN, ALGOL, COBOL.

Services Available
Advice, operators, preparation of data, programming, systems analysis. Operate on a closed shop basis.

Fields of Application
Scientific, commercial, production control, operational research.

AUTOMATION CENTER INTERNATIONAL*
CA-5430 Wettingen
Telephone: (056) 6-11-22

European offices: Vienna (Austria); Brussels (Belgium); Paris (France); Düsseldorf, Frankfurt, Hamburg, Munich and Stuttgart (Germany); Milan (Italy); The Hague (Netherlands).

Officers
H. Waldburger, *General Manager*
H. Birrer, *Treasurer*
S. Jaksetich, *Technical Manager*
F. Orth, *Marketing Manager*

Computer Installation
IBM 1401 (2) and IBM 1410—internal storage: 16K bits each (1401) and 40K bits (1410); magnetic tapes: 6 IBM 729-04, 3 IBM 729-02; magnetic discs: 2 IBM 1311-02/04.

BULL GENERAL ELECTRIC GE 415 (5)—internal storage: 16K bits; magnetic tapes: 6.

Coding Languages
COBOL, FORTRAN, MAKRO, (GE) Autocoder

Contemplated Equipment
Time-sharing installation and Cope.

Services Available
Advice, operators, preparation of data, programming, systems analysis. Operate on a closed shop basis.

Fields of Application
Statistical, commercial, production control, accounting, management, technical, scientific.

BERNISCHE DATENVERARBEITUNG A.G.
Parkterrasse 12, 3012 Berne
Telephone: 031-65 85 11

Officers
Prof. W. Nef and Prof. R. Huesser, *Joint Managers*

Computer Installation
IBM 370/155—operating system: OS-MVT-HASP-TSO; internal storage: 8,000K bits; magnetic tapes: 6 3420; magnetic discs: 8 3330; 2 line printers. *Remote processing features*: about 80 terminals through 3705.

BULL GENERAL ELECTRIC Gamma 30 (= RCA 301)—operating system: IOCS; internal storage: 240K bits; magnetic tapes: 6; 1 line printer. *Remote processing features*: MDS 2400.

Coding Languages
Assembler, FORTRAN, PL/1, COBOL.

Contemplated Equipment
IBM 370/158, 2 IBM 3333 magnetic discs.

Services Available
Advice, programming, education and training. Operate on a closed shop and time-sharing basis.

Fields of Application
Scientific, statistical, commercial, accounting, management, systems analysis, operational research.
Specialized areas: Analysis, payroll, medical research.

Training
Lecture courses at the University of Berne in EDP (technique, organization and applications) and in programming and exercises.

BULL GENERAL ELECTRIC (SCHWEIZ)*
Lagerstrasse 47, 8004 Zürich
Telephone: 051-236760

Also at:
Basle, Berne, Geneva.

Officer
A. Huber, *Time-sharing Manager*

Computer Installation
BULL GENERAL ELECTRIC GE 265—operating system: TS; internal storage: 640K bits; magnetic tapes: 5; magnetic discs: 2 DSU 204; 1 line printer. *On-line satellite computers* TTY, Olivetti, Friden. *Remote processing features*: time-sharing.

Services Available
Consultation, programming, education and training, software packages, documentation, preparation of data, systems analysis. Operate on a self-service, remote access, closed shop and time-sharing basis.

Fields of Application
Scientific, statistical, production control, accounting, management, systems analysis, operational research.

Training
Courses in BASIC, FORTRAN, ALGOL, EDIT, applications; short introductory courses in BASIC and FORTRAN.

BUREAU JUNG*
St Albanvorstadt 80, 4000 Basle

Officer
K. W. Jung

Services Available
Education and training, preparation of data.

Fields of Application
All.

Training
Training of punch operators.

CENTRE CANTONAL D'INFORMATIQUE
Promenade des Bastions, 1211 Geneva 4
Telephone: 022/24-13-38

Officers
Dr. J. F. Renevey, *Computer Manager for the State of Geneva*
Prof. B. Levrat, *for the University*

Computer Installation
CDC 3800—operating system: Tape-Scope; internal storage: 65K 48-bit words; magnetic tapes: 8 7-track; 1 line printer.
IBM 1620—internal storage: 20K × 6 bits; magnetic discs: 1 IBM 1311.
CDC 160/A—internal storage: 8K 12-bit words; magnetic tapes: 2 7-track; 1 line printer.

Coding Languages
FORTRAN, COBOL, COMPASS, ALGOL, PERT, SIMSCRIPT, INFOL.

Contemplated Equipment
3 discs CDC 854.

Services Available
Advice, operators. Operate on a closed shop and block time basis.

Fields of Application
Scientific, statistical, commercial, accounting.
Specialized areas: Data processing for high-energy physics, astronomy, econometry, payroll, medical research.

Training
Courses in computer programming, practical work on the computer, knowledge of computers, administrative programming; diploma "de calcul numérique" can be obtained by post-graduates in one year; also a two-week course in COBOL.

COMPUTER AG ZÜRICH*
Computer-Haus, Badenerstrasse 551, 8048 Zürich

Officers
R. P. Walti, *President and Executive Manager* (Foreign Relations)
J. Schreiber, *Director of Computer Centre*

Computer Installations
ZUSE Z25 (2)—internal storage: 400K bits; magnetic tapes: 5; magnetic drums; 2 line printers.
RAYTHEON 706—internal storage: 512K bits; magnetic tapes: 2; magnetic discs: 1; 1 line printer.

Coding Languages
Assembler, FORTRAN IV.

Services Available
Consultation, programming, education and training, operators, software packages, documentation, preparation of data, systems analysis. Operate on a self-service, closed and open shop basis.

Fields of Application
Scientific, statistical, commercial, production control, accounting, management, systems analysis.

Switzerland – Service Bureaux

CYBERNA S.A.*
Route des Jeunes 23, Genève
Téléphone: (022) 43-93-20

Succursale: Valais

Dirigeants
Joseph Hideg, *Directeur général*
A. Varaa, *Dir. Technique*
M. Tharin

Equipement
Genève:
ICL 1904–système d'opération: GEORGE; mémoire interne: 32K bits; bandes magnétiques: 1 1973/1, 1 1973/2; 1 imprimante.

Langages de Programmation
COBOL, FORTRAN, ALGOL, PLAN.

Services Fournis
Conseils, opérateurs, préparation des données, programmation, systems analysis. Fonctionnement en self-service, en porte fermée, en porte ouverte et en abonnement machine.

Domaines d'Applications
Scientifique, statistique, commercial, comptabilité, gestion.

Formation
Introduction au Traitement de l'Information; Introduction à la mécanographie (4 semaines–6 mois).

DATA CENTER LUZERN
AG für Datenverarbeitung and Betriebsberatung
Pilatusstrasse 60, 6002 Luzern
Telephone: (041) 22-13-13

Officers
Ernst Erb, *General Manager*
Robert Amrein, *Sales Manager*
Marcus Michelotti, *Software Manager*
Marcel Weber, *EDP Manager*

Computer Installation
IBM 360/30–operating system: DOS; internal storage: 600K bits; magnetic tapes: 3 2401/5; magnetic discs: 4 2311; 1 line printer. *Remote processing features*: Olivetti 308.

Coding Languages
RPG, Assembler, COBOL, FORTRAN IV.

Contemplated Equipment
More internal storage and two magnetic discs.

Services Available
Advice, programming, education and training, software packages, preparation of data, systems analysis, data service. Operate on a self-service, closed shop and open shop basis.

Fields of Application
Scientific, statistical, commercial, production control, accounting, management, systems analysis.
Specialized areas: Sales analysis, analysis, payroll, mail-order work.

Training
Courses in EDP programming and techniques and in management techniques.

DATENVERARBEITUNGS DIENST AG*
Schützengraben 20, Schaffhausen

Computer Installation
ICL 1300.

Services Available
Advice, programming, preparation of data.

Fields of Application
Commercial, industrial, payroll, stock control.

DIGITAL AG
P.O. Box 2246, 8023 Zürich

Also at:
Leonhardshalde 21, 8001 Zürich

Officers
Dr. P. Humbel, *Vice-Chairman*
Dr. A. Frey, *Managing Director*

Computer Installations
UNIVAC 1106/1107/1108.
IBM 1620.

Coding Languages
FORTRAN, COBOL, Assembler.

Services Available
Consultation, programming, operators, software packages, documentation, preparation of data, systems analysis.

Fields of Application
Structural engineering programmes, survey programmes, highway construction programmes, constructional costing programmes.

Training
Three-day course on structural engineering calculations by STRIP (Structural Integrated Programmes); 1-day training in all other activities.

ELECTRO-CALCUL S.A.
9 Chemin des Délices, 1000 Lausanne 13
Telephone: (021) 277285

Officers
P.-A. Meystre, *Director*
Claude Brossy and Ygal Fishman, *Chief Engineers*

Computer Installation
ELECTROLOGICA X8–internal storage: 884,736 bits; 1 line printer. *On-line satellite computer*: Input-output processor.

PDP-11/20–internal storage: 131,072 bits.

Coding Languages
FORTRAN, ALGOL, BASIC.

Contemplated Equipment
Extensions to PDP-11/20: increase of 131,072 bits in storage, a magnetic disc and DOS.

Services Available
Advice, programming, software packages, preparation of data, systems analysis. Operate on a closed shop basis.

Fields of Application
Scientific, systems analysis, operational research, process control.
Specialized area: Structural engineering.

ELEKTRONISCHE DATENVERARBEITUNG AG. (ELDAG)*
Birsstrasse 58, 4000 Basle 28
Telephone: 061/41 99 75

Officers
Dr. P. Nabholz, *President*
Dr. V. Ziegler, *General Manager*
C. Schilling, *Systems Manager*

Computer Installation
ICL 1500/1900—internal storage: 20K bits; magnetic tapes: 4; 1 line printer. *Remote processing features*: off-line (MDS).

Coding Languages
COBOL, FAS-Assembler.

Services Available
Consultation, preparation of data, programming, systems analysis, data processing. Operate on a closed shop basis.

Fields of Application
Statistical, commercial, production control, accounting, management, systems analysis.
Specialized areas: Software packages (commercial), billing, accounting, stock control, sales analysis, production planning, type setting.

Training
Two-day course in applications of data services.

GESTRONIC S.A.
4-6 boulevard des Promenades, 1227 Carouge-Genève
Téléphone: (022) 43-39-20

Dirigeants
M. Rieben, *responsable software*
M. Falquet, *responsable administration*
M. Jacquerioz, *responsable service commercial*

Equipement
HONEYWELL H200—mémoire interne: 32K bits; bandes magnétiques: 4; 1 imprimante; 2 lecteurs de bandes papiers.
HONEYWELL H115/2—mémoire interne: 32K bits; bandes magnétiques: 4; disques magnétiques: 1; 1 imprimante.

Langages de Programmation
Easycoder, COBOL, FORTRAN.

Equipement Projeté
Time-sharing centre.

Services Fournis
Conseils, organisation, préparation des données, programmation, software packages, analyse de systèmes. Fonctionnement en self-service et en abonnement machine.

Domaines d'Applications
Scientifique, commercial, contrôle des processus, etc.
Domaines spécialisés: PERT, gestion commerciale, gestion hospitalière, gestion bancaire.

Formation
Stages de courte durée en PERT (1 semaine); Entreprises de construction (1 semaine); Hôpitaux (1 semaine).

HONEYWELL AG*
Dufourstrasse 47, 8034 Zürich
Telephone: 051-474400

Officers
A. Schaffer, *Supervisor of Data Centre*
F. Koller, *Subsidiary Systems Manager*

Computer Installation
HONEYWELL—operating systems: MOD I TR, MOD I TSR; magnetic tapes: 5; magnetic discs: 4; 1 line printer.

Coding Languages
COBOL, FORTRAN IV, RPG, Easycoder.

Services Available
Consultation, programming, education and training, operators, software packages, preparation of data, systems analysis. Operate on a block time and closed shop basis.

Fields of Application
Scientific, statistical, commercial, production control, accounting, management, systems analysis.

Training
Customer-tailored courses available.

IBM (SWITZERLAND)*
Data Center Services
Talstrasse 66, 8022 Zürich
Telephone: (051) 35-88-10

Also at:
Zürich, St Gallen, Basle, Berne and Geneva

Officers
H. Senn, *Manager (Country)*
M. G. Hoffman, *Manager (Zürich)*
P. Koch, *Manager (Basle)*
H. Lüthi, *Manager (Berne)*
M. Jeanneret, *Manager (Geneva)*

Computer Installations
Zürich:
IBM 360/50—internal storage: 348K bits; magnetic tapes: 8.
IBM 360/40—internal storage: 128K bits; magnetic tapes: 6; magnetic discs: 6.
IBM 360/20—internal storage: 16K bits; magnetic tapes: 2; magnetic discs: 2; switched line link to IBM 360 65 at Basle.
Basle:
IBM 360/65—internal storage: 1,024K bits; magnetic tapes: 8.
IBM 1401—internal storage: 16K bits; magnetic tapes; magnetic discs.
Berne:
IBM 360/40—internal storage: 256K bits; magnetic tapes: 6; magnetic discs: 6.
IBM 360/20—internal storage: 16K bits; magnetic tapes: 2; magnetic discs: 2; switched line link to IBM 360 65 at Basle.
Geneva:
IBM 360/40—internal storage: 256K bits; magnetic tapes: 7; magnetic discs: 6.
IBM 360/40—internal storage: 128K bits; magnetic tapes: 5; magnetic discs: 4.
IBM 1401—internal storage: 16K bits; magnetic discs: 2.
St. Gallen:
IBM 2780—terminal lease link to IBM 360/65 at Basle.

Coding Languages
COBOL, FORTRAN, PL/1.

Contemplated Equipment
Network of all four DCs.

Switzerland – Service Bureaux

Services Available
Advice, preparation of data, programming, processing, packages, time-sharing, remote job entry, teleprocessing. Operate on a closed shop basis (IBM Service), open and closed shop basis (Customer Responsibility Usage) and open shop basis (System Usage); also self-service terminal usage for RAX, CRBE and RJE Remote Services.

Fields of Application
Scientific, statistical, commercial, production control, accounting, management, systems analysis, operational research.

INDUSTRIE AND BANK AUTOMATION AG*
Postgasse 15-21, 3000 Berne
Telephone: 031-221401

Officer
Josef Vonarburg

Computer Installation
IBM 360/30—operating system: DOS; internal storage: 64K bits; magnetic tapes: 2 2401; magnetic discs: 3 2311; 1 line printer.

Coding Languages
COBOL, Assembler.

Services Available
Consultation, programming, operators, preparation of data, systems analysis. Operate on a self-service, remote access and closed shop basis.

Fields of Application
Statistical, commercial, production control, accounting, bank applications.

INFORMATICS S.A.
12A route de Meyrin, 1202 Geneva
Telephone: (022) 34-42-42

Officer
Jeffrey Milton, *Managing Director (Europe)*

Coding Languages
MARK IV.

Services Available
Software packages (the MARK IV file management system); presently available on IBM 360s, model 25 upwards (minimum 32K core, 1 disc device and OS or DOS operating systems), IBM 370, Siemens (DOS operating system), Spectra 70 (TDOS operating system) and Univac 9400 and 9700.

Fields of Application
Management, systems analysis, programming.
Specialized areas: Proprietary software packages and real time systems.

Training
Training in the use of the MARK IV file management system for DP and non-DP personnel.

INTERDATA AG, BASEL
Henric-Petri Strasse 35, 4000 Basel
Telephone: 061-22-01-22

Also at:
Zürich, Baden, Bern, Johannesburg, Brussels, Beirut.

Officers
Hans-Peter Unger, *Director*
Niklaus L. Krattiger, *Vice-Director*

Computer Installation
IBM 1401 Tape—internal storage: 119K bits; magnetic tapes: 729/II, 5 7330; 1 line printer.

Coding Languages
SPS, Autocoder, FORTRAN.

Contemplated Equipment
IBM 360/30 or equivalent.

Services Available
Consultation, programming, preparation of data, systems analysis. Operate on an open shop basis.

Fields of Application
Scientific, statistical, commercial, accounting.
Specialized areas: Sales accounting, accounts receivable, salaries accounting, production accounting.

INTERDATA AG, ZÜRICH
Zürich
Telephone: 01/60-30-44, 01/46-90-95

Also at:
Basle, Baden, Berne and Zürich (Digital AG). Centres in Brussels, Johannesburg and Beirut.

Officers
Dr. Peter M. Humbel, *General Manager*
Dr. Arthur A. Frey, *Managing Director*
D. Luethy, *Managing Director of Interdata-international*
G. Schelling, *Managing Director*

Computer Installation
CDC 3100—operating system: MSOS; internal storage: 896K bits; magnetic tapes: 5 604; magnetic discs: 3 854; 1 line printer.

CDC 3170—operating system: MASTER; internal storage: 2,016K bits; magnetic tapes: 9; magnetic discs: 1 841; 2 line printers.

IBM 1401—internal storage: 112K bits; magnetic tapes: 5 729/5; 1 line printer. *Remote processing features*: MDS.

UNIVAC 1005—internal storage: 27K bits; magnetic tapes: 2; 1 line printer. *On-line satellite computer*.

Coding Languages
COBOL, FORTRAN IV, ALGOL.

Contemplated Equipment
UNIVAC 1106 and 6 terminals by 1974.

Services Available
Advice, programming, education and training, operators, software packages, documentation, preparation of data. Operate on a remote access, closed shop, block time and time-sharing basis.

Fields of Application
Scientific, statistical, commercial, accounting, management, systems analysis, operational research.
Specialized areas: Sales analysis, investment, analysis, payroll, structural engineering, STRIP (statics), survey programmes.

Training
Seminars and EDP courses at the INTERDATASCHULE, Sekretariat Weinbergstr. 149, 8006 Zürich. No diplomas.

Switzerland – Service Bureaux

MAISON CH. VEILLON S.A.
Case Postale 1032, 1001 Lausanne
Telephone: 89.23.11

Officer
Michel Emer, *Director*

Computer Installation
IBM 370/145–operating system: MFT-OS; internal storage: 384K bits; magnetic tapes: 3; magnetic discs: 1 3330, 1 3333, 1 2314; 2 line printers. *Remote processing features*: Local visual displays– 14 2260, 8 3270.

Coding Languages
Assembler, FORTRAN, COBOL.

Services Available
Service Bureau. Operate on a closed shop basis.

Fields of Application
Commercial, management.
Specialized areas: Sales analysis, payroll.

OREG A.G.
Hegibachstrasse 47, 8032 Zürich
Telephone: 01-535800

Officer
Dr. Hans-Rudolf Fenner, *Manager*

Computer Installation
BULL GENERAL ELECTRIC GE 120–operating system: EDOS; internal storage: 32K bits; magnetic tapes: 3 MTH 163; magnetic discs: 1 DSS 157; 1 line printer.

Coding Language
COBOL.

Services Available
Advice, programming, operators, preparation of data, systems analysis. Operate on a closed shop basis.

Fields of Application
Statistical, commercial, production control, accounting, management, systems analysis.
Specialized areas: Sales analysis, analysis, payroll.

PAILLARD S.A.
Centre Informatique Paillard
Rue des Pêcheurs, 1400 Yverdon
Telephone: 024 2 23 31

Officer
Gérard Kemper, *Manager*

Computer Installation
IBM 360/40–operating system: DOS; internal storage: 128K bytes; magnetic tapes: 2 2415; magnetic discs: 8 2314; 1 line printer.
IBM 360/20–operating system: BOS; internal storage: 8K bits; magnetic tapes: 2 2415; 1 line printer.

Coding Languages
COBOL, Assembler, RPG.

Services Available
Advice, programming, software packages, preparation of data. Operate on a closed shop basis.

Fields of Application
Commercial, production control, accounting, management.

RATIONAL AG
Forchstrasse 36, 8008 Zürich
Telephone: 328408

Officer
Dr. S. Hollai, *Director*

Contemplated Equipment
Third generation 32K computer with 4 discs.

Services Available
Consultation, programming, preparation of data, systems analysis.

Field of Application
Commercial.

REBER DATENVERARBEITUNGSSERVICE*
Quartiergasse 25, 3000 Berne
Telephone: 031-416877, 425600

Officer
Urs Reber

Services Available
Consultation, programming, software packages, preparation of data, systems analysis. Operate on a closed shop basis.

Fields of Application
Scientific, statistical, commercial, production control, management, systems analysis.

RECHEN-CENTER RAPPERSWIL AKTIENGESELL-SCHAFT (RCR)*
Untere Bahnhofstrasse 11, 8640 Rapperswil
Telephone: 055-2 44 88

Officer
M. W. Schmid, *Director*

Computer Installation
HONEYWELL H125–operating system: MOD 1; internal storage: 32K bits; magnetic tapes: 3; magnetic discs: 4 273; 1 line printer.

Coding Languages
COBOL, Easycoder.

Services Available
Consultation, programming, operators, preparation of data, systems analysis. Operate on a block time and closed shop basis.

Fields of Application
Commercial, production control, BOM, accounting, management, systems analysis.
Specialized area: Cost accounting for textile industry.

RECHENZENTRUM AG, BERN*
Dufourstrasse 45, 3000 Berne
Telephone: (031) 44-03-51

Officers
W. Weber, *General Manager*
G. Gretener, *Manager, Analysis and Programming*
Mr. Baumann, *Production Manager*

Computer Installation
HONEYWELL H120–operating system: Tape Resident; internal storage: 32K bits; magnetic tapes: 4; 1 line printer.

Coding Languages
COBOL, FORTRAN, Easycoder.

Services Available
Advice, operators, programming, systems analysis, punching, key tape, software packages. Operate on a closed shop and block time basis.

Fields of Application
Commercial, scientific, statistical, production control, accounting, management.
Specialized areas: Payroll, stock control.

SEDAB AG
(Servicebüro für Datenverarbeitung und Betriebsberatung)
Hirschengraben 43, 6002 Luzern
Telephone: (041) 227-227

Also at:
17 rue des Pierres-du-Niton, 1207 Genève
Telephone: (022) 35 2889

Winzerstrasse 112, 8049 Zürich
Telephone: (051) 56-39-70

SEDAB Stockholm, Sundsvall, Kristianstad, Malmö, Göteborg, Helsinki, Amsterdam.

Officers
Fred Lundholm, Börje Werneborg, *General Managers*
Ernst Erb, *Manager (Switzerland)*

Computer Installation
IBM 360/20.
IBM 360/30.
IBM 360/40.

Coding Languages
Assembler, RPG, COBOL, PL/1.

Services Available
Consultation, operators, preparation of data, programming, systems analysis. Operate on a self-service basis.

Fields of Application
Commercial, statistical, accounting, systems analysis.

SIEMENS ELEKTRIZITÄTSERZEUGNISSE AG*
8953 Dietikon 2 H/Fahrweid
Telephone: (051) 88-66-11

Officers
Dr. H. Wiedenkeller, *Country Sales Manager*
Ernst Gächter, *Manager of the Service Bureau*

Computer Installation
SIEMENS 4004/15 and 4004/45—operating systems: BOS, TOS, TDOS, DOS; internal storage: 16K bytes and 131K bytes; magnetic tapes: 8 9-track; magnetic discs: 4; 2 line printers.

Coding Languages
Assembler, COBOL, FORTRAN, ALGOL, RPG.

Services Available
Consultation, operators, preparation of data, programming, software packages, systems analysis. Operate on a closed shop and block time basis.

Fields of Application
Scientific, statistical, commercial.

SOCIÉTÉ ANONYME DES ATELIERS DE SECHERON
Case Postale, 1211-Genève 21
Téléphone: (022) 32-67-50

Dirigeant
J. Binggeli, *Chef du centre de calcul électronique*

Equipement
IBM 1131/2C—mémoire interne: 16K bits; disques magnétiques: 3 2310/B02; 1 imprimante. Calculatrice analogique OME P2-SEA (48 amplif) et nombreux éléments non linéaires.

Langages de Programmation
SAP, FORTRAN, COBOL.

Services Fournis
Conseils, opérateurs, préparation des données, programmation, software packages, systems analysis. Fonctionnement en porte fermée.

Domaines d'Application
Mathématiques appliquées, gestion.
Domaine spécialisé: Electrotechnique.

SOCIÉTÉ D'EXPLOITATION D'UTIMACO SA ET COMPTABILITÉS-STATISTIQUES SA (UCS)*
39 rue Peilloneux, 1225 Chêne-Bourg, Genève

Dirigeants
Hugo Bernard, *Directeur*
Serge Pictet, *Directeur*
Serge Noel, *Fondé de pouvoir*

Equipement
BULL GENERAL ELECTRIC GE 115—mémoire interne: 16K bits; bandes magnétiques: 3 MT 107; disques magnétiques: 2 D 5; 1 imprimante.

BULL GENERAL ELECTRIC Gamma 10—mémoire interne: 4K bits; bandes magnétiques: à carte.

Langages de Programmation
Autocode, TAB, COBOL.

Services Fournis
Conseils, opérateurs, préparation des données, programmation. Fonctionnement à porte ouverte.

Domaines d'Application
Tous les domaines en fonction de la machine.
Domaines spécialisés: Comptabilite, statistiques, cartes de versement P.T.T., payes et gestion.

SPERRY RAND AG UNIVAC, WISSENSCHAFT UND TECHNIK*
Konradstrasse 58, 8005 Zürich
Telephone: 444080

Officer
A. Schmid

Computer Installations
UNIVAC 1107—operating system: EXEC II; internal storage: 2,340K bits; magnetic tapes: 7 Uniservo IIIC; 2 line printers. *On-line satellite computer*: Univac 1004. *Remote processing features*: 4 Data Line Terminals 1200/2400 baud.

UNIVAC 1108—operating system: EXEC 8; internal storage: 7,020K bits; magnetic tapes: 9 Uniservo VIC, 3 Uniservo VIIIC. *On-line satellite computer*: Univac 1004. *Remote processing features*: 32-channel Communications Terminal Module Controller.

Services Available
Consultation, programming, education and training, software packages, documentation. Operate on a self-service, remote access and closed shop basis.

Fields of Application
Scientific, operational research.
Specialized areas: Electronics, numerical control, civil engineering, critical path methods, simulation, linear programming.

Training
Education in the use of application programmes; short courses (3-10 days) in Analysis of Electronic Circuits, STRESS, PERT, Powerflow Analysis, APT, EXAPT I and II, SIMULA, Linear Programming.

SYSTEMSERVICES
Eichstrasse 23, 8045 Zürich
Telephone: 35 47 10

Officer
K. Grässle, *Manager*

Computer Installation
IBM 360/50—operating system: OS-MFT II; internal storage: 384K bytes; magnetic tapes: 6; magnetic discs: 8 2314; 2 line printers.

Coding Languages
Assembler, PL/1.

Services Available
Advice, programming, operators, preparation of data, systems analysis. Operate on a closed shop basis.

Field of Application
Commercial.

TELEDATA A.G.
Steinerstrasse 35, 3006 Berne
Telephone: 031 44 24 24

Seefeldstrasse 108, 8034 Zürich
Telephone: 01 34 16 16

Officers
Dr. Peter Schnyder, *Director*
Hans-Jörg Berger, *Deputy Director and Manager of Berne Data Centre*
Eckart Koschenz, *Manager of Zürich Data Centre*
Dr. Peter Appel, *Deputy Director*

Computer Installation
IBM 370/135—operating system: DOS; internal storage: 192K bytes; magnetic tapes: 4 3420; magnetic discs: 1 2318/2319; 1 line printer. *On-line satellite computers*: IBM 5985. *Remote processing features*: POWER/RJE.

Coding Languages
Assembler, COBOL, PL/1.

Services Available
Advice, programming, operators, software packages, documentation, preparation of data, systems analysis. Operate on a remote access, closed shop and block time basis.

Fields of Application
Statistical, commercial, production control, accounting, management, systems analysis.
Specialized areas: Sales analysis, investment, analysis, payroll, structural engineering.

VERWALTUNGSRECHENZENTRUM AG
Rathaus, 9001 St. Gallen
Telephone: 071-21-54120

Officers
H. Gabathuler, *Manager*
H. Vetsch, *Authorized Manager*

Computer Installation
IBM 1410—internal storage: 40K bits; magnetic tapes: 5 729/V; 1 line printer.

Coding Languages
Autocoder, PL/1.

Contemplated Equipment
IBM 370/158 with operating system OS/VSI, 512K bits internal storage, 4 3420/003 tape units, 3333/001 and 3330/001 disc units and 1 line printer. Also remote processing equipment.

Services Available
Advice, programming, systems analysis. Operate on a time-sharing basis. Available to government offices only.

Fields of Application
Statistical, commercial, accounting.
Specialized areas: Payroll, population, taxes.

SYRIA

GOVERNMENT ESTABLISHMENT

CENTRAL BUREAU OF STATISTICS
EDP Directorate
Telephone Exchange Building, Baghdad Street, Damascus
Telephone: 446190, 446197.

Officers
Dr. A. Radjai, *Director of Bureau*
F. Eid, *EDP Manager*

Computer Installation
NCR Century 100—operating system: B1-1; internal storage: 256K bits; magnetic tapes: 3 633-119; magnetic discs: 1 655-101; 1 line printer.

Coding Languages
NEAT/3, FORTRAN II, COBOL.

Contemplated Equipment
A high-speed printer and a high-speed card reader.

Services Available
Advice, programming, preparation of data, systems analysis.

Fields of Application
Statistical, commercial.

TANZANIA

UNIVERSITY

UNIVERSITY OF DAR-ES-SALAAM
Box 35062, Dar-es-Salaam
Telephone: 53611, extension 516

Officer
D. Cappitt, *Acting Head, Mathematics Dept.*

Computer Installation
ICL 1901—internal storage: 384K bits; magnetic tapes: 4; 1 line printer.

Coding Languages
FORTRAN, ALGOL, PLAN, COBOL.

Services Available
Consultation, programming, education and training, preparation of data, systems analysis. Service available to University and Government Ministries.

Fields of Application
Scientific, statistical, operational research.
Specialized areas: Statistical surveys and analysis.

Training
Information Processing plays a part in the University's Mathematics, Statistics and Economics courses. Short courses in Scientific Programming.

THAILAND

NATIONAL CENTRE

NATIONAL STATISTICAL OFFICE
Data Processing Centre of Thailand (DPCT)
Larn Luang Road, Bangkok
Telephone: 810779, 818619

Officers
Rojanakorn Laowanich, *Director of DPCT*
Thavisakdi Thangsuphanich, *Assistant Director*

Computer Installation
IBM 360/40—operating systems: DOS, POWER II; internal storage: 128K bytes; magnetic tapes: 5; magnetic discs: 4; 1 line printer.
IBM 1401—internal storage: 8K bytes; magnetic tapes: 4; 1 line printer.

Coding Languages
COBOL, FORTRAN IV, Assembler, RPG, PL/1, Autocoder, FORTRAN II.

Services Available
Advice, programming, education and training, software packages, preparation of data, systems analysis. Operate on a self-service basis. Available only to government agencies, state enterprises and international organizations.

Fields of Application
Scientific, statistical, accounting.

Specialized area: Census and surveys.

Training
Courses in programming languages (COBOL, FORTRAN, Assembler) and in systems analysis and design.

UNIVERSITY

CHULALONGKORN UNIVERSITY*
Computer Science Laboratory, Graduate School
Bangkok
Telephone: 55955

Officer
Dr. Ittipon Padunchewit

Computer Installations
IBM 1620—operating system: TSS; internal storage: 20K BCD; 1 line printer.
IBM 1800—operating system: TTS; internal storage: 32K words; magnetic tapes: 2 2401; magnetic discs: 2 2310; 1 line printer. *Remote processing features*: 2470s; Shinko teleprinters.
NIPPON ELECTRIC NEAC 2200/200—operating system: TOS; internal storage: 24K words; magnetic tapes: 5 N404-3; 1 line printer.
ICL 1902A—operating system: DOS; internal storage: 16K words; magnetic tapes: 4; magnetic discs: 2; 1 line printer.

Coding Languages
Assembler, RPG, COBOL, FORTRAN (BASIC and IV), PLAN, ASA.

Services Available
Consultation, programming, education and training, operators, software packages, documentation, preparation of data, systems analysis. Operate on a self-service, remote access, block time, closed shop (classified), open shop (non-classified) and time-sharing basis. Available for research and education.

Fields of Application
Education and research in: science and engineering, social science, system science/operating research, MIS, commercial fields.

Training
M.S. and Ph.D. degree courses in Computer Science; Associate Degree in Computer Science and Data Processing (2 years).

RESEARCH INSTITUTION

NATIONAL INSTITUTE OF DEVELOPMENT ADMINISTRATION
Huamark, Bankok 10
Telephone: 777-400

Officer
Dr. Boonserm Weesakul

Coding Language
FORTRAN IV.

Contemplated Equipment
Varian 620-F.

Services Available
Advice, programming, education and training, preparation of data. Operate on a remote access basis.

Field of Application
Statistical.

Training
Various courses as part of requirements for Master's degree in Applied Statistics.

CONSULTANT

COMPUTER THAILAND LIMITED PARTNERSHIP*
5 Trok Watrachnadda, Dinso Street, Bangkok

Officer
Sanguan Phonphaibulya

Service Available
Consultation.

Fields of Application
Commercial, accounting.

SERVICE BUREAU

IBM THAILAND CO. LTD.
P.O. Box 1354, Bangkok

Computer Installation
IBM 360/30.

Services Available
Advice, operators, preparation of data, programming, software packages, systems analysis, education and training, documentation.

Fields of Application
Scientific, statistical, accounting, commercial.

TRINIDAD AND TOBAGO

UNIVERSITY

UNIVERSITY OF THE WEST INDIES*
St. Augustine, Trinidad
Telephone: 662 5511

Officer
K. A. Cazabon, *Manager of the Computer Centre*

Computer Installation
IBM 1620/1 – internal storage: 20K digits.

Coding Languages
SPS, FORTRAN with FORMAT.

Contemplated Equipment
ICL 1901A with internal storage of 16K bits.

Services Available
Advice, programming, education and training, preparation of data. Operate on a self-service basis.

Fields of Application
Scientific, statistical.

Training
Short course (12 hours) on the introduction to programming the FORTRAN language.

CONSULTANT

PEAT, MARWICK, MITCHELL AND CO.
P.O. Box 1328, 20 Abercromby Street, Port of Spain
Telephone: 62-31081

Officers
John H. Hilton, *Partner*
Ian G. Bertrand, *Principal*

Services Available
Advice, education and training, systems analysis.

Fields of Application
Commercial, accounting, management, systems analysis, operational research.
Specialized areas: Sales analysis, linear programming, analysis, payroll.

SERVICE BUREAUX

IBM WORLD TRADE CORPORATION*
Port of Spain

Computer Installation
IBM 1401.

Services Available
Advice, operators, preparation of data, programming.

Fields of Application
Statistical, commercial.

INTERNATIONAL COMPUTERS LTD.*
ICL House, 46 Park Street, Port of Spain
Telephone: 62-32826

Officers
D. J. Yeo, *Caribbean Manager*
M. Daniel, *Bureau Manager*

Computer Installation
ICL 1902A – operating system: ICL Executive; internal storage: 64K characters; magnetic tapes: 6; 1 line printer.

Coding Languages
COBOL, PLAN.

Contemplated Equipment
Extra core, discs.

Services Available
Advice, operators, preparation of data, programming, software packages, systems analysis. Operate on an open shop and block time basis.

Fields of Application
All fields.
Specialized area: PERT (critical path).

Training
Courses in systems analysis, programming, operating and management appreciation.

A. M. PROVAN AND ASSOCIATES (AMPA)
Data Services
31 Frederick Street, Port of Spain

Officers
Alasdair C. Macleod Provan, *Principal*
Donald N. Ali, *Supplies Manager*
Vishnu Ramsarran, *Data Centre Manager*

Computer Installation
IBM 360/25–operating system: DOS; internal storage: 48K bits; magnetic tapes: 4; magnetic discs: 2; 1 line printer.

Coding Language
COBOL IV.

Contemplated Equipment
Microfilming – CALCOMP 2100.

Services Available
Advice, programming, operators, software packages, documentation, preparation of data, systems analysis. Operate on a closed shop basis. Preference given to industrial and commercial customers.

Fields of Application
Scientific (petroleum), statistical, commercial, production control, accounting, management, systems analysis, operational research.
Specialized areas: Sales analysis, linear programming, investment, analysis, payroll, structural engineering.

TUNISIA

GOVERNMENT ESTABLISHMENT

MINISTÈRE DES POSTES, TÉLÉGRAPHES ET TÉLÉPHONES
5 rue d'Angleterre, Tunis

Computer Installation
IBM 360/30–operating system: DOS; internal storage: 64K bits; magnetic tapes: 2 2401; magnetic discs: 3 2311; 1 line printer.

Coding Languages
Assembler, COBOL, FORTRAN IV.

Services Available
Advice, programming, operators, preparation of data. Operate on a closed shop and open shop basis.

Fields of Application
Commercial, accounting, management.
Specialized areas: Investment, payroll.

Training
Courses for engineering diplomas.

TURKEY

UNIVERSITIES

BOĞAZİÇİ ÜNİVERSİTESİ
Bebek, P.K.8, Istanbul
Telephone: 635650

Officer
Dr. Semih Tezcan, *Acting Director*

Computer Installation
IBM 1620–operating system: Monitor I; internal storage: 40K decimal digits; magnetic discs: 1 1311; 1 line printer.

Coding Languages
FORTRAN IID, SPS IID.

Services Available
Consultation, operators. Operate on an open shop basis.

Fields of Application
Scientific, statistical, accounting.

Training
Short courses in FORTRAN programming.

EGE ÜNİVERSİTESİ*
Bornova, Izmir
Telephone: 29033, 29325, 29326

Officers
Prof. Dr. Selma Karhan
Mühendislik Bilimleri Fakültesi

Computer Installation
IBM 1130–internal storage: 8K bits; 1 line printer.

HACETTEPE ÜNİVERSİTESİ*
Bigli Islem Merkezi, Ankara
Telephone: 108540/1069

Officer
Aydin Köksal, *Manager, Information Processing Centre*

Computer Installation
BURROUGHS B3500–operating system: MCP (DATA-COM); internal storage: 737,280 bits; magnetic tapes: B9381-2; magnetic discs: 1 B9370-2, 3 B9376-2; 1 line printer. *Remote processing features*: 2 teletypes, 8 Cathode ray tubes (B9352).

Coding Languages
COBOL, FORTRAN IV, Assembler.

Services Available
Consultation, programming, education and training, documentation, preparation of data, systems analysis. Operate on a self-service, closed and open shop basis. Services to customers outside the University are provided jointly with SISAG Ltd.

Training
Graduate level credit courses: Introduction to data processing, COBOL programming, FORTRAN IV programming, Introduction to systems analysis.

Turkey – Universities

İSTANBUL DEVLET MÜHENDİSLİK VE MİMARLIK AKADEMİSİ
Yildiz, Istanbul
Telephone: 47 34 30

Officers
Dr. Muzaffer Sağisman, *Head of the Mechanical Engineering Department*
Dr. M. Yahya Karsligil, *Assistant Head of Department*

Computer Installation
IBM 1130–operating system: Card-Disc; internal storage: 8K 16-bit bytes; magnetic discs: 3 2310; 1 line printer.

Coding Languages
FORTRAN, RPG, Assembler.

Contemplated Equipment
IBM 1627 plotter; 1231 optical mark page reader.

Services Available
Advice, programming, education and training, preparation of data, systems analysis. Operate on a self-service basis.

Fields of Application
Scientific, statistical, accounting, management, systems analysis, operational research.
Specialized areas: Linear programming, analysis, structural engineering.

İSTANBUL TEKNİK ÜNİVERSİTESİ
(Technical University of Istanbul)
Institute of Computer Sciences
Taşkişla 114, Istanbul
Telephone: 452258-452150-9/2173

Officers
Günay Ozmen, *Director*
Muzaffer Ipek, *Engineer, Chief of Technical Section*
Nadir Yücel, *Engineer, Chief of Educational Section*
Fevzican A. Akyüz, *Engineer, Chief of Research and Development Section*
Selma Şener, *Programming Adviser*
Cahit Çetinler, *Engineer, System Programmer*.

Computer Installation
IBM 1620–operating system: Monitor 1; internal storage: 40K bits; magnetic discs: 2 1311, Model 2 and 3; 1 line printer.

Coding Languages
FORTRAN II, FORTRAN IID, SPS IID.

Services Available
Advice, programming, software packages. Operate on a self-service and open shop basis. Not available for customers with routine jobs.

Fields of Application
Scientific, statistical, mathematical, engineering, operational research.
Specialized area: Structural engineering.

Training
FORTRAN IID and Monitor I courses every semester; seminars on other related subjects.

ORTA DOĞU TEKNİK ÜNİVERSİTESİ
(Middle East Technical University)
Computation Center
Ankara
Telephone: Ankara 232120/401-402-403

Officer
Bülent Epir, *Chairman*

Computer Installation
IBM 360/40F–operating system: DOS; internal storage: 64K bytes; magnetic tapes: 1 2401; magnetic discs: 2 2311; 1 line printer.

Coding Languages
FORTRAN IV, Assembly, PL/1, COBOL.

Contemplated Equipment
Increase in core storage to 256K bits with additional disc storage and 8 tape drives; multiprogramming and time-sharing capabilities.

Services Available
Consultation, systems analysis, programming, preparation of data, software packages, operators, education and training. Operate on a remote access and closed shop basis. Priority to university teaching and research.

Fields of Application
Scientific and technical research, education, administration, systems analysis, commercial.

Training
M.Sc. in Computer Science, service courses (9 undergraduate, 14 graduate).

SERVICE BUREAU

IBM WORLD TRADE CORPORATION*
Istanbul

Computer Installation
IBM 1401.

Services Available
Advice, operators, preparation of data, programming.

Fields of Application
Statistical and commercial.

UGANDA

UNIVERSITY

MAKERERE UNIVERSITY*
P.O. Box 7062, Kampala
Telephone: 56661-380

Officer
C. P. Welter, *Professor of Mathematics*

Computer Installation
IBM–operating systems: BPS, TOS; internal storage: 128K bits; magnetic tapes: 4; 1 line printer.

Coding Languages
FORTRAN, RPG.

Services Available
Advice, programming. Operate on a closed shop basis. Available for scientific programmes only.

Fields of Application
Scientific, statistical.
Specialized areas: Instruction, research projects in science, research projects in computing.

Training
Courses in FORTRAN (1-4 weeks).

UNION OF SOVIET SOCIALIST REPUBLICS

RESEARCH INSTITUTION

ACADEMY OF SCIENCES OF THE U.S.S.R.*
Siberian Department
Computing Center
Novosibirsk 90
Telephone: E 5-56-50

Officers
G. I. Marchuk, *Director (Computational methods in partial differential equations, especially in dynamic methodology and nuclear energetics)*
M. K. Fage, *Computational methods in Nuclear Physics*
N. N. Yanenko, *Numerical Methods*
M. M. Laurentiev, *Computational Methods in Potential Theory, especially in Geophysics Problems*
A. P. Ershov, *Theory of Programming, Translator Construction*
M. L. Nechepurenko, *Computer and Mathematical Simulation, Simulation Languages, Systems Design.*

Computer Installation
BESM 6–operating system: Standard; internal storage: 32K 48-bit words; magnetic tapes: 16; magnetic drums: 4; 2 line printers. *On-line satellite computer*: M-220 for compilation of ALGOL programmes. *Remote processing features*: 24 low speed channels.

MINSK 220–operating systems: IS-2 + ALPHA; internal storage: 4K 45-bit words; magnetic tapes: 4; magnetic drum: 1; 1 line printer.

MINSK 20–internal storage: 4K bits; magnetic tapes: 4 8-track magnetic drums: 3; 1 line printer.

Coding Languages
ALGOL and Input language for ALPHA- translator; EPSYLON and SYGMA systems for symbol manipulation and software production.

Contemplated Equipment
Experimental time-sharing systems AIST-0 and AIST-1.

Services Available
Advice, operators, preparation of data, software packages. Operate on an open shop basis.

Fields of Application
Numerical methods, nuclear energy, nuclear physics, geophysics, theory of programming, translator construction.

UNITED KINGDOM AND ISLE OF MAN

NATIONAL CENTRE

COMPUTER POWER
Cannock, Staffordshire, WS11 3HZ
Telephone: Cannock 2581

Also at:
Doncaster, Edinburgh, Gateshead, Lowton and Tredomen.

Officers
R. A. Hitchcock, *Managing Director*
G. M. Bannerman, *Deputy Managing Director*
D. Black, *Manager, Cannock*
L. Vickers, *Manager, Doncaster*
W. Penman, *Manager, Edinburgh*
G. A. D. English, *Manager, Gateshead*
W. A. Downes, *Manager, Lowton*
W. D. Davies, *Manager, Tredomen*

Computer Installations
Cannock:
IBM 360/50–operating system: OS; internal storage: 512K bits; magnetic tapes: 4 2401; magnetic discs: 5 2314; 1 line printer. *Remote processing features*: CPS RJE.

IBM 360/50–operating system: OS; internal storage: 512K bits; magnetic tapes: 7 2401, 2 2311; magnetic discs: 9 2314; 2 line printers.

IBM 360/65–operating system: OS; internal storage: 512K bits; magnetic tapes: 7 2301; magnetic discs: 9 2314; 1 line printer. *Remote processing features*: CPS, RJE.

Doncaster:
ICL 1904A–internal storage: 64K words; magnetic tapes: 8 1973/1; magnetic discs: 4 2802/2; two line printers.

ICL 1904–internal storage: 32K words; magnetic tapes: 10 1974/1; magnetic discs: 2 2802/2; 2 line printers.

IBM 360/40–operating system: DOS; internal storage 128K bits; magnetic tapes: 7 2401, 1 2415; magnetic discs: 4 2311; 1 line printer.

Edinburgh:
ICL 1904–internal storage: 32K words; magnetic tapes: 8 1974/1; magnetic discs: 2 2802/2; 2 line printers.

Gateshead:
ICL 1906–internal storage: 64K words; magnetic tapes: 10 1973/1; magnetic discs: 4 2802/2; 3 line printers.

Lowton:
ICL 1902A–internal storage: 32K words; magnetic tapes 6 1971/2; magnetic discs: 2 2801/2; 1 line printer.

Tredomen:
IBM 360/30–operating system: DOS; internal storage: 64K bits; magnetic tapes: 7 2402; magnetic discs: 3 2311; 1 line printer.

Coding Languages
COBOL, Assembler, ALGOL, FORTRAN, PL/1, RPG, CPS.

Contemplated Equipment
2 CTL Modular 1 computers.

Services Available
Advice, programming, education and training, operators, software packages, documentation, preparation of data, systems analysis. Operate on a self-service, remote access, block time and time-sharing basis.

Fields of Application
Scientific, statistical, commercial, production control, management, systems analysis, sales invoicing and suppliers, stock and general accounting.
Specialized areas: Linear programming, sales analysis, investment, analysis, payroll, structural engineering, medical research.

Training
Various training schemes to meet the specific needs of individual businesses.

EDUCATIONAL AND TRAINING INSTITUTIONS

ALTERGO LTD.
7 Lower James Street, London, W1R 3PL
Telephone: 01-437 8802

Officers
David A. Redclift, *Manager of Education*
R. Thomas, *Managing Director*
R. Mannering, *Marketing Director*

Coding Language
PL/1.

Services Available
Advice, programming, education and training, software packages, systems analysis.

Fields of Application
Commercial, systems analysis.

Training
Courses in all aspects of the PL/1 language.

INSTITUTE OF DATA PROCESSING
418-422 Strand, London WC2
Telephone: 01-240 3106

Officer
D. W. Bradley, *General Secretary*

Service Available
Education and training.

Fields of Application
Commercial and Business.

Training
Institute of Data Processing Examination Parts I–IV.

INTERNATIONAL COMPUTERS LTD. (ICL)
Beaumont, Old Windsor, Windsor, SL4 2JJ
Telephone: 68181

Officers
G. J. Morris, *Manager, Education and Training Organization*
R. Chamberlain, *Manager, Customer Training Advisory Service*

Computer Installation
ICL 1904–operating system: EXEC; internal storage: 32K words.

Coding Languages
PLAN, COBOL, FORTRAN, ALGOL.

Service Available
Education and training.

Fields of Application
Scientific, statistical, commercial, production control, accounting, management, systems analysis, operational research and operating.

Training
Courses in management, systems and applications, programming, data preparation and control.

ICL COMPUTER EDUCATION IN SCHOOLS
Computer House, Euston Centre, 322 Euston Road, London, NW1 3BD
Telephone: 01-387 7030

Officers
C. Hampson-Evans, *Manager*
A. R. Ward, *Overseas Relations*

Computer Installation
About 70 installations are involved, mostly ICL 1900 series, with storage ranging from 384K to 1,536K bits.

Coding Languages
CESIL, SIR, BASIC, ALGOL, FORTRAN, COBOL.

Services Available
Advice, programming, education and training, software packages and documentation. Operate on a self-service, remote access, block time, open shop and time-sharing basis. Available to any educational institution.

Field of Application
Educational.
Specialized area: Computer education.

Training
Twelve-day residential course for teachers, lecturers and education advisers on the teaching of computer studies in schools. Five-day advanced residential course (usually taken about one year after the initial 12-day course).

KATE LTD.
Concord House (2nd floor), The Centre, Feltham, Middlesex, TW13 4BG
Telephone: 01-890 4717

Officers
Dennis Conroy, *Director*
Mrs. P. Noterman, *Director*

Services Available
Education and training.

Training
Courses in on-site keypunch training (English, German and Dutch).

LONDON BOROUGH OF HAVERING
Educational Computer Centre
Teachers' Centre Annexe, Tring Gardens, Harold Hill, Romford, Essex, RM3 9QX
Telephone: Ingrebourne 49115

Officer
W. R. Broderick

Computer Installation
HEWLETT PACKARD 2116/C—operating system: DOS-M; internal storage 24K 16-bit words; magnetic discs: 1 HP 2870; 1 line printer. *Remote processing features*: Terminal to GEIS SYSTEM.

Coding Languages
ALGOL, FORTRAN, Assembler, BASIC.

Services Available
Advice, education and training, software packages. Operate on an open shop basis.

Fields of Application
Scientific, educational, research.
Specialized area: Computer-aided learning.

Training
Programming and teaching computer studies (8 to 10 courses per year).

SCHOOL OF COMPUTER PROGRAMMING*
Computer Training Centre
6 Park Mansions Arcade, 134A Knightsbridge,
London SW1
Telephone: 01-589 6691

Also at:
Prudential Buildings, St Philips Square, Birmingham
Telephone: 021-236 3623

Officers
E. Fich, *Director*
J. Miller, *Manager (London)*
R. Ragan, *Manager (Birmingham)*

Coding Languages
PLAN, COBOL.

Services Available
Consultation, programming, education and training, preparation of data, systems analysis. Operate on a self-service and time-sharing basis.

Training
16 training courses provided.

SCOTTISH COUNCIL FOR COMMERCIAL, ADMINISTRATIVE AND PROFESSIONAL EDUCATION
22 Great King Street, Edinburgh, EH3 6QH, Scotland

Officers
C. A. Oakley, *Chairman*
D. M. H. Starforth, *Secretary*

Coding Language
COBOL.

Services Available
Advice, education and training.

Fields of Application
Commercial, accounting, management and systems analysis.

Training
Courses for diploma in Systems Analysis and Design (1 year), diploma in Data Processing (2 years), and certificate in Data Processing (2 years, day-release).

UNIVERSITIES AND COLLEGES

BELFAST COLLEGE OF TECHNOLOGY
College Square East, Belfast, BT1 6DJ, Northern Ireland
Telephone: Belfast 27244

Officer
G. E. Robinson, *Head of Department, Mathematics and Computer Studies*

Computer Installation
ELLIOTT 803B—operating system: manual; internal storage: 320K bits.

Coding Languages
Elliott ALGOL, Autocode, Machine Code, City and Guilds.

Services Available
Education and training, operators, preparation of data. Operate on a self-service and open shop basis.

Fields of Application
Scientific, statistical, management.

Training
RSA course in Computer Appreciation for Management; City and Guilds courses for Basic Certificate in Programming, Certificate for Programming and Information Processing.

BIRKBECK COLLEGE, UNIVERSITY OF LONDON*
Department of Computer Science
Malet Street, London, WC1E 7HX

Officers
Andrew D. Booth, *Honorary Director*
M. Levison, *Acting Head of Department*
W. A. Sentance, *Lecturer*
S. A. Evans, *Lecturer and Systems Programmer*

Computer Installation
ICL 1400—magnetic tapes: 2 Ampex; 1 line printer.

Coding Language
Special Autocode.

Services Available
Unlimited applications. Computer time may be hired by arrangement. Programming and advice at cost.

Field of Application
Specialized area: Mechanized linguistic analysis.

Training
B.Sc. and M.Sc. degree courses in Computer Science; M.Phil., Ph.D. of the University of London.

BLACKBURN COLLEGE OF TECHNOLOGY AND DESIGN
Feilden Street, Blackburn, Lancashire
Telephone: Blackburn 64321

Officers
J. Brown, *Head of Department of Mathematics, Computing and Statistics*
J. Tomlinson, *Computer Manager*
R. J. Owen, *Chief Systems Programmer*

Computer Installation
ICL 1903—operating system: GEORGE 1; internal storage: 768K bits; magnetic tapes: 4; magnetic discs: 3; 1 line printer. *Remote processing features*: 4 teletypes ASR33 (multiplexor).

Coding Languages
FORTRAN, ALGOL, COBOL, PLAN, BASIC, and (for schools) City and Guilds 319, ICL— CES, SIR, CESIL.

Services Available
Education and training. Operate on a remote access, closed shop and time-sharing basis. Available only to schools and colleges in the Local Education Authority area and the County, with limited overflow use to the Local Authority.

Fields of Application
Scientific, statistical, commercial, management, systems analysis, operational research, numerical analysis.
Specialized area: Linear programming.

Training
HND in Mathematics, Statistics and Computing; Part II of the BCS exams; Diploma in Computer Techniques (post-HND); Courses for other Departments are: HND in Management; Diploma in Management; HND in Mechanical Engineering and Production Engineering; HNC in Electrical Engineering.

BLACKPOOL COLLEGIATE GRAMMAR SCHOOL
Blackpool Old Road, Blackpool, Lancashire, FY3 7LS
Telephone: Blackpool 34911

Officers
G. Batty, *in charge of Computer Science*
E. Makin, *Head of Mathematics and Computer Science*

Computer Installation
PDP-8/E—operating system: EDUSYSTEM 10; internal storage: 49,152 bits.

Coding Languages
PAL III, BASIC, FORTRAN, ALGOL, FOCAL.

Contemplated Equipment
Increased storage of 98,304 bits; 2 magnetic tapes; 2 teletypes units.

Services Available
Education and training. Operate on a self-service basis.

Field of Application
Educational.

Training
GCE 'A' Level in Computer Science.

BOREHAM WOOD COLLEGE OF FURTHER EDUCATION
Elstree Way, Boreham Wood, Hertfordshire
Telephone: 01-953 6024/6

Officer
K. Staple, *Head of Engineering Department*

Computer Installations
ELLIOTT 803—internal storage: 8K 39-bit words.

Coding Languages
ELLIOTT T1 Code, ALGOL, BASIC, Autocode.

Services Available
Advice, programming, education and training. Operate on an open shop and time-sharing basis. Available to students and some industrial firms.

Fields of Application
Scientific, statistical, commercial.
Specialized area: General educational.

Training
GCE 'A' Level in Computer Science, City and Guilds 747 and 748, RSA Computer Appreciation.

BOURNEMOUTH COLLEGE OF TECHNOLOGY
Lansdowne, Bournemouth, Hampshire
Telephone: Bournemouth 20844

Officer
J. Sanger, *Head of Mathematics and Computing Department*

Computer Installation
IBM 1440—internal storage: 100K bits; magnetic discs: 2; 1 line printer. *On-line satellite computers*: Honeywell/GE.

Coding Languages
FORTRAN, COBOL, Autocoder.

Contemplated Equipment
Multi-access on-line system.

Services Available
Advice, programming, education and training. Operate on a closed shop basis. Available for educational purposes only.

Fields of Application
Scientific, statistical, commercial, operational research.
Specialized area: Linear programming.

Training
B.Sc. degree and several diploma courses in Computer Studies and Data Processing.

BRIGHTON POLYTECHNIC
Department of Computing and Cybernetics
Moulsecoomb, Brighton, Sussex, BN2 4GJ
Telephone: Brighton 67304

Officers
Dr. D. Longley, *Head of Department*
A. H. Warburton, *Head of Computer Centre*

Computer Installation
ICL 1905E—operating system: GEORGE 2, MAXIMOP; internal storage: 64K 24-bit words; magnetic tapes: 4; magnetic discs: 4; 1 line printer. *Remote processing feature*: 9-line multiplexer.

IBM 1130—internal storage: 4K 16-bit words; magnetic disc; console/printer.

Coding Languages
FORTRAN, ALGOL, BASIC, City and Guilds, Assembler, CECIL, JEAN.

Services Available
Advice, education and training, preparation of data. Operate on a closed-shop basis. Available on a standby basis to ICL customers and to customers where contact has arisen through student work or staff consultancy.

Fields of Application
Scientific, commercial, statistical, operational research.

Training
B.Sc. in Computer Science; Post-graduate Diploma in Computer Science, HND in Mathematics, Statistics and Computing; HNC in Computer Studies; NCC systems analysis course.

BRISTOL POLYTECHNIC
Unity Street, City, Bristol, BS1 5HP
Telephone: 0272 23016

Also at:
Ashley Down, Bristol 7
Telephone: 0272 41241

Officers
Mrs. K. Anstey, *Computer Manager*
Dr. C. T. Chudley, *Head of Department of Computer Studies and Mathematics*
Dr. K. W. Bolland, *Director*

Computer Installation
ICL 1902A—internal storage: 393K bits; magnetic discs: 2; 1 line printer.

Coding Languages
BASIC, PLAN, FORTRAN IV, COBOL, ALGOL, City and Guilds, SIR, CESIL.

Contemplated Equipment
Further 393K bits store, scanner and terminals.

Services Available
Education and training. Operate on a self-service basis. Available only for educational purposes.

Fields of Application
Scientific, statistical, management, systems analysis, operational research.
Specialized areas: Linear programming, analysis.

Training
HND and HNC courses in Mathematics, Statistics and Computing; NCC basic course in Systems Analysis; NCC courses for Higher Certificate in Systems Analysis; BCS Part I course; short courses in COBOL and FORTRAN programming.

BROOKLANDS COUNTY TECHNICAL COLLEGE*
Department of Science
Heath Road, Weybridge, Surrey
Telephone: Weybridge 43286

Officers
A. N. Hobbs, *Senior Lecturer in charge (Systems)*
A. Beake, *Lecturer (Programming, Data Processing)*
Dr. W. Parker, *Assistant Lecturer (Statistics, Operational Research)*
I. Mann, *Lecturer (Mathematics, Statistics)*
L. Williams, *Engineer in Charge (Hardware, Programming)*

Computer Installation
ICL Pegasus—internal storage: 8K bits; magnetic tapes: 4.

Coding Languages
COBOL, FORTRAN, Autocode, City and Guilds 319, ALGOL.

Contemplated Equipment
ICL 1903 with internal storage of 16K bits; disc and tape orientated.

Services Available
Advice, programming. Operate on an open shop basis. Equipment not suited to commercial work.

Fields of Application
Calculations for mechanical engineers, scientific laboratories, statistics. Also deal with training in commercial techniques, including systems work and operational research.

Training
HNC Computer Studies; BCS part I; GCE 'A' level Computer Science; City and Guilds 319, 320, 383; appreciation courses; programming courses.

BRUNEL UNIVERSITY*
Computer Science Department
Kingston Lane, Uxbridge, Middlesex

Officer
M. L. V. Pitteway, *Professor of Computer Science*

Computer Installations
ICL 1903A—operating system: GEORGE 2; internal storage: 786,432 plus 196,608 bits; magnetic tapes: 4; magnetic discs: 2 CDC type; 1 line printer. *On-line satellite computers*: ICL 1901A and Elliott 803B.

CTL Modular 1—experimental operating system only; internal storage: 131,072 bits; 1 mini-disc.

Coding Languages
ALGOL, COBOL, FORTRAN, PLAN.

Contemplated Equipment
Universal Scanner, 64K bits core, ICL 1904A.

Services Available
Consultation, programming, education and training, operators, software packages, documentation. Operate on a block time, closed shop and time-sharing basis.

Fields of Application
Full university range.
Specialized area: Computer graphics.

Training
Bachelor of Technology and Master of Technology Honours Degree courses.

CAMBRIDGESHIRE COLLEGE OF ARTS AND TECHNOLOGY
Collier Road, Cambridge, CB1 2AJ
Telephone: 0223-63271

Officers
D. E. Mumford, *Principal*
J. D. Irwin, *Vice-Principal*
F. P. Wright, *Director of Computer Centre*

Computer Installation
IBM 1130—operating system: DMS; internal storage: 128K bits; magnetic discs: 1 1131, 1 2310; 1 line printer.

Coding Languages
FORTRAN, COBOL, CESIL, BASIC, Assembler.

Contemplated Equipment
1 line printer, 1 disc drive.

Services Available
Advice, education and training, preparation of data. Operate on a self service and block time basis.

Fields of Application
Scientific, statistical, commercial.

Training
Day release courses for BCS, GCE 'A' level, City and Guilds, RSA and HNC qualifications, and a full-time 'A' level course in Computer Science.

CARLISLE TECHNICAL COLLEGE
Carlisle, Cumberland

Officers
G. H. Vick, *Principal*
R. Hogg, *Head of Computer Science Department*

Computer Installation
The College has access by time-sharing to Bull General Electric GE 625.

Coding Languages
FORTRAN, BASIC, ALGOL.

Contemplated Equipment
NCR Century 100 or IBM 1130 with storage of 16K bits.

Services Available
Advice, education and training. Operate on a time-sharing basis.

Fields of Application
Scientific, statistical, commercial, production control, accounting, management, systems analysis, operational research.

Training
GCE 'A' level in Computer Science, City and Guilds 459, NCC Certificate in Systems Analysis.

CHELSEA CENTRE FOR SCIENCE EDUCATION, UNIVERSITY OF LONDON
Bridges Place, London, SW6 4HR
Telephone: 01-736 3401

Officer
R. Lewis, *Lecturer in Education*

Computer Installation
DATA GENERAL 1220–operating system: DOS; internal storage: 384K bits; magnetic tapes: 1 cassette; magnetic discs: 1.

Coding Language
BASIC.

Contemplated Equipment
Moving head disc, high speed paper tape reader, line printer.

Services Available
Advice, programming, education and training, software packages. Operate on a time-sharing basis. Restricted to educational users.

Field of Application
Education.
Specialized area: Simulation.

Training
Post-graduate certificate in Science and Mathematics Education with computer education options.

CITY OF LEICESTER POLYTECHNIC
School of Mathematics, Computing and Statistics
P.O. Box 143, Leicester, LE1 9BH
Telephone: Leicester 50181

Officer
A. H. Wise, *Head of Computer Centre*

Computer Installation
HONEYWELL H200–operating system: Mod 1 (TR and MSR); internal storage: 8K x 24 bits; magnetic tapes: 5 204B; magnetic discs: 1 259; 1 line printer. *On-line satellite computer:* DDP 516–operating system: BOS; internal storage: 16K x 16 bits; magnetic discs: 1 259. *Remote processing features:* P.M.L.C. 16 lines.

Coding Languages
Easycoder, FORTRAN, COBOL CSL, WORDCOM, ALEX, PL516.

Services Available
Operate on a time-sharing basis, on a closed shop basis (H 200) and on an open shop basis (DDP 516).

Fields of Application
Scientific, statistical, commercial, systems analysis, operational research.
Specialized areas: Linear programming, computer-aided design.

Training
Full-time courses in computer science up to honours degree level; diplomas to BCS Part II level; part-time day and evening courses.

THE CITY UNIVERSITY*
St. John Street, London, EC1V 4PB
Telephone: 01-253 4399

Officer
B. Girling, *Manager of Hybrid Computing System*

Computer Installation
EAI 690–internal storage: 128K bits. *On-line satellite computer:* ICL 1905, with 4 magnetic tape units, 2 magnetic discs and 1 line printer.

Coding Languages
FORTRAN IV, Hybrid Operations Interpreter, Assembler

Contemplated Equipment
Double the amount of store, own discs and line printer.

Services Available
Consultation, programming, education and training, systems analysis. Operate on a self-service and open shop basis. Services available to staff, undergraduates and post-graduate students of the university, and to industrial organization for research only.

Field of Application
Scientific.
Specialized areas: Optimization and control.

Training
B.Sc. and M.Sc. degree courses in Computer Science.

COLLEGE OF TECHNOLOGY, LETCHWORTH*
Broadway, Letchworth, Hertfordshire
Telephone: Letchworth 3911

Officer
A. F. Woodhurst, *Lecturer in Charge*

Computer Installation
NHECTA II—internal storage: 40, 960 bits.

Coding Languages
PEARL, FORTRAN.

Contemplated Equipment
Increased internal storage; small magnetic tape deck; hardware floating-point decimal arithmetic unit.

Services Available
Advice, programming and data punching service, special lectures, subroutine packages. Operate on an open shop basis.

Fields of Application
Teaching programming and operating at varying levels—Nhecta II is specifically designed to facilitate instruction of this type.
Specialized areas: Logical design, design of machine code, circuit design, compiler writing.

Training
HND and HNC in Mathematics, Statistics and Computing and in Computer Studies. Special short courses in programming and computer appreciation.

COVENTRY TECHNICAL COLLEGE
Butts, Coventry, Warwickshire, CV1 3GD
Telephone: Coventry 57221

Officer
R. A. Arculus, *Principal*

Coding Languages
ALGOL, FORTRAN, COBOL, BASIC.

Services Available
Education and training. Operate on a closed shop basis.

Fields of Application
Commercial, management.

Training
Courses in systems analysis, computer programming and data processing.

CRANFIELD INSTITUTE OF TECHNOLOGY
Cranfield Computing Centre
Cranfield, Bedford
Telephone: Bedford 51551, extension 334

Officers
Professor D. R. Bland, *Professor of Mathematics and Head of Department of Mathematics*
K. G. Beauchamp, *Computer Director*
Miss M. E. Williamson, *Principal Programmer*
P. G. Thowasson, *Senior Programmer*

Computer Installation
ICL 1905—operating system: Executive; internal storage: 32K bits; magnetic tapes: 4; magnetic discs: 2; 2 line printers.
DIGICO M16/P (2) and M16/V linked to form hybrid unit.

Coding Languages
FORTRAN IV, ALGOL, COBOL, PLAN.

Contemplated Equipment
ICL 1903/T to replace 1905.

Services Available
Advice, operators, preparation of data, programming, research. Operate on a closed shop basis. Available for education and research only.

Fields of Application
Scientific engineering and business applications of digital and analogue computers.
Specialized areas: Signal processing and simulation.

Training
Courses in Symbolic programming, data processing, digital, analogue and hybrid techniques.

EDGE HILL COLLEGE OF EDUCATION
St. Helen's Road, Ormskirk, Lancashire

Officer
P. K. C. Millins, *Principal*

Computer Installation
Off-line link to ICL 1901A.

Coding Languages
BASIC, FORTRAN.

Contemplated Equipment
A computer with storage of 8K bits and remote access terminals.

Service Available
Education and training. Operate on a time-sharing basis.

Fields of Application
Scientific, statistical.

Training
Courses provided as part of Certificate in Education and Bachelor of Education Degree, and in-service courses for teachers.

ETON COLLEGE
Windsor, Berkshire
Telephone: 63697

Officers
M. McCrum, *Headmaster*
R. G. Prior, *Head of Computing Department*

Computer Installation
ELLIOTT 903—operating system: CPU; internal storage: 147,456 bits.

Coding Languages
ALGOL, FORTRAN, SIR, MASIR, City and Guilds.

Services Available
Operate on a self-service basis. Available only to schools.

Field of Application
Education.

Training
Only general courses within the normal school curriculum.

FALKIRK TECHNICAL COLLEGE
Grangemouth Road, Falkirk, Stirlingshire, FK2 9AD, Scotland
Telephone: Falkirk 22766

Officers
Dr. W. W. Easton, *Principal*
N. Ferguson, *Head of Mathematics and Computing Department*

United Kingdom – Universities and Colleges

Computer Installation
ICL 1901A – operating system: GEORGE 1S; internal storage: 196,608 bits; magnetic discs: 1 twin EDS; 1 line printer.

Coding Languages
FORTRAN, ALGOL, BASIC, COBOL, TAM, City and Guilds Mnemonic, PLAN, NICOL.

Services Available
Education and training, schools service. Operate on a closed shop and time-sharing basis.

Fields of Application
Scientific, statistical, commercial, management, systems analysis and operational research.
Specialized area: Analysis.

Training
Courses for ONC in Mathematics, Statistics and Computing (day release and evening), HNC in Mathematics, Statistics, and Computing (evening), BCS Part 1 (evening), Computer Studies (day release and evening), SNC in Business Studies (with computer options) (full-time), SHNC in Data Processing (day release), SHND in Data Processing (day release), SHND in Data Processing (full-time), Computer Programming and Computer Processing (full-time), short programming courses in FORTRAN, ALGOL, COBOL and PLAN (day release and evening), Computer Appreciation Courses.

FARNBOROUGH COLLEGE OF TECHNOLOGY
Boundary Road, Farnborough, Hampshire
Telephone: 45061

Officers
Dr. T. D. H. Baber, *Principal*
V. A. Williams, *Vice Principal*

Computer Installation
IBM 1131/2B – operating system: Monitor; internal storage: 8,192 16-bit words; magnetic discs: 5 2315; 1 line printer.

Coding Languages
FORTRAN, COBOL, SL/1, RPG, APL, Assembler.

Services Available
Education and training. Operate on a block time, open shop and time-sharing basis. Available only to students and staff under training.

Fields of Application
Scientific, statistical, commercial, production control, accounting, management, systems analysis, operational research.
Specialized areas: Sales analysis, linear programming, investment.

Training
HNC course in Mathematics, Statistics and Computing.

FLINTSHIRE COLLEGE OF TECHNOLOGY*
Connah's Quay, Deeside, Flintshire, Wales

Computer Installation
ICL 1903 – operating system: GEORGE; internal storage: 768K bits; magnetic discs: 2; 1 line printer. *Remote processing features*: 8 teletypes.

Coding Languages
PLAN, ALGOL, FORTRAN, COBOL, JEAN, City and Guilds.

Services Available
Consultation, education and training, software packages, documentation, systems analysis. Operate on a self-service basis.

Fields of Application
Scientific, statistical, commercial, management, accounting, systems analysis, etc.

Training
BCS 1, BCS 2, HND in Computer Studies, HND in Business (Computing). Also short courses in systems, operational research, programming techniques.

FOREST GRAMMAR SCHOOL
Winnersh, Wokingham, Berkshire
Telephone: Wokingham 781626

Officers
A. T. Pomeroy
D. L. A. Hooper

Computer Installation
PDP-8/E – internal storage: 4K bits.

Coding Languages
BASIC, ALGOL, FORTRAN, FOCAL, PAL III.

Services Available
Education and training. Operate on a self-service basis.

Field of Application
Educational.

GLAMORGAN POLYTECHNIC
Llantwit Road, Treforest, Pontypridd, Glamorgan, Wales
Telephone: Pontypridd 3284

Officer
D. J. Green

Computer Installation
IBM 1130/2C – internal storage: 16K 16-bit words; magnetic discs: 3 IBM 2315; 2 line printers. *Remote processing features*: IBM 870.
PDP-11/10.

Coding Languages
FORTRAN, Assembler, RPG, PL/1, COBOL.

Services Available
Advice, operators, preparation of data, programming, software packages, systems analysis. Operate on a closed shop basis.

Fields of Application
Scientific, statistical, commercial, management, operational research.

Training
CNAA B.Sc. degree in Computer Sciences; CNAA B.Sc. degree in Mathematics and Computer Sciences; HND in Mathematics, Statistics and Computing; HND in Computer Studies; HNC in Computer Studies.
Evening classes (course of 10 two-hour sessions) in computer programming, computer applications, computers in management and computers in engineering.

United Kingdom – Universities and Colleges

HATFIELD POLYTECHNIC
Computer Centre
P.O. Box 109, College Lane, Hatfield, Hertfordshire,
AL10 9AB
Telephone: Hatfield 68100

Officer
Miss D. A. Nelson, *Director of the Computer Centre*

Computer Installation
PDP-10–operating system: Monitor 5; internal storage: 240K 36-bit words; magnetic tapes: 7 DEC; magnetic discs: 1 FH, 1 drum, 6 exchange; 1 line printer. *On-line satellite computer*: PDP-8/I. *Remote processing features*: 66 ASR33 teletypes.

Coding Languages
ALGOL, BASIC, FORTRAN, COBOL, MACRO-10, BBCX, POP-2, SNOBOL, LISP.

Services Available
Advice, preparation of data, programming. Operate on a remote access, closed shop and time-sharing basis. Available to staff and students, to schools and colleges in Hertfordshire, and to other users by special arrangement.

Fields of Application
Scientific, statistical, commercial, management, teaching, research.
Specialized areas: Linear programming, structural engineering and teaching packages.

Training
M.Sc., B.Sc. and HND courses in Computer Science offered by the Department of Computer Science.

HERIOT-WATT UNIVERSITY
Computer Centre
37/39 Grassmarket, Edinburgh, EH1 2HW, Scotland
Telephone: 031-226 5601

Officer
Prof. A. Balfour, *Director*

Computer Installation
ELLIOTT 4130–operating systems: DES 1, DES 2; internal storage: 2,359K bits; magnetic tapes: 4; magnetic discs: 4; 2 line printers. *Remote processing features*: 8 on-line teletypes.

Coding Languages
NEAT Assembly Language, ALGOL, FORTRAN, COBOL, POP, BASIC.

Contemplated Equipment
On-line satellite computer.

Services Available
Advice, programming, education and training, software packages, documentation, preparation of data, systems analysis. Operate on a closed shop basis.

Fields of Application
Scientific, statistical, commercial, production control, accounting, management, system analysis.

Training
B.Sc. (Ord. & Hons.) in Computer Science; M.Sc. in Computer Science; short courses in Computer Appreciation, ALGOL, FORTRAN, COBOL.

HUDDERSFIELD POLYTECHNIC
Queensgate, Huddersfield, Yorkshire, HD1 3DH
Telephone: Huddersfield 30501

Officers
R. Shaw, *Head of Department of Computer Studies and Mathematics*
A. F. Nightingale, *Computer Manager*

Computer Installation
ICL 4120–operating system: NICE; internal storage: 528K bits; magnetic tapes: 4; 1 line printer.

IBM 1130–operating system: DMS; internal storage: 512K bits; magnetic discs: 2 2310; 1 line printer.

Coding Languages
NEAT, ALGOL, COBOL, FORTRAN, BASIC, RPG, Assembler.

Services Available
Advice, operators, preparation of data. Operate on a closed shop and open shop basis.

Fields of Application
Scientific, statistical, commercial, management.

Training
HND and HNC in Computer Studies; BCS Parts I and II Examinations; National Computing Centre Basic Systems Analysis Course.

IMPERIAL COLLEGE OF SCIENCE AND TECHNOLOGY, UNIVERSITY OF LONDON
Computer Centre
South Kensington, London, SW7 2BX
Telephone: 01-589 5111

Officers
S. G. W. Nordanholt, *Director*
J. L. Benbow, *Computer Manager*
P. Whitehead, *Programming Manager*
T. E. Mitchell, *Operations Manager*

Computer Installations
CDC 6400–operating system: KRONOS; internal storage: 3,932,160 bits; magnetic tapes: 6 604; magnetic discs: 7 841; 2 line printers. *On-line satellite computer*: CDC 1700. *Remote processing features*: up to 64 teletypewriters.

CDC 1700–operating system: MSOS; internal storage: 524,288 bits; magnetic tapes: 2 608; magnetic disc: 1 CDC5; 1 line printer. *Remote processing features*: Graphics.

Coding Languages
COMPASS, BASIC, COBOL, FORTRAN, ALGOL 60, SNOBOL, APL.

Service Available
Education and training. Operate on a self-service, remote access, closed shop and time-sharing basis.

Field of Application
Scientific.

Training
Courses relating to computing facilities.

IMPERIAL COLLEGE OF SCIENCE AND TECHNOLOGY, UNIVERSITY OF LONDON
Department of Computing and Control
London SW7
Telephone: 01-589 5111

Officers
Prof. J. H. Westcott, *Head of Department*
Prof. M. M. Lehman, *Prof. of Computing Science and Head of Computing Science Section*
S. G. W. Nordanholt, *Director of Computing Services*

Computer Installation
CDC 6400—operating system: KRONOS; internal storage: 65,536 x 60 bits; magnetic tapes: 6 604; magnetic discs: 6 841, 2 6638; 2 line printers. *Remote processing features*: 64 teletypewriter terminals.

IBM 7094—operating system: IBSYS; internal storage: 32K bits; magnetic tapes: 10 729; magnetic disc: 1 1301; 2 line printers. *On-line satellite computers*: 1 1460, 1 1401.

Coding Languages
All standard languages.

Contemplated Equipment
IBM 360/40 and 370/135.

Services Available
Advice, education and training. Operate on a self-service, remote access, time-sharing, closed and open shop basis. Available generally to members of UK universities and in particular to members of the University of London.

Fields of Application
Scientific, and statistical.

Training
Courses for B.Sc. (Eng) and M.Sc. in Computing Science and research courses leading to M.Phil, or Ph.D.

JORDANHILL COLLEGE OF EDUCATION
76 Southbrae Drive, Glasgow, G13 1PP, Scotland
Telephone: 041-959 1232

Officers
Dr. T. R. Bone, *Principal*
J. O. Hawthorn, *Senior Lecturer – Computer Education*

Computer Installation
IBM 1130 (1131 B); internal storage: 8K bits; magnetic disc: 1 2315; 1 line printer.

Coding Languages
FORTRAN, BASIC, SL/1, ALGOL, COBOL, RPG.

Contemplated Equipment
Mark sense card reader.

Services Available
Advice, programming, education and training, operators, software packages, documentation and preparation of data. Operate on a closed shop basis. Available to local schools.

Training
Courses for B.Ed. (Ordinary Standard – Computing). In-service courses for teachers.

KINGSTON POLYTECHNIC
Computer Unit
Penrhyn Road, Kingston upon Thames, Surrey
Telephone: 01-549 1366

Officers
L. M. Newall, *Director*
K. S. H. Halstead, *Programming Manager*
Miss E. Law, *Computer Manager (1905)*
W. A. Cockett, *Computer Manager (4120)*

Computer Installation
ICL 1905—operating system: GEORGE 2; internal storage: 768K bits; magnetic tapes: 2 7-track; magnetic discs: 2; 1 line printer.

ICL 4120—operating system: BATCH; internal storage: 768K bits; magnetic tapes: 4 7-track; 1 line printer.

Coding Languages
ALGOL, FORTRAN, COBOL, NEAT (4120), PLAN (1905).

Contemplated Equipment
Multiplexer for 1905.

Services Available
Education and training. Operate on a self-service and closed shop basis. Outside use limited.

Fields of Application
Scientific, statistical, commercial.

Training
Honours and Ordinary degrees in Computer Science.

KING'S COLLEGE, UNIVERSITY OF LONDON
Computer Unit
The Strand, London, WC2R 2LS
Telephone: 01-836 5454

Officers
D. C. Knight, *Computing Manager*
R. Kingslake, *Systems Programmer*

Computer Installation
CDC 1700—operating system: MSOS; internal storage: 32K x 16 bits; magnetic discs: 2 CDC 854; 1 line printer. *Remote processing features*: 12 on-line teletypes.

Coding Language
FORTRAN.

Services Available
Operate on a closed shop basis. Restricted to staff and student members of the College.

Fields of Application
Scientific, statistical, educational.

Training
Science and engineering degree courses have computing options.

LANCHESTER POLYTECHNIC
Priory Street, Coventry, Warwickshire, CV1 5FB
Telephone: Coventry 24166

Officers
K. Legg, *Director*
K. Normington, *Computer Manager*
J. E. Sellars, *Head of Department of Computer Science*

Computer Installation
ICL 1903A—operating system: GEORGE 3; internal storage: 64K 24-bit words; magnetic tapes: 4 7-track; magnetic discs: 3 EDS8; 1 line printer. *Remote processing features*: 2 7020 terminals with 9MOP teletypes.

Coding Languages
ALGOL, FORTRAN, COBOL, PLAN, CESIL, SIR, CSL, SIMON, SLAM, BASIC.

Contemplated Equipment
Extra core store of 32K words and an extra EDS8 disc.

Services Available
Advice, education and training, systems analysis. Operate on a closed shop and time-sharing basis. Available for non-continuing work, particularly of a research nature.

Fields of Application
Scientific, statistical, education.

Training
Degree course in Computer Science, HND course in Computer Studies and in Mathematics, Statistics and Computing.

LEEDS POLYTECHNIC*
Calverley Street, Leeds, Yorkshire, LS1 3HE
Telephone: Leeds 36191

Officers
J. J. Kiely, *Head of Department of Mathematics and Computing*
B. J. Vokes, *Principal Lecturer*
M. S. James, *Senior Lecturer*
D. Owen, *Senior Lecturer*
J. A. Webster, *Senior Lecturer*

Computer Installation
ICL 1901—internal storage: 393,216 bits; magnetic disc: ICL 2801; 1 line printer.

Coding Languages
ALGOL, COBOL, FORTRAN IV, PLAN.

Services Available
Advice, preparation of data, programming. Operate on a closed shop basis. Not available for large scale commercial use.

Fields of Application
Teaching computer programming and applications.
Specialized areas: Numerical analysis, statistical analysis, operational research.

Training
HND in Computer Methods (3 years' full-time study); HNC in Mathematics, Statistics and Computing (2 years' part-time study); B.Sc. Ordinary Degree in Operational Research with Computing (4 years' full-time study).

LIVERPOOL POLYTECHNIC
Computer Centre
Byrom Street, Liverpool 3, Lancashire
Telephone: 051-207 3581

Officers
P. D. Potts, *Head of the Department of Mathematics and Computing*
F. W. Royle, *Computer Manager*

Computer Installation
ICL 1902A—operating system: GEORGE 2 and 3; internal storage: 790K bits; magnetic tapes: 4 1971; magnetic discs: 1 EDS8; 1 line printer. *Remote processing features*: graph plotter.

ELLIOTT 803B—internal storage: 319K bits.

Coding Languages
ALGOL, FORTRAN, COBOL, PLAN, Assembler.

Contemplated Equipment
Another EDS8; 1350 LPM line printer; card punch.

Services Available
Advice, programming, education and training, operators, software packages, documentation, preparation of data, systems analysis. Operate on a closed shop basis.

Fields of Application
Scientific, statistical, production control, accounting, management, systems analysis, operational research.
Specialized areas: Linear programming, structural engineering, medical research, teaching.

Training
HND and HNC courses in Mathematical Statistics Computing; HND course in Computer Studies; BCS Part I.

LLANDAFF COLLEGE OF TECHNOLOGY
Western Avenue, Cardiff, CF5 2YB, Wales
Telephone: Cardiff 561241

Officers
J. Cotterell, *Principal of College*
P. B. Williams, *Head of the Department of Physical Sciences and Mathematics*

Computer Installation
The college operates on ICL 7020 RJE terminal connected to an ICL 1903A computer with an internal storage of 64K bits.

Coding Languages
PLAN, CESIL, SIR, ALGOL, FORTRAN, COBOL, BASIC.

Services Available
Advice, education and training. Operate on a self-service and remote access basis. Available only to local educational establishments, including the training of school teachers.

Fields of Application
Scientific, statistical, commercial, production control, management, systems analysis.
Specialized area: Computing in schools.

Training
Courses provided: BCS Part I; City and Guilds 747; Teacher Training in Computing; also short specialist courses in systems analysis, programming, etc.

LLANELLI TECHNICAL COLLEGE
Alban Road, Llanelli, Carmarthenshire, SA15 ING, Wales
Telephone: Llanelli 59165

Officer
Leonard A. Jones, *Principal*

Computer Installation
ELLIOTT 903—internal storage: 147,456 bits.

Coding Languages
ALGOL, FORTRAN, Workshop, SIR.

Contemplated Equipment
A multi-access mini-computer.

Services Available
Advice, programming, education and training, preparation of data. Operate on an open shop basis.

Fields of Application
Scientific, statistical.
Specialized areas: Linear programming, analysis.

Training
Courses provided: GCE 'A' level in Computer Science; RSA Digital Computer Appreciation; OND Business Studies, Elements of Computers.

LONDON GRADUATE SCHOOL OF BUSINESS STUDIES (LONDON BUSINESS SCHOOL)
Sussex Place, Regent's Park, London, NW1 4SA
Telephone: 01-262 5050

Officers
Prof. R. J. Ball, *Principal*
J. R. Eaton, *Director of Computing*

Computer Installation
INTERDATA 70—operating system: RJE; internal storage: 1,024K bits; 1 magnetic disc; 1 line printer. *Remote processing features*: 4800 baud link to an IBM 360/65.

HEWLETT PACKARD 2000E—operating system: time-sharing; internal storage: 172K bits; 2 magnetic discs.

Coding Languages
Assembler, BASIC.

Services Available
Advice, programming. Operate on a time-sharing basis. Available only to students and staff of the School.

Fields of Application
Commercial, accounting, management, operational research.
Specialized areas: Linear programming, investment.

Training
A two-year course in Business Studies, leading to an M.Sc. degree of the University of London.

LONDON POLYTECHNICS COMPUTER UNIT
Polytechnic of North London, Holloway Road, London, N7 8DB
Telephone: 01-607 6767

Officers
B. C. Rowe, *Head of Unit*
Mrs. B. J. Farmer, *Chief Programmer*

Computer Installation
ICL 1905E—operating system: GEORGE 2 and 3; magnetic tapes: 4; magnetic discs: 3; 1 line printer. *Remote processing features*: Multiplexor and 4 7020 terminals.

Coding Languages
ALGOL, FORTRAN IV, COBOL, PLAN.

Contemplated Equipment
Replacement of Multiplexor by Communications Processor.

Services Available
Advice, operators, software packages. Operate on a closed shop and remote access basis. Priority to educational establishments.

Fields of Application
Scientific and software research, teaching, data processing, systems development, college administration, statistical.

LONDON SCHOOL OF ECONOMICS, UNIVERSITY OF LONDON
Computer Services Unit
Houghton Street, Aldwych, London, WC2A 2AE
Telephone: 01-405 7686, extension 597

Officer
P. Wakeford, *Computer Unit Manager*

Computer Installation
The Unit has 2 CDC 200 terminals linked to a CDC 6600.

Coding Languages
FORTRAN, BASIC, ALGOL, SNOBOL, COBOL.

Contemplated Equipment
A programmable terminal.

Services Available
Advice, programming, education and training, software packages, documentation, preparation of data. Operate on an open shop and time-sharing basis. Not available for commercial purposes.

Fields of Application
Statistical, systems analysis, operational research, information retrieval.
Specialized area: Survey analysis.

Training
Computing as a special subject in B.Sc. (Econ.) course. Other courses arranged as necessary, including programming courses, lectures on specific computer topics and general introductions.

LOUGHBOROUGH UNIVERSITY OF TECHNOLOGY*
Loughborough, Leicestershire, LE 11 3TU
Telephone: Loughborough 3171

Officer
D. C. Hogg, *Manager of the Computer Centre*

Computer Installation
ICL 1904A.

Services Available
Available to outside users for research, etc.

Fields of Application
Problems arising in aeronautical, automotive, chemical, civil, electrical, industrial, mechanical and production engineering, physical education, industrial fitness, ergonomics and cybernetics and applied science.

MANCHESTER POLYTECHNIC*
John Dalton Faculty of Technology
Chester Street, Manchester
Telephone: 061-236 7784

Officer
G. Blundell, *Senior Lecturer*

Computer Installation
ELLIOTT 803—internal storage: 8,192 39-bit words; 3 magnetic film units.

Coding Languages
ALGOL, Elliott Autocode, Language H, Machine Code, Assembly, City and Guilds.

Services Available
Consultation, education and training. Operate on a block time basis.

Field of Application
Scientific.

Training
HND in Mathematics, Statistics and Computing; HND in Computer Studies; 2-week courses in Computer Appreciation, ALGOL, FORTRAN, COBOL, Computing for Hospital Personnel.

MEDWAY AND MAIDSTONE COLLEGE OF TECHNOLOGY*
Horsted, Maidstone Road, Chatham, Kent
Telephone: Medway 41001-2-3-4

Officer
D. M. Esterson, *Director*

Computer Installation
ELLIOTT 903C—internal storage: 8K bits; magnetic tapes: 3 TM7; 1 line printer.

ICL 1901A—internal storage: 16K bits; magnetic tapes: 2; twin EDS; 1 line printer.

Coding Languages
ALGOL, FORTRAN, SIR, PLAN, COBOL.

Services Available
Advice, operators, preparation of data, programming, systems analysis. Operate on an open shop basis.

Fields of Application
Education and research in mathematics, engineering and electronics.

Training
Courses in computer appreciation, computer applications for commercial data processing, programming and systems analysis and design; C and G Data Processing for Computer Uses; C and G Certificate in Business Studies; HNC in Mathematics, Statistics and Computing, and in Computer Studies; HND in Computer Studies; RSA Computer Appreciation for Management.

MIDDLESEX POLYTECHNIC AT ENFIELD
Computing Centre
Queensway, Enfield, Middlesex, EN3 4SF
Telephone: 01-804 8131

Officer
Derek J. Bush, *Head of the Computing Centre*

Computer Installation
HONEYWELL H120—operating system: Disc and Tape; internal storage: 294,912 bits; magnetic tapes: 4 204B; magnetic discs: 2 259; 1 line printer. *Remote processing features*: Off-line links.

ICL 1903—operating system: GEORGE 1; internal storage: 819,200 bits; magnetic tapes: 4; magnetic discs: 2; 1 line printer.

Coding Languages
FORTRAN, Easycoder, ALGOL, WORDCOM, COBOL, City and Guilds Mnemonic Code, ECSL, PLAN.

Contemplated Equipment
Multi-access system.

Services Available
Education and training, software packages. Operate on a remote access, closed shop and time-sharing basis.

Fields of Application
Scientific, statistical, commercial, operational research.
Specialized areas: Structural engineering, educational, computer-aided design.

Training
Courses provided: B.Sc. in Mathematics for Business; B.Sc. in Society and Technology; NCC courses in systems analysis; BCS, Part I and II; HNC in Mathematics, Statistics and Computing; HNC in Computer Studies; B.A. in Business Studies; B.A. in Accounting and Finance; HND in Business Studies.

MORAY HOUSE COLLEGE OF EDUCATION
Centre for Computer Education
Holyrood Road, Edinburgh, EH8 8AQ, Scotland
Telephone: 031-556 4415

Officer
P. J. Barker, *Director*

Computer Installation
IBM 1130—operating system: Monitor; internal storage: 128K bits; magnetic discs: 1 2311; 1 line printer.

Coding Languages
FORTRAN, COBOL, ALGOL, BASIC, SL/1, City and Guilds 319, TAM.

Contemplated Equipment
A faster line printer.

Services Available
Advice, programming, education and training, operators, software packages, preparation of data, systems analysis. Operate on an open shop basis. Available only to College students and staff and to schools in south-east Scotland served by the Centre.

Fields of Application
Statistical, educational.
Specialized areas: Student training, secondary education.

Training
Courses for trainee and serving teachers.

NAPIER COLLEGE OF SCIENCE AND TECHNOLOGY*
Colinton Road, Edinburgh, EH10 5DT, Scotland
Telephone: 031-447 1011

Officer
D. F. Leach, *Head of Department of Mathematics*

Computer Installation
ELLIOTT 4120—operating system: B20; internal storage: 393,216 bits.

Coding Languages
ALGOL, FORTRAN, NEAT, City and Guilds Mnemonic.

Contemplated Equipment
3 magnetic tapes; extra 196,608 bits internal storage; 1 line printer.

Services Available
Consultation, programming, education and training. Operate on a closed shop basis. Service available to educational and industrial establishments in the Edinburgh area.

Fields of Application
Scientific, statistical, production control, operational research, engineering software programming, computer-assisted typesetting.

Training
ONC/HNC in Mathematics, Statistics and Computing. BCS Part I course.
Short courses in Computer Studies (Technological); ALGOL Programming and Computer Appreciation; Introduction to Information Retrieval.

NEW UNIVERSITY OF ULSTER
Coleraine, County Londonderry, Northern Ireland
Telephone: Coleraine 4141, extension 530

Officers
R. D. Atherley, *Computing Services Manager*
R. H. Blackwood, *Senior Computer Officer*
B. McDowell, *Senior Computer Officer*

Computer Installation
ICL 1903A–operating system: GEORGE 2; internal storage: 32K 24-bit words; magnetic tapes: 1 1971/2; magnetic discs: 2 2802/3; 1 line printer.

Coding Languages
ALGOL, FORTRAN, PLAN, COBOL.

Contemplated Equipment
An increase in storage to 64K words; communications scanner 7930; EDS 60.

Services Available
Primarily for University use, both academic and administrative.

Fields of Application
Scientific, statistical, management.

Training
Units of computing are available as parts of a degree course.

NEWCASTLE UPON TYNE POLYTECHNIC
Ellison Place, Newcastle upon Tyne, NE1 8ST
Telephone: Newcastle 26002

Officer
R. Fleeting, *Director of Computing*

Computer Installation
IBM 1620–internal storage: 60K bits; magnetic discs: 1; 1 line printer.

IBM 360/67–internal storage: 1 million bytes. *On-line satellite computer*: IBM 1130.

Coding Languages
FORTRAN, ALGOL, PL/1, COBOL.

Services Available
Advice, operating and programming services. Available to outside users for business and research purposes.

Fields of Application
Scientific, statistical.
Specialized areas: Geophysics, crystallography, mechanical vibrations.

Training
Twelve-week programming courses.

NEWPORT AND MONMOUTHSHIRE COLLEGE OF TECHNOLOGY*
Allt-Yr-Yn Avenue, Newport, Monmouthshire, NPT 5XA
Telephone: Newport 51525/6/7

Officer
B. Robins, *Principal*

Computer Installation
ELLIOTT 803.

Coding Languages
Elliott Autocode, ALGOL.

Services Available
Limited availability.

Training
Twelve-week programming courses; HNC in Mathematics, Statistics and Computing; L.I.M.A. systems analysis; 'A' level computer science; data processing.

NORTH-EAST LONDON POLYTECHNIC
Barking Precinct
Department of Systems Engineering and Computer Studies
Longbridge Road, Dagenham, Essex, RM8 2AS

Officers
J. R. Thompson, *Head of Department*
A. C. Causon, *Head of Computer Centre*

Computer Installation
IBM 1130–operating system: Monitor 2; internal storage: 256K bits; magnetic discs: 1 2315; 2 line printers.

ICL 4120–internal storage: 384K bits.

Coding Languages
FORTRAN, COBOL, ALGOL, Assembler, NEAT.

Services Available
Advice, programming, education and training, systems analysis. Operate on a closed shop and time-sharing basis.

Fields of Application
Scientific, statistical, management, systems analysis.

Training
Courses available: HND in Computer Studies; special short courses in languages, systems analysis, data processing and numerical methods.

NORTH GLOUCESTERSHIRE COLLEGE OF TECHNOLOGY
The Park, Cheltenham, Gloucestershire, GL50 2RR
Telephone: Cheltenham 28021

Officer
A. N. Barber, *Principal*

Computer Installation
ICL 1904E–internal storage: 1,570K bits; magnetic tapes: 4 1971; magnetic discs: 2 2802; 1 line printer.

Coding Languages
PLAN, COBOL, FORTRAN, ALGOL.

Services Available
Advice, programming, education and training, preparation of data, systems analysis. Operate on a closed shop basis.

Fields of Application
Scientific, statistical, commercial, management, systems analysis.
Specialized area: Education.

Training
Courses available: HND in Mathematics, Statistics and Computing; HND and HNC in Computer Studies; BCS Part I; GCE 'A' level in Computer Science.

NORTH STAFFORDSHIRE POLYTECHNIC
Blackheath Lane, Stafford
Telephone: Stafford 53511

Also at:
Beaconside, Stafford; College Road, Stoke-on-Trent, Staffordshire.

Officer
D. M. Melluish, *Head of Computer Centre*

Computer Installations
ICL 4/50—operating system: 5J and own multiaccess; internal storage: 256K bytes; magnetic tapes: 4; magnetic discs: 4 EDS8; 1 line printer. *On-line satellite computer*: PDP-8. *Remote processing features*: 7020 remote batch terminals, 10 teletypes, 2 visual display units.

PDP-8/E—operating system: OS8; internal storage: 8K x 12 bits; magnetic tapes: 2 DEC; 1 line printer.

PDP-8/E—internal storage: 4K bits.

PDP-8—internal storage: 4K bits; *Remote processing features*: 3 teletypes.

Coding Languages
ALGOL, COBOL, FORTRAN, CSL, RPG, Usercode, City and Guilds Mnemonic, Alphacode, PL/1, PAL 8.

Contemplated Equipment
Second main-frame; two satellite midicomputers.

Services Available
Advice, programming, education and training, software packages, documentation. The ICL 4/50 operates on a remote access, closed shop and time-sharing basis. The PDP-8s operate on a self-service basis. Available only for educational purposes.

Fields of Application
Scientific, statistical, commercial, accounting, management, systems analysis.
Specialized areas: Compiler writing, operating systems, software packages for education.

Training
B.Sc. and M.Sc. degrees in Computer Science; HND in Computer Science; short courses in programming and systems analysis, and operating system design.

NORWICH CITY COLLEGE
Department of Mathematics and Computer Studies
Ipswich Road, Norwich, Norfolk, NOR 67D

Officers
V. F. Thomas, *Head of Department*
D. Ruse, *Computer Manager*

Computer Installation
ICL 1901A—operating system: Auto Operator; internal storage: 393,216 bits; magnetic tapes: 4 1971/2; 1 line printer.

Coding Languages
COBOL, FORTRAN, ALGOL, PLAN, City and Guilds, CESIL, SIR, EMA.

Contemplated Equipment
ICL 1902S with internal storage of 32K words; discs; on-line facilities.

Services Available
Advice, programming, education and training, preparation of data. Operate on a closed shop basis.

Fields of Application
Scientific, statistical, commercial, accounting.

Training
Courses available: HND in Business Studies; HNC in Mathematics; Computing and Statistics; HNC in Computer Studies; BCS Part I and Part II; City and Guilds 271, 747 and 748; GCE 'A' level in Computer Studies; RSA Computer Operator's Certificate; RSA Computer Appreciation; short courses in ALGOL, FORTRAN, COBOL, and Logical Design.

PAISLEY COLLEGE OF TECHNOLOGY
High Street, Paisley, Renfrewshire, Scotland
Telephone: 041-887 1241

Officer
A. G. Wilson, *Computer Manager*

Computer Installation
ICL 1901S—operating system: GEORGE 1S; internal storage: 16K 24-bit words; magnetic tapes: 2; magnetic discs: 2; 1 line printer.

PDP-8/E—internal storage: 12K 12-bit words; *Remote processing features*: 8 on-line terminals.

Coding Languages
ICL 1901, ALGOL, FORTRAN, PLAN, COBOL; PDP-8/E: BASIC, FOCAL.

Services Available
Advice, programming. Operate on an open shop basis. No routine tasks for industry and commerce.

Fields of Application
Scientific, operational research, research.
Specialized areas: Linear programming, payroll, student records.

Training
Short programming courses in ALGOL, FORTRAN, and BASIC; B.Sc. in Computing with Operational Research.

POLYTECHNIC OF CENTRAL LONDON
Computer Centre
115 New Cavendish Street, London, W1M 8JS
Telephone: 01-486 5811

Officer
Mrs. O. Routledge, *Computer Manageress*

Computer Installation
ICL 1902A—operating system: GEORGE 2; internal storage: 32K words; magnetic tapes: 1; magnetic discs: 2 2801/2; 1 line printer.

Coding Languages
PLAN, FORTRAN, COBOL, ALGOL, BASIC.

Services Available
Education and training. Operate on a closed shop basis.

Fields of Application
Educational and research, scientific, commercial, statistical, business management, systems analysis.

Training
B.Sc. in Applied Computing (part-time); HND in Computer Studies; HND in Computer Studies-Indorsement; several 12-week evening courses in various programming languages and computer applications.

POLYTECHNIC OF NORTH LONDON
Holloway, London, N7 8DB
Telephone: 01-607 6767

Officer
B. Rowe, *Head of the Computer Unit*

Computer Installation
ICL 1905E–operating system: GEORGE 2 and 3; internal storage: 64K 24-bit words; magnetic tapes: 4 7-track; magnetic discs: 3 EDS 4; 1 line printer.
Remote processing features: 4 ICL 7020.

Coding Languages
FORTRAN, ALGOL, PLAN, COBOL, City and Guilds, SNOBOL 3, ALGOL 68, CCSU, EMA.

Contemplated Equipment
An additional 32K words of core; one more EDS 4 disc.

Services Available
Advice, operators, preparation of data. Operate on a remote access and closed shop basis. Unrestricted access to staff and students of Inner London Educational Authority institutions. Available to outside customers only in special circumstances.

Fields of Application
Scientific, statistical, educational.

Training
Courses in the Departments of Mathematics and of Management.

THE POLYTECHNIC, WOLVERHAMPTON
Wolverhampton, Staffordshire, WV1 1LY

Officers
B. M. J. Kavanagh, *Director of Digital Computing Unit*
G. B. Hamer, *Computer Manager*

Computer Installations
ICL 1903A–operating system: GEORGE 2; internal storage: 1,052 bits; magnetic tapes: 4 1971/2; magnetic discs: 2 2802/2; 1 line printer.

IBM 1620–internal storage: 40K characters; magnetic discs: 1 1311; 1 line printer.

Coding Languages
FORTRAN, COBOL, PLAN, ALGOL, City and Guilds, SPS.

Services Available
Consultation, education and training, operators, systems analysis. Operate on a self-service (IBM 1620) and closed shop (ICL 1903A) basis. Service available to educational establishments and local industry.

Fields of Application
Scientific, statistical, commercial, production control, accounting, management, systems analysis, operational research.

Training
B.Sc. Computer Science (CNAA), B.A. Business Studies (CNAA), HND Computer Studies, HND Business Studies (D.P. option), Adv. Dip. Computer Technology (grad. I.M.A.). Short courses on Introduction in Computing, Introduction to Programming Languages.

PORTSMOUTH POLYTECHNIC*
Department of Computer Science
Mercantile House, Portsmouth, Hampshire
Telephone: Portsmouth 21371

Officer
P. F. Mills, *Head of Department*

Computer Installation
ELLIOTT 4130–operating system: Batch; internal storage: 32K 24-bit words; magnetic tapes: 4 Handless; 1 line printer.

ELLIOTT 803.

Coding Languages
ALGOL, FORTRAN, COBOL, NEAT.

Contemplated Equipment
2 magnetic disc units on 4130 and 32K bits additional internal storage.

Service Available
Advice, programming, software packages, systems analysis. Operate on a closed shop basis.

Fields of Application
Research in pure science and engineering, business studies and management, teaching.
Specialized area: Mathematical modelling.

Training
Courses in programming Autocode and ALGOL; Numerical Methods for Computers, etc.

PRESTON POLYTECHNIC
Preston, Lancashire

Officers
Dr. H. Wilkinson, *Principal*
W. Woodcock, *Head of Department, Mathematics and Computer Studies*

Computer Installations
ICL 1901A–operating system: own: internal storage: 384K bits; 1 line printer.

PDP-8/E; internal storage: 48K bits; 1 line printer.

Coding Languages
FORTRAN, ALGOL, COBOL, PLAN, BASIC.

Services Available
Advice, education and training. Operate on an open shop basis.

Fields of Application
Scientific, statistical, commercial.
Specialized area: Education.

Training
Courses for Computer Science (University Entrance Level), HNC courses in Mathematics, Statistics, Computing Data Processing. Specialist short courses in programming, computer techniques, etc.

QUEEN ELIZABETH COLLEGE, UNIVERSITY OF LONDON
Campden Hill Road, London, W8 7AH
Telephone: 01-937 5411

Officer
B. L. Meek, *Director of Computer Unit*

Computer Installation
ELLIOTT 903B – internal storage: 8,192 18-bit words.

CTL Modular 1 – operating system: Modus 4; 24,576 16-bit words; 1 line printer. *Remote processing features*: system used as satellite to University of London CDC complex.

Coding Languages
ALGOL 60, FORTRAN IV, 903 SIR.

Service Available
Software packages. Operate on a self-service basis. Priority given to educational needs.

Fields of Application
Scientific, statistical.

Training
Course leading to B.Sc. degree.

QUEEN MARY COLLEGE, UNIVERSITY OF LONDON
Mile End Road, London, E1 4NS
Telephone: 01-980 4811

Officer
Prof. I. M. Khabaza, *Director of the Computer Centre*

Computer Installation
ICL 1904S – operating system: GEORGE 2 and MAXIMOP; internal storage: 3,072K bits; magnetic tapes: 4; magnetic discs: 5 EDS 4, 5 EDS 30, 1 drum; 2 line printers. *On-line satellite computers*: PDP-8, PDP-11. *Remote processing features*: 7903 communications processor; 40.8Kb link to CDC 6400, 6600, 7600 system.

Coding Languages
FORTRAN, ALGOL, PLAN, COBOL, JEAN, BASIC, POP-2, BCPL, LISP.

Services Available
Advice, software packages, documentation, preparation of data, systems analysis. Operate on a remote access, closed shop and time-sharing basis.

Fields of Application
Scientific, statistical.

Training
Courses provided: B.Sc. in Computer Science; other courses in programming and computer science.

QUEEN'S UNIVERSITY OF BELFAST
Computer Centre
University Road, Belfast, BT7 1NN, Northern Ireland
Telephone: 0232-45133, extension 484

Officers
Dr. F. J. Smith, *Director*
D. B. Shields, *Computer Manager*
R. A. McLaughlin, *Systems Manager*

Computer Installation
ICL 1907 – operating system: IMP; internal storage: 96K 24-bit words; magnetic tapes: 8; magnetic discs: 8; 2 line printers. *Remote processing features*: 30 remote teletypewriter units.

ICL 1906S – operating system: GEORGE 4; internal storage: 128K 24-bit words; magnetic tapes: 6; magnetic discs: 4; 2 line printers. *On-line satellite computer*: CTL Modular 1.

Coding Languages
FORTRAN, ALGOL, COBOL, PLAN, QUBAL.

Contemplated Equipment
Further satellite processors for attachment to the ICL 1906S.

Services Available
Advice, programming, education and training, operators, software packages, documentation, preparation of data, systems analysis. Operate on a remote access, closed shop, block time and time-sharing basis. Available to all academic departments of the University for research and teaching.

Fields of Application
Scientific, statistical, systems analysis, information retrieval.
Specialized areas: Linear programming, structural engineering, medical research.

Training
Graduate and post-graduate courses in computer programming and the applications of computers.

ROYAL HOLLOWAY COLLEGE, UNIVERSITY OF LONDON
Department of Statistics and Computer Science
Englefield Green, Surrey, TW20 0EX
Telephone: Egham 4455

Officers
Prof. H. J. Godwin, *Head of Department*
Dr. F. G. Kingston, *Lecturer in charge of Computing Services*

Computer Installation
CDC 1700 – operating system: MSOS; internal storage: 458,752 bits; magnetic discs: 2; 1 line printer. *Remote processing features*: Linked to CDC 7600, 6600 and 6400.

Coding Languages
FORTRAN, ALGOL, SNOBOL, COBOL, LISP, PL/1, BCPL.

Services Available
Usually available only to members of the College.

Field of Application
Scientific.
Specialized area: Number theory.

Training
Course units for B.Sc. degree; programming courses.

SALISBURY COLLEGE OF TECHNOLOGY
Southampton Road, Salisbury, Wiltshire
Telephone: Salisbury 6877

Officer
R. H. Wood, *Lecturer in Computing*

United Kingdom – Universities and Colleges

Computer Installation
The College has access to a Honeywell computer on a time-sharing basis.

Coding Languages
ALGOL, BASIC, FORTRAN.

Services Available
Advice, education and training. Operate on a time-sharing basis. Available only to educational users.

Fields of Application
Scientific, educational.

Training
GCE 'A' level course in Computer Science; short introductory computing courses.

SCOTTISH COLLEGE OF TEXTILES
Galashiels, Selkirkshire, TD1 3HF, Scotland

Officer
J. G. Martindale, *Principal*

Computer Installation
ELLIOTT 903–operating system: FAS; internal storage: 18K bits; magnetic tapes: 4.

Coding Languages
ALGOL 60, FORTRAN IV, Machine Code (SIR).

Services Available
Advice, education and training, systems analysis. Operate on a closed shop basis.

Fields of Application
Scientific and statistical.

Training
HND courses in Business Studies, Data Processing, Accounting and Textile Technology.

SHEFFIELD POLYTECHNIC
Pond Street, Sheffield, Yorkshire, S1 1WB
Telephone: 0742-29671

Officer
G. Tolley, *Principal*

Computer Installation
IBM 1130/2B–operating system: DMS/V2; internal storage: 16,384 16-bit words; magnetic discs: 3 2310; 1 line printer.

IBM 1130/2A–operating system: DMS/V2; internal storage: 4,096 16-bit words; magnetic discs: 1.

Coding Languages
FORTRAN IV, RPG, 1130 Assembler.

Services Available
Range of services available. Operate on a block time basis.

Fields of Application
Education, research.

Training
B.Sc. degree in Computing Science (sandwich course); HND in Mathematics, Statistics and Computing (sandwich course) and in Computer Studies (sandwich course); short courses in FORTRAN, COBOL and PL/1 programming.

SLOUGH COLLEGE OF TECHNOLOGY*
William Street, Slough, Buckinghamshire
Telephone: Slough 27511

Computer Installation
ICL 1901–internal storage: 8K x 24 bits; magnetic tapes: 4; 1 line printer.

Coding Languages
PLAN, COBOL, FORTRAN, ALGOL.

Contemplated Equipment
Another 8K bits storage; card reader.

Services Available
Consultation, programming, education and training, operators, software packages, preparation of data, systems analysis. Operate on a closed shop basis. Service mainly restricted to educational users.

Fields of Application
Scientific, statistical, commercial, production control, accounting, management, systems analysis, operational research.

Training
Two-year courses in computer programming and information processing, data processing for computer users; HNC in Computer Studies.
Short courses in introduction to computers and programming, commercial programming, FORTRAN, ALGOL. Computer fundamentals for management, principles of programming planning; also courses on mathematics, statistics and operational research.

SOUTH EAST LONDON TECHNICAL COLLEGE*
25 Bromley Road, London SE6
Telephone: 01-698 7311

Also at:
Lewisham Way, London SE13
Telephone: 01-692 7296

Officer
P. Kilgannon, *Senior Lecturer*

Computer Installation
ELLIOTT 4120–operating system: ETHOS B20; internal storage: 432K bits.

Coding Languages
BASIC, FORTRAN, ALGOL, COBOL.

Services Available
Education and training. Operate on a closed shop basis. Service available to College students and local schools.

Fields of Application
Scientific, statistical, commercial, production control, accounting, management, systems analysis, operational research.
Specialized area: Computer education.

Training
One-term courses in compact systems analysis, programming for beginners, practical ALGOL programming and practical COBOL programming.

SOUTH WEST LONDON COLLEGE*
196 Garratt Lane, London SW18

Officer
J. Allen, *Principal Lecturer*

Services Available
Education and training.

Fields of Application
Statistical, commercial, accounting, management, systems analysis, operational research.

Training
Courses in computer techniques, systems analysis, COBOL programming, business orientation, fundamentals of EDP; NCC Basic Systems Analysis course; short courses (1 to 5 days) in data processing management development, FORTRAN programming, computer appreciation for managers and supervisors, the computer and the auditor, audit requirements in computer-based systems.

SOUTHAMPTON COLLEGE OF TECHNOLOGY
East Park Terrace, Southampton, Hampshire

Officers
Mr. Bocklem, *Principal*
Mr. Dowding, *Head of Mathematics and Computing*

Computer Installation
IBM 1130—operating system: 1130; internal storage: 8K bits; magnetic discs: 2; 1 line printer.

Coding Languages
FORTRAN, COBOL, BASIC, City and Guilds, CESIL, Assembler, RPG.

Services Available
Advice and education and training. Operate on a remote access basis. Available to all students and staff.

Fields of Application
Scientific, statistical, commercial, accounting, management, systems analysis, operational research.
Specialized areas: Linear programming, structural engineering.

Training
Courses for HNC in Computer Studies; HNC in Mathematics, Statistics and Computing; BCS Part I; BSC CNAA in Mathematics. Short courses in FORTRAN, COBOL, computer appreciation and systems analysis. Institute of Data Processing Parts 1, 2, 3 and 4.

STAFFORD COLLEGE OF FURTHER EDUCATION
Tenterbands, Stafford, ST16 2QR
Telephone: Stafford 2361

Officer
D. G. Blake, *Lecturer in charge*

Computer Installation
The College has off-line and on-line access to the ICL 4/50 at North Staffordshire Polytechnic.

Coding Languages
COBOL, ALGOL, City and Guilds, Alphacode.

Services Available
Education and training. Operate on a remote access basis.

Fields of Application
Educational, scientific, statistical, commercial.

Training
City and Guilds 319 Course in Computer Programming and Information Processing; RSA Computer Appreciation course; G.C.E. 'A' level in Computer Science with Associated Subjects.

SUNDERLAND POLYTECHNIC*
Chester Road, Sunderland, County Durham, SR1 3SD
Telephone: 71675

Officers
J. F. Reed, *Head of Department of Mathematics*
B. R. Meech, *Director of Computing*

Computer Installations
ICL 1902A—operating system: GEORGE 1S; internal storage: 16,384 x 24 bits; magnetic discs: 2; 1 line printer.
Remote processing features: 3 Westrix type 33 terminals.

ELLIOTT 803B—internal storage: 8,192 x 39 bits.

Coding Languages
ALGOL, FORTRAN IV, COBOL, PLAN, Autocode.

Services Available
Consultation, education and training, software packages. Operate on a closed shop basis. Service available to industry, commerce, colleges and schools; work accepted only with an educational research or development basis; no routine repetitive work accepted.

Fields of Application
All.

Training
B.Sc. General degree including mathematics with computer science option; HND in Computer Studies; part-time courses leading to BCS and City and Guilds qualifications; part-time courses in programming languages, systems analysis, etc. Occasional short courses on systems analysis and on specific computer applications.

TEESSIDE POLYTECHNIC
Computer Centre
Borough Road, Middlesbrough, Teesside, Yorkshire, TS1 3BA
Telephone: 0642-44176

Officers
A. J. Dunning, *Director of Computer Centre*
F. Mosedale, *Operations Manager*
C. J. Brown, *Chief Programmer/Analyst*

Computer Installations
ICL 1905E—operating systems: GEORGE 2 and 3, MAXIMOP; internal storage: 64K 24-bit words; magnetic tapes: 4 7-track; magnetic discs: 3 EDS; 1 line printer.
On-line satellite computer: ICSL ALP2. *Remote processing features*: 19 remote terminals (TTY, VDU, Graphics).

IBM 1620/II—operating system: Monitor; internal storage: 40K 6-bit digits; magnetic discs: 2 EDS; 1 line printer.

Coding Languages
ALGOL, BASIC, COBOL, FORTRAN, JEAN, PLAN, PASCAL, POP-2, SNOBOL, LISP, SPS, SNAP.

Contemplated Equipment
1905/E: core to 128K words, 2 tape units, 2 disc units, another line printer, extensions to the ALP2 front-end processor to enable 30/32 multiaccess interactive terminals.

Services Available
Advice, programming, education and training, preparation of data, systems analysis. Operate on a self-service, remote access, closed shop, block time, open shop and time-sharing basis. Only limited service to customers outside educational field; a certain amount of research and development computing support for business customers, but no production work.

Fields of Application
Scientific, statistical, commercial, management, systems analysis, operational research.
Specialized areas: Analysis, structural engineering, medical research.

Training
BCS Parts I and II; B.Sc. degrees, Honours and Ordinary, in Computer Science; HND in Computer Studies and Mathematics, Statistics and Computing; Advanced Diploma in Mathematics, Statistics and Computing.

THAMES POLYTECHNIC
Wellington Street, Woolwich, London, SE18 6PF
Telephone: 01-854 2030

Officers
Dr. D. E. R. Godfrey, *Director*
P. C. Oxlade

Computer Installations
ICL 1902A—operating system: GEORGE 2; internal storage: 768K bits; magnetic tapes: 2; magnetic discs: 2 2801 EDS; 1 line printer. *Remote processing features*: 7920 scanner.

Services Available
Operate on a closed shop basis. Services available only to students and staff of the Polytechnic and to local schools.

Fields of Application
Scientific, statistical, commercial, systems analysis, operational research.

Training
B.Sc. in Mathematics, Statistics and Computing; HND in Mathematics, Statistics and Computing; HND and HNC in Computer Studies; NCC Basic and Higher Certificates in Systems Analysis; BCS Parts I and II; many shorter courses.

TRENT POLYTECHNIC
Burton Street, Nottingham, NG1 4BU
Telephone: 0602-48248

Officer
D. R. Judd, *Computer Director*

Computer Installation
ICL 1905—operating system: GEORGE 2; internal storage: 196,608 bits; magnetic tapes: 4 7-track; magnetic discs: 2 EDS; 1 line printer.

Coding Languages
PLAN, FORTRAN, ALGOL, COBOL.

Services Available
Advice, programming, education and training, systems analysis. Operate on a closed shop basis.

Fields of Application
Scientific, statistical, commercial, systems analysis.

Training
Courses for HND in Computer Studies (3 years full-time) and HNC in Computer Studies (2 years part-time).

TWICKENHAM COLLEGE OF TECHNOLOGY*
Division of Cybernetics and Data Processing
Egerton Road, Twickenham, Middlesex

Officer
John Moss, *Head of Division*

Computer Installation
ELLIOTT 803B—internal storage: 160K bits.

Coding Language
Autocode.

Services Available
Advice, systems analysis. Operate on an open shop basis. Limited availability to other educational and research establishments, and commercial concerns.

Fields of Application
Educational work within the College.
Specialized areas: Computer typesetting, programmed learning, system simulation.

Training
A variety of special courses covering computer appreciation, programming, advanced programming, compiler writing, computer typesetting and systems analysis. Full-time and part-time courses such as Postgraduate Diploma in Systems Analysis and Design.

UNIVERSITY COLLEGE, UNIVERSITY OF LONDON
Computer Centre
19 Gordon Street, London, WC1 0AH
Telephone: 01-387 0858/9

Officers
Prof. P. A. Samet, *Director*
D. A. Sturt, *Manager*
C. J. Kennington, *Head of Systems*
Dr. A. C. Day, *Head of Applications*

Computer Installation
IBM 360/65—operating system: OS 260; internal storage: 512K bytes; magnetic tapes: 2 7-track, 3 9-track; magnetic discs: 2314, 5 2311; 2 line printers. *Remote processing features*: RJE 6 lines.

Coding Languages
FORTRAN IV, ALGOL, PL/1, COBOL, etc.

Service Available
Advice. Operate on a closed shop basis. Service available to London University only.

Field of Application
Scientific.

UNIVERSITY COLLEGE, CARDIFF, UNIVERSITY OF WALES*
Cathays Park, P. O. Box 78, Cardiff, CF1 1XL, Wales
Telephone: Cardiff 44211

Officers
Dr. D. H. McLain, *Director of Computing Centre*
A. F. Damodaran, *Computer Manager*
Dr. W. F. B. Jones, *Lecturer in Computing*

Computer Installation
ICL 4/50—operating system: 5J; internal storage: 1 million bits; magnetic tapes: 3; magnetic discs: 3; 1 line printer. *Remote processing features*: 40 teletype 33, videos.

Coding Languages
FORTRAN, ALGOL, etc.

Services Available
Advice, operators. Operate on a closed shop basis.

Fields of Application
Normal University computations.

Training
Courses in programming and computer science for undergraduates and others.

UNIVERSITY COLLEGE OF SWANSEA, UNIVERSITY OF WALES
Computer Centre
Singleton Park, Swansea, Glamorgan, SA2 8PP, Wales
Telephone: Swansea 25678

Officers
Dr. D. C. Cooper, *Professor of Computer Science*
A. Gilmour, *Director of the Computer Centre*

Computer Installation
ICL 1904S–operating system: GEORGE 3; internal storage: 2,304K bits; magnetic tapes: 6; magnetic discs: 7; 2 line printers. *Remote processing features*: Teletypes and 4002 Tektronic Display.

Coding Languages
FORTRAN, ALGOL, COBOL, PLAN, POP-2.

Contemplated Equipment
Links with the University of Manchester Regional Centre and St. David's College, Lampeter.

Services Available
Advice, machine time. Operate on a closed shop and time-sharing basis. Priority given to College departments.

Fields of Application
Scientific, statistical, operational research.
Specialized area: Structural engineering.

UNIVERSITY COLLEGE OF SWANSEA, UNIVERSITY OF WALES
Department of Electrical Engineering
Singleton Park, Swansea, Glamorgan, SA2 8PP, Wales
Telephone: Swansea 25678

Officer
Prof. D. Aspinall, *Head of Department*

Computer Installation
PDP-8–internal storage: 49,152 bits; magnetic tapes: 2 TU55. *On-line satellite computers*: Link to Solartron 247 analogue computer.

PDP-11–operating system: DOS; internal storage: 131,072 bits; magnetic discs: 1 RS64.

IBM 1620–operating system: Monitor 1; internal storage: 80K bits; magnetic discs: 1 1311; 1 line printer.

Coding Languages
PAL, FOCAL, FORTRAN, BASIC.

Services Available
Operate on a self-service basis.

Field of Application
Scientific.
Specialized area: Electrical engineering.

Training
B.Sc. courses: Electrical engineering; Computer Technology; Computer Science (with Physics, Pure Mathematics or Applied Mathematics). M.Sc. Course in Instrumentation.

UNIVERSITY OF ABERDEEN
Computing Centre
12 Sunnybank Road, Aberdeen, AB9 2UY, Scotland
Telephone: 0244-40241

Officers
B. Rule, *Director*
N. Griffith, *Computer Room Manager*
M. Goodland, *Information Officer*

Computer Installation
ICL 4/70–operating system: J 1600; internal storage: 512K bytes; magnetic tapes: 6 9-track; magnetic discs: 10; 1 line printer. *On-line satellite computers*: 2 Modular.

Coding Languages
FORTRAN, COBOL, ALGOL, Assembler.

Services Available
Advice, operators. Operate on a self-service, open shop and closed shop basis. Limited availability for non-University users.

Fields of Application
Scientific research in a wide variety of fields. Most extensive use has been by departments of physics and statistics.

Training
Programming courses given in March/April and September/October each year.

UNIVERSITY OF ABERDEEN
Department of Engineering
Marischal College, Aberdeen, AB9 1AS
Telephone: 0244-40241

Officer
Dr. W. W. Bell

Computer Installation
ELLIOTT 4120–internal storage: 32K 24-bit words; magnetic discs: 2; 1 line printer.

Coding Languages
ALGOL, FORTRAN, NEAT.

Service Available
Advice. Operate on a self-service basis.

Field of Application
Scientific.

UNIVERSITY OF ASTON IN BIRMINGHAM
Computer Centre
15 Coleshill Street, Birmingham, B4 7PA
Telephone: 021-359 3611

Officers
K. J. Bowcock, *Head of Department*
P. Abbott, *Computer Manager*

Computer Installation
ICL 1905E–operating system: GEORGE 3; internal storage: 96K 24-bit words; magnetic tapes: 6; magnetic discs: 4 exchangeable; 1 line printer.

Coding Languages
ALGOL, COBOL, FORTRAN, PLAN, POP-2, SNOBOL.

Contemplated Equipment
Multiplexor and teletype terminals.

United Kingdom – Universities and Colleges

Services Available
Advice, preparation of data, programming, systems analysis. Operate on a closed shop basis.

Fields of Application
Scientific, statistical, commercial, operational research, systems analysis.
Specialized areas: Structural engineering, linear programming, simulation.

Training
Programming courses (3 days); M.Sc. in Computer Science with applications.

UNIVERSITY OF BIRMINGHAM
Computer Centre
Elms Road, North Campus, P.O. Box 363, Birmingham, B15 2TT
Telephone: 021-472 1301, extension 2112

Officers
Dr. S. H. Hollingdale, *Director*
P. G. Walling, C. Oliver, *Assistant Directors*

Computer Installation
ICL 1906A–operating system: GEORGE 4; internal storage: 256K bits; magnetic tapes: 2 7-track, 6 9-track; magnetic discs: 8 EDS 60; 2 line printers. *On-line satellite computer*: Modular One. *Remote processing features*: 2 7020 RJE stations.

Coding Languages
FORTRAN, ALGOL, COBOL.

Services Available
Education and training. Operate on a closed shop and time-sharing basis. Free access to University staff and students; limited time sold to other bodies.

Fields of Application
Scientific, operational research.
Specialized areas: Medical research, numerical analysis.

Training
One-year M.Sc. course in Computer Science.

UNIVERSITY OF BRADFORD*
Computing Laboratory
Great Horton Road, Bradford 7, Yorkshire
Telephone: 0274-33466

Officers
Prof. M. G. Mylroi, *Chairman of Computer Services Advisory Committee*
Dr. R. J. Ord-Smith, *Director of Computing Laboratory*

Computer Installation
ICL 1909–operating system: GEORGE 2E; internal storage: 786,436 bits; magnetic tapes: 4; magnetic discs: 4; 2 line printers. *On-line satellite computers*: link to ICL Argus 400 process control computer. *Remote processing features*: multiplexor, line printers, terminals, Westrex terminals.

Coding Languages
Stantec Simple Code, FORTRAN, ALGOL, LISP, PLAN, COBOL, etc.

Services Available
Advice, data preparation, programming, software packages. Operate on a closed shop basis. Limited service usually arising from industrial consultancy activity.

Fields of Application
Wide range of scientific, engineering and commercial applications for University users. Scientific and commercial applications arising from industrial consultancy.
Specialized area: Nuclear power calculations.

Training
Many courses run internally and externally. Wide range of languages, methods, computer appreciation.

UNIVERSITY OF BRISTOL
Computer Centre
Bristol, BS8 1TH
Telephone: Bristol 24161

Officers
Prof. M. H. Rogers, *Director*
Dr. P. J. Marcer, *Computer Manager*

Computer Installation
ICL 4/75–operating system: ICL Multijob; internal storage: 768K bytes; magnetic tapes: 4; magnetic discs: 12 EDS 30; 1 line printer. *Remote processing features*: 2 RJE, 40 teletypes, included in South West Universities Computer Network.

ICL 4/50–operating system: ICL J 1600; internal storage: 128K bits; magnetic discs: 1 RDU; 1 line printer.

Coding Languages
FORTRAN IV, ALGOL W, WATFOR, BASIC.

Services Available
General university service. Operate on a cafeteria basis (4/50) and a closed shop and time-sharing basis. Available to students (4/50 only), research workers and staff.

Fields of Application
Scientific, statistical.

Training
Joint degree in Mathematics and Computer Science; short courses on coding languages (1 week).

UNIVERSITY OF BRISTOL
Computer Science Department
School of Mathematics, University Walk, Bristol, BS8 1TW

Computer Installation
ICL 4/75–operating system: Multijob; internal storage: 768K bytes; magnetic tapes: 4; magnetic discs: 13; 1 line printer. *On-line satellite computers*: 2. *Remote processing feature*: video terminal.

ICL 4/50–operating system: 5J; internal storage: 228K bits; magnetic discs: 2; 1 line printer.

Coding Languages
ALGOL W, FORTRAN, BASIC, COBOL, Usercode.

Services Available
Advice, programming, education and training, software packages, documentation, preparation of data. Operate on a remote access, closed shop and time-sharing basis. Available only to staff and students.

Fields of Application
Scientific, statistical, operational research.
Specialized areas: Linear programming, structural engineering, medical research.

Training
B.Sc. degree in Mathematics with Computer Science.

UNIVERSITY OF CAMBRIDGE
Department of Applied Mathematics and Theoretical Physics
Silver Street, Cambridge, CB3 9EW

Officer
R. D. Harding, *Senior Assistant in Computing Research*

Computer Installation
PDP-8/I—operating system: TSS/8; internal storage: 24K 12-bit words; magnetic tapes: 4 DEC; magnetic discs.

CTL Modular 1—operating system: E2; internal storage: 32K 16-bit words. Linked to the PDP-8/I above.

Coding Languages
FOCAL, PAL-D, BASIC.

Services Available
Operate on a time-sharing basis. Available only to students taking courses or members of the department.

Fields of Application
Scientific, educational.

Training
Two courses, both for undergraduates reading for mathematical degrees: Elementary Programming and Numerical Analysis for 2nd-year students, Further Numerical Analysis and Computational Mathematics for 3rd-year students.

UNIVERSITY OF DUNDEE
Mathematics Department
Dundee, Angus, DD1 4HN, Scotland
Telephone: 0382-23181, extension 335

Officer
Prof. A. K. Mitchell, *Head of Department*

Computer Installation
ELLIOTT 4130—operating systems: T30C, DES 1, DES 2; internal storage: 96K 24-bit words; magnetic tapes: 4, magnetic discs: 4; 1 line printer.

Coding Languages
ALGOL, FORTRAN, COBOL, BASIC, NEAT.

Contemplated Equipment
CTL Modular 1 enhancement.

Services Available
Advice, programming, education and training. Operate on a self-service and time-sharing basis.

Fields of Application
Scientific, statistical, operational research.
Specialized areas: Linear programming, medical research, scientific research.

Training
Courses in computer programming, computer applications, computer science.

UNIVERSITY OF DURHAM
Computer Unit
Science Laboratories, South Road, Durham
Telephone: Durham 4971

Officers
Dr. John Hawgood, *Director*
A. A. Young, *Computing Services Manager*

Computer Installation
IBM 360/67 (owned jointly with the University of Newcastle upon Tyne)—operating systems: OS, MFT 2, MTS; internal storage: 8 million bits; magnetic tapes: 4; magnetic discs: 2 2314; 2 line printers. *On-line satellite computers*: IBM 1130, etc. *Remote processing features*: 9 IBM 2741 terminals.

IBM 1130 (linked to 360/67 in Newcastle)—internal storage: 128K bits; magnetic discs: 1 2315; 1 line printer.

PDP-11 (linked to IBM 1130). *Remote processing features*: 4 Beehive character display terminals.

Coding Languages
ALGOL, PL/1, FORTRAN, APL, 360 Assembler, 1130 Assembler, etc.

Services Available
All services available. Operate on a closed shop batch basis with open access to terminals. Priority given to internal use.

Fields of Application
Scientific engineering, operational research, research data processing, educational.
Specialized areas: Structural engineering, simulation, library automation, economic evaluation of computer-based systems, cost-benefit analysis.

Training
Short courses in PL/1 and FORTRAN programming; one-year courses in computer applications in science and social science.

UNIVERSITY OF DURHAM
Department of Geology
Science Laboratories, South Road, Durham
Telephone: Durham 4971

Officer
Dr. R. E. Long

Computer Installation
CTL Modular 1—operating system: specialized; internal storage: 8K plus 4K bits; magnetic tapes: 1 CTL; magnetic discs: 1 CTL.

Coding Languages
Special purpose modified FORTRAN for use in time series analysis.

Service Available
Preparation of data. Operate on a block time and open shop (by agreement) basis. Available only by agreement.

Field of Application
Scientific.
Specialized area: Seismic record processing.

UNIVERSITY OF EAST ANGLIA*
Computing Centre
University Plain, Norwich, Norfolk, NOR 88C
Telephone: 0603-56161

Officer
Professor P. M. Stocker, *Director*

Computer Installation
ICL 1905E—operating systems: GEORGE 2, MINIMOP; internal storage: 768K bits; magnetic tapes: 4; magnetic discs: 2; 1 line printer. *Remote processing features*: 6 remote teletypewriters.

Coding Languages
FORTRAN, ALGOL.

Contemplated Equipment
Further 768K bits of store, further 9 million characters of disc store, graphics terminals.

Services Available
Consultation, programming, education and training. Operate on a closed shop and time-sharing basis.

Field of Application
Scientific.
Specialized areas: Nuclear magnetic resonance spectroscopy, computer assisted learning, input of data from graphic sources, data structures.

Training
Courses leading to degrees of Master of Philosophy and Doctor of Philosophy; a Computing Science minor is available with Mathematics, Social Studies and Environmental Science courses; short course on Computers in a Management Context (5 weeks).

UNIVERSITY OF EDINBURGH
School of Artificial Intelligence
Forest Hill, Edinburgh, EH1 2QL, Scotland
Telephone: 031-226 3101

Officers
Dr. J. C. P. Schwarz, *Convenor, School Co-Ordinating Committee*
C. A. Mckinder, *Projects Manager*
I. A. Adie, *Computer Manager*

Computer Installation
ELLIOTT 4130—operating system: Multi-POP; internal storage: 3,072K bits; magnetic discs: 3; 1 line printer.
On-line satellite computers: 2 Honeywell H316. *Remote processing features*: remote terminals for 8 possible users.

Coding Languages
POP-2, NEAT.

Services Available
Software packages, documentation. Operate on a time-sharing basis.

Field of Application
Scientific.
Specialized areas: Research in artificial intelligence.

UNIVERSITY OF ESSEX
Computing Centre
Wivenhoe Park, Colchester, Essex, CO4 3SQ
Telephone: 0206-44144

Officer
Professor R. A. Brooker, *Director*

Computer Installation
PDP-10—internal storage: 128K 38-bit words; magnetic tapes: DEC. *Remote processing features*: approximately 25 teletypes and visual display units.

ICL 1909—serves as frontend to PDP-10, giving access to line printer, card readers and 4 7-track IBM compatible tapes.

Coding Languages
ALGOL, FORTRAN, BASIC, BCPL, LISP, COBOL, POP-2, PAL, SNOBOL.

Contemplated Equipment
Faster magnetic tape (including 9-track) units attached directly to the PDP-10. "Cafeteria" facilities via the 1909.

Services Available
Consultation, programming, education and training, documentation, preparation of data. Operate on a closed shop basis. Available only to members of the university.

Fields of Application
Scientific, social sciences.

Training
B.A. in Computing Science and Computer Systems; M.Sc. in Computer Studies (including Programme Linguistics); B.A. and M.Sc. in Mathematical Computation; M.Phil. and Ph.D. in Computing Science; short courses in programming and computing applications for students in physical sciences and humanities.

UNIVERSITY OF EXETER
Computer Unit
Mathematics and Geology Building, Exeter, Devon
Telephone: Exeter 77911, extension 474

Officers
D. J. Stone, *Director*
R. Palmer, *Manager*

Computer Installation
ICL 4/50—operating systems: 5J and Multijob; internal storage: 262,144 bytes; magnetic tapes: 4; magnetic discs: 4; 1 line printer.

Coding Languages
ALGOL, FORTRAN, COBOL, Usercode.

Services Available
Advice, operators, programming preparation of data. Operate on a closed shop basis.

Field of Application
Scientific research.

Training
Variety of programming courses.

UNIVERSITY OF GLASGOW
Computing Department
Glasgow, G12 8QQ, Scotland
Telephone: 041-339 8855, extensions 484 and 478

Officer
D. C. Gilles, *Professor of Computing Science*

Computer Installation
ICS Multum—operating system: self-designed; internal storage: 64K x 16 bits; magnetic discs: 1 cartridge disc; 1 line printer.

Coding Languages
PASCAL, ALGOL, FORTRAN.

Contemplated Equipment
Extension of core store and disc storage.

Services Available
Advice, education and training and software packages. Operate on a remote access and open shop basis.

Field of Application
Scientific.

Training
B.Sc. and postgraduate diploma in Computing Science.

UNIVERSITY OF GLASGOW
Computing Service
Glasgow, G12 8QQ, Scotland

Officer
Dr. G. K. S. Browning, *Director*

Computer Installation
ICL KDF/9–operating system: EGDON; internal storage: 1,570K bits; magnetic discs: 1; 1 line printer. *On-line satellite computer*: PDP-8. *Remote processing features*: teletype interactive network.

CTL Modular 1 (3)–operating system: E2; internal storage: 260K bits each; magnetic discs: 2 (on 1 machine); 1 line printer (on 2 machines). *Remote processing features*: RJE terminals to IBM 370/155.

Coding Languages
FORTRAN, ALGOL, COBOL, PL/1, etc.

Contemplated Equipment
ICL 1906S.

Services Available
Advice, software packages and preparation of data. Operate on a remote access, closed shop and time-sharing basis. Available only to certain classes of user if demand heavy.

Fields of Application
Scientific, statistical.
Specialized areas: Linear programming, structural engineering, medical research.

UNIVERSITY OF HULL*
Cottingham Road, Kingston-upon-Hull, Yorkshire, HU6 7RX
Telephone: Hull 408960

Officers
Dr. D. W. Beard, *Director, Centre for Computer Studies*
T. Cornall, *Computer Manager*

Computer Installation
ICL 1905E–operating systems: GEORGE 2 and GEORGE 3; internal storage: 1,179,648 bits; magnetic tapes: 4; magnetic discs: 2 ICL 2801; 1 line printer. *Remote processing features*: 9 teletype terminals.

ELLIOTT 803B–internal storage: 319,488 bits.

Coding Languages
ALGOL, FORTRAN, PLAN, CSL, COBOL.

Contemplated Equipment
Internal storage: 393,216 bits; 2 magnetic disc drives, ICL 2801.

Services Available
Advice, preparation of data, programming. Operate on a closed shop and remote access basis.

Fields of Application
Scientific, statistical, operational research, linear programming, administration, teaching.

Training
Programming courses in FORTRAN, ALGOL, and PLAN; computation courses.

UNIVERSITY OF KEELE
Computer Centre
Keele, Staffordshire, ST5 5BG
Telephone: 0782-71 371

Officer
Dr. H. H. Greenwood, *Director*

Computer Installation
ELLIOTT 4130–operating systems: DES Batch, KOS, Multi-Pop; internal storage: 64K bits; magnetic tapes: 4 Elliott/NCR; magnetic discs: 2; 1 line printer. *On-line satellite computer*: PDP-11. *Remote processing features*: Teletype terminals.

ELLIOTT 803B–internal storage: 4K bits; 1 line printer.

Coding Languages
FORTRAN, ALGOL, NEAT, BASIC.

Contemplated Equipment
1 disc unit, 32K bits store for 4130.

Services Available
Advice, programming, education and training, operators, software packages, documentation, preparation of data. Operate on a self-service, remote access, closed shop and time-sharing basis. Available to university users and local colleges and schools.

Fields of Application
Scientific, statistical, operational research, teaching.
Specialized areas: Linear programming, analysis, medical research.

Training
Honours degree courses.

UNIVERSITY OF KENT AT CANTERBURY
Computing Laboratory
Canterbury, Kent
Telephone: 66822

Officer
Dr. E. B. Spratt, *Director*

Computer Installation
ELLIOTT 4130–operating system: DES 2; internal storage: 131,072 bits; magnetic tapes: 4; magnetic discs: 4; 2 line printers. *On-line satellite computer*: PDP-11. *Remote processing features*: 34 teletypes.

Coding Languages
ALGOL, FORTRAN IV, NEAT, ML1, MACRO 11.

Contemplated Equipment
Storage Tube Displays (Tektronic).

Services Available
Advice, programming, education and training, operators, software packages, documentation, preparation of data, systems analysis. Operate on a remote access, closed shop and time-sharing basis.

Fields of Application
Scientific, statistical, accounting, management, systems analysis, operational research.

Training
Various courses (details on application).

United Kingdom – Universities and Colleges

UNIVERSITY OF LANCASTER
Computer Service
Computer Laboratory, Lancaster
Telephone: 0524-65201

Officer
J. W. Anderson, *Computer Manager*

Computer Installation
ICL 1905F—operating system: local; internal storage: 128K 24-bit words; magnetic tapes: 4 7-track, 2 9-track; magnetic discs: 6; 2 line printers. *On-line satellite computer:* CTL Modular 1.

Coding Languages
FORTRAN, ALGOL, POP-2, COBOL.

Services Available
Operate on a closed shop and time-sharing basis. Not available to outside customers.

Fields of Application
Scientific, statistical, operational research.
Specialized area: Linear programming.

UNIVERSITY OF LEEDS
Computer-Based Learning Project
Leeds, Yorkshire, LS2 9JT

Officers
J. R. Hartley, Prof. K. Lovell, Dr. D. H. Sleeman, *Directors*

Computer Installation
CTL Modular 1—operating system: Base Control; internal storage: 32K x 16 bits; magnetic discs: 2.

Coding Languages
LOGO, BASIC, L^6, Assembly

Contemplated Equipment
Tektronix cathode ray tube, increased store, processor, teletypes and random access audiovisual terminals.

Services Available
Education and training. Operate on a remote access, open shop and time-sharing basis. Available only in certain teaching areas and to designated University Departments and Schools.

Fields of Application
Scientific, statistical.
Specialized area: Computer-based learning.

Training
Undergraduate optional course in Computational Science and post-graduate courses relating to education.

UNIVERSITY OF LEEDS
Electronic Computing Laboratory
Leeds, Yorkshire, LS2 9JT
Telephone: 0532-31751

Officer
Dr. M. Wells, *Professor and Director*

Computer Installation
ICL KDF9—operating system: Eldon 2; internal storage: 32K 48-bit words; magnetic tapes: 5 1081, 1 TM4; magnetic discs: Data Products; 2 line printers. *On-line satellite computer:* PDP-8. *Remote processing features:* 32 on-line teletypes.

ICL 1906A—operating system: GEORGE 4; internal storage: 256K 24-bit words; magnetic tapes: 8; magnetic discs: 2 EDS 8, 3 EDS 60; 2 line printers. *On-line satellite computer:* ICL 7903. *Remote processing features:* 6 7020, 40 teletypes.

Coding Languages
ALGOL, FORTRAN, KDF9, Assembler, PLAN, SNOBOL, ALGOL 68.

Contemplated Equipment
Further fast drums, EDS 60 for 1906A.

Service Available
Advice. Operate on a closed shop and remote access basis. Very limited services are available to outside customers.

Fields of Application
Scientific, technical, operational research.
Specialized areas: Operating systems, numerical analysis.

Training
Undergraduate and postgraduate courses at all levels.

UNIVERSITY OF LEICESTER*
University Road, Leicester, LE1 7RH
Telephone: Leicester 50000

Officer
Dr. J. R. Thompson, *Director of Computer Centre*

Computer Installation
ELLIOTT 4130—internal storage: 65K bits; magnetic tapes: 8; magnetic discs: disc store; 1 line printer.

Coding Languages
ALGOL 60, FORTRAN IV, Language H.

Services Available
Operators, programming. Operate on a closed shop basis. Available on a limited basis. Inexperienced customers are expected to have taken professional advice elsewhere.

Fields of Application
General scientific applications.

Training
Programming for undergraduates, postgraduates and staff.

UNIVERSITY OF LIVERPOOL
Centre for Computer-Aided Building Design
P.O. Box 147, Liverpool, Lancashire, L69 3BX
Telephone: 051-709 6022, extension 761

Officer
A. L. Britch, *Director*

Computer Installation
ELLIOTT 905/928—operating system: RADOS; internal storage: 18K x 16 bits; magnetic tapes: 2; magnetic discs: 1 Burroughs. *On-line satellite computer:* ICL Argus 600.

Coding Languages
FORTRAN, Assembler.

Contemplated Equipment
Elliott 905/928 with line printer.

Services Available
Advice, programming, education and training, software packages, documentation. Operate on a self-service, remote access basis.

Field of Application
Computer aided design.
Specialized area: Computer-aided building design.

Training
Postgraduate course in computer-aided building design (CABD) leading to Diploma in CABD.

UNIVERSITY OF LIVERPOOL
Computer Laboratory,
P.O. Box 147, Liverpool, Lancashire, L69 3BX
Telephone: 051-709 6022

Officer
Dr. J. L. Alty, *Director*

Computer Installation
ICL KDF9—operating systems: EGDON 3, Standard Time-sharing; internal storage: 1,536K bits; magnetic tapes: TM 4, 8 ICL 1081; magnetic discs: DP 5023; 1 line printer. *On-line satellite computer*: PDP-8. *Remote processing features*: 24 teletypes.

CTL Modular 1—operating system: E2; internal storage: 76,800 bits; 2 line printers. *On-line satellite computer*: CTL Modular 1. *Remote processing features*: connection to CDC 7600.

Coding Languages
ALGOL 60, FORTRAN IV, KDF9, Usercode.

Contemplated Equipment
ICL 1906A, 8 tapes, 6 EDS 60 disc units, 2 line printers, 50 remote teletypes, 6 remote batch terminals.

Services Available
Education and training. Operate on a remote access, closed shop and time-sharing basis. Service available to members of the University.

Field of Application
Scientific.

Training
Courses in FORTRAN, ALGOL, Optimization, etc.

UNIVERSITY OF LIVERPOOL
Department of Computational and Statistical Science and Data Processing
Research Unit
Victoria Building, Brownlow Hill, Liverpool
Telephone: 051-709 6022

Officers
Prof. L. M. Delves, *Head of Department*
Dr. P. G. Hibbard, *Director of Data Processing Research Unit*
P. H. Leng, *Computer Officer*

Computer Installation
CTL Modular 1—operating system: E2; internal storage: 512K bits; magnetic discs: 1 double spindle EDS; 1 line printer.
PDP-8/S—internal storage: 48K bits.

Coding Languages
Assembler, FORTRAN, FOCAL, BASIC, ALGOL 68, WISP, etc.

Contemplated Equipment
Cassette tapes, data link to large twin-processor CTL Modular 1 installation.

Services Available
Advice, programming, education and training. Operate on a self-service, open shop and time-sharing basis.

Fields of Application
Scientific, statistical, commercial, computer science teaching.
Specialized area: Language implementation.

Training
B.Sc., M.Sc., Ph.D. and Diploma courses.

UNIVERSITY OF LONDON
Management Systems Department
Senate House, Malet Street, London, WC1E 7HU
Telephone: 01-636 8000, extension 363

Officer
Peter Holwell, *Head of Department*

Computer Installation
ICL 1904E—operating system: GEORGE 2; internal storage: 48K 24-bit words; magnetic tapes: 6; magnetic discs: 4; 3 line printers.

Coding Languages
PLAN, COBOL.

Contemplated Equipment
ICL 1903T, including on-line communications system.

Services Available
Operate on a closed shop basis. Available only to the member institutions of the University.

Fields of Application
Accounting, university administration.
Specialized areas: Payroll, examination processing.

UNIVERSITY OF LONDON COMPUTER CENTRE
20 Guilford Street, London WC1
Telephone: 01-405 8400

Officers
Neil Spoonley, *Director*
K. D. Mackenzie, *Operations Manager and Assistant Director*
R. Alpiar, *Technical Liaison Manager*
H. J. Zell, *Programming Manager*

Computer Installation
CDC 7600—operating system: SCOPE; internal storage: 1,536K bits; magnetic tapes: 8 7-track; magnetic discs: 1 7638, 1 6638, 8 multispindle; 3 line printers. *On-line satellite computers*: 8 CTL Modular 1. *Remote processing features*: 17 CDC 200 user terminals.

CDC 6600—operating system: SCOPE; internal storage: 768K bits. *On-line satellite computers*: 2 CDC 1700.

CDC 6400—operating system: SCOPE; internal storage: 384K bits. *On-line satellite computer*: ICL 1904S.

Coding Languages
FORTRAN, ALGOL, COBOL, BASIC, COMPASS (Assembler), SNOBOL, SIMSCRIPT, SIMULA, MIMIC, BCPL, LISP, BALM.

Contemplated Equipment
Unspecified front-end system.

United Kingdom – Universities and Colleges

Services Available
Advice, software packages, documentation, preparation of data, courier service. Operate on a self-service and remote access basis. Restricted to research and educational users, primarily the University of London and 13 other universities in southern England.

Field of Application
Scientific.
Specialized area: Medical research.

UNIVERSITY OF NEWCASTLE UPON TYNE
Computing Laboratory
Claremont Tower, Claremont Road, Newcastle upon Tyne, NE1 7RU
Telephone: Newcastle 29233/4/5

Officers
Dr. E. S. Page, *Director, Professor of Computing and Data Processing*
B. Randall, *Professor of Computing Science*
Miss E. D. Barraclough, *Computing Manager*

Computer Installation
IBM 360/67 (owned jointly with the University of Durham)–operating systems: OS/HASP, MTS; internal storage: 8 million bits; magnetic tapes: 4; magnetic discs: 2 2314; 2 line printers. *On-line satellite computer*: IBM 1130 (in Durham). *Remote processing features*: 9 IBM 2741 terminals.

ICL KDF9–operating system: POST; internal storage: 768K bits; magnetic tapes: 4; 1 line printer.

IBM 1130–internal storage: 131,072 bits; magnetic disc: 1131-2B.

HEWLETT PACKARD 2000E–internal storage: 256K bits; magnetic disc: 1.

Coding Languages
Many.

Contemplated Equipment
Burroughs B1700.

Services Available
Advice, operators, preparation of data, programming, software packages, systems analysis. Operate on a closed shop basis (IBM 360/67, ICL KDF9) and open shop basis (IBM 1130).

Fields of Application
Numerical and non-numerical analysis, scientific research and data processing.
Specialized areas: Operating systems, programming theory, combinatorics, graph theory, simulation, operational research, numerical analysis, information retrieval.

Training
Postgraduate research for Ph.D. and M.Sc. and courses leading to Diploma or M.Sc. in Computing Science. Honours courses in Computing Science.

UNIVERSITY OF NOTTINGHAM
Cripps Computing Centre
Nottingham, NG7 2RD
Telephone: 0602-56101

Officers
Dr. E. Foxley, *Director*
S. A. Goold, *Head of Services*
C. W. Atkinson, *Manager*

Computer Installation
ICL 1906A–operating system: GEORGE 3; internal storage: 6,400K bits; magnetic tapes: 6 ICL 2505, 2 ICL 1973; magnetic discs: 8 ICL 2815 EDS, 2 ICL 2802 EDS; 2 line printers. *On-line satellite computer*: ICL 7903. *Remote processing features*: 8 ICL 7020 terminals, 60 teletypes.

Coding Languages
ALGOL 60, FORTRAN, PLAN, ALGOL 68, COBOL.

Services Available
Advice, education and training, software packages, documentation. Operate on a remote access, closed shop and time-sharing basis.

Fields of Application
Scientific, systems analysis, design engineering, compatibility with other computers, automatic operating systems.

UNIVERSITY OF OXFORD
Computing Laboratory
19 Banbury Road, Oxford, OX2 6NN
Telephone: Oxford 56727

Officers
Prof. L. Fox, *Director*
F. A. Scott, *Computer Manager*
Dr. C. E. Phelps, *Service Group Manager*

Computer Installation
ICL 1906A–operating systems: GEORGE 3 and 4; internal storage: 6 million bits; magnetic tapes: 6 9-track, 2 7-track; magnetic discs: 7 ICL EDS 30; 3 line printers. *On-line satellite computers*: PDP-8, ICL 7902, 2 Modular 1. *Remote processing features*.

Coding Languages
ALGOL, FORTRAN, ALGOL 68.

Contemplated Equipment
Magnetic tapes and discs, line printer.

Services Available
Advice, education and training, operators, software packages, documentation. Operate on a self-service, remote access, open shop and time-sharing basis. Junior members of University restricted to self-service at a remote terminal.

Fields of Application
Scientific, statistical.

Training
Courses in ALGOL, FORTRAN, Computer Appreciation (1 week), application courses on demand.

UNIVERSITY OF READING*
Computer Unit
Reading, Berkshire

Officer
Dr. L. A. G. Dresel, *Director*

Computer Installation
ELLIOTT 4130–internal storage: 786,432 bits; magnetic tapes: 4; 1 line printer.

Coding Languages
ALGOL, FORTRAN, NEAT.

United Kingdom – Universities and Colleges

Services Available
Advice, operators. Operate on a closed shop and remote access basis.

Fields of Application
Scientific programming in various departments of the University.
Specialized areas: Statistical analysis, calculation of force constants from molecular spectra.

Training
Courses in ALGOL programming; computer science.

UNIVERSITY OF READING
Department of Applied Physical Sciences
Division of Cybernetics
3 Earley Gate, Whiteknights, Reading, Berkshire, RG6 2AL

Officer
Dr. P. B. Fellgett, *Professor of Cybernetics and Instrument Physics*

Computer Installation
PDP-8–internal storage: 48K bits; magnetic discs: 1 J102 drum.
PDP-8/L–internal storage: 48K bits.
CTL Modular 1–internal storage: 256K bits.

Coding Languages
Assembler, FORTRAN, SUBSET ALGOL, CORAL.

Service Available
Consultancy.

Field of Application
Computer-aided design, especially of closed-loop control systems.
Specialized area: Sampled-data, multi-loop and non-linear control system synthesis.

UNIVERSITY OF ST. ANDREWS
Computing Laboratory
North Haugh, St. Andrews, Fife, Scotland
Telephone: St. Andrews 1906

Officer
D. Erskine, *Computer Manager*

Computer Installation
IBM 360/44–operating system: 44 MFT, OS, RAX; internal storage: 2 million bits; magnetic tapes: 2 IBM 2400; magnetic discs: 5 2311; 1 line printer. *On-line satellite computer*: Honeywell 316.
HONEYWELL H316–operating system: local; internal storage: 128K bits; magnetic discs: 1 4610.

Coding Languages
FORTRAN, ALGOL, PL/360, Assembler, etc.

Services Available
Advice, programming, education and training. Operate on a closed shop and time-sharing basis. Available only to University users.

Fields of Application
Scientific, management.
Specialized area: Linear programming.

Training
Courses leading to B.Sc., M.Sc. and Ph.D. degrees in Computational Science.

UNIVERSITY OF SALFORD
Computing Laboratory
Salford, Lancashire, M5 4WT
Telephone: 061-736 5843

Officers
P. Jarratt, *Director*
J. Lindley, *Deputy Director*

Computer Installation
ICL KDF9–operating system: EGDON; internal storage: 1,600K bits; magnetic tapes: 8; magnetic disc: 1 5023; 1 line printer. *On-line satellite computer*: 1 PDP-8.
Remote processing features: 22 teletypes.

Coding Languages
ALGOL, FORTRAN, KDF9 Usercode.

Contemplated Equipment
CTL Satellite 1; ICL KDF9 to be replaced.

Services Available
Advice, programming, education and training, preparation of data. Operate on a closed shop basis.

Field of Application
Scientific.

Training
Numerous courses at all levels.

UNIVERSITY OF SHEFFIELD
Computing Services
Western Bank, Sheffield, Yorkshire, S10 2TN
Telephone: 0742-78555

Officers
Dr. D. H. McLain, *Director of Computing Services*
Dr. S. Wardle, *Systems Manager*

Computer Installation
ICL 1907–operating system: GEORGE 2; internal storage: 2,359,296 bits; magnetic tapes: 4; magnetic discs: 2 EDS 8, 3 EDS 30; 1 line printer. *On-line satellite computer*: Micro 16P. *Remote processing features*: teletypes, 2 card reader/line printer links.

Coding Languages
FORTRAN, ALGOL, COBOL, ALGOL 68, PLAN.

Services Available
Advice, programming, preparation of data. Operate on a remote access, closed shop and time-sharing basis.

Fields of Application
Scientific, statistical.

Training
Courses in Computer Science as part of curriculum for B.Sc.

UNIVERSITY OF SOUTHAMPTON
Data Analysis Centre
Highfield, Southampton, Hampshire, SO9 5NH
Telephone: 559122

Officers
Prof. D. W. Barron, *Director*
J. R. Reeves, *Computer Manager*
A. Schulkins, *Head of User Services*

Computer Installation
ICL 1907—operating system: COOP3; internal storage: 2,304K bits; magnetic tapes: 6; magnetic discs: 9; 2 line printers. *On-line satellite computer*: CTL Modular 1. *Remote processing features*: teletypes, remote job entry.

ICL 1901—internal storage: 384K bits; magnetic tapes: 4; 1 line printer.

Coding Languages
FORTRAN, ALGOL 60, ALGOL 68, PLAN, COBOL, POP-2, BASIC.

Services Available
Advice, education and training, operators, documentation. Operate on a remote access, closed shop and time-sharing basis.

Fields of Application
Scientific, statistical, accounting, management, operational research.
Specialized areas: Linear programming, analysis, payroll, structural engineering, medical research.

Training
Full-time postgraduate course (M.Sc. in Computing); short courses in FORTRAN and ALGOL programming.

UNIVERSITY OF STRATHCLYDE
Department of Computer Science
George Street, Glasgow, G1 1XW, Scotland
Telephone: 041-552 4400

Officers
J. G. Fraser, *Director of Computer Services*
A. J. T. Colin, *Professor of Computer Science*

Computer Installation
ICL 1904S—operating system: GEORGE 3; internal storage: 128K words; magnetic tapes: 4; magnetic discs: 3 EDS 60, 2 EDS 58; 2 line printers. *Remote processing features*: 18 teletypes.

BULL GENERAL ELECTRIC GE415—operating system: TSO; internal storage: 32K words; magnetic tapes: 6; magnetic discs: 3; 1 line printer. *Remote processing features*: 9 teletype lines.

Coding Languages
FORTRAN, ALGOL, COBOL.

Contemplated Equipment
Extension of multiplexer on ICL 1904S.

Service Available
Advice. Operate on a remote access, closed shop and time-sharing basis.

Fields of Application
Scientific, statistical, operational research.

Training
B.Sc. degree course in Computer Science; occasional language and operating systems courses.

UNIVERSITY OF SURREY*
Computing Unit
Stag Hill, Guildford, Surrey
Telephone: 0483-71281

Officers
T. F. Goodwin, *Director*
B. Deaville, *Senior Programmer*

Computer Installation
ICL 1905F—operating system: GEORGE 2; internal storage: 64K words; magnetic tapes: 4; magnetic discs: 4; 1 line printer. *On-line satellite computer*: Digico Micro 16 P. *Remote processing features*: teletype terminals.

ICL Sirius—internal storage: 7K bits.

Coding Languages
ALGOL, FORTRAN, PLAN and others.

Services Available
By arrangement. Operate on a closed shop and time-sharing basis.

Fields of Application
Scientific, engineering, mathematics.
Specialized area: Scientific research.

Training
Training in computing methods and programming as part of standard courses.

UNIVERSITY OF WALES
Institute of Science and Technology
Cathays Park, Cardiff, CF1 1XL, Wales
Telephone: Cardiff 37374

Officer
E. Stuart, *Senior Lecturer in Computing*

Computer Installation
ELLIOTT 803B—internal storage: 312K bits.

Coding Languages
ALGOL 60, Autocode.

Contemplated Equipment
The University is to participate in an integrated computer network with four other Universities.

Services Available
Advice, programming, systems analysis. Operate on a self-service and open shop basis. Preference is given to scientific/technical customers as opposed to commercial interests.

Fields of Application
All fields of University disciplines.
Specialized areas: Numerical analysis, simulation.

Training
Full-time undergraduate courses in Computer and Data Processing are in course of preparation. Short courses in Programming at frequent intervals; courses on specific fields of application.

UNIVERSITY OF WARWICK
Coventry, Warwickshire, CV4 7AL
Telephone: 0203-24011

Officers
H. S. P. Jones, *Computer Unit*
J. N. Buxton, *Department of Computer Science*

United Kingdom – Universities and Colleges

Computer Installation
ELLIOTT 4130–operating system: DES 2; internal storage: 128K bits; magnetic tapes; magnetic discs; 1lline printer. *Remote processing features*: graphical display unit.

ELLIOTT 4120–operating system: DES 1; internal storage: 64K bits; magnetic discs; 1 line printer. *Remote processing features*: graphical display unit.

CTL Modular 1–internal storage: 32K bits; magnetic discs; 1 line printer.

Coding Languages
ALGOL, FORTRAN, NEAT, BASIC.

Services Available
Advice, operators. Operate on a closed shop basis.

Fields of Application
Numerical analysis, D.D.C. of processes.

UNIVERSITY OF YORK
Department of Computer Science
Heslington, York, YO1 5DD
Telephone: 0904-59861

Officers
I. C. Pyle, *Professor*
D. G. Burnett-Hall, *Director*
P. D. Roberts, *Computer Manager*

Computer Installation
ELLIOTT 4130–operating system: DES 2; internal storage: 2,359,296 bits; magnetic tapes: 4; magnetic discs: 4; 2 line printers. *Remote processing features*: 8 teletype terminals.

CTL Satellite 1–internal storage: 131,072 bits; 1 line printer.

Coding Languages
FORTRAN, ALGOL 60, BASIC, NEAT, ML/1.

Services Available
Advice, operators, documentation, preparation of data. Operate on a closed shop and time-sharing basis.

Fields of Application
Scientific, statistical, accounting.
Specialized area: Payroll.

Training
B.A. degree in Mathematics/Computation, Physics/Computation, Biology/Computation, Computer Science/Economics; B.Phil. in Computation in the Life Sciences.

VICTORIA UNIVERSITY OF MANCHESTER
Administrative Computer Unit
Main Building, Oxford Road, Manchester, M13 9PL
Telephone: 061-273 3333

Officers
J. C. F. Hayward, *Senior Administrative Assistant in the Registrar's Department*
G. Longworth, *Senior Systems Analyst*
K. J. W. Setchfield, *Systems Accountant in the Bursar's Department*

Computer Installation
ICL 1901A–operating system: EXEC; internal storage: 393,216 bits; magnetic tapes: 4 1971/2; 1 line printer.

Coding Languages
COBOL, PLAN.

Contemplated Equipment
ICL 1902S.

Services Available
Operate on an open shop basis. Primarily for the Registrar's and Bursar's Departments.

Field of Application
Commercial.
Specialized area: Library applications.

VICTORIA UNIVERSITY OF MANCHESTER
Department of Computer Science
Oxford Road, Manchester, M13 9PL
Telephone: 061-273 3333

Officer
Prof. T. Kilburn, *Head of Department*

Computer Installation
MU 5–operating system: in-house: internal storage: 9,216K bits; magnetic discs: 2 fixed-head.

ICL 1905E–operating system: in-house; internal storage: 768K bits; magnetic discs: 2 EDS, 1 file disc.

Note: The MU 5 and ICL 1905E are the Department's two main installations. They are linked to each other and form part of a multi-computer system.

Coding Languages
SPG, XPL, ALGOL, FORTRAN, PL/1, Atlas Autocode.

Services Available
Operate on a closed shop basis. Mainly for large computer research and evaluation.

Training
A three-year course for a B.Sc. degree in Computer Science; a one-year M.Sc. course in Computer Science.

VICTORIA UNIVERSITY OF MANCHESTER
Department of Psychology
Hopkinson Laboratories, Oxford Road, Manchester, M13 9PL
Telephone: 061-273 3333

Officers
Prof. J. Cohen, *Head of Department*
Dr. A. Reader, *Lecturer in Computing*

Computer Installation
CTL Modular 1–operating system: on-line experimental control; internal storage: 16K bits.

Coding Languages
CTL Assembler, CORAL, Easycode (in-house).

Services Available
Operate on a self-service and closed shop basis.

Field of Application
Scientific.

Training
Psychology undergraduates receive familiarization courses in computer programming and control.

United Kingdom – Universities and Colleges

VICTORIA UNIVERSITY OF MANCHESTER
Regional Computer Centre
Oxford Road, Manchester, M13 9PL

Officers
Prof. G. Black, *Director*
J. Clegg, *Assistant Director*

Computer Installations
ICL 1906A–operating system: GEORGE 3; internal storage: 196K 24-bit words; magnetic tapes: 4 7-track, 6 9-track; magnetic discs: 4 EDS8, 1 FDS; 2 line printers. *Remote processing features*: 2 RJE terminals, 2 MOPs.

ICL 1904A–operating system: GEORGE 3; internal storage: 128K 24-bit words; magnetic tapes: 2 7-track, 4 9-track; magnetic discs: 6 EDS8; 2 line printers. *On-line satellite computer*: CDC 7600. *Remote processing features*: 6 RJE terminals, 4 MOPs.

CDC 7600–operating system: SCOPE 2; internal storage: 32K × 60 plus 256K × 60 bits; magnetic tapes: 2 7-track; magnetic discs: 2 EDS8; 2 line printers.

Coding Languages
ALGOL 60, COBOL, FORTRAN, COMPASS, PLAN.

Contemplated Equipment
7 EDS60, 6 RJE terminals, 12 MOPs.

Services Available
Advice, training, operators, software packages, documentation, preparation of data. Operate on a remote access, closed shop and time-sharing basis. Restricted to university users.

Fields of Application
Scientific, statistical, management, operational research, student teaching.
Specialized areas: Sales analysis, linear programming, analysis, structural engineering, medical research, other academic research.

Training
Training given on using the Centre's facilities.

WANDSWORTH TECHNICAL COLLEGE
Wandsworth High Street, London, SW18 2PP
Telephone: 01-870 2241

Officer
K. G. Lavender, *Principal*

Computer Installation
IBM 1620–operating system: Monitor I; internal storage: 120K bits; magnetic discs: 1 IBM 1311.

The College also has an ICL 7020 terminal–operating system: GEORGE 3.

Coding Languages
Assembler, FORTRAN II, SNOBOL.

Contemplated Equipment
Terminals to bureaux; card to line printer off-line facility.

Services Available
Education and training. Operate on a closed shop basis.

Field of Application
Teaching.

Training
Courses provided: City and Guilds 746, 747 and 748; RSA Digital Computer Appreciation (Stages II and III), Computer Operator's Certificate; GCE 'A' level in Computer Science; College diploma in Computer Studies; short evening courses on computer topics.

WARLEY COLLEGE OF TECHNOLOGY
Chance Building, Crocketts Lane, Smethwick, Warley, Worcestershire
Telephone: 021-558 4121

Officer
G. F. Sims, *Head of Computing, Mathematics and Physics*

Computer Installation
ELLIOTT 905–internal storage: 294,912 bits. *Remote processing feature*: on-line teleprinter.

Coding Languages
ALGOL, FORTRAN, SIR, City and Guilds.

Contemplated Equipment
PDP-8/F with 8K bits; 2 DECtapes; on-line teleprinters.

Services Available
Consultation, education and training, software packages. Operate on an open shop basis. Service available to teachers and industry.

Fields of Application
Scientific, engineering, operational research.

Training
HNC Computer Studies A1, A2, A3; 'A'-level Computer Science; City and Guilds 747, 746, 743; RSA Computer Appreciation. Short courses in ALGOL, FORTRAN, COBOL, Operational Research, City and Guilds Mnemonic Code, systems analysis.

WATFORD COLLEGE OF TECHNOLOGY
Hempstead Road, Watford, Hertfordshire, WD1 3EZ
Telephone: Watford 41211

Officer
Lieut.-Col. L. F. Ball, *Computer Manager*

Computer Installation
PDP-10–operating system: DEC Monitor 505; internal storage: 112K bits; magnetic tapes: 7 TU-56; magnetic discs: 4 RPO-8; 1 line printer. *On-line satellite computers*: 70 ASR/KSR 33. *Remote processing features*: DC 71D at Watford.

PDP-8/I–operating system: DEC Monitor 505; internal storage: 8K bits; 1 line printer. *On-line satellite computers*: 5 Data Dynamics 390.

Note: This computer is installed as a terminal on the PDP-10.

Contemplated Equipment
Two TU-56 tape units; Calcomp 563 drum plotter; four Data Dynamics 390 units; additional internal storage of 64K bits in the PDP-10.

Services Available
Education and training. Operate on a remote access basis.

Fields of Application
Scientific, statistical, management, systems analysis, operational research.
Specialized area: Sales analysis.

Training
Courses provided: B.Sc. in Print Technology; HND in Business Studies; HNC in Computer Studies; HNC in Mathematics, Statistics and Computing; National Computer Centre's Basic Certificate in Systems Analysis.

WEST LONDON COLLEGE
Greyhound Road, London W14

Officer
R. J. Savage, *Senior Lecturer in Data Processing*

Coding Languages
BASIC, FORTRAN, COBOL.

Contemplated Equipment
A central processing unit with internal storage of 2,496K bits; card reader; line printer; 20 teletype terminals; 4 visual display units.

Services Available
Advice, education and training. Operate on a remote access basis.

Fields of Application
Statistical, commercial, production control, accounting, management, operational research.
Specialized areas: Sales analysis, investment.

Training
Courses provided: HND and HNC in Business Studies (with a data processing option) and in Business Data Processing.

WESTFIELD COLLEGE, UNIVERSITY OF LONDON
Kidderpore Avenue, Hampstead, London, NW3 7ST
Telephone: 01-435 7141

Computer Installation
CTL Modular 1–operating system: E2; internal storage: 24K 16-bit words; 1 line printer.
ARCTURUS 18C–internal storage: 8K 18-bit words; magnetic tapes: 1; magnetic discs: 1; 1 line printer.

Coding Languages
FORTRAN, ALGOL, NAL, BALSA.

Contemplated Equipment
Additional storage of 16K words, and two magnetic discs, for the Modular 1.

Services Available
Operate on a self-service and closed shop basis.

Field of Application
Scientific.

Training
Courses in Computer Science for B.Sc., M.Phil. and Ph.D. degrees.

WIDNES AND RUNCORN COLLEGE OF FURTHER EDUCATION
Kingsway, Widnes, Lancashire
Telephone: 051-424 3666

Officer
A. C. Shotton, *Principal*

Computer Installation
ELLIOTT 903–internal storage: 8K bits.

Coding Languages
ALGOL, FORTRAN, SIR.

Contemplated Equipment
A magnetic disc.

Services Available
Advice, education and training. Operate on a self-service basis.

Field of Application
Scientific.
Specialized area: Education.

Training
Courses provided: City and Guilds 747; GCE 'A' level in Computer Science.

GOVERNMENT ESTABLISHMENTS

CENTRAL ELECTRICITY GENERATING BOARD
85 Park Street, London SE1
Telephone: 01-248 1202

Officers
S. R. Gallop, *Manager, Management Services Department*
A. G. Oughton, *Head, Systems Development Division*
F. J. Linger, *Head, Bureau Services*

Computer Installations
IBM 370/165–operating system: RELEASE; internal storage: 8,192K bits; magnetic tapes: 7 3420/3; magnetic discs: 8 3330.

IBM 370/155–operating system: RELEASE; internal storage: 8,192K bits; 3 line printers. *On-line satellite computers*: 17 1130. *Remote processing features*: 14 2740.

Coding Languages
FORTRAN, COBOL, PL/1, Assembler.

Services Available
Consultation, programming, education and training, operators, software packages. Operate on a self-service, remote access, block time and closed shop basis.

Fields of Application
Scientific, statistical, commercial, production control, management, systems analysis, operational research, engineering stress analysis, nuclear, forward planning, transmission, etc.
Specialized areas: System operation (electricity grid network)–digital; Power station simulation and control –hybrid.

Training
Short courses in elementary appreciation, job control languages, introductory programming and elementary, advanced and practical FORTRAN/COBOL and PL/1.

CENTRAL ELECTRICITY GENERATING BOARD
North West Region Computer Branch
Carrwood Road, Bramhall, Cheshire
Telephone: 061-485 4466

Officers
M. B. Jackson, *Computer Manager*
J. Hardman, *Section Head*
G. D. Scott, *Section Head*

United Kingdom – Government Establishments

Computer Installation
ICL 1905–operating system: GEORGE 2; internal storage: 32K bits; magnetic tapes: 6; magnetic discs: 2 EDS8; 1 line printer. *Remote processing feature*: interrogating typewriter.

Coding Languages
FORTRAN, COBOL, PLAN.

Contemplated Equipment
ICL 1903T with 96K bits storage and 4 tapes. 2 EDS60 disc units, 2 EDS8, 2 line printers, ICR, ITR, ITP, document reader, remote terminals.

Services Available
Advice, programming, education and training, operators, software packages, documentation, preparation of data, systems analysis, liaison. Operate on a closed shop basis. Available to internal regional customers.

Fields of Application
Scientific, statistical, commercial, accounting, management, systems analysis, operational research, packages. *Specialized areas*: Payroll, data processing, PERT, power systems.

COMMUNITY HEALTH INFORMATION PROJECT
107 Sydney Street, London, SW3
Telephone: 01-352 6663, 01-352 9600

Officers
H. C. Price, *Project Director*
J. Macdonald Ross, *Project Leader*

Services Available
Advice, preparation of data. Operate on a remote access and time-sharing basis. Available to general medical practitioners in their surgeries, to medical out-patients in District General Hospitals and to Social Service Departments of Local Authorities.

Fields of Application
Management, patient record summary.
Specialized area: Medical research.

COMPUTER-AIDED DESIGN CENTRE
Madingley Road, Cambridge, CB3 OHB
Telephone: Cambridge 63125

Officers
A. I. Llewelyn, *Director*
B. Gott, *Chief Consultant*
J. S. W. Chilvers, *Centre Manager*

Computer Installation
ICL Atlas–operating system: Cambridge Multi-Access System; internal storage: 128K bits; magnetic tapes: 6; magnetic discs: 2; 2 line printers. *On-line satellite computers*: PDP-11/20, PDP-9, 6 MECSL 905, Imlac. *Remote processing features*: teletypes, storage tubes, etc.
CTL Modular 1–operating system: CADC; internal storage: 56K bits; magnetic tapes: 1; magnetic discs: 4. *On-line satellite computer*: SM4. *Remote processing features*: teletypes, storage tubes, etc.
ICL 1904A–operating system: GEORGE 3; internal storage: 128K bits; magnetic tapes: 4 ICL PE 1600; magnetic discs: 1 drum, 2 EDS 60; 1 line printer. *On-line satellite computer*: PDP-11. *Remote processing features*: teletypes, storage tubes, etc.

Coding Languages
FORTRAN, ALGOL, SAL, IIT, PLAN, Modular 1 Code, DEC Code, BCPL 90S Code.

Contemplated Equipment
Plotter for 1904A, terminal equipment, time division multiplexing equipment.

Services Available
Advice, programming, education and training, software packages, documentation. Operate on a remote access and time-sharing basis. Available only for customers involved in computer-aided design.

Field of Application
Computer-aided design.

Training
User training only.

DEPARTMENT OF HEALTH AND SOCIAL SECURITY
47/57 Queens Road, Reading, Berkshire, RG1 4BQ

Officers
D. J. Francis, *Head of Computer Project*
K. C. Cudby, *Operations Manager*
J. M. Fraser, M. S. Dunbar, *Chief Programmers*

Computer Installations
ICL 1904–operating system: manual; internal storage: 32K bits; magnetic tapes: 4; magnetic discs 1 FDS, 4 EDS; 6 line printers. *Remote processing features*: on-line terminals.

ICL 1906–operating system: manual; internal storage: 128K bits; magnetic tapes: 8; magnetic discs: 3 FDS, 12 EDS; 3 line printers. *Remote processing features*: on-line terminals.

Coding Language
PLAN.

Contemplated Equipment
2 ICL 1904S.

Services Available
Preparation of data. Operate on an open shop basis. Available to government departments only.

Field of Application
Government.

DEPARTMENT OF TRADE AND INDUSTRY
Business Statistics Office
Cardiff Road, Newport, Monmouthshire, NPT 1XG
Telephone: Newport 56111, extension 2104

Officers
M. C. Fessey, *Director*
J. A. Tiffin, *Head of Management Services*

Computer Installations
ICL 1906A–operating system–GEORGE 3; internal storage: 3,072K bits; magnetic tapes: 9; magnetic discs: 4 EDS8 and 4 EDS30; 3 line printers. *On-line satellite computers*: 7903 front-end processor.

Coding Languages
COBOL, FORTRAN, PLAN.

Contemplated Equipment
Increased storage of 3,072K bits, 6 MTU, 12 EDS 60, 2 HS drums.

Services Available
Advice, programming, education and training, preparation of data, systems analysis. Operate on a closed shop and time-sharing basis.

United Kingdom – Government Establishments

Field of Application
Statistical.
Specialized area: Analysis.

Training
Courses for BCS Part I; National Computing Centre's course in Basic Systems Analysis.

DEPARTMENT OF TRADE AND INDUSTRY
National Engineering Laboratory
East Kilbride, Lanarkshire, Scotland
Telephone: East Kilbride 20222

Officers
Dr. J. H. Ludley, *Head of Computer Services Division*
J. T. McKinlay, *Computer Operations Manager*

Computer Installation
UNIVAC 1108–operating system: EXEC VIII; internal storage: 7 million bits; magnetic tapes: 6 VI C; magnetic discs: 6 FH432, 2 F-11; 3 line printers. *On-line satellite computers*: 2 Elliott 905. *Remote processing features*: 40 teletypes, 5 Tektronix.

Coding Languages
FORTRAN, Assembler, ALGOL, COBOL.

Contemplated Equipment
3 Univac 8440 discs.

Services Available
Advice, software packages, preparation of data. Operate on a self-service, remote access, closed shop, block time and time-sharing basis.

Fields of Application
Scientific, statistical, production control, mechanical engineering.
Specialized areas: Structural engineering, numerical control.

DONCASTER RURAL DISTRICT COUNCIL
Treasurer's Department
Nether Hall, Doncaster, Yorkshire
Telephone: Doncaster 68465

Officers
W. J. Jackson, *Treasurer*
K. Horsfield, *Deputy Treasurer*

Computer Installation
ICL 1901–internal storage: 16K bits; magnetic tapes: 4; 1 line printer.

Coding Languages
COBOL, PLAN.

Service Available
Preparation of data. Operate on a self-service basis. Available only to other local authorities.

Fields of Application
Scientific, accounting.
Specialized area: Payroll.

EASTERN REGIONAL HOSPITAL BOARD (SCOTLAND)
"Vernonholme", Riverside Drive, Dundee, DD2 1QF, Scotland

Officers
J. K. Johnston, *Secretary*
R. C. Graham, *Senior Administrative Medical Officer*
H. J. Pilling, *Treasurer*

Computer Installation
ICL 1901A–internal storage: 384K bits; magnetic tapes: 4 1971/2; magnetic discs: 1 2821/1; 1 line printer.
Remote processing features: 1 ICL 7070/5, 5 Teletype terminals.

Coding Languages
PLAN, COBOL.

Contemplated Equipment
ICL 1903T processor with storage of 1,536K bits, 2 EDS 60 disc units, 1 7930 Scanner system, 2 visual display units.

Services Available
Operators, preparation of data. Operate on an open shop basis.

Fields of Application
Statistical, commercial, accounting.
Specialized area: Medical research.

EDINBURGH CORPORATION
City Chambers, Edinburgh 1, Scotland
Telephone: 031-225 2424

Officers
E. G. Glendinning, *Town Clerk*
A. L. Imrie, *City Chamberlain*
G. R. Waddell, *Computer Controller*

Computer Installation
ICL 4/50–operating system: J; internal storage: 2,048K bits; magnetic tapes: 5; magnetic discs: 3 EDS 8, 5 EDS 30; 2 line printers. *Remote processing features*: ICL Mk II VDU terminals.

Coding Languages
System 4 Usercode, COBOL, FORTRAN, ALGOL.

Services Available
Advice, programming, preparation of data, systems analysis. Operate on a closed shop, block time and time-sharing basis. Available mainly to other local authorities and public boards.

Fields of Application
Statistical, commercial, accounting, management, operational research, technical.
Specialized areas: Analysis, payroll, structural engineering, urban data bases.

LONDON BOROUGHS' JOINT COMPUTER COMMITTEE
John Humphries House, Stockwell Street, Greenwich, London SE10
Telephone: 01-858 7041

Officers
P. G. Bell, *Computer Manager*
R. J. Mountford, *Deputy Computer Manager – Training.*

Computer Installation
ICL Leo III–operating system: Master Routine; internal storage: 750K × 6 bits; magnetic tapes: 10 Ampex; 2 line printers.

ICL 4/70–operating system: J. Level; internal storage: 2,300K x 6 bits; magnetic tapes: 6 ICL; magnetic discs: 8 EDS/30; 2 line printers.

Coding Languages
Intercode, CLEO, COBOL, ALGOL, FORTRAN, Usercode RPS.

Contemplated Equipment
ICL 4/70 Communications Control Unit, all-round expansion with remote access; 8 EDS 60 disc units.

Services Available
Consultation, programming, operators, software packages, documentation, preparation of data, systems analysis. Operate on a closed shop basis. Service available to quasi Local Government bodies, e.g. Hospital Service. Priority to work for Joint Committee members.

Fields of Application
All local government fields.
Specialized area: Finance.

NATIONAL COAL BOARD*
Bridgtown, Cannock, Staffordshire
Telephone: 2581

Also at: Doncaster, Yorkshire; Edinburgh, Scotland; Gateshead, Northumberland; Lowton, Lancashire; Mansfield, Nottinghamshire; Tredomen, Cardiff, Wales.

Officers
R. A. Hitchcock, *Managing Director*
R. Leigh, *Head of Administration*
E. Wille, *Head of Training and Information*

Computer Installation
Cannock:
IBM 360/50 tape/disc.
IBM 360/130 tape/disc.

Doncaster:
ICL 1904 tape/disc (2). *Remote processing features*.

Edinburgh:
ICL 1904 tape/disc.

Gateshead:
ICL 1906 tape/disc. *Remote processing features*.

Lowton:
ICL 1902A tape/disc.

Mansfield:
IBM 360/40 tape/disc.

Tredomen:
IBM 360/30 tape/disc.

Coding Languages
PLAN, FORTRAN, COBOL, Assembler.

Services Available
Service bureau facilities are available at each of the seven computer centres. This has developed from the hire of machine time to a bureau service providing consultancy, analysis and programming facilities for commercial or management science applications.

Fields of Application
Commercial applications include payroll/wages costs, sales invoicing/statistics, stores control, supplier accounting, pension payments and staff records.
Specialized areas: Action networks, action estimates, surveyor's traverse calculations and ventilation networks.

Training
Courses held are not confined to Board employees. Details of training and fee charged may be obtained on application.

PORTSMOUTH CORPORATION
1 Clarence Parade, Southsea, Hampshire, PO5 3NW

Officer
R. Tomlinson, *Computer Manager*

Computer Installation
IBM 370/135–operating system: DOS; internal storage: 168K bits; magnetic tapes: 2 2415; magnetic discs: 6 2319; 1 line printer. *Remote processing features*.

Coding Languages
BAL, COBOL, FORTRAN.

Service Available
Preparation of data. Operate on a closed shop and remote access basis.

Fields of Application
All local government fields.

POST OFFICE DATA PROCESSING SERVICE
Edinburgh Computer Centre
57 Craiglockhart Avenue, Edinburgh, EH14 1AQ, Scotland
Telephone: 031-443 6141

Officer
J. T. Forbes, *Manager*

Computer Installation
ICL Leo 326–operating system: Master Program; internal storage: 32K 40-bit words; magnetic tapes: 15; 2 line printers.

Coding Languages
CLEO, Intercode.

Services Available
Operators, preparation of data. Operate on a closed shop basis.

Fields of Application
Commercial, management.

SCOTTISH OFFICE COMPUTER SERVICE
Broomhouse Drive, Edinburgh, EH11 3XD, Scotland
Telephone: 031-443 4040

Officers
J. S. Robertson, *Manager*
J. Wheeler, *Deputy Manager*

Computer Installation
IBM 360/40–operating system: OS 360; internal storage: 256K bytes; magnetic tapes: 8 9-track, 3 7-track; magnetic discs: 8 2314, 8 2319; 4 line printers. *Remote processing features*: interactive terminal facility.

IBM 360/50–operating system: OS 360; internal storage: 256K bits.

Coding Languages
IBM Assembler, COBOL, FORTRAN.

Services Available
Advice, programming, operators, software packages, preparation of data, systems analysis, ITF terminals. Operate on a closed shop and time-sharing basis. Available to (a) Scottish Education Department, (b) Scottish Home and Health Department, (c) Scottish Development Department, (d) Department of Agriculture and Fisheries for Scotland and certain other Government Departments and allied bodies.

Fields of Application
Some scientific work for marine laboratory, management, systems analysis, model building.
Specialized area: Payroll.

SOUTH OF SCOTLAND ELECTRICITY BOARD
Cathcart House, Inverlair Avenue, Glasgow, G44 4BE, Scotland

Officer
John S. Macfarlane, *Computer Services Manager*

Computer Installations
ICL 4/70–operating system: J1600; internal storage: 262K bits; magnetic tapes: 8; magnetic discs: 10 RDS; 3 line printers. *Remote processing features*: 7181 VDUs and 7020 system.

ICL 4/72–operating system: J1600; internal storage: 262K bits; magnetic tapes and discs, line printers and remote processing features as 4/70 above.

Coding Languages
COBOL, FORTRAN, Usercode.

Contemplated Equipment
A four-spindle ICL EDS 60 disc unit.

Service Available
Operators. Operate on a remote access, closed shop and time-sharing basis.

Fields of Application
Scientific, commercial, accounting, management.

SURREY COUNTY COUNCIL
Penrhyn Road, Kingston upon Thames, Surrey
Telephone: 01-546 1050

Officer
F. L. Partington, *Computer Services Manager*

Computer Installation
UNIVAC 1106–operating system: EXEC 8; internal storage: 131K bits; magnetic tapes: 2 7-track NRZI, 2 9-track PE; magnetic discs: 4 8440; 1 line printer. *Remote processing features:* visual display unit, RJE, teletype.

Coding Languages
COBOL, FORTRAN, 1106 Assembler.

Contemplated Equipment
Additional internal storage of 131K bits, extra 8440 disc units and continuous expansion of terminals.

Services Available
Software packages and documentation. Operate on a remote access, closed shop and time-sharing basis. Available to all departments of the County Council, and technical computing facilities to Highway Engineers.

Fields of Application
Scientific, statistical, commercial, accounting, systems analysis, operational research.
Specialized areas: Linear programming, analysis, payroll.

TEESSIDE COUNTY BOROUGH COUNCIL
Computer Section
Treasurer's Department, Municipal Buildings, Middlesbrough, Teesside, Yorkshire
Telephone: 44255

Officer
G. Woodley, *Computer Manager*

Computer Installations
IBM 370/145–operating systems: DOS and MFT; internal storage: 256K bytes; magnetic tapes: 2 2415; magnetic discs: 8 2319; 1 line printer.

IBM 1130–operating system: MONITOR 2; internal storage: 16K 16-bit words; magnetic discs: 3 2310 drives; 1 line printer.

Coding Languages
COBOL, FORTRAN, PL/1 and Assembler.

Contemplated Equipment
3270 and 3275 terminals, faster tapes, increased storage, 3330 drives.

Service Available
Advice. Operate on a remote access and closed shop basis with terminals on premises for data base.

Fields of Application
Statistical, commercial, accounting, management, systems analysis, operational research, data base.
Specialized areas: Analysis, payroll, civil engineering, quantity surveying.

UNITED KINGDOM ATOMIC ENERGY AUTHORITY
Culham Laboratory
Abingdon, Berkshire, OX14 3DB

Officers
Alan Price, *Computing Services Manager*
Leon A. J. Verra, *Computer Operations Manager*

Computer Installation
ICL 4-70–operating system: Multijob; internal storage: 640K bytes; magnetic tapes: 3 4452, 1 4450; magnetic discs: 14 EDS30; 3 line printers. *On-line satellite computer*: CTL Modular 1.

Coding Languages
FORTRAN, COBOL, ALGOL, Usercode.

Services Available
Programming, software packages, systems analysis. Operate on a remote access and time-sharing basis.

Fields of Application
Scientific, commercial.

WEST SUSSEX COUNTY COUNCIL
County Hall, Chichester, Sussex
Telephone: Chichester 85100

Officer
C. K. Davie, *Data Processing Manager*

United Kingdom – Government Establishments

Computer Installation
IBM 370/155–operating system: MFT 2; internal storage: 512K bits; magnetic tapes: 6 2400; magnetic discs: 1 2314, 1 3330; 2 line printers. *Remote processing features*: 9 3270 visual display units.

Coding Languages
COBOL, Assembler, FORTRAN, PL/1.

Contemplated Equipment
Two more 3270 visual display units; a 3330 disc unit with four drives; two ADS Modulflex terminal systems.

Service Available
Computer time. Operate on a remote access and time-sharing basis.

Fields of Application
Statistical, accounting, management.
Specialized area: Local government.

RESEARCH INSTITUTIONS

BRITISH AIRCRAFT CORPORATION (OPERATING) LTD.*
Engineering Management Services
G.P.O. Box No. 77, Filton House, Bristol
Telephone: 693831

Officers
J. M. Hahn, *Head of Engineering Management Services*
B. M. A. Scott, *Chief Systems Analyst*
M. D. P. Fasey, *Chief Application Engineer*
R. Kerr, *Chief Programmer*
J. K. Haynes, *Group Leader, Computer Operations*

Computer Installation
ICL KDF9–internal storage: 16K bits; magnetic tapes: 5; 1 line printer. *Remote processing features*: Marconi-data data link, custom-built data link.

Coding Languages
ALGOL, KDF9 Usercode.

Services Available
By arrangement.

Fields of Application
Engineering and scientific computation, data reduction, management information and control systems.
Specialized areas: Computing techniques pertinent to the aerospace industry including matrix algebra and differential equations.

BRITISH AIRCRAFT CORPORATION (OPERATING) LTD.*
Warton Aerodrome, near Preston, Lancashire
Telephone: St. Annes 21255

Officers
Dr. T. A. Duerden, *Chief of Management Services*
J. H. McDonnell, *Mathematical Services and Computer Programming*
G. Pitt, *Administration Services*
G. Barnes, *Analogue Computing*

Computer Installation
IBM 360/50–operating system: OS 360; internal storage: 2,048K bits; magnetic tapes: 4 2403; magnetic discs: 6 2311; 1 line printer.

Coding Languages
FORTRAN IV, MAP.

Services Available
Advice, operators, preparation of data, programming, systems analysis. Operate on a closed shop and open shop basis.

Fields of Application
Airframe design and testing, labour accounting, spares control.
Specialized areas: Flight dynamics (including flight simulation), aerodynamics, structural analysis, reduction of test data aided design.

BRITISH LAUNDERERS' RESEARCH ASSOCIATION*
Hill View Gardens, London NW4
Telephone: 01-203 2143

Officer
C. F. Tinworth

Computer Installation
ELLIOTT 903–operating system: FAS; internal storage: 147,456 bits; magnetic tapes: 2.

Coding Languages
SIR, ALGOL, FORTRAN.

Services Available
Consultation, programming, software packages, documentation, systems analysis. Operate on a self-service and open shop basis.

Fields of Application
Scientific, accounting, management information, costing, budgetary control.
Specialized area: Laundry applications.

BRITISH RAIL
Research and Development Division
Technical Centre, London Road, Derby
Telephone: Derby 49203

Officers
P. E. West, *Project Manager, Computing*
D. R. Berz, *Head, Systems and Services*

Computer Installations
IBM 370/145–operating systems: OS, MFT2, HASP; internal storage: 512K bytes; magnetic tapes: 4 IBM 2401; magnetic discs: 8 BASF 6214; 1 line printer. *On-line satellite computer*: Elliott 905. *Remote processing feature*: IBM 2770 terminal.

Coding Languages
FORTRAN, PL/1, Assembler.

Contemplated Equipment
Increase in storage to 768K bytes; teletypes for remote job entry.

Services Available
Consultation, programming, operators, preparation of data. Operate on a closed shop and block time basis.

Fields of Application
Scientific, statistical, production control, management, operational research.
Specialized areas: Linear programming, analysis, structural engineering.

BRITISH SCIENTIFIC INSTRUMENT RESEARCH ASSOCIATION*
South Hill, Chislehurst, Kent
Telephone: 01-467 2636

Officers
S. S. Carlisle, R. E. Fishbacher, T. P. Flanagan, W. H. Simmonds.

Computer Installation
ELLIOTT 4120–internal storage: 384K bits; magnetic tapes: 3; 1 line printer.

Coding Languages
ALGOL, NEAT.

Services Available
Advice, operators, preparation of data, programming. Operate on an open shop basis. Mainly for members of the Research Association and staff of other research associations and government research establishments.

Fields of Application
Instrument research, computer applications in industrial production.

BRITISH SHIP RESEARCH ASSOCIATION*
Wallsend Research Station,
Wallsend, Northumberland
Telephone: Wallsend 625242

Officers
Dr. R. Hurst, *Director of Research*
J. C. Asher, *Administrative Director*
M. N. Parker, *Head of Computer Division*
L. F. Walker, *Head of Computer Services*

Computer Installations
ICL 1903A–operating system: GEORGE 3; internal storage: 1.5 million bits; magnetic tapes: 4 7-track; magnetic discs: 2 EDS; 2 line printers. *Remote processing features*: 4 keyboard terminals.

DDP 116–operating system: drives automatic draughting system; internal storage: 131,072 bits; magnetic tapes: 1.

Coding Languages
FORTRAN IV, ALGOL, EMA, PLAN, DAP.

Contemplated Equipment
Interactive graphics terminal.

Services Available
Operators, software packages, preparation of data. Operate on a closed shop and time-sharing basis.

Fields of Application
Scientific, statistical, production control.
Specialized areas: Ship design, numerical control, numerical lofting, automatic draughting.

Training
Short courses by arrangement for member firms only.

BUREAU OF INFORMATION SCIENCE
Grove House, Grove Road, Beaconsfield, Buckinghamshire
Telephone: 6868, 3358

Officer
Prof. F. H. George, *Chairman*

Services Available
Advice, programming, education and training, software packages, systems analysis, heuristic programming.

Fields of Application
Scientific, statistical, commercial, production control, management, systems analysis, management information systems.

Training
Course in computer programming and training for diagnostic computer engineers.

DEPARTMENT OF TRADE AND INDUSTRY
Warren Spring Laboratory
Gunnels Wood Road, Stevenage, Hertfordshire
Telephone: Stevenage 3388

Officers
Dr. A. J. Robinson, *Director*
P. H. Hammond, *Head of Control Engineering Division*

Computer Installation
ICL 1903–operating systems: executive and automatic; internal storage: 32K bits; magnetic tapes: 4; 1 line printer. *Remote processing features*: Off-line DATEL 600, data link to ICL 1905E.

ICL Argus 500/II–internal storage: 32K bits; fixed disc.

IBM 1130/APPLIED DYNAMICS 4 hybrid–internal storage: 8K bits; interchangeable disc.

Coding Languages
ALGOL, PLAN, FORTRAN, etc.

Services Available
Advice, operators, preparation of data, programming, systems analysis. Operate on a closed shop basis. Restricted to problems related to the laboratory's experience and interests.

Fields of Application
Chemical and mineral process engineering, process control and instrumentation, general scientific.

Training
Courses for industry on practical computer control, general courses on process control, courses on hybrid computing.

ELLIOTT BROTHERS (LONDON) LTD.*
Chobham Road, Frimley, Surrey

Officer
D. C. Sellen, *Computer Manager*

Computer Installation
ELLIOTT 4130–operating system: T20/30; internal storage: 32,768 x 24 bits; magnetic tapes: 4 4276/4277; 1 line printer.

Coding Languages
NEAT, ALGOL, FORTRAN, SLANG.

Services Available
Programming, systems analysis. Operate on a closed shop basis. Internal service only.

Fields of Application
Scientific, engineering.
Specialized area: Mathematical modelling.

FORESTRY COMMISSION
Research Division
Alice Holt Lodge, Wrecclesham, Farnham, Surrey
Telephone: Bentley 2255

United Kingdom – Research Institutions

Officers
R. S. Howell, *Principal Statistician*
D. H. Stewart, *Statistician*

Computer Installation
IBM 1130–operating system: Disk Monitor II; internal storage: 8K 16-bit words; integral exchangeable disc; 1 line printer.

Coding Language
FORTRAN.

Contemplated Equipment
Extension of computing facilities.

Services Available
Advice, preparation of data, programming, computing. Operate on a closed shop basis. Services restricted to research institutions with biometric interests.

Fields of Application
Biometric, statistical and operational research.

MARCONI COMPANY
Research and Development Laboratories
West Hanningfield Road, Great Baddow, Chelmsford, Essex, CM2 8HN
Telephone: Chelmsford 73331

Officers
G. D. Speake, *Technical Director*
H. U. M. Adler, *Computer Bureau Manager*

Computer Installation
ICL 4/70–operating system: Multijob and J; internal storage: 3,072K bits; magnetic tapes: 6 4452, 1 KD; magnetic discs: 7 EDS 4420, 3 EDS 4425; 2 line printers. *Remote processing features*: 10 Teletype, 2 visual display units, 8 Datel 200 lines.

MARCONI Myriad 1 (3)–internal storage: 8K, 16K and 32K 24-bit words.

MARCONI Myriad 2–internal storage: 32K 24-bit words.

Note: The four Marconi computers share 4 magnetic discs and 3 line printers. *Remote processing features*: Full graphics and tabular.

Coding Languages
COBOL, FORTRAN IV, ALGOL 60, BASIC, RPG, FORTRAN II, MINI CORAL, CORAL.

Services Available
Advice, programming, operators, software packages, preparation of data, graphics. Operate on a self-service, remote access, open shop and time-sharing basis.

Fields of Application
Scientific, statistical, systems analysis, operational research, CAD.
Specialized areas: Linear programming, analysis (data, graphical), structural engineering, propagation prediction, filter design, printed board layout, integrated cot masks.

NATIONAL INSTITUTE OF OCEANOGRAPHY
Brook Road, Wormley, Godalming, Surrey
Telephone: Wormley 2122

Officers
Prof. H. Charnock, *Director*
B. J. Hinde, *Head of Data Processing Group*

Computer Installation
IBM 1800 (2)–operating system: MPX; internal storage: 512K bits each; magnetic tapes: 2 7-track IBM 2401 (one computer only); magnetic discs: 3 IBM 1810 each; 1 line printer (one computer only).

HEWLETT PACKARD 2100A–operating system: MOS; internal storage: 256K bits; magnetic tapes: 1 9-track.

Coding Languages
FORTRAN, Assembler.

Service Available
Data retrieval. Operate on a closed shop basis.

Field of Application
Scientific.
Specialized area: Oceanography.

NATIONAL PHYSICAL LABORATORY
Central Computer Unit
Teddington, Middlesex
Telephone: 01-977 3222

Officers
T. Vickers, *Senior Staff*
B. A. Wichmann, *Senior Staff*
N. F. Bird, *Operations Manager*

Computer Installation
ICL KDF9 (2)–operating system: PROMPT; internal storage: 1,572,864 bits; magnetic tapes: 6 1081; magnetic disc: Data Products 5023; 1 line printer. *On-line satellite computer*: PDP-8. *Remote processing features*: ELDON system via PDP-8 acting as multiplexer.

ELLIOTT 4120–graphics research.
ELLIOTT 905–interferometry.
PDP-8 (3)–special purpose.

Coding Languages
ALGOL, Autocode, FORTRAN, BASIC, Matrix scheme.

Services Available
Advice, programming (limited). Operate on a closed shop basis. Available to scientific users only.

Fields of Application
Scientific computation, data handling, solution of problems of classical applied mathematics and modern theoretical physics.
Specialized areas: Linear algebra, error analysis, data fitting, making of mathematical tables, application of Chebyshev polynomials.

THE NUCLEAR POWER GROUP*
Radbroke Hall, Knutsford, Cheshire
Telephone: Knutsford 3800

Officers
A. G. Bradshaw, *Computer Manager*
D. McIntosh, *Programme Information*

Computer Installation
IBM 360/65–operating system: OS; internal storage: 512K bits; magnetic discs: 1 2314; 2 line printers.

Coding Languages
ALGOL, FORTRAN, COBOL, PL/1.

Services Available
Advice, operators, preparation of data, programming, software packages, systems analysis. Operate on a self-service and closed shop basis. Availability limited.

Fields of Application
Problems in the fields of engineering, physics and economics arising in the design of large nuclear power stations.
Specialized areas: Reactor physics, Monte Carlo methods, nuclear reactor gas/steam cycles, reactor shielding; various methods of numerical analysis in connection with the above.

PLANNING AND TRANSPORT RESEARCH AND COMPUTATION CO. LTD.*
40 Grosvenor Gardens, London SW1
Telephone: 01-730 0767

Officers
W. Oxburgh, *Manager*
C. Stevenson, *In charge of foreign relations*

Services Available
Consultation, programming, education and training, software packages, documentation, systems analysis.

Fields of Application
Scientific, statistical, management science, systems analysis, operational research, model building, econometrics, information science.
Specialized areas: Road design, traffic and transportation planning, urban and regional planning, local and central government data banks and information systems.

Training
In conjunction with the University of London Institute of Computer Science, M.Sc. (Computer Science), optional courses in: (1) Road location and design computational methods; (2) Transportation planning and model building. One week courses: Use of computers in road design; Use of computers in transportation planning; Use of computers in urban planning.

ROTHAMSTED EXPERIMENTAL STATION*
Harpenden, Hertfordshire
Telephone: Harpenden 62271

Officers
D. H. Rees, *Head of Computer Department*

Computer Installation
ICL Orion–operating system: Orion Monitoring System; internal storage: 16,384 x 48 bits; magnetic tapes: 7 Ampex TM2; 1 line printer.

ICL 4/70–operating system: Multijob; internal storage: 262,144 bytes; magnetic tapes: 4 ICL 4452; magnetic discs: 4 ICL 4452; 2 line printers. *Remote processing features*: consoles.

Coding Languages
EMA, FORTRAN IV, Usercode.

Contemplated Equipment
High speed terminals and satellite computer.

Services Available
Consultation, programming, operators, software packages, documentation, preparation of data. Operate on a remote access, closed shop and time-sharing basis. Service available to agricultural research institutes.

Fields of Application
Scientific, statistical.
Specialized area: Biological problems.

SCIENCE RESEARCH COUNCIL
Atlas Computer Laboratory
Chilton, near Didcot, Berkshire
Telephone: Abingdon 1900

Officers
Dr. J. Howlett, *Director*
D. G. House, *Head of Operations Group*
J. E. Hailstone, *Head of User Services*

Computer Installation
ICL 1906A–operating system: GEORGE 4, Mk. 7; internal storage: 1,024K characters; magnetic tapes: 8 9-track, 4 7-track; magnetic discs: 9 EDS30, 5 EDS60, 2 drums; 2 line printers. *Remote processing features*: 4, 32 teletypes.

PDP-15–internal storage: 64K words; magnetic tapes: 3 DEC, 2 drives; magnetic discs. *Remote processing features*: Stromberg–Datagraphix microfilm recorder, DEC VT 15 programmable display.

Coding Languages
FORTRAN, PLAN, ALGOL.

Services Available
Advice, operators, preparation of data, software packages. Free service to all universities in the U.K. and to the Science Research Council's laboratories; service to all other government research laboratories charged to cost.

Fields of Application
System programming, numerical analysis, statistical programming, survey analysis, crystallographic computation, number theory, information retrieval, literary text analysis, computer graphics.

SCIENCE RESEARCH COUNCIL
Daresbury Nuclear Physics Laboratory
Daresbury, Warrington, Lancashire
Telephone: 65000

Officers
Prof. A. Ashmore, *Director*
Dr. B. Zacharov, *Head of Computer/Electronics Division*

Computer Installations
IBM 370/165–operating system: MVT with TSO; internal storage: 16 million bits; magnetic tapes: 8 3420; magnetic discs: 6 3330, 9 2319; 2 line printers. *On-line satellite computers*: PDP-8, PDP-11, Honeywell H516, Honeywell H316, ICL Argus 400, Honeywell H112. *Remote processing features*: TSO terminals and RJE.

IBM 1802–operating system: locally developed multi-programming; internal storage: 512K bits; magnetic tapes: 2 2400; 1 line printer. *On-line satellite computers*: PDP-8, PDP-11, Honeywell H112, Honeywell H316, Honeywell H516, ICL Argus 400.

Coding Languages
FORTRAN, PL/1 COBOL, Assembler.

Service Available
Advice. Operate on a remote access, open shop and time-sharing basis. Available only to authorized users.

Field of Application
Scientific.
Specialized areas: Nuclear physics, on-line links, operating systems.

SHOE AND ALLIED TRADES RESEARCH ASSOCIATION (SATRA)*
Management and Computer Services
Rockingham Road, Kettering, Northamptonshire

Officer
A. W. N. Ede, *Manager*

Computer Installation
ELLIOTT 4120–internal storage: 576K bits; magnetic tapes: 4; 1 line printer.

Coding Languages
ALGOL, COBOL, NEAT.

Services Available
Consultation, programming, education and training, software packages, documentation, preparation of data, systems analysis. Operate on a closed shop basis. Service available to the shoe industry (principally to SATRA members).

Fields of Application
Commercial (finished stock control, sales analysis and invoicing, sales forecasting, raw material control, production planning, market research); statistical (data retrieval and statistical analysis); research into computer-aided design.

SHORT BROTHERS AND HARLAND LTD.
Queen's Island, Belfast, BT3 9D2, Northern Ireland

Officer
P. F. Foreman, *Managing Director*

Computer Installation
ICL 1903A–operating system: GEORGE 2; internal storage: 1,180,128 bits; magnetic tapes: 4 1972; magnetic discs: 5 EDS8; 1 line printer.

ELLIOTT 803C–internal storage: 319,488 bits; magnetic tapes: 3 Ampex; 1 line printer.

ELLIOTT 803B–internal storage: 159,744 bits.

PDP-8–operating system: OS/8; internal storage: 245,760 bits; magnetic tapes: 1 DEC; magnetic discs: 1 RSK 1.

PDP-15–operating system: ASS; internal storage: 295K bits; magnetic tapes: 4 DEC.

Fields of Application
Scientific, statistical, commercial, production control, accounting, management, systems analysis, operational research.
Specialized areas: Sales analysis, payroll, structural engineering, aeronautical engineering.

CONSULTANTS

ANNAN IMPEY MORRISH
Oldbourne Hall, 43 Shoe Lane, London EC4
Telephone: 01-583 0154

Officer
G. C. Child, *Data Processing Partner*

Services Available
General management consultancy, feasibility studies, specification writing, systems analysis and design, facilities management, staff selection, computer audit.

Fields of Application
All commercial applications involving visible record computers to medium scale systems. Also terminal systems.

BELLARD INVESTMENTS LTD.*
Adelphi, 1 John Adam Street, London WC2
Telephone: 01-930 5833

Officers
J. M. Gilbert, *Computer Centre*
J. R. Atkinson, *Training and Consultancy*

Computer Installations
HONEYWELL H400 (2)–internal storage: 4K bits each; magnetic tapes: 12; 2 line printers.

HONEYWELL H1250–internal storage: 81,920 characters; magnetic tapes: 7; magnetic discs: 1; 1 line printer.

Coding Languages
EASY II Assembly, Easycoder Assembly, COBOL H & I High Level Language.

Contemplated Equipment
Honeywell H3200.

Services Available
Consultation, programming, education and training, operators, software packages, documentation, preparation of data, systems analysis. Operate on a closed shop basis. Service available to industry and commerce.

Fields of Application
Commercial, accounting, management, systems analysis.
Specialized areas: Hire purchase, printing and publishing industries.

Training
Various courses.

M. J. BEVAN LTD.
14-15 High Street, Hitchin, Hertfordshire

Also at:
8 Cavendish Place, London W1
40–42 Washway Road, Sale, Cheshire

Officers
M. J. Bevan, *Managing Director*
C. R. Corder, *Foreign Relations and Training*

Coding Languages
COBOL, FORTRAN, ALGOL, PL/1, RPG, Assembler, PLAN.

Services Available
Consultation, programming, education and training, software packages, documentation, systems analysis.

Fields of Application
Commercial, scientific.
Specialized areas: Report generator, vehicle scheduling.

Training
Short courses in computer languages and systems analysis.

BISHOPS ASSOCIATES*
Allweather House, High Street, Edgware, Middlesex
Telephone: 01-952 7308, 01-958 6965

Officer
F. Bishops, *Principal*

Coding Languages
All major coding languages including the high level languages.

United Kingdom – Consultants

Services Available
Management consultancy covering computer installations and projects on site.

Field of Application
Commercial, including all accountancy applications, stock and production control, standard costing, statistical analysis, management information and scientific work.

Training
In-house training for all levels of management, both in data processing and non-technical areas.

BOOZ, ALLEN & HAMILTON INTERNATIONAL
New Bond Street House, 1-5 New Bond Street, London, W1Y 0DB
Telephone: 01-499 8971

Services Available
Consultation, programming, systems analysis, systems and procedures.

Fields of Application
Engineering, research and development management, finance/accounting, marketing, systems planning and design, general management, etc.
Specialized areas: Equipment evaluation, systems planning and design, information retrieval, data communication, data-based management, project management.

BRANDON APPLIED SYSTEMS LTD.*
Brandon House, 79-80 Blackfriars Road, London S.E.1
Telephone: 01-928 9511

Officers
G. M. R. Graham, *Managing Director*
R. B. Yearsley, *Director*

Coding Languages
Various Assembly languages, COBOL, ALGOL, PL/1, etc.

Services Available
Consultation, programming, systems analysis, aptitude tests, personnel selection.

Fields of Application
Commercially oriented applications, D.P. consulting, real time and transaction processing.
Specialized areas: Inventory management systems, standard development, training (D.P.), real time computer installation audit.

Training
Computer operations management, management standards for D.P., basic business systems analysis, decision tables, data base management, executive guide to D.P., real time communication systems and practical systems design.

BUSINESS OPERATIONS RESEARCH (SERVICES) LTD.
New Bond Street House, 1-5 New Bond Street, London W1Y 0DB
Telephone: 01-499 8971

Services Available
Consultation, systems analysis.

Fields of Application
Stock and production control, optimum mix, rationalization and mergers, company models, transport and distribution, corporate planning, operational research, etc.

BUSINESS SOFTWARE LTD.*
Broadway House, The Broadway, Wimbledon, London SW19
Telephone: 01-542 4202

Officers
R. W. F. Rice, *Chairman*
M. J. Hayward, *General Projects Manager*
A. R. Gill, *Bureau Manager*

Services Available
Systems design, programming, software packages,

Fields of Application
Statistical, commercial, projection control, accounting, management, systems analysis, operational research.
Specialized areas: Management information systems, linear programming.

C.I. SOFTWARE LTD.*
Brunel Road, Churchfields, Salisbury, Wiltshire
Telephone: 6938

Officers
A. R. V. Roberts, *Managing Director*
Miss E. N. Evans, *Marketing Director*
A. R. Jackman, *Technical Director*

Services Available
Consultation, programming, software packages, documentation, systems analysis.

Fields of Application
Scientific, technical, systems analysis.
Specialized areas: On-line applications, real time data communications, message switching.

COMPUTER AID FOR MANAGEMENT LTD.*
45 Albemarle Street, London W1
Telephone: 01-499 0770

Also at:
102a Westbourne Grove, London W2
Telephone: 01-727 1315

Officers
C. J. Bowyer, *Chairman*
J. S. Godfrey, *Foreign relations*

Coding Languages
All second and third generation, including 360 BAL, 1900 PLAN, COBOL, FORTRAN, RPG, ALGOL, etc.

Services Available
Consultation, programming, software packages, documentation, preparation of data, systems analysis. Operate on a self-service, remote access and closed shop basis. Provision of contract systems analysis and programming on a timed or fixed-fee basis; consultants available with proficiency in French, German, Spanish, Italian, Swedish and Danish.

Fields of Application
Commercial data processing; development and marketing of software.

United Kingdom – Consultants

COMPUTER ANALYSTS & PROGRAMMERS LTD.
CAP House, 14/15 Great James Street, London, WC1N 3DY
Telephone: 01-242 0021

Also:
Computer Analysts & Programmers (Reading) Ltd.,
New Oxford House, 1 Station Road, Reading, Berkshire, RG1 1LL
Telephone: Reading 580264

Computer Analysts & Programmers (Northern) Ltd.,
67 London Road, Alderley Edge, Cheshire, SK9 7DY
Telephone: Alderley Edge 4420

Computer Analysts & Programmers (Products) Ltd.,
CAP House, 14/15 Great James Street, London WC1N 3DY
Telephone: 01-242 0021

Overseas offices:
Paris (France); Brussels (Belgium); Basle (Switzerland); Amsterdam (Netherlands); Düsseldorf, Munich (Germany); Stockholm (Sweden); Vienna (Austria); Madrid (Spain); Copenhagen (Denmark).

Officers
A. d'Agapeyeff, *Managing Director*
B. J. Gibbens, *Executive Director*
D. T. Sheahan, *Executive Director*
K. W. Clark, *Executive Director*
L. J. Russell, *Executive Director*
D. G. N. Hunter, *Technical Director*
J. M. MacLeod, *Technical Director*

Coding Languages
PL/1, COBOL, FORTRAN, ALGOL, CORAL, NELIAC and many Assembler and other low-level codes.

Services Available
Consulting advice, installation reviews, system design, project implementation, tailored software, compilers, operating systems and software packages.

Fields of Application
Scientific, statistical, commercial, production control, accounting, etc.
Specialized areas: Software development, commercial applications, on-line and real time systems, etc.

COMPUTER ASSOCIATES*
28 Kingsway, London WC2
Telephone: 01-242 0941

Also at:
11 Muswell Hill, London N10

Officers
D. J. Dormer, *Chief Executive*
S. Fishman, *General Manager*
C. Woodham, *Senior Consultant*

Services Available
Consultation, programming, operators, systems analysis.

COMPUTER PROFESSIONALS CONSULTANCY LTD.
Albany Buildings, 47 Victoria Street, Westminster, London, SW1H 0RE
Telephone: 01-222 6226

Officers
M. J. Brawn, *Managing Director*
M. V. S. Stammers, *Marketing Director*
D. W. Brawn, *Director*

Services Available
Advice, programming, software packages, systems analysis.

Fields of Application
Commercial, accounting, management, systems analysis.
Specialized areas: Payroll, NCR computers, used computers.

COMPUTER SCIENCES INTERNATIONAL UNITED KINGDOM LTD. (CSI UK)*
Portland House, Stag Place, London SW1
Telephone: 01-828 8211

Officers
Dr. M. I. Montana, *President and General Manager*
K. R. Barge, *Managing Director*
R. O. Needham, *Manager of Programme Development*

Services Available
Advice, programming, education and training, operators, software packages, preparation of data, systems analysis.

Fields of Application
Management, systems analysis.
Specialized areas: Compiler writing, management information systems.

Training
Standard courses: Computer Concepts for Management; Management Utilization of the Computer; Systems and Programming Project Management; Systems Analysis and Design.

COMPUTER SYSTEMS INTERNATIONAL INC. (GB) LTD.*
Station House, Harrow Road, Wembley, Middlesex

Also at:
ITS Building, Jonathan Industrex, Chaska, Minnesota 55218, U.S.A.

Officers
Dr. A. L. Reed, *Chairman*
A. G. Stuck, *Managing Director*
M. W. H. Thomson, *Foreign Relations*

Services Available
Consultation, programming, education and training, operators, software packages, documentation, preparation of data, systems analysis.

Fields of Application
All commercial and business applications.
Specialized areas: Systems analysis and design standards, modular programming standards and associated module test packages.

Training
Courses in systems analysis; programme specification; programming standards and techniques; computer appreciation for management.

CONSTRUCTIVE MANAGEMENT SERVICES LTD.*
38 Wilson Street, London EC2
Telephone: 01-247 6213

Officers
R. H. Thorpe, *Managing Director*
T. A. Howard, *Technical Director*

Computer Installations
UNIVAC 9400—operating systems: TOS/DOS 2; internal storage: 94K bits; magnetic tapes: 6; magnetic discs: 6 8411; 1 line printer.

UNIVAC 9300—internal storage: 32K bits core.

Contemplated Equipment
120 Cossor VDUs; 2 425 control units.

Services Available
Consultation, programming, software packages, preparation of data, systems analysis. Operate on a closed shop and time-sharing basis.

Fields of Application
Commercial, statistical, accounting, management, systems analysis, etc.
Specialized area: Real time applications.

CONTRACT COMPUTING LTD.*
Nicholas House, 78/86 Brigstock Road,
Thornton Heath, Croydon, Surrey
Telephone: 01-684 9557, 01-684 8382

Also at:
Newspaper House, 8/16 Great New Street, London EC4

Officers
Dr. D. A. Eyeions, *Managing Director*
A. M. McLaren, R. W. Forbes, *Executive Directors*
J. de Bage, S. McKibbin, *Senior Officers*

Computer Installation
CDC 3200—operating system: Tape Scope; internal storage: 32K 24-bit words; magnetic tapes: 8; 1 line printer.

Coding Languages
FORTRAN, COBOL, COMPASS.

Contemplated Equipment
CDC 3300.

Services Available
Consultation, programming, operators, software packages, documentation, preparation of data, systems analysis. Operate on a self-service, block time, open and closed shop basis.

Fields of Application
Scientific, commercial, operational research, survey analysis.
Specialized area: Market research.

CONTRACT PROGRAMMING COMPANY*
30 Baker Street, London W1
Telephone: 01-486 5353/4

Also at:
34 Valley Way, Knutsford, Cheshire
Telephone: Knutsford 3691

Officers
M. G. O'Connell, M. R. O'Connell, M. C. Rees

Services Available
Programming, software packages, documentation, preparation of data, systems analysis.

Fields of Application
Commercial, production control, accounting, management, systems analysis.

COOPERS AND LYBRAND ASSOCIATES LTD.
Shelley House, Noble Street, London, EC2V 7DQ
Telephone: 01-606 4040

Also at: Birmingham and Glasgow

Officers
R. V. Fabian, *Director of EDP London*
E. P. Morris, *Director of EDP London*
F. Mitchell, *Birmingham*

Coding Languages
ALGOL, COBOL, FORTRAN, PLAN, PL/1, Assembler.

Services Available
Advice, programming, education and training, software packages, documentation, preparation of data, systems analysis, selection of equipment, management effectiveness reviews, organization structure, personnel services.

Fields of Application
Scientific, statistical, commercial, production control, accounting, management, systems analysis, operational research.

Training
Short courses in effective computer management and effective work management.

CORPORATE COMPUTER SERVICES LTD.*
37/38 Margaret Street, London W1
Telephone: 01-629 2611

Also at:
Corporate Computer Management, Pangbourne
CCS Engineering, Hounslow

Officers
R. Tomlin, *Managing Director, Corporate Computer Services*
R. C. Ferguson, *Managing Director, Corporate Computer Management*
S. Hastings, *Director in charge of Foreign Relations*

Contemplated Equipment
Large ICL 1904A.

Services Available
Consultation, programming, education and training, documentation, systems analysis.

Fields of Application
Scientific, statistical, commercial, production control, accounting, management, systems analysis, operational research.
Specialized areas: Management information and control systems.

DATA CONSULTANTS LTD.
56 High Street, Sutton Coldfield, Warwickshire
Telephone: 021-354 2440, 021-355 3551

Officers
R. Smith, *Managing Director*
M. V. Bunting, *Administration*
A. G. Thompson, *Director of Management Science*
C. T. Dillon, *Director of Systems*

Coding Languages
Autocoder, BEST, CLEO, COBOL, Easycoder, FORTRAN, Language H, NEAT, PLAN, TAS.

Services Available
Consultation, operators, preparation of data, programming, software packages, systems analysis.

Fields of Application
Statistical, commercial, production control, accounting, management, systems analysis, operational research, management science, contract programming and software programming.

DATA EXPRESS (D.P.) LTD.*
Marlborough House, 151 Uxbridge Road, London W12
Telephone: 01-743 2129, 01-743 0044

Coding Languages
FORTRAN, COBOL, Assembler.

Services Available
Consultation, programming, preparation of data.

DIGITAL APPLICATIONS INTERNATIONAL LTD.
Axtell House, 24 Warwick Street, London, W1R 5RB
Telephone: 01-734 5486

Officers
A. J. Kisiel, *Managing Director*
S. Kisiel, *Director*

Coding Languages
Assembly, FORTRAN.

Services Available
Consultation, programming, systems analysis.

Field of Application
Industrial automation.
Specialized areas: Process control, industrial data acquisition.

EMERSON CONSULTANTS LTD.
8 Grafton Street, London W1
Telephone: 01-493 1087

Officers
R. G. Marriott, *Director*
T. B. Foster, *Vice-President (U.S.)*
D. Devereux, *President (U.S.)*

Service Available
Systems analysis.

Fields of Application
Management, systems analysis.
Specialized area: Plant maintenance control.

ENGINEERING COMPUTATIONS*
72 Newman Street, London W1
Telephone: 01-636 6228

Officer
Dr. E. W. Solomon

Coding Languages
ALGOL, FORTRAN, E.M.A., Atlas Basic Languages (ABL), TELCOMP.

Services Available
Consultation, preparation of data, programming, software packages, systems analysis. Commercial data processing is not undertaken.

Fields of Application
All branches of engineering technology and operations research.
Specialized areas: Optimization, design of computer systems for technical applications, structural-engineering applications.

EUROPLEX LTD.
Theory Analysis Group Sector
6 Conduit Street, London, W1R 9TG

Also at:
22 East Elm Street, Chicago, Illinois 60611, U.S.A.
Telephone: (312) 751-2747

Officer
W. J. Rago, *Managing Director*

Computer Installation
On-line satellite computer: Bull General Electric Mark I and II.

Coding Languages
BASIC, FORTRAN IV, Assembler, Simulation: GPSS.

Contemplated Equipment
Analog type computer.

Services Available
Advice, programming and contract computing. Operate on on a time-sharing basis. Available to persons with investment portfolios greater than £50,000 (U.S.$ 120,000), e.g. financial institutions, banks and financial corporate officers.

Fields of Application
Statistical, commercial, operational research.
Specialized areas: Sales analysis, linear programming, investment.

FARM PLANNING & COMPUTER SERVICES LTD.*
1 Exeter Road, Newmarket, Suffolk
Telephone: Newmarket 3275/6

Officers
B. M. Camm, *Managing Director*
M. E. Daw, *Senior Consultant*
D. M. Castle, *Senior Consultant*
R. J. Govier, *Senior Consultant*

Service Available
Consultation. Generally restricted to clients concerned with agricultural and horticultural production and marketing.

Fields of Application
Feasibility studies, investment appraisals, long term plans, operational research, management, accounting and recording.

FRASER, WILLIAMS & CO. LTD.
61-63 Dale Street, Liverpool, Lancashire

Also at:
London, Sheffield and Birmingham

Officers
E. R. Williams, T. McCafferty, *Joint Managing Directors*

Coding Languages
All current commercial languages; also FORTRAN.

Services Available
Consultation, programming, systems analysis. Service available to commerce and industry.

Fields of Application
Commercial, industrial.
Specialized areas: Information retrieval, actuarial and insurance.

GENERAL COMPUTING SERVICES LTD.
65-67 Western Road, Hove, Sussex
Telephone: 0273-778161/2

Coding Languages
COBOL, FORTRAN, ALGOL, RPG, PL/1, PLAN, etc.

Officers
S. Crane, *Managing Director*
B. Grill, *Director*

Services Available
Advice, education and training, preparation of data, raw data digitising for research, self-instructional packages. Operate on a closed shop basis.

Fields of Application
Scientific, statistical, commercial, general research.
Specialized areas: Structural engineering, medical research, geophysical raw data handling.

Training
Basic computer training; keyboard training.

GENERAL INFORMATION AND CONTROL SYSTEMS LTD.*
Adelphi, John Adam Street, London WC2
Telephone: 01-930 5833

Officers
J. R. Atkinson, *Managing Director*
K. R. London, *Director of Training and Personnel*

Services Available
Consultation, programming, education and training, systems analysis.

Training
Senior management seminars; D. P. management techniques seminars; systems and programming techniques courses.

GENERAL PRECISION SYSTEMS LTD.*
Abbey House, 282-292 Farnborough Road, Farnborough, Hampshire
Telephone: Farnborough 44321

Officers
P. C. Haines, *Managing Director*
C. Evans, *General Manager*
J. Nokes, *Programming Manager*

Coding Languages
FORTRAN, ALGOL, ALGOL R, COBOL, PL/1, DAP 16, NEAT Assembly, SAP Assembly, FIXPAC.

Contemplated Equipment
SIA remote terminal to CDC 6600.

Services Available
Consultation, programming, software packages, systems analysis.

Fields of Application
Operational research, systems analysis and design, scientific programming, real time systems programming.
Specialized areas: Computer-based fast time simulation of air and surface; transportation systems.

J. HARWELL DATA PROCESSING LTD.
Radnor House, 93-97 Regent Street, London, W1R 7TD

Officers
J. Harwell, *Director and Supervising Consultant*
M. Lewis, *General Manager*
F. Chambers, *Co-ordinating Consultant*
M. Nickolay, *Marketing Manager*

Coding Languages
PLAN, COBOL, FORTRAN, System 4 Usercode, 360 Assembler, NICOL, ALGOL, BASIC.

Services Available
Advice, programming, software packages, documentation, compilers. Operate on a time-sharing basis.

Field of Application
Software.
Specialized areas: Compilers, software aids, languages.

HILTI (GREAT BRITAIN) LTD.*
Faulkner House, Faulkner Street, Manchester 1

Officer
P. L. Campbell, *Management Services Manager*

Computer Installation
HONEYWELL H200—internal storage: 24K characters; magnetic tapes: 6; 1 line printer.

Coding Languages
Easycoder, COBOL, FORTRAN.

Services Available
Consultation, programming, operators, software packages, documentation, preparation of data, systems analysis. Operate on a self-service and block time basis.

Fields of Application
Statistical, commercial, production control, accounting, management, systems analysis, etc.
Specialized areas: Payroll, stock recording control, sales ledgers.

HOSKYNS GROUP LTD.*
Boundary House, Furnival Street, London EC4

Officer
A. L. Helman

Services Available
Consultation, programming, education and training, software packages, systems analysis.

Fields of Application
Manufacturing, distribution, financial, government.
Specialized area: Real time systems.

Training
10 short courses of 3-20 days' duration.

T.C. HUDSON ASSOCIATES LTD.*
28 Crawford Street, London, W1H 1PL

Officers
T. C. Hudson (Canada), *Managing Director*
P. C. Harbridge, *Director*
E. Newman, *Director*
F. M. Trapnell (U.S.A.), *Director*

Services Available
Consultation, programming, software packages, systems analysis.

Fields of Application
Commercial, management systems, production control, software design.
Specialized areas: Computer performance measurement and analysis; design of communication based systems.

Training
Introduction to systems programming (4-week course).

INTEGRATED SYSTEMS AND DESIGN LTD.*
Stephenson Way, Crawley, Sussex
Telephone: Crawley 29831

Also at:
Boston (U.S.A.), Geneva (Switzerland).

Officers
J. N. Chapple, *Managing Director, Computer Systems Division*
S. E. White, *Marketing Director, Computer Services Division*

Computer Installation
PDP-8 (2).

Services Available
Consultation, education and training, software packages, systems analysis. Operate on an open shop basis.

Fields of Application
Management Assistance Systems: stock control, order processing, etc.; Engineering: road construction programmes.
Specialized area: Reservation systems (e.g. hotels, shipping, railways).

Training
Short courses in computer operating; management for computers; FOCAL programming.

INTERNATIONAL PROGRAMMING SERVICES LTD.*
5B Market Hill, Saffron Walden, Essex

Officer
Dr. A. J. Hirsh

Services Available
Consultation, programming, software packages, systems analysis.

JEANTEX INTERNATIONAL LTD.*
'Stranraer House', Stoney Road, Bracknell, Berkshire

Officer
S. W. Graham, *Managing Director (in charge of foreign relations)*

Services Available
Consultation, programming, education and training, systems analysis. Operate on a self-service basis.

Fields of Application
Scientific, statistical, commercial, production control, accounting, management, systems analysis.
Specialized area: Computer security and privacy.

JEFFREYS & HILL LTD.*
4 Half Moon Street, London W1
Telephone: 01-629 3445

Also at:
17 King Street, Luton, Bedfordshire

Coding Languages
All widely used languages, including Machine Code, Assembler, COBOL, PL/1, FORTRAN, ALGOL.

Services Available
Consultation, programming, documentation, systems analysis.

Fields of Application
Process control, commercial, production control, accounting, management information systems, general statistics.
Specialized areas: Message switching software, software programme convertors.

KNIGHT WEGENSTEIN LTD.*
47 Berkeley Square, London W1
Telephone: 01-629 3831

Also at:
75 Mosley Street, Manchester, M23 HR
Telephone: 061-228 1393

Officers
L. J. Pedicini, *Managing Director*
N. K. Hopkins, *Director*
A. J. Crook, *Director*

Computer Installation
IBM 1130.

Services Available
Systems analysis, hardware evaluation, configuration, operations audit.

Fields of Application
Management, foundry, production control.
Specialized areas: Banking, automated warehousing, integration of information systems for management.

Training
Specialized tailored courses in computer facilities, management, systems analysis, planning, decision tables for clients.

JOHN LANG COMPUTER PROGRAMMING SERVICE*
19 The Close, Great Dunmow, Essex
Telephone: Great Dunmow 3167

Officer
J. E. Lang

Coding Languages
PL/1, COBOL, System 360 Assembler and RPG, 360/20 BAL and RPG, IBM 1401 Autocoder and SPS, ICL 1900 series PLAN.

Services Available
Consultation, programming, software packages, documentation, systems analysis.

United Kingdom – Consultants

Fields of Application
Commercial, production control, accounting, management information systems, systems analysis, etc.
Specialized areas: Mail order specialized systems; upgrading IBM 360/20 systems and programmes for use on larger 360s; systems and programmes for card, tape or disc IBM 360/20s.

LEA ASSOCIATES LTD.
P.O. Box 1024, Westminster, London, SW1P 2JL
Telephone: 01-222 7305

Officer
G. Lea, *Managing Director*

Contemplated Equipment
Terminal to Univac 1108.

Services Available
Consultation, programming, education and training, software packages, documentation, systems analysis, phototypesetting. Operate on a self-service basis.

Field of Application
Scientific.
Specialized areas: Bibliographies, computer-aided indexing and phototypesetting.

Training
Courses in bibliographical phototypesetting by computer, automatic indexing and thesaurus construction.

LEASCO SOFTWARE LTD.
197 Knightsbridge, London SW7
Telephone: 01-584 7040

Officers
J. P. B. Stevens, *President*
P. M. Hunt, *Managing Director*

Services Available
Advice, programming, education and training, software packages, documentation, preparation of data, systems analysis. Operate on a time-sharing basis.

Fields of Application
Commercial, production control, accounting, management, systems analysis.
Specialized areas: Sales analysis, analysis, payroll.

ARTHUR D. LITTLE LTD.
Berkeley Square House, Berkeley Square, London, W1X 6EY
Telephone: 01-493 6801

Officers
H. A. Riker, *Managing Director*
J. L. Felker, *Director*

Computer Installation
In U.K., remote access to HIS.
In U.S., several in-house and remote access computers.

Services Available
Advice on hardware and software design and appraisal, systems analysis and consultants in systems design and implementation.

Fields of Application
Systems analysis, systems design, hardware appraisal, computer department organization, systems implementation.
Specialized areas: Scientific and commercial systems and applications. Large multi-access, time sharing, systems for government, industry and services. Multi-computer systems, national and international date communication between computers, application of minicomputers.

LOGICA LTD.
31-36 Foley Street, London, W1P 7LB
Telephone: 01-637 1511

Officers
P. A. B. Hughes, *Chairman*
L. A. Taylor, *Managing Director*
P. J. Coen, *Director, International Operations*
J. McNeil, *Director, Computer Sciences Group*
P. C. Harbridge, *Director, Management Systems Group*

Coding Languages
COBOL, FORTRAN, PL/1, ALGOL, Simulation.

Services Available
Advice, programming, education and training, software packages, documentation, systems analysis, total system supply, computer market studies, hardware consultancy and design, computer performance analysis.

Fields of Application
Scientific, statistical, commercial, production control, accounting, management, systems analysis, operational research, corporate computer policy studies, marketing, real time systems, communications systems.
Specialized area: Linear programming.

Training
The company advises on course structure and content and provides lectures for numerous conference and training course organizers.

D. G. LOWES MANAGEMENT SERVICES*
128 Park Lane, London W1
Telephone: 01-629 7353

Officers
D. G. Lowes, *Chairman*
E. C. Parkin, *Services Director*

Coding Languages
COBOL, FORTRAN, 360 Assembler, PLAN, RPG, FORTRAN.

Contemplated Equipment
Remote data terminals; keyboard terminals; 2314 Mass Storage D.A.S.D.

Services Available
Consultation, programming, operators, software packages, documentation, preparation of data, systems analysis. Operate on a self-service, block time open shop basis.

Fields of Application
General commercial and accounting, production/inventory control, M.I.S.

McKINSEY & COMPANY INC.*
74 St. James's Street, London SW1
Telephone: 01-839 8040

Services Available
Management consulting, systems analysis.

Fields of Application
Operations research, simulation, statistical analysis, management.

McLINTOCK MANN & WHINNEY MURRAY
95 Southwark Street, London SE1

Officers
C. A. del Tufo, *Partner in charge of Computer Bureau*
P. G. Richardson, *Managing Partner*

Computer Installation
IBM 360/30—operating system: DOS; internal storage: 64K bits; magnetic tapes: 2 2415; magnetic discs: 4 2311; 2 line printers.

Coding Languages
MARK IV, COBOL, Assembler.

Contemplated Equipment
IBM 370/125.

Services Available
Advice, programming, software packages, preparation of data, systems analysis. Operate on a block time and closed shop basis.

Fields of Application
Statistical, commercial, accounting, management, systems analysis, operational research.
Specialized areas: Sales analysis, analysis, payroll.

MANAGEMENT DYNAMICS SOFTWARE SERVICES*
Heathrow House, Bath Road, Cranford, Hounslow, Middlesex
Telephone: 01-759 9191

Also at:
Calthorpe House, Hagley Road, Edgbaston, Birmingham 15
213 Oxford Street, London, W1R 1AH

Officer
R. D. Phillips, *General Manager*

Computer Installation
ICL 1905—internal storage: 32K words; magnetic tapes: 8; 2 line printers.

Coding Languages
PLAN, COBOL, NICOL, FORTRAN, ALGOL, BAL, PL/1, RPG, Assembler.

Services Available
Consultation, programming, education and training, software packages, documentation, systems analysis, contract systems and programming. Prepared to work on an off-site, fixed price or time hire basis.

Fields of Application
Commercial, production control, accounting, management, systems analysis.

Training
Customer designed training programmes.

MANAGEMENT SCIENCES LTD.*
Grove Chambers, Green Lane, Wilmslow, Cheshire
Telephone: Wilmslow 29121

Also at:
Hadley House, 79 Uxbridge Road, Ealing, London W5

Officers
Dr. A. Hodkin, *Managing Director*
R. J. Taylor, *Operations Director*
G. E. Phizaclea, *Commercial Director*

Services Available
Consultation, programming, education and training, software packages, documentation, systems analysis.

Fields of Application
Production, accounting, operational research, management systems, econometrics, regional planning, transportation.
Specialized area: Environmental studies.

MARINE AND GENERAL COMPUTER CONSULTANCY (I.O.M.) LTD.
Mill Lane, Greeba, St. Johns, Isle of Man
Telephone: 0624 71-356

Officers
Capt. J. S. McKenzie, *Managing Director*
Mrs. M. McKenzie, *Director in charge of Personnel and Training*

Coding Languages
FORTRAN, BASIC, ALGOL, COBOL, FOCAL, Assembler.

Contemplated Equipment
A time-sharing computer with 32 terminals on site.

Services Available
Advice, programming, education and training, software packages, documentation, systems analysis. Operate on a time-sharing basis.

Fields of Application
Scientific, statistical, commercial.
Specialized areas: Marine and surveying projects.

Training
Short courses in computer appreciation, loading programmes and the marine applications of computers.

MASTER REGISTER LTD.
Royal Buildings, 2 Mosley Street, Manchester, M2 3AN
Telephone: 061-228 1601

Officers
R. J. McQuaker, *Managing Director*
J. H. W. Pickard, *Manager of Programming Services*

Coding Languages
Usercode, FORTRAN, COBOL, PLAN, BAL, PL/1, ALGOL, CLEO, ASTRAL, GIN, RPG, NICOL, FILETAB, APRIL.

Services Available
Advice, programming, education and training, software packages, systems analysis.

Fields of Application
Scientific, statistical, commercial, production control, accounting, management, systems analysis.
Specialized areas: Sales analysis, analysis, payroll, structural engineering.

Training
Courses in programming languages and management training on site.

MIPS INTERNATIONAL*
Suites 11-12, 52 Shaftesbury Avenue, London, W1U 7DE
Telephone: 01-693 3689, 01-734 8862

Also at:
Paris, Lagos, Stuttgart, Vienna, New York.

Officers
F. Savage, *Marketing Director*
K. Savage

Coding Languages
COBOL, ALGOL, FORTRAN, RPG, PLAN, PL/1, BEST.

Services Available
Consultation, programming, education and training, software packages, documentation, systems analysis. Operate on a block time and open shop basis.

Fields of Application
Scientific, statistical, commercial, production control, accounting, management, systems analysis, operational research.
Specialized areas: Software design, feasibility studies, software research and development, software marketing and advice, financing project services, management science, linear programming, market studies, bio-medical services.

Training
Programmer Training Course (6 weeks); COBOL (basic and advanced), FORTRAN (basic and advanced) and ALGOL (basic and advanced) (all 3 weeks); Keyboard operating (2 weeks).

MOUNCEY & PARTNERS LTD.*
York House, Empire Way, Wembley, Middlesex
Telephone: 01-903 4901

Also at:
Royal Oak House, Prince Street, Bristol, BS1 4QH
Telephone: 0272-20981

Officers
R. F. C. McKay, *Managing Director*
D. R. Garfoot, *Sales Manager, Software House*
R. G. Evans, *General Manager, Data Preparation Bureau*

Services Available
Consultation, programming, education and training, software packages, documentation, preparation of data, systems analysis.

Fields of Application
General commercial, specializing in Building Societies, banking, insurance, Trustee Savings Banks.

T. WILLIAM OLLE
15 Weymede, Byfleet, Surrey, KT14 7DG
Telephone: Byfleet 47530

Officer
Dr. T. William Olle

Services Available
Advice, education and training.

Fields of Application
Commercial, management, systems analysis.
Specialized area: Data base management.

Training
Courses on data base management, systems theory and application.

OMICRON*
56 Wilbury Road, Hove, Sussex, BN3 3PA
Telephone: OBR3–735587

Officers
L. R. Greybourne, *Systems Analyst and Planning Consultant*
S. M. Greybourne, *Systems Analyst*
C. L. G. Bell, *Mathematical Economist*

Services Available
Consultation, programming, software packages, systems analysis.

Fields of Application
Statistical, management, systems analysis, software development.
Specialized areas: Computer-language translation, technological forecasting, economic and social planning, system simulation, economic model building, management games.

P. A. MANAGEMENT CONSULTANTS LTD.
2 Albert Gate, Knightsbridge, London, SW1X 7JU
Telephone: 01-235 6060

Also at:
6 Highfield Road, Edgbaston, Birmingham, B15 3DJ
Telephone: 021-454 5791

Royal London Buildings, 42 Baldwin Street, Bristol 1
Telephone: 0272-294581

Holbeck House, Albion Street, Leeds, Yorkshire, LS1 5AU
Telephone: 0532-36572

Pearl Assurance House, 55 Castle Street, Liverpool, L2 9TW
Telephone: 051-227 3521

St. James's House, Charlotte Street, Manchester, M1 4DZ
Telephone: 061-237 4531

Bank Chambers, 51 Grainger Street, Newcastle upon Tyne, NE1 5JE
Telephone: 0632-28038

93 Talbot Street, Nottingham, NG1 5GN
Telephone: 0602-47475

70 Clarkehouse Road, Sheffield, Yorkshire, S10 2LJ
Telephone: 0742-67281

6 Manor Place, Edinburgh, EH3 7DH, Scotland
Telephone: 031-225 4481

Fitzpatrick House, Cadogan Street, Glasgow C.2, Scotland
Telephone: 041-221 3954

Ulster Bank House, Shaftesbury Square, Belfast, BT2 7DL, Northern Ireland
Telephone: 0232-27467

1A South Mall, Cork, Republic of Ireland
Telephone: Cork 21184

Hume House, Ballsbridge, Dublin, Republic of Ireland
Telephone: Dublin 684346

United Kingdom – Consultants

Overseas Offices:
Sydney, Adelaide, Brisbane, Melbourne, Perth (Australia); Brussels (Belgium); Copenhagen (Denmark); Helsinki (Finland); Paris (France); Düsseldorf, Frankfurt, Stuttgart (Germany); Athens (Greece); Hong Kong; Milan (Italy); Tokyo (Japan); Amsterdam (Netherlands); Auckland, Wellington (New Zealand); Singapore; Barcelona, Madrid (Spain); Stockholm (Sweden); Zürich (Switzerland); Los Angeles (U.S.A.).

Officers
H. Holman Hunt, *Director, Computer and Management Sciences Group*
A. C. Glass, *Divisional Director, Computer Division*
J. Cameron Low, *Divisional Director, Systems and Programming Division*
M. A. Aczel, *Divisional Manager, Operational Research Division*

Coding Languages
COBOL, FORTRAN, PLAN, PL/1, Assembler, RPG, NICOL, Easycoder, BASIC, NEAT, MARK IV.

Services Available
Advice, programming, education and training, software packages, documentation, preparation of data, systems analysis.

Fields of Application
Statistical, commercial, production control, accounting, management, systems analysis, operational research.
Specialized areas: Sales analysis, linear programming, analysis, payroll, design and implementation of large systems, real time, etc.

Training
In-house training for systems analysts, programmers and computer appreciation.

P-E CONSULTING GROUP LTD.*
12 Grosvenor Place, London SW1
Telephone: 01-235 5444

Also at: Egham, Birmingham, Bristol, Leeds, Manchester, Newcastle, Glasgow, Belfast.
Overseas: South Africa, Australia, Ireland, Spain, France, Italy, U.S.A., Canada, Denmark, Netherlands, India, Lebanon

Officers
J. G. Donaldson, *Manager, Data Processing Services*
M. F. Grove, *European Operations Manager*
W. H. F. Lovett, *Manager, Training Division*

Coding Languages
COBOL, FORTRAN, PL/1.

Services Available
Consultation, programming, education and training, software packages, systems analysis.

Fields of Application
Commercial, industrial, operational research.
Specialized areas: Production control, simulation, automatic warehousing.

Training
2-week course in computer systems and management.

PEAT, MARWICK, MITCHELL & CO.
Austral House, Basinghall Avenue, London EC2
Telephone: 01-606 8888

Officers
A. W. Howitt, *Senior Partner*
D. W. Moore, *Data Processing Partner*
D. J. Bishop, *Operational Research Partner, Land Use, Traffic and Transportation Partner*
J. C. Percival, *Head of Training*
J. Fielden, *Head of Education*

Services Available
Consultancy, systems architecture and planning, analysis, design and implementation.

Fields of Application
Organization and general management, profit planning and control, data processing, purchasing, production, warehousing and transport, marketing, project evaluation, office management, operations research, personnel and training.

Training
Appreciation courses for management in data processing, organization and methods, engineering and accounting. These courses are each of one week's duration. Systems analysts' course (1 month).

PLYMOUTH COMPUTER SYSTEMS INTERNATIONAL LTD.
20 Soho Square, London W1
Telephone: 01-580 3461

Officers
R. J. McGregor, *Chairman*
E. M. Robertson, *Managing Director*

Computer Installation
BURROUGHS B4000.

Coding Languages
COBOL, PLAN, FORTRAN, RPG.

Services Available
Advice, programming, software packages, documentation, systems analysis, facilities management.

Fields of Application
Commercial, production control, accounting, management, systems analysis.
Specialized areas: Sales analysis, investment, analysis, payroll, management, data base, real time.

P.M.A. CONSULTANTS LTD.
Imperial Buildings, Victoria Road, Horley, Surrey
Telephone: Horley 71361/5

Officer
M. G. R. Flexen, *Marketing Executive*

Contemplated Equipment
Time-sharing terminal or small computer.

Services Available
Consultation, programming, preparation of data, systems analysis.

Fields of Application
Scientific, including surveys and statistical analysis, commercial, including general accounting, banking, etc., industrial, e.g. production control, operational research, integrated business systems.
Specialized areas: Biomedical, real time systems, specialized projects (e.g. extraction and recording of map elevations), factory floor data collection, on-line order entry systems.

Training
Seminars and lectures given as required.

PUNCHED CARD SERVICES LTD.*
49 Wellington Street, London WC2
Telephone: 01-836 5539

Officer
Dr. J. S. Spring

Services Available
Consultation, programming, preparation of data.
Operate on a closed shop basis.

Field of Application
Survey analysis.

REDAC SOFTWARE LTD.*
Newtown, Tewkesbury, Gloucestershire
Telephone: Tewkesbury 2476

Officer
K. Wyatt, *Marketing Director*

Computer Installations
ELLIOTT 4130–operating system: DES 2; internal storage: 1,500K bits; magnetic tapes: 3; magnetic discs: 2; 1 line printer. *Remote processing features*: 4280 interactive graphic terminal.

ICL 1904A–operating system: GEORGE 3; internal storage: 1,500K bits; magnetic tapes: 4; magnetic discs: 3; 1 line printer. *Remote processing features*: remote teletypes attached to G.P.O. networks.

Coding Languages
FORTRAN, ALGOL, Assembler languages.

Services Available
Programming, education and training, software packages for computer-aided design (CAD) in electronics. Operate on a remote access, block time and closed shop basis.

Fields of Application
Specialized areas: Circuit analysis, microelectronics design, printed circuit board design, component databank.

Training
Short course in CAD in electronics.

REED COMPUTER SERVICES*
143 New Bond Street, London W1
Telephone: 01-499 9793

Also at:
18th Floor, The Rotunda, Birmingham 2
Telephone: 021-643 7226

Officers
N. R. C. John (London)
F. A. Swain (Birmingham)

Services Available
Consultation, programming.

Fields of Application
Scientific, statistical, commercial, management, systems analysis, etc.

KURT SALMON & P. E. ASSOCIATES LTD.*
10 Hertford Street, London W1
Telephone: 01-493 9233

Officers
S. D. Hollander, R. S. Clarke, *Joint Managing Directors*

Services Available
Computer consultancy, programming, software packages, systems analysis.

Fields of Application
Management information systems, production control and planning, overall systems analysis, incentives and payroll, forecasting, industrial engineering, advanced analytical methods training, quality control, material utilization, marketing, etc.
Specialized area: Clothing and textiles industries exclusively.

SCAN DATA LTD.*
Abbey House, Farnborough Road, Farnborough, Hampshire
Telephone: 49226

Officer
N. J. Twilley, *Managing Director*

Computer Installations
ICL 1901A–operating system: manual; internal storage: 393,216 bits; magnetic tapes: 6 7-track; 1 line printer.

INTERDATA 4 (2)–operating system: manual; internal storage: 131,072 bits each; magnetic tapes: 2; 1 magnetic drum. *Remote processing features*: on-line data preparation system.

Coding Languages
ICL PLAN, COBOL, simplified IBM 360 Assembler.

Contemplated Equipment
Upgrading computer to 1902A or similar.

Services Available
Consultation, programming, software packages, documentation, preparation of data, systems analysis. Operate on a self-service and block time basis.

Fields of Application
Statistical, commercial, management, production control, accounting, systems analysis.
Specialized area: Share registration.

SOFTWARE SCIENCES LTD.
27 Gloucester Place, London W1
Telephone: 01-486 4692

Officers
Sir Cecil Mead, *Chairman*
C. G. Southgate, *Managing Director*
W. E. Ellis, *Marketing Director*
P. C. Haines, *Director*

Computer Installation
The company is linked by Data 100 to an IBM 360/65; 1 line printer.

Coding Languages
COBOL, FORTRAN, PL/1, 360 Assembler, etc.

Contemplated Equipment
Mini configuration, Arcturus 18D with storage of 16K bits, printer, CR, PTR.

Services Available
Advice, programming, education and training, software packages, systems analysis, transportation consultancy. Operate on a remote access basis.

Fields of Application
Scientific, commercial, production control, management, systems analysis, operational research, airport planning.
Specialized areas: Structural and software engineering.

Training
Courses in GEORGE 3 operating system (ICL 1900 series).

SPL INTERNATIONAL
25 St. James's Street, Nottingham
Telephone: 0602-45011

Officer
James W. Baker, *Education Manager*

Coding Languages
PL/1, COBOL, FORTRAN, Assembler, PLAN.

Services Available
Advice, programming, education and training, systems analysis.

Fields of Application
Scientific, commercial, production control, accounting, systems analysis.
Specialized areas: Sales analysis, investment, payroll, medical research.

Training
Courses in systems analysis, systems design and real time design.

STEVENSON, JORDAN & HARRISON LTD.
Brook House, Park Lane, London, W1Y 4JQ
Telephone: 01-629 4912

Also at: Glasgow, Scotland

Officer
K. G. Kenrick, *Managing Director*

Services Available
Advice, education and training, systems analysis.

Fields of Application
Commercial, production control, accounting, management, systems analysis, operational research.
Specialized areas: Sales analysis, payroll.

SYSTEMS AND SERVICES LTD.*
42 Russell Hill, Purley, Croydon, Surrey, CR2 2JA
Telephone: 01-668 2105/6

Officers
S. Z. Brown, *Marketing Director*
J. A. Kemp, *Director of Consultancy Services*
R. C. Mogg, *Projects Manager*

Services Available
Consultation, analytical and programming contracting services, machine and system conversion and/or upgrading, organization and methods, hardware and software feasibility studies, design and installation of manual systems.

Fields of Application
Commercial, industrial, accounting, banking.

SYSTEMS PROGRAMMING LTD.*
75 Grosvenor Street, London W1
Telephone: 01-493 9301

Also at: Hitchin, Nottingham, Edinburgh

Overseas offices: Stockholm (Sweden); Geneva (Switzerland)

Officer
K. R. Barnes, *Managing Director*

Services Available
Consultation, programming, software packages, systems analysis.

Fields of Application
Feasibility studies, systems design, software and development, management training.

TOUCHE, ROSS AND CO.
27 Chancery Lane, London WC2
Telephone: 01-242 9451

Officers
M. J. Blackburn, *Managing Director*
W. Braithwaite, *Principal, Management Services*

Coding Languages
ASSEMBLER, PL/1, COBOL, FORTRAN, CSL, GPSS, Honeywell, COBOL, Easycoder, PLAN.

Services Available
Advice, programming, education and training, software packages, systems analysis.

Fields of Application
Commercial, production control, accounting, management, systems analysis, operational research.

URWICK DYNAMICS LTD.
9 Monmouth Road, London, W2 4UT
Telephone: 01-229 7246

Officers
P. T. Bridgman, *Managing Director*
J. F. Green, *Director*
C. B. B. Grindley, *Director*

Services Available
Advice, programming, education and training, software packages, systems analysis.

Fields of Application
Scientific, statistical, commercial, production control, accounting, management, systems analysis, operational research.
Specialized areas: Analysis, computer performance appraisal, management information systems, business modelling, computer policy studies.

Training
Courses in Computer Systems Analysis, Management Information Systems, Business Modelling; bespoke courses; one-day seminars for management.

WHITEHEAD CONSULTING GROUP*
21 Wigmore Street, London, W1H 9LA

Officer
Dr. G. Fraser

United Kingdom – Service Bureaux

Services Available
Consultation. Operate on a time-sharing basis.

Fields of Application
Commercial, management, operational research.

1900 MANAGEMENT CONTROLS LTD.*
11-13 Melton Street, London NW1

Officers
J. Rozier, *Managing Director*
B. A. Cooper, *Technical Director*
M. F. Gale, *Marketing Director*

Services Available
Consultation, education and training, feasibility studies, implementation project management, installation review.

Training
DP management training, management appreciation course.

1900 PROGRAMMING LTD.
11-13 Melton Street, London NW1
Telephone: 01-387 8013

Also at:
Peter House, Oxford Street, Manchester 1

Officers
P. Basson, *Technical Director*
W. Pears, *Technical Services Manager*

Computer Installation
ICL 1904–operating system: GEORGE 2; internal storage: 785,472 bits; magnetic tapes: 10; magnetic discs: 4 2802; 2 line printers.

Coding Languages
PLAN, NICOL, COBOL, FORTRAN.

Contemplated Equipment
ICL 1904A under GEORGE 3 with remote ICL 7020 terminals.

Services Available
Consultation, programming, education and training, software packages, documentation, preparation of data, systems analysis. Operate on a remote access and block time basis.

Fields of Application
Production control, accounting, stock control, payroll and similar commercial work.

Training
2-3 week courses in PLAN and 1900 COBOL.

SERVICE BUREAUX

ABACUS COMPUTER SERVICES LTD.*
3 Queen Square, Brighton, Sussex

Officer
F. A. Lane

Coding Languages
COBOL, PL/1.

Services Available
Programming, systems analysis.

Fields of Application
Commercial, insurance.

AJAX DATA PROCESSING LTD.*
21-25 Tabernacle Street, London EC2
Telephone: 01-628 6161

Officer
D. O. Wyatt, *Manager*

Computer Installation
IBM 360/30–internal storage: 64K bits; magnetic tapes: 4; magnetic discs: 2; 1 line printer.

Coding Languages
COBOL, FORTRAN, RPG.

Services Available
Advice, operators, preparation of data, programming, software packages.

Field of Application
General commercial.
Specialized areas: Payroll, insurance, sales accounting.

A.K.S. LTD.*
4 Half Moon Street, London W1
Telephone: 01-499 2184

Contemplated Equipment
IBM System/3.

Service Available
Preparation of data.

APPLIED COMPUTER TECHNIQUES LTD.
Dudley Road, Halesowen, Worcestershire
Telephone: 021-550 7411

Also at: Birmingham, Leicester, Bristol, London

Officers
R. K. Foster, *Managing Director*
B. M. Androlia, *Director, Midlands Division*
A. G. Bryan, *Director, Southern Division*

Computer Installation
Birmingham:
ICL 1903–internal storage: 16K words; magnetic tapes: 6; 1 line printer. *Remote processing features*: remote batch terminal.

Leicester:
ICL 1902A–internal storage: 32K words; magnetic tapes: 4; magnetic discs: 2; 1 line printer. *Remote processing features*: remote batch terminal.

Bristol:
ICL 1902A–internal storage: 16K words; magnetic tapes: 4; 1 line printer. *Remote processing features*: remote batch terminal.

London:
ICL 1901–internal storage: 16K words; magnetic tapes: 4; 1 line printer. *Remote processing features*: remote batch terminal.

Coding Language
PLAN.

Services Available
Software packages, preparation of data. Operate on a self-service basis.

Fields of Application
Commercial, accounting, management.
Specialized areas: Sales analysis, analysis, payroll.

APPLIED SYSTEMS AND PERSONNEL LTD.*
11 Waterloo Place, Pall Mall, London SW1
Telephone: 01-839 6155

Also at:
Calthorpe House, Hagley Road, Edgbaston, Birmingham 15
Telephone: 021-454 7811

Faulkner House, Faulkner Street, Manchester 2
Telephone: 061-236 3828

Officer
J. V. Wheelwright, *Director and General Manager*

Services Available
Staff selection within management services, including organization and methods, operational research, accounting, electronic and industrial engineering, and sales and marketing.

Fields of Application
Job evaluation, client staff evaluation, institution and review of performance standards, aptitude testing, organization analysis and design, training advisory service, salary administration and career structuring, market salary surveys.

ATKINS COMPUTING SERVICES LTD.
Woodcote Grove, Ashley Road, Epsom, Surrey
Telephone: Epsom 24981

Officers
P. M. Worthington, *Chairman*
D. B. Chandler, *Managing Director*
R. B. Wallhouse, *Marketing Manager*

Computer Installations
XDS Sigma 5—operating system: BTM; internal storage: 320K bytes; magnetic tapes: 3 9-track, 1 7-track; magnetic discs; EDS, RADS; 1 line printer. *On-line satellite computers*: ICS Multum PDP-11. *Remote processing features*.

XDS Sigma 7—operating system: BTM; internal storage: 320K bytes; magnetic tapes: 4 9-track; magnetic discs: EDS, RADS; 1 line printer. *On-line satellite computers*: ICS Multum PDP-II. *Remote processing features*: time-sharing, remote job entry.

Coding Languages
FORTRAN IV, ALGOL 60, COBOL, 68, BASIC, Assembler.

Contemplated Equipment
XDS Sigma 9.

Services Available
Advice, programming, education and training, software packages, documentation, preparation of data, systems analysis, facilities management. Operate on a remote access, block time, open shop and time-sharing basis.

Fields of Application
Scientific, statistical, commercial, production control, accounting, management, systems analysis, operational research.
Specialized areas: Sales analysis, linear programming, analysis, payroll, structural engineering, finance modelling.

AUTOMATIC DATA PROCESSING LTD.*
Heathrow House, Bath Road, Cranford, Hounslow, Middlesex
Telephone: 01-759 9191

Also at:
London, Northampton, Bradford, Leeds, Manchester, St Helens, Derby, Birmingham, Bristol.

Officer
A. E. King, *General Manager*

Computer Installation
ICL 1905—internal storage: 32K words; magnetic tapes: 8; 2 line printers.

Service Available
Preparation of data. Operate on a closed shop basis.

Fields of Application
Scientific, statistical, commercial, production control, accounting, management, systems analysis, operational research.

AVERY PUNCHING BUREAU LTD.*
49 Wellington Street, London WC2
Telephone: 01-836 7495

Officer
Miss S. Avery

Service Available
Preparation of data. Operate on a closed shop basis.

BARIC COMPUTING SERVICES LTD.
68 Newman Street, London, W1P 4EH
Telephone: 01-636 5040

Also at:
Hartree House, Queensway, London, W1P 4EH
Telephone: 01-229 3422

Alanbrooke Road, Belfast, BT6 9HE, Northern Ireland
Telephone: 0232-59415/6/7

Bridge House, 121 Smallbrook Ringway, Birmingham, B5 4LA
Telephone: 021-643 9061

36/38 Baldwin Street, Bristol, BS1 1LS
Telephone: 0272-21406

Monument Buildings, Grand Parade, Cork, Republic of Ireland
Telephone: Cork 20435

ICL House, Adelaide Road, Dublin 2, Republic of Ireland
Telephone: Dublin 58904

8 Walker Street, Edinburgh, Scotland
Telephone: 031-226 2716

134 Renfrew Street, Glasgow C3, Scotland
Telephone: 041-332 3603

Kidsgrove, Stoke-on-Trent, Staffordshire, ST7 1TL
Telephone: 0782-29681

Tithe House, Horsforth, Leeds, Yorkshire, LS18 5LL
Telephone: 0973-44678

2nd Floor, Cunard Building, Water Street, Liverpool, L3 1BS

Petersfield House, 29 Peter Street, Manchester, M2 5QJ
Telephone: 061-832 9511

Bridgford House, West Bridgford, Nottingham
Telephone: 0602-82011

St. James House, Vicar Lane, Sheffield, Yorkshire, S1 1LS
Telephone: 0472-27186

Officer
R. Woolf, *Managing Director*

Computer Installation
A wide range of ICL machines including ICL 1903 (2), 1904A, 1904E, 1905 (3), 1905F, 4/50, 4/75, 1500, Atlas, Leo III, KDF8, KDF9 and ELLIOTT 4120.

Coding Languages
FORTRAN, ALGOL, COBOL, Autocode, PLAN, JEAN.

Contemplated Equipment
ICL 1904A.

Services Available
Programming, preparation of data, systems analysis, processing. Operate on a remote access, closed shop and block time basis.

Fields of Application
Scientific, statistical, commercial, production control, accounting, management, systems analysis, operational research.
Specialized areas: Sales analysis, linear programming, investment, analysis, payroll, structural engineering, share registration, stock and production control, sales and purchase accounting.

BEDFORD COMPUTER SERVICE LTD.*
Kingsway House, Kingsway, Bedford
Telephone: Bedford 62538/9

Officer
D. H. Budd, *Managing Director*

Computer Installation
ELLIOTT 803B–internal storage: 4K bits; magnetic film: 4.
ELLIOTT 803B–internal storage: 8K bits; magnetic film: 2.
IBM 360/30E–internal storage: 32K bits; magnetic discs: 3 2311; 1 line printer. *Remote processing features*: teleprinters, Telex data transmission link.
HONEYWELL H120–internal storage: 24K bits; magnetic tapes: 4; 1 line printer.

Coding Languages
COBOL, Autocode, Easycoder, ALGOL, FORTRAN, Language H.

Contemplated Equipment
Data transmission links to major centres.

Services Available
Advice, operators, preparation of data, programming, software packages, systems analysis. Operate on a self-service, closed shop, open shop and block time basis.

Fields of Application
Scientific, statistical, commercial, production control, accounting, management, systems analysis. There are also numerous package programmes available, e.g. payroll, printers' costing, hospital management services, architects' and general accounting.

Specialized areas: Production control, i.e. budgetary control and requirements schedule, raw materials and finished goods control, optimized machine loading and scheduling using heuristic programming techniques. Development of modular programming with indexed parameter definition for general computer use.

Training
Short courses in management, specialized programming, computer appreciation, Autocoder and COBOL.

B.I.E.T. COMPUTER TRAINING*
24/32 Kilburn High Road, London NW6
Telephone: 01-624 1194; 01-734 9395

Officers
J. B. Young, *Director of Studies*
G. M. Vaughan, *Marketing Manager*
M. A. Aston, *EDP Manager*

Computer Installation
HONEYWELL H120–operating system: B.O.S.; internal storage: 8K bits; magnetic tapes: 3; 1 line printer.

Coding Languages
COBOL, Easycoder.

Services Available
Preparation of data, programming, systems analysis. Operate on a self-service, open shop and block time basis.

Fields of Application
Specialized areas: Payroll, sales analysis, market analysis.

Training
Computer programming courses of six weeks' full-time duration covering the basis of flowcharting and programming in COBOL with practical work.

BRITISH WOOL MARKETING BOARD*
Kew Bridge House, Kew Bridge Road, Brentford, Middlesex
Telephone: 01-560 0551

Officers
C. A. Pain, *D. P. Manager*

Computer Installation
HONEYWELL H125–operating system: MOD 1 MSR; internal storage: 32K bits; magnetic tapes: 4 204B; magnetic discs: 2 259.

Coding Languages
Easycoder, COBOL, FORTRAN.

Services Available
Preparation of data, programming, systems analysis, machine hire.

Fields of Application
Accounting, statistical, commercial.

BUSINESS ACCOUNTING SERVICES*
Broadway House, The Broadway, London SW19
Telephone: 01-542 4202

Computer Installations
PHILIPS P352 (2)–internal storage: 1,000 16-position locations each; 1 line printer.

Coding Languages
Philips machine language.

Services Available
Consultation, programming, education and training, software packages, documentation, preparation of data, systems analysis. Operate on a closed shop basis.

Fields of Application
Commercial, accounting, management, systems analysis.
Specialized area: Management information systems.

Fields of Application
Scientific, statistical, commercial, production control, accounting, management, systems analysis, operational research.
Specialized areas: Payroll, sales/purchase accounting, construction industry.

Training
Courses arranged in collaboration with Watford College of Technology.

CAMBRIDGE COMPUTER SERVICES LTD.
Jupiter House, Station Road, Cambridge
Telephone: Cambridge 66111

Officers
P. W. West, *General Manager*
P. R. Rolph, *Sales Director*
D. P. Bilby, *Production Director*

Computer Installations
ICL 1903A—operating system: GEORGE 2 (opt); internal storage: 770K bits; magnetic tapes: 4 1972; magnetic discs: 2; 2 line printers. *Remote processing feature*: MDS transmission link.

Coding Languages
PLAN, COBOL.

Services Available
Advice, programming, education and training, software packages, documentation, preparation of data, systems analysis. Operate on an open shop basis.

Fields of Application
Commercial, production control, accounting, management, systems analysis.
Specialized areas: Sales analysis, analysis, payroll.

CAPITAL COMPUTER APPLICATIONS LTD.*
Audley House, 10 Margaret Street, London, W1N 7LF
Telephone: 01-637 2591

Also at:
Archway Computing Centre, Stanhope House,
2a Fairbridge Road, London N19
Telephone: 01-272 6983

Officers
J. E. Halder, *Director*
G. K. Findlay, *Director (Service Bureau)*
D. B. Wilkinson, *Director (Training)*
V. M. Wyman, *Director (Foreign Relations)*

Services Available
Consultation, programming, education and training, operators, software packages, preparation of data, systems analysis. Operate on a block time basis.

Fields of Application
Commercial, administrative, production control, engineering, computer control and supporting software.

Training
Short courses in systems analysis to clients' requirements.

CAPITAL CITIES COMPUTER CENTRES LTD.
St. Martin's House, 31-35 Clarendon Road, Watford, Hertfordshire
Telephone: 01-834 9181

Officers
B. R. Mustoe, *Managing Director*
H. N. Wilkinson, *Sales Director*

Computer Installation
ICL 1904S—operating system: GEORGE 2; internal storage: 96K 24-bit words; magnetic tapes: 8 9-track, 2 7-track; magnetic discs: 3 EDS60, 2 EDS8; 2 line printers. *Remote processing features*: remote batch terminal.

ICL 1905F—operating system: GEORGE 2; internal storage: 64K 24-bit words; magnetic tapes: 8 9-track, 2 7-track; magnetic discs: 3 EDS30; 2 line printers. *Remote processing features*: remote batch terminal.

Coding Languages
PLAN, COBOL, FORTRAN.

Contemplated Equipment
Front-end processor to 1904S.

Services Available
Advice, programming, education and training, documentation, preparation of data, systems analysis, consultancy. Operate on a remote access, closed shop, block time and open shop basis.

CENTRAL COMPUTER SERVICES (HIGHLANDS) LTD.*
Harbour Road, Inverness, Scotland
Telephone: 0463-36222

Officers
R. Simpson, *Managing Director*
J. Durham, *Technical Director*

Computer Installation
ICL 1902A—internal storage: 16K 24-bit words; magnetic tapes: 4; 1 line printer.

Contemplated Equipment
2 disc stores; data links to major cities; extra 16K words store.

Services Available
Consultation, programming, education and training, operators, software packages, documentation, preparation of data, systems analysis. Operate on a closed shop basis.

Fields of Application
Statistical, commercial, production control, accounting, management, systems analysis.
Specialized areas: Payroll, sales ledger, purchase ledger, incomplete records and mailing labels packages.

Training
Short courses in COBOL and FORTRAN.

United Kingdom – Service Bureaux

CENTRE-FILE LTD.*
16 Park House, Finsbury Circus, London EC2
Telephone: 01-638 6161

Officer
C. Townsend, *Managing Director*

Computer Installations
IBM 360/50–operating system: MFT II; internal storage: 512K bytes; magnetic tapes: 8 2401; magnetic discs: 2 2314, 8 2311; 3 line printers. *Remote processing features*: 1050 terminals.

IBM 360/50–operating system: MFT II; internal storage: 512K bytes; magnetic tapes: 4 2401; magnetic discs: 2 2314, 4 2311; 3 line printers. *Remote processing features*: 3940 terminals.

Coding Languages
PL/1, 360 Assembler.

Contemplated Equipment
Microfilm and OCR equipment.

Services Available
Consultation, programming, software packages, systems analysis.

Fields of Application
Statistical, commercial, production control, accounting, management, systems analysis.
Specialized area: Financial.

CENTRE-FILE (NORTHERN) LTD.
Westinghouse Road, Trafford Park, Manchester, M17 1PY

Officers
T. Smith, *Managing Director*
J. W. Stilling, *Systems and Development Manager*

Computer Installation
ICL 1904E–operating system: GEORGE 3; internal storage: 65,536 bits; magnetic tapes: 4; magnetic discs: 4 EDS; 1 line printer. *Remote processing features*: 7020, etc.

Coding Languages
PLAN, COBOL.

Services Available
Software packages, preparation of data, systems analysis. Operate on a closed shop and block time basis.

Fields of Application
Commercial, accounting, management.
Specialized areas: Sales Analysis, payroll, PERT, bills of quantities, direct debits.

C.I. DATA CENTRE LIMITED
Eelmoor Road, Farnborough, Hampshire
Telephone: Farnborough 513834/5/6

Officer
J. Heyes, *Managing Director*

Computer Installation
PDP-11/40–operating system: DOS/BATCH 11; internal storage: 262,144 bits; magnetic tapes: 1; magnetic discs: 1; 1 line printer.

Coding Languages
FORTRAN IV, PAL 11, MACRO 11, IBM 1130 Assembler, FORTRAN II.

Contemplated Equipment
LPS Interface, second 7-track magnetic tape unit.

Services Available
Advice, programming, software packages, preparation of data, systems analysis, project management, hardware systems, interface design. Operate on a closed shop and block time basis.

Fields of Application
Scientific, statistical, commercial, systems analysis, research and development.
Specialized areas: Analysis of experimental work through the stages of measurement of film or trace recordings or direct digitisation of F/M and digital tapes into computer storage, programming, computing and presentation of results in tabular or graphical form.

COMMERCIAL COMPUTER CONSULTANTS (DIGITAL) LTD.*
Ramsmead, Biddenham, Bedford

Coding Languages
COBOL, Autocode, Easycoder, ALGOL, FORTRAN, Language H.

Services Available
Consultation, preparation of data, programming, software packages, systems analysis.

Fields of Application
Scientific, statistical, commercial, production control, accounting, management, systems analysis.

COMPREHENSIVE COMPUTER SERVICES LTD.*
P.O. Box 2, Bradford Road, Cleckheaton, Yorkshire
Telephone: 4 707/8

Computer Installation
HONEYWELL H1200–magnetic tapes: 6.

Services Available
Advice, operators, preparation of data, programming.

Fields of Application
Commercial, industrial.

COMPRITE LTD.
Boreham Hill, Bishopstrow, Warminster, Wiltshire
Telephone: 09852-2922

Officers
C. R. E. Hillyer, *Managing Director*
A. E. Salt, *Director of Marketing*
G. Muir, *Technical Manager*
E. Sims, *Commercial Manager*

Computer Installation
PDP-8/L–internal storage: 12K bits; magnetic discs: DF32.

DIGICO Micro 16–internal storage: 16K bits; magnetic drum: MD 102/32.

DIGITAL EQUIPMENT 112–internal storage: 12K bits; magnetic discs.

Coding Languages
MACRO 8, MACRO 16, Assembly.

Contemplated Equipment
Micro 16 with 8K bits core and 64K bits drum.

United Kingdom – Service Bureaux

Services Available
Advice, programming, education and training, software packages, systems analysis. Operate on an open shop basis. Available only to customers within the graphic arts industry.

Fields of Application
Commercial, production control, management, systems analysis.
Specialized areas: Computer-aided typesetting.

COMPUTATION RESEARCH AND DEVELOPMENT
12 Dartmouth Street, London SW1
Telephone: 01-930 0665

Officers
D. A. Meyers, *Managing Director*
P. J. O'Donnell, *Applications Consultant*

Computer Installation
CDC 3300–operating system: Master; internal storage: 131,072 24-bit words; magnetic tapes: 6 7-track; magnetic discs: 5; 2 line printers.

Coding Languages
ALGOL, COMPASS, FORTRAN, COBOL.

Services Available
Advice, operators, preparation of data, programming, software packages, systems analysis. Operate on a block time and time-sharing basis.

Fields of Application
Scientific, statistical, commercial.
Specialized areas: Transportation, civil engineering problems, critical path techniques, data mapping and all commercial packages.

Training
Short courses in programming languages, Respond time-sharing system, Master operating system.

COMPUTECH SYSTEMS & PERSONNEL LTD.
168 Finchley Road, London NW3
Telephone: 01-794 0202

Officer
L. G. Payne, *Manager*

Services Available
Consultation, programming, education and training, operators, software packages, systems analysis.

Fields of Application
Scientific, statistical, commercial, production control, accounting, management, systems analysis, operational research.

Training
On-site educational courses for business methods and practice in D.P. systems analysis, and programmer instruction in any computer language.

COMPUTEL LTD.
Eastern Road, Bracknell, Berkshire
Telephone: 0344-23031/6

Registered Office: 111 Westminster Bridge Road, London SE1

Officer
W. B. Cousins, *General Manager*

Computer Installation
ICL 1904A–operating system: GEORGE 3; internal storage: 4,608K bits; magnetic tapes: 16 1972/2; magnetic discs: 16 2802/2; 3 line printers. *Remote processing features*: teletype and remote batch.

Coding Languages
PLAN, COBOL, FORTRAN, ALGOL, FORCON, BASIC, JEAN.

Services Available
Advice, programming, education and training, software packages. Operate on a time-sharing basis.

Fields of Application
Scientific, statistical, commercial, management.
Specialized areas: Structural engineering, network planning.

COMPUTER AID LTD.*
Commercial Avenue, Cheadle Hulme, Cheshire
Telephone: 061-485 7191

Officers
R. Craig-Wood, *Chairman*
I. Craig-Wood, *Managing Director*
D. Graig-Wood, *Marketing Director*
J. Loh, *Production Director*

Computer Installation
ICL 4/50; operating system: 55; internal storage: 128K bits; magnetic tapes: 6 4454; magnetic discs: 2 4425; 1 line printer.

Coding Languages
Usercode, COBOL.

Services Available
Advice, data preparation, data processing, programming, software packages, systems analysis, education, time hire. Operate on a block time basis, with contracted routine processing.

Fields of Application
Commercial, production control, accounting, management.
Specialized area: Production control.

Training
Six-day residential course on computing for directors.

COMPUTER BUREAU SERVICES (CARDIFF) LTD.*
Wroughton Place, Ely, Cardiff, Wales
Telephone: 0222-72382

Officer
P. R. Evans, *Manager*

Computer Installation
BURROUGHS B383–magnetic tapes.

Coding Language
COBOL.

Services Available
Advice, preparation of data, programming.

Fields of Application
Commercial, accounting, industrial.
Specialized area: Stock control.

United Kingdom – Service Bureaux

COMPUTER DYNAMICS
Blue Star House, Highgate Hill, London, N19 5NU
Telephone: 01-263 1387

Officers
L. A. Reed, *General Manager*
P. W. A. Edwards-Rebbitt, *Sales Manager*

Computer Installation
IBM 360/40–operating system: DOS; internal storage: 128K bits; magnetic tapes: 4 3420; magnetic discs: 8 660; 1 line printer.

Coding Languages
COBOL, BAL, RPG, FORTRAN.

Contemplated Equipment
IBM 370/145.

Services Available
Advice, programming, education and training, operators, software packages, documentation, preparation of data, systems analysis. Operate on a self-service, block time and open shop basis.

Fields of Application
Statistical, commercial, production control, accounting, management, systems analysis.
Specialized areas: Sales analysis, analysis, payroll.

Training
Training given to clients' staff.

COMPUTER MANAGEMENT GROUP LTD. (CMG)
Lennig House, Masons Avenue, Croydon, Surrey, CRO 1EH
Telephone: 01-688 2261

Also at:
Sunley House, Bedford Park, Croydon, Surrey, CRO 2AP
Telephone: 01-686 8251

Highland House, 58 Waterloo Street, Glasgow C2, Scotland
Telephone: 041-221 8193/6

Overseas: Amsterdam (Netherlands).

Officers
P. J. Robbins, *Director (Croydon)*
D. W. van Til, *Director (Croydon)*
D. W. Brown, *Director (Scotland)*
M. T. Francis, *Director (Scotland)*

Computer Installation
HONEYWELL H1200 (2)–operating system: MOD 1; internal storage: 32K 6-bit characters; magnetic tapes: 5 each; 1 line printer each. *Remote processing features*: paper tape and card readers.
BURROUGHS B3500–operating system: MCP; internal storage: 100K bytes; magnetic tapes: 6; magnetic discs: 2 line printers. *On-line satellite computers*: TC 500s. *Remote processing features*: TTY adaptors.

Coding Languages
COBOL, FORTRAN, ALGOL, most Assemblers.

Services Available
Advice, programming operators, software packages, documentation, preparation of data, systems analysis. Operate on a self-service, remote access, block time, closed and open shop basis.

Fields of Application
Statistical, commercial, production control, accounting, management, systems analysis.
Specialized area: Financial.

COMPUTER PAYROLLS LTD.*
58 Blakemere Road, Welwyn Garden City, Hertfordshire

Services Available
Advice, operators, preparation of data, programming.

Field of Application
Accounting.

COMPUTER PROJECTS LTD.
14 Old Park Lane, London W1
Telephone: 01-499 7099

Also at:
Temple House, Temple Avenue, London EC4

Officer
D. A. Eyeions, *Managing Director*

Computer Installation
IBM 360/40–operating system: SUPER DOS; internal storage: 128K bytes; magnetic tapes: 5 2430; magnetic discs: 6 2314; 2 line printers.

Contemplated Equipment
IBM 370/145

Services Available
Advice, programming, operators, software packages, documentation, preparation of data, systems analysis. Operate on a self-service, closed shop, block time and open shop basis.

Fields of Application
Statistical, commercial, accounting, management, systems analysis.
Specialized areas: Sales analysis, investment, analysis, payroll.

COMPUTER SERVICES (SOUTH WEST) LTD.
2 Wedgwood Villas, Mutley, Plymouth, Devon, PL4 6RH
Telephone: Plymouth 68814

Officer
F. G. Knight, *Managing Director*

Computer Installation
ICL 1901A–internal storage: 16K bits; magnetic tapes: 4; 1 line printer.

Coding Languages
PLAN, FORTRAN, COBOL.

Contemplated Equipment
ICL 1902A.

Services Available
Advice, preparation of data, programming, systems analysis. Operate on a self-service, closed shop, block time and open shop basis.

Fields of Application
Statistical, commercial, accounting, management.
Specialized areas: Sales analysis, payroll, construction engineering.

United Kingdom – Service Bureaux

COMPUTER SYSTEMS IMPLEMENTATIONS LTD.
3 Park Gardens, Glasgow C3, Scotland

Officers
F. Duckworth, *General Manager*
J. Ellis, *Operations Manager*

Computer Installation
ICL 1902A–internal storage: 16K bits; magnetic tapes: 4; 1 line printer.

Coding Languages
COBULT, PLAN.

Services Available
Advice, programming, software packages, preparation of data, systems analysis. Operate on a self-service basis.

Fields of Application
Commercial, production control, accounting, systems analysis.
Specialized areas: Sales analysis, analysis, payroll, structural engineering, sales and purchase ledgers.

COMPUTERISED BUSINESS SYSTEMS LTD.*
Wroughton Place, Ely, Cardiff, Wales
Telephone: 562382

Officer
I. A. Monro, *Managing Director*

Computer Installation
BURROUGHS B383–internal storage: 19,200 words; magnetic tapes: 4; 1 line printer.

Coding Language
Burroughs Basic Assembler.

Services Available
Advice, programming, software packages, preparation of data, systems analysis. Operate on a block time and closed shop basis.

Fields of Application
Scientific, statistical, commercial, production control, accounting, management, systems analysis, operational research.
Specialized areas: Incomplete records for accountants, professional job costing, licensed premises inventory and stock control, sales/purchase ledger inventory and stock control, payroll.

COMPUTERS IN BUSINESS LTD.*
89 Wigmore Street, London W1
Telephone: 01-935 8908, 01-486 3503

Officer
A. L. Shaw, *Executive Director*

Computer Installation
ICL 1901–magnetic tapes: 6; 1 line printer.

Coding Languages
COBOL, ALGOL, FORTRAN.

Services Available
Advice, operators, preparation of data, programming.

Field of Application
Commercial data processing.

COMTIME (MANCHESTER) LTD.*
Thomas Street, Stretford, Lancashire
Telephone: 061-865 2202

Officer
J. R. Walshe, *General Manager*

Computer Installation
ICL 1902–internal storage: 384K bits; magnetic tapes: 4; magnetic discs: 2 2808; 1 line printer.

Services Available
Programming, preparation of data, systems analysis. Operate on an open shop basis.

Fields of Application
Commercial, stock control, accounting.

CONTRACT COMPUTING LTD.*
Nicholas House, 78-86 Brigstock Road, Thornton Heath, Surrey
Telephone: 01-653 4461

Officers
B. F. M. Adamczewski, G. G. E. Money, J. P. Erskine, N. J. W. Browne, *Directors*

Computer Installation
CDC 3200– magnetic tapes: 8; 1 line printer.

Coding Languages
COBOL, FORTRAN, ALGOL, COMPASS, PERT, SORT, SIMSOL.

Contemplated Equipment
Disc file.

Services Available
General bureau for commercial scientific use, systems advice, programming, operating, full input punching facilities.

Fields of Application
Commercial, simulation surveys.
Specialized area: Market research.

CSS EUROPE LTD.
232-242 Vauxhall Bridge Road, London, SWIV 1AU.
Telephone: 01-828 2906

Officers
Alan P. Brigish, *Managing Director*
R. H. Orenstein, J. T. McCarthy, A. C. Rievman, *Directors*

Computer Installation
IBM 360/67 (6)–operating system: VP/CSS/OS; internal storage: 2 million bytes; magnetic tapes: 20; magnetic discs: over 100; 5 line printers. *On-line satellite computer*: PDP 11. *Remote processing features*: full capability including interactive, remote job entry.

Coding Languages
FORTRAN, COBOL, PL/1, Assembler, BASIC.

Contemplated Equipment
IBM 370/154, IBM 370/168, Honeywell H6180.

Services Available
Advice, programming, education and training, software packages. Operate on a self-service, remote access and time-sharing basis.

Fields of Application
Scientific, statistical, commercial, production control, accounting, management, systems analysis, operational research.
Specialized areas: Sales analysis, linear programming, investment, analysis, structural engineering.

CYBERNETICS INTERNATIONAL (U.K.) LTD.*
Thames Bridge Road, 59½ Southwark Street, London SE1
Telephone: 01-928 9477

Officers
D. A. Thompson, *Managing Director*
M. Tucker, *Marketing Director*

Computer Installation
IBM 360/40–operating systems: DOS III/GRASP, OS MFT II; internal storage: 256K bits; magnetic tapes: 6 2401; magnetic discs: 2314; 2 line printers.

Coding Languages
PRISM Data Management System, COBOL, PL/1, Assembler.

Contemplated Equipment
Remote terminals.

Services Available
Consultation, programming, education and training, operators, software packages, documentation, systems analysis. Operate on a self-service, remote access, block time and open shop basis.

Fields of Application
Financial, commercial.
Specialized areas: Transportation, on-line systems.

D-A COMPUTER SERVICES LTD.
Moorfoot House, 2 Clarence Lane, Sheffield, Yorkshire, S3 7UZ
Telephone: 0742-71201

Officers
R. J. Watt, *Chief Executive*
P. G. Henry, *Technical Director and Contracts Manager*
E. A. Cook, *Sales Manager*

Computer Installation
ICL 1903A–operating system: GEORGE 2; internal storage: 64K bits; magnetic tapes: 4 1972; magnetic discs: 3 EDS30; 1 line printer. *Remote processing features*: 2 7020 on-line link.

Coding Languages
FORTRAN, COBOL, PLAN, EUCLID.

Services Available
Advice, programming, education and training, operators, software packages, documentation, preparation of data, systems analysis. Operate on a remote access, closed shop, block time and open shop basis.

Fields of Application
Scientific, statistical, commercial, production control, accounting, management, systems analysis, operational research, engineering.
Specialized areas: Sales analysis, analysis, payroll, structural engineering, contracting, PERT.

DANACO COMPUTER SERVICES
Woodlands Road, Birmingham, B8 3BD
Telephone: 021-772 8331

Officers
J. A. Mudge, *General Manager*
J. Davis, *Marketing Support Executive*
D. Roberts, *Marketing Planning Executive*
N. Wood, *Head of Operations*

Computer Installation
HONEYWELL H600/6000–operating system: GCOS III; internal storage: 128K 36-bit words; magnetic tapes: 6 9-track; magnetic discs: 3 fixed drive, 6 replaceable; 1 line printer. *On-line satellite computers*: 2 Honeywell H105/115. *Remote processing features*: run as satellite CR, CP, LP.

Coding Languages
BASIC, FORTRAN, ALGOL, COBOL, GMAP, SIMSCRIPT, JOVIAL, GPSS III.

Services Available
Programming, education and training, software packages, documentation, systems analysis. Operate on a remote access and time-sharing basis.

Fields of Application
Scientific, statistical, commercial, production control, accounting, management, systems analysis, operational research.
Specialized areas: Sales analysis, linear programming, investment, analysis, payroll, structural engineering.

Training
Various courses (information available on application).

DATA DYNAMICS SERVICES LTD.
11 Bancroft, Hitchin, Hertfordshire
Telephone: 0462-52761

Officer
D. Hofford, *General Manager*

Coding Languages
COBOL, ALGOL, FORTRAN, PL/1, Assembly languages.

Service Available
Preparation of data.

DATA SCIENCES INTERNATIONAL LTD.*
DSI House, Sheepscar Street South, Leeds, Yorkshire, LS7 1AW
Telephone: 41541/4

Also at:
Bradford, Leeds, Manchester, Norwich, Teesside.

Officer
D. G. H. Geddes, *Marketing Director*

Computer Installations
ICL 1902A (3)–internal storage: 32K bits each; magnetic tapes: 4-8 each; magnetic discs: 2-4 each; line printers.

BURROUGHS–internal storage: 19,200 bits; magnetic tapes: 4; 1 line printer.

Coding Language
Assembler, PLAN, NICOL, ALGOL, FORTRAN, COBOL.

Services Available
Consultation, programming, education and training, operators, software packages, documentation, preparation of data, systems analysis, computer processing. Operate on a self-service, block time and closed shop basis with remote access facilities and time-sharing terminals on premises if required.

Fields of Application
Payroll, sales purchase and nominal accounting, parts inventory control for motor trade, estate management, order processing, etc.

Training
Short courses for customer personnel; seminar for management on computer techniques and applications.

DATA SCIENCES INTERNATIONAL LTD.*
Norwich Computer Centre, Norvic House, 29-33 Chapelfield Road, Norwich, Norfolk, NOR 67E

Also at:
Leeds and Manchester

Officer
K. Davies, *Manager*

Computer Installation
ICL 1902A—internal storage: 16,364 x 24 bits; magnetic tapes: 6; 1 line printer.

Coding Languages
PLAN, FORTRAN, COBOL, ALGOL.

Services Available
Consultation, programming, software packages, documentation, preparation of data, systems analysis. Operate on a closed and open shop basis.

Fields of Application
Statistical, commercial, accounting, management information, stock control, production control, payroll, sales, sales/purchase/nominal ledger, estate management.

DATA SERVICE CENTRE LTD.*
Clive House, India Street, Glasgow C2, Scotland
Telephone: 041-221 1357

Officers
R. J. Hamilton, *Director*
J. Robertson, *Operations Manager*

Computer Installation
IBM 360/20—internal storage: 16K bits; magnetic discs: 2.

Coding Languages
RPG, Basic Assembler.

Services Available
Systems analysis, programming, preparation of data and processing.

Fields of Application
Commercial, statistical, production control, accounting, engineering, payroll.

DATAPRON SERVICES LTD.
114 High Street, Erdington, Birmingham, B23 6RS
Telephone: 021-373 8293

Officers
B. L. Pagett, *Managing Director*
O. Findlay, *Director*

Service Available
Preparation of data.

DATASKIL LTD.
Reading Bridge House, Reading Bridge Approach, Reading, Berkshire, RG1 8PN
Telephone: Reading 581253

Officers
P. D. R. Simpson, *Chairman*
A. R. Roustell, *Managing Director*
M. Tucker, *Marketing Manager*

Services Available
Advice, programming, operators, software packages, documentation, systems analysis, facilities management. Available to users or prospective users of ICL computers.

Fields of Application
Scientific, statistical, commercial, production control, accounting, management, systems analysis, operational research.
Specialized areas: Sales analysis, linear programming, investment, analysis, payroll, structural engineering, medical research.

DATASOLVE INTERNATIONAL LTD.
88 Old Street, London EC1
Telephone: 01-251 1121

Also at:
Cavridy House, Ladymead, Guildford, Surrey
Telephone: Guildford 64691

Officers
W. S. C. Richards, *Chairman*
M. J. Brooke, *Managing Director*
G. R. Pinkus, *Sales and Marketing Director*
G. Horton, *Production Director*

Computer Installation
ICL 1904A—operating system: GEORGE 2; internal storage: 64K words; magnetic tapes: 8 7-track; magnetic discs: 4 EDS8; 1 line printer. *Remote processing feature*: ICL 7010.

ICL 1902S—operating system: GEORGE 2; internal storage: 48K words; magnetic tapes: 4 7-track; magnetic discs: 2 EDS8; 1 line printer. *Remote processing feature*: ICL 7010.

IBM 360/40—operating system: DOS; internal storage: 128K bits; magnetic tapes: 6 9-track; magnetic discs: 8 2314; 2 line printers. *Remote processing feature*: Olivetti DE 523 terminal.

IBM 360/30—operating system: DOS; internal storage: 64K bits; magnetic tapes: 3 9-track, 1 7-track; magnetic discs: 3 2314; 1 line printer. *Remote processing feature*: Olivetti DE 523 terminal.

ICL 4/50—operating system: DOS; internal storage: 128K bits; magnetic tapes: 6; magnetic discs: 3 EDS8; 2 line printers. *Remote processing feature*: Olivetti DE 523 terminal.

Coding Languages
PLAN, COBOL, Assembler, FORTRAN, Usercode.

Contemplated Equipment
ICL 1903T, IBM 370/145, EDS60.

Services Available
Advice, programming, operators, software packages, documentation, preparation of data, systems analysis. Operate on a remote access, closed shop, block time and time-sharing basis.

Fields of Application
Statistical, commercial, production control, accounting, management, systems analysis.
Specialized areas: Sales analysis, medical research.

D. J. COMPUTER SERVICES LTD.*
47 Hatton Garden, London EC1
Telephone: 01-242 0687

Officer
D. H. Brown, *Managing Director*

Computer Installation
IBM 360/25–operating system: DOS; internal storage: 48K bits; magnetic tapes: 4 2415; magnetic discs: 3 2311; 1 line printer.

Coding Languages
COBOL, RPG, PL/1, Basic Assembler.

Contemplated Equipment
IBM 360/40 or equivalent with real time applications.

Services Available
Software packages, consultancy, systems analysis, programming, contract programming, made to measure schemes, data preparation, computer time brokerage, education. Operate on a self-service, closed and open shop, remote access and block time basis.

Fields of Application
Commercial, production control, accounting, systems analysis.
Specialized areas: Payroll, sales analysis, purchase ledger.

Training
Training of IBM punch operators and programmers.

DUNFORD HADFIELDS LTD.*
East Hecla Works, Sheffield, Yorkshire, S9 1TZ
Telephone: 41001

Also at:
Claywheels Lane, Sheffield 6
Chippingham Street, Sheffield 9

Officers
C. H. Day, *Management Services Controller*

Computer Installation
HONEYWELL H200–operating system: MOD 1 MSR; internal storage: 49,151 characters; magnetic tapes: 3 204B; magnetic discs: 2 259; 1 line printer.

Coding Languages
COBOL, Easycoder, FORTRAN.

Contemplated Equipment
Keytape data preparation equipment; on-line visual display units.

Services Available
Consultation, programming, documentation, preparation of data, systems analysis. Operate on a block time basis.

Fields of Application
Scientific, statistical, commercial, production control, accounting, management, systems analysis, operational research, etc.

DYCHURCH BUSINESS SERVICES*
12 Gold Street, District Bank Chambers, Northampton
Telephone: 33394

Officers
L. Hunt, *Managing Director*

Computer Installations
UNIVAC 9300–operating system: BASIC; internal storage: 32K bytes; magnetic tapes: 6; 1 line printer.
UNIVAC 9300–operating system: BASIC; internal storage: 16K bytes; magnetic tapes: 8; 1 line printer.

Coding Languages
RPG, COBOL, BAL.

Contemplated Equipment
Univac 9400.

Services Available
Consultation, preparation of data, systems analysis. Operate on a closed shop basis.

Fields of Application
Statistical, commercial, accounting.

EAST MIDLANDS COMPUTER SERVICES*
34-50 Rutland Street, Leicester
Telephone: Leicester 57222

Officers
D. J. Castledine, M. N. Cockayne, D. J. Cowtan, J. R. Fisher.

Coding Languages
PLAN, COBOL.

Services Available
Advice, programming, systems analysis.

Fields of Application
Commercial, production control, accounting, management systems.

EASTERN COMPUTER SERVICES LTD.
Wool Hall Computer Centre, Wykeham, Spalding, Lincolnshire
Telephone: Spalding 4706/7

Officer
P. E. Wainwright

Computer Installation
IBM 360/25–operating system: D/S; internal storage: 48K bits; magnetic discs: 4 2314; 1 line printer.

Coding Languages
PL/1, Basic Assembler, COBOL, FORTRAN.

Contemplated Equipment
IBM 370/125, IBM 370/135, 2 line printers.

Services Available
Advice, programming, software packages, documentation, preparation of data, systems analysis. Operate on a block time and open shop basis.

Fields of Application
Commercial, accounting, management, systems analysis, operational research.
Specialized areas: Sales analysis, payroll.

EDGWARE COMPUTER BUREAU*
18-24 High Street, Edgware, Middlesex
Telephone: 01-952 7397

Officer
G. Kramer, *Managing Director*

Computer Installation
NCR 315—internal storage: 240K bits; magnetic tapes: 1 334/132, 3 334/131; 1 line printer.

Coding Languages
NEAT.

Services Available
Advice, programming, preparation of data, systems analysis. Operate on a block time and open shop basis.

Fields of Application
Commercial, accounting, management.
Specialized areas: Hire purchase accounting, stock control, plant hire profitability analyses, mailing lists and subscription accounting.

EDINBURGH REGIONAL COMPUTING CENTRE
James Clerk Maxwell Building, Kings Buildings, Mayfield Road, Edinburgh, EH9 3JZ, Scotland
Telephone: 031-667 1081

Officer
Dr. G. E. Thomas, *Director*

Computer Installation
ICL 4-75—operating system: EMAS; internal storage: 1 million bytes; magnetic tapes: 4 9-track, 1 7-track; magnetic discs: 6 4425, CDC 700; 2 line printers. *On-line satellite computer*: PDP-11. *Remote processing features*: interactive, about 100 teletypes.

IBM 370/155—operating system: OS 370 (MVT/HASP); internal storage: 512K bytes; magnetic tapes: 3 3420; magnetic discs: 8 3330; 1 line printer. *On-line satellite computers*: CTL Modular 1, IBM 1130, PDP-8, PDP-11. *Remote processing features*: Batch.

Coding Languages
FORTRAN, IMP.

Services Available
Advice, programming, education and training, operators, software packages, documentation, preparation of data, systems analysis. Operate on a remote access, closed shop and time-sharing basis. Available to commercial users only via a university department.

Fields of Application
Scientific, statistical, management, systems analysis, operational research.
Specialized areas: Linear programming, structural engineering, medical research.

Training
Programme language training and packages.

E. J. V. DATA SERVICES LTD.*
92-94 Tooley Street, London SE1
Telephone: 01-407 4174

Computer Installation
IBM 360/20—magnetic discs: 2 2311.

Services Available
Programming, preparation of data, systems analysis.

Field of Application
Accounting.

ELECTRONIC ASSOCIATES LTD.*
United Kingdom Computation Centre
Victoria Road, Burgess Hill, Sussex
Telephone: Burgess Hill 5101

Officer
J. B. Swainston, *Group Manager, Analogue/Hybrid Division*

Computer Installation
EAI 640 (2)—internal storage: 16K bits; magnetic tape: paper tape, card reader; 1 line printer.
EAI 680 (2).
EAI 48.
EAI 580.

Coding Languages
FORTRAN, DOI.

Services Available
Operators, programming, software packages, systems analysis. Operate on an open shop basis.

Fields of Application
Aircraft, missile, automobile, railway, steel, chemical water transmission, nuclear, medical, hydraulic, servo and process industries, economic, structural and gas pipeline simulation and computation.
Specialized area: Hybrid simulation.

Training
Courses in analogue simulation and computation; parallel hybrid programming; 640 and 693 programming and operation; hybrid simulation and computation; maintenance courses on all EAI equipment.

ELECTRONIC DATA PROCESSING LTD.*
88 Solly Street, Sheffield 1, Yorkshire
Telephone: Sheffield 28094

Officers
J. Neill, *Managing Director*
F. M. Slinn, *Director and General Manager*

Computer Installation
BURROUGHS B383—internal storage: 9,600 bits; magnetic tapes: 2; magnetic discs: 1; 1 line printer.

BURROUGHS B3500—internal storage: 60K bits; magnetic tapes: 4; magnetic disc: 1; 1 line printer.

Coding Languages
Basic Assembler, COBOL, FORTRAN.

Services Available
Advice, operators, preparation of data, programming, software packages, systems analysis. Operate on a closed shop basis.

Field of Application
Commercial.
Specialized areas: Invoicing, sales ledger, payroll.

Training
Courses in the analysis and programming of commercial computer systems (3 days).

EXTEL COMMUNICATIONS LTD.
Lowndes House, 1-9 City Road, London EC1

Officers
M. W. Warburg, *Managing Director*
J. S. Rouse, *Sales Executive*

Computer Installation
IBM 370/135—operating system: DOS/GRASP; internal storage: 196,068 8-bit words; magnetic tapes: 3 3420; magnetic discs: 8 2319; 1 line printer. *Remote processing feature*: 3270 visual display unit.

Coding Languages
BAL, PL/1, COBOL, FORTRAN IV.

Contemplated Equipment
4 IBM 3330 disc units.

Services Available
Investment accounting service, FOCUS (Financially Oriented Computer Updating Service). Operate on a self-service basis. Specialized services available to the financial community and for mailing and typesetting.

Field of Application
Financial.
Specialized area: Investment.

F2 LTD.
The Old Schoolhouse, Chestnut Lane, Amersham, Buckinghamshire, HP6 6DZ
Telephone: Amersham 4651

Officers
Mrs. V. S. Shirley, *Managing Director*
A. H. Lines, *Director*
Mrs. D. A. Shermer, *Marketing Executive*

Services Available
Advice, documentation and systems analysis.

Fields of Application
Scientific, statistical, commercial, production control, accounting, systems analysis, operational research and small business systems.
Specialized areas: Systems consultancy and bilingual documentation.

FARRINGTON DATA PROCESSING LTD.*
New Lane, Havant, Hampshire
Telephone: Havant 6444

Officer
D. G. Wright

Service Available
Preparation of data.

FENI DATA SERVICES LTD.*
17 Hinton Road, Bournemouth, Hampshire
Telephone: Bournemouth 28455

Also at:
Computer Centre, Hollybrook Road, Southampton, Hampshire.
Telephone: Southampton 74799

Officer
R. J. Hoare, *Managing Director*

Computer Installation
UNIVAC 1050—operating system: OPR; internal storage: 96K bits; magnetic tapes: 4 Uniservo VIC; 1 line printer.

UNIVAC 9400—operating system: TOS/DOS/5; internal storage: 384K bits; magnetic tapes: 5; 1 line printer.

Coding Languages
Assembler, COBOL, FORTRAN IV.

Contemplated Equipment
Discs for Univac 9400.

Services Available
Advice, preparation of data, programming consultancy, systems analysis. Operate on a self-service and closed shop basis.

Field of Application
Commercial.

FINANCIAL ACCOUNTING SERVICE BUREAU (DATA PROCESSING) LTD.*
P.O. Box 31, Bective Road, Alverthorpe, Wakefield, Yorkshire
Telephone: 75031

Officer
M. J. Biglin, *Director*

Computer Installation
HONEYWELL—operating system: MOD I; internal storage: 256K bits; magnetic tapes: 3; magnetic discs: 3; 1 line printer.

FLETCHER COMPUTER SERVICES LIMITED
2113-2117 Coventry Road, Sheldon, Birmingham 26
Telephone: 021-743 8721

Officers
M. A. Reeves, *Managing Director*

Computer Installation
BURROUGHS B500—operating system: MCP; internal storage: 19,200 bits; magnetic tapes: 5; magnetic discs: 2; 1 line printer. *Remote processing feature*: Data Com. TC500.

BURROUGHS B500—operating system: MCP; internal storage: 19,200 bits; magnetic tapes: 4; magnetic discs: 2; 1 line printer. *Remote processing feature*: Data Com. TC500.

Coding Languages
COBOL, Assembler.

Services Available
Advice, programming, software packages, preparation of data, systems analysis. Operate on a closed shop basis.

Fields of Application
Commercial, production control, accounting, management, systems analysis.
Specialized areas: Sales analysis, payroll.

FORGE BUSINESS SERVICES LTD.*
11 Pleasant Place, Hersham, Walton-on-Thames, Surrey
Telephone: Walton-on-Thames 29880

Service Available
Preparation of data.

United Kingdom – Service Bureaux

Fields of Application
General.
Specialized area: Market research.

FREELANCE PROGRAMMERS LIMITED
16 Station Road, Chesham, Buckinghamshire
Telephone: Chesham 4999

Officers
F. C. Knight, *Chairman*
Mrs. Steve Shirley, *Managing Director*
W. Griffiths, *Director*
Mrs. S. M. T. Harold, *Marketing Executive*

Services Available
Advice, programming, documentation.

Fields of Application
Scientific, statistical, commercial, production control, accounting, management, operational research.
Specialized areas: Fixed price programming services to schedule, bilingual documentation.

GEC-ELLIOTT SPACE AND WEAPON SYSTEMS LTD.*
Space and Guided Weapons Division
Frimley Road, Camberley, Surrey
Telephone: Camberley 63311

Officers
A. J. Nelson, P. Jones

Computer Installation
ELLIOTT 503 (2)–internal storage: 24K bits each; magnetic tapes: 4 Elliott TM4; 3 line printers. *On-line satellite computer*: Elliott 920M.

Coding Languages
ALGOL, SLANG, SAP. Autocode.

Services Available
Advice, programming, operators, systems analysis. Operate on an open shop basis.

Fields of Application
Scientific, statistical, production control, accounting, management, systems analysis, operational research.
Specialized areas: Simulation, digital modelling.

GENERAL ELECTRIC CO. LTD.*
Computer Unit
Erith, Kent
Telephone: Erith 36933

Officers
J. S. Gatehouse, *Director*
G. C. Hatcher, *Applications*
B. M. Scott, *Programming and Systems Analysis*

Computer Installation
ICL Mercury.
HONEYWELL H800–internal storage: 16K bits; magnetic tapes: 8; 1 line printer. *Remote processing features*: 4 terminals for data communication over public networks.
EAI 231 R.

Coding Languages
Autocode, FORTRAN IV, COBOL.

Services Available
Available to outside customers for scientific and engineering problems on an open shop basis. Assistance can be given at any level.

Fields of Application
Scientific, statistical, commercial, operational research, technical.
Specialized areas: Mechanical engineering design, critical path studies.

GMS COMPUTER SERVICES
Atlas House, Savile Street, Sheffield, Yorkshire, S4 7US
Telephone: 0742-24292

Officers
G. E. Clayton, *Manager*
R. Little, *Production Manager*
G. Aizlewood, *Development Manager*

Computer Installation
ICL 1902A–operating system: GEORGE 2; internal storage: 32K words; magnetic tapes: 6; magnetic discs: 2; 1 line printer. *Remote processing features*: off-line terminal.

Coding Languages
PLAN, COBOL, FORTRAN.

Services Available
Programming, software packages, preparation of data and systems analysis. Operate on a closed shop and block time basis.

Fields of Application
Statistical, commercial, production control, accounting, management, systems analysis.
Specialized areas: Sales analysis, analysis, payroll.

HAMWORTHY ENGINEERING LTD.
Powell Duffryn Computer Services
Fleets Corner, Poole, Dorset
Telephone: Poole 5123, extension 294

Officer
R. W. Batchelor, *D. P. Manager*

Computer Installation
HONEYWELL H200–operating system: MOD 1 MSR; internal storage: 32K bits; magnetic tapes: 4 204; magnetic discs: 2 273; 1 line printer.

Coding Languages
Easycoder, COBOL.

Contemplated Equipment
DC 72 remote batch terminal (PDP-8/E) linked to PDP-10.

Services Available
Advice, programming, preparation of data, systems analysis. Operate on a block time and time-sharing basis.

Fields of Application
Commercial, production control, accounting, management.

HERMES COMPUTING SERVICES LTD.*
8-9 Giltspur Street, London EC1
Telephone: 01-248 2814

Also at:
71 Great Portland Street, London W1
Telephone: 01-636 7131

187-189 St. Alban's Road, Watford, Hertfordshire
Telephone: Watford 43630

United Kingdom – Service Bureaux

Officers
D. Pasea, *Director*
Mrs. M. Smith, *Branch Manager* (Watford)
Mrs. J. Beaton, *Branch Manager* (W1)

Computer Installation
ICL 1902–internal storage: 16K bits; magnetic tapes: 4; 1 line printer.

Coding Languages
PLAN, COBOL.

Services Available
Programming, preparation of data, systems analysis, computer time hire, service bureau processing. Operate on a block time basis.

Fields of Application
Commercial, accounting, management.
Specialized areas: Sales analysis, general accounting services.

HONEYWELL INFORMATION SYSTEMS LTD.
Honeywell House, Great West Road, Brentford, Middlesex
Telephone: 01-568 9191

Officers
L. R. Price, *Chairman*
D. E. Clark, *Director, Data Processing Group*
R. Gilchrist, *Director, Computer Operations*
D. F. Brosnan, *Vice-President and Managing Director*

Computer Installation
HONEYWELL H3200 and H1200.
BULL GENERAL ELECTRIC GE635.
BULL GENERAL ELECTRIC GE265 (7) and HONEYWELL H1648–available for time-sharing.

Coding Languages
Various languages available.

Services Available
Advice, operators, preparation of data, programming, software packages, systems analysis.

Fields of Application
Advice, operators, preparation of data, programming, software packages, systems analysis.

Fields of Application
All fields of industry, commerce, government, science and services.

Training
A full range of computer training courses and executive courses provided by the Honeywell Education Group.

HOSKYNS SYSTEMS LTD.
143 Tennant Street, Birmingham 15

Officers
M. S. Owen, *Midland Area Manager*
D. Burgoyne, *Systems Centre Manager*
A. Manson, *Area Sales Manager*

Computer Installation
ICL 1902; internal storage: 32K words; magnetic tapes: 6; magnetic discs: 3 2802/3; 1 line printer.

Coding Languages
PLAN, COBOL, TABN.

Services Available
Advice, programming, education and training, software packages, documentation, preparation of data and systems analysis.

Fields of Application
Commercial, production control, accounting.

Training
Courses provided by Hoskyns Education Division, 91 Farringdon Road, London EC1.

HUDDERSFIELD AND SPEN VALLEY INCORPORATED CHAMBER OF COMMERCE*
Commerce House, 112 Fitzwilliam Street, Huddersfield, Yorkshire
Telephone: 26591/2

Officers
B. Whitley, J. S. Marsden

Services Available
Programming, documentation, preparation of data, systems analysis. Operate on a block time basis. Service available to members of Chamber of Commerce.

Fields of Application
Management accounting, wages, production control.

IBM UNITED KINGDOM LTD.*
IBM Data Services Centre
389 Chiswick High Road, London W4
Telephone: 01-995 1441

Also at:
London Data Centre
58 Newman Street, London W1
Telephone: 01-636 7788

CALL/360 Branch
40 Basinghall Street, London EC2
Telephone: 01-628 7700

1 Katherine Street, Croydon, Surrey, CR9 1LQ
Telephone: 01-688 7799

Rosanne House, Bridge Road, Welwyn Garden City, Hertfordshire
Telephone: Welwyn Garden 22801

Birmingham Data Centre
62 Hagley Road, Birmingham 15
Telephone: 021-455 9737

5 Queens Avenue, Bristol 8
Telephone: Bristol 23241

Crossford Court, Dane Road, Sale, Cheshire
Telephone: 061-962 2231

55 Blythswood Street, Glasgow C2, Scotland
Telephone: 041-221 4681

3 Leazes Park Road, Newcastle upon Tyne
Telephone: Newcastle 611200

46 Maid Marion Way, Nottingham, NG1 6GJ

Officers
J. S. McCracken, *Manager, Data Centre Services*
O. Williams, *Manager, DCS London District*
T. B. Crammond, *Manager DCS Southern District*
B. Chilver, *Manager, DCS Northern District*

O. Williams, *Manager, London Data Centre*
W. Carslake, *Manager, CALL/360 Branch*
G. A. Pearce, *Manager, Welwyn Garden City Branch*
E. Sutcliffe, *Manager, Croydon Branch*
E. S. Deane, *Manager, Birmingham Service Bureau*
F. C. Ham, *Manager, Newcastle Branch*
M. Thompson, *Manager, Manchester (Sale) Branch*
I. B. Gillies, *Manager, Glasgow Branch*
T. Pinnell, *Manager, Bristol Branch*
C. Chambers, *Manager, Nottingham Branch*

Computer Installation
London Data Centre:
IBM 360/65–operating system: ASP; magnetic tapes: magnetic discs: 2 2301.

IBM 360/50–operating system: ASP; magnetic tapes; magnetic discs: 2 2301.

IBM 360/30.

IBM 360/40.

CALL/360:
IBM 360/50–internal storage: 233.4 million bytes; magnetic tapes: 2 2401/1; 1 line printer.

Birmingham:
IBM 360/40–internal storage: 128K bits; magnetic tapes: 4 2402; magnetic discs: 5 2311; 2 line printers.

IBM 360/30–internal storage: 64K bits; magnetic tapes: 2 2402; magnetic discs: 6 2311; 1 line printer.

Bristol:
IBM 360/30–internal storage: 64K bits; magnetic discs: 3 2311.

IBM 1401–internal storage: 16K bits; magnetic tapes: 4 7330; magnetic discs: 2 1311; 1 line printer.

Croydon:
IBM 360/40–internal storage: 128K bits; magnetic tapes: 5; magnetic discs: 5 2311; 1 line printer.

Glasgow:
IBM 360/30–operating system: DOS; internal storage: 64K bits; magnetic tapes: 4 7-track, 3 9-track; magnetic discs: 3 2311.

IBM 360/20–internal storage: 16K bits.

Manchester (Sale):
IBM 360/30–internal storage: 64K bits; magnetic tapes; magnetic discs: 4 2311; 1 line printer.

IBM 360/30–internal storage: 64K bits; magnetic discs: 4 2311, 1 2314; 1 line printer.

Newcastle:
IBM 360/30–internal storage: 64K bits.

Nottingham:
IBM 1401–internal storage: 16K bits; magnetic tapes: 6 729/6; magnetic discs: 2 1311; 1 line printer.

Welwyn Garden City:
IBM 360/40–internal storage: 128K bits; magnetic tapes: 2; magnetic discs: 3 2311; 2 line printers.

Coding Languages
COBOL, FORTRAN, RPG, PL/1, Basic Assembler, BAL.

Services Available
Computer time, complete custom service, terminal services, preplanned applications. Systems usage with customer or IBM operators, total custom service, remote job entry, CALL/360 conversational time sharing service.

Fields of Application
Mathematical programming system, survey analysis, sales forecasting, statistics, depot siting, project management system, civil engineering, traffic planning system, storm sewer design, co-ordinate geometry, bar cutting, pipe stress, shop scheduling system, stock control and costing, single depot stock control, spares stock control packages for motor manufacturers, motor dealer accounting, insurance broker accounting, portfolio valuation, share registration, branch accounting, retail information system, sales accounting.

Training
Numerous training facilities.

ILFORD LTD.*
Computer Services
23 Roden Street, Ilford, Essex
Telephone: 01-478 3000

Computer Installation
HONEYWELL H200 (2)–magnetic tapes.

Coding Languages
COBOL, FORTRAN, Easycoder.

Services Available
Advice, operators, preparation of data, programming (limited).

Fields of Application
Statistical, accounting.
Specialized area: Payroll.

IMPERIAL CHEMICAL INDUSTRIES LTD.*
Central Management Services
Sunley Building, Piccadilly Plaza, Manchester 1
Telephone: 061-236 8555

Officers
Dr. J. A. Payne, *Business Manager*
M. A. Browitt, *Service Manager*

Computer Installation
IBM 360/65–operating system: MFT2/HASP2; internal storage: 4,096K bits; magnetic tapes: 8 2401; magnetic discs: 2 2314; 2 line printers. *On-line satellite computers*: IBM 1130, 2 XL6, 5 IBM 2780 terminals.

Coding Languages
PL/1, FORTRAN, K Code, COBOL, Assembler.

Services Available
Consultation, programming, operators, software packages, preparation of data, systems analysis. Operate on a remote access and block time basis.

Fields of Application
Commercial, production control, operational research, technical applications.

United Kingdom – Service Bureaux

INDEPENDENT COMPUTER SERVICES LTD.
Queen's Road, Belfast, BT3 9DT, Northern Ireland
Telephone: Belfast 56435/8

Officers
T. Winter, *Managing Director*
N. J. Millar, *Executive Director*

Computer Installation
ICL 1902A – internal storage: 32K words; magnetic tapes: 4; magnetic discs: 2 EDS30; 2 line printers. *Remote processing features*: 7020 data-link to ICL 1904E.

Coding Languages
PLAN, COBOL, FORTRAN.

Services Available
Advice, operators, preparation of data, programming, software packages, systems analysis. Operate on a closed shop and block time basis.

Fields of Application
Scientific, statistical, commercial, production control, accounting, management, systems analysis.
Specialized areas: Construction industry, shipbuilding, PERT.

INDUSTRIAL & COMMERCIAL DATA PROCESSING LTD.*
Blackburn House, London Road, Whitley, Coventry, Warwickshire, CV3 4AN
Telephone: 0203-27226

Computer Installation
HONEYWELL H200 – internal storage: 32K bits; magnetic tapes: 5; 1 line printer.

Coding Languages
Easycoder, COBOL, FORTRAN.

Services Available
Advice, data processing, contract systems, preparation of data, programming packages.

Fields of Application
Commercial, accounting, production control.
Specialized areas: Direct mailing, payroll ledgers, parts list, bills of quantity, costing, production scheduling.

INTEGRANT COMPUTER BUREAU*
Cobham Park, Cobham, Surrey
Telephone: Cobham 2862

Officers
R. Sherman, *Manager*
R. D. Greenwood, *Training*

Computer Installation
ICL 1901A – internal storage: 16K bits; magnetic tapes: 4 Calcomp.

Coding Languages
FORTRAN, ALGOL.

Services Available
Advice, operators, preparation of data, programming, software packages, systems analysis. Operate on a self-service, open shop and block time basis.

Fields of Application
Scientific, technical
Specialized areas: Civil/structural engineering, original programmes and research.

INTERFILE COMPUTER SERVICES LTD.
Data House, Cadbury Road, Sunbury-on-Thames, Middlesex
Telephone: Sunbury-on-Thames 85611

Officers
N. J. T. Munro, *Chairman*
D. L. Greetham, *Managing Director*

Computer Installation
NCR Century 100 (2) – operating system: batch processing B1; internal storage: 262,144 bits; magnetic tapes: 2 9-track; magnetic discs: 4 NCR 655; 1 line printer.

Coding Languages
COBOL, NEAT 3, FORTRAN, BASIC.

Contemplated Equipment
NCR Century 200.

Services Available
Advice, programming, education and training, operators, software packages, documentation, preparation of data, systems analysis, facilities management. Operate on a self-service, block time and open shop basis.

Fields of Application
Statistical, commercial, production control, accounting, management, systems analysis.
Specialized areas: Sales analysis, linear programming, investment, analysis, payroll, mailing systems.

INTERNATIONAL COMPUTERS LTD.

(*See* under **Baric Computing Services Ltd.**)

INTERNATIONAL DATA HIGHWAYS LTD.*
83 Clerkenwell Road, London EC1
Telephone: 01-242 0747

Officers
W. C. Dunlop, *Chief Executive*
L. Jordan, *Customer Services*

Computer Installation
UNIVAC 418/II (2) – operating system: EXEC; internal storage: 64K bits each; magnetic tapes: 11; magnetic discs: 2 Fostrand II; 2 line printers. *On-line satellite computer*: Elliott Arch 102. *Remote processing features*: potential for 250 remote terminals.

Coding Languages
Assembler, Basic FORTRAN, COBOL.

Services Available
Advice, operators, preparation of data, programming, software packages, systems analysis, real time bureau services, time-sharing services, matching systems, stock-market computer answering networks, stock management service. Operate on a closed shop, remote access and time-sharing basis.

Fields of Application
On-line information dissemination for commercial, statistical, scientific and management purposes, on-line stockbroker service.

ISIS COMPUTER SERVICES LTD.
Forum House, 15/18 Lime Street, London EC3
Telephone: 01-405 1331

United Kingdom – Service Bureaux

Officers
L. Jacoby, *Manager Director*
D. D. O. Jones, *General Manager*
G. Herring, *Manager, Facilities Management Division*
W. E. Matthews, *Manager, Customer Services Division*

Computer Installation
ICL 1903–operating system: Automatic Operator; internal storage: 64K words; magnetic tapes: 6; 1 line printer.

Coding Languages
ALGOL, COBOL, FORTRAN, PLAN, BAL, PL/1, RPG.

Contemplated Equipment
Discs for ICL 1903.

Services Available
Advice, programming, education and training, software packages, documentation, preparation of data, systems analysis. Operate on a closed shop and block time basis.

Fields of Application
Statistical, commercial, accounting, management, mailing.
Specialized areas: Analysis, insurance, publishing, transportation.

ITT DATA SERVICES
153-155 East Barnet Road, East Barnet, Hertfordshire
Telephone: 01-440 5161

Officers
N. Bark, *General Manager*
D. Stern, *Director, Marketing and Sales*
M. Collis, *Production Director*

Computer Installation
IBM 360/65–internal storage: 512K bits.
IBM 360/50
IBM 370/145
Remote processing features: 1130 remote terminal, 5 DATA 100 terminals, RJE, CRJE, ATS.

Coding Languages
All 360 languages.

Contemplated Equipment
IBM 360/65, IBM 370/158

Services Available
Advice, operators, preparation of data, programming, software packages, systems analysis. Operate on a closed shop, open shop, remote access, block time and time-sharing basis.

Fields of Application
Scientific, statistical, commercial, production control, accounting, management, systems analysis, operational research.
Specialized areas: Sales analysis, linear programming, investment analysis, payroll, structural engineering, media scheduling.

K & H BUSINESS CONSULTANTS LTD.
53 Victoria Street, London SW1
Telephone: 01-799 5351

Officers
J. Harvey, D. A. Barrett, S. Phelan, *in charge of Programming, Training and Home Sales*

Coding Languages
FORTRAN, IBM 360 Assembler.

Services Available
Programming, software packages.

Fields of Application
Project control (PERT, CPM); stock control (staple and fashion merchandise).

Training
Short courses in project control and stock control.

KALAMAZOO COMPUTER CENTRE
Kalamazoo Ltd., Northfield, Birmingham, B31 2RW
Telephone: 021-475 7411

Officer
P. J. Rex, *General Manager*

Computer Installations
ELLIOTT 4120 (2)–internal storage: 16K 24-bit words; magnetic tapes: 9; 2 line printers.

NCR Century 200–operating system: BI; internal storage: 64K bytes; magnetic tapes: 8; magnetic discs: 2 dual disc units; 2 line printers.

BURROUGHS B3500–internal storage: 120K bytes; magnetic tapes: 6; 2 line printers.

Coding Languages
COBOL, 4100 NEAT, NEAT 3.

Services Available
Programming, education and training, software packages, preparation of data. Operate on a closed and open shop basis.

Fields of Application
Management, accounting.
Specialized area: Motor trade applications.

Training
Short courses related to packages on offer for directors, accountants and staff.

KASAD COMPUTER SERVICES LTD.*
123/124 The Stow, Harlow, Essex
Telephone: 33231/2, 25339

Also at:
Sigma-Kasad Ltd., 78 Church Street, Dunstable, Bedfordshire
Telephone: Dunstable 66233

Kasad Equipment Ltd., 21 Mill Road, Royston, Hertfordshire
Telephone: Royston 42084

Officer
K. A. C. Smith, *Managing Director*

Computer Installation
ICL 1902–operating system: GEORGE 2; internal storage: 32K words; magnetic tapes: 6 1972.

Coding Languages
PLAN, COBOL, Autocoder, Usercode, Easycoder.

Services Available
Consultation, programming, software packages, documentation, preparation of data, systems analysis. Operate on a self-service and block time basis.

Fields of Application
Statistical, commercial, production control, accounting, management, systems analysis, banking, stock control.

KELLOGG INTERNATIONAL CORPORATION*
62/72 Chiltern Street, London W1
Telephone: 01-486 4444

Officer
A. V. Dyke

Computer Installations
IBM 360/30 (2)–operating system: DOS; internal storage: 64K bits each; magnetic tapes: 4 each; magnetic discs: 3 2311 each; 2 line printers.

Coding Languages
COBOL, RPG, FORTRAN IV.

Services Available
Consultation, operators, preparation of data. Operate on a block time basis.

Fields of Application
Commercial, accounting, production control, scientific.

Training
Several IBM courses.

KENT DATA SERVICES LTD.
134 Biscot Road, Luton, Bedfordshire, LU3 1AL
Telephone: Luton 32483

Officers
J. E. Swadling, *Managing Director*
B. H. Ashworth, *Sales Manager*

Computer Installations
IBM 360/40–operating system: DOS/GRASP; internal storage: 128K bits; magnetic tapes: 4 2401; magnetic discs: 8 2311; 1 line printer.

Coding Languages
COBOL, FORTRAN, Assembler.

Contemplated Equipment
IBM 370/135.

Services Available
Programming, software packages, preparation of data, systems analysis. Operate on a self-service and block time basis.

Fields of Application
Systems analysis, commercial, production control, accounting, management.
Specialized areas: Sales analysis, payroll, N/C machine tool tape preparation.

LEASCO RESPONSE LTD.
197 Knightsbridge, London, SW7 1RT
Telephone: 01-589 4577

Officers
K. D. Boardman, *Managing Director*
J. C. Hampshire, *Sales Manager*
A. J. Sanders, *Operations Manager*

Computer Installations
HEWLETT PACKARD 2116 (4)–operating system: Leasco Response I; internal storage: 500K bits; magnetic tapes; magnetic discs: 4 CDC 9433; 1 line printer. *Remote processing features*: 24-line time-sharing.

Coding Language
BASIC.

Contemplated Equipment
Further systems as above.

Services Available
Programming, education and training, software packages, advice, documentation, systems analysis. Operate on a self-service, remote access and time-sharing basis.

Fields of Application
Scientific, statistical, commercial, production control, accounting, management.
Specialized areas: Sales analysis, linear programming, analysis, payroll, business control, business planning.

Training
Programming courses by arrangement; user training for business applications provided during installation.

LONDON UNIVERSITY COMPUTING SERVICES LTD.
39 Gordon Square, London, WC1H 0PD
Telephone: 01-387 4344

Officers
F. Gordon, *Managing Director*
J. Cox, *Company Secretary*

Computer Installation
CDC 6500–operating system: SCOPE; internal storage: 131K 60-bit words; magnetic tapes: 6 7-track 659/4, 1 9-track 659/1; magnetic discs: 3 841; 2 line printers.

Coding Languages
ALGOL, FTN, FORTRAN, BASIC, COBOL, COMPASS, BCPL, SNOBOL-4, POP-2.

Services Available
Advice, programming, education and training, operators, software packages, documentation, preparation of data, systems analysis. Operate on a self-service, remote access, block time, open shop and time-sharing basis.

Fields of Application
Scientific, statistical, commercial, production control, accounting, management, systems analysis, operational research.
Specialized areas: Sales analysis, linear programming, analysis, payroll, structural engineering.

Training
Courses in management, introduction to computers, introduction to systems analysis, programming and special interest courses.

LOWNDES-AJAX COMPUTER SERVICE LTD.
Philip House, Lansdowne Road, Croydon, Surrey, CR9 2XG
Telephone: 01-686 3661

Officers
P. N. W. Merrick, *Managing Director*
Dr. M. D. Bigg, *General Manager*
J. E. Spalding, *Director of Systems and Programming*

Computer Installation
IBM 370/145–operating system: OS/VS1; internal storage: 512K bits; magnetic tapes: 6 3420; magnetic discs: 6 2314, 5 Telex 5314; 3 line printers. *On-line satellite computer*: IBM System/3. *Remote processing features*: IBM 2780, Olivetti DE523.

Coding Languages
COBOL, PL/1, RPG, Assembler.

Services Available
Advice, programming, software packages, documentation, preparation of data, systems analysis, computer output microfilm. Operate on a self-service, remote access and block time basis.

Fields of Application
Commercial, production control, accounting, management, systems analysis.
Specialized areas: Sales analysis, analysis, payroll, management accounting, project control.

M. & G. COMPUTER SERVICES LTD.
91/99 New London Road, Chelmsford, Essex
Telephone: 0245-51651

Officers
R. Morrison, *Director and Secretary*
B. Beavis, *E. D. P. Manager*

Computer Installation
ELLIOTT 4120–operating system: EXEC; internal storage: 393,216 bits; magnetic tapes: 5; 1 line printer.

Coding Languages
NEAT, Language H.

Services Available
Preparation of data, programming, systems analysis. Operate on a self-service and closed shop basis.

Fields of Application
Commercial, accounting.

MAGNET COMPUTER BUREAU LTD.
P.O. Box 214, Electric Avenue, Witton, Birmingham, B6 7JW
Telephone: 021-327 1216

Officer
O. S. Lumb, *General Manager and Director*
B. T. Smith, *Commercial Manager*
S. J. Taylor, *Technical Manager*

Computer Installation
HONEYWELL H800–operating system: EXEC; internal storage: 768K bits; magnetic tapes: 8. *On-line satellite computer*: Honeywell H200.

HONEYWELL H200–operating system: MOD 1TR; internal storage: 96K bits; magnetic tapes: 4; 2 line printers.

HONEYWELL H1648–operating system: STD OS; internal storage: 1,088K bits; magnetic tapes: 2; magnetic discs: 6. *Remote processing features*: 48 simultaneous teletypes.

ELLIOTT 503–operating system: RAP; internal storage: 936K bits; magnetic tapes: 4; 1 line printer.

HONEYWELL H1250–operating system: MOD 1MSR; internal storage: 584K bits; magnetic tapes: 6; magnetic discs: 3 859; 1 line printer.

Coding Languages
COBOL, FORTRAN, ARGUS, Easycoder, SAP, BASIC, DAP.

Contemplated Equipment
ICL 4/72.

Services Available
Programming, preparation of data, systems analysis, total bureau service. Operate on a closed shop and time-sharing basis.

Fields of Application
Scientific, commercial, production control, accounting, management, systems analysis.
Specialized areas: Sales analysis, payroll, power systems analysis.

MANAGEMENT COMPUTING SERVICES LTD.*
The Adelphi, 1 John Adam Street, London WC2
Telephone: 01-930 5833

Also at:
Warner House, 48 Upper Thames Street, London EC4

Computer Installation
HONEYWELL H400–magnetic tapes.
HONEYWELL H1250–magnetic tapes and discs.
HONEYWELL H3200–magnetic tapes and discs.

Coding Languages
COBOL, FORTRAN, Easycoder.

Services Available
Advice, preparation of data, programming.

Fields of Application
Commercial, accounting.

MANAGEMENT DYNAMICS LTD.*
213 Oxford Street, London, W1R 1AH
Telephone: 01-437 9481

Also at:
Heathrow House, Bath Road, Cranford, Hounslow, Middlesex, TW5 9QP
Telephone: 01-759 9191

Officer
D. Boyt, *General Manager*

Computer Installations
London:
ICL 1905–operating system: GEORGE 2; internal storage: 32K words; magnetic tapes: 8; magnetic discs: 4; 2 line printers.

Hounslow:
ICL 1905–internal storage: 32K words; magnetic tapes: 8; 2 line printers.

Coding Languages
PLAN, COBOL, FORTRAN, ALGOL, CSL.

Services Available
Consultation, programming, software packages, documentation, preparation of data, systems analysis. Operate on a block time and closed shop basis.

Fields of Application
Scientific, statistical, commercial, accounting, management, systems analysis, production control, operational research.
Specialized areas: Payroll, nominal and budgetary control ledger, sales ledger, SCRIBE service for subscription accounting, share registration, MAILFLOW for direct mailing.

Training
Installation services, PLUM (Program Library and Update Maintenance).

MANAGEMENT DYNAMICS SOFTWARE SERVICES
Heathrow House, Bath Road, Cranford, Hounslow, Middlesex, TW5 9QP
Telephone: 01-759 9191

Also at:
7A Grafton Street, London, W1X 3OA

Officer
P. L. Rothwell, *Director of Software Services*

Coding Languages
PLAN, COBOL, NICOL, FORTRAN, ALGOL, PL/1, RPG, Assembler.

Services Available
Advice, preparation of data, programming, software packages, analysis. Operate on an off-site, fixed price or time hire basis.

Fields of Application
Statistical, commercial, production control, accounting, management, systems analysis.

Training
Customer designed training programme (available on request).

MANAGEMENT SYSTEMS AND PROGRAMMING LTD.
71 Gloucester Place, London, W1H 3PF
Telephone: 01-486 3947

Also at:
The Crescent, King Street, Leicester
Telephone: 0533-56935

Officer
D. Gomes da Costa, *Manager*

Coding Languages
COBOL, FORTRAN, ALGOL, PL/1, BAL, PLAN, FAS, NEAT, Easycoder, Autocoder.

Services Available
Software development, installation management, applications programming, proprietary software, complete project implementation.

Fields of Application
Commercial and industrial systems development and programming; software development, including compilers and real time systems.
Specialized areas: Module testing system, project management and control system, COBOL programme Analyser.

Training
Course in the use of MTS and MPTC modular programming techniques.

MANCHESTER COMPUTER CENTRE LTD.*
P.O. Box 474, 21 Spring Gardens, Manchester, M60 2BX
Telephone: 061-834 0116

Officers
J. C. Masters, *Director and General Manager*
S. Snowball, *Technical Manager*
J. A. Thomas, *Operations Manager*
J. H. Marshall, *Sales Manager*

Computer Installation
ICL 1903—operating system: EXEC; internal storage: 32K words; magnetic tapes: 8; 1 line printer.

Coding Languages
COBOL, PLAN.

Contemplated Equipment
ICL 1902A with storage of 32K words, 8 tape units, 1 line printer.

Services Available
Consultation, preparation of data, programming, software packages, systems analysis. Operate on a closed shop and block time basis.

Fields of Application
Commercial, statistical, production control, accounting.
Specialized areas: Motor trade, payroll, sales purchase and nominal accounting, estate management.

Training
Two-day management appreciation courses.

MEDWAY DATA SERVICES LTD.*
Medway House, Star Mill Lane, Chatham, Kent
Telephone: 01-458 5011

Officer
C. J. Messer, *Manager*

Computer Installation
ICL 1902.

HONEYWELL H200.

Coding Languages
COBOL, FORTRAN, ALGOL.

Services Available
Consultation, operators, preparation of data, programming.

Fields of Application
Scientific, commercial, management, industrial.

METALOGIC LTD.
1 Redcliff Street (2nd floor), Bristol, BS99 7JS

Officer
Dr. A. M. Bigwood, *Managing Director*

Computer Installation
ICL 4-30

Coding Language
COBOL.

Contemplated Equipment
Univac 9380.

Services Available
Advice, programming, software packages, documentation, preparation of data, systems analysis. Operate on a block time basis.

Fields of Application
Statistical, commercial, accounting, management, systems analysis, operational research.
Specialized areas: Sales analysis, linear programming, analysis, payroll.

MIDAS LTD.*
Midas House, 368 Old Street, London EC1
Telephone: 01-739 5481

United Kingdom – Service Bureaux

Computer Installation
ICL 1903.
BURROUGHS B383.

Coding Languages
PLAN, FORTRAN, COBOL, Assembler.

Services Available
Advice, preparation of data, programming, software packages.

Fields of Application
Commercial, stock control, accounting.
Specialized area: Feasibility studies.

MIDLAND DATA PROCESSING SERVICES LTD.
39 York Road, Northampton
Telephone: Northampton 32508/9

Also at:
214 St. Nicholas Circle, Leicester
Telephone: Leicester 57785

Officers
S. Wise, *Managing Director*
H. C. Jones, *Sales Director*

Computer Installation
UNIVAC 9200–internal storage: 8K bits.

Services Available
Advice, preparation of data, programming, software packages, systems analysis.

Fields of Application
Accounting, commercial, management, systems analysis, production control.
Specialized areas: Analysis, payroll.

MIDLANDS COMPUTING CENTRE LTD.
Lichfield House, 85 Smallbrook, Ringway, Birmingham, B5 4JF
Telephone: 021-643 4743

Officers
J. H. Marshall, *Managing Director*
A. J. Gough, *Sales Manager*

Computer Installation
HONEYWELL H200–operating system: MOD I; internal storage: 120K bits; magnetic tapes: 5; 1 line printer.

Coding Languages
Easycoder, COBOL, FORTRAN, PM3.

Contemplated Equipment
Honeywell H1250 with discs and tapes.

Services Available
Advice, operators, preparation of data, programming, software packages, systems analysis. Operate on a self-service, closed shop and block time basis.

Fields of Application
Commercial, production control, accounting, management, systems analysis.
Specialized areas: Single company and multi-company processing systems for payroll, sales ledger/statements, purchase ledger.

MILLS ASSOCIATES LTD.
Wonastow Road, Monmouth, NP5 4YE
Telephone: 2131

Also at:
Alexandra House, 307/315 Cowbridge Road East, Cardiff, CF5 1JD, Wales
Telephone: 397345

13/15 Pembroke Road, Clifton, Bristol, BS8 3BA
Telephone: 37631

7 Clinton Terrace, Derby Road, Nottingham, NG7 1NA
Telephone: 46219

Cobham Park, Cobham, Surrey
Telephone: 5265

Sedgley Buildings, Market Street, Droylsden, Manchester, M35 6DL
Telephone: Droylsden 9207

Officers
R. G. Mills, *Managing Director*
P. Wilson, *Manager, Monmouth*
M. W. Thomas, *Manager, Cardiff*
R. R. Lawrence, *Manager, Bristol*
T. W. Mansworth, *Manager, Nottingham*
P. Burnett, *Manager, Cobham*
J. Harrison, *Manager, Droylsden*

Computer Installation
ICL 1901 (2 in Monmouth, 1 at each bureau)–internal storage: 16K bits; magnetic tapes: 4; 1 line printer.

ELLIOTT 803 (1 each in Cardiff and Nottingham)–internal storage: 8K bits; magnetic tapes: 3; 1 line printer.

Coding Languages
COBOL, ALGOL, PLAN, FORTRAN.

Contemplated Equipment
ICL 1901 to be installed in projected bureau in Edinburgh.

Services Available
Advice, programming, education and training, preparation of data, systems analysis. Operate on a self-service and open shop basis.

Fields of Application
Statistical, commercial, production control, accounting, management, operational research.
Specialized areas: Analysis, payroll.

Training
Internal programming courses (COBOL) and engineering courses (for ICL equipment).

MP DATA PREP.*
York House, Empire Way, Wembley, Middlesex
Telephone: 01-903 4901

Officer
R. G. Evans

Services Available
Preparation of data. Restricted to users of 6-, 7-, and 8-channel paper tape.

Fields of Application
Banking, insurance, building societies, government departments, most other commercial and industrial organizations.

United Kingdom – Service Bureaux

NATIONAL CASH REGISTER LTD.
London Data Processing Centre
St. Alphage House (West Wing),
St. Alphage Garden, Fore Street, London EC2
Telephone: 01-638 6200

Also at:
NCR Scottish Data Processing Centre
227/237 West George Street, Glasgow, Scotland
Telephone: 041-221 3603

NCR Birmingham Data Processing Centre
236-239 Broad Street, Birmingham
Telephone: 021-643 8091

Officers
H. E. W. Bristow, *Manager, U.K. Data Processing Centres*
T. Chellew, *Manager, London Centre*
G. S. Brown, *Manager, Glasgow Centre*
R. W. H. Longhurst, *Manager, Birmingham Centre*

Computer Installations
London:
NCR 315 (2)–operating system: NOF; internal storage: 40K characters each; magnetic tapes: 5 each; magnetic discs: 4 CRAM each; 1 line printer each. *Remote processing features*: off-line transmission.

Glasgow:
NCR Century 200–operating system: paper tape punched cards; internal storage: 32,000K bits; magnetic tapes: 5; magnetic disc: 1; 1 line printer. *Remote processing features*: off-line transmission.

Birmingham:
NCR 315 (details as for London).

Coding Languages
NEAT, BEST.

Contemplated Equipment
Third NCR 315 in London.

Services Available
Advice, limited data preparation, programming, systems analysis, package applications. Operate on open shop, block time and self-service basis.

Fields of Application
Commercial, industrial, financial.
Specialized areas: All forms of analysis, invoicing, stock control, statistical etc.

NATIONAL COMPUTING CENTRE LTD.
Quay House, Quay Street, Manchester, M3 3HU
Telephone: 061-832 9731

Officers
Dr. A. A. Robinson, *Director*
J. Lloyd, *Controller*

Computer Installation
ICL 1905F–operating system: GEORGE 3; internal storage: 1,500K bits; magnetic tapes: 6 7-track NRZ1; magnetic discs: 3; 1 line printer. *Remote processing features*: 10 ASR 33.

Coding Languages
FORTRAN, COBOL, ALGOL, PLAN, JEAN, Basic.

Services Available
Advice, programming, education and training, operators, software packages, documentation, preparation of data. Operate on a remote access, block time, open shop and time-sharing basis.

Fields of Application
Scientific, commercial, accounting.
Specialized areas: Payroll, information science.

Training
Courses related to data processing for professionals, managers and users, also for education in schools, colleges and universities.

NATIONAL DATA PROCESSING SERVICE
Tenter House, 45 Moorfields, London, EC2Y 9TH
Telephone: 01-432 9258

Also at:
26-28 Glasshouse Yard, London, EC1A 4JY
National Giro Centre, Bootle, Lancashire, GIR OAA
Filton Road, Bristol, BS7 OBH
Maes-y-Coed Road, Cardiff, CF4 4UY, Wales
Curzon Road, Derby, DE2 7BX
Post Office Research Station, Brook Road, London, NW2 7DT
57 Craiglockhart Avenue, Edinburgh, EH14 1AQ, Scotland
2-12 Gresham Street, London, EC2V 7AG
Colnbrook by-pass, Harmondsworth, West Drayton, Middlesex
Charles House, Kensington High Street, London, W14 8QX
Computer House, Dewsbury Road, Leeds, Yorkshire, LS11 5UQ
Central Telephone Exchange, King Henry I Street, Portsmouth, Hampshire, PO1 2BZ
25 Grosvenor Road, St. Albans, Hertfordshire

Officers
F. J. M. Laver, *Post Office Board Member*
N. O. Johnson, *Director of Project and Technical Development*
P. J. Smith, *Director of National Data Processing Service*

Computer Installation
ICL 4-70 (8)–operating systems: J1600, Multijob, Monitor; internal storage: 2,048K, 2,048K, 2,048K, 2,048K, 4,028,416, 2,048K, 2,877,440 and 3,542,928 bits; magnetic tapes: 5, 4, 4, 2, 2, 2, 2 and 4 control units, 13, 19, 19, 11, 12, 10, 10 and 12 9-track decks, 2, 3, 3, none, none, none, none and 1 7-track decks; magnetic discs: 2, 1, 1, 4, 2, 1, 1 and 4 replaceable disc store units, 8, 5, 5, 12, 8, none, none and 4 replaceable disc stores; 3, 4, 5, 2, 2, 1, 2 and 4 line printers.

ICL 4-72 (2)–operating systems: Monitor, J1600; internal storage: 3,452,928 bits each; equipment shared with eighth 4/70 listed above.

ICL Leo 326 (10)–operating system: Master; internal storage: 287,744 bits (9) and 143,872 bits; magnetic tapes: 17, 13, 12, 16, 15, 13, 15, 15, 15 and 7; 2, 1, 2, 2, 2, 2, 1, 2, 2 and 1 line printers.

RCA Spectra 70/45 (2)–operating systems: J1600, BASIC; internal storage: 2,048K bits each; magnetic tapes: 2 control units each, 10 (and 8) decks; magnetic discs: 2 (and 4) replaceable disc store control units, 8 (and 12) replaceable disc stores; 1 (and 2) line printers.

ELLIOTT 503 (2)–operating systems: Reserved Area Program; internal storage: 71,936 bits each; magnetic tapes: 2 control units each, 6 (and 4) decks; 1 line printer each.

ELLIOTT 803B–operating system: Reserved Area Program; internal storage: 71,936 bits.

BURROUGHS B5500 (2)–operating system: Master; internal storage: 287,744 bits each; magnetic tapes: 4 each; magnetic discs: 2 control units each, 10 file modules each; 1 line printer each. *On-line satellite computers*: 2 Interdata 5 (to one B5500 only).

Coding Languages
COBOL, Usercode, Inter-code, FORTRAN, CLEO.

Services Available
Programming, education and training, software packages, preparation of data, systems analysis, computer output to microfilm. Operate on a self-service, remote access and open shop basis.

Fields of Application
Scientific, commercial, accounting, management, systems analysis, technical.
Specialized areas: Sales analysis, payroll, stock control.

NATIONAL WESTMINSTER BANK LTD.*
Computer Centre
33 Piccadilly, Manchester, M1 1LR

Also at:
Warrington, Lancashire

Officer
S. G. Martlew, *Data Processing Manager (Manchester)*

Computer Installation
Manchester:
BURROUGHS B3500–internal storage: 180K bytes; magnetic tapes: 1 7-track, 8 9-track; magnetic discs: 3; 3 line printers.

Warrington:
BURROUGHS B300 (2)–internal storage: 19,200 bits; magnetic tapes: 5 7-track; magnetic discs: 2; 1 line printer.

Coding Language
Advanced Assembler.

Fields of Application
Commercial, accounting.

OLDACRES COMPUTERS LTD.*
48 Hatton Garden, London EC1

Officers
D. A. Smart

Computer Installation
ELLIOTT 803B–internal storage: 8K 39-bit words; 5 803 magnetic film units.

Coding Languages
ALGOL, Basic Machine Code, Autocode.

Services Available
Consultation, programming, education and training, operators, documentation, preparation of data, systems analysis. Operate on a self-service, block time and open shop basis.

Fields of Application
Building industry (mainly for architects, quantity surveyors and contractors offering complete service for production of bills of quantities, preliminaries and preambles, repair and alteration specifications, valuations, elemental and operational cost re-analysis, engineering specifications, Ministry of Housing cost yardstick calculations).

PRACTICAL COMPUTER SYSTEMS*
Garratt Mills, Trewint Street, Earlsfield, London SW18
Telephone: 01-946 8822

Officers
J. T. Gould, *General Manager*
R. D. Read, *European Operations Manager*
K. Rodgers, *International Contracts Manager*

Coding Languages
COBOL, PLAN, FORTRAN, ALGOL, EMA.

Contemplated Equipment
ICL 1900-series computer.

Services Available
Consultation, programming, education and training, software packages, documentation, systems analysis.

Fields of Application
Commercial, accounting, management, systems analysis.
Specialized areas: Local government, real time systems.

Training
Courses held as required.

RANDAX EDP LTD.
10-14 Macklin Street, London WC2
Telephone: 01-246 6291

Officers
C. G. Webb, *D. P. Manager*
P. M. Lambert, *Sales Manager*
B. Riman, *General Manager*

Computer Installations
BURROUGHS B3500–operating system: MCP; internal storage: 120K bytes; magnetic tapes: 6 9-track; magnetic discs: 1 fixed; 2 line printers.

Coding Language
COBOL.

Contemplated Equipment
Burroughs B3500.

Services Available
Advice, operators, programming, education and training, software packages, documentation, preparation of data, systems analysis. Operate on a batch processing basis.

Fields of Application
Statistical, commercial, production control, accounting, management, systems analysis.
Specialized areas: Sales analysis, analysis, payroll, purchase accounting, stock recording, costing.

REDAL SOFTWARE LTD.*
Newtown, Tewkesbury, Gloucestershire
Telephone: Tewkesbury 2476

Officers
E. Wolfendale, *Managing Director*
K. Wyatt, *Marketing Director*

Computer Installation
ELLIOTT 4130–internal storage: 583K bits; magnetic tapes: 3; magnetic disc: 2 interactive graphics.

ICL 1904A–internal storage: 5 million bits; magnetic tapes: 4; magnetic discs: 3;

Coding Languages
ALGOL, FORTRAN, NEAT.

Services Available
Advice, operators, preparation of data, programming, software packages. Operate on a closed shop and time-sharing basis. Design service is available for outside users.

Fields of Application
Research into electronic equipment design by computer.

Training
Training courses on computer-aided design of electronic circuits available on a very limited basis.

SCIENTIFIC CONTROL SYSTEMS LTD. (SCICON)
49/57 Berners Street, London, W1P 4AQ
Telephone: 01-580 5599

Also at:
Milton Court, Ropemaker Street, London, EC2Y 9BH
Telephone: 01-920 8313

Albany House, Hurst Street, Birmingham
Telephone: 021-622 2575

Fisons House, Princes Street, Ipswich, Suffolk
Telephone: Ipswich 53112, 52867

67 Maid Marion Way, Nottingham
Telephone: 0602-40883

4 Burners Way, Kiln Farm, Stony Stratford, Buckinghamshire
Telephone: 09082-71121

Northcliffe House, Colston Avenue, Bristol, BS1 4XB
Telephone: 0272-299842

Queen's House, Queen Street, Manchester 2
Telephone: 061-832 2232

Officers
J. Brennan, *Chairman*
B. Elson, *Managing Director*

Computer Installation
UNIVAC 1108 (2)—operating system: EXEC 8; internal storage: 7,056K and 4,716K bits; magnetic tapes: 16 Uniservo VIC; magnetic discs: 4 FH 1782 and 7 FH 432 drums; 5 line printers. *On-line satellite computers*: PDP-11 front end, DCT 132, DCT 2000. *Remote processing features*: IBM 360/22.

Coding Languages
FORTRAN, CFOR, ALGOL, COBOL, BASIC, PL/1, Assembler, etc.

Contemplated Equipment
A third Univac 1108, IBM 370/145.

Services Available
Advice, programming, education and training, operators, software packages, documentation, systems analysis. Operate on a self-service, remote access, closed shop, block time and time-sharing basis.

Fields of Applications
Scientific, statistical, commercial, production control, accounting, management, systems analysis, operational research.
Specialized areas: Sales and investment analysis, linear programming, payroll, structural engineering, medical research.

Training
Courses in basic systems analysis (6 weeks); advanced systems analysis (28 days); operational research (5 weeks); management appreciation of computers (3 days); management in a computer department (3 days); network techniques (5 days) and forecasting techniques (2 days).

SCOTTISH COMPUTER SERVICES LIMITED
1395 South Street, Glasgow, G14 OXJ, Scotland
Telephone: 041-954 5944

Officer
J. Allan, *General Manager*

Computer Installation
ICL 1903—operating systems: EXEC, GEORGE, UDAS; internal storage: 32K words; magnetic tapes: 4; magnetic discs: 3 EDS8; 2 line printers.

HONEYWELL H200; internal storage: 24K characters; magnetic tapes: 4; 1 line printer.

Coding Languages
PLAN, Easycoder, COBOL, FORTRAN,

Contemplated Equipment
Large computer with random access and terminal facilities.

Services Available
Advice, programming, software packages, preparation of data, systems analysis. Operate on a self-service, closed shop and block time basis.

Fields of Application
Scientific, statistical, commercial, production control, accounting, management, systems analysis.
Specialized areas: Sales analysis, investment, analysis, payroll, share registration.

J. SHORT DATA CENTRE*
92—94 Newman Street, London W1

Also at:
15 St. George's Walk, Croydon, Surrey
15 Broad Street, London EC2

Officers
V. F. Reader, J. D. Reader, *Partners*

Computer Installation
ICL 1902A—internal storage: 32K bits; magnetic tapes: 8 1971; magnetic discs: 2; 2 line printers. *Remote processing features*: visual display units.

Coding Languages
PLAN, COBOL, FORTRAN.

Contemplated Equipment
UDUS, disc, ICL 1904A.

Services Available
Consultation, programming, education and training, operators, software packages, documentation, preparation of data, systems analysis. Operate on a self-service, remote access, block time, open and closed shop and time-sharing basis.

Fields of Application
Scientific, statistical, commercial, production control, accounting, management, systems analysis, operational research.

United Kingdom – Service Bureaux

Training
Short IBM course for punch operators.

SIGMA DATA SERVICES*
3-7 Albemarle Road, Beckenham, Kent, BR3 2HZ

Officers
K. R. Leaver, B. E. Safey, *Managers*

Service Available
Preparation of data.

S.I.A. LTD.
23 Lower Belgrave Street, London, SW1W ONW
Telephone: 01-730 4544

Officers
Dr. P. C. Hooper, *Managing Director*
R. W. Daniels, *General Sales Manager*

Computer Installation
CDC 6600–operating system: SCOPE; internal storage: 131K 60-bit words; magnetic tapes: 6 7-track, 2 9-track; magnetic discs: 8 CDC 841, 1 CDC 808; 3 line printers. *On-line satellite computers*: IBM 1130, Myriad, CTL Satellite 2. *Remote processing features*: CDC 200, DATA 100, DCT 132, teletypes.
CDC 3200–internal storage: 16K 24-bit words; magnetic tapes: 4 7-track, 1 21-track; magnetic discs: 2; 1 line printer.

Coding Languages
FORTRAN, COBOL, ALGOL, COMPASS.

Services Available
Advice, programming, education and training, software packages, preparation of data, systems analysis. Operate on a self-service, remote access, block time, open shop and time-sharing basis.

Fields of Application
Scientific, statistical, commercial, production control, accounting, management, systems analysis, operational research, engineering.
Specialized areas: Linear programming, analysis, structural engineering, chemical engineering.

W. H. SMITH & SON LTD.
Head Office: Strand House, Portugal Street, London, WC2A 2HS
Telephone: 01-405 4343

Also at:
Drake's Way, Greenbridge Trading Estate, Swindon, Wiltshire
Telephone: 0793-6271

Officers
P. H. Bagnall, *Director of Management Information Services*
A. F. Boyce, *Systems Manager*
A. T. Young, *Accounting and Computer Services Manager*

Computer Installation
Swindon:
ICL 2904A–operating system: GEORGE 2; internal storage: 2,304K bits; magnetic tapes: 8; magnetic discs: 5 EDS30; 3 line printers. *Remote processing features*: MODEM/Terminal.

London:
ICL 1903A–operating system: GEORGE 1; internal storage: 768K bits; magnetic tapes: 6; magnetic discs: 4 EDS8; 1 line printer. *Remote processing features*: MODEM/Terminal link to Swindon.

Coding Languages
PLAN, COBOL, FORTRAN.

Contemplated Equipment
30 on-line visual display units, terminal links with regional offices.

Services Available
Operators, computer time and datagraphix C.O.M. Operate on a block time basis. Services negotiable by contract.

Fields of Application
Statistical, commercial, accounting, management, systems analysis, operational research.
Specialized areas: Sales analysis, distribution, warehouse management.

SPL INTERNATIONAL*
75 Grosvenor Street, London, W1X 0DT
Telephone: 01-493 9301

Officers
K. R. Barnes, *Managing Director*
A. A. Benjamin, *Financial Director*
K. L. Davis, *Marketing Director*
D. B. Rodway, *Technical Director*

Services Available
Consultation, programming, operators, software packages, documentation, preparation of data, systems analysis.

Fields of Application
Partial or total management information systems in business, commerce and manufacturing industry, real time on-line systems, including process control, retail and distributive trades, science and engineering, medical science and services.
Specialized areas: Real time applications, medical.

SUN ALLIANCE AND LONDON INSURANCE LTD.
Computer Service
Sun Alliance House, North Street, Horsham, Sussex, RH12 1BT

Also at:
Beacon Building, 1301 Stratford Road, Hall Green, Birmingham, B28 9AP

Officers
W. W. R. Hill, *Group Computer Manager*
E. H. Fray, *Superintendent, Horsham*
A. J. Dancey, *Controller, Birmingham*

Computer Installation
Horsham:
IBM 370/155 (2)–operating systems: MFT and DOS; internal storage: 512K bytes each; magnetic tapes: 12 3420; magnetic discs: 14 3330, 8 2314; 5 line printers. *Remote processing features*: IBM 3270 and Datapoint 2200.

Birmingham:
IBM 360/50–operating systems: MFT and DOS; internal storage: 256K bytes; magnetic tapes: 5 2400; magnetic discs: 8 2314; 1 line printer. *Remote processing features*: Datapoint 2200.

Coding Languages
COBOL, Assembler.

Services Available
Advice, programming, education and training, software packages.

Fields of Application
Commercial, production control, accounting.
Specialized areas: Sales analysis, payroll.

Training
Three-day course in Operations Management; basic operations course in operating system and job control language (2 weeks), operating systems utilities (1 week), machine room training (1-3 weeks) and systems programmer training (as required).

SYSTEMATICS INTERNATIONAL LTD.
Northgate House, Town Square, Basildon, Essex
Telephone: Basildon 25288/9

Officers
R. A. Young, *Managing Director*
R. B. Pickering, *General Manager*

Computer Installation
IBM 370–operating system: DOS; magnetic tapes: 4; magnetic discs: 18; 2 line printers.

Coding Languages
COBOL, FORTRAN, Assembler.

Services Available
Consultation, programming, preparation of data, systems analysis, documentation, printing.

Fields of Application
Accounting, management, commercial, systems analysis.
Specialized areas: Sales analysis, investment, analysis.

SYSTEMSHARE LTD.
Pilton Drive, Edinburgh, EH5 2XT, Scotland
Telephone: 031-552 7601

Officers
I. Christie, *Managing Director*
R. G. Buxton, *Sales and Marketing Manager*

Computer Installation
BULL GENERAL ELECTRIC GE 430 (2)–operating system: TSPS; internal storage: 1,536K bits; magnetic tapes: 5 9-track; magnetic discs: 9 DSU 167, 8 DSU 160; 2 line printers. *Remote processing features*: 60 on-line terminals.

Coding Languages
FORTRAN IV, BASIC, COBOL.

Services Available
Programming, education and training, software packages, documentation, preparation of data, systems analysis. Operate on a closed shop and time-sharing basis.

Fields of Application
General purpose.
Specialized areas: Linear programming, civil and structural engineering, shipbuilding, integrated circuits.

TYLIN MANAGEMENT SYSTEMS LTD.
Fernbrook, The Square, Pangbourne, Reading, Berkshire, RG8 7AL
Telephone: Pangbourne 3838

Also at:
Leon House, High Street, Croydon, Surrey, CR9 3NH

Officers
D. L. J. Tomkins
P. Marks, *Computer Manager*
D. T. Wyke

Computer Installation
IBM 370/135–operating system: DOS; internal storage: 240K bytes; magnetic tapes: 7 BASF; magnetic discs: 8 2314, 3 2319; 2 line printers. *On-line satellite computers*: Raytheon PTS 100 System 3. *Remote processing features*: IBM 2780, 3270 or compatible machines.

Coding Languages
COBOL, BAL, FORTRAN.

Contemplated Equipment
IBM 370/145.

Services Available
Advice, programming, education and training, operators, software packages, documentation, preparation of data, systems analysis. Operate on a remote access, closed shop and time-sharing basis.

Fields of Application
Statistical, commercial, management systems, accounting.
Specialized areas: Teleprocessing, telecommunications, mixed manufacturer systems, design and software, transport and distribution.

UNILEVER COMPUTER SERVICES LTD.
Station House, Harrow Road, Wembley, Middlesex, HA9 6EB
Telephone: 01-903 4851

Also at:
55/57 Clarendon Road, Watford, Hertfordshire, WD1 1SP
Telephone: Watford 28591

Unilever House, Blackfriars, London, EC4P 4BQ
Telephone: 01-353 7474

Bromborough Port, Wirral, Cheshire, L62 4SU
Telephone: 051-645 2060

BOCM Silcock House, Basing View, Basingstoke, Hampshire
Telephone: 0256-29211

Officers
L. J. Rawle, *Chairman*
P. C. Jones, *Marketing Director*
C. P. Dear, *Commercial Director*
M. C. Hopping, *Manager, Watford*
C. W. Bush, *Manager, Unilever House*
M. J. Savage, *Manager, Wirral*

Computer Installation
IBM 360/65–operating system: MFT2/HASP2; internal storage: 768K bytes; magnetic tapes: 6 2401/5; magnetic discs: 3 2314, 8 2316; 3 line printers. *On-line satellite computer*: IBM 1130. *Remote processing features*: 14 terminals.

IBM 360/50–operating system: MFT2/HASP2; internal storage: 512K bytes; magnetic tapes: 3 2401/5; magnetic discs: 1 2314, 8 2316. Line printers, on-line computers and remote processing features shared with IBM 360/65 above.

Coding Languages
PL/1, FORTRAN, COBOL, Assembler, RPG, Informatics Mark IV.

Services Available
Advice, programming, operators, software packages, documentation, preparation of data, systems analysis, support remote fast terminals. Operate on a remote access, closed shop, block time and time-sharing basis.

Fields of Application
Scientific, statistical, commercial, accounting, management, systems analysis, operational research.
Specialized areas: Sales analysis, linear programming, investment, payroll, vehicle scheduling, market research.

UNIROYAL LTD.
Management Information Centre
Newbridge, Midlothian, Scotland
Telephone: 031-337 2468

Officer
T. B. Simpson, *Data Processing Manager*

Computer Installation
IBM 360/30—operating system: DOS; internal storage: 64K bytes; magnetic tapes: 4 4822; magnetic discs: 3 5314; 1 line printer.

Coding Languages
ANS COBOL, FORTRAN, RPG.

Services Available
Programming, operators, preparation of data, systems analysis, standard packages for payroll, payables, receivables, stock control. Operate on an open shop basis.

Fields of Application
Scientific, commercial, production control, accounting, management.

UNIVERSITY COMPUTING COMPANY (GREAT BRITAIN) LTD.
143 Bromsgrove Street, Birmingham 5
Telephone: 021-692 1041

Also at:
343/348 Euston Road, London NW1
Telephone: 01-387 9660

37 The Mall, Eccles, Manchester
Telephone: 061-789 5963

Officers
C. E. Weston, *Centre Director, Birmingham*
J. Kason, *Centre Director, London*
W. T. Watts, *Terminal Manager, Manchester*

Computer Installation
UNIVAC 1107—operating system: EXEC; internal storage: 2,359,296 bits; magnetic tapes: 7 IIIA, 2 IIIC; magnetic drum: 1 FH880.

UNIVAC 1108 (dual system)—operating system: EXEC; internal storage: 2 x 2,359,296 bits; magnetic tapes: 16 VIIIC; magnetic drums: 13 FH432, 2 1782, 3 Fastrand II; 3 line printers. *Remote processing features*: 3 1004, 1005, 1050, 9300, 8 Cope 32, 6 Cope 45.

PDP-9—operating system: EXEC; internal storage: 589,824 bits; connected to Dual 1108 above.

PDP-8—operating system: EXEC; internal storage: 98,304 bits; connected to Dual 1108 above.

Coding Languages
COBOL, FORTRAN, CASH, SLEUTH, ALGOL.

Services Available
Advice, operators, preparation of data, programming, software packages, systems analysis, installation of terminals. Operate on a closed shop and block time basis.

Fields of Application
Scientific, statistical, commercial, production control, accounting, management, systems analysis, operational research.
Specialized areas: Linear programming, APT, structural engineering.

UPPER CLYDE SHIPBUILDERS LTD.*
Linthouse Division, Holmfauld Road, Glasgow SW1, Scotland
Telephone: 041-445 2421

Officer
P. E. A. Green

Computer Installation
ICL 1903A—internal storage: 32K bits; magnetic tapes: 8 1971; magnetic discs: 2 2802; 2 line printers.

Services Available
Consultation, programming, operators, software packages, preparation of data, systems analysis. Operate on a self-service and block time basis.

Fields of Application
Commercial, accounting, management, statistical.
Specialized areas: PERT, AUTOKON.

WATES COMPUTER SERVICES LTD.
1258 London Road, Norbury, London SW16
Telephone: 01-764 1006

Officer
M. Sands, *General Manager*

Computer Installation
UNIVAC 1106—operating system: EXEC 8; internal storage: 131K 36-bit words; magnetic tapes: 8 Uniservo 12; magnetic discs: 8 8414; 2 line printers. *On-line satellite computer*: Univac 9300. *Remote processing features*: 110 to 2400 baud. Dial Up.

Coding Languages
ALGOL, APL, BASIC, COBOL, FORTRAN, Assembler.

Contemplated Equipment
4 8424 disc drives.

Services Available
Advice, programming, education and training, operators, software packages, documentation, preparation of data, systems analysis. Operate on a remote access, closed shop, block time and time-sharing basis.

Fields of Application
Scientific, statistical, commercial, accounting, management, systems analysis, operational research.
Specialized areas: Linear programming, payroll.

WESSEX COMPUTER SERVICES LTD.*
Wessex House, 121 London Road, Waterlooville, Portsmouth, Hampshire

Computer Installations
ICL Pegasus (2)—internal storage: 300K bits each; magnetic tapes: 3.

Coding Languages
Pegasus Order Code and Usercode.

Contemplated Equipment
Honeywell H200.

Services Available
Consultation, programming, preparation of data, systems analysis. Operate on an open shop basis.

Fields of Application
Commercial, scientific.

WESTERN PROGRAMMING SERVICES*
51 Catherine Street, Frome, Somerset
Telephone: Frome 3838

Officers
J. Everson
B. Williams

Coding Languages
COBOL, ALGOL, PLAN, NEAT.

Services Available
Programming, software packages. Operate on a block time basis.

Fields of Application
Scientific, statistical, commercial, production control, accounting, management, systems analysis, operational research.
Specialized area: Management information.

WILFORD COMPUTER GROUP LTD.
52 Princess Street, Manchester, M1 6HX
Telephone: 061-236 1922

Also at:
233 Kentish Town Road, London, NW5 2JT
Telephone: 01-267 3581

27 St. Paul's Street, Leeds, Yorkshire, LS1 2JG
Telephone: 0532 32511

Chapel Field East, Norwich, Norfolk, NOR 43A
Telephone: 0603 60655

117/119 Portland Street, Manchester, M1 6FD
Telephone: 061-236 3682

Haxby Road, York, YO1 1XY
Telephone: 0904 53071

Officers
Alan Wilford, *Managing Director*
R. J. Flint, *Director*

Computer Installation
IBM 370/155–operating system: OS RJE; internal storage: 512K bits; magnetic tapes: 8 2401/6; magnetic discs: 12 2314; 2 line printers.

IBM 360/30–operating system: DOS; internal storage: 64K bits; magnetic tapes: 2 2415; magnetic discs: 4 2314; 1 line printer.

IBM 1287/2.

Services Available
Advice, programming, education and training, operators, software packages, documentation, preparation of data, systems analysis. Operate on a self-service, remote access, block time, open shop and time-sharing basis.

Fields of Application
Scientific, statistical, commercial, production control, accounting, management, systems analysis, operational research.
Specialized areas: Sales analysis, linear programming, analysis, payroll.

WOODALL-DUCKHAM COMPUTING SERVICES LTD.*
65/67 Western Road, Hove, Sussex
Telephone: 0273-778161

Officers
R. D. Haxby, *Chairman*
S. Crawe, *Managing Director*
J. D. Woodhouse, *Marketing Manager*
W. R. Knighton, *Director of Computer Operations*

Computer Installation
ICL 1901–internal storage: 384K bits; magnetic tapes: 6 7-track; 1 line printer.

Coding Languages
PLAN, COBOL, FORTRAN, ALGOL.

Contemplated Equipment
ICL 1902A with storage of 32K words and 4 magnetic tapes.

Services Available
Advice, preparation of data, programming, software packages, systems analysis, educational services. Operate on an open shop and block time basis.

Fields of Application
Scientific, statistical, commercial, production control, accounting, management, systems analysis, operational research, project planning, PERT, stock control.
Specialized area: Project planning.

Training
Basic computer training, keypunch training; course in preparation custom planned.

UNITED STATES OF AMERICA

NATIONAL CENTRE

NATIONAL CENTER FOR ATMOSPHERIC RESEARCH (NCAR)
1850 Table Mesa Drive, Boulder, Colorado 80302
Telephone: 494-5151

Officers
John W. Firor, *Director*
Philip D. Thompson, *Associate Director*

Computer Installation
CDC 6600–internal storage: 3.9 million bits; magnetic tapes: 6 607; magnetic discs: 1 6603; 2 line printers.

CDC 7600–internal storage: 3.9 million + 30.7 million bits; magnetic tapes: 6 607; magnetic discs: 2 7638; 2 line printers. *Remote processing features*: on line-remote batch terminal.

Coding Languages
FORTRAN, ASCENT.

Contemplated Equipment
Mass storage device.

Services Available
Advice, operators, documentation, systems analysis.
Operate on a remote access and closed shop basis.

Field of Application
Scientific.
Specialized area: Atmospheric research.

Training
Courses in Assembly language and elementary, intermediate and advanced FORTRAN. Short course in Programme Development. Summer fellowship programme.

EDUCATIONAL AND TRAINING INSTITUTIONS

ADELPHI BUSINESS SCHOOLS INC.*
1712 Kings Highway, Brooklyn, New York 11229
Telephone: 336-7200

Also at:
47 Mineola Boulevard, Mineola, New York
Telephone: (516) 248-8900

Officer
Jerry Katzeff, *Director*

Computer Installation
IBM 360/20–operating system: BPS; internal storage: 8K bits; 1 line printer.

Coding Languages
RPG, BAL.

Services Available
Education and training.

Training
Course in programming, systems, console operation, and operating systems (650 hours).

AMERICAN COMPUTER SCHOOLS
1627 Main Street, Kansas City, Missouri 64108
Telephone: (816) 221-2044

Officers
R. Nowlin, *Director of Admissions*
E. Minor, *Director of School*

Computer Installation
IBM 360/20–internal storage: 4K bits; 1 line printer.

Coding Languages
RPG, BAL, PL/1, COBOL, FORTRAN.

Services Available
Education and training. Operate on a self-service basis. Available for student training only.

Fields of Application
Accounting, statistical, systems analysis.

Training
Courses in data processing operations and programming. Short courses for key punch operations (4-6 weeks).

AUTOMATION INSTITUTE OF TOLEDO*
1220 Madison Avenue, Toledo, Ohio 43624
Telephone: 255-0060

Officer
T. R. Worley, *Vice-President*

Computer Installation
IBM 360/20–internal storage: 16K bits; magnetic discs: 2; 1 line printer.

Coding Languages
RPG, BAL, COBOL, PL/1.

Services Available
Consultation, programming, education and training, operators, preparation of data, systems analysis.
Operate on a closed shop basis.

Fields of Application
Commercial, educational.

Training
Courses in concepts, systems, and programming – RPG, BAL, COBOL, PL/1.

AUTOMATION TRAINING CENTER
1930 Isaac Newton Square East, Reston, Virginia 22070
Telephone: (703) 471-5751

Officers
Harold Weiss, *Director*
Sylvia M. Geller, *Registrar*

Services Available
Education and training.

Fields of Application
Accounting, management, systems analysis.
Specialized areas: Auditing EDP.

Training
Short courses in EDP Audit and Control (5-7 days). Data processing risk management (1 day), Management control of EDP (3-5 days), Advanced EDP audit and control conference (2 days).

BARNETT DATA SYSTEMS
Suite 507-1010 Rockville Pike, Rockville, Maryland 20852
Telephone: (301) 762-1288

Officer
Arnold Barnett, *President*

Services Available
Consultation, education and training.

Fields of Application
Commercial, systems analysis and design, management information systems.

Training
Data Systems Development (3-day in-house seminars).

BRYANT AND STRATTON EDUCATION CENTER*
23 East Jackson Boulevard, Chicago, Illinois 60604
Telephone: (312) 939-7090

Also at:
The Emery School Inc., 120 Boylston Street, Boston, Massachusetts 02116
Telephone: (617) 542-8012

Officers
Leonard Levin, *Personnel*
Donald Kerins, *Director of Automation*

United States of America – Educational and Training Institutions

Computer Installation
IBM 360/20–internal storage: 8K bits.
IBM 360/20–operating system: 1130; internal storage: 8K bits; magnetic discs: 1 2315; 1 line printer.

Coding Languages
RPG, BAL, FORTRAN, COBOL, BML.

Contemplated Equipment
IBM 360/30.

Services Available
Education and training. Available only to students.

Fields of Application
Statistical, accounting, management, systems analysis, operations research.
Specialized areas: Accounting, management.

Training
Courses in mathematics, English, accounting, programming and systems. Short courses in mathematics, English, accounting and programming.

CAREER EDUCATIONAL INSTITUTE
1200 Walnut Street, Philadelphia, Pennsylvania 19107
Telephone: (215) KI6-3377

Officers
Martin Austin, *President*
Cesare L. Cosenza, *Administrative Vice-President*

Computer Installation
IBM 360–operating system: DOS; internal storage: 12,288 bits; magnetic tapes: 2; 1 line printer.

Coding Languages
BAL, RPG.

Contemplated Equipment
IBM 360/30.

Services Available
Programming, education and training, systems analysis. Operate on an open shop basis. Available to students only

Field of Application
Commercial.
Specialized area: Payroll.

Training
Two-year Computer Programming Course: RPG Programming, COBOL Programming, BAL Programming, Systems Analysis, Assoc. in Computer Science.

COLLEGE OF AUTOMATION*
3001 Grand Avenue, Des Moines, Iowa 50312
Telephone: 243-8696

Officer
John D. LeCroy, *Director Education*

Computer Installation
IBM 360/30–operating system: DOS; internal storage: 64K bits; magnetic tapes: 2 2301; magnetic discs: 4 2311; 1 line printer

IBM 360/20–operating system: TPS; internal storage: 16K bits; magnetic tapes: 4; 1 line printer.

Coding Languages
RPG, BAL, COBOL, FORTRAN.

Services Available
Education and training. Operate on a self-service basis. Available only for student use.

Field of Application
Business.

Training
Certificates in data processing, key punch operation, console operation. Short course in key punch operation (1 month).

COLLEGE OF DATA PROCESSING*
8451 South Vermont Avenue, Los Angeles, California 90044
Telephone: 778-1925

Officer
Bill Anderson, *Director of Computer Center*

Computer Installation
IBM 360/30–operating system: DOS; internal storage: 64K bits; magnetic tapes: 4; magnetic discs: 2; 1 line printer.

Coding Languages
ALGOL, FORTRAN, FAP, MAP, JOVIAL, Autocoder, COBOL.

Contemplated Equipment
CMC Key Tape/Disc system.

Services Available
Consultation, programming, education and training, software packages, systems analysis. Operate on remote access, closed shop, block time and time-sharing basis.

Fields of Application
Scientific, executive, management information systems.
Specialized areas: Hybrid simulation, software services.

Training
A. A. and B. S. Degree in consortium with Pepperdine College. Courses in key training, computer operations and programming. Short courses in EDP for accountants, engineers, educators, social workers, community leaders.

COMMERCIAL PROGRAMMING UNLIMITED*
853 Broadway, New York, New York 10003
Telephone: (212) 982-4000

Officer
Noel Prager, *Assistant Director of Education*

Services Available
Consultation, programming, education and training, software packages.

Training
Certificates in Introduction to System 360, 360 computer programming, 360 console operations. Short course in IBM Key punch (3-8 weeks).

COMPUTER COMMAND AND CONTROL COMPANY
1717 Pennsylvania Avenue, N.W., Washington, D.C. 20006

Also at:
Philadelphia, Pennsylvania

Officer
W. E. Wallace, *President*

Services Available
Consultation, programming, education and training, operators, software packages, documentation, preparation of data, systems analysis. Operate on time-sharing basis.

Fields of Application
Systems analysis.
Specialized areas: Management, logistic, personnel, financial, chemical, and health information systems, command and control systems, intelligence and data management systems.

Training
Short courses in management information systems, data management systems survey, third generation systems techniques, OS 360 seminars, advanced file structures for on-line systems, systems programming principles, privacy and security (1 day-3 weeks).

CONTROL DATA COMPUTER TRAINING SCHOOL*
105 Madison Avenue, New York, New York 10016
Telephone: (212) 889-1210

Officer
Howard Binnick, *Director*

Computer Installation
CDC 3150—operating system: MSOS; internal storage: 16K bits; magnetic tapes: 4 CDC 604; magnetic discs: 2 CDC 853; 1 line printer.

Coding Languages
COBOL, FORTRAN, COMPASS

Services Available
Education and training. Operate on an open shop basis. Available only to students.

Training
Courses in programming (600 hours), computer maintenance (1000 hours), console operations (350 hours).

CONTROL DATA EDUCATION CENTERS*
8100 34th Avenue South, Minneapolis, Minnesota 55440
Telephone: 888-5555, extension 4177

Also at:
8616 LaTijiera Blvd., Los Angeles, California 90045
5630 Arbor Vitae Blvd., Los Angeles, California 90045
675 North First St., San José, California 95112
500 Interstate Pike, Rockville, Maryland 20852
7200 France Avenue South, Minneapolis, Minnesota 55435
4940 Viking Drive, Minneapolis, Minnesota 55435
277-12th Avenue North, Minneapolis, Minnesota 55411
2 Penn Plaza, New York, New York 10001
Fannin Bank Bldg., Suite 302, 1010 Holcombe Blvd., Houston, Texas.

Officers
Layton G. Kinney, *General Manager*
Brian J. Roth, *Director, International Operations*

Services Available
Education and training. Applicants from the general public must pass the appropriate aptitude tests.

Training
Courses in programming technology, computer hardware technology, systems analysis. Various seminars on computer sciences, management sciences, mathematical and statistical sciences.

CONTROL DATA INSTITUTE
1780 West Lincoln Avenue, Anaheim, California 92801
Telephone: (714) 635-2770

Officers
D. E. Scherer, *Director*
Jack Katz, *Sales Manager*

Computer Installation
IBM 360/20—operating system: DPS; internal storage: 96K bits; magnetic discs: 1; 1 line printer.

The Institute also has a CDC 200 User terminal to a CDC 6600.

Coding Languages
RPG, BAL, FORTRAN, COBOL.

Services Available
Education and training. Operate on a self-service and time-sharing basis.

Fields of Application
Scientific, statistical, commercial, production control, accounting, management, systems analysis.
Specialized areas: Analysis, payroll.

Training
Diploma course in Computer Technology; Diploma and A.S. degree courses in Programming Technology; short courses in computer operations, card punch and machine operations.

CONTROL DATA INSTITUTE*
20 North Avenue, Burlington, Massachusetts 01803
Telephone: (617) 272-4070

Officers
Leonard Traugott, *Director*
Donald J. Matuszek, *Manager of Administration*

Computer Installation
CDC 3150—operating system: MSOS; internal storage: 384K 16-bit words; magnetic tapes: 2 CDC 607; magnetic discs: 2 CDC 854; 1 line printer.

Coding Languages
Machine, Assembly (COMPASS), FORTRAN, COBOL.

Services Available
Education and training. Operate on a closed shop and open shop basis. Available only for student training.

Training
Courses in programming technology (600 hours) and computer technology (1,000 hours). Also a short mathematics course (100 hours).

CONTROL DATA INSTITUTE*
3605 Long Beach Boulevard, Long Beach, California 90807
Telephone: (213) 426-9381

Officers
James E. McCormick, *Director*
Charles A. Culver, *Dean*

Computer Installation
IBM 360/20—internal storage: 4K bytes; 1 line printer.

Coding Languages
FORTRAN, COBOL, RPG, BAL.

United States of America – Educational and Training Institutions

Services Available
Consultation, education and training. Operate on an open shop and time-sharing basis. Students must be high school graduates and pass an aptitude test.

Fields of Application
Commercial training.

Training
Course in computer programming and systems, a non-degree certificate programme, and a course for card punch operators.

CONTROL DATA INSTITUTE
Kossman Building, Forbes and Stanwix, Pittsburgh, Pennsylvania 15222
Telephone: (412) 471-1810

Officers
F. R. Haberkorn, *Director*
E. K. Dunham, *Marketing Manager*

Computer Installation
CDC 3100–operating system: MSOS, Tape, SCOPE; internal storage: 16K 24-bit words; magnetic tapes: 3 CDC 604; magnetic discs: 2 CDC 854; 1 line printer. *Remote processing features*: Can connect to a satellite terminal and to a satellite computer.

Coding Languages
COMPASS, COBOL, FORTRAN, RPG.

Services Available
Programming, education and training. Operate on a self-service, closed shop and open shop basis. Available to staff and students only.

Fields of Application
Commercial, accounting and training.

Training
Courses in computer technology, programming technology, digital computer operations, total data processing, business machines services. Short courses in key punch (7 weeks).

CONTROL DATA INSTITUTE*
14003 Ventura Blvd., Sherman Oaks, California 91403
Telephone: (213) 981-5100

Officers
Leon Cooper, *Director*
Ian Murray, *Education Director*

Computer Installation
IBM 360/20–operating system: card; internal storage: 4K bits; 1 line printer.

Coding Languages
RPG, BAL, COBOL.

Services Available
Education and training. Operate on an open shop basis. Available only to students.

Contemplated Equipment
IBM 360/20: 12K storage; 1 2311 disc drive. CDC 200 User Terminal, linked to a nationwide Cybernet Data Center.

Fields of Application
Commercial, accounting.

Training
Course in computer programming/systems analysis and design (540 hours).

CONTROL DATA INSTITUTE*
601 James Street, Syracuse, New York 13203
Telephone: 474-5316

Computer Installation
IBM 360/20–operating system: DOS; internal storage: 96 million bits; magnetic discs: 1 2311; 2 line printers. *On-line satellite computers*: CDC 3700. *Remote processing features*: BATCH.

Services Available
Programming, operators, preparation of data, systems analysis. Operate on a self-service, remote access and time-sharing basis.

Field of Application
Commercial.

Training
Courses in computer programming and systems design.

DATA PROCESSING MANAGEMENT ASSOCIATION
505 Busse Highway, Park Ridge, Illinois 60068
Telephone: (312) 825-8124

Officers
Herbert B. Safford, *CDP International President*
Donn W. Sanford, *Executive Director*

Computer Installation
HONEYWELL H120.

Services Available
Education and training.

Training
Annual Certificate in Data Processing (CDP) and the Registered Business Programmer (RBP) examination or certification programmes.

DETROIT COLLEGE OF BUSINESS*
4801 Oakman Boulevard, Dearborn, Michigan 48126
Telephone: 582-6983

Officer
G. R. Lamphere, *Chairman, Data Processing*

Computer Installation
IBM 360/20–operating system: OS; internal storage: 8K bits; 1 line printer.

Coding Languages
RPG, BAL.

Services Available
Programming, education and training, operators, systems analysis. Operate on a self-service basis.

Fields of Application
Statistical, commercial, accounting, scheduling.

Training
A.S. degree course in Data Management. B.S. degree course in Data Processing.

United States of America – Educational and Training Institutions

EDUTRONICS SYSTEMS INTERNATIONAL INC.*
3345 Wilshire Blvd., Los Angeles, California 90005

Also at:
New York, N.Y.; San Francisco, California; Chicago, Illinois; Dayton, Ohio.

Officers
Sherman Titens, *President*
Richard A. Green, *Vice-President*

Services Available
Education and training. Operate on a self-service basis.

EL PASO DATA SERVICES INC.*
Data Processing School of El Paso,
815 E Yandell Dr., El Paso, Texas 79902
Telephone: (915) 542-1701

Officer
William R. Fletcher, *President and Director of School*

Computer Installation
IBM System/3–internal storage: 12K bits; magnetic discs: 2 54444. *Remote processing features*: Data phone.

Services Available
Consultation, programming, education and training, operators, documentation, preparation of data, systems analysis. Operate on a self-service basis.

Fields of Application
Commercial, accounting, systems analysis.
Specialized areas: Education.

Training
Courses in data preparation, computer operation and basic programming, advanced computer programming and systems. Short courses in input management control (two days), systems writing of DP (one day), participation management of EDP systems (two days).

ELECTRONIC COMPUTER PROGRAMMING INSTITUTE*
111 East 4th Street, Dayton, Ohio 45402

Computer Installation
IBM 360/20–operating system: TOS; internal storage: 131,072 bits; magnetic tapes: 2 2415; 1 line printer.

Services Available
Education and training. Operate on an open shop basis.

Field of Application
Commercial analysis.

Training
Courses in UR, RPG, BAL, COBOL, DOS.

ELECTRONIC COMPUTER PROGRAMMING INSTITUTE*
49 N. Progress Avenue, Harrisburg, Pennsylvania 17109
Telephone: (717) 545-4231

Officer
Arthur Mark, *Director*

Computer Installation
UNIVAC 9200–internal storage: 8K bits; 1 line printer.

Coding Languages
RPG, BAL, COBOL.

Services Available
Consultation, programming, education and training, software packages, systems analysis. Operate on a closed shop basis.

Fields of Application
Commercial, accounting, management.
Specialized areas: Mortgage loans.

Training
Short courses in data processing and computer programming (308 hours).

ELECTRONIC COMPUTER PROGRAMMING INSTITUTE
722 Walnut St., Kansas City, Missouri 64106
Telephone: (816) 842-0877

Officer
N. E. Capps, *Director*

Computer Installation
UNIVAC 9200–internal storage: 80K bits; 1 line printer.

Coding Languages
RPG, BAL, COBOL.

Services Available
Programming, education and training. Operate on a closed shop basis.

Training
Course in data processing and programming.

ELECTRONIC COMPUTER PROGRAMMING INSTITUTE*
2024 J St., Suite 2500, Sacramento, California 95814
Telephone: 444-0433

Officers
H. M. Wilchek, *President*
Anita K. Minier, *Executive Director*

Computer Installation
IBM 360/20–operating system: DPS; internal storage: 12,188 × 8 bits; magnetic tapes: 1 2415, 1 2311.

Coding Languages
RPG, BAL, PL/1.

Contemplated Equipment
Key to tape devices.

Services Available
Consultation, programming, education and training, operators, preparation of data. Operate on a self-service basis. Not available during student class hours.

Fields of Application
Commercial, accounting, management, system analysis.
Specialized area: Student training.

Training
Courses in data processing and computer programming, computer operations, key entry. Short courses in COBOL (40 hours), introduction to data processing (28 hours), basic assembly language (200 hours).

ELECTRONIC COMPUTER PROGRAMMING INSTITUTE OF TIDEWATER
416 Janaf Office Building, Norfolk, Virginia 23502
Telephone: (703) 855-0191

Officer
Alfred Dreyfus, *President*

Computer Installation
IBM 360/20—internal storage: 8K bits; 1 line printer.

Coding Languages
BAL, RPG, COBOL, FORTRAN, DOS, ANSI COBOL, RPG III.

Contemplated Equipment
IBM 360/30.

Services Available
Advice, programming, education and training, operators, systems analysis. Operate on a self-service, block time and open shop basis.

Fields of Application
Statistical, commercial, production control, accounting, management, systems analysis.
Specialized areas: Sales analysis, investment, analysis, payroll.

Training
Computer Programming (basic and advanced), Computer Electronics, Computer Technology.

HERZING INSTITUTES INC.*
174 West Wisconsin Avenue, Milwaukee, Wisconsin 53203
Telephone: (414) 271-8103

Also at:
2011 North Richmond Street, Appleton, Wisconsin 54911
1218 South 20th Street, Birmingham, Alabama 35209
4040 Charles Street, Rockford, Illinois 61108

Officers
Henry G. Herzing, *President*
William J. Herzing, *Vice President Finance*
Gerald Morearty, *Vice President Education*

Computer Installation
IBM 360/20—internal storage: 8K bits.
UNIVAC 9200—internal storage: 8K bits.

Coding Languages
Assembly, RPG.

Services Available
Consultation, programming, education and training, systems analysis. Operate on a self-service and block time basis.

Fields of Application
Accounting, commercial and production control.

Training
Courses in data processing and 360 programming. Short courses in key punch, RPG programming, COBOL programming, Assembly language programming and introduction to data processing.

INSTITUTE FOR ADVANCED TECHNOLOGY
Control Data Corporation, 5272 River Road, Washington, D.C. 20016
Telephone: (301) 652-2268

Officer
Frederick J. Karch, *Director*

Services Available
Education and training.

Training
Seminars in computer sciences, management sciences, mathematical and statistical sciences.

INTERNATIONAL DATA PROCESSING INSTITUTE*
Division of Data Science Corporation, 1253 Griswold, Detroit, Michigan 48226
Telephone: 963-0609

Officers
V. J. Bronsing, *President*
W. J. Bronsing, *Secretary-Treasurer*
H. D. Merrell, *Director of Education*

Computer Installation
IBM 360/20—internal storage: 64K bits; 1 line printer.

Coding Languages
Assembler, COBOL, Report Program Generator.

Services Available
Consultation, education and training. Operate on a closed shop basis. Available only to educational staff and students.

Fields of Application
Scientific, statistical, commercial, production control, accounting, management, systems analysis, operational research.
Specialized areas: Commercial applications.

Training
Various courses in computer programming, and operations ranging in duration from 4 to 10 months.

KINMAN BUSINESS UNIVERSITY
The Bon Marche Building, North 214 Wall Street, Spokane, Washington, 99201
Telephone: 838-3521

Officers
Harold E. Leffel, *Director*
Robert E. Falkner, *Head of Programming Department*

Computer Installation
IBM 360/20—internal storage: 16K bits; magnetic discs: 2; 120 line printers.

Services Available
Education and training.

Field of Application
Educational.

Training
Courses in computer programming and computer operations. Short IBM card punch course.

MANPOWER BUSINESS TRAINING INSTITUTION*
105 N. 7th Street, St. Louis, Missouri 63101
Telephone: (314) 241-5588

Also at:
826 N. Plankinton, Milwaukee, Wisconsin 53203
1614 Fannin, Houston, Texas 77002

Officers
Ronald E. Purcell, *Director*
Raymond H. Bakken, *Educational Director*

Computer Installation
IBM 360/20—internal storage: 12K bits; magnetic tapes: 1 2311.

Coding Languages
RPG, BAL, COBOL.

Services Available
Education and training. Operate on a self-service basis. Available only to students.

Field of Application
Commercial.

Training
Courses in data processing.

MATA COLLEGE OF AUTOMATION*
415 East Broad Street, Columbus, Ohio 43215
Telephone: (614) 224-8263

Officer
D. R. Broyles

Computer Installation
IBM 360/20—operating system: CPS; internal storage: 8K bits; 1 line printer.
IBM 360/30—operating system: DOS; internal storage: 64K bits; magnetic tapes: 2 2401; magnetic discs: 4 2311; 1 line printer.

Coding Languages
COBOL, BAL, RPG, PL/1.

Services Available
Programming, education and training. Operate on a self-service and block time basis.

Field of Application
Commercial.

Training
Courses in electronic data processing. Short courses in keypunch operation, computer operations.

METROPOLITAN JUNIOR COLLEGE DISTRICT*
560 Westport Road, Kansas City, Missouri 64111
Telephone: (816) 753-4949

Officer
L. Don Frazier, *Manager, Data Services*

Computer Installation
IBM 1410—operating system: DOS; internal storage: 16K bits; magnetic tapes: 2 7330; magnetic discs: 2 1311; 1 line printer.

Coding Languages
COBOL, FORTRAN, RPG, Autocoder, FARGO, BAL.

Contemplated Equipment
IBM 360/40 with 256K-bit store.

Services Available
Programming, education and training, operators, documentation, systems analysis. Operate on an open shop basis. Available only to administrators, faculty and students.

Fields of Application
Educational, administrative.

Training
Courses in electro mechanical machines, data processing, computer programming, IBM 360 Systems, FORTRAN, Assembly, COBOL.

M.T.I. BUSINESS COLLEGES*
2731 Capitol Avenue, Sacramento, California 95816

Officers
A. E. Zimmerman, *President*
H. Haase, *Manager*

Computer Installation
IBM 360/20—internal storage: 8K bits; 1 line printer.

Contemplated Equipment
IBM 360/25.

Services Available
Consultation, programming, education and training, operators. Operate on a closed shop basis.

Field of Application
Commercial.

Training
Courses in computer operation, COBOL, RPG, BAL, PCU and card punch operating.

NATIONAL COLLEGE OF BUSINESS
P.O. Box 1628, Rapid City, South Dakota 57701
Telephone: (605) 348-1200

Officers
John W. Hauer, *President*
Harold Buckingham, *Chairman of the Board*

Computer Installation
NCR Century 101—operating system: BATCH; internal storage: 131,072 bits; magnetic discs: 2; 1 line printer.

Coding Languages
FORTRAN, COBOL, NEAT/3, RPG, BAL, BASIC.

Services Available
Consultation, programming, education and training, operators, documentation, preparation of data, systems analysis. Operate on a self-service, closed shop and time-sharing basis.

Fields of Application
Commercial, accounting, management, education.
Specialized areas: Student scheduling, grade reporting, student programmes, student instruction, census reports.

Training
B.S. degree course in computer science; A.S. degree course in computer programming; IBM course in clerical and office machines.
Short courses in principles of data processing, computer programming (BASIC, RPG, FORTRAN, COBOL, BAL, NEAT/3), computer operators functions, data processing management, systems development and design, linear programming (all of 12 weeks duration).

PHILLIPS INFORMATION TECHNOLOGY INC.*
1049 Park Avenue, New York, New York 10028
Telephone: (212) 427-3979

Services Available
Education and training.

United States of America – Educational and Training Institutions

Field of Application
Management.

Training
Short course in computer-aided management; self-instructional audio-visual course for managers.

RENO JUNIOR COLLEGE OF BUSINESS*
258 Wonder, Reno, Nevada 89502
Telephone: 322-4071

Officer
Don S. Thompson, *Systems Administrator*

Computer Installation
IBM System/3–operating system: Card; 1 line printer.

Coding Language
RPG.

Services Available
Education and training. Operate on an open shop basis.

Fields of Application
Accounting, commercial.
Specialized area: Accounts receivable.

Training
Courses in computer programming and systems management. Short courses in computer operations (3-6 months) and junior programming (6-9 months).

SALT CITY BUSINESS COLLEGE*
Ave A & Walnut, Hutchinson, Kansas 67501
Telephone: (316) 663-4488

Officer
R. L. Conard, *President*

Computer Installation
BURROUGHS B4000–internal storage: 2,400 bits.

Coding Language
Symbolic.

Services Available
Programming, education and training, operators.

Training
Diploma course in machine accounting and computer programming.

SOUTHWEST COMPUTER COLLEGE INC.
525 San Pedro Drive, N.E., Albuquerque, New Mexico 87108
Telephone: (505) 265-5904

Officer
H. C. Harenberg, *President*

Computer Installation
IBM System/3–operating system: DOS; internal storage: 16K bits; magnetic discs: 2 5444; 1 line printer.
IBM 1130–operating system: DOS; internal storage: 8K bits; magnetic tapes: 1 2313; 1 line printer.

Coding Languages
COBOL, FORTRAN, Assembly, RPG.

Services Available
Programming, education and training, software packages, preparation of data, systems analysis. Operate on a self-service and block time basis.

Fields of Application
Commercial, accounting.
Specialized areas: Linear programming, medical research.

Training
Courses in business administration and computer science, computer programming.

TECHNICAL EDUCATION CORPORATION*
Automation Training Division
5701 Waterman Avenue, St. Louis, Missouri 63112
Telephone: (314) 727-7212

Officer
C. R. Johnson, *President*

Computer Installation
UNIVAC 9200–internal storage: 16K bits; magnetic tapes: 4; 1 line printer.

Coding Languages
RPG, BAL, COBOL.

Services Available
Consultation, programming, education and training. Operate on a block time basis.

Fields of Application
Commercial, accounting, instruction.

Training
Courses in keypunch, computer operation and computer programming.

UNITED STATES NAVAL ACADEMY*
Academic Computing Center
Room 111, Ward Hall, U.S. Naval Academy, Annapolis, Maryland 21402
Telephone: (301) 268-7711, extension 550

Officer
Lieutenant Roy N. Poust, *Director*

Computer Installation
IBM 7094–operating system: IBSYS; internal storage: 2,340K bits; magnetic tapes: 10 729/IV, 2 799/V; 1 line printer. *On-line satellite computer*: IBM 1401.
IBM 1620–operating system: 1620 Monitor; internal storage: 120K bits; magnetic discs: 1 1311.

Coding Languages
MAP, FAP, FORTRAN, Autocoder, BASIC, COBOL, SPS.

Services Available
Education and training, operators, software packages. Operate on a closed shop, open shop and time-sharing basis. Available only to midshipmen and faculty of U.S.N.A.

Fields of Application
Scientific, academic and research.
Specialized areas: Course and examination scheduling.

Training
Courses in computing and advanced programming. Short courses in computing and FORTRAN IV.

United States of America – Educational and Training Institutions

WESTERN BUSINESS UNIVERSITY*
812 S.W. 10th Avenue, Portland, Oregon 97205
Telephone: 226-7004

Officers
Don Grulke, *President*
John Stocklem, *Director of Education*

Computer Installation
IBM 360/20–operating system: DPS; internal storage: 12,288 bits; magnetic discs: 1 2311; 1 line printer.

Coding Languages
RPG, COBOL, FORTRAN, BAL.

Services Available
Education and training. Operate on a closed and open shop and time-sharing basis.

Fields of Application
Statistical, educational, accounting.

Training
Short courses in computer concepts (30 hours), unit record equipment (90 hours), FORTRAN (30 hours), COBOL (210 hours), RPG (90 hours), BAL (120 hours), systems design (70 hours).

UNIVERSITIES AND COLLEGES
(In alphabetical order by State)

ALABAMA

AUBURN UNIVERSITY
Computer Center
Auburn, 36830
Telephone: (205) 826-4285

Officers
Dr. Ben B. Barnes, *Director*
Dr. Donald L. Hartford, *Manager of Consulting and Programming*
Dr. H. Troy Nagle, *Manager of Mini-computer Operations*
Mr. J. Lee Franklin, *Manager of Operations and Administration*

Computer Installation
IBM 370/155–operating system: OS/MVT with HASP; internal storage: 4,194,304 bits; magnetic tapes: 3 3420; magnetic discs: 4 3330; 2 line printers.
HEWLETT PACKARD 2000E–operating system: 2120A DOS-M; internal storage: 262,144 bits; magnetic tapes: 1 7970B; magnetic discs: 1 HP cartridge; 1 line printer.
Remote processing features: 22 teletype terminals.

Coding Languages
FORTRAN, PL/1, COBOL, BASIC.

Services Available
Advice, programming, education and training, operators, software packages, documentation, preparation of data, systems analysis. Operate on a closed shop and time-sharing basis.

Fields of Application
Scientific, statistical, commercial, instruction.
Specialized areas: Linear programming, structural engineering.

Training
Computer Science options in B.S. degrees.

GADSDEN STATE JUNIOR COLLEGE
George Wallace Drive, Gadsden, 35903
Telephone: (205) 546-0484

Officers
Dr. Allan D. Naylor, *President*
Chad B. Hawkins, *Dean of Instruction*
H. D. Ponder, *Director, Computer Center*

Computer Installation
IBM 1130–internal storage: 130,892 bits; magnetic discs: 2 2310; 1 line printer.

Coding Languages
FORTRAN, RPG, COBOL, PL/1, Assembler.

Contemplated Equipment
IBM System/3.

Services Available
Advice, programming, preparation of data. Operate on a self-service basis.

Fields of Application
Scientific, accounting, management.
Specialized areas: Linear programming, student accounting.

Training
Courses in data processing, introduction to computers, computer programming, electronic computers. A.S. degree.

TUSKEGEE INSTITUTE*
Computer Center, School of Engineering
Tuskegee, 36088
Telephone: (205) 727-8357

Officer
A. V. Jett, Jr., *Assistant Professor and Manager*

Computer Installation
IBM 1620–internal storage: 60K bits.
IBM 1401–internal storage: 12K bits; magnetic tapes: 2 tape drives; magnetic discs: 2; 1 line printer.

Coding Languages
SPS, FORTRAN.

Services Available
Limited availability to agencies outside the institute.

Fields of Application
Analysis and programming in areas of interest to an academic institution.
Specialized areas: Scientific programming, numerical analysis.

Training
Courses in elementary computer techniques (FORTRAN), numerical methods and digital computation.

UNIVERSITY OF ALABAMA IN HUNTSVILLE
Research Institute
P.O. Box 1247, Huntsville, 35807
Telephone: (205) 895-6120

Officer
Dr. Benjamin B. Graves, *President*

United States of America – Universities and Colleges

Computer Installation
UNIVAC 1108–operating system: EXEC VIII; internal storage: 9,437,184 bits; magnetic tapes: 11 7-track, 2 9-track; magnetic discs: 3 Fastrand II; 4 line printers.
On-line satellite computers: 1 Univac 9200. *Remote processing features*: batch and demand.
PDP-8–internal storage: 49,152 bits; magnetic tapes: 1 Hewlett Packard. *Remote processing features*: TTY.

Coding Languages
COBOL, FORTRAN V, BASIC, CFOR, Assembler, ALGOL.

Services Available
Advice, programming, education and training, documentation, systems analysis. Operate on a remote access, on-site batch, closed shop and time sharing basis.

Fields of Application
Scientific, statistical, commercial, accounting, systems analysis, operational research.
Specialized areas: Linear programming, analysis, solar physics, atmospheric dynamics, aero and fluid mechanics.

Computer Installation
CDC 6400–operating system: SCOPE; internal storage: 4 million bits; magnetic tapes: 5 607; magnetic discs 2 6603; 2 line printers.
UNIVAC 9300–internal storage: 32,768 bits; 1 line printer.

Coding Languages
FORTRAN, COBOL, ALGOL, SIMSCRIPT, COMPASS, MIMIC, LISP, SNOBOL.

Contemplated Equipment
Additional direct access devices; communications capability.

Services Available
Consultation, programming, education and training, operators, software packages, documentation, preparation of data, systems analysis. Operate on a closed shop basis.

Fields of Application
Scientific, statistical, commercial, accounting, management, systems analysis, operational research.

Training
M.S. and Ph.D. courses in Computer Science. Short courses in FORTRAN and COBOL.

ALASKA

UNIVERSITY OF ALASKA
Computer Center
College, Fairbanks, 99701
Telephone: (907) 479-7665

Officer
Edward J. Gauss, *Director*

Computer Installation
IBM 360/40–operating system: DOS/POWER; internal storage: 1,048K bits; magnetic tapes: 3 2401; magnetic discs: 6 2314; 1 line printer.
IBM 1620–internal storage: 200K bits.
EAI 380 Analog.

Coding Languages
FORTRAN IV, COBOL, RPG, PL/1.

Services Available
Advice, operators, preparation of data, programming, software packages, systems analysis. Operate on a closed shop basis.

Fields of Application
Scientific analysis, computer models, numerical analysis, data acquisition, data systems.
Specialized areas: Spectral analysis, permafrost soil models, geophysics.

Training
Associate Degree offered in Computer Science.

ARIZONA

UNIVERSITY OF ARIZONA
Tucson, 85721
Telephone: (602) 884-2915

ARKANSAS

ARKANSAS STATE UNIVERSITY*
Drawer AAA, State University, 72467
Telephone: (501) 972-2100

Also at:
Jonesboro, Arkansas

Officer
C. Yauger, *Director*

Computer Installation
IBM 360/20–operating system: DOS; magnetic tapes: 2 2415; magnetic discs: 3 2311; 1 line printer.

Coding Languages
COBOL, FORTRAN, BAL, RPG PL/1.

Services Available
Consultation, programming, education and training, operators, documentation, preparation of data, systems analysis. Operate on a self-service and open shop basis.

Fields of Application
Scientific, statistical, commercial, accounting.

UNIVERSITY OF ARKANSAS*
Computing Center
SE 301, Fayetteville, 72701
Telephone: (501) 575-2905

Officers
Dr. J. Wray Wilkes, *Supervisor and Professor*
Dr. James E. Dunn, *University Statistical Consultant and Associate Professor*

Computer Installation
IBM 360/50–operating system: OS; internal storage: 2,097,152 bits; magnetic tapes: 4 2401; magnetic discs: 4 2314; 2 line printers. *On-line satellite computer*: IBM 360/20. *Remote processing features*: 12 2741 terminals.
IBM 7040–operating system: IBSYS: internal storage: 1,179,648 bits; magnetic tapes: 3 729, 4 7330; 1 line printer.

Coding Languages
FORTRAN, COBOL, PL/1, GPSS, Assembly, BASIC, MAP, MAD, ALGOL.

Contemplated Equipment
Additional core for 360/50.

Services Available
Advice, software packages. Operate on a closed shop, self-service and time-sharing basis.

Fields of Application
Scientific research, education in computer science and programming, statistical computation.

Training
Computer science programme leading to M.S. in Computer Science.

UNIVERSITY OF ARKANSAS AT LITTLE ROCK
33rd and University Avenue, Little Rock, 72204
Telephone: (501) 565-7531

Computer Installation
IBM 1130–operating system: DOS; internal storage: 262,144 bits; magnetic discs: 3 2310; 1 line printer.

Coding Languages
FORTRAN, COBOL, APL, RPG, BNL, Assembler.

Services Available
Advice, programming, education and training, operators, software packages, documentation, preparation of data, systems analysis. Operate on a closed shop and block time basis.

Fields of Application
Scientific, statistical, accounting, management, systems analysis.
Specialized area: Linear programming.

Training
All courses designed to assist students in their major area.

CALIFORNIA

CALIFORNIA STATE UNIVERSITY, FULLERTON*
800 North State College Boulevard, Fullerton, 92631
Telephone: (714) 870-2625

Officer
E. Dippel, *Director of Computer Center*

Computer Installation
CDC 3150–operating system: MSOS; internal storage: 384K bits; magnetic tapes: 2; magnetic discs: 2; 1 line printer.

Coding Languages
COMPASS, COBOL, FORTRAN, ALGOL.

Services Available
Consultation, programming, education and training, operators, software packages, documentation, preparation of data, systems analysis. Operate on an open shop basis. Available only to College staff and students.

Fields of Application
Scientific, statistical, management, operational research, student records.

CALIFORNIA STATE UNIVERSITY, LONG BEACH*
6101 East Seventh Street, Long Beach, 90801
Telephone: (213) 433-0951

Officer
Dr. R. T. Littrell, *Director*

Computer Installation
Remote job entry terminals to Univac 1108 and CDC 3300.

Coding Languages
ALGOL, COBOL, FORTRAN, Symbolic Assembly.

Services Available
Education and training. Operate on a closed shop basis. Available only to students and faculty of college.

Fields of Application
Scientific, statistical, accounting, management, operational research.

Training
B.S. course in Operations Research and Statistics.

CALIFORNIA STATE UNIVERSITY, NORTHRIDGE
18111 Nordhoff, Northridge, 91324
Telephone: (213) 885-2787

Officers
Jerry Boles, *Director*
Wes Hampton, *Data Processing Manager*
Jeff Craig, *Operations Supervisor*
Russ Sprouse, *Academic Applications*

Computer Installation
CDC 3170–operating system: MASTER/ITS; internal storage: 2,752,512 bits; magnetic tapes: 4 CDC 604; magnetic discs: 4 CDC 841; 1 line printer.
CDC 3170–operating system: MASTER/ITS; internal storage: 2,359,296 bits; magnetic discs: 3 CDC 841; 1 line printer.

Coding Languages
COMPASS, COBOL, FORTRAN IV, ALGOL.

Services Available
Advice, programming, education and training, operators, software packages, documentation, preparation of data, systems analysis. Operate on a closed shop basis. Available only to faculty and students of the California State University and College System.

Fields of Application
Scientific, statistical, commercial, systems analysis, instructional.
Specialized area: Computer-aided instruction.

Training
B.S. degree course in Computer Science. Courses in most disciplines.

CLAREMONT COLLEGES
Institute for Educational Computing
McConnell Center, Claremont, 91711

Officer
William Koteff, *Acting Director*

Computer Installation
PDP-10–operating system: TOPS 10; internal storage:
2,880K bits; magnetic tapes: 2 9-track; magnetic discs:
2 RPO2; 1 line printer. *Remote processing features*:
40 remote time-sharing terminals.

Coding Languages
BASIC, ALGOL, FORTRAN, COBOL, APL, SNOBOL,
LISP, POP-2.

Services Available
Advice, programming, education and training, preparation
of data. Operate on a remote access basis. Services are
available to non-profit, educational users only.

Field of Application
Education.

Training
Basic introductory courses for undergraduates.

FOOTHILL COMMUNITY COLLEGE DISTRICT*
12345 El Monte, Los Altos Hills, 94022
Telephone: (415) 948-8590

Officer
R. B. Henderson Jr., *Data Processing Manager*

Computer Installation
IBM 360/40–operating system: DOS; internal storage:
128K bytes; magnetic discs: 1 2314; 2 line printers.

Coding Languages
COBOL, Assembler, FORTRAN, RPG, PL/1.

Services Available
Computer operation. Operate on a block time basis.
Available to local non-profit organizations only.

Fields of Application
Statistical, accounting, management, student
processing.

Training
Three general courses, eight programming courses, one
systems analysis course.

FULLERTON JUNIOR COLLEGE
321 East Chapman Avenue, Fullerton, 92632
Telephone: (714) 871-8000

Officer
Hal Beddows, *Co-ordinator of Data Processing*

Computer Installation
IBM 1130–internal storage: 8K bits; magnetic discs: 2;
1 line printer.

Coding Languages
ALC, COBOL, FORTRAN IV, RPG.

Contemplated Equipment
Possibly IBM 360/30.

Services Available
Advice, operators, preparation of data, programming.
Operate on a self-service and block time basis.

Fields of Application
Statistical, commercial, research, education.

Training
Survey of data processing; introduction to data processing;
beginning computer programming; COBOL programming;
computer programming project; data processing systems;
keypunch training, FORTRAN for business programming.

LOYOLA MARYMOUNT UNIVERSITY
Computer Science Center
7101 West 80th Street, Los Angeles, 90045
Telephone: (213) 776-0403

Officers
Rev. D. P. Merrifield, *President*
E. H. Spitz, *Director, Data Processing*

Computer Installation
IBM 360/22–operating system: DOS; internal storage:
262,136 bits; magnetic tapes: 2 2415; magnetic discs:
2 2311; 1 line printer.
DATA GENERAL Nova 1200–internal storage: 131,072
bits; magnetic discs: 2 DFABLO; 1 line printer. *Remote
processing features*: 4 time sharing terminals.

Coding Languages
FORTRAN, BASIC, ALGOL, COBOL, RPG, PL/I,
Assembler.

Contemplated Equipment
A larger IBM 360 computer.

Services Available
Programming, education and training, software packages,
data preparation, systems analysis. Operate on a self-
service, open shop and time-sharing basis.

Fields of Application
Accounting, management, operational research, instruction.
Specialized areas: Education.

Training
Courses in programming, systems analysis and computer
circuit design. Options in computer science available
from Engineering, Mathematics and Business Schools.

MONTEREY PENINSULA COLLEGE
980 Fremont, Monterey, 93940
Telephone: (408) 375-9821

Officer
Philip Nash, *Associate Dean of Instruction*

Computer Installation
IBM 1620–internal storage: 20K.
BURROUGHS B1726–magnetic disc; 1 line printer.

Coding Languages
FORTRAN, COBOL, Autocoder, RPG, BASIC.

Services Available
Operate on a self-service basis.

Fields of Application
Educational data processing and research.

Training
Courses in business data processing and computer science.

United States of America – Universities and Colleges

OCCIDENTAL COLLEGE
1600 Campus Road, Los Angeles, 90041
Telephone: (213) 255-5151, extension 280

Officer
Ronald J. Bennett, *Supervisor, Data Processing*

Computer Installation
IBM 1401–internal storage: 8K bits; magnetic tapes: 2 7330; magnetic discs: 3 1311; 1 line printer.

Coding Languages
COBOL, Autocoder.

Contemplated Equipment
Burroughs B1726.

Services Available
Advice, programming, software packages. Operate on an open shop basis. Available to non-profit organizations only.

Fields of Application
Accounting, management, administrative.

PACIFIC UNION COLLEGE
Angwin, 94508
Telephone: (707) 965-7278

Officers
Eugene H. Lambert, *Director of Data Services*
V. K. Juler, *Assistant Director*

Computer Installation
IBM 1401–internal storage: 8K bits; magnetic discs: 3 1311; 1 line printer.
HEWLETT PACKARD 2000–operating system: DOS; internal storage: 16K bits; magnetic discs: 2. *Remote processing features*: 7 TTY terminals.

Coding Languages
Autocoder, COBOL, BASIC, FORTRAN II.

Contemplated Equipment
Two 1311 disc drives.

Services Available
Advice, programming, operators, preparation of data. Operate on a closed shop basis.

Fields of Application
Commercial, accounting, management.
Specialized areas: Payroll, administrative accounting.

Training
Courses in data processing techniques, IBM key punch and computer programming (FORTRAN II, COBOL and BASIC).

POMONA COLLEGE
Computer Center
6th and College, Claremont, 91711
Telephone: (714) 626-8511, extension 3312

Officers
F. W. Weingarten, George H. Clark, *Directors*

Computer Installations
IBM 360/40–operating system: DOS; internal storage: 1,024K bits; magnetic tapes: 4; magnetic discs: 4 2311; 1 line printer.

Coding Languages
COBOL, FORTRAN, PL/1.

Services Available
Consultation, programming, education and training, operators, software packages, documentation, systems analysis, preparation of data. Operate on a closed shop and block time basis (1130 self-service). Available only to faculty, students and staff.

Fields of Application
Scientific research, education, administration.

Training
Non-credit courses in FORTRAN, COBOL, PL/1.
Credited courses in APL.

RIVERSIDE CITY COLLEGE*
3650 Fairfax Avenue, Riverside, 92506
Telephone: (714) 684-3240

Officer
John M. Matulich, *Dean of Admissions*

Computer Installation
IBM 1620–operating system: Disk; internal storage: 20K bits; magnetic discs: 3 1311; 1 line printer.

Coding Languages
SPS, FORTRAN.

Contemplated Equipment
Management Information System through a multi-programming teleprocessing computer system.

Services Available
Programming, education and training, operators, documentation, preparation of data, systems analysis. Operate on a self-service and block time basis.

Fields of Application
Commercial as related to educational institution, accounting, systems analysis, programming.

Training
Courses leading to an A.A. degree in data processing, data processing operations, computer concepts, electromechanical machines, language programming (Assembler, FORTRAN, COBOL, PL/1, RPG), data processing systems, internship in data processing, problems in data processing,

SAN MATEO JUNIOR COLLEGE DISTRICT
1700 West Hillsdale Boulevard, San Mateo, 94402
Telephone: 341-6161, extension 505

Also at:
2040 Pioneer Court, San Mateo, California 94402

Officers
Ronald B. Smith, *Manager of Data Processing Services*
Thomas W. George, *Chairman, Business Division*

Computer Installation
HONEYWELL H200–operating system: MOD I; internal storage: 20K bits; magnetic tapes: 5 204B; 1 line printer.

Coding Languages
COBOL, Easycoder, FORTRAN.

Services Available
Education and training. Operate on a block time basis. Available only for use of District, students and faculty.

Fields of Application
Statistical, administrative educational services.

United States of America – Universities and Colleges

Training
Introductory courses in data processing, punch card equipment operation and wiring; basic and advanced programming courses in RPG, COBOL, PL/1; courses in basic and advanced System 360 ALP; data processing for managers; key punch instruction.

SANTA ANA COLLEGE
17th and Bristol Streets, Santa Ana, 92706
Telephone: (714) 547-9566

Officer
Jack Breglio, *Director of Computer Center*

Computer Installation
BURROUGHS B3500–operating system: M.C.P.; internal storage: 180K bytes; magnetic tapes: 6; magnetic discs; 1 line printer. *On-line satellite computers*: On-line admin. system. *Remote processing features*: 3 CRT, Multiple Teletype.

Coding Languages
COBOL, FORTRAN, BASIC, Advanced Assembler.

Contemplated Equipment
Disc, CRTs, PDP-8.

Services Available
Education and training, software packages, documentation. Operate on a self service, open shop and time-sharing basis.

Field of Application
Educational.

Training
Introductory course to data processing and courses in FORTRAN, BASIC and COBOL programming leading to C.A or A.A. degree.

STANFORD UNIVERSITY
Computation Center
Stanford, 94305
Telephone: (415) 321-2300, extension 3082

Officers
C. R. Dickens, *Director*
T. D. Phillips, *Deputy Director*

Computer Installation
IBM 360/50–operating system: OS; internal storage: 128K bytes; magnetic tapes: 1; magnetic discs: 16; 1 line printer. *On-line satellite computer*: IBM 1800. *Remote processing features*: 53 2741 terminals, cathode ray tube displays.
IBM 360/67–operating system: OS; internal storage: 1,000K bytes; magnetic tapes: 4; magnetic discs: 24; 3 line printers. *Remote processing features*: 143 2741 terminals, card readers.
IBM 360/91–operating system: OS; internal storage: 2,000K bytes; magnetic tapes: 10; magnetic discs: 29; 3 line printers. *On-line satellite computer*: IBM 1800. *Remote processing features*: Typewriter terminals, Cathode ray tube displays.

Coding Languages
All OS/360 languages, SIMSCRIPT II, ACME PL.

Contemplated Equipment
2 IBM 370/165; 1 IBM 370/168; 1 IBM 370/158.

Services Available
Advice, programming, education and training, operators, software packages, documentation. Operate on a self-service, remote access, open shop and time-sharing basis. Educational and research applications only.

Fields of Application
Scientific, statistical, management, systems analysis, educational.
Specialized area: Medical research.

Training
Courses leading to M.A. and Ph.D. degrees in Computer Science; also short courses.

UNIVERSITY OF CALIFORNIA, BERKELEY*
Computer Center
Berkeley, 94720
Telephone: 642-2521

Officer
K. J. Hebert, *Acting Director*

Computer Installation
CDC 6400–operating system: SCOPE; internal storage: 65K 60-bit words; magnetic tapes: 5 604; magnetic discs: 1 6638; 3 line printers. *On-line satellite computer*: PDP-8. *Remote processing features*: TTY 33,35,37.
CDC 6400–operating system: CAL Time sharing system; internal storage: 32K 60-bit words; magnetic tapes: 1 604; magnetic discs: 1 6638; 1 line printer. *Remote processing features*: TTY 33, 35, 37.
IBM 360/40–operating system: OS; internal storage: 256K bytes; magnetic tapes: 4 2403; magnetic discs: 1 2314; 1 line printer.

Coding Languages
ALGOL 60, FORTRAN, COMPASS, SNOBOL, ARIEL.

Contemplated Equipment
Additional remote stations for present system and a new computing system capable of providing greater capacity for interactive and real time computing services.

Services Available
Advice, operators, preparation of data, programming, systems analysis. Operate on a closed shop, open shop, remote access and time-sharing basis.

Fields of Application
Research in computer systems, numerical analysis and language translation.

UNIVERSITY OF CALIFORNIA, BERKELEY
Information Systems Division
Office of the Vice-President for Administration,
417 University Hall, Berkeley, 94720
Telephone: (415) 642-7515

Officers
Dr. George Turner, *Director, Information Systems Division*
W. R. Kilcourse, *Associate Director*

Computer Installation
Berkeley:
IBM 360/65–operating system: OS MFT with HASP; internal storage: 12,582,912 bits; magnetic tapes: 8 2401/2; magnetic discs: 16 2314; 2 line printers. *Remote processing features*: 360/30 connected via HASP on 50KB telephone line to Los Angeles.

Los Angeles:
IBM 360/40–operating system: OS/PCP; internal storage: 1,572,864 bits; magnetic tapes: 4 2401/2; magnetic discs: 8 2314; 1 line printer.
IBM 360/30–magnetic tapes: 4; 1 line printer.

Coding Languages
PL/1, Assembler, COBOL, FORTRAN.

Services Available
Advice, programming, education and training, operators, software packages, documentation, preparation of data, systems analysis. Operate on a remote access, closed and open shop basis. In general, instruction and research computing is not handled.

Fields of Application
Statistical, commercial, accounting, management. *Specialized area*: Payroll.

Training
In-house training usually related to hardware or software being used. Training for outside customers in applications systems developed by the University, or software packages developed or acquired by the University.

Computer Installation
PDP-10–operating system: TOPS-10; internal storage: 4,032K bits; magnetic tapes: 4 7-track; magnetic discs: 3 2314; 2 line printers. *On-line satellite computer*: PDP-10 CPU. *Remote processing feature*: terminal service.
XDS Sigma 7–operating system: UTS; internal storage: 2,460K bits; magnetic tapes: 2 9-track; magnetic discs: 5; 1 line printer. *Remote processing feature*: terminal service.

Coding Languages
Assembly, BASIC, FORTRAN IV, COBOL, APL, LISP, LOGO, SNOBOL, ALGOL.

Services Available
Advice. Operate on a remote access and open shop basis with time sharing terminals on premises. Primary service commitment to University of California users. Services also available to other educational institutions and some public agencies.

Fields of Application
Scientific, statistical, instructional.
Specialized area: Computer graphics.

Training
The Department of Information and Computer Science grants a B.Sc. and a Ph.D. degree.

UNIVERSITY OF CALIFORNIA, DAVIS
Computer Center
Davis, 95616
Telephone: (916) 752-0233

Officers
Dr. D. R. Ojakangas, *Director*
J. B. Burdette, *Chief Programmer*
N. R. Smith, *Operations Supervisor*

Computer Installations
BURROUGHS B6700–operating system: MCP; internal storage: 132K 52-bit words; magnetic tapes: 5; magnetic discs; 2 line printers. *Remote processing features*: teletype network, remote batch.

Coding Languages
ALGOL, COBOL, FORTRAN, PL/1.

Services Available
Consultation, education and training, operators, software packages, preparation of data, systems analysis. Operate on a closed shop, block time and time-sharing basis. Generally restricted to staff and students of the University of California.

Training
Courses on computer applications in the following fields: mathematics (3 courses), engineering (2 courses), sociology (1 course), human physiology (1 course), medical education (1 course). Short courses in FORTRAN IV, ALGOL II, TAPE I/O.

UNIVERSITY OF CALIFORNIA, IRVINE
Irvine, 92664
Telephone: (714) 833-7303

Officers
D. G. Aldrich, *Chancellor*
J. Feldman, *Assistant Chancellor for Computing*

UNIVERSITY OF CALIFORNIA, LOS ANGELES (UCLA)
Campus Computing Network
Math-Science Addition, 405 Hilgard Avenue, Los Angeles, 90024

Officers
W. Kehl, *Director*
R. Bell, *User Relations*

Computer Installation
IBM 360/91–operating system: OS; internal storage: 4 million bytes; magnetic tapes: 4 2401, 4 3420; magnetic discs: 5 2314; 4 line printers. *Remote processing features*: RJS, IBM 2922, ARPA.

Coding Languages
Assembler, FORTRAN, PL/1, ANS, COBOL, SNOBOL, ALGOL, PL/C, SIMSCRIPT, SPASM.

Services Available
Consultation, programming, software packages, documentation, preparation of data. Operate on a self-service, remote access and closed shop basis. Service restricted to accredited universities and research institutions.

Training
Scientific, statistical.

UNIVERSITY OF CALIFORNIA, RIVERSIDE
Computing Center
P.O. Box 112, Riverside, 92502

Officer
James C. Henshaw, *Computing Center Director*

Computer Installation
IBM 360/50–operating systems: OS, DOS; internal storage: 3,145,728 bits; magnetic tapes: 3 2401; magnetic discs: 6 2311; 1 line printer. *Remote processing features*: Serves 10 2741, 2 1050, 1 1070, 1 Data 100.

Coding Languages
FORTRAN IV, PL/1, COBOL, APL, RPG, ATS, Assembly.

United States of America – Universities and Colleges

Services Available
Keypunching, programming and computer usage, all on a limited basis. Operate on a closed shop and time-sharing basis.

Fields of Application
All fields of university disciplines.
Specialized areas: User dependent fields of interest in instruction, research and administration.

Training
Formal courses in computer methodology, programming and applications.

UNIVERSITY OF CALIFORNIA, SAN DIEGO
Computer Center
La Jolla, 92037
Telephone: (714) 453-2000

Officer
Edward H. Coughran, *Director*

Computer Installations
CDC 3600–operating systems: PRESTO, SCOPE; internal storage: 32K 48-bit words; magnetic tapes: 14 607; magnetic discs: 3 854; 1 line printer. *On-line satellite computer:* CDC 1704. *Remote processing features:* RJE.
BURROUGHS B6700–operating system: MCP; internal storage: 246K 48-bit words; magnetic tapes: 4 B9394/1, 6 B9394/2; magnetic discs; 2 line printers. *Remote processing features:* RJE, interactive graphics.

Coding Languages
FORTRAN, ALGOL, COBOL, PL/1, BASIC APL, POL, SNOBOL, LISP, SIMULA, DYNAMO.

Services Available
Consultation, programming, operators, preparation of data, systems analysis. Operate on remote access and closed shop basis.

Fields of Application
All fields of university disciplines, research, educational and administrative.

UNIVERSITY OF CALIFORNIA, SAN FRANCISCO MEDICAL CENTER
Office of Information Systems – Computer Center
Room 76U, 3rd and Parnassus Avenues, San Francisco, 94122
Telephone: (415) 666-2012

Officers
John A. Starkweather, *Director*
Joseph B. Yeaton, *Assistant Director*
David R. Gomberg, *Manager of User Services*

Computer Installation
IBM 360/50–operating system: MVT/HASP 2; internal storage: 10 million bits; magnetic tapes: 2 2400 9-track, 1 7-track; magnetic discs: 2314; 1 line printer. *Remote processing features:* RJE from multiple 2780, 2741/2702 support for CPS, ATS and PILOT.

Coding Languages
PL/1, FORTRAN, COBOL, ALGOL, RPG, BASIC.

Services Available
Advice, preparation of data, programming, software packages, systems analysis, statistical consulting. Operate on an open shop, time-sharing and remote access basis. Services restricted to non-profit making, educational, medical or government users.

Fields of Application
Scientific, statistical, hospital accounting systems.
Specialized area: PILOT (Programmed inquiry, Learning or Teaching) – a conversational language for natural language handling.

Training
Occasional programming courses.

UNIVERSITY OF CALIFORNIA, SANTA BARBARA
Computer Centre
North Hall 1214, Santa Barbara, 93106
Telephone: 961-2261

Officers
C. R. Loepkey, *Director*
W. Holsten, *Assistant Director*

Computer Installations
IBM 360/75–operating system: OS (MVT); internal storage: 20,576K bits; magnetic tapes: 2 2415, 4 2405; magnetic discs: 2314, 4 2311; 2 line printers. *On-line satellite computer:* Honeywell RP 61R. *Remote processing features:* UCSB (Culler Fried Time Sharing System).
IBM 360/20–internal storage: 64K bits; magnetic tapes: 2 2415; 1 line printer.

Coding Languages
FORTRAN, PL/1, BAL, RPG, SNOBOL, COBOL, ALGOL.

Services Available
Consultation, programming, education and training, operators, software packages, documentation, preparation of data, systems analysis. Operate on a remote access, block time, closed shop and time-sharing basis. Available only to students, faculty and staff.

Fields of Application
Scientific, statistical, accounting, management, systems analysis, operational research.

UNIVERSITY OF CALIFORNIA, SANTA CRUZ
Computer Center
Santa Cruz, 95060

Officer
H. D. Huskey, *Director*

Computer Installations
IBM 360/40–operating system: MFT/HASP; internal storage: 1 million bits; magnetic tapes: 3; magnetic discs: 4 2311, 1 Calcomp; 1 line printer.
PDP-11/45 with 30 CRT and TTY terminals; interfaced to 360/40 via a PDP-11/20.
Varian 620/I.

Coding Languages
FORTRAN, PL/1, ALGOL, COBOL, SPL, XPL, BASIC.

Contemplated Equipment
PDP-8/L with 5-teletype system.

Services Available
Consultation, education and training, operators, software packages. Operate on remote access, open and closed shop and time-sharing basis. Available only to academic institutions.

Fields of Application
Scientific, educational.

Training
Upper and lower division and graduate courses in cybernetics; short courses in programming languages.

United States of America – Universities and Colleges

UNIVERSITY OF REDLANDS
Educational Data Processing Center
1200 East Colton Avenue, Redlands, 92373
Telephone: (714) 793-2121

Officers
Dr. Robert D. Engel, *Director*
Thomas J. Stokes, *Manager*

Computer Installation
IBM 1130–operating system: DMV2; internal storage: 256K bits; magnetic tapes: 4 9-track; magnetic discs: 1 2310; 1 line printer.
HEWLETT PACKARD 2000B–operating system: Timeshare; internal storage: 256K plus 128K bits; magnetic tapes: 1 9-track; magnetic discs: 1. *On-line satellite computers*: 10 terminals.

Coding Languages
FORTRAN, COBOL, RPG, Assembler, BASIC.

Contemplated Equipment
Hewlett Packard 3000.

Services Available
Advice, programming, education and training, software packages, documentation, preparation of data, systems analysis. Operate on an open shop basis. Priority given to students and faculty.

Fields of Application
Scientific, commercial, accounting, management, systems analysis.

Training
Degree course in Computer Science.

UNIVERSITY OF SANTA CLARA
Santa Clara, 95053
Telephone: (408) 984-4242

Officer
John H. Hosemann, *Director of Computer Service*

Computer Installation
IBM 360/25–internal storage: 32K bytes; magnetic discs: 3 2319.
IBM 1130–internal storage: 16K bytes; magnetic discs: 2 2301.

Coding Languages
FORTRAN, COBOL.

Services Available
Advice, programming, education and training, preparation of data, systems analysis. Operate on a self-service, open shop basis (1130) and closed shop basis (360) with time-sharing terminals on premises.

Fields of Application
Scientific, statistical, accounting, management, systems analysis, operational research.

WEST COAST SCHOOLS
Computer Center
451 South Hill Street, Los Angeles, 90013

Officer
James Sanchez, *School Director*

Computer Installation
IBM 360/22–operating system: DOS; internal storage: 32K bits; magnetic tapes: 2 2415; magnetic discs: 2 2311; 1 line printer.
IBM System/3–operating system: OCL; internal storage: 16K bits; magnetic discs: 2 5444; 1 line printer.

Coding Languages
RPG, RPG II, COBOL, FORTRAN, PL/1, ALC.

Contemplated Equipment
IBM 370/125.

Services Available
Education and training, computer time. Operate on a self-service, remote access and closed shop basis.

Fields of Application
Commercial.

Training
Courses in keypunch operation, computer operation and computer programming fundamentals.

WEST COAST UNIVERSITY
440 Shatto Place, Los Angeles, 90020
Telephone: (213) 487-4433

Officers
Dr. Victor Elcouin, *President*
Fred Mintz, *Vice President*

Computer Installation
IBM 1130/2B–operating system: Disc Monitor V2 M11; internal storage: 131,072 bits; magnetic discs: 1 2516; 1 line printer.
EAI TR 20.

Coding Languages
FORTRAN, COBOL, RPG, APL, Assembly.

Contemplated Equipment
IBM 360/30.

Services Available
Education and training. Operate on a self-service basis. Available to students and employees of the University; other non-profit universities at a nominal fee.

Fields of Application
Scientific, statistical, commercial, accounting, operational research.
Specialized areas: Linear programming, structural engineering.

Training
B.S. and M.S. in Computer Science.

COLORADO

ADAMS STATE COLLEGE
Alamosa, 81101
Telephone: 589-7541

Officer
D. G. Perko, *Director of Computer Center*

Computer Installation
IBM 360/30–operating system: DOS; internal storage: 32K bits; magnetic tapes: 2 units; magnetic discs: 2 2311; 1 line printer.

Coding Languages
COBOL, FORTRAN, RPG, PL/1, Assembly.

Services Available
Programming, education and training, preparation of data, systems analysis. Operate on an open shop basis. Available only for state-supported activities.

Fields of Application
Accounting, scientific and statistical support.

Training
Support courses for all academic fields; short courses in FORTRAN, numerical analysis, digital computers.

COLORADO STATE UNIVERSITY
University Computer Center
E-12 Engineering Building, Fort Collins, 80521
Telephone: (303) 491-5136

Officers
Dr. B. Marschner, *Director*
Dr. G. R. Johnson, *Associate Director*

Computer Installation
CDC 6400–operating system: SCOPE; internal storage: 4; magnetic tapes: 5; magnetic discs: 6603; 2 line printers. *Remote processing features*: 2 user remote CDC 200.

Coding Languages
FORTRAN, COBOL, ALGOL, SIMSCRIPT, SIMULA, MIMIC, BASIC, COMPASS.

Contemplated Equipment
Additional remote processing facilities; disc; extended core storage.

Services Available
Consultation, programming, education and training, operators, software packages, documentation, preparation of data, systems analysis. Operate on a remote access and closed shop basis.

Fields of Application
Scientific, statistical, commercial, production control, accounting, management, systems analysis, operational research.
Specialized areas: Numerical weather forecasting, simulation, artificial intelligence, advanced ADP techniques, numerical analysis.

Training
Master's and Doctor's degree in computer science. Short courses in FORTRAN, numerical analysis, SCOPE, computer modelling and simulation.

TRINIDAD STATE JUNIOR COLLEGE
Trinidad, 81082
Telephone: 846-5660

Officers
Dr. Thomas Sullivan, *President*
Mr. Melvin Langshaw, *Director of Computer Center*

Computer Installation
IBM 1401–internal storage: 8K bits; magnetic discs: 1 1311; 1 line printer.
IBM 1620–internal storage: 32K bits.
The College is also linked by CDC User 200 terminal to a CDC 6400.

Coding Languages
SPS, Autocoder, FORTRAN, COBOL, BAL, ALGOL.

Contemplated Equipment
IBM System/3.

Services Available
Programming, education and training, operators. Operate on a self-service, remote access, and open shop basis. Available to state institutions only.

Fields of Application
Accounting, education.

Training
Courses to prepare students as Unit Record and Computer Programmers and Supervisors.

UNIVERSITY OF COLORADO
University Computing Center
Boulder, 80302
Telephone: (303) 443-2211, extension 8031

Officer
Dr. E. R. Krueger, *Director*

Computer Installation
CDC 6400 (2)–operating system: KRONOS; internal storage: 64K bits each; magnetic tapes: 8 607; magnetic discs: 2 6603; 2 line printers. *On-line satellite computers*: 1700/274 digigraphics, 280 film processor. *Remote processing features*: 2 8231, 6 User 200 terminals.

Coding Languages
FORTRAN, COMPASS, Assembler, WISP, SNOBOL, SIMSCRIPT, FORWARD 2.0 MATRIX, ECAP, SORT-MERGE, BMD, COBOL, ALGOL, MIMIC.

Services Available
Advice, operators, preparation of data, programming, software packages, systems analysis, documentation. Operate on a closed shop and time sharing basis.

Fields of Application
General scientific.

Training
Periodic short courses given in FORTRAN and COBOL.

UNIVERSITY OF DENVER
Computer Center,
University Park, Denver, 80210
Telephone: 753-2787

Officer
W. H. Eichelberger, *Director*

Computer Installation
BURROUGHS B6700–operating system: MCP; internal storage: 6,288K bits; magnetic tapes: 4 9-track; magnetic discs: 2; 1 line printer. *Remote processing features*: CRT, RJE, teletypes.

Coding Languages
ALGOL, COBOL, FORTRAN IV, BASIC, PL/1.

Services Available
Advice, operators, programming, software packages. Operate on a closed shop, remote access and time-sharing basis.

Fields of Application
Physical sciences research, instruction, data processing.

United States of America – Universities and Colleges

Training
Introductory courses in digital computers and digital computer technology, and non-credit programming courses in ALGOL.

UNIVERSITY OF NORTHERN COLORADO*
Carter Hall, Greeley, 80631
Telephone: (303) 351-2336

Officer
D. L. Myers, *Director*

Computer Installation
IBM 360/30–operating system: DOS; internal storage: 32K bits; magnetic tapes: 2 2402, 2 2404; magnetic discs: 2 2311; 1 line printer.

Coding Languages
COBOL, FORTRAN, RPG, Assembler.

Contemplated Equipment
Additional 32K core storage, 3 2314.

Services Available
Education and training. Operate on an open shop basis. Available only to faculty and students, area High Schools.

Fields of Application
Statistical, accounting, some scientific and operational research.
Specialized area: Academic administration.

CONNECTICUT

CENTRAL CONNECTICUT STATE COLLEGE*
1615 Stanley Street, New Britain, 06050
Telephone: 225-7481, extensions 211, 212

Officer
M. J. Jannace, *Director*

Computer Installation
IBM 360/25–DOS; internal storage: 32,768 bytes; magnetic discs: 2 2311; 1 line printer.

Coding Languages
FORTRAN, COBOL, Assembler.

Services Available
Consultation, programming, education and training, operators, software packages, documentation, preparation of data, systems analysis. Operate on a closed shop basis. Available only to college departments and students.

Fields of Application
Education, college administration.

Training
Introduction to Computers; courses in FORTRAN and COBOL.

FAIRFIELD UNIVERSITY
Computer Center
North Benson Road, Fairfield, 06430
Telephone: 255-1011, extension 381

Officer
Dr. J. J. Schurdak, *Director*

Computer Installations
IBM 1500–internal storage: 64K bytes; magnetic discs: 4 2310; 1 line printer. *Remote processing features*: 16 1510 CRTs; 9 2741 terminals.
IBM 360/50–operating system: DOS; internal storage: 256K bytes; magnetic tapes: 4 2415; magnetic discs: 2314; 1 line printer. *Remote processing features*: 14 2741 terminals.

Coding Languages
APL, Coursewriter, FORTRAN, COBOL.

Services Available
Consultation, programming, education and training, systems analysis. Operate on a remote access, block time and time-sharing basis.

Fields of Application
Educational, university administration, elementary and secondary school administration, municipal administration. *Specialized areas*: Computer assisted instruction, computer aided mathematics.

Training
Five courses; 2 short courses.

UNIVERSITY OF CONNECTICUT
University Computer Center
Storrs, 06268
Telephone: (203) 429-3311

Officer
John L. C. Löf, *Director and Professor of Electrical Engineering*

Computer Installation
IBM 360/65–operating systems: OS (MVT), HASP, CPS; internal storage: 6,291,456 bits plus 8,388,608 bits; magnetic tapes: 4 3420; magnetic discs: 12 2314; 2 line printers. *Remote processing features*: 35 2741 and 8 2260 terminals using CPS and RJE, 2 2780, 1 2770 and 1 1130 using RJE.
IBM 1620–operating system: MONITOR I; internal storage: 240,000 bits; magnetic discs: IBM 1311.

Coding Languages
FORTRAN, PL/1, COBOL, Assembler, FORGO, SPS.

Contemplated Equipment
Additional memory, disc storage, communication terminals and CPU to provide dual system.

Services Available
Advice, operators, systems analysis. Operate on a self-service, closed shop (360) and open shop (1620) basis. Time-sharing terminals on premises. Available to limited number of staff and students from neighbouring educational institutions, and occasional research work by a few industries in Connecticut.

Fields of Application
Scientific computation and list processing procedures are carried out for all academic fields of the University and a few external researchers.

Training
Graduate and undergraduate courses related to digital and analog computers are taught by twenty-four departments of the University. Workshops are conducted by the University Computer Center to train the University staff.

United States of America – Universities and Colleges

WESLEYAN UNIVERSITY*
Computer Laboratory
High Street, Middletown, 06457
Telephone: 347-4421, extension 511

Officer
James M. McFarlane, *Manager*

Computer Installation
IBM 1130–operating system: DM 2; internal storage: 262K bits; magnetic discs: 2 2315; 1 line printer.
IBM 1620–internal storage: 40K bits.

Coding Languages
FORTRAN IV, APL, RPG.

Services Available
Programming, education and training. Operate on open shop and time-sharing basis. Available only to students, faculty, administration.

Fields of Application
Scientific research (faculty) and education.

YALE UNIVERSITY*
Computer Center
175 Whitney Avenue, New Haven, 06520
Telephone: (203) 787-3131

Officer
Robert M. Woodruff, *Director*

Computer Installation
IBM 7094/7044 direct coupled system–operating system: IBSYS; internal storage: 2,560K bits; magnetic tapes: 8 729; magnetic disc: 1301; 2 line printers.

IBM 360/50–operating system: CYTOS; internal storage: 1.5 million bits; magnetic tapes: 8 2402; magnetic discs: 2 2314; 2 line printers. *On-line satellite computer*: IBM 1130. *Remote processing features*: 2741, TTY 35, 2260.
IBM 1401–internal storage: 4K bits; magnetic tapes: 2.

Coding Languages
FORTRAN, MAP, FAP, MAD, MADTRAN, UMAP, ALGOL, SNOBOL, IPL-V, LISP, SLIP, SIMSCRIPT, GPSS, Autocoder.

Contemplated Equipment
IBM 360/50 with 512K-bit store; various remote devices.

Services Available
Advice, operators, software packages and some systems analysis. Operate on an open shop and remote access basis.

Fields of Application
All areas of numerical analysis, statistical programming and construction of languages.
Specialized areas: Photocomposition of printed texts.

Training
A number of courses are given in several departments in programming, numerical analysis and the hardware of computers.

DELAWARE

UNIVERSITY OF DELAWARE*
Newark, 19711
Telephone: 738-2000

Computer Installation
IBM 1620–internal storage: 40K bits; magnetic discs: 2 1311.
SDS 9300–internal storage: 32K bits; magnetic tapes: 4 SDS 7-track; magnetic discs: 2; 1 line printer.
IBM 1401–internal storage: 12K bits; magnetic tapes: 4 729; 1 line printer.

Coding Languages
FORTRAN, METASYMBOL, Autocoder, SPS, COBOL.

Contemplated Equipment
Connection to PACE analog computer for process control simulation; additional medium-priced digital computer with four or more magnetic tapes; time-sharing facilities are in planning stage.

Services Available
Advice, operators, programming and software packages. Operate on a closed and open shop basis.

DISTRICT OF COLUMBIA

AMERICAN UNIVERSITY*
Computation Center
209 McKinley Building, Washington, 20016
Telephone: (202) 244-6800, extensions 470 and 350

Officer
James Mark III

Computer Installation
IBM 1130–internal storage: 32K bits; 1 magnetic disc: 1 line printer.

Services Available
Consultation, programming, education and training, operators, software packages, systems analysis. Operate on a block time basis. Service available to American university professors and students primarily for academic and research purposes.

Fields of Application
Scientific, statistical, accounting.

Training
Short courses in FORTRAN IV; seminars on new equipment.

CATHOLIC UNIVERSITY OF AMERICA*
Computer Center
620 Michigan Avenue, N.E., Washington, 20017
Telephone: (202) 529-6000, extension 661

Officers
Dr. Andrew G. Favret, *Director*
Kevin B. Casey, *Assistant Director*

Computer Installation
IBM 1620–operating system: Card; internal storage: 20K words.

PDP-10–operating system: 4S72 Swapping Monitor; internal storage: 4,800 36-bit words; magnetic tapes: 2 7-channel, 8 Dectapes; magnetic discs: 12; 1 line printer.

Computer Installation
IBM 1620–operating system: Card; internal storage: 20K words.

United States of America — Universities and Colleges

PDP-10—operating system: 4S72 Swapping Monitor; internal storage: 4,800 36-bit words; magnetic tapes: 2 7-channel, 8 Dectapes; magnetic discs: 12; 1 line printer.

Coding Languages
Assembly, BASIC, AID, COBOL, SNOBOL, ALGOL, FORTRAN, SPS.

Contemplated Equipment
Remote batch station.

Services Available
Programming, systems analysis, software packages. Operate on a closed shop and time-sharing basis.

Fields of Application
Numerical analysis, statistics, general mathematical methods, operating systems.

Training
Courses in computer science. Short courses in many aspects of computer usage.

GALLAUDET COLLEGE*
7th Street and Florida Avenue, N.E., Washington, 20002
Telephone: (202) 386-6551

Officers
Jerald M. Jordan, *Director, Computer Center*
Robert J. Herbold, *Assistant Director*

Computer Installation
IBM 360/30—internal storage: 64K; magnetic tapes: 2 2415; magnetic discs: 3 2311; 1 line printer. *Remote processing features*: 5 2740.

Coding Languages
PL/1, BAL, FORTRAN, COBOL, Coursewriter, BASIC.

Services Available
Limited to area of information on deafness. Operate on an open shop basis with remote access.

Fields of Application
Research on deafness and related subjects, training of deaf programmers, computer assisted instruction.

Training
Courses in the language and structure of computers, FORTRAN, COBOL, and problem solving.

GEORGE WASHINGTON UNIVERSITY
2013 G Street, N.W., Washington, 20006
Telephone: (202) 676-6140

Officer
Raymond E. Thomas, *Director*

Computer Installation
IBM 370/145—operating system: OS/VS1; internal storage: 2.7 million bits; magnetic tapes: 4 2400; magnetic discs: 4 3330; 1 line printer. *Remote processing features*: 2 video displays.

Coding Languages
FORTRAN, PL/1, Assembler, COBOL, SNOBOL, ALGOL.

Services Available
Consultation, operators, programming, software packages, systems analysis, education and training, documentation, education in conjunction with University sponsored courses. Operate on self-service basis. Available to University affiliated students, faculty, staff and sponsored projects which are education-related.

Fields of Application
Scientific, social sciences, systems analysis, theses, dissertations and faculty research.

Training
Ten courses in computer programming, 20 courses in pure computer training, 10 courses in applied computer training.

GEORGETOWN UNIVERSITY
Academic Computation Center
37th and O Streets, N.W., Washington, 20007
Telephone: (202) 625-4338

Officer
Dr. Herbert Maisel, *Director*

Computer Installation
IBM 360/40—operating system: OS/PCP; internal storage: 1,048K bits; magnetic tapes: 3 2400; magnetic discs: 5 2314; 1 line printer.

Coding Languages
FORTRAN, PL/1, COBOL, GPSS, ALGOL, Assembly.

Contemplated Equipment
IBM 370/135 with IBM 3330 disc drives and 1,820K bits of main storage.

Services Available
Advice, programming, education and training, operators, software packages, documentation, preparation of data, systems analysis. Operate on a closed shop and block time basis. Available to the university community only.

Fields of Application
Scientific, statistical, commercial, management, systems analysis, operational research, student training.

Training
Computer Science courses run by the Department of Mathematics are offered as part of a Master's level programme, in Applied Mathematics.

FLORIDA

CHIPOLA JUNIOR COLLEGE*
College Street, Marianna, 32446
Telephone: (904) 482-4935

Officer
J. A. Lewis

Computer Installation
IBM 1130—operating system: 1130; internal storage: 8,192 16-bit words; magnetic discs: 2315.

Services Available
Education and training. Operate on an open shop basis. In-house service only.

Fields of Application
Accounting, educational.

United States of America — Universities and Colleges

FLORIDA STATE UNIVERSITY
Computing Center
Tallahassee, 32306
Telephone: (904) 599-4770

Officers
Dr. J. H. Poore, Jr., *Director*
H. C. Huff, *Manager of User Services*
P. Spivey, *Manager of Systems Programming*
A. B. Williams, *Manager of Operations*
D. McEwen, *Manager of Applications Programming*

Computer Installation
CDC 6500—operating system: KRONOS; internal storage: 7,864,320 bits; magnetic tapes: 6 604; magnetic discs: 1 6638, 1 841/8; 2 line printers. *On-line satellite computers*: CDC 200-user terminals. *Remote processing features*: 92 remote terminals.
IBM 1401—internal storage: 48K bits; magnetic tapes: 4 7330; 1 line printer.

Coding Languages
FORTRAN, COBOL, COMPASS, MARS VI, SIMSCRIPT, PERT-TIME, SNOBOL, MIX, LISP, BALM, PASCAL, BASIC.

Contemplated Equipment
CDC 844 disc system; teletypes.

Services Available
Advice, programming. Operate on a remote access, closed shop and time sharing basis. Services available to university and other state agencies only.

Fields of Application
Scientific, statistical, data base management.

Training
Courses in FORTRAN, COBOL, BASIC and COMPASS. Computer Science courses in operating systems, data structures, compilers and information systems.

NORTHEAST REGIONAL DATA CENTER
233 Space Sciences Research Building, University of Florida, Gainesville, 32601
Telephone: (904) 392-2061

Officers
Dr. C. V. Shaffer, *Director*
R. H. Schoenau, *Associate Director*
Dr. J. B. Conklin, Jr., *Associate Director*

Computer Installation
IBM 370/165—operating system: OS/MVT; internal storage: 2 million bytes; magnetic tapes: 5 3420; magnetic discs: 6 3330, 1 2311; 2 line printers. *Remote processing features*: 130 2741, RJE, 5 interactive services.
IBM 1401—internal storage: 8K characters; magnetic tapes: 4 7330; 1 line printer.

Coding Languages
FORTRAN, COBOL, APL, SNOBOL, Assembler, PL/1, BASIC, ALGOL.

Services Available
Advice, programming, education and training, software packages, documentation, data preparation, systems analysis. Operate on a self-service, remote access and time sharing basis. Services are restricted to education and research, except that administrative computing services are provided to the Universities of Florida and North Florida.

Fields of Application
Scientific, statistical, accounting, management, systems analysis, operational research.
Specialized area: Medical research.

UNIVERSITY OF MIAMI
Computing Center
Box 8011, Coral Gables, 33124
Telephone: (305) 284-3961

Officer
R. T. Huxtable, *Director of Computer Services*

Computer Installation
UNIVAC 1106—operating system: EXEC 8; internal storage: 9,432K bits; magnetic tapes: 8; magnetic discs: 14 8414; 2 line printers. *On-line satellite computers*: PDP-11, IBM 1130, Data 100-78s. *Remote processing features*: 35 conversational terminals, 6 VDUs.

Coding Languages
FORTRAN, COBOL, BASIC, APL, Assembler.

Contemplated Equipment
Univac communications/symbiont processor.

Services Available
Advice, programming, education and training, operators, software packages, documentation, data preparation, systems analysis, time sharing. Operate on a remote access, open shop and time-sharing basis.

Fields of Application
Scientific, statistical, accounting, management, systems analysis.
Specialized areas: Analysis, medical research, oceanographic research.

Training
Training in Computer Sciences available through Academic Departments. The Center offers various seminars.

UNIVERSITY OF SOUTH FLORIDA
4202 Fowler Avenue, Tampa, 33620
Telephone: (813) 974-2930

Officer
Dr. William Miller, *Acting Director of Computer Research Center*

Computer Installation
IBM 360/65—operating systems: OS, DOS; internal storage: 264,144 bytes; magnetic tapes: 4 2401, 2 2415; magnetic discs: 1 2314; 1 line printer. *Remote processing features*: 7 2740 terminals.
IBM 1410—operating system: DOS; internal storage: 80K bits; magnetic tapes: 6 729; magnetic discs: 1 1301; 1 line printer.

Coding Languages
FORTRAN, COBOL, PL/1, ALGOL, Autocoder.

Services Available
Consultation, programming, education and training, operators, software packages, documentation, preparation of data, systems analysis. Operate on a closed shop and time-sharing basis. Available only to administration, faculty and students.

Fields of Application
Scientific, statistical, accounting, systems analysis, management.
Specialized areas: Simulation, student records, teaching, mathematical.

Training
Several introductory courses.

UNIVERSITY OF TAMPA*
401 West Kennedy Boulevard, Tampa, 33606
Telephone: 253-8861

Officer
Joseph H. Diaz, *Director of Computer Centre*

Computer Installation
IBM 1401—internal storage: 8K bits; 1 line printer.

Coding Language
Autocoder.

GEORGIA

EMORY UNIVERSITY
Computing Center
Uppergate House, Atlanta, 30322
Telephone: (404) 377-2411, extension 7751

Officers
Dr. W. B. Evans, *Director*
B. A. Blumenstein, *Coordinator of Digital Computing*
F. Schmidt, *Manager, Special Data Acquisition*

Computer Installation
UNIVAC 70/7—operating system: UMOS; internal storage: 40 million bits; magnetic tapes: 8; magnetic discs: 13; 2 line printers.
RCA Spectra 70/46—operating systems: TDOS, UMOS; internal storage: 20 million bits; tapes, discs and line printers shared with 70/7 above. *On-line satellite computers*: Univac 70/1600, PDP-8, GT40. *Remote processing features*: 70 interactive, 2 remote batch.
DIGITAL EQUIPMENT GT40—operating system: DOS; internal storage: 128K bits; magnetic discs: 1.

Coding Languages
BASIC, FORTRAN, COBOL, SNOBOL, Assembly.

Contemplated Equipment
Increased store, another magnetic drum, more communications lines.

Services Available
Advice, programming, education and training, operators, software packages, documentation, data preparation, systems analysis, statistical consulting. Operate on a self-service, remote access, block time and time-sharing basis.

Fields of Application
Scientific, statistical, commercial, management, systems analysis.
Specialized areas: Medical research, on-line information systems.

GEORGIA INSTITUTE OF TECHNOLOGY
School of Information and Computer Science
225 North Avenue, N.W., Atlanta, 30332
Telephone: (404) 894-3152

Officer
Dr. Vladimir Slamecka, *Professor and Director*

Computer Installations
BURROUGHS B5500—operating systems: time-sharing, Master Control Program; internal storage: 8 x 4,096 48 bits; magnetic tapes: 10; magnetic discs: 3; 2 line printers.
Remote processing features: 13 data communication telephone adaptors for Model 33 and 35 Teletype Terminals.
PDP-8/L—operating system: PS-8 OS; internal storage: 8,192 12-bit words; magnetic tapes: 2 Dectape; magnetic discs: 2 RPO8; 1 line printer. *Remote processing features*: 2 PTO8 teletype data lines.
PDP-11/45—internal storage: 4K 16-bit words. *Remote processing features*: direct memory access channels, teletypewriter control console, two DC11-DA full duplex interface module sets.

Coding Languages
ALGOL, FORTRAN, COBOL, BASIC, APL, GTL, Assembly.

Services Available
Education and training, systems analysis. Operate on a closed shop (B5500) open shop (PDP-8, PDP-11) and time-sharing basis. Available only to the School of Information and Computer Science.

Fields of Application
Scientific, systems analysis, operational research, instruction.
Specialized areas: Medical research, information and computer science research.

Training
B.S., M.S., Ph.D. degree courses in information, computer and systems sciences.

GEORGIA STATE UNIVERSITY*
Computer Center
33 Gilmer Street, Atlanta, 30303
Telephone: 658-2639

Officers
William H. Wells, *Director, Computer Center*
Monroe Jones, *Manager Data Processing*

Computer Installation
IBM 7094—internal storage: 32K bits; magnetic tapes: 14; magnetic discs.
RCA Spectra 70/46.

Coding Languages
FORTRAN, COBOL, ALGOL, MAP, BASIC.

Services Available
Available to business outside the college.

Training
Introductory course in computer science and data processing, and courses in programming languages and advanced programming. Master of Business Information Systems degree.

UNIVERSITY OF GEORGIA*
Athens, 30601
Telephone: 542-3030

Officer
James L. Carmon, *Director*

Computer Installation
IBM 360/65.

IBM 7094 – internal storage: 32K bits; magnetic tapes: 12 729/V.

IBM 1401 (2) – internal storage: 8K bits and 16K bits; magnetic tapes: 2 729/V, 4 7330.

IBM 1620 – internal storage: 60K bits.

Coding Languages
FORTRAN, COBOL, MAP, Autocoder, FORGO.

Contemplated Equipment
CDC 6400.

Services Available
The IBM 7094 is available for commercial use (advice, operators, preparation of data, programming).

Fields of Application
General statistical data processing, system design, numerical analysis, operating systems design.
Specialized areas: Multiple regression and analysis of varians of data with disproportionate subclass numbers; stochastic modelling and simulation.

Training
Degree programme leading to a M.S. in Computer Sciences.

HAWAII

UNIVERSITY OF HAWAII
Computing Center
2525 Correa Road, Honolulu, 96822
Telephone: (808) 948-7351

Officers
Walter S. Yee, *Director*
Albert M. Higashi, *Assistant Director*

Computer Installation
IBM 360/65 – operating system: OS/MVT; internal storage: 20,971,520 bits; magnetic tapes: 2 7-track, 5 9-track (IBM 2400); magnetic discs: 24 2314; 2 line printers.
On-line satellite computers: 5 IBM 1130, 1 Westinghouse 2550.

Coding Languages
FORTRAN, PL/1, COBOL, ALGOL, SNOBOL, WATFIV, etc.

Contemplated Equipment
IBM 370/168.

Services Available
Advice, programming, education and training, operators, software packages, documentation, preparation of data, systems analysis. Operate on a self-service, remote access, block time, closed and open shop, and time-sharing basis.

Fields of Application
Scientific, statistical, commercial, production control, accounting, management, systems analysis, operational research.
Specialized areas: Sales analysis, linear programming, investment, analysis, payroll, structural engineering, medical research.

Training
M.S. course in Information Science.

IDAHO

IDAHO STATE UNIVERSITY*
Pocatello, 83201
Telephone: (208) 236-0211

Officers
Dr. H. Fechter, *Director*
D. Brick, *Training of Scientific Personnel*
S. Frazier, *Training of Scientific Personnel*

Computer Installation
IBM 360/20 – magnetic tapes: 4.
IBM 1130.
IBM 1620.

Coding Languages
FORTRAN, SPS, M.L.

Services Available
Some outside work is done.

Fields of Application
Chemistry, physics, sociology, education, industry.
Specialized areas: Data processing of high energy physics, space reconstructions, kinematics, phase spaces.

Training
FORTRAN, SPS, M.L. courses.

UNIVERSITY OF IDAHO*
Moscow, 83843
Telephone: 208-3511, extension 6721

Officer
W. Crowley, *Director, Computer Services*

Computer Installations
IBM 360/40 – operating system: DOS; internal storage: 1,048,576 bits; magnetic tapes: 2 2415; magnetic discs: 2 2314; 1 line printer.

IBM 360/40 – internal storage: 106,608 bits; 1 line printer.

Coding Languages
FORTRAN, PL/1, COBOL, RPG.

Contemplated Equipment
IBM 360/50.

Services Available
Consultation, programming, education and training. Operate on a closed shop basis. Available only to university researchers and classes, Federal and State agencies, public education.

Fields of Application
Scientific, statistical, management, accounting, systems analysis.

Training
Various computer science courses at present available; courses leading to Master's degrees in Computer Science and Applied Statistics are planned.

United States of America – Universities and Colleges

ILLINOIS

BRADLEY UNIVERSITY
Computer Center
Peoria, 61606
Telephone: 676-7611

Officer
Marian Frobish, *Manager*

Computer Installation
IBM 370/135–operating system: DOS; internal storage: 144K bits; magnetic tapes: 1 3410, 1 3411; magnetic discs: 4 2314; 1 line printer.

Coding Languages
FORTRAN, COBOL, PL/1, Assembly.

Services Available
Advice, programming, preparation of data. Operate on a closed shop basis.

Fields of Application
Statistical, scientific, operational research.

Training
Bachelor and Master's degree courses in Computer Science.

CHICAGO STATE COLLEGE*
95th Street at King Drive, Chicago, 60621
Telephone: (312) 995-2517

Officer
H. Hook, *Director of Computer Services*

Computer Installation
IBM 360/40–operating system: DOS; internal storage: 128K bytes; magnetic tapes: 2415; magnetic discs: 2314; 1 line printer.

Coding Languages
FORTRAN, COBOL, RPG, APL, PL/1, Assembler.

Contemplated Equipment
IBM 2260 CRTs for teleprocessing.

Services Available
Consultation, programming, education and training, operators, documentation, preparation of data, systems analysis. Operate on a self-service and closed shop basis. Available only for college staff, students and administration.

Fields of Application
Statistical, scientific, accounting, systems analysis, management.

Training
Courses in computing, computers and programming.

CONCORDIA TEACHERS COLLEGE
7400 Augusta Street, River Forest, 60305
Telephone: (312) 771-8300

Computer Installation
UNIVAC 70/2–operating system: DOS TDOS; internal storage: 262K bits; magnetic tapes; magnetic discs; 1 line printer. *Remote processing features*: 1 TTY.

Coding Languages
Assembly, COBOL, FORTRAN, RPG, IITRAN.

Services Available
Advice, programming, operators, software packages, preparation of data, systems analysis. Operate on a closed shop basis.

Fields of Application
Scientific, statistical, commercial, accounting, management, research.
Specialized areas: Payroll, education, research.

EASTERN ILLINOIS STATE UNIVERSITY
Charleston, 61920
Telephone: (217) 581-3227

Officers
Dr. Gilbert Fite, *President*
Dr. Roland Spaniol, *Director of Computer Services*

Computer Installation
IBM 360/50–operating system: OS/MFT with HASP; internal storage: 256K bits; magnetic tapes: 2 2401/1; magnetic discs: 2 2314; 1 line printer. *Remote processing features*: 15 IBM 3277 VDTs, 8 IBM 1030, Data Collection.

Coding Languages
PL/1, COBOL, FORTRAN, RPG, BAL, ALGOL, SNOBOL, SIMSCRIPT, WATFIV.

Contemplated Equipment
4 IBM 3277 VDTs, 1 IBM 2401 Tape Drive, 1 IBM 2702 Control Unit, 4 IBM 2741 Communication Terminals.

Services Available
Advice, programming, education and training, operators, software packages, documentation, preparation of data, systems analysis. Operate on a closed shop basis. Available only through established university functions and offices.

Fields of Application
Scientific, statistical, commercial, accounting, management.
Specialized areas: Student record systems, library circulation systems.

Training
Major in automated information systems for business data processing.

ILLINOIS STATE UNIVERSITY
Eastgate Hall, Normal, 61761
Telephone: (309) 438–3611

Officer
T. A. Brigham, *Director*

Computer Installations
IBM 360/50–operating system: OS/MVT; internal storage: 512K bytes; magnetic tapes: 4 Telex 4862; magnetic discs: 8 Memorex 3660; 2 line printers.

Coding Languages
COBOL, RPG, FORTRAN, PL/1, WATFIV, ALGOL.

Services Available
Programming, education and training, operators, software packages, documentation, preparation of data, systems analysis.

Fields of Application
Scientific, statistical, commercial, systems analysis, operational research, accounting.

United States of America – Universities and Colleges

Training
Courses covering computer applications offered by various Departments of the university; several short courses such as operating system overview. Keypunch training and fundamentals of programming.

NORTHERN ILLINOIS UNIVERSITY
Computer Services Department
Altgeld Hall 223, DeKalb, 60115

Computer Installation
IBM 360/67–operating system: OS, MVT, HASP; internal storage: 1.5 million bits; magnetic tapes: 4 IBM 3420; magnetic discs: 18 IBM 2319; 2 line printers. *Remote processing features*: 3 RJE stations, EBCDIC terminals, teletypes.

IBM 360/20–internal storage: 8K bits; magnetic tapes: 2 2415; 1 line printer. *Remote processing features*: DATA 100, REMCOM 4780.

Contemplated Equipment
Teleprocessing Control Unit; additional disc storage; faster core.

Services Available
Advice, programming, education and training, operators, software packages, documentation, preparation of data, systems analysis. Operate on a closed shop basis.

Fields of Application
Scientific, statistical, accounting, management, operational research.
Specialized area: Linear programming.

NORTHWESTERN UNIVERSITY
Vogelback Computing Center
Evanston, 60201
Telephone: (312) 492-3682

Officer
B. Mittman, *Director*

Computer Installation
CDC 6400–operating system: Scope 3.3; internal storage: 65,536 plus 250K 60-bit words; magnetic tapes: 4 607; magnetic discs: 1 6603, 2 844-2; 3 line printers. *Remote processing features*: 4 CDC 200 user terminals; 40 teletype terminals.

Coding Languages
FORTRAN, ALGOL, COBOL, SIMSCRIPT, etc.

Services Available
Advice, operators, software packages. Operate on a closed shop and remote access basis.

Fields of Application
General applied programming and University service research computations.
Specialized areas: Information retrieval, computer graphics, statistical packages for social sciences.

ROOSEVELT UNIVERSITY
430 South Michigan Avenue, Chicago, 60605
Telephone: 341-3500

Officer
Theodore J. Mlsna

Computer Installation
IBM 1401–internal storage: 8K bits. *On-line satellite computer*: IBM 1401. *Remote processing features*: 2 terminals to a Bull General Electric GE 235, 1 Honeywell 1642, 2 terminals to an IBM 360/40.

Coding Languages
SPS, Autocoder, FORTRAN, COBOL, BASIC, BAL.

Services Available
Education and training, operators, documentation, preparation of data, systems analysis. Operate on a self-service, remote access, block time, open shop basis.

Fields of Application
Statistical, commercial, accounting, management, systems analysis.

Training
Courses in computer technology, including B.G.S. degree in Computer Sciences. Short courses in IBM data processing machines, computer concepts and programming.

SOUTHERN ILLINOIS UNIVERSITY, CARBONDALE
Information Processing Department
Carbondale, 62901
Telephone: (618) 453-4361

Officers
Thomas D. Purcell, *Director*
B. D. Cross, *Director of Management Systems*
George A. Flummer, *Assistant Director*

Computer Installation
IBM 370/155–operating system: OS/MVT with HASP; internal storage: 768K bits; magnetic tapes: 5 3420; magnetic discs: 2 3330; 2 line printers. *On-line satellite computer*: IBM 1130. *Remote processing features*: 2741 magnetic card typewriter.

IBM 1130–internal storage: 16K bits; 1 line printer.

Coding Languages
FORTRAN, ALGOL, COBOL, PL/1, SNOBOL 3, GPSS, BAL.

Contemplated Equipment
IBM 370/158.

Services Available
Operate on a closed shop and time-sharing basis. Priority given to University business, faculty and students.

Fields of Application
Administrative, research, instruction.

Training
Courses leading to an M.S. degree in Applied Science with a major in information processing.

UNIVERSITY OF CHICAGO*
Computation Center
5640 South Ellis Avenue, Chicago, 60637
Telephone: (312) 667-4700, extension 8400

Officer
F. H. Harris, *Director*

Computer Installations
IBM 360/65—operating system: OS MVT with ASP; internal storage: 512K plus 1,024K bytes; magnetic tapes: 5 2401; magnetic discs: 2 2314; 3 line printers.

IBM 7094—operating systems: FMS, IBSYS; internal storage: 32K 36-bit words; magnetic tapes: 729/V 12 729/VI; 1 line printer.

Coding Languages
FORTRAN, WATFOR, COBOL, PL/1, ALGOL, SNOBOL, LISP, SIMSCRIPT, Assembler.

Contemplated Equipment
IBM 370/165.

Services Available
Consultation, programming, education and training, operators, software packages, documentation, preparation of data, systems analysis. Operate on a remote access, closed shop and time-sharing basis. Priority given to academic research; some outside users.

Fields of Application
Academic research, university administration, on-line applications for hospital and library.

Training
Master's and Doctor's degree courses in Information Sciences; short courses in practical aspects of computing.

UNIVERSITY OF CHICAGO
Institute for Computer Research
5640 South Ellis Avenue, Chicago, 60637
Telephone: (312) 753-8764

Computer Installation
DEC-11/45—operating systems: DOS, BOSOM; internal storage: 1,048,576 bits; magnetic tapes: 2 TU10/9; magnetic discs: 4 RKO5; 1 line printer. *On-line satellite computer*: NOVA 820. *Remote processing features*: facilities for connection to remote minicomputers.

MANIAC III (built at University of Chicago)—operating system: DCP/JOBCOP; internal storage: 786,500 bits; magnetic discs: 2 IBM 1301; 1 line printer. *On-line satellite computers*: PDP-8, EAI-680 Analog Computer.

Services Available
Operate on an open shop basis. Available to members of the University of Chicago and to those affiliated to it.

Fields of Application
Scientific, experimentation.

Training
The Committee on Information Sciences sponsors S.M. and Ph.D. degrees.

WESTERN ILLINOIS UNIVERSITY
Computer Center
Macomb, 61455
Telephone: (309) 295-6444

Officers
Christian L. Brix, *Director*
Tate F. Lindahl, *Assistant to Director*

Computer Installation
IBM 360/50—operating system: DOS; internal storage: 256K bytes; magnetic tapes: 2 2415 MI; magnetic discs: 4 2314; 2 line printers.

Coding Languages
ANS COBOL, BAL, FORTRAN IV, RPG.

Services Available
Advice, education and training, operators, software packages. Operate on a closed shop and block time basis. Available to staff, students and ADM users.

Fields of Application
Scientific, statistical, commercial, management, systems analysis.
Specialized areas: Linear programming, analysis, payroll.

Training
B.B.A. course in Information Science; courses in languages, systems analysis, programming, numerical analysis, operational research.

INDIANA

ANDERSON COLLEGE
Anderson, 46011
Telephone: (317) 644-0951

Officer
T. R. Harbron, *Director of the Computing Center*

Computer Installation
HEWLETT PACKARD 3000—operating system: MPE; internal storage: 1 million bits; magnetic tapes: 1 9-track; magnetic discs: 1; 1 line printer. *Remote processing features*: 16 terminals.

Coding Languages
FORTRAN, BASIC, COBOL, SPL.

Services Available
Advice, programming, education and training, operators, software packages, documentation, data preparation, systems analysis. Operate on a self-service, remote access, closed and open shop, block time and time-sharing basis.

Fields of Application
Scientific, statistical, commercial, accounting, systems analysis, instructional.
Specialized areas: Linear programming, analysis, payroll.

Training
Courses in elementary computing, programme structures, information structures, machine structures, systems analysis, quantitive business methods, numerical analysis. Majors are offered in Computer Science, Business, and Computer Science, and Mathematics. A minor is offered in Computer Science.

BALL STATE UNIVERSITY*
Muncie, 47306
Telephone: (317) 285-7411

Officer
Dr. Hubert Austin, *Director*

Computer Installation
IBM 360/40—operating systems: DOS, OS; internal storage: 192K bytes; magnetic tapes: 2 2415; magnetic discs 2314; 2 line printers. *Remote processing features*: 2701.

IBM 360/20—operating system: card system; internal storage: 8K bytes; 1 line printer.

Coding Languages
COBOL, FORTRAN IV, PL/1, Assembler.

Contemplated Equipment
IBM 360/50 with 256K-bit storage.

Services Available
Education and training. Operate on a closed shop and block time basis. Service available mainly within the University at the discretion of the Director.

Fields of Application
Scientific, statistical, commercial, accounting, systems analysis.

Training
A Computer Science major is available from the Math Sciences Department at undergraduate and master's level.

INDIANA INSTITUTE OF TECHNOLOGY*
1600 Washington Boulevard, Fort Wayne, 46803
Telephone: (219) 422-5561

Officer
Professor Charles R. Carr, *Director*

Computer Installation
IBM 1130—magnetic disc: 1; 1 line printer.

Coding Language
FORTRAN.

Services Available
Available to outside customers as time permits.

Fields of Application
Education in engineering and scientific areas. Some research in scientific areas.
Specialized area: Numerical analysis.

Training
Introductory courses in programming and data processing.

INDIANA UNIVERSITY*
Research Computing Center
Bloomington, 47401
Telephone: (812) 337-191, 337-9143

Officers
Dr. Dale J. Hall, *Director*
Stephen W. Young, *Operating Systems Manager*

Computer Installation
CDC 6600—internal storage: 98K 60-bit words; magnetic tapes: magnetic disc: 1; 2 line printers. *Remote processing features*: typewriter via IBM 1050s, teletype to Honeywell H200, IBM 1130 and Univac 9200. CDC 3400.

Coding Languages
FORTRAN, COMPASS, ALGOL, COBOL, SIMSCRIPT, SNOBOL, OPTIMA.

Service Available
Operators. Operate on a closed shop basis. Available for non-continuing work at commercial rates. Service is subject to approval by the Policy Committee. Limited personnel services — programming and consulting.

Fields of Application
Analysis and programming in all fields of interest to the University. Simulation, physical chemistry, high energy physics, statistical analysis, selective dissemination of information.

Training
Courses in the theory and application of digital computers and a survey of electronic data processing.

PURDUE UNIVERSITY*
Computer Sciences Center
Engineering Adm. Building, West Lafayette, 47907
Telephone: (317) 749-8111

Officers
Dr. S. D. Conte, *Director*
J. Steele, *Associate Director*

Computer Installation
CDC 6500—operating system: SCOPE; internal storage: 65K 60-bit words; magnetic tapes: 4; magnetic discs: 2 6638; 3 line printers. *On-line satellite computers*: IBM 360/20. *Remote processing features*: 4 mod. 20s.

IBM 7094—operating system: IBSYS-13; internal storage: 32K 36-bit words; magnetic tapes: 8; magnetic discs: 1302; 2 line printers. *On-line satellite computer*: IBM 1401.

Coding Languages
FORTRAN, MAP, COBOL, ALGOL, SNOBOL, SLIP.

Services Available
Advice, operators, software packages and systems analysis. Operate on a closed shop, remote access and time-sharing basis. Available on a limited basis for research.

Fields of Application
General numerical analysis, compiler writing, time-sharing. *Specialized areas*: Scheduling and inventory, linear programming, space trajectory computations, automatic numerical analysis.

Training
Introductory course in computers and courses in advanced programming systems and commercial data processing.

ROSE-HULMAN INSTITUTE OF TECHNOLOGY*
5500 Wabash Avenue, Terre Haute, 47803
Telephone: Crawford 0271

Officer
Dr. D. E. Criss, *Administrative Director of Computing Center*

Computer Installation
IBM 1130—operating system: MONITOR; internal storage: 131,072 bits; magnetic disc: 2310; 1 line printer.

CDC G15—operating system: INTERCOM; internal storage: 60,900 bits.

Coding Languages
Floating Point Interpretive Routines, ALGOL, FORTRAN, Assembler.

Services Available
Operate on a closed and open shop basis. Available only on a staff consulting basis.

Fields of Application
Scientific and engineering computations, educational work in computing, administrative information processing. *Specialized areas*: System analysis and simulation in chemical and electrical engineering.

Training
Elective courses in computer methods of computation and computer technology; B.S. degree in Computer Science.

UNIVERSITY OF NOTRE DAME*
Computing Center
Notre Dame, 46556
Telephone: 284-6547

Officers
Dr. Don Mittleman, *Director and Professor of Computing Science*
Dr. Henry C. Thacher, Jr., *Professor of Computing Science*

Computer Installation
UNIVAC 1107—operating system: EXEC 2; internal storage: 2,359,296 bits; magnetic tapes: 8 Uniservo IIA; magnetic drum: 1 FH880; 1 line printer. *Remote processing features*: 3 remote terminals.

Coding Languages
SLEUTH II, FORTRAN IV, COBOL, ALGOL.

Contemplated Equipment
Additional remote stations and I/O devices of experimental design.

Services Available
Advice, operators and programming. Operate on a closed shop and remote access basis. Available on a limited scale to other universities, research organizations and industrial organizations.

Fields of Application
Analysis and programming of research problems in science, engineering, and data processing.

Training
Introductory courses in computers and programming, FORTRAN and COBOL programming; other courses in advanced computer programming, computer organization and programming, computers and computability, algorithmic languages and compilers, semantic theory of programming languages, syntactic theory of programming languages, design of computer and programming systems, design of multi-programming and multi-processor systems, current advances in computing science. Also an undergraduate seminar in computing science, special studies in computing science and special topics in computing science.

IOWA

COE COLLEGE*
Computer Center
Cedar Rapids, 52402
Telephone: (319) 364-1511, extension 313

Officer
C. R. Nicolaysen, *Director, Computer Center*

Computer Installation
IBM 1130—operating system: DOS/OS; internal storage 132,136 bits; magnetic discs: 2315; 1 line printer.

Coding Language
FORTRAN IV, Assembler.

Services Available
Consultation, programming, education and training, operators, software packages, documentation, preparation of data. Operate on a self-service, block time, closed and open shop basis. Available only to students, faculty and staff.

Fields of Application
Scientific, statistical, commercial, accounting, educational, records control.

Training
Introductory course in computers.

CORNELL COLLEGE
Mount Vernon, 52314
Telephone: (319) 895-8811

Officer
Samuel Enoch Stumpf, *President*

Computer Installation
IBM 1130—internal storage: 131,072 bits; magnetic discs: 1 2315; 1 line printer.

Coding Languages
FORTRAN, APL, Assembler, RPG.

Services Available
Available on an open shop basis to the college's students and faculty only.

Fields of Application
Scientific, statistical, accounting, management.
Specialized area: Payroll.

Training
Basic instruction in computing systems and computer programming.

EASTERN IOWA COMMUNITY COLLEGE*
601 West 2nd Street, Davenport, 52801
Telephone: (319) 326-4401

Officers
L. E. Stone, *Program Chairman*
D. Smith, *Deputy Head*

Computer Installation
IBM 360/30—operating system: DOS; internal storage: 256K bits; magnetic tapes: 2 2415; magnetic discs: 3 2311; 1 line printer.

Coding Languages
RPG, Basic Assembler, COBOL, FORTRAN IV.

Services Available
Education and training.

Training
Two-year Associate in Applied Science degree programme, comprising 19 courses. Short evening courses in FORTRA COBOL, key punch; Assembler and small business accounting.

IOWA STATE UNIVERSITY OF SCIENCE AND TECHNOLOGY
Computation Center
Ames, 50010
Telephone: (515) 294-3402

Officers
Dr. Clair G. Maple, *Professor of Computer Science; Chief, Mathematics and Computer Science Division*
Dr. Robert M. Stewart, *Professor of Physics, Professor of Computer Science*
Professor C. C. Mosier, *Assoc. Professor of Computer Science; Head, Admin. Data Systems*.

Computer Installation
IBM 360/65–operating system: OS; internal storage: 2 million bytes; magnetic tapes: 8 2402; magnetic disc: 2 2314; 2 line printers.

IBM 370/145.
IBM 1401.
SDS 910 (2).
ASI 6050.
PDP-11/20 (6).
PDP-15 (3).
PDP-12 (2).
PDP-8 (2).

Coding Languages
FORTRAN IV, COBOL, PL/1, ALGOL.

Services Available
Advice, operators, preparation of data, software packages. Operate on a closed shop basis.

Fields of Application
All fields of university research, education and administration. Numerical analysis, statistical analysis, systems programming, control systems.

Training
Computer science curriculum leading towards B.S., M.S. and Ph.D. in Computer Science.

MARYCREST COLLEGE*
1607 West 12th Street, Davenport, 52804
Telephone: (319) 326-9512

Officers
Marie Ven Horst
Phyllis Stanger

Coding Languages
FORTRAN IV, COBOL, SNOBOL.

Services Available
Education and training. Operate on a remote access basis.

Fields of Application
Educational, statistical.

Training
Courses in FORTRAN IV programming.

MORNINGSIDE COLLEGE
Jacobsen Computer Centre
1501 Morningside Avenue, Sioux City, 51106
Telephone: (712) 277-5153/4

Officer
J. C. McDonald, *Director*

Computer Installation
IBM 1130–operating system: DOS; internal storage: 8K bits; magnetic discs: IBM 2315, Memorex 3610/5; 1 line printer.

Coding Languages
FORTRAN, RPG, Assembler, APL, COBOL, SL/1.

Contemplated Equipment
Remote terminals.

Services Available
Education and training. Operate on a self-service, block time and open shop basis. Available only to educational institutions.

Fields of Application
Scientific, statistical.

Training
Courses in computer programming, computer workshop, and an introductory course in data processing.

PARSONS COLLEGE*
Fairfield, 52556
Telephone: (515) 699-8512

Officers
Dr. Carl W. Kreisler, *President*
Larry G. Nixon, *Director of Data Processing*

Computer Installation
IBM 1460–internal storage: 12K bits; magnetic discs: 3 1311; 1 line printer.

Coding Languages
Autocoder.

Services Available
Advice, preparation of data, programming. Operate on a closed shop basis. All classes of customers on a limited basis.

Fields of Application
Student data, accounting, payroll, institutional research. *Specialized areas*: Manufacturing, sales analysis.

Training
Short introductory course to data processing in manufacturing.

UNIVERSITY OF IOWA
Computer Center
Lindquist Building, Iowa City, 52240
Telephone: (319) 353-3170

Officers
G. P. Weeg, *Director*
J. Esbin, *Operations Manager*
P. Trotter, *Non-University Applications*
J. Inghram, *Head, Special Services*

Computer Installation
IBM 360/65–operating system: OS/MVT; internal storage: 6,144K plus 8,192K bits; magnetic tapes: 5 2400; magnetic discs: 2 2314; 2 line printers. *On-line satellite computers*: 2 1130, 360/20. *Remote processing features*: total of 15 batch terminals.

Coding Languages
BAL, FORTRAN, COBOL, PL/1, ALGOL, GPSS, SIMSCRIPT, BASIC, WATFOR, PL/C, Assembler.

Contemplated Equipment
IBM 370/168 and several Hewlett Packard 2000Fs.

Services Available
Consultation, programming, education and training. Operate on a remote access, closed shop and time-sharing basis.

Fields of Application
Scientific, statistical, commerce, research.

Training
Master's and Doctor's degrees in Computer Science; many other courses in computer science; 10 short courses.

KANSAS

KANSAS STATE COLLEGE OF PITTSBURG*
1700 South Broadway, Pittsburg, 66762
Telephone: 231-7000

Officer
W. A. Gray, *Director, Data Processing Center*

Computer Installation
IBM 1401–internal storage: 16K bits; magnetic discs: 2 1311; 1 line printer.

Coding Languages
Autocoder, FORTRAN IV, COBOL.

Services Available
Advice, systems analysis. Available only to educational establishments.

Training
B.S. course in Business Administration with a major in Data Processing and 3-week courses for teachers.

KANSAS STATE UNIVERSITY OF AGRICULTURE AND APPLIED SCIENCE
Computing Center
Cardwell Hall, Manhattan, 66506
Telephone: (913) 532-6311

Officers
T. L. Gallagher, *Director*
Elizabeth A. Unger, *Associate Director*
M. H. Miller, *Assistant Director*

Computer Installation
IBM 360/50–operating systems: OS, HASP; internal storage: 128K plus 1 million bytes; magnetic tapes: 1 7-track, 1 9-track; magnetic discs: 9 2314; 2 line printers. *Remote processing features*: 12 2741, 3780, 2780, 2770.

Coding Languages
FORTRAN IV, Assembler, COBOL, PL/1.

Contemplated Equipment
IBM 370/158.

Services Available
Keypunching and verifying, programming, consulting, library of software and documentation, tape and disc pack rental, sale and storage, non-credit seminars on software and languages. Operate on a closed shop and time-sharing basis. Services restricted to university community.

Fields of Application
Computer course instruction, faculty and graduate research involving scientific and statistical applications.

Training
Non-credit seminars for all users; courses from Department of Computer Science leading to B.S., B.A., M.S. and Ph.D. in Computer Science; courses in specialized areas of computing offered by various departments including mathematics, education, agriculture, chemistry and industrial engineering.

UNIVERSITY OF KANSAS
Lawrence, 66044
Telephone: (913) 864-4291

Officers
P. J. Wolfe, *Director*
J. Magnuson, J. E. Kocourek, Dr. P. M. Neely, Dr. D. I. Rummer, *Associate Directors*

Computer Installation
BULL GENERAL ELECTRIC GE635–operating system: GECOS III; internal storage: 7,800K bits; magnetic tapes: 8; magnetic discs; 2 line printers. *On-line satellite computers*: GE-DN/30. IBM 1130, 2 HP 2116B, PDP-15/20. *Remote processing features*: remote batch and time sharing.

IBM 1401–internal storage: 48K bits; magnetic tapes: 4 units; 1 line printer.

Coding Languages
ALGOL, SIMSCRIPT, FORTRAN IV, GMAP, COBOL, SNOBOL, JOVIAL, IDS, KUICC, SORT/MERGE, BASIC.

Contemplated Equipment
Additional disc storage; more flexible communication computer; terminals.

Services Available
Administrative: Systems analysis, programming, production control. *Academic*: Statistical consulting, application programming assistance, software packages development. *All*: Data preparation, unit record services. Operate on a closed shop basis; extensive time-sharing and remote batch. Available only to educational agencies, State of Kansas agencies and other research groups by arrangement

Fields of Application
Scientific research, statistical analysis, administrative information systems, instructional.
Specialized areas: On-line data acquisition and control.

Training
Short courses in programming, laboratories in academic computing, seminars and workshops on specific topics.

WICHITA STATE UNIVERSITY
1845 Fairmount, Wichita, 67208
Telephone: (316) 689-3630

Officer
Prof. J. B. O'Loughlin, *Director, Digital Computing Cente*

Computer Installation
IBM 360/44–operating system: Disc.

IBM 1130–operating system: DMS/V2 (modified); internal storage: 128K bits; magnetic drive: 1; 1 line printer.

Coding Languages
FORTRAN IV, COBOL, PL/1, ALGOL, BAL, GPSS, GASP, BMD, SPSS, Assembler, RPG.

Contemplated Equipment
IBM 370/145.

Services Available
Consultation, operators, preparation of data, programming software packages, systems analysis, education and training, documentation. Operate on self-service, closed shop and time-sharing basis. Available only for student course and laboratory work, student and faculty unsponsored research, university administrative work, sponsored research projects and local community commercial work.

Fields of Application
Undergraduate and graduate educational course work, scientific, statistical and commercial batch work, university accounting and management systems, registration systems, aerospace and computer software systems research, masters and doctoral dissertation studies, programming and systems analysis.

Specialized areas: Aeronautical, mechanical and electrical engineering, computer system evaluations, software operating systems, analysis of socia-economic data systems.

Training
A department of Computer Science will shortly be established. Short courses are given in 6 subjects.

KENTUCKY

EASTERN KENTUCKY UNIVERSITY*
Richmond, 40475
Telephone: (606) 622-3496

Officers
Dr. J. Young, *Dean, College of Business*
P. E. Ridgley, *Director, Data Processing Division*

Computer Installation
HONEYWELL H200–operating system: Mod. 1; internal storage: 24K characters; magnetic tapes: 5 240B; 1 line printer.

Coding Languages
COBOL, FORTRAN, Assembly.

Contemplated Equipment
H1250; communications controller.

Services Available
Consultation, programming, education and training, preparation of data, systems analysis. Available only to faculty, staff and students.

Fields of Application
Scientific, commercial, accounting, systems analysis and design, educational.

Training
Bachelor's degree course in Data Processing.

THOMAS MORE COLLEGE
P.O. Box 85, Fort Mitchell, 41017
Telephone: (606) 341-5800

Officers
Margaret M. Geis, *Director of the Computer Center*
Richard A. DeGraff, *President*

Computer Installation
IBM 1130–operating system: 1130; internal storage: 16K bits; magnetic discs: 3 2310; 1 line printer.

Coding Languages
FORTRAN IV, COBOL, RPG, Assembler.

Services Available
Advice, programming, education and training. Operate on a closed shop basis. Available primarily to educational customers.

Fields of Application
Scientific, statistical, accounting.
Specialized area: Educational.

Training
Associate Degree or a Certificate in Computer Science with specific courses in basic computer technology, FORTRAN IV, COBOL, business programming techniques, linear programming, systems analysis and advanced programming techniques.

UNIVERSITY OF KENTUCKY
Computing Center
Lexington, 40506
Telephone: (606) 258-2916

Officers
Dr. Martin Solomon, *Director*
Forrest E. Hahn, *Manager of Data Processing*
L. Thrailkill, *Manager, Research and Development*
Selwyn Zerof, *Manager, Systems Programming and Operations*

Computer Installation
IBM 7040–internal storage: 32K bits; magnetic tapes: 9 7330.

IBM 1410–internal storage: 40K bits; magnetic tapes: 5 7330.

Coding Languages
FORTRAN, SPS, Autocoder, COBOL, MAP, IOCS.

Contemplated Equipment
IBM 360/65.

Services Available
Advice, programming, education and training, operators, software packages, documentation, data preparation, systems analysis. Operate on a remote access, closed shop, and time-sharing basis. Priority is given to the needs of the University, but available for a limited number of non-university users.

Fields of Application
Scientific, statistical, administrative data processing.
Specialized areas: Electric network analysis, computer assisted instruction.

Training
Computer Science Department offers M.S. degree; 2-year computation course; short courses.

UNIVERSITY OF LOUISVILLE*
Engineering Computing Laboratory
Speed Scientific School, South Third Street,
Louisville, 40208
Telephone: (502) 636-4426

Officer
Alfred T. Chen, *Associate Professor*

Computer Installation
IBM 1800–operating system: TSX; internal storage: 256K bits; magnetic discs: 1810; 1 line printer.

Coding Languages
FORTRAN IV, Assembly.

Contemplated Equipment
XDS 7670 remote batch terminal to Sigma 7 at Vanderbilt University.

United States of America – Universities and Colleges

Services Available
Advice, systems analysis. Operate on a closed shop basis.
Restrictions: Available for research activities only.

Fields of Application
Scientific, statistical, engineering analysis and computation.
Specialized areas: Process control, hybrid computation.

Training
Master of Engineering in Computer Science (5-year professional degree programme).

LOUISIANA

LOUISIANA STATE UNIVERSITY*
Computer Research Center
Baton Rouge, 70803
Telephone: 388-2348

Officers
Olen A. Nance, *Director*
Mrs. Patricia Nettles, *Assistant Director*
John Tyler, *Assistant Director*

Computer Installation
IBM 360/30–internal storage (to 512K bytes); IBM 3 330 disc magnetic discs: LCS.

Coding Languages
FORTRAN, COBOL, WATFOR, PL/1.

Services Available
On a limited basis so as not to conflict with university research or instruction.

Training
Credit and non-credit seminar-type programming courses.

TULANE UNIVERSITY OF LOUISIANA*
School of Medicine
Division of Medical Computing Sciences
134 La Salle Street, New Orleans, 70112
Telephone: (504) 525-8708

Officers
Bernard Saltzberg, *Director*
Wilson J. Nettleton, Jr., *Associate Director*
Vernon P. Gurske, *Assistant Director*

Computer Installation
IBM 1410–operating system: PR 155; internal storage: 40K bits; magnetic tapes: 7 729; magnetic disc: 1301.

IBM 1401–internal storage: 4K bits; magnetic tapes: 2 729; 1 line printer. *Remote processing features*: Hybrid A/D D/A capabilities on-line through a Pace TR48.

IBM 360/30–operating system: DOS; internal storage: 64K bits; magnetic tapes: 2 2415; magnetic discs: 4 2311; 1 line printer. *Remote processing features*: 2260 CRT.

Coding Languages
FORTRAN IV, Autocoder, BAL, COBOL.

Services Available
Advice, operators, preparation of data, programming, software packages, systems analysis. Operate on a closed shop basis.

Fields of Application
Comparative analysis of I/O devices; automating medical records, evaluation of EEG's, evaluation of dietary surveys; application of DP equipment in hospitals – specifically I/O devices.

UNIVERSITY OF SOUTHWESTERN LOUISIANA
P.O. Box 2770, U.S.L. Station, Lafayette, 70501
Telephone: (318) 234-7349

Computer Installation
RCA Spectra 70/46–operating system: VMOS 9.3; internal storage: 2,048K bits; magnetic tapes: 4; magnetic discs: 6; 2 line printers. *Remote processing features*: 15 teletypes.

Coding Languages
FORTRAN IV, COBOL (ANSI), BAL, BASIC, FASTFOR.

Services Available
Advice, education and training. Operate on a remote access, closed shop and time-sharing basis.

Fields of Application
Scientific, statistical, commercial, accounting, management, systems analysis, operational research.

Training
Courses leading to M.S., Ph.D. and B.S. degrees in Computer Science.

XAVIER UNIVERSITY OF LOUISIANA
7325 Palmetto Street, New Orleans, 70125
Telephone: (504) 486-7411

Officer
Sister P. Marshall, *Director of Computer Center*

Computer Installation
IBM 1130–operating system: DMS/V2; internal storage: 16K 16-bit words; magnetic discs: 1 2310, 1 Memorex 660; 1 line printer.

Coding Languages
FORTRAN IV, COBOL, APL, BASIC, RPG.

Contemplated Equipment
Teletype multiplexer and 8 ASR33 teletypes.

Services Available
Advice, programming, education and training, operators, data preparation. Operate on a closed and open shop and time-sharing basis. Services are not available to commercial users outside the University community.

Fields of Application
Scientific, statistical, commercial, accounting.
Specialized area: Student information system.

Training
Minor in Computer Science (10 courses).

MAINE

UNIVERSITY OF MAINE
Computing and Data Processing Services
Wingate Hall, Orono, 04473
Telephone: (207) 581-7876

Officers
Dr. D. R. McNeil, *Chancellor*
H. L. Fowle, Jr., *Vice-Chancellor for Business and Financial Affairs*
J. E. Johnson, *Director of Computing and Data Processing Services*

Computer Installation
IBM 370/145–operating systems: DOS OS VM/370; internal storage: 392K bytes; magnetic tapes: 3 3420; magnetic discs: 8 2319; 1 line printer. *Remote processing features*: 2 3780 unit record terminals, 25 keyboard terminals.

Coding Languages
BAL, FORTRAN, COBOL, PL/1, WATFIV, CUPL, PL/C, HYCOMP, ASAP, RPG, BASIC, PL/1, Coursewriter.

Contemplated Equipment
Increased core storage (to 512K bytes); IBM 3 330 disc units.

Services Available
Advice, programming, education and training, operators, software packages, documentation, preparation of data, systems analysis. Operate on a self-service, remote access, closed shop, and time-sharing basis.

Fields of Application
Scientific, statistical, commercial, accounting, management, systems analysis, operation research.
Specialized areas: Linear programming, analysis, payroll, structural engineering.

Training
Each of the eight constituent campuses offers at least one programming course. Approximately 25 "computer science" courses are offered by the various academic units.

MARYLAND

HOOD COLLEGE*
Frederick, 21701
Telephone: (301) 663-3131

Officer
Dr. Phyllida M. Willis

Services Available
Education and training. Operate on a remote access basis. Available only to students, faculty, administration.

Fields of Application
Scientific, statistical.

Training
Introductory course in computer science.

JOHNS HOPKINS UNIVERSITY
University Computing Center
34th and Charles Streets, Baltimore, 21218
Telephone: (301) 366-3300

Officer
Steven Muller, *President*

Computer Installation
IBM 7094–operating systems: IBSYS; internal storage: 1 million bits; magnetic tapes: 12 IBM 729; 1 line printer.

IBM 1401–internal storage: 16K characters; magnetic tapes: 4 729; magnetic disc: 1 1311; 1 line printer.

Coding Languages
FORTRAN, GPSS, Autocoder, COBOL, LISP, ALGOL, SNOBOL.

Services Available
Advice, programming, systems analysis and software packages, education and training, operators, documentation, data preparation. Operate on a closed shop and time-sharing basis. Available only to other educational institutions.

Fields of Application
Scientific, statistical, accounting, management, systems analysis, operational research.
Specialized areas: Payroll, medical research.

Training
Non-credit FORTRAN course; computer related seminars.

UNIVERSITY OF MARYLAND
Computer Science Center
College Park, 20742
Telephone: (301) 454-4259

Officers
William F. Atchison, *Director*
John P. Menard, *Associate Director*

Computer Installation
IBM 7094–operating system: IBSYS; internal storage: 1,152K bits; magnetic tapes: 14 729; 2 line printers.

UNIVAC 1108–operating system: EXEC 8; internal storage: 9216K bits; magnetic tapes: 11 Uniservo VIIIC; 4 line printers. *On-line satellite computer*: Univac 9400. *Remote processing features*: demand remote on site.

Coding Languages
FORTRAN, COBOL, ALGOL, SNOBOL, APL, BASIC, OMNITAB, SIMSCRIPT, XL-6.

Contemplated Equipment
Univac 1106 time-sharing system planned.

Services Available
Consultation, programming, education and training, documentation, preparation of data, systems analysis. Operate on a closed shop remote access basis with time-sharing terminals on premises. Services available only for faculty-sponsored projects of benefit to State and the University.

Fields of Application
Scientific, statistical, management, systems analysis, operational research.

Training
M.S. and Ph.D. degree courses in Computer Science; also short courses in Computer Science (1 to 3 weeks).

United States of America – Universities and Colleges

MASSACHUSETTS

BOSTON COLLEGE*
611 Higgins Hall, Commonwealth Avenue, Chestnut Hill, 02167
Telephone: 969-0100, extension 2460

Officers
Dr. John J. Sopka, *Director of University Computation Programs*
William J. Kealy, *Head of Computing Center*
Rev. Stanley J. Bezuszka, *Director of Mathematics Institute*

Computer Installations
Computing Center:
IBM 360/40–internal storage: 252K bytes; magnetic tapes: 5 2401; magnetic discs: 1 2314; 1 line printer. *Remote processing features*: RAX system.

Mathematics Institute:
IBM 1620–internal storage: 40K bits.

IBM 1130–internal storage: 8K bits.

Coding Languages
FORTRAN, COBOL, BAL, PL/1, FORGO, SPS.

Contemplated Equipment
RCA Spectra 70/46 or IBM 360/50.

Services Available
Advice, programming, data processing, design systems. Operate on a closed shop, batch and remote access (Computing Center), open shop and processing service (Mathematics Institute) basis.

Fields of Application
Scientific, statistical, academic research, administrative records processing, academic teaching.
Specialized areas: Social sciences and natural science research.

Training
Introductory courses in computer science including programming in FORTRAN, COBOL and PL/1.

BOSTON UNIVERSITY*
Computing Center
147 Bay State Road, Boston, 02215
Telephone: (617) 353-2200

Officer
Mr. John E. Alman, *Director*

Computer Installation
IBM 360/50–operating systems: OS, RAX; internal storage: 256K bits; magnetic tapes: 2 2415; magnetic discs: 7 2314; 1 line printer. *Remote processing features*: 50 2741 terminals under RAX.

Coding Languages
FORTRAN, PL/1, BASIC, BAL, COBOL.

Services Available
Advice, operators, preparation of data, programming, software packages. Operate on a closed shop and time-sharing basis.

Fields of Application
Educational, scientific and statistical data analysis.

Training
Courses in computer science.

BRANDEIS UNIVERSITY*
415 South Street, Waltham, 02154
Telephone: (617) 894-6000

Officer
Mr. Max Chrétien, *Director*

Computer Installation
IBM 1130–internal storage: 16K bits; magnetic discs: 2 2310.

Coding Languages
FORTRAN, ALGOL.

Services Available
Advice, operators, preparation of data, programming. Operate on a closed and open shop basis.

Fields of Application
Scientific, educational, research.

Training
Short FORTRAN programming courses (5 evenings each), credit courses in computer science and numerical methods.

HARVARD UNIVERSITY
Computing Center
33 Oxford Street, Cambridge, 02138
Telephone: (617) 868-7600

Officer
Dr. Norman Zachary, *Director*

Computer Installation
IBM 360/65–operating system: OS/MVT; internal storage: 16 million bits; magnetic tapes: 9 2401; magnetic discs: 2 2314; 4 line printers. *On-line satellite computer*: 360/20. *Remote processing features*: 2780 remote terminals.

Services Available
Consultation, programming, education and training, software packages, preparation of data, systems analysis. Operate on a remote access, closed shop and time-sharing basis. Available only to members of Harvard University and affiliated educational institutions.

Fields of Application
Scientific, statistical, accounting, management, systems analysis, operational research.

Training
Short course in FORTRAN.

LOWELL TECHNOLOGICAL INSTITUTE
Lowell, 01854
Telephone: (617) 454-7811

Officers
Dr. Everett V. Olsen, *President*
Dr. Leon E. Beghian, *Provost*

Computer Installation
CDC 3100–operating system: MSOS; internal storage: 384K bits; magnetic discs: 2 854; 1 line printer.

PDP-9–operating system: foreground/background; internal storage: 576K bits; magnetic tapes: 6 Dectapes; magnetic discs: 2; 1 line printer.

Coding Languages
Assembler, FORTRAN, COBOL, ALGOL, FOCAL.

Contemplated Equipment
Interactive time-sharing computer system.

Services Available
Education and training. Operate on a closed shop basis. Computer use available only to members of the faculty, students and administrative departments of the Institute.

Fields of Application
Scientific, statistical, accounting, management.

Training
Undergraduate courses offered in computer programming, business data processing, numerical analysis, statistics, etc.; M.S. programme in computer engineering.

MASSACHUSETTS INSTITUTE OF TECHNOLOGY
Education Research Centre
Cambridge, 02139
Telephone: 253-7772

Officer
Professor J. R. Zacharias, *Director*

Computer Installation
PDP-7—internal storage: 8K bits; magnetic tapes: 4; magnetic discs: 1.

Coding Languages
Assembler, FORTRAN, BASIC.

Services Available
Operate on a self-service basis. Not available to outside users.

Field of Application
Scientific.
Specialized area: Graphics.

MASSACHUSETTS INSTITUTE OF TECHNOLOGY
Information Processing Center
39-559, 77 Massachusetts Avenue, Cambridge, 02139
Telephone: (617) 253-7849

Officer
W. J. burner

Computer Installations
IBM 360/165—operating system: ASP/OS/MVT; internal storage: 16 million bits; magnetic tapes: 6 3420; magnetic discs: 12 3330, 10 Memorex 3660. *Remote processing features*: RJE, TSO.

BULL GENERAL ELECTRIC GE 645—operating system: Multics; internal storage: 14,191,776 bits; magnetic tapes: 10; magnetic discs: 15 DSU 270; 1 line printer. *On-line satellite computer*: dual processor. *Remote processing features*: typewriter terminals.

Services Available
Consultation, programming, education and training, operators, software packages, documentation, preparation of data, systems analysis. Operate on a closed shop, remote access and time-sharing basis. Available only to New England universities.

Fields of Application
Scientific, statistical, commercial, production control, accounting, management, systems analysis, operational research.
Specialized area: Engineering.

Training
Various short introductory courses.

NORTHEASTERN UNIVERSITY
360 Huntingdon Avenue, Boston, 02155
Telephone: (617) 137-2335

Officer
Richard I. Carter, *Director, Computation Center*

Computer Installation
CDC Cyber 72/14—operating system: KRONOS; internal storage: 65K 60-bit words; magnetic tapes: 3 604; magnetic discs: 3 841; 2 line printers.

Coding Languages
FORTRAN, COBOL.

Services Available
Consultation, education and training, operators, software packages, documentation. Operate on a closed shop basis.

Fields of Application
Research, student education.

Training
A variety of courses offered.

UNIVERSITY OF MASSACHUSETTS*
Amherst, 01002
Telephone: (413) 545-2690

Officers
Dr. C. A. Wogrin, *Director and Professor of Computer Science*
R. H. Gonter, *Associate Director*

Computer Installation
CDC 3600—operating system: SCOPE; internal storage: 1,572,864 bits; magnetic tapes: 5 604; magnetic discs: 2 854; magnetic drums: 2 861; 2 line printers.

CDC 3600—operating system: UMASS; internal storage: 3,145,728 bits; magnetic tapes: 3 604; magnetic discs: 841; magnetic drums: 2 861; *On-line satellite computer*: PDP-8/680. *Remote processing features*: 94 simultaneous remote user terminals (dial-in).

Coding Languages
FORTRAN, COBOL, ALGOL, COMPASS, PERT, COM IV, KWIC, COGO, ECAP, UMFF, SMALL, BASIC, JOBSHOP, MIX, APL, CDM 4, LISP, MIMIC, SIMSCRIPT, SPSS, GPSS, SNOBOL.

Services Available
Operate on a closed shop and time-sharing basis. Available only for the research and educational needs of the university, local colleges, and other state institutions of higher education.

Fields of Application
Education, research.

Training
Courses in basic FORTRAN, advanced languages, compiler design, linguistics, numerical analysis.

WORCESTER POLYTECHNIC INSTITUTE*
Worcester, 01609

Officer
Dr. Elliott L. Buell, *Director of Computation Facility*

Computer Installation
IBM 1620—internal storage: 40K bits; magnetic disc: 1.

Coding Languages
FORGO, FORTRAN, SPS.

Services Available
Outside use is available only when time allows and by special permission of the Director.

Fields of Application
Education and service to engineering and scientific users among faculty and students.

Training
Non-credit short programming courses are offered to faculty and students.

MICHIGAN

EASTERN MICHIGAN UNIVERSITY*
Ypsilanti, 48197

Officers
J. N. Finzel, *Director of Administrative Data Processing*
E. Goings, *Professor, Instructional Computer Center*

Computer Installation
IBM 360/40—operating system: DOS; internal storage: 131K bytes; magnetic tapes: 3 2401; magnetic discs: 5 2314; 1 line printer.

IBM 1130—internal storage: 162,144 bits; magnetic discs: 3 2315; 1 line printer.

Coding Languages
PL/1, COBOL, FORTRAN, RPG.

Services Available
Consultation, programming, education and training, operators, documentation, preparation of data, systems analysis. Operate on a closed shop basis. In-house service only.

Fields of Application
Statistical, commercial, accounting, management, systems analysis, scientific, instructional.

Training
Seven undergraduate courses.

GENESEE COMMUNITY COLLEGE
1401 East Court Street, Flint, 48503
Telephone: (313) 238-1631

Officers
Charles Pappas, *President*
Russell Waltmire, *Business Manager*
Joseph Sloboder, *Director of the Computer Center*

Computer Installation
IBM 1130—operating system: Monitor; magnetic discs: 5 2315; 1 line printer.

Coding Languages
Assembler, FORTRAN, COBOL, RPG.

Contemplated Equipment
IBM 370/125.

Service Available
Documentation. Operate on a closed shop, block time, and open shop basis. Available only to certain areas of the college.

Fields of Application
Scientific, statistical, education administrative support, instructional support.

Training
Courses in all programming languages. Two-year Associate degree course in Business Data Processing.

LAWRENCE INSTITUTE OF TECHNOLOGY*
21000 West Ten Mile Road, Southfield, 48075
Telephone: (313) 444-1340

Officer
Bernard Lis, *Director*

Computer Installation
IBM 1130—internal storage: 16K bits; magnetic discs: 4; 1 line printer.

Coding Languages
FORTRAN, RPG, SL/1, COBOL, ECAP, DYSTAL, Assembler.

Services Available
Advice, operators, preparation of data, programming, software packages, systems analysis. Operate on an open shop basis.

Fields of Application
All fields of college disciplines.
Specialized areas: Batch processing student FORTRAN problems, academic record keeping, administrative and accounting functions.

Training
B.S. course in Mathematics and Computer Science, and courses in computers in business systems, computer techniques in engineering, computer technology associate degree program.

MICHIGAN STATE UNIVERSITY
Computer Laboratory
East Lansing, 48823
Telephone: (517) 355-3600

Officers
L. W. Von Tersch, *Director, Computer Laboratory*
J. Kateley, Jr., *Associate Director, Computer Laboratory*

Computer Installation
CDC 3600—operating system: SCOPE; internal storage: 3,145,728 bits; magnetic tapes: 10 606; 2 line printers.

CDC 6500—operating system: SCOPE; internal storage: 3,981,312 bits; magnetic tapes: 4 607; magnetic discs: 8 844; 2 line printers. *Remote processing features*: remote batch and interactive.

Coding Languages
FORTRAN, COBOL, COMPASS, ALGOL, BASIC, APL, SIMULA.

Services Available
Advice, programming, education and training, operators, software packages, documentation, data preparation, systems analysis, computation. Operate on a self-service, remote access, closed shop, block time and time-sharing basis.

Fields of Application
Scientific, statistical, commercial, accounting, management, systems analysis.
Specialized areas: Linear programming, structural engineering.

Training
Non-credit courses in FORTRAN and COBOL programming are offered by the Computer Laboratory. Undergraduate and graduate academic programmes leading to B.S., M.S. and Ph.D. degrees are offered by Department of Computer Science.

MICHIGAN TECHNOLOGICAL UNIVERSITY*
Digital Computer Laboratory
Houghton, 49931
Telephone: 487-2110

Officers
T. Scott Johnston, *Director*
W. J. de Blaubien, *Manager of Academic Services*

Computer Installation
IBM 360/44–operating system: OS/MFT; internal storage: 256K bits; magnetic tapes: 2 9-track, 1 7-track; magnetic discs: 5 2314; 1 line printer. *Remote processing features*: HASP.

Coding Languages
FORTRAN IV, Assembler, PL/1, COBOL, RPG, ALGOL.

Services Available
Advice, operators, preparation of data, programming, software packages, systems analysis. Operate on a closed shop basis.

Fields of Application
Scientific, statistical, accounting, systems analysis, scheduling.
Specialized areas: X-Ray analysis, contour mapping, application software development.

Training
Full set of courses in FORTRAN, Assembler and data structures.

UNIVERSITY OF DETROIT
Computer Center
4001 West McNichols Road, Detroit, 48221
Telephone: (313) 342-1000

Officer
Michael Byrne, *Director*

Computer Installation
BURROUGHS B5500–magnetic tapes: 4; magnetic discs: 8; 1 line printer.

Coding Languages
FORTRAN, COBOL, BASIC, ESPOL, ALGOL, SNOBOL.

Services Available
Limited availability to business outside the University.

Training
Programming courses.

UNIVERSITY OF MICHIGAN
Computing Center
1075 Beal Avenue, Ann Arbor, 48104
Telephone: (313) 764-9595

Officer
Prof. R. C. F. Bartels, *Director*

Computer Installation
IBM 360/67–operating system: Michigan Terminal System; internal storage: 1.5 million bytes; magnetic tapes: 8 9-track, 2 7-track; magnetic discs: 28 Telex Double-Density; 3 line printers. *On-line satellite computers*: about 20 of various types. *Remote processing features*: RJE, about 200 terminals.

Coding Languages
FORTRAN, PL/1, APL, BASIC, SNOBOL, GPSS, ALGOL, etc.

Services Available
Advice, education and training, operators, software packages, documentation, systems analysis. Operate on a remote access, closed shop and time-sharing basis. Services restricted to University community.

Fields of Application
Scientific, statistical, commercial, management, systems analysis, operational research.
Specialized areas: Linear programming, analysis, structural engineering, medical research, all fields relevant to university affairs.

Training
Courses leading to undergraduate and graduate degrees. Departments include Computer and Communication Sciences, Electrical and Computer Engineering, Mathematics, Industrial Engineering and Business Administration.

WAYNE STATE UNIVERSITY*
Computing and Data Processing Center
5925 Woodward Avenue, Detroit, 48202
Telephone: (313) 833-1400, (313) 831-5070

Officers
Dr. Walter Hoffman, *Director*
Dr. Charles F. Briggs, *Associate Director*
Roger C. Hardenberg, *Assistant Director*

Computer Installation
IBM 360/50–operating system: OS 360; internal storage: 512K bytes; magnetic tapes: 3 2400 7-track, 5 2400 9-track; magnetic discs: 4 2311, 1 2314; 2 line printers.

IBM 360/67.

IBM 7074–operating system: Scamper; internal storage: 10K bits; magnetic tapes: 7 729, 4 729; magnetic disc: 1301.

IBM 1460–internal storage: 8K bits; magnetic tapes: 4 729. System switchable to 7074.

Coding Languages
Autocoder, FORTRAN, COBOL, DYSTAL.

Services Available
Advice, preparation of data, programming, software packages, systems analysis. Operate on a self-service, remote access and time-sharing basis.

Fields of Application
Research in computing, instruction, and University administration.
Specialized areas: Large-scale processing student programmes (WASPS); FORTRAN, COBOL, Autocoder, Russian character chain.

Training
The Department of Mathematics has elementary and graduate courses in programming using the current programming facilities.

MINNESOTA

BEMIDJI STATE COLLEGE*
Bemidji, 56601
Telephone: (218) 755-2056

Officer
L. Dally, *Director of Data Processing*

Computer Installations
IBM 1401–internal storage: 12K bits; magnetic discs: 2 1311; 1 line printer.
PDP-8/I–magnetic discs: 1. *Remote processing features*: ASR 33 teletype terminals.

Coding Languages
Autocoder, COBOL, FORTRAN, SPS, FOCAL, PAL 3, BASIC.

Services Available
Consultation, education and training. Operate on a closed shop (1401), self-service, remote access and time-sharing (PDP-8) basis.

Fields of Application
Accounting, management, statistical, educational.

Training
Minors in Data Processing and Computer Science.

CARLETON COLLEGE
Computation Center
Northfield, 55057
Telephone: 645-4431

Officer
Graham L. Kimble, *Director*

Computer Installation
IBM 1620–internal storage: 20K bits.
PDP-11/20–operating systems: time sharing, 1401 simulation, DOS; internal storage: 28K bits; magnetic tapes: 4 DEC; magnetic discs: 1 RCII, 4 RKO3; 1 line printer.
PDP-8/1–operating system: time-sharing; internal storage: 4K bits; magnetic tapes: 2 DEC; magnetic discs: 2 RS08; 1 line printer. *On-line satellite computers*: 4 PDP-8/L. *Remote processing features*: graphical displays.
PDP-8/L (2)–internal storage: 4K bits each.

Coding Languages
FORTRAN, Autocoder, BASIC, FOCAL, PAL, TRAC, ALGOL, SPS.

Services Available
Advice, operators, programming. Operate on a closed and open shop and time-sharing basis.

Fields of Application
Instruction in programming and numerical methods, general faculty research, administration.
Specialized area: Computer assisted learning.

Training
Introduction to computer science, computer science seminars, independent study.

CONCORDIA COLLEGE*
920 South 7th Street, Moorhead, 56560
Telephone: (218) 299-4617

Officer
Arne Garness

Computer Installation
IBM 1620–internal storage: 20K bits.

Coding Languages
FORTRAN II, SPS.

Contemplated Equipment
Diskpack.

Services Available
Advice, preparation of data, programming. Operate on a closed shop basis. Available only for scientific computations and research.

Field of Application
Mathematics.

Training
Elementary FORTRAN and SPS programming courses.

MACALESTER COLLEGE*
St. Paul, 55101
Telephone: (612) 647-6544

Officer
R. W. Paulson, *Director of Computing Services*

Computer Installations
NCR Century 200–operating system: B-2; internal storage: 65K bytes; magnetic discs: 3; 1 line printer. *Remote processing features*: 4 on-line CRTs.
IBM 1130–internal storage: 8K 16-bit words; magnetic discs: 1; 1 line printer.

Coding Languages
COBOL, FORTRAN.

Services Available
Consultation, programming, operators, software packages, preparation of data, systems analysis. Operate on an open shop (1130) and closed shop basis (NCR 200).

Fields of Application
Academic and administrative on-line processing.

MANKATO STATE COLLEGE
5th and Jackson, Mankato, 56001
Telephone: 389-6651

Officers
James Nickerson, *President*
Kent Alm, *Executive Vice-President*

Computer Installation
UNIVAC 1106–operating system: EXEC 8; internal storage: 262K 36-bit words; magnetic tapes: 4 6C; magnetic discs; 4 line printers. *On-line satellite computer*: Univac 9200. *Remote processing features*: 22 ASR 33, 7 remote batch on CTM controller.

United States of America – Universities and Colleges

Coding Languages
FORTRAN, COBOL, SNOBOL, ALGOL, BASIC.

Services Available
Advice, programming, education and training, operators, software packages, documentation, preparation of data. Operate on a self-service, remote access, closed and open shop, and time-sharing basis. Available to educational customers only.

Fields of Application
Scientific, statistical, accounting, management, systems analysis.
Specialized areas: Linear programming, analysis, payroll.

Training
B.S. degree with computer science major.

ST. JOHN'S UNIVERSITY*
Collegeville, 56321
Telephone: (612) 363-7761

Officer
Fintan Bromenshenkel

Computer Installation
IBM 1620 – internal storage: 20K bits; magnetic discs: 2 1311.

Coding Languages
SPS, FORTRAN.

Services Available
Consultation, programming, education and training, operators. Operate on an open shop and self-service basis.

Fields of Application
Management, educational, accounting, research.
Specialized areas: Registrar and alumni records.

Training
Courses in computer science and numerical analysis. Short courses in TAB equipment and programming.

SAINT MARY'S COLLEGE*
Winona, 55987
Telephone: (507) 452-4430

Officer
Brother John D. Grover

Computer Installation
IBM 1130 – operating system: DMS; internal storage: 8K bits; magnetic discs: 20 2315; 1 line printer. *On-line satellite computer*: IBM 360/40.
IBM 1401 – internal storage: 4K bits; 1 line printer.

Coding Languages
FORTRAN IV, RPG, COBOL, Autocoder, Assembler.

Contemplated Equipment
IBM 360/40.

Services Available
Consultation, programming, education and training, operators, software packages, documentation, preparation of data, systems analysis. Operate on an open and closed shop basis.

Fields of Application
Scientific, statistical, commercial accounting, management, systems analysis.
Specialized area: Education.

Training
Various programming and system courses.

UNIVERSITY OF MINNESOTA
Management Information Systems Research Center
Blegen 93, Minneapolis, 55455

Officers
Gordon B. Davis, *Director*
Gary W. Dickson, *Associate Director*
Robert Henry, *Assistant Director*

Computer Installation
The Center has access to the CDC 6600, and CDC 3200 of the University.

Coding Languages
FORTRAN, COBOL.

Services Available
Education and training. Operate on a self-service, remote access, closed shop, and time-sharing basis.

Fields of Application
Commercial, systems analysis, operational research.
Specialized area: Management information systems.

Training
Masters degree and Ph.D. in Business Administration with specialization in Management Information Systems (in association with the Graduate School of Business Administration).

UNIVERSITY OF MINNESOTA
University Computer Center
Room 227, Experimental Engineering Building,
Minneapolis, 55455
Telephone: (612) 373-4360

Officers
P. C. Patton, *Director*
A. Franck, *Assistant Director, Engineering*
R. L. Hotchkiss, *Assistant Director, Applications*
L. A. Liddiard, *Assistant Director, Systems*

Computer Installation
CDC 6600 – operating system: MOMS; internal storage: 65K plus 256K words; magnetic tapes: 8 607; magnetic discs: 2 6603, 5 844; 3 line printers. *Remote processing features*: CDC 8231 remote terminal, CDC 3200 (MSOS) UofM terminal, CDC 1700 terminal, 8 CDC 200 UT, 12 Univac 1004, 3M EBR (microfilm processing).
CDC 6400 – operating system: KRONOS; internal storage: 32K words; magnetic disc: 6638. *Remote processing features*: 128 time-sharing terminals. This system is operated by the University as a statewide computer time-sharing service under the auspices of the Minnesota Higher Education Coordinating Commission.

Coding Languages
FORTRAN, ALGOL, COBOL, SIMSCRIPT.

Services Available
Advice, operators. Operate on a closed shop and remote access basis.

Fields of Application
Research in the use and applications of computers and the design of computer systems.

Training
Computer Science degree programme. Courses in general computer programming. Special courses in FORTRAN, COBOL, ALGOL, etc.

United States of America – Universities and Colleges

WINONA STATE COLLEGE*
Winona, 55987
Telephone: 507-2951

Officers
Robert A. DuFresne, *President*
David E. Hamerski, *Computer Consultant*

Computer Installation
IBM 1130–operating system: MINITOR; internal storage: 128,100 bits; magnetic disc: 2315; 1 line printer.

Coding Languages
Assembler, FORTRAN, SL/1.

Contemplated Equipment
IBM 2310 disc storage.

Services Available
Advice, operators, preparation of data. Operate on a self-service and open shop basis.

Fields of Application
Scientific, administrative functions, statistical, accounting.
Specialized areas: Physics, mathematics, library science, registration procedures.

Training
Courses in computer science (2 weeks) and scientific numerical techniques (2 weeks).

MISSISSIPPI

ALCORN AGRICULTURAL AND MECHANICAL COLLEGE
Lorman, 39096
Telephone: (601) 877-3711

Officers
Dr. Walter Washington, *President*
Mr. Harold E. Spencer, *Director of Computing Center*

Computer Installation
IBM 1130–internal storage: 32,768 bits; magnetic discs: 3 2310; 1 line printer.

Coding Languages
FORTRAN, RPG.

Contemplated Equipment
IBM System/3.

Services Available
Education and training. Operate on a self-service basis. Available to institutes only.

Fields of Application
Scientific, statistical, accounting, management, research projects.
Specialized area: Payroll.

Training
Courses in FORTRAN, COBOL.

HINDS JUNIOR COLLEGE
Box 1166, Raymond, 39154
Telephone: (601) 857-5261

Officers
Dr. Robert Mayo, *President*
Lester F. Martin, *Director of Computer Center*

Computer Installation
IBM System/3–operating system: disc; internal storage: 128K bits; magnetic discs: 1; 1 line printer.
IBM 1620–operating system: card; internal storage: 110K bits.

Coding Languages
Assembler, FORTRAN, RPG, COBOL.

Services Available
Education and training, operators. Operate on an open shop basis. Available to students and administration only.

Fields of Application
Scientific, statistical, commercial, accounting, management.
Specialized areas: Analysis, payroll.

Training
Twenty-seven semester hours of programming languages and systems analysis leading to a degree of Associate of Applied Science in Data Processing.

JACKSON STATE COLLEGE
1325 Lynch Street, Jackson, 39217
Telephone: (601) 948-8533

Officer
Dr. Jesse C. Lewis

Computer Installation
IBM 360/40–operating system: DOS; internal storage: 512K bits; magnetic discs: 3 2311; 1 line printer.

Coding Languages
FORTRAN IV, COBOL, Assembler, RPG.

Services Available
Advice, programming, education and training, operators software packages, documentation, preparation of data. Operate on a closed shop basis. Available for College use only.

Fields of Application
Scientific, statistical, accounting and management.
Specialized areas: Instruction of students.

Training
B.S. degree course in computer science.

MISSISSIPPI STATE UNIVERSITY*
Drawer CC, State College, 39762
Telephone: (601) 323-4321

Officer
Gerald A. Matthews

Computer Installation
IBM 360/40–operating systems: OS; internal storage: 264K bits; magnetic tapes: 4 2415; magnetic discs: 3 2311; 2 line printers.

Coding Languages
FORTRAN, AL.

Contemplated Equipment
IBM 360/50.

Services Available
Advice, programming, systems analysis. Operate on a closed and open shop basis. Not available for work which could be normally done by service bureaus.

Fields of Application
Scientific, statistical.
Specialized areas: Forest inventory and cruises.

Training
B.S. and M.S. degree courses in computer science.

UNIVERSITY OF MISSISSIPPI
Computer Center
University P.O., Lafayette County, 38677
Telephone: (601) 232-7206

Officer
Dr. Howard L. Dockery, *Director*

Computer Installation
DIGITAL EQUIPMENT System 10/77–internal storage: 131K 36-bit words; magnetic tapes: 4 TM10; magnetic discs: 6 RP03; 2 line printers. *Remote processing features*: 3 remote batch terminals, time-sharing (VT05), 14 teletypes.

Coding Languages
FORTRAN, COBOL, BASIC, ALGOL.

Services Available
Advice, preparation of data, programming, software packages, systems analysis. Available to university faculty, staff and students, and co-operative agencies of the university and state. Operate on a closed shop basis. Not available to customers outside Mississippi state agencies.

Fields of Application
Scientific, statistical, accounting, systems analysis, operational research.
Specialized areas: Payroll, pharmacy, accounting research, school bus routing, numerical analysis, linear programming.

Training
Courses in programming for digital computing, business data processing, introduction to computers and operational research.

UNIVERSITY OF SOUTHERN MISSISSIPPI
Box 106, Southern Station, Hattiesburg, 39401
Telephone: 266-7298

Officers
Danny R. Carter, *Academic Director*
Billy L. Green, *Director of Operations*
Ric O. Stewart, *Chief of Systems*

Computer Installation
XDS Sigma 9–operating system: UTS (CP-V); internal storage: 512K bytes; magnetic tapes: 5; magnetic discs: 4; 2 line printers. *Remote processing features*: 10 TI terminals, 3 cathode ray tubes, 1 graphics unit, 1 on-line plotter.

Coding Languages
FORTRAN, COBOL, Meta-Symbol, RPG, BASIC, APL, USM HELP.

Services Available
Advice, programming, education and training. Operate on an open shop and time-sharing basis. Availability to outside institutions is limited.

Fields of Application
Scientific, statistical, commercial, systems analysis, operational research.
Specialized areas: Linear programming, menu planning, student training.

Training
Courses leading to B.S. degrees in Computer Science and Business Data Processing; courses in COBOL, BAL, FORTRAN, BASIC, RPG, linear programming, simulation, numerical analysis, process control, hardware design, etc.

MISSOURI

DRURY COLLEGE*
Springfield, 65802
Telephone: (417) 865-8731

Officer
Mrs. M. Voss

Computer Installations
NCR Century 100–internal storage: 128K bits; magnetic discs: 2; 1 line printer.

Coding Languages
FORTRAN, COBOL, NEAT 3.

Services Available
Consultation, education and training, operators, software packages, documentation, systems analysis. Operate on a block time and closed shop basis. Available for education, business, industry.

Fields of Application
Education, operational research, production control, commercial.
Specialized area: Operational research statistics.

Training
Courses in COBOL, FORTRAN, numerical analysis and digital computers.

KANSAS CITY (MISSOURI) PUBLIC SCHOOLS
Bingham Junior High School
7618 Wyandotte, Kansas City, 64114
Telephone: (816) 363-4482

Officers
Dr. Andrew Adams, *Superintendent*
Dr. Gordon Wesner, *General Director of Instructional Services*
Thomas A. Hartley, Jr., *CAI Project Director*

Computer Installation
IBM 1500(1130 CPU)–operating system: 1500; internal storage: 32K bits; magnetic tapes: 2 2415; magnetic discs: 4 2310; 1 line printer.

Coding Languages
COURSEWRITER II, Assembly, APL, FORTRAN IV, RPG.

Contemplated Equipment
IBM 370/135 eventually to be used with 64 IBM 3270 CRTs at 8 different school locations.

Service Available
Computer time. Operate on a block time basis.

Fields of Application
Computer-assisted instruction.

Training
Series of 65 lessons in the area of mathematics and science primarily for 8th-grade students.

LINDENWOOD COLLEGES*
St. Charles, 63301
Telephone: 723-7152

Officer
Aaron Konstam, *Director, Computer Center.*

Computer Installation
IBM 1130/2A–operating system: MONITOR 2; internal storage: 64K bits; magnetic discs: 1 2315.

Coding Languages
FORTRAN, Assembler.

Contemplated Equipment
Line printer, plotter.

Services Available
Operate on an open shop basis.

Fields of Application
Scientific, statistical, commercial.

Training
Introductory course in computer sciences.

MISSOURI SOUTHERN COLLEGE*
Newman and Duquesne Roads, Joplin, 64801
Telephone: (417) 624-8100

Officer
Robert D. Carpenter, *Director, Computer Center*

Computer Installation
IBM 1130–internal storage: 8,192 16-bit words; magnetic disc: 1; 1 line printer.

Coding Languages
FORTRAN, BAL.

Contemplated Equipment
Disc drive, 1403 line printer.

Services Available
Advice, programming, systems analysis. Operate on a closed shop basis. Available only for FORTRAN Language.

Fields of Application
Management, scientific, statistical.

Training
A.S. course in computer science.

MISSOURI VALLEY COLLEGE
500 East College, Marshall, 65340
Telephone: 886-6183

Officers
Dr. W. L. Tompkins, *President*
Dr. George Brock, *Interim Academic Dean*

Computer Installation
The College is connected by means of a time-sharing terminal to the Bull General Electric GE 265 installation of United Computing Systems, Inc. in Kansas City, Missouri.

Coding Languages
BASIC, FORTRAN.

Services Available
Education and training. Operate on an open shop and time-sharing basis. Available to all students, faculty, and staff of the college.

Fields of Application
Scientific, statistical, accounting, educational.

Training
Introduction to computing and advanced computer programming courses.

NORTHEAST MISSOURI STATE COLLEGE*
Kirksville 63501
Telephone: 665-5121

Officer
Robert J. Bradley, *Director of the Data Processing Center*

Computer Installation
IBM 1401–internal storage: 16K bits; magnetic tapes: 4 729; magnetic discs: 1 1311; 1 line printer.

Coding Languages
Autocoder, FORTRAN, RPG, COBOL.

Contemplated Equipment
IBM 360.

Services Available
Advice, operators, preparation of data, programming, software packages, systems analysis. Operate on a closed shop and block time basis.

Fields of Application
Academic services: Language processing, best scoring, research.
Administrative services: Alumni system, facilities system, finance system, library, student system.

Training
Courses in programming business computers, business information systems and computers, numerical analysis (utilizing FORTRAN) and linear programming (utilizing FORTRAN).

NORTHWEST MISSOURI STATE UNIVERSITY
Department of Statistics and Computer Science
Maryville, 64468
Telephone: (816) 582-3004

Officers
Dr. Ronnie L. Moss. *Department Chairman*
Mr. William Churchill, *Director, Computer Center*

Computer Installation
IBM 360/30–operating system: Disk; internal storage: 64K bits; 1 line printer.
HEWLETT PACKARD 2115A–operating system: OS; internal storage: 8K bits; 4 line printers. *Remote processing features*: teletypes.

Coding Languages
FORTRAN, BASIC, COBOL, PL/1, RPG, ALGOL, Assembler.

Contemplated Equipment
Tape drives, more remote terminals.

Services Available
Advice, programming, education and training, systems analysis. Operate on a closed shop and time-sharing basis. Priority lists are set up with administrative and instructional priorities highest on list.

Fields of Application
Statistical, management, instructional.

Training
B.S. in Computer Science, B.S. in Mathematics with emphasis on Computer Science, B.S. in Business (Computer Science).

SOUTHEAST MISSOURI STATE UNIVERSITY
900 Normal, Cape Girardeau, 63701
Telephone: (314) 334-4811

Officer
James R. Briney, *Director of Data Processing*

Computer Installation
IBM 360—operating system: Disk; internal storage: 262,144 bytes; magnetic tapes: 2 2415; magnetic discs: 3 2311, 1 2314; 2 line printers. *Remote processing features*: 8 2260 display stations, 1 1053 printer, 5 2741 terminals.

Coding Languages
Assembly, PL/1, RPG, FORTRAN IV, COBOL, BASIC.

Contemplated Equipment
IBM 370/135, 2314 disc, 8 2260 display stations, 1030 data collection system.

Services Available
Consultation, programming, operators, preparation of data, systems analysis. Operate on a closed shop basis. Available to area high schools only.

Fields of Application
Statistical, accounting.
Specialized areas: Institutional research, student scheduling, instruction, inventory, payroll.

Training
Sixteen courses of 3 semester hours credit.

SOUTHWEST MISSOURI STATE COLLEGE*
901 South National, Springfield, 65801

Officer
Fred O. Turner, *Director of Computers*

Computer Installation
IBM 1401—internal storage: 12K bits; magnetic discs: 2 1311; 1 line printer.

Coding Languages
FORTRAN, Autocoder.

Services Available
Consultation, programming, education and training, operators, software packages, documentation, preparation of data, systems analysis. Operate on a closed and open shop basis.

Fields of Application
Statistical, accounting.
Specialized areas: Administration reports, simulation games.

Training
Courses in programming, systems analysis, numerical analysis.

UNIVERSITY OF MISSOURI, COLUMBIA
Computational Service Center
Math Sciences Building, Columbia, 65201
Telephone: 449-8376

Officers
Dr. D. R. Shurtleff, *Director*
C. Burton and L. L. Johnson, *Assistant Directors*

Computer Installation
IBM 360/65—operating system: HASP/OS/MVT; internal storage: 3 million bytes; magnetic tapes: 6 3420; magnetic discs: 1 2314, 2 Memorex 660; 2 line printers.
On-line satellite computers: IBM 1130, 3 IBM 360/20.
Remote processing features: HASP, RJE.

Coding Languages
FORTRAN, COBOL, PL/I, PL/C, WATFIV, WATBOL.

Contemplated Equipment
IBM 370/165.

Services Available
Remote job entry. Operate on a self-service basis.

Field of Application
Scientific.

Training
Courses in computer and programming languages, numerical analysis, data storage and retrieval, topics in Computer Science. Degree obtainable: M.S. in Electrical Engineering or Applied Mathematics with an emphasis on Computer Science.

UNIVERSITY OF MISSOURI, ROLLA
Mathematics-Computer Science Building, Rolla, 65401
Telephone: (314) 341-4841

Officers
R. E. Lee, *Director of Computer Center*
D. W. Dearth, *Assistant Director*
J. W. Hamblen, *Chairman of Computer Science Department*

Computer Installation
IBM 360/50—operating system: OS-MVT; internal storage: 12 million bits; magnetic tapes: 2 2415; magnetic discs: 9 2314; 1 line printer. *On-line satellite computers*: 6 Data General Nova 800. *Remote processing features*: interactive, RJE, graphics.

Coding Languages
FORTRAN IV, COBOL, PL/1, BASIC, WATFIV, ALGOL, LISP, SNOBOL 4.

Contemplated Equipment
A seventh Data General Nova 800.

Services Available
Advice, programming, education and training, software packages, documentation, data preparation, systems analysis. Operate on a remote access and closed shop basis.

Fields of Application
Scientific, statistical, systems analysis, operational research.
Specialized areas: Linear programming, sales analysis, structural engineering.

Training
Over 50 undergraduate and graduate courses in computer science and computer engineering.

United States of America – Universities and Colleges

WASHINGTON UNIVERSITY*
Computing Facilities
Skinker and Lindell Boulevards, St. Louis, 63130
Telephone: 803-0100

Officer
T. L. Gallagher, *Director of Computing Facilities*

Computer Installation
IBM 360/50–internal storage: 1,256K bits; magnetic tapes: 4; magnetic discs: 2 2314. *Remote processing features*: 2780 high speed terminals and 2741 low speed terminals.
IBM 1401–internal storage: 8K bits; magnetic tapes: 4; magnetic disc: 1.
IBM 1710–internal storage: 40K bits; magnetic disc: 1 1311.
PDP-5–used with EAI TR-48 (analog).

Coding Languages
FORTRAN, Autocoder, COBOL, SPS, PL/1.

Contemplated Equipment
High speed data transmission equipment, IBM 360/65.

Services Available
Available for business research, providing problem is of mutual interest to faculty and industrial user.

Fields of Application
Statistics, engineering analysis, mathematical programming, medical data processing.
Specialized areas: Non-linear and integer programming, text processing.

Training
Twenty-nine formal courses are offered in computer programming, applications, and mathematical and statistical techniques. M.Sc. and D.Sc. offered by Department of Applied Mathematics and Computer Science.

MONTANA

EASTERN MONTANA COLLEGE*
Billings, 59101
Telephone: (406) 657-2235

Officer
J. C. Hall, *Director*

Computer Installation
IBM 360/20–operating systems: CPS, DPS; internal storage: 16K bits; magnetic discs: 2 2311; 1 line printer.

Coding Languages
BAL, RPG.

Contemplated Equipment
IBM 1130.

Services Available
Programming, education and training, operators, documentation, preparation of data, systems analysis. Operate on a closed shop basis. Available only to faculty, students and all departments of the College.

Fields of Application
Accounting, college records, statistical, management information, mailing.

Training
Courses in BAL, RPG, FORTRAN and data processing. Short course in key punch training.

MONTANA STATE UNIVERSITY
Computing Center
Bozeman, 59715
Telephone: (406) 994-3092

Officer
Lou Lucke, *Director of Computing Center*

Computer Installation
XDS Sigma 7–operating system: UTS; internal storage: 96K 32-bit words; magnetic tapes: 3 9-track; magnetic discs: 3 RADS, 4 removable; 2 line printers. *Remote processing features*: 50 terminals, time-sharing, remote batch.
HEWLETT PACKARD 2114.
HEWLETT PACKARD 2115.
HEWLETT PACKARD 2116.

Coding Languages
FORTRAN, COBOL, BASIC, APL, RPG, COGO.

Services Available
Advice, preparation of data, programming, systems analysis. Operate on a remote access basis. Priority is given to the University.

Fields of Application
Statistical analysis, engineering calculations, scientific computation, administrative data processing.

Training
Introductory course in programming; courses in machine methods of calculation, electronic processing of scientific data, digital computer applications, business data processing. Complete range of programming courses offered by Engineering and Computer Science Departments.

UNIVERSITY OF MONTANA
Computer Center
Missoula, 59801
Telephone: 543-7241

Officers
Frank Greenwood, *Director*
Leonard L. Lewis, *Assistant Director*

Computer Installation
PDP-10–operating system: DEC MONITOR; internal storage: 96K 36-bit words; magnetic tapes: 3; magnetic discs: 3; 1 line printer. *Remote processing features*: 35 remote terminals.
IBM 1620–internal storage: 40K bits; 1 line printer.

Coding Languages
FORTRAN, BASIC, COBOL, ALGOL, SNOBOL.

Services Available
Advice, programming, education and training, software packages, systems analysis. Operate on a remote access, closed shop and time-sharing basis.

Fields of Application
Scientific, statistical, commercial, accounting, management, systems analysis, operational research.
Specialized areas: Linear programming, analysis, payroll, medical research.

Training
Courses in FORTRAN and programming digital computers.

United States of America — Universities and Colleges

NEBRASKA

UNIVERSITY OF NEBRASKA*
Lincoln, 68508
Telephone: 472-7211

Officers
Dr. Don J. Nelson, *Director*
Don Costello, *Assistant Director*
Roy Hallquist, *Assistant Director*

Computer Installation
IBM 360/65—operating system: OS/MVT; internal storage: 1 million bytes; magnetic tapes: 7 9-track; magnetic discs: 2 2314; 2 line printers. *Remote processing features*: 50 remote devices of various kinds.

Coding Languages
FORTRAN, COBOL, GPSS, Assembly, PL/1.

Services Available
Advice, operators, preparation of data, programming, software packages, systems analysis. Operate on a closed shop, time-sharing and remote access basis.

Fields of Application
Scientific, statistical, commercial, production control, accounting, management, systems analysis, operational research.
Specialized areas: Linear programming, investment analysis.

Training
Handled by Computing Science Department.

UNIVERSITY OF NEBRASKA AT OMAHA*
60th & Dodge Street, P.O. Box 688, Omaha, 68101
Telephone: (402) 553-4700

Officers
R. J. Robinson, *Director*
J. Ray, *In charge of Training, User Services, etc.*

Computer Installations
NCR 315—internal storage: 40K x 12 bits; magnetic tapes: 1; magnetic discs: 1; 1 line printer. *Remote processing features*: 16 teletypes.
IBM 360/20—operating system: DPS; internal storage: 32K bytes; magnetic tapes: 2; magnetic discs: 3; 1 line printer.

Coding Languages
FORTRAN, COBOL, NEAT, RPG, BAL.

Contemplated Equipment
Univac 1106, 9300.

Services Available
Consultation, programming, education and training, operators, software packages, documentation, preparation of data, systems analysis. Operate on a closed shop, remote access and time-sharing basis. Available to outside uses only with approval of the project.

Fields of Application
Scientific, statistical, educational, administrative.

Training
Nine courses available.

NEVADA

UNIVERSITY OF NEVADA*
Data Processing Center
Reno, 89507
Telephone: 323-2081

Officer
Dr. Craig A. Magwire, *Director of Data Processing Center*

Computer Installation
IBM 1620—internal storage: 360K bits; magnetic discs: 4 1311; 1 line printer. *Remote processing features*: TTY 33 ASR remote to Tymshare SDS 940 computer in Palo Alto, California.
PDP-8—internal storage: 48K bits. *Remote processing features*: analogue to digital convertor for telemetered data.

Coding Languages
FORTRAN II, SPS.

Contemplated Equipment
XDS Sigma 7.

Services Available
Advice, operators, preparation of data, software packages. Operate on a closed shop and limited open shop basis.

Field of Application
Statistical analysis.

Training
Introductory courses in computer programming.

UNIVERSITY OF NEVADA AT LAS VEGAS*
4505 Maryland Parkway, Las Vegas, 89109
Telephone: (702) 736-6111

Officer
Mona Wecksung, *Acting Director of the Computer Center*

Computer Installation
IBM 1130—operating system: Monitor; internal storage: 131,074 bits; magnetic tapes: 2 2415; magnetic disc: 2315; 1 line printer.

Coding Languages
FORTRAN IV.

Services Available
Operators, preparation of data. Operate on a block time basis.

Fields of Application
Administration, scientific, statistical, research and education.

Training
Introductory courses in business data processing and computer languages; FORTRAN programming for business and scientific applications.

NEW HAMPSHIRE

DARTMOUTH COLLEGE*
Kiewit Computation Center
Hanover, 03755
Telephone: (603) 646-2643

Officers
Thomas E. Kurtz, *Director*
Robert F. Hargraves, Jr., *Associate Director*

Computer Installation
BULL GENERAL ELECTRIC GE 635–operating system: Dartmouth Time Sharing System; internal storage: 160K 36-bit words; magnetic tapes: 6 7-track; magnetic discs: 3 2314; 1 line printer. *On-line satellite computers*: 2 Datanet-30. *Remote processing features*: Access by means of teletypes and other remote time-sharing terminals.

Coding Languages
GMAP, BASIC, FORTRAN, LISP, TRAC, ALGOL.

Services Available
Documentation, telecommunications service, programming assistance, time-sharing service, background service, batch service. Operate on a closed shop and time-sharing basis. Remote customers may not usually use on-line printer, card punch, card reader.

Fields of Application
Scientific, statistical, management information, investment analysis, data retrieval, and analysis, simulation, instruction, editing, computer science research, clinical medicine, engineering.

Training
Informal courses in BASIC and FORTRAN.

PLYMOUTH STATE COLLEGE
Plymouth, 03264
Telephone: (603) 536-1550

Officers
Harold E. Hyde, *President*
Richard J. Brook, *Associate Dean of Instruction*
F. Glynn Rodean, *Director, Computer Center*

Computer Installation
IBM System/3/10–operating system: DOS; internal storage: 128K bits; magnetic discs: 1 5444; 1 line printer.

Coding Languages
COBOL, FORTRAN.

Contemplated Equipment
Binary Synchronous Communications Adapter.

Services Available
Operate on a block time basis.

Field of Application
Management.
Specialized area: Applied computer science.

Training
Introductory course in computer programming (FORTRAN IV), and advanced programming course in IBM 1130 Assembly language.

UNIVERSITY OF NEW HAMPSHIRE*
Computation Center
Kingsbury Hall, Durham, 03824
Telephone: (603) 868-5511

Officer
Dr. Shan S. Kuo, *Director*

Computer Installation
IBM 360/40–operating systems: OS, RAX; internal storage: 128K; magnetic tapes: 2403 and 2402 9-track, 2401 7-track; magnetic discs: 3 2311; 1 line printer. *Remote processing features*.
IBM 1620–internal storage: 40K bits; magnetic tapes: 2 7330; 1 line printer.

Coding Languages
FORTRAN, Load and Go.

Services Available
Advice, operators, software packages. Operate on a closed shop (360/40), open shop (1620), remote access and time-sharing basis. Limited availability to outside users.

Field of Application
Space data processing.

Training
Introductory courses in FORTRAN programming, numerical methods and computers.

NEW JERSEY

FAIRLEIGH DICKINSON UNIVERSITY*
Rutherford, 07070

Officer
David T. Northrop, *Computer Center Director*

Computer Installation
IBM 1401–internal storage: 128K bits; magnetic discs: 3.
IBM 1311–1 line printer.
IBM 1620–internal storage: 120K bits.

Coding Languages
FORTRAN, Autocoder.

Contemplated Equipment
IBM 360/30 with 65K-bit storage.

Services Available
Advice, operators, preparation of data, programming, software packages, systems analysis. Operate on a closed shop and block time basis. Limited to projects of educational interest.

Fields of Application
Scientific, statistical, commercial, accounting, systems analysis, operational, computer science.

MONMOUTH COLLEGE*
Cedar Avenue, West Long Branch, 07764
Telephone: (201) 222-6600

Officer
W. A. Richards, *Director of Computer Center*

Computer Installation
HONEYWELL H200–internal storage: 32K bits; magnetic tapes: 4; 1 line printer.

Coding Languages
Easycoder, FORTRAN IV, COBOL.

Services Available
Programming, education and training, operators, preparation of data. Operate on a self-service and time-sharing basis. Available for educational use only.

Fields of Application
Accounting, management, scientific, statistical, educational.

Training
Courses in Assembly language programming, FORTRAN and COBOL.

NEWARK COLLEGE OF ENGINEERING*
Computing Center
323 High Street, Newark, 07102
Telephone: (201) 264-2424, 224-2424

Officers
Dr. Frederick G. Lehman, *Director*
Dr. Phyllis Fox, *Associate Director*

Computer Installation
RCA Spectra 70/35–operating systems: TOS, DOS; internal storage: 599,824 bits; magnetic tapes: 4 40/432; magnetic discs: 2 70/564; 1 line printer. *Remote processing features*: Communication control for 6 teletypewriters on "first come service".
IBM 1620–internal storage: 20K bits.

Coding Languages
FORTRAN, SPS.

Contemplated Equipment
RCA Spectra 70-45 time-sharing system.

Services Available
Advice, operators, preparation of data, programming, systems analysis. Operate on a closed shop, remote access and time-sharing basis.

Field of Application
Traffic simulation.

Training
Introductory and advanced programming courses.

PRINCETON UNIVERSITY
Historical Data Center
Department of History, Princeton, 08540
Telephone: (609) 452-4159

Officer
Theodore K. Rabb, *Director*

Computer Installation
IBM 360/91.

Coding Languages
FORTRAN, PL/1.

Services Available
Advice, education and training. Operate on a self-service basis.

Field of Application
Statistical.
Specialized area: Analysis.

RUTGERS, THE STATE UNIVERSITY
Center for Computer and Information Services
Hill Center for Mathematical Sciences, New Brunswick, 08903

Officers
Edward Bloustein, *President*
David Freeman, *Director of University Computing and Information Processing*

Computer Installation
IBM 360/67–operating system: OS/360; internal storage: 20 million bits; magnetic tapes: 7 3420/5; magnetic discs: 4 2314/A1; 3 line printers. *On-line satellite computers*: 25 total – 1130, 360/20, 360/30, 360/40, 2770, etc. *Remote processing features*: 20 RJE lines, 110 time-sharing lines.
IBM 370/135–operating system: DOS/VS; internal storage: 2 million bits; magnetic tapes: 5 3420/3; magnetic discs: 3 3330; 2 line printers.

Coding Languages
FORTRAN, PL/I, COBOL, RPG, BAL, ALGOL, BASIC, SNOBOL.

Contemplated Equipment
IBM 370/168.

Services Available
Advice, education and training, software packages, documentation. Operate on a remote access, closed shop, and time-sharing basis.

Fields of Application
Scientific, statistical, operational research.
Specialized areas: Linear programming, structural engineering, medical research.

SAINT PETER'S COLLEGE*
Kennedy Boulevard, Jersey City, 07306
Telephone: 333-4400, extension 311

Officer
Robert Harrington, *Manager, Data Processing Department*

Computer Installation
IBM 360/25–operating system: DOS, internal storage: 192K bits; magnetic tapes: 2; magnetic discs: 2 2311; 1 line printer.

Coding Languages
BAL, RPG, COBOL, FORTRAN.

Services Available
Education and training. Operate on a closed shop basis.

Fields of Application
Scientific, statistical, accounting, commercial, management, systems analysis.

SETON HALL UNIVERSITY*
South Orange, 07079
Telephone: South Orange 2-9000

Officers
Dr. Richard F. Gabriel, *Director*
George Germann, *Instructor in Computer Science*
Harry P. Wujciak, *Data Processing Supervisor*

Computer Installation
IBM 1620–operating system: Monitor; internal storage: 20K bits; magnetic discs: 1311; 1 line printer.

Coding Languages
FORTRAN, SPS, LOAD AND GO, SNOBOL.

Contemplated Equipment
Remote terminals, time-sharing facilities.

Services Available
Advice, operators, preparation of data, programming, software packages, systems analysis. Operate on a closed and open shop basis. Available only to those people whose projects are deemed compatible with the University education and research.

Fields of Application
General University research as well as administrative data processing.
Specialized areas: Bio-medical computation, numerical analysis.

Training
Computer programming and numerical methods.

STEVENS INSTITUTE OF TECHNOLOGY*
Hoboken, 07030
Telephone: (201) 792-2700

Officer
Dr. Irving N. Rabinowitz, *Director, Computer Center*

Computer Installation
IBM 360/40—operating system: OS; internal storage: 2 million bits; magnetic tapes: 2 2415; magnetic discs: 3 2311; 1 line printer. *Remote processing features*: typewriter terminals.

Coding Languages
FORTRAN, PL/1, COBOL, ALGOL, OSA.

Services Available
Advice, operators, software packages. Operate on a closed shop and remote access basis.

Fields of Application
Numerical analysis, hydrodynamics, numerous research projects in science and engineering.
Specialized areas: Numerical solution of differential equations; various special topics in hydrodynamics; symbol processing; programming languages.

Training
Courses in computer fundamentals and programming, and in the theory and practice of the use of digital computers.

NEW MEXICO

NEW MEXICO HIGHLANDS UNIVERSITY
Computer Center
Las Vegas, 87701
Telephone: 425-7511

Officer
T. Q. King, *Director*

Computer Installation
IBM 360/25—operating system: DOS; internal storage: 32,768 bytes; magnetic tapes: 2 2415; magnetic discs: 3 2311; 1 line printer.
IBM 1620-1—internal storage: 240K bits.

Coding Languages
PL/1, COBOL, FORTRAN, RPG, Assembler.

Services Available
Consultation, programming, education and training, operators, software packages, documentation, preparation of data, systems analysis. Operate on a closed shop basis. Available to all members of the university community.

Fields of Application
Scientific computing and research, statistical analysis, accounting, payroll, student records, management information.

Training
Computer Science option under Mathematics B.S. degree.

NEW MEXICO STATE UNIVERSITY
Physical Science Laboratory
P.O. Box 3548, Las Cruces, 88003
Telephone: (505) 524-2851

Also at:
University Computer Center
P.O. Box 3AT, Las Cruces, 88003
Telephone: (505) 646-3439

Officers
Gerald W. Thomas, *President*
Carl R. Hall, *Vice-President, Administration*
Harold R. Lawrence, *Director, Physical Science Laboratory*
Don Cartlidge, *Director, Computer Center*

Computer Installation
Physical Science Laboratory:
IBM 370/135—operating systems: DOS, OS/VSI; internal storage: 192K bits; magnetic tapes: 2 9-track, 2 7-track; magnetic discs: 2 2319; 1 line printer. *Remote processing features*: 2 2741 terminals.

University Computing Center:
IBM 360/65—operating system: OS/MVT/HASP; internal storage: 256K plus 2 million bytes; magnetic tapes: 2 Ampex 9-track; magnetic discs: 14 Ampex DS314 spindles; 2 line printers. *Remote processing features*: 15 2741 terminals, 4 Datel portable terminals.

Coding Languages
FORTRAN, FORTRAN IV, COBOL, PL/1, Assembler, ALGOL, SIMSCRIPT, WATFOR, BASIC, SNOBOL, WATBOL, APL.

Services Available
Advice, preparation of data, programming, software packages, systems analysis. Operate on a closed and open shop and remote access basis. Physical Science Laboratory offers complete computation service to selected outside agencies and customers. University Computer Center facilities available to all faculty, staff and students on shared basis.

Fields of Application
Scientific, statistical, commercial, accounting, management, systems analysis, operational research, numerical analysis, data analysis.
Specialized areas: Rocket simulation, payroll, voter records, records, student on-line academic records, APL applications.

Training
Bachelor's and Master's programmes in Computer Science; Associate degree course in data processing; Bachelor's degree course in business systems analysis; introductory courses in programming and computer design.

United States of America – Universities and Colleges

UNIVERSITY OF ALBUQUERQUE
St. Joseph's Place, N.W., Albuquerque, 87105
Telephone: (505) 243-9461

Officers
Frank A. Kleinhenz, *President*
Andrew Imrik, *Administrative Vice-President*
J. Peter Carey, *Academic Dean*

Computer Installation
IBM System/3–operating system: DSM; internal storage: 131,072 bits; magnetic discs: 4 5444; line printer.

Coding Languages
COBOL, FORTRAN IV, RPG II.

Contemplated Equipment
Additional main storage, CTR terminal.

Services Available
Advice, programming, education and training. Operate on a closed shop basis.

Fields of Application
Accounting, management, educational.
Specialized area: Payroll.

Training
Programming courses in FORTRAN, COBOL, RPG; course in system design.

UNIVERSITY OF NEW MEXICO*
Computing Center
2706 Lomas Boulevard, N.E., Albuquerque, 87106
Telephone: (505) 277-4822

Officer
S. Bell, *Director, Computer Center*

Computer Installations
IBM 360/67–operating systems: CP67, OS, RAX, CMS; internal storage: 512K bytes; magnetic tapes: 5; magnetic discs: 6; 1 line printer. *Remote processing features*: 30 terminals.

IBM 360/40–operating system: OS; internal storage: 2 million bits; magnetic tapes: 4; magnetic discs: 2314; 1 line printer.

NEW YORK

ADELPHI UNIVERSITY*
Garden City, 11530
Telephone: (516) 747-2200

Officer
Mary Louise Buchanan, *Director*

Computer Installation
CDC 3300–internal storage: 64K bits; magnetic tapes: 3 601; magnetic discs: 2 854; 1 line printer.

Coding Languages
FORTRAN, COBOL.

Fields of Application
Scientific, administrative programmes (financial, registration, etc.), education.

BROOME COMMUNITY COLLEGE
907 Upper Front Street, Binghamton, 13902
Telephone: 772-5000

Officer
D. Copeland, *Director*

Computer Installation
IBM 1130–internal storage: 8K bits; magnetic disc: 2315; 2 line printers. *Remote processing features*: IBM 2741 communications terminal.
IBM 360/20–internal storage: 8K bits; 1 line printer.

Coding Languages
FORTRAN IV, RPG, APL, Assembler, COBOL.

Services Available
Advice, operators, programming. Operate on a self-service and time-sharing basis. Limited outside time available.

Fields of Application
All fields of college disciplines.

Training
Courses in computer programming and systems analysis.

CITY UNIVERSITY OF NEW YORK*
Board of Higher Education Central Office
535 East 80th Street, New York, 10021

Officer
R. Spock, *Associate Dean*

Computer Installation
IBM 360/20–operating system: Monitor; internal storage 100K bits; magnetic tapes: 4 2415; 2 line printers.
Remote processing features.

Contemplated Equipment
RCA Spectra 70/46.

Services Available
Consultation, programming, education and training, operators, documentation, preparation of data, systems analysis. Operate on a remote access and closed shop basis.

Fields of Application
Accounting, management, systems analysis.

CITY UNIVERSITY OF NEW YORK
Graduate School and University Center
33 West 42nd Street, New York, 10036
Telephone: (212) 790-4401

Officers
S. Fisher, *Acting Director*
W. Bradley, *Associate Director*

Computer Installation
IBM 1130–operating system: CUNY-Partitioned; internal storage: 16K 16-bit words; magnetic tapes: 2; magnetic discs: 3 2310, 1 2311; 1 line printer. *Remote processing features*: serves as RJE station.
PDP-8–operating systems: TSS-8, DS-8; internal storage: 16K 12-bit words; magnetic tapes: 4; magnetic discs: 2 DEC. *On-line satellite computer*: IMLAC PDS-I; *Remote processing features*: 4 telephone ports; AD/DA port.

Coding Languages
FORTRAN, Assembly, BASIC, LISP, SNOBOL, BALM, PL/1,

Contemplated Equipment
PDP-11.

United States of America – Universities and Colleges

Services Available
Advice, programming, education and training, software packages, documentation, systems analysis. Operate on a self-service open and closed shop and time-sharing basis.

Fields of Application
Scientific, statistical, systems analysis, operational research.
Specialized areas: Analysis, non-numeric models, computer assisted instruction.

Training
Ph.D. course in Educational Psychology with a concentration in computer applications. Special courses in the use of computers in research.

CITY UNIVERSITY OF NEW YORK*
Hunter College
695 Park Avenue, New York, 10021
Telephone: 360-2771

Officer
B. Shlasko, *Manager, Computer Center*

Computer Installation
IBM 360/40–operating system: DOS; internal storage: 128K bits; magnetic tapes: 4 2415; magnetic discs: 5 2314; 1 line printer.

Contemplated Equipment
Additional reader-printer; terminals.

Services Available
Consultation, programming, education and training, operators, software packages, preparation of data. Operate on a remote access basis. Available only to City University of New York.

Fields of Application
Scientific, statistical, teaching, accounting, administration.

Training
Four computer-orientated courses. 2 short courses.

CITY UNIVERSITY OF NEW YORK
Kingsborough Community College
2001 Oriental Boulevard, Brooklyn, 11235
Telephone: (212) 769-9200

Officer
H. Reznikoff, *Director, Computer Center*

Computer Installation
IBM 360/30–operating system: DOS; internal storage: 524,288 bits; magnetic tapes: 2415; magnetic discs: 3 2311; 1 line printer.

Coding Languages
COBOL, Assembler, RPG, FORTRAN, PL/1.

Services Available
Consultation, programming, education and training, operators, software packages, documentation, preparation of data, systems analysis. Operate on an open shop and block time basis. Available only to administration, faculty, students.

Fields of Application
Scientific, commercial, management, research.

Training
Courses as part of A.S. degree programme (4 courses), and A.A.S. degree programme (7 courses). Two short courses.

CITY UNIVERSITY OF NEW YORK
Staten Island Community College
715 Ocean Terrace, Staten Island, 10301
Telephone: (212) 390-7580

Officer
Ethem R. Kok, *Director of Computer Center*

Computer Installation
IBM 360/30–operating systems: DOS, RMTDOS; internal storage: 64K bits; magnetic tapes: 3 3420, 1 2403; magnetic discs: 3 2311, 2 Memorex 630; 2 line printers. *Remote processing features*: RJE to IBM 360/50 and 370/165.

Coding Languages
RPG, BAL, COBOL, PL/1, FORTRAN, PLC, SPASM, WATBOL.

Contemplated Equipment
IBM 3270, PDP-11.

Services Available
Programming, education and training, systems analysis, preparation of data. Operate on a closed shop basis. Available only to students, faculty members and administrators.

Fields of Application
Accounting, statistical, scientific, educational, management, systems analysis.
Specialized areas: Student Data Base and Transcripts.

Training
Nineteen courses in Computer Technology and Business Departments are offered. A.A.S. course in computer technology.

CLARKSON COLLEGE OF TECHNOLOGY
Computer Center
Potsdam, 13676
Telephone: 268-7721

Officer
W. H. Lyman, *Director*

Computer Installation
IBM 360/44–operating system: 44MFT; internal storage: 1,056K bits; magnetic discs: 4 1316; 1 line printer.

Coding Languages
FORTRAN, Assembler, L6, SNOBOL, LISP, GPSS.

Services Available
Advice, operators, programming. Operate on a closed shop basis.

Fields of Application
Education, analysis and programming in all scientific fields.

Training
Computer Science options on several courses.

COLGATE UNIVERSITY*
Hamilton, 13346
Telephone: (315) 824-1000

Officers
James H. Reynolds, *Director of Computer Center*
Peter J. Angell, *Director of Administrative Data Processing Services, Administration Building Facility*

United States of America – Universities and Colleges

Computer Installation
Computer Center:
IBM 1130–operating system: MONITOR; internal storage: 32K bits; magnetic discs: 3 2315; 1 line printer. *Remote processing features:* link to IBM 360/65.
IBM 1401–internal storage: 12K bits; magnetic discs: 2 1311; 1 line printer.

Administration Building Facility:
IBM 1620–operating system: MONITOR; internal storage: 20K bits; magnetic discs: 1 1311. *Remote processing features:* teletype terminals to A-GE 645 IBM 2741 terminal to IBM 360/65.

Coding Languages
FORTRAN, Assembler, SPS, BASIC, APL, Autocoder, RPG.

Services Available
Operate on an open and closed shop basis. Computers in Computer Center used for academic purposes only; Administration Building Facility computer used only for administration.

Fields of Application
Education and research in sciences, social sciences and humanities; accounting student records and alumni records.

CORNELL UNIVERSITY
Office of Computer Services
Langmuir Laboratory, Ithaca, 14850
Telephone: (607) 256-3325

Officers
John W. Rudan, *Acting Director*
Robert R. Blackmun, *Business Manager*
Richard Cogger, *Assistant Director*

Computer Installation
IBM 360/65–operating systems: OS(MVT), HASP, TSO; magnetic tapes: 8 3420; magnetic discs: 23 2314; 2 line printers. *Remote processing features:* 5 remote work stations.

Coding Languages
FORTRAN, PL/1, WATFIV, PL/C, Assembler.

Services Available
Advice, preparation of data, documentation.

FORDHAM UNIVERSITY*
Computing Center
East Fordham Road, Bronx, 10458
Telephone: (212) 933-2233

Officers
Charles Bowman, *Director of Data Processing*
Mrs. Susan Kliavkoff, *Director of Computer Center*
Mrs. Carmen Stanley, *Programming Supervisor*

Computer Installation
IBM 360/40–operating system: DOS; internal storage: 65K bytes; magnetic tapes: 1 2415; magnetic discs: 3 2311; 1 line printer.

Coding Languages
ALP, COBOL, FORTRAN, PL/1, RPG.

Contemplated Equipment
Additional 65K memory; 2311 magnetic discs to be replaced with 4 2314 disc drives; 1 2780 remote batch terminal.

Services Available
Advice and limited programming service for University academic community, systems analysis, programming, preparation of data, processing for administration. Operate on a closed shop basis. Limited service available for non-university users.

Fields of Application
Scientific for academic users; commercial applications for university administration.

Training
Several six-hour seminars in FORTRAN each semester.

LONG ISLAND UNIVERSITY
Money Management Institute
C.W. Post Center, Treenvale, Long Island, 11548
Telephone: (516) 299-2861

Officer
Sigmund Rothschild, *President*

Computer Installation
NCR–magnetic tapes: 2; magnetic discs: 2.

Contemplated Equipment
Microfilming by means of aperture cards.

Services Available
Advice, documentation, preparation of data. Operate on time-sharing basis.

Field of Application
Educational.
Specialized areas: Sales analysis, investment, analysis, cataloguing works of art.

MANHATTAN COLLEGE*
Bronx, 10471
Telephone: 548-1400

Officers
Brother H. W. Hogan, *Director*
Norbert Hart, *Supervisor*

Computer Installation
CDC 8090–internal storage: 8,192 12-bit words; magnetic tapes: 4 603; 1 line printer.

Coding Languages
FORTRAN, AUTOCOMM, OSAS.

Services Available
Advice, operators, preparation of data, programming, systems analysis. Operate on a closed shop basis. Available to educational users only.

Fields of Application
Engineering research, scientific research (nuclear).
Specialized area: Numerical analysis.

Training
Programming courses for students only. Introductory FORTRAN programming.

MARIST COLLEGE
North Road, Poughkeepsie, 12601
Telephone: (914) 471-3240

Officers
V. J. Donnelly, *Director of Computer Center*
E. Gumierry, *Operations Manager*

Computer Installation
IBM 1401—internal storage: 16K bits; magnetic discs: 2; 1 line printer. *Remote processing features*: 3 2741 communications terminals.

Coding Languages
Autocoder, FORTRAN, COBOL, APL, Coursewriter III.

Services Available
Education and training. Operate on a self-service and time-sharing basis.

Fields of Application
Scientific, statistical, commercial, accounting, management, systems analysis, operational research.

Training
Computer internship, computer organization and programming.

NASSAU COMMUNITY COLLEGE
Stewart Avenue, Garden City, 11530
Telephone: (516) 712-0600

Officer
T. A. Corr, *Director*

Computer Installation
IBM 360/25—operating system: DOS; internal storage: 49,152 bits; magnetic tapes: 4 2401; magnetic discs: 2 2311; 1 line printer.

Contemplated Equipment
IBM 370/135.

Services Available
Consultation, programming, education and training, operators, preparation of data. Operate on an open shop basis. Available only to students, faculty, administration.

Fields of Application
Scientific, statistical, commercial, accounting.

Training
A.A.S. course in Data Processing.

NEW YORK INSTITUTE OF TECHNOLOGY
Advanced Systems Laboratory
Wheatley Road, Old Westbury, 11568
Telephone: (516) 626-3400, extension 289

Officers
Dr. Alexander Schure, *President*
Dr. Alan Roseblum, *Director of ASL*

Computer Installation
XDS Sigma 6—operating system: Universal Time Sharing; internal storage: 3,072K bits; magnetic tapes: 4; magnetic discs: 8; 1 line printer. *Remote processing features*: 50 time-sharing terminals.

Coding Languages
FORTRAN, COBOL, BASIC, APL, META SYMBOL.

Contemplated Equipment
Tape drives, line printer.

Services Available
Programming, education and training, software packages. Operate on a time-sharing basis.

Fields of Application
Scientific, statistical, commercial.
Specialized area: CMI/CAI.

Training
Courses in programming, system design and logic design leading to a four-year accredited degree in Computer Science Technology.

NEW YORK UNIVERSITY
Courant Institute of Mathematical Sciences
AEC Computing and Applied Mathematics Center
Warren Weaver Hall, 251 Mercer Street, New York, 10012
Telephone: (212) 460-7100

Officers
Prof. P. D. Lax, *Director of Institute*
Prof. P. Garabedian, *Director of Center*
Prof. M. Goldstein, *Director of Computing*

Computer Installation
CDC 6600—operating system: SCOPE 3.4; internal storage: 8,355,840 bits; magnetic tapes: 6 CDC 607, 2 CDC 626; magnetic discs: 1 CDC 6603, 1 CDC 6638, 1 CDC 814; 2 line printers. *On-line satellite computers:* 2 Honeywell DDP-516. *Remote processing features:* varied terminals and speeds, interactive start-stop terminals.

Coding Languages
FORTRAN, BALM, COMPASS, SETL.

Services Available
Advice, education and training, operators. Operate on a closed shop, remote access and time-sharing basis.

Field of Application
Scientific.
Specialized areas: Applied mathematics, computer science.

Training
The University's Computer Science Department offers a full range of courses leading to degrees of B.A., M.S. and Ph.D.

NEW YORK UNIVERSITY
Department of Electrical Engineering and Computer Science
University Heights, Bronx, 10453

Officer
Prof. H. Freeman, *Chairman*

Computer Installation
ADAGE AGT-30—operating system: AMOS; internal storage: 480K bits; magnetic tape: 1; magnetic discs: 2; 1 line printer.
UNIVAC 1108—operating system: EXEC 8; internal storage; 4,752K bits; magnetic tapes: 8; 3 line printers. *Remote processing features:* Remote batch and teletype terminals.

Coding Languages
FORTRAN IV.

Services Available
Education and training. Operate on a remote access, closed shop, block time, and time-sharing basis. Available for educational use only.

Field of Application
Scientific.

Training
B.S., M.S. and Ph.D. courses in Computer Science.

United States of America — Universities and Colleges

PACE COLLEGE*
Pace College Plaza, New York, 10038
Telephone: (212) 285-3000

Officers
Dr. E. J. Mortola, *President*
Prof. A. Varanelli, Jr., *Computer Center Director*

Computer Installation
IBM 360/25—operating system: DOS; internal storage: 32K bytes; magnetic tapes: 4 2415; magnetic discs: 2 2314; 1 line printer.

Coding Languages
BAL, COBOL, FORTRAN, PL/1, RPG.

Contemplated Equipment
IBM 360/40 with 196K-bit store, RJE and interactive terminal use.

Services Available
Programming, consultation, provision of computer services to graduate and undergraduate students. Operate on a closed shop and block time basis. Programming support not available to undergraduate students.

Fields of Application
Commercial, scientific, statistical.
Specialized areas: Data base design, information retrieval, integrated systems.

Training
Undergraduate courses in EDP and the computer in auditing and accounting; graduate courses in business information systems, electronic computer programming, electronic computer systems development and advanced computer programming.

PRATT INSTITUTE
Computer Education and Research Center (CERC)
215 Ryerson Street, Brooklyn, 11205
Telephone: (212) 636-3600

Officer
Dr. C. E. Grosch, *Director of the Center*

Computer Installation
PHILCO 2000/210(2)—operating system: SYS; internal storage: 1·5 million bits each; magnetic tapes: 13 Philco TM/2; magnetic discs: Philco 272; 1 line printer.
IBM 1620—operating system: MONITOR I; internal storage: 120K bits; magnetic discs: 1 1311.

Coding Languages
FORTRAN, COBOL, TAC Assembler, SIMSCRIPT, GPSS, MIMIC, MIX, ALTAC, PERT, APT, OPAL, STAT, SPS.

Services Available
Operate on a closed shop basis.

Fields of Application
Scientific, statistical, operational research.
Specialized areas: Linear programming.

QUEENSBOROUGH COMMUNITY COLLEGE*
Springfield Blvd. and 56th Ave., Bayside, 11364
Telephone: 428-0200

Officer
Dr. G. C. Goulandris, *Director*

Computer Installation
IBM 360/30—internal storage: 32K bits; magnetic tapes: 3 2401; magnetic discs: 3.
IBM 1130—internal storage: 8K bits.

Contemplated Equipment
32K additional core.

Services Available
Programming, operators, software packages, documentation, preparation of data, systems analysis. Operate on a closed shop and time-sharing basis.

Fields of Application
College administration, educational, scientific.

RENSSELAER POLYTECHNIC INSTITUTE*
110 8th Street, Troy, 12181
Telephone: (518) 270-6279

Officers
Dr. Richard G. Folsom, *President*
Dr. C. O. Dohrenwend, *Vice President*

Computer Installation
IBM 360/50—operating system: OS/MVT; internal storage: 12 million bits; magnetic tapes: 5 9-track; magnetic discs: 4 2311, 1 2314; 2 line printers.
Remote processing features: 2702.

Coding Languages
FORTRAN, ALGOL, COBOL, Assembler, GPSS, PL/1, RPG, LISP.

Services Available
Advice, programming, computer time. Operate on a closed and open shop and time-sharing basis.

Field of Application
Education.

Training
Graduate programmes in computer science; courses in computing on all levels for other academic programmes.

STATE UNIVERSITY OF NEW YORK, ALBANY
1400 Washington Avenue, Albany, 12222
Telephone: (518) 457-1895

Officer
R. J. Robinson, *Director of Computer Center*

Computer Installation
UNIVAC 1108—operating system: EXEC 8; internal storage: 7 million bits; magnetic tapes: 6 Uniservo VIIIC; magnetic discs: 5 8414; 2 line printers. *Remote processing features:* time-sharing with TTYs and CRTs; on-line graphics.

Coding Languages
FORTRAN, ALGOL, COBOL, BASIC, GPSS, SNOBOL, LISP.

Services Available
Consultation, programming, education and training, operators, software packages, documentation, preparation of data, systems analysis. Operate on a remote access block time basis with time-sharing terminals on premises. Available to educational and public institutions on a contractual basis. Other private concerns may purchase services on an "occasional usage" basis.

Fields of Application
Scientific, statistical, systems analysis.

United States of America – Universities and Colleges

Training
The Department of Computer Science offers an undergraduate minor and a master's degree.

STATE UNIVERSITY OF NEW YORK, BROCKPORT
Brockport, 14420
Telephone: (716) 395-2211

Officers
N. V. Plyter, *Director of Computing Center*
D. Meyers, *Director, International Education Programs*

Computer Installations
IBM 1130–operating system: DMS; internal storage: 256K bits; magnetic discs: 3; 1 line printer. *Remote processing features:* RJE to CDC 6400, IBM 360/65.
IBM 1401–internal storage: 76K bits; magnetic tapes: 2 729; magnetic discs: 3 1311; 1 line printer.

Coding Languages
FORTRAN, COBOL, APL, ALGOL, LISP, SIMSCRIPT, SNOBOL.

Services Available
Consultation, programming, education and training. Operate on a self-service, remote access, open shop and time-sharing basis. Available only to educational institutions.

Fields of Application
Scientific research, educational data processing, computer assisted instruction.

Training
Numerous courses.

STATE UNIVERSITY OF NEW YORK, BUFFALO*
Computing Center
4250 Ridge Lea Road, Amherst, 14226
Telephone: (716) 831-1245

Officers
Gordon Lilly, *Director*
Charles Allan, *Associate Director, Data Processing*
John Hale, *Associate Director, Computing Center*

Computer Installation
CDC 6400–operating system: SCOPE; internal storage: 3,932,160 bits; magnetic tapes: 4 604 7-track; magnetic discs: 1 6603; 2 line printers. *On-line satellite computers:* 4 IBM 360/20, 2 Univac 9200, 2 IBM 1130. *Remote processing features:* time-sharing regional network of state university units within 100 mile radius.
IBM 360/40–operating system: DOS; internal storage: 2,048K bits; magnetic tapes: 6 2400; magnetic discs: 8 2314; 1 line printer. *Remote processing features:* administrative terminal system for text editing and message switching using IBM 2741 communications terminal.

Coding Languages
FORTRAN IV, ALGOL, COBOL, SNOBOL, PL/1, COMPASS.

Services Available
Advice, preparation of data, programming, software packages, systems analysis. Operate on a self-service, closed shop, remote access and time-sharing basis.

Fields of Application
Scientific research, education.

Training
Short programming courses given regularly. University Computer Science curriculum at graduate level.

STATE UNIVERSITY OF NEW YORK, STONY BROOK
Stony Brook, 11790
Telephone: 246-7170

Officer
R. Franciotti, *Director of Computing Center*

Computer Installation
IBM 370/155–internal storage: 1 million bytes; magnetic tapes: 6 2401; magnetic discs: 8 3330, 8 2314; 3 line printers. *Remote processing features:* 5 high-speed RJE stations.
DIGITAL EQUIPMENT System 10–internal storage: 128K 36-bit words; magnetic tapes: 2; magnetic discs: 4 2314. *Remote processing features:* 60 terminal ports.

Coding Languages
FORTRAN, COBOL, PL/1, ALGOL, APL, GPSS, SNOBOL, CROSSTABS.

Services Available
Consultation, programming, education and training, operators, software packages, documentation, preparation of data, systems analysis. Operate on a remote access, open shop and time-sharing basis. Available only to faculty, administration, students.

Fields of Application
Scientific research, general administrative, systems analysis, educational, statistical.

Training
Graduate programme in Computing Science leading to Master's and Ph.D. degrees. Short courses.

STATE UNIVERSITY OF NEW YORK
Agricultural and Technical College
Alfred, 14802
Telephone: (607) 871-6235

Officers
Dr. D. Huntington, *President*
Dr. R. Rawe, *Vice President*
Dr. R. Close, *Director of Computing Center*

Computer Installation
BURROUGHS B3500–operating system: MCP; internal storage: 120K bytes; magnetic tapes: 2; magnetic discs: 2; 1 line printer. *Remote processing features:* up to 4 terminals.

Coding Languages
FORTRAN, COBOL, BASIC, Assembler.

Contemplated Equipment
More terminals.

Services Available
Advice, programming, education and training, data preparation, systems analysis. Operate on an open shop and time-sharing basis.

Fields of Application
Scientific, statistical, commercial, accounting, management, education.

Training
A.A.S. degree course in Data Processing.

STATE UNIVERSITY OF NEW YORK
College of Arts and Sciences
Plattsburgh, 12901
Telephone: (518) 564-2025

United States of America – Universities and Colleges

Officer
J. Matasovsky, *Director*

Computer Installation
BURROUGHS B3500 – operating system: MCP; internal storage: 90K bits; magnetic tapes: 2; magnetic discs: 5; 1 line printer. *Remote processing features:* 10 TC 500 units.

Coding Languages
FORTRAN, COBOL, BPL, PASS IV, SIMULATION.

Services Available
Advice, education and training, software packages, documentation, data preparation. Operate on a closed shop and time-sharing basis. Available for educational purposes only.

Fields of Application
Scientific, statistical, accounting, management, systems analysis, system design.
Specialized areas: Analysis, payroll.

Training
Courses in COBOL, FORTRAN, BPL and information theory basics. There is a computer science emphasis within the Science and Mathematics Division.

STATE UNIVERSITY OF NEW YORK
Maritime College
Fort Schuyler, New York 10465
Telephone: (212) 892-3000

Officers
A. E. Kinney, *Director, Computer Center*
J. D. Vierno, *Manager, Computer Center*

Computer Installation
IBM 1130 – internal storage: 8K 16-bit words; magnetic discs: 1; 1 line printer.

Coding Languages
FORTRAN, COBOL, APL, Assembler.

Services Available
Education and training. Operate on an open shop basis. Available only to students, faculty, administration.

Fields of Application
Scientific, engineering, administration.

Training
Seven courses.

STATE UNIVERSITY OF NEW YORK
School of Advanced Technology
Binghamton, 13901
Telephone: (607) 798-2793

Officer
Walter Lowen, *Dean*

Computer Installation
IBM 370/155 – operating system: OS 360, TSO, APL; internal storage: 8 million bits; magnetic tapes: 4 9-track; magnetic discs: 12 3330; 2 line printers. *Remote processing features:* 60 typewriter ports, RJE.

Coding Languages
APL, PL/I, FORTRAN, COBOL, SNOBOL, GPSS, Assembler.

Services Available
Advice, programming, education and training, software packages, documentation. Operate on a remote access and time-sharing basis. Available mainly to educational users.

Fields of Application
Scientific, statistical, commercial, accounting, management, operational research, education.

Training
The School offers a Master's degree to students who have completed an agreed course of study. Specializations include courses of study in computer systems, applied mathematics, and general systems.

UNION COLLEGE*
Schenectady, 12308
Telephone: (346) 8751-376

Officers
Harold C. Martin, *President*
James D. Palmer, *Dean of Science and Engineering*
Theodore G. Schuarz, *Director of Information Systems*

Computer Installation
BULL GENERAL ELECTRIC GE 415 – operating systems: BOS/MT, DPS; internal storage: 409,600 bits; magnetic tapes: 5 7-track; magnetic discs: 3 DSU 160; 1 line printer.

Coding Languages
FORTRAN IV, CARD, BASIC, SAP, IOS COBOL, COBOL BAP, MAP, SORT/MERGE.

Contemplated Equipment
Separate dedicated time-sharing system.

Services Available
Advice, programming, software packages, preparation of data, systems analysis. Operate on a self-service, time-sharing, closed and open shop basis. External customers have lower priority than internal work, but normally receive 3-6 hour turn-around.

Fields of Application
Scientific, statistical, accounting, systems analysis.
Specialized areas: Educational administrative software, academic software, compilers.

Training
Courses in FORTRAN, BASIC and COBOL programming, machine language programming, information system design, compiler courses, automata theory, logical design.

UNIVERSITY OF ROCHESTER
Computer Center
727 Elmwood Avenue, Rochester, 14620
Telephone: (716) 275-4181

Officers
Dr. Vincent H. Swoyer, *Director*
Bruce W. Van Atta, *Associate Director*

Computer Installation
IBM 360/65 – operating system: OS/MVT with HASP; internal storage: 512K plus 1,024 K bytes; magnetic tapes: 5 3420; magnetic discs: 16 2314 and 2319; 2 line printers. *On-line satellite computers:* IBM 360/20, 2 UCC 1225. *Remote processing features:* 35 remote terminals.

Coding Languages
WATFIV, FORTRAN, PL/1, PL/C, Assembler, SNOBOL, APL, WYLBUR, ALGOL, COBOL, GPSS, MPS, CUPL.

United States of America – Universities and Colleges

Services Available
Advice, programming, education and training, operators, software packages, documentation, preparation of data, systems analysis. Operate on a remote access, closed shop and time-sharing basis. Generally restricted to problems of research and education.

Fields of Application
Scientific, statistical.
Specialized areas: Research, educational computing.

Training
Frequent courses in programming languages and systems.

WESTCHESTER COMMUNITY COLLEGE
75 Grasslands Road, Valhalla, 10595
Telephone: (914) 946-1616

Officer
Mark S. Gesoff, *Director of the Computer Center*

Computer Installation
RCA Spectra 70/35–operating system: DOS; internal storage: 524,288 bits; magnetic tapes: 4 70/432; magnetic discs: 4 70/564; 1 line printer.

Coding Languages
BAL, FORTRAN, COBOL, RPG.

Services Available
Education and training. Operate on closed shop basis. Available only to students and staff.

Fields of Application
Scientific, statistical, accounting, management.

Training
A.A.S. degree course in business data processing.

NORTH CAROLINA

DUKE UNIVERSITY
Computation Center
Durham, 27706
Telephone: 684-3695

Officer
R. A. Schroeder, *Director*

Computer Installation
IBM 370/135–operating systems: OS/MFT, HASP; internal storage: 240K bytes; magnetic tapes: 3 3420; magnetic discs: 6 2314; 2 line printers.
IBM 370/165–operating systems: OS/MVT, HASP; internal storage: 2,097K bytes; magnetic tapes: 5 3420; magnetic discs: 24 2314, 8 3330; 1 line printer.

Coding Languages
TSAR, FORTRAN IV, PL/1, COBOL, ALGOL, RPG, Assembler.

Services Available
Advice, operators, preparation of data, programming, software packages and systems analysis. Operate on an open shop and remote access basis.

Fields of Application
Information retrieval, statistics, numerical analysis, medical applications.

NORTH CAROLINA STATE UNIVERSITY AT RALEIGH
Computing Center
P.O.B. 5445, Raleigh, 27607
Telephone: (919) 737-2518

Officer
LeRoy B. Martin Jr., *Director*

Computer Installation
IBM 360/40–operating system: OS/MFT; internal storage: 256K bytes; magnetic tapes: 2; magnetic discs: 1 2314; 2 line printers. *Remote processing features:* connected via wide band communication to IBM 370/165 at Triangle University Computation Center. Data 100 terminals.

Coding Languages
Assembly, ALGOL, FORTRAN, PL/1, COBOL, ECAP, SNOBOL etc.

Services Available
Use of computer facilities available only to University members or to those with contacts with the University. Operate on an open and closed shop basis.

Fields of Application
All fields of university interest.

Training
Department of Computer Science offers B.S. degree in Computer Science; graduate programme under development.

TRIANGLE UNIVERSITIES COMPUTATION CENTER
P.O. Box 12076, Research Triangle Park, 27709
Telephone: (919) 549-8291

Officer
Dr. Leland Williams, *President and Director*

Computer Installation
IBM 370/165–operating system: OS/HASP/MVT; internal storage: 16 million bits; magnetic tapes: 5; magnetic discs: 2 2314, 1 3330; 1 line printer. *On-line satellite computers:* IBM 360/75, 360/40, 370/135. *Remote processing features:* remote batch and conversational computing using teletypes, IBM 2741, IBM 1050, IBM 2780, IBM 1130, 360, 370 and Data 100, UCC, etc. equivalents.

Coding Languages
PL/1, FORTRAN IV, WATFIV, COBOL, ALGOL, SNOBOL, SLIP, SIMSCRIPT, Assembler, PL/C, WATBOL.

Services Available
Remote access basis and time-sharing basis. Available to education in North Carolina and some local industry.

Fields of Application
Scientific, statistical, commercial, management, systems analysis, programming systems research and development.
Specialized area: Operating systems research and development.

UNIVERSITY OF NORTH CAROLINA AT CHAPEL HILL*
Computation Center
Chapel Hill, 27514
Telephone: (919) 933-2018

Officers
J. Batter, *Director*
W. F. Evans and W. Hetzel, *Associate Directors*

Computer Installation
IBM 360/40–operating system: OS; internal storage: 256K bytes; magnetic tapes: 2 2401; magnetic discs: 1 2314; 2 line printers. *Remote processing features:* connected by land lines to IBM 360/75.

Coding Languages
Assembler, COBOL, FORTRAN IV, PL/1.

Services Available
Advice, operators, preparation of data, limited programming, software packages. Operate on an open shop and remote access basis.

Fields of Application
Analysis and programming in all fields of interest to the university; statistical work dominates.

Training
Department of Information Science offers graduate-level instruction and opportunities for research in information science.

UNIVERSITY OF NORTH CAROLINA AT CHAPEL HILL
Department of Computer Science
New West Hall, Chapel Hill, 27514
Telephone: (919) 933-2148

Officers
Ferebee Taylor, *Chancellor*
F. P. Brooks, Jr., *Chairman, Department of Computer Science*

Computer Installation
IBM 370/165–operating system: OS/360; internal storage: 16 million bits; magnetic tapes: 5; magnetic discs: 16 2, 8 3330; 1 line printer. *Remote processing features:* all work remote – over 100 lines.
IBM 360/75–operating system: OS/360; internal storage: 10 million bits; magnetic tapes: 2; magnetic discs: 8; 2 line printers. *On-line satellite computers:* Interdata 3, PDP-11.

Coding Languages
PL/1, FORTRAN, COBOL, ALGOL, RPG, Assembler.

Contemplated Equipment
Increased storage of 8 million bits.

Services Available
Advice, education and training, software packages. Operate on a remote access, closed shop, and time-sharing basis.

Fields of Application
Scientific, statistical.

Training
M.S. professional programme, and Ph.D. programme, in Computer Science.

Computer Installation
IBM 1620–operating system: Monitor I; internal storage: 40K bits; magnetic disc: 1311.
IBM 360/50–operating system: OS; internal storage: 131K bits; magnetic tapes: 2 3420; magnetic discs: 6 2319; 1 line printer.

Coding Languages
FORTRAN, RPG, COBOL, PL/1.

Contemplated Equipment
Increased storage.

Services Available
Advice, operators, preparation of data, programmers, utilization of major statistical packages. Operate on a closed shop basis. Limited availability to business outside University.

Fields of Application
Statistics, educational and administrative usage.

Training
B.S. degree courses in computer science.

UNIVERSITY OF NORTH DAKOTA
Computer and Data Processing Center
Grand Forks, 58201
Telephone: 777-3171

Officer
Conrad Dietz, *Director*

Computer Installation
IBM 370/135–operating system: DOS; internal storage: 1,920K bits; magnetic tapes: 2 2415; magnetic discs: 2 2319; 1 line printer.
PDP-8/I–operating system: Edusystem 20; internal storage: 64K bits.

Coding Languages
FORTRAN IV, COBOL, RPG, Assembler, PL/1.

Contemplated Equipment
2 remote terminals, 1100 1pm printer.

Services Available
Advice, operators, preparation of data, programming (limited), software packages, systems analysis. Operate on a closed shop basis. Available to outside users with restrictions on time limitations.

Fields of Application
All University administrative and academic work.
Specialized areas: Numerical analysis and statistical analysis.

Training
Mechanized data processing, electronic data processing and programming, digital computer logic, electronic computing systems, fundamentals of computer programming, computer science.

NORTH DAKOTA

NORTH DAKOTA STATE UNIVERSITY
Fargo, 58102
Telephone: (701) 237-7505

Officer
Prof. Donald E. Peterson, *Director*

OHIO

BOWLING GREEN STATE UNIVERSITY
Office of Computational Services
Bowling Green, 43403
Telephone: (419) 372-2911

Officer
Hal Eckel, *Director*

United States of America – Universities and Colleges

Computer Installation
IBM 360/75–internal storage: 750K plus 1 million bits; magnetic tapes: 4 2400; magnetic discs: 20 2314; 1 line printer. *Remote processing features:* 4 UT/1, 1 Data Nova 800, 65 TTYs and 2741s, 8 2260s.

Coding Languages
FORTRAN, ALGOL, BAL, SNOBOL, BASIC, RPG, PL/1, PL/C, COBOL, WATFIV, ASSIST, ALGOL W.

Services Available
Operate on a remote access, closed shop and time-sharing basis.

Fields of Application
Scientific, statistical, commercial, accounting, management, systems analysis.
Specialized area: Education.

Training
B.S. and M.S. courses in Computer Sciences, B.A. courses in Information Sciences.

CASE WESTERN RESERVE UNIVERSITY
Andrew R. Jennings Computing Center
University Circle, Cleveland, 44106
Telephone: (216) 368-2800

Officer
Edward L. Glaser, *Director of the Center*

Computer Installation
UNIVAC 1108–operating system: CHIOS; internal storage: 10·8 million bits; magnetic tapes: 15; magnetic drums: 7; 8 line printers. *Remote processing features:* UNIVAC 1004, teletypes, telephone lines.
PDP-10–operating system: Tenex; internal storage: 5·6 million bits; magnetic tapes: 9; magnetic discs: 10 DEC; 1 line printer. *On-line satellite computers:* 1 PDP-8, 4 PDP-11, 1 TI 960A. *Remote processing features:* Graphic and ASCI terminals, telephone lines TIP processor.

Coding Languages
ALGOL, FORTRAN, COBOL, BASIC, SAIL.

Contemplated Equipment
Computer graphics, speech processing, and smaller, more efficient data base storage systems.

Services Available
Advice, education and training. Operate on a self-service, remote access, block time, open shop, and time-sharing basis. Univac 1108 available to all customers; PDP-10 available to faculty and students in the computing and information sciences only.

Fields of Application
Scientific, statistical, accounting, management, systems analysis, operational research, computer-aided design of computing systems.

Training
B.S., M.S. and Ph.D. in Computer Engineering; M.S. and Ph.D. in Computing and Information Sciences.

CINCINNATI TECHNICAL COLLEGE
3520 Central Parkway, Cincinnati, 45223
Telephone: (513) 681-3320

Officer
Richard D. Brown, *Data Processing Co-ordinator*

Computer Installation
HONEYWELL H200–operating system: DOS; internal storage: 32K bits; magnetic tapes: 4; magnetic discs: 2; 1 line printer.

Coding Languages
Easycoder, COBOL, FORTRAN, RPG.

Services Available
Advice, education and training, co-operative employment. Operate on a self-service and closed shop basis.

Field of Application
Education.

Training
Associate degree course in Business Data Processing.

CLEVELAND STATE UNIVERSITY*
24th and Euclid Avenue, Cleveland, 44115
Telephone: (216) 771-0250

Officers
C. William Marcy III, *Director*
John H. Hsu, *Administrative Programming Manager*
Hugo J. Kringel, *Systems Programming Manager*
David Willow, *Operations Manager*

Computer Installation
IBM 360/40–operating system: OS/MFT; internal storage: 2,097,152 bits; magnetic tapes: 4 2401; magnetic discs: 1 2314; 2 line printers.

Coding Languages
COBOL, FORTRAN, ALGOL, SNOBOL, WATFOR.

Contemplated Equipment
IBM 360/50.

Services Available
Operators, programming, software packages. Operate on a block time basis.

Fields of Application
Scientific, commercial, accounting, instructional.

JOHN CARROLL UNIVERSITY
20700 North Park Boulevard, University Heights, 44124
Telephone: (216) 491-4261

Officer
D. F. Grazko, *Director of Computer Center*

Computer Installation
BURROUGHS B5700–operating system: MCP; internal storage: 1,571,864 bits; magnetic tapes: 4; magnetic discs: 3; 1 line printer. *Remote processing features:* 6 Model 33 ASR and 1 CRT teletypes, etc.

Coding Languages
COBOL, ALGOL, FORTRAN, BASIC.

Services Available
Operate on a remote access, time-sharing and closed shop basis. Restricted to in-house use only.

Training
Unrelated courses are offered by Natural Science Departments and Business School.

United States of America – Universities and Colleges

OBERLIN COLLEGE
N. Professor Street, Oberlin, 44074
Telephone: (216) 774-1221

Officer
Don Mittleman, *Director, Computer Center*

Computer Installation
IBM 360/44–operating systems: DOS, CP/44; internal storage: 1 million bits; magnetic tapes: 2 Potter 2405; magnetic discs: 6 Potter 4314; 1 line printer. *Remote processing features:* 4 digital analog converters.
PDP-11/20–operating system: RSTS; internal storage: 450K bits; magnetic tapes: 1 DEC TU10; magnetic discs: 2 DEC RK05, RF11. *Remote processing features:* 16 low-speed TTY/CRT.

Coding Languages
FORTRAN, BASIC, COBOL, Assembly, FOCUS.

Services Available
Advice, programming, education and training, operators, software packages, documentation, preparation of data, systems analysis. Operate on an open shop and time-sharing basis.

Fields of Application
Scientific, statistical, commercial, accounting, management, systems analysis, operational research.
Specialized area: Payroll.

OHIO STATE UNIVERSITY
Department of Computer and Information Science
Columbus, 43210

Officer
Dr. M. C. Yovits, *Chairman of the Department*

Computer Installation
IBM 370/165.

IBM 360/50.

PDP-10.

XDS Sigma 5.

Coding Languages
FORTRAN, ALGOL, COBOL, PL/1, XPL, PL/C, SPL, Assembly.

Contemplated Equipment
Microdata, IBM VM computers.

Services Available
Advice, education and training. Operate on a remote access, closed shop and time-sharing basis.

Fields of Application
Scientific, education.

Training
Courses leading to a Ph.D. or an M.S. degree in Computer and Information Science.

OHIO STATE UNIVERSITY
Instruction and Research Computer Center
1971 Neil Avenue, Columbus, 43210
Telephone: (614) 422-4843

Officer
Roy F. Reeves, *Director*

Computer Installation
IBM 370/165–operating systems: OS/MVT with HASP, TSO; internal storage: 3,072K bits; magnetic tapes: 8 3420; magnetic discs: 8 3330/1; 2 line printers.

Coding Languages
FORTRAN IV, PL/1F, Assembler F, Assembler G, COBOL F, SNOBOL 4, RPG, SIMSCRIPT, SORT, CSMP, MPS, GPSS, PMS, OMNITAB, CPS, PL/1, WATFIV, SPITBOL, WATBOL, ALGOL.

Services Available
Consultation, data preparation, software packages, systems analysis. Programming and keypunching services available on a limited basis. Operate on an open and closed shop, remote access and time-sharing basis. Available mainly to members of other universities for sponsored research, to non-university users on a selective basis at special rates, and to all users for consultation and advice.

Field of Application
Scientific computations.
Specialized areas: Algebraic language compilers, design of monitor system for time-sharing with real time applications, data transmission to and from remote stations.

Training
Introductory courses to digital computer programming, digital computer programming and systems programming.

OHIO UNIVERSITY
Science Complex
Athens, 45701
Telephone: 594-5511

Officers
Robert W. Lilley, *Director*
Robert L. McGee, *Associate Director (Resources)*
Richard L. Davis, *Associate Director (Services)*

Computer Installation
IBM 360/44–operating systems: OUIJI (O.U. system), OS/360; internal storage: 262K bits; magnetic tapes: 3 IBM 3420/2; magnetic discs: 1 IBM 2319; 1 line printer.
IBM 360/20–operating system: O.U.-written I/O utility system; internal storage: 4K bits.

Coding Languages
FORTRAN IV (G), SNOBOL, OULP, COBOL, BASIC, GPSS, PL/1, WATFIV, Assembler.

Contemplated Equipment
Teleprocessing gear.

Services Available
Operate on a closed shop basis. Primarily for University use.

Fields of Application
All fields of University research and teaching.
Specialized areas: Systems programming, statistical work.

Training
Higher languages programming courses oriented to numerous disciplines; also courses in systems programming and operation.

United States of America – Universities and Colleges

UNIVERSITY OF AKRON*
Computer Center
302 East Buchtel Avenue, Akron, 44304
Telephone: (216) 762-2441

Officers
Robert S. Hathaway, *Director*
Michael Klein, *Computer Scientist*
Carl R. Kieffer, *Data Processing Production Manager*
Philip Manthey, *Management Science Senior Associate*

Computer Installation
IBM 360/40–operating systems: OS, RAX; internal storage: 2,097,152 bits; magnetic tapes: 5 2402; magnetic discs: 4 2311; 1 line printer. *Remote processing features:* 1050 and 2260 terminals plus 1070 equipment.
IBM 1130–operating system: DMS; internal storage: 131,072 bits; magnetic discs: 1; 1 line printer.
IBM 1620–operating system: DMS; internal storage: 360K bits; magnetic tapes: 2 7330; magnetic discs: 3 1311; 1 line printer.
IBM 1401–internal storage: 32K bits; 1 line printer.

Coding Language
FORTRAN.

Contemplated Equipment
IBM 360/44, IBM 360/65.

Services Available
Advice, operators, preparation of data, programming, systems analysis. Operate on a self-service, semi-closed shop, remote access and time-sharing basis.

Fields of Application
Business and scientific system analysis and programming, consulting, instruction, and data processing.

Training
Courses in computer science, programming, data processing, and systems.

UNIVERSITY OF DAYTON
Office for Computing Activities
Dayton, 45409
Telephone: (513) 229-3511

Officers
Dr. M. J. Gee, *Director*
R. L. McAdams, *Assistant Director*
J. A. Pugh, *Manager of Systems Programming*
A. J. Roemer, *Manager of Administrative Systems*
Dr. A. M. May, *Manager of Academic Services*
W. A. Honingford, *Manager of Operations*

Computer Installation
RCA Spectra 70/46–internal storage: 262K bytes; magnetic tapes: 6 9-track; magnetic discs: 1 590 5; 2 line printers. *Remote processing features:* 70/668 communication controller; 53 33-TTY, 5 752 VDT, 3 2741 terminals.
UNIVAC 70/7–internal storage: 512K bytes; magnetic disc: 1 590/8. *Remote processing features:* 62 33-TTY, 5 752 VDT, 7 Portacom, 1 Novar, 1 300-Execuport, 1 NCR-260.

Coding Languages
COBOL, FORTRAN, PL/1, BASIC, TIFOR, WATFIV, File Editor, ICES, ECAP.

Services Available
Programming, systems analysis. Operate on a closed shop and time-sharing basis.

Fields of Application
Research, instruction, and administration.

Training
B.S. and M.S. courses in Computer Science, introductory courses in data processing, principles of systems and procedures; programming courses in FORTRAN, BASIC, PL/1, COBOL and Machine Language.

UNIVERSITY OF CINCINNATI
Computing Center
Beecher Hall, Cincinnati, 45221
Telephone: (513) 475-3033

Officer
R. R. Caster, *Director*

Computer Installation
IBM 370/165–operating system: OS/MVT; internal storage: 524,288 bits; magnetic tapes: 10 3420; magnetic discs: 2 3330; 3 line printers. *Remote processing features:* teleprocessing, data entry.

Coding Languages
FORTRAN IV, COBOL, PL/I.

Contemplated Equipment
IBM 370/168.

Services Available
Advice, programming, operators, software packages, documentation, data preparation. Operate on a remote access and closed shop basis. Services restricted to non-profit organizations.

Fields of Application
Scientific, medical, business.
Specialized areas: Linear programming, medical research.

UNIVERSITY OF TOLEDO
2801 W. Bancroft Street, Toledo, 43606
Telephone: (419) 531-5711

Officer
Dr. L. Bellamy, *Director of Computer Services*

Computer Installation
IBM 360/50–operating system: OS/MFT; internal storage: 256K bytes; magnetic tapes: 2 2415; magnetic discs: 9 2319; 1 line printer.
IBM 1130–operating system: Monitor I; internal storage: 16 x 8K bits; magnetic discs: 1 2310; 1 line printer.

Coding Languages
PL/1, FORTRAN, COBOL, BAL.

Contemplated Equipment
IBM 370/145.

Services Available
Programming, systems analysis. Operate on a closed shop basis.

Fields of Application
Scientific, statistical, commercial, accounting.

Training
Courses from each college.

United States of America – Universities and Colleges

WITTENBERG UNIVERSITY
North Wittenberg Avenue, Springfield, 45501
Telephone: (513) 327-6231

Officers
Dr. Byron W. Thorsen, *Director of Research and Planning*
William Barnes, *Director, Administrative Computer Services*
Marvin Philpott, *Director, Academic Computer Services*

Computer Installation
IBM 360/30–operating system: DOS; internal storage: 65K bits; magnetic tapes: 2 2415; magnetic discs: 3 2311; 1 line printer.

Coding Languages
COBOL, FORTRAN, RPG.

Services Available
Education and training. Operate on a closed shop and open shop (evenings only) basis.

Fields of Application
Scientific, statistical, accounting, management.
Specialized area: Payroll.

Training
Mathematics 125 course – Introduction to Computer Programming with emphasis on FORTRAN.

YOUNGSTOWN STATE UNIVERSITY*
Computer Center
410 Wick Avenue, Youngstown, 44503
Telephone: (216) 747-1492

Officers
Dr. A. L. Pugsley, *President*
Dr. R. W. Jonas, *Director of Computer Center*

Computer Installation
IBM 360/50–operating system: ASP; internal storage: 1,256K bits; magnetic tapes: 2 2415; magnetic discs: 12 2314; 2 line printers. *On-line satellite computer:* 360/40.

Coding Languages
FORTRAN, COBOL, PL/1, Assembler.

Services Available
Analysis and programming for university administration; consultation only for faculty and students. Batch-processing on closed shop basis.

Fields of Application
Commercial, instructional, research.

Training
Minor in Computer Science offered by Mathematics department (8 courses).

OKLAHOMA

CENTRAL STATE UNIVERSITY
Edmond, 73034
Telephone: (405) 341-2980

Officers
Prof. Raymond Beasley, *Chairman of the Department of Mathematics, Computer Science and Statistics*
Bill Jenkens, *Chairman of the Data Processing Department*

Computer Installation
IBM 360/40–operating system: DOS; internal storage: 192K bytes; magnetic tapes: 2; magnetic discs: 1 IBM 2314; 1 line printer. *Remote processing features:* cathode ray tube units for student enrolment.

Coding Languages
FORTRAN, COBOL, PL/1, RPG, 360 Assembly.

Services Available
Education and training. Operate on a closed shop and block time basis.

Fields of Application
Scientific, commercial, accounting.

Training
B.S. in Computer Science, including courses in coding languages, systems analysis and data structures; courses in numerical analysis, linear programming, etc.

OKLAHOMA STATE UNIVERSITY
Computer Center
Stillwater, 74074
Telephone: (405) 372-6211

Officer
Dr. Robert Gumm, *Director and Assistant Professor of Computer Science*

Computer Installation
IBM 360/65–operating system: OS(MVT); internal storage: 1,024K plus 1,024K bits; magnetic tapes: 3 3420; magnetic discs: 15 2314; 3 line printers. *Remote processing features:* CPS time-sharing system, remote 3270 visual display terminals.

Coding Languages
FORTRAN IV, COBOL, PL/1.

Services Available
Advice, preparation of data, programming, software packages, systems analysis, consulting services. Operate on a closed shop, self-service and time-sharing basis.

Fields of Application
Scientific, statistical, commercial, production control, accounting, management, systems analysis, operational research.

Training
Introductory courses in FORTRAN, CPS(PL/1), PL/1 for FORTRAN users; JCL seminar; graduate student seminar, advanced FORTRAN; linkage editor.

SOUTHWESTERN STATE COLLEGE
Weatherford, 73096
Telephone: (405) 772-6611

Officer
George E. Atkins, *Director of Computer Center*

Computer Installation
IBM 1130/2B–operating system: Disc Monitor; internal storage: 131,136 bits; magnetic discs: 1; 1 line printer.

Coding Languages
FORTRAN, COBOL, Assembly, AMTRAN, RPG, SL/1, APL.

United States of America – Universities and Colleges

Services Available
Advice, programming, education and training, operators, software packages, documentation, preparation of data, systems analysis. Operate on an open shop basis. Outside customers are served on a closed shop basis.

Fields of Application
Scientific, statistical, commercial, systems analysis, operational research, computer science.
Specialized area: Linear programming.

Training
Introduction to computer programming (FORTRAN), and courses in scientific programming (FORTRAN), business programming (COBOL), data structures, advanced computer concepts, programming languages, numerical analysis and operations research.

OREGON

LEWIS AND CLARK COLLEGE*
Portland, 97219
Telephone: (503) 246-8251

Officer
Clifford R. Burns, *Director*

Computer Installation
IBM 1130 2B–operating system: DOS; internal storage: 313,072 bits; magnetic tapes: 2310; 1 line printer.

Contemplated Equipment
Graphics display, time-sharing facilities.

Services Available
Consultation, programming, education and training, operators, systems analysis. Operate on an open shop basis.

Fields of Application
Scientific, statistical, commercial, accounting.

Training
Introductory course in computer science (FORTRAN IV), and course in computer organization and structure (Assembler).

OREGON STATE UNIVERSITY
Computer Center
Corvallis, 97331
Telephone: (503) 754-2494

Officer
Dr. Larry C. Hunter, *Director*

Computer Installation
CDC 3300–operating systems: OS3 Time-Sharing; internal storage: 98K bits; magnetic tapes: 4 604; magnetic discs: 5 854, 2 841; 1 line printer. *On-line satellite computer:* PDP-8. *Remote processing features:* Network of teletypewriters and CRT terminals.

Coding Languages
FORTRAN, ALGOL, COBOL, EDITOR, OSCAR, BASIC, COMPASS.

Services Available
Advice, preparation of data, programming, software packages, systems analysis. Operate on a closed shop, remote access and time-sharing basis.

Fields of Application
Support of instructional and research projects.
Specialized areas: On-line use of computers and computer-driven displays in experimental research.

Training
Short courses in major programming languages.

PORTLAND STATE UNIVERSITY*
P.O. Box 751, Portland, 97207
Telephone: (503) 226-7271, extension 1501

Officer
C. A. Magwire, *Director of Computer Center*

Computer Installation
IBM 1130–internal storage: 128K bits; magnetic discs: 1; 1 line printer.
HONEYWELL H200–internal storage: 112K bits; magnetic tapes: 5; 1 line printer.

Coding Languages
SYMBOLIC, FORTRAN IV, COBOL, BASIC.

Services Available
Consultation, programming, education and training, operators, documentation, preparation of data, systems analysis. Operate on a closed shop, open shop and time-sharing basis. Available only to members of the university.

Fields of Application
Almost all areas of university instruction, research and administration (scientific, statistical, accounting, management, systems analysis, operational research).
Specialized areas: Urban studies, environmental studies, system science.

Training
Courses in mathematics and business administration.

UNIVERSITY OF OREGON
Computing Center
Eugene, 97403
Telephone: (503) 686-4394

Officer
Dr. George Struble, *Director*

Computer Installation
IBM 360/50–operating system: OS/360; internal storage: 256K bytes; magnetic discs: 1 2316; 1 line printer.
PDP-10–operating system: DEC time-sharing monitor; internal storage: 64K 36-bit words; 1 line printer. *On-line satellite computer:* Varian 620. *Remote processing features:* 40 Teletypes.

Coding Languages
FORTRAN, COBOL, Assembler, WATFOR, WATBOL, PL/1, PLC, MACRO-10, AID, BASIC.

Services Available
Advice, programming, education and training, operators, software packages. Operate on a remote access, closed shop and time-sharing basis.

Fields of Application
Scientific, statistical, accounting, management.
Specialized area: Computer science.

Training
Courses leading to a B.A. or M.S. in Computer Science.

United States of America – Universities and Colleges

PENNSYLVANIA

BUCKNELL UNIVERSITY*
Freas – Rooke Computer Center
Lewisburg, 17837
Telephone: (717) 524-1436

Officers
Edward F. Staiano, *Director, Office of Computer Activities*
Alan L. Mitchell, *Manager, Computer Systems Division*
William D. Gold, *Manager, Administrative Systems*
Lee I. Frantz, *Manager, Operations Division*

Computer Installation
XDS Sigma 7–operating system: BPM/BTM; internal storage: 64K words; magnetic tapes: 2 9-track; magnetic discs: 6; 1 line printer. *Remote processing features:* remote batch, time-sharing users.

Coding Languages
BASIC, ALGOL, LISP, FORTRAN IV, COBOL, SOL, SYMBOL, METASYMBOL.

Contemplated Equipment
32K word core increase; several remote batch terminals; time-sharing expansion; digital-analog interfaces; additional line printer.

Services Available
Advice, programming, preparation of data, systems analysis, software packages. Operate on a closed shop, remote batch and time-sharing basis. Available on a limited basis to industry and other educational institutions.

Fields of Application
Engineering, scientific, mathematics (statistics), university oriented programming in general.
Specialized areas: Highway and bridge design, stellar model research, ballistic missile trajectory simulation, structural analysis and university administrative processing.

Training
Courses in the philosophy of computation, introduction to computing, computers and programming, numerical calculus, data structures and a consortium course for Social Science students.

CARNEGIE-MELLON UNIVERSITY*
Department of Computer Science
5000 Forbes Avenue, Pittsburgh, 15213
Telephone: (412) 621-2600

Officers
Professor A. J. Perlis, *Head, Department of Computer Science*
Professor A. Newell, *Institute Professor of Systems and Communication Sciences*
David H. Nickerson, *Director, Computer Center*

Computer Installation
IBM 360/67–internal storage: 128K bits. *Remote processing features:* 100 teletypes time-sharing.

CDC G-21–internal storage: 4K bits; magnetic tapes: 8; magnetic discs: 2; 2 line printers. *On-line satellite computers:* 2 G-20. *Remote processing features:* 30 model 35 teletypewriters.

IBM 7040–internal storage: 32K bits; magnetic tapes: 12; 1 line printer.

IBM 1407–internal storage: 4K bits; magnetic tapes: 4.

CDC G-15.

RCA 301.

Coding Languages
FORTRAN, GATE, ALGOL, IPL-V, FORMAL, FSL, SCADS, BOOLE.

Services Available
Limited access to commercially sponsored research in advanced areas.

Fields of Application
Design of programming operating systems; design of general process programming languages and construction of translators; scientific and data processing computations; complex problem solving by machines.
Specialized areas: Computer education and management games; special programmes in heuristic programming; theory of programming: man machine interaction.

Training
Four-semester sequence in programming. One-semester course in computer systems. Doctoral programme in the department of computer science.

CHEYNEY STATE COLLEGE
Cheyney, 19319
Telephone: (215) 399-6880

Officers
Dr. Wade Wilson, *President*
Dr. Bernard S. Proctor, *Vice-President, Academic Affairs*
Mr. Herbert E. Balian, *Director, Computer Center*

Computer Installation
RCA Spectra 70/35–operating system: DOS; internal storage: 65K bits; magnetic tapes: 4 442; magnetic discs: 3 564; 1 line printer.

Coding Languages
COBOL, FORTRAN, RPG.

Services Available
Education and training. Operate on an open shop basis.

Fields of Application
Statistical, commercial, accounting, management, systems analysis.

Training
Courses in the basic principles of computers and computer programming.

CLARION STATE COLLEGE
Clarion, 16214
Telephone: (814) 226-6000, extension 345

Officers
Dr. James Gemmell, *President*
Dr. George R. Lewis, *Director, Computer Center*

Computer Installation
IBM 360–operating system: DOS; internal storage: 256K bits; magnetic tapes: 4 9-track; magnetic discs: 6 2319; 1 line printer.

Coding Languages
BAL, FORTRAN, ANS COBOL, APL, BASIC.

Contemplated Equipment
Additional visual displays and teletypes.

Services Available
Advice, programming, education and training, software packages, documentation, preparation of data, systems analysis. Operate on a closed shop and time-sharing basis. Available to educational institutions only.

United States of America – Universities and Colleges

Fields of Application
Scientific, statistical, commercial, management, systems analysis, operational research.
Specialized areas: Linear programming, analysis, payroll.

Training
Five courses in computer science.

DICKINSON COLLEGE*
Carlisle, 17013
Telephone: (717) 243-5121

Officer
G. A. Stegink, *Director*

Computer Installation
IBM 1130–operating system: DOS; internal storage: 131,136 bits; magnetic discs: 2; 2 line printers.

Coding Languages
FORTRAN, RPG.

Services Available
Operate on a closed shop basis.

Fields of Application
Scientific, management.

Training
Introductory course in computer science.

DUQUESNE UNIVERSITY*
600 Forbes Avenue, Pittsburgh, 15219
Telephone: (412) 434-6000

Officers
James F. Acklin, *Director*
James R. Hayes, *Associate Director*

Computer Installation
CDC 3200–operating system: MSOS; internal storage: 768K bits; magnetic tapes: 4 601; magnetic discs: 4 854; 1 line printer. *Remote processing features:* RESPOND.

Coding Languages
COMPASS, FORTRAN IV, COBOL, BASIC.

Services Available
Advice, operators, preparation of data, systems analysis. Operate on a closed shop basis.

Fields of Application
Design and programming of systems.
Specialized area: Management information systems.

Training
FORTRAN and COBOL programming.

FRANKLIN AND MARSHALL COLLEGE
Merc Pentamation Data Center
Lancaster, 17604
Telephone: (717) 393-0748

Officers
Donald V. Appleton, *Data Center Co-ordinator*
William M. Parsons, *Systems/Programming Manager*

Computer Installation
RCA Spectra 70/46–operating system: VMOS; internal storage: 262K bytes; magnetic tapes: 4; magnetic discs: 4; 1 line printer. *Remote processing features:* TTY 33/35, IBM 2741.

Coding Languages
BASIC, FORTRAN, COBOL, Assembler.

Contemplated Equipment
Optical scanning.

Services Available
Advice, programming, education and training, operators, software packages, documentation, preparation of data, systems analysis, facilities management. Operate on a remote access, closed shop, block time, and time-sharing basis. Available to educational and other non-profit organizations and also to local businesses and industry.

Fields of Application
Scientific, statistical, commercial, production control, accounting, management, systems analysis, operational research.
Specialized areas: Sales analysis, linear programming, analysis, payroll, structural engineering, medical research.

Training
Courses in BASIC, COBOL, FORTRAN, EDP Concepts, Math-Statistical.

GROVE CITY COLLEGE
Grove City, 16127
Telephone: (412) 458-6600

Officer
Professor D. O. Smock

Computer Installation
IBM 1130–internal storage: 8K words; magnetic discs: 2315.

Coding Languages
Assembly, RPG, FORTRAN IV.

Services Available
Education and training. Operate on a closed shop basis.

Fields of Application
Scientific, engineering, statistical.

LAFAYETTE COLLEGE*
Computer Center
Easton, 18042
Telephone: 253-6281

Officer
Prof. James P. Schwar, *Director*

Computer Installation
IBM 1130–internal storage: 8K bits; magnetic disc: 2315; 1 line printer.

Coding Languages
FORTRAN, Assembly, CSMP.

Services Available
Advice, operators, programming. Operate on a closed shop basis.

Fields of Application
Student programming, analysis of student grades, faculty and student research.
Specialized areas: Statistical analysis, digital simulation.

Training
Introductory course in digital computation and programming for engineers (part of a first year course).

United States of America — Universities and Colleges

LEHIGH UNIVERSITY
Computing Center
Room 119, Packard Laboratory, Bethlehem, 18015
Telephone: 691-7000

Officer
Dr. J. E. Walker, *Director*

Computer Installation
CDC 6400—operating system: SCOPE; internal storage: 3·9 million bits; magnetic tapes: 4 604; magnetic discs: 1 808, 1 821; 2 line printers. *On-line satellite computer:* Varian 620/F. *Remote processing features:* Batch and interactive.
VARIAN 620/F—operating system: Special; internal storage: 320K bits. *Remote processing features:* communications control.

Coding Languages
FORTRAN, COBOL, COMPASS, ALGOL, LISP, WIZARD, SIMULA, SNOBOL, APT, SIMSCRIPT.

Contemplated Equipment
Varian 620/F—021 and F—011; increased core storage; 7054 disc controller; 844-2 disc drives; 881 disc packs.

Services Available
Advice, programming, education and training, operators, software packages, documentation, data preparation, systems analysis. Operate on a remote access, closed shop, block time and time-sharing basis.

Fields of Application
Scientific, statistical, commercial, accounting, management, systems analysis, operational research.
Specialized areas: Linear programming, investment, analysis, payroll, structural engineering, medical research.

Training
Computer Science curriculum.

LOCK HAVEN STATE COLLEGE
Lock Haven, 17745
Telephone: (717) 748-5351

Officer
Dr. W. H. Billhartz, *Director, Computer Center*

Computer Installation
IBM 360/30—operating system: DOS; internal storage: 520K bits; magnetic tapes: 2 2415; magnetic discs: 3 2319; 1 line printer. *Remote processing features:* TTY 33 ASR interactive.
IBM 1130—operating system: MONITOR 2; internal storage: 128K bits; magnetic discs: 2 2310; 1 line printer.

Coding Languages
FORTRAN IV, COBOL, Assembler, RPG, PL/1, APL.

Contemplated Equipment
IBM 370/125.

Services Available
Advice, programming, education and training, operators, software packages, documentation, preparation of data, systems analysis, time-sharing I.T.F. Operate on a self-service, open shop basis (1130), remote access and closed shop (360/30) basis. Service available to students, faculty, administration.

Fields of Application
Statistical, commercial, accounting, management, systems analysis, operational research.
Specialized areas: Linear programming, analysis, payroll.

Training
B.S. degree: 21 courses available. Short introductory course to computers.

MILLERSVILLE STATE COLLEGE
Millersville, 17551
Telephone: (717) 872-5411

Officers
Thomas J. Houser, *Director of Computer Services*
William H. Duncan, *President*

Computer Installation
RCA Spectra 70/35E—operating system: DOS; internal storage: 524,288 bits; magnetic tapes: 4 9-track; magnetic discs: 3 70/564; 1 line printer.

Coding Languages
Assembly, COBOL, FORTRAN, RPG, IITRAN.

Contemplated Equipment
Univac 70/3.

Services Available
Advice, programming, education and training, operators, software packages, documentation, preparation of data, systems analysis. Operate on a closed shop and time-sharing basis. Available to University faculty, staff, students, and other educational agencies.

Fields of Application
Scientific, statistical, commercial, accounting, management.

Training
Computer sciences courses at undergraduate level.

PENNSYLVANIA STATE UNIVERSITY
Computation Center
Computer Building, University Park, 16802
Telephone: (814) 863-0422

Officer
Dr. Donald T. Laird, *Director, Computation Center*

Computer Installation
IBM 370/165—operating system: OS/MVT with HASP; internal storage: 20·9 million bits; magnetic tapes: 8 3420; magnetic discs: 14 2316, 4 3330; 4 line printers. *On-line satellite computers:* about 24.
IBM 360/50—operating system: OS/MVT with HASP; internal storage: 12·6 million bits; magnetic tapes: 2 3420; magnetic discs: 16 2316; 2 line printers. *On-line satellite computers:* 4 IBM 360/20.
ADAGE AGT-30—operating system: AMOS/2; internal storage: 983,046 bits; magnetic tapes: 2; 1 line printer.
IBM 1401—internal storage: 24,576 bits; magnetic tapes: 2 729; 1 line printer.

Coding Languages
Almost all that run on Systems 360 and 370.

Services Available
Advice, education and training, operators. Operate on a self-service, remote access, closed shop, and time-sharing basis. Time-sharing access to students is restricted to courses which require it.

Fields of Application
Scientific, statistical, commercial, management, systems analysis, operational research.
Specialized areas: Linear programming, investment, structural engineering.

United States of America – Universities and Colleges

Training
Computer Science Programme.

PENNSYLVANIA STATE UNIVERSITY
Computer Assisted Instruction (CAI) Laboratory
201 Chambers Building, University Park, 16802
Telephone: (814) 865-0471

Officer
Dr. Keith A. Hall, *Director*

Computer Installation
IBM 1130–operating system: 1500; internal storage: 512K bits; magnetic tapes: 2 2415; magnetic discs: 5 2310; 1 line printer. *Remote processing features:* 32 remote stations.

Coding Languages
Coursewriter II, FORTRAN, TACL, Assembler.

Contemplated Equipment
Intercomp 114/115; 2314 type disc unit.

Services Available
Advice, programming, education and training, operators, software packages, documentation, preparation of data. Operate on a time-sharing basis.

Field of Application
Education.

Training
Course material is offered providing approximately 10 credits of college work in a CAI environment.

POINT PARK COLLEGE*
201 Wood Street, Pittsburgh, 15222
Telephone: (412) 391-4100

Officer
John David Canter, *Director of the Computer Center*

Computer Installation
IBM 360/30–operating system: DOS; internal storage: 32K bytes; magnetic tapes: 2 2415; magnetic discs: 2 2311; 1 line printer.
ADAGE AGT/10–operating system: AMOS; internal storage: 240K bits; magnetic tapes: 1.

Coding Languages
Assembler, PL/1, COBOL, FORTRAN, SIMPLIST/70, SIMPLTON, RPG, ADEPT.

Services Available
Education and training. Operate on a self-service and closed shop basis. Available only to students, faculty, staff, administration of college.

Fields of Application
Education, information storage and retrieval research, list processing research, linguistics, heuristics, management information systems.
Specialized areas: Information storage and retrieval, theoretical turing machines, list processing and heuristic programming, election analysis.

Training
Courses in information science.

ST. FRANCIS COLLEGE*
Loretto, 15940
Telephone: (814) 472-7000

Officer
Richard M. Bender, *Director of Computer Center*

Computer Installation
IBM 1130–operating system: DOS; internal storage: 131K bits; magnetic discs: 1 2315; 1 line printer.

Coding Languages
FORTRAN IV, Assembly, RPG, APL.

Services Available
Education and training. Operate on a closed shop basis.

Fields of Application
Educational, student records, commercial.

Training
Courses in numerical methods, FORTRAN IV programming, Assembly language programming.

SCHOOL DISTRICT OF PHILADELPHIA
Division of Instructional Systems
5th and Luzerne Streets, Philadelphia, 19140
Telephone: (215) 229-9492

Officers
Dr. Sylvia Charp, *Director*
Henry R. Altschuler, Richard J. D'Orazio, Harris Kay, *Supervisors*

Computer Installation
HEWLETT PACKARD 2000F (3)–operating system: DOS internal storage: 128K bits (each); magnetic tapes: 1 9-track (each); magnetic discs: 2 (each); 1 line printer (each). *Remote processing features:* 32 on-line ports per system.
HEWLETT PACKARD 2000C–operating system: DOS; internal storage: 128K bits; magnetic tapes: 1 9-track; magnetic discs: 1. *Remote processing features:* 32 on-line ports.

Coding Languages
BASIC, COBOL, FORTRAN.

Contemplated Equipment
2000F to be replaced by 3000.

Services Available
Advice, programming, education and training, operators, software packages. Operate on a remote access and time-sharing basis. Available to Philadelphia schools only.

Fields of Application
Scientific, education.

SHIPPENSBURG STATE COLLEGE*
Shippensburg, 17257
Telephone: (717) 532-2184

Officer
William C. Snyder, *Director, Computer Center*

Computer Installation
RCA Spectra 70/45–operating system: TDOS; magnetic tapes: 6; magnetic discs: 3; 1 line printer.

Coding Languages
FORTRAN IV, COBOL, Assembly.

Services Available
Advice, programming, operators, software packages, documentation, preparation of data, systems analysis. Operate on a remote access, closed shop basis and time-sharing basis.

Fields of Application
Scientific, statistical, commercial, production control, systems analysis.
Specialized areas: Student information processing.

Training
Six credit courses.

TEMPLE UNIVERSITY*
Computing Activity
Broad Street and Montgomery Avenue, Philadelphia, 19122
Telephone: 787-7402

Officer
Dr. Leonard J. Garrett, *Director*

Computer Installation
CDC 6400–operating system: SCOPE; internal storage: 65K bits; magnetic tapes: 4 607; magnetic disc: 6603; 2 line printers. *Remote processing features:* Teletype.

Coding Languages
FORTRAN IV, COMPASS.

Contemplated Equipment
Increased memory and Random Access Devices.

Services Available
Advice, programming, software packages, systems analysis. Operate on an open shop, remote access and time-sharing basis.

Fields of Application
Business data processing; standard university research.
Specialized area: Administrative files.

THIEL COLLEGE*
Greenville, 16125
Telephone: (412) 588-7700

Officer
Dr. Chauncey G. Bly, *President*

Computer Installation
NCR Century 100–operating system: DOS; internal storage: 32K bits; magnetic discs: 2; 1 line printer.

Coding Languages
NEAT 3, COBOL, FORTRAN IV.

Services Available
Education and training, internal applications. Operate on self-service and open shop basis. Available to data processing personnel, selected faculty and authorized students for College use only.

Fields of Application
Administrative: accounting, student grades, student registration, other student records.
Academic: Teaching in business, mathematics, science and other disciplines is contemplated.

UNIVERSITY OF PENNSYLVANIA*
Computer Center
3401 Market Street, Philadelphia, 19104
Telephone: (215) 594-5841

Officers
Dr. John F. Lubin, *Director for Computing Activities*
Dr. George Schrenck, *Associate Director*
James E. Guertin, *Manager and Assistant Director*

Computer Installation
IBM 360/65 and 40–operating systems: PHAST, HASP, OS; internal storage: 512K; magnetic tapes: 6 2401; magnetic discs: 6 2311, 1 2314; 6 line printers. *On-line satellite computers:* 2 M20. *Remote processing features:* IBM 2741 terminal, teletypewriters, M20, 1130.
IBM 7040/1401–operating system: IBSYS; internal storage: 32K 36-bit words; magnetic tapes: 12 709; magnetic discs: 1301. *On-line satellite computer:* PDP-8.

Coding Languages
FORTRAN IV, MAP, COBOL, SORT, SIFT, ALGOL, LISP, SLIP, SIMSCRIPT, GPSS, LP, SNOBOL, MAD, DYNAMAT, PL/1.

Contemplated Equipment
IBM 360/67.

Service Available
Advice. Operate on a closed shop and remote access basis. Time-sharing terminals on premises. Available to local institutions when such use does not appreciably interfere with the educational and research needs of the University.

Fields of Application
Research and education.
Specialized areas: Scientific programming text-manipulation, file systems, information retrieval.

Training
Short programming courses on the use of FORTRAN, MAP, IBSYS, Intermediate FORTRAN, OS 360, PL/1, and other programming systems.

UNIVERSITY OF PENNSYLVANIA
Moore School of Electrical Engineering
Philadelphia, 19104

Officer
Dr. Harvey L. Garner, *Director*

Computer Installation
RCA Spectra 70/46–operating system: VMOS 9; internal storage: 2,096K bits; magnetic tapes: 4 70/432; magnetic discs: 8 70/594; 1 line printer. *On-line satellite computers:* DEC-338 display, PDP-8. *Remote processing features:* 13 interactive terminals.
DIGITAL EQUIPMENT 338–operating system: DMS; internal storage: 98,304 bits; magnetic tape: 1 TU-65; magnetic disc: 1 DF32.

Coding Languages
FORTRAN IV, WATFOR, COBOL, SNOBOL, LISP, STAR 1, ALGOL, BASIC, XPL, Assembly.

Services Available
Advice, programming, education and training, operators, software packages, documentation. Operate on a time-sharing basis. Free to Moore School students and faculty; available to outside customers on a commercial basis.

Fields of Application
Scientific, systems analysis, operational research.
Specialized areas: Linear programming, analysis, payroll, structural engineering, medical research.

Training
B.S., M.S. and Ph.D. in Computer and Information Science.

UNIVERSITY OF PITTSBURGH*
Computer Center
800 Cathedral of Learning, Fifth Avenue, Pittsburgh, 15213
Telephone: (412) 621-3500

Officers
Dr. Orrin E. Taulbee, *Director*
Siegfried Treu, *Assistant Director*

Computer Installation
IBM 7090–operating system: Michigan; internal storage: 32K bits; magnetic tapes: 10 729; magnetic disc: 1301; 1 line printer. *On-line satellite computers:* 2 IBM 1401.

IBM 360/50–operating system: Pittsburgh; internal storage: 128K bits; magnetic tapes: 6 2403; magnetic discs: 2 2311, 1 2314; 1 line printer. *On-line satellite computers:* 2 PDP-8. *Remote processing features:* 25 terminals.
IBM 360/40.
IBM 1620.
PDP-4, -7 and -8.

Coding Languages
FORTRAN, MAD Autocoder, FAP, Penelope, Pittsburgh Interpretive Language (PIL).

Contemplated Equipment
IBM 360/50.

Services Available
Advice, operators, preparation of data. Operate on a closed shop, remote access and time-sharing basis.

Field of Application
System design.
Specialized areas: Compilers, automatic operator, systems, natural text processing.

UNIVERSITY OF PITTSBURGH
Information Science Department
Room 408, LIS Building, Pittsburgh, 15213
Telephone: (412) 621-3500, extension 6352

Officers
Professor Allen Kent, *Chairman*
Professor Anthony Debons, *Vice-Chairman*

Computer Installation
PDP-10/55–operating system: T/S and Batch; internal storage: 7,274,496 bits; magnetic tapes: 6 9-track, 2 7-track; magnetic discs: 15 RPO3; 1 line printer. *On-line satellite computers:* 6 Honeywell 316, 1 PDP-8. *Remote processing features.*
PDP-10/70–operating system: T/S and Batch; internal storage: 3,637,248 bits; magnetic tapes: 2 9-track, 2 7-track; magnetic discs: 6 RPO2; 1 line printer. *On-line satellite computers:* 1 1401. *Remote processing features.*

Coding Languages
FORTRAN, ALGOL, BASIC, COBOL, AID, PIL, MACRO-10.

Contemplated Equipment
Replacement of current systems with DEC 1077s.

Operational Basis
Self-service, remote access, and time-sharing basis. Restrictions are based on account type and range from limits on CPU time to a type of system access.

Fields of Application
Scientific, statistical.
Specialized areas: Linear programming, structural engineering, medical research, social science research.

Training
Computer Science – M.S. and Ph.D. degrees; Information Science – M.S. degree.

UNIVERSITY OF PITTSBURGH
Media Research and Communications Center
Graduate School of Library and Information Science
135 North Bellefield, Pittsburgh, 15213

Officers
Dr. Patrick R. Penland, *Director*
Dr. Clark D. Rogers, *Researcher*

Computer Installation
PDP-10–magnetic tapes: 3; 5 line printers. *Remote processing features:* CRT; typewriters.

Coding Languages
PIL (Pitt Interpretive Language), FORTRAN IV.

Services Available
Advice, education and training, documentation, systems analysis. Operate on a self-service, remote access, and time-sharing basis. Available to graduate students and faculty of the University and to visiting faculty.

Fields of Application
Systems analysis, operational research.
Specialized areas: Linear programming, instructional research.

Training
M.S. and Ph.D. in Communication, Library and Information Science and in Urban Affairs.

UNIVERSITY OF SCRANTON
Scranton, 18510
Telephone: 347-3321

Officer
Rev. Paul J. Casey, S.J., *Director of Computer Center*

Computer Installation
XDS Sigma 5–operating systems: DOS, TOS; internal storage: 128K bits; magnetic tapes: 2; magnetic discs: 1; 1 line printer.

Coding Languages
FORTRAN, COBOL, PL/1, Assembler, RPG.

Contemplated Equipment
Time-sharing terminals on the premises.

Services Available
Advice, programming, education and training, software packages, systems analysis. Operate on an open shop and self-service basis.

Fields of Application
Scientific research, student, academic and financial management, educational research.

Training
B.S. degree in Computer Science; short courses in programming languages: FORTRAN, COBOL, PL/1.

United States of America – Universities and Colleges

VILLANOVA UNIVERSITY*
Computer Center
Villanova, 19085
Telephone: 527-2200

Officer
John M. Halloran, *Director, Villanova Computing Center*

Computer Installation
IBM 360/30–operating system: DOS; internal storage: 65K bits; magnetic tapes: 3; 2 line printers.

Coding Languages
FORTRAN, COBOL, PL/1, BAL, RPG.

Service Available
Operators. Operate on a closed shop and time-sharing basis. Available only to a limited extent to outside customers for research purposes.

Fields of Application
Instruction and scientific problems.

RHODE ISLAND

BROWN UNIVERSITY
Computing Laboratory
Providence, 02912
Telephone: (401) 863-2221, 2222

Officers
Roger Jette, *Director, Computing Laboratory*
Richard Martira, *Operations Manager*
Joy Elliot, *Manager of Systems programming*
Nathan Williamson, *Manager, User Services*

Computer Installation
IBM 360/67–operating system: CP/67; internal storage: 1 million bits; magnetic tapes: 3; magnetic discs: 17 Memorex 3660; 2 line printers. *On-line satellite computers:* 2 1130 DDP.

Coding Languages
FORTRAN, PL/1, APL, ALC.

Services Available
Advice, operators, programming and software packages. Operate on a closed shop, remote access and time-sharing basis.

Fields of Application
Research, education general scientific, statistical, commercial, operational research.
Specialized area: Computer science.

Training
Courses in programming.

SOUTH CAROLINA

THE CITADEL*
Charleston, 29409
Telephone: (803) 723-0611

Officers
Major G. L. Crumley, *Director of Computer Center*
W. P. Banks, *Manager of Data Processing*

Computer Installations
IBM 1130–operating system: DOS; internal storage: 131,072 bits; magnetic discs: 2; 1 line printer.
NCR Century 100–operating system: DOS; internal storage: 131,072 bits; magnetic discs: 2 655; 1 line printer.

Coding Languages
FORTRAN, Assembler, RPG, AMTRAN, APL, NEAT 3.

Services Available
Consultation, programming, education and training, operators, software packages, documentation, preparation of data, systems analysis. Operate on an open shop basis. Available to outside users when time permits.

Fields of Application
Scientific, statistical, commercial, accounting, management, systems analysis, operational research.

Training
B.Sc. degree course.

UNIVERSITY OF SOUTH CAROLINA
Computer Services Division
Columbia, 29208
Telephone: (803) 777-5211

Officer
Jack Cooper, *Director of the Division*

Computer Installation
IBM 360/45–operating system: OS/MVT; internal storage: 1,756K bits; magnetic tapes: 8; magnetic discs: 24; 2 line printers. *On-line satellite computers:* 6. *Remote processing features:* 3705.

Coding Languages
FORTRAN, COBOL, PL/1, RPG, APL, BASIC.

Services Available
Advice, programming, education and training, operators, software packages, documentation, preparation of data, systems analysis. Operate on a self-service, remote access, closed shop and block time basis.

Fields of Application
Scientific, statistical, commercial, accounting, management, systems analysis, operational research.
Specialized areas: Linear programming, analysis, payroll, structural engineering, medical research.

SOUTH DAKOTA

AUGUSTANA COLLEGE*
29 and Summit, Sioux Falls, 57102
Telephone: (605) 336-4918

Officer
G. N. Wika, *Director of Computer Services*

Computer Installations
IBM 1130–operating system: MTR; internal storage: 8K 16-bit words; magnetic discs: 1; 1 line printer.
IBM 360/20–internal storage: 8K 8-bit bytes; 1 line printer.

Coding Languages
FORTRAN, RPG, Assembler, BAL.

Services Available
Operate on an open shop (1130) and closed shop (360/20) basis.

Fields of Application
Instruction, research, administration.

Training
Courses in computing, computers and programming.

SOUTH DAKOTA STATE UNIVERSITY
Department of Research and Data Processing
Brookings, 57006
Telephone: (605) 688-6136

Officers
Dr. H. M. Briggs, *President*
Dr. Paul L. Koepsell, *Director of Research and Data Processing*

Computer Installation
IBM 370/145–operating system: VS1; internal storage: 1,048,576 bits; magnetic tapes: 4 2415; magnetic discs: 6 2319; 1 line printer. *Remote processing features:* 1 Analogue to Digital Input line, 6 TP lines.

Coding Languages
RPG, FORTRAN, COBOL, ALGOL, Assembler.

Contemplated Equipment
Expansion of disc, core and TP facilities.

Services Available
Advice, programming, education and training, operators, software packages, documentation, preparation of data, systems analysis. Operate on an open shop basis. Services available to all components of the University and to staff members engaged in consulting arrangements with a wide variety of private and governmental agencies.

Fields of Application
Scientific, statistical, commercial, accounting, management, systems analysis, operational research.

Training
Courses include Introduction to Computers, FORTRAN Programming, Assembler Programming, Numerical Methods, Operations Research and Digital Circuit Theory; option in Computer Science at B.S. level in Electrical Engineering.

UNIVERSITY OF SOUTH DAKOTA
Computer Center
Vermillion, 57069
Telephone: (605) 677-5258

Officers
Richard Larue, *Director*
Lanny Hoffmann, *Systems Manager*

Computer Installation
IBM 360/40–operating system: OS; internal storage: 3,072K bits; magnetic tapes: 2 2415; magnetic discs: 9 2314; 1 line printer. *Remote processing features:* 8 terminals.
IBM 1620–operating system: MON 43; internal storage: 240K bits; magnetic discs: 1 1311; 1 line printer.

Coding Languages
FORTRAN, PL/1, BAL, COBOL.

Contemplated Equipment
IBM 370/145.

Services Available
Advice, programming, education and training, operators, software packages, documentation, preparation of data, systems analysis. Operate on a remote access, closed shop and time-sharing basis.

Fields of Application
Scientific, statistical, accounting, management, systems analysis, operational research.
Specialized areas: Analysis, data bases.

Training
Courses leading to B.A. and B.S. degrees in computer science.

TENNESSEE

AUSTIN PEAY STATE UNIVERSITY
College Street, Clarksville, 37040
Telephone: (615) 648-7588

Officer
Dr. Joe Morgan, *President*

Computer Installation
IBM 360/25–operating system: DOS; internal storage: 32K bits; magnetic tapes: 2 2415; magnetic discs: 4 2311; 1 line printer.

Coding Languages
COBOL, BAL, FORTRAN IV.

Services Available
Operate on an open shop basis.

Fields of Application
Scientific, statistical, commercial, accounting, management.
Specialized areas: Payroll, student records.

MEMPHIS STATE UNIVERSITY
Memphis, 38152
Telephone: (901) 321-1406

Officer
D. M. Vaught, *Director of Computing Center*

Computer Installation
XDS Sigma 9–operating system: UTS; internal storage: 1,048,576 bits; magnetic tapes: 2 9-track, 1 7-track; magnetic discs: 9 7242; 1 line printer. *Remote processing features:* 3 remote batch terminals; 24 time-sharing lines.
XDS Sigma 9–operating system: UTS; internal storage: 524,288 bits; magnetic tapes: 1 9-track; magnetic discs: 4 7242; 1 line printer. *Remote processing features:* 3 remote batch terminals, 8 time-sharing lines.

Coding Languages
FORTRAN, COBOL, META-SYMBOL.

Services Available
Advice, programming, education and training, operators, software packages, data preparation. Operate on a remote access, closed shop and time-sharing basis.

Fields of Application
Scientific, statistical.
Specialized areas: Analysis, payroll.

United States of America – Universities and Colleges

SOUTHWESTERN AT MEMPHIS
2000 North Parkway, Memphis, 38112
Telephone: (901) 274 1800

Officer
William C. Nemitz, *Director, Computer Center*

Computer Installation
IBM 1620–internal storage: 240K bits; 1 line printer.

Coding Languages
FORTRAN, SNOBOL.

Services Available
Consultation, programming, education and training. Operate on a self-service, block time and open shop basis.

Fields of Application
Scientific.
Specialized areas: Numerical analysis, artificial intelligence.

Training
Introductory courses in computer programming.

TENNESSEE AGRICULTURAL AND INDUSTRIAL STATE UNIVERSITY*
Computer Center
3500 Centennial Boulevard, Nashville, 37203
Telephone: 242-4311, extensions 377, 392

Officers
Clinton E. Jones, *Professor of Mathematics and Director*
Mrs. Pazetta B. Mallette, *Systems Supervisor – 1620 Center*
Wiley Lynch, *Systems Supervisor – 1401 Center*

Computer Installation
IBM 1620–operating system: Monitor I; internal storage: 40K bits; magnetic disc: 1311.
IBM 1401–internal storage: 12K bits; magnetic tapes: 2; magnetic discs: 2; 1 line printer.
IBM 360/30.

Coding Languages
FORTRAN II, SPS.

Service Available
Preparation of data. Operate on a self-service basis.

Fields of Application
Scientific disciplines in the University.
Specialized area: Numerical analysis.

Training
Two programming courses.

TENNESSEE TECHNOLOGICAL UNIVERSITY
Box 5071, T.T.U., Cookeville, 38501
Telephone: 526-9541

Officer
H. B. Kerr

Training
Programming courses are run in the Departments of Management, Mathematics, Civil Engineering and Electrical Engineering.

Computer Installation
XDS Sigma 6–operating system: BPM/BTM; internal storage: 2,048K bits; magnetic tapes: 2 9-track; magnetic discs: 4; 1 line printer. *Remote processing features:* Remote batch terminals, Timeshare.

Coding Languages
COBOL, FORTRAN, BASIC, Meta-Symbol.

Services Available
Advice, education and training, software packages, preparation of data, systems analysis. Operate on a remote access, closed shop and time-sharing basis.

Fields of Application
Scientific, statistical, commercial, accounting, management, systems analysis.
Specialized areas: Linear programming, analysis, payroll, structural engineering.

UNIVERSITY OF TENNESSEE, CHATTANOOGA
Computer Center
Chattanooga, 37403
Telephone: 755-4551

Officer
Lloyd D. Davis, *Director*

Computer Installation
IBM 360/30–internal storage: 65K bits; magnetic tapes: 1 2415; magnetic discs: 1 2319, 1 2501; 2 line printers.

Coding Languages
FORTRAN, Assembly, PL/1, COBOL.

Services Available
Advice. Operate on a closed shop basis. Available for University administration, faculty research and student instruction only.

Fields of Application
Scientific, statistical, commercial, educational, administrative.

Training
Six courses in computer science.

UNIVERSITY OF TENNESSEE, KNOXVILLE
Computing Center
Knoxville, 37916
Telephone: 974-0111

Officer
Dr. Gordon R. Sherman, *Director*

Computer Installation
IBM 360/65–operating system: OS HASP-MVT; internal storage: 1,750K bits; magnetic tapes: 4 3420; magnetic discs: 14 2319; 4 line printers. *Remote processing features:* Batch RJE.

Coding Languages
FORTRAN, COBOL, PL/I, ALGOL, SNOBOL.

Services Available
Advice, programming, education and training, operators, software packages, documentation, preparation of data, systems analysis. Operate on a self-service, remote access, block time, closed and open shop, and time-sharing basis.

United States of America — Universities and Colleges

Fields of Application
Scientific, statistical, commercial, accounting, management, systems analysis, operational research.
Specialized areas: Linear programming, analysis, medical research.

Training
Computer Science Department offers many courses pertaining to modern computing including an M.S. in Computer Science.

VANDERBILT UNIVERSITY*
Nashville, 37203
Telephone: (615) 254-5411

Officers
Dr. George E. Haynam, *Director*
James F. Petznick, *Manager*

Computer Installation
IBM 1401—internal storage: 16K bits; magnetic discs: 3 1311.

Coding Languages
FORTRAN, Autocoder, COBOL.

Services Available
Available for research and business.

Field of Application
Research.

TEXAS

AUSTIN COLLEGE
Sherman, 75090
Telephone: (214) 892-9101, extension 278

Officer
D. A. McBlain, *Director of Computer Services*

Computer Installation
IBM 1130—operating system: Disk Monitor; internal storage: 131,072 bits; magnetic discs: 2315; 1 line printer.

Coding Languages
FORTRAN IV, ALC, APL, APL PLUS.

Services Available
Consultation, programming, education and training. Operate on an open shop and time-sharing basis. Available only for academic and community service purposes.

Fields of Application
Scientific, educational, administrative.

Training
Courses in programming and computer applications.

BAYLOR UNIVERSITY*
Casey Computation Center
Waco, 76706
Telephone: 753-1101

Officer
Mrs. Helen Ligon, *Director*

Computer Installation
IBM 1620—internal storage: 20K bits.

Coding Languages
FORTRAN, SPS.

Services Available
Operators, programming. Operate on an open shop basis.

Fields of Application
Physics, business, psychology, counselling.
Specialized areas: Statistical studies on private behaviour data.

LAMAR STATE COLLEGE OF TECHNOLOGY*
Computer Center
Beaumont, 77710
Telephone: 838-6671

Officer
Dr. Frank A. Thomas Jr., *Vice-President of Academic Affairs*

Computer Installation
CDC 3300—operating system: MSOS; internal storage: 393,216 bits; magnetic discs: 2 853; 1 line printer.

Services Available
Advice, operators, preparation of data, programming, software packages, systems analysis. Operate on a closed shop basis. Priority is given to research and development programmes.

Fields of Application
Preparation of programmes for performance calculations in the fields of chemistry, chemical engineering, mechanical engineering, industrial engineering, civil engineering and electrical engineering, business and other areas.

Training
Undergraduate courses in computer methods.

NORTH TEXAS STATE UNIVERSITY*
Computer Center
N.T. Station, Denton, 76203
Telephone: (817) 387-4511

Officers
Richard A. Harris, Jr., *Director*
Jerry H. Waldon, *Associate Director*

Computer Installation
IBM 360/50—operating systems: OS/MFT, HASP; internal storage: 256K bits; magnetic tapes: 4 2415; magnetic discs: 5 2314; 1 line printer.

Coding Languages
ALC, COBOL, FORTRAN IV, PL/1.

Services Available
Limited availability to other schools and business.

Fields of Application
All fields of University disciplines.
Specialized areas: Statistics and numerical analysis.

Training
Courses in scientific programming, data processing, systems analysis and problems in electronic data processing.

United States of America – Universities and Colleges

RICE UNIVERSITY
Electrical Engineering Department
Laboratory for Computer Science and Engineering
P.O. Box 1892, Houston, 77001
Telephone: (713) 528-4141

Officers
Robert C. Minnick, *Director and Professor of Electrical Engineering and Computer Science*
Edward A. Feustel, *Assistant Professor of Computer Science*
J. Robert Jump, *Assistant Professor of Electrical Engineering*
Sigsby K. Rusk, *Lecturer*

Computer Installation
R2 (Rice Research Computer, under construction)–internal storage: 1·5 million bits; magnetic discs: 1 2317; 1 line printer. *On-line satellite computer:* 1 PDP-11.

Coding Languages
FOCAL, APL, PAL 11.

Contemplated Equipment
Intelligence terminals, new processors.

Services Available
Advice, programming, education and training. Operate on a self-service basis. Available for research use by students and faculty.

Field of Application
Scientific.

Training
Courses leading to B.S., M.S. and Ph.D. degrees.

ST. EDWARD'S UNIVERSITY*
3001 South Congress Avenue, Austin, 78704
Telephone: 444-2621

Officer
Brother Elmer Brummer, *Director*

Computer Installation
IBM 1620–internal storage: 20K bits.

Coding Languages
FORTRAN, SPS.

Contemplated Equipment
1311 disc pack.

Service Available
Operators. Operate on a self-service basis. Limited to use when machine is not being used for educational or administrative purposes for the school.

Training
Introduction to digital computer programming and operations.

ST. MARY'S UNIVERSITY OF SAN ANTONIO*
2700 Cincinnati Avenue, San Antonio 78228
Telephone: (512) 433-2311

Officers
Neil Kammer, *Director, Computer Center*
Paul Laplante, *Assistant Director*

Computer Installation
NCR Century 200–operating system: B1; internal storage: 32K bits; magnetic tapes: 2 9-track; magnetic discs: 2; 1 line printer.

Coding Languages
COBOL, FORTRAN, NEAT/3.

Services Available
Advice, limited programming, systems analysis, operating, sale of computer time. Operate on a closed shop basis.

Fields of Application
Student records, accounting, research support, support of computer-oriented classes.
Specialized area: Regression analysis.

Training
Academic minor in Computer Science of 18 semester hours.

SOUTHERN METHODIST UNIVERSITY
Dallas, 75275
Telephone: (214) 692-2000

Computer Installation
CDC Cyber 72–operating system: KRONOS; internal storage: 4·5 million bits; magnetic tapes: 2 657, 1 659; magnetic discs: 3 854, 1 6638; 2 line printers. *Remote processing features:* 32 time-sharing terminals.
CDC 1604–operating system: CO-OP; internal storage: 1·5 million bits; magnetic tapes: 8 1607; 1 line printer.

Coding Languages
Assembler, FORTRAN, COBOL, ALGOL, SNOBOL, PASCAL, TMG.

Services Available
Advice, programming, operators, software packages. Operate on a closed shop and time-sharing basis. Available only to non-profit organizations.

Fields of Application
Scientific, statistical, systems analysis, operational research.

Training
Computer science courses leading to degrees of B.A.S., M.A.S. and Ph.D; courses leading to M.S. and D.E. degrees with computer science specialization; other courses at all levels.

STEPHEN F. AUSTIN STATE UNIVERSITY
Box 6083, S.F.A., Nacogdoches, 75961
Telephone: (713) 569-3201

Officer
Al. F. Trussell, *Director University Computer Center*

Computer Installation
IBM 360/50–operating system: OS/HASP; internal storage: 2,048K bits; magnetic tapes: 2 3410; magnetic discs: 9 2314; 2 line printers.

Coding Languages
COBOL, FORTRAN, PL/1.

Services Available
Advice, programming, education and training, operators, software packages, documentation, preparation of data, systems analysis. Operate on a closed shop basis.

Fields of Application
Scientific, statistical, commercial, accounting, management, systems analysis, operational research.

Training
B.S. course in Computer Science.

TEXAS AGRICULTURAL AND MECHANICAL UNIVERSITY
Data Processing Center
College Station, 77843
Telephone: (713) 845-4211

Officer
Dr. D. B. Simmons, *Director*

Computer Installation
IBM 360/65—operating systems: OS/MVT with HASP, BEST TP, APLPLUS; internal storage: 512K bytes; magnetic tapes: 6 Ampex 1624; magnetic discs: 24 Ampex DM 312, 3 CDC 23122; 4 line printers. *On-line satellite computers:* 8 remote high-speed terminals on leased line. *Remote processing features:* connected through HASP.

Coding Languages
FORTRAN IV, ALC, COBOL, PL/1, WATFIV, WATBOL, SPASM, APL.

Services Available
Advice, programming, education and training, operators, software packages, documentation, data preparation, systems analysis. Operate on a remote access, closed shop and time-sharing basis. Services primarily for Texas A & M University system but also provided to State and Federal governments; regular commercial work only under special approval.

Fields of Application
Scientific, statistical, data processing.
Specialized areas: Linear programming, payroll.

Training
Courses in computing science, computer organization, data structures, programming languages, compiler design, systems programming, information processing, scientific programming, mechanical languages, data processing systems organization, data processing management, time-sharing computer systems, computer language design, formal languages and automata theory, advanced computer structures.

TEXAS TECHNOLOGICAL UNIVERSITY
P.O. Box 4519, Lubbock, 79409
Telephone: (806) 742-1201

Officer
R. C. Gray, *Director, Computer Services*

Computer Installation
IBM 360/50—operating system: OS/MFT; internal storage: 384K bytes; magnetic tapes: 4 3420; magnetic discs: 2 2319; 2 line printers.

Coding Languages
FORTRAN IV, COBOL, PL/1, RPG, ALGOL.

Services Available
Advice, education and training, operators, documentation, administrative data processing. Operate on a closed shop basis.

Fields of Application
Scientific, statistical, commercial, production control, accounting, management, operational research, instructional.
Specialized areas: Linear programming, investment analysis, payroll, structural engineering.

Training
Seminars in programming.

TRINITY UNIVERSITY
715 Stadium Drive, San Antonio, 78284
Telephone: (512) 736-7401

Officer
C. D. Johnson, *Director, Computer Center*

Computer Installation
IBM 370/155—operating system: OS/MVT; internal storage: 1 million bytes; magnetic tapes: 4 3420, 2 2401; magnetic discs: 8 3330; 2 line printers. *On-line satellite computer:* MOD 20/1130. *Remote processing features:* APL and CRJE.

Coding Languages
BAL, COBOL, FORTRAN, APL, PL/1, PL/C.

Services Available
Advice, programming, education and training, operators, software packages, documentation, data preparation, systems analysis. Operate on a remote access, closed shop and time-sharing basis.

Fields of Application
Scientific, statistical, commercial, production control, accounting, management, systems analysis, operational research.

Training
Department of Information and Computing Sciences offers an undergraduate major in Information and Computing Sciences.

UNIVERSITY OF ST. THOMAS
3812 Montrose Boulevard, Houston, 77006
Telephone: (713) 522-7911, extension 329

Officer
Rev. P. O. Braden, *President*

Computer Installation
PDP-8/E—internal storage: 8K bits.

Coding Language
BASIC.

Service Available
Documentation. Operate on an open shop basis.

Fields of Application
Scientific, statistical, accounting.
Specialized area: Instruction.

Training
Courses in basic programming and numerical analysis.

UNIVERSITY OF TEXAS, ARLINGTON*
Arlington, 76010
Telephone: (817) 273-2011

Officer
L. Pierce, *Professor in charge, Computer Laboratory*

Computer Installation
IBM 1620/I—operating system: FORGO; internal storage: 60K bits.
IBM 1620/II—operating system: MONITOR I; internal storage: 60K bits; magnetic discs: 2 1311.
IBM 1401—internal storage: 16K bits; magnetic tapes: 3; magnetic discs: 2 1311; 1 line printer.

United States of America — Universities and Colleges

Coding Languages
FORTRAN, Autocoder, SPS.

Contemplated Equipment
XDS Sigma 5 with 20K word memory.

Service Available
Advice. Operate on a self-service basis. Primarily for education and research. Available to outside customers when not in use for above.

Field of Application
Education.

Training
Two introductory programming courses using FORTRAN language; one junior level course (Symbolic programming).

UNIVERSITY OF TEXAS, AUSTIN
Computation Center
Austin, 78712
Telephone: (512) 471-7242

Officers
Dr. Charles H. Warlick, *Director*
Edwin P. Shaw, *Assistant Director*
Robert J. Baker, *Manager of Operations and User Services*

Computer Installation
CDC 6600—operating system: UT2D; internal storage: 7,864,320 bits; magnetic tapes: 6 607; magnetic discs: 2 6638, 1 841/8; 3 line printers. *On-line satellite computers:* CDC 3100, CDC 8231, CDC 1700, XDS 930, PDP-11/20 (6), Nova 1200. *Remote processing features:* Local batch, remote batch entry, interactive time-sharing.
CDC 6400—operating system: UT2D; internal storage: 3,932,160 bits; magnetic tapes: 6 607; magnetic discs: 2 6638, 1 841/8. *On-line satellite computers:* CDC 3100, CDC 8231, CDC 1700, XDS 930, PDP-11/20 (6), Nova 1200. *Remote processing features:* Local batch, remote batch entry, interactive time-sharing.

Coding Languages
OPTIMA, SIMSCRIPT, SPSS, OMNITAB II, FUN, COMPASS, COBOL, L6, MIX, SCALLOP, SYMBAL, UTECAP, RFMS, CLIC, System 2000, TAURUS, ALGOL, BASIC, LISP, SNOBOL, EDITOR, MIMIC, MODIFY, UPDATE, BRUTE, PASCAL.

Contemplated Equipment
Communication front end processor; additional disc storage (CDC 844); additional extended core storage.

Services Available
Advice, programming, education and training, operators, software packages, documentation, preparation of data, systems analysis. Operate on a remote access, open shop and time-sharing basis. Not available for commercial computing.

Fields of Application
Scientific, statistical, educational.
Specialized area: Development of operating systems.

Training
The Computer Science Department offers 16 undergraduate courses (no degree programmes) and 19 graduate courses.

UNIVERSITY OF TEXAS, EL PASO*
Campus Administration Building,
El Paso, 79999
Telephone: (915) 542-5011

Officers
Semih Yildirim
Robert L. Schumaker

Computer Installation
IBM 360/25—operating systems: DOS, TPS; internal storage: 32K bits; magnetic tapes: 4 2415; magnetic discs: 2311; 1 line printer. *Remote processing features:* optical page reader.
CDC 3100—operating system: BOS; internal storage: 32K words; magnetic tapes: 3 604; magnetic discs: 2 854; 1 line printer. *Remote processing features:* communication channel.

Coding Languages
COBOL, RPG, FORTRAN, BAL.

Services Available
Consultation, operators, preparation of data, programming, software packages, systems analysis, education and training, documentation. Operate on self-service, closed and open shop basis. Available only to administration departments, faculty for research, students for education. IBM 360/25 is restricted to administrative data processing.

Fields of Application
Analysis of data received from the weather satellites, student academic evaluations, management reports, etc.

Training
Introductory courses in data processing and computers; courses in FORTRAN programming and computer and operator research; short adult education courses in computer fundamentals and programming.

UNIVERSITY OF TEXAS, EL PASO*
Schellenger Research Laboratories
El Paso, 79999
Telephone: (915) 542-5011

Officers
Dr. T. G. Barnes, *Director*
Professor Robert L. Schumaker, *Director of Data Analysis*

Computer Installation
CDC 3100—operating systems: SCOPE, Real Time SCOPE, MSOS; internal storage: 384K bits; magnetic tapes: 4 604; magnetic disc: 853; 1 line printer.

Coding Languages
ALGOL, ALTRAN.

Services Available
Advice, operators, preparation of data, programming, software packages, systems analysis. Operate on a closed shop basis.

Fields of Application
Acoustics, electronics.
Specialized areas: Upper atmosphere acoustics, rocket grenade sound ranging, frequency distribution of temperature, pressure, scalar winds, wind shear, etc.

WEST TEXAS STATE UNIVERSITY
Computer Center
Canyon, 79015
Telephone: (806) 055-7141

Officer
L. Durwood Henderson, *Director*

United States of America – Universities and Colleges

Computer Installation
IBM 360/40–operating system: DOS; internal storage: 256K bits; magnetic tapes: 2; magnetic disc: 1 2319. *Remote processing features:* 6 3270 CRTs and 4 typewriter terminals.

Coding Languages
FORTRAN, COBOL, ALC, PL/1.

Contemplated Equipment
Additional terminals.

Services Available
Preparation of data, programming, software packages, systems analysis. Operate on a closed shop basis. Primary service is to University Departments in Education, Research and Administration. Some time available to outside business.

Fields of Application
Administration, research and education.

Training
Courses in the principles of computer and information systems, techniques of computer programming, advanced programming techniques, Assembler language programming, contemporary programming method, computer system development and design, computer center management, data structures, computer hardware and software development, logic and algorithms, management information systems, applied problems in computer and information systems; graduate seminar in compiler writing.

UTAH

BRIGHAM YOUNG UNIVERSITY
Provo, 84601
Telephone: (801) 374-1211

Officers
Dr. Gary Carlson, *Director*
Willard H. Gardner, *Assistant Director*

Computer Installation
IBM 360/50–operating system: OS/MVT with HASP; internal storage: 384K bytes; magnetic tapes: 6; magnetic discs: 18 Calcomp; 2 line printers. *Remote processing features:* 16 3270.
IBM 1130–internal storage: 8K bytes; magnetic disc; 1 line printer.

Coding Languages
BAL, PL/1, GPSS, FORTRAN IV, COBOL.

Contemplated Equipment
IBM 2314, 1 Calcomp 563 plotter, RJE devices, IBM 2741's.

Services Available
Advice, software packages. Operate on a closed shop basis. Services available to students and faculty.

Fields of Application
Scientific, statistical and accounting.
Specialized areas: Payroll, processing genealogical files, performance measurement on computer monitoring.

Training
Courses in basic and advanced programming, applications in science, business, industrial control and behavioral sciences, information structure, systems and formal languages.

SNOW COLLEGE
Ephraim, 84627
Telephone: (801) 283-4611

Officer
Ross P. Findlay, *Registrar*

Computer Installation
IBM 1620–operating system: card; internal storage: 40K bits.

Coding Language
FORTRAN.

Services Available
Advice, programming, education and training, operators, software packages, documentation, preparation of data, systems analysis. Operate on a self-service and open shop basis.

Fields of Application
Scientific, statistical, commercial.
Specialized area: Linear programming.

Training
Courses in COBOL, FORTRAN, Unit-Record and General ADP Survey.

UNIVERSITY OF UTAH
Computer Center
3116 Merrill Engineering, Salt Lake City, 84112
Telephone: (801) 581-6802

Officer
E. M. Sharp, *Director*

Computer Installation
UNIVAC 1108–operating system: EXEC 8; internal storage: 262K 36-bit words; magnetic tapes: 9 Uniservo VIIIC; magnetic drums: 6 FH432 and 2 Fastrand II; 5 line printers. *On-line satellite computers:* Univac 9200, 9300. *Remote processing features:* Teletype, Univac 1004, 9200, 9300.

Coding Languages
FORTRAN, COBOL, ALGOL, SLEUTH, SIMULA.

Services Available
Advice, operators, preparation of data, programming, software packages and systems analysis. Operate on a closed shop, time-sharing and remote access basis.

Fields of Application
Scientific research and education, limited commercial.
Specialized areas: Statistics and numerical analysis.

Training
Formal degrees in computer science are offered.

UTAH STATE UNIVERSITY OF AGRICULTURE AND APPLIED SCIENCE
Computer Center
Logan, 84322
Telephone: (801) 752-4100, extension 7286

Officers
W. L. Pope, *Director*
K. A. Fugal, *Assistant Director*

Computer Installation
BURROUGHS B6700–operating system: MCP; internal storage: 6,291,456 bits; magnetic tapes: 4; magnetic discs: 13; 2 line printers. *Remote processing features:* Univac 9200 linked to Univac 1108 in Salt Lake City.

Coding Languages
FORTRAN IV, COBOL, ALGOL, PL/1, BASIC, ESPOL.

Services Available
Advice, programming, data preparation, systems analysis. Operate on a self-service, closed shop and time-sharing basis.

Fields of Application
Scientific, statistical, commercial, accounting, management, systems analysis.
Specialized areas: Payroll, structural engineering.

WEBER STATE COLLEGE*
Ogden, 84403
Telephone: 399-5941, extension 360

Officer
L. A. Nicholas

Computer Installation
IBM 360/40—operating system: DOS; internal storage: 128K bits; magnetic tapes: 4 2401; magnetic discs: 3 2311; 1 line printer.

Coding Languages
BAL, COBOL, FORTRAN, PL/1, RPG.

Services Available
Consultation, programming, systems analysis, educational training. Operate on closed shop and block time basis.

Fields of Application
Commercial, systems analysis.

Training
B.S. data processing courses.

VERMONT

UNIVERSITY OF VERMONT*
Computation Center
Burlington, 05401
Telephone: (802) 656-3480

Officers
Dr. David B. Hill, *Director*
Norbert Charbonneau, *Operations Manager*

Computer Installation
IBM 360/30—operating system: DOS/OS; internal storage: 64K bits; magnetic tapes: 4 2415; magnetic discs: 3 2311; 1 line printer.
IBM 1130—internal storage: 8K bits; magnetic disc: 2315; 1 line printer.
IBM 1620—internal storage: 40K bits; magnetic disc: 1311.

Coding Languages
FORTRAN, SPS, ALGOL, BAL, COBOL, RPG, PL/1.

Contemplated Equipment
IBM 360/40.

Services Available
Advice, operators, programming. Operate on a closed shop basis.

Fields of Application
All fields of interest to the University.
Specialized area: Numerical analysis.

Training
Programming courses.

VIRGINIA

BRIDGEWATER COLLEGE
C.E. Schull Computing Center
Bridgewater, 22812
Telephone: (703) 828-2501, extension 57

Officers
Dean Neher, *Director*
Ted W. Flory, *Manager*

Computer Installation
IBM 1130—internal storage: 128K bits; magnetic discs: 1 IBM 2315; 1 line printer.

Coding Languages
FORTRAN, RPG, Assembler.

Services Available
Operate on a self-service basis. Used primarily for administrative processing, educational applications and student learning.

Fields of Application
Scientific, accounting, management.
Specialized areas: Payroll, student training.

Training
Courses in programming, data processing, numerical analysis, simulation.

COLLEGE OF WILLIAM AND MARY IN VIRGINIA
Williamsburg, 23185
Telephone: (703) 229-3000

Officers
Dr. Thomas A. Graves, Jr., *President*
Dr. George R. Healy, *Vice President for Academic Affairs*
William J. Carter, *Vice President for Business Affairs*

Computer Installation
IBM 360/50—operating systems: OS, MFT; internal storage: 10,485,760 bits; magnetic tapes: 4 3420; magnetic discs: 12 Memorex 660; 1 line printer. *On-line satellite computers:* IBM 1130, IBM System/3, Data 100. *Remote processing features:* HASP, APL.

Coding Languages
FORTRAN, COBOL, RPG, PL/1, SNOBOL, LISP, Assembler.

Services Available
Advice, programming, education and training, preparation of data. Operate on a remote access, closed shop, and time-sharing basis. Only a small amount of commercial time is available.

Fields of Application
Scientific, accounting, management, educational.

United States of America – Universities and Colleges

Training
B.A. course in Computer Science within the Mathematics Department; M.S. course in Computer Science; undergraduate and graduate courses in programming, numerical analysis, automatation, etc.

NORTHERN VIRGINIA COMMUNITY COLLEGE
8333 Little River Turnpike, Annandale, 22003
Telephone: (703) 280-4000, extension 466

Officer
Dr. Richard Ernst, *President*

Computer Installation
Honeywell H1250–internal storage: 32K bits; magnetic tapes: 4; magnetic discs: 2; 1 line printer.

Coding Languages
Easycoder, FORTRAN IV, COBOL.

Services Available
Programming, operators, systems analysis. Operate on a closed shop basis. Available only to state educational institutions.

Fields of Application
Statistical, accounting, teaching.

Training
Associate in Applied Science (Computer Programming).

RANDOLPH-MACON COLLEGE*
Ashland, 23005
Telephone: (703) 798-8372

Officers
Luther W. White III, *President*
Dr. Harris Burns, Jr., *Director, Computer Center*
Thomas E. Vaughan, *Operations Manager*
Harry L. Heckel, *Programmer-Analyst*

Computer Installation
IBM 1800–operating system: TSX; internal storage: 24K bits; magnetic discs: 3 2315; 1 line printer.

Coding Languages
FORTRAN, NUTRAN, Assembler.

Services Available
Operate on an open shop and remote access basis. Available only to college members.

Fields of Application
Natural and social sciences, mathematics, administrative records.

Training
Eighteen hours of academic credit offered in computer science including an introduction to digital computation, programming, information structures, programming languages and selected topics in computer science.

UNIVERSITY OF VIRGINIA
Computer Science Center
Gilmer Hall, Charlottesville, 22903
Telephone: 295-1447

Officers
C. A. Plesums, *Associate Director for Research and Instructional Systems*
E. Grabman, *Manager of Operations*

Computer Installation
CDC 6400–operating system: SCOPE; internal storage; 3,932,160 bits; magnetic tapes: 4 607; magnetic discs: 5 841; 1 line printer. *On-line satellite computer:* Unitech RJE station. *Remote processing features:* Remote batch.

HEWLETT PACKARD 2000C (2)–operating system: TSB; internal storage: 524,288 bits each; magnetic tapes: 1 each. *Remote processing features:* 32 time-sharing terminals each.

Coding Languages
FORTRAN, COBOL, BASIC, ALGOL and others.

Contemplated Equipment
Additional peripherals, interactive graphics.

Services Available
Advice, programming, operators, software packages. Operate on a remote access, closed shop, block time and time-sharing basis. Available primarily to non-profit organizations.

Fields of Application
Scientific, statistical, computer science research. *Specialized areas:* Operating systems, simulation.

Training
M.S. and Ph.D. degrees are offered by the Department of Applied Mathematics and Computer Science.

VIRGINIA COMMONWEALTH UNIVERSITY
901 West Franklin Street, Richmond, 23220
Telephone: (703) 770-7256

Officer
E. E. Blanks, *Director of Administrative Services*

Computer Installation
HONEYWELL H200–operating system: MOD 1; internal storage: 20K bits; magnetic tapes: 4 B15 & 16; 1 line printer.
IBM 370/145–operating system: OS/HASP; internal storage: 512K bytes; magnetic tapes: 3 2415; magnetic discs: 1 2314; 1 line printer.

Coding Languages
COBOL, FORTRAN, Easycoder, PL/1, Assembler.

Services Available
Programming, systems analysis, education and training, advice, operators, software packages, documentation, data preparation. Operate on closed shop basis.

Fields of Application
Education, finance, management.

Training
Two year Associate degree in Business Data Processing.

VIRGINIA POLYTECHNIC INSTITUTE AND STATE UNIVERSITY
126 Burruss Hall, Blacksburg, 24061
Telephone: (703) 951-6381

Officer
Dr. R. C. Heteric, Jr., *Director of Computing Center*

United States of America – Universities and Colleges

Computer Installation
IBM 370/155–operating systems: OS/MVT, ASP; internal storage: 3,072K bytes; magnetic tapes: 5 3420; magnetic discs: 12 3330, 3 2319; 3 line printers. *On-line satellite computers:* 2 1130. *Remote processing features:* ASP-RJP, TSO, IMS, IBM 2260, 3270, 2770, 2780, 2741, Data 100.

Coding Languages
FORTRAN, COBOL, PL/1, BASIC, Assembler, ALGOL, RPG.

Contemplated Equipment
IBM 370/158 (2).

Services Available
Advice, programming, education and training, operators, software packages, documentation, preparation of data, systems analysis. Operate on a remote access basis. Available only to State and Federal Agencies.

Fields of Application
Scientific, commercial.

Training
B.S. and M.S. courses in Computer Science and Applications.

VIRGINIA STATE COLLEGE*
Petersburg, 23803
Telephone: 526-5111

Officers
Dr. Walter H. Quarles, Jr., *Acting President*
Charles R. Cone, *Interim Director of the Computer Center*

Computer Installation
IBM 360/30–internal storage: 32K bits; magnetic tapes: 2 2415; magnetic discs: 2 2311; 1 line printer.

Coding Languages
FORTRAN IV, PL/1, COBOL, RPG, Assembly.

Services Available
Advice, operators, preparation of data, programming. Operate on a closed shop basis. Commercial customers are restricted by an IBM educational allowance.

Fields of Application
Education and administration.

Training
Courses in basic computer concepts and basic computer programming.

WASHINGTON AND LEE UNIVERSITY*
Lexington, 24450
Telephone: (703) 463-2181

Officers
Robert B. Brownell, *Director Computer Center*
Lee Dudley, *Manager, Data Processing*

Computer Installation
IBM 1130–internal storage: 8K bits; 1 line printer.

Coding Languages
FORTRAN, RPG, APL, Assembler.

Service Available
Advice. Operate on an open shop basis. Available only to educational institutions.

Fields of Application
All disciplines in the University.

Training
One semester course in programming.

WASHINGTON

CENTRALIA COLLEGE
P.O. Box 639, Centralia, 98531
Telephone: 736-9391

Officer
Victor E. Lattin, *Director of Data Processing*

Computer Installation
IBM 1620–internal storage: 20K; magnetic discs: 2 1311.

Coding Languages
SPS, FORTRAN, COBOL, BAL, RPG, PL/1.

Contemplated Equipment
IBM 360/30–internal storage: 32K bits; 1 line printer.

Services Available
Advice, operators, programming, software packages, systems analysis. Operate on a closed shop basis. Available only for high schools in our service area.

Fields of Application
All College functions that need the use of a computer centre.

Training
Courses in data processing, computer design, BAL, COBOL, RPG, systems design and operations.

EASTERN WASHINGTON STATE COLLEGE
Cheney, 99004
Telephone: (509) 359-2391

Officer
Wade M. Harris, *Director*

Computer Installation
RCA Spectra 70/46–operating system: VMOS; internal storage: 8 x 256K bits; magnetic tapes: 4 9-track; magnetic discs: 5 70/590; 2 line printers. *On-line satellite computers:* 70/668 communication controller *Remote processing features:* 12 terminals.

Coding Languages
BAL, COBOL, FORTRAN.

Services Available
Programming, education and training, operators, software packages, preparation of data, systems analysis, teleprocessing services. Operate on a closed shop basis. Priority to in-house requirements; limited availability to non-profit and governmental agencies; no programmers supplied to outside agencies.

Fields of Application
Scientific, statistical, software development.

Training
B.A. degree course in Mathematics/Computer Sciences; short courses.

United States of America – Universities and Colleges

PACIFIC LUTHERAN UNIVERSITY*
Tacoma, 98447
Telephone: 531-6900

Officer
Dr. Dwight J. Zulauf, *Director of Data Processing*

Computer Installation
IBM 1401–operating system: Card; internal storage: 8K bits; 1 line printer.

Coding Languages
Autocoder, FORTRAN II.

Services Available
Consultation, programming, preparation of data. Operate on an open shop basis. No commercial work unless it is in the nature of pure research of interest to the institution.

Fields of Application
Accounting and registration systems for the University.

Training
Courses in programming and computers, data processing systems, systems analysis and design.

SEATTLE UNIVERSITY*
10th & East Madison, Seattle, 98122
Telephone: (206) 626-6200

Officers
George G. Town, *Director of Personnel*
Jeremy W. Reed, *Director of Administration Data Systems*
Joseph Burgher, *Director of Personnel*

Computer Installation
IBM 1620–operating system: Monitor I; internal storage: 120K bits; magnetic discs: 2 1311; 1 line printer.

Coding Languages
FORTRAN, SPS.

Services Available
Consultation, programming, education and training, operators, software packages, documentation, preparation of data, systems analysis. Operate on an open shop and time-sharing basis. Priority given to internal educational users.

Fields of Application
Engineering, student applications, scientific, statistical, administrative, records.

Training
Courses in elementary computer programming, principles of computer programming and computer operating systems. Occasional seminars on programming.

UNIVERSITY OF WASHINGTON
Computer Center
Seattle, 98105
Telephone: (206) 543-5970

Officer
R. G. Gillespie, *Director*

Computer Installation
CDC 6400–operating system: SCOPE, version 7; internal storage: 3·9 million bits; magnetic tapes: 6 607; magnetic discs: 1 6638; 3 line printers. *Remote processing features:* 2 remote 211, remote 200.
BURROUGHS B5500–operating system: MCP; internal storage: 1·6 million magnetic tapes: 8 magnetic discs; 2 line printers. *Remote processing features:* 8 ports for teletype access.

Coding Languages
BASIC, ESPOL, TSPOL, MAP, FORTRAN IV, COBOL, ALGOL, SNOBOL, RUNT.

Services Available
Advice, operators, preparation of data, programming. Operate on open shop, remote access and closed shop basis.

Fields of Application
Scientific, statistical, commercial, accounting, management, systems analysis, operational research.
Specialized areas: Sales analysis, linear programming, investment analysis, payroll, structural engineering, medical research.

Training
Programming courses in ALGOL, COBOL, FORTRAN IV, NPS and systems architecture are given each quarter.

WASHINGTON STATE UNIVERSITY
Pullman, 99163
Telephone: (509) 335-5536

Officers
Dr. W. E. Walden, *Director, Systems and Computing*
H. C. Fischer, *Director, Office of Systems Services and Development*
Dr. G. R. Ingram, *Director, Computing Center*
Dr. O. W. Rechard, *Chairman, Computer Science Department*

Computer Installation
IBM 360/67–operating system: OS/MVT/HASP; internal storage: 750K plus 1 million bytes; magnetic tapes: 4 2402, 1 2403; magnetic discs: 20 Calcomp 22/14, 7 1015; 2 line printers. *On-line satellite computers:* IBM 1130, IBM 360/20, IBM System/3.

Coding Languages
FORTRAN, PL/1, COBOL, ALGOL, LISP, SNOBOL, MPS, Assembler, WATFIV, WATBOL, BASIC, COMIT, RPG, GPSS, CSMP, STAR I.

Services Available
Advice, education and training, software packages, documentation. Operate on a remote access, closed shop and time-sharing basis. Services available to educational institutions and government agencies. Rate structure separate for other classes of users.

Fields of Application
Scientific, statistical, accounting, management, systems analysis, operational research, educational research.
Specialized area: Library applications.

Training
B.S., M.S. and Ph.D. degrees offered in Computer Science.

WESTERN WASHINGTON STATE COLLEGE
Bellingham, 98225
Telephone: (206) 676-3360

Officer
Melvin Davidson, *Director*

United States of America — Universities and Colleges

Computer Installation
IBM 360/40—operating system: OS; internal storage: 256K bytes; magnetic tapes: 2 2415; magnetic discs: 2 2314; 2 line printers. *Remote processing features:* 7 2741 terminals.
IBM 7090—operating system: IBSYS; internal storage: 32K words.

Coding Languages
PL/1, FORTRAN, COBOL, GSS, BASIC, RPG.

Contemplated Equipment
7 3270 terminals.

Services Available
Advice, programming, education and training, software packages, documentation, preparation of data, systems analysis. Operate on a closed shop and time-sharing basis. Limited availability for non-College rental.

Fields of Application
Scientific, accounting, management, systems analysis, instructional.
Specialized area: payroll.

Computer Installation
IBM 1130—operating system: DOS; internal storage: 8K 16-bit words; magnetic discs: CPU disc drive; 1 line printer.
PDP-8/E—operating system: PT; internal storage: 8K 8-bit words. *Remote processing features:* 3 TTY terminals.

Coding Languages
FORTRAN IV, BASIC, RPG, APL, Assembler, COBOL.

Services Available
Consultation, programming, education and training, operators, software packages, documentation, preparation of data, systems analysis. Operate on a block time and time-sharing basis. Service available to faculty, students, administration.

Fields of Application
Scientific, educational, statistical, accounting, management.

Training
Courses in scientific programming, business programming and assembly language programming; short introductory course in basic FORTRAN IV.

WEST VIRGINIA

BETHANY COLLEGE
Bethany, 26032
Telephone: (304) 829-7000

Officers
Cecil H. Underwood, *President*
Barrie Richardson, *Vice-President and Dean of the Faculty*

Computer Installation
IBM System/3—internal storage: 98,304 bits; 1 line printer.
DATA GENERAL Supernova—operating system: time-shared; internal storage: 327,680 bits; magnetic tapes: 2 Potter; magnetic discs: 1 Honeywell DSC 200; 1 line printer. *On-line satellite computers:* 1 General Mills AD/ECS 37A. *Remote processing features:* 2000 baud port.

Coding Languages
BASIC, FORTRAN IV, ALGOL 60, Assembler.

Contemplated Equipment
Additional line printer.

Services Available
Advice, programming, education and training, software packages, documentation. Operate on a time-sharing basis.

Fields of Application
Scientific, statistical, instruction.
Specialized area: Simulation.

Training
Courses in introductory and advanced computer science, and facilities for independent study in computer science.

CONCORD COLLEGE
Athens, 24712
Telephone: (304) 384-3115

Officer
C. James Burkhart, *Director, Office of Computing Services*

WEST VIRGINIA UNIVERSITY*
Computer Center
837 Chestnut Ridge Road, Morgantown, 26505
Telephone: (304) 293-5192

Officer
Dr. Wayne A. Muth, *Director*

Computer Installation
IBM 360/75—operating system: OS/MVT/HASP II; internal storage: 1,536K bytes; magnetic tapes: 3; magnetic discs: 1 2314, 2 2303 drums; 4 line printers. *On-line satellite computers:* 2 1130. *Remote processing features:* RJE w/2714, ASR 33, ASR 35, 2780, 1130 and 2260 CRT.

Coding Languages
COBOL, FORTRAN IV, ALGOL, RPG, CPS, PL/1 with FORMAC, MPS, SIMSCRIPT, ECAP, MIDAS, CSMP, SNOBOL, WATFIV, Assembler.

Contemplated Equipment
2314 disc controller (8 drives).

Services Available
Consultation, data preparation, programming, software packages, training. Operate on a closed shop basis.

Fields of Application
Scientific, statistical, commercial, accounting, management, systems analysis.
Specialized areas: Medical, music and transportation research.

Training
Courses in COBOL, FORTRAN, PL/1, CPS.

WEST VIRGINIA UNIVERSITY
Potomac State College
Fort Avenue, Keyser, 26726
Telephone: (304) 788-3012

Officers
Dr. H. C. Doster, *Dean of College*
E. Hartman, *Director, Computer Center*

United States of America — Universities and Colleges

Computer Installation
NCR Century 100—operating system: Monitor; internal storage: 262,144 bits; magnetic discs: 2 NCR 655; 1 line printer. *Remote processing features:* terminal to IBM 360/75.

Coding Languages
COBOL, FORTRAN, BASIC, NEAT/3, RPG, Assembler, PL/1.

Contemplated Equipment
NCR Century 101 with tape and disc.

Services Available
Advice, programming, education and training, data preparation, systems analysis. Operate on a closed shop basis. Services restricted to state agencies.

Fields of Application
Scientific, statistical, commercial, systems analysis, operational research.

Training
A.A. degree in Computer Programming Technology; B.S. degree in Computer Science; degree course in Computer Technology planned.

WISCONSIN

CARROLL COLLEGE
Waukesha, 53186
Telephone: (414) 547-1211

Officers
Robert V. Cramer, *President*
H. Glander, *Director of Computer Services*

Computer Installation
IBM 1130—operating system: Disk Monitor; internal storage: 131,072 bits; magnetic discs: 1 2310; 1 line printer;
GENERAL AUTOMATION SPC-12—internal storage: 65,536 bits.

Coding Languages
BASIC, FORTRAN IV, ASM, RPG, COBOL, APL.

Services Available
Advice, programming, education and training. Operates on a self-service and closed shop basis. Services restricted to schools and companies with scientific rather than commercial problems.

Fields of Application
Scientific, statistical, administrative.

Training
Various courses in computer science. Minor offered in computer science; soon to offer combined computer science - physics major.

MARQUETTE UNIVERSITY*
Computing Center
1515 West Wisconsin Avenue, Milwaukee, 53233
Telephone: (414) 224-7250

Officers
Robert Miller, *Acting Director*
James Tobin, *Operations Manager*
Prof. William Weidman, *Research Associate*

Computer Installation
IBM 7040—operating system: IBSYS; internal storage: 16K 36-bit words; magnetic tapes: 2 729 and 4 733; 1 line printer.
IBM 360/30—internal storage: 64K bits; magnetic discs: 6. *Remote processing features:* 8 2741 terminals.

Coding Languages
FORTRAN IV, MAP Assembly, COBOL, COGO SIMSCRIPT, IPL-V, MAD.

Contemplated Equipment
Small computer for data acquisition in biomedical engineering.

Services Available
Advice, operators, some programming, software packages and some systems analysis. Operate on a closed shop and open shop basis.

Fields of Application
Computer education, statistical data processing, other research orientated computation, medical research data processing.
Specialized areas: Statistical analysis of medical and biomedical engineering data, such as fetal electrocardiogram, respiratory simulation.

UNIVERSITY OF WISCONSIN, EAUCLAIRE
Schofield Hall, Eauclaire, 54701
Telephone: (715) 836-4428

Officer
Rudolph C. Polenz, *Director, Computer Center*

Computer Installation
BURROUGHS 3500—operating systems: MCP; internal storage: 180K bytes; magnetic tapes: 3; 2 line printers. *Remote processing features:* Burroughs DC1100, 7 TWX, 2 CRTs.

Coding Languages
COBOL, FORTRAN, Assembler, BASIC.

Contemplated Equipment
BURROUGHS B4700, additional disc, additional CRTS and TWX.

Services Available
Education and training. Operate on a remote access, closed shop and time-sharing basis.

Training
Minor degree courses are offered in computer science and data processing.

UNIVERSITY OF WISCONSIN, GREEN BAY
Green Bay, 54305

Officer
A. W. Cronk, *Director*

Computer Installation
XDS Sigma 6—operating system: BTM; internal storage: 2,048K bits; magnetic tapes: 2; magnetic discs: 4; 1 line printer. *Remote processing features:* several time-sharing ports, 1 dedicated line to Univac 1108.

Coding Languages
FORTRAN, COBOL, META-SYMBOL, Data Base Language (DMS).

United States of America – Universities and Colleges

Services Available
Consultation, operators, programming, software packages, systems analysis, education and training. Operate on closed shop basis. Available only to faculty, staff, students and limited consultation, education and training to local business.

Fields of Application
Scientific, statistical, operational research, administration, registration, financial aid, admissions, business offices, university library automation system.

Training
Credit courses and non-credit seminars.

UNIVERSITY OF WISCONSIN, MADISON*
Computing Center
1210 West Dayton Street, Madison, 53706

Officer
Professor Dr. Mervin E. Muller, *Director*

Computer Installation
BURROUGHS B5500–operating system: MCP; internal storage: 1,572,864 bits; magnetic tapes: 3 B425, 2 B475; 1 line printer. *Remote processing features:* model 33 and 35 teletypes.
CDC 3600–operating system: SCOPE; internal storage: 3,145,728 bits; magnetic tapes: 10 607; 2 line printers. *On-line satellite computers:* CDC 924/15, Liac. *Remote processing features:* remote card reader and line printer.
CDC 1604–operating system: COOP Monitor; internal storage: 1,572,864 bits; magnetic tapes: 4 1607, 6 606; 1 line printer. *On-line satellite computers:* CDC 160, Univac 1004.
IBM 1460–internal storage: 49,152 bits; magnetic tapes: 3 7330; magnetic disc: 1 1311; 1 line printer.

Coding Languages
FORTRAN, CODAP, DITRAN, ALGOL, SLIP, COMPASS, SIMSCRIPT, LISP, COBOL, INTERP, WIPL.

Contemplated Equipment
Burroughs B8500.

Services Available
Application programmes, library routines, documentation, programming, systems analysis, advice.

Fields of Application
Numerical analysis, statistics, remote multi-access computing, data processing.

Training
Introductory courses in computing machines and data processing methods; other courses in computer programming in the physical sciences and the theory and operation of computers.

UNIVERSITY OF WISCONSIN, MILWAUKEE
3200 North Cramer Street, Milwaukee, 53201
Telephone: (414) 963-4424

Officers
L. P. Levine, *Director*
A. Glasberg, *Associate Director*

Computer Installation
UNIVAC 9200–internal storage: 8K bytes; 1 line printer. *Remote processing features:* satellite to Univac 1108.
UNIVAC 9300–internal storage: 8K bytes; 1 line printer. *Remote processing features:* satellite to Univac 1108.
IBM 360/40–internal storage: 256K bits.
IBM 360/20.

Coding Languages
All.

Contemplated Equipment
Univac 1106.

Services Available
Advice, programming, education and training, operators, software packages, documentation, data preparation, systems analysis. Operate on a self-service, remote access, closed shop, block time and time-sharing basis.

Fields of Application
Scientific, statistical, commercial, production control, accounting, management, systems analysis, operational research.

Training
A variety of short courses. Computer science programme under development.

UNIVERSITY OF WISCONSIN, OSHKOSH*
800 Algoma Boulevard, Oshkosh, 54901
Telephone: (414) 235-6220

Officer
D. L. Melin, *Director*

Computer Installation
IBM 360/40–operating systems: DOS, OS; internal storage: 256K bytes; magnetic tapes: 3 2401; magnetic discs: 1 2314; 1 line printer.

Coding Languages
COBOL, FORTRAN, PL/1, RPG, Assembler.

Contemplated Equipment
IBM 360/50.

Services Available
Consultation, preparation of data, programming, software packages, systems analysis, education and training, documentation. Operate on closed shop and time-sharing basis. Available only to faculty and students.

Fields of Application
Scientific, statistical, accounting, student records.

Training
Courses in FORTRAN, Assembler, COBOL, PL/1 programming and introduction to data processing.

UNIVERSITY OF WISCONSIN, STEVENS POINT*
2100 Main Street, Stevens Point, 54481

Officer
W. Eggert, *Director of Computer Center*

Computer Installation
IBM 1401–operating system: IOCS; internal storage: 16K bits; magnetic discs: 2 1311; 1 line printer.
IBM 1130–internal storage: 8K bits; 1 magnetic disc: 1 line printer.

United States of America – Universities and Colleges

Coding Languages
FORTRAN, RPG, APL, Autocoder.

Contemplated Equipment
Burroughs B2500.

Services Available
Consultation, operators, preparation of data, programming, software packages, systems analysis. Operate on closed shop basis. Available only to faculty and students.

Fields of Application
Assistance in student instruction and management information for administration.

Training
Elementary mathematical programming, introduction to computer programming. Short courses in FORTRAN programming.

UNIVERSITY OF WISCONSIN, WHITEWATER
Whitewater, 53190
Telephone: (414) 472-1325

Officer
D. J. Fleckenstein, *Computer Center Director*

Computer Installation
IBM 1130–operating systems: Monitor 2; internal storage: 131,072 bits; magnetic disc: 1; 1 line printer.
IBM 360/25–operating system: DOS; internal storage: 393,216 bits; magnetic tapes: 2 2415; magnetic discs: 3 2319; 1 line printer.

Coding Languages
FORTRAN, COBOL, PL/1, BAL, APL.

Contemplated Equipment
IBM 370/135.

Services Available
Consultation, operators, preparation of data, programming, software packages, systems analysis, education and training, documentation. Operate on closed shop basis.

Fields of Application
University administration, instruction and research.
Specialized areas: Student records, finances, facilities, academic programmes, staff, mathematic instruction, computer science instruction, business data processing instruction, physical science instruction.

Training
Minor degree course in computer science. Major in general business, with emphasis on computer center administration.

UNIVERSITY OF WISCONSIN CENTER, SHEBOYGAN COUNTY
P.O. Box 719, Sheboygan, 53081
Telephone: (414) 458-5566

Officers
James F. Gross, *Director of Computing Center*
Kenneth L. Bailey, *Dean*

Computer Installation
UNIVAC 9200–internal storage: 64K bits; 1 line printer.
Remote processing features: 9200 used as terminal to UNIVAC 1108.

Coding Languages
9200 Assembly, RPG, FORTRAN, ALGOL, COBOL, SNOBOL, LISP, BASIC, STATJOB.

Services Available
Advice, operators. Operate on a remote access and open shop basis. Available to all customers but academic and non-profit users pay less than commercial users do.

Field of Application
Instructional.

Training
Courses provided: Introduction to Computing Machines; Algebraic Language Programming.

WYOMING

UNIVERSITY OF WYOMING*
Division of Computer Sciences
Box 3945, University Station, Laramie, 82070
Telephone: 766-6160

Officer
Dr. Winkel, *Director, Computing Services*

Computer Installation
PHILCO 2000–operating system: SYS; internal storage: 32K bits; magnetic tapes: 10 Ampex TM 2; 1 line printer.
XDS Sigma 5–operating system: BPM/BTM; internal storage: 48K bits; magnetic tapes: 1 XDS; magnetic discs: 2 XDS 7204; 1 line printer. *Remote processing features:* real time and time-sharing.
IBM 1401–internal storage: 8K bits.

Coding Languages
FORTRAN, COBOL, Metasymbol, TAC, Basic, Manage, Autocoder.

Contemplated Equipment
XDS Sigma 7.

Services Available
Advice, operators, systems analysis, software packages. Operate on a closed shop and time-sharing basis.

Fields of Application
Scientific, statistical, administrative.

Training
Academic computer science courses available through the University.

GOVERNMENT ESTABLISHMENTS

AGENCY FOR INTERNATIONAL DEVELOPMENT (AID)
State Dept. SA-12 Room 725, Washington, D.C.20523
Telephone: (202) 632-7962

Officers
Maury D. Brown, *Director, Office of Data Management*
John H. Chamberlayne, *Deputy Director*
William C. Ruotola, *Chief, Information Systems Division*
Willard Lee, *Chief, Computer Center*

Computer Installations
IBM 360/50–operating system: OS - MFT II; internal storage: 512K bytes; magnetic tapes: 5 2420/5, 1 2415/2; magnetic discs: 14 2314; 2 line printers.

United States of America – Government Establishments

Coding Languages
COBOL, FORTRAN.

Contemplated Equipment
IBM 360/65.

Services Available
Advice, programming, documentation, systems analysis. Operate on remote access and closed shop basis.

Fields of Application
Statistical, commercial, accounting, management.
Specialized areas: Linear programming, analysis, payroll.

LAWRENCE BERKELEY LABORATORY
Berkeley, California 94720
Telephone: (415) 843-2740

Officers
E. M. McMillan, *Director*
J. A. Baker, *Mathematics and Computing Department Head*
E. R. Beals, *Mathematics and Computing User Services Head*

Computer Installation
CDC 7600–operating system: SCOPE; internal storage: 33,932,160 bits; magnetic discs: 2 7638, 1 844. *On-line satellite computers:* CDC 6600, CDC 6200.
CDC 6600–operating system: BKY 52; internal storage: 7,864,320; magnetic tapes: 10 607, 2 657; magnetic discs: 3 6603; 1 844. *On-line satellite computers:* CDC 7600, CDC 6200. *Remote processing features:* locally developed teletype system.

Coding Languages
FORTRAN, COBOL, SNOBOL, COMPASS, ALGOL.

Services Available
Advice, programming, education and training, operators, software packages, documentation, preparation of data, systems analysis. Operate on a self-service, remote access, open shop and time-sharing basis.

Field of Application
Scientific.

NATIONAL AERONAUTICS AND SPACE ADMINISTRATION (NASA)
Jet Propulsion Laboratory (operated by California Institute of Technology)
4800 Oak Grove Drive, Pasadena, California 91103

Officers
Dr. William H. Pickering, *Director*
Charles H. Terhune, *Deputy Director*
Dr. Aaron Finerman, *Manager, Office of Computing and Information Systems*

Computer Installation
UNIVAC 1108 (2)–operating system: EXEC 8; internal storage: 196K bits (each); magnetic tapes: Univac 20 859-08; magnetic discs: 16 Intranet 351; 2 line printers. *On-line satellite computers:* 6 UNIVAC 9300. *Remote processing features:* 96 keyboard terminals.
IBM 360/75 (3)–operating systems: JPLOS, OS/MVT; internal storage: 1 million + 2 million bytes (each); magnetic tapes: 10 2401/2, 16 2401/3, 10 3420/7; magnetic discs: 14 2319/B1, 2 3330; 12 line printers. *Remote processing features:* 34 IBM 2260/2 display keyboards.

Coding Languages
FORTRAN, BASIC, COBOL, ALGOL 60, GPSS, SIMULA, MATH, Assembly.

Contemplated Equipment
IBM 370/165, UNIVAC 1230.

Services Available
Advice, programming, operators, software packages, documentation, systems analysis. Operate on a remote access, closed shop, block time, and time-sharing basis. Permission to use facilities required from NASA, Pasadena Office.

Fields of Application
Scientific, systems analysis, research and development.
Specialized areas: Structural engineering, medical research, spacecraft navigation, tracking data acquisition, unmanned spacecraft.

NATIONAL AERONAUTICS AND SPACE ADMINISTRATION (NASA)*
Lewis Research Center
Plum Brook Station, Sandusky, Ohio 44870
Telephone: (419) 625-1123

Computer Installation
IBM 1620–operating system: Monitor; internal storage: 20K characters; magnetic tapes: 2 556; magnetic discs: 1; 1 line printer.

Coding Languages
FORTRAN, SPS.

Services Available
Operate on an open shop basis. Available to other NASA installations, also other Government installations through General Services Administration, on a time-available basis.

Fields of Application
All general fields.
Specialized area: Data reduction.

NATIONAL BUREAU OF STANDARDS
Computer Services Division
Room A225, Administration Building, Washington, D.C. 20234
Telephone: (301) 921-3424

Officers
W. Bruce Ramsay, *D. P. Manager*
H. S. Peiser, *Office of International Relations*

Computer Installation
UNIVAC 1108/418 intercoupled–operating system: EXEC 8; internal storage: 9,437,184 bits (1108), 737,280 bits (418); magnetic tapes: 10 VIIIC (1108), 1 VIC (418); magnetic drums: 7 FH 432 (1108), 1 Data Products (1108), 1 Fastrand (418); line printers: 3 (1108), 1 (418). *Remote processing features:* simultaneous remote access to 18 high-speed batch terminals and 4 low-speed interactive terminals.

Coding Languages
FORTRAN, COBOL, SIMSCRIPT, OMNITAB.

Fields of Application
Scientific, statistical.
Specialized areas: Payroll, equipment inventory, accounting and personnel.

United States of America – Government Establishments

NATIONAL CLIMATIC CENTER
Federal Building, Asheville, North Carolina 28801
Telephone: (704) 254-0961

Officers
William H. Haggard, *Director*
Raymond L. Joiner, *Digital Systems Advisor*
William M. McMurray, *Chief, Applied Climatology Division*
Grady F. McKay, *Chief, Data Reduction Branch*

Computer Installation
RCA Spectra 70/45 (2)–operating system: TDOS; internal storage: 195K bytes each; magnetic tapes: 8 70/445-2 each; magnetic discs: 3 70/590 each; 1 line printer each.

Coding Languages
COBOL, FORTRAN.

Services Available
Advice, operators, preparation of data, programming, systems analysis. Operate on a closed shop basis.

Fields of Application
Environmental data processing.

NATIONAL SCIENCE FOUNDATION (NSF)
Office of Computing Activities
1800 G Street, N.W., Washington, D.C. 20550
Telephone: (202) 632-7346

Officers
Dr. H. Guyford Stever, *Director of NSF*
John Pasta, *Head, Office of Computing Activities*
Kent Curtis, *Head, Computer Science and Engineering*
D. D. Aufenkamp, *Head, Computer Applications to Research*

Service Available
Support of research. Operate on a time-sharing basis.

Fields of Application
Scientific, statistical, commercial, production control, accounting, management, systems analysis, operational research.
Specialized areas: Research in computer science and engineering; applications of computers to scientific research and to problems of society.

OAK RIDGE NATIONAL LABORATORY
P.O. Box X, Oak Ridge, Tennessee 37830
Telephone: (615) 483-8611

Officers
A. M. Weinberg, *Director*
F. L. Culler, *Deputy Director*
H. P. Carter, *Director, Mathematics Division*

Computer Installation
IBM 360/91–operating system: OS/360; internal storage: 16 million bits; magnetic tapes: 5; magnetic discs: 16 2314; 3 line printers. *Remote processing features:* numerous RJE terminals.
IBM 360/75–operating system: OS/360; internal storage: 20 million bits; magnetic tapes: 4; magnetic discs: 16 2314; 2 line printers. *Remote processing features:* numerous RJE, CRT and TTY terminals.
PDP-10–operating system: DEC Monitor; internal storage: 4 million bits; magnetic tapes: 2 IBM Compatible, 3 DEC; magnetic discs: 16 RPO2; 1 line printer. *On-line satellite computers:* PDP-15 (5). *Remote processing features:* many.

Coding Languages
FORTRAN, PL/1, ALGOL, COBOL, Assembly, BASIC.

Services Available
Advice, programming, operators, software packages. Operate on a remote access and open shop basis. Services restricted to the U.S. Government and its contractors.

Fields of Application
Scientific, statistical.
Specialized areas: Nuclear engineering, information science.

SOCIAL AND ECONOMIC STATISTICS ADMINISTRATION
Bureau of the Census
Washington, D.C. 20233
Telephone: (301) 763-5190

Officers
George H. Brown, *Director*
Robert L. Hagan, *Deputy Director*
Walter E. Simonson, *Associate Director for Electronic Data Processing.*

Computer Installation
UNIVAC 1108 (2)–operating system: EXEC 8; internal storage: 4,716K bits (each); magnetic tapes: 14 Uniservo IIIA 9-track, 3 VIIIC 7-track (each); 2 line printers (each). *Remote processing features:* DCT 2000.
UNIVAC 1106 (2)–operating system: EXEC 1; internal storage: 2,340K bits (each); magnetic tapes: 14 Uniservo IIIA; 2 IVC (each); 2 line printers (each).
IBM 360/40–operating system: DOS; internal storage: 520K bits; magnetic tapes: 3 2400 9-track, 4 2400 7-track; magnetic discs: 5 2314; 1 line printer.

Coding Languages
FORTRAN, COBOL, SLEUTH, Assembly, RPG, PL/1.

Contemplated Equipment
IBM 360/65. Core modules, 1782 drums, tape drives and discs for the Univac installation.

Services Available
Advice, programming, software packages, documentation, preparation of data, systems analysis. Operate on remote access, closed shop, and time-sharing basis.

Fields of Application
Statistical, social and economic and demographic.
Specialized areas: Medical research, census surveys and analyses of statistical data.

Training
Training for computer programmers, operators and EDP managers, and courses in systems analysis and statistics.

SOCIAL SECURITY ADMINISTRATION
Bureau of Data Processing
6401 Security Blvd., Room 2-A-10 Operations Building,
Baltimore, Maryland 21235

Officers
William E. Hanna, Jr., *Director*
Louis Lazarus, *Assistant Bureau Director, Operations*
Edward Coady, *Chief EDP Branch*

United States of America – Government Establishments

Computer Installation
IBM 360/65J (4)–operating system: OS/MVT; internal storage: 8,388,608 bits (each); magnetic tapes: 20 9-track (each), 4 7-track (each); magnetic discs: 16 (each); 3 line printers (each). *Remote processing features:* 2 test plus 1 batch entry facility.
IBM 360/65I (9)–operating system: OS/MFT; internal storage: 4,194,304 bits (each); magnetic tapes: 10 9-track (each), 8 7-track (each); magnetic discs: 8 (each); 1 line printer (each).
IBM 370/165K–operating system: OS/MVT LASP; internal storage: 16,777,216 bits; magnetic tapes: 54 9-track, 10 7-track; magnetic discs: 14; 3 line printers. *On-line satellite computers:* TEMPO II Front End Concentrator.
UNIVAC 1108 (2)–operating system: EXEC 8; internal storage: 9,432K bits (each); magnetic tapes: 13 9-track (each), 2 7-track (each); magnetic discs: 27 (each); 4 line printers (each). *Remote processing features:* 4 label processing stations.

Coding Languages
COBOL, FORTRAN, PLI, RPG, ALC.

Contemplated Equipment
IBM 370/168.

Services Available
Advice, education and training, documentation, preparation of data. Operate on a remote access, closed shop and time-sharing basis. Customers outside the Administration would generally be restricted to other governmental agencies, commercial insurance companies associated with the Medicare phase of social security and trade unions.

Field of Application
Social security.

Fields of Application
Scientific, statistical, commercial, accounting, systems analysis, operational research.
Specialized areas: Linear programming, payroll, structural engineering, critical path method.

Training
Multi-media training courses in IBM 360 and 370 job control language, operating systems, FORTRAN, COBOL, etc.

UNITED NATIONS
Public Administration Division
First Avenue, New York, New York 10017
Telephone: (212) 754-1234, extension 2493

Officers
Emil J. Sady, *Acting Director*
Michael A. Bentil, *Chief, Section for Organization & Methods*
Henry L. Willis, *Public Administration Officer* (Data Processing)

Services Available
Advice, education and training, publications, technical assistance. Services provided at requests of governments.

Field of Application
Government.

TENNESSEE VALLEY AUTHORITY (TVA)
Computing Services Branch
101 Old Post Office Building, Chattanooga, Tennessee 37401

Officers
Martin Hochdorf, *Branch Chief*
L. G. Payne, *Assistant Branch Chief*

Computer Installation
IBM 370/165–operating system: OS/MVT/HASP; internal storage: 8,388,608 bits; magnetic tapes: 6 3420; magnetic discs: 6 3330, 2 2311; 3 line printers. *On-line satellite computers:* IBM 360/30, IBM 360/20, Mohawk 2420.
IBM 360/50–operating system: OS/MVT; internal storage: 4,194,304 bits; magnetic tapes: 8 2400 (six 9-track, two 7-track); magnetic discs: 9 2314, 4 2311; 1 line printer.
BULL GENERAL ELECTRIC GE 225–internal storage: 163,840 bits; 1 line printer.

Coding Languages
FORTRAN IV, COBOL, PL/1, FORTRAN II, RPG.

Services Available
Advice, programming, education and training, operators, documentation, preparation of data, systems analysis. Operate on a remote access, open shop and time-sharing basis. Available to outside customers subject to prior use by TVA and only if services requested are not readily available through commercial services.

UNITED STATES GEOLOGICAL SURVEY
Computer Center Division
18th and East Streets, Washington, D.C. 20242

Officers
Carl E. Diesen, *Chief*
Charles H. Tyler, *Assistant Chief*

Computer Installation
IBM 360/65–operating system: HASP/OS; internal storage: 1 million + 1 million bits; magnetic tapes: 8 9-track, 2 7-track; magnetic discs: 8 IBM, 24 Calcomp; 3 line printers. *Remote processing features:* 70 terminals on line, teletype to IBM 360/30.

Coding Languages
FORTRAN, PL/1, COBOL.

Contemplated Equipment
Additional IBM 360/65 or 370/155.

Services Available
Advice, programming, education and training operators, software packages, documentation, preparation of data, systems analysis. Operate on a remote access and closed shop basis.

Fields of Application
Scientific, statistical, commercial, production control, accounting, management, systems analysis, operational research.
Specialized areas: Linear programming, analysis, payroll.

Training
Courses in Programming and JCL.

RESEARCH INSTITUTIONS

ABACUS COMPUTER CORPORATION
110 East Granada Ave., Suite 222, Ormond Beach, Florida 32074
Telephone: (904) 672-5672

Officer
Donald D. Spencer, *President*

Coding Languages
BASIC, FORTRAN, PL/1.

Contemplated Equipment
Data General Nova 1220.

Services Available
Advice, programming, education and training, software packages, systems analysis, preparation of reference books.

Fields of Application
Scientific, educational.
Specialized area: Medical research.

Training
Seminars offered to teachers about instruction on how to use computers in secondary schools.

AEROJET ELECTROSYSTEMS COMPANY
1100 West Hollyvale, Azusa, California 91702
Telephone: (213) 334-6211

Officers
G. W. Leisz, *President*
B. G. Walker, *Chief Engineer, Data Systems*
W. J. Meyer, *Manager, Data Processing*

Computer Installation
IBM 360/75–operating system: OS/MVT; internal storage: 1 million plus 2 million bytes; magnetic tapes: 14 3420, 1 2415; magnetic discs: 2 2314; 3 line printers. *Remote processing features:* 1030, 1050, 2740, 2741, 2260, 3277.
IBM 360/75–operating system: OS/MVT; internal storage: 1 million plus 2 million bytes; magnetic tapes: 4 2420; magnetic discs: 1 2314; 2 line printers. *On-line satellite computer:* special design. *Remote processing features:* teletype, 2741.

Coding Languages
COBOL, FORTRAN.

Contemplated Equipment
IBM 370/158 with 3331 discs.

Services Available
Programming, systems analysis, batch processing. Operate on a remote access, closed shop and time-sharing basis.

Fields of Application
Scientific, statistical, commercial, production control, accounting, management, systems analysis, operational research.

ARGONNE NATIONAL LABORATORY
Applied Mathematics Division
Building 221, Room A-241, 9700 South Cass Avenue, Argonne, Illinois 60439
Telephone: (312) 739-7711, extension 4201

Officers
R. V. Laney, *Acting Director*
R. J. Royston, *Director, Applied Mathematics Division*

Computer Installation
IBM 360/75–operating system: OS; internal storage: 6 million bytes; magnetic tapes: 1 2401, 2 2402, 2 2403, 5 3420; magnetic discs: 3 2314, 7 3330; 4 line printers.
Remote processing features: RJE network, 13 terminals.

Coding Languages
FORTRAN, PL/I, COBOL.

Contemplated Equipment
Additional discs, communications equipment and graphics facilities.

Services Available
Operate on a remote access, open shop and time-sharing basis.

Fields of Application
Scientific, statistical, management, systems analysis.
Specialized area: Atomic energy research.

AVCO CORPORATION*
Avco Systems Division
201 Lowell Street, Wilmington, Massachusetts 01887
Telephone: (617) 729-7700

Officers
Dr. William F. Brown, *Director*
Joseph S. DeNatale, *Manager, Computing Systems Department*

Computer Installation
IBM 360/75–operating system: OS/MVT; internal storage: 8,388,608 bits; magnetic tapes: 4 2402; magnetic discs: 2 2314; 3 line printers. *Remote processing features:* IBM 2701.

Coding Languages
FORTRAN, COBOL.

Services Available
Advice, operators, preparation of data, programming, software packages. Operate on a self-service basis.

Fields of Application
Scientific, engineering, management information analyses and programming.
Specialized areas: Research and solution of re-entry phenomena problems.

BATTELLE MEMORIAL INSTITUTE*
505 King Avenue, Columbus, Ohio 43201

Also at:
Richland, Washington

Officers
R. L. Merrick, *Director, Columbus*
F. W. Albaugh, *Director, Northwest*

Computer Installation
Columbus:
CDC 6400.
Northwest:
UNIVAC 1108.

Services Available
Programming, education and training, software packages, documentation, preparation of data, systems analysis. Available only as a research and development tool.

Fields of Application
Research and development programmes and studies in the physical, life and behavioral sciences.

United States of America – Research Institutions

BELL LABORATORIES
6200 East Broad Street, Columbus, Ohio 43213
Telephone: (614) 868-2392

Officer
R. J. Spires, *Head*

Computer Installation
IBM 370/155–operating system: OS/MVT with HASP; internal storage: 16 million bits; magnetic tapes: 3 3420; magnetic discs: 3330; 3 line printers. *On-line satellite computer:* IBM 2250/4. *Remote processing feature:* remote link to other computer centers within Bell Laboratories.

Coding Languages
PL/1, FORTRAN, Assembler, COBOL, SNOBOL, Internal Written Assembler.

Contemplated Equipment
IBM 370/158.

Services Available
Advice, programming, education and training, operators, software packages, documentation, preparation of data, systems analysis. Operate on a remote access, closed shop, block time and time-sharing basis.

Fields of Application
Scientific, statistical, systems analysis, operational research.

Training
Extensive internal educational programme - no formal recognition outside Bell Laboratories.

BOLT, BERANEK & NEWMAN, INC.
50 Moulton Street, Cambridge, Massachusetts 02138
Telephone: (617) 491-1850

Officers
Sam Labate, *President*
John Swets, *Senior Vice-President*

Computer Installation
PDP-10 (2)–operating system: TENEX; internal storage: 192K 36-bit words; magnetic tapes: 2 7-track; magnetic discs: 8 CD215; 1 line printer. *On-line satellite computers:* several PDP 11 units.
Many Honeywell H516 computers, special software for Arpa Network.

Coding Languages
Machine Language, BEN-LISP, ALGOL, FORTRAN, BLISS, BCPL, etc.

Contemplated Equipment
500K 36-bit words MOS memory, Data Products Line Printer, another PDP 10 processor.

Services Available
Advice, software packages, documentation, systems analysis. Operate on a time-sharing basis.

Fields of Application
Scientific, commercial, accounting, systems analysis, research.
Specialized areas: Speech recognition, network distributed operating systems.

BROWN ENGINEERING CO.*
300 Sparkman Drive, Huntsville, Alabama 35807
Telephone: (205) 532-1285

Officers
Dr. George Schussel, *Information Systems Division Manager*
Lee H. Cushman, *Computer Center Manager*

Computer Installation
IBM 360/50, IBM 360/30–operating system: OS 360; internal storage: 2,097,152 bits; magnetic tapes: 15 IBM; magnetic discs: 8 2311, 1 2314; 2 line printers. *Remote processing features:* capability for remote processing time sharing.

Coding Languages
FORTRAN, COBOL.

Services Available
Advice, operators, preparation of data, programming, software packages and systems analysis. Operate on a self-service, closed shop, open shop, remote access, block time and time-sharing basis.

Fields of Application
Scientific, statistical, commercial, production control, accounting, management, systems analysis, operational research, etc.
Specialized area: Information storage and retrieval.

COMPUTER COMMAND AND CONTROL COMPANY*
No. One University City, 4025 Chestnut Street, Philadelphia, Pennsylvania 19104
Telephone: (215) 387-1500

Also at:
Suite 1305, 1717 Pennsylvania Avenue N.W., Washington, D.C. 20006
Telephone: (202) 298-8300

Officers
Dr. Noah S. Prywes, *Chairman*
J. E. Gustaferro, *President*

Coding Languages
FORTRAN, COBOL, JOVIAL, ALGOL, PL/1.

Services Available
Consulting, programming, software packages, systems analysis.

Fields of Application
Research and development with information and control systems, educational.
Specialized areas: On-line systems, real time systems, naval command and control systems, personnel systems, chemical information systems, data management systems.

Training
Courses in mathematics for managers (40 hours lecture), design and analysis of statistical experiments (10 days), file structures for on-line systems (1 or 2 days).

CALSPAN CORPORATION
P.O. Box 235, Buffalo, New York 14221
Telephone: (716) 632-7500

Officers
R. S. Kelso, *President*
M. G. Spooner, *Senior Vice President*

Computer Installation
IBM 370/165–operating system: OS/MVT; internal storage: 2,048K bytes; magnetic tapes: 8 3420; magnetic discs: 8 3330; 3 line printers. *On-line satellite computers:* 2 Comcor CI5000 analog consoles.

Coding Languages
FORTRAN, COBOL, Assembler, F & H.

Contemplated Equipment
IBM 370/168; additional 3330 discs and tape drive units.

Services Available
Advice, programming, education and training, software packages, data preparation, systems analysis. Operate on an open shop basis.

Fields of Application
Scientific, statistical, commercial, accounting, management, systems analysis, operational research.
Specialized areas: Linear programming, investment analysis, payroll.

FELS RESEARCH INSTITUTE
800 Livermore Street, Yellow Springs, Ohio 45387
Telephone: (513) 767-7331

Officers
Dr. F. Falkner, *Director*
F. E. Lowe, *Chief, Computer Facility*

Computer Installation
IBM 360/44–operating system: PS 44; internal storage: 520K bits; magnetic tapes: 2 2401; magnetic discs: 2 2315; 1 line printer.
PDP-12/30–operating system: OS-8; internal storage: 128K bits; magnetic tapes: 2 Linctapes; magnetic discs: 2 DF32.

Coding Languages
FORTRAN, Assembler, BASIC, FOCAL.

Services Available
Advice, programming, systems analysis. Operate on an open shop and block time basis.

Fields of Application
Scientific, statistical.
Specialized area: Medical research.

FRANKEL ENGINEERING LABORATORIES INC.*
207 South Fifth Street, Reading, Pennsylvania 19603
Telephone: (215) 373-1858

Officers
Samuel R. Frankel, *President*
E. Thomas Sheetz, *Treasurer*

Computer Installation
CDC 160A.

Coding Language
FORTRAN.

Services Available
Computer time and programming time available to all.

Fields of Application
Engineering and scientific.
Specialized areas: Numerically controlled machine tools, steel industry, chemical industries.

GENERAL APPLIED SCIENCE LAB. INC.*
Merrick and Stewart Avenues, Westbury, New York 11590
Telephone: 333-6960

Officers
Dr. A. Ferri, *President of Company*
R. W. Byrne, *Vice-President of Research*
D. E. Magnus, *Head of Numerical Analysis and Programming Group*

Computer Installation
CDC 160A–1 line printer.

Coding Languages
FORTRAN, OSAS-A, SICOM.

Contemplated Equipment
High speed data link to IBM 7094 or IBM 360/67.

Services Available
Available to outside customers for scientific and data processing programming.

Fields of Application
Research and development.
Specialized areas: Analytical studies in aerodynamics and structures; digital programming and numerical analysis; experimental and analytical studies of scram jets.

ILLINOIS INSTITUTE OF TECHNOLOGY (IIT)*
IIT Research Institute
10 West 35th Street, Chicago, Illinois 60616
Telephone: (312) 225-9630

Officers
E. H. Schultz, *Executive Vice-President*
R. M. Janowiak, *Director, Computer Sciences Division*

Coding Languages
FORTRAN IV, PL/1, APL, ALGOL, COBOL.

Services Available
Computing services available to Institute research projects. Programming and analysis services are available on contract

Fields of Application
Physical sciences, life sciences, social sciences, management.

INTERUNIVERSITY COMMUNICATIONS COUNCIL, INC. – EDUCOM
P.O. Box 364, Rosedale Road, Princeton, New Jersey 08540
Telephone: (609) 921-7575

Officers
Dr. Henry Chauncy, *President*
H. Eugene Kessler, *Executive Director and Treasurer*
Dr. William Atchison, *Council Chairman*

Computer Installation
IBM 360/65–operating systems: OS/MVT, HASP; internal storage: 20 million bits; magnetic tapes: 23 2400 series; magnetic discs: 40 2314; 5 line printers. *Remote processing features:* 360/20 RJE, terminals.

Coding Languages
COBOL, PL/1, FORTRAN, BAL.

Contemplated Equipment
XDS Sigma 6.

Services Available
Advice, education and training, systems analysis, consultation on educational computing problems. Operate on a closed shop and time-sharing basis. Services available to institutions of higher education and other non-profit organizations.

Fields of Application
Education, computer networks.
Specialized area: Library automation.

Training
Seminar on Computer Management for college and university presidents and vice presidents; general working seminars on a National Science Computer Network.

LITTON INDUSTRIES*
Mellonic Systems Development Division
1001 West Maude Avenue, Sunnyvale, California 94086
Telephone: (408) 245-0795

Also at:
Mellonics Information Center, 6701 Varvel Avenue, Canoga Park, California 91303
Telephone: (213) 887-4372
55 Abrego Street, Monterey, California 93940
Telephone: (408) 373-0484
and at Munich, Federal Republic of Germany

Officers
C. E. Holmquist, *President*
A. R. Sult, *Vice-President (Sunnyvale)*
R. Neal, *Vice-President (Monterey)*

Computer Installation
Canoga Park
IBM 360/65—internal storage: 1,028K bytes.
IBM 360/65—internal storage: 768K bytes.
IBM 360/40—internal storage: 128K bytes.
IBM 360/20.
CDC 1700 (2).

Coding Languages
FORTRAN, COBOL, Assembler, PL/1, RPG, SORT, DL-1, IMS.

Services Available
All phases of computer-based systems design, implementation, management and services.

Fields of Application
Data processing services, management information services (Canoga Park); environmental sciences, operations analysis, behavioural sciences and military sciences compiler development (Monterey); real-time command/control systems and software, communications system engineering, space technology (Sunnyvale).

MASSACHUSETTS COMPUTER ASSOCIATES, INC.
Lakeside Office Park, Door 10, Wakefield, Massachusetts 01880
Telephone: (617) 245-9540

Officer
Stephen Warshall, *President*

Services Available
Advice, programming, software packages, systems analysis. Operate on a time-sharing basis.

Fields of Application
Scientific, commercial, systems analysis.
Specialized area: Linear programming.

MEASUREMENT RESEARCH CENTER*
321 East Market Street, Iowa City, Iowa 52240
Telephone: (319) 351-4300

Officers
Dr. Burdette Hanse, *Director*
Walter Goodrich, *Director, Systems and Computer Operations*

Computer Installation
IBM 360/50—operating system: DOS/MFT II; internal storage: 256K bits; magnetic tapes: 8 2401; magnetic discs: 5 2314; 1 line printer. *Remote processing features:* 2740 terminals, 2703 control unit.
IBM 360/30—operating system: DOS; internal storage: 64K bits; magnetic tapes: 6 2401; magnetic discs: 2 2311; 1 line printer.
IBM 360/30—operating system: TOS; internal storage: 16K bits; magnetic tapes: 4; 1 line printer.
IBM 360/25—operating system: TOS; internal storage: 16K bits; magnetic tapes: 4 2401; 1 line printer.
HEWLETT PACKARD 2116B—operating system: TOS; internal storage: 8K bits; magnetic tapes: 2; 1 line printer. *Remote processing features:* remote TP batch entry.
CDC 160—internal storage: 4K bits; magnetic tapes: 6 shared; 1 line printer.

Coding Languages
Autocoder, COBOL, Assembler, PL1, FORTRAN, BASIC, RPG.

Services Available
Consultation, programming, education and training, operators, software packages, documentation, preparation of data, systems analysis. Operate on a remote access and closed shop basis. Available to educational systems, publishers and general research and service bureau work; priority to academic needs.

Fields of Application
General.
Specialized area: Statistical analysis.

NATIONAL INFORMATION RESEARCH INSTITUTE*
P.O. Box 3358, Santa Monica, California 90403
Telephone: (213) 653-1992

Also at:
8444 Wilshire Blvd., 7th Floor, Beverly Hills, California 90211

Officer
Dr. E. J. Schubert, *President*

Computer Installation
BULL GENERAL ELECTRIC GE 265—internal storage: 18·5 million bits; magnetic tapes: 4; magnetic discs: 1; 1 line printer.

Coding Languages
BASIC, FORTRAN.

Contemplated Equipment
IC 7000.

Services Available
Programming, education and training, software packages, systems analysis. Operate on a remote access, time sharing basis. Available only to members.

Field of Application
Performance analysis.

Training
Short courses in business data processing, data organization, comparative evaluation of EDP.

PETTY GEOPHYSICAL ENGINEERING
P.O. Drawer 2061, San Antonio, Texas 78206
Telephone: (512) 226-5131

Officers
W. H. Mayne, *Vice-President Technical Services*
L. T. Nicol, *Vice-President Data Processing*
H. J. Jones, *Marketing Manager*

Computer Installation
CDC 3200 (2)–operating system: MSOS; internal storage: 786,432 bits each; magnetic tapes: 8 607, 1 627, 2 604; magnetic discs: 3 854; 2 line printers.

Coding Languages
FORTRAN, COMPASS.

Services Available
Advice, operators. Operate on a closed shop basis.

Field of Application
Scientific.
Specialized area: Seismic data processing.

RAND CORPORATION
1700 Main Street, Santa Monica, California 90406
Telephone: (213) 393-0411

Officers
D. B. Rice, *President*
R. M. Fredrickson, *Director, Rand Computation Center*

Computer Installation
IBM 360/65–operating system: OS; internal storage: 800 million bits; magnetic tapes: 8 2401/6; magnetic discs: 20 2314; 2 line printers. *On-line satellite computer:* IBM 1800. *Remote processing features:* Memorex Controler.
PDP-6–operating system: JOSS; internal storage: 576K bits; magnetic tapes: 2 7-track; magnetic discs: 1.

Coding Languages
FORTRAN, COBOL, BAL, CPS, JOSS, SIMSCRIPT, MARK IV, ECSS.

Contemplated Equipment
General configuration changes, 8 more discs spindles, printer – smaller but faster core, channel changes, remote batch station; PDP-6 to be replaced by IBM 360/40 (tentative).

Services Available
Advice, programming, education and training, operators, software packages, documentation, preparation of data, systems analysis. Operate on a self-service, remote access, block time and open shop basis. Services made available to outside users are limited in aggregate.

Fields of Application
Scientific, statistical, commercial, accounting, systems analysis.
Specialized area: Simulation.

Training
User language and "how to do it" courses covering services offered by the center.

RESEARCH TRIANGLE INSTITUTE
P.O. Box 12194, Research Triangle Park, North Carolina 27709
Telephone: (919) 549-8311

Officers
George R. Herbert, *President*
S. C. Ashton, *Corporate Vice-President*

Computer Installation
IBM 370/165–operating system: OS-MVT-HASP; internal storage: 2 million 36-bit words; magnetic tapes: 4 9-track; 1 7-track; magnetic discs: 16 2314, 8 3330; 1 line printer. *On-line satellite computers:* 1 360/75, 2 360/50. *Remote processing features:* Support high, medium, and low speed terminals.

Coding Languages
FORTRAN, COBOL, PL/1, ALGOL, Assembler.

Services Available
Advice, programming, software packages, documentation, systems analysis. Operate on a remote access and time-sharing basis.

Fields of Application
Scientific, statistical, systems analysis, operational research.
Specialized areas: Linear programming, analysis, population projection, simulation models.

SCIENTIFIC CALCULATIONS INC.
110 Allen's Creek Road, Rochester, New York 14618
Telephone: (716) 442-7660

Officers
Dr. Gordon Spencer, *President*
Herbert D. Weimer, *Vice-President*
Joseph J. Cameron, *Vice-President, Marketing*

Coding Languages
FORTRAN, COBOL.

Contemplated Equipment
Mini computer.

Services Available
Advice, programming, software packages. Operate on a remote access and time-sharing basis.

Fields of Application
Scientific, statistical, commercial, production control, accounting, management, systems analysis, operational research.
Specialized areas: Sales analysis, linear programming, investment, analysis, structural engineering, optics lens design, printed circuit layout.

SERENDIPITY INC.*
15433 Ventura Boulevard, Sherman Oaks, California 91401
Telephone: (213) 981-8330

Officers
S. E. Medall, *President*
D. R. Einhorn, *Vice-President (Sales)*

Coding Languages
FORTRAN, BAL, COBOL, ALGOL, MAP, FAP.

Contemplated Equipment
Remote job entry and/or time-sharing terminals.

Services Available
Consultation, preparation of data, programming, software packages, systems analysis. Operate on a self-service basis.

Fields of Application
Engineering services for earth sciences (soil engineering, engineering geology, etc.), environmental sciences, systems analysis.

SMITHSONIAN ASTROPHYSICAL OBSERVATORY
60 Garden Street, Cambridge, Massachusetts 02138
Telephone: (617) 864-7910

Officer
Robert W. Martin, *Manager, Data Processing*

Computer Installation
CDC 6400—operating system: SCOPE; internal storage: 3,981,312 bits; magnetic tapes: 6 607, 1 609; magnetic discs: 1 6603, 1 6638, 3 853; 2 line printers. *On-line satellite computers:* 1 Honeywell H200, 1 Honeywell H1250. *Remote processing features:* Data General Nova 1220 interface for time-sharing.

Coding Languages
FORTRAN, COBOL, COMPASS.

Services Available
Programming, preparation of data.

Field of Application
Scientific.
Specialized areas: Astrophysics, geophysics.

STANFORD RESEARCH INSTITUTE*
333 Ravenswood Avenue, Menlo Park, California 94025
Telephone: (415) 326-6200

Officer
D. B. Parker, *Director of Computer Planning and Operations*

Services Available
Consultation, programming, education and training, operators, software packages, documentation, preparation of data, systems analysis.

Fields of Application
General.
Specialized area: Research.

Training
Basic orientation seminars, non-scheduled programming training.

SYSTEMS, SCIENCE AND SOFTWARE
P.O. Box 1620, La Jolla, California 92037
Telephone: (714) 453-0060

Officers
Robert A. Kruger, *President*
Kedar D. Pyatt, *Vice-President*
Robert C. Boe, *Director of Marketing*

Computer Installation
UNIVAC 1108—operating system: EXEC 8; internal storage: 132K words; magnetic tapes: 7; magnetic discs: Fastran; 4 line printers. *Remote processing features:* graphics, 1004.
DATA GENERAL Nova 800—operating system: SSS; internal storage: 56K 16-bit words; magnetic tapes: 2; magnetic discs: 2; 1 line printer. *Remote processing features:* interactive graphics.

Services Available
Programming, software packages. Operate on a self-service, remote access, block time, and time-sharing basis.

Field of Application
Scientific.
Specialized areas: Analysis, physics, mechanics.

TELEDYNE EXPLORATION*
P.O. Box 36269, 5825 Chimney Rock Road, Houston, Texas 77036
Telephone: (713) 666-2561

Also at:
Calgary (Canada)

Officers
J. H. Frasher, *General Manager*
K. Barry, *Manager, Data Processing Division*
P. Savage, *Regional Manager, Data Processing (Canada)*

Computer Installation
Houston and Calgary:
IBM 360/44—internal storage: 131K bytes; magnetic tapes: 4 2401; magnetic discs: 2 2311; 1 line printer.
Houston only:
IBM 1800—operating system: TSX; internal storage: 8K bytes; magnetic tapes: 1401.

Coding Languages
FORTRAN, Assembly, COBOL.

Services Available
Advice, preparation of data, programming, software packages, systems analysis. Operate on a self-service basis.

Fields of Application
Scientific, accounting.
Specialized areas: Seismic data processing, medical research.

WOLF RESEARCH AND DEVELOPMENT CORPORATION*
6801 Kenilworth Avenue, Riverdale, Maryland 20840
Telephone: (301) 779-2800

Officers
John A. Dudley, *President and General Manager*
W. T. Wells, *Vice-President*

Services Available
Consultation, preparation of data, programming, software packages, systems analysis.

Fields of Application
Information systems, management systems, mathematical-statistical analysis.
Specialized areas: Space sciences, planetary physics.

WYLE LABORATORIES*
7800 Governors Drive West, Huntsville, Alabama 35800
Telephone: (205) 837-4411

Officers
D. Bozich
A. Jolly

Computer Installation
CDC 3300—operating system: SCOPE; internal storage: 65,536 24-bit words; magnetic tapes: 6 607; magnetic discs: 2 854; 1 line printer.

Coding Languages
FORTRAN, COMPASS.

Services Available
Preparation of data, programming, software packages, systems analysis. Operate on an open shop and block time basis. Not available for purely business or accounting work.

Fields of Application
Scientific and statistical mainly.
Specialized areas: Analog-to-digital on-line data acquisition, analysis of special time history data, R and D of tape recorded analog data for time varying phenomena.

Training
On special demand, systems or complex data analysis problems are treated as "short courses".

Fields of Application
Complex operating system research and development, compilers and assemblers, systems analysis.
Specialized areas: Time-sharing, remote graphic displays, simulation, computer graphics, communications, computer security.

Training
One - three week course in computer security.

CONSULTANTS

(In alphabetical order by State)

ARIZONA

NEIL F. BLAIR AND ASSOCIATES, INTERNATIONAL*
P.O. Box 747, Prescott, 86301
Telephone: (602) 778-0386

Officer
Neil F. Blair, *Principal Consultant and President*

Coding Languages
RPG, COBOL, NEAT 3.

Services Available
Consultation, programming.

Fields of Application
Accounting, management, systems analysis.
Specialized areas: Accounting systems for Universities and businesses.

Training
On-the-job training of personnel in systems installed by the group.

GRAPHTEK CORPORATION*
700 West Campbell Avenue, Phoenix, 85013
Telephone: (602) 277-7434

Also at:
2133 W. Chapman Avenue, Orange, California
Telephone: 633-8240
and at: Los Angeles, California

Officer
Walter F. Cook, *Vice-President*

Coding Languages
All high-level languages and machine languages for most systems.

Services Available
Consultation, programming, education and training, software packages, documentation, systems analysis.

CALIFORNIA

BASIC COMPUTING ARTS INC.*
2680 E. Bayshore Frontage Road, Mountain View, 94040
Telephone: (415) 964-3138

Officer
Michael P. Burwen, *President*

Coding Language
FORTRAN IV.

Services Available
Consultation, programming, software packages, systems analysis.

COMPUTER COMMUNICATIONS INC.*
701 West Manchester Boulevard, Inglewood, 90301
Telephone: (213) 674-5300

Officers
Dominick Nigro, *Vice-President, Marketing*
Papken Sassouni, *Vice-President, Programming Sciences*

Computer Installation
IBM 360/40–operating systems: OS, DOS; internal storage: 131K bytes; magnetic tapes: 4 2401; magnetic discs: 4 2361; 1 line printer. *On-line satellite computers:* CC-701. *Remote processing features:* CC-30 stations.
IBM 1130 (3)–operating system: DMS/V2; internal storage: 8K x 16 bits (2) and 16K x 16 bits; magnetic discs: 1 1316; 1 line printer. *On-line satellite computers:* CC-701. *Remote processing features:* CC-30 communications stations.

Coding Languages
Assembly, FORTRAN, COBOL, CAP/1130, CAP/360.

Services Available
Consultation, programming, software packages, systems analysis, hardware systems, computer communications equipment. Operate on a self-service, remote access and time-sharing basis.

Fields of Application
Scientific, commercial, systems analysis, integrated systems.
Specialized areas: Computer communications equipment and systems, real time programming, compilers, processors, interpreters, assemblers.

Training
Special short courses to CCI customers.

United States of America – Consultants

COMPUTER FINANCIAL INC.*
1111 Wilshire Boulevard, Los Angeles, 90017
Telephone: (213) 481-2287

Officers
William R. Lennartz, *President*
Robert M. Miller, *Vice-President*

Contemplated Equipment
IBM 360/40.

Services Available
Software packages, computer leasings and brokerage consulting.

COMPUTER MICRO-IMAGE SYSTEMS INC.*
9600 DeSoto Avenue, Chatsworth, 91311
Telephone: (213) 882-8900

Services Available
Consultation, education and training, systems analysis. Available only to computer output microfilm users.

COMPUTER PROCESSES INC.*
Kirkeby Center, Suite 500, 10889 Wilshire Boulevard, Los Angeles, 90024

Officer
Jesse H. Katz, *President*

Coding Languages
COBOL, PL/1, RPG, FORTRAN, JOVIAL, GPSS, SIMSCRIPT, Assembly.

Services Available
Consultation, programming, education and training, software packages, documentation, preparation of data.

Fields of Application
Commercial, management, military, operational research etc.

Training
Short courses in simulation applications (3 days), Simscript modelling and programming (3 days) and PL/1 programming (3 days).

DANIEL, MANN, JOHNSON AND MENDENHALL*
3325 Wilshire Boulevard, Los Angeles, 90005
Telephone: DU1-3663

Officers
S. Moe, *General Manager*
V. Khachooni, *Manager of Computer Services*

Computer Installation
UNIVAC 9300—internal storage: 32K bits; magnetic tapes: 6; 1 line printer.

Coding Languages
RPG, Assembly, FORTRAN, COBOL.

Services Available
Consultation, systems analysis. Operate on an open shop basis.

Fields of Application
Scientific, engineering, statistical.

DARZINS MATHEMATICAL AND ECONOMETRIC CONSULTANTS*
1911 46th Avenue, San Francisco, 94116
Telephone: (415) 661-6265

Officer
Dr. A. Luis Darzins, *Director*

Services Available
Consultation, systems analysis. Operate on an open shop basis.

Fields of Application
Scientific, statistical, management, operational research.
Specialized areas: Scientific methodology studies and applications— "the polylectic method".

EDUCATION AND TRAINING CONSULTANTS CO.
Box 49899, Los Angeles, 90049
Telephone: (213) 472-2444

Officer
Dr. Leonard C. Silvern, *President*

Coding Languages
FORTRAN, LYRIC, Coursewriter II & III.

Services Available
Consultation, programming, education and training, software packages, systems modelling and simulation. Operate on a remote access basis and time-sharing basis.

Fields of Application
Education, management.

Training
Brochure of courses available.

GEORGE GLASER
225 Warren Road, San Mateo, 94402
Telephone: (415) 343-6746

Service Available
Advice.

Fields of Application
Commercial, organization and management in Data Processing Industry.

INFO CONSULTING COMPANY*
429 South Western Avenue, Los Angeles, 90005

Officer
Lawrence M. Gentry, *Owner*

Fields of Application
Financial and manufacturing systems.

INFORMATION CONSULTANTS, INC.
3740 South Grand Avenue, Los Angeles, 90007
Telephone: (213) 747-0536

Officer
Arthur R. Dansby, *President*

Computer Installation
IBM 360/30—operating system: DOS or OS; internal storage: 524,288 bits; magnetic tapes: 4 2400; magnetic discs: 4 2314; 1 line printer.

Coding Languages
COBOL, FORTRAN, PL/1.

Services Available
Advice, programming, education and training, operators, software packages, documentation, preparation of data, systems analysis. Operate on a self-service, block time and open shop basis.

Fields of Application
Statistical, commercial, accounting, management, systems analysis.
Specialized areas: Sales analysis, payroll.

INFOSCI INC.
Box 464, Menlo Park, 94025
Telephone: (415) 365-5811

Officer
Dr. Ned Chapin, *Consultant in Charge*

Services Available
Consultation, education and training, documentation, systems analysis. Operate on a closed shop basis.

Fields of Application
Statistical, commercial, production control, accounting, management, systems analysis, operational research.
Specialized areas: File organization, data structures, data management, structured programming.

Training
Courses designed to suit client's requirements.

WILBUR C. MYERS AND COMPANY
27620 Eastvale Road, Rolling Hills, 90274
Telephone: (213) 377-7941, 377-2551

Officer
Wilbur C. Myers, *President*

Services Available
Advice, education and training, systems analysis, micrographics systems, information retrieval.

Fields of Application
Commercial, management, systems analysis, new product analysis.
Specialized areas: High-reduction micrographics, laser-based systems.

Training
Lectures and seminars are offered to customers on basic micrographics systems, computer output microfilm (COM) systems, laser recording and information handling systems and advanced business management principles and practices.

PROFIMATICS INC.
6355 Topanga Canyon Boulevard, Woodland Hills, 91364
Telephone: (213) 883-6530

Officers
Dr. T. M. Stout, *President*
R. P. Cline, *Vice-President*

Services Available
Consultation, programming, systems analysis.

Fields of Application
Industrial process control – all tasks involved in planning, design, installation, and evaluation of advanced control systems, including process control. Computer applications: Feasibility studies, simulation, system design, instrument engineering, specifications, bid evaluations, project management, programming, installation, project appraisal, recruiting.
Specialized areas: Petroleum refining, petrochemicals production, chemicals, cement, pulp and paper, iron and steel.

Training
Theory and practice of modern process control. Courses are usually arranged upon request and designed to meet the specific requirements of the client and the education and experience levels of the students.

PROGRAMMING SERVICES INC.*
6355 Topanga Canyon Boulevard, Suite 231, Woodland Hills, 91364
Telephone: (213) 884-9480

Officers
Donald F. Ford, *President*
Wayne M. Aamoth, *Vice-President*
Charles P. Bourne, *Vice-President*

Coding Languages
FORTRAN, COBOL, ALGOL, PL/1, JOVIAL, APT, CS-1, NELIAC, Assembler.

Services Available
Consultation, programming, software packages, systems analysis.

Fields of Application
Scientific, production control, information storage and retrieval, library sciences, management information systems, systems analysis, system sciences.
Specialized areas: Process control, information storage and retrieval.

Training
Four-day course in process control.

SYSTEMS AND COMPUTER INFORMATION INC.*
1621 Centinelo Avenue, Inglewood, 90302
Telephone: (213) 641-3380

Officer
Martin A. Rubin, *President*

Computer Installation
UNIVAC 1004/1108–operating system: EXEC 8; internal storage: 130K bits; magnetic tapes: 12; magnetic discs: 4; 1 line printer. *On-line satellite computer*: 1004.

Coding Languages
COBOL, FORTRAN, Assembly.

Services Available
Advice, programming, software packages, systems analysi turnkey hardware/software systems. Operate on a self-service, remote access, block time and time-sharing basis.

Fields of Application
All scientific and commercial fields.
Specialized areas: Oceanology, military data systems.

United States of America – Consultants

UNITED COMPUTING CORPORATION
22500 S. Avalon Blvd., Carson, 90745
Telephone: (213) 830-7720

Officers
J. H. Wright, *President*
M. L. Simon, *Director of Marketing*

Computer Installation
PDP-8–operating system: OS-8; internal storage: 192K bits; magnetic discs: 1 RK8; 1 line printer.
GENERAL AUTOMATION SPC 16–operating system: RTOS; internal storage: 420,864 bits; magnetic discs: 1 3347; 1 line printer.

Coding Languages
FORTRAN, BASIC, UPL, Assembly, APT, UNIAPT.

Services Available
Advice, programming, education and training, software packages, systems analysis. Operate on a self-service basis.

Fields of Application
Scientific, production control, accounting, systems analysis.
Specialized area: Numerical control.

COLORADO

AUTO-TRONIX UNIVERSAL CORPORATION*
444 Sherman Street, Denver, 80203
Telephone: (303) 744-3381

Officer
R. L. Subry, *President*

Services Available
Consultation, programming, operators, software packages, documentation, preparation of data, systems analysis. Operate on a closed shop basis.

Fields of Application
Statistical, commercial, accounting, management, systems analysis, operational research, engineering, education.
Specialized areas: Highways, public works, education.

CONNECTICUT

COMPUTER ASSISTANCE INC.*
298 Park Road, West Hartford, 06119

Also at:
New York City, Springfield, Massachusetts, and Boston, Massachusetts.

Officer
Thomas P. McDonagh, Jr., *President*

Services Available
Consultation, programming, education and training, software packages, documentation, systems analysis.

Fields of Application
Wide range of applications with emphasis on commercial.
Specialized areas: Insurance data processing, manufacturing applications, OEM software.

Training
Project management seminar (3 days), intermediate and advanced programming courses.

TURNKEY SYSTEMS, INC.
111 East Avenue, Norwalk, 06851
Telephone: 838-4581

Officers
Howard G. Pontius, *President*
Ernest E. Keet, *Vice-President*

Services Available
Consultation, programming, education and training, software packages, documentation, systems analysis.

Fields of Application
Manufacturing, distribution, scientific, software packages for control of on-line display terminals and for manufacturing planning.
Specialized areas: Design and implementation of manufacturing and distribution information systems, and on-line terminal data entry and inquiry systems.

DELAWARE

INTERNATIONAL TELECONTROL CORPORATION
Suite 86, 1601 Concord Pike, Independence Mall, Wilmington, 19803
Telephone: (302) 655-7285

Officers
William T. Fary, *President*
Warner J. Sharkey, *Vice-President*
Richard Worth, *Treasurer*

Coding Languages
Assembler, COBOL, FORTRAN, BASIC, APL, GPSS, SIMSCRIPT.

Services Available
Advice, programming, education and training, software packages.

Fields of Application
Scientific, commercial, systems analysis, operational research, data communications.
Specialized areas: Medical research, teleprocessing.

Training
Courses in the Fundamentals of Data Communications, Advanced Data Communications, Analysis and Design of Teleprocessing Systems, Data Communications Engineering, Systems Simulation.

DISTRICT OF COLUMBIA

COMARECS INC.*
1701 Pennsylvania Avenue, N.W., Washington 20006
Telephone: (202) 298-6255

Officers
H. C. Leipold, *President*
J. S. McFarland, *Systems Analyst*

Services Available
Consultation, software packages.

United States of America – Consultants

Field of Application
Banking.

EDP TECHNOLOGY INC.*
2600 Virginia Avenue, N.W., Suite 707, Washington, 20037
Telephone: (202) 965-0090

Also at:
7115 Leesburg Pike, Falls Church, Virginia 22043
363 S. Taaffe Avenue, Sunnyvale, California 94086

Services Available
Consultation, programming, software packages, systems analysis.

Fields of Application
Scientific, commercial, accounting, management, operational, research.

EDUCATIONAL INFORMATION SERVICES, INC.
Air Rights Building, Suite 520E, Washington, 20014
Telephone: (301) 770-6440

Officer
James J. Prevel, *President*

Services Available
Advice, education and training, systems analysis.

Fields of Application
Systems analysis, educational.

PHILIP C. PIPHER ASSOCIATES INC.*
1000 16th Street, N.W., Washington, 20036
Telephone: 659-2055

Officers
Philip C. Pipher, *President*
Gary G. Van Winkle, *Vice-President for Administration*
Donald P. Kahn, *Vice-President for Finance*
Ronald S. Ontko, *Secretary*

Computer Installation
HONEYWELL H200–internal storage: 20K bits; magnetic tapes: 5; 1 line printer.

Coding Languages
All major coding languages.

Services Available
Consultation, operators, preparation of data, programming, software packages, systems analysis. Operate on a self-service, closed shop and block time basis.

Fields of Application
Real time, scientific, statistical, communication industry processing, systems analysis.
Specialized areas: Telephone toll billing, rating and interlining, telephone local service billing–complete, telephone separations studies, medicare programme, railroad freight car accounting.

KURT SALMON ASSOCIATES*
4301 Connecticut Avenue, N.W., Washington, 20008
Telephone: (202) EM3-1281

Also at:
350 Fifth Avenue, Suite 1800, New York, New York 10001
Telephone: (212) CH4-6244

and at: London, U.K., Paris, France, Darmstadt, Federal Republic of Germany.

Officer
S. A. Kry, *Vice-President, Systems Division*

Services Available
Consultation, programming, software packages, systems analysis.

Fields of Application
Management information systems, production control and planning, overall systems analysis, incentives and payroll, forecasting, industrial engineering, advanced analytical methods training, quality control, material utilization, marketing, etc.
Specialized areas: Clothing and textiles industries exclusively.

FLORIDA

EASTERN AIR LINES INC.
Miami International Airport, Miami, 33148
Telephone: (305) 873-3123

Officers
Floyd Hall, *Chairman of the Board*
Samuel Higgenbottom, *President and Chief Operating Officer*
C. J. Simons, *Executive Vice-President for Finance and Administration*
F. M. Heinzmann, *Vice-President for Computer Sciences*

Computer Installation
IBM 360/65–operating system: OS/7074 Emulator; internal storage: 256K bytes; magnetic tapes: 10 2401-6, 1 2401-4; magnetic discs: 2 2314.
IBM 360/65–operating system: OS/7074; internal storage: 768K plus 2,000K bytes; magnetic tapes: 13 2401-6, 2 2401-4; magnetic discs: 5 2314; 2 line printers. *On-line satellite computer*: 1 4-Phase.
IBM 360/65–operating system: OS/ASP; internal storage: 768K plus 1,000K bytes; magnetic tapes: 7 2401-6, 3 2401-4; magnetic discs: 6 2314; 2 line printers. *On-line satellite computers*: 3 4-Phase. *Remote processing features*: TSO.
IBM 360/65–operating system: OS; internal storage: 768K bytes; magnetic tapes: 13 2401-6, 3 2401-4; magnetic discs: 5 2314; 3 line printers.
IBM 360/195–operating system: ACP; internal storage: 1 million bytes; magnetic tapes: 12; magnetic discs: 8 IBM 3330; 3 line printers.
IBM 360/195–operating system: OS; internal storage: 1 million bytes; magnetic tapes: 4; magnetic discs: 2 2314; 2 line printers.
IBM 360/65–operating system: ACP; internal storage: 256K bytes; magnetic tapes: 6; magnetic discs: 4 23.
IBM 360/165–operating system: OS; internal storage: 512K bytes; magnetic tapes: 4; magnetic discs: 1 2314; 1 line printer.

Coding Languages
Assembler, COBOL, SABRETALK, FORTRAN.

Contemplated Equipment
DVA-168's MP.

Services Available
Advice, programming, education and training, software packages. Operate on a self-service, remote access, block time and time-sharing basis.

United States of America – Consultants

Fields of Application
Commercial, accounting.

Training
Courses in communications system design and analysis, programming, concepts and facilities.

ELECTRONIC DATA PREPARATION CORPORATION
1390 Main Street, Sarasota, 33577
Telephone: (813) 366-2600

Also at:
Indianapolis, Indiana

Officers
David A. Jones, *Chairman of the Board*
James O. Mathis, *President*

Computer Installation
NCR Century 300–operating system: B-4; internal storage: 256K bytes; magnetic tapes: 4 240KB 633-311; magnetic discs: 10 NCR 657; 1 line printer. *On-line satellite computer*: NCR 720. *Remote processing features*: CRT-printers.
NCR Century 200 (3)–operating system: B-3; internal storage: 128K bytes each; magnetic tapes: 4 each; magnetic discs: 4 655-102 each; 1 line printer each. *Remote processing features*: CRAM (5) 653-101.

Coding Languages
COBOL, FORTRAN, NEAT 3.

Services Available
Programming, software packages, documentation, preparation of data, systems analysis. Operate on a closed shop basis. On-line services limited primarily to financial institutions.

Fields of Application
Commercial, accounting, systems analysis, facility management.
Specialized areas: Payroll, financial institutions.

NUS CORPORATION
Southern Nuclear Department
P.O. Box 10, Dunedin, 33528
Telephone: (813) 733-3138

Officer
N. B. McLeod, *President*

Computer Installation
CDC 6600 (2) and IBM 360/1130 with extensive capacity and ancillary hardware, including plotters, printers and memories.

Coding Languages
COBOL, FORTRAN IV.

Services Available
Advice, programming, software packages, documentation, preparation of data. Operate on a closed shop, block time and time-sharing basis.

Fields of Application
Scientific, statistical, systems analysis, operational research.
Specialized areas: Nuclear engineering, heat transfer, fluid flow physics.

SCHULTZ INSTRUMENTS, INC.*
P.O. Box 13385, Gainesville, 32601
Telephone: (904) 378-1750

Officers
Charles Schultz, Jr., *President and Computer Center Director*
David Lee Johnson, *Secretary-Treasurer*
Karl Skadowski, *Director of Marketing*

Computer Installation
PDP-12–internal storage: 4K bits; magnetic tapes: 2 LINC tapes.

Coding Languages
FOCAL, DIAL, PAL 111, FORTRAN.

Services Available
Consultation, programming, software packages, documentation, systems analysis. Operate on a closed shop basis.

Fields of Application
Scientific, management, systems analysis, computer aid design and manufacturing.
Specialized area: Computer interfacing.

GEORGIA

TILLINGHAST & CO., INC.
3400 Peachtree Road, N.E., Atlanta, 30326
Telephone: (404) 261-5420

Officers
Vic Reinhold, *Manager*
Rolph Masecar, *Senior Officer*

Computer Installation
HONEYWELL H115–internal storage: 196,608 bits; magnetic tapes: 5; magnetic discs: 1 172; 1 line printer.

Coding Languages
COBOL, FORTRAN IV, Easycoder.

Services Available
Advice, programming, systems analysis. Operate on a self-service basis. Available only to insurance and actuarial companies.

Fields of Application
All actuarial calculations and related data processing.

ILLINOIS

ESPO DATA CONSULTANTS INC.*
5334 West 65th Street, Chicago, 60638
Telephone: 581-0123

Also at:
Covina, California; Addison, Illinois; Boston, Massachusetts.

Officers
Donald J. Esposito, *President*
Eugene G. Esposito, *Vice-President*

Computer Installation
IBM 360/Special – 1 line printer.

Services Available
Consultation, programming, education and training, operators, software packages, documentation, preparation of data, systems analysis. Operate on a remote access and block time basis.

Fields of Application
Scientific, commercial, production control, accounting, systems analysis.
Specialized areas: Packaging systems, audio-visual EDP systems.

DANIEL D. HOWARD ASSOCIATES INC.*
307 N.Michigan, Chicago, 60601

Officer
Daniel D. Howard, *President*

Services Available
Consultation, education and training, systems analysis. Time-sharing terminals on the premises.

Fields of Application
Systems analysis and design, organizational studies, data processing audits.
Specialized areas: Local and state governments.

Training
Two-week course in systems and methods.

INDECON INC.*
30 N. LaSalle Street, Chicago, 60602
Telephone: (312) 641-6397

Also at:
Indianapolis, San Francisco

Officer
Phillip G. Iversen, *Vice-President*

Computer Installation
HONEYWELL H1250—operating system: MOD I; internal storage: 256K bits; magnetic tapes: 4; magnetic discs: 1; 1 line printer. *Remote processing features*: teletype communications, CRT communications.

Services Available
Consultation, programming, software packages, systems analysis.

Fields of Application
Manufacturing, health services, insurance, banking.

JACOBS COMPANY INC.
1100 Jorie Boulevard, Oak Brook, 60521
Telephone: (312) 887-9450

Officers
Martin D. Miller, *President*
Alf Moody, *Vice-President, Operations*
Paul E. Smith, *Vice-President, Marketing and Research*
Earl W. Holtz, *Secretary and Treasurer*

Services Available
Advice, education and training, software packages, preparation of data, systems analysis.

Fields of Application
Statistical, production control, management, systems analysis.
Specialized areas: Sales analysis, linear programming, analysis.

LESTER B. KNIGHT AND ASSOCIATES INC.*
549 W. Randolph Street, Chicago, 60606
Telephone: (312) 346-2100

Also at:
666 5th Avenue, New York, New York 10019
Telephone: (212) 581-1221
560 Mission Street, San Francisco, California 94105
Telephone: (415) 397-2385

and at: Vienna, Austria, Frankfurt/Main and Düsseldorf, Federal Republic of Germany, Florence, Italy, Karlstad, Stockholm, Goteborg, Malmo, Karlshan, Vasteras and Ludvika, Sweden, Zug and Zurich, Switzerland, London and Leeds, United Kingdom.

Officers
L. B. Knight, *Chairman*
C. F. Knight, *President*
C. E. Fausel, *Executive Vice-President*
C. G. Rummel, *Executive Vice-President*
A. E. Suter, *Executive Vice-President*

Computer Installation
IBM 1130—internal storage: 128K bits; magnetic disc: 2315; 1 line printer. *Remote processing features*: Teleprocessing.
IBM 360/30—operating systems: DOS, TOS; internal storage: 500K bits; magnetic tapes: 4 2415; magnetic discs: 4 2311; 1 line printer.

Coding Languages
COBOL, FORTRAN.

Services Available
Consultation, operators, preparation of data, programming, systems analysis. Operate on a self-service, closed shop, open shop and block time basis.

Fields of Application
Scientific, commercial, production control, accounting, management information systems, operational research, linear programming, CPM.
Specialized areas: CPM, STRESS, COGO, production control, M.I.S.

Training
Short courses in computer concepts (1½ day), COGO, STRESS (1 day each) and FORTRAN (3 days).

PANSOPHIC SYSTEMS, INC.
1211 West 22nd Street, Suite 720, Oak Brook, 60521
Telephone: (312) 325-9600

Officers
J. A. Piscopo, *President*
W. W. Luke, *Vice-President and Director of Marketing*
D. R. Landgraf, *Vice-President and Director of Technical Services*

Contemplated Equipment
IBM 370/135.

Services Available
Software packages, consultation.

Fields of Application
Commercial, production control, accounting, management

Training
Training provided with software packages (half-day to 2-day courses).

United States of America – Consultants

PUBLIC ADMINISTRATION SERVICE*
1313 East 60th Street, Chicago, 60637
Telephone: (312) 324-3400

Also at:
1619 Massachusetts Avenue, N.W., Washington, D.C. 20036
Telephone: (202) 265-5355

Services Available
Consultation, systems analysis.

Fields of Application
Provide consulting services in the areas of systems analysis and design, computer feasibility surveys, development and installation of information systems and related consulting services.

Training
Courses in the field of governmental data processing, use of modern techniques, etc., for all levels of management.

MARYLAND

COMPUTER CAREERS INCORPORATED*
4720 Montgomery Lane, Suite 503, Bethesda, 20014
Telephone: (301) 654-9225

Officer
Edward W. MacLaren, Jr., *President*

Contemplated Equipment
Terminal equipment on a time-sharing basis.

Services Available
Consultation.

Fields of Application
Management, industrial, engineering, commercial, institutional.

COMRESS, INC.
Two Research Court, Rockville, 20850
Telephone: (301) 948-8000

Officers
F. C. Ihrer, *President*
E. J. Clark, *Vice-President, American Operations*
P. T. Clisura, *Vice-President, Overseas Operations*

Computer Installation
IBM 360/50–operating system: OS/HASP; internal storage: 512K bytes; magnetic tapes: 6; magnetic discs: 8 2314; 2 line printers.

Coding Languages
All.

Service Available
Software packages. Operate on a closed shop basis.

Field of Application
Management.
Specialized areas: Simulation, performance monitoring, systems software.

Training
Complete training available for all software and hardware products.

MARVIN M. WOFSEY
2407 Eccleston Street, Silver Spring, 20902
Telephone: (301) 681-6427

Officer
Marvin M. Wofsey, *President*

Services Available
Education and training, management of data processing consultants. Operate on a self-service basis.

Fields of Application
Commercial, management, systems analysis, government.

Training
Training in computer management, computer selection and acquisition and systems analysis and design.

MASSACHUSETTS

AGRIPPA-ORD CORPORATION*
Monument Square, Carlisle, 01743
Telephone: (617) 369-2912

Officer
N. David Culven, *President*

Coding Languages
Wide variety of languages.

Services Available
Consultation, programming, software packages, systems analysis.

Fields of Application
Scientific, statistical, systems analysis, real time, time-sharing.
Specialized areas: Operating systems, scientific, process control, assemblers, compilers.

AMERICAN USED COMPUTER CORPORATION
712 Beacon Street, Boston, 02215
Telephone: (617) 261-1100

Officers
Adolf F. Monosson, *President*
William S. Grinker, *Executive Vice-President*

Service Available
Advice.

Field of Application
Specialized area: Buying and selling used computer equipment.

APPLIED GEODATA SYSTEMS INC.*
675 Massachusetts Avenue, Cambridge, 02139
Telephone: (617) 868-8168

Officers
Donald Cox, *President*
Laurence N. Beckreck, *Vice-President, Software Systems*

Coding Languages
ICES, FORTRAN.

Services Available
Consultation, software packages. Services restricted to civil engineers.

Field of Application
Civil engineering.
Specialized area: Soil engineering.

BEDFORD ASSOCIATES INC.*
75 Wiggins Avenue, Bedford, 01730
Telephone: (617) 275-0740

Officer
Richard E. Morley, *President*

Computer Installation
PDP-8L (2)–operating system: DEC library; internal storage: 48K bits each; magnetic discs: 1 Memorex 630.

Coding Language
SYMBOLIC.

Services Available
Consultation, programming, systems analysis. Operate on a block time basis.

Fields of Application
Digital control systems for industry, electronics and product development.
Specialized areas: Machine tool control, transportation system control, process control.

CAMBRIDGE COMPUTER ASSOCIATES INC.
222 Alewife Brook Parkway, Cambridge, 02138
Telephone: (617) 868-1111

Officers
Victor Oppenheimer, *President*
Michael Joblin, *Executive Vice-President*

Computer Installation
PDP-11.

Coding Languages
FORTRAN, COBOL, PL/1, Utility-Coder/360, Assembler.

Services Available
Advice, programming, software packages, documentation, systems analysis, turn-key systems. Operate on a remote access, closed shop and time-sharing basis.

Fields of Application
Statistical, commercial, systems analysis.
Specialized areas: Sales analysis, analysis, medical research, social science research, health care data systems, software packages.

Training
Short courses in use of proprietary products CROSSTAB, Utility-Coder, AUTOGRAF, PROFILE and DATA-TEXT.

COMPUTEC ASSOCIATES*
P.O. Box 174, Cambridge, 02138
Telephone: (617) 926-3128

Officer
Nelson Hanover, *Technical Services Manager*

Services Available
Consultation, economic analysis, systems analysis.

Fields of Application
Real time data processing systems design and analysis, communications systems.
Specialized areas: Industry studies, telecommunications systems planning.

DESIGN AUTOMATION INC.
809 Massachusetts Avenue, Lexington, 02173
Telephone: (617) 862-8998

Officer
Nathan O. Sokal, *President*

Coding Languages
NET-1, SCEPTRE, CIRCUS, ECAP.

Services Available
Consultation, education and training, software packages, simulation. Operate on a closed shop basis.

Field of Application
Scientific: computer-aided electronic circuit and systems analysis.
Specialized areas: Semiconductor modelling for computer analysis.

Training
Courses in NET-1, CIRCUS and SCEPTRE programmes for non-linear DC and transient analysis (3 days), ECAP computer programme for linear DC, frequency and transient analysis (3 days).

ENGINEERING COMPUTER INTERNATIONAL, INC.
1033 Massachusetts Avenue, Cambridge, 02138
Telephone: (617) 864-5810

Officers
Richard V. Goodman, *President*
Joseph M. Sussman, Daniel Roos, Robert D. Logcher, *Directors*

Computer Installation
IBM 360/195–operating system: OS; internal storage: 4 million bytes; magnetic tapes: 39 3420/7; magnetic discs: 7 2314, 2 3330; 6 line printers. *Remote processing features*: full RJE support.

Coding Languages
FORTRAN, ICETRAN, PL/1, COBOL, SNOBOL.

Services Available
Advice, programming, software packages, documentation, system analysis. Operate on a remote access and open shop basis.

Fields of Application
Scientific, statistical, commercial, production control, accounting, management, systems analysis, operational research.
Specialized areas: Linear programming, payroll, structural engineering, project management, transportation consulting.

ENTELEK INC.
42 Pleasant Street, Newburyport, 01950
Telephone: (617) 465-3000

Officer
Dr. Albert E. Hickey, *President*

Services Available
Education and training, software packages, information exchange.

Fields of Application
Management, systems analysis, operational research, computer-assisted instruction.
Specialized area: Education.

United States of America – Consultants

Training
Short correspondence courses in linear programming, sales forecasting, inventory management, etc. Seminar in computer-assisted instruction.

HEFFELFINGER ASSOCIATES, INC.
888 Washington Street, Dedham, 02026
Telephone: (617) 329-1040

Officer
Thomas V. Heffelfinger, *President*

Services Available
Advice, executive search. Consultation available only to the computer industry.

INFORMATION & SYSTEMS INSTITUTE INC.*
14 Concord Lane, Cambridge, 02138
Telephone: (617) 491-4471

Officers
Larry L. Constantine, *President*
David Bamberger, *Senior Consultant*

Coding Languages
COBOL, FORTRAN, ALGOL, PL/1, SLIP, LISP, SNOBOL, OLCADD, etc.

Services Available
Consultation, programming, systems analysis.

Fields of Application
Integral hardware/software design, systems analysis, operations research, management information systems, real-time control, artificial language and translator design.

Training
Short courses in programme systems design (5 days), real-time systems design (5 days), management information systems (5 days), and 12 others.

ARTHUR D. LITTLE INC.*
Acorn Park, Cambridge, 02140
Telephone: (617) 864-5770

Also at:
Prudential Plaza, Suite 1912, Chicago, Illinois 60601
Telephone: (312) 346-7575
630 Fifth Avenue, New York, New York 10020
Telephone: (212) 586-2300
500 Sansome Street, San Francisco, California 94111
Telephone: (415) 981-2500
1735 Eye Street, N.W., Washington, D.C. 20006
Telephone: (202) 223-4400
and at: Toronto, Canada; Athens, Greece; Brussels, Belgium; Caracas, Venezuela; London, United Kingdom; Mexico City, Mexico; Paris, France; Rio de Janeiro, Brazil; Zürich, Switzerland.

Services Available
Consultation, software packages, systems analysis and development, feasibility studies, data processing, hardware design reviews and evaluations, computer graphics, simulation and modelling, project management.

Fields of Application
For industry, public institutions, government agencies, financial intermediaries, transportation, communications: scientific, statistical, commercial, production control, operational research, management information systems, market research, inventory control, physical distribution.

MITECH SYSTEMS INC.*
49 Hampshire Street, Cambridge, 02139
Telephone: (617) 646-3446

Officers
I. Marshall McCloskey, Jr., *President*
Alberto M. Rivas, *Foreign Relations*

Coding Languages
FORTRAN, COBOL, PL/1, Assembly.

Services Available
Consultation, programming, software packages, systems analysis. Operate on an open shop and self-service basis.

Fields of Application
Scientific Systems, real time data processing systems, systems software.

PROJECT PLANNING ASSOCIATES*
19 Houston Avenue, Milton, 02187
Telephone: (617) 696-6295

Officer
Isadore Halzel, *President*

Service Available
Consultation.

Fields of Application
Advanced management planning and scheduling techniques through the utilization of PERT and CPM.
Specialized areas: Application of above techniques to construction projects and other large industrial projects.

Training
One- or two-day courses in advanced management planning and scheduling techniques.

SCIENTIFIC ANALYSIS CORPORATION*
97 Lincoln Road, Wayland, 01778
Telephone: (617) 358-7400

Officers
K. C. Black, *Chairman*
M. R. Black, *President*

Services Available
Consultation, systems analysis.

Fields of Application
Systems analysis, operations research, market planning, management consulting.
Specialized areas: Communications systems, general electronic systems, convention planning.

EDWARD STARK ASSOCIATES, LTD.
31 Hazelton Avenue, Needham, 02192
Telephone: (617) 444-7837

Also at:
Research and Study Facility, Baker Hill, P.O. Box 45, Newbury, New Hampshire 03255
Telephone: (603) 763-5354

Officers
Edward J. Stark, *President (also responsible for international operations)*
K. Esser, *Secretary*

United States of America – Consultants

Services Available
Consultation, operators, preparation of data, programming, software packages, systems analysis. Operate at client's location.

Fields of Application
Commercial, production control, finance, management, systems analysis, organization, marketing, sales forecasting, warehousing, payroll and labour distribution, standard cost systems.
Specialized areas: Management information services, institutional information systems.

Training
One- to three-day seminars on executive introduction to management information systems.

VIATRON PROGRAMMING, INC.*
3 New England Executive Park, Burlington, 01803
Telephone: 272-2345

Also at:
1 California Street, San Francisco, California 94111
Telephone: 989-3160

Officer
Robert Dockser, *President*

Computer Installation
IBM 360/30–operating system: DOS; internal storage: 65K bits; magnetic tapes: 4; magnetic discs: 3; 1 line printer. *Remote processing features*: 2701.

Coding Languages
BAL, COBOL, FORTRAN, RPG, PL/1.

Contemplated Equipment
Viatron 2150.

Services Available
Consultation, programming, education and training, systems analysis. Operate on a closed shop basis.

Training
Operator and systems training for system 21.

MICHIGAN

APPLIED SYSTEMS CORPORATION*
18325 W. McNichols Road, Detroit, 48219
Telephone: 535-5800

Officers
Martin W. Wyrod, *President*
L. J. Hughes, *Vice-President*

Computer Installation
IBM 360/30 and 40–operating system: OS 360; magnetic tapes: 6; magnetic discs: 6; 1 line printer.

Coding Languages
FORTRAN, COBOL. PL/1.

Services Available
Consultation, preparation of data, programming, software packages, systems analysis. Operate on a closed shop basis.

Fields of Application
Development of scientific, commercial and process control applications.
Specialized areas: Systems development and computation.

Training
Two-five-day course in scientific computing.

BRUCE ERTS AND ASSOCIATES INC.*
24489 Telegraph, Southfield, 48075
Telephone: (313) 353-3361

Officers
Bruce R. Erts, *President*
Alan J. Shepherd, *Executive Vice-President (Foreign Relations Officer)*

Computer Installation
IBM 1130–internal storage: 129,600 bits; magnetic discs: 11 2315; 1 line printer.

Coding Language
FORTRAN.

Services Available
Consultation, operators, preparation of data, programming, software packages, systems analysis. Operate on a self-service and open shop basis.

Fields of Application
Scientific, statistical, commercial, production control, accounting, management, systems analysis, operational research.
Specialized area: CPM/PERT project management.

MISSOURI

AERO TECHNICAL APPLICATIONS INC.*
8011 Clayton Road, Suite 315, St. Louis, 63117

Officers
J. A. Wiggins, *President*
Chester B. Hein, *Executive Vice-President*

Coding Languages
APT III, COBOL, FORTRAN IV, BAL, SPS, ACL, RPG, PL/1.

Contemplated Equipment
Time-sharing terminals.

Services Available
Consultation, programming, software packages, documentation, systems analysis. Operate on a self-service basis.

Fields of Application
Management, systems analysis, operational research.
Specialized area: Transportation.

LAWRENCE-LEITER & COMPANY
114 West Tenth Street, Kansas City, 64105
Telephone: (816) 474-8340

Officer
Norman J. Heying, *Manager of Data Processing*

Services Available
Consultation, systems analysis.

Fields of Application
Commercial (governmental), accounting, management, systems analysis.

United States of America – Consultants

NEW JERSEY

COMPUTER CONSULTANTS CORPORATION*
Route 46, East Denville, 07834
Telephone: (201) 625-1213

Officer
Jon Gould

Services Available
Consultation, software packages, systems analysis.

Fields of Application
Real time and multiprocessing, data communication systems, scientific and engineering applications, commercial applications, software development.

Training
Orientation seminars on the design and applications of on-line real time systems.

CYBERMATICS INC.
560 Sylvan Avenue, Englewood Cliffs, 07632
Telephone: (201) 871-1300, (212) 868-7255

Also at:
5249 Duke Street, Alexandria, Virginia 22304
Telephone: (703) 370-5926

Officers
J. Roy Morris, *Chairman of the Board and President*
T. E. Farrell, *Vice-President, Finance*
Peter J. Ryan, *General Manager*

Computer Installations
PDP-8–operating system: TIN CAN; internal storage: 16K bits; magnetic discs: 1; 2 line printers. *Remote processing features*: full communications capability.
PDP-11–operating system: TIN CAN; internal storage: 32K bits; magnetic discs: 2; 2 line printers. *Remote processing features*: full communications capability.
VARIAN 620F–operating system: TIN CAN; internal storage: 32K bits; magnetic discs: 5; 1 line printer. *Remote processing features*: full communications capability.

Coding Languages
Machine languages, FORTRAN, ALGOL, COBOL, etc.

Contemplated Equipment
PDP-11/40.

Services Available
Advice, programming, education and training, software packages, documentation, systems analysis. Operate on a closed shop basis.

Fields of Application
Scientific, commercial, management, systems analysis, operational research, on-line communications.
Specialized area: Communications.

Training
Courses in programming, operating and management.

DATAMATICS MANAGEMENT SERVICES, INC.
120 Sylvan Avenue, Englewood Cliffs, 07632
Telephone: (201) 947-6100

Officers
Norman C. Heinle, Jr., *President*
L. Van Dyke, *Vice-President*

Coding Languages
COBOL, FORTRAN, PL/1, BAL, Autocoder, RPG.

Contemplated Equipment
IBM 360/30.

Services Available
Consultation, operators, programming, systems analysis, education, package evaluation.

Fields of Application
Commercial, management information systems, control, education, etc.
Specialized area: Quantitative techniques.

Training
Organize, develop and conduct courses and developmental programmes for many client companies. Seminars conducted throughout North America and Europe, principally in electronic data processing and computer methodology.

FISHER-STEVENS INC.*
120 Brighton Road, Clifton, 07012
Telephone: (201) 471-4000

Officer
Robert J. Atkins, *Vice-President*

Computer Installation
IBM 360/30 (2).
IBM 360/40.

Services Available
Consultation, programming, software packages, systems analysis.

HAVERLY SYSTEMS INC.
4 Second Avenue, Denville, 07834
Telephone: (201) 627-1424

Also at:
St. Albans, United Kingdom.

Officers
C. A. Haverly, *President*
George M. Lowell, *Vice-President*

Coding Languages
BAL, FORTRAN, COBOL, RPG.

Services Available
Consultation, programming, education and training, software packages, systems analysis, linear programming. Operate on a remote access and time-sharing basis.

Fields of Application
Scientific, commercial, production control, systems analysis, operational research, linear programming.
Specialized areas: Linear programming, matrix/report generator.

Training
Workshops on mathematical programming (1 to 5 days) and advanced mathematical programming tutorial.

I.S.E.C.
Route 206 Center, Princeton, 08540
Telephone: (609) 924-3366

Officers
Fredrik J. Ranney, *President, Director of Research*
George E. Wilson, *Vice President, Director of Sales*

Services Available
Consultation, software packages, preparation of data.

Fields of Application
Investment analysis, stock exchange forecasting.

JOHN A. KEANE AND ASSOCIATES
20 Nassau Street, Princeton, 08540
Telephone: (609) 924-7904

Officer
John A. Keane, *President*

Services Available
Advice, software packages, systems analysis. Time-sharing terminals on the premises.

Fields of Application
Scientific, production control, management, systems analysis, operational research.
Specialized area: Analysis.

ARTHUR S. KRANZLEY AND COMPANY, INC.*
1110 Wynwood Avenue, Cherry Hill, 08034
Telephone: (609) 665-4447

Coding Languages
Assembler, RPG, COBOL, PL/1.

Services Available
Consultation, programming, software packages, systems analysis.

Fields of Application
Commercial systems and applications programming: production control, accounting (all aspects), management, information systems; systems analysis, design and development; business, product and market planning.
Specialized areas: Banking, credit, hospitals, retailing, steel, electronic equipment manufacturing, government.

MANAGEMENT SCIENCE AMERICA, INC.
580 Sylvan Avenue, Englewood Cliffs, 07632
Telephone: (201) 871-4700

Officers
John Imlay, *President*
William Graves, *Executive Vice-President*

Coding Language
COBOL.

Services Available
Education and training, software packages, documentation.

Field of Application
Accounting.
Specialized areas: General ledger, financial statement, accounts payable, inventory control, fixed asset accounting.

Training
Training of clerical and computer staff in the use of the above systems.

META SYSTEMS CORPORATION
32 Scotch Road, Trenton, 08628

Officers
B. Gray III, *Chairman*
L. H. Ray, *President*
G. Friet, Jr., *Vice-President*

Coding Languages
PL/1, COBOL, FORTRAN, ALGOL, JOVIAL, TACPOL.

Services Available
Consultation, programming, systems analysis.

Fields of Application
Commercial, systems evaluation, software.
Specialized areas: Simulators, operating systems, compilers, systems evaluation, feasibility studies.

Training
Seminars in computer specialties.

DAVID A. NELSON
127 Forrest Road, Moorestown, 08057
Telephone: (609) 235-4322

Officer
David A. Nelson, *Proprietor*

Services Available
Consultation, systems analysis.

Fields of Application
Systems analysis.
Specialized areas: COBOL compiler design, operating system design, product planning.

PERFORMANCE DEVELOPMENT CORPORATION
32 Scotch Road, Trenton, 08628

Officers
Leo J. Cohen, *President*
K. Cohen, *Vice-President*

Coding Languages
PL/1, COBOL, FORTRAN, JOVIAC, ALGOL.

Contemplated Equipment
Time-sharing terminal.

Services Available
Advice, education and training, systems analysis.

Fields of Application
Scientific, statistical, management, systems analysis, operational research.
Specialized areas: Analysis, data base management analysis, systems performance measurements.

Training
"Systems Performance Measurement Analysis" (self-contained cassette/workbook course); "Data Base Management Systems: A Critical and Comparative Analysis" (an in-depth report with periodic updates); Seminars: Data Base, Systems Performance, Measurement, Network Techniques, Modelling and Simulation.

United States of America – Consultants

NEW YORK

AGS COMPUTERS INC.*
485 Fifth Avenue, New York, 10017
Telephone: (212) 661-4588

Officers
Lawrence J. Schoenberg, *President*
Joseph Abrams, *Vice-President*

Coding Languages
COBOL, FORTRAN, ALGOL, PL/1, NELIAC, NEAT, RPG, COMTRAN.

Services Available
Consultation, programming, software packages, systems analysis.

Fields of Application
Systems design, real-time systems evaluation, management information systems, accounting, scientific, statistical and financial analysis, information retrieval.

BOOZ, ALLEN & HAMILTON INC.*
245 Park Avenue, New York, 10017

Also at:
Room 401, Cafritz Building, 1625 Eye Street, N.W., Washington, D.C. 20006
Suite 600, Union Commerce Building, 925 Euclid Avenue, Cleveland, Ohio 44115
Penobscot Building, Room 1617, Detroit, Michigan 48226
Room 1700, 135 South LaSalle Street, Chicago, Illinois 60603
Room 2210, Republic National Bank Tower, 325 North Street, Paul Street, Dallas, Texas 75201
Crocker-Citizens Plaza, 611 W. Sixth Street, Los Angeles, California 90017
Suite 3980, Bank of America, 555 California Street, San Francisco, California 94014
and at: London, United Kingdom, and Düsseldorf, Federal Republic of Germany.

Computer Installation
IBM 360/30—operating system: DOS; internal storage: 65K bits; magnetic tapes: 6; magnetic discs: 3 1316; 1 line printer.

Coding Languages
All major languages.

Services Available
Consultation, preparation of data, programming, systems analysis.

Fields of Application
Engineering, R & D management, finance/accounting, marketing, systems planning and design, general management, etc.
Specialized areas: Equipment evaluation, systems planning and design, information retrieval, data communication, PERT.

BRANDON APPLIED SYSTEMS, INC.
BRANDON SYSTEMS INSTITUTE, INC.
BRANDON TECHNICAL SERVICES, INC.
1700 Broadway, New York, 10019
Telephone: (212) 757-2100

Also at:
1611 North Kent Street, Arlington, Virginia 22209
3210 Geary Street, San Francisco, California 94118
and at: London and Birmingham, United Kingdom.

Officers
D. H. Brandon, *President*
N. Rand, *Chairman*

Computer Installation
IBM 370/145—operating systems: OS/VS 1, OS/MVT/HASP; internal storage: 512K bytes; magnetic tapes: 4 3420; magnetic discs: 4 3330; 1 line printer.

Coding Languages
COBOL, FORTRAN, PL/1, etc.

Contemplated Equipment
IBM 370/158 with 1 million bytes internal storage.

Services Available
Advice, programming, education and training, software packages, documentation, systems analysis, conversion programmes. Operate on a remote access and closed shop basis.

Fields of Application
Statistical, commercial, accounting, management, systems analysis, operational research.

Training
A wide variety of data processing seminars (2-12 days).

COMPUTER APPLICATIONS INC.*
555 Madison Avenue, New York, 10022
Telephone: (212) 759-1310

Officer
J. A. DeVries, *President and Chairman of the Board*

Computer Installation
IBM 360/30.
IBM 1401.
CDC 160A.

Services Available
Consultation, programming, systems analysis.

Fields of Application
Programme design and development, systems modelling and simulation, systems engineering, systems design, computer facility management, data processing, educational institutes, market research, direct mail, graphic arts, publishing.

Training
Seminars in linear programming, simulation and modelling and multivariate analysis.

COMPUTER METHODS CORPORATION*
470 Mamaroneck Avenue, White Plains, 10605
Telephone: (914) 428-0400

Officers
Albert Chiappinelli, Jr., *President*
Jay G. Wilson, *Vice-President, Operations*
Lee Rydell, *Vice-President, Sales*

Coding Languages
COBOL, ALC, PL/1, FORTRAN.

Services Available
Consultation, programming, systems analysis, facilities management, proprietary software.

Fields of Application
Systems programming and consulting services for commercial real-time and batch-type systems. Specialists in turn-key commercial systems development. Tutorial films and texts of EDP topics for programmers and systems personnel. Commercial application packages for Revolving Credit and On-line Brokerage System for Over-the-Counter Brokers. Management consulting services. TESTPAK-proprietary testing system for IBM 360 and RCA Spectra 70.

COMPUVISOR INC.*
P.O. Box 381, Ithaca, 14850
Telephone: (607) 272-3269

Also at:
P.O. Box 113, Village Station, New York, New York 10014
Telephone: (212) 533-1470

Officer
Howard Lee Morgan, *President*

Services Available
Consultation, software packages.

Fields of Application
Commercial, operational research.
Specialized areas: File management and information retrieval, job shop simulation, scheduling, hardware simulation.

CRESAP, McCORMICK AND PAGET INC.
245 Park Avenue, New York, 10017
Telephone: (212) 661-4600

Also at:
Chicago, Illinois; Los Angeles, California; San Francisco, California; Washington, D.C.; Mexico City, Mexico; Brussels, Belgium; Melbourne, Australia; São Paulo, Brazil.

Officers
Albert Kushner, *Director of EDP Services*
Georges Petitpas, *Vice-President and Director, Europa*
Rodney F. Beckwith, *Vice-President and Director, Australia*

Services Available
Advice, systems analysis.

Fields of Application
Management of systems and data processing, systems and procedures studies, equipment evaluation and selection, communications, information systems.

Training
Executive seminars on EDP and systems.

R. N. DAILEY INC.*
300 Madison Avenue, New York, 10017
Telephone: (212) 986-6740

Officer
R. N. Dailey, *President*

Coding Languages
COBOL, FORTRAN, PL/1, Autocoder, MAP, FAP, BAL.

Services Available
Programming, systems analysis.

Fields of Application
Scientific, commercial, operations research, management information systems, systems analysis.

DATASONICS, INC.
663 Fifth Avenue, New York, 10022
Telephone: (212) 682-0326

Officer
Martin Burack, *President*

Services Available
Advice, programming, software packages, systems analysis.

Fields of Application
Commercial, accounting, management, systems analysis.
Specialized areas: Sales analysis, investment, analysis.

DESIGNERS AND BUILDERS OF INFORMATION SYSTEMS (DBIS)*
35 West 53rd Street, New York, 10019
Telephone: 581-2490

Officer
Edward Baron

Coding Languages
Autocoder, COBOL, PL/1, APL, Assembly, Job Control.

Services Available
Consultation, programming, software packages, documentation, systems analysis.

Fields of Application
Statistical, commercial, accounting, administrative, systems analysis, programming, implementation.
Specialized areas: Medical and hospital industries.

DIEBOLD GROUP INC.*
430 Park Avenue, New York, 10022
Telephone: (212) PL5-0400

Also at:
John Diebold & Associates
33 North Michigan Avenue, Chicago, Illinois 60602
Telephone: (312) RA6-3686
Griffenhagen-Kroeger Inc.
1543 West Olympic Boulevard, Los Angeles, California 90015
Telephone: (213) 381-7058
Griffenhagen-Kroeger Inc.
64 Pine Street, San Francisco, California 94111
Telephone: (413) GA1-3412
The Diebold Group Inc.
1616 H Street, N.W., Washington, D. C. 20006
Telephone: (202) 737-1164
Griffenhagen-Kroeger Inc.
Park Building, Portland, Oregon
Telephone: (503) 222-3365

Overseas:
Brussels (Belgium); Paris (France); Frankfurt am Main (Federal Germany); Amsterdam and Hengelo (Netherlands); London (U.K.).

Services Available
Consultation, software packages, systems analysis.

Fields of Application
Management planning and control, information systems, communications, public and institutional management, etc.
Specialized area: Management information systems.

Training
Two-week course in advanced systems analysis; seminars on various topics.

EBS MANAGEMENT CONSULTANTS INC.*
100 Church Street, New York, 10007
Telephone: (212) 344-4400

Also at:
Chicago, Illinois; Cleveland, Ohio; Dallas, Texas; Los Angeles and San Francisco, California.

Officers
K. W. Reece, *President*
R. E. Sibson, *Executive Vice-President*
J. S. Wilde, Sr., *Vice-President*
T. J. Johnson, *Managing Director, Management Sciences*
R. L. Schlesinger, *Managing Director, International Operations*

Computer Installation
BURROUGHS B5500—internal storage: 24K bits; magnetic tapes: 4; magnetic discs: 2; 1 line printer.

Coding Languages
FORTRAN, ALGOL, COBOL.

Services Available
Consultation, programming, software packages, systems analysis.

Fields of Application
Management sciences, operations research, accounting and management systems analysis, financial tax and insurance services, marketing studies, manufacturing and operations, (including production control), economic research, transportation and distribution, organization and personnel management, actuarial and employee benefit services, public planning and development.

ECONOMIC INFORMATION SYSTEMS INC.
21 West 38th Street, New York, 10018
Telephone: (212) 239-7090

Officers
Dr. Jay M. Gould, *President*
Bentley H. Paykin, *Vice-President*

Services Available
Software packages, preparation of data. Operate on a time-sharing basis.

Fields of Application
Statistical, management.
Specialized areas: Sales analysis, analysis, development of databanks of sales and purchases of U.S. companies.

EDP ASSOCIATES INC.*
1250 Broadway, New York, 10001
Telephone: (212) 695-6630

Officers
Sheldon Danziger, *President*
Will G. Hale, III, *Executive Vice-President*

Coding Languages
COBOL, ALP, PL/1, Easycoder.

Services Available
Consultation, programming, systems analysis, education and training, documentation.

Fields of Application
Commercial, statistical, production control, accounting, management, systems analysis.

EMERSON CONSULTANTS INC.*
30 Rockefeller Plaza, New York, 10020
Telephone: (212) 245-5738

Also at:
16 California Street, San Francisco, California 94111
Telephone: (415) 433-2319
and at London, United Kingdom.

Officers
E. G. Fremont, Jr., *Chairman*
W. R. Sorensen, *President*
A. R. White, *Principal*
C. H. Kruse, *Principal*

Services Available
Consultation, systems analysis. Consulting service only: major railroads, utilities, steel industry, coal mining, hospitals.

Fields of Application
Management systems, organization, cost control.

E.P.G. COMPUTER SERVICES INC.*
269 Lexington Avenue, New York, 10017
Telephone: (212) 682-5255/6

Officer
Erich P. Gurtner, *President*

Coding Languages
COBOL, FORTRAN, RPG, ALGOL.

Contemplated Equipment
IBM 360/50.

Services Available
Consultation, programming, software packages, systems analysis.

Fields of Application
Consulting, systems analysis, programming.

GENESEE COMPUTER CENTER, INC.
20 University Avenue, Rochester, 14605
Telephone: (716) 232-7050

Officers
Kurt Enslein, *President*
R. T. MacIntyre, *Vice-President and General Manager*

Computer Installation
UNIVAC 9200 used as remote batch terminal to 8 CDC 660 sites in the U.S.A. and Canada.

Coding Languages
FORTRAN, COBOL, SIMSCRIPT, SLIP, COMPASS.

Services Available
Consultation, programming, statistical analysis, remote batch processing. Operate on a remote access, closed shop basis and time-sharing basis.

Fields of Application
Biomedical statistics, optics, inventory control, numerical control, simulation, computer communications, business methods.
Specialized areas: Multivariate analysis, interactive optics, compressed plotting routines, computer to computer software, pattern recognition, sophisticated simulation, electrocardiograms.

Training
Customer-tailored courses in programming and system usage.

JOHN GILMORE & ASSOCIATES INC.*
90 Park Avenue, New York, 10016
Telephone: (212) 697-8218

Officers
John Gilmore
Daniel Davis

Computer Installation
IBM 1130—operating system: Monitor; internal storage: 32K bits; magnetic discs: 4; 1 line printer.

Coding Languages
FORTRAN, PL/1, ALGOL.

Services Available
Consultation, programming, software packages, systems analysis. Operate on an open shop basis.

Fields of Application
Simulation, operational research, real-time, process control, computer graphics.
Specialized areas: Programming packages for personnel, organizational simulation, information retrieval, graphics.

Training
Short courses in computer graphics (3 days) and OS/360 for scientific programmers (3 days).

HALCON COMPUTER TECHNOLOGIES, INC.
2 Park Avenue, New York, 10016
Telephone: (212) 689-7357

Officers
T. W. Stein, *President*
S. M. Krusch, *Director of Engineering Services*

Computer Installation
IBM 360/40—operating system: OS; internal storage: 128K bytes; magnetic discs: 3 2311; 1 line printer.

Coding Languages
FORTRAN, COBOL, RPG.

Services Available
Advice, programming, education and training, operators, software packages, documentation, preparation of data, systems analysis, computer graphics. Operate on an open shop basis.

Fields of Application
Scientific, statistical, production control, management, systems analysis, operational research.
Specialized areas: Chemical and mechanical engineering.

INFOTEC, INC.*
70 Newtown Road, Plainview, 11803
Telephone: (516) 694-9633

Officers
Henry R. Seppanen, *Technical Director*
Richard Johnson, *Manager*

Computer Installation
IBM 1130—operating system: DMS; internal storage: 256K bits; magnetic tapes: 5 IBM Compatible; magnetic discs: 1 2310; 1 line printer. *Remote processing features*: data transmission.
PDP-8/L—operating system: Executive Real Time; internal storage: 96K bits; magnetic tapes: 4 IBM Compatible; 1 line printer. *On-line satellite computers*: communicates with system 360. *Remote processing features*: RJE, BSC, STR, Batch.

Coding Languages
FORTRAN, COBOL, RPG, APL.

Contemplated Equipment
IBM 360/30.

Services Available
Consultation, programming, software packages, systems analysis. Operate on a remote access and time-sharing basis.

Fields of Application
Commercial, management, systems analysis.
Specialized areas: Business communications, data collection, store and forward, inquiry response, graphics, statistical, scientific, management.

INFOTRAN INC.
860 Fifth Avenue, New York, 10021
Telephone: (212) 628-4240

Officers
Rudy C. Stiefel, *President*
Dr. F. Assadourian, *Communications Specialist*
Arthur Belefant, *Chief Engineer*

Services Available
Advice, documentation.

Fields of Application
Scientific, commercial, accounting.
Specialized area: Payroll.

LOWENTHAL PROGRAMMING CORPORATION
30 Rock Ridge Drive, Port Chester, 10573
Telephone: (914) 939-8298

Officer
Mark J. Lowenthal, *President*

Coding Languages
COBOL, Assembly, RPG.

Services Available
Programming, systems analysis.

Fields of Application
Commercial, systems analysis.
Specialized areas: Analysis, systems programming.

United States of America — Consultants

McKINSEY AND COMPANY INC.*
245 Park Avenue, New York, 10017
Telephone: (212) 687-3600

Also at:
Chicago, Illinois; Cleveland, Ohio; Los Angeles and San Francisco, California; Washington, D.C.
and at: Amsterdam, Netherlands; Düsseldorf, Federal Republic of Germany; Milan, Italy; London, U.K.; Melbourne, Australia; Paris, France; Toronto, Canada; Zürich, Switzerland.

Officer
C. L. Walton, Jr., *Managing Director*

Computer Installation
IBM 1130—operating system: Monitor II; internal storage: 16,384 16-bit words; magnetic disc: 2310; 1 line printer. *Remote processing features*: dataphone hookup with Univac 1108.

Coding Languages
FORTRAN, BASIC, ALGOL.

Services Available
Consultation, programming, software packages, systems analysis. Operate on a self-service and time-sharing basis. All services are entirely for internal use by consultants and supporting staff members in solving client problems.

Fields of Application
Operations research, linear programming, simulation, statistical analysis.

MANAGEMATICS, INC.
2 Penn Plaza, New York, 10001
Telephone: (212) 594-7199

Officers
Erving Katz, *President*
Raymond P. Wenig, *Vice-President, Operations and Training*

Coding Languages
COBOL, FORTRAN, BAL, GPSS, Autocoder.

Services Available
Consultation, programming, education and training, software packages, documentation, systems analysis.

Fields of Application
Management, scientific, systems analysis, commercial, statistical, industrial engineering (production scheduling, control, inventory control), operations research.
Specialized areas: Management sciences, services for data processing management.

Training
Short courses in systems analysis (4 days), EDP administration (1 day), management for data processing projects (3 days) and introduction to management sciences (2 days).

NAREMCO SERVICES INC.*
555 Fifth Avenue, New York, 10017
Telephone: (212) OX7-0290

Officer
Robert A. Shiff, *President*

Services Available
Consultation, systems analysis.

Fields of Application
Research, design and installation of advanced systems, administrative and office management, records management, information retrieval.

OFFICE OF GRAHAM PARKER INC.
100 Park Avenue, New York, 10017
Telephone: MU4-0548

Also at:
Paris, France; Milan, Italy; Tokyo, Japan.

Officers
Graham Parker, *President*
Dr. M. Rivard, *European General Manager*

Services Available
Consultation, systems analysis.

Fields of Application
Consulting services in commercial, production control, management and systems analysis.

PEAT, MARWICK, MITCHELL & CO.*
70 Pine Street, New York, 10005
Telephone: (212) 944-7900

Also at:
Tower Building, Prudential Center, Boston, Massachusetts 02199
Telephone: (617) 266-3000
Peat, Marwick, Livingston & Co., Tower Building, Prudential Center, Boston, Massachusetts 02199
Telephone: (617) 266-7100
111 West Monroe Street, Chicago, Illinois 60603
Telephone: (312) F16-7200
211 North Ervay Building, Dallas, Texas 75201
Telephone: (214) R17-8911
Chamber of Commerce Building, Houston, Texas 77002
Telephone: (713) CA7-6561
629 South Spring Street, Los Angeles, California 90014
Telephone: (213) 625-7464
Peat, Marwick, Livingston & Co., 6151 West Century Boulevard, Los Angeles, California 90045
Telephone: (213) 776-4720
Peat, Marwick, Livingston & Co., 275 Fifth Street, San Francisco, California 94103
Telephone: (415) 362-3141
Peat, Marwick, Livingston & Co., 1140 Connecticut Avenue, N.W., Washington, D.C. 20036
Telephone: (202) 223-1012
C.P.O. Box 4089, San Juan, Puerto Rico 00936
Telephone: 767-7840
Kates, Peat, Marwick & Co., Prudential Building, 4 King Street West, Toronto 1, Ontario (Canada)
Telephone: (416) 362-2371
and at: Mexico City; Rio de Janeiro, Brazil; Bogota, Columbia; Caracas, Venezuela; Kingston, Jamaica; Paris, France; Frankfurt, Federal Republic of Germany; Milan, Italy; London and Liverpool, U.K.; Johannesburg, South Africa; Sydney, Australia; Tokyo, Japan.

Officer
Walter E. Hanson, *Senior Partner, Executive Office*

Services Available
Consultation, systems analysis.

United States of America – Consultants

Fields of Application
Economic studies, general management, scientific management, operations research, project management, corporate policies and strategies, organization and manpower management, training, industrial engineering, marketing, executive recruitment, production and inventory control, information systems, general and cost accounting systems, data processing and transmission systems and related areas.
Specialized areas: Banking, transportation, insurance, government, petroleum production, refining and marketing, and others.

Training
A variety of training services designed specifically to match the clients' needs. Short courses in behavioral science, education science, executive development, training development, and visual programs.

REALTIME SYSTEMS INC.*
866 Third Avenue, New York, 10022
Telephone: (212) 421-2250

Also at:
London, United Kingdom.

Officer
J. C. Lindley, *President*

Computer Installations
BURROUGHS B5500 (dual processor)–operating system: MCP; internal storage: 1,568K bits; magnetic tapes: 4; magnetic discs; 1 line printer. *Remote processing features*: terminals.
Burroughs B5500 (single processor)–details as above.

Coding Languages
FORTRAN, ALGOL, COBOL, BASIC.

Contemplated Equipment
BURROUGHS B6500.

Services Available
Consultation, programming and software support in business simulation, forecasting, operations research finance. Operate on time sharing, remote batch processing and batch processing basis.

Fields of Application
Scientific, engineering and commercial applications, business systems, software development, time-sharing, management, operations research.
Specialized areas: Linear programming, investment analysis, simulation.

PAUL ROSENBERG ASSOCIATES
330 Fifth Avenue, Pelham, 10803
Telephone: (914) 738-2266

Officer
Dr. Paul Rosenberg, *President*

Service Available
Consultation.

RSI COMPUTER SERVICES CORPORATION*
475 Fifth Avenue, New York, 10017
Telephone: (212) 689-4190

Officers
R. F. Canaday, *Executive Vice-President, External Relations Officer*
T. W. Wade, Jr., *Director Data Processing Operations*

Coding Languages
PL/1, COBOL, FORTRAN, Autocoder.

Services Available
Advice, operators, preparation of data, programming, software packages, systems analysis.

Fields of Application
Commercial, scientific, accounting, management.
Specialized areas: Linear programming, information retrieval educational DPS.

SDA INFORMATION SCIENCES, INC.*
1540 Broadway, New York, 10036

Officers
Robert E. Spinner, *President*
Edward J. Brady, *Vice-President*
Joseph A. Romanello, *Vice-President*

Services Available
Consultation, systems analysis.

Fields of Application
Data acquisition and data communications.

R. DIXON SPEAS ASSOCIATES INC.
47 Hillside Avenue, Manhasset, 11030
Telephone: (516) 627-7460

Also at:
Miami, Florida; Atlanta, Georgia; Minneapolis, Minnesota; Los Angeles, California; London, United Kingdom.

Officers
R. Dixon Speas, *President*
D. R. Bornemann, *Vice-President*

Computer Installation
IBM 360/30–operating system: DOS; internal storage: 64K bits; magnetic discs: 3 2311; 1 line printer.
On-line satellite computer: PDP 11. *Remote processing features*: interactive 2741/TTY terminals.
IBM 360/30–operating system: DOS; internal storage: 32Kbits; magnetic discs: 2 2311; 1 line printer.
On-line satellite computer: PDP 11. *Remote processing features*: on-line TTYs.

Coding Languages
Assembly, PL/1, FORTRAN.

Contemplated Equipment
IBM 370/125 central processor.

Services Available
Consultation, programming, software packages, documentation, preparation of data, systems analysis. Operate on a semi-closed shop basis.

Fields of Application
Scientific, simulation of airports and airline operations, flight crew scheduling, equipment evaluation, systems design and program package development; management information and consultation.
Specialized areas: Flight planning and cargo documentation services.

SPECIAL STUDIES INSTITUTE*
122 East 42nd Street, New York, 10017
Telephone: (212) 697-6643

Officers
Dr. Nachman Bench, *President*
Leonard H. Aptman, *Director*

Services Available
Consultation, preparation of data, programming, software packages, systems analysis.

Fields of Application
Management science, operations research, systems analysis, computer application.
Specialized areas: Simulation for management decisions, forecasting and inventory control, management information systems.

Training
Short courses in new tools for management, PERT-CPM, implementing on-line, real time systems, the use of computers in personnel management, the use of computers in maintenance management.

THEODORE STEIN*
400 Madison Avenue, New York, 10017
Telephone: (212) HA1-1434

Services Available
Consultation, programming, software packages, systems analysis.

Field of Application
Commercial.

STEVENSON, JORDAN & HARRISON MANAGEMENT CONSULTANTS INC.*
200 Park Avenue (Pan Am Building), New York, 10017
Telephone: (212) 687-1280

Also at:
St. Louis, Missouri
and at: Caracas, Venezuela

Officers
Edward H. Jube, *President*
L. M. Matthews, *Vice President*
N. Robert, *Vice President*

Services Available
Consultation, systems analysis, requirements analysis, systems design.

Fields of Application
Statistical, commercial, production control, management, operational research, accounting, financial management.

Training
Courses in management of computer systems projects, management of projects, production control, developing sales forecasts, scheduling, cost analysis and control.

STEWARD, DOUGALL & ASSOCIATES INC.*
415 Madison Avenue, New York, 10017
Telephone: (212) 755-2900

Officers
Arthur B. Dougall, *Chairman of the Board*
Harrison M. Rainie, Jr., *President*
Robert C. Montgomery, *Vice-President – Foreign Relations*

Services Available
Consultation, preparation of data.

Fields of Application
Management, marketing consulting, marketing research.

SYSTEMS PROGRAMMING INC.*
175 Main Street, White Plains, 10601
Telephone: (914) 428-0494

Officer
Norbert Jay, *President*

Coding Languages
Autocoder, Easycoder, ARGUS, COBOL, BAL, RPG.

Services Available
Consultation, programming, software packages, systems analysis.

Fields of Application
Commercial business applications, systems design and analysis, feasibility studies.
Specialized areas: Services of automatic translator package for conversion of programmes from IBM 705/7080 and 1401 Autocoder to COBOL.

TIME SHARING SCIENCES INC.*
1180 Avenue of the Americas, New York, 10036

Officer
Hal Lamster, *President*

Services Available
Consultation, programming, education and training, software packages, documentation, systems analysis. Operate on a remote access and time-sharing basis.

Fields of Application
Information systems, management services, business systems.

Training
Courses designed to suit individual client's requirements.

WERNER ASSOCIATES INC.*
1450 Broadway, New York, 10018
Telephone: (212) 565-1280

Also at:
Brussels, Belgium.

Officers
Herbert L. Werner, *Chairman of the Board*
Jack C. Werner, *President*
Frank Paul, *Treasurer*

Service Available
Consultation.

Fields of Application
General management, manufacturing and technical, marketing services, administration – EDP feasibility studies, personnel management information systems.
Specialized areas: Services to the textile industry.

WORLDWIDE COMPUTER SERVICES INC.*
Fortune Building, Hartsdale, 10530
Telephone: (914) 428-0284

Officer
Jerald Greenberg

Contemplated Equipment
IBM System/3.

Services Available
Consultation, programming, education and training, software packages, systems analysis.

Field of Application
Commercial.

OHIO

ADVANCED COMPUTER SYSTEMS INC.*
3131 South Dixie Drive, Suite 201, Dayton, 45439
Telephone: (513) 294-0586

Officers
Peter D. Senkiw, *Director*
Tod A. Rapp, *Personnel Training*

Coding Languages
FORTRAN, COBOL, BAL, SPS, NEAT/3, NEAT, PL/1, etc.

Services Available
Consultation, programming, software packages, documentation, preparation of data, systems analysis.

Fields of Application
Scientific, statistical, commercial, production control, accounting, management, systems analysis, operations research.
Specialized areas: Manufacturing systems, inventory control, bill of materials, production scheduling, numerical control, management information systems, data collection, direct numerical control, math modelling etc.

BROWNING ASSOCIATES INC.*
4536 Imperial Drive, Toledo, 43623
Telephone: (419) 882-4196

Officers
Thomas H. Browning, *President*
Lillian D. Browning, *Vice-President*
William MacDaniels, *Secretary*

Services Available
Consultation, systems analysis.

Fields of Application
Commercial, production control, accounting, management, systems analysis, operational research.

Training
Short course in the design of management information systems (two half days).

COMPUTER SYSTEMS CO., INC.*
1470 Saint Charles Avenue, Cleveland, 44107
Telephone: (216) 228-4100

Also at:
1150 North Shadeland Avenue, Indianapolis, Indiana 46219
Telephone: (317) 357-1117

Officers
J. J. Celesnik, *Director of Systems*
R. B. Polhemus, *Director of Marketing*

Coding Languages
COBOL, PL/1, ALP, FORTRAN, BASIC, GAP, ALGOL, Easycoder, Autocoder, SPS, NEAT.

Contemplated Equipment
Remote terminal for general communication and batch processing from 1108, 360/67, CDC 6600 and other large systems.

Services Available
Consultation, preparation of data, programming, systems design, documentation, microfilm service, feasibility studies.

Fields of Application
Statistical, commercial, numerical control, operational research.

Training
Courses covering management, applications development, systems analysis, programming techniques and specialized areas to customer requirements.

ELECTRONIC SERVICE ASSOCIATES CORPORATION*
21877 Euclid Avenue, Cleveland, 44117
Telephone: (216) 692-1919

Officers
Manuel Salabounis, *President*
Dr. Laurence G. Brown, *Vice President*

Contemplated Equipment
IBM 360/40.

Services Available
Consultation, programming, education and training, software packages, documentation, systems analysis. Operate on a self-service and block time basis.

Fields of Application
General.
Specialized areas: Marketing information systems.

RAK ASSOCIATES
11820 Edgewater Drive, Cleveland, 44107
Telephone: (216) 228-2045

Officer
Richard A. Kuehn, *President*

Service Available
Consultation.

Fields of Application
Design of telecommunications facilities for efficient economical access of central processors from remote terminals.

REILAND, PAGE AND ASSOCIATES INC.*
1521 East Broad Street, Columbus, 43205
Telephone: (614) 258-3903

Officer
W. F. Reiland, *President*

Services Available
Consultation, programming, systems analysis.

Field of Application
Systems design.

United States of America – Consultants

E. RALPH SIMS JR. AND ASSOCIATES, INC.
919 East Fair Avenue, Lancaster, 43130
Telephone: (614) 654-1091

Also at:
2 The Shrubberies, George Lane, London E18, United Kingdom.
Telephone: 01-989 1974

Officer
E. Ralph Sims Jr., *President*

Computer Installation
IBM 360/30–operating system: DOS; internal storage: 64K bits; magnetic discs: 4; 2 line printers.
IBM 1620–internal storage: design programmes.

Coding Languages
NS COBOL, PL/1.

Services Available
Advice, systems design. Programming computers are used only for support on client projects.

Fields of Application
Statistical, management, design.
Specialized areas: Investment analysis, physical distribution.

Training
Special training to suit each individual client's needs.

OKLAHOMA

ICM COMPUTER CORPORATION
P.O. Box 7220, Tulsa, 74105
Telephone: (918) 587-2333

Officers
Daniel B. McDuvitt, *Chairman and President*
Willard Mason, *Vice-President and Director*
Mary Ann McDevitt, *Secretary and Director*

Computer Installation
IBM 360/40–operating system: DOS; internal storage: 128K bits; magnetic tapes: 8 2401; magnetic discs: 6 2311; 2 line printers. *On-line satellite computer*: PDP-11. Remote processing features.
HONEYWELL H425–internal storage: 256K bits; magnetic tapes: 8 9-track; magnetic discs: 6; 2 line printers. *On-line satellite computer*: Honeywell H700. Remote processing features.

Coding Languages
COBOL, ALGOL, FORTRAN, BASIC.

Contemplated Equipment
Communications equipment.

Services Available
Advice, programming, education and training, operators, software packages, documentation, preparation of data, systems analysis, communications design, facilities management. Operate on a remote access, closed shop and time-sharing basis. Available only to those who accept the conditions and advice.

Fields of Application
Scientific, statistical, commercial, production control, accounting, management, systems analysis, operational research, control and operations.
Specialized areas: Sales analysis, linear programming, investment, analysis, payroll, structural engineering, medical research, retail operations, optical scanning, document conversion.

PENNSYLVANIA

ATLANTIC SOFTWARE INC.
5th and Chestnut Streets, Philadelphia, 19106
Telephone: (215) 925-8424

Officers
Richard Thatcher Jr., *President*
Robert P. Wolk, *Vice-President*

Coding Languages
COBOL, Assembly, RPG.

Service Available
Software packages.

Fields of Application
Commercial, management information systems.
Specialized area: Project management software (accounting, scheduling, planning, etc.).

Training
Project management courses.

AUERBACH CORPORATIONS
121 North Broad Street, Philadelphia, 19107
Telephone: (215) 491-8200

Also at:
150 East 58th Street, New York, New York 10022
1501 Wilson Boulevard, Arlington, Virginia 22209
Center Professional Bldg., 280 Washington Street, Brighton, Massachusetts 02135
780 Welch Road, Palo Alto, California 94304

Overseas affiliate:
Attwood-Auerbach Ltd., Attwood House, West Halkin Street, London SW1, United Kingdom.

Officers
Isaac L. Auerbach, *President*
Raymond LeKashman, *Executive Vice-President, Auerbach Associates Inc.*
Arnold B. Shafritz, *Vice President and Technical Director*
Howard I. Morrison, *Vice-President and General Manager, Auerbach Publishers Inc.*
Lawrence I. Boonin, *Vice-President*

Services Available
Advice, programming, education and training, software packages, documentation, preparation of data, systems analysis.

Fields of Application
Commercial, management, systems analysis, operational research.

CIMS GROUP INC.*
Penn Sheraton, William Penn Place, Pittsburgh, 15230
Telephone: (412) 281-9800

Officers
R. B. Tomlinson, *President*
T. A. Van Wormer, *Executive Vice-President*

Computer Installation
IBM 1130–internal storage: 128K bits; magnetic disc: 1; 1 line printer.

Coding Language
FORTRAN.

Services Available
Consultation, programming, software packages, systems analysis.

Fields of Application
Operations research and advanced computer sciences.

Training
Courses in systems analysis, operations research and advanced programming (specially tailored to client requirements).

CONSENTIVE INC.*
3525 Lancaster Avenue, Philadelphia, 19104
Telephone: (215) 382-6715

Officer
Peter Kuner, *President*

Coding Languages
FORTRAN, PL/1, METASYMBOL, BAL.

Services Available
Consultation, programming, software packages, preparation of data, systems analysis. Operate on a self-service, remote access and time-sharing basis.

Fields of Application
Statistical, simulation in social sciences, information retrieval.

ECCO CONSULTING INC.
607 Washington Road, Pittsburgh, 15228
Telephone: (412) 561-5509

Officers
Joseph C. Ott, *President*
Horace C. Miles, *Vice-President*
Thomas S. Marchese, *Vice-President*
Roger D. Cripe, *Vice-President*

Services Available
Consulting, programming, software packages, systems analysis.

Fields of Application
Operations research, language and other software development, systems analysis and programming primarily in the scientific area, engineering applications.
Specialized areas: Development of management information systems for Metropolitan Governments, development of computer languages.

Training
Train management personnel in use of our high-level language (ECCO-CODER).

GANNETT FLEMING CORDDRY & CARPENTER INC.*
P.O. Box 1963, Harrisburg, 17105
Telephone: (717) 238-0451

Officer
J. Douglas Berry, *Director, Computing Center*

Computer Installation
IBM 360/44–operating system: DOS; internal storage: 128K bits; magnetic tapes: 2415; magnetic discs: 3 2314; 1 line printer.

Coding Languages
FORTRAN IV, BAL, RPG, COBOL.

Services Available
Consultation, preparation of data, programming, systems analysis. Operate on an open shop basis.

Fields of Application
Civil engineering, statistical, accounting, management reports.
Specialized areas: Data processing for large multi-store retail department stores.

INFORMATION ENGINEERING*
3401 Market Street, Philadelphia, 19104
Telephone: (215) 387-5150

Officer
Philip R. Bagley, *President*

Coding Languages
PL/1, COBOL, FORTRAN, APL.

Services Available
Consultation, preparation of data, programming, systems analysis, software packages, documentation. Operate on a closed shop basis.

Fields of Application
Commercial, systems analysis, statistical, scientific.
Specialized areas: Information retrieval (law), accounting, computer typesetting.

KEYSTONE COMPUTER ASSOCIATES, INC.
1055 Virginia Drive, Fort Washington, 19034
Telephone: (215) 643-3800

Also at:
1700 Broadway, New York, New York 10019

Officers
John E. Brennan, *President*
Leon Ellerson, *Manager, Philadelphia Operations*
Harold A. Steiner III, *Manager, New York Operations*

Coding Languages
COBOL, FORTRAN, PL/1, BAL, RPG, most Assembly languages.

Services Available
Consultation, programming, documentation, systems analysis.

Fields of Application
Scientific, statistical, commercial, production control, accounting, management, systems analysis, operational research, microcomputer software and technology.
Specialized areas: Sales analysis, investment, analysis, payroll.

SYSTEMS TECHNOLOGY CORPORATION*
530 West Street Road, Warminster, 18974
Telephone: (215) 672-9220

Officer
Walter F. Mruk, Ph.D., *President*

Computer Installation
IBM 360/40.

Services Available
Consultation and systems analysis. Operate on an open shop basis.

Fields of Application
Scientific and engineering studies, instrumentation, automation, and controls for the process and manufacturing industries.
Specialized areas: Automated process and manufacturing systems.

RICHARD M. WALSH ASSOCIATES
310 Jefferson Avenue, Scranton, 18510
Telephone: (717) 346-3856

Officer
Richard M. Walsh

Computer Installation
IBM 360/30–operating system: DOS; internal storage: 65K bits; magnetic tapes: 2; magnetic discs: 4; 1 line printer.

Services Available
Consultation, programming, education and training, software packages, documentation, systems analysis. Operate on a block time and time-sharing basis.

Fields of Application
Commercial, management, systems analysis, programming.
Specialized area: Educational administrative systems.

Training
Introductory course in data processing for management and administrators.

RHODE ISLAND

COMPUTER SERVICE CONSULTANTS INC.*
59 West Shore Road, Warwick, 02889
Telephone: (401) 739-9100

Computer Installation
IBM 1401–internal storage: 8K bits; magnetic tapes: 4.

Services Available
Consultation, operators, preparation of data, programming, systems analysis.

Fields of Application
Systems design and development, accounting, inventory control, critical path network solution, accounts receivable, payroll.

TENNESSEE

COMPASS COMPUTER SYSTEMS INC.*
2950 Foster Creighton Drive, Nashville, 37204
Telephone: (615) 259-2741

Officer
Harold W. Black, *President*

Computer Installation
IBM 360/50–operating system: OS; internal storage: 524,288 bytes; magnetic tapes: 3 2401; magnetic discs: 5 2314; 1 line printer. *Remote processing features*: 2 2780; 2741.

Coding Languages
FORTRAN, COBOL, BASIC, Assembler, RPG, PL/1.

Contemplated Equipment
IBM 370/155.

Services Available
Consultation, programming, systems analysis, remote processing, batch processing. Operate on a closed shop and remote access basis.

Fields of Application
Commercial, scientific, systems analysis.
Specialized areas: Actuarial services, market research and demographic services.

MANAGEMENT COMPUTER CONTROLS INC. (MC^2)
Suite 302, 2714 Union Ave. Extd., Memphis, 38112
Telephone: (901) 323-2651

Officer
W. Cole Early, *President*

Computer Installation
IBM 370/135.

Coding Languages
Autocoder, COBOL.

Services Available
Consultation, preparation of data, programming, software packages, systems analysis, construction cost consulting. Operate on a closed shop basis.

Fields of Application
Applications pertain to the construction field of architects, contractors, owners, engineers and reinforcing steel fabricators.
Specialized areas: Quantity surveying and cost estimating; reinforcing steel estimating and detailing; construction cost accounting; planning and scheduling.

Training
Seminars on fee basis describing the MC^2 approach to construction using the electronic computer.

TEXAS

ASSOCIATED COMPUTER SERVICES*
6420 Hillcroft, Houston, 77036
Telephone: (713) 771-3561

Officer
R. D. McCullough, *President*

Coding Languages
Assembly, FORTRAN, COBOL.

Services Available
Consultation, programming, software packages, systems analysis, turnkey installations.

Fields of Application
Scientific, process control, telecommunications, seismic.
Specialized area: Petrochemicals.

United States of America – Consultants

COMPUTER AID COMPANIES INC.*
Fidelity Union Life Building, Dallas, 75201

Officer
G. A. Zimmermann, *President*

Services Available
Consultation, systems analysis.

Fields of Application
Systems analysis, operational research, statistical, environmental control, mailing lists, management Studies, commercial.

COMPUTER TECHNICAL SERVICES INC. (COMTECH)*
5615 Daniels Avenue, Dallas, 75206
Telephone: (214) 363-6461

Also at:
Suite 720, 4151 Southwest Freeway, Houston, Texas

Officers
Tom L. Irby, *President*
Ken F. Sellers, *Operations Manager*

Computer Installation
UNIVAC 9300–operating system: NCOS-Tape; internal storage: 256K bits; magnetic tapes: 4 Uniservo VIC 9-track; 1 line printer. *Remote processing features*: C-4 with MILGO Modem to Univac 1108, 201-A Bell set to any central.
UNIVAC 1004–internal storage: 64K bits; 1 line printer. *Remote processing features*: C-4 with MILGO Modem to Univac 1108.

Coding Languages
FORTRAN, COBOL, RPG, BAL.

Services Available
Consultation, programming, operators, software packages, preparation of data, systems analysis. Operate on an open shop and remote access basis.

Fields of Application
Business, scientific.
Specialized areas: Petroleum reservoir mathematical modelling, traffic engineering, civil engineering – STRESS II.

FIRST BUSINESS COMPUTING*
Suite 1020 Houston Bank and Trust Tower, Houston, 77002
Telephone: (713) 227-3429

Officer
Lee M. Green, *President*

Computer Installation
IBM 360/25–operating system: DOS; internal storage: 256K bits; magnetic tapes: 4 2401; magnetic discs: 3 2311; 1 line printer.

Coding Languages
COBOL, FORTRAN, ALC, ABL, PL/1, PL/360, ALGOL.

Services Available
Consultation, programming, operators, software packages, preparation of data, systems analysis. Operate on a self-service basis.

Fields of Application
Scientific, commercial, accounting.

H. J. GRUY AND ASSOCIATES INC.
2501 Cedar Springs Road, Dallas, 75201
Telephone: (214) 742-1421

Also at:
Houston, Texas

Officers
H. J. Gruy, *President*
Forrest A. Garb, *Executive Vice-President*

Computer Installation
UNIVAC 1004 terminal.

Coding Languages
FORTRAN.

Services Available
Consultation, programming, software packages, systems analysis. Operate on a block time basis.

Field of Application
Scientific.
Specialized area: Petroleum engineering.

MANAGEMENT SYSTEMS CORPORATION*
7007 Preston Road, Dallas, 75205
Telephone: (214) LA1-0370

Officers
Robert L. McIntire, *President*
F. I. O'Dell, *Vice-President*
O. B. Lane, *Vice-President*

Coding Languages
Autocoder, COBOL, FORTRAN, S360 ALC, MAP and BAP, SPS, Easycoder, Tabsim, SOAP, BASIC, etc.

Services Available
Consultation, programming, software packages, systems analysis, data preparation batch and on-line data processing. Operate on a closed shop basis.

Fields of Application
Scientific and commercial systems design and programming, production control systems, data processing education, standards development and installation, management consulting.
Specialized areas: Payroll and cost distribution, production control systems, language compilers, generalized reporters, EDP audits, documentation standards installation, batch and on-line processing of medical, accounting and manufacturing data. Hospital and clinic systems, petroleum systems.

Training
System and programming documentation standards.

M.R.I. SYSTEMS CORPORATION*
12575 Research Blvd., Austin, 78758
Telephone: (512) 258-5171

Officers
Alfred A. King, *Chairman*
Robert L. Brueck, *President*

Contemplated Equipment
CDC 6000.

Services Available
Consulting, programming, software packages, systems analysis, education and training. Operate on an open shop, remote access, block time and time-sharing basis. Service not available for small-scale routine jobs.

Fields of Application
Commercial, management science, operational research, systems analysis, marketing planning information systems design, development and implementation, management information systems.
Specialized areas: Linear programming, computer modelling, real estate evaluation, marketing planning and strategy.

Training
Computer-oriented executive education programme; symposia on census data usage.

HUB S. RATLIFF*
Computer Systems Consultants
3600 W. Alabama, Houston, 77027
Telephone: (713) 622-1192

Officer
Hub S. Ratliff

Coding Languages
FORTRAN, COBOL, MAP, FAP, BASIC, Assembly, SOAP, SPS.

Services Available
Consultation, programming, software packages, systems analysis.

Fields of Application
Systems analysis, operations research, scientific and commercial systems and applications, information retrieval.
Specialized areas: Information retrieval, management information systems.

VIRGINIA

PRC COMPUTER CENTER, INC.
Planning Research Corporation
7670 Old Springhouse Road, McLean, 22101
Telephone: (703) 893-4880

Officer
J. D. Tupac, *President*

Computer Installation
IBM 360/65 (2)—internal storage: 512K bytes each.
IBM 370/155—internal storage: 1 million bytes; magnetic tapes: 27 2401-216 tape drives; magnetic discs: 6 2314; 4 line printers. *Remote processing features*: RJE with 2780, 1130, 2741, etc.

Coding Languages
Assembly, FORTRAN, COBOL, PL/1, ALGOL, SIMSCRIPT.

Services Available
Consultation, programming, software support, systems analysis. Operate on remote access, block time, time-sharing and closed shop basis.

Fields of Application
Systems analysis, operational research, management, scientific, commercial, accounting, traffic and transportation, simulation.

SAID INC.*
645 Oakley Avenue, Lynchburg, 24501
Telephone: (703) 845-8036

Also at:
1243 W. Broad Street, Falls Church, Virginia
Telephone: (703) 532-9190
5415 Patterson Avenue, Richmond, Virginia 23226
Telephone: (703) 532-9190
98 North Main Street, Keyser, West Virginia 26726
Telephone: (304) 788-2951
1717 York Road, Lutherville, Maryland 21093
Telephone: (301) 252-4810

Officer
R. O. Beach, *President*

Computer Installation
UNIVAC 9300—operating system: TOS; internal storage: 64K bits; magnetic tapes: 5; 1 line printer. *On-line satellite computer*: 9200. Remote processing features.

Contemplated Equipment
Univac 9400.

Services Available
Advice, preparation of data, programming, software packages, systems analysis, facilities management. Operate on a closed shop basis.

Fields of Application
Commercial, accounting, management.

WASHINGTON

ARCE CORPORATION*
N 4407 Division Street, Suite 801, Spokane, 99207
Telephone: (509) 489-1122

Officers
Manuel Th. Arce, *President*
John Cladwell, *Vice-President*
H. Halvorson, *Vice-President*

Coding Languages
FORTRAN IV, RPG, ALGOL, COBOL.

Services Available
Consultation, preparation of data, programming, software packages, systems analysis.

Fields of Application
Cost control, production control, systems statistical work, scientific and minor accounting.
Specialized areas: Cost control, productivity analysis, equipment control, cask flow for construction industry scheduling.

Training
Short courses in the general approach to construction control by computers, PERT, CPM, and Cost Analysis.

R. W. BECK AND ASSOCIATES*
200 Tower Building, Seattle, 98101
Telephone: (206) 622-5000

Officer
L. F. Mahoney

Computer Installation
IBM 1130–operating system: DMS; internal storage: 16K bits; magnetic discs: 1; 1 line printer. *Remote processing feature*: TWX.
IBM 1130–operating system: V2M7; internal storage: 16K bits; magnetic discs: 1; 1 line printer. *Remote processing feature*: TWX.

Coding Languages
Assembler, FORTRAN, RPG, COBOL.

Services Available
Consultation, programming, education and training, software packages, documentation, preparation of data, systems analysis. Operate on a self-service, open shop, block time, remote access and time-sharing basis.

Fields of Application
Scientific, statistical, commercial, accounting, process control, analysis, research, engineering.
Specialized areas: Engineering, scheduling, control computers.

Training
Seminars for business, industry and public agencies. Also hands-on training in the shop.

DATA CENTER INC.*
Room 306, 120 Sixth Avenue North, Seattle, 98109
Telephone: (206) MU2-8366

Officers
Edwin V. Hanson, *President and General Manager*
Alan C. Cline, *Vice-President*

Computer Installation
IBM 360/20–operating system: Tape Programming System; internal storage: 124K bits; magnetic tapes: 4 9-track; 1 line printer.

Coding Languages
RPG, BAL.

Services Available
Operators, preparation of data, programming, software packages, systems analysis. Operate on a self-service, open shop and block time basis.

Fields of Application
Statistical, commercial, production control, accounting, management.

DATA SYSTEMS CONSULTANTS*
1204 Old National Bank Building, Spokane, 99201
Telephone: (509) 747-0020

Officer
Earl H. Martinson, *Owner-Manager*

Services Available
Consultation, programming, education and training, documentation, systems analysis.

Fields of Application
Commercial, accounting, management, systems analysis.
Specialized areas: Government, industry, commerce, finance.

Training
Courses arranged for particular requirements. Short courses in input development, control development and use, operating requirements, project planning.

M. HARVEY SEGALL & ASSOCIATES*
1019 Rust Building, Tacoma, 98402
Telephone: (206) 383-4848

Officer
M. Harvey Segall, *President*

Services Available
Consultation, programming, education and training, software packages, documentation, systems analysis.

Fields of Application
Commercial, production control, accounting, management, systems analysis.

Training
Short courses in management and all data processing related subjects.

SERVICE BUREAUX

(In alphabetical order by State)

ALABAMA

CONTROL DATA CORPORATION*
Huntsville Center
7800 Governors Drive West, Huntsville, 35805
Telephone: (205) 837-0400
(*See* under Minnesota)

ELECTRONIC PROCESSORS INC.*
2101 Magnolia Avenue South, Suite 216, Birmingham, 35205
Telephone: 322-2551

Officers
Andy W. Rogers, *President*
R. L. Standridge, *Vice-President*

Computer Installation
BURROUGHS B3500–internal storage: 50K bits; magnetic tapes: 4; 1 line printer.

Coding Languages
Advanced Assembler, COBOL.

Services Available
Advice, operators, preparation of data, programming, software packages, systems analysis. Operate on an open shop basis.

Fields of Application
Statistical, commercial, production control, accounting, management, systems analysis, and operational research.
Specialized areas: Establishing master numbering system for central offices.

FIRST NATIONAL BANK OF MONTGOMERY*
8 Commerce Street, Montgomery, 36104
Telephone: 262-5711

Officers
James D. Pate, *Data Processing Manager*
Charles Jager, *Market Research*

United States of America – Service Bureaux

Computer Instalaltion
IBM 360/30–operating system: DOS; internal storage: 64K bits; magnetic tapes: 4 2400; magnetic discs: 4 2311; 2 line printers.

Coding Languages
BAL, COBOL.

Contemplated Equipment
IBM 360/30, teleprocessing.

Services Available
Preparation of data, programming, systems analysis. Operate on an open shop basis.

Fields of Application
Commercial, accounting.

GENERAL COMPUTER SERVICES, INC.
P.O. Box 5148, Huntsville, 35805
Telephone: (205) 539-9492

Coding Languages
COBOL, FORTRAN, PL/1, BASIC.

Services Available
Advice, programming, operators, software packages, documentation, preparation of data, systems analysis.

Fields of Application
Commercial, accounting, systems analysis, banking.

Training
Complete training supplied with all applications software offered.

GENERAL ELECTRIC COMPANY*
Information Service Department
2151 Highland Avenue, Room 214, Birmingham, 35202
Telephone: (205) 322-7683

McDILL CORPORATION
116 Catoma Street, P.O. Box 98, Montgomery, 36101
Telephone: (205) 262-6401

Officers
Ray B. McLure, *President*
Tom C. Cantey, Jr., *Vice-President and Secretary*
John N. Prim, *Vice-President (Marketing)*

Computer Installations
HONEYWELL H1250–internal stoage: 32K bits; magnetic tapes: 5; magnetic discs: 1. *Remote processing feature*: NCR 735-301.
NCR 420.

Coding Languages
COBOL, Easycoder, RPG.

Services Available
Advice, programming, operators, software packages, documentation, preparation of data, systems analysis.

Fields of Application
Statistical, commercial, production control, accounting, management, systems analysis.
Specialized areas: Sales analysis, analysis, payroll, medical research.

NATIONAL CASH REGISTER COMPANY*
Data Processing Center
1900 20th Avenue, South, Birmingham, 35209
Telephone: (205) 871-9611

Officer
R. R. Lower, *Manager*
(For details, *see* under Ohio)

SERVICE BUREAU CORPORATION*
2015 Highland Avenue, Birmingham, 35205
Telephone: (205) 322-5677
(*See* under New York)

SOUTHERN COMPUTER SERVICE*
P.O. Box 100, Dothan, 36301
Telephone: (205) 794-3166

Computer Installation
IBM 1440–internal storage: 16K bits; magnetic tapes; magnetic discs: 1 line printer.

Field of Application
Commercial.

ARIZONA

GENERAL ELECTRIC COMPANY*
Information Service Department
2725 North Central Avenue, Phoenix, 85004
Telephone: (602) 263-3229

GENERAL ELECTRIC COMPANY
Process Computer Department
2255 West Desert Cove Road, Phoenix, 85029
Telephone: (602) 943-2341

Officers
L. E. Bret, *General Manager*
C. G. O'Bryan, *Manager Customer Training*

Computer Installation
GE-PAC 4010–operating system: RTMOS; internal storage: 800K bits; magnetic discs: 4; 1 line printer. *On-line satellite computers*: GE-PAC 30. *Remote processing features*: remote CRT terminals.
GE-PAC 4020–operating systems: RTMOS; internal storage: 800K bits; magnetic tapes; magnetic discs: 4; 1 line printer. *On-line satellite computers*: GE-PAC 30. *Remote processing features*: remote analog scanner and CRT terminals.

Coding Languages
FORTRAN, PAL, BPL.

Services Available
Consultation, programming, education and training, software packages, documentation, systems analysis. In-house computing equipment available on fee basis in conjunction with system order. Services available to any industrial or power utility application.

Fields of Application
Manufacturing processes, industrial laboratory operations, transportation surveillance, electric power stations and distribution systems.

United States of America – Service Bureaux

Training
Short courses in programming, software analysis, software packages, computer equipment maintenance.

SERVICE BUREAU CORPORATION*
3136 N. Third Avenue, Phoenix, 85013
Telephone: (602) 274-3679
(*See* under New York)

SOUTHWEST COMPUTING SERVICE INC.*
635 W. Indian School Road, Suite 204, Phoenix, 85013
Telephone: (602) 264-0466

Officers
R. Glen Ryden, *President*
M. A. Goebel, *Vice President*

Services Available
Consultation, preparation of data, programming.

Field of Application
Engineering (civil, structural, highways).
Specialized area: Earthwork computations.

TRANSDATA CORPORATION*
4808 N. Central, Phoenix, 85012
Telephone: (602) 279-2301

Also at:
2030 E. Speedway, Suite 116, Tucson, 85719
Telephone: (602) 327-4554

Officer
William E. DeLair, *President*

Computer Installation
XDS Sigma 5–operating system: BPM/BTM; internal storage: 64K 32-bit words; magnetic tapes: 2; magnetic discs: 5 fixed head, 1 removeable medium; 1 line printer. *Remote processing features*: timesharing and remotely initiated batch via low speed terminals; high speed batch via DCT 2000.

Coding Languages
Extended BASIC, FORTRAN, COBOL 65, SYMBOL, METASYMBOL, MANAGE.

Contemplated Equipment
XDS Sigma 7.

Services Available
Consultation, programming, education and training, operators, software packages, documentation, preparation of data, systems analysis. Operate on a closed shop, block time, remote access and time-sharing basis.

Fields of Application
Scientific, statistical, commercial, accounting, management, systems analysis, education.
Specialized areas: Telecommunications, software and hardware systems design, consulting, applications programming, keypunching.

Training
Short programming course in BASIC.

UNIVAC DATA PROCESSING CENTER*
3443 North Central Avenue, Tucson, 85012
Telephone: (602) 264-9211
(*See* under California)

ARKANSAS

DATA-TRONICS CORPORATION*
310 Towson Avenue, Fort Smith, 72901
Telephone: (501) 782-8987

Officer
David E. Stubblefield, *President*

Computer Installation
IBM 360/40–operating system: DOS-QTAM; internal storage: 128K bits; magnetic tapes: 4 2401; magnetic discs: 2314; 1 line printer. *Remote processing features*: 2 2701 controls with 37-2740 Mod 2.
IBM 360/40–operating system: DOS; internal storage: 128K bits; magnetic tapes: 2 2415; magnetic discs: 2314; 1 line printer. *Remote processing features*: Mohawk Data Sciences 6403s.

Coding Languages
COBOL, BAL, QTAM.

Contemplated Equipment
IBM 2770's with MICR capability.

Services Available
Systems design, preparation of data, programming, education. Operate on an open shop, remote access and block time basis.

Fields of Application
Statistical, commercial, accounting, management, education.
Specialized areas: Order entry, revenue accounting and sales analysis, communications and billing, motor carrier reporting.

Training
Courses in programming, keypunch and data recording.

SYSTEMATICS INC.
411 Victory Street, Little Rock, 72201
Telephone: (501) 372-7158

Also at:
Locations throughout Arkansas

Officer
Walter V. Smiley, *President*

Computer Installation
IBM 360/30 (4)–operating system: DOS; internal storage: 96K bits each; magnetic tapes: 12 2401; magnetic discs: 10 2314; 4 line printers.

Coding Languages
COBOL, FORTRAN, RPG, PL/1, Autocoder, Assembler.

Services Available
Consultation, programming, education and training, operators, software packages, documentation, preparation of data, systems analysis. Operate on a block time and open shop basis.

Fields of Application
Statistical, commercial, production control, accounting, management, systems analysis.
Specialized areas: Sales analysis, investment, analysis, payroll.

Training
Courses run by the Systematics Institute.

CALIFORNIA

A.D.P. OF CALIFORNIA*
6505 Wilshire Boulevard, Los Angeles, 90048
Telephone: (213) 653-6230

Officer
E. H. Kramer

Computer Installation
IBM 360–operating system: DOS; internal storage: 32K bits; magnetic tapes: 3; magnetic discs: 3; 1 line printer.

Coding Languages
COBOL, RPG, BAL.

Services Available
Advice, preparation of data, software packages, systems analysis. Operate on a closed shop basis.

Fields of Application
Commercial, accounting, systems analysis.
Specialized area: Optical font.

ACCOUNTING CORPORATION OF AMERICA*
1929 First Avenue, San Diego, 92101
Telephone: (714) 232-6823

Also at:
39 Brighton Avenue, Boston, Massachusetts 02134
Telephone: (617) 254-7743
2222 West Olympic Boulevard, Los Angeles, California 90006
Telephone: (213) 387-6174

Officer
Nat Colker, *President*

ALLIED COMPUTER TECHNOLOGY INC.*
3112 Penn Avenue, Santa Monica, 90404
Telephone: (213) 828-7471

Officer
Mark J. McGrew, *Executive Vice-President*

Computer Installation
IBM System/3–internal storage: 12K bytes; magnetic discs: 1; 1 line printer.

Coding Languages
RPG, Assembler.

Services Available
Consultation, programming, education and training, operators, software packages, documentation, preparation of data, systems analysis. Operate on a self-service, open shop and block time basis.

Fields of Application
All business applications.

Training
RPE programming courses.

APPLIED CYBERNETICS CORPORATION*
1285 Forgewood, Sunny Vale, 94086
Telephone: (408) 734-1900

Officer
R. J. Destefanis, *Director*

Computer Installation
IBM 360/50–operating systems: OS, DOS; internal storage: 256K bits; magnetic tapes: 7; magnetic discs: 6 2311, 1 2314; 1 line printer. *Remote processing features*: RJE.

Coding Languages
COBOL, PL/1, Assembly.

Contemplated Equipment
IBM 360/30 with 1 million byte store and teleprocessing by 2701-2-3 or equivalent.

Services Available
Consultation, programming, education and training, operators, software packages, documentation, preparation of data, systems analysis. Operate on an open shop, block time and remote access basis.

Fields of Application
Complete range.
Specialized areas: Data processing, systems programming, management consulting.

BUSINESS DATA PROCESSING*
3760 State Street, Santa Barbara, 93105

Services Available
Advice, preparation of data, programming.

Field of Application
Commercial.
Specialized areas: Inventory, payroll, accounts receivable, sales analysis.

CAL-WESTERN DATA SYSTEMS, INC.
12345 Ventura Blvd., Suite X, Studio City, 91604
Telephone: (213) 980-3700

Officer
M. E. Knorr, *President*

Computer Installation
IBM 360/20–internal storage: 131,056 bits; magnetic discs: 2 2311; 1 line printer. *Other processing features*: paper tape reader IBM 3903, Card MFLM IBM 2560.

Coding Languages
BAL, RPG.

Services Available
Advice, programming, software packages. Operate on a closed shop basis. Available to licensed accountants only. Customers must have P.A. or C.P.A. certificate and be engaged in public accounting.

Field of Application
Accounting.
Specialized area: Financial statements.

CENTUREX CORPORATION
Suite 1100, 5959 West Century Boulevard, Los Angeles, 90045

Officers
Howard Lester, *President*
Jack Crane, *Vice-President for Finance*
Ron Wilson, *Vice-President for Facilities Management Marketing*
Robert Grant, *Vice-President for Systems Sales*

Computer Installation
IBM 360/30 (2)–operating system: DOS; internal storage: 65K bits; magnetic tapes: 4 2401; magnetic discs: 4 2311, 1 2314; 1 line printer.
IBM 370/135–operating system: DOS/OS; internal storage: 96K bits; magnetic tapes: 3 3411-3; magnetic discs: 4 2319-A1; 1 line printer.

Coding Languages
BAL, COBOL.

Services Available
Programming, software packages, systems analysis, facilities management. Operate on a self-service basis.

Field of Application
Commercial.
Specialized area: Banking.

Training
Courses for users of software packages.

CIMSCO DATA PROCESSING COMPANY*
5600 Paramount Boulevard, Long Beach, 90805
Telephone: (213) 634-0606

Officer
Marc A. Frederick, *President*

Computer Installation
IBM 360/20–operating system: OS 360; internal storage: 16K bits; magnetic discs: 2; 1 line printer.
UNIVAC 9300–internal storage: 32K bits; magnetic tapes: 4; magnetic discs: 3. *On-line satellite computer*: 1.

Coding Languages
Assembler, COBOL, FORTRAN IV, RPG.

Services Available
Advice, preparation of data, programming, software packages, systems analysis. Operate on a closed shop and block time basis.

Fields of Application
Mainly commercial, accounting and management.

C.M.I. COMPUTER MICROGRAPHICS, INC.
5345 W. 102nd Street, Los Angeles, 90015
Telephone: (213) 776-6820

Officer
David S. Shanks, *President*

Computer Installation
III FR80–internal storage: 148K bits.
DATAGRAPHIX 4460–internal storage: 148K bits.
GOULD BETACOM 700–internal storage: 192K bits.

Services Available
Advice, programming, education and training, software packages, systems analysis, magtape to microfilm conversion. Operate on an open shop basis.

Fields of Application
Scientific, statistical, commercial, production control, accounting, management, systems analysis, operational research.

COMPUTER MICROFILM SYSTEMS INC.*
1310 Air Way, Glendale, 91201
Telephone: (213) 245-5119

Officers
C. J. Taylor, *President*
Bruce E. Thyden, *Vice-President of Operations*

Computer Installation
IBM 360/30–operating system: DOS; internal storage: 65K; magnetic tapes: 5 2401; magnetic discs: 4 2311; 1 line printer.

Coding Languages
COBOL, RPG, Autocoder, BAL.

Services Available
Programming, operators, software packages, documentation, preparation of data, systems analysis. Operate on a self-servece, closed shop and remote access basis. No scientific services available.

Fields of Application
Commercial, accounting, production control, logistics documentation, manufacturing management, etc.
Specialized areas: Technical documentation and logistics support.

COMPUTER SCIENCES CORPORATION
650 North Sepu Iveda Boulevard, El Segundo, 90245
Telephone: (213) 678-0311

Also at:
Huntsville, Alabama, San Diego and San Francisco, California, New York, Washington, D.C., Falls Church, Virginia, Chicago, Illinois, Richland, Washington, Silver Spring, Maryland.

Officers
William R. Hoover, *President*
Roy Nutt, *Vice-President*

Coding Languages
FORTRAN, COBOL, ALGOL, PL/1, JOVIAL, SYMPL, BAL, GENESIS, and others.

Services Available
Requirements analysis, programming, consultation, software packages, network time-sharing services.

Fields of Application
Scientific, commercial, process control, management.
Specialized areas: Military and aerospace systems, data acquisition, information storage and retrieval, real time and on-line applications, command-and-control, intelligence, satellite and terrestrial communications, design and development of total software systems for computer manufacturers, including operating systems, compilers, assemblers and related systems software.

CONTROL DATA CORPORATION*
3330 Hillview Avenue, Palo Alto, 94304
Telephone: 321-8920

Officer
M. E. Hetherington, *Center Manager*

Computer Installation
CDC 6613–internal storage: 131K 60-bit words; magnetic tapes: 10 607 units; magnetic discs: 1 6638, 4 854; 3 line printers. *Remote processing features*: 2 16-201B data sets.
CDC 160–internal storage: 32K 12-bit words; magnetic tapes: 3; 2 line printers. *Remote processing features*: 1 wide band, 1 201 data set.

Coding Languages
FTN, COBOL, APT, Simscript, Compuss.

United States of America – Service Bureaux

Services Available
Consultation, operators, software packages, documentation preparation of data, systems analysis. Operate on a closed shop, remote access and block time basis.

Fields of Application
Scientific, statistical, commercial, production control, accounting, management, systems analysis, operational research, etc.
Specialized areas: Scientific, commercial.

COOPER COMPUTER SERVICES*
14003 Ventura Boulevard, Sherman Oaks, 91403
Telephone: (213) 981-5100

Officer
Leon Cooper, *President*

Computer Installation
IBM 360/20—internal storage: 4K bits; 1 line printer.

Contemplated Equipment
Increased store, 1 2311 disc drive, CDC 200 terminal.

Services Available
Consultation, programming, operators, software packages, documentation, preparation of data, systems analysis. Operate on an open shop basis.

Fields of Application
Accounting, management, systems analysis, inventory management.
Specialized areas: Life insurance production and accounting systems.

DATA CORPORATION
1111 West 6th Street, Los Angeles, 90017
Telephone: (213) 482-1300

Officers
E. Hobbs, *President*
R. G. Elzinga, *General Manager*

Computer Installation
IBM 360/30—operating system: DOS; internal storage: 768K bits; magnetic tapes: 6 9-track, 1 7-track; magnetic discs: 5 2314; 1 line printer.

Coding Languages
COBOL, BAL, ADPAC.

Contemplated Equipment
IBM 360/40 with 128K-bit storage.

Services Available
Programming, software packages, preparation of data, systems analysis. Operate on a closed shop and block-time basis.

Field of Application
Sale of packaged insurance services.

DIVERSIFIED COMPUTER APPLICATIONS
2525 E. Bayshore Road, Palo Alto, 94303
Telephone: (415) 324-2523

Officers
S. Kalt, *President*
J. M. Lantz, *Vice-President*

Computer Installation
BURROUGHS B3500—operating system: MCP; internal storage: 720K bits; magnetic tapes: 4; magnetic discs: 4; 1 line printer. *Remote processing features*: 4 lines.
BURROUGHS B2500—operating system: MCP; internal storage: 720K bits; magnetic tapes: 2; magnetic discs: 3; 1 line printer.
BURROUGHS B3500—operating system: MCP; internal storage: 960K bits; magnetic tapes: 7; 2 line printers.
BURROUGHS B300—operating system: MCP; internal storage: 120K bits; magnetic tapes: 4; 1 line printer.

Coding Language
COBOL.

Services Available
Programming, operators, software packages, data preparation, systems analysis. Operate on an open shop basis.

Fields of Application
Commercial, production control, accounting, management, systems analysis.
Specialized areas: Sales analysis, payroll, hospital statistics.

ELECTRONIC ASSOCIATES INC.*
Analysis and Computation Centers
1500 East Imperial Highway, El Segundo, 90245
Telephone: (213) 322-3220

Also at:
4151 Middlefield Road, Palo Alto, California 94303
Telephone: (415) 321-0363
12260 Wilkins Avenue, Rockville, Maryland 2085
Telephone: (301) 933-4100
U.S. Route No. 1, P.O. Box 582, Princeton, New Jersey 08541
Telephone: (609) 452-2900

Officers
Donald Darms, *Director of Computer Center (El Segundo)*
T. C. Sammons, *Manager, Customer Services (El Segundo)*
J. Brue Mawson, *Director of Computer Center (Rockville)*

Computer Installation
El Segundo:
EAI Hybrid—internal storage: 32K bits; magnetic tapes: 4; 2 line printers.

Rockville:
EAI 690 Hybrid—operating systems: COS, TOS; internal storage: 16K bits; 1 line printer. *On-line satellite computers*: EAI 680 (Analog) and EAI 693 (Hybrid).

Coding Languages
FORTRAN, EAI Assembly, HYTRAN Operations Interpreter.

Contemplated Equipment
Disc operating system (Rockville).

Services Available
Advice, operators, preparation of data, programming, software packages, systems analysis. Operate on a self-service, open shop and block time basis.

Fields of Application
Scientific, commercial, operational research.
Specialized areas: Simulation (El Segundo); Hybrid studies of aerospace vehicles (Rockville).

United States of America – Service Bureaux

Training
Short courses in analog computation, hybrid computation, digital computation (1 week each). All types of service courses.

ELECTRONIC BUSINESS SERVICE*
219 N. Encina Street, Visalia, 93277

Officer
John C. Crawford, *Manager*
Telephone: (209) 732-8601

Computer Installation
IBM 360—internal storage: 16K bits; magnetic tapes: 6 2415; magnetic discs: 2; 1 line printer.

Coding Languages
BAL, RPG.

Services Available
Preparation of data, programming, systems analysis. Operate on an open shop basis.

Field of Application
Commercial.
Specialized area: Accounts receivable, accounts payable, payroll, etc.

GENERAL ELECTRIC COMPANY*
Information Service Department
2118 Milvia Street, Berkeley, 94704
Telephone: (415) 848-8390

GENERAL ELECTRIC COMPANY*
Information Service Department
9550 Flair Drive, Suite 504, El Monte, 91731
Telephone: (213) 579-0322

GENERAL ELECTRIC COMPANY*
Information Service Department
3605 Long Beach Boulevard, Suite 333, Long Beach, 90807
Telephone: (213) 426-9345

GENERAL ELECTRIC COMPANY*
Information Service Department
3550 Wilshire Boulevard, Suite 1410, Los Angeles, 90005
Telephone: (213) 385-9411

GENERAL ELECTRIC COMPANY*
Information Service Department
1120 San Antonio Road, Palo Alto, 94301
Telephone: (415) 969-3772

GENERAL ELECTRIC COMPANY*
Information Service Department
18040 Sherman Way, Reseda, 91335
Telephone: (213) 881-1602

GENERAL ELECTRIC COMPANY*
Information Service Department
P.O. Box 1677, 2407 "J" Street, Sacramento, 95808
Telephone: (916) 442-3696

GENERAL ELECTRIC COMPANY*
Information Service Department
2560 First Avenue, Suite 110, San Diego, 92103
Telephone: (714) 232-7167

GENERAL ELECTRIC COMPANY*
Information Service Department
425 California Street, San Francisco, 94104
Telephone: (415) 989-1100

GENERAL ELECTRIC COMPANY*
Information Service Department
812 Anacapa Street, Suite 5, Santa Barbara, 93101
Telephone: (805) 963-7796

GENERAL RESEARCH CORPORATION
5383 Hollister Avenue, Santa Barbara, 93111
Telephone: (805) 964-7724

Officer
T. C. Bazemore, *President*

Computer Installation
CDC 6400—operating system: Goleta; internal storage: 5,898,240 bits; magnetic tapes: 5 604; magnetic discs: 2 6603; 2 line printers. *Remote processing features*: RJE, interactive.

Coding Languages
FORTRAN, COBOL, COMPASS.

Services Available
Programming, data preparation, systems analysis. Operate on a remote access and open shop basis.

Fields of Application
Scientific, commercial, systems analysis.

HELM DATA PROCESSING INC.
1190 Eighth Street, P.O. Box 147, Arcata, 95521
Telephone: (707) 822-0386

Officer
Robert R. Helm, *President*

Computer Installation
BURROUGHS B500—operating system: MCP II; internal storage: 115,200 bits; magnetic tapes: 3; magnetic discs: 1; 1 line printer.

Coding Languages
COBOL, Burroughs Advanced Assembler.

Services Available
Advice, preparation of data, programming, systems analysis. Operate on an open shop and block time basis.

Fields of Application
Commercial, statistical, production control.
Specialized area: Forest products industry applications.

INFORMATICS INC.
21050 Vanowen Street, Canoga Park, 91303
Telephone: (213) 887-9121

Also at:
River Edge, New Jersey, Rome, New York, Los Angeles, Palo Alto and San Francisco, California, Omaha, Nebraska, Chicago, Illinois, Rockville, Maryland, Olympia, Washington, Honolulu, Hawaii.
and at: Geneva, Switzerland, and Tokyo, Japan.

Officers
Dr. W. F. Bauer, *President and Chairman*
F. V. Wagner, *Executive Vice-President*
R. E. Kaylor, *Executive Vice-President*
A. S. Kaplan, *Vice-President and Treasurer*

Services Available
Programming, software packages, documentation, data preparation, systems analysis.

Fields of Application
Scientific, commercial, production control, accounting, management, systems analysis, operational research.
Specialized areas: Investment analysis, payroll, medical research, message switching, data base services.

Training
Annual symposium on data processing applications; customer classes for MARK IV users.

METACOMPUTER SCIENCES INC.*
17791 Sky Park Circle, Irvine, 92664
Telephone: (714) 557-6767

Officer
Willis Marsing, *Executive Vice-President*

Computer Installation
IBM 360/40–operating system: DOS 21; internal storage: 256K bits; magnetic tapes: 5 9-track, 1 7-track; magnetic discs: 3 2311, 4 2314; 1 line printer.
VARIAN 5201/6201–operating system: 620 MOS; internal storage: 16K bits; magnetic tapes: 2 9-track; magnetic discs: 1 EDP. *Remote processing features*: 64 terminal capacity.

Service Available
Preparation of data.

Field of Application
IBM 2680 photocomposition.

MILNER BROTHERS PRODUCTS
8000 Blackburn Avenue, Los Angeles, 90048

Officer
Arnold Milner

Computer Installation
IBM 1401–internal storage: 4K bits; 1 line printer.
IBM 360/30–internal storage: 64K bits; magnetic tapes: 4; magnetic discs: 2; 1 line printer.

Services Available
Consultation, programming, education and training, operators, software packages, documentation, preparation of data, systems analysis.

Fields of Application
Scientific, statistical, commercial, production control, accounting, management, systems analysis, operational research etc.

Training
General programming, operating and systems courses.

NATIONAL CASH REGISTER COMPANY*
Data Processing Center
3348 West El Segundo Boulevard, Hawthorne, 90250
Telephone: (213) 777-7372

Officer
H. R. Intemann, *Manager*

Also at:
9 Peter Yorke Way, San Francisco, 94109
Telephone: (415) 771-1141

Officer
C. E. Chapman, *Manager*
(For details, *see* under Ohio)

PROGRAMMATICS INC.
11661 San Vicente Boulevard, Los Angeles, 90049
Telephone: (213) 826-6503

Officer
David E. Ferguson, *President*

Coding Languages
FORTRAN, COBOL, PL/1, Assembly.

Services Available
Programming, software packages, systems analysis.

Fields of Application
Software systems (e.g. compilers, assemblers, operating systems), scientific applications, commercial applications.
Specialized areas: Assemblers and meta-assemblers, compilers and meta-compilers, operating systems.

RECORDING & STATISTICAL COMPANY*
447 Battery Street, San Francisco, 94111
Telephone: (415) 981-7011
(*See* under New York)

REMOTE COMPUTING CORPORATION
One Wilshire Building, Suite 1400, Los Angeles, 90017
Telephone: (213) 629-2532

Officer
Charles Calderaro, *President*

Computer Installation
BURROUGHS B5700 (4)–operating system: modified TSS/MCP; internal storage: 32K 48-bit words (each); magnetic tapes: 6 7-track (each); magnetic discs; 1 line printer (each). *On-line satellite computer*: Interdata 50. *Remote processing features*: Time-sharing.

Coding Languages
FORTRAN, COBOL, ALGOL, BASIC.

Contemplated Equipment
Burroughs B6700.

Services Available
Advice, programming, education and training, software packages, documentation, systems analysis, time sharing. Operate on a remote access and time-sharing basis.

Fields of Application
Scientific, statistical, commercial, accounting, management, systems analysis, operational research.
Specialized areas: Sales analysis, linear programming, investment, structural engineering.

Training
Three-day introductory course on BASIC; Programming Languages and Techniques (½ day), Foresight I (½ day).

United States of America – Service Bureaux

SERVICE BUREAU CORPORATION
5151 West Imperial Highway, Inglewood, 90304
Telephone: (213) 776-5900

Also at:
2450 Watson Court, Palo Alto, 94303
Telephone: (415) 327-0500
3730 Fifth Avenue, San Diego, 92103
Telephone: (714) 298-8241
1 Maritime Plaza, San Francisco, 94111
Telephone: (415) 982-3441
111 West St. John Street, San Jose, 95113
Telephone: (408) 286-9100
(*See* under New York)

SOFTWARE RESOURCES CORPORATION*
6399 Wilshire Boulevard, Los Angeles, 90048
Telephone: 653-2704

Officers
R. V. Head, *President*
D. C. Nigro, *Vice-President*

Coding Languages
COBOL, FORTRAN, Assembler.

Services Available
Software packages, consultation.

Fields of Application
Systems programming, commercial applications.
Specialized area: Banking systems.

SUPERIOR DATA PROCESSING SERVICE*
5429 East Beverly Boulevard, Los Angeles, 90022
Telephone: (213) 685-5470

Computer Installation
IBM 1401 (on premises).
IBM 360/30 (off premises).

Services Available
Advice, preparation of data, programming, systems analysis.

Fields of Application
All commercial applications.

SYSTEMS DATA PROCESSING CORPORATION
701 Howe Avenue, Sacramento, 95825
Telephone: (916) 927-5371

Officers
R. W. Johnson, *President*
R. H. Stranford, *Vice-President, Sales*
M. L. Shoemaker, *Vice-President, Operations*

Computer Installation
NCR Century 200–operating system: DOS; internal storage: 32K bits; magnetic tapes: 2; magnetic discs: 2; 1 line printer.
BURROUGHS B260–internal storage: 4,800 bits; 1 line printer.

Coding Languages
COBOL, SPS.

Services Available
Programming, data preparation, systems analysis. Operate on an open shop basis.

Fields of Application
Commercial, accounting, management.
Specialized areas: Sales analysis, payroll, accounts received, accounts payable, inventory.

TABULATING CONSULTANTS INC.
1011 West Alameda Avenue, Burbank, 91506
Telephone: 843-3043, 849-7264

Computer Installation
RCA Spectra 70/35–internal storage: 64K bits; magnetic tapes: 6; magnetic discs: 2 2311; 1 line printer.
NCR Century 200 (2)–operating systems: B1, B2; internal storage: 64K bits each; magnetic tapes: 6; magnetic discs: 12 657; 2 line printers each.

Coding Languages
COBOL, BAL, NEAT/3.

Contemplated Equipment
NCR Century 300 (2) with 24 657 discs and 12 NRL tapes.

Services Available
Programming, operators, documentation, data preparation, systems analysis. Operate on a closed shop basis. No one-time jobs and no prime defence contracts.

Fields of Application
Statistical, commercial, production control, accounting, management, systems analysis, operational research.
Specialized areas: Negotiated employee benefit plans, subscription fulfilment applications, list maintenance functions.

TECHNICAL COMPUTING CENTER*
515 Market Street, San Francisco, 94105
Telephone: (415) 362-2375

Computer Installation
IBM 360/30–internal storage: 65K bits; magnetic tapes: 2; magnetic discs: 2; 1 line printer.

Services Available
Advice, preparation of data, programming.

Fields of Application
Engineering, commercial.

TRI-DEX DATA SERVICES
2146 E. Main Street, Visalia, 93277
Telephone: (209) 732-7415

Officer
K. B. Howard, *Owner*

Coding Language
COBOL.

Services Available
Consultation, programming, education and training, software packages, documentation, preparation of data, systems analysis. Operate on a remote access and time-sharing basis.

Fields of Application
Commercial, production control, accounting, management.
Specialized areas: Programming for large machines used on interactive basis for time-shared and remote-batch service.

TYMSHARE INC.
10340 Bubb Road, Cupertino, 95014
Telephone: (408) 257-6550

Officers
T. J. O'Rourke, *President*
A. R. Heintz, *Vice-President*
E. J. Field, *Treasurer*

Computer Installation
XDS 940–operating system: Tymshare; internal storage: 64K 24-bit words. *On-line satellite computer*: 104 (Tymshare designed). *Remote processing features*: Interactive time-sharing.
PDP-10–operating system: Tymshare modified. *On-line satellite computer*: 104. *Remote processing features*: Interactive time-sharing and RJE.

Coding Languages
FORTRAN, SUPER BASIC, COBOL, EDITOR and several hundred application programmes.

Contemplated Equipment
IBM 370/158.

Services Available
Programming, computer services. Operate on a remote access and time-sharing basis.

Fields of Application
Scientific, statistical, commercial, production control, management, systems analysis, operational research, marketing.
Specialized areas: Sales analysis, linear programming, investment analysis, structural engineering.

URS DATA SCIENCES COMPANY*
155 Bovet Road, San Mateo, 94402
Telephone: (415) 574-5000

Also at:
7245 Arlington Boulevard, Falls Church, Virginia 22042
Telephone: (703) 532-5500

Officers
William Plette, *President, San Mateo Data Center*
Richard Jensky, *General Manager, San Mateo Data Center*

Computer Installation
UNIVAC 9300–operating system: TOS; internal storage: 32K bits; magnetic tapes: 8; magnetic discs: 4 8410; 1 line printer.
UNIVAC 9400–operating systems: TOS, DOS; internal storage: 65K bits; magnetic tapes: 5; magnetic discs: 4 8411; 1 line printer.

Services Available
Consultation, programming education and training, operators, software packages, documentation, preparation of data, systems analysis. Operate on a self-service and remote access basis. Available to commercial and government contractors.

Fields of Application
Commercial, systems analysis, operational research, accounting management, systems design, logistics systems.
Specialized areas: Conversion, medical information systems, transportation and maintenance information systems, inventory management, programming support services.

UNIVAC DATA PROCESSING CENTERS*
2520 West Sixth Street, Los Angeles, 90057
Telephone: (213) 381-7821

Also at:
3443 N. Central Avenue, Tucson, Arizona 85012
Telephone: (602) 264-9211
612 Howard Street, San Francisco, California 94105
Telephone: (415) 781-7388
1038 Bannock Street, Denver, Colorado 80204
Telephone: (303) 255-0447
1776 Peachtree Road, N.W. Atlanta, Georgia 30309
Telephone: (404) 874-4493
444 N. Michigan Avenue, Chicago, Illinois 60611
Telephone: (312) 527-3000
818 Roeder Road, Silver Spring, Maryland 20910
Telephone: (301) 587-3210
Wellesley Office Park, William Street, Wellesley, Massachusetts 02181
Telephone: (617) 237-1515
2978 West Grand Boulevard, Detroit, Michigan 48202
Telephone: (313) 874-3000
3300 University Avenue, S.E. Minneapolis, Minnesota 55414
Telephone: (612) 335-6487
1901 Baltimore, Kansas City, Missouri 64108
Telephone: (816) 471-0477
531 Delaware Avenue, Buffalo, New York 14202
Telephone: (716) 882-2171
60 Herricks Road, Mineola, Long Island 11501
Telephone: (516) 248-5544
1290 Avenue of the Americas, New York, New York 10019
Telephone: (212) 956-3378
3645 Warrensville Center Road, Cleveland, Ohio 44122
Telephone: (216) 752-7000
1303 S.W. 16th Avenue, Portland, Oregon 97207
Telephone: (503) 226-3541
1624 Locust Street, Philadelphia, Pennsylvania 19103
Telephone: (215) 546-5300
Stanwix at 4th Avenue, Pittsburgh, Pennsylvania 15222
Telephone: (412) 391-2000
3311 Richmond Avenue, Houston, Texas 77006
Telephone: (713) 528-2881

Officers
D. B. Hunt, *Branch Manager (Los Angeles)*
C. A. Kinkel, *Manager of Computer Operations (Los Angeles)*

Computer Installation
UNIVAC 1004.
UNIVAC 1107.
UNIVAC 1108.
UNIVAC 9300.

Coding Languages
FORTRAN, COBOL, SALT.

Services Available
Advice, operators, preparation of data, programming, software packages, systems analysis, on-line computing.

Fields of Application
Commercial and scientific applications.
Specialized areas: Numerical control, accounting, payroll and inventory applications.

UNIVERSITY COMPUTING COMPANY*
Computer Utilities Group
888 North Sepulveda Boulevard, El Segundo, 90245
Telephone: (213) 322-3093

Also at:
1740 Stanford Street, P.O. Box 655, Santa Monica, California 90406
Data-Link Group, Los Angeles, California
(*See* under Texas)

VALLEY COMPUTER CENTER*
8155 Van Nuys Boulevard, Suite 950, Panorama City, 91402
Telephone: 781-6000

Officer
Alan C. Cline, *Manager*

Computer Installation
IBM 360/30—operating system: DOS; internal storage: 65K bits; magnetic tapes: 6 2401; magnetic discs: 3 2311; 2 line printers.

IBM 360/40—operating systems: DOS, OS-MFP; internal storage: 198K bits; magnetic tapes: 7 2401; magnetic discs: 4 2314. *Remote processing features*: 32 IBM 2260.

Contemplated Equipment
IBM 360/40—internal storage: 256K bits; 2321s and additional 2260s.

Services Available
Consultation, programming, operators, software packages, documentation, preparation of data, systems analysis. Operate on a self-service, block time and remote access basis.

Fields of Application
Commercial, production control, accounting, systems analysis.
Specialized areas: Facilities management, on-line systems.

WOLF AND COMPANY*
1545 Wilshire Boulevard, Los Angeles, 90017

Also at:
Other principal cities of the U.S.A.

Officer
E. H. Kramer

Computer Installation
IBM 360/30—internal storage: 65K bits; magnetic tapes: 5; magnetic discs: 3; 1 line printer.

Services Available
Consultation, education and training, software packages, preparation of data, systems analysis. Operate on an open shop basis.

Fields of Application
Commercial, accounting, management, systems analysis.
Specialized area: Accounting.

Officers
Richard L. Subry, *President*
J. Stever Ott, *Executive Vice-President*
Charles A. Atler, *Vice-President and Treasurer*
Fred A. Nagel, *Vice-President and Secretary*

Computer Installation
HONEYWELL H120—internal storage: 24K bits; magnetic tapes: 4; 1 line printer.
IBM 360/30—operating systems: TOS, DOS; internal storage: 16K bits; magnetic tapes: 4; magnetic discs: 2; 1 line printer.

Coding Languages
Assembler, Easycoder, BAL, FORTRAN, COBOL.

Services Available
Consultation, operators, preparation of data, programming, software packages, systems analysis. Operate on an open shop and block time basis.

Fields of Application
Commercial, banking, statistical, investment accounting, engineering, research and development.
Specialized areas: Banking, investment accounting, engineering — highway, civil, mining, geological.

Training
Computer operator, computer programmer, unit record operator, critical path methods, management seminars, in house training. Short courses in CPM, linear programming, management systems, management training.

COMPUTE AMERICA CORPORATION (COMERICA)*
1038 Bannock Street, Denver, 80204
Telephone: (303) 255-0447

Also at:
1515 Classen Boulevard, Oklahoma City, Oklahoma 73106

Officers
Richard M. Deaton, *Executive Vice-President*
John W. Cormack, *Director of Personnel*

Computer Installation
UNIVAC 9300—operating systems: NCOS, COS; internal storage: 288K; magnetic tapes: 6 Uniservo IV; 1 line printer.
UNIVAC 1004—operating systems: EXEC; internal storage: 6,608 bits; magnetic tapes: 2 Uniservo IV; 1 line printer. *On-line satellite computers*: Univac 1108.

Coding Languages
RPG, COBOL, Assembler, FORTRAN.

Services Available
Programming, operators, documentation, preparation of data, systems analysis. Operate on a closed shop and block time basis.

Fields of Application
Scientific, statistical, commercial, production control, accounting, management and systems analysis.

COLORADO

AUTO-TRONIX UNIVERSAL CORPORATION*
44 Sherman Street, Denver, 80203
Telephone: (303) 744-3381

GENERAL ELECTRIC COMPANY*
Information Service Department
201 University Boulevard, Denver, 80201
Telephone: (303) 388-5751

United States of America — Service Bureaux

JEFFERSON COUNTY BANK OF LAKEWOOD*
7590 West Colfax Avenue, Lakewood, 80215
Telephone: (303) 233-6561

Officer
Owen E. Thomas, *Manager of Data Processing*

Computer Installation
NCR 315/100–internal storage: 120K bits; magnetic tapes: 5 NCR 334; 1 line printer.

Coding Languages
NCR, NEAT, some COBOL.

Services Available
Advice, programming, software packages, systems analysis. Operate on a self-service and open shop basis.

Fields of Application
General financial and business data processing.
Specialized areas: Internal banking operations, outside billing and accounts receivable.

KAMAN SCIENCES CORPORATION
1500 Garden of the Gods Road, Colorado Springs, 80907
Telephone: (303) 598-5880

Officers
Dr. A. P. Bridges, *President*
R. E. W. Smith, *Vice-President; Director, Computing Center*

Computer Installation
CDC Cyber 72/14 and 73/14–operating system: SCOPE; internal storage: 65,536 60-bit words each; magnetic tapes: 7 607; magnetic discs: 2 841/4; 2 line printers. *On-line satellite computer*: PDP-8/E. *Remote processing features*: CDC, DEC and others.
BURROUGHS B344 (MICR processing only)–operating systems: Special Bank Processing, KSC; internal storage: 16K words; magnetic tapes: 2; 1 line printer.

Coding Languages
FORTRAN, COBOL, COMPASS, PERT.

Contemplated Equipment
Up-grading of peripherals on the twin CDC Cybers; more PDP-8/E minicomputers and additional CDC 200 User Terminals and 731 Minicomputers.

Services Available
Advice, programming, operators, software packages, documentation, data preparation, systems analysis, nation-wide remote terminals and complete information processing centre. Operate on a remote access, closed shop and block time basis.

Fields of Application
Scientific, statistical, commercial, accounting, management, systems analysis, operational research, specialized radio and TV traffic-accounting software and services.
Specialized areas: Sales analysis, linear programming, investment analysis, payroll, information processing for secondary schools and school administration.

Training
Training provided to all customers on all systems operational and used at the Computing Center.

MCDONNELL AUTOMATION CO.*
360 Western Federal Building, Denver, 80202
Telephone: (303) 534-6291

(*See* under Missouri)

NATIONAL CASH REGISTER COMPANY*
Data Processing Center
1455 Champa Street, Denver, 80202
Telephone: (303) 244-4408

Officer
R. J. Prestin, *Manager*

(For details, *see* under Ohio)

SCIENTIFIC SOFTWARE CORPORATION*
5300 S. Ulster, Englewood, 80110

Officer
Dr. Allen Breitenbach, *President*

Computer Installation
BURROUGHS B5500–operating system: MCP; internal storage: 32K words; magnetic tapes: 5 B426; magnetic discs: 2 B475; 1 line printer. *On-line satellite computer*: TC-500. *Remote processing features*: TC-500 teletype.

Coding Languages
ALGOL, COBOL, FORTRAN, PL/1, BASIC.

Contemplated Equipment
BURROUGHS B6500.

Services Available
Consultation, programming, operators, software packages, preparation of data, systems analysis. Operate on a closed shop and block time basis.

Fields of Application
Scientific, commercial, operations research, proprietary software.
Specialized areas: Large scale complex systems for oil, gas and mining industries, education and economic planning systems; mutual fund accounting systems; operational research.

SERVICE BUREAU CORPORATION*
7826 East Prentice Avenue, Denver, 80222
Telephone: (303) 771-5510

(*See* under New York)

UNIVAC DATA PROCESSING CENTER*
1038 Bannock Street, Denver, 80204
Telephone: (303) 255-0447
(*See* under California)

CONNECTICUT

APPLIED DATA PROCESSING INC.*
155 Whitney Avenue, New Haven, 06510
Telephone: 787-4107

Officers
David W. Chaffin, *President*
Robert S. Seelig, *Vice-President Sales*
F. Kells-Murphy, *Vice-President Operations*
Elmer E. Barth, *Treasurer*

Computer Installation
IBM 360/20–internal storage: 16K bits; magnetic tapes: 4; 1 line printer.

Coding Languages
RPG, BAL.

Contemplated Equipment
UNIVAC 9300 with 32K-bit store and 5 tape units.

Services Available
Advice, operators, preparation of data, programming. Operate on a closed shop basis.

Fields of Application
Commercial of all types.

COMPUTER SYSTEMS AND EDUCATION CORPORATION*
111 Ash Street, East Hartford, 06108
Telephone: 528-9216

Officer
D. S. Shefrin, *President*

Computer Installation
IBM 360–operating system: DOS; internal storage: 32K bits; magnetic tapes: 3 2400; magnetic discs: 2 2311; 1 line printer.

Coding Languages
COBOL, BAL.

Contemplated Equipment
IBM 360/40.

Services Available
Advice, operators, preparation of data, programming, software packages, systems analysis. Operate on a closed shop basis.

Fields of Application
Scientific, statistical, commercial, production control, accounting, management, systems analysis.

Training
800-hour programmer training.

COMPUTER USAGE CORPORATION*
Corporate Headquarters
100 Putnam Green, Greenwich, 06830
Telephone: (203) 661-4100

Also at:
Presidential Park Suite 123, 3781 N.E. Expressway, Atlanta, Georgia 30040
Telephone: (404) 451-4643
22 West Road, Towson, Baltimore, Maryland, 21204
Telephone: (301) 823-1300
387 Elliot Street, Newton Upper Falls, Massachusetts, 02164
Telephone: (617) 969-4000
600 So. Michigan Avenue, Chicago, Illinois
Telephone: (312) 427-1404
30233 Southfield Road, Southfield, Michigan, 48075
Telephone: (313) 647-8313
454 Gulf Life Tower, Jacksonville, Florida, 32207
Telephone: (904) 396-2225
8939 South Sepulveda Blvd., Los Angeles, California, 90045
Telephone: (213) 670-7246
655 Madison Avenue, New York City, New York, 10021
Telephone: (212) 752-5900
3181 Porter Drive, Palo Alto, California, 94304
Telephone: (415) 321-6754

Barclay Bldg., City Line & Belmont Avenues, Bala-Cynwyd, Pennsylvania, 19004
Telephone: (215) 839-4185
7315 Wisconsin Avenue, N.W., Washington, D.C., 20014
Telephone: (301) 656-0200

Officers
Cuthbert C. Hurd, *Chairman of the Board*
Victor E. Bartoletti, *President and Chief Executive Officer*

Computer Installation
Computer Usage Development Corporation, New York:
IBM 360/40–operating systems: DOS, OS/360 PCP and MFT-II, BPS, BOS, COS; internal storage: 128K bits; magnetic tapes: 2400 series (4 9-track, 2 7-track); magnetic discs: 4 2311; 1 line printer.
IBM 360/30–operating systems: DOS, BOS, BPS, COS; internal storage: 64K bits; magnetic tapes: 2400 series (4 9-track, 2 7-track); magnetic discs: 3 2311; 1 line printer.
Computer Usage Development Corporation, Chicago:
IBM 360/30–operating systems: DOS, CID; internal storage: 64K; magnetic tapes: 3 2404, 1 2401; magnetic discs: 5 2311; 1 line printer.

Coding Languages
COBOL, FORTRAN, Assembly, PL/1; all major programming languages as well as many specialized languages.

Contemplated Equipment
Additional large-scale computer equipment.

Services Available
Consultation, operators, preparation of data, programming, software packages, systems analysis. Operate on a closed shop and block time basis.

Fields of Application
Management, applications, programming, education and operations in all major fields of computational requirements.
Specialized areas: Compiler development, simulation, time shared systems, multiprogramming and multiprocessing systems, management information systems, applied scientific calculations.

Training
Computer usage study course; home study programming course; short courses in computer education and training programmes for business, industry and government.

DATA INSTITUTE INC.*
248 Farmington Avenue, Hartford, 06105
Telephone: (203) 249-9649

Coding Languages
BAL, COBOL, PPG, RCA 501, 301.

Contemplated Equipment
IBM 360/20 and 360/30.

Services Available
Advice, operators, preparation of data, programming, software packages, systems analysis. Operate on a closed shop basis.

Fields of Application
Production control, scientific and commercial systems analysis, design and programming.

Training
Computer programming, operation, installation management, systems analysis and design.

United States of America − Service Bureaux

GENERAL ELECTRIC COMPANY*
Information Service Department
One Prestige Drive, Meriden, 06450
Telephone: (203) 238-1201

SERVICE BUREAU CORPORATION*
964 Asylum Avenue, Hartford, 06105
Telephone: (203) 249-5864

Also at:
97 Whitney Avenue, New Haven, Connecticut 06510
Telephone: (203) 562-4149
(*See* under New York)

SPECIALIZED MANAGEMENT SERVICE INC.*
1144 East Main Street, Torrington, 06790
Telephone: (203) 482-7535

Also at:
618 Warburton Avenue, Hastings, New York

Officer
Walter L. J. Adorno, *President*

Computer Installation
IBM 360−internal storage: 12K bits; 1 line printer.

Coding Language
RPG.

Services Available
Consultation, programming, software packages, documentation, preparation of data. Operate on a self-service basis.

Fields of Application
Accounting and management systems.

UNITED DATA CENTERS INC.
Park Two, Greenwich, 06830

Also at:
Syracuse, Birmingham, Springfield, Salem, Benton Harbor, Decatur, Madison, Minneapolis, Norristown, Jacksonville, Lexington, Wichita, Southfield, St. Louis.
and at: Montreal, Canada.

Officer
Bernard Goldstein, *President*

Computer Installation
BURROUGHS B3500 (3).
IBM 360/30 (3).
IBM 360/25.
IBM 360/40.
HONEYWELL H200.
HONEYWELL H115 (3).

Services Available
Processing − commercial data.

Fields of Application
Accounting, fuel oil distribution, banking.
Specialized area: Computer tax preparation, accounts receivable.

WINGATE COMPUTING CENTER*
80 Farmington Avenue, Hartford, 06105
Telephone: (203) 522-2187
(*See* under Rhode Island)

DELAWARE

ELECTRONIC DATA SERVICE INC.*
18 Germay Drive, Wilmington, 19804
Telephone: (302) 652-3901

Also at:
Bermuda Computer Services Ltd.,
P.O. Box 1632, Hamilton, Bermuda

Officer
W. A. Cover, *President*

Computer Installation
IBM 1401−internal storage: 8K bits; magnetic tapes: 2 729 IV; 1 line printer.
IBM 360/40−operating system: DOS; internal storage: 256K bits; magnetic tapes: 4 2400 V; magnetic discs: 2314; 1 line printer. *Remote processing features.*

Coding Languages
COBOL, RPG, BAL, SPS.

Services Available
Preparation of data, systems and software development, data center time sales. Operate on an open shop and block time basis.

Fields of Application
Statistical, commercial, production control, accounting, management, systems analysis.
Specialized areas: Payroll, billing and accounts receivable.

SCI-TEK INC.
1707 Gilpin Avenue, Wilmington, 19899
Telephone: (302) 658-2431

Officers
W. H. du Pont, *Chairman of the Board*
W. G. Verge, *President*
W. H. Rapley, *Vice-President*

Computer Installation
UNIVAC 1108−operating system: EXEC 8; internal storage: 9,216K bits; magnetic tapes: 9; magnetic drums: 13; 1 line printer. *On-line satellite computer*: Univac 1104. *Remote processing features*: Model 33 or 35 TTY, IBM 2780, Univac 900 Series, DCT 2000, Remcom 2780, Mohawk 2400 and 7208, Data 100 Model 70, 74 and 78, Westinghouse 2550, Cope 1200 Series.

Coding Languages
ALGOL, BASIC, FORTRAN, COBOL, JOVIAL, SNOBOL, LISP, RALPH.

Contemplated Equipment
A second Univac 1108.

Services Available
Advice, programming, education and training, software packages, documentation, data preparation, systems analysis. Operate on a remote access, block time and time-sharing basis.

Fields of Application
Scientific, statistical, commercial, systems analysis, operational research.
Specialized areas: Linear programming, structural engineering, numerical control.

Training
Customer training as required.

DISTRICT OF COLUMBIA

CONTROL DATA CORPORATION*
C.E.I.R. Professional Services Division
5272 River Road, Washington, 20016
Telephone: (301) 652-2268

Also at:
1725 K Street, Northwest Washington, D.C. 20006
Telephone: (202) 296-9155
1180 Avenue of Americas, New York, New York 10036
Telephone: (212) 582-6640
186 Alewife Brook Parkway, Cambridge,
Massachusetts 02138
Telephone: (617) 491-3050
9171 Wilshire Boulevard, Beverly Hills, California 90210
Telephone: (213) 273-0810
100 Bush Street, San Francisco, California 94104
Telephone: (415) 397-1205

Officers
Dr. Herbert W. Robinson, *President*
H. E. Owens, *Secretary*
R. J. Niederriter, *Vice-President, Finance and Treasurer*

Computer Installation
Washington:
IBM 7090.
IBM 360/30 (5).
BULL GENERAL ELECTRIC GE 625-Datanet 30.
BULL GENERAL ELECTRIC GE 420-Datanet 30.
RCA 501.
RCA 301.
New York:
IBM 360/65.
IBM 360/30 (2).
Boston:
IBM 7094.
IBM 360/30.
IBM 1401 (2).
San Francisco:
IBM 360/65.
IBM 360/44.
IBM 360/30 (2).
Los Angeles:
IBM 7094.
IBM 360/30.

Coding Languages
PL/1, FORTRAN, LP/90, LP/90/94, LP/94, FAP, MAP, JOVIL, COBOL, ALGOL, SIMSCRIPT, COMTRAN, GPSS, DYNAMO, Autocoder, SPS.

Services Available
Advice, operators, preparation of data, programming, software packages, systems analysis. Operate on a closed shop, open shop, remote access and time-sharing basis.

Fields of Application
Analysis and programming in all major fields of interest.
Specialized areas: Linear programming, compilers and special programming systems, statistics, time series, information retrieval, various management information systems.

Training
Special courses designed for and provided to industry and government.

INSTITUTE OF COMPUTER TECHNOLOGY INC.*
Suite 100, 2600 Virginia Avenue, N.W.,
Washington, 20037
Telephone: (202) 337-7200

Officers
Albert M. Kreger, *President*
Charles Agre, *Director, Washington School*

Coding Languages
Autocoder, 360 Assembly, 360/TOS/DOS, COBOL, FORTRAN IV, RPG.

Services Available
Advice, operators, programming, software packages, systems analysis.

Fields of Application
Statistical, commercial, accounting, management.

Training
Certificate in Computer Programming; Certificate in Computer Systems Operations. Short courses: Special purpose training for employers in specific types of machines; management seminars—both executive and middle management level; systems analysis course for experienced programmers.

INTEGRATED BUSINESS METHODS*
2135 Wisconsin Avenue, Washington, 20007
Telephone: (202) 965-5015

Officer
D. W. Gregg, *Executive Vice-President*

Services Available
Consultation, operators, preparation of data, programming, systems analysis.

PHOTO DATA INC.*
601 G Street, N.W., Washington, 20001
Telephone: (202) ST3-6245

Officer
Kenneth B. Ludwig

Computer Installation
IBM 1130—internal storage: 8K bits; magnetic disc: 1; 1 line printer.

Coding Languages
Assembler, FORTRAN.

Service Available
Preparation of data.

Fields of Application
Scientific, statistical.
Specialized area: Graphic arts — computerized photo-typesetting.

SERVICE BUREAU CORPORATION*
2251 Wisconsin Avenue, N.W., Washington, 20007
Telephone: (202) 337-2900
(*See* under New York)

UNIVAC*
2121 Wisconsin Avenue, N.W., Washington, 20007

Officers
S. Grady Putnam, *Vice-President*
Fred Anderson, *Director, Education*

United States of America – Service Bureaux

Computer Installation
UNIVAC 1108–operating systems: EXEC 8; internal storage: 5 million bits; magnetic tapes: 10 VIIIC; magnetic discs: 2 Fastrand drums, 6 FH432 drums; 4 line printers. *On-line satellite computer*: Univac 418. *Remote processing features*: Time-sharing on Univac 9200, Univac 9300, etc.

Coding Languages
Assembly, FORTRAN IV, COBOL, ALGOL, GPSS, SIMSCRIPT, GASP, MIMIC, etc.

Contemplated Equipment
Graphics terminals.

Services Available
Consultation, programming, education and training, operators, software packages, documentation, preparation of data, systems analysis. Operate on a closed shop, block time, remote access and time-sharing basis. Not available for commercial sales.

Fields of Application
Scientific, engineering, operations research, customers' business applications.

Training
Extensive customer training; also a wide range of short courses (2 days – 4 weeks).

V.I.P. SYSTEMS*
1145 19th Street, N.W., Washington, 20036
Telephone: 296-1430

Also at:
Boston, New York, Chicago, Cleveland, Philadelphia

Officer
J. M. Van Horn, *President*

Computer Installation
IBM 360/40–operating system: DOS, OS/360; internal storage: 2,097,152 bits; magnetic tapes: 4 2401/2; magnetic discs: 2 2314; 1 line printer.

Coding Languages
COBOL, FORTRAN, PL/1, Assembler.

Contemplated Equipment
IBM 360/50.

Services Available
Consultation, programming, software packages, documentation, preparation of data, systems analysis. Operate on a remote access, block time and time-sharing basis.

Fields of Application
Information services, publications, information systems.
Specialized area: Text-orientated information systems.

FLORIDA

AUTOMATIC DATA PROCESSING OF FLORIDA, INC.*
7007 N.W. 77th Avenue, Miami, 33133
Telephone: (305) 885-0181

Officer
D. L. Perlman, *President*

CITY NATIONAL BANK OF MIAMI
P.O. Box 3280, Miami, 33101

Officers
D. K. Gill, *President*
M. B. Mitchell, *Senior Vice-President and Cashier*

Computer Installation
NCR Century 200 (2)–operating system: B2; internal storage: 64K bits; magnetic tapes: 2 633; magnetic discs: 4 655; 1 line printer.
NCR 315–internal storage: 45K bits; magnetic tapes: 1 323; magnetic discs: 4 CRAM units; 1 line printer.

Coding Languages
NEAT 3, COBOL.

Contemplated Equipment
NCR 251 (2).

Service Available
Preparation of data. Operate on a closed shop basis. Services restricted to commercial banks.

Field of Application
Commercial.
Specialized area: Finance.

Training
Programming School: NEAT 3, COBOL; Special courses on Operating Software; Debugging Shop; on-line programming.

COMPUTER CENTER INC. OF MIAMI
4141 N. Miami Avenue, Miami, 33127
Telephone: (305) 576-1960

Officer
Frank O. Nichols, *President*

Computer Installation
BURROUGHS B3500–operating system: MFCP; internal storage: 2,400K bits; magnetic tapes: 4; magnetic discs; 1 line printer. *On-line satellite computers*: 12 TC500.

Coding Language
COBOL.

Services Available
Programming, operators, software packages, preparation of data, systems analysis. Operate on a closed shop, block time and time-sharing basis.

Field of Application
Commercial.
Specialized area: Specialized Accounts Receivable.

COMPUTER POWER INC.
30 South Laura Street, Jacksonville, 32202
Telephone: 353-0953

Officers
T. L. Dent, *Chairman of the Board*
D. M. Hicks, *President*
M. Kahler, *Manager, Computer Operations*

Computer Installation
IBM 360/50–operating system: DOS 360; internal storage: 128K bits; magnetic tapes: 6 2403, 2 2402; magnetic discs: 6 2413; 2 line printers.

Coding Languages
COBOL, FORTRAN, Autocoder, BAL.

Contemplated Equipment
IBM 370/145.

Services Available
Advice, preparation of data, programming, software packages, systems analysis. Operate on a closed shop and remote access basis.

Fields of Application
Scientific, statistical, commercial, accounting.
Specialized areas: Mortgage servicing, insurance.

COMPUTER CENTER INC.*
400 Royal Palm Way, Palm Beach, 33480
Telephone: (305) 655-3711

Also at:
4141 North Miami Avenue, Miami
Telephone: 305-754-5441

Officer
H. Jefferson Mills, Jr., *President and Chairman of the Board*

Computer Installation
HONEYWELL H1201–operating systems: TOS, DOS; internal storage: 64K bits; magnetic tapes: 6 204-B; magnetic discs: 1 259-A; 1 line printer.
IBM 360/30–operating system: DOS; internal storage: 32K bits; magnetic tapes: 4 2314; magnetic discs: 3 2311; 1 line printer.

Coding Languages
COBOL, Autocoder, Easycoder, BAL.

Services Available
Consultation, programming, operators, software packages, documentation, preparation of data, systems analysis. Operate on an open shop, remote access and block time basis.

Fields of Application
Commercial, production control, accounting, management, systems analysis.

COMPU-TIME INC.*
2455 East Sunrise Boulevard, Fort Lauderdale, 33304
Telephone: (305) 563-4311

Also at:
Orlando, Tampa, Jacksonville, Daytona Beach

Officer
Drew F. Burton, *President*

Computer Installation
BULL GENERAL ELECTRIC GE 430–operating systems: TSOS, DPS, MTPS; internal storage: 786,432 bits; magnetic tapes: 2; magnetic discs: 7; 1 line printer. *On-line satellite computer*: Datanet 30. *Remote processing features*: terminals.

Coding Languages
BASIC, FORTRAN, COBOL, SORT, Machine Assembly Language.

Contemplated Equipment
Bull General Electric GE 435.

Services Available
Consultation, programming, education and training, software packages, documentation, systems analysis. Operate on a block time and remote access basis.

Fields of Application
Statistical, commercial, accounting, management, systems analysis, time-sharing, contract programming, software development, computer facilities management.
Specialized areas: Banking, engineering applications, contract programming design, development and implementation.

Training
Programming courses in BASIC (9 hours) and FORTRAN IV (9 hours).

DATA PROCESSING INC.*
744 Gulf Life Tower, Jacksonville, 32207
Telephone: (904) 398-6815

Officer
John D. Zoller, *President*

Computer Installation
HONEYWELL H1250–operating system: OS-200; internal storage: 114K bits; magnetic tapes: 6 204B-4: magnetic discs: 3 259; 1 line printer. *Remote processing features*: Teletype ASR-33 into 281-1B communications control on computer.

Coding Languages
COBOL, FORTRAN IV, Easycoder.

Services Available
Advice, preparation of data, programming, systems analysis, management services. Operate on an open shop and block time basis.

Fields of Application
Commercial, accounting, management, statistical.
Specialized areas: Payroll, accounts receivable, accounts payable, general ledger mail lists, sales analysis, daily invoicing, job costing.

DATA CORPORATION OF AMERICA
411 Avenue K.S.E., Winter Haven, 33880
Telephone: (813) 294-5913

Officers
A. Lacerte, *President*
G. Lacerte, *Vice-President*

Computer Installation
BURROUGHS B300.

Coding Language
COBOL.

Contemplated Equipment
10 Burroughs B1700.

Services Available
Advice, programming, education and training, software packages, preparation of data, systems analysis.

Fields of Application
Commercial, accounting, management, systems analysis.
Specialized areas: Sales analysis, payroll.

FEDDER DATA CENTER OF FLORIDA*
P.O. Box E, Clearwater, 33518
Telephone: (813) 581-1538
(*See* under Maryland)

United States of America – Service Bureaux

FLORIDA COMPUTER SYSTEMS COMPANY*
P.O. Box 44, Winter Park, 32789

Officers
Robert L. Cramer, *Vice-President and Comptroller*
William B. Stratman, *General Manager*

Computer Installation
IBM 360/30–operating system: DOS; internal storage: 524,288 bits; magnetic tapes: 4 IBM 2400/2; magnetic discs: 2 IBM 2311; 1 line printer.

Coding Languages
COBOL, Assembler, FORTRAN, 1401 Autocoder.

Contemplated Equipment
RCA Spectra 70/45.

Services Available
Consultation, programming, operators, software packages, preparation of data, systems analysis. Operate on a block time and open shop basis.

Fields of Application
Tax roll systems, junior college student registration, commercial, financial systems, public utility billing.

GENERAL ELECTRIC COMPANY*
Information Service Department
5950 Washington Street, Hollywood, 33023
Telephone: (305) 621-1196

GENERAL ELECTRIC COMPANY*
Information Service Department
3165 McCrory Place, Orlando, 32803
Telephone: (305) 841-9380

GTE DATA SERVICES INC.
First Financial Tower, Tampa, 33601
Telephone: (813) 224-3131

Also at:
Bloomington, Illinois; Durham, North Carolina; Erie, Pennsylvania; Everett, Washington; Fort Wayne, Indiana; Grinnell, Iowa; Johnstown, New York; Lexington, Kentucky; Los Angeles, California; Madison, Wisconsin; Marion, Ohio; Muskegon, Michigan; Owosso, Michigan; San Angelo, Texas.

Officers
J. B. Renwick, *President*
D. E. Peeples, *Vice-President, Operations*
W. R. Wofford, *Vice-President and Controller*
B. H. Scott, *Vice-President, Systems Development*
J. V. Carideo, *Vice-President and General Counsel*

Computer Installation
Several computers, including IBM 360 and IBM 370. Operating systems include DOS and OS.

Coding Languages
ANS COBOL, ALC, BASIC, FORTRAN.

Contemplated Equipment
IBM 360 and 370 series.

Services Available
Advice, programming, software packages, data preparation, systems analysis. Operate on a self-service, remote access, block time and time-sharing basis.

Fields of Application
Commercial, accounting, management.
Specialized areas: Applications for the telephone industry, several business and data centre management software applications, processing for financial institutions, time-sharing services and cable television management services.

INFORMATION PROCESSING INC.
6237 North Edgewater Drive, Orlando, 32810
Telephone: (305) 293-9431

Officers
T. D. Tyra, *President*
R. F. Roycroft, *Vice-President*
M. W. Williams, *Comptroller*

Computer Installation
VARIAN 73–operating system: VORTEX; internal storage: 32K × 8 bits; magnetic tapes: 1; magnetic discs: 1; 1 line printer.

Contemplated Equipment
Data General Nova with 1·25 million words disc drive.

Services Available
Advice, programming, education and training, operators, software packages, documentation, data preparation, systems analysis.

Fields of Application
Scientific, commercial, production control, management, systems analysis.

MARINE BANK & TRUST CO.*
Data Processing
Systems and Software Corporation
4720 Cypress Street, Tampa, 33607
Telephone: 224-2261

Officer
H. M. Cooper, *President*

Computer Installation
IBM 360–operating systems: DOS, COS; internal storage: 65K bits; magnetic tapes: 4; magnetic discs: 3; 1 line printer.
NCR 315 (2)–internal storage: 10K bits each; magnetic tapes: 10; 1 line printer each.

Coding Languages
COBOL, FORTRAN.

Contemplated Equipment
IBM 360.
BURROUGHS B3500.

Services Available
Preparation of data, programming, software packages, systems analysis. Operate on a closed shop basis.

Fields of Application
Banking services, commercial, system analysis.
Specialized area: Banking services.

NATIONAL CASH REGISTER COMPANY*
Data Processing Center
2915 Biscayne Boulevard, Miami, 33137
Telephone: (305) 377-8461

Officer
T. W. Thornton, *Manager*

Also at:
4404 North Tamiami Trail, Sarasota, 33580
Telephone: (813) 959-2011

Officer
B. V. Alton, *Manager*
(For details, *see* under Ohio)

SCIENTIFIC SYSTEMS SERVICES
476 Highway Ala, P.O. Box 2519, Satellite Beach, 32935
Telephone: (305) 262-7527

Officers
W. Dan DuPont, *President*
V. Lamb, *Vice-President*
R. Iennaco, *Director of Marketing*

Computer Installation
DCC-116—operating system: RTX; internal storage: 131,072 bits.

Coding Languages
BASIC, FORTRAN, Assembler.

Contemplated Equipment
Diablo cartridge disc storage unit.

Services Available
Programming, education and training, systems analysis. Operate on a closed shop and block time basis.

Field of Application
Production control.
Specialized area: Industrial automation.

Training
One-week courses are offered in an introduction to real time minicomputer systems and a survey of popular minicomputers.

SERVICE BUREAU CORPORATION*
955 N.E. 125th Street, No. 1, Miami, 33161
Telephone: (305) 754-4647
(*See* under New York)

SYSTEMS PROGRAMMING SERVICES INC.*
2500 S.W. 3rd Avenue, Miami, 33129
Telephone: (305) 358-0761

Officer
Henry W. Meyer, *President*

Computer Installation
NCR 315—internal storage: 120K bits; magnetic tapes; 1 line printer.
UNIVAC 1005—internal storage: 24K bits; magnetic tape; 1 line printer.

Coding Languages
BEST, COBOL, FORTRAN II.

Contemplated Equipment
IBM 360/40.
RCA 70/35.

Services Available
Advice, preparation of data, programming, software packages, systems analysis. Operate on a closed shop basis.

Fields of Application
Statistical, commercial, production control, accounting, management, operational research, etc.
Specialized areas: Department store sales analysis and inventory control; accounts receivable.

WEST FLORIDA DATA PROCESSING CENTER INC.*
P.O. Box 1460, Panama City, 32401
Telephone: (904) 763-6510

Officers
H. M. Lewis, *President*
T. M. Dailey, *Vice-President*
Donald R. Grace, *Vice-President and Manager*

Computer Installation
BURROUGHS B500—internal storage: 19,200 bits; magnetic tapes: 4; 1 line printer.

Coding Languages
Burroughs Basic Assembler, Burroughs Advanced Assembler, COBOL.

Contemplated Equipment
Second BURROUGHS B500 to be dedicated on line.

Services Available
Preparation of data, programming, systems analysis. Operate on a closed shop basis.

Fields of Application
Accounting, financial, A/R, payroll, inventory. All types of commercial applications
Specialized areas: Utility billing, banking, grocery wholesale business, hospital billing and accountants' work, cable TV billing.

XIOX INTERNATIONAL INC.*
119 N.E. 79th Street, Miami, 33138
Telephone: (305) 758-1836

Computer Installation
IBM 360/40G—operating systems: DOS, OS; internal storage: 256K bits; magnetic tapes: 5 IBM 2401; magnetic discs: 7 2314; 1 line printer.

Coding Languages
BAL, COBOL, PL/1, RPG.

Contemplated Equipment
IBM 360/50.

Services Available
Consultation, programming, software packages, systems analysis. Operate on a self-service, open and closed shop and block time basis.

Fields of Application
Commercial, accounting, management, systems analysis, banking, processing for land development companies and local government.
Specialized areas: Land development processing, utility billing systems, software package marketing.

United States of America – Service Bureaux

GEORGIA

COMPUTE AMERICA CORPORATION (COMERICA)*
8 Executive Park West, N.E., Atlanta, 30329
Telephone: (404) 634-6388

Also at:
Corporate Headquarters, 1515 Classen Boulevard,
Oklahoma City, Oklahoma 73106

Officers
Richard M. Deaton, *Executive Vice-President*
John W. Cormack, *Director of Personnel*
Carlisle T. Smith, *Branch Manager*

Computer Installation
UNIVAC 9300–operating systems: NCOS, COS; internal storage: 288K bits; magnetic tapes: 6 Uniservo IV; 1 line printer.
UNIVAC 1004–operating systems: EXEC, 11 8; internal storage: 6,608 bits; magnetic tapes: 2 Uniservo IV; 1 line printer. *On-line satellite computer*: Univac 1108.

Coding Languages
RPG, COBOL, Assembler, FORTRAN.

Services Available
Programming, operators, documentation, preparation of data, systems analysis. Operate on a closed shop and block time basis.

Fields of Application
Scientific, statistical, commercial, production control, accounting, management, systems analysis.

COMPUTONE SYSTEMS INC.
361 E. Paces Ferry Road, Atlanta, 30305
Telephone: (404) 261-0070

Officer
W. O. Robeson, *President*

Computer Installation
IBM 360/50–operating system: DOS; internal storage: 394K bits; magnetic tapes: 3; magnetic discs: 6 Memorex 660; 1 line printer. *Remote processing features*: Audio Response, Memorex 1240, TI Silent 725.

Coding Languages
COBOL, Assembler.

Services Available
Operate on a remote access and block time basis.

Fields of Application
Scientific, management, sales.
Specialized areas: Linear programming, analysis, insurance.

GENERAL ELECTRIC COMPANY*
Information Service Department
1800 Peachtree Road N.W., Atlanta, 30309
Telephone: (404) 351-3400

GEORGIA DATA CORPORATION*
P.O. Box 514, 207 West York Street, Savannah, 31402
Telephone: (912) 236-0279

Officers
Harris Slotin, *President and General Manager*
Donald R. Coomer, *Vice-President, Production*
Michael Sievers, *Vice-President, Sales*

Computer Installation
UNIVAC 1050 III–internal storage: 8K bits; 1 line printer.

Coding Languages
REGENT, PAL.

Contemplated Equipment
IBM 360/20.

Services Available
Advice, operators, preparation of data, programming, systems analysis. Operate on a closed shop basis.

Field of Application
Commercial.
Specialized areas: Payroll, accounts receivable and payable.

Training
Basic programming.

NATIONAL CASH REGISTER COMPANY*
Data Processing Center
5 Executive Park Drive, N.E., Atlanta, 30329
Telephone: (404) 633-6308

Officer
D. L. Parsons, *Manager*
(For details, *see* under Ohio)

SERVICE BUREAU CORPORATION*
1332 West Peachtree Street, N.W., Atlanta, 30309
Telephone: (404) 875-7835
(*See* under New York)

SOUTHERN DATA PROCESSING SERVICES INC.*
P.O. Box 123, Augusta, 30903
Telephone: (404) 722-0468

Officer
Alexander H. Von Pinsky, Jr., *President*

Computer Installation
IBM 360/20–internal storage: 8K bits.

Services Available
Advice, preparation of data, programming, systems analysis. Operate on a closed shop basis.

Fields of Application
Statistical, commercial, accounting, management, municipal.
Specialized areas: Data bank construction and maintenance for municipal operations.

Training
Courses in data processing systems and procedures; short courses in related subjects and required.

UNIVAC DATA PROCESSING CENTER*
1776 Peachtree Road, N.W., Atlanta, 30309
Telephone: (404) 874-4493
(*See* under California)

HAWAII

COMPUTAB INC.
700 Bishop Street, Suite 200, P.O. Box 3886, Honolulu, 96812
Telephone: 521-4734

Also at:
P.O. Box 5076, Walnut Creek, California 94596
Telephone: 837-4734

Officers
D. W. Fitzgerald, *Board Chairman*
R. Jones, *President*

Computer Installation
IBM 360/50–operating system: OS; internal storage: 1 million bits; magnetic tapes: 4; magnetic discs: 8 IBM 2314, 5 Ampex DS324; 2 line printers. *Remote processing features*: RJE, TSO.
IBM 360/30–operating system: DOS; internal storage: 64K bits; magnetic tapes: 2; magnetic discs: 1 2314; 1 line printer.

Coding Languages
COBOL, RPG, BASIC, FORTRAN.

Contemplated Equipment
IBM 360/65.

Services Available
Advice, programming, education and training, operators, software packages, documentation, data preparation, systems analysis. Operate on a remote access, block time, open shop and time-sharing basis.

Fields of Application
Statistical, commercial, accounting, management, systems analysis, operational research.
Specialized areas: Sales analysis, investment analysis, payroll.

FEDDER DATA CENTER OF THE PACIFIC LTD.*
800 Kawailani Street West, Hilo, 96720
Telephone: 56-618
(*See* under Maryland)

NATIONAL CASH REGISTER COMPANY*
Data Processing Center
606 Coral – 2nd Floor, Honolulu, 96813
Telephone: (808) 955-1543

Officer
R. H. Thompson, *Manager*
(For details, *see* under Ohio)

SERVICE BUREAU CORPORATION*
606 Coral Street, Honolulu, 96813
Telephone: (808) 531-0241
(*See* under New York)

TELECHEK INTERNATIONAL INC.*
1481 South King Street, Honolulu, 96814
Telephone: 962-867

Officer
Harry M. Flagg, *President*

Computer Installation
HONEYWELL H200–internal storage: 20K bits; magnetic tapes: 5; 1 line printer.

Service Available
Operate on a time-sharing basis.

Fields of Application
Statistical, engineering, accounting.
Specialized areas: On-line and real time inquiry service for airlines, hotels, etc.

ILLINOIS

BEVERLY BANCORPORATION*
1357 West 103rd Street, Chicago, 60643

Officers
A. C. Herzog, *Manager*
J. D. Nieds, *Foreign Relations*

Computer Installation
IBM 360/40–operating system: DOS; internal storage: 128K bits; magnetic tapes: 4 IBM 2400; magnetic discs: 2 2314; 2 line printers. *Remote processing features*: Teleprocessing.
IBM 360/30–operating system: DOS; internal storage: 65K bits; magnetic discs: 2 2314. *Remote processing features*: Teleprocessing.

Coding Languages
COBOL, BAL, BTAM.

Contemplated Equipment
IBM 360/40.

Services Available
Consultation, programming, education and training, software packages, preparation of data, systems analysis. Operate on a remote access and closed shop basis. Available only to client banks.

Fields of Application
Banking, accounting.
Specialized area: Bank-orientated teleprocessing.

COMPUTER USAGE DEVELOPMENT CORPORATION*
200 South Michigan Avenue, Chicago, 60604
Telephone: (312) 427-8934
(*See* under New York)

CONTROL DATA CORPORATION*
Chicago Center
223 West Jackson Boulevard, Chicago, 60606
Telephone: (312) 427-8270
(*See* under Minnesota)

DPS INC.*
1800 Longview Road, Waukegan, 60085
Telephone: (312) 662-3333

Services Available
Advice, preparation of data, programming, systems analysis.

Fields of Application
Commercial, banking.

FEDDER DATA CENTER OF CHICAGO*
First National Bank Building, 38 South Dearborn Street, Chicago, 60603
Telephone: (312) 372-7586
(*See* under Maryland)

GENERAL ELECTRIC COMPANY*
Information Service Department
110 North Wacker Drive, Chicago, 60606
Telephone: (312) 663-3900

GRAPHIC IMAGE CORPORATION*
549 West Washington Boulevard, Chicago, 60606
Telephone: (312) 332-0693

Officer
Joseph D. Owen, Jr., *Vice-President*

Computer Installation
IBM 1130–operating system: TOS; internal storage: 8K bits; magnetic discs: 1 IBM 2315; 1 line printer.

Services Available
Consultation, programming, software packages, preparation of data, systems analysis. Operate on a closed shop and block time basis. Available primarily for the graphic arts industry.

Fields of Application
Typesetting and related graphic arts applications, including manuscript compilation/preparation.
Specialized area: Buying guides.

INPUT INC.*
640 North La Salle Street, Chicago, 60610
Telephone: (312) 751-0100

Officers
Irwin Schier, *President*
J. E. Kovetz, *Executive Vice-President*

Computer Installation
HONEYWELL H1200–internal storage: 32K bits; magnetic tapes: 5; 1 line printer.

Coding Languages
Easycoder, COBOL.

Contemplated Equipment
Honeywell H2200.

Services Available
Advice, operators, preparation of data, programming, software packages, systems analysis. Operate on an open shop and block time basis.

Fields of Application
General accounting, subscription fulfilment, stockbroker appraisal reporting.
Specialized areas: Stockbroker, security analysis and portfolio appraisal.

Training
Short courses as part of a key punch training programme.

INTERSTATE DATA SERVICES*
118 East Washington Street, Monticello, 61856
Telephone: (217) 762-2557

Services Available
Consultation, preparation of data, programming, systems analysis.

MAY & SPEH DATA PROCESSING CENTER*
(Division of Computing and Software, Inc.)
4020 West Division Street, Chicago, 60651
Telephone: 384-3823

Officers
Roland C. May, *Associate General Manager*
Albert J. Speh, Jr., *General Manager*
J. Edward Wilmotte, Jr., *General Sales Manager*
Carmen A. Ranieri, *Operations Manager*

Computer Installation
IBM 360/30–operating system: DOS; internal storage: 65K bits; magnetic tapes: 5 2400/II; magnetic discs: 2 2311; 1 line printer.
IBM 360/30–operating system: DOS; internal storage: 65K bits; magnetic tapes: 4 2400/II; magnetic discs: 2 2311; 1 line printer.
IBM 360/25–operating system: BPS; internal storage: 16K bits; magnetic tapes: 4 2400/II; 1 line printer.

Coding Languages
RPG, Basic Assembler, COBOL, FORTRAN, 1401 Autocoder (compatibility).

Contemplated Equipment
IBM 360/40.

Services Available
Advice, preparation of data, programming, systems analysis. Operate on a self-service, open shop and block time basis.

Fields of Application
Statistical, commercial, accounting, systems analysis.
Specialized areas: Cost control reports, inventory reports (fiscal and perpetual), machine load analysis, engineering reports, production scheduling, labour distribution, special statistical reports, sales and cost of sales analysis, order studies, payroll distribution and market research tabulations.

MIDWEST BUSINESS STATISTICS*
6945 North Avenue, Oak Park, 60302
Telephone: VI8-9700

Officer
George Early, *Systems Manager*

Services Available
Available only to the medical and dental fields.

Fields of Application
Scientific, commercial.
Specialized areas: Medical, dental.

NATIONAL CASH REGISTER COMPANY*
Chicago Data Processing Center
3075 Tollview Drive, Rolling Meadows, 60008
Telephone: (312) 259-6010

Officer
G. M. Cormack, *Manager*
(For details, *see* under Ohio)

PUBLIC DATA PROCESSING CORPORATION*
640 North La Salle Street, Chicago, 60610
Telephone: (312) 751-0100

Computer Installation
HONEYWELL H1200–internal storage: 32K bits; magnetic tapes: 5; 1 line printer.

Services Available
Consultation, programming, education and training, software packages, preparation of data. Operate on a closed shop basis.

Field of Application
Commercial.
Specialized areas: Publishing (circulation fulfilment/ management), transportation (vehicle maintenance).

RECORDING AND STATISTICAL COMPANY*
223 West Jackson Boulevard, Chicago
Telephone: (312) 427-2380
(*See* under New York)

SERVICE BUREAU CORPORATION
8501 West Higgins Road, Chicago, 60631
Telephone: (312) 693-3021

Also at:
4040 Charles Street, Rockford, Illinois 61108
Telephone: (815) 398-5994
(*See* under New York)

STATISTICAL TABULATING CORPORATION
104 South Michigan Avenue, Chicago, 60603
Telephone: (312) 332-2484

Officers
M. R. Notaro, Sr., *President and Chairman of the Board*
E. C. Becker, Sr., *Executive Vice-President*

Computer Installation
IBM 360/65–operating system: OS/MVT/HASP; internal storage: 1,768K bits; magnetic tapes: 12; magnetic discs: 28 2314; 3 line printers. *Remote processing features*: various.
IBM 360/30–operating system: DOS; internal storage: 65K bits; magnetic tapes: 8; magnetic discs: 4; 1 line printer.

Coding Languages
ADPAC, COBOL, RPG, FORTRAN, Assembler, PL/1.

Contemplated Equipment
IBM 370/158.

Services Available
Advice, programming, operators, software packages, documentation, preparation of data, systems analysis. Operate on a self-service, remote access, block time and time-sharing basis.

Fields of Application
Scientific, statistical, commercial, production control, accounting, management, systems analysis.
Specialized areas: Sales analysis, investment, analysis, payroll, commercial packages.

UNIVAC DPS MIDWEST COMPUTER CENTER*
1211 West 22nd Street, Oak Brook, 60521
Telephone: (312) 654-4680

Computer Installation
UNIVAC 1108–operating system: EXEC 8; internal storage: 196K 36-bit words; magnetic tapes: 16 Uniservo VIIIC; magnetic discs: 12 FH432 drums, 1 Fastrand 11 drum; 3 line printers. *Remote processing features*: 110 bps, 2000 bps, 2400 bps, 4800 bps.

Contemplated Equipment
Fastrand 11 drum.

Service Available
Consultation. Operate on a self-service, remote access and closed shop basis.

Fields of Application
Scientific, statistical, commercial, numerical control.

UNIVERSITY COMPUTING COMPANY*
Data-Link Group
323 South Franklin, Chicago, 60606
Telephone: (312) HA7-1355
(*See* under Texas)

INDIANA

ANACOMP INC.*
6161 North Hillside Avenue, Indianapolis, 46220
Telephone: (317) 257-6555

Officers
Ronald D. Palamara, *President*
Thomas G. Ulsas, *Vice-President*

Computer Installation
BURROUGHS B3500–operating system: MPS; internal storage: 1,200K bits; magnetic tapes: 6 9-track, 2 7-track; magnetic discs: 3; 1 line printer. *Remote processing features*: 12 lines with mixed terminals.
NCR 315–operating system: "on-line"; internal storage: 140K bits; magnetic tapes: 5 7-track; magnetic discs: 3 CRAM; 1 line printer. *Remote processing features*: NCR 42 window machines.

Contemplated Equipment
Viatron data preparation and terminal equipment.

Services Available
Consultation, programming, education and training, software packages, systems analysis. Operate on a remote access basis. Available only to savings and loan associations, credit unions, commercial banks and wholesale distributors.

Fields of Application
Financial institution accounting, commercial, production control.
Specialized areas: Savings and loan associations, credit unions, commercial banks, wholesale distributors.

ANROCOR INDUSTRIES INC.
5949 Hohman Avenue, Hammond, 46320
Telephone: (312) 721-1900, (219) 931-0750

Also at:
2015 Western Avenue, South Bend, Indiana
Telephone: (219) 289-7891

Officers
S. M. Kleinman, *President*
F. R. Ryan, *Vice-President, Treasurer*
A. Rosen, *Vice-President of Operations*

Computer Installation
HONEYWELL H115–operating systems: Mod 1, MSR, TR; internal storage: 32K bits; magnetic tapes: 4; magnetic discs: 1; 1 line printer. *On-line satellite computer*: paper tape reader. *Remote processing features*: communications controller.
HONEYWELL H115–operating systems: Mod. 1, MSR, TR; internal storage: 24K bits; magnetic tapes: 4; magnetic discs: 1; 1 line printer.

United States of America – Service Bureaux

Coding Languages
COBOL, FORTRAN, ALGOL, BAL, RPG, Autocoder, SPS, Easycoder.

Services Available
Advice, programming, education and training, operators, software packages, documentation, data preparation, systems analysis, remote processing services. Operate on a self-service, remote access, open and closed shop, block time and time-sharing basis.

Fields of Application
Statistical, commercial, production control, accounting, management, systems analysis, operational research.
Specialized areas: Sales analysis, investment analysis, payroll, building management retail systems.

AUTOMATED SERVICES INC.*
7009 North River Road, Fort Wayne, 46805
Telephone: (219) 749-9681

Services Available
Advice, operators, preparation of data, programming.

Fields of Application
Commercial, accounting.

GENERAL ELECTRIC COMPANY*
Information Service Department
3969 Meadows Drive, Suite 102, Indianapolis, 46205
Telephone: (317) 545-7591

INTERNATIONAL COMPUTER PROGRAMS INC. (ICP)
2506 Willowbrook Parkway, Indianapolis, 46205
Telephone: (317) 257-4274

Officer
L. A. Welke, *President*

Services Available
Consultation, education and training.

Training
ICP Sales Training Seminar – a three-day sales training course for computer software salesmen.

NORTHERN INDIANA FINANCIAL SERVICE CORPORATION*
315 South Adams, Marion, 46952
Telephone: (317) 664-0533

Officer
Robert Gray, *Executive Vice-President and General Manager*

Computer Installation
BURROUGHS B300–operating system: EXEC; internal storage: 57,600 bits; magnetic tapes: 4; magnetic discs: 2; 1 line printer. *On-line satellite computer*: Varian 6201. *Remote processing features*: 4 Western Union telex lines.

Services Available
Consultation, programming, software packages, systems analysis. Operate on a remote access and closed shop basis. Available to financial institutions only.

Fields of Application
Complete bank book keeping with on-line central file.

Training
Courses in Introductory Computer Science in conjunction with Marion College.

SERVICE BUREAU CORPORATION*
1923 North Meridian Street, Indianapolis, 46202
Telephone: (317) 924-4301
(*See* under New York)

IOWA

COMPUTER CONSULTING SERVICE
Box 1278, 840 Dubuque Building, Dubuque, 52001
Telephone: (319) 556-3131

Officers
Jim Houtz, *President*
Dick Burgmeier, *Vice-President*

Computer Installation
IBM 360/30 (2)–internal storage: 65K bits; magnetic tapes: 5 2401/V; magnetic discs: 8 2311; 2 line printers. *Remote processing features*: 1 4200 Datagraphix Com. Unit (On-line); 1 Data Card 750 Embossing system (plastic plates).

Coding Languages
RPG, BAL, COBOL.

Services Available
Consultation, programming, software packages, preparation of data, systems analysis. Operate on a block time basis.

Fields of Application
Commercial, production control, management.
Specialized areas: Medical clinic accounting, route accounting for bakeries.

COMPUTER SERVICES CORPORATION*
2501 Grand, Des Moines, 50312
Telephone: (515) 288-9777

Also at:
P.O. Box 3594, Davenport, Iowa
Telephone: (319) 323-8094

Officers
E. W. Abbott, *President*
Frank M. Myers, *Executive Vice-President*
Annalou Myers, *Administrative Vice-President*
Joseph Dorzweiler, *Director of Education*

Computer Installation
Des Moines:
HONEYWELL H200–internal storage: 16K bits; magnetic tapes: 4; 1 line printer.

Davenport:
HONEYWELL H120–internal storage: 16K bits; magnetic tapes: 5; 1 line printer.

Coding Languages
COBOL, Easycoder, 360 BAL, 360 COBOL.

Services Available
Consultation, operators, preparation of data, programming, software packages, systems analysis. Operate on a self-service basis (occasionally).

Fields of Application
Commercial, production control, accounting, management analysis, systems analysis.
Specialized areas: Hospital programme, county programmes, municipal government programmes and insurance programmes.

United States of America – Service Bureaux

Training
Courses in programming and administrative systems.

EXECUTIVE DATA SYSTEMS
4403 First Avenue S.E., Cedar Rapids, 52402
Telephone: (319) 393-9400

Officer
D. C. Olson, *President*

Computer Installation
BURROUGHS B3500–operating system: MCP; internal storage: 150K bits; magnetic tapes: 6; magnetic discs: 7; 1 line printer. *On-line satellite computer*: Datapoint 2200.
IBM 370/145–operating system: OS; internal storage: 128K bits; magnetic tapes: 5; magnetic discs: 2; 1 line printer.

Coding Language
COBOL.

Services Available
Advice, programming, education and training, operators, software packages, documentation, preparation of data, systems analysis. Operate on a time-sharing basis. Services restricted to health care applications.

FEDDER DATA CENTER OF SIOUX CITY*
600 Toy National Bank Building, Sioux City, 51101
Telephone: (712) 262-2354
(*See* under Maryland)

GENERAL ELECTRIC COMPANY*
Information Service Department
1039 State Street, Bettendorf, 52722
Telephone: (319) 355-0231

NETWORK DATA PROCESSING CORPORATION
321 Third Street, S.E., Cedar Rapids, 52407
Telephone: (319) 365-8691

Officers
Robert H. Taylor, *Chairman of the Board*
Daniel C. Benner, *President*

Computer Installation
NCR Century 200–operating system: B1 EXEC; internal storage: 64K bytes; magnetic tapes: 2 624, 4 633; magnetic discs: 1 655; 1 line printer.
HONEYWELL H120–operating system: Mod 1 TR; internal storage: 32K bits; magnetic tapes: 5 204B-7; 1 line printer.

Coding Languages
COBOL, NEAT 3, FORTRAN, Easycoder, COMAT.

Contemplated Equipment
IBM 370/125, Honeywell H2040.

Services Available
Advice, programming, education and training, operators, software packages, documentation, preparation of data, systems analysis. Operate on an open shop basis.

Fields of Application
Commercial, accounting, insurance.
Specialized areas: Sales analysis, insurance, actuarial computing.

Training
Three week, 8-part training seminar in the implementation and use of the LILA System for life insurance companies; 3-week, 6-part training seminar in the implementation and use of the CILA System for property and casualty insurance companies; 2-day training course in the use of the IAA System for insurance agents; special training courses in insurance data processing.

PIONEER DATA SYSTEMS INC.*
606 Merle Hay Tower, Des Moines, 50310
Telephone: (515) 276-6746

Officer
L. H. Baker, *President*

Computer Installation
IBM 360/40–operating system: OS/MFT-HASP; internal storage: 2,048K bits; magnetic tapes: 9-track; magnetic discs: 8 2314; 1 line printer. *Remote processing features*: RJE support.

Coding Languages
Univac Assembly, IBM Symbolic, Autocoder, ALGOL, PL/1, COBOL, FORTRAN II and IV, BASIC, APL, JCL. GPSS, BAL.

Services Available
Consultation, programming, software packages, documentation, systems analysis. Operate on a self-service and remote access basis.

Fields of Application
Scientific, statistical, commercial, accounting, systems analysis, operational research.
Specialized areas: Agriculture, file management.

KANSAS

CENTRAL COMPUTING INC.*
2627 East Central, Wichita, 67214
Telephone: (316) 685-9207

Officers
Joe Mamary, *President*
Robert T. Cornwell, *Secretary*
Donald J. Grommesh, *Treasurer*

Computer Installation
BULL GENERAL ELECTRIC GE 415–operating systems: MTPS SDL7, DPS SDL4, TSPS SDL2; internal storage: 786,432 bits; magnetic tapes: 5 1 MTH 403, 4 MTH 200; magnetic discs: 4 DSU 160; 1 line printer. *Remote processing features*: GE time-sharing.

Coding Languages
COBOL, BASIC, FORTRAN, MAP, BAP.

Services Available
Consultation, programming, education and training, software packages, systems analysis. Operate on a self-service, block time, open shop and time-sharing basis.

Fields of Application
Scientific, management, systems analysis, commercial.
Specialized areas: Government tax services, time-sharing, feedlot accounting.

Training
Courses in FORTRAN IV time-sharing (12 sessions).

United States of America – Service Bureaux

KENTUCKY

GENERAL ELECTRIC COMPANY*
Information Service Department
2100 Gardiner Lane, Louisville, 40205
Telephone: (502) 452-4211

LOUISVILLE TABULATING SERVICE BUREAU*
118 South 5th Street, Louisville, 40202
Telephone: (502) 587-0728

Officer
Vern Ferguson

NATIONAL CASH REGISTER COMPANY*
Data Processing Center
630 E. Broadway, Louisville, 40202
Telephone: (502) 587-0713

Officer
G. W. Coffing, *Manager*

(For details, *see* under Ohio)

SERVICE BUREAU CORPORATION*
844 South Fourth Street, Louisville, 40203
Telephone: (502) 584-5261
(*See* under New York)

LOUISIANA

DELTA DATA SERVICES INC.*
4720 Dixon Street, New Orleans, 70125
Telephone: 486-6414

Officer
Joseph D. Bryant, *General Manager*

Computer Installation
HONEYWELL H120–operating system: Modular 1; internal storage: 16K bits; magnetic tapes: 4; 1 line printer.

Coding Language
COBOL.

Services Available
Advice, preparation of data, programming, software packages, systems analysis. Operate on a closed shop basis.

Fields of Application
Commercial, accounting.

GENERAL ELECTRIC COMPANY*
Information Service Department
3525 North Causeway Boulevard, Metairie, 70002
Telephone: (504) 837-0722.

NATIONAL CASH REGISTER COMPANY*
Data Processing Center
2315 N. Causeway Boulevard, New Orleans, 70001
Telephone: (504) 834-3740

Officer
E. J. Simokat, *Manager*

(For details, *see* under Ohio)

MARYLAND

ERNEST E. BLANCHE & ASSOCIATES INC.*
10335 Kensington Parkway, Kensington, 20795
Telephone: (301) 949-0500

Officers
Ernest E. Blanche, *President*
B. A. Ferguson, *Executive Vice-President*
Thomas C. Johannes, *Vice-President for Operations*

Computer Installation
IBM 360/30–operating systems: TOS, DOS; internal storage: 32K bits; magnetic tapes: 4 9-track, 2 7-track; magnetic discs: 2 2311; 1 line printer.
IBM 1401 (2)–internal storage: 16K and 8K bits; magnetic tapes: 4 7330 each; 1 line printer.

Coding Languages
360 Assembler, Autocoder, COBOL, RPG, SPS.

Services Available
Preparation of data, programming, systems analysis. Operate on an open shop and block time basis.

Fields of Application
Commercial, statistical, accounting, operations research, scientific, management.

CENTRAL INFORMATION PROCESSING CORPORATION
The Quadrangle/Village of Cross Keys, Baltimore, 21210

Officers
R. E. Brindley, *President*
G. E. Moore, *Vice-President, Client Services*
N. M. Belin, *Director, Product Development*
P. E. Souzis, *Controller*

Computer Installation
CDC 3300–operating system: MASTER; internal storage: 3,072K bits; magnetic tapes: 10 607; magnetic discs: 1 841; 3 line printers. *On-line satellite computers*: 4 8090.
CDC 3500–operating system: MASTER; internal storage: 3,072K bits; magnetic tapes: 10 607; magnetic discs: 1 841; 3 line printers. *On-line satellite computers*: 4 8090, 4 U-200.

Coding Languages
COBOL, FORTRAN, Assembly, BASIC.

Contemplated Equipment
CDC 6600.

Services Available
Software packages, preparation of data. Operate on a remote access basis.

Fields of Application
Commercial, accounting, management.
Specialized area: Payroll.

COMPRESS INC.*
2 Research Court, Rockville, 20850
Telephone: (301) 948-8000

COMPUTE AMERICA CORPORATION (COMERICA)*
818 Roeder Road, Silver Spring, 20910
Telephone: (301) 587-3210

Also at:
Corporate Headquarters, 1515 Classen Boulevard,
Oklahoma City, Oklahoma 73106

Officers
Richard M. Deaton, *Executive Vice-President*
John W. Cormack, *Director of Personnel*
John J. Starzec, *Branch Manager*

Computer Installation
UNIVAC 9300—operating systems: NCOS, COS; internal storage: 288K bits; magnetic tapes: 8 Uniservo IV; 1 line printer.
UNIVAC 1004—operating systems: EXEC 11 and 8; internal storage: 6,608 bits; magnetic tapes: 2 Uniservo IV; 1 line printer. *On-satellite computer*: Univac 1108.

Coding Languages
RPG, COBOL, FORTRAN, Assembler.

Services Available
Programming, operators, documentation, preparation of data, systems analysis. Operate on a closed shop and block time basis.

Fields of Application
Scientific, statistical, commercial, production control, accounting, management, systems analysis.

COMPUTER CENTER INC.*
423 West Monument Street, Baltimore, 21201
Telephone: (301) 728-3883

Officer
Jerome Markman, *President*

COMPUTER USAGE DEVELOPMENT CORPORATION*
22 West Road, Towson, 21204
Telephone: (301) 823-1300
(*See* under New York)

COMTECH*
4318 Hamilton Street, Hyattsville, 20781
Telephone: (301) 779-0111

Services Available
Advice, programming.

Field of Application
Scientific.

CONTROL DATA CORPORATION*
Rockville Center
11428 Rockville Pike, Rockville, 20852
Telephone: (301) 881-5800
(*See* under Minnesota)

ELECTRONIC ASSOCIATES INC.*
12260 Wilkins Avenue, Rockville, 20852
Telephone: (301) 933-4100
(*See* under California)

FEDDER DATA CENTERS, INC.*
307 South Sharp Street, Baltimore, 21201
Telephone: (301) 685-6773

Also at:
10 East 39th Street, New York, New York 10016
Telephone: (212) 686-6252
800 Kawailani Street, West Hilo, Hawaii 96720
Telephone: (808) 959-7618
20 Crest Drive, Briarcliffe Manor, New York 10510
Telephone: (914) 762-0741
8719 W. Greenfield Avenue, West Allis, Wisconsin 53214
Telephone: (414) 258-4800
10024 Carnegie Avenue, Cleveland, Ohio 44104
Telephone: (216) 229-5240
141 Kaye Vue Drive, Hamden, Connecticut 06514
Telephone: (203) 288-7529
230 Houston Street, N.E., Atlanta, Georgia 30303
Telephone: (404) 523-3351
P.O. Box 386, Schenectady, New York 12301
P.O. Box 386, East Brunswick, New Jersey 08816
Telephone: (609) 665-1243
101 Richmond Street W., Suite 110, Toronto 1, Ontario, Canada
Telephone: (416) 362-3090
19 West Flagler Street, Miami, Florida 33130
Telephone: (305) 377-3100
110 Place Cremazie, Suite 322, Montreal, Quebec, Canada
Telephone: (514) 382-2563
Post Office Box 1458, Gadsden, Alabama 35902
Telephone: (205) 547-8276
40-10 National Street, Corona, New York 11386
Telephone: (212) 446-3131
G.P.O. Box 4602, San Juan, Puerto Rico 99036
Telephone: (809) 765-0733
327 South LaSalle Street, Rooms 1045 and 1046, Chicago, Illinois 60604
Telephone: (312) 427-5119
308 Antoine Street, Wyandotte, Michigan 48190
Telephone: (313) 283-2000
300 Main Street, Orange, New Jersey 07051
Telephone: (201) 676-0970
505 Burwell Building, Knoxville, Tennessee 37902
Telephone: (615) 525-1912
7015 Gulf Freeway, Houston, Texas 77017
Telephone: (713) 649-0083

Officers
D. E. Fedder, *President and Chief Executive Officer*
H. F. Horowitz, *Executive Vice-President and Treasurer*
E. Peyton Fuller, *Secretary*

Computer Installations
IBM 360/40—operating system: DOS; internal storage: 132K bits; magnetic tapes: 4; magnetic discs: 4 2311; 1 line printer; interfaced for Fedder remote terminals.
NCR 615-100—internal storage: 32K bits; magnetic tapes: 2; magnetic discs: 2; 1 line printer.

Coding Languages
COBOL, ALC, RPG.

Contemplated Equipment
IBM 2314; additional tape drives; IBM 2701 communications adaptor; Data Collection Station; PDP-8.

Services Available
Programming, preparation of data, systems analysis and design, input conversion service, etc. Operate on a remote access and conventional batch processing basis.

Fields of Application
Commercial, accounting, statistical, systems analysis, order processing, retail management.
Specialized areas: Accounts receivable, payroll, job costing, professional time and record keeping.

Training
Available to meet customer requirements.

United States of America – Service Bureaux

GENERAL ELECTRIC COMPANY*
Information Service Department
5100 Falls Road, Suite 346, Baltimore, 21210
Telephone: (301) 323-8700

GENERAL ELECTRIC COMPANY*
Information Service Department
7735 Old Georgetown Road, Bethesda, 20014
Telephone: (301) 654-9360

Also at:
Birmingham, Ala., Phoenix, Ariz., Berkeley, Cal., El Monte, Cal., Long Beach, Cal., Los Angeles, Cal., Palo Alto, Cal., Reseda, Cal., Sacramento, Cal., San Diego, Cal., San Francisco, Cal., Santa Barbara, Cal., Denver, Colo., Meriden, Conn., Hollywood, Fla., Orlando, Fla., Atlanta, Ga., Chicago, Ill., Indianapolis, Ind., Bettendorf, Iowa, Louisville, Ky., Metairie, La., Baltimore, Md., Bethesda, Md., Waltham, Mass., Pittsfield, Mass., Detroit, Mich., Grand Rapids, Mich., Minneapolis, Minn., St. Louis, Mo., Omaha, Nebr., Highland Park, N.J., Teaneck, N.J., Albuquerque, N.M., Binghampton, N.Y., Buffalo, N.Y., New York, N.Y., Rochester, N.Y., Schenectady, N.Y., Syosset, N.Y., Syracuse, N.Y., Greensboro, N.C., Cincinnati, Ohio, Cleveland, Ohio, Columbus, Ohio, Dayton, Ohio, Oklahoma City, Okla., Tulsa, Okla., Portland, Ore., Bala Cynwyd, Pa., Pittsburgh, Pa., York, Pa., Greenville, S.C., Memphis, Tenn., Dallas, Texas, Houston, Texas, Midland, Texas, Salt Lake City, Utah, Hampton, Va., Seattle, Wash., Milwaukee, Wis.

Officers
P. R. Leadley, *General Manager*
E. A. Bescherer, *Manager of Finance and Administration Dept.*
E. L. McCleary, *Manager of Marketing Dept.*

Computer Installation
BULL GENERAL ELECTRIC GE 265–operating system: Time-sharing EXEC; internal storage: 320K bits; magnetic discs: GE 3520 system.
BULL GENERAL ELECTRIC GE 635–operating system MARK II AX; internal storage: 302.7 million 10-bit characters; magnetic discs: 20 DSU 270. *On-line satellite computers*: 1 GEPAC 4020, 8 COMPAT H 416. *Remote processing features*: Real time time-sharing.

GENERAL ELECTRIC COMPANY*
Information Service Department
4815 Rugby Avenue, Bethesda, 20014
Telephone: (301) 657-2132

LEASCO SYSTEMS & RESEARCH CORPORATION
4833 Rugby Avenue, Bethesda, 20014
Telephone: (301) 656-9723

Officers
W. T. Brandhorst, *Director*
D. S. Price, *Deputy Director*

Coding Language
Assembly (ALC).

Services Available
Advice, programming, education and training, operators, documentation, preparation of data, systems analysis. Operates on a closed shop basis. Available only to the National Institute of Education/Educational Resources Information Centre (ERIC).

Field of Application
Education.

NATIONAL CASH REGISTER COMPANY*
Data Processing Center
940 Madison Avenue, Baltimore, 21201
Telephone: (301) 728-8900

Officer
J. K. Yochum, *Manager*

(For details, *see* under Ohio)

OPERATIONS RESEARCH INC.
1400 Spring Street, Silver Spring, 20910
Telephone: (301) 588-6180

Officers
Dr. J. Emory Cook, *President*
Dr. Walter G. Wadey, *Director of the Computer Center*

Computer Installation
CDC 3100–operating system: MSOS; internal storage: 32K bits; magnetic tapes: 3 608; magnetic discs: 2 854; 1 line printer.

Coding Languages
FORTRAN IV, COBOL, COMPASS.

Services Available
Advice, operators, preparation of data, programming, software packages, systems analysis. Operate on a closed shop basis.

Fields of Application
Operations research, management systems, information systems.

SERVICE BUREAU CORPORATION*
Wheaton Plaza Off. Building, Wheaton, 20902
Telephone: (301) 933-2600

Also at:
1350 Avenue of the Americas, New York, N.Y. 10019

Officers
Benjamin Ocampo, *Manager of Programming Center*
Richard Sanford, *Manager of Time-Sharing Center*

Coding Languages
360 ALC, PL/1, FORTRAN, COBOL, RPG, etc.

Services Available
Consultation, programming, education and training, operators, software packages, documentation, preparation of data, systems analysis. Operate on a remote access, block time and time-sharing basis.

Fields of Application
Scientific, statistical, commercial, production control, accounting, management, systems analysis, operational research, etc.

Training
Courses in systems, languages or applications as required.

UNIVAC DATA PROCESSING CENTER*
818 Roeder Road, Silver Spring, 20910
Telephone: (301) 587-3210
(*See* under California)

WESTAT, INC.
11600 Nebel Street, Rockville, 20852
Telephone: (301) 881-5310

Officers
Dr Edward C. Bryant, *President*
Matthew D. Lee, *Director, Data Processing*

Coding Languages
COBOL, FORTRAN.

Services Available
Advice, programming, software packages, documentation, preparation of data, systems analysis. Operate on a remote access, block time, and time-sharing basis.

Fields of Application
Statistical, commercial, accounting, management, systems analysis, operational research.
Specialized areas: Sales analysis, linear programming, analysis.

MASSACHUSETTS

ACCOUNTING CORPORATION OF AMERICA
39 Brighton Avenue, Boston, 02134
Telephone: (617) 254-7743
(*See* under California)

BIZ-MATIC DATA CONTROL CENTERS INC.*
232 Summer Street, Boston, 02210
Telephone: (617) 426-6863

Officer
Peter G. Sicurella

Computer Installation
IBM 360/30–internal storage: 64K bits; magnetic tapes: 3 9-track, 1 7-track; magnetic discs: 3 2311; 1 line printer.

Cooling Languages
COBOL, BAL, RPG.

Services Available
Advice, operators, preparation of data, programming, software packages, systems analysis. Operate on a self-service and open shop basis.

Fields of Application
Scientific, commercial.
Specialized areas: Retail and manufacturing control.

COMPUTER FULFILLMENT*
225 East Street, Winchester, 01890
Telephone: (617) 729-4650

Officers
William J. McMillan, *President*
Beman G. Davis, *Vice-President*
Mrs. Dolores Genchi, *Vice-President*

Computer Installation
IBM 360/30–operating system: DOS; internal storage: 65K bits; magnetic tapes: 4; magnetic discs: 4 2311; 1 line printer.

Coding Language
360 Assembler.

Services Available
Advice, preparation of data, programming, software packages, systems analysis. Operate on an open shop basis.

Fields of Application
Specialized areas: Magazine subscription, mailing list maintenance, data bank management.

COMPUTER SERVICES INC.*
47 Congress Street, Salem, 01970
Telephone: (617) 745-3550

Officers
Stanley A. Ferbank, *President*
N. F. Beebe, *Vice-President*

Computer Installations
HONEYWELL H120–internal storage: 24K bits; magnetic tapes: 5; 1 line printer.
HONEYWELL H120–internal storage: 4K bits; magnetic tapes: 1; 1 line printer.

Coding Languages
COBOL, FORTRAN, Easycoder.

Contemplated Equipment
Honeywell H1250.

Services Available
Consultation, preparation of data, application packages, system design, data processing. Operate on a block time basis.

Fields of Application
Commercial, management, scientific.
Specialized area: Petroleum distribution.

CONDON CORPORATION
11 De Angelo Drive, Bedford, 01730
Telephone: (617) 275-2000

Officers
E. S. Walter, *President*
E. F. Gregory, *Vice-President, Marketing*
S. M. Fisch, *Vice-President, Marketing Services*

Computer Installation
CB-100–operating system: DEAL; internal storage: 384K bits; magnetic tapes: 1; magnetic discs: 4; 4 line printers. *On-line satellite computer*: CB-100R. *Remote processing features*: Video data terminals for data and order entry.

Coding Languages
DEAL, Assembler, RPG.

Services Available
Programming, software packages, preparation of data, systems analysis.

Fields of Application
Commercial, inventory control.
Specialized areas: Sales analysis, distribution management.

CONTROL DATA CORPORATION*
Cambridge Center
545 Technology Square, Cambridge, 02139
Telephone: (617) 354-6200

Also at:
CEIR Inc. Subs. of Control Data
186 Alewife Brook Parkway, Cambridge, Massachusetts 02138
Telephone: (617) 491-3050
Waltham Center
60 Hickory Drive, Waltham, Massachusetts 02154
Telephone: (617) 891-4600
(*See* under Minnesota)

United States of America – Service Bureaux

DATA OPERATIONS INC.*
2464 Massachusetts Avenue, Cambridge, 02140
Telephone: (617) 868-0500

Officer
Richard N. Marks, *President*

Computer Installation
HONEYWELL H120–internal storage: 16K bits; magnetic tapes: 4; 1 line printer.

Coding Languages
COBOL, FORTRAN, Easycoder.

Services Available
Advice, operators, preparation of data, programming, software packages, systems analysis. Operate on a self-service, open shop, remote access, block time and time-sharing basis.

Fields of Application
Commercial, accounting, systems analysis.

DIAL-DATA INC.*
429 Watertown Street, Newton, 02158
Telephone: (617) 244-2560

Computer Installation
XDS 940.

Coding Languages
CAL, FORTRAN, SNOBOL, QED.

Service Available
Time-sharing. Operate on a remote access basis.

Fields of Application
Scientific, commercial.

EDUCATORS CONSULTANT SERVICE INC.*
(Subsidiary of Simplicity Pattern Corp., 200 Madison Avenue, New York)
56 Chandler Street, Worcester, 01609
Telephone: 757-3838

Officers
Dr. John Torosian, *President*
Dr. John Magee, *Treasurer*

Computer Installation
IBM 1130–internal storage: 16K bits; magnetic discs: 2 2315; 1 line printer.

Coding Languages
COBOL, FORTRAN IV, RPG, Assembly.

Contemplated Equipment
IBM 360/30.

Services Available
Advice, operators, preparation of data, programming, software packages, systems analysis. Operate on a closed shop basis.

Fields of Application
Computer applications, systems analysis.
Specialized area: Educational applications.

FEDDER DATA CENTER OF THE NORTHEAST*
824 Boylston Street, Chestnut Hill
Telephone: (617) 734-2033
(*See* under Maryland)

GENERAL ELECTRIC COMPANY*
Information Service Department
400 Totten Pond Road, Waltham, 02154
Telephone: (617) 891-1313/0306

GENERAL ELECTRIC COMPANY*
Information Service Department
766 Tyler Street, Pittsfield, 01201
Telephone: (413) 443-4711

INFORMATION DYNAMICS CORPORATION*
80 Main Street, Reading, 01201
Telephone: (617) 944-2224

Computer Installation
IBM 360/30.

Services Available
Advice, preparation of data, programming.

Fields of Application
Scientific, commercial.

INTERACTIVE DATA CORPORATION*
486 Totten Pond Road, Waltham, 02154
Telephone: (617) 891-6250

Computer Installation
IBM 360/67 (2)–internal storage: 512K bits each; magnetic tapes: 14 IBM 2401; magnetic discs: 3 IBM 2314; 4 line printers.

Services Available
Education and training. Operate on a time-sharing basis.

Fields of Application
Financial, management systems, statistical, scientific, economic.

Training
Courses on various computer languages as required.

INTERACTIVE SCIENCES CORPORATION
60 Brooke Drive, Braintree, 02184

Officers
Richard Reut, *President and Treasurer*
Alfred Jorgensen, *Vice-President, Marketing*
Karl Reiter, *Vice-President, Engineering*

Computer Installation
PDP-10 (2)–internal storage: 3,500K bits (and 2,360K bits); magnetic tapes: 4 (and 2) TU20; magnetic discs: 8 DS3; 1 line printer (each). *Remote processing features*: 64 simultaneous 110, 134, 300 B/S.

Coding Languages
FORTRAN, COBOL, LISP, BASIC, MACRO (Assembly).

Contemplated Equipment
Increased storage, magnetic discs, a third computer system (all during 1973).

Services Available
Advice, programming, education and training, operators, software packages, documentation, systems analysis, time-sharing service. Operate on a remote access, block time off prime, and time-sharing basis.

United States of America – Service Bureaux

Fields of Application
Scientific, statistical, commercial, production control, accounting, management, operational research, data management.
Specialized areas: Sales analysis, linear programming, investment, logic design.

Training
System and application user training.

INTER-COMERICA COMPUTING COMPANY INC.*
A division of Compute America Corporation (COMERICA)
375 Harrison Avenue, Boston, 02118
Telephone: (617) 542-5365

Also at:
Corporate Headquarters, 1515 Classen Boulevard, Oklahoma City, Oklahoma 73106

Officers
Richard M. Deaton, *Executive Vice-President*
John W. Cormack, *Director of Personnel*
James B. Fitzgerald, *Branch Manager*

Computer Installation
UNIVAC 9300–operating system: NCOS, COS; internal storage: 288K bits; magnetic tapes: 6 Uniservo IV; 1 line printer.
UNIVAC 1004–operating systems: EXEC 11 and 8; internal storage: 6,608 bits; magnetic tapes: 2 Uniservo IV; 1 line printer. *On-line satellite computer*: Univac 1108.

Coding Languages
RPG, COBOL, FORTRAN, Assembler.

Services Available
Programming, operators, documentation, preparation of data, systems analysis. Operate on a closed shop and block time basis.

Fields of Application
Scientific, statistical, commercial, production control, accounting, management, systems analysis.

KEYDATA CORPORATION*
108 Water Street, Watertown, 02172
Telephone: (617) 924-1200

Also at:
1700 Broadway, New York, N.Y. 10019
Telephone: (212) 586-5500
1 Gateway Plaza, Newton, Massachusetts
5725 East River Road, O'Hare Plaza, Suite 545, Chicago, Illinois 60631

Officers
John T. Gilmore, *President*
Allen F. Rousseau, *Vice-President*
John S. Hermistone, *General Manager, Computer Operations*

Computer Installations
UNIVAC 494–operating system: Omega VI; internal storage: 65K 30-bit words; magnetic tapes: 7 Univac VIII-C; 1 line printer. *On-line satellite computer*: Honeywell H516.
IBM 360/40–operating system: DOS; internal storage: 128K 8-bit bytes; magnetic tapes: 2 2311; 2 line printers.

Coding Languages
KOP III, Keydata Proprietary Language.

Contemplated Equipment
Additional Univac 494.

Service Available
Business utility.

Fields of Application
Commercial, accounting.
Specialized areas: Accounts, inventory control.

MARK/OPS
(Division of Northeastern Systems Associates, Inc.)
475 Commonwealth Avenue, Boston, 02216
Telephone: (617) 266-1930

Officer
Homer W. Cates, *President*

Computer Installation
PDP-10–internal storage: 160K bits; magnetic tapes: 3; magnetic discs: 16; 1 line printer. *On-line satellite computer*: Card I/O. *Remote processing features*: PPT I/O.

Coding Languages
FORTRAN, BASIC, ALGOL, LISP, TECO, BBL.

Contemplated Equipment
Another PDP-10.

Services Available
Consultation, programming, education and training, software packages, documentation, systems analysis. Operate on a remote access and time-sharing basis.

Fields of Application
Scientific, statistical analysis, production control, business packages, numerical control, engineering applications.

Training
Courses available through Data Education, Inc., Totten Pond Road, Waltham, Massachusetts.

NAMAC INC.*
534 Boston Post Road, Wayland, 01778
Telephone: (617) 899-5560

Computer Installation
HONEYWELL H200–internal storage: 16K bits; magnetic tapes: 5.

Services Available
Consultation, preparation of data, programming.

NATIONAL CASH REGISTER COMPANY
Boston Data Processing Center
135 Pennsylvania Avenue, Framingham, 01701
Telephone: (617) 875-0657

Officer
R. V. Jordan, *Manager*
(For details, *see* under Ohio)

PRODUCTION SYSTEMS INC.*
242 Second Avenue, Waltham, 02154
Telephone: (617) 893-2356

Officers
Mitchell J. Marcus, *President*
Herbert D. Marcus, *Vice-President*
L. Gerald Marcus, *Vice-President*
John M. White, *Manager*

United States of America – Service Bureaux

Computer Installation
BULL GENERAL ELECTRIC GE 225 (2)–internal storage: 180K bits each; magnetic tapes: 4 each; 2 line printers. *Remote processing features*: GE Datanet 30 with complete time-sharing ability.

Coding Languages
Assembly, GECOM, COBOL, FORTRAN-RPG.

Services Available
Advice, operators, programming, software packages, systems analysis. Operate on a closed shop basis.

Fields of Application
Statistical, commercial, production control, accounting, management systems, CPM, PERT.
Specialized areas: Business data processing, systems design and programming.

PROGRAMS AND ANALYSIS INC.
21 Ray Avenue, Burlington, 01803
Telephone: (617) 272-7723

Also at:
144 Moody Street, Waltham, Massachusetts 02154
Telephone: (617) 891-6508
1372 Broadway, 20th Floor, New York, N.Y. 10018
Telephone: (212) 354-6055

Officers
B. Blumberg, Jr., *President*
P. J. Brighton, *Vice-President*

Computer Installation
IBM 360/30–operating system: DOS; internal storage: 128K bits; magnetic tapes: 5 2401/3; magnetic discs: 9 2314; 2 line printers. *On-line satellite computer*: IBM 360/20. *Remote processing features*: 2701.
HONEYWELL H6050–operating system: GECOS; internal storage: 192K words; magnetic tapes: 5 MTH500; magnetic discs: 18 DSU180; 2 line printers. *On-line satellite computers*: MDS2400 (2). *Remote processing features*: 50 lines.

Coding Languages
COBOL, RPG, Autocoder, FORTRAN, BAL, BASIC.

Services Available
Advice, programming, education and training, operators, software packages, documentation, data preparation, systems analysis. Operate on a self-service, remote access, block time and time-sharing basis.

Fields of Application
Scientific, statistical, commercial, production control, accounting, management, systems analysis, operational research.

RECORDING AND STATISTICAL COMPANY
556 Atlantic Avenue, Boston, 02210
Telephone: (617) 542-5365
(*See* under New York)

SDK MEDICAL COMPUTER SERVICES CORPORATION*
68 Harvard Street, Brookline, 02147
Telephone: 566-1139

Officer
S. David Kaufman, *President*

Computer Installation
HONEYWELL H1200–operating system: MOD 1; internal storage: 32K bits; magnetic tapes: 5; 1 line printer.

Coding Language
COBOL.

Service Available
Preparation of data. Operate on an open shop and remote access basis. Available only to hospitals and nursing homes.

Fields of Application
Accounting, management.
Specialized areas: Hospitals and nursing homes.

SERVICE BUREAU CORPORATION*
140 Federal Street, Boston, 02110
Telephone: (617) 542-2380

Also at:
147 Milk Street, Boston Massachusetts 02110
Telephone: (617) 542-5891
(*See* under New York)

SYSTEK INC.*
621 Pittsfield-Lenox Road, P.O. Box N, Pittsfield, 01201
Telephone: (413) 445-4793

Officers
Edward O. Brutsch, *President*
John W. Neff, *Vice-President, Technical Development*

Computer Installation
IBM 360/30–operating system: TOS; internal storage: 261,888 bits; magnetic tapes: 6 2415 9-track; 1 line printer.

Coding Languages
BAL, COBOL, FORTRAN, PL/1, RPG.

Services Available
Consultation, programming, software packages, documentation, preparation of data, systems analysis. Operate on a closed shop basis.

Fields of Application
Scientific, engineering, accounting, commercial, management information sciences, publishing and mailing lists, systems analysis and design, statistical and survey.

TELCOMP CORPORATION OF AMERICA*
(Subsidiary of Bolt Beranek and Newman Inc.)
50 Moulton Street, Cambridge, 02138
Telephone: (617) 491-1850

Officers
J. E. Stratton, *President*
S. Labate, *Vice-President*
R. L. Fish, *Treasurer*

Computer Installation
PDP-10–internal storage: 128K 36-bit words; magnetic tapes: 10; magnetic discs: 6 drives; 1 line printer. *Remote processing features*: 64-user capacity, Calcomp 663 on-line plotter.
PDP-8 (2)–magnetic tapes: 2; magnetic drum: Fastrand. *On-line satellite computers*: PDP-8, PDP-10. *Remote processing features*: 32-user capacity.

Coding Languages
TELCOMP II and III, FORTRAN IV, Advanced BASIC, MACRO-10.

Contemplated Equipment
Additional PDP-10s of similar configuration; front-end communications processor.

United States of America – Service Bureaux

Services Available
Advice, preparation of data, programming, software packages. Operate on a time-sharing basis. No batch or remote-batch processing.

Fields of Application
Scientific, engineering, research, statistical, operational research, management, financial, accounting, production control.
Specialized areas: Circuit analysis, highway design, structural engineering, filter design and analysis, analog simulation, PERT, linear programming, financial forecasting, merger analysis, journal entry, SORT/MERGE, information storage and retrieval applications.

Training
Customer-tailored courses.

UNIVAC NORTHEAST REGIONAL OFFICE*
55 William Street, Wellesley, 02181
Telephone: (617) 237-2780
(*See* under California)

WANG LABORATORIES, INC.
Phi Computer Services Division
836 North Street, Tewksbury, 01876
Telephone: (617) 851-4111

Officers
Dr. An Wang, *President*
Ned Chang, *General Manager*

Computer Installation
IBM 360/65–operating system: OS/MVT; internal storage: 2.5 million bytes; magnetic tapes: 8 9-track; magnetic discs: 5 2314; 4 line printer. *On-line satellite computers*: PDP-11 frontend, Tempo 270X emulator. *Remote processing features*: RJE/HASP, Wylbur Conversational RJE.

Coding Languages
COBOL, BAL, PL/1, BASIC, FORTRAN, ALGOL.

Contemplated Equipment
IBM 370/158.

Services Available
Advice, programming, operators, software packages, documentation, preparation of data, systems analysis. Operate on a remote access, block time and time-sharing basis.

Fields of Application
Payroll, structural engineering, teleprocessing, data communications.

WINGATE COMPUTING CENTER*
River Park and Barik Street, Attleboro, 02703
Telephone: (617) 222-5400

Also at:
151 Rock Street, Fall River, Massachusetts 02720
Telephone: (617) 674-8421
(*See* under Rhode Island)

MICHIGAN

BURROUGHS CORPORATION*
6071 2nd Avenue, Detroit, 48232
Telephone: (313) 972-7000

Also at:
Detroit Data Center, 13001 Eckles Road, Plymouth, Michigan 48075
Charlotte Data Center, 731 Central Avenue, Charlotte, North Carolina 28204
San Francisco Data Center, 447 Battery Street, San Francisco, California 94111

Service Available
Time-sharing on various applications.

COM-SHARE INC.
2395 Huron Parkway, Ann Arbor, 48105
Telephone: (313) 761-4040

Officer
R. L. Crondall, *President*

Computer Installation
XDS 940 (11)–internal storage: 64K 24-bit words; magnetic discs; magnetic drum; 1 line printer. *Remote processing features*: 40-user capacity.
XDS Sigma 9 (3)–internal storage: 128K 32-bit words.

Coding Languages
COBOL, FORTRAN, BASIC, NEWBASIC, XTRAN, SNOBOL, QED, TAP, DDT.

Services Available
Consultation, programming, software packages, systems analysis. Operate on a remote access and time-sharing basis.

Fields of Application
Scientific, statistical, commercial, production control, accounting, management, systems analysis, operational research.

Training
Short initial courses in system capabilities and its use.

CONTROL DATA CORPORATION*
Detroit Center
23775 Northwestern, Southfield, 48075
Telephone: (313) 353-3600
(*See* under Minnesota)

GENERAL ELECTRIC COMPANY*
Information Services Department
Kyle Building, 22150 Greenfield Road, Detroit, 48237
Telephone: (313) 398-9000

GENERAL ELECTRIC COMPANY*
Information Service Department
3206 Eastern Avenue, Grand Rapids, 49508
Telephone: (616) 241-5441

MODERN BUSINESS RECORDS*
6030 Chase Road, Dearborn, 48126
Telephone: (313) 584-7330

Officer
Howard Hyatt, *President*

United States of America – Service Bureaux

NATIONAL CASH REGISTER COMPANY*
Data Processing Center
2875 West Grand Boulevard, Detroit, 48202
Telephone: (313) 873-5500

Officer
D. B. Kerwin, *Manager*

(For details, *see* under Ohio)

SERVICE BUREAU CORPORATION*
1550 Howard Street, Detroit, 48216
Telephone: 961-9688

Also at:
1422 West Court Street, Flint, Michigan 48503
Telephone: (313) 232-3143
415 Cherry Street, S.E., Grand Rapids, Michigan 49502
Telephone: (616) 458-1527
2201 East Grand River Avenue, Lansing, Michigan 48912
Telephone: (517) 485-5495
(*See* under New York)

TECHNICAL ADVISORS, INC.
4455 Fletcher Street, Wayne, 48184
Telephone: (313) 722-5010

Officers
Edwin W. Miller, *President*
Thomas A. Weyand, *Vice-President*

Computer Installation
VARIAN 620/I–operating system: TECH-MAC; internal storage: 216K bits; magnetic discs: 1 fixed head; 1 line printer. *Remote processing features*: 16 ports.

Coding Language
Assembly.

Services Available
Programming, education and training, software packages, preparation of data. Operate on a remote access, open shop, and time-sharing basis.

Field of Application
Surveying (horizontal geometry).

S. J. TESAURO & CO.*
Data Processing Center
5435 West Fort Street, Detroit, 48209
Telephone: (313) 842-4200

Officer
Jerome J. Havrda, *Vice-President and General Manager*

Computer Installation
IBM 360/30–operating system: DOS; internal storage: 32K bits; magnetic tapes: 4 2401; magnetic discs: 1 2311; 1 line printer.
IBM 360/20–operating system: DOS; internal storage: 12K bits; 1 line printer.

Coding Languages
BAL, Autocoder, RPG.

Contemplated Equipment
IBM 360/30.

Services Available
Preparation of data, programming, systems analysis. Operate on a closed shop and block time basis.

Fields of Application
Statistical, commercial, accounting, management.
Specialized areas: File maintenance, sales analysis.

UNIVAC DATA PROCESSING CENTER*
2978 West Grand Boulevard, Detroit, 48202
Telephone: (313) 874-3000
(*See* under California)

MINNESOTA

BUSINESS PUBLISHERS CIRCULATION SERVICES
1 East First Street, Duluth, 55802
Telephone: (218) 727-8511

Officers
Lars Fladmark, *President*
Joe Bilderbach, *Vice-President and General Manager*

Computer Installation
NCR Century 200 (2)–internal storage: 32K bits each; magnetic tapes: 3 each; magnetic discs: 1 657-202 each; 1 line printer each.

Coding Language
NEAT 3.

Services Available
Advice, programming, preparation of data, systems analysis. Operate on a closed shop basis.

Fields of Application
Specialized areas: Circulation fulfilment, reader inquiry processing, comparative space advertising reporting.

COMPUTER SYSTEMS INTERNATIONAL INC.*
Jonathan Industries, Chaska, 55318

Overseas:
London (U.K.)

Officer
A. L. Reed, *Director*

Coding Languages
All high level languages, particularly COBOL.

Services Available
Advice, operators, preparation of data, programming, software packages, systems analysis.

Fields of Application
Scientific, statistical, commercial, production control, management, operational research, etc.
Specialized areas: Commercial applications, time-sharing and real time.

CONTROL DATA CORPORATION*
Data Centers Division
8100 34th Avenue South, Minneapolis, 55440
Telephone: (612) 888-5555

Also at:
7800 Governors Drive West, Huntsville, Alabama 35805
Telephone: (205) 837-0400
5630 Arbor Vitae, Los Angeles, California 90045
Telephone: (213) 670-3640
3330 Hillview Avenue, Palo Alto, California 94304
Telephone: (415) 321-8920

United States of America – Service Bureaux

Fox Plaza Suite 235, San Francisco, California 94102
Telephone: (415) 626-2790
223 West Jackson Boulevard, Chicago, Illinois 60606
Telephone: (312) 427-8270
11428 Rockville Pike, Rockville, Maryland 20852
Telephone: (301) 949-8800
545 Technology Square, Cambridge, Massachusetts 02139
Telephone: (617) 354-6200
60 Hickory Drive, Waltham, Massachusetts 02154
Telephone: (617) 891-4600
23775 Northwestern, Southfield, Michigan 48075
Telephone: (313) 353-3600
575 Lexington Avenue, New York, New York 10022
Telephone: (212) 752-3840
295 Northern Boulevard, Great Neck, New York 11021
Telephone: (212) 886-0411
140 Broadway, New York, New York 10005
Telephone: (212) 422-7400
1014 Vine Street, Cincinnati, Ohio 44115
Telephone: (513) 381-4520
1450 Leader Building, Cleveland, Ohio 44114
Telephone: (216) 696-4515
P.O. Box 45409, Dallas, Texas 75235
Telephone: (214) 358-4277
7135 Office City Drive, Houston, Texas 77017
Telephone: (713) 644-2221
2000 L Street, Northwest, Washington, D.C. 20036

Overseas centres:
Frankfurt am Main (Germany); Genoa, Milan, Rome (Italy).

Computer Installation
A wide range of CDC computers.

Coding Languages
COBOL, COMPASS, APT III, ALLEGRO, INFOL.

Services Available
Consultation, operators, preparation of data, programming, systems analysis. Operate on a self-service, closed shop, open shop and block time basis.

Fields of Application
All computer-related fields.
Specialized areas: Numerical control, linear programming, transportation networks, information and retrieval, structural engineering, PERT/TIME, nuclear applications, seismic applications, investment analysis.

Training
Courses in programming and computer technology; courses for digital computer operators. Short courses covering hardware, software and operational aspects are taught at the specific request of customers.

DATA SYSTEMS INC.*
434 Stinson Boulevard, Minneapolis, 55413
Telephone: (612) 331-9435

Officers
R. Dean Caldwell, *President*
Edward W. Shimek, *Vice-President, including computer center operation management*
Robert O. Polzak, *Vice-President, including management of staff education*

Computer Installation
BURROUGHS B300–operating system: Burroughs B300 basic; internal storage: 19,200 characters; magnetic tapes: 5; 1 line printer. *Remote processing features*: Card reader, card punch, paper tape reader.

Coding Languages
Advanced Assembler, COBOL.

Contemplated Equipment
Burroughs B3500, 4 tapes, 1 disc, 2 printers.

Services Available
Advice, operators, preparation of data, programming, software packages, systems analysis. Operate on an open shop and block time basis.

Fields of Application
Data processing consultants in systems and applications; contract programming; computing services and time sales; complete bureau service.
Specialized areas: Application programme packages; PERT; CPM; contract programming, systems design and analysis.

Training
Short courses: Introduction and applications of network planning techniques (3-5 days); management information systems design (3 days).

GENERAL ELECTRIC COMPANY*
Information Service Department
1500 Lilac Drive South, Minneapolis, 55416
Telephone: (612) 544-6699

NATIONAL CASH REGISTER COMPANY*
Data Processing Center
2523 Wayzata Boulevard, Minneapolis, 55405
Telephone: (612) 377-3110

Officer
J. E. Hite, *Manager*
(For details, *see* under Ohio)

SCIENTIFIC COMPUTERS INC.*
919 2nd Ave. South, Minneapolis, 55402
Telephone: 339-0544

Officer
L. J. Cooke, *President*

Computer Installation
IBM 360–operating systems: DOS, QTAM; internal storage: 128K bits; magnetic tapes: 4 2400; magnetic discs: 2314; 1 line printer.

Coding Languages
COBOL, Assembly, ADPAC.

Contemplated Equipment
IBM 360/50.

Services Available
Advice, preparation of data, programming, software packages, systems analysis. Batch and on-line services.

Fields of Application
Statistical, commercial, production control, accounting, management.
Specialized areas: Manufacturing, financial, construction and distribution industry.

Training
All courses specially designed.

SERVICE BUREAU CORPORATION*
8901 Wayzata Boulevard, Minneapolis, 55426
Telephone: (612) 544-1571
(*See* under New York)

United States of America – Service Bureaux

SIGMA PROCESSING INC.*
10130 Highway 55, Minneapolis, 55427
Telephone: (612) 544-4611

Officer
James R. Loux

Computer Installation
IBM 360–internal storage: 16K bits; magnetic tapes: 4; magnetic discs: 2; 1 line printer. *Remote processing features*: Teleprocessing.

NCR Century 100–magnetic discs: 2; 1 line printer.

Coding Languages
BAL, RPG, COBOL, NEAT 3.

Services Available
Advice, operators, preparation of data, programming, systems analysis. Operate on a self-service, remote access and block time basis.

Fields of Application
Commercial, production control, accounting, management. *Specialized areas*: Labour management, production job costing, inventory control.

UNIVAC DATA PROCESSING CENTER*
3300 University Avenue, South-east, Minneapolis, 55414
Telephone: (712) 335-6487
(*See* under California)

MISSOURI

DATA CENTRAL INC.*
200 South Hanley Road, SU 600, St. Louis, 63105
Telephone: (314) 863-4000

Officer
Donald G. Hogan, *President*

FIRST NATIONAL BANK IN ST. LOUIS*
510 Locust Street, St. Louis, 63101
Telephone: GA1-2000

Officer
Anton Burkhartsmier, *Vice-President, EDP*

Computer Installation
IBM 360/30 (1); IBM 360/40 (2); IBM 360/50–operating system: DOS; internal storage: 196K, 256K and 131K bits; magnetic tapes: 23; magnetic discs: 5 IBM 2311, 1 IBM 2314; 6 line printers. *Remote processing features*: 2703 communications control for on-line terminals at remote locations; tally paper tape and magnetic tape transmission from remote locations.

Coding Languages
Basic Assembler, COBOL, RPG.

Services Available
Operators, preparation of data, software packages, systems analysis. Operate on a closed shop basis. Generally restricted to financial institutions.

Field of Application
Bank accounting.

FIRST-UNION AUTOMATION SERVICE, INC. (FAS)*
515 Olive Street, St. Louis, 63101

Officers
A. Borkhartsmeier, *President*
P. Mozola, *Vice-President*

Computer Installation
IBM 360/40–operator system: DOS; internal storage: 196K bits; magnetic tapes: 6; magnetic discs: 1 2314; 2 line printers.

Services Available
Software sales, systems and programming services. Operate on a closed shop basis.

Field of Application
Commercial.
Specialized areas: Optical reading, COM.

GENERAL ELECTRIC COMPANY*
Information Service Department
1015 Locust Street, Suite 505, St. Louis, 63101
Telephone: (314) 436-4343

INFORMATION MANAGEMENT ASSOCIATES INC.*
4221 Lindell, St. Louis, 63108
Telephone: JE5-2544

Officer
Robert W. Gehlert, *President*

Computer Installation
IBM 360/20–internal storage: 8K bits; 1 line printer.

Coding Languages
RPG, BAL.

Contemplated Equipment
Univac 9200.

Services Available
Advice, operators, preparation of data, programming, systems analysis. Operate on a closed shop basis.

Field of Application
Commercial.

McDONNELL AUTOMATION COMPANY
A Division of McDonnell Douglas Corp.
P.O. Box 516, St. Louis, 63166
Telephone: (314) 232-8021

Also at:
666 Park Avenue, East Orange, New Jersey 07017
Telephone: (201) 676-4222
2990 Telestar Court, Falls Church, Virginia 22042
Telephone: (703) 573-4100
1124 North Berkeley Avenue, Peoria, Illinois 61603
Telephone: (309) 674-0637
Suite 400, 500 Jefferson Building, Houston, Texas 77002
Telephone: (713) 224-5921
360 Western Federal Building, Devner, Colorado 80202
Telephone: (303) 534-6291
Suite 806, 3711 Long Beach Boulevard, Long Beach, California 90807
Telephone: (213) 593-8221

Officers
W. R. Orthwein, Jr., *President*
R. L. Harmon, *Executive Vice-President*
A. J. Quackenbush, *Executive Vice-President*

United States of America – Service Bureaux

Computer Installation
IBM 195 (2); IBM 360/20 (8); IBM 360/22; IBM 360/25;
IBM 360/30 (6); IBM 360/40 (2); IBM 360/50; IBM 370/
135; IBM 370/145 (2); IBM 370/155 (5); IBM 370/165 (3);
IBM 1800 (3); IBM 7094 (3); IBM 1130 (3); CDC 6400;
CDC 6500; CDC 6600; CDC 915; CDC 1700; UNIVAC
1004 (2); UNIVAC 9300; HONEYWELL DDP 516;
XDS Sigma 5 (2); XDS Sigma 7 (3); XDS 930 (5);
XDS 9300.

Coding Languages
All languages.

Services Available
Consultation, preparation of data, programming, software
packages, systems analysis. Operate on a closed shop,
open shop, remote access, block time and time-sharing
basis.

Fields of Application
Scientific, statistical, commercial, production control,
accounting, engineering, management, operational
research, hospital data processing.

NATIONAL CASH REGISTER COMPANY*
Data Processing Center
1601 Broadway, Kansas City, 64108
Telephone: (816) 421-6642

Officer
L. H. Logan, *Manager*

Also at:
3744 Lindell Boulevard, St. Louis, 63108
Telephone: (314) 371-1900

Officer
G. E. Brothers, *Manager*
(For details, *see* under Ohio)

SERVICE BUREAU CORPORATION*
2911 Main Street, Kansas City, 64108
Telephone: (816) 753-2141

Also at:
2360 Hampton Avenue, St. Louis, Missouri 63139
Telephone: (314) 647-5444
(*See* under New York)

UNITED COMPUTING SYSTEMS, INC. (UCS)*
(Subsidiary of United Utilities Inc.)
3130 Broadway, Kansas City, 64111
Telephone: (816) 753-4500

Also at:
418 West 26th Street, Kansas City, Missouri 64108.
Also 12 sales offices throughout the U.S.A.

Officers
G. J. Lorenz, *President*
J. D. Howard, *Vice-President, Treasurer*
G. W. Elstun, *Marketing Manager*

Computer Installation
CDC 6000 series–operating system: MAX; internal
storage: 7,864,320 bits; magnetic tapes: 7 7-track;
magnetic discs: 1 814, 1 808; 2 line printers. *On-line
satellite computer*: CDC 6411. *Remote processing
features*: conversational time-sharing and remote batch.
BULL GENERAL ELECTRIC GE 265–internal storage:
327,680 bits; magnetic tapes: 4 7-track; magnetic discs:
1 GE DSU204; 1 line printer. *On-line satellite computer*:
GE DN-30. *Remote processing features*: conversational
time-sharing.

Coding Languages
BASIC, FORTRAN IV, COBOL, COMPASS, ALGOL.

Contemplated Equipment
Additional CDC 6000 series.

Services Available
Consultation, programming, education and training
(to UCS customers only), software packages, preparation
of data, systems analysis. Operate on remote access,
closed shop and time-sharing basis.

Fields of Application
Scientific, statistical, commercial, production control,
accounting, management, systems analysis, operational
research.
Specialized areas: Engineering, file management and data
retrieval, business accounting applications.

UNIVAC DATA PROCESSING CENTER*
1907 Baltimore, Kansas City, 64108
Telephone: (816) 471-0477
(*See* under California)

NEBRASKA

AMERICAN KEY PUNCH*
Wow Building, Omaha, 68102

Officers
William Wurgler, Sr., *President*
William Wurgler, Jr., *Vice-President*

Computer Installation
CDC 8092/915–internal storage: 32,768 bits; magnetic
tapes: 1 608, 1 609.

Coding Languages
GRASP, LIST Processor, NIMP, Keypunch Simulator,
TAS Assembly Language.

Service Available
Preparation of data. Operate on an open shop basis.

Field of Application
Commercial.
Specialized areas: Volume key punching, OCR typing and
optical scanning.

AUTOMATION INC.*
1904 Farnam Street, Omaha, 68102
Telephone: (402) 342-3346

Officer
D. R. Dale, *President*

United States of America – Service Bureaux

GENERAL ELECTRIC COMPANY*
Information Service Department
409 South 17th Street, Omaha, 68102
Telephone: (402) 341-4455

SERVICE BUREAU CORPORATION*
3119 Dodge Street, Omaha, 68131
Telephone: (402) 342-1678
(*See* under New York)

NEVADA

NATIONAL CASH REGISTER COMPANY*
Data Processing Center
1270 East Plumb Lane, Reno, 89502
Telephone: (702) 786-0510

Officer
J. D. Wise, *Manager*
(For details, *see* under Ohio)

NEW JERSEY

APPLIED DATA RESEARCH INC.
(Home Office)
Route 206 Center, Princeton, 08540
Telephone: (609) 921-8550

Also at:
(Service Bureau Office)
2425 Wilson Boulevard, Arlington, Virginia 22201
Telephone: (703) 524-9650
11661 San Vicente Boulevard, Los Angeles, California 90049
Telephone: (213) 826-6503
Lakeside Office Park, Wakefield, Massachusetts 01880
Telephone: (617) 245-9540

Officers
John R. Bennett, *President*
Warren F. Spalding, *Vice-President*
Martin A. Goetz, *Vice-President*
Robert V. Smith, *Treasurer*

Computer Installation
IBM 360/50 (2).

Coding Languages
BAL, COBOL, FORTRAN.

Services Available
Advice, operators, programming, software packages, systems analysis. Operate on a closed shop basis.

Fields of Application
Systems analysis design and programming for all types of computer users exclusive of scientific applications.

Training
Short courses conducted in training programmers to third generation equipment, random access methods and other specialized subjects.

AUTOMATED DATA ASSOCIATES INC.*
1333 Lawrence Street, Rahway, 07065
Telephone: (201) 382-3900

Officers
R. L. Campbell, *President*
N. S. Nolan, *Vice-President*

Computer Installation
HONEYWELL H120–internal storage: 20K bits; magnetic tapes: 4; 1 line printer.
HONEYWELL H110–internal storage: 16K bits; magnetic tapes: 2; 1 line printer.

Coding Language
COBOL.

Services Available
Software packages, systems analysis, preparation of data, programming.

Fields of Application
Commercial, accounting.
Specialized areas: Sales analysis, accounts receivable.

AUTOMATIC DATA PROCESSING INC.*
405 Route 3, Clifton, 07015

Also at:
Automatic Computer Services, Inc.
Brokerage Processing Center, Inc. (BPC)
50 Broadway, New York, New York 10004
Independent Blueprint & Supply Co., Inc. and Affiliates
215 East 42nd Street, New York, New York 10017
Analytic Computing Services, Inc.
405 Route 3, Clifton, New Jersey 07015
Automatic Data Processing of Florida, Inc.
2525 S.W. 27th Avenue, Miami, Florida 33133
Automatic Data Processing of Maryland, Inc.
1718 E. Northern Parkway, Baltimore, Maryland 21239
Automatic Data Processing of Massachusetts, Inc.
1040-50 Commonwealth Avenue, Boston, Massachusetts 02215
Automatic Data Processing of Michigan, Inc.
5435 W. Fort Street, Detroit, Michigan 48209
Automatic Data Processing of Missouri, Inc.
8794 Manchester Road, St. Louis, Missouri 63144
Automatic Data Processing of Pennsylvania, Inc.
1700 Benjamin Franklin Parkway, Philadelphia, Pennsylvania 19103
Automatic Data Processing of Pittsburgh, Inc.
1930 West Liberty Avenue, Pittsburgh, Pennsylvania 15226
I.D.R. Co.
325 Chestnut Street, Philadelphia, Pennsylvania 19106
Automatic Remote Computer Services
42 Broadway, New York, New York 10004

Officers
Frank R. Lautenberg, *President (Clifton)*
Henry Taub, *Chairman (New York)*

Computer Installation
IBM 360/40–magnetic tapes: 31.

Services Available
Advice, programming, software packages.

Field of Application
Commercial.
Specialized area: Payroll.

COMPUTER USAGE DEVELOPMENT CORPORATION*
37 North Fullerton Avenue, Montclair, 07042
Telephone: (201) 746-3200
(*See* under New York)

COMSONIC CORPORATION*
123 Pleasant Avenue, Upper Saddle River, 07458
Telephone: (201) 825-1800

Officers
A. Dale Mayo, *President*
C. Desimone, Sr., *Vice-President – Marketing*
F. Heiss, Sr., *Vice-President – Operations*

Computer Installation
PDP-8–operating system: TSS-8; internal storage: 192K bits; magnetic tapes: 2 DEC; magnetic discs: 1 RSO8; 1 line printer. *Remote processing features*: interactive terminals.

Coding Languages
BASIC, FORTRAN II, FOCAL, Assembly.

Services Available
Consultation, programming, software packages, systems analysis. Operate on a remote access and time-sharing basis.

Fields of Application
Accounting, file management system, statistical, commercial, scientific, systems analysis, cargo handling, text editing.

DATA SYSTEMS ANALYSTS INC.
North Park Drive, Cooper Parkway Office Building, Pennsauken, 08109
Telephone: (609) 665-6088; (215) WA5-9550

Officers
Charles H. Margolin, *President*
T. N. Scambia, *Vice-President*
Irwin J. Fredman, *Director of European Operations*

Services Available
Advice, preparation of data, programming, software packages, systems analysis, systems design, technical consulting, turnkey message switching systems, feasibility studies, product planning, research studies. Operate on a time-sharing basis.

Fields of Application
On-line systems, communications switching systems, airline and aviation systems, management information systems, information storage and retrieval, commercial operations research, production control.
Specialized area: Design of store-and-forward message switching systems.

Training
Seminars on message-switching and data communications.

DATA USAGE CORPORATION
2460 Lemoine Avenue, Fort Lee, 07024
Telephone: (201) 461-6242

Officers
Gary Mokotoff, *President*
Stan Smillie, *Vice-President*

Computer Installation
IBM 360/20–operating system: DPS; internal storage: 24K bits; magnetic tapes: 2 2145; magnetic discs: 2 2311; 1 line printer.
IBM System/3–internal storage: 16K bits; magnetic tapes: 2 3411; magnetic discs: 1 5444.

Coding Languages
BAL, RPG, COBOL, FORTRAN, PL/1.

Contemplated Equipment
IBM 370/115.

Services Available
Consultation, programming, software packages, preparation of data, systems analysis. Operate on a closed shop basis.

Fields of Application
Commercial, production control, accounting, management.

DATATROL CORPORATION*
32 Brand Avenue, Clementon, 08021

Officers
Herb B. Brooks, *President*
Ray W. Schlunk, *Vice-President*

Services Available
Consultation, programming, education and training, systems analysis. Operate on a self-service basis. Service available to industry and government.

Fields of Application
Hardware and software services for computer control systems, information systems and other real time applications.
Specialized area: Process control simulation.

Training
Courses in basic control experiments using the Model 60 process control simulator.

ELECTRONIC ASSOCIATES INC.*
P.O. Box 582, Princeton, 08541
Telephone: (609) 452-2900
(*See* under California)

ELI COMPUTER SYSTEMS INC.*
319 East 54th Street, East Paterson, 07407
Telephone: (212) 594-1010

Also at:
2 Penn Plaza, New York City, N.Y. 10001

Officer
C. Bernard Pistilli, *Vice-President*

Computer Installation
BURROUGHS B5500–internal storage: 32K bits; magnetic tapes: 4; magnetic discs: 4; 1 line printer.

Coding Languages
ALGOL, FORTRAN, COBOL.

Services Available
Consultation, programming, education and training, operators, software packages, documentation, preparation of data, systems analysis. Operate on remote access, block time and time-sharing basis.

Fields of Application
Commercial, production control, statistical, accounting, management, systems analysis.
Specialized area: Garment/textile industry.

EQUIMATICS INC.
6 Kingsbridge Road, Fairfield, 07006
Telephone: (201) 575-9610

Officers
Werner L. Frank, *President*
G. M. Perry, *Vice-President, Application Development*
H. W. Richmond, *Vice-President, Custom Services*
J. A. Grady, *Vice-President, Administration and Finance*

Computer Installation
IBM 360/40–operating system: DOS/OS; internal storage: 128K bits.

Coding Languages
ALC, COBOL, FORTRAN.

Contemplated Equipment
IBM 360/145.

Services Available
Advice, programming, education and training, software packages, systems analysis. Operate on an open shop basis.

Field of Application
Commercial.
Specialized area: Insurance.

Training
CFO II and ALIS courses.

GENERAL ELECTRIC COMPANY*
Information Service Department
320 Raritan Avenue, Highland Park, 08904
Telephone: (201) 545-6314

GENERAL ELECTRIC COMPANY*
Information Service Department
1500 Palisades Avenue, Teaneck, 07666
Telephone: (201) 833-8300

INSCO SYSTEMS CORPORATION
3501 State Highway 66, Neptune, 07753
Telephone: (201) 922-1100

Officers
F. B. Wadelton, *President*
W. Leslie, *Executive Vice-President*
W. A. Power, *Executive Vice-President*

Computer Installation
IBM 370/155–operating systems: OS-MVT, HASP; internal storage: 1,024K bytes; magnetic tapes: 24 3420/7; magnetic discs: 4 3330, 24 2314; 3 line printers. *Remote processing features:* HASP RJE.
IBM 370/145–operating systems: OS-MVT, OS-VSII; internal storage: 512K bytes; magnetic tapes: 18 3420/7; magnetic discs: 4 3330, 12 2319; 1 line printer. *Remote processing features*: HASP RJE.
IBM 360/67–operating system: CP67/CMS, OS, DOS, BPS; internal storage: 768K bytes; magnetic tapes: 16 3420/7; magnetic discs: 24 2319; 2 line printers. *Remote processing features*: HASP RJE, CMS.
IBM 350/50–operating system: OS-MVT; internal storage: 512K bytes; magnetic tapes: 18 3420/7; magnetic discs: 12 2319; 1 line printer. *Remote processing features*: HASP RJE.

Coding Languages
COBOL, Assembler, FORTRAN IV.

Contemplated Equipment
IBM 370/158, IBM 370/168.

Services Available
Advice, programming, education and training, operators, software packages, documentation, preparation of data, systems analysis, time-sharing-RJE. Operate on a self-service, remote access, block time, open shop and time-sharing basis.

Fields of Application
Statistical, commercial, accounting, management, systems analysis, operational research.
Specialized areas: Sales analysis, medical research, insurance and general business applications.

ITT DATA SERVICES
Eastern Regional Computer Center
P.O. Box 402, Route 17 and Garden State Parkway, Paramus, 07652
Telephone: (201) 262-8700

Overseas:
Stuttgart (Germany); Barnet, Basildon and Cockfosters (U.K.).

Officers
W. J. Ernst, *General Manager and Executive Vice-President*
A. S. Gianoplus, *Vice-President and Director*
R. Madsen, *Vice-President and Director*

Computer Installation
IBM 370/155–operating system: OS/MVT/HASP; internal storage: 1,500 million bits; magnetic tapes: 16 9-track 3420/VII; magnetic discs: 26 2314, 3660, 3330; 2 line printers. *On-line satellite computers*: 1 IBM 360/40, 7 Data 100. *Remote processing features*: RJE, CRJE, TSO.
IBM 360/67–operating system: RTS; internal storage: 750K bits; magnetic tapes: 13 3420/VII, 2401/111; magnetic discs: 25 2314; 2 line printers. *On-line satellite computers:* 10: *Remote processing features:* 100 simultaneous users.

Coding Languages
FORTRAN IV, COBOL, Assembler, BASIC, PL/1, ALGOL, RPG, GPSS, MPSX.

Contemplated Equipment
IBM 370/168.

Services Available
Advice, programming, education and training, operators, software packages, documentation, preparation of data, systems analysis. Operate on a self-service, remote access, block time and time-sharing basis.

Fields of Application
Scientific, statistical, commercial, production control, accounting, management, systems analysis, operational research.
Specialized areas: Investment, inventory control, portfolio accounting, consumer finance.

ARTHUR S. KRANZLEY AND COMPANY, INC.*
1010 South Kings Highway, Cherry Hill, 08034
Telephone: (609) 795-1515

Also at:
Suite 1318, 405 Montgomery Street, San Francisco, California 94104

Officers
Arthur S. Kranzley, *President*
Harlow B. Ladd, *Vice-President*

Computer Installation
IBM 360/40–operating system: DOS; internal storage: 131K bytes; magnetic tapes: 5 2401; magnetic discs: 1 2314; 1 line printer. *Remote processing features*: 2260 video display stations.

Services Available
Consultation, programming, software packages, systems analysis. Operate on a block time basis.

Fields of Application
Commercial, accounting, on-line credit authorization.
Specialized areas: Charge card, instalment loan, certificate of deposit and overdraft accounting.

United States of America – Service Bureaux

McDONNELL AUTOMATION COMPANY*
666 Park Avenue, East Orange, 07017
(*See* under Missouri)

NATIONAL COMPUTER ANALYSTS INC.
U.S. Highway One, Princeton, 08540
Telephone: (609) 452-2800

Officers
John J. Sheehan, *President*
Donald R. Nothstein, *Vice-President and Director of International Marketing*
Irving S. Schechtman, *Secretary-Treasurer*

Computer Installation
RCA 301–internal storage: 140K bits; magnetic tapes: 6 381 drives; 1 line printer. *Remote processing features*: 2 on-line sorters, 1 off-line sorter.

UNIVAC System 70–operating system: DOS; internal storage: 118K bits; magnetic tapes: 6; magnetic discs: 3; 2 line printers.

Coding Languages
COBOL, 370 Assembler, RCA Assembler, Assembler, RPG, FORTRAN.

Services Available
Advice, programming, software packages, documentation, preparation of data, systems analysis. Operate on a closed shop basis.

Fields of Application
Commercial, systems analysis, financial data processing.
Specialized areas: Proprietary software, data communications.

PRINCETON TIME-SHARING SERVICES, INC.*
U.S. Highway No. 1, Princeton, 08540
Telephone: (609) 452-7877

Officers
T. A. Dolotta, *President*
S. S. Witonsky, *Marketing Manager*

Computer Installation
IBM 360/65–operating system: OS/360 MVT, CPS; internal storage: 1,500K bits; magnetic tapes: 6 IBM 2420; magnetic discs: 2 2314-A1; 2 line printers. *Remote processing features*: low and high speed remote job entry, conversational/interactive system.

Coding Languages
FORTRAN, COBOL, PL/1, SNOBOL, WATFOR, RPG, GPSS, ECAP, MPS, ACCAP, QUICK-DRAW, CSMP, Autocode, IMPACT, Assembly.

Services Available
Consultation, programming, education and training, operators, software packages, documentation, preparation of data, systems analysis. Operate on a self-service, remote access, block time and time-sharing basis.

Fields of Application
Scientific, statistical, commercial, production control, accounting, management, systems analysis, operational research.
Specialized areas: Large data base maintenance and inquiry systems; facilities management.

Training
Courses in Conversational PL/1 at introduction level (1 day), at advanced level (1 day), Remote Job Entry (1/2 days), Remote FORTRAN (1 day), Remote COBOL (1 day), Remote PL/1 (1 day), Remote GPSS (1 day).

RAPIDATA, INC.*
20 New Dutch Lane, Fairfield, 07006
Telephone: (201) 227-0035

Officer
Stewart B. Gold, *President*

Computer Installation
BULL GENERAL ELECTRIC GE 420–internal storage: 786,432 bits; magnetic tapes: 4; magnetic discs: 1; 1 line printer. *Remote processing features:* Teletype.

Coding Languages
BASIC, FORTRAN IV.

Services Available
Consultation, software packages. Operate on a time-sharing basis.

Fields of Application
Scientific, statistical, commercial, operational research.

SERVICE BUREAU CORPORATION*
68 South Harrison Street, East Orange, 07018
Telephone: (201) 676-3434

Also at:
1440 Pennington Road, Trenton, New Jersey 08618
Telephone: (609) 883-2990
(*See* under New York)

TELE-DATA CORPORATION*
130 U.S. Highway 22, North Plainfield, 07060
Telephone: (201) 755-1124

Officer
Charles Whittle, *President*

Computer Installation
IBM 360/25–operating systems: DOS, CS; internal storage: 32K bits; magnetic discs: 3 2311; 1 line printer.

Coding Languages
COBOL, RPG, Basic Assembler.

Contemplated Equipment
IBM 360/30.

Services Available
Consultation, programming, education and training, operators, software packages, documentation, preparation of data, systems analysis. Operate on a self-service and open shop basis.

Fields of Application
Commercial, production control, management, accounting, systems analysis.
Specialized areas: Banking, education, facilities management, food distribution.

TRENTON NASSAU SERVICE BUREAU*
2309 Brunswick Avenue, Trenton, 08638

Officer
F. Glenn Heins, *President*

Computer Installation
HONEYWELL H120–internal storage: 16K bits; magnetic tapes: 4.

Coding Languages
COBOL, Easycoder.

United States of America – Service Bureaux

Services Available
Consultation, programming, education and training, software packages, documentation, preparation of data, systems analysis. Operate on an open shop, self-service and block time basis.

Field of Application
Basic commercial systems.

UNIVERSITY COMPUTING COMPANY*
Computer Utilities Group
P.O. Box 279, East Brunswick, 08816
Telephone: (201) 828-3900
(*See* under Texas)

NEW MEXICO

COMPUSYS INC.*
P.O. Box 11104, Albuquerque, 87112
Telephone: (505) 255-2165

Also at:
Las Cruces, New Mexico, 88001

Officers
C. S. Hwa, *President*
Tom Lidstone, *Manager, Data Processing Services*

Computer Installation
HONEYWELL H115–operating system: Mod. 1 MSR; internal storage: 28K bits; magnetic discs: 2; 1 line printer.

Coding Languages
COBOL, Easycoder.

Contemplated Equipment
Honeywell H115.

Services Available
Consultation, programming, education and training, operators, software packages, documentation, preparation of data, systems analysis. Operate on a block time basis.

Fields of Application
Scientific, commercial, systems analysis, statistical, management, production control.
Specialized areas: Commercial and government accounting systems.

GENERAL ELECTRIC COMPANY*
Information Service Department
5301 Central Avenue N.E., Albuquerque, 87108
Telephone: (505) 265-3494

NEW YORK

AAA DATA PROCESSING CENTER*
15 East 41st Street, New York, 10016
Telephone: (212) 687-8005

Computer Installation
UNIVAC 1050.

Services Available
Advice, operators, preparation of data, programming.

Fields of Application
Commercial, market research.

ALPHA COMPUTER SERVICE CORPORATION
226 West 37th Street, New York, 10018
Telephone: (212) 695-1824

Officers
Nicolina Lamagese, *Manager-Director*
J. Porretta, *Director*

Computer Installation
CDC 6600–internal storage: 512K bits; magnetic tapes: 4; magnetic discs: 8; 1 line printer.
UNIVAC 1108.
IBM 370/145.

Coding Languages
COBOL, BAL, FORTRAN.

Services Available
Advice, programming, software packages, documentation, preparation of data, systems analysis.

Fields of Application
Scientific, statistical, commercial, accounting, management, systems analysis.
Specialized areas: Sales analysis, analysis, payroll.

ALPHANUMERIC INC.*
10 Nevada Drive, Lake Success, 11040
Telephone: (516) 437-9000

Also at: Los Angeles, Cal.

Officers
S. Manber, *President*
J. McMahon, *Executive Vice-President*
C. Sullivan, *Vice-President*
G. White, *Vice-President*

Computer Installation
New York:
IBM 360/50–internal storage: 256K bits.
Los Angeles:
IBM 360/40–internal storage: 256K bits.

Services Available
ATS, computer composition, CRT photoprinting.

Field of Application
Computer typesetting.

Training
One-day course in computerized typesetting.

ALTRO WORK SHOP INC.*
1021 Jennings Street, Bronx, 10460
Telephone: (212) K12-1550

Officer
Helen Warren, *Manager*

Computer Installation
IBM 360/20–internal storage: 16K bits; magnetic tapes: 2 2311; 1 line printer.

Coding Language
RPG.

United States of America – Service Bureaux

Contemplated Equipment
IBM 360/25.

Services Available
Advice, preparation of data, programming, systems analysis, software packages. Operate on an open shop, block time and time-sharing basis.

Fields of Application
Statistical, accounting, commercial, management, systems analysis.
Specialized areas: Medical research, hospital accounting, market research.

Training
Training in computer operations and programming.

ANALYTIC COMPUTING SERVICES*
1140 Broadway, New York, 10001
Telephone: (212) 679-4087

Officer
Ira Silverman, *President*

Computer Installation
IBM 360.

Services Available
Advice, operators, preparation of data, programming.

AUDITEK INC.*
866 Sixth Avenue, New York, 10001
Telephone: (212) 689-8999

Officer
G. Kahn, *President*

Computer Installation
IBM 360/30–operating system: DOS; internal storage: 64K; magnetic tapes: 4; magnetic discs: 2; 1 line printer.

Coding Languages
BAL, Autocoder.

Services Available
Advice, operators, preparation of data, programming, software packages, systems analysis. Operate on a closed shop basis.

Fields of Application
Commercial, accounting.
Specialized area: Steamship accounting systems.

AUTOMATED BOOKKEEPING CORPORATION*
55 West 42nd Street, 10036
Telephone: (212) 695-6893

Officer
Sigmund Bahr, *President*

Computer Installation
UNIVAC 9200–operating system: CARD; internal storage: 8K bits; 1 line printer.

Coding Language
RPG.

Contemplated Equipment
IBM System/3, Univac 9300.

Services Available
Consultation, programming, software packages, preparation of data, systems analysis. Operate on a self-service basis.

Fields of Application
Commercial, accounting, management, systems analysis.

AUTOMATIC DATA PROCESSING INC.*
50 Broadway, New York, 10007
Telephone: (212) 425-8940
(*See* under New Jersey)

CALL-A-COMPUTER*
425 Broadhollow Road, Melville, 11746
Telephone: (516) 293-9660

Also at:
1500 South Lilac Drive, Minneapolis, Minnesota

Officers
Michael P. Lowery, *Branch Manager*
James Rude, *Chairman of the Board*
Warren Prince, *President*

Computer Installation
BULL GENERAL ELECTRIC Datanet 30–operating system: Dartmouth Time-sharing; internal storage: 369,264 bits; magnetic discs: 1. *On-line satellite computer:* PDP-8/I. *Remote processing features:* time-sharing.
BULL GENERAL ELECTRIC GE235–operating system: Dartmouth Time-sharing; magnetic tapes: GE 4; magnetic discs: 1; 1 line printer. *Remote processing features:* other half of Dartmouth time-sharing system.

Coding Languages
BASIC, FORTRAN, ALGOL, LISP, Advanced BASIC.

Services Available
Programming, education and training, software packages. Operate on a remote access and time-sharing basis.

Fields of Application
Scientific, statistical, commercial, production control, accounting management, systems analysis, operational research.

Training
Short introductory courses in BASIC (3 hours), FORTRAN (3 hours) and general information procedures for the use of time-sharing (3 hours).

CCM INFORMATION CORPORATION*
909 Third Avenue, New York, 10022
Telephone: (212) 935-7998

Officer
Richard Kollin

Computer Installation
IBM 360/25–operating system: DOS; internal storage: 32K bits; magnetic tapes: 4; magnetic discs: 2; 1 line printer.

Coding Languages
COBOL, PL/1.

Services Available
Programming, software packages, documentation, preparation of data. Operate on a block time basis.

Fields of Application
Publishing of scientific and technical information.
Specialized areas: Input programmes for bibliographic material in viosocomp photo-composition, special indexing programmes.

CEIR INC.*
Subsidiary of Control Data Corporation
1180 Avenue of Americas, New York, 10036
Telephone: (212) 582-6640

Also at:
Lexington Avenue Center
575 Lexington Avenue, New York, 10022
Telephone: (212) 752-3840
Long Island Center
295 Northern Boulevard, Great Neck, 11021
Telephone: (212) 886-0411
Wall Street Center
140 Broadway, New York, 10005
Telephone: (212) 422-7400
(See under Control Data Corporation, Minnesota)

CELESTRON ASSOCIATES INC.*
844 Commerce Street, Thornwood, 10594
Telephone: (914) RO9-3458

Officers
Henry Oswald, *President*
Mrs. Florence Jeanne Oswald, *Executive Vice-President*
Peter Colgon, *Vice-President—Marketing*

Coding Languages
FORTRAN, COBOL, JOVIAL.

Services Available
Advice, programming, software packages, systems analysis.

Fields of Application
Scientific, commercial, software.
Specialized area: Automatic programme translation.

COMBINED DATA GROUP INC.*
180 Broadway, New York, 10038
Telephone: (212) WO4-1084

Officers
Davis Newman, *President*
George Smith, *Manager of Service Bureau*

Computer Installation
IBM 360/30—operating system: OS; internal storage: 65K bits; magnetic tapes: 4; magnetic discs: 4; 1 line printer. *Remote processing feature:* telecommunications.

Coding Languages
COBOL, ALP, PL/1, FORTRAN, RPG.

Services Available
Advice, operators, preparation of data, programming, software packages, systems analysis. Operate on a self-service and time-sharing basis.

Fields of Application
Systems Range in both commercial and scientific, from applications such as inventory control, market research to patter recognition, etc.
Specialized areas: Data banks, data reduction, telecommunications, operations research, MIS systems, operations research, etc.

COMPUTER FULFILLMENT CORPORATION*
200 Levittown Parkway, Hicksville, Long Island, 11050
Telephone: (516) 938-4620

Officer
Hush Fullerton

Computer Installation
IBM 360/30—internal storage: 65K bits; magnetic tapes: 5; magnetic discs: 3 2311; 1 line printer.

Contemplated Equipment
IBM 360/30.

Services Available
Consultation, programming, software packages. Operate on a self-service and remote access basis.

Field of Application
Commercial.

COMPUTERWARE INC.*
131 East 23rd Street, New York, 10010
Telephone: OR3-2791

Officers
Ichiro Murase, *President*
P. Casvikes, *Director of Education*

Computer Installation
IBM 360/50—operating system: DOS; internal storage: 512K bits; magnetic tapes: 8; magnetic discs: 1 2314; 1 line printer.
IBM 360/40—operating system: DOS; internal storage: 256K bits; magnetic tapes: 8; magnetic discs: 5 2311; 1 line printer.

Coding Languages
COBOL, BAL, PL/1.

Services Available
Consultation, programming, education and training, operators, software packages, documentation, preparation of data, systems analysis. Operate on a self-service basis.

Fields of Application
Statistical, accounting, scientific, commercial.

Training
Courses in introduction to data processing, concepts of data processing, architecture of 360, introduction to BAL, advanced BAL, introduction to Cobol, advanced COBOL, PL/1.

COMPUTING EFFICIENCY INC.*
35 Orville Drive, Bohemia, Long Island, 11716
Telephone: (516) 567-3600

Also at:
Manhattan, Chicago, Philadelphia

Officers
Donald E. Lees, *President*
Louis J. Desiderio, *Marketing Vice President*
John J. McElroy, *Executive Vice President*
John J. Guidice, *Technical Vice President*

Computer Installation
IBM 360/40—operating systems: DOS, OS/MFT 11; internal storage: 128K bits; magnetic tapes: 4 2415; magnetic discs: 6 2311; 1 line printer.

Coding Languages
BAL, COBOL, FORTRAN, PL/1, RPG.

United States of America – Service Bureaux

Contemplated Equipment
4 2402/V tapes.

Services Available
Programming, software packages. Operate on a self-service basis.

Fields of Application
Commercial, management.

COMSPACE CORPORATION*
350 Great Neck Road, Farmingdale, 11735
Telephone: (516) 293-5525

Officer
Irving Becker, *Officer in charge of Foreign Relations and Training of Personnel*

Coding Language
Machine.

Services Available
Education and training. Operate on a self-service basis.

Fields of Application
Training and learning.

Training
Courses in the craft of computer technology; short courses in data processing (1 semester), computer orientation (20 hours) and basic programming (80 hours).

DATATAB INC.*
315 Park Avenue South, New York, 10010
Telephone: (212) 677-4601

Officer
Richard Scotson

Computer Installation
IBM 360–operating system: DOS; internal storage: 65K bits; magnetic tapes: 3 9-track, 1 7-track; magnetic disc: 1311; 1 line printer.
IBM 360–operating system: OS; internal storage: 128K bits; magnetic tapes: 6 9-track; magnetic discs: 3 2311; 1 line printer.

Services Available
Advice, preparation of data, programming.

Fields of Application
Commercial, accounting.

ELECTRONIC ACCOUNTING SYSTEMS INC.*
339 East Avenue, Rochester, 14604
Telephone: (716) 546-8237

Officers
Edward B. Reagan, *President*
James S. Doyle, *Secretary-Treasurer*

Computer Installation
HONEYWELL H200–operating system: MOD 1; internal storage: 20K bits; magnetic tapes: 5; 1 line printer.

Coding Languages
COBOL, Easycoder.

Contemplated Equipment
Additional 8K-bit store.

Services Available
Advice, preparation of data, programming, software packages, systems analysis. Operate on an open shop and block time basis.

Fields of Application
Commercial, educational.
Specialized areas: Payroll, accounts receivable, accounts payable, general ledger.

ELECTRONIC TABULATING CORPORATION
P.O. Box 728, Newburgh, 12550
Telephone: (914) 564-6000

Officers
Walter A. Ruhlen, *President*
Thomas G. Mason, *Vice-President*

Computer Installation
IBM 360/30 (2)–operating system: DOS; internal storage: 64K bits; magnetic tapes: 4 2401; magnetic discs: 4 2311; 1 line printer.

Coding Languages
PL/1, COBOL.

Services Available
Programming, preparation of data, systems analysis. Operate on an open shop basis.

Fields of Application
Commercial, accounting.
Specialized areas: Sales analysis, payroll, insurance agents, A/R and A/P, municipal taxes, pari-mutuel reports, property management.

ERDOS AND MORGAN INC.*
114 Fifth Avenue, New York, 10011
Telephone: (212) 691-3150

Officers
Dr. P.L. Erdos, *President*
F. Boone, *Vice-President*

Computer Installation
IBM 1130.

Service Available
Preparation of data.

Field of Application
Commercial.

FEDDER DATA CENTER OF NEW JERSEY*
8 West 40th Street, New York, 10018
Telephone: (212) 695-6155
(*See* under Maryland)

FULFILLMENT CONSULTANTS CORPORATION*
1937 Williamsbridge Road, Bronx, 10461
Telephone: (212) 792-8155

Officers
George Tizzano, *President*
Anthony Annunziata, *Vice-President*

Computer Installation
IBM 360/20–internal storage: 8K bits; 1 line printer.

Coding Languages
RPG, BAL.

United States of America – Service Bureaux

Contemplated Equipment
Tape and disc drives.

Services Available
Preparation of data, programming, application packages, systems analysis. Operate on a closed shop basis.

Fields of Application
Commercial and charitable.

GENERAL ELECTRIC COMPANY*
Information Service Department
30 West State Street, Binghamton, 13901
Telephone: (607) 772-0546

GENERAL ELECTRIC COMPANY*
Information Service Department
3343 Harlem Road, Buffalo, 14225
Telephone: (716) 837-7752

GENERAL ELECTRIC COMPANY*
Information Service Department
110 East 59th Street, New York, 10022
Telephone: (212) 486-1700

GENERAL ELECTRIC COMPANY*
Information Service Department
339 East Avenue, Suite 411, Rochester, 14604
Telephone: (716) 325-4450

GENERAL ELECTRIC COMPANY*
Information Service Department
650 Franklin Street, Schenectady, 12305
Telephone: (518) 372-5471

GENERAL ELECTRIC COMPANY*
Information Service Department
175 Jericho Turnpike, Syosset, 11791
Telephone: (516) 921-9521

GENERAL ELECTRIC COMPANY*
Information Service Department
202 Twin Oaks Drive, Syracuse, 13206
Telephone: (315) 456-1539

GRAPHIC CONTROLS CORPORATION*
Computer Systems Division
189 Van Rensselaer Street, Buffalo, 14210
Telephone: (716) 853-7500

Officers
M. B. E. Clarkson, *President*
Norman M. Schueckler, *General Manager – Computer Systems Division*
Robert E. Tannehill, *General Manager – Training and Development Services Division*

Computer Installation
BULL GENERAL ELECTRIC GE235/Datanet 30– operating systems: GE235 EXEC, Datanet 30, Batch Monitor; internal storage: 655,360 bits; magnetic tapes: 6 MTH-690; magnetic disc: GE D20; 1 line printer. *On-line satellite computer:* Datanet 30. *Remote processing features:* composition, compilation and execution of a maximum of 40 users' programs simultaneously in several different languages, plus permanent read and write file capability.

Coding Languages
BASIC, ALGOL, FORTRAN, EDIT, EVA-LISP, GAP, LAFFF, PACER.

Contemplated Equipment
2 Bull General Electric GE235.

Services Available
Advice, operators, preparation of data, programming, software packages, systems analysis. Operate on a self-service, closed shop, open shop, remote access, block time and time-sharing basis.

Fields of Application
Scientific, research, management, statistical, commercial consulting.

Training
Short courses in BASIC, FORTRAN and ALGOL programming (30 hours or longer).

INFODATA SYSTEMS INC.*
680 Ridge Road, Webster, 14580
Telephone: (716) 671-7700

Also at:
1901 N. Fort Myer Drive, Arlington, Virginia 22209
Telephone: (703) 524-6700

Officers
Donald H. Stromberg, *Vice-President, Marketing*
Harry Kaplowitz, *Director Operations*

Computer Installation
IBM 360/40–operating system: DOS/OS; internal storage: 131K bits; magnetic tapes: 4 9-track, 1 7-track; magnetic discs: 4 2311; 1 line printer. *Remote processing features:* teletype compatible.

Coding Languages
COBOL, PL/1, FORTRAN, Assembly.

Contemplated Equipment
2314 disk storage.

Services Available
Consultation, programming, education and training, operators, software packages, documentation, systems analysis. Operate on a remote access, block time, open shop and time-sharing basis.

Fields of Application
Commercial, information storage and retrieval, statistical and financial management.
Specialized areas: Information retrieval, engineering software, teleprocessing.

Training
Training in the use of a proprietary system for information processing.

INTER-COMERICA COMPUTING COMPANY INC.*
1040 Avenue of the Americas, New York, 10018
Telephone: (212) 239-6600

Also at:
361 Delaware Avenue, Buffalo, 14202
Telephone: (716) 853-7850
Corporate Headquarters, 1515 Classen Blvd., Oklahoma City, Oklahoma 73106

Officers
Richard M. Deaton, *Executive Vice President*
John M. Cormack, *Director of Personnel*
Charles P. Sweeney, *Branch Manager*

United States of America – Service Bureaux

Computer Installation
New York:
UNIVAC 9300–operating systems: NCOS, COS; internal storage: 288K bits; magnetic tapes: 6 Uniservo IV; 1 line printer.
UNIVAC 1050–internal storage: 96K bits; magnetic tapes: 2 Uniservo IV; 1 line printer.

Buffalo:
UNIVAC 1004–operating systems: EXEC; internal storage: 6,608 bits; magnetic tapes: 2 Uniservo IV; 1 line printer. *On-line satellite computer:* Univac 1108.

Coding Languages
RPG, COBOL, FORTRAN, Assembler.

Services Available
Programming, operators, documentation, preparation of data, systems analysis. Operate on a closed shop and block time basis.

Fields of Application
Scientific, statistical, commercial, production control, accounting, management and systems analysis.

INTERNATIONAL DATA PROCESSING CORPORATION*
15 East 26th Street, New York, 10010
Telephone: (212) 683-6115

Officer
John B. Harding, Jr., *President*

Coding Languages
COBOL, FORTRAN IV.

Contemplated Equipment
IBM 360/30.

Services Available
Advice, operators, preparation of data, programming, software packages, systems analysis. Operate on a closed shop and time-sharing basis.

Fields of Application
Commercial and scientific consulting and services.

Training
Short courses in FORTRAN and IBM 360 programming.

INTERNATIONAL SYSTEMS ASSOCIATES LTD.*
350 5th Avenue, New York, 10001
Telephone: (212) 736-2924

Also at:
London and Bradford, U.K.

Officers
Nat Rothenberg, *Chairman*
Paul A. Goldner, *President*

Computer Installation
IBM 360/30–internal storage: 65K bits; magnetic tapes: 5; magnetic discs: 3 2311; 1 line printer.

IBM 1460–internal storage: 12K bits; magnetic tapes: 4; magnetic discs: 1; 1 line printer.

IBM 1401–internal storage: 8K bits; magnetic tapes: 4 7330; 1 line printer.

PDP-8/L–magnetic tapes: magnetic discs. *Remote processing features:* terminals.

Coding Languages
Autocoder, BAL, COBOL, FORTRAN.

Services Available
Consultation, operators, preparation of data, programming, software packages, systems analysis. Operate on an open shop basis.

Fields of Application
Statistical, commercial, production control, accounting management, mail order fulfillment, subscription fulfillment, mail marketing services.
Specialized areas: Data conversion, distribution systems.

INTERSTATE COMPUTER SERVICES
754 Fourth Avenue, Brooklyn, 11232
Telephone: (212) 965-2500

Officer
Max Houss, *President*

Computer Installation
CDC 3200–operating system: MSOS; internal storage: 65K bits; magnetic tapes: 4 604; magnetic discs: 2 854; 1 line printer.
SCAN OPTICS 2020–operating system: NANOSCAN; internal storage: 8K bits; magnetic tapes: 1 9-track, 1 7-track; 1 line printer.

Coding Language
COBOL

Services Available
Preparation of data, data conversion.

Field of Application
Direct mail.

MACRO-PAK BUSINESS SYSTEMS, INC.
132 West 31st Street, New York, 10001
Telephone: (212) 868-4520

Officers
Arnold B. Schacknow, *President*
Robert H. Schwartz, *Vice President*

Computer Installation
IBM 370/155–OS RELEASE; internal storage: 1·5 million bytes; magnetic tapes: 2 2420, 17 3420; magnetic discs: 16 2314, 8 3330; 4 line printers. *Remote processing features:* TSO, RJE(HASP).
IBM 370/145–operating system: DOS; internal storage: 256K bytes; magnetic tapes: 7 2420, 6 2415; magnetic discs: 8 2314; 2 line printers.

Coding Languages
PL/1, COBOL, BAL, FORTRAN.

Contemplated Equipment
Additional 512K storage for the 370/155; replacement of 2314s by 3330s.

Services Available
Advice, operators. Operate on a remote access and block time basis. Do not service customers who require applications programming support. Sell computer time to OS and DOS users.

Fields of Application
General.

MATHEMATICAL APPLICATIONS GROUP INC.
3 Westchester Plaza, Elmsford, 10523
Telephone: (914) 592-46446

United States of America — Service Bureaux

Officers
P. Mittelman, *President*
R. Davis, *Vice-President Research and Development*
M. Elsbach, *Vice-President Direct Marketing*
A. Levine, *Vice-President, Finance*
L. Malin, *Vice-President, Corporate Development*

Computer Installation
IBM 360/65–operating system: OS; internal storage: 2,048K bits; magnetic tapes: 7 2420; magnetic discs: 8 2314; 2 line printers.
DATA GENERAL Supernova–operating system: BASIC; internal storage: 1,310,720 bits; magnetic tapes: 2 Pertec 7000.

Coding Languages
COBOL, FORTRAN, BAL, PL/I, GLYPNIR.

Services Available
Advice, programming, software packages, systems analysis, operational research, direct mail services.
Specialized area: Direct mail.

MATRIX CORPORATION*
380 Madison Avenue, New York, 10017
Telephone: (212) 697-0800

Also at:
635 Hawai Street, El Segundo, California 90245
Telephone: (213) 679-8211

Officers
Dr. J. P. Walsh, *President*
Eugene C. Murphy, *Divisional Manager Computer Services East*

Computer Installation
New York:
IBM 360/65–internal storage: 512K bits; magnetic tapes: 12; magnetic discs: 5 2311, 1 2314; 1 line printer. *Remote processing features:* IBM 2702.
IBM 360/40–internal storage: 128K bits; magnetic tapes: 5; magnetic discs: 4 2311.

El Segundo:
IBM 7094 (2).
IBM 1401 (2).
IBM 360/65.
IBM 360/40 (3).
IBM 360/30 (2).
BULL GENERAL ELECTRIC GE 635.
BULL GENERAL ELECTRIC GE 115.
UNIVAC 1004 (9).

Coding Languages
FORTRAN, COBOL, PL/1.

Services Available
Advice, operators, preparation of data, programming, software packages, systems analysis. Operate on an open shop, remote access and block time basis.

Fields of Application
Matrix provides a complete range or data processing services to the scientific, commercial and government communities.

Training
Short courses in automated design (1 day), numerical control (1 week) and systems programming (1-6 weeks).

MNEMOTECH COMPUTER SYSTEMS INC.*
55 Liberty Street, New York, 10005
Telephone: (212) 267-8762

Also at:
130 Front Street, Hempstead
Telephone: (516) 481-0766

Officers
George P. Elgar, *President*
A. A. Calamari, *Director of Operations*

Computer Installation
IBM 360/40–operating system: DOS; internal storage: 128K bits; magnetic tapes: 8 2401; magnetic discs: 5 2311; 2 line printers.

Coding Languages
Assembler, COBOL, FORTRAN, MNEMOSYS, PL/1.

Services Available
Consultation, programming, education and training, operators, software packages, systems analysis. Operate on a closed shop basis.

NATIONAL CASH REGISTER COMPANY*
Data Processing Center
138-150 Queens Boulevard, Jamaica, Long Island, 11435
Telephone: (212) 291-7105

Officer
E. G. Burton, *Manager*

Also at:
660 Madison Avenue, New York, 10021
Telephone: (212) 832-9000

Officer
P. O. Peterson, *Manager*

(For details *see* under Ohio)

And at:
742 James Street, Syracuse, 13203
Telephone: (315) 474-6811

Officer
W. R. Wall, *Manager*

(For details, *see* under Ohio)

PAYTRONICS INC.*
425 Genesee Building, Buffalo, 14202
Telephone: (716) 853-0243

Officers
David B. Thomas, *President*
John P. Maley, *Vice-President*
Thomas Pitman, *Secretary-Treasurer*

Computer Installation
HONEYWELL H200–internal storage: 16K bits; magnetic tapes: 4; 1 line printer.

Fields of Application
Commercial, accounting.

PCS DATA PROCESSING INC.*
140 Cedar Street, New York, 10006
Telephone: (212) 964-4646

Officer
S. Berger, *Managing Officer*

Computer Installation
IBM 360/30—operating system: DOS; internal storage: 65K bits; magnetic tapes: 8; magnetic discs: 3; 2 line printers.
IBM 360/20—internal storage: 12K bits.

Coding Language
COBOL.

Contemplated Equipment
IBM 360/40 and IBM 360/50.

Services Available
Advice, preparation of data, programming, software packages, systems analysis. Operate on a self-service, closed shop and block time basis.

Fields of Application
Commercial, accounting, production.

PREFERED TABULATING SERVICE*
41 East 28th Street, New York, 10016
Telephone: 889-3100

Officers
Sy. Linett, *President*
Stephan J. Cohen, *Executive Vice-President*

Computer Installation
Remote processing features: 1050 terminals, portable TTY's.

Coding Languages
COBOL, FORTRAN.

Contemplated Equipment
Computer for time-sharing.

Services Available
Advice, preparation of data, programming, systems analysis. Operate on an open shop, remote access and time-sharing basis.

Field of Application
Commercial.
Specialized areas: Accounting, list processing, real time systems.

Training
Short courses in COBOL, operating systems, fundamentals (20-40 hours each).

PROGRAMMING & SYSTEMS INC.*
151 West 51st Street, New York, 10019
Telephone: (212) 245-1900

Officers
Emanuel Wunsch, *Director of Education*
Carmine Dieli, *Director of Admissions*
Frank Anello, *Manager, Service Bureau*

Computer Installation
IBM 360 (2)—operating system: DOS; internal storage: 65K bits each; magnetic tapes: 1 2401, 4 2402 each; magnetic discs: 3 2311 each; 2 (and 1) line printers.

Coding Languages
BAL, COBOL, RPG.

Services Available
Consultation, programming, education and training, software packages, systems analysis. Operate on a self-service, block time and open shop basis.

Fields of Application
Commercial, systems analysis, education.
Specialized areas: Programming education, computer letters, small-medium business applications, publishers.

Training
Courses in 360 programming.

PROGRAMMING METHODS INC.*
51 Madison Avenue, New York, 10010
Telephone: (212) 889-4200

Officers
George Langnas, *President*
Joseph Levy, *Secretary*

Services Available
Consultation, programming, software packages, systems analysis.

Fields of Application
Software development, real time and communications, management information systems, scientific and engineering, commercial applications.

Training
Management seminar and courses in system design and programming and computer system operations.

RECORD PROCESSING CORPORATION*
111 Fourth Avenue, New York, 10003
Telephone: 682-4333

Officers
W. E. Halliday, *President*
H. J. MacDonald, *Vice-President*
J. J. Judge, *Vice-President*

Computer Installation
UNIVAC 1005—internal storage: 4K bits; 2 line printers.

Contemplated Equipment
UNIVAC 9300/9400; 1108.

Services Available
Advice, preparation of data, programming, systems analysis. Operate on a closed shop basis.

Fields of Application
Commercial, accounting.

ROCHESTER COMPUTER SERVICE INC.*
908 Avenue D. Rochester, 14621
Telephone: (716) 342-8280

Officers
Dr. H. E. Paddock, *President*
R. E. Myrick, *Vice President*
E. A. Beth, Jr., *Operations Manager*

Computer Installation
BURROUGHS B3500—internal storage: 90K bits; magnetic tapes: 4; magnetic discs: B9372; 1 line printer.
Remote processing features: direct transmission with TC-500 terminals.

Coding Languages
COBOL, FORTRAN, Advanced Assembler.

Services Available
Advice, preparation of data, programming, systems analysis. Operate on a block time and open shop basis.

United States of America – Service Bureaux

Fields of Application
Scientific, statistical, commercial, production control, accounting, management, systems analysis, sales analysis.

SERVICE BUREAU CORPORATION*
Division of IBM
1350 Avenue of the Americas, New York, 10019
Telephone: (212) 262-5189

Also at:
2015 Highland Avenue, Birmingham, Alabama 35205
Telephone: (205) 322-5677
3136 N. Third Avenue, Phoenix, Arizona 85013
Telephone: (602) 274-3679
*5151 West Imperial Highway, Inglewood, California 90304
Telephone: (213) 776-5900
3630 Atlantic Avenue, Long Beach, California 90807
Telephone: (213) 424-0761
2511 West Third Street, Los Angeles, California 90057
Telephone: (213) 385-8201
650 East 14th Street, Oakland, California 94606
Telephone: (415) 893-1387
*2450 Watson Court, Palo Alto, California 94303
Telephone: (415) 327-0500
375 North Garey Avenue, Pomona, California 91766
Telephone: (714) 629-4045
3730 Fifth Avenue, San Diego, California 92103
Telephone: (714) 298-8241
One Maritime Plaza, San Francisco, California 94111
Telephone: (415) 982-3441
1493 Park Avenue, San Jose, California 95126
Telephone: (408) 298-1200
1931 Wilshire Boulevard, Santa Monica, California 90403
Telephone: (213) 393-0281
7826 East Prentice Avenue, Denver, Colorado 80222
Telephone: (303) 771-5510
964 Asylum Avenue, Hartford, Connecticut 06105
Telephone: (203) 249-5864
97 Whitney Avenue, New Haven, Connecticut 06510
Telephone: (203) 562-4149
2251 Wisconsin Avenue, N.W., Washington, D.C. 20007
Telephone: (202) 337-2900
955 N.E. 125th Street, North Miami, Florida 33161
Telephone: (305) 754-4647
1332 W. Peachtree Street, N.W., Atlanta, Georgia 30309
Telephone: (404) 875-7835
606 Coral Street, Honolulu, Hawaii 96813
Telephone: (808) 510-241
*8501 West Higgins Road, Chicago, Illinois 60631
Telephone: (312) 693-3021
4040 Charles Street, Rockford, Illinois 61108
Telephone: (815) 398-5994
1923 North Meridian Street, Indianapolis, Indiana 46202
Telephone: (317) 924-4301
427 North St. Francis Avenue, Wichita, Kansas 67202
Telephone: (316) 264-9328
844 South Fourth Street, Louisville, Kentucky 40203
Telephone: (502) 584-5261
2310 North Charles Street, Baltimore, Maryland 21218
Telephone: (301) 235-8110
*Wheaton Plaza Office Building, Wheaton, Maryland 20902
Telephone: (301) 933-2600
140 Federal Street, Boston, Massachusetts 02110
Telephone: (617) 542-2380
*147 Milk Street, Boston, Massachusetts 02110
Telephone: (617) 542-5891
1550 Howard Street, Detroit, Michigan 48216
Telephone: (313) 961-9688
1422 West Court Street, Flint, Michigan 48503
Telephone: (313) 232-3143
415 Cherry Street S.E., Grand Rapids, Michigan 49502
Telephone: (616) 458-1527
2201 E. Grand River Avenue, Lansing, Michigan 48912
Telephone: (517) 485-5495
8901 Wayzata Boulevard, Minneapolis, Minnesota 55426
Telephone: (612) 544-1571
2911 Main Street, Kansas City, Missouri 64108
Telephone: (816) 753-2141
2360 Hampton Avenue, St. Louis, Missouri 63139
Telephone: (314) 647-5444
3119 Dodge Street, Omaha, Nebraska 68131
Telephone: (402) 342-1678
68 S. Harrison Street, East Orange, New Jersey 07018
Telephone: (201) 676-3434
1440 Pennington Road, Trenton, New Jersey 08618
Telephone: (609) 883-2990
Stuyvesant Plaza, Executive Park South, Albany, New York 12203
Telephone: (518) 489-5561
584 Delaware Avenue, Buffalo, New York 14202
Telephone: (716) 884-8311
850 Old Country Road, Garden City, Long Island, New York 11530
Telephone: (516) 741-5242
61 Broadway, New York, New York 10004
Telephone: (212) 262-5000
2522 Monroe Avenue, Rochester, New York 14618
Telephone: (716) 442-9940
528 W. Onondaga Street, Syracuse, New York 13204
Telephone: (315) 476-7948
360 Mamaroneck Avenue, White Plains, New York 10605
Telephone: (914) 949-8877
1228 E. Morehead Street, Charlotte, North Carolina 28201
Telephone: (704) 377-3661
1519 Central Parkway, Cincinnati, Ohio 45214
Telephone: (513) 721-2551
14701 Detroit Avenue, Cleveland, Ohio 44107
Telephone: (216) 228-1200
2111 E. Main Street, Columbus, Ohio 43209
Telephone: (614) 237-7404
2181 Embury Park Road, Dayton, Ohio 45414
Telephone: (513) 278-7365
1215 Madison Avenue, Toledo, Ohio 43624
Telephone: (419) 248-6616
3920 N. Lincoln, Oklahoma City, Oklahoma 73105
Telephone: (405) 528-7441
907 S. Main Street, Tulsa, Oklahoma 74119
Telephone: (918) 584-6195
1976 S.W. Sixth Avenue, Portland, Oregon 97201
Telephone: (503) 277-3676
3507 Poplar Street, Erie, Pennsylvania 16508
Telephone: (814) 864-4944
2135 N. Front Street, Harrisburg, Pennsylvania 17105
Telephone: (717) 236-5051
1617 J. F. K. Boulevard, Philadelphia, Pennsylvania 19103
Telephone: (215) 568-3457
526 Penn Avenue, Pittsburgh, Pennsylvania 15222
Telephone: (412) 261-1316
*2025 Greentree Road, Pittsburgh, Pennsylvania 15220
Telephone: (412) 343-5444
117 Eleanor Roosevelt, Hato Rey, Puerto Rico 00918
Telephone: (809) 765-5050
160 Wayland Avenue, Providence, Rhode Island 02906
Telephone: (401) 331-3875
2829 Millwood Avenue, Columbia, South Carolina 29205
Telephone: (803) 254-1636
1418 Madison Avenue, Memphis, Tennessee 38104
Telephone: (901) 276-4446
8200 John Carpenter Freeway, Dallas, Texas 75247
Telephone: (214) 631-1010
2910 W. Lancaster Street, Fort Worth, Texas 76107
Telephone: (817) 335-9365
*4665 S.W. Freeway, Houston, Texas 77027
Telephone: (717) 766-0331
1222 N. Main Street, San Antonio, Texas 78212
Telephone: (512) 226-6295
3228 W. Carey Street, Richmond, Virginia 23221
Telephone: (703) 355-5788

United States of America – Service Bureaux

2308 Sixth Avenue, Seattle, Washington 98121
Telephone: (206) 682-6474
2040 W. Wisconsin Avenue, Milwaukee, Wisconsin 53233
Telephone: (414) 344-4121
Includes Scientific Computing Center

Computer Installation
A wide range of IBM computers.

Coding Languages
RPG, Autocoder, FORTRAN, COBOL, AL, etc.

Services Available
Advice, operators, preparation of data, programming, software packages, systems analysis.

Fields of Application
Scientific, commercial, management, engineering, economics, statistics, operations research, etc.

SPORTS DATA CORPORATION*
150 West 52nd Street, New York, 10019
Telephone: (212) LT1-9480

Officers
Franklin Knobel, *President*
Ira Weinman, *Comptroller*
Bernard Winokur, *E.D.P. Manager*

Computer Installation
HONEYWELL H200–internal storage: 20K; magnetic tapes: 4.

Coding Languages
Easycoder, COBOL.

Service Available
Preparation of data. Operate on a self-service basis. Available only to those engaged in country club operations in computing handicaps and billing systems, and to individuals in computing golf handicaps.

Field of Application
Commercial.

STANDARD DATA CORPORATION
1540 Broadway, New York, 10036
Telephone: (212) 586-3100

Officers
Mark W. Iobst, *President*
Kenneth W. Hammond, *Manager*

Computer Installation
IBM–internal storage: 32K; magnetic tapes: 6; 1 line printer.
IBM–internal storage: 16K; magnetic tapes: 2; 1 line printer.

Coding Languages
BAL, RPG, COBOL, ALP.

Services Available
Preparation of data, programming, systems analysis. Operate on a closed shop basis.

Fields of Application
Commercial, production control, accounting, management.
Specialized areas: Pension and welfare.

STANDARD PROGRAMS CORPORATION*
342 Madison Avenue, New York, 10017
Telephone: (212) 986-9250

Computer Installation
PDP-8–internal storage: 96K bits; magnetic tapes: 3 DEC; magnetic discs: 2. *Remote processing features:* 4 typewriter terminals.

Coding Language
PAL.

Services Available
Advice, operators, preparation of data, programming, software packages, systems analysis. Operate on a self-service, closed shop and time-sharing basis. Available primarily for corporate operations.

Fields of Application
Marketing, manufacturing, distribution, retailing, banks, accounting, management information systems.

UNIVAC DATA PROCESSING CENTERS*
1290 Avenue of the Americas, New York, 10019
Telephone: (212) 946-3378

Also at:
531 Delaware Avenue, Buffalo, New York 14202
Telephone: (716) 882-2171
60 Herricks Road, Mineola, Long Island, New York 11501
Telephone: (516) 248-5544
(*See* under California)

WATERTOWN COMPUTER SERVICE INC.
153 J. B. Wise Place, Watertown, 13601
Telephone: (315) 788-1451

Officers
Edward Behan, Jr., *President*
Noah Prior, *Director*

Computer Installation
IBM 1130 - 1 line printer.

Coding Language
FORTRAN IV.

Services Available
Advice, programming, education and training, software packages, systems analysis.

Fields of Application
Commercial, production control, accounting, management, systems analysis.
Specialized areas: Sales analysis, payroll.

NORTH CAROLINA

COMPUTER SERVICENTERS, INC.*
1020 E. Wendover Avenue, Greenboro, 27405
Telephone: (919) 273-0856

Officer
F. C. Rick Berry, *President*

Computer Installation
BURROUGHS B300–internal storage: 19,200 bits; magnetic tapes: 4; 1 line printer.

United States of America – Service Bureaux

Coding Language
Assembly.

Contemplated Equipment
Disc; on line.

Services Available
Advice, operators, preparation of data, programming, software packages, systems analysis. Operate on a closed shop basis.

Fields of Application
Statistical, commercial, production control, accounting, management.
Specialized areas: Payroll, A/R, inventory.

DIXIE DATA PROCESSING, INC.
Box 395, Warsaw, 28398
Telephone: (919) 293-7136

Officers
Douglas H. Pigford, *Co-ordinator*
Brent Hodges, *President*
John B. Hall, *Treasurer*

Computer Installation
UNIVAC 9300–operating system: MCS; internal storage: 24K bits; magnetic tapes: 4; 1 line printer.
IBM System/3–operating system: DOS; internal storage: 16K bits; magnetic discs: 2; 1 line printer. *Remote processing feature:* SYCOR.

Coding Language
RPG.

Contemplated Equipment
Remote on-line and off-line terminals including line printers.

Services Available
Advice, programming, education and training, operators, documentation, preparation of data, systems analysis, service bureau. Operate on a self-service, closed and open shop basis.

Fields of Application
Commercial, production control, accounting, management, systems analysis, operational research.
Specialized areas: Sales analysis, analysis, payroll, county and municipal governments.

GENERAL ELECTRIC COMPANY*
Information Service Department
801 Summit Avenue, Greensboro, 27405
Telephone: (919) 275-2561

HYDRA COMPUTER CORPORATION*
P.O. Box 17883, Raleigh, 27609
Telephone: (919) 782-1051

Officer
Fred C. Tarbox, Jr.

Computer Installation
CDC 1700–operating system: MSOS; internal storage: 524,288 bits; magnetic tapes: 2 601; magnetic discs: 1 853; 1 line printer. *Remote processing features:* teletype I/0 via paper tape.
CDC 1700–internal storage: 524,288 bits.

Coding Languages
FORTRAN, Assembler.

Services Available
Consultation, programming, software packages, preparation of data, systems analysis. Operate on a closed shop basis.

Fields of Application
Business data processing, scientific computation, software systems development (compilers, assemblers, operating systems, communication systems).

NATIONAL DATA PROCESSING INC.*
716 South 17th Street, Wilmington, 28401
Telephone: 763-1559

Officer
J. Sherwood Thompson, *General Manager*

Computer Installation
NCR Century 100–internal storage: 128K bits; magnetic tapes: 2 NCR 736; magnetic discs: 2 NCR 655 101; 1 line printer. *Remote processing features:* 736 tape transmit/receive units using voice grade phone lines.

Services Available
Consultation, programming, education and training, systems analysis. Operate on a closed shop basis.

Fields of Application
Commercial, accounting, management, systems analysis.

SERVICE BUREAU CORPORATION*
1228 E. Morehead Street, Charlotte, 28201
Telephone: (704) 377-3661
(*See* under New York)

NORTH DAKOTA

DAKOTA DATA INC.*
410 E. Thayer Avenue, Bismarck, 58501
Telephone: 223-2026

Officers
Wayne Schnell, *President*
Lee Hanson, *Vice-President*

Computer Installation
IBM 1440–internal storage: 8K bits; magnetic discs: 2 1311; 1 line printer. *Remote processing features:* Bell system 35 ASR.

Coding Language
ICOS.

Contemplated Equipment
CDC 1700/3300 system.

Services Available
Operators, preparation of data, programming, software packages, systems analysis. Operate on a closed shop and remote access basis.

Fields of Application
Scientific, statistical, commercial, accounting, production control.

United States of America – Service Bureaux

OHIO

THE ANDERSONS*
Data Processing Division
1015 Conant Street, Maumee, 43537
Telephone: (419) 893-6551

Officer
F. L. Grindle, Jr., *Division Manager*

Computer Installation
HONEYWELL H120–internal storage: 20K bits; magnetic tapes: 4 204B; 1 line printer.

Coding Languages
COBOL, Easycoder, FORTRAN.

Services Available
Advice, preparation of data, programming, software packages, systems analysis. Operate on an open shop basis.

Fields of Application
Commercial, statistical, production control, accounting, operations control.
Specialized areas: Sales analysis, payroll, medical research.

Training
On job programming and systems training for outside customers' employees.

BARRON DATA SYSTEMS INC.*
5810 Monroe Street, Sylvania, 43560
Telephone: (419) 882-0525

Officer
H. Gene Barron, *Executive Director*

Computer Installation
IBM 360/40–operating system: DOS; internal storage: 128K bits; magnetic tapes: 2 2415; magnetic discs: 1 2314, 1 2311; 1 line printer. *On-line satellite computers:* 3 2770. *Remote processing features:* 2701.
IBM 360/20–operating system: BASIC; internal storage: 12K bits; magnetic tapes: 2 2415; magnetic discs: 1 2311; 1 line printer. *Remote processing features:* TP interface to remote model 65.

Coding Languages
BAL, RPG, COBOL, Basic FORTRAN.

Services Available
Consultation, programming, software packages, documentation, systems analysis (TP only). Operate on a remote access, block time and open shop basis.

Fields of Application
Commercial, accounting management.
Specialized areas: Banking and other financial institutions, and software.

CHI CORPORATION
Suite 200, 11000 Cedar Avenue, Cleveland, 44106
Telephone: (216) 229-6400

Also at:
Room 1210 East Ohio Building, Cleveland, 44114
Telephone: (216) 861-1557
1110 Morse Road, Columbus
Telephone: (614) 846-7581

Officers
Francis E. Ilein, *President*
Jack L. Stones, *Executive Vice President*

Computer Installation
UNIVAC 1108–operating system: EXEC; internal storage: 4,718,592 bits; magnetic tapes: 10 Uniservo VIII C 7-track, 4 Uniservo VIII C 9-track; magnetic discs: 2 Fastrand 11 drums, 6 FH-432 drums, 2 FH-1782 drums; 3 line printers. *Remote processing features:* capable of handling remote job entry through reader printers and teletype compatible terminals.

Coding Languages
SIMULA, ALGOL, COBOL, FORTRAN V, plus many special purpose languages.

Contemplated Equipment
UNIVAC 1110.

Services Available
Consultation, programming, education and training, software packages, systems analysis, hardware development. Operate on a remote access, open shop and time-sharing basis.

Fields of Application
Scientific, statistical, commercial, accounting, management, systems analysis, operational research.
Specialized areas: Sales analysis, linear programming, investment, analysis, payroll, structural engineering, medical research.

CALTEC INC.*
3023 Sylvania Avenue, Toledo, 43613
Telephone: (419) 475-3501

Officers
W. P. Sanzenbacher, *President*
W. C. Sparman, *Vice President*
F. C. Miller, *Vice President and Secretary*

Computer Installation
IBM 1130–internal storage: 128K bits; magnetic discs: 2315; 1 line printer.

Coding Languages
FORTRAN, RPG, Assembler.

Contemplated Equipment
IBM 360/25.

Services Available
Preparation of data, programming, systems analysis, software packages, consultation. Operate on an open shop basis.

Fields of Application
Scientific, accounting, financial data processing, systems analysis, commercial, statistical, engineering.
Specialized areas: Engineering analysis and design, payroll, cost accounting.

Training
Training in keypunching and programming.

CHAMPION SERVICE CORPORATION*
19001 Villaview Road, Cleveland, 44119
Telephone: 486-9300

Officers
E. Seymour, Jr., *Chairman of the Board*
John R. Hall, *President*

554

United States of America – Service Bureaux

Computer Installation
IBM 360/30–operating system: DOS; internal storage: 65K bits; magnetic tapes: 4 2415; magnetic discs: 8 2311; 2 line printers.

IBM 1401–internal storage: 8K bits; magnetic tapes: 4; 729; 2 line printers.

Coding Language
BAL.

Contemplated Equipment
IBM 360/40.

Services Available
Preparation of data, programming, software packages, systems analysis. Operate on a remote access basis.

Fields of Application
Accounting, financial.
Specialized area: Banking.

CONTROL DATA CORPORATION*
Cincinnati Center
1014 Vine Street, Cincinnati, 44115
Telephone: (513) 381-4520

Also at:
Cleveland Center
1450 Leader Building, Cleveland, 44114
Telephone: (216) 696-4515
(*See* under Minnesota)

DATA CONTROL SERVICES*
948 High Avenue, S.W. Canton, 44707
Telephone: (216) 456-73333

Officers
James E. Boocestone, *Manager*
Gregor W. Leatherman, *Assistant Manager*

Computer Installation
IBM 360/20–internal storage: 8K bits; 1 line printer.

Coding Languages
RPG, BAL.

Contemplated Equipment
IBM 360/30.

Services Available
Advice, preparation of data, programming, systems analysis.

Fields of Application
Commercial, accounting, production control, statistical, general data processing services.

DATA SERVICES CORPORATION*
2835 Springboro Road, P.O.B. 1007, Dayton, 45401
Telephone: (513) 294-0406/0564

Officers
D. D. Brubaker, *President*
D. E. Burrowes, *Vice-President, Operations*

Computer Installation
IBM 360/30–operating system: DOS; internal storage: 32K 8-bit bytes; magnetic tapes: 6 2415; magnetic disc: 2311; 1 line printer.
IBM 1401–internal storage: 12K 6-bit bytes; magnetic tapes: 4 7330; 1 line printer.

Coding Languages
Autocoder, COBOL, PL/1, Assembler.

Services Available
Advice, preparation of data, programming, software packages, systems analysis. Operate on a block time basis.

Fields of Application
Commercial, accounting.
Specialized areas: Package processing of payroll and accounting, facilities management, systems design.

DATALOGICS INC.
12025 Shaker Blvd., Cleveland, 44120
Telephone: 721-9035

Officers
Benson P. Lee, *President*
David G. Shields, *Executive Vice President*

Computer Installation
XDS Sigma 7–operating system: BTM time-sharing; internal storage: 2,432K bits; magnetic tapes: 2 9-track; magnetic discs: 10; 1 line printer. *Remote processing features:* teletype and all other ASCII.
IBM 1401–operating system: IOCS; internal storage: 128K bits; magnetic tapes: 4 729; 1 line printer.

Coding Languages
BASIC, FORTRAN, COBOL, Assembler, Autocoder, SPS.

Contemplated Equipment
Additional 640K bit store, 2 removable discs.

Services Available
Advice, programming, education and training, operators, software packages, documentation, preparation of data, systems analysis. Operate on a remote access, block time and time-sharing basis.

Fields of Application
Scientific, statistical, commercial, production control, accounting, management, systems analysis, operational research, education.

Training
Short courses in BASIC and FORTRAN.

FEDDER DATA CENTER OF OHIO*
10024 Carnegie Avenue, Cleveland, 44106
Telephone: (216) 229-5240
(*See* under Maryland)

GENERAL ELECTRIC COMPANY*
Information Service Department
8620 Winton Road, Cincinnati, 45231
Telephone: (513) 243-7361

GENERAL ELECTRIC COMPANY*
Information Service Department
5755 Granger Road, Cleveland, 44131
Telephone: (216) 398-5062/5066

GENERAL ELECTRIC COMPANY*
Information Service Department
1495 Morse Road, Room 206, Columbus, 43224
Telephone: (614) 262-4043

GENERAL ELECTRIC COMPANY*
Information Service Department
3430 South Dixie Highway, Dayton, 45439
Telephone: (513) 298-0311

United States of America – Service Bureaux

NATIONAL CASH REGISTER COMPANY*
Data Processing Centers
Main & K Streets, Dayton, 45409
Telephone: (513) 449-2000

Also at:
3950 Euclid Avenue, Cleveland, 44115
Telephone: (216) 881-9500
3095 Kettering Boulevard South, Dayton, 45439
Telephone: (513) 298-4381

and at:
Atlanta, Georgia; Baltimore, Maryland; Birmingham, Alabama; Boston, Massachusetts; Brooklyn, New York; Chicago, Illinois; Denver, Colorado; Detroit, Michigan; Hawthorne, California; Honolulu, Hawaii; Houston, Texas; Kansas City, Missouri; Louisville, Kentucky; Lubbock, Texas; Miami, Florida; Minneapolis, Minnesota; New Orleans, Louisiana; New York; Norfolk, Virginia; Pittsburgh, Pennsylvania; Reno, Nevada; Richmond, Virginia; St. Louis, Missouri; San Francisco, California; Sarasota, Florida; Seattle, Washington; Syracuse, New York.

and 31 centres in Europe and other parts of the world.

Computer Installation
A wide range of NCR computers.

Coding Languages
FORTRAN, COBOL, NEAT.

Services Available
Advice, operators, preparation of data, programming, software packages, systems analysis. On-line facilities.

Fields of Application
Scientific, commercial, industrial and financial.

SERVICE BUREAU CORPORATION*
1519 Central Parkway, Cincinnati, 45214
Telephone: (513) 721-2551

Also at:
14701 Detroit Avenue, Cleveland, 44107
Telephone: (216) 228-1200
2111 E. Main Street, Columbus, 43209
Telephone: (614) 237-7404
2181 Embury Park Road, Dayton, 45414
Telephone: (513) 278-7365
1215 Madison Avenue, Toledo, 43624
Telephone: (419) 248-6616
(*See* under New York)

UNIVAC DATA PROCESSING CENTER*
3645 Warrensville Center Road, Cleveland, 44122
Telephone: (216) 752-7000
(*See* under California)

OKLAHOMA

AFFILIATED COMPUTER SYSTEMS INC.*
8118 East 46th Street, Tulsa, 74145
Telephone: (918) NA7-5013

Officer
Raleigh W. Wright, *President*

Computer Installation
HONEYWELL H200 (2)–operating system: Mod 1; internal storage: 147,456 bits each; magnetic tapes: 10; 1 line printer each. *Remote processing features:* DCT-2000 printer (communication).

Coding Languages
COBOL, FORTRAN, Easycoder.

Services Available
Advice, operators, programming, systems analysis. Operate on a closed shop basis.

Field of Application
Commercial.
Specialized area: Banking.

Training
Courses are organized only for individual companies, generally on equipment selection and systems planning.

COMPUTE AMERICA CORPORATION (COMERICA)*
2811 N.W. 36th Street, Oklahoma City, 73112
Telephone: (405) 943-8521

Also at:
Corporate Headquarters, 1515 Classen Blvd., Oklahoma City, 73106

Officers
Richard M. Deaton, *Executive Vice President*
John W. Cormack, *Director of Personnel*
James R. Veitch, *Branch Manager*

Computer Installation
UNIVAC 9300–operating systems: NCOS, COS; internal storage: 288K bits; magnetic tapes: 6 Uniservo IV; 1 line printer.

Coding Languages
RPG, COBOL, FORTRAN, Assembler.

Services Available
Programming, operators, documentation, preparation of data, systems analysis. Operate on a closed shop and block time basis.

Fields of Application
Scientific, statistical, commercial, production control, accounting, management and systems analysis.

GENERAL ELECTRIC COMPANY*
Information Service Department
2000 Classen Road, Suite 616, Oklahoma City, 73112
Telephone: (405) 528-4521

GENERAL ELECTRIC COMPANY*
Information Service Department
3315 East 47th Place, Suite 100, Tulsa, 74135
Telephone: (918) 743-9761

DALE L. GULLEY & ASSOC., INC.*
2302 14th Street, Tulsa, 74104
Telephone: (918) 932-3628

Officer
Dale L. Gulley

Computer Installation
IBM 1130–operating systems: Monitor; internal storage: 128K bits; magnetic discs: 1 2310; 1 line printer.

United States of America – Service Bureaux

Coding Languages
Assembler, FORTRAN, RPG.

Services Available
Consultation, programming, software packages, systems analysis. Operate on an open shop basis.

Fields of Application
Scientific, statistical, commercial, production control, accounting, management, systems analysis, operational research.
Specialized areas: Chemical engineering, heat transfer equipment design.

INTERNATIONAL DIGITIZING CORPORATION*
Suite 189, London Square, Tulsa, 74105
Telephone: (918) 742-4543

Officer
R. E. Bickham, *President*

Services Available
Consultation, preparation of data, programming. Also operate a well log digitizing service.

Field of Application
Scientific.
Specialized area: Petroleum industry (well log digitizing).

SERVICE BUREAU CORPORATION*
3920 N. Lincoln, Oklahoma City, 73105
Telephone: (405) 528-7441

Also at:
907 S. Main Street, Tulsa, 74119
Telephone: (918) 584-6195
(*See* under New York)

UNIVERSITY COMPUTING COMPANY*
Computer Utilities Group
823 South Detroit, Tulsa, 74120
Telephone: (918) LU2-0975

Also at:
3535 N.W. 58th Street, Oklahoma City, 73112
Telephone: (405) W16-0577
(*See* under Texas)

OREGON

AUTOMATED INFORMATION INC.*
309 S.W. Fourth Avenue, Portland, 97204
Telephone: (503) 223-2139

Coding Languages
FORTRAN, SPS, 360 Assembler.

Services Available
Advice, operators, preparation of data, programming, systems analysis.

Fields of Application
Scientific, statistical, engineering, management, surveying.

COMPUTER SYSTEMS
Wing Building, Grants Pass, 97526
Telephone: (503) 476-6557

Officer
Gene T. McMenamy, *Manager*

Computer Installation
NCR 315–operating system: NEAT; internal storage: 120K bits; magnetic tapes: 5; 1 line printer.

Coding Languages
NEAT, BEST, COBOL.

Services Available
Consultation, programming, education and training, software packages, documentation, systems analysis. Operate on an open shop basis.

Field of Application
Commercial.
Specialized area: Municipal accounting.

GENERAL ELECTRIC COMPANY*
Information Service Department
2154 North East Broadway, Portland, 97232
Telephone: (503) 228-6915

SERVICE BUREAU CORPORATION*
1976 S.W. Sixth Avenue, Portland, 97201
Telephone: (503) 277-3676
(*See* under New York)

UNIVAC DATA PROCESSING CENTER*
1303 S.W. 16th Avenue, Portland, 97207
Telephone: (503) 226-3541
(*See* under California)

PENNSYLVANIA

ABINGTON KEYPUNCH INC.
920 Fox Chase Road, Rockledge, 19111
Telephone: (215) ES9-3718

Officers
Agnes R. Kraus, *President*
William J. Kraus, *Vice President*

Service Available
Preparation of data.

Field of Application
Commercial.
Specialized areas: Data conversions, inventories, daily bank transactions, payrolls, programs, subscription fulfillment, mailing lists.

AUTOMATIC DATA PROCESSING INC.*
3 Penn Center Plaza, Philadelphia, 19102
Telephone: (215) 564-6030
(*See* under New Jersey)

CDI COMPUTER SERVICES
Department DM, 5 Penn Center Plaza, Philadelphia, 19103
Telephone: (215) 569-2200

Services Available
Advice, operators, preparation of data, programming.

Fields of Application
Business and scientific.

COMPUTE AMERICA CORPORATION (COMERICA)*
1951 New Hope Street, Norristown, 19401
Telephone: (215) 753-1993

Also at:
Corporate Headquarters, 1515 Classen Blvd., Oklahoma City, Oklahoma 73106

Officers
Richard M. Deaton, *Executive Vice President*
John W. Cormack, *Director of Personnel*
Harry A. Matthias, *Branch Manager*

Computer Installation
UNIVAC 9300—operating systems: NCOS, COS; internal storage: 288K bits; magnetic tapes: 6 Uniservo IV; 1 line printer.
UNIVAC 1004—operating systems: EXEC; internal storage: 6,608 bits; magnetic tapes: 2 Uniservo IV; 1 line printer. *On-line satellite computers:* UNIVAC 1108.

Coding Languages
RPG, COBOL, FORTRAN, Assembler.

Services Available
Programming, operators, documentation, preparation of data, systems analysis. Operate on a closed shop and block time basis.

Fields of Application
Scientific, statistical, commercial, production control, accounting, management and systems analysis.

COMPUTER RESEARCH INC.
Seven Parkway Center, Pittsburgh, 15220
Telephone: (412) 922-4114

Also at:
P.O. Box 532, Boston, Massachusetts 02102
Telephone: (617) 742-8199
132 Nassau Street, New York, New York 10038
Telephone: (212) 233-0890
4 Kings Highway East, Haddonfield, New Jersey 08033
Telephone: (609) 428-0020
3024 Central Avenue, St.Petersburg, Florida 33712
Telephone: (813) 894-4961
509 Siteman Building, 111 South Bemiston Avenue, St. Louis, Missouri 63105
Telephone: (314) 725-0445
The Ten South LaSalle Street Building, Room 1048, Chicago, Illinois 60603
Telephone: (312) 726-0654
Suite 110, 919 18th Street, N.W., Washington, D.C. 20006
Telephone: (202) 785-4040
802 Dermon Building, 46 North Third Street, Memphis, Tennessee 38102
Telephone: (901) 527-7159
Airport Imperial Building, 999 North Sepulveda Boulevard, El Segundo, California 90245
Telephone: (213) 640-0314
813 Cascade Building, 529 Southwest Sixth Avenue, Portland, Oregon 97204
Telephone: (503) 222-1231

Officers
O. E. Nemitz, *President*
James L. Schultz, *Vice-President*

Computer Installation
HONEYWELL H3200 (2)—operating system: OS/200; internal storage: 196K bits; magnetic tapes: 6; magnetic discs: 5; 1 line printer.

Coding Languages
Easycoder, COBOL.

Services Available
Operate on a closed shop basis.

Fields of Application
Commercial, accounting.
Specialized areas: Back office accounting for investment securities firms.

COMPUTER SERVICENTERS, INC.*
F & M Bank Building, St. Mary's, 15857
Telephone: (814) 834-2893

Officer
J. C. Caimi, *Vice-President and Managing Director*

COMPUTER USAGE DEVELOPMENT CORPORATION*
Barclay Building, City Line and Belmont Avenues, Bala-Cycwyd, 19004
Telephone: (215) 839-4185
(*See* under New York)

COMSERV*
One University City, 4025 Chestnut Street, 19104

Officer
Dr. Noah S. Prywes

Computer Installation
XDS Sigma 7—operating system: BTM, Time Sharing and Remote Batch; internal storage: 2,560K bits; magnetic tapes: 4 9-track; magnetic discs: 12; 1 line printer.
Remote processing features: TTY's, IBM 2741, Univac DCT 2000, Burroughs TC 500.

Coding Languages
FORTRAN IV, BASIC, COBOL 65, SNOBOL.

Contemplated Equipment
XDS Sigma 9.

Services Available
Consultation, programming, education and training, software packages, systems analysis. Operate on a remote access and time-sharing basis.

Fields of Application
Scientific, statistical, commercial, accounting, systems analysis, operational research.
Specialized area: Comserv on line transaction system.

Training
Short courses in any of the above programming languages.

CONDATA INC.
1809 Walnut Street, Philadelphia, 19103
Telephone: (215) LO9-4240

Officers
Daniel R. Moore, *President*
Cornelius J. Deegan, *Vice-President*
Donald White, *Vice-President*

Computer Installation
IBM 370/135—operating system: DOS/OS; internal storage: 245K bits; magnetic tapes: 8 9-track; magnetic discs: 3 2311, 16 2314; 1 line printer.

Coding Languages
COBOL, FORTRAN, BAL, RPG, PL/1.

Services Available
Advice, programming, operators, software packages, preparation of data, systems analysis. Operate on a block time, open shop and time-sharing basis.

Field of Application
Commercial.
Specialized area: Payroll.

DATA SYSTEMS INTERNATIONAL INC.
1701 Arch Street, Philadelphia, 19103
Telephone: (215) 665-0120

Officer
Daniel J. Devine, *President*

Computer Installation
IBM 360/50—operating system: OS/DOS; internal storage: 384K bits; magnetic tapes: 8 3420; magnetic discs: 8 2314; 2 line printers. *Remote processing features:* 2700 Type interface.
IBM 360/30—operating system: DOS; internal storage: 96K bits; magnetic tapes: 4; magnetic discs: 4 2311; 1 line printer.

Contemplated Equipment
IBM 370.

Services Available
Consultation, programming, education and training, operators, software packages, documentation, preparation of data, systems analysis. Operate on a remote access, block time, time-sharing terminals when available.

Fields of Application
Most commercial business and management applications.
Specialized area: Facilities management.

Training
Custom Client Courses in Data Processing Management, Data Processing Operations and Programming.

DATANETICS
3512 Fifth Avenue, Pittsburgh, 15213
Telephone: (412) 621-7358

Officer
Jerome V. Lisovich, *Director*

Computer Installation
Minicomputer.

Coding Languages
All common higher level languages and machine language for most machines produced by major manufacturers.

Services Available
Advice, programming, operators, software packages, documentation, preparation of data, systems analysis, statistical analysis.

Fields of Application
Scientific, statistical, production control, management, systems analysis, statistical analysis.

EASTERN COMPUTER SERVICES INC.*
920 Fox Chase, Rockledge, 19111

Officers
Francis X. O'Brien, *President*
Charles W. Via, *Vice-President*

Coding Languages
Assembly, COBOL, FORTRAN, PL/1.

Services Available
Consultation, programming, software packages, documentation, preparation of data, systems analysis.

Fields of Application
Varied.

EUR DATACENTER INC.*
65 N. Fifth Street, Lemoyne, 17043
Telephone: (717) 761-0630

Officer
G. F. Patterson, *President*

FEDDER DATA CENTER OF CENTRAL PENNSYLVANIA*
715 North Second Street, Harrisburg, 17102
Telephone: (717) 238-0869

Also at:
Fedder Data Center of Pittsburgh
915 Saxonburg Boulevard, Pittsburgh, Pennsylvania 15220
Telephone: (412) 792-1311
(*See* under Maryland)

FIMACO INC.
230 West Washington Square, Philadelphia, 19106
Telephone: (215) WA3-1930

Also at:
Burlington, New Jersey, Kingston Jamaica.

Officers
Julius T. Cocozza, *President, Chief Executive Officer, Director of Marketing*
Frank T. Barclay, *Executive Vice-President, Treasurer, Director of Finance*
Louis O. Colburn, *Executive Vice-President*

Computer Installation
HONEYWELL H2200 (2)—internal storage: 65K bits; magnetic tapes: 7; 1 line printer.
HONEYWELL H120—internal storage: 16K bits; magnetic tapes: 2; 1 line printer.
RCA Spectra 70/35—operating system: DOS; internal storage: 32K bytes; magnetic tapes: 7; 1 line printer.

Coding Languages
Easycoder, COBOL, BOCOL (Fimaco's proprietary package).

Contemplated Equipment
IBM 370/135.

Services Available
Consultation, programming, software packages, preparation of data, systems analysis. Operate on a closed shop and block time basis.

Field of Application
Commercial.
Specialized areas: Circulation fulfillment, list maintenance, book club, computer type setting and composition.

United States of America – Service Bureaux

FIRST NATIONAL BANK OF PENNSYLVANIA*
717 State Street, Erie, 16512
Telephone: 456-2011

Officer
Ralph C. Lantzy, *Vice-President and Director of Data Processing*

Computer Installation
BULL GENERAL ELECTRIC GE 415—operating system: MIT; internal storage: 16K bits; magnetic tapes: 6; 1 line printer.

Coding Languages
COBOL, MAP, BAP, FORTRAN.

Services Available
Advice, preparation of data, programming, software packages, systems analysis. Operate on a closed shop and block time basis.

Fields of Application
Business, commercial.
Specialized area: Banking.

GENERAL ELECTRIC COMPANY*
Information Service Department
2 Decker Square, Bala-Cynwyd, 19004
Telephone: (215) 839-7700

GENERAL ELECTRIC COMPANY*
Information Service Department
One Allegheny Square, Suite 265, Pittsburgh, 15212
Telephone: (412) 322-8700

GENERAL ELECTRIC COMPANY*
Information Service Department
110 Haines Road, York, 17402
Telephone: (717) 755-9661

JOHNSON COMPUTING INC.*
120 South 17th Street, Philadelphia, 19101
Telephone: 585-5000

Officers
Victor L. Johnson, *Chairman*
Saul Lapp, *President*
William R. Scott, *General Manager*

Computer Installation
IBM 360/40 (5)—operating system: C.S.; internal storage: 265K bits; magnetic tapes: 10 each; magnetic discs: 2314; 1 line printer each. *Remote processing features:* audio response and video remote.
IBM 360/30 (4)—internal storage: 65K bits; magnetic tapes: 4 each; magnetic discs: 2311.

Coding Languages
Autocoder, BAL, COBOL.

Services Available
Advice, preparation of data, programming, systems analysis. Operate on a remote access, open shop and block time basis.

Fields of Application
Statistical, commercial, production control, accounting, management, systems analysis.
Specialized areas: Sales analysis, investment analysis, payroll, medical research.

KEYSTONE COMPUTER ASSOCIATES INC.*
1055 Virginia Drive, Fort Washington, 19034
Telephone: (215) 643-3800

Officers
J. Guernaccini, *President*
R. T. Cottrill, *Secretary*

Coding Languages
FORTRAN, COBOL, PL/1, Assembly.

Contemplated Equipment
COPE.

Services Available
Advice, programming, operations research, systems analysis.

Fields of Application
Scientific, commercial, process control, management, operations research.
Specialized areas: Executive programmes, input/output systems, sort/merge packages, utility programmes, assemblers, compilers, problem-oriented languages, real-time applications, hardware diagnostics.

KIDDE COMPUTER SERVICES COMPANY
Fairway Plaza, Philmont and Red Lion Road, Huntingdon Valley, 19006
Telephone: (215) 947-6400

Officers
Lonnie Sciambi, *Executive Vice-President*
Carl Reifeis, *Vice-President, Systems*
Arthur Randal, *Vice-President, Marketing*
S. Weston Heritage, *Vice-President, Administration*

Computer Installation
IBM 360/50—operating systems: OS, DOS, HASP, POWER; internal storage: 384K bits; magnetic tapes: 4; magnetic discs: 11; 1 line printer. *Remote processing features:* RJE/HASP.
IBM 370/135—operating systems: OS, DOS, HASP, POWER; internal storage: 240K bits; magnetic tapes: 5; magnetic discs: 8; 1 line printer. *Remote processing features:* RJE/HASP.

Coding Languages
PL/1, BAL, COBOL, FORTRAN.

Services Available
Advice, programming, education and training, operators, software packages, documentation, preparation of data, systems analysis, facilities management. Operate on a self-service, remote access, block time and open shop basis.

Fields of Application
Scientific, statistical, commercial, production control, accounting, management, systems analysis, retail.
Specialized areas: Sales analysis, analysis, payroll, manufacturing, retail.

Training
OS and DOS training.

MANAGEMENT DATA CORP.
1845 Walnut Street, Suite 2300, Philadelphia, 19103

Officers
Gilbert N. Zitin, *President*
Ian J. Berg, *Vice-President*

Computer Installation
IBM 360/40–operating system: DOS; internal storage: 128K bits; magnetic tapes: 4 2401; magnetic discs: 2314; 1 line printer. *Remote processing features:* 2780 terminals.
IBM 360/40–operating system: DOS; internal storage: 128K bits; magnetic tapes: 6 2401; magnetic discs: 2314; 1 line printer. *Remote processing features:* 1052, 1092 terminals.

Services Available
Consultation, programming, education and training, operators, software packages, documentation, preparation of data, systems analysis. Operate on a self-service, remote access basis.

Fields of Application
Commercial, management, accounting, operational research, hospitals.

MECHANIZED BUSINESS INC.*
430 7th Avenue (Koppers Building), Pittsburgh, 15219
Telephone: (412) 391-1324

Officers
Robert Rupert, *Owner*
Tony Dan, *Manager*

Computer Installation
IBM 1410–internal storage: 40K bits; magnetic tapes: 5 729; 1 line printer.

Coding Languages
Autocoder, FORTRAN.

Contemplated Equipment
IBM 360/30.

Services Available
Advice, operators, preparation of data, programming, systems analysis. Operate on an open shop basis.

Fields of Application
Commercial, statistical, etc.

MEGASYSTEMS, INC.*
1 Bala Avenue, Bala-Cynwyd, 19004
Telephone: (215) 667-1700

Also at:
640 West 40th Street, New York, New York 10018
Telephone: (212) 594-2500
127 North Broadway, Hicksville, New York, 10018
Telephone: (516) 931-1314
3918 Jonestown Road, Harrisburg, Pennsylvania, 17109
Telephone: (717) 545-3741

Officers
J. J. Callanan, *President*
R. B. Wallach, *Vice-President, Finance*
J. G. Scarry, *Vice-President, Marketing*
S. Listman, *Vice-President, Operations*

Computer Installation
Bala-Cynwyd:
XDS 940 (2)–internal storage: 65K 24-bit words each; magnetic discs: 1; magnetic drums: 3.
New York:
BULL GENERAL ELECTRIC GE 430–internal storage: 32K 24-bit words; magnetic tapes; magnetic disc.
IBM 360/67–internal storage: 128K 32-bit words; magnetic tapes: 15 2401; magnetic discs: 3 2314; magnetic drums: 2 2301; 2 line printers.

Coding Languages
BASIC, FORTRAN, CAL, TAP, BAL, COBOL, SCRIPT, PL/1, SNOBOL, BRUIN.

Services Available
Consultation, documentation, preparation of data, programming, software packages, systems analysis. Time-sharing terminals on premises.

Fields of Application
Scientific, statistical, educational, accounting, commercial, management.
Specialized areas: Numerical control, computer assisted instruction, electronic circuit analysis, corporate accounting.

Training
Courses in time-sharing languages and periodic seminars covering major application areas.

MSADP INC.*
835 E. Germantown Pike, Norristown, 19401
Telephone: (215) 279-7500

Computer Installation
BURROUGHS B283–magnetic tapes: 4.

Services Available
Advice, operators, preparation of data, programming.

NATIONAL CASH REGISTER COMPANY*
Data Processing Center
100 Fleet Street, Pittsburgh, 15520
Telephone: (412) 922-5000

Officer
J. L. Bangs, *Manager*

(For details, *see* under Ohio)

NATIONAL INFORMATION SYSTEMS CORPORATION*
150 Allendale Road, Valley Forge, 19481
Telephone: (215) 265-5000

Officer
Keith D. Quackenbush, *Director, Systems Center*

Computer Installation
IBM 360/50–operating system: DOS/OS; internal storage: 512K bytes; magnetic tapes: 8 2401; magnetic discs: 1 2314; 2 line printers.
IBM 360/30–operating system: DOS; internal storage: 64K bytes; magnetic tapes: 6 2401; magnetic discs: 2 2311; 1 line printer.

Coding Languages
BAL, COBOL, PL/1.

Contemplated Equipment
IBM 360/65.

Services Available
Consultation, programming, education and training, operators, software packages, documentation, preparation of data, systems analysis. Operate on a closed shop and block time basis. Available primarily for business applications under total facilities management service.

United States of America — Service Bureaux

Fields of Application
Commercial, production control, accounting management, systems analysis, statistical, distribution, inventory control, mass marketing, insurance.
Specialized areas: Accounting, insurance, manufacturing distribution, mass marketing, business management consulting.

ON-LINE SYSTEMS, INC.
115 Evergreen Heights Drive, Pittsburgh, 15229

Computer Installation
PDP-10/40 (5)—internal storage: 192K 36-bit words each; magnetic tapes: 4 each; magnetic discs: 8 each; 1 line printer each. *On-line satellite computers:* 2 PDP-11 each. *Remote processing features:* Remote batch — Data 100 (each).

Coding Languages
FORTRAN, BASIC, COBOL, ARL.

Services Available
Advice, programming, education and training, software packages, documentation, preparation of data, systems analysis. Operate on a self-service, remote access, open shop, and time-sharing basis.

Fields of Application
Scientific, statistical, commercial, production control, accounting, management, systems analysis, operational research, data management, information retrieval.
Specialized areas: Sales analysis, linear programming, investment, analysis, structural engineering, materials handling.

Training
Programming courses on demand.

PENNDATA INC.*
1729 Cedar Avenue, Scranton, 18510
Telephone: (717) 346-7348

Officer
Lewis L. Cosor, *Executive Vice-President*

Services Available
Advice, operators, preparation of data, programming, systems analysis.

Fields of Application
Accounting, payroll, sales analysis, production control.

SERVICE BUREAU CORPORATION*
1617 J.F.K. Boulevard, Philadelphia, 19103
Telephone: (215) 568-3457

Also at:
3507 Poplar Street, Erie, 16508
Telephone: (814) 864-4944
2135 N. Front Street, Harrisburg, 17105
Telephone: (717) 236-5051
526 Penn Avenue, Pittsburgh, 15222
Telephone: (412) 261-1316
2025 Greentree Road, Pittsburgh, 15220
Telephone: (412) 343-5444
(*See* under New York)

UNI-COLL CORPORATION
3401 Market Street, Philadelphia, 19104
Telephone: (215) 387-3890

Officers
Dr. Randall M. Whaley, *President*
Robert L. Logan, *Executive Vice-President*

Computer Installation
IBM 370/165—operating systems: OS/MVT, HASP; internal storage: 16,384K bits; magnetic tapes: 5 9-track, 2 7-track; magnetic discs: 16 3330, 13 2314, 1 2305; 3 line printers. *Remote processing features:* remote RJE, interactive time-share.

Coding Languages
BASIC, COBOL, FORTRAN, PL/1, Assembler, APL.

Services Available
Advice, programming, education and training, operators, software packages, documentation, preparation of data, systems analysis, application consultation. Operate on a self-service, remote access, closed shop, block time and time-sharing basis.

Fields of Application
Scientific, statistical, commercial, production control, accounting, management, systems analysis, operational research, engineering.
Specialized areas: Linear programming, investment, analysis, structural engineering, statistical analysis, medical research, financial management, student records.

Training
Basic and advanced course in all languages available on the system.

UNIVAC DATA PROCESSING CENTERS*
1624 Locust Street, Philadelphia, 19103
Telephone: (215) 546-5300

Also at:
Stanwix at 4th Avenue, Pittsburgh, 15222
Telephone: (412) 391-2000
(*See* under California)

RHODE ISLAND

INDUSTRIAL NATIONAL BANK OF RHODE ISLAND*
822 Industrial Bank Building, 111 Westminster Street, Providence, 02903
Telephone: 861-6100

Computer Installation
BULL GENERAL ELECTRIC GE 415 (2)—internal storage: 768K bits; magnetic tapes: 6 7-channel; 3 line printers.
IBM 360/30—internal storage: 520K bits; magnetic tapes: 4 9-track, 1 7-track; magnetic discs: 4.

Coding Languages
COBOL, GE Macro, GE Basic.

Services Available
Advice, operators, preparation of data, programming, software packages, systems analysis. Operate on a closed shop, remote access and time-sharing basis.

United States of America – Service Bureaux

Fields of Application
Emphasis on commercial accounting, management, systems analysis. Also, equipment leasing, personnel and educational division.

INFORMATION SCIENCES INC.*
14 Jefferson Boulevard, Warwick, 02888

Officer
M. Arthur Gillis, *Vice-President*

Computer Installation
IBM 360/30 (2)–operating system: DOS; internal storage: 65K bits each; magnetic tapes: 10 2401; magnetic discs: 10 2311; 2 line printers.
BULL GENERAL ELECTRIC GE 415 (2)–operating systems: MTPS, EOS; internal storage: 32K bits each; magnetic discs: 16; 4 line printers.

Coding Languages
COBOL, BAL, MACRO, BAP.

Contemplated Equipment
2 IBM 360/40.

Services Available
Consultation, programming, operators, software packages, documentation, preparation of data, systems analysis. Operate on a remote access, closed shop and block time basis.

Fields of Application
Statistical, commercial, production control, accounting, management, systems analysis, consulting.
Specialized areas: Municipal systems, banking systems, health/medical systems.

SOUTH CAROLINA

COMPUTER SERVICENTRES INC.*
Daniel Building, Greenville, 29602
Telephone: (803) 242-5742

Officer
K. G. Robinson II, *President*

GENERAL ELECTRIC COMPANY*
Information Service Department
252 Pleasantburg Drive, Room 110, Greenville, 29607
Telephone: (803) 233-7467

MANAGEMENT INFORMATION CENTER*
10th Floor, Daniel Building, Greenville, 29702
Telephone: (803) 242-5500

Officers
Henry B. Young, *President*
Paul S. Crowder, *Director*
James G. Lane, *Director*

Computer Installation
BURROUGHS B300–operating system: DOS; internal storage: 19,200 bits; magnetic tapes: 4; magnetic discs: 4; 1 line printer. Remote processing features.

Coding Language
Assembler.

Contemplated Equipment
Burroughs B3500.

Services Available
Preparation of data, programming, systems analysis. Operate on a closed shop basis.

Fields of Application
Statistical, commercial, production control, accounting.
Specialized area: Garment industry.

SERVICE BUREAU CORPORATION*
2829 Millwood Avenue, Columbia, 29205
Telephone: (803) 254-1636
(*See* under New York)

TENNESSEE

DATA SERVICE CORPORATION*
1907 Division Street, Nashville, 37203
Telephone: (615) 327-4471

Officer
F. I. Nebhut, Jr., *President*

Computer Installation
IBM 360/30–operating system: DOS; internal storage: 65K bits; magnetic tapes: 4; magnetic discs: 3; 1 line printer.

Coding Language
COBOL.

Services Available
Advice, preparation of data, programming, software packages, systems analysis. Operate on a closed shop basis.

Fields of Application
Statistical, commercial, production, control, accounting, management, systems analysis, operational research.

FEDDER DATA CENTER OF TENNESSEE*
216 Mercantile Building, Knoxville, 37092
Telephone: (615) 525-9339
(*See* under Maryland)

GENERAL ELECTRIC COMPANY*
Information Service Department
3385 Airways Boulevard, Memphis, 38116
Telephone: (901) 332-3900

GUARDIAN DATA SERVICE & SUPPLY*
44 N. 2nd Street, Memphis, 38103

Officer
Hank Cocozza, *Data Processing Director*

Computer Installation
IBM 360/30–operating system: DOS/COS; internal storage: 32K bits; magnetic tapes: 2 2415; magnetic discs: 3 2311; 1 line printer.

Coding Languages
RPG, BAL, PL/1, Autocoder.

Contemplated Equipment
2314 disk drive.

Services Available
Consultation, programming, preparation of data. Operate on an open shop basis.

Fields of Application
Commercial, financial.
Specialized areas: Banking, parts inventory.

MEMPHIS METHODS & TABULATING SERVICE*
56 North Main Street, Memphis, 38103
Telephone: (901) 527-4913

Officer
C. H. Norvell

Service Available
Preparation of data.

SERVICE BUREAU CORPORATION*
1418 Madison Avenue, Memphis, 38104
Telephone: (901) 276-4446
(*See* under New York)

TEXAS

A.I.D. COMPUTING INC.*
P.O. Box 12613, Fort Worth, 76101
Telephone: (817) 732-8841

Officer
M. C. Matson, *President*

Computer Installation
IBM 360/30–operating system: DOS; internal storage: 32K bits; magnetic tapes: 1 2403, 1 2402, 2 2401; magnetic discs: 4 2311.

Coding Languages
Autocoder, RPG, COBOL, ALP.

Services Available
Advice, operators, preparation of data, programming, software packages, systems analysis. Operate on a self-service, open shop and block time basis.

Fields of Application
Statistical, commercial, accounting, management.

COMPUTER DIMENSIONS, INC.*
Corporate Offices and Dallas Regional Center
511 North Akard, Dallas, 75201
Telephone: (214) 742-2131

Also at:
Detroit, Michigan; Los Angeles, California

Officers
J. T. Verdesca, Sr., *President*
C. C. Miller, *Secretary-Treasurer*

Computer Installation
HONEYWELL H2200 (2)–operating system: DOS; internal storage: 49K bits each; magnetic tapes: 6 tapes each; magnetic discs: 2 H208; 3 line printers.
IBM 360/30–operating system: DOS; internal storage: 32K bits; magnetic discs: 2 2311; 1 line printer.
HONEYWELL H200.
BURROUGHS B500.
IBM 360/40 (2).

Coding Languages
COBOL, ALC, Easycoder, FORTRAN.

Services Available
Consultation, operators, preparation of data, programming, systems analysis. Operate on a self-service, remote access and block time basis.

Fields of Application
Commercial applications (payroll, accounting, inventory and oil industry applications), scientific processing and programming (math. models), systems design.
Specialized areas: Optical scanning and key punching (high volume), computerized typesetting, payroll applications, accounting system for law firms, distribution accounting system (on-line) for beer and liquor distributors, automated inventory control system for automobile dealerships, insurance industry applications, banking applications.

CONTROL DATA CORP.*
Dallas Center
P.O. 45409, Dallas, 75235
Telephone: (214) 358-4277

Also at:
Houston Center
7135 Office City Drive, Houston, 77017
Telephone: (713) 644-2221
(*See* under Minnesota)

GENERAL ELECTRIC COMPANY*
Information Service Department
8100 Carpenter Freeway, Dallas, 75247
Telephone: (214) 631-0910

GENERAL ELECTRIC COMPANY*
Information Service Department
6300 Hillcroft Road, Suite 412, Houston, 77006
Telephone: (713) 771-7292

GENERAL ELECTRIC COMPANY*
Information Service Department
122 North "N" Street, Midland, 79071
Telephone: (915) 682-1032

MCDONNELL AUTOMATION COMPANY*
Suite 400/500 Jefferson Building, Houston, 77002
Telephone: (813) 224-5921
(*See* under Missouri)

NATIONAL CASH REGISTER COMPANY*
Data Processing Center
6806 Hornwood Drive, Houston, 77036
Telephone: (713) 771-4611

Officer
J. J. Knoblauh, *Manager*

Also at:
2203 34th Street, Lubbock, 79412
Telephone: (806) 747-2721

Officer
A. T. Barber, *Manager*
(For details, *see* under Ohio)

SERVICE BUREAU CORPORATION*
8200 John Carpenter Freeway, Dallas, 75247
Telephone: (214) 631-1010

Also at:
2910 W. Lancaster Street, Fort Worth, 76107
Telephone: (817) 335-9365
4665 S.W. Freeway, Houston, 77037
Telephone: (717) 766-0331
1222 N. Main Street, San Antonio, 78212
Telephone: (512) 226-6295
(*See* under New York)

UNITAB COMPANY OF ABILENE
P.O. Box 2499, Abilene, 79604
Telephone: (915) 673-3779

Officer
B. Jack Williams, *President*

UNIVAC DATA PROCESSING CENTER*
3311 Richmond Avenue, Houston, 77006
Telephone: (713) 528-2281
(*See* under California)

UNIVERSITY COMPUTING COMPANY*
Computer Utilities Group and Data-Link Group
1949 N. Stemmons Freeway, Dallas, 75207
Telephone: (214) R17-6351

Also at:
Computer Utilities Group:
400 Fannin Bank Building, Houston, Texas 77025
888 North Sepulveda Boulevard, El Segundo, California 90245
Telephone: (213) 322-3093
1740 Stanford Street, P.O. Box 655, Santa Monica, California 90406
823 South Detroit, Tulsa, Oklahoma 74120
Telephone: (918) LU2-0975
P.O. Box 279, East Brunswick, New Jersey 08816
Telephone: (201) 828-3900

Data-Link Group:
22 Waugh Drive, Houston, Texas
Telephone: (713) UN9-6636
323 South Franklin, Chicago, Illinois 60606
Telephone: (312) HA7-1355
3535 N.W. 58th Street, Oklahoma City, Oklahoma 73112
Telephone: (405) W16-0577
and at: Los Angeles, California, Birmingham and London, United Kingdom, Shannon, Ireland, The Hague, Netherlands.

Officers
B. G. Grubbs, *President*
Sy. Joffe, *Vice-President*

Computer Installation
Computer Utilities Group:
UNIVAC 1108–operating system: EXEC II (modified); internal storage: 65K bits; magnetic tapes: 8; magnetic drums: 9 432, Fastrand II. *On-line satellite computers:* 2 univac 1004. *Remote processing features:* telephone lines or Telpak microwave, COPE 45, 1004, DCI 2000, H200 and IBM 1130 as remote terminals.
UNIVAC 1007 (El Segundo only).

Data-Link Group:
Equipped with HONEYWELL H200 computers. Serve also as remote terminals to the UNIVAC 1108 Centers.

Services Available
Advice, operators, preparation of data, programming, software packages, systems analysis. Operate on a self-service, closed shop, block time and time-sharing basis.

Fields of Application
All scientific and commercial applications.

Training
Computer programming and computer application courses and management seminars.

UTAH

GENERAL ELECTRIC COMPANY*
Information Service Department
431 South 3rd East, Salt Lake City, 84110
Telephone: (801) 364-1891

VIRGINIA

APPLIED DATA RESEARCH INC.*
2425 Wilson Boulevard, Arlington, 22201
(*See* under New Jersey)

ARIES CORPORATION*
Westgate Research Park, McLean, 22101
Telephone: (703) 893-4400

Also at:
4930 West 77th Street, Minneapolis, Minnesota 55435
Telephone: (612) 920-2966
15 Spinning Wheel Road, Hinsdale, Illinois 60521
Telephone: (312) 325-4160

Officers
C. A. Clark II, *Chairman and President*
R. C. Foote, *Secretary*

Coding Languages
All commercially available machine and problem oriented languages.

Services Available
Consultation, preparation of data, programming, software packages, systems analysis.

Fields of Application
Scientific, commercial, accounting, management, real time reservations, message switching, equipment software.
Specialized areas: Financial management systems, data organization and retrieval systems, on-line real time reservation systems, message switching, facility management.

DATA INC.*
4620 Lee Highway, Arlington, 22207
Telephone: (703) 524-0400

Officer
Donald W. Tobias, *President*

Computer Installation
IBM 360/30.

Services Available
Consultation, preparation of data, programming.

United States of America – Service Bureaux

GENERAL ELECTRIC COMPANY*
Information Services Department
2017 Cunningham Drive, Hampton, 23366
Telephone: (703) 838-5500

HELIODYNE CORPORATION*
KMS Technology Center
1401 Wilson Boulevard, Arlington, 22209
Telephone: (703) 528-5003

Officers
James Healey, *President*
Dominic Laiti, *Vice-President*

Coding Languages
ALGOL, FORTRAN, COBOL, FAP, MAP, Autocoder, SPS, GAP, BAL, etc.

Services Available
Advice, preparation of data, programming, software packages, systems analysis.

Fields of Application
Scientific, statistical, commercial, accounting, management, systems analysis.
Specialized areas: Re-entry physics, management information systems, data correlation, advanced programming.

Training
Short courses in the application of computers to management and government, management of systems development and management of programming.

MCDONNELL AUTOMATION COMPANY
7115 Leesburg Pike, Falls Church, 22043
(*See* under Missouri)

NATIONAL CASH REGISTER COMPANY*
Data Processing Center
6300 Virginia Beach Boulevard, Norfolk, 23502
Telephone: (703) 499-2321

Officer
B. J. Dean, *Manager*

Also at:
7001 West Broad Street, Richmond, 23220
Telephone: (703) 288-0091

Officer
P. S. Terrell, *Manager*
(For details, *see* under Ohio)

SERVICE BUREAU CORPORATION*
3228 West Carey Street, Richmond, 23221
Telephone: (703) 355-5788
(*See* under New Yrok)

WASHINGTON

ALLIED DATA
P.O. Box 2406, Olympia, 98507
Telephone: (206) 456-3535

Officer
Robert Lovely, *General Manager*

Computer Installations
IBM 360/20–operating system: COS; internal storage: 8K bytes; 1 line printer.
IBM 360/30–operating system: DOS; internal storage: 32K bytes; magnetic tapes: 4 Potter SC2402; magnetic discs: 3 Potter DD4311; 1 line printer. *Remote processing features:* NCR 736.

Coding Languages
RPG, COBOL, Assembler.

Services Available
Advice, programming, education and training, software packages, documentation, preparation of data, systems analysis. Operate on a remote access and block time basis.

Fields of Application
Commercial, accounting, management.

GENERAL ELECTRIC COMPANY*
Information Service Department
5900 Fourth Avenue South, Seattle, 98108
Telephone: (206) 763-0850

NATIONAL CASH REGISTER COMPANY*
Data Processing Center
500 Fairview Avenue, Seattle, 98109
Telephone: (206) 682-4343

Officer
P. C. Baker, *Manager*
(For details, *see* under Ohio)

NORTHWEST COMPUTING SERVICE*
1260 Mercer Street, Seattle, 98109
Telephone: (206) 623-5711

Officer
Richard I. Normann, *Manager*

Computer Installation
IBM 1130's–internal storage: 2 million bits each; magnetic discs: 20; 1 line printer. *Remote processing features:* telecommunication, batch time-sharing through telecommunications.

Coding Language
FORTRAN.

Contemplated Equipment
IBM 360/40.

Services Available
Advice, operators, preparation of data, programming, software packages, systems analysis. Operate on a self-service, closed shop, open shop, remote access, block time and time-sharing basis.

Fields of Application
Scientific and engineering.
Specialized areas: Linear programming, structural analysis, CPM network analysis, computer system analysis.

Training
Courses in civil engineering applications (2 weeks) and structural analysis (2 weeks).

NORTHWEST MANAGEMENT SERVICES INC.*
2300 East Lake Ave. E., Seattle, 98102
Telephone: EA9-9990

Officer
Warren R. Chapin, *Vice-President and Executive Director*

United States of America – Service Bureaux

Computer Installation
BURROUGHS B300 (2)–operating system: DOS; internal storage: 115,200 bits each; magnetic tapes: 6 B421; magnetic discs: 7; 2 line printers.

Services Available
Advice, operators, processing of data, programming, on-line, real time applications.

Fields of Application
Financial, commercial, management, etc.

PROFESSIONAL DATA PROCESSING INC.*
820 Third Avenue, Seattle, 98104
Telephone: (206) 624-7442

Officer
Robert B. Foster, *President*

Computer Installation
IBM 360/30–operating system: OS; internal storage: 32K bits; magnetic tapes: 4 2415; 1 line printer.

Coding Languages
Autocoder, BAL, ADPAC.

Contemplated Equipment
Univac 9400.

Services Available
Advice, preparation of data, programming. Operate on a closed shop and block time basis. Not available for scientific work.

Fields of Application
Commercial: receivables, payroll, inventory, payables, general ledger.

SERVICE BUREAU CORPORATION*
2308 Sixth Avenue, Seattle, 98121
Telephone: (206) 682-6474
(*See* under New York)

UNITED STATES COMPUTERS INC.
P.O. Box 3396, 8815 South Tacoma Way, Tacoma, 98499
Telephone: (206) 584-7211

Officers
Robert Gerth, *President*
Jack Babbit, *Chairman*

Computer Installation
HONEYWELL H200–operating system: MOD 1 (MSR); internal storage: 32,768 bits; magnetic tapes: 3 204B-4; magnetic discs: 2 173; 1 line printer.
HONEYWELL DDP-516–operating system: MIKON; internal storage: 8,192 bits; magnetic discs: 2 259.

Coding Languages
Easycoder, COBOL, RPG, FORTRAN.

Contemplated Equipment
Honeywell H2040 or IBM 360/65.

Services Available
Preparation of data, processing of data. Operate on a closed shop basis.

Fields of Application
Commercial, production control, accounting, management.
Specialized areas: Insurance accounting, college records.

WEST VIRGINIA

BUSINESS COMPUTER SERVICE
1027 Virginia Street E., Charleston, 25301
Telephone: (304) 343-9471

Officer
Robert C. Payne

Computer Installation
NCR 315 (2)–operating system: CRAM; internal storage: 60K bits; 1 line printer.
NCR Century 200.

Coding Languages
NEAT, COBOL.

Services Available
Advice, software packages, systems analysis. Operate on a self-service basis.

Fields of Application
Commercial, accounting.

WISCONSIN

GENERAL ELECTRIC COMPANY*
Information Service Department
615 East Michigan Street, Milwaukee, 53202
Telephone: (414) 271-7900

MIDLAND NATIONAL BANK
Data Processing Division
201 West Wisconsin Avenue, Milwaukee, 53203
Telephone: (414) 278-6030

Officer
George D. Dalton, *Vice-President*

Computer Installation
BURROUGHS B3500 (2)–operating system: MCP; internal storage: 240K (and 190K) bytes; magnetic tapes: 4 each; magnetic discs; 1 line printer each. *Remote processing features* (on one machine only): multi-line control, 100 terminals.

Coding Languages
Assembler, COBOL.

Contemplated Equipment
Front end mini.

Services Available
Advice, programming, education and training, software packages, preparation of data, systems analysis. Operate on a remote access, block time, open shop and time-sharing basis.

Fields of Application
Statistical, commercial, accounting, management, systems analysis, financial.
Specialized areas: Sales analysis, analysis, payroll.

SERVICE BUREAU CORPORATION*
2040 West Wisconsin Avenue, Milwaukee, 53233
Telephone: (414) 344-4121
(*See* under New York)

URUGUAY

SERVICE BUREAU

IBM WORLD TRADE CORPORATION*
Montevideo

Computer Installation
IBM 1401 (2).

Services Available
Advice, operators, preparation of data, programming.

Fields of Application
Statistical, commercial.

VENEZUELA

UNIVERSITIES

UNIVERSIDAD CENTRAL DE VENEZUELA*
Facultad de Ciencias
Departamento de Computación
Apartado 59002, Ciudad Universitaria, Caracas
Telephone: 726748-724226

Officer
Manuel Bemporad, *Head of the Department*

Computer Installation
IBM 360/50–operating system: OS/MVT; internal storage: 512K bits; magnetic tapes: 4 2420/5, 1 2401/5; magnetic discs: 2314 A1; 2 line printers. *Remote processing features:* 1050 (CRBE).

Coding Languages
FORTRAN IV, COBOL, Assembler, GPSS, ALGOL, PL/1.

Services Available
Advice, operators, preparation of data, programming, software packages. Operate on an open shop basis.

Fields of Application
Teaching, scientific, statistical.
Specialized areas: Numerical calculus, mathematical models.

Training
"Licenciado en Computación" after 5 years of courses.
Short courses in FORTRAN IV (5 weeks), PL/1 (6 weeks), Computers in Management (8 weeks).

UNIVERSIDAD DE LOS ANDES
Edificio Administrativo, Avenida Tulio Febres, Mérida

Officers
Dr. Ramón Vicente Cassnova, *President*
Dr. Hernán Hernández, *Secretary*
Dr. Freddy Reveron Osio, *Director of Computer Centre*

Computer Installation
IBM 360/40–operating system: DOS/25; internal storage: 512K bits; magnetic discs: 3 2314; 1 line printer.

Coding Languages
Assembler, RPG, COBOL, PL/I, FORTRAN IV.

Contemplated Equipment
IBM 370/135.

Services Available
Advice, programming, education and training, documentation, preparation of data, systems analysis. Operate on a self-service, closed shop, block time, and open shop basis.

Fields of Application
Scientific, statistical, commercial, accounting, systems analysis.
Specialized areas: Linear programming, payroll, structural engineering.

Training
Systems Engineer course.

UNIVERSIDAD DE ORIENTE
Instituto Tecnologico
Centro de Computación
Apartado 4327, Puerto La Cruz
Telephone: 22424-29

Officer
Ing. Ignacio Cavero, *Director*

Computer Installation
IBM 1130–operating system: DS; internal storage: 16K bits; magnetic discs: 3 2320; 1 line printer.

Coding Languages
FORTRAN IV, RPG, APL, ALGOL 1130, AMTRAN, Assembler.

Contemplated Equipment
IBM 370/125.

Services Available
Education and training. Operate on a self-service basis. Available for student training, internal administrative and academic control only.

Fields of Application
Commercial, operational research.

Training
Courses in Basic FORTRAN for engineers and RPG for commercial courses.

CONSULTANT

PEAT, MARWICK, MITCHELL & CO.*
Edificio Parsa, 5° piso, Plaza La Castellana, Apartado 11572, Caracas
Telephone: 324981

Officer
F. W. Southerland

Services Available
Consultation, systems analysis.

Fields of Application
Economic studies, general and scientific management, operations research, project management, industrial engineering, marketing, production and inventory control, information systems, general and cost accounting systems, data processing and transmission systems, etc.

SERVICE BUREAU

IBM WORLD TRADE CORPORATION*
Caracas

Also at:
Valencia

Computer Installation
Caracas:
IBM 360/30.
IBM 7070.
IBM 1620.
IBM 1401.
Valencia:
IBM 1401.

Services Available
Advice, operators, preparation of data, programming, software packages, systems analysis.

Fields of Application
Scientific, statistical, commercial.

REPUBLIC OF VIET-NAM

NATIONAL CENTRE

DIRECTORATE OF DATA PROCESSING
1 Throng Nhut Street, Saigon

Officer
Lieut.- Col. Truong Van Tuc, *Director*

Computer Installation
IBM 360/50—operating system: OS; internal storage: 4,194,304 bits; magnetic tapes: 8 2420, 3 2401; magnetic discs: 2 2314; 3 line printers.

Coding Language
COBOL.

Services Available
Advice, programming, education and training, software packages, documentation, systems analysis. Operate on a closed and open shop basis. Available to all Vietnamese governmental agencies and ministries as requested.

Fields of Application
Scientific, statistical, commercial, accounting, management, systems analysis, operational research.
Specialized areas: Linear programming, analysis, payroll.

Training
Courses in systems analysis, computer programming, computer operation and control.

SERVICE BUREAU

HEURISTIC SYSTEMS INTERNATIONAL*
269/1, duong Truong-min-Ký, Tân-son-hoa, Gia-dinh

Officer
Harold S. Hunt, *President*

Coding Languages
COBOL, FORTRAN, IPL, PL/1, SLIP, SNOBOL, Machine-oriented and RPG languages.

Contemplated Equipment
Unit Record (EAM) Service Bureau.

Services Available
Consultation, programming education and training, software packages, documentation, systems analysis, market research, sales representation.

Fields of Application
Engineering, social and behavioral sciences, humanities, management and data processing, information retrieval.
Specialized area: Software documentation.

YUGOSLAVIA

EDUCATIONAL AND TRAINING INSTITUTIONS

INSTITUT "JOŽEF STEFAN"
Jamova 39, 61001 Ljubljana
Telephone: 061-63261

Officers
C. Trampuz, *General Manager*
T. Turnsek, *Systems Analysis Manager*
Y. Grad, *Operations Manager*
T. Kalin, *Systems Manager*

Computer Installation
CDC Cyber 72/24—operating system: SCOPE 3·3: internal storage: 3,932,160 bits; magnetic tapes: 8 604, 2 657, 2 659; magnetic discs: 2 841/6; 2 line printers. *On-line satellite computers:* 2 IBM 1130. *Remote processing features:* 9 RJE terminals, CDC 200 user terminal.

Coding Languages
COMPASS, COBOL, FORTRAN, ALGOL.

Contemplated Equipment
6671 communication multiplexer.

Services Available
Advice, education and training, operators, software packages. Operate on a remote access and closed shop basis.

Fields of Application
Scientific, statistical, commercial.

Training
Courses in advanced programming, systems analysis, FORTRAN and COBOL.

SOCIETY FOR CYBERNETICS
Trg P. Togliatti 4/1, 51000 Rijeka
Telephone: 22095

Officers
Pavle Dragojlović, *President*
Ranko Smokvina, *Secretary*

Computer Installation
IBM 360/40–operating system: DOS: internal storage: 713,240 bits; magnetic tapes: 4; magnetic discs: 2; 1 line printer.
NCR Century 100–operating system: DOS; internal storage: 356,620 bits; magnetic discs: 2 Twin Exchangeable Disc Store; 1 line printer.

Coding Languages
COBOL, PL/I, FORTRAN IV, Assembler, RPG, NEAT 3.

Contemplated Equipment
Terminals to a UNIVAC 1106 in Zagreb, an ICL 1903S in Rijeka and a minicomputer time sharing basic system.

Services Available
Advice, programming, education and training. Operate on a block time basis. Available only to members (individual or organizations).

Fields of Application
Scientific, commercial.
Specialized Areas: Linear programming, medical research.

Training
Diplomas in EDP, programming languages, systems analysis, PERT, linear programming, microfilm and reproduction techniques.

UNIVERSITIES AND COLLEGES

BORIS KIDRIČ EKONOMSKA ŠKOLA
33 Medulićeva ulica, 41000 Zagreb
Telephone: 447-598, 442-289

Officers
Stjepan Blažeković, *Principal*
Mrs. Slavica Knežević, *Head of Course*

Coding Languages
COBOL, PARIS.

Services Available
Programming, education and training, operators.

Fields of Application
Commercial, accounting.
Specialized area: Payroll.

Training
Courses for programmers and operators.

SVEUČILIŠTE U ZAGREBU
Elektronicko Računalo Elektrotehnickog Fakulteta
Unska b.b., 41000 Zagreb
Telephone: 515-411/133

Officer
Petar Maćašović

Computer Installation
IBM 1130–internal storage: 32K 16-bit words; magnetic discs: 1; 1 line printer.

Coding Languages
FORTRAN, SAP, COBOL.

Services Available
Advice, programming, education and training, software packages, preparation of data. Operate on a self-service basis.

Fields of Application
Scientific, statistical, operational research.
Specialized areas: Linear programming, medical research.

VIŠA EKONOMSKA ŠKOLA VARAŽDIN
I.L. Ribara 2, 42000 Varaždin
Telephone: (042) 44-199

Officers
Teodor Abramić
Smiljko Job

Computer Installation
BULL GENERAL ELECTRIC GE150.

Coding Language
COBOL.

Contemplated Equipment
Burroughs B1714.

Services Available
Programming, education and training.

VIŠJA TEHNIŠKA ŠOLA MARIBOR
Smetanova 17, 62000 Maribor
Telephone: 062-25530

Officer
Milan Kac, *Professor*

Computer Installation
IBM 1130–operating system: Monitor: internal storage: 128K bits; magnetic discs: 1 2315/1.

Coding Languages
Assembler, FORTRAN.

Contemplated Equipment
CDC 731/12 terminal.

Services Available
Advice, programming, education and training, software packages. Operate on an open shop basis.

Fields of Application
Scientific, statistical, production control.
Specialized areas: Linear programming, structural engineering.

Training
Subjects covered include analysis, numerical methods and programming techniques in technical and scientific applications.

UNIVERZA V LJUBLJANI
Computer Centre
Hajdrihova 28, 61000 Ljubljana
Telephone: (061) 62-182

Officer
Janez Grad, *Head of the Centre*

Computer Installation
CDC Cyber 72/24—operating system: SCOPE 3·3; internal storage: 3,932,160 bits; magnetic tapes: 12; magnetic discs: 8 CDC; 4 line printers.
IBM 1130—operating system: DOS; internal storage: 262,144 bits; magnetic discs: 2; 1 line printer.
IBM 1130—operating system: DOS 1130/5; internal storage: 131,072 bits; magnetic discs: 1; 1 line printer.
On-line satellite computer: IBM System/7.

Coding Languages
Assembler, FORTRAN, COBOL.

Contemplated Equipment
CDC 1700 Digigraphics.

Services Available
Advice, programming, education and training, software packages, documentation. Operate on a self-service and remote access basis.

Fields of Application
Scientific, statistical, commercial, operational research.
Specialized areas: Linear programming, analysis, structural engineering.

UNIVERZITET KIRIL I METÓDIJ VO SKOPLJE*
Faculty of Electrical and Mechanical Engineering
Karpoš 11, P.fah 105, Skopje 91000
Telephone: 091-53-218

Computer Installation
IBM 1130—internal storage: 8K bits; magnetic discs: 1 IBM 2315; 1 line printer.

Coding Languages
FORTRAN IV, Assembler. 1130 RPG

Services Available
Education and training. Operate on a closed shop basis.

Field of Application
Scientific.

UNIVERZITET U BEOGRADU
Civil Engineering Faculty, Engineering Computing Centre
Bulevar Revolucije 73/1, 11000 Belgrade
Telephone: 29-302

Officers
Dr. N. Hajdin
Dr. M. Sekulović

Computer Installation
IBM 1130—operating system: DMS; internal storage: 8K bits; magnetic discs: 1 2315; 1 line printer.

Coding Languages
FORTRAN IV, SAP.

Contemplated Equipment
A computer with storage of 16K bits.

Services Available
Advice, programming, education and training, software packages, documentation. Operate on a self-service basis. Available for civil engineering only.

Field of Application
Scientific.
Specialized areas: Linear programming, structural engineering.

Training
Graduate and post-graduate courses.

GOVERNMENT ESTABLISHMENTS

FEDERAL INSTITUTE FOR STATISTICS
Kneza Miloša 20, 11000 Belgrade
Telephone: 681-999

Computer Installation
IBM 360/50—operating system: OS/MFT; internal storage 256K bits; magnetic tapes: 8 2401; magnetic discs: 6 2319, 3 2311; 2 line printers.

Coding Languages
PL/1, FORTRAN, Assembler.

Services Available
Advice, operators, software packages, preparation of data. Operate on a self-service and closed shop basis. Available to government agencies and scientific institutes.

Fields of Application
Scientific, statistical, operational research.
Specialized area: Statistics.

GRADSKI ZAVOD ZA STATISTIKU BEOGRAD
Tirsova 1, Belgrade
Telephone: 011-644-863

Officer
Miloš Serčić, *EDP Director*

Computer Installation
IBM 360/40—operating system: DOS; internal storage: 131K bits; magnetic tapes: 6 2401; magnetic discs: 3 2311; 2 line printers.
IBM 360/20—internal storage: 16K bits; magnetic tapes: 2 2145; 1 line printer.

Coding Languages
RPG, Assembler, FORTRAN IV, PL/1.

Contemplated Equipment
6 IBM 2319 disc units.

Services Available
Programming, operators, preparation of data, systems analysis. Operate on a block time basis.

Fields of Application
Statistical, commercial, accounting.
Specialized area: Payroll.

INDUSTRIJA MOTORA RAKOVICA (IMR)
Patrijarha Dimitrija 7, 11000 Belgrade

Officers
Dobrivoje Azanjac, *General Manager*
Branko Miler, *Development and DP Manager*

Computer Installation
IBM 360/25—operating system: DOS: internal storage: 32K bits; magnetic discs: 3 2311; 1 line printer.

Coding Languages
Assembler, PL/1, RPG.

Contemplated Equipment
1 magnetic tape, 3 2314 magnetic discs.

Services Available
Advice, preparation of data. Operate on an open shop basis. Available only to similar industries.

Fields of Application
Statistical, commercial, production control.
Specialized area: Structural engineering.

JUGOSLOVENSKI CENTAR ZA TECHNIČKU I NAUČNU DOKUMENTACIJU
Slobodana Peneziča 29-31, 11000 Belgrade
Telephone: 644-184

Officer
Natalija Vasović, *Director*

Coding Language
UDC.

Services Available
Advice, education and training, documentation, preparation of data, systems analysis. Operate on an open shop basis.

Fields of Application
Scientific, commercial, management, systems analysis, operational research.
Specialized areas: Analysis, information science.

Training
Short courses, seminars, symposia.

SLUŽBA DRUŠTVENOG KNJIGOVODSTVA JUGOSLAVIJE
Pop-Lukina 7-9, Belgrade

Officer
Svetozar Ivanković, *Chief Systems Engineer*

Computer Installation
IBM 370/145—operating system: DOS; internal storage: 144K 8-bit bytes; magnetic tapes: 4 IBM 3420/3; magnetic discs: 5 IBM 2319; 2 line printers.
BURROUGHS B1726—operating system: MCP-II; internal storage: 64K 8-bit bytes; magnetic tapes: 2 A-9480/2; magnetic discs: 4 A-9491/2; 1 line printer.

Coding Languages
Assembler, PL/1, COBOL, RPG, BASIC.

Contemplated Equipment
Singer System 10—operating system: DMF; internal storage: 30K 6-bit bytes; 1 magnetic tape; 2 magnetic discs; 1 line printer.

Services Available
Advice, programming, education and training, software packages, documentation. Operate on a closed shop basis.

Fields of Application
Statistical, accounting, systems analysis.
Specialized areas: Investment, payroll.

SVILA TEKSTILNA TOVARNA
Ob Dravi 6, 62000 Maribor

Officer
Milan Brecl, *Programmer*

Computer Installation
PHILIPS P359—operating system: MLC; internal storage: 6K bits.

Coding Language
BASIC.

Contemplated Equipment
Card, discs, magnetic tape cassettes.

Services Available
Operate on a self-service basis.

Field of Application
Commercial.

Training
BASIC programming course.

RESEARCH INSTITUTIONS

CENTAR ZA AUTOMATIZACIJU POSLOVANJA ZAVOD ZA UNAPREAENJE PRODUKTIVNOSTI RADA
Trg Republike 1/1, Zagreb
Telephone: 34-335

Officer
Mrakoučić Tihoraj, *Director*

Computer Installation
IBM 360/25—operating system: DOS; internal storage: 32K bits; magnetic tapes: 1 2415 M4; magnetic discs: 3 2311 M1; 1 line printer.
ZUSE Z23—internal storage: 32K bits.

Coding Languages
IBM 360/25: Assembler, RPG, COBOL, FORTRAN, PL/1; ZUSE Z23: Formelübersätzer, ALGOL.

Services Available
Preparation of data, programming, software packages, advice.

Fields of Application
Commercial, scientific.
Specialized areas: Sales analysis, payroll, research.

Training
Courses for IBM 360.

ELEKTRONSKO-NUNERIČKI CENTAR
Bijenička cesta 54 (Zgrada Instituta Rugjer Bošković) 41000 Zagreb, P.O. Box 171

Officers
Krešimir Klaužer, *Manager of Centre*
Vladimir Vranić, *Professor of Mathematics at the University of Zagreb*

Computer Installation
CII 9040—internal storage: 16K bits; 3 line printers.

Coding Language
FORTRAN II.

Services Available
Advice, operators, preparation of data, programming, systems analysis. Operate on a closed shop and block time basis. Available only to scientific institutions.

Training
Courses in programming.

ENERGOINVEST*
Centre de Calcul
Ulica JNA 20, Sarajevo
Telephone: 45-505

Dirigeants
Cico Muhamed, *Directeur*
Kontic Milan
Silijeg Marijan

Equipement
BULL GENERAL ELECTRIC Gamma 30—mémoire interne: 40K bits; bandes magnétiques: 6; disques magnétiques: 1; 1 imprimante.
PACE 231R.

Langages de Programmation
Autocode, FORTRAN.

Services Fournis
Conseils, programmation, analyse de systèmes.
Fonctionnement en porte ouverte.

Domaines d'Applications
Scientifique, statistique.

INDUSTROPROJEKT
Savska 88a, Zagreb
Telephone: 516-022

Officer
Vilko Žiljak, *Chief of Programming Department*

Computer Installation
IBM 1130—internal storage: 524,288 bits; magnetic discs: 3 2310; 1 line printer.

Coding Languages
FORTRAN, RPG.

Contemplated Equipment
IBM 370.

Services Available
Advice, programming, education and training, software packages, systems analysis.

Fields of Application
Scientific, statistical, production control, systems analysis, operational research, simulation.
Specialized areas: Sales analysis, linear programming, investment analysis, medical research.

INSTITUT EKONOMSKIH NAUKA*
(Institute of Economic Sciences)
Zmaj Jovina 12, Belgrade
Telephone: 629-950

Officers
Dr. Branko Horvat, *Director*
Mihailo Jauković, *Computer Supervisor*
Tatjana Basigalupo, *Programmer*

Computer Installation
ELLIOTT 803B—internal storage: 4K plus 4K words.

Coding Languages
Autocode 3, Elliott ALGOL.

Service Available
Research (social sciences) for the requirements of the Institute and other institutions.

Fields of Application
All fields of postgraduate school disciplines and social science.
Specialized area: Statistical analysis.

INSTITUT "RUDJER BOŠKOVIĆ"
Bijenička cesta 54, P.O. Box 1016, 41001 Zagreb
Telephone: 37067

Officer
Dr. Vinko Škarić, *Director*
Prof. Dr. Branko Soucek, *Head of Data Processing*

Computer Installation
XDS 930—internal storage: 16K bits; magnetic tapes: 2; magnetic discs: 1; 1 line printer.
PDP-8 (2)—internal storage: 4K bits.
PDP-11—internal storage: 8K bits.

Coding Languages
FORTRAN, Assembler.

Services Available
Programming, education and training. Operate on a self-service and open shop basis.

Field of Application
Scientific.
Specialized areas: Structural engineering, medical research, nuclear research.

INSTITUT ZA NUKLEARNE NAUKE "BORIS KIDRIČ"
P.O. Box 522, 11000 Belgrade
Telephone: 444-961

Officer
Dr. Miodrag Petrovič, *Director of the Computer Centre*

Computer Installation
CDC 3600—operating system: SCOPE; internal storage: 3·2 million bits; magnetic tapes: 5 CDC 604; magnetic discs: 2 CDC 854; 1 line printer. *On-line satellite computer:* ZUSE Z23. *Remote processing features.*
CDC 1700—operating system: MSOS; internal storage: 350K bits; magnetic discs: 1 CDC 853.

Coding Languages
3600 FORTRAN, ALGOL, COBOL, INFOL, 3600 COMPASS.

Services Available
Advice, programming, education and training, preparation of data, systems analysis. Operate on a remote access and open shop basis.

Fields of Application
Scientific, statistical, systems analysis, operational research.
Specialized areas: Linear programming, analysis, structural engineering.

Training
Advanced courses in applied mathematics and numerical analysis; introduction to information systems.

INSTITUTE OF TRANSPORTATION
Moše Pijade 39, 61000 Ljubljana
Telephone: 320-844

Officer
Dr. Janez Dekleva, *Director*

Computer Installation
IBM 360/30—operating system: DOS; internal storage: 128K bits; magnetic tapes: 4 IBM 2415/5; magnetic discs: 3 2314, 2 2311; 1 line printer.

Coding Languages
PL/1, Assembler, FORTRAN, RPG.

Services Available
Programming, software packages, systems analysis. Operate on an open shop basis.

Fields of Application
Scientific, statistical, commercial, systems analysis.
Specialized areas: Sales analysis, linear programming, payroll.

MULTIMEDIJSKI NASTAVNO-INFORMACIONI CENTAR ZAVODA ZA UNAPREDJIVANJE STRUČNOG OBRAZOVANJA S.R.H. I REFERALNOG CENTRA SVEUČILIŠTA U ZAGREBU
Trg Maršala Tita 3, 41000 Zagreb

Officer
Branimir Makanec, *Chairman*

Computer Installation
HEWLETT PACKARD 2100A–operating system: HP 2000E; internal storage: 16K bits; magnetic tapes: 1 HP 30115A; magnetic discs: 1 HP 30110A. *Remote processing features:* 2 modems ITT GH–1151.

Coding Languages
HP Time-shared Basic, HP Assembler.

Contemplated Equipment
Hewlett Packard 2000F extension.

Services Available
Education and training, software packages, documentation. Operate on a time-sharing basis. Available only for educational purposes.

Field of Application
Educational research.
Specialized areas: Computer-aided instruction, CMI.

ZAVOD ZA EKONOMIJU*
Vlaska 11, Zagreb

Computer Installation
ICT 1902A.

Services Available
Consultation, programming, systems analysis.

Fields of Application
Statistics, stock control, accounting.

ZAVOD ZA EKONOMSKE EKSPERTIZE*
(Institute for Expert Economic Analyses)
Palmira Toljatija 3, Belgrade
Telephone: 604-022

Officer
Borislav Bakić

Computer Installation
UNIVAC 9300–operating systems: CARD and MOS; internal storage: 16K bytes; magnetic tapes: 4 Uniservo VIC; 1 line printer.

Coding Languages
RPG, Assembler, COBOL, FORTRAN.

Services Available
Advice, programming, systems analysis. Operate on an open shop basis.

Fields of Application
Statistical, commercial, production control, accounting, management.

ŽTP BEOGRAD
Centar za Organizaciju i Kibernetiku
Zdravka Čelara 14a, Belgrade
Telephone: 762-136

Officers
Ljubomir Stamenković, *General Director*
Branko Djokić, *Computer Centre Director*

Computer Installation
IBM 370/145–operating system: OS/MFT; internal storage: 160K bits; magnetic tapes: 1 2401/2, 2 2401/5; magnetic discs: 2 2319, 1 2318; 1 line printer.
UNIVAC 1050–1 line printer.

Coding Languages
Assembler, COBOL, FORTRAN IV, PL/1.

Contemplated Equipment
Increased storage of 48K bits.

Services Available
Programming, education and training, preparation of data. Operate on a self-service basis. Available primarily for railway operations; to outside customers when time is available.

Fields of Application
Statistical, commercial, accounting.
Specialized areas: Payroll, structural engineering.

SERVICE BUREAUX

ELEKTRONSKI RAČUNSKI CENTAR
Korzo Narodne Revolucije 16, 51000 Rijeka
Telephone: 31-011

Officers
Marijan Starčević, *General Manager*
Boris Čabrijan, *ADP Manager*

Computer Installation
ICL 1903 S–operating system: GEORGE 3; internal storage: 1,572,864 bits; magnetic tapes: 4; magnetic discs: 2; 1 line printer.

Coding Languages
PLAN, COBOL, FORTRAN.

Services Available
Advice, programming, education and training, operators, software packages, documentation, systems analysis. Operate on a block time and open shop basis.

Fields of Application
Statistical, commercial, accounting, management, systems analysis, operational research.
Specialized areas: Linear programming, investment, payroll, structural engineering, medical research.

Training
Courses in systems analysis and programming.

INDUSTRIJA DRVETA, CELULOZE, PAPIRA I VLAKNA (INCEL)
Banjaluka
Telephone: 21944, 23990

Officer
Nada Adamović, *Manager*

Computer Installation
IBM 360/25 – operating system: DOS; internal storage: 261,144K bits; magnetic tapes: 2 2145; magnetic discs: 3 2314; 1 line printer.

Coding Languages
PL/1, Assembler, COBOL, RPG, FORTRAN.

Services Available
Advice, programming, education and training, operators, software packages, documentation, preparation of data, systems analysis. Operate on a self-service and closed shop basis.

Fields of Application
Commercial, accounting, management.

INDUSTRIJSKO POLJOPRIVREDNI KOMBINAT (IPK)
Sektor za EOP
ul. Republike 45, 54000 Osijek
Telephone: 054-25455

Officers
Aron Nagyvegi, *Director*
Stipan Topalic, *Head of Systems Analysis Department*
Josip Kovač, *Head of Programming Department*

Computer Installation
IBM 360/30 – operating system: DOS; internal storage: 64K bits; magnetic tapes: 1 2715; magnetic discs: 5 2311; 1 line printer.

Coding Languages
Assembler, PL/1, COBOL, FORTRAN, RPG.

Contemplated Equipment
A 2317 magnetic disc; increased storage of 32K bits.

Services Available
Advice, programming, education and training, operators, software packages, documentation, preparation of data, systems analysis. Operate on a block time and open shop basis.

Fields of Application
Statistical, commercial, accounting, management, systems analysis, operational research.
Specialized areas: Sales analysis, linear programming, analysis.

INTERTRADE
Moša Pijade 29, 61000 Ljubljana
Telephone: 322-844

Officers
Ljubo Knop, *Director*
Miran Železnik, *Director*

Computer Installation
IBM 360/40 – operating system: DOS; internal storage: 256K bytes; magnetic tapes: 5 IBM 2401/5; magnetic discs: 1 IBM 2314; 2 line printers.

IBM 1130 – operating system: Monitor; internal storage: 16K words; magnetic discs: 3 2310; 1 line printer.

Coding Languages
PL/1, FORTRAN, RPG.

Contemplated Equipment
IBM 360/50 and IBM System/3.

Services Available
Advice, programming, education and training, software packages, preparation of data. Operate on a closed shop and block time basis.

Fields of Application
Commercial, accounting.
Specialized areas: Sales analysis, payroll.

JUGOMONT-JUGOBETON
Horvaćanska 11, 41000 Zagreb
Telephone: 513-855

Computer Installation
IBM 1130 – operating system: DMS; internal storage: 8K 16-bit words; magnetic discs: 3 2310; 1 line printer.

Coding Languages
RPG, FORTRAN, Assembler.

Service Available
Programming. Operate on an open shop basis.

Field of Application
Commercial.
Specialized areas: Analysis, payroll, structural engineering.

JUGOMONTAZA - VENTILATOR (JUVENT)
Elektronsko Racunski Odjel
Veslacka b.b., 41000 Zagreb
Telephone: 517-099

Officer
Antun Vresk, *Head of Department*

Computer Installation
IBM System/3 – operating system: DMS; internal storage: 32K bits; magnetic discs: 1 5444/A2, 1 5445; 1 line printer.

Coding Language
RPG II.

Service Available
Machine time. Operate on a self-service basis.

Field of Application
Commercial.

MEHANOGRAFSKI CENTER - EMO
Mariborska c.86, 63000 Celje

Officer
Ing. Ferdinand Lupše, *Chief*

Computer Installation
IBM 360/25 – operating system: DOS; internal storage: 24K bytes; magnetic discs: 3 2311; 1 line printer.

Coding Languages
RPG, Assembler, FORTRAN.

Contemplated Equipment
Magnetic tapes; increased storage of 16K bytes.

Services Available
Advice, programming, education and training, operators, documentation, preparation of data, systems analysis. Operate on an open shop basis.

Fields of Application
Statistical, commercial, production control, systems analysis.
Specialized area: Analysis.

Yugoslavia – Service Bureaux

RAČUNSKI CENTER
Kidričeva 66, Škofja Loka

Officers
I. Gorenc
J. Ločniškar

Computer Installation
UNIVAC 9700–operating system: OS/4; internal storage: 1,024K bits; magnetic tapes: 2 UNI; magnetic discs: 4 Univac 8414; 1 line printer.
IBM 360/20–operating system: DOS; internal storage: 108K bits; magnetic discs: 2 2311; 1 line printer.

Coding Languages
COBOL, RPG, Assembler.

Contemplated Equipment
Additions to the Univac 9700: six Uniscope 100 terminals, additional memory of 1,024K bits, large disc units and two more tape units.

Services Available
Advice, education and training, operators. Operate on a remote access, block time and open shop basis.

Fields of Application
Commercial, production control, operational research.
Specialized areas: Sales analysis, linear programming (including production scheduling), payroll.

RAPID
Elektronki Računski Centar
Studentski Trg 4, 11000 Belgrade

Officer
Dačić Živojin, *Manager of Computer Centre*

Computer Installation
NCR Century 100–operating system: B1; internal storage: 32K bytes; magnetic discs: 1 655-101, 1 655-102; 1 line printer.

Coding Language
NEAT/3.

Contemplated Equipment
Three magnetic tape units and a control unit.

Services Available
Programming, preparation of data, systems analysis, data processing. Operate on an open shop basis.

Fields of Application
Accounting, management.

TOVARNA AVTOMOBILOV IN MOTORJEV MARIBOR
Ptujska c. 184, 62000 Maribor
Telephone: (062) 32330

Officer
Stojan Perhavc, *General Director*

Computer Installation
IBM 1401–internal storage: 84K bits; magnetic tapes: 4 7330; 1 line printer.

Coding Language
Autocoder.

Services Available
Programming, preparation of data, systems analysis. Operate on a closed shop basis.

Fields of Application
Statistical, commercial, accounting.
Specialized area: Payroll.

ZAIRE

GOVERNMENT ESTABLISHMENT

BANQUE DU ZAÏRE
Département Organisation et Informatique
B.P. 2697, Kinshasa

Officers
Sambwa Pida Nbagui, *Governor*
Lundu Mpongo Ntueto, *Head of Organization and Informatics Department*

Computer Installation
IBM 370/145–operating system: DOS/VS; internal storage: 256K bits; magnetic tapes: 4 3420 /5; magnetic discs: 4 3330; 1 line printer. *Remote processing features:* 4 IBM 2260 (display stations).

Coding Languages
COBOL, Assembler, RPG.

Services Available
Operate on a block time basis. Available only to government and state bodies.

Field of Application
Management.
Specialized area: Operations of the Central Bank.

SERVICE BUREAU

IBM WORLD TRADE CORPORATION*
6, Avenue du Port, Kinshasa

Principal Officers
R. Mazuir, *General Manager*
E. Wattier, *Sales Manager*

Computer Installation
IBM 360/40–operating system: DOS; internal storage: 64K bits; magnetic tapes: 4 2400; magnetic discs: 4 2314; 1 line printer.
IBM 1410–internal storage: 16K bits; magnetic tapes: 5 729; 1 line printer.

Coding Languages
Autocoder, PL/1, RPG.

Services Available
Advice, operators, preparation of data, programming, etc. Operate on a self-service, closed and open shop and block time basis.

Field of Application
Commercial.
Specialized areas: Sales analysis, payroll.

Training
Courses in key punching, operation and programming.

ZAMBIA

NATIONAL CENTRE

MINISTRY OF FINANCE
Data Processing Unit
P.O. Box 1998, Lusaka
Telephone: Lusaka 50155

Officers
A. E. Darlington, *Data Processing Manager*
C. G. Lester, *Systems Manager*
G. P. A. Mills, *Operations Manager*
J. Whitehead, *Programming Manager*

Computer Installation
ICL 1904—operating system: Basic EXEC; internal storage: 40K 24-bit words; magnetic tapes: 10; 2 line printers.
IBM 360/30—operating system: DOS; internal storage: 96K bytes; magnetic tapes: 7 2401; magnetic discs: 3 2311; 1 line printer.

Coding Languages
ANS, COBOL, FORTRAN, BAL, COBOL, PLAN.

Contemplated Equipment
IBM 370/145 with storage of 160K bytes, 4 IBM 3420/5 tapes, 2 IBM 3420/3 tapes, 2 IBM 3330 disc drives and 2 line printers; 2 1627 graph plotters; 1 1287 OCR.

Services Available
Advice, programming, education and training, complete system development and operating. Available mainly to governmental and semi-governmental organizations.

Fields of Application
Scientific, statistical, commercial, production control, accounting, management, systems analysis, operational research.

Training
Courses in programming and operations.

GOVERNMENT ESTABLISHMENTS

CITY OF NDOLA
P.O. Box 197, Ndola

Officers
G. Z. Sikananu, *City Treasurer*
J. Clark, *Computer Manager*

Computer Installation
ICL 1901A—internal storage: 393,216 bits; magnetic tapes: 4 1972; magnetic discs: 1 2821; 1 line printer.

Coding Language
COBOL.

Contemplated Equipment
ICL, KEY-EDIT.

Service Available
The computer is hired to ICL on a self-service and block time basis for bureau use after normal hours.

Fields of Application
Statistical, commercial, accounting, management.
Specialized area: Payroll.

Training
Joint Lusaka/Kitwe/Ndola city councils training scheme could eventually lead to B.C.S. qualifications.

NATIONAL AGRICULTURAL MARKETING BOARD OF ZAMBIA
Kwacha House, P.O. Box 122, Lusaka
Telephone: Lusaka 75191

Officers
R. B. Banda, *General Manager*
P. L. Wiles, *Data Processing Manager*

Computer Installation
ICL 1901A—internal storage: 384K bits; magnetic tapes: 4; magnetic discs: 2 Twin Exchangeable Disc Store; 1 line printer.

Coding Language
COBOL.

Services Available
Programming, operators, preparation of data, systems analysis. Operate on a self-service and open shop basis. Available to government bodies only.

Fields of Application
Commercial, accounting.

INDEX OF INSTITUTIONS

AAA Data Processing Center, New York, 543
AC-Service GmbH, Offenbach, 132
AC-Service Gesellschaft für Automatische Datenverarbeitung mbH, Düsseldorf, 132
ADB Centralen AB, Copenhagen, 78
ADB Konsult AB, Skärholmen, 265
ADB-System AB, Göteborg, 271
A.D.P. of California, Los Angeles, 505
ADV/ORGA Unternehmensberatung, Wilhelmshaven, 132-3
AGS Computers Inc, New York, 489
A.I.D. Computing Inc, Fort Worth, 564
AIV-Institut, Darmstadt, 127-8
A.K.S. Ltd, London, 353
APS Computer Centrum N.V., Arnhem, 208
AR Service i Sundsvall AB, Sundsvall, 271
A.T.M., Milano, 178-9
Abacus Computer Corporation, Ormond Beach, 470
Abacus Computer Services Ltd, Brighton, 353
Abington Keypunch Inc, Rockledge, 557
Åbo Akademi, Åbo, 86
Åbo Akademi School of Economics, Åbo, 86
Academia Republicii Socialiste România, Cluj, 244
Academy of Sciences of the U.S.S.R., Novosibirsk, 299
Accounting Corporation of America, Boston, 530
Accounting Corporation of America, San Diego, 505
Acta Pty. Ltd, Sydney, 15
Adams State College, Alamosa, 398-9
Adaps Ltd, St Kilda, 15-16
A-Data, Copenhagen, 77
Adelphi Business Schools Inc, New York, 382
Adelphi University, Garden City, 431
A/S Administrativ Data Behandling, Oslo, 228
Administrativ Rationalisering AB, Stockholm, 265
Advanced Computer Systems Inc, Dayton, 496
Advanced Technology Ltd, Tel-Aviv, 167
Adviesbureau R. Aronson N.V., Breda, 205
Aero Technical Applications Inc, St Louis, 486
Aerojet Electrosystems Company, Azusa, 470
Affiliated Computer Systems Inc, Tulsa, 556
Agder Distriktshøskole, Kristiansand, 224

Agency for International Development, Washington, 466-7
Agrippa-Ord Corporation, Carlisle, 483
Ahmadu Bello University, Zaria, 221-2
Ahmedabad Electricity Co. Ltd., Ahmedabad, 158
Ahmedabad Textile Industry's Research Association, Ahmedabad, 154
Ajax Data Processing Ltd, London, 353
Aktiengesellschaft für Datenverarbeitung und Betriebswirtschaftliche Organisation, Zürich, 287
Aktuelldata AB, Mölnlycke, 265-6
Albert-Ludwigs-Universität Freiburg, Freiburg-im-Breisgau, 117
Alcan Aluminium of South Africa Ltd, Pietermaritzburg, 167
Alcorn Agricultural and Mechanical College, Lorman, 422
Alef Research and Development Ltd, Haifa, 167
Alembic Chemical Works Company Ltd, Baroda, 158
Alfa Nummerisk Data Bureau, Copenhagen, 78
Algemeen Reken Centrum N.V., Amsterdam, 208
Allgemeine Elektricitäts-Gesellschaft, Konstanz, 133
Allied Computer Technology, Santa Monica, 505
Allied Data, Olympia, 566
Allmäna Ingenjörsbyrän AB, Stockholm, 266
Alpha Computer Centre (Cape) (Pty) Ltd, Parow East, 250
Alpha Computer Centre (Pty) Ltd, Mobeni, 250
Alpha Computer Service Corporation, New York, 543
Alphanumeric Inc, Lake Success, 543
Altergo Ltd, London, 300
Altro Work Shop Inc, Bronx, 543-4
American Computer Schools, Kansas City, 382
American Key Punch, Omaha, 538
American University, Washington, 401
American University of Beirut, Beirut, 190-91
American Used Computer Corporation, Boston, 483
An Foras Talúntais, Dublin, 162
Anacomp Inc, Indianapolis, 524
Análisis y Sistematización Electrónica Ltda, Bogotá, 72
Analytic Computing Services, New York, 544
Karl E. Andermatt Management Consultants, Zürich, 285
Anderson College, Anderson, 408
The Andersons, Maumee, 554

Ångpanneföreningen, Stockholm, 266
Annan Impey Morrish, London, 340
Anrocor Industries Inc, Hammond, 524-5
Apoteksbolaget AB, Stockholm, 264
Applied Computer Techniques Ltd, Halesowen, 353-4
Applied Cybernetics Corporation, Sunny Vale, 505
Applied Data Processing Inc, New Haven, 513-4
Applied Data Research Inc, Arlington, 565
Applied Data Research Inc, Princeton, 539
Applied Dynamics Europe, Rotterdam, 205
Applied Dynamics' European Computation Centre, Rotterdam, 208
Applied Geodata Systems Inc, Cambridge, 483-4
Applied Systems and Personnel Ltd, London, 354
Applied Systems Corporation, Detroit, 486
Arbeitsstelle für Wirtschaftliche Datenverarbeitung AG, Zürich, 287
Arce Corporation, Spokane, 510
Argonne National Laboratory, Argonne, 470
Århus Universitet, Århus, 75-6
Aries Corporation, McLean, 565
Aristoteleion Panepistimion Thessalonikis, Thessaloniki, 143
Arithma AG, Zürich, 287
Arkansas State University, Arkansas, 391
Asbjörn Habberstad AB, Göteborg, 266
Associated Business Consultants, Calcutta, 157
Associated Business Consultants Ltd, Beirut, 191
Associated Computer Services, Houston, 499
Associated Computer Services, Melbourne, 16
Association pour le Développement de l'Informatique de Gestion, Marseille, 91
Association pour le Développement de l'Informatique dans la Region Rhône-Alpes, Grenoble, 91
Atkins Computing Services Ltd, Epsom, 354
Atlantic Software Inc, Philadelphia, 497
AB Atomenergi, Nyköping, 262
Atomenergikommissionens Forsøgsanlaeg Risø, Risø, 77
Atomic Energy Board, Pretoria, 248
Atomic Energy Centre, Dacca, 24
Auburn University, Auburn, 390
Auditek Inc, New York, 544

Auerbach Corporations, Philadelphia, 497
Augustana College, Sioux Falls, 451-2
AB Auriga, Stockholm, 271
Austin College, Sherman, 454
Austin Peay State University, Clarksville, 452
Australian Atomic Energy Commission, Sutherland, 13
Australian National University, Canberra, 6
Autinform, GmbH & Co, Wiesbaden, 128
Autocode AB, Solna, 271
Automated Book-keeping Corporation, New York, 544
Automated Business Systems (PTY) Ltd, Marshalltown, 248-9
Automated Data Associates Inc, Rahway, 539
Automated Information Inc, Portland, 557
Automated Services Inc, Fort Wayne, 525
Automatic Data Processing Inc, Clifton, 539
Automatic Data Processing Inc, New York, 544
Automatic Data Processing Inc, Philadelphia, 557
Automatic Data Processing Ltd, Hounslow, 354
Automatic Data Processing of Florida, Inc, Miami, 517
Automation Center International, Wettingen, 287
Automation Center, S.p.A., Milan, 179
Automation Centre AB, Johanneshov, 271
Automation Inc, Omaha, 538
Automation Institute of Toledo, Toledo, 382
Automation Training Center, Reston, 382
N.V. Automatiseringsmaatschappij Yselbrein, Deventer, 208
Auto-Tronix Universal Corporation, Denver, 479, 512
Avco Corporation, Wilmington, 470
Avery Punching Bureau Ltd, London, 354
Aviner Weisener U. Galler KG, Hamburg, 133
Axel Boje Unternehmensberatung, Düsseldorf, 128

B.I.E.T. Computer Training, London, 355
B.I.T.S.A., Barcelona, 254
B.O.G., Frankfurt am Main, 133
'Badal' Computer and Management Services Ltd, Tel Aviv, 169
Bairesco, Buenos Aires, 5
T.Bak-Jensen A/S, Copenhagen, 77
Ball State University, Muncie, 408-9
Ballarat Institute of Advanced Education, Ballarat, 6
Banco Cafetero, Bogotá, 70
Bank of Canada, Ottawa, 55
Banque du Zaïre, Kinshasa, 576

Baric Computing Services Ltd, Dublin, 163
Baric Computing Services Ltd, London, 354-5
Barnestado S.A., Curitiba, 40-41
Barnett Data Systems, Rockville, 382
Barron Data Systems Inc, Sylvania, 554
Basic Computing Arts Inc, Mountain View, 476
Battelle Memorial Institute, Columbus, 470
Bayerische Akademie der Wissenschaften, Munich, 117
Bayerisches Julius-Maximilians-Universität, Würzburg, 117
Bayerisches Staatsministerium für Ernährung, Landwirtschaft und Forsten, Munich, 124
Baylor University, Waco, 454
R.W. Beck and Associates, Seattle, 501-2
Bedaux Consultants S.p.A., Milano, 177
Bedaux Nederlands N.V., Amsterdam, 205
Bedford Associates Inc, Bedford, 484
Bedford Computer Service Ltd, Bedford, 355
Belfast College of Technology, Belfast, 301
Belkereskedelmi Ügyvitelszervezesi es Informaciofeldolgozasi Intezet Kerinforg, Budapest, 148
Bell Laboratories, Columbus, 471
Bell-Northern Research, Ottawa, 56
Bellard Investments Ltd, London, 340
Bemidji State College, Bemidji, 420
Bendigo Institute of Technology, Bendigo, 6
Berenschot-Diebold B.V., Utrecht, 205-6
A/S Bergen Datasenter, Bergen, 228
Bernische Datenverarbeitung AG, Berne, 287-8
Bertels N.V. Mail Order, Rotterdam, 208
Bethany College, Bethany, 463
M.T. Bevan Ltd, Hitchin, 340
Beverly Bancorporation, Chicago, 522
Bhabha Atomic Research Centre, Bombay, 155
Birkbeck College, University of London, London, 301
Bishops Associates, Edgeware, 340-41
Biuro Projektow i Realizacji Inwestycji Przemysłu Syntezy Chemicznej, Gliwice, 238
Biz-matic Data Control Centers Inc, Boston, 530
Blackburn College of Technology and Design, Blackburn, 301-2
Blackpool Collegiate Grammar School, Blackpool, 302
Neil F. Blair & Associates International, Prescott, 476
Ernest E Blanche & Associates Inc, Kensington, 527
Boğaziçi Universitesi, Istanbul, 297

Bogføringsforeningen Automationscentralen, Naestved, 78
Johan F.Böhmer, Oslo, 228
Bolt Beranek & Newman, Inc, Cambridge, 471
Bombay Suburban Electric Supply Ltd, Bombay, 158
Bonnierdata AB, Stockholm, 271-2
Booz Allen & Hamilton Inc, New York, 489
Booz Allen & Hamilton International B.V., Düsseldorf, 128
Booz Allen & Hamilton International, London, 341
Boreham Wood College of Further Education, Boreham Wood, 302
Bosboom C.O.P.I.C. GmbH, Düsseldorf, 128
Boston College, Chestnut Hill, 416
Boston University, Boston, 416
Bournemouth College of Technology, Bournemouth, 302
Bowling Green State University, Bowling Green, 439-40
Bradley University, Peoria, 406
Brandeis University, Waltham, 416
Brandon Applied Systems Ltd, London, 341
Brandon Applied Systems Inc, New York, 489
Brandon Systems Institute Inc, New York, 489
Brandon Technical Services Inc, New York, 489
Bransch-Konsult Aktiebolag, Stockholm, 266
Bridgewater College, Bridgewater, 459
Brigham Young University, Provo, 458
Brighton Polytechnic, Brighton, 302-3
Brisbane City Council, Brisbane, 13
Bristol Polytechnic, Bristol, 303
British Aircraft Corporation (Operating) Ltd, Preston, 336
British Aircraft Corporation (Operating), Ltd, Bristol, 336
British Launderers Research Association, London, 336
British Rail, Derby, 336
British Scientific Instrument Research Association, Chislehurst, 337
British Ship Research Association, Wallsend, 337
British Wool Marketing Board, Brentford, 355
Brooklands County Technical College, Weybridge, 303
Broome Community College, Binghampton, 431
Bror Andersson AB, Skärholmen, 266
Brostrom Shipping Company, Göteborg, 272
Brown Engineering Company, Huntsville, 471
Brown University, Providence, 451
Browning Associates Inc, Toledo, 496
Bruce Erts and Associates Inc, Southfield, 486

Index of Institutions

Brunel University, Uxbridge, 303
Bryant and Stratton Education Center, Chicago, 382-3
Bucknell University, Lewisburg, 445
Bulgarian Academy of Sciences, Sofia, 46
Bull General Electric, Buenos Aires, 5
Bull General Electric, Copenhagen, 78
Bull General Electric S.A., Madrid, 255
Bull General Electric (Nederland) N.V., Amsterdam, 209
Bull General Electric (Schweiz), Zürich, 288
Bundesministerium der Justiz, Bonn, 125
Bundesministerium für Arbeit und Sozialordnung, Bonn-Duisdorf, 125
Bundesanstalt für Strassenwessen, Cologne, 124
Bunker Ramo Electronic Data Systems GmbH, Munich, 128-9
Bureau Dr B.J.M. van Spaendonck, Tilburg, 209
Bureau for Computation and for Mechanisation of Building Administration, Budapest, 146
Buerau Jung, Basle, 288
Bureau of Information Science, Beaconsfield, 337
Bureau of Statistics, Tokyo, 185
Büro für Datenverarbeitung GmbH, Hamburg, 134
Burroughs Corporation, Detroit, 534
Burroughs Electrônica Ltda, Rio de Janeiro, 40
Burroughs AB, Stockholm, 272
Burroughs Ltd, Sydney, 16
Business Accounting Services, London, 355-6
Business Computer Service, Charleston, 567
Business Data Processing, Santa Barbara, 505
Business Operations Research (Services) Ltd, London, 341
Business Publishers Circulation Services, Duluth, 535
Business Software Ltd, London, 341
AB Bygg-ADB, Solna, 272

CAE Datenverarbeitungssysteme für Wissenschaft und Wirtschaft GmbH, Frankfurt am Main, 134
CBC Byggeadminstration A/S, Kokkedal, 78
CCM Information Corporation, New York, 544-5
CDI Computer Services, Philadelphia, 557-8
CERN, Genève, 284
C.I. Data-Centre Ltd, Farnborough, 357
CIMS Group Inc, Pittsburgh, 497-8
C.I. Software Ltd, Salisbury, 341
C.M.I. Computer Micrographics Inc, Los Angeles, 506
CSS Europe Ltd, London, 360-61
Cabinet Giles, Brussels, 28

Cabinet P. de Los Rios, Montpellier, 103
Caja de Ahorros de Granada, Granada, 255
Caja de Ahorros y Monte de Piedad de Cádiz, Cádiz, 255
Caja Provincial de Ahorros, Córdoba, 255-6
Caisse Générale d'Épargne et de Retraite, Brussels, 26-7
Caisse Régionale de Crédit Agricole Mutuel d'Avignon et de Vaucluse, Avignon, 108
Calculo y Tratamiento de la Información S.A., Madrid, 256
California State University, Fullerton, 392
California State University, Long Beach, 392
California State University, Northridge, 392
Cal-Western Data Systems Inc, Studio City, 505
Call-a-Computer, Melville, 544
Calspan Corporation, New York, 471-2
Caltec Inc, Toledo, 554
Cambridge Computer Associates, Cambridge, 484
Cambridge Computer Services Ltd, Cambridge, 356
Cambridgeshire College of Arts and Technology, Cambridge, 303-4
Canadian General Electric Co Ltd, Toronto, 59-60
Canadian General Electric Co Ltd, Vancouver, 60
Canberra College of Advanced Education, Canberra, 7
Capital Cities Computer Centres Ltd, Watford, 356
Capital Computer Applications, Århus, 77
Capital Computer Applications Ltd, London, 356
Capricornia Institute of Advanced Education, Rockhampton, 7
Card Punching Service, Copenhagen, 78
Career Educational Institute, Philadelphia, 383
Carleton College, Northfield, 420
Carleton University, Ottawa, 47-8
Carlisle Technical College, Carlisle, 304
Carnegie-Mellon University, Pittsburgh, 445
Carroll College, Waukesha, 464
Case-Cegos, Brussels, 28
Case Western Reserve University, Cleveland, 440
Catholic University of America, Washington, 401-2
Cati-Cofigat, Nantes, 108-9
Cati-Mécanorga-Ergem, Paris, 109
Caulfield Institute of Technology, Caulfield East, 7
Cedis, Besançon, 109
Cegos-Informatique, St.Cloud, 103-4
Cegos Institut für Datenverarbeitung, Munich, 129
Ceir Inc, New York, 545
Celestron Associates Inc, Thornwood, 545

Centar za Automatizaciju Poslovanja Zavod za Unapreaenje Produktivnosti Rada, Zagreb, 572
Centi (Canada) Ltée, Montréal, 56-7
Centrais Elétricas do Sul do Brasil S.A. (Eletrosul), Rio de Janeiro, 36-7
Central Bureau of Statistics, Damascus, 294
Central Bureau of Statistics, Djakarta, 159-60
Central Computer Services (Highlands) Ltd, Inverness, 356
Central Computing Inc, Wichita, 526
Central Conneticut State College, New Britain, 400
Central Electricity Board, Curepipe, 194
Central Electricity Generating Board, Branhall, 331-2
Central Electricity Generating Board, London, 331
Central Information Processing Corporation, Baltimore, 527
Central Institute for Computing Techniques, Sofia, 46
Central Mechanical Engineering Research Institute, Durgapur, 155
Central State University, Edmond, 443
Central Statstical Office, Warszawa, 238
Centrala Folkbokförings-Och Uppbordsnamnden, Stockholm, 262
Centralia College, Centralia, 461
Centralny Osrodek Doskonalenia Kadr Kierowniczych, Warsaw, 238-9
Centralny Osrodek Informatyki Gornictwa i Energetyki, Katowice, 240
Centre Académique de Traitement de l'Information, Paris, 91-2
Centre d'Analyse et de Programmation Belgique S.A., Brussels, 28
Centre d'Analyse et de Programmation, Paris, 109
Centre Cantonal d'Informatique, Geneva, 288
Centre de l'Étude de l'Énergie Nucléaire, Brussels, 27
Centre de Techniques d'Organisation et de Direction, Paris, 104
Centre de Traitement Automatique de l'Information, Louvain, 24-25
Centre de Traitement de l'Information, Asnières, 109
Centre de Traitement des Informations, Aix-en Provence, 109
Centre Électronique de Gestion, Blois, 110
Centre d'Études et de Traitement sur Ordinateur, Courbevoie, 109
Centre d'Études Pratiques d'Informatique et d'Automatique, Le Chesnay, 92
Centre d'Études Techniques de l'Equipement Aix-en-Provence, 100
Centre Expérimental de Recherches et d'Études du Batiment et des Travaux Publics, Paris, 101

Centre Expérimental Eurocontrol, Brétigny, 101
Centre-File Ltd, London, 357
Centre-File (Northern) Ltd, Manchester, 357
Centre for Educational Technology, Herzlia, 164
Centre Français de Recherche Opérationelle, Paris 110
Centre d'Information Générale, S.A., Brussels, 30
Centre Interuniversitaire de Calcul de Grenoble, Grenoble, 94
Centre Interuniversitaire de Traitement de l'Information, Paris, 94
Centre National de la Recherche Scientifique Bellevue-Meudon, 101
Centre National de la Recherche Scientifique, Marseille, 94-5
Centre National de la Recherche Scientifique, Marseille, 101-2
Centre of Economic Computation and Economic Cybernetics, Bucharest, 244
Centre pour le Traitement de l'Information (Centi Benelux), Brussels, 29
Centre pour le Traitement de l'Information Paris, 104
Centre Universitaire de Formation et d'Education Permanente, Poitiers, 92
Centres Informatique Philips, Fontenay-aux-Roses, 110
Centro S.p.A., Verona, 179
Centro de Calculo Cientifico, Lisboa, 240-41
Centro de Información y Cómputo S.A Cali, 72
Centro de Informações Para o Desenvolvimento Urbano e Local, Rio de Janeiro, 37
Centro de Investigacion de Tecnicas Matematical Aplicadas a la Direccion de Empresas, Buenos Aires, 4
Centro de la Informática, Técnica y Material Administrativos, Madrid, 254
Centro de Prestacão de Servicos Técnicos do Estado de Pernambuco, Pernambuco, 37
Centro Distrital de Sistematización y Servicios Técnicos, Bogotá, 70
Centro Electrônico Walmap S.A., Rio de Janeiro, 41
Centro Informazioni Studi Esperienze, Milan, 175
Centro Italiano Studi e Richerche S.p.A., Roma, 175
Centro Nacional de Cálculo, Mexico, 194
Centro Nazionale Universitario di Calculo Elettronico, Pisa, 172
Centro Studi e Applicazioni in Technologie Avanzate, Bari, 175
Centro Superior De Procesamiento De La Informacion, La Plata, 1
Centro Técnico de Proceso de Datos S.A., Alicante, 256
Centrum voor Automatisering Bredatilburg, Tilburg, 202-3
Centrum voor Automatisering Noord-Holland, Haarlem, 203

Centrum voor Informatie Management N.V., Antwerp, 30
Centrum voor Informatieverwerking N.V., Utrecht, 209
Centurex Corporation, Los Angeles, 505-6
Century Computer Deutschland GmbH, Offenbach, 134
Certa AB, Stockholm, 266
Cetel, Lisboa, 241
Challenge Corporation Ltd, Wellington, 219
Chalmers Tekniska Högskola, Göteborg, 260
Chambre de Commerce et d'Industrie, Paris, 92
Champion Service Corporation, Cleveland, 554-5
Chelsea Centre for Science Education, University of London, London, 304
Cheyney State College, Cheyney, 445
Chi Corporation, Cleveland, 554
Chicago State College, Chicago, 406
China Data Processing Centre, Taipei, 67
Chipola Junior College, Marianna, 402
Christain-Albrechts-Universität, Kiel, 117-8
Chulalongkorn University, Bangkok, 295
Chung Shan Institute of Science and Technology, Lungtan, 67
Cie Fse Thomson Houston-Hotchkiss Brandt, Le Plessis Robinson, 103
Cimsco Data Processing Company, Long Beach, 506
Cincinnati Technical College, Cincinnati, 440
The Citadel, Charleston, 451
City National Bank of Miami, Miami, 517
City of Leicester Polytechnic, Leicester, 304
City of Ndola, Ndola, 577
City Treasurer's Department, Port Elizabeth, 247
The City University, London, 304
City University of New York, Board of Higher Education Central Office, New York 431
City University of New York Graduate School and University Center, New York, 431-2
City University of New York Hunter College, New York, 432
City University of New York, Kingsborough Community College, Brooklyn, 432
City University of New York Staten Island Community College, Staten Island, 432
Claremont Colleges. Claremont, 393
Clarion State College, Clarion, 445-6
Clarkson College of Technology, Potsdam, 432
Cleveland State University, Cleveland, 440
Coboeking N.V., Amsterdam, 210
Coe College, Cedar Rapids, 410
Colgate University, Hamilton, 432-3
Collège de France, Paris, 95

College of Automation, Des Moines, 383
College of Data Processing, Los Angeles, 383
College of Technology, Letchworth, 304-5
College of William and Mary in Virginia, Williamsburg, 459-60
Colorado State University, Fort Collins, 399
Com-Share Inc, Ann Arbor, 534
Combined Data Group Inc, New York, 545
Combit (Israel) Ltd, Ramat-Gan, 167
Combyte Software GmbH, Hanau, 134
Comi, Saint Cyr l'Ecole, 104
Comitato Nazionale per l'Energia Nucleare, Bologna, 175
Comitato Nazionale per L'Energia Nucleare, Roma, 176
Comitati Nazionale per l'Energia Nucleare, Gruppo Calcoli Numerici dei Laboratori Nazionali di Frascati, Roma, 176
Commercial and Industrial Computer Services (Pty) Ltd, Johannesburg, 250
Commercial Computer Centre Pty Ltd, Parramatta, 16
Commercial Programming Unlimited, New York, 383
N.V. Commercieel Computer Centrum, The Hague, 210
Commercial Computer Consultants (Digital) Ltd, Bedford, 367
Commonwealth Scientific and Industrial Research Organisation, Canberra, 13
Community Health Information Project, London, 332
Compagnie Amienoise de Mécanographie, Amiens, 110
Compagnie des Systèmes et Services d'Informations, Paris, 105
Compagnie Française d'Organisation, Paris, 104
Compagnie Générale d'Informatique, Paris, 104
Compagnie IBM France, Boulogne/ Billancourt, 92
Compagnie IBM France, Casablanca, 197
Compagnie Internationale pour l'Informatique, Grenoble, 102
Compagnie Internationale pour l'Informatique, Louveciennes, 110-111
Compagnie Parisienne d'Ingénieurs-Conseils, Paris, 104
Companhia de Processamento de Dados do Estado do Rio Grande do Sul, Rio Grande do Sul, 27
Companhia de Processamento de Dados do Maranhão, Maranhão, 37-8
Companhia de Processamento de Estado de São Paulo, São Paulo, 41
Companhia do Metropolitano de São Paulo, São Paulo, 38
Companhia Estadual de Aguas da Guanabara, Guanabara, 38

Index of Institutions

Compañía Colombiana de Sistemas, Bogotá, 71
Compañía Cuyana de Cómputos, Mendoza, 4
Comparecs Inc, Washington, 479-80
Compass Computer Systems Inc, Nashville, 499
Competance EDB-Service A/S, Copenhagen, 78-9
Comprehensive Computer Services Ltd, Cleckheaton, 357
Compress Inc, Rockville, 483,527
Comprite Ltd, Warminster, 357-8
Comptabilité Statistique Informatic, Paris, 111
Compumar, Soest, 206
Compunet Ltd, Artarmon, 16
Computab Inc, Honolulu, 522
Computação e Planejamento S.A., Rio de Janiero, 40
A.S.Computas, Oslo, 228
Computation Research and Development, London, 358
Compute America Corporation, Atlanta, 521
Compute America Corporation, Denver, 512
Compute America Corporation, Norristown, 558
Compute America Corporation, Oklahoma City, 556
Compute America Corporation, Silver Spring, 528
Computec Associates, Cambridge, 484
Computech Consulting Canada Ltd, Vancouver, 57
Computech Systems and Personnel Ltd, London, 358
Computel Ltd, Bracknell, 358
Computel Systems Ltd, Ottawa, 60
Computer Accounting Services Pty Ltd, Camperdown, 17
Computer AG Zürich, 288
Computer Aid Companies Inc, Dallas, 500
Computer Aid for Management Ltd, London, 341
Computer Aid Ltd, Cheadle Hulme, 358
Computer-Aided Design Centre, Cambridge, 332
Computer Analyse en Programmering N.V., Amsterdam, 206
Computer Analysts & Programmers Ltd, London, 342
Computer and Mechanographic Centre for Data Processing, Bucharest, 243
Computer Applications Inc, New York, 489
Computer Assistance Inc, West Hartford, 479
Computer Associates, London, 342
Computer Bureau Ltd, Christchurch, 219
Computer Bureau Services (Cardiff) Ltd, Cardiff, 358
Computer Bureau (Waikato) Ltd, Hamilton, 219
Computer Careers Incorporated, Bethesda, 483
Computer Center Inc, Baltimore, 528

Computer Center Inc of Miami, Miami, 517
Computer Center Inc, Palm Beach, 518
Computer Centrum 'Europort' N.V., Rotterdam, 210
Computer Command and Control Company, Philadelphia, 471
Computer Command and Control Company, Washington, 383-4
Computer Consulting Service, Dubuque, 525
Computer Consultants Corporation, East Denville, 487
Computer Dimensions Inc, Dallas, 564
Computer Dynamics, London, 359
Computer Engineering Applications Pty Ltd, Sydney, 14
Computer Enterprises AG, Zug, 285
Computer Financial Inc, Los Angeles, 477
Computer Fulfillment Corporation, Long Island, 545
Computer Fulfillment, Winchester, 530
Computer Management Group, Ltd, Croydon, 359
Computer Methods Corporation, White Plains, 489-90
Computer Micro-Image Systems Inc, Chatsworth, 477
Computer Microfilm Systems Inc, Glendale, 506
Computer Payrolls Ltd, Welwyn Garden City, 359
Computer Power, Cannock, 299
Computer Power Inc, Jacksonville, 517-8
Computer Processes Inc, Los Angeles, 477
Computer Professionals Consultancy Ltd, London, 342
Computer Projects Ltd, London, 359
Computer Research Inc, Pittsburgh, 558
Computer Sciences Canada, Ltd, Don Mills, 60-61
Computer Sciences Corporation, El Segundo, 506
Computer Sciences International S.A., Brussels, 29
Computer Sciences International Deutschland, GmbH, Frankfurt-am-Main, 129
Computer Sciences International France S.A., Paris, 105
Computer Sciences International Italia, Rome, 177-8
Computer Sciences International Nederland N.V., Amstelveen, 210-11
Computer Sciences International United Kingdom Ltd, London, 342
Computer Sciences of Australia Pty Ltd, Milsons Point, 17
Computer Sciences S.A. Ltd., Johannesburg, 250-51
Computer Service Consultants Inc, Warwick, 499
Computer Service Holland B.V., Rotterdam, 210

Computer Servicenters Inc, Greenboro, 522-3
Computer Servicenters Inc, Greenville, 563
Computer Servicenters Inc, St Mary's, 558
Computer Services Corporation, Des Moines, 525-6
Computer Services Inc, Salem 530
Computer Services International, Bombay, 158
Computer Services Ltd, Dublin, 163-4
Computer Services Ltd, Lagos, 223
Computer Services (South West) Ltd, Plymouth, 359
Computer Systems Advisers (Pte) Ltd, Singapore, 244
Computer Systems and Education Corporation, East Hartford, 514
Computer Systems Co Inc, Cleveland, 496
Computer Systems, Grants Pass 577
Computer Systems Implementations Ltd. Glasgow, 360
Computer Systems Internationl Inc, Chaska, 535
Computer Systems International AB, Solna, 267
Computer Systems International Inc, (GB) Ltd, Wembley, 342
Computer Technical Services Inc, Dallas, 500
Computer Thailand Ltd Partnership, Bangkok, 296
Computer Usage Corporation, Greenwich, 514
Computer Usage Development Corporation, Bala-Cycwyd, 558
Computer Usage Development Corporation, Chicago, 522
Computer Usage Development Corporation, Montclair, 539
Computer Usage Development Corporation, Towson, 528
Computing Efficiency Inc, Long Island, 545-6
Computer Utilities (Brookvale) Pty Ltd, Brookvale, 17
Computer Utilities (Industrial) Pty Ltd, Sydney, 17
Computerised Business Systems Ltd, Cardiff, 260
Computers and Organisation Ltd, Tel-Aviv, 167
Computers in Business Ltd, London, 360
Computerware Inc, New York, 545
Compu-Time Inc, Fort Lauderdale, 518
Computone Systems Inc, Atlanta, 521
Compuvisor Inc, Ithaca, 490
Compuysus Inc, Albuquerque, 543
Comserv, University City, 558
Comsonic Corporation, Upper Saddle River, 540
Comspace Corporation, Farmingdale, 546
Comtech, Hyattsville, 528
Comtime (Manchester) Ltd, Stretford, 360
Concord College, Athens, 463
Concordia College, Moorhead, 420

Concordia Teachers College, River Forest, 406
Condata Inc, Philadelphia, 558-9
Condon Corporation, Bedford, 530
Conseil National de la Recherche Scientifique, Beirut, 190
Conseils et Engineering d'Affaires, Monaco-Ville, 197
Consentive Inc, Philadelphia, 498
Conservatoire National des Arts et Metiers, Paris, 100
Consiglio Nazionale delle Richerche, Istituto di Elaborazione della Informazione, Pisa, 176
Consiglio Nazionale delle Richerche, Istituto Nazionale per le Applicazione del Calcolo, Roma, 176
Consiglio Nazionale delle Richerche, Laboratorio Cibernetica, Napoli, 176-7
Consolidated Brick and Pipe Investments Ltd, Auckland, 219
Consolidated Computer Services Ltd, Toronto, 61
Constructive Management Services Ltd, London, 342-3
Consulta AB, Lidingö, 267
Consultdata Nederland N.V., Amsterdam, 206
Consultee S.R.L., Ascunción, 234
Consulting Engineers, Leidschendam, 206
Consultmar S.A., Mar del Plata, 4
Consultoria e Serviços Técnicos Aplub Ltda, Rio Grande do Sul, 41
Contahal Ltd, Tel Aviv, 168
Contract Computing Ltd, Croydon, 343
Contract Computing Ltd, Thornton Heath, 360
Contract Programming Company, London, 343
Control Data Australia Pty Ltd, Sydney, 17-18
Control Data Canada Ltd, Ottawa, 61
Control Data Computer Training School, New York, 384
Control Data Corporation, Cambridge, 530
Control Data Corporation, Chicago, 522
Control Data Corporation, Cincinnati, 555
Control Data Corp., Dallas, 564
Control Data Corporation, Detroit, 534
Control Data Corporation, Huntsville, 502
Control Data Corporation, Minneapolis, 535-6
Control Data Corporation, Palo Alto, 506-7
Control Data Corporation, Rockville, 528
Control Data Corporation, Washington, 516
Control Data Education Centers, Minneapolis, 384
Control Data GmbH, Frankfurt-am-Main, 134
Control Data Holland N.V., Rijswijk, 211
Control Data Institute, Anaheim, 384
Control Data Institute, Burlington, 384
Control Data Institute, Long Beach, 384-5
Control Data Institute, Pittsburgh, 385
Control Data Institute, Sherman Oaks, 385
Control Data Institute, Syracuse, 385
Control Data Institute, Willowdale, 46-7
Control Data Italia S.p.A., Roma, 179
Control Data Sweden AB, Stockholm, 272-3
Contruções e Comércio Camargo Corrêa S.A., Vila Olímpia, 41
Cooper Computer Services, Sherman Oaks, 507
Cooperativa Agricola de Cotia-Cooperativa Central, São Paulo, 41-2
Coopers and Lybrand Associates Ltd, London, 343
Coranord, Paris, 111
Cornell College, Mount Vernon, 410
Cornell University, Ithaca, 433
Corporación de Obras Sanitarias, Ascunción, 234
Corporate Computer Services Ltd, London, 343
Corporation of the District of Surrey, Surrey, 56
Council of Scientific and Industrial Research, Hyderabad, 155
Council of Scientific and Industrial Research, Uttar Pradesh, 155
Counter-Data AB, Stockholm, 273
Coventry Technical College, Coventry, 305
Cover-All Computer Services Ltd, Toronto, 61
E.H. Cowled Pty Ltd, Seaforth, 14
Cranfield Institute of Technology, Cranfield, 305
Crefidata, S.A., Rio Grande do Sul, 42
Cresap McCormick and Paget Inc, New York, 490
Cybermatics Inc, Englewood Cliffs, 487
Cyberna S.A., Genève, 289
Cybernetics International AB, Danderyd, 267
Cybernetics International (U.K.) Ltd, London, 361
Cybernetion Consultants Ltd, Edmonton, 57

D-A Computer Services Ltd, Sheffield, 361
DBO Systeme für Datenverarbeitung und Betriebswirtschaftliche Organisation, Düsseldorf, 129
DIPL-ING Wolfram Erdlen, Seefeld/Obb, 130
DIPL-KFM Helmut Blau, Gauting, 128
DIPL-KFM Wolfgang Brezina, EDP-Consulting, München, 128
D. J. Computer Services Ltd, London, 363
DPS Inc, Waukegan, 522
R.N.Dailey Inc, New York, 490
Dakota Data Inc, Bismarck, 553
Dalhousie University, Halifax, 48
Danaco Computer Services, Birmingham, 361
Dâneshgâhé Isfahan, Isfahan, 160
Dâneshgâhé Pahlavi, Shiraz, 160
Dâneshgâhé Sanati Arya-Mehr, Teheran, 161
Daniel Mann Johnson & Mendenhall, Los Angeles, 477
Danish EDP Council, Copenhagen, 75
Danmarks Statistik, Copenhagen, 77
Danmarks Tekniske Højskole, Copenhagen, 76
Dansk-Siemens, Copenhagen, 79
Dartmouth College, Hanover, 428
Darzins Mathematical and Econometric Consultants, San Fransisco, 477
A/S Data-Automasion, Oslo, 229
Data Automation Ltd, Tel Aviv, 169
Data Center Luzern, Luzern, 289
Data Center Inc, Seattle, 502
Data Central Inc, St Louis, 537
Data Consultants Ltd, Sutton Coldfield, 343-4
Data Control Services, Canton, 555
Data Corporation, Los Angeles, 507
Data Corporation of America, Winter Haven, 518
Data Dynamics Services Ltd, Hitchin, 361
Data Express (D.P.) Ltd, London, 344
Data Inc, Arlington, 565
Data-Inform A/S, Risskov, 79
Data Institute Inc, Hartford, 514
Data Ljunggen, Malmö, 267
Data Logic A/S, Oslo, 229
Data Logic AB, Solna, 273
Data Operations Inc, Cambridge, 531
Data Processing Inc, Jacksonville, 418
Data Processing Management Association, Park Ridge, 385
Data Processing Research Demonstration Centre for the Blind and Otherwise Handicapped, Jerusalem, 166-7
Data Råd A/S, Oslo, 227
Data Sciences International Ltd, Leeds, 361-2
Data Sciences International Ltd, Norwich, 362
Data Service Centre Ltd, Glasgow, 362
Data Service Corporation, Nashville, 563
Data Services Corporation, Dayton, 555
AB Data-Service, Danderyd, 273-4
AB Data-Service, Stockholm, 274
Data Systems Analysts Inc, Pennsauken, 540
Data Systems Consultants, Spokane, 502
Data Systems Inc, Minneapolis, 536
Data Systems International Inc, Philadelphia, 559

Data-Tjeneste A/S, Oslo, 229
Data-Tronics Corporation, Fort Smith, 504
Data Usage Corporation, Fort Lee, 540
Dataanlyse AB, Stockholm, 267
AB Databyrån Cassemar & Hallman, Farsta, 267
Datacard Computer Services Pty Ltd, Sydney, 18
I/S Datacentralen, Copenhagen, 77
Datacraft International, Brussels, 30
Datalogics Inc, Cleveland, 555
Datamatic A/S, Copenhagen, 79
Datamatics Management Services Inc, Englewood Cliffs, 487
Datanetics, Pittsburgh, 559
AB Datorganisation, Stockholm, 273
Dataprojekt AB, Stockholm, 273
Datapron Services Ltd, Birmingham, 362
Datarutin AB, Stockholm, 273
Datasentralen A/S, Oslo, 229
Dataskil Ltd, Reading, 362
Dataskolen, Copenhagen, 79
Datasolve International Ltd, London, 362-3
Datasonics, New York, 490
Datatab Inc, New York, 546
Datatrol Corporation, Clementon, 540
Datema AB, Solna, 274
Daten-Service Beck GmbH, Neckarsulm, 133
Datenverarbeitungs-Dienst, A.G., Schaffhausen, 289
Datenverarbeitungsdeinst der Stadt Bern, Berne, 283
Datenzentrale Schleswig-Holstein, Kiel, 125
Datorg, Budapest, 146-7
Datron AG Für Datenverarbeitung und Organisation, St Gallen, 285
Decca Radar Canada (1967) Ltd, Toronto, 57
Defence Research and Development Laboratory, Hyderabad, 152
Delta Data Services Inc, New Orleans, 527
Delta Informática S.A., Madrid, 256-7
Delta-Institut für Arbeitsvereinfachung, Vienna, 21
Demag EDV Service GmbH, Duisburg, 134-5
Departamento Nacional de Estadística, Bogotá, 70
Departamento Nacional de Planeación, Bogotá, 70
Department of Health and Social Security, Reading, 332
Department of Public Works, Djakarta, 160
Department of Scientific and Industrial Research, Wellington, 218
Department of Statistics, Kuala Lumpur, 192-3
Department of Statistics, Pretoria, 247
Department of Trade and Industry, East Kilbride, 333
Department of Trade and Industry, Newport, 332-3
Department of Trade and Industry, Stevenage, 337

Design Automation Inc, Lexington, 484
Designers and Builders of Information Systems, New York, 490
Detroit College of Business, Dearborn, 385
Deutsche Bau- und Boden AG, Mainz, 135
Deutsche Baugruppe GmbH & Co, Munich, 135
Deutsche Bedaux, GmbH, Frankfurt-am-Main, 129
Deutsche Forschungs und Versuchanstalt für Luft und Raumfahrt E.V. Braunschweig, 126
Deutsche Forschungs- und Versuchsanstalt für Luft und Raumfahrt, Oberpfaffenhofen, 126
Deutsche Utimaco GmbH, Frankfurt-am-Main, 135
Deutsches Rechenzentrum, Darmstadt, 117
Dial-Data Inc, Newton, 531
Dickinson College, Carlisle, 446
Diebold Deutschland GmbH, Frankfurt-am-Main, 129
Diebold France S.A., Paris, 105
Diebold Group Inc, New York, 490-91
N.V. Dienstverlening Overheids Administrative en Automatiserings Service Centrum van N.Samson N.V., Alphen, 211
Digital AG, Zürich, 289
Digital Applications International Ltd, London, 344
Digitron AG, Nidau, 285
Direction Centrale de la Statistique, Beirut, 191
Directorate of Data Processing, Saigon, 569
Diversified Computer Applications, Palo Alto, 507
Dixie Data Processing Inc, Warsaw, 553
Dobiess, Hannover, 129
Documentations Automatiques des Textes Juridiques de l'Université de Montréal, Montréal, 48
Dolnóslakie Biuro Projektów Gorniczych, Wrocław, 239
Doncaster Rural District Council, Doncaster, 333
Doxiadis Associates Computer Centre Ltd, Athens, 144
Drammensvassdragets Datasentral, Hønesfoss, 229
Drury College, Springfield, 423
Dublin Health Authority, Dublin, 163
Duke University, Durham, 438
Dunfold Hadfields Ltd, Sheffield, 363
Duquesne University, Pittsburgh, 446
Dychurch Business Services, Northampton, 363

EBS Management Consultants Inc, New York, 491
EDB-Centralen, Herning, 79
EDB Service A/S, Oslo, 229-30

EDP Assistance Ltd, Basel, 285
EDP Associates Inc, New York, 491
E.D.P. (Aust.) Pty Ltd, Melbourne, 18
EDP Industries Ltd, Vancouver, 61-2
EDP Resources Deutschland AG, Bad Homburg, 135
EDP Technology Inc, Washington, 480
EF Management Consultants Oy, Helsingfors, 89
E.J.V. Data Services Ltd, London, 364
EPG Computer Services Inc, New York, 491
ESPO Data Consultants Inc, Chicago, 481-2
EUR Data Center Inc, Lemoyne, 559
EWP Computer Services Ltd, Karachi, 232-3
East Midlands Computer Services, Leicester, 363
Eastern Air Lines Inc, Miami, 480-81
Eastern Computer Services Inc, Rockledge, 559
Eastern Computer Services Ltd, Spalding, 363-4
Eastern Illinois State University, Charleston, 406
Eastern Iowa Community College, Davenport, 410
Eastern Kentucky University, Richmond, 413
Eastern Michigan University, Ypsilanti, 418
Eastern Montana College, Billings, 426
Eastern Railway, Mughalsarau, 152-3
Eastern Regional Hospital Board, Scotland, Dundee, 333
Eastern Washington State College, Cheney, 461
Eberhard-Karls-Universität, Tübingen, 118
Eberhard-Karls-Universität Zentrum für neue Lernverfahren, Tübingen, 118
Ecco Consulting Inc, Pittsburgh, 498
École Centrale des Arts et Manufactures, Paris, 95
École Nationale d'Ingénieurs, Metz, 95
École Nationale Supérieure de la Métallurgie et de l'Industrie des Mines, Nancy, 95-6
École Polytechnique Fédérale de Lausanne, Lausanne, 281-2
École Professionelle Supérieure de l'Informatique, Paris, 92
École Royale Militaire, Brussels, 25
École Supérieure d'Electricité, Malakoff, 96
École Supérieur d'Ingenieurs de Beyrouth, Beirut, 191
Economic Information Systems Inc, New York, 491
Edge Hill College of Education, Ormskirk, 305
Edgeware Computer Bureau, Edgeware, 364
Edinburgh Corporation, Edinburgh, 333
Edinburgh Regional Computing Centre, Edinburgh, 364

Education and Training Consultants, Los Angeles, 477
Educational Information Services Inc, Washington, 480
Educators Consultant Service Inc, New York, 531
Edutronics Systems International Inc, Los Angeles, 386
Eidgenössisches Statistisches Amt, Bern, 283
Eidgenössische Technische Hochschule, Zurich, 282
Ekonomisk Data Behandling AB, Bromma, 274
Ekonomisk Företagsledning AB, Solna, 267
El Paso Data Services Inc, El Paso, 386
Elaborazione Automatica Dati S.R.L., Milan, 179
Electrical Communication Laboratory, Tokyo 185
Electro-Calcul S.A., Lausanne, 289
Electro-Misrad, Tel-Aviv 168
N.V. Electrologica, Rijswijk, 211
Electronic Accounting Systems Inc, Rochester, 546
Electronic Associates Ltd, Burgess Hill, 364
Electronic Associates Inc, Brussels, 30
Electronic Associates Inc, El Segundo, 507-8
Electronic Associates Pty Ltd, Melbourne, 18
Electronic Associates Inc, Princeton, 540
Electronic Associates Inc, Rockville, 528
Electronic Business Services, Visalia, 508
Electronic Computer Programming Institute, Dayton, 386
Electronic Computer Programming Institute, Hamilton, 47
Electronic Computer Programming Institute, Harrisburg, 386
Electronic Computer Programming Institute, Kansas City, 386
Electronic Computer Programming Institute, London, 47
Electronic Computer Programming Institute of Montreal, Montreal, 47
Electronic Computer Programming Institute of Tidewater, Norfolk, 387
Electronic Computer Programming Institute, Sacramento, 386
Electronic Data Preparation Corporation, Sarasota, 481
Electronic Data Processing Ltd, Sheffield, 364-5
Electronic Data Service Inc, Wilmington, 515
Electronic Data Systems Ltd, Auckland, 220
Electronic Processors Inc, Birmingham, 502
Electronic Service Associates Corporation, Cleveland, 496
Electronic Tabulating Corporation, Newburgh, 546
Electronisch Communicatie Centrum, The Hague, 211

Electronisch Reken en Administratiecentrum, Hertogenbosch, 211
Electrotechnical Laboratory, Tokyo, 185-6
Elektro Data Bolaget, Stockholm, 274-5
Elektronische Datenverarbeitung AG, Basle, 290
Elektronische Datenverarbeitungsgesellschaft mbH, Wuppertal-barmen, 135
Elektronisches Rechenzentrum, Bayreuth, 136
Elektronisches Rechenzentrum GmbH, Bielefeld, 136
Elektronisk Bogføring for Revisorer, Copenhagen, 79
Elektronsko-Nunerički Centar, Zagreb, 572
Elektronski Računski Centar, Rijeka, 574
Eli Computer Systems Inc, East Paterson, 540
Elliott Brothers (London) Ltd, Frimley, 337
Elgave, Budapest, 148-9
Elniv Software, Haifa, 168
Emerson Consultants Ltd, London, 344
Emerson Consultants Inc, New York, 491
Emory University, Atlanta, 404
Empire Data Centers Ltd, St-Laurent, 62
Empresa Colombiana de Petróleos, Bogotá, 70-71
Empresa de Sistemas de Computadores Ltda, São Paulo, 32
Empresa Nacional de Computación e Informatica Ltda, Santiago, 66
Energoinvest, Sarajevo, 572-3
Engenharia de Seguros Ltda, São Paulo, 42
Engehharia Processamentos Electrônicos Ltda, Minas Gerais, 42
Engineering Computations, London, 344
Engineering Computer International Inc, Cambridge, 484
Entelek Inc, Newburyport, 484-5
Equimatics Inc, Fairfield, 540-41
Equitable Life & General Insurance Co Ltd, Sydney, 18
Erdos and Morgan, Inc, New York, 546
L.M. Ericsson Pty Ltd, Broadmeadows, 18
Escola de Engenharia de Maranhao, São Luís, 32
Escola de Engenharia Mauá, São Caetano do Sul, 33
Escuela de Arquitectura, Barcelona, 252-3
Escuela Técnica Superior de Ingenieros de Minas, Madrid, 253
Esselte AR-Konsult AB, Stockholm, 267
Estudos e Processamentos Ltda, Rio de Janeiro, 42
Ethnikon Kai Kapodistriakon Panepistimion Athinon, Athens, 143-4
Ethnikon Metsovion Polytechneion Athinai, Athens, 144
Eton College, Windsor, 305

Études et Traitement des Données (Montreal) Inc, Montreal, 62
Europe Informatique, Paris, 111
European Computer Services S.p.A., Roma, 178
European Space Research Institute, Frascati, 174
Europlex Ltd, London, 344
Ex Data GmbH, Nürnberg, 136
Executive Data Systems, Cedar Rapids, 526
Extel Communications Ltd, London, 365

F2 Ltd, Amersham, 365
Fabricato S.A., Medellín, 72
Fachhochschule Ulm, Ulm, 118
Facta N.V., The Hague, 211
Faculté des Sciences de St Jérôme, Marseille, 96
Faculté Polytechnique de Mons, Mons, 25
Fairfield University, Fairfield, 400
Fairleigh Dickinson University, Rutherford, 428
Falkirk Technical College, Falkirk, 305-6
Farm Planning & Computer Services Ltd, Newmarket, 344
Farnborough College of Technology, Farnborough, 306
Farrington Data Processing Ltd, Havant, 365
Fedder Data Center of Central Pennsylvania, Harrisburg, 559
Fedder Data Center of Chicago, Chicago, 523
Fedder Data Center of Florida, Clearwater, 518
Fedder Data Center of New Jersey, New York, 546
Fedder Data Center of Ohio, Cleveland, 555
Fedder Data Center of Tennessee, Knoxville, 563
Fedder Data Center of the Northeast, Chestnut Hill, 531
Fedder Data Center of the Pacific Ltd, Hilo, 522
Fedder Data Center of Sioux City, Sioux City, 526
Fedder Data Centers Inc, Baltimore, 528
Federal Institute for Statistics, Belgrade, 571
Armin E Fehr, Thalwil, 285
Fellesdata/SIS, Oslo, 230
Fels Research Institute, Yellow Springs, 472
Feni Data Services Ltd, Bournemouth, 365
Fimaco Inc, Philadelphia, 559
Financial Accounting Service Bureau (Data Processing) Ltd, Wakefield, 365
Finnish State Computer Centre, Helsinki, 88
First Business Computing, Houston, 500
First National Bank in St Louis, St Louis, 537
First National Bank of Montgomery, Montgomery, 502-3

Index of Institutions

First National Bank of Pennsylvania, Erie, 560
First-Union Automation Service Inc, St Louis, 537
Fisher-Stevens Inc, Clifton, 487
Fletcher Computer Services Ltd, Birmingham, 365
Flintshire College of Technology, Deeside, 306
Florida Computer Systems Company, Winter Park, 519
Florida State University, Tallahasee, 403
Flygtekniska Försöksanstalten, Bromma, 264
Foothill Community College District, Los Altos Hills, 393
Fordham University, Bronx, 433
Forest Grammar School, Wokingham, 306
Forestry Commission, Farnham, 337-8
Forge Business Services Ltd, Walton-on-Thames, 365-6
Forskningsinstitutet för Atomfysik, Stockholm, 264
Forsikringsselskabernes Data Central, Copenhagen, 80
Forstaedernes Bank Akts, Glostrup, 80
Försvarets Civilförvaltning, Stockholm 262
Fövárosi Epitöipari Üzemgazdasági és Ugyviteltechnikai Iroda, Budapest, 149
Frankel Engineering Laboratories, Inc, Reading, 472
Franklin and Marshall College, Lancaster, 446
Franlab Informatique, Rueil Malmaison, 111
Fraser Williams & Co Ltd, Liverpool, 344-5
Freelance Programmers Ltd, Chesham, 366
Friedrich-Alexander-Universität, Erlangen-Nürnberg, Erlangen, 118
Fulfillment Consultants Corporation, Bronx, 546-7
Fullerton Junior College, Fullerton, 393
A/S Fyns Data Service, Odense, 80

GEC-Elliott Space and Weapons Systems Ltd, Camberley, 366
GMS Computer Services, Sheffield, 366
GTE Data Services Inc, Tampa, 519
Gadsden State Junior College, Gadsden, 390
Gallaudet College, Washington, 402
Gannett Fleming Corddry & Carpenter Inc, Harrisburg, 498
Gemeentelijk Centrum voor Elektronische Informatieverwerking, Amsterdam, 203
Gemini Computer Systems Deutschland, Frankfurt-am-Main, 136
General Applied Science Lab.Inc., New York, 472
General Computer Services Inc, Huntsville, 503
General Computing Services Ltd, Hove, 345

Général de Service Informatique, Massy, 111-112
Général de Service Informatique, Paris, 111
Général de Service Informatique, GSI-Entreprises, Paris, 112
General Electric Company, Albuquerque, 543
General Electric Company, Atlanta, 521
General Electric Company, Bala-Cwnwyd, Pittsburgh, York, 560
General Electric Company, Baltimore, Bethesda, 529
General Electric Company, Berkeley, El Monte, Long Beach, Los Angeles, Palo Alto, Reseda, Sacramento, San Diego, San Francisco, Santa Barbara, 508
General Electric Company, Bettendorf, 526
General Electric Company, Binghampton, Buffalo, New York, Rochester, Schenectady, Syosset, Syracuse, 547
General Electric Company, Birmingham, 503
General Electric Company, Chicago, 523
General Electric Company, Cincinnati, Cleveland, Colombus, Dayton, 555
General Electric Company, Dallas, Houston, Midland, 564
General Electric Company, Denver, 512
General Electric Company, Detroit, Grand Rapids, 534
General Electric Co Ltd, Erith, 366
General Electric Company, Greensboro, 553
General Electricity Company, Greenville, Memphis, 563
General Electric Company, Hampton, Seattle, 566
General Electric Company, Highlands Park, Teaneck, 541
General Electric Company, Hollywood, 519
General Electric Company, Indianapolis, 525
General Electric Company, Louisville, Metairie, 527
General Electric Company, Meriden, 515
General Electric Company, Milwaukee, 567
General Electric Company, Minneapolis, 536
General Electric Company, Oklahoma City, Tulsa, 556
General Electric Company, Omaha, 539
General Electric Company Phoenix, 503-4
General Electric Company, Pittsfield, Waltham, 531
General Electric Company, Portland, 557
General Electric Company, St Louis, 537
General Electric Company, Salt Lake City, 565

General Electric do Brasil S.A., Santo André, 42-3
General Information and Control Systems Ltd, London, 345
General Precision Systems Ltd, Farnborough, 345
General Research Corporation, Santa Barbara, 508
Genesee Community College, Flint. 418
Genesse Computer Center Inc, Rochester, 491-2
Geodata A/S, Copenhagen, 80
George Washington University, Washington, 402
Georges et Gilbert Castellanet, Paris, 103
Georgetown University, Washington, 402
Georgia Data Corporation, Savannah, 521
Georgia Institute of Technology, Atlanta, 404
Georgia State University, Atlanta, 404
Gertzberg Oren & Co Ltd, Tel-Aviv, 168
Gesellschaft für Marktforschung Hamburg, 125
Gesellschaft für Mathematik und Datenverarbeitung mbH, St Augustin-Birlinghoven, 126
Gesellschaft für Organisations- und Programmierungssysteme mbH, Wiesbaden, 130
Gesellschaft für Prozesssteuerungs- und Informationssysteme, mbH, Berlin, 130
Gestelec, Paris, 112
Gestronic SA, Genève, 290
John Gilmore and Associates Inc, New York, 492
Glamorgan Polytechnic, Pontypridd, 306
George Glaser, San Mateo, 477
Gordon Institute of Technology, Geelong, 7
Göteborgs Datacentral, Göteborg, 260
Gradski Zavod za Statistiku Beograd, Belgrade, 571
Graficom B.V., Amsterdam, 212
Grafisch Administratie Centrum, Amsterdam, 212
Graphic Controls Corporation, Buffalo, 547
Graphic Image Corporation, Chicago, 523
Graphtek Corporation, Phoenix, 476
Groupe Opéra, Paris, 105
Grove City College, Grove City, 446
H.J. Gruy and Associates Inc, Dallas, 500
Guardian Data Service & Supply, Memphis, 563-4
Dale L. Gulley & Assoc. Inc, Tulsa, 556-7
Gunma University, Gunma, 183
Gutacker EDV Beratung GmbH, Stuttgart, 130

Ha-Technion, Haifa, 164-5
Ha-Universita Ha-Ivrit Bi-Yerushalayim, Jerusalem, 165

Haags Computer Service Centrum, The Hague, 212
Hacettepe Üniversitesi, Ankara, 297
Haile Sellassie I University, Addis Ababa, 86
Halcon Computer Technologies Inc, New York, 492
Halmstad Dataservice AB, Halmstad, 275
Hamashbir Hamerkazi Israel Cooperative Wholesale Society Ltd, Tel Aviv, 169-70
Hamworthy Engineering Ltd, Poole, 366
Handelshøjskolen, i Århus, Århus, 76
Hans Freibichler Ausbildungsplanung und Didaktische Programmierung, Heidelberg, 130
Harvard University, Cambridge, 416
H. Harvey Segall & Associates, Tacoma 502
J. Harwell Data Processing Ltd, London, 345
Hatfield Polytechnic, Hatfield, 307
Bernard Haus, Paris, 105
Haverly Systems Inc, Denville, 487
Heffelfinger Associates Inc, Dedham, 485
Heliodyne Corporation, Arlington, 566
Helm Data Processing Inc, Arcata, 508
Helsingin Yliopisto Computing Centre, Helsinki, 86-7
Helsingin Yliopisto Dept. of Nuclear Physics, Helsinki, 87
Henkel et Cie AG, Pratteln, 136-7
Heriot-Watt University, Edinburgh, 307
Hermes Computing Services Ltd, London, 366-7
Herzing Institutes Inc, Milwaukee, 387
Herzing Institutes of Canada Ltd, Toronto, 47
Heuristics Systems International, Gia-Dinh, 569
Hewlett-Packard France, Orsay, 112
Hewlett-Packard Vertriebsgesellschaft mbH, Frankfurt-am-Main, 137
Hifab Aktiebolog, Stockholm, 268
Hilti (Great Britain) Ltd, Manchester, 345
Hinds Junior College, Raymond, 422
Hindustan Aeronautics Ltd, Bangalore, 156
Hindustan Motors Ltd, Hooghly, 158-9
Hobart Technical College, Hobart, 8
Hochschule für Bodenkultur in Wien, Vienna, 21
Hochschule für Sozial- und Wirtschaftwissenschaften, Linz, 21
Hokushin Electric Works Ltd, Tokyo, 187
Honeywell AG, Zürich, 290
Honeywell Bull, Brussels, 30
Honeywell Bull do Brasil S.A., São Paulo, 43
Honeywell-Bull GmbH, Köln, 137
Honeywell Bull AB, Stockholm, 275

Honeywell Bull AG, Vienna, 23
Honeywell Information Systems Ltd, Brentford, 367
Honeywell Information Systems Italia, Milano, 179
Honeywell Pty Ltd, Edgecliff, 19
Hood College, Frederick, 415
Horsens Datacentral, Horsens, 80
Hoskyns Group Ltd, London, 345
Hoskyns Systems Ltd, Birmingham, 367
Housing Commission, Victoria, Melbourne, 13
Daniel H. Howard Associates Inc, Chicago, 482
Huddersfield and Spen Valley Incorporated Chamber of Commerce, Huddersfield, 367
Huddersfield Polytechnic, Huddersfield, 307
T. C. Hudson Associates Ltd, London, 346
Human Sciences Research Council, Pretoria, 248
Hungarian Computer Education Centre, Budapest, 146
Huygens Lyceum Voorburg, Voorburg, 198
Hydra Computer Corporation, Raleigh, 553
Hydro-University Computing Centre, Hobart, 8

IBM Australia Ltd, Sydney, 19
IBM Chile S.A.C. Ltda, Santiago, 66
IBM Co Ltd, Toronto, 62
IBM Colombia Ltda, Bogotá, 72-3
IBM A/S, Copenhagen, 80
IBM de Guatemala S.A., Guatemala City, 144-5
IBM de Mexico S.A., Mexico, 196-7
IBM de Panamá S.A., Panamá, 233
IBM del Ecuador, Quito, 85
IBM do Brasil, Rio de Janeiro, 43
IBM France, Neuilly-sur-Seine, 112
IBM Finland, Helsinki, 89-90
IBM Ireland Ltd, Dublin, 164
IBM Israel Data Centre Services, Tel Aviv, 170
IBM Italia S.p.A., Milano, 180
IBM Japan Ltd, Tokyo, 187
IBM, Madrid, 257
IBM Nederland N.V., Amsterdam, 212
IBM New Zealand Ltd, Wellington, 220
IBM Nigeria Ltd, Lagos, 223
IBM of Belgium S.A., Brussels, 31
IBM A/S, Oslo, 230
IBM Philippines Inc, Rizal, 235-6
IBM Portuguesa SARL, Lisboa, 241
IBM Service Bureau, Abidjan, 182
IBM South Africa (Pty) Ltd, Johannesburg, 251
IBM Svenska AB, Stockholm, 275-6
IBM Switzerland, Zürich, 290-91
IBM Systems Development Institute, Canberra, 14
IBM Taiwan Corporation, Taipei, 68
IBM Thailand Co Ltd, Bangkok, 296
IBM United Kingdom Ltd, London, 367-8

IBM World Trade Corporation, Accra, 143
IBM World Trade Corp., Algiers, 1
IBM World Trade Corporation, Bombay, 159
IBM World Trade Corp., Buenos Aires, 5
IBM World Trade Corporation, Cairo, 85
IBM World Trade Corporation, Caracas, 569
IBM World Trade Corporation, Curaçao, 217
IBM World Trade Corporation, Hong Kong, 145
IBM World Trade Corporation, Karachi, 233
IBM World Trade Corporation, Kinshasa, 576
IBM World Trade Corporation, Kingston, 183
IBM World Trade Corporation, Kuala Lumpur, 193
IBM World Trade Corporation, Lima, 235
IBM World Trade Corporation, Montevideo, 568
IBM World Trade Corporation, Nassau, 24
IBM World Trade Corporation, Port of Spain, 296
IBM World Trade Corporation, Salisbury, 242
IBM World Trade Corporation, San José, 73
IBM World Trade Corporation, San Salvador, 85
IBM World Trade Corporation, Singapore, 244-5
IBM World Trade Corporation, Tegucigalpa, 145
IBM World Trade Corporation, Teheran, 161
ICL Computer Education in Schools, London, 300
ICL Data AB, Solna, 275
ICM Computer Corporation, Tulsa, 497
ID Anwendungs-Software Forschungszentrum, Bad Gandersheim, 137
IFU, Hamburg, 137
IKO Software Service A/S, Oslo, 227
IKO Software Service GmbH, Stuttgart, 130
ISEC, Princeton, 488
ITT Data Services, East Barnett, 370
ITT Data Services, Paramus, 541
ITT Data Services, Rio de Janeiro, 44
ITT Datenservice, Stuttgart, 139
Ianus S.p.A., Roma, 180
Ibadan University, Ibadan, 222
IBAT-Büro für Elektronische Datenverarbeitung-A Triestram, Essen, 137
Ibérica de Racionalización, Automación y Calculo, Madrid, 254
Idaho State University, Pocatello, 405
Idan Computers Ltd, Tel Aviv, 170
Ilford Ltd, Ilford, 368
Illinois Institute of Technology, Chicago, 472

Index of Institutions

Illinois State University, Normal, 406-7
Ilmatieteen Iaitos, Helsinki, 89
Iltam Corporation for Planning and Research Ltd, Jerusalem, 167
Imar Consult Nr. Nordisk Rationalisering A/S, Albertslund, 77
Imar Consult RN, Stockholm, 268
Imperial Chemical Industries Ltd, Manchester, 368
Imperial College of Science and Technology, Computer Centre, London, 307
Imperial College of Science and Technology, Dept. of computing and Control, London, 307-8
Inbucon Services Ltd, Etobicoke, 57
Indecon Inc, Chicago, 482
Independent Computer Services Ltd, Belfast, 369
Independent Computing Services Pty Ltd, Melbourne, 19
Indian Council of Agricultural Research, Delhi, 156
Indian Institute of Management, Ahmedabad, 150
Indian Institute of Science, Bangalore, 150
Indian Institute of Technology, Bombay, 150
Indian Institute of Technology, Delhi, 150-1
Indian Institute of Technology, Kanpur, 151
Indian Institute of Technology, Madras, 151
Indian Posts and Telegraphs Department, Delhi, 156
Indian Space Research Organisation, Thumba, 156-7
Indian Statistical Institute, Calcutta, 153
Indiana Institute of Technology, Fort Wayne, 409
Indiana University, Bloomington, 409
Industri-Matamatik AB, Bromma, 268
Industria Electrica Brown Boveri S.A., São Paulo, 44
Industrial and Commercial Data Processing Ltd, Coventry, 369
Industrial National Bank of Rhode Island, Providence, 562-3
Industridata AB, Solna, 276
Industrie and Bank Automation AG, Berne, 291
Industries Development Corporation, Jerusalem, 168
Industrija Drveta, Celuloze, Papira i Vlakna, Banjaluka, 574-5
Industrija Motora Rakovica, Belgrade, 571-2
Industrijsko Poljoprivredni Kombinat, Osijek, 575
Industroprojekt, Zagreb, 573
Infelor Rendszertechnikai Vallalat, Budapest, 147
Info Consulting Company, Los Angeles, 477
Infodata Systems Inc, Webster, 547
Infonet B.V., Amsterdam, 212
Inforama S.A., Geneva, 285-6
Informatics Inc, Canoga Park, 508-9

Informatics S.A., Geneva, 291
Information and Systems Institute Inc, Cambridge, 485
Information Consultants, Inc, Los Angeles, 477-8
Information Dynamics Corporation, Reading, 531
Information Engineering, Philadelphia, 498
Information Management Associates Inc, St Louis, 537
Information Processing Inc, Orlando, 519
Information Sciences Inc, Warwick, 563
Information System AB, Solna, 268
Inforsystem AB, Bromma, 268
Infosci Inc, Menlo Park, 478
Infotec Inc, Plainview, 492
Infotran Inc, New York, 492
Ingenieursbureau Rescona, Amstelveen, 213
Ingenieursbureau Sandwijk N.V., Haarlem, 206
Ingenjörsfirma Nordisk ADB AB, Solna, 268-9
Innenministerium des Landes Nordrhein-Westfalen, Düsseldorf, 125-6
Input B.V., Alphen aan den Rijn, 206
Input Inc, Chicago, 523
Insco Systems Corporation, Neptune, 541
Institut Bedaux International S.A., Lausanne, 286
Institut Blaise Pascal, Paris, 102
Institut de Gestion et d'Organisation S.A., Brussels, 29
Institut de Recherche d'Informatique et d'Automatique, Le Chesnay, 102
Institut de Recherches Technico-Economiques, Genève, 284
Institut D'Etudes Nucleaires, Alger, 1
Institut Ekonomskih Nauka, Beograd, 573
Institut Français de Gestion, Paris, 93
Institut Français des Experts Comptables, Paris, 93
AG Institut für Automation, Zürich, 286
Institut für Datensystem-Entwicklung EDV-Beratung, Bremen, 139
Institut für Deutsche Sprache, Mannheim, 126-7
Institut für Informatik, Stuttgart, 119
Institut für Medizinische Datenverarbeitung der Gesellschaft für Strahlen- und Umweltforschung mbH, München, 127
Institut Géographique National, Paris, 100
Institut d'Informatique et de Gestion, Paris, 93
Institut International d'Informatique, Grenoble, 93
Institut "Jožef Stefan", Ljubljana, 569
Institut National de Statistique, Brussels, 27
Institut National des Sciences Apliquées, Villeurbanne, 93-4

Institut Royal Météorologique de Belgique (I.R.M.), Brussels, 27
Institut 'Rudjer Bosković', Zagreb, 573
Institut Teknologi Bandung, Bandung, 159
Institut Universitaire de Technologie, Paris, 96
Institut Universitaire de Technologie, Villeurbanne, 94
Institut Universitaire de Technologie-Informatique, Nancy, 96
N.V. Institut voor Electronische Administratie, Rotterdam, 213
Institut Za Nuklearne Nauke 'Boris Kidric', Belgrade, 573
Institute of Computer Technology, Washington, 516
Institute of Data Processing, London, 300
Institute of Fundamental Technical Research, Warsaw, 239
Institute of Information Technology, Tokyo, 186
Institute of Solid State Physics, Prague, 75
Institute of Transportation, Ljubljana, 573-4
Institute for Advanced Technology, Washington, 387
Institute for Petroleum Research and Geo-Physics, Holon, 165-6
Institute for Rationalisation of Production and Management in the Engineering Industry, Prague, 75
Institute TNO for Mathematics, Information Processing and Statistics, The Hague, 203
Instituto Brasileiro de Informática, Rio de Janeiro, 38
Instituto de Pesquisas Espaciais, São José dos Campos, 39
Instituto de Pesquisas Tecnológicas, Centro de Pesquisas Informaticas, São Paulo, 39
Instituto de Pesquisas Tecnológicas, São Paulo, 39
Instituto Deusto S.A., Bilbao, 257
Instituto Mexicano del Seguro Social, Mexico, 196
Instituto Tecnológico de Aeronáutica, São José des Campos, 38
Instituto Tecnológico y de Estudios Superiores de Monterrey, Monterrey, 194-5
Institutt for Atomenergi, Halden, 226
Instytut Elektrotechniki-Zakad Techniki Obliczenidwej, Warszawa, 240
Instytut Energetyki, Warsaw, 239
Integral Coach Factory, Madras, 153
Integrant Computer Bureau, Cobham, 369
Integrata GmbH, Tübingen, 131
Integrated Business Methods, Washington, 516
Integrated Systems and Design Ltd, Crawley, 346
Inter-Comerica Computing Company Inc, Boston, 532
Inter-Comerica Computing Company Inc, New York, 547-8

Interactive Data Corporation, Waltham, 531
Interactive Sciences Corporation, Braintree, 531-2
Interconsult S.A., Bogotá, 71
Intercontinental Data Services Ltd, Buenos Aires, 5
Interdata AG Basel, Basel, 291
Interdata AG Zürich, Zürich, 291
Interfile Computer Services Ltd, Sunbury-on-Thames, 369
Intergret Databehandling A/S, Oslo, 230
Interlogic Gesellschaft für Computer- und Programm-Service mbH & Co., Sennestadt, 137
International Büromaschinen GmbH, Vienna, 23
International Computer Programs Inc, Indianapolis, 525
International Computer Services, S.A., Bogotá, 71-2
International Computers and Tabulators A/S, Copenhagen, 80-81
International Computers (Australia) Pty Ltd, Sydney, 19
International Computers (Central Africa) (Private) Ltd, Salisbury, 242
International Computers (East Africa) Ltd, Nairobi, 189-90
International Computers Ltd, Port Louis, 193-4
International Computers Ltd, Port of Spain, 296
International Computers Ltd, Singapore, 245
International Computers Ltd, Windsor, 300
International Computers (New Zealand) Ltd, Wellington, 220
International Computers S.A. (Pty) Ltd, Johannesburg, 251
International Data Highways Ltd, London, 369
International Data Processing Corporation, New York, 548
International Data Processing Institute, Detroit, 387
International Digitizing Corporation, Tulsa, 557
International Institute for Aerial Survey and Earth Sciences, Enschede, 204
International Programming Services Ltd, Saffron Walden, 346
International Systems Associates Ltd, New York, 548
International Systems Research N.V., Amsterdam, 206-7
International Telecontrol Corporation, Wilmington, 479
Internationale Atomreaktorbau, Köln, 127
Internationale Büro Maschinen GmbH, Sindel-Fingen-Wuerrt, 138-9
Interstate Computer Services, Brooklyn, 548
Interstate Data Services, Monticello, 523
Intertrade, Ljubljana, 575
Interuniversity Communications Council, Princeton, 472-3

Intomart, Hilversum 213
Iowa State University of Science and Technology, Ames, 410-411
Ipar gazdaszgi Szervezesi es Szamitastechnikai Intezet, Budapest, 147
Iraqi Republic Railways, Baghdad, 161-2
Irodagéptechnika Vállalat, Budapest, 149
Isis Computer Services Ltd, London 369-370
Israel Institute of Productivity, Tel-Aviv, 167
Istanbul Devlet Mühendislik ve Mimarlik Akademisi, Istanbul, 298
Istanbul Teknik Universitesi, Istanbul, 298
Istituto Centrale di Statistica, Roma, 177
Istituto Meschini, Genova, 181
Istituto Universitario di Venezia, Venezia, 172
Iva Software N.V., Schiedam, 207

Jackson State College, Jackson, 422
Jacobs Company Inc, Oak Brook, 482
Jadavpur University, Calcutta, 151
James Cook University of North Queensland, Townsville, 8
Japan Computer Usage Development Institute, Tokyo, 186
Japan Information Processing Development Center, Tokyo, 183,186
Jeantex International Ltd, Bracknell, 346
Jefferson County Bank of Lakewood, Lakewood, 513
Jeffreys & Hill Ltd, London, 346
Johannes-Gutenberg-Universität, Mainz, 119
John Carroll University, University Heights, 440
John Hopkins University, Baltimore, 415
Johnson Computing Inc, Philadelphia, 560
Johnston Terminals Ltd, Vancouver, 62-3
Joint Plant Committee, Calcutta, 153
Jordanhill College of Education, Glasgow, 308
Jugomont-Jugobeton, Zagreb, 575
Jugomontaza-Ventilator, Zagreb, 575
Jugoslovenski Centar za Tehničku i Naučnu Dokumentaciju, Belgrade, 572
A/S Jydsk Data Centre, Vejle,81
Jyväskylän Yliopisto, Jyväskylä, 87

KG Karl Heinz Both GmbH & Co, Düsseldorf, 134
K & H Business Consultants Ltd, London, 370

Kalamazoo Computer Centre, Birmingham, 370
Kalle Anttila Oy, Helsinki, 90
Kaman Sciences Corporation, Colorado Springs, 513
Kanawaga Prefectural Government, Yokohama, 186
Kancelarske Srtoje, Prague, 74
Kansas City (Missouri) Public Schools, Kansas City, 423
Kansas State College of Pittsburgh, Pittsburgh, 412
Kansas State University of Agriculture and Applied Science, Manhattan, 412
Kasad Computer Services Ltd, Harlow, 370-71
Kate Ltd, Feltham, 300
Kates, Peat, Marwick and Co, Toronto, 57-8
Katholieke Universiteit te Leuven, Afdeling Toegepaste Wiskunde en Programmatie, Louvain, 25
Katholieke Universiteit te Leuven, Centre for Operations Research and Econometrics, Louvain, 25
Katholieke Universiteit te Leuven, Institute of Applied Economics, Louvain, 25-6
Katholieke Universiteit te Leuven, Rekencentrum, Louvain, 26
Katholieke Universiteit te Nijmegen, Nijmegen, 198-9
Kauppakorkeakoulu, Helsinki, 87
John A. Keane and Associates, Princeton, 488
Kellogg International Corporation, London, 371
Kempthorne Information Services, Melbourne, 19
Kent Data Services Ltd, Luton, 371
Kenya Commercial Bank, Nairobi, 189
Keydata Corporation, Watertown, 532
Keystone Computer Associates Inc, Fort Washington, 498, 560
Kezev Statistical Consultancy and Data Processing Ltd, Jerusalem, 170
Kidde Computer Services Company, Huntingdon Valley, 560
Boris Kidrič Ekonomska Škola, Zagreb, 570
Kienbaum Unternehmensberatung GmbH, Gummersbach, 131
King's College, University of London, London, 308
Kingston Polytechnic, Kingston, 308
Kinman Business University, Spokane, 387
Kirloskar Oil Engines Ltd, Poona, 159
Klynveld Kraayenhof & Co, Amsterdam, 207
AB Knight, Karlstad, 269
Lester B. Knight & Associates Inc, Chicago, 482
Knight Wegenstein SRL, Florence, 178
Knight Wegenstein GmbH, Frankfurt-am-Main, 131

Index of Institutions

Knight Wegenstein Ltd, London, 346
Knight Wegenstein GmbH, Vienna, 22
Knight Wegenstein AG, Zürich, 286
Kφbenhavns Universitet, Copenhagen, 76
Kolynos S.A.C.I., Quilmes, 5
Komisja Planowania Przy Radzie Ministrow, Warsaw, 239
Kommersiell Databehandling AB, Frölunda, 276
Kommun-Data AB, Stockholm, 276
I/S Kommunernes EDB-Central, Copenhagen, 81
Konsulterande Byrån i Örebro AB, Örebro, 269
Korea Computer Centre, Seoul, 190
Korea Institute of Science and Technology, Seoul, 190
König-Unternehmensberatung, Stuttgart, 131
Központi Statisztikai Hivatal Szamitokozpont, Budapest, 147
Arthur S. Kranzley and Company Inc, Cherry Hill, 488, 541
Kungliga Tekniska Högskolan, Department of Speech Communication, Stockholm, 260
Kungliga Tekniska Högskolan, Library-Documentation Centre, Stockholm, 260-1
Kurz and Steel Ltd, Sheridan Park, 58
Kurt Salmon Associates GmbH, Darmstadt, 132
Kyoto University, Kyoto, 184

L & W Data Systems Ltd, Toronto, 58
Laboratorio Nacional de Engenharia Civil, Lisboa, 240
Lafayette College, Easton, 446
Lakehead University, Thunder Bay, 48
Lamar College of Technology, Beaumont, 454
Lanchester Polytechnic, Coventry, 308-9
Landbouwhogeschool to Wageningen, Wageningen, 199
Landbrugets EDB-Centraler, Risskov, 81
Landmäteristyrelsen Tekniska Byrån, Stockholm, 263
John Lang Computer Programming Service, Great Dunmow, 346-7
Lantbruksdata, Eskilstuna, 276-7
Lappeenrannan Teknillinen Korkealuolu, Lappeenranta, 87
Larc, Zutphen, 213
Laskentakeskus Oy, Helsinki, 90
Lawrence Berkeley Laboratory, Berkeley, 467
Lawrence Institute of Technolgoy, Southfield, 418
Lawrence Leiter & Company, Kansas City, 486
Lea Associates Ltd, London, 347
Leasco Response Ltd, London, 371
Leasco Software Ltd, London, 347

Leasco Systems and Research Corporation, Bethesda, 529
Lebon Informatique, Rueil, 112-3
Leeds Polytechnic, Leeds, 309
Lehigh University, Bethlehem, 447
Leo Computer Bureaux (Pty) Ltd, Johannesburg, 251-2
Leopold-Franzens Universität Innsbruck, Innsbruck, 21
Les Ingénieurs Associés, Paris, 105
Lewis and Clark College, Portland, 444
Liceul de Informatică, Cluj, 243
Lindenwood Colleges, St Charles, 424
Linköpings Högskola, Linköping, 261
Arthur D. Little de Mexico S.A., Mexico, 196
Arthur D. Little–Hellas S.A., Athens, 144
Arthur D. Little Inc, Cambridge, 485
Arthur D. Little Ltd, London, 347
Arthur D. Little S.A., Brussels, 29
Arthur D. Little S.A./AG, Zürich, 286
Arthur Little of Canada Ltd, Toronto, 58
Litton Business Systems AB Dataservice, Solna, 277
Litton Industries, Brussels, 28
Litton Industries, Sunnyvale, 473
Liverpool Polytechnic, Liverpool, 309
Llandaff College of Technology, Cardiff, 309
Llanelli Technical College, Llanelli, 309-310
Local Authorities Data Processing Centre, Tel Aviv, 170
Local Government Superannuation Board, Sydney, 13
Lock Haven State College, Lock Haven, 447
Logica Ltd, London, 347
Logisterion, Rotterdam, 213
London Borough of Havering, Romford, 300-301
London Boroughs Joint Computer Committee, London, 333-4
London Graduate School of Business Studies, London, 310
London Polytechnics Computer Unit, London, 310
London School of Economics, University of London, London, 310
London University Computing Services Ltd, London, 371
Long Island University, Long Island, 433
Loughborough University of Technology, Loughborough, 310
Louisiana State University, Baton Rouge, 414
Louisville Tabulating Service Bureau, Louisville, 527
Lowndes-Ajax Computer Service Ltd, Croydon, 371-2
Lowell Technological Institute, Lowell, 416-7
Lowenthal Programming Corporation, Port Chester, 492
D.G. Lowes, Management Services, London, 347

Loyola College, Montreal, 48
Loyola Marymount University, Los Angeles, 393
B. Ludwigson Ingenjörsbyrå AB, Göteborg, 269
Lunds Universitet Computing Centre, Lund, 261
Lunds Universitet Department of Computer Sciences, Växjö, 261

M & G Computer Services Ltd, Chelmsford, 372
MHD Computers, Tel Aviv, 171
MIPS International, London, 349
MLL Statistics Institute and Office Efficiency Ltd, Tel Aviv, 171
MP Data Prep, Wembley, 374
MRI Systems Corporation, Austin, 500-1
MSADP Inc, Norristown, 561
M.T.I. Business Colleges, Sacramento, 388
Macalester College, St Paul, 420
McDill Corporation, Montgomery, 503
McDonnell Automation Co, Denver, 513
McDonnell Automation Company, East Orange, 542
McDonnell Automation Company, Falls Church, 566
McDonnell Automation Company, Houston, 564
McDonnell Automation Company, St Louis, 537-8
McGill University, Montreal, 48-9
McKinsey & Co, Amsterdam, 207
McKinsey & Company Inc, London, 347-8
McKinsey & Co. Inc, Melbourne, 15
McKinsey and Company Inc, New York, 493
McKinsey & Co. Inc., Paris, 106
McKinsey & Co, Zürich, 286
McLintock Mann & Whinney Murray, London, 348
McMaster University, Hamilton, 49
Macquarie University, North Ryde, 8
Macro-Pak Business Systems Inc, New York, 548
Magnet Computer Bureau Ltd, Birmingham, 372
Magyar Tudományos Akadémia, Budapest, 147-8
Magyar Tudományos Akadémia, Institute for Computation and Automation, Budapest, 148
Magyar Vegyipari Egyesüles, Budapest, 149
Maison des Sciences de l'Homme, Paris, 100-101
Maison Ch. Veillon S.A., Lausanne, 292
Makere University, Kampala, 298-9
Malawi Railways Ltd, Limbe, 192
Managematics Inc, New York, 493
Management Accounting and EDP Consultants Ltd, Tel-Aviv, 168

Management Centre Europe-Brussels, Brussels, 25
Management Computer Controls Inc, Memphis, 499
Management Computer Services South Africa (Pty) Ltd, Marshalltown, 252
Management Computing Services Ltd, London, 372
Management Data Corp., Philadelphia, 560-61
Management Dynamics Ltd, London, 372
Management Dynamics Software Services, Hounslow, 348, 373
Management Information Center, Greenville, 563
Management Science America Inc, Englewood Cliffs, 488
Management Sciences Ltd, Wilsmlow, 348
Management Systems and Programming Ltd, London, 373
Management Systems Corporation, Dallas, 500
Management Training Centre, Budapest, 146
Manchester Computer Centre Ltd, Manchester, 373
Manchester Polytechnic, Manchester, 310-11
Manhattan College, Bronx, 433
Mankato State College, Mankato, 420-21
Manpower Business Training Instituion, St Louis, 387-8
Marconi Company, Chelmsford, 338
Marine and General Computer Consultancy (I.O.M.) Ltd, St Johns, 348
Marine Bank & Trust Co, Tampa, 519
Marist College, Poughkeepsie, 433-4
Mark/Ops, Boston, 532
Marquette University, Milwaukee, 464
Paul Marthouret S.A., Sainte Foy Les Lyon, 106
Marycrest College, Davenport, 411
Massachusetts Computer Associates Inc, Wakefield, 473
Massachusetts Institute of Technology, Cambridge, 417
Master Register Ltd, Manchester, 348
Mata College of Automation, Colombus, 388
Mathematical Applications Group Inc Elmsford, 548-9
Mathematischer Beratungs- und Programmierungsdienst GmbH, Dortmund, 139
Matrix Corporation, New York, 549
Mauritius Computing Services Ltd, Port Louis, 194
May & Speh Data Processing Center, Chicago, 523
May Roberts Ltd, Dublin, 164
Measurement Research Center, Iowa City, 473
Mécanorga, St. Ouen, 113
Mechanized Business Inc, Pittsburgh, 561
Medway and Maidstone College of Technology, Chatham, 311
Medway Data Services Ltd, Chatham, 373

Megasystems Inc, Bala-Cynwyd, 561
Mehanografski Center-Emo, Celje, 575
Mem Alef Electronic Computers Ltd, Ramat Gan, 170
Memphis Methods and Tabulating Service, Memphis, 564
Memphis State University Memphis, 452-3
Messerschmitt-Boelkow-Blohm GmbH, Munich, 140
Meta Systems Corporation, Trenton, 488
Metacomputer Sciences Inc, Irvine, 509
Metalogic Ltd, Bristol, 373
Metra Divo, Frankfurt-am-Main, 140
Metron Datenverarbeitung AG, Brugg, 286
Metropolitan Junior College District, Kansas City, 388
Chr Michelsens Institutt for Videnskap og Aandsrihet Bergen, 226-7
Michigan State University, East Lansing, 418-9
Michigan Technological University, Houghton, 419
Midas Ltd, London, 373-4
Middlesex Polytechnic, Enfield, 311
Midland Data Processing Services Ltd, Northampton, 374
Midland National Bank, Milwaukee, 567
Midlands Computing Centre Ltd, Birmingham 374
Midwest Business Statistics, Oak Park, 523
Millersville State College, Millersville, 447
Mills Associates Ltd, Monmouth, 374
Milner Brothers Products, Los Angeles, 509
Ministère de l'Économie et des Finances, Libreville 116
Ministère des Postes, Télégraphes et Téléphones, Tunis, 297
Ministère des Travaux Publics, Borgerhout, 27-8
Ministerie van Openbare Werken, Brussels, 28
Ministerio de Educación y Ciencia, Madrid, 254
Ministerio de Hacienda y Créditoo Público, Bogotá, 71
Ministerio de Justicia, Madrid, 254
Ministry of Finance, Jerusalem, 166
Ministry of Finance, Kingstown, 244
Ministry of Finance, Lusaka, 577
Ministry of Finance, Nicosia, 74
Ministry of Finance, Port Louis, 193
Ministry of Finance, Teheran, 161
Ministry of Planning, Tripoli, 192
Mississippi State University, Mississippi, 422-3
Missouri Southern College, Joplin, 424
Missouri Valley College, Marshall, 424
Mitech Systems Inc, Cambridge, 485

Mitsubishi Office Machinery Co Ltd, Tokyo, 187-8
I. E. Mittwoch & Sons Ltd, Tel Aviv, 171
Mnemotech Computer Systems Inc, New York, 549
Modern Business Records, Dearborn, 534
Mohawk College of Applied Arts and Technology, Hamilton 49
Monaco International Management Services, La Ruche, 197
Monash University, Clayton, 8
Monmouth College, West Long Branch, 428-9
Monsanto Research, S.A., Zürich, 284
Montana State University, Bozeman, 426
Montedata S.A., Pôrto Alegre, 44
Monterey Peninsula College, Monterey, 393
Moray House College of Education, Edinburgh, 311
Møre og Romsdal Distriktshøgskole, Molde, 223-4
Morningside College, Sioux City, 411
Morris & Elliott S.A. de C.V., Mexico, 196
Mouncey and Partners Ltd, Wembley, 349
Mount Lawley Technical College, Perth 9
Multimedijski Nastovno-Infomacioni Centar Zavoda za Unpredjivanje Strucnog Obrazovanja S.R.H. Referalnog Centra Sveucilista, Zagreb, 574
Municipal and Water Computer Services, Kingston, 182-3
Municipality of Tel Aviv, Tel Aviv, 171
Municipio de Medellín. Medellín, 71
Wilbur C. Myers & Company, Rolling Hills, 478

NCR Argentina S.A., Buenos Aires, 5
NCR Central Africa (PVT) Ltd, Salisbury, 242-3
N.C.R. France, Paris, 113
NCR Rekencentrum, Gravenhage, 213-4
NIM Igüszi, Budapest, 148
NUS Corporation, Dunedin, 481
Namac Inc, Wayland, 532
Napier College of Science and Technology, Edinburgh, 311-2
Naremco Services Inc, New York, 493
Nassau Community College, Garden City, 434
Natal Oil and Soap Industries (Pty) Ltd, Jacobs, 252
Natam-Systems Analysis & Operations Research Ltd, Jerusalem, 168-9
Nationaal Instituut voor de Ontwikkeling van Wiskundige Opvoeding, Utrecht, 198
National Aeronautical Laboratory, Bangalore, 153
National Aeronautics and Space Administration, Pasadena, 467

Index of Institutions

National Aeronautics and Space Administration, Sandusky, 467
National Agricultural Marketing Board of Zambia, Lusaka, 577
National Board of Survey, Helsinki, 89
National Bureau of Standards, Washington, 467
National Cash Register Company, Atlanta, 521
National Cash Register Co Ltd, Auckland, 220-21
National Cash Register Company, Baltimore, 529
National Cash Register Company, Birmingham, 503
National Cash Register Co., Copenhagen, 81-2
National Cash Register Company, Dayton, 556
National Cash Register Company, Denver, 513
National Cash Register Company, Detroit, 535
National Cash Register Company, Framingham, 532
National Cash Register Company, Hawthorne, 509
National Cash Register Company, Honolulu, 522
National Cash Register Company, Houston, 564
National Cash Register Company, Johannesburg, 252
National Cash Register Company, Kansas City 538
National Cash Register Co..pany, Long Island, 549
National Cash Register Company, Louisville, 527
National Cash Register Company, Miami, 519-20
National Cash Register Company, Minneapolis, 536
National Cash Register Company, New Orleans, 527
National Cash Register Company, Norfolk, Seattle, 566
National Cash Register Company of Sweden AB, Stockholm, 277
National Cash Register Company Pittsburgh, 561
National Cash Register Company, Reno, 539
National Cash Register Company, Rolling Medows, 523
National Cash Register Co Ltd, Sydney, 19-20
National Cash Register Ltd, London, 375
National Center for Atmospheric Research, Boulder, 381-2
National Chiao Tung University, Hsinchu, 67
National Climatic Center, Asheville 468
National Coal Board, Cannock, 334
National College of Business, Rapid City, 388
National Computer Analysts Inc, Princeton, 542
National Computer Centre, Baghdad, 161
National Computing Centre Ltd, Manchester, 375

National Data Centre for Administrative Data Processing, Bromma, 259
National Data Processing Inc, Wilmington, 553
National Data Processing Service, London, 375-6
National Datacentre Corporation Ltd, Vancouver, 63
National Electricity Administration, Baghdad, 162
National Information Research Institute, Santa Monica, 473
National Information Systems Corporation, Valley Forge, 561-2
National Institute for Scientific and Technical Information and Documentation, Bucharest, 243
National Institute of Development Administration, Bangkok, 295-6
National Institute of Oceanography, Wormley, 338
National Insurance Institute, Jerusalem, 166
National Kassa Register A/S, Oslo, 230
National Physical Laboratory, Teddington 338
National Registrier Kassen GmbH, Frankfurt-am-Main, 140
National Science Foundation, Washington, 468
National Statistical Office, Bangkok, 295
National Taiwan University, Taipei, 67
National University of Ireland, Cork, 162
National University of Ireland, Dublin, 162-3
National University of Ireland, Galway, 163
National Westminster Bank Ltd, Manchester, 376
Nederlands Instituut voor Praeventieve Geneeskunde TNO, Leiden, 204
Nederlands Organ voor de Bevordering van de Informatieverzorging, The Hague, 203
Nederlands Scheepsbouwkundig Proefstation, Wageningen, 204
Nederlandse Accountants Maatschap, Rotterdam, 214
Nehèzipari Müszaki Egyetem, Miskolc, 146
David A Nelson, Moorestown, 488
Network Data Processing Corporation, Cedar Rapids, 526
New Mexico Highlands University, Las Vegas, 430
New Mexico State University, Las Cruces, 430
New South Wales Institute of Technology, Broadway, 9
New University of Ulster, Londonderry, 312
New York Institute of Technology, Old Westbury, 434
New York University, New York, 434
New Zealand Post Office, Wellington, 218-9
Newark College of Engineering, Newark, 429
Newcastle upon Tyne Polytechnic, Newcastle, 312

Newport and Monmouthshire College of Technology, Newport, 312
Josef Niedermair München, Munich, 140-1
Nigerian Ports Authority, Lagos, 222
Nippon Electric Company Ltd, Tokyo, 188
Nippon Software Company Ltd, Tokyo, 188
A/S Nor-Data, Trondheim, 230
Nord Data A/S, Nivä, 82
A/L Nord-Norges Hull Kortsentral, Tromsø, 230
Nordined N.V., Utrecht, 214
Nordisk ADB AB, Stockholm, 269
Nordostschweiz Kraftwerke, Baden, 283-4
A/S Nordsk Data Elektronikk, Oslo, 227
Norrdata AB, Sundsvall, 277
A/S Norsk Hullkort Service, Oslo, 231
Norsk Regensentral, Oslo, 225
North Carolina State University, Raleigh, 438
North Dakota State University, Fargo, 439
North-East London Polytechnic, London, 312
North Gloucestershire College of Technology, Cheltenham, 312-3
North Staffordshire Polytechnic, Stafford, 313
North Texas State University, Denton, 454
Northeast Missouri State College, Kirksville, 424
Northeast Regional Data Center, Gainesville, 403
Northeastern University, Boston, 417
Northern European University Computing Centre, Copenhagen, 76
Northern Illinois University, DeKalb, 407
Northern Indiana Financial Service Corporation, Marion, 525
Northwest Computing Service, Seattle, 566
Northwest Management Services Inc, Seattle, 566-7
Northwest Missouri State University, Maryville, 424-5
Northwestern University, Evanston, 407
Norwegian Water Resources and Electricity Board, Oslo, 225-6
Norwich City College, Norwich, 313
Nova Scotia Technical College, Halifax, 49

OK Data, Copenhagen, 82
Oak Ridge National Laboratory, Oak Ridge, 468
Oberlin College, Oberlin, 441
Observatoire de Marseille, Marseille, 102-3
Occidental College, Los Angeles, 394
Office Centrale de la Mécanographie, Adibjan, 182
Office Mechanization Centre, Jerusalem, 166

Office of Graham Parker, Milan, 178
Office of Graham Parker Inc, New York, 493
Office of Graham Parker, Paris, 106
Office of the National Redemption Council, Accra, 143
Ohio State University, Colombus, 441
Ohio University, Athens, 441
Oklahoma State University, Stillwater, 443
Oldacres Computers Ltd, London, 376
Olivetti Africa (Pty) Ltd, Johannesburg, 252
T. William Olle, Byfleet, 349
Omicron, Hove, 349
On-Line Systems Inc, Pittsburgh, 562
Ontario Institute for Studies in Education, Toronto, 49-50
Operaatiotutkimustoimisto Seppälä Ky, Helsinki, 90
Operations Research Inc, Silver Spring, 529
Opetusministerio, Helsinki, 89
Orda-B, Korbeek, 31
Ordina, Paris, 106
Orega AG, Zürich, 292
Oregon State University, Corvallis, 444
Organisation Maurice Bressy, Rhône, 106
Organisation Service S.C., Brussels, 29
Organisation Yves Bossard et Pierre Michel, Paris, 106
Orta Doğu Teknik Universitesi, Ankara, 298
Osaka Institute of Technology, Osaka, 184
Osaka University, Osaka, 184
Oslo Datasenter A/S, Oslo, 231
H. H. Osterbye, Copenhagen, 82
Osterreichisches Statistisches Zentralamt, Vienna, 22
Osterreichische Studiengesellschaft für Atomenergie, Vienna, 21
Oulun Yliopisto, Oulu, 87
Oy Nokia AB, Helsinki, 90
Oy Paragon AB, Helsinki, 90-91

P.A. Consulenza Direzionale, Milano, 178
P.A. Consultores de Dirección, Madrid, 255
P.A. Management Consultants Ltd, Auckland, 219
P.A. Management Consultants S.A., Brussels, 29
P.A. Management Consultants Ltd, Dublin, 163
P.A. Management Consultants GmbH, Frankfurt am Main, 131
P.A. Management Consultants Ltd, London, 349-50
P.A. Management Consultants S.A., Paris, 106
P.A. Management Consultants Pty Ltd, Melbourne, 15
PCS Data Processing Inc, New York, 549-50

P.E. Consulting Group (Aust) Pty Ltd, Sydney, 15
P.-E. Consulting Group Ltd, Dublin, 163
P.-E Consulting Group, London, 350
P.E. Consulting Group (Rhodesia) (PVT) Ltd, Salisbury, 242
P.E. Consulting Group S.A. (Pty) Ltd, Cape Town, 249
P.E. Consulting Group (West Africa) Ltd, Ikeja, 223
P.E. Italia, S p.A., Milan, 178
P.M.A. Consultants Ltd, Horley, 350-51
PN-Data AB & ACO . Data-Bolagen, Solna, 277
PRC Computer Center Inc, McLean, 501
Pabst Hulkort service, Copenhagen, 82
Pace College, New York, 435
Pacific Lutheran University, Tacoma, 462
Pacific Union College, Angwin, 394
Pakistan Computer Bureau, Rawalpindi, 232
Paillard S.A., Yverdon, 292
Paisley College of Technology, Paisley, 313
Panjab University, Chandigarh, 151-2
Pansophic Systems Inc, Oak Brook, 482
Parsons & Williams Inc., Copenhagen, 78
Parsons & Williams Inc, Stockholm, 269
Parsons College, Fairfield, 411
Paytronics Inc, Buffalo, 549
Peat Marwick Livingstone de México, Mexico City, 196
Peat Marwick Mitchell & Co, Caracas, 568-9
Peat Marwick Mitchell & Co, Frankfurt-am Main, 131
Peat Marwick Mitchell & Co, Johannesburg, 249
Peat Marwick Mitchell & Co, Kingston, 183
Peat Marwick Mitchell & Co, London, 350
Peat Marwick Mitchell & Co, Milan, 178
Peat Marwick Mitchell & Co, New York, 493-4
Peat Marwick Mitchell & Co, Paris, 106-7
Peat Marwick Mitchell & Co, Port of Spain, 296
Peat Marwick Mitchell & Co, Rio de Janeiro, 40
Peat Marwick Mitchell & Co, Sydney, 15
Peat Marwick Mitchell & Co, Tokyo, 187
Penndata Inc, Scranton, 562
Pennsylvania State University Computation Center, University Park, 447-8
Pennsylvania State University Computer Assisted Instruction Laboratory, University Park, 448
Performance Development Corporation, Trenton, 488

Perrot-Desnoix et Cie S.A., Paris, 107
Perscombinatie, Amsterdam, 214
Perth Technical College, Perth, 9
Petty Geophysical Engineering, San Antonio, 474
Phillips Information Technology, Inc, New York, 388-9
Photo Data Inc, Washington, 516
Physical Research Laboratory, Ahmedabad, 157
Pioneer Data Systems Inc, Des Moines, 526
Philip C. Pipher Associates Inc, Washington, 480
Planning and Transport Research and Computation Co,Ltd., London, 339
Plymouth Computer Systems International Ltd, London, 350
Plymouth State College, Plymouth, 428
Point Park College, Pittsburgh, 448
Polgat Woollen Industries Ltd, Kiriat-Gat, 171-2
Politechnika Gdańska, Gdańska, 236
Politechnika Wrokawska, Wrocaw, 236
Politecnico di Milano, Milano, 172-3
Politecnico di Torino, Torino, 173
Polska Akademia Nauk, Warsaw, 236-7
Polytechnic of Central London, London, 313-4
Polytechnic of North London, London, 314
The Polytechnic, Wolverhampton, 314
Pomona College, Claremont, 394
Pontificia Universidad Católica del Peru, Lima, 234-5
Pontificia Universidad Javeriana, Bogotá, 68
Pontifícia Universidade Católica de Campinas, Campinas, 33
Pontificia Universidade Católica do Rio de Janeiro, Rio de Janeiro, 33
Pope, Evans and Robbins International Ltd, Djakarta, 160
Portland State University, Portland, 444
Portsmouth Corporation, Portsmouth, 334
Portsmouth Polytechnic, Portsmouth, 314
Post Office Data Processing Service, Edinburgh, 334
Postnabken, Stockholm, 263
Potchefstroom University for Christian Higher Education, Potchefstroom, 245
Practical Computer Systems, London, 376
Prakla GmbH, Hannover, 141
Pratt Institute, Brooklyn, 435
Praxis Calcolo S.p.A., Milan, 178
Prefered Tabulating Service, New York, 550
Preston Institute of Technology, Preston, 9
Preston Polytechnic, Preston, 314
Princeton Time-Sharing Services Inc, Princeton, 542

Index of Institutions

Princeton University, Princeton, 429
Proceda S.R.L., Buenos Aires, 6
Procesamientos Electronicos S.A.C., Santiago, 66
Processamento de Dados S.A., Pernambuco, 40
Processamento Electrônico Ltda, Pôrto Alegre, 44
Procomputos Ltda, Barranquilla, 72
Prodata International Datenverarbeitung GmbH, Frankfurt, 141
Production Systems Inc, Waltham, 532-3
ADB Produktion AB, Stockholm, 270-71
Produktionstenik AB, Helsinki, 89
Professional Data Processing Inc, Seattle, 567
Profimatics Inc, Woodland Hills, 478
AB Programator, Stockholm, 269
Programma Nederland N.V., The Hague, 214
Programmatics Inc, Los Angeles, 509
Programme Evaluation Organisation, Delhi, 154-5
Programming & Systems Inc, New York, 550
Programming Methods Inc, New York, 550
Programming Services Inc, Woodland Hills, 478
Programs and Analysis Inc, Burlington, 533
Progress Rationaliserings AB, Solna, 277
Progresso e Desenvolvimento de Santos, Santos, 44-5
Project Planning Associates, Milton, 485
A. M. Provan and Associates, Port of Spain, 297
Public Administration Service, Chicago, 483
Public Data Processing Corporation, Chicago, 523-4
H. S. Pühlhorn, Kulmbach 131
Punch Card Service Centre, Dublin, 164
Punched Cards Services Ltd, London, 351
Purdue University, West Lafayette, 409

Quaternaire Informatique S.A. Paris, 113
Queen Elizabeth College, University of London, London, 315
Queen Mary College, University of London, London, 315
Queen's University at Kingston, Kingston, 50
Queen's University of Belfast, Belfast, 315
Queensborough Community College, Bayside, 435
Queensland State Treasury, Brisbane, 13-14

RAK Associates, Cleveland, 496
RDB Databyrå AB, Stockholm, 278

RSI Computer Services Corporation, New York, 494
Raadgevend Bureau Drs D. van der Lelie N.V., Groningen, 207
Raadgevend Efficiency Bureau Bosboom En Hegener N.V., Amsterdam 207
Računski Center, Skofja Loka, 576
Raet Automation Consultancy and Service Bureau, Arnhem, 214
Rand Corporation, Santa Monica, 474
Randax EDP Ltd, London, 376
Randolph-Macon College, Ashland, 460
Rapid, Belgrade, 576
Rapid Data Computer Services (Hamilton) Ltd, Hamilton, 63
Rapidata Inc, Fairfield, 542
Rational AG, Zürich, 292
Rationel Databehandling A/S, Glostrup, 82
Rationell Planering AB, Solna, 269
Rationella Data AB, Luleå, 277-8
Hub S. Ratliff, Houston, 501
Real Time Corporation Ltd, Don Mills, 63
Realtime Systems Inc, New York, 494
Reber Datenverarbeitungsservice, Berne, 292
Rechen-Center Rapperswil Aktiengesellschaft, Rapperswil, 292
Rechen- und Entwicklungsinstitut für EDV im Bauwesen, Stuttgart, 141
Rechenzentrale für Wirtschaft und Verwaltung, Essen, 141
Rechenzentrum AG, Bern, 292-3
Rechenzentrum Graz, Graz, 22
Rechenzentrum Koch, Heidelberg, 139
Record Processing Corporation, New York, 550
Recording and Statistical Company, Boston, 533
Recording and Statistical Company, Chicago, 524
Recording and Statistical Company, San Francisco, 509
Redac Software Ltd, Tewkesbury, 351
Redal Software Ltd, Tewkesbury 376-7
Reed Computer Services, London, 351
Reelltids-Data AB, Stockholm, 278
Refinerías de Maiz S.A.I.C., Buenos Aires, 6
Régie T. T. Informatique, Brussels, 31
Regneanlegget Blindern-Kjeller, Kjeller, 227
A/S Regnecentralen, Copenhagen, 82-3
Reiland Page and Associates Inc, Columbus, 496
Rekencentrum C. van de Velden, N.V., Arnhem, 214-5
Rekencentrum 'Informatron' N.V., Amsterdam, 215
B.V. Rekencentrum Ogem, Rotterdam, 215
Rekencentrum voor Administratie Efficiency en Techniek, Arnhem, 215

N.V. Rekencentrum voor Handel en Industrie, Rotterdam, 215
Remote Computing Corporation, Los Angeles, 509
Reno Junior College of Business, Reno, 389
Rensselaer Polytechnic Institute Troy, 435
Research Institute of National Defence (1), Stockholm, 264
Research Institute of National Defence (2), Stockholm, 265
Research Institute of National Defence (3), Stockholm, 265
Research Institute of National Defence (4), Stockholm, 265
Research Triangle Institute, Triangle Park, 474
Rheinisch-Westfälische Technische Hochschule, Aachen, 119
Rheinische Friedrich-Wilhelms-Universität, Bonn, 119
Rhodes University, Grahamstown, 245
Rice University, Houston, 455
Rijks Computercentrum Apeldoorn, 204
Rijksuniversiteit te Gent, Gent, 26
Rijksuniversiteit te Groningen, Groningen, 199
Rijksuniversiteit te Leiden, Leiden, 199
Rijksuniversiteit te Utrecht, Utrecht, 199-200
Rijksuniversiteit te Utrecht, Department of Medical and Physiological Physics, Utrecht, 200
Rijksuniversiteit te Utrecht, Department of Physiology, Utrecht, 200
Rijksuniversiteit te Utrecht, Flektronisch Rekencentrum, Utrecht, 200
Riverside City College, Riverside, 394
Rochester Computer Service Inc, Rochester, 550-1
Rogaland College, Stavanger, 224
Roosevelt University, Chicago, 407
Rose-Hulman Institute of Technology, Terre Haute, 409
Paul Rosenberg Associates, New York, 494
P. S. Ross & Partners, Montreal, 58
Rothamsted Experimental Station, Harpenden, 339
Christian Rovsing A/S, Herlev, 83
Royal Holloway College, University of London, Englefield Green, 315
Royal Scientific Society, Amman, 189
Ruhr-Universität, Bochum, 119-120
Rutgers, The State University, New Brunswick, 429

SDA Information Sciences Inc, New York, 494
SDK Medical Computer Services Corporation, Brookline, 533
S.E.T.M., Paris, 114
S.I.A. Ltd, London, 378
SIA International, Paris, 114
SPL International, London, 378

SPL International, Nottingham, 352
SPS A/S, Copenhagen, 83
S.V.Z. Computer Centre, Rotterdam, 216
Saab-Scania AB, Linköping, 278
Said Inc, Lynchburg, 501
St Edward's University, Austin, 455
St Francis College, Loretto, 448
St Francis Xavier University, Antigonish, 50
St John's University, Collegeville, 421
Saint Louis University, Baguio City, 235
Saint Mary's College, Winona, 421
St Mary's University, Halifax, 50
St Mary's University, San Antonio, 455
Saint Peter's College, Jersey City, 429
Salisbury College of Technology, Salisbury, 315-6
Kurt Salmon & P.E. Associates Ltd, London, 351
Kurt Salmon Associates, Washington, 480
Salt City Business College, Hutchinson, 389
AB Sam Sjöberg, Fröllinda, 270
Samkontor AB, Malmö, 278
Samson Automatiserings Service Centrum N.V., Alphen, 215-6
San Mateo Junior College District, San Mateo, 394-5
Santa Ana College, Santa Ana, 395
Scan Data, Copenhagen, 83
Scan Data Ltd, Farnborough, 351
Schema Processamento de Dados Comércio e Importaçao Ltda, São Paulo, 45
School District of Philadelphia, Philadelphia, 448
School of Computer Programming, London, 301
Schulz Instruments Inc, Gainesville, 481
Schwarz Fine Kane & Co, Johannesburg, 249
Sci-Tek Inc, Wilmington, 515
Science Research Council, Chilton, 339
Science Research Council, Daresbury, 339
Scientific Analysis Corporation, Wayland, 485
Scientific Calculations Inc, Rochester, 474
Scientific Computation Centre, Cairo, 85
Scientific Computers Inc, Minneapolis, 536
Scientific Control Systems Ltd, London, 377
Scientific Software Corporation, Englewood, 513
Scientific Systems Services, Satellite Beach, 520
Scottish College of Textiles, Galashiels, 316
Scottish Computer Services Ltd, Glasgow, 377
Scottish Council for Commercial Administrative and Professional Education, Edinburgh, 301
Scottish Office Computer Service, Edinburgh, 334-5

Seattle University, Seattle, 462
Secretaría de Recursos Hidráulicos, Mexico, 196
Secretaría del Consejo Provincial de Desarrollo, Corrientes, 4
Sedab AG, Luzern, 293
Seguros Bolívar, Bogotá, 73
Semka AB, Sundbyberg, 270
Serendipity Inc, Sherman Oaks, 474-5
Seresco S.A., Barcelona, 257
Serescodata S.A., Sevilla, 257-8
Serete S.A., São Paulo, 40
Service Bureau Corporation, Atlanta, 521
Service Bureau Corporation, Birmingham, 503
Service Bureau Corporation, Boston, 533
Service Bureau Corporation, Charlotte, 553
Service Bureau Corporation, Chicago, 524
Service Bureau Corporation, Cincinnati, 556
Service Bureau Corporation, Dallas, 564-5
Service Bureau Corporation, Denver, 513
Service Bureau Corporation, Detroit, 535
Service Bureau Corporation, East Orange, 542
Service Bureau Corporation, Hartford, 515
Service Bureau Corporation, Honolulu, 522
Service Bureau Corporation, Indianapolis, 525
Service Bureau Corporation, Inglewood, 510
Service Bureau Corporation, Kansas City, 538
Service Bureau Corporation, Louisville, 527
Service Bureau Corporation, Memphis, 564
Service Bureau Corporation, Miami, 520
Service Bureau Corporation, Milwaukee, 568
Service Bureau Corporation, Minneapolis, 536
Service Bureau Corporation, New York, 551-2
Service Bureau Corporation, Oklahoma City, 557
Service Bureau Corporation, Omaha, 539
Service Bureau Corporation, Philadelphia, 562
Service Bureau Corporation, Phoenix, 504
Service Bureau Corporation, Portland, 557
Service Bureau Corporation, Richmond, 566
Service Bureau Corporation, Seattle, 567
Service Bureau Corporation, Washington, 516
Service Bureau Corporation, Wheaton, 529
Service Informatique Honeywell Bull, Neuilly-sur-Seine, 113-4

Services Electrônicos de Contabilidade Ltda, São Paulo, 45
Servico Federal de Processamento de Dados, Rio de Janeiro, 38-9
Servicios Informática de Honeywell Bull, Mexico City, 197
Servimec S.A., São Paulo, 45
Servizio Internazionale Elaborazione Dati S.p.A., Roma, 181
Setak Computing Services Corporation Ltd, Toronto, 63
Seton Hall University, South Orange, 429-30
I. P. Sharp Associates, Ltd, Toronto, 58
Sheffield Polytechnic, Sheffield, 316
Shekem Ltd, Jaffa, 169
Shippensburg State College, Shippensburg, 448-9
Shoe and Allied Trades Research Association, Kettering, 340
Short Brothers and Harland Ltd, Belfast, 340
J. Short Data Centre, London, 377-8
S. A. Siemens N.V., Brussels, 31-2
Siemens S.A., Madrid, 258
Siemens AG, München, 141
Siemens Nederland N.V., The Hague, 216
Siemens S.A.F., Saint-Denis, 114
Siemens GmbH, Vienna, 23
Siemens Data Skandinavien, Stockholm, 280
Siemens Elektrizitätserzeugnisse AG, Fahrweid, 293
Siffer-Service Datacentral AB, Stockholm, 278-9
Sigma Data Services, Beckenham, 378
Sigma Processing Inc, Minneapolis, 537
Silkeborg Datacentral A/S, Silkeborg, 83
Simon Fraser University, Burnaby, 50
K. Lund Simonsen A/S, Vaerløse, 83
E. Ralph Sims Jr & Associates, Inc, Lancaster, 497
Singer Business Machines, Berg en Dal, 198
Singer Friden Division, Milano, 181
Sir George Williams University, Montreal, 50-51
Sistemas Analíticos, San José, 73
Sivillingeniör Rolf Höyer A/S, Oslo, 228
Skogbrukets Datasentral A/S, Oslo, 231
Skogsbrukets Datacentral Sundsvall, 279
Skýrsluvélar Ríkisins og Reykjavíkurborgar, Reykjavík, 149
Slagelse Data Service A/S, Slagelse, 83-4
Slough College of Technology, Slough, 316
Služba Društvenog Knjigovodstva Jugoslavije, Belgrade, 572
W. H. Smith & Son Ltd, London, 378
Smithsonian Astrophysical Observatory, Cambridge, 475
Snam Progetti S.p.A., Milan, 177
Snow College, Ephraim, 458
Social and Economic Statistics Administration, Washington, 468

Index of Institutions

Social Security Administration, Baltimore, 468-9
Sociedade Lusitana de Organizacões LDA, Lisboa, 241
Società Sispre, Roma, 177
Société Anonyme des Ateliers de Secheron, Genève, 293
Société d'Applications det de Méthodes Mécanographiques, Paris, 115
Société de Gestion Électronique, Neuilly-sur-Seine, 115
Société d'Engineering Appliqué au traitement de l'Information, Paris, 107
Société d'Etudes des Systèmes d'Automation, Paris, 107
Société d'Etudes des Systèmes d'Automation, Paris, 115
Société d'Exploitation d'Utimaco SA et Compatibilités-Statistiques SA, Genève, 293
Société Générale de Recherche et Programmation, Marseille, 107
Société Industrielle de Travaux de Bureaux, Paris, 115
Société Infor, Chassieu, 107-8
Société d'Ingénieurs Conseils en Organisation, Parjs, 107
Société Nationale d'Etudes de Construction de Moteurs d'Avion, Suresnes, 103
Société Nationale Terrienne, Brussels, 28
Société Perforas, Saint Maur, 116
Society for Cybernetics, Rijeka, 570
Carl Soderberg AB, Stockholm, 279
Södertalje Data AB, Nacka, 279
Sofemasa, Madrid, 255
The Software House (Pty) Ltd, Pretoria, 249
Software Resources Corporation, Los Angeles, 510
Software Sciences Ltd, London, 351-2
Sogecim, Paris, 116
Sonatrach, Algiers, 1
Sorpra, Annecy, 108
South African Council for Scientific and Industrial Research, Pretoria, 248
South African Railways, Durban, 248
South African Railways, Johannesburg, 248
South Australian Institute of Technology, Adelaide, 10
South Australian Institute of Technology, Ingle Farm, 9
South Australian Public Service ADP Centre, Adelaide, 14
South Central Railway Secunderabad, 154
South Dakota State University, Brookings, 452
South East London Technical College, London, 316
South of Scotland Electricity Board, Glasgow, 335
South West London College, London, 316-7
Southampton Technical College, Southampton, 317

Southeast Missouri State University, Cape Giradreau, 425
Southern Computer Service, Dothan, 503
Southern Cross Computer Pty Ltd, Toowoomba, 20
Southern Data Processing Services Inc, Augusta, 521
Southern Illinois University, Carbondale, 407
Southern Methodist University, Dallas, 455
Southern Railway, Madras, 154
Southwest Computer College Inc, Albuquerque, 389
Southwest Computing Service Inc, Phoenix, 504
Southwest Missouri State College, Springfield, 425
Southwestern at Memphis, Memphis, 453
Southwestern State College, Weatherford, 443-4
Spaarbank voor de Stad Amsterdam, Amsterdam, 216
Sparbankernas Datacentraler AB, Stockholm, 279
Sparekassernes Datacentraler, Copenhagen, 84
R. Dixon Speas Associates Inc, Manhasset, 494
Special Studies Institute, New York, 495
Specialized Management Service Inc, Torrington, 515
Spencer Stuart and Associés S.A., Paris, 108
Sperry Rand GmbH, Frankfurt-am-Main, 142
Sperry Rand Univac, Vienna, 23
Sperry Rand AG Univac Wissenschaft und Technik, Zürich, 293-4
Sports Data Corporation, New York, 552
Stafford College of Further Education, Stafford, 317
Standard Bank Nigeria Ltd, Lagos, 223
Standard Data Corporation, New York, 552
Standard Programs Corporation, New York, 552
Stanford Research Institute, Menlo Park, 475
Stanford University, Stanford, 395
Stansrutin AB, Stockholm, 279-80
Edward Stark Associates Ltd, Needham, 485-6
State Bank of India, Bombay, 154
State Bank of Pakistan, Karachi, 232
State Engineering Corporation, Colombo, 258
State University of New York Agricultural and Technical College, Alfred, 436
State University of New York, Albany, 435-6
State University of New York, Brockport, 436
State University of New York, Buffalo, 436
State University of New York College of Arts and Sciences, Plattsburgh, 436-7
State University of New York Maritime College, New York, 437

State University of New York, School of Advanced Technology, Binghampton, 347
State University of New York, Stony Brook, 436
Statens Driftssentrale for Administrativ Databehhandling, Oslo, 226
Statens Järnvägar, Stockholm, 263
Statens Vägwerk, Stockholm, 259
Statistical Reporting and Tabulating Ltd, Toronto, 64
Statistical Tabulating Corporation, Chicago, 524
Statistics Canada, Ottawa, 56
Statistisk Sentralbyrå, Oslo, 226
Statisska Centralbyråns, Stockholm, 259
"Stefan Gheorghiu" Academy, Bucharest, 243
Theodore Stein, New York, 495
Stephen F. Austin State University, Nacogdoches, 455-6
Stevens Institute of Technology, Hoboken, 430
Stevenson & Kellogg Ltd, Toronto, 59
Stevenson, Jordan & Harrison, Copenhagen, 78
Stevenson, Jordan & Harrison Ltd, London, 352
Stevenson Jordan & Harrison Management Consultants Inc, New York, 495
Stewart Dougall & Associates Inc, New York, 495
Stichting Academisch Rekencentrum, Amsterdam, 200-1
Stichting Bevordering Computertoepassing Bouwwezen, Rotterdam, 205
Stichting Het R. K. Gasthuis, Tilburg, 216
Stichting Mathematisch Centrum, Amsterdam, 205
AB Stockholms Datajänst AB, Stockholm, 270, 280
Stockholms Datamaskincentral, Stockholm, 259
Stockholms Universitet, Department of Administration Information Processing, Stockholm, 261
Stockholms Universitet Department of Information Processing, Stockholm, 261-2
Stroede AB, Torslanda, 280
Studiecentrum Novi, Amsterdam, 198
Dr Suchan Ratio-Data GmbH, Weinheim, 142
Sun Alliance and London Insurance Ltd, Horsham, 378-9
Sunderland Polytechnic, Sunderland, 317
Suomen Sedab Oy, Helsinki, 91
Superdata S.A., Guanabara, 45
Superior Data Processing Service, Los Angeles, 510
Surrey County Council, Kingston, 335
Survey Department, Kuala Lumpur, 193
Svenska Elektroniska Data AB, Johanneshov, 280
Svenska Stadsfördbundet, Stockholm, 259-60

Sveriges Kreditbank ADB Service, Stockholm, 280-81
Sveučilište u Zagrebu, Zagreb, 570
Svila Tekstilna Tovarna, Maribor, 572
Swedish Meteorological and Hydrological Institute, Stockholm, 265
Swedish Planning and Rationalization Institute of the Health and Social Services, Stockholm, 263
Swinburne College of Technology, Hawthorn, 10
Swiss Federal Railways, Bern, 284
Sydfyns Datacentral, Svendborg, 84
Symbionics Systems Ltd, Winnipeg, 64
Synthèsedes Techniques de l'Organisation, Le Chesnay, 108
Systek Inc, Pittsfield, 533
System Dynamics Ltd, Dublin, 163
System Printing Italiana S.p.A., Roma, 181
Systematics Inc, Little Rock, 504
Systematics International Ltd, Basildon, 379
Systemberatung GmbH, Karlsruhe, 132
Systemkonsult Aktiebolag, Hälsingborg, 270
Systems Advisers (Pty) Ltd, Johannesburg, 249
Systems Analysis Corp A/S, Copenhagen, 84
Systems and Computer Information Inc, Inglewood, 478
Systems and Research (Nederland) N.V., Rotterdam, 208
Systems and Services Ltd, Croydon, 352
Systems Data Processing Corporation, Sacramento, 510
Systems Dimensions Ltd, Ottawa, 64
Systems Programming S.A., Geneva, 286-7
Systems Programming Ltd, London, 352
Systems Programming Services Inc, Miami, 520
Systems Programming Ltd Svenska AB, Stockholm, 270
Systems Programming Inc, White Plains, 495
Systems, Science and Software, La Jolla, 475
Systems Technology Corporation Ltd, Tel Aviv, 169
Systems Technology Corporation, Warminster, 498-9
Systemshare Ltd, Edinburgh, 379
Syntax S.p.A., Milano, 181-2
Számitástechnikai és Ugyvietszervezö Vállalat, Budapest, 149

TEA-Informática, Madrid, 255
Tabulating Consultants Inc, Burbank, 510
Tahal Consulting Engineers Ltd, Tel Aviv, 169
Taikoo Dockyard and Engineering Company of Hong Kong Ltd, Hong Kong, 145

Tampereen Teknillinen Korkeakoulu, Tampere, 88
Tampereen Yliopisto, Tampere, 88
Tata Consultancy Services, Bombay, 157
Tata Institute of Fundamental Research, Bombay, 157
Technical Advisers Inc, Wayne, 535
Technical Computing Center, San Fransisco, 510
Technical Education Corporation, St Louis, 389
Technical University of Ostrava, Ostrava, 74
Technicomps Pty Ltd, Chatswood, 20
Technikum Winterthur (Ingenieurschule), Winterthur, 282
Techniques et Systèmes Informatique, Paris, 108
Technische Hochschule, Darmstadt, 120
Technische Hochschule in Wien, Abeilung Prozessrechenanlage, Vienna, 22
Technische Hochschule in Wien, Rechenzentrum, Vienna, 22
Technische Hogeschool Eindhoven, Eindhoven, 201
Technische Hogeschool te Delft, Delft, 201
Technische Hogeschool te Delft, Department of Mathematics, Delft, 201
Technische Hogeschool Twente, Enschede, 201-2
Technische Universität, Berlin, 120
Technische Universität Berlin, Institut für Informationsverabteilung, Berlin, 120
Technische Universität Berlin, Recheninstitut, Berlin, 120
Technische Universität Carolo-Wilhelmina zu Braunschweig, Braunschweig, 121
Technische Universität Carolo-Wilhelmina zu Braunschweig, Institut für Datenverarbeitungsanlagen, Braunschweig, 120-1
Technische Universität Clausthal, Clausthal, 121
Technische Universität Hannover, Hannover, 121
Technische Universität München, München, 121
Technische Universität München, Geodätisches Institut, München, 121
Technisches Universität München, Institut für Angewandte Mathematik, München, 122
Teesside County Borough Council, Teesside, 335
Teesside Polytechnic, Teesside, 317-8
'Tehavot' Israel Mortgage Bank Ltd, Jerusalem, 166
Tekn. Lic Johan F. Böhmer Konsultrande Ingenjörsbyrå AB, Stockholm, 266
Teknillinen Korkeakoulu, Helsinki, 88
Telcomp Corporation of America, Cambridge, 533-4
Tele-Data Corporation, North Plainfield, 542

Telechek International Inc, Honolulu, 522
Teledata AG, Berne, 294
Teledyne Corporation, Houston, 475
Teledyne Exploration, Calgary, 56
AB Teleplan, Solna, 270
Televerkets Industriavdelning, Nynäshamm, 281
Temple University, Philadelphia, 449
Tennessee Agricultural and Industrial State University, Nashville, 453
Tennessee Technological University, Cookeville, 453
Tennessee Valley Authority, Chattanooga, 469
S.J. Tesauro & Co, Detroit, 535
Texas Agricultural and Mechanical University, College Station, 456
Texas Technological University, Lubbock, 456
Thames Polytechnic, London, 318
The Nuclear Power Group, Knutsford, 338-9
Thiel College, Greenville, 449
Thomas More College, Fort Mitchell, 413
Thomas Nationwide Transport Computer Centre, St Peters, 20
Tietotehdas Oy, Kilo, 91
Tilastollinen Päätoimisto, Helsinki, 86
Tilburg School of Economics, Social Sciences and Law, Tilburg, 202
Tillinghast & Co Inc, Atlanta, 481
Time-Sharing A/S, Oslo, 231
Time Sharing Sciences Inc, New York, 495
Tohoku University, Sendai, 184-5
Tokyo Shibaura Electric Co Ltd, Tokyo, 188
Tom Gilb, Kolbotn, 227
Touche Ross and Co, London, 352
Tovarna Avtomobilov in Motorjev Maribor, Maribor, 576
Transdata Corporation, Phoenix, 504
Trask Datasystem AB, Stocksund, 281
Trent Polytechnic, Nottingham, 318
Trenton Nassau Service Bureau, Trenton, 542-3
Tretorn Datacenter, Hälsingborg, 281
Treuga Datenservice Neuy KG, Wiesbaden, 142
Tri-Dex Data Services, Visalia, 510
Triangle Universities Computation Centre, Triangle Park, 438
Trinidad State Junior College, Trinidad, 399
Trinity University, San Antonio, 456
A/S Trønder-Data, Trondheim, 231
Trygg-Hansa, Stockholm, 281
Tulane University of Louisiana, New Orleans, 414
Turnkey Systems Inc, Norwakk, 479
Tuskegee Institute, Tuskegee, 390
Twickenham College of Technology, Twickenham, 318

Index of Institutions

Tylin Management Systems Ltd, Reading, 379
Tymshare Inc, Cupertino, 511

UCC-Automation Centre S.A., Brussels, 32
URS Data Sciences Company, San Mateo, 511
Uni-Coll Corporation, Philadelphia, 562
Unid. Processamento de Dados (FEAUSP), São Paulo, 32
Unidata AG, Wetzikon, 287
Unilever Computer Service Ltd, Wembley, 379-80
Union College, Schenectady, 437
Uniroyal Ltd, Newbridge, 380
Unitab Company of Abilene, Abilene, 565
United Bank Ltd, Karachi, 233
United Computing Corporation, Carson, 479
United Computing Systems Inc, Kansas City, 538
United Data Centers Inc, Greenwich, 515
United Data Centres Pty Ltd, Sydney, 20
United Kingdom Atomic Energy Authority, Abingdon, 335
United Nations, New York, 469
United Nations Development Programme, Bratislava, 74-5
United Nations Educational Scientific and Cultural Organization, Paris, 101
United States Computers Inc, Tacoma, 567
United States Geological Survey, Washington, 469
United States Naval Academy, Annapolis, 389
Univac Canada Ltd, Toronto, 64
Univac DPS Midwest Computer Centre, Oak Brook, 524
Univac Data Processing Center, Atlanta, 521
Univac Data Processing Center, Cleveland, 556
Univac Data Processing Center, Denver, 513
Univac Data Processing Center, Detroit, 535
Univac Data Processing Center, Houston, 565
Univac Data Processing Center, Kansas City, 538
Univac Data Processing Centers, Philadelphia, 563
Univac Data Processing Center, Portland, 557
Univac Data Processing Center, Silver Spring, 529
Univac Data Processing Center, Tucson, 504
Univac Data Processing Centers, Los Angeles, 511
Univac Data Processing Centers, New York, 552
Univac Northeast Regional Office, Wellesley, 534
Univac, Washington, 516-7

Universal Design Systems (India) Private Ltd, Delhi, 159
Universidad Autónoma de Guadalajara, Guadalajara, 195
Universidad Católica Argentina "Santa María de los Buenos Aires", Buenos Aires, 1
Universidad Católica de Chile, Programa Interdisciplinario de Investigaciones en Educación, Santiago, 66
Universidad Católica de Chile, Santiago, 64-5
Universidad Católica de Córdoba, Córdoba, 2
Universidad Central de Venezuela, Caracas, 568
Universidad de Antioquía, Medellín, 68
Universidad de Barcelona, Barcelona, 253
Universidad de Buenos Aires, Centro de Cómputos, Buenos Aires, 2
Universidad de Buenos Aires, Instituto de Cálculo, Buenos Aires, 2
Universidad de Chile, Santiago, 65
Universidad de Concepción, Concepción, 65
Universidad de Costa Rica, San José, 73
Universidad de la Patagonia "San Juan Bosco", Comodoro Rivadavia, 2
Universidad de los Andes, Biblioteca General, Bogotá, 68
Universidad de los Andes, Centro de Cómputo, Bogotá, 68-9
Universidad de los Andes, Mérida, 568
Universidad de Madrid, Madrid, 253
Universidad de Navarra, San Sebastián, 253
Universidad de Oriente, Puerto La Cruz, 568
Universidad de Panamá, Panamá, 233
Universidad del Cauca, Cauca, 69
Universidad del Norte, Antofagasta, 65
Universidad del Salvador, Buenos Aires, 2
Universidad del Valle, Cali, 69
Universidad Iberoamericano, Mexico, 195
Universidad Industrial de Santander, Santander, 69
Universidad La Salle de Mexico, Mexico, 195
Universidad Nacional Autónoma de Mexico, Mexico, 195
Universidad Nacional Autónoma de Nicaragua, Managua, 221
Universidad Nacional de Asunción, Asunción, 234
Universidad Nacional de Córdoba, Centro de Cálculo, Córdoba, 3
Universidad Nacional de Córdoba, Centro de Computación y Procesamiento de Datos, Córdoba, 3

Universidad Nacional de Ingeniería, Lima, 235
Universidad Nacional de Tucumán, San Miguel de Tucumán, 3
Universidad Nacional del Litoral, Sante Fe, 3
Universidad Pontificia Bolivariana, Medellín, 69
Universidad Técnica del Estado, Santiago, 65
Universidad Técnica "Federico Santa María", Valparaíso, 65-6
Universidad Tecnológica de Pereira, Pereira, 69-70
Universidad Tecnológica Nacional, Buenos Aires, 3
Universidade de São Paulo, Centro de Computação Electrônica, São Paulo, 33
Universidade de São Paulo, Centro de Processamento de Dados, São Carlos, 34
Universidade de São Paulo, Nuclear Physics Department, São Paulo, 33-4
Universidade do Porto, Porto, 240
Universidade Estadual de Campinas, Campinas, 34
Universidade Federal de Minas Gerais, Minas Gerais, 34
Universidade Federal de Paraíba, Paraíba, 34
Universidade Federal de Pernambuco, Pernambuco, 34-5
Universidade Federal de Sergipe, Sergipe, 35
Universidade Federal de São Carlos, São Carlos, 35
Universidade Federal do Paraná, Curitiba, 35
Universidade Federal de Rio de Janeiro, Instituto Biofísica, Rio de Janeiro, 39
Universidade Federal do Rio de Janeiro, Rio de Janeiro, 35
Universidade Federal do Rio Grande do Sul, Rio Grande do Sul, 36
Universidade Federal Fluminense, Niterói, 36
Universidade Federal Rural de Pernambuco, Pernambuco, 36
Universidade Mackenzie, São Paulo, 36
Universita Bar-Ilan, Ramat-Gan, 165
Università degli Studi di Bari, Bari, 173
Università degli Studi di Milano, Milano, 173
Università degli Studi di Trieste, Trieste, 173
Università di Napoli, Napoli, 173-4
Università di Padova, Padova, 174
Università di Roma, Centro di Calculo Interfacolta, Roma, 174
Università di Roma, Facolta di Ingegneria, Rome, 174
Universität Basel, Basel, 282
Universität des Saarlandes, Saarbrücken, 123

599

Universität Fridericiana, Karlsruhe, 122
Universität Hamburg, Institut für Informatik, Hamburg, 122
Universität Hamburg, Rechenzentrum, Hamburg, 122
Universitat Hanegev, Beer-Sheva, 165
Universität Konstanz, Konstanz, 123
Universität Rostock, Rostock, 116
Universität Stuttgart, Stuttgart, 123-4
Universitat Tel-Aviv, Tel-Aviv, 165
Universität Ulm, Ulm-Wiblingen, 124
Universität zu Köln, Betreibswirtschaftliches Institut für Organisation und Automation, Cologne, 122-3
Universität zu Köln, Rechenzentrum, Cologne, 123
Universität Zürich, Zürich, 282
Université Catholique de Louvain, Louvain, 26
Université de Bescançon, Bescançon, 96-7
Université de Bordeaux I, Talence, 97
Université de Caen, Caen, 97
Université de Fribourg, Fribourg, 282-3
Université de Grenoble, Grenoble, 97
Université de Lausanne, Lausanne, 283
Université de Montréal, Montréal, 51
Université de Nancy I et de Nancy II, Nancy, 97-8
Université de Neuchâtel, Neuchâtel, 283
Université de Nice, Nice, 98
Université d'Orléans, Orléans, 98
Université de Paris VI, Paris, 98
Université de Paris IX, Paris, 98
Université de Poitiers, Poitiers, 98-9
Université de Rennes, Rennes, 99
Université de Sherbrooke, Sherbrooke, 51
Université de Strasbourg, Strasbourg, 99
Université de Toulouse III, Toulouse, 99
Université de Tours, Tours, 99-100
Université Laval, Sainte-Foy, 51
Universiteit van Amsterdam, Amsterdam, 202
Universitet i Umeå, Umeå, 262
Universitet i Uppsala, Uppsala, 262
Universitetet i Bergen, Bergen, 224
Universitetet i Oslo, Oslo, 224-5
Universitetet i Oslo, Student Administration, Oslo, 225
Universitetet i Tromsø, Tromsø, 225
Universitetet i Trondheim, Trondheim, 225
Universiti Malaya, Kuala Lumpur, 192
University College, Cardiff, University of Wales, Cardiff, 318-9
University College of Swansea, University of Wales, Swansea, 319

University College, University of London, London, 318
University Computing Company, Chicago, 524
University Computing Company, Dallas, 565
University Computing Company, East Brunswick, 543
University Computing Company, El Segundo, 512
University Computing Company, (Great Britain) Ltd, Birmingham, 380
University Computing Company (Nederland) N.V., The Hague, 216-7
University Computing Company, Tulsa, 557
University Hospital, Utrecht, 202
University of Aberdeen Computing Centre, Aberdeen, 319
University of Aberdeen Dept. of Engineering, Aberdeen, 319
University of Adelaide, Adelaide, 10
University of Akron, Akron, 442
University of Alabama, Huntsville, 390-91
University of Alaska, Fairbanks, 391
University of Alberta, Edmonton, 51-2
University of Albuquerque, Albuquerque, 431
University of Arizona, Tucson, 391
University of Arkansas, Fayetteville, 391-2
University of Arkansas, Little Rock, 392
University of Aston in Birmingham, Birmingham, 319-20
University of Auckland, Auckland, 217
University of Baghdad, Baghdad, 161
University of Birmingham, Birmingham, 320
University of Bradford, Bradford, 320
University of Bristol Computer Centre, Bristol, 320
University of Bristol Computer Science Department, Bristol, 320
University of British Columbia, Vancouver, 52
University of Calcutta, Calcutta, 152
University of Calgary, Calgary, 52
University of California Computer Centre, Berkeley, 395
University of California Information Systems Division, Berkeley, 395-6
University of California, Davis, 396
University of California, Irvine, 396
University of California, Los Angeles, 396
University of California, Riverside, 396-7
University of California, San Diego, 397
University of California, San Francisco Medical Center, San Francisco, 397
University of California, Santa Barbara, 397

University of California, Santa Cruz, 397
University of Cambridge, Cambridge, 321
University of Canterbury, Christchurch, 218
University of Cape Town, Cape Town, 245
University of Chicago, Chicago, 407-8
University of Chicago Institute for Computer Research, Chicago, 408
University of Cincinnati, Cincinnati, 442
University of Colorado, Boulder, 399
University of Conneticut, Storrs, 400
University of Dar-es-Salaam, Dar-es-Salaam, 295
University of Dayton, Dayton, 442
University of Delaware, Newark, 401
University of Delhi, Delhi, 152
University of Denver, Denver, 399-400
University of Detroit, Detroit, 419
University of Dublin, Trinity College, Dublin, 163
University of Dundee, Dundee, 321
University of Durban-Westville, Durban, 246
University of Durham, Durham, 321
University of Durham Department of Geology, Durham, 321
University of East Anglia, Norwich, 321-2
University of Edinburgh, Edinburgh, 322
University of Essex, Colchester, 322
University of Exeter, Exeter, 322
University of Georgia, Athens, 404-5
University of Ghana, Accra, 142
University of Glasgow Computing Department, Glasgow, 322-3
University of Glasgow Computing Service, Glasgow, 323
University of Hawaii, Honolulu, 405
University of Hong Kong and the Chinese University of Hong Kong, Kowloon, 145
University of Hull, Kingston upon Hull, 323
University of Idaho, Moscow, 405
University of Ife, Ile-Ife, 222
University of Iowa, Iowa City, 411
University of Kansas, Lawrence, 412
University of Keele, Keele, 323
University of Kent, Canterbury, 323
University of Kentucky, Lexington, 413
University of Khartoum, Khartoum, 258
University of Kurukshetra, Kurukshetra, 152
University of Lagos, Lagos, 222
University of Lancaster, Lancaster, 324
University of Leeds, Computer-Based Learning Project, Leeds, 324
University of Leeds Electronic Computing Laboratory, Leeds, 324
University of Leicester, Leicester, 324
University of Libya, Tripoli, 192

Index of Institutions

University of Liverpool Centre for Computer-Aided Building Design, Liverpool, 324-5
University of Liverpool Computer Laboratory, Liverpool, 325
University of Liverpool Department of Computational and Statistical Sciences and Data Processing, Liverpool, 325
University of Louisville, Louisville, 413-4
University of London Computer Centre, London, 325-6
University of London Management Systems Department, London, 325
University of Maine, Orono, 414-5
University of Manitoba, Computer Centre, Winnipeg, 52
University of Manitoba, Faculty of Medicine, Winnipeg, 52-3
University of Maryland, College Park, 415
University of Massachusetts, Amherst, 417
University of Mauritius, Réduit, 193
University of Melbourne, Melbourne, 10
University of Miami, Coral Gables, 403
University of Michigan, Ann Arbor, 419
University of Minnesota, Minneapolis, 421
University of Mississippi, Lafayette County, 423
University of Missouri, Columbia, 425
University of Missouri, Rolla, 425
University of Montana, Missoula, 426
University of Montreal, École Polytechnique, Montreal, 53
University of Nairobi, Nairobi, 189
University of Natal, Durban, 246
University of Nebraska, Lincoln, 427
University of Nebraska, Omaha, 427
University of Nevada, Las Vegas, 427
University of Nevada, Reno, 427
University of New Brunswick, Fredericton, 53
University of New England, Armidale, 11
University of New Hampshire, Durham, 428
University of New South Wales Computing Services Unit, Kensington, 11
University of New South Wales, Wollongong University College, Wollongong, 11
University of Newcastle, Newcastle, 11
University of Newcastle Upon Tyne, Newcastle, 326
University of North Carolina, Chapel Hill, 438-9
University of North Dakota, Grand Forks, 439
University of Northern Colorado, Greeley, 400

University of Notre Dame, Notre Dame, 410
University of Nottingham, Nottingham, 326
University of Oregon, Eugene, 444
University of Otago, Dunedin, 218
University of Ottawa, Computing Centre, Ottawa, 53
University of Ottawa, Linguistics Documentation Centre, Ottawa, 53
University of Oxford, Oxford, 326
University of Pennsylvania Computer Center, Philadelphia, 449
University of Pennsylvania Moore School of Electrical Engineering, Philadelphia, 449
University of Pittsburgh Computer Center, Pittsburgh, 450
University of Pittsburgh Information Science Dept., Pittsburgh, 450
University of Pittsburgh Media Research and Communications Center, Pittsburgh, 450
University of Port Elizabeth, Port Elizabeth, 246
University of Pretoria, Pretoria, 246
University of Puerto Rico, Puerto Rico, 241-2
University of Queensland, Brisbane, 11-12
University of Reading Computer Unit, Reading, 326-7
University of Reading Dept. of Applied Physical Sciences, Reading, 327
University of Redlands, Redlands, 398
University of Rhodesia, Salisbury, 242
University of Rochester, Rochester, 437-8
University of St. Andrews, St. Andrews, 327
University of St Thomas, Houston, 456
University of Salford, Salford, 327
University of Santa Clara, Santa Clara, 398
University of Santo Tomas, Manila, 235
University of Saskatchewan, Computation Centre, Saskatoon, 54
University of Saskatchewan, Computer Centre, Regina, 53-4
University of Science and Technology, Ashanti, 142
University of Scranton, Scranton, 450
University of Sheffield, Sheffield, 327
University of South Africa, Pretoria, 246
University of South Carolina, Columbia, 451
University of South Dakota, Vermillion, 452
University of South Florida, Tampa, 403-4
University of Southampton, Southampton, 327-8
University of Southern Mississippi, Hattiesburg, 423
University of Southwestern Louisiana, Lafayette, 414

University of Sri Lanka, Colombok, 258
University of Stellenbosch, Stellenbosch, 247
University of Strathclyde, Glasgow, 328
University of Surrey, Guildford, 328
University of Sydney, Basser Computing Centre, Sydney, 12
University of Sydney, School of Physics, Sydney, 12
University of Tampa, Tampa, 404
University of Tennessee, Chattanooga, 453
University of Tennessee, Knoxville, 453-4
University of Texas, Arlington, 456-7
University of Texas, Austin, 457
University of Texas, El Paso, 457
University of the Orange Free State, Bloemfontein, 347
University of the Panjab, Lahore, 232
University of the West Indies, Kingston, 182
University of the West Indies, Trinidad, 296
University of the Witwatersrand, Johannesburg, 247
University of Toledo, Toledo, 442
University of Tokyo, Tokyo, 185
University of Toronto, Toronto, 54
University of Utah, Salt Lake City, 458
University of Vermont, Burlington, 459
University of Virginia, Charlottesville, 460
University of Wales, Cardiff, 328
University of Warwick, Coventry, 328-9
University of Washington, Seattle, 462
University of Waterloo, Waterloo, 54
University of Western Australia, Nedlands, 12
University of Western Ontario, Althouse College of Education, London, 55
University of Western Ontario, London, 54-5
University of Windsor, Windsor, 55
University of Wisconsin Center, Sheboygan, 466
University of Wisconsin, Eauclaire, 464
University of Wisconsin, Green Bay, 464-5
University of Wisconsin, Madison, 465
University of Wisconsin, Milwaukee, 465
University of Wisconsin, Oshkosh, 465
University of Wisconsin, Stevens Point, 465-6
University of Wisconsin, Whitewater, 466
University of Wyoming, Laramie, 466
University of Yaoundé, Yaoundé, 46
University of York, York, 329
Univerza v Ljubljani, Ljubljana, 570-71

Univerzitet u Beogradu, Belgrade, 571
Univerzitet Kiril i Metódij vo Skoplje, Skopje, 571
Univest S.A., Administração e Participações, São Paulo, 45-6
Uniwersytet Im Adama Mickiewicza w Poznaniu, Poznań, 237
Uniwersytet Marii Curie-Skodowskiej, Lublin, 237
Uniwersytet Slaski, Katowice, 237
Uniwersytet Warszawski, Warszawa, 237
Uniwersytet Wrocawski, Wrocaw, 238
Unternehmensberatung Dr. Parisini, Vienna, 22-3
Upper Clyde Shipbulders Ltd, Glasgow, 380
Urwick, Currie & Partners Ltd, Toronto, 59
Urwick Dynamics Ltd, London, 352
Urwick International, Brussels, 29
Urwick International (Pty) Ltd, Johannesburg, 249-50
Urwick International Pty Ltd, Sydney, 15
Utah State University of Agriculture and Applied Science, Logan, 458-9

V.I.P. Systems, Washington, 517
Valley Computer Center, Panorama City, 512
Robert J. Van Der Graaff Laboratorium, Utrecht, 200
Vanderbilt University, Nashville, 454
Värnpliktsverket, Solna, 263-4
Varvsindunstrins Datacentral AB, Göteborg, 264
Verein Deutscher Eisenhüttenleute/ Betriebsforschungs-institut, Düsseldorf, 127
Vereniging voor Centrale Electronische Administratie, Apeldoorn, 217
Vereinigte Osterreichische Eisen- und Stahlwerke AG, Linz, 24
Verwaltungsrechenzentrum, AG, St Gallen, 294
Vestdata A/S, Bergen, 231
Vestjydsk Data Bureau, Esbjerg, 84
Vestjydsk EDB-Center, Esbjerg, 84-5
Viatron Programming Inc, Burlington, 486
Victoria University of Manchester, Administrative Computer Unit, Manchester, 329
Victoria University of Manchester Dept. of Computer Science, Manchester, 329
Victoria University of Manchester Dept. of Psychology, Manchester, 329-30
Victoria University of Manchester, Regional Computer Centre, Manchester, 330
Victoria University of Wellington, Wellington, 218
André Vidal & Associés, Paris, 108
Vierhand Reclamediensten N.V., Haarlem, 217
Villanova University, Villanova, 451

Virginia Commonwealth University, Richmond, 460
Virginia Polytechnic Institute and State University, Blacksburg, 460-61
Virginia State College, Petersburg, 461
Viša Ekonomska Škola Varaždin, Varaždin, 570
Višja Tehniška Sola Maribor, Maribor, 570
Vive-Stans AB, Stockholm, 281
Volán Tröszet Elektronika, Budapest, 147
'Volmac' Automation Centre B.V., Rotterdam, 217
Voralberger Rechenzentrum GmbH, Dornbirn, 24
Vrij Hoger Technisch Instituut (VHTI), Kortrijk, 26
Vrije Universiteit te Amsterdam, Amsterdam, 202
Vysoká Škola Ekonomická, Prague, 74
Vyzkumný Ústav Matematických Stroju, Prague, 75

W. Data AB, Huskvarna, 281
Richard M. Walsh Associates, Scranton, 499
Wandsworth Technical College, London, 330
Wang Laboratories Inc, Tewksbury, 534
Warley College of Technology, Warley, 330
Waseda University, Tokyo, 185
Washington and Lee University, Lexington, 461
Washington State University, Pullman, 462
Washington University, St Louis, 426
Watertown Computer Service Inc, Watertown, 552
Watford College of Technology, Watford, 330-31
Wates Computer Services Ltd, London, 380
Wayne State University, Detroit, 419-20
Weber State College, Ogden, 459
Weizmann Institute of Science, Rehovot, 167
Welby Computer Services Ltd, Ottawa, 64
Werkwinkel, Lekkerkerk, 208
Werner Associates Inc, Brussels, 30
Werner Associates Inc, New York, 495
Wesleyan University, Middletown, 401
Wessex Computer Services Ltd, Waterlooville, 380-81
West African Examinations Council, Accra, 143
West Coast Schools, Los Angeles, 398
West Coast University, Los Angeles, 398
West Florida Data Processing Center Inc, Panama City, 520

West London College, London, 331
West Pakistan University of Engineering and Technology, Lahore, 232
West Sussex County Council, Chichester, 335-6
West Texas State University, Canyon, 457-8
West Virginia University, Keyser, 463-4
West Virginia University, Morgantown, 463
Westat Inc, Rockville, 529-30
Westchester Community College, Valhalla, 438
Western Australia Institute of Technology, South Bentley, 12-13
Western Business University, Portland, 390
Western Illinois University, Macomb, 408
Western Programming Services, Frome, 381
Western Railway, Bombay, 154
Western Washington State College, Bellingham, 462-3
Westfälische Wilhelms-Universität, Münster, 124
Westfield College University of London, London, 331
Westinghouse Management Systems S.A., Paris, 108
Whitehead Consulting Group, London, 352-3
Wichita State University, Wichita, 412-13
Widnes and Runcorn College of Further Education, Widnes, 331
Wilford Computer Group Ltd, Manchester, 381
Wingate Computing Center, Attleboro, 534
Wingate Computing Center, Hartford, 515
Winona State College, Winona, 422
Winstone Ltd, Auckland, 221
Wittenberg University, Springfield, 443
Wolf and Company, Los Angeles, 512
Wolf Research and Development Corporation, Riverdale, 475
Woodall-Duckham Computing Services Ltd, Hove, 381
Woods Gordon & Co, Vancouver, 59
Marvin M. Woofsey, Silver Spring, 483
Worcester Polytechnic Institute, Worcester, 417-8
Worldwide Computer Services Inc, Hartsdale, 495-6
Wright, Stephenson and Co Ltd, Wellington, 221
Wyle Laboratories, Huntsville, 475-6
Wyzsza Szkoa Ekonomiczna, Wrocaw, 238

Xavier University of Louisiana, New Orleans, 414
Xiox International Inc, Miami, 520

Index of Institutions

Yael Management Automation Co, Tel-Aviv, 172
Yale University, New Haven, 401
York University, Downsview, 55
Youngstown State University, Youngstown, 443

ZTP Beograd, Belgrade, 574
Zakad Elektronicznej Techniki Obliczeniowej, Szczecin, 236
Zavod za Ekonomiju, Zagreb, 574
Zavod za Ekonomske Eksprtize, Belgrade, 574

Zéro Un Informatique, Paris, 116
1900 Management Controls Ltd, London, 353
1900 Programming Ltd, London, 353

INDEX OF COMPUTER INSTALLATIONS

A D-4/IBM 1800
Technische Hogeschool te Delft, Delft, 201

AD-4/PDP-11
Technische Hogeschool te Delft, Delft, 201

ASI 6050
Iowa State University of Science and Technology, Ames, 410-11

Adage AGT 10
Point Park College, Pittsburgh, 448

Adage AGT 30
New York University, Dept. of Electrical Engineering and Computer Science, Bronx, 434
Pennsylvania State University, Computation Center, University Park, 447-8

Arcturus 18C
Westfield College, University of London, London, 331

BESM 6
Academy of Sciences of the U.S.S.R., Novosibirsk, 299

Bull General Electric Datanet 30
Call-a-Computer, Melville, 544

Bull General Electric Gamma 10
Bull General Electric S.A., Madrid, 255
Bull General Electric (Nederland) N.V., Amersfoort, Groningen, The Hague, Tilburg, 209
Compagnie Amienoise de Mécanographie, Amiens, 110
Coranord, Lille, 111
Coranord, Paris, 111
AB Data-Service, Danderyd, 273-4
Deutsche Utimaco Gmbh, Frankfurt-am-Main, 135
Drammensdragets Datasentral, Hønefoss, 229
Bull General Electric do Brasil S.A., Santo André, 42-3
Honeywell Bull do Brasil, S.A., São Paulo, 43
Mitsubishi Office Machinery Co. Ltd, Tokyo, 187-8
Nederlandse Accountants-Maatschap, Rotterdam, 214
A/S Norsk Hullkort Service, Oslo, 231
Organisation Maurice Bressy, Rhône, 106
Samkontor AB, Malmö, 278
Service Informatique Honeywell-Bull, Neuilly-sur-Seine, 113-4
Servicios Informatica Honeywell Bull, Mexico, 197
Société d'Exploitation d'Utimaco SA et Compatibilités-Statistiques, Genève, 293
Svenska Elektroniska Daya AB, Sundsvall, 280

Bull General Electric Gamma 30
Bernische Datenverarbeitung AG, Berne, 287-8
Bull General Electric (Nederland) N.V., Amsterdam, 209
Compatabilité Statistique Informatic, Paris, 111
Coranord, Lille, 111
Energoingvest, Sarajevo, 572-3
Halmstad Dataservice AB, Halmstad, 275
Honeywell Bull AB, Stockholm, 275
Larc, Zutphen, 213
Office Central de la Mécanographie, Abidjan, 182
Service Informatique Honeywell Bull, Neuilly-sur-Seine, 113-4
Sparbankernas Datacentraler AB, Linköping, 279
Sparekassernes Datacentraler, Copenhagen, 84

Bull General Electric GE 55
Bull General Electric, Buenos Aires, 5
Mitsubishi Office Machinery Co Ltd, Tokyo, 187-8
Rekencentrum "Informatron" N.V, Amsterdam, 215

Bull General Electric GE 58
Consultdata Nederland N.V., Amsterdam, 206

Bull General Electric GE 100
Service Informatique Honeywell Bull, Neuilly-sur-Seine, 113-4

Bull General Electric GE 115
Bairesco, Buenos Aires, 5
Canadian General Electric Co. Ltd, Toronto, 59-60
Compania Cuyana de Computos, Mendoza, 4
Consultmar, Mar del Plata, 4-5
Elgave, Budapest, 148-9
Ipargazdaszgi, Szervezesi es Számitastechnikai Intezet, Budapest, 147
Matrix Corporation, El Segundo, 549
Mitsubishi Office Machinery Co Ltd, Tokyo, 187-8
Oslo Datasenter A/S, Oslo, 231
Oy Nokia AB, Helsinki, 90
Société d'Exploitation D'Utimaco SA et Compatibilités-Statistiques, Genève, 293
Universidad Católica de Córdoba, Córdoba, 2

Bull General Electric GE 120
Bull General Electric (Nederland) N.V., Amersfoort, 209
Bull General Electric (Nederland) N.V., The Hague, 209
Coranord, Paris, 111
Direction Centrale de la Statistique, Beirut, 191
Honeywell Bull, Brussels, 30-31
Honeywell Bull do Brasil S.A., São Paulo, 43
Orega AG, Zürich, 292
Svenska Elektroniska Data AB, Sundsvall, 280

Bull General Electric GE 130
Mitsubishi Office Machinery Co Ltd, Tokyo, 187-8

Bull General Electric GE 150
Viša Ekonomska Škola Varaždin, Varaždin, 570

Bull General Electric GE 225
Cie FSE Thomson Houston-Hotchkiss Brandt, Le Plessis Robinson, 103
Production Systems Inc, Waltham, 532-3
Tennessee Valley Authority, Chattanooga, 469
University of Queensland, Brisbane, 11-12

Bull General Electric GE 235
Call-a-Computer, Melville, 544
Graphic Controls Corporation, Buffalo, 547
OK Data, Copenhagen, 82

Bull General Electric GE 265
Bull General Electric (Schweiz), Zürich, 288
Canadian General Electric Co Ltd, Toronto, 59-60
General Electric Company, Bethseda 265
Honeywell Bull, Brussels, 30-31
Honeywell Bull AG, Vienna, 23

Index of Computer Installations

Honeywell Information Systems
  Ltd, Brentford, 367
Honeywell Information Systems
  Italia, Milano, 179
Honeywell Pty Ltd, Melbourne, 19
Honeywell Pty Ltd, Sydney, 19
National Information Research
  Institute, Santa Monica, 473
United Computing Systems Inc,
  Kansas City, 538

Bull General Electric GE 400
Honeywell Bull do Brasil S.A.,
  São Paulo, 43
Service Informatique Honeywell
  Bull, Neuilly-sur-Seine, 113-4

Bull General Electric GE 415
AC Service GmbH, Offenbach,
  132
AC-Service Gesellschaft für Auto-
  matische Datenverarbeitung
  mbH, Frankfurt am Main,
  132
AC-Service Gesellschaft für
  Automatische Datenverarbeitung
  mbH, Munich, 132
Automation Centre, S.p.A.,
  Milan, 179
Automation Centre International,
  Wettingen, 287
Central Computing Inc, Wichita,
  526
Centro S.p.A., Verona, 179
Data-Tjeneste A/S, Oslo, 229
Datacard Computer Services Pty
  Ltd, Sydney, 18
First National Bank of Pennsyl-
  vania, Erie, 560
General Electric do Brasil S.A.,
  Santo André, 42-3
Industrial National Bank of
  Rhode Island, Providence, 562-3
Information Sciences Inc., Warwick,
  563
Institut National de Statistique,
  Brussels, 27
Nederlandse Accountants-Maatschap,
  Rotterdam, 214
A/S Norsk Hullkort Service, Oslo,
  231
Oy Nokia AB, Helsinki, 90
Serescodata S.A., Sevilla, 257-8
A/S Trønder-Data, Trondheim, 231
Union College, Schenectady, 437
University of Strathclyde, Glasgow,
  328
UCC-Automation Centre S.A.,
  Brussels, 32
Vestdata A/S, Bergen, 231

Bull General Electric GE 420
Control Data Corporation,
  Washington, 516
Rapidata Inc, Fairfield, 542

Bull General Electric GE 425
Canadian General Electric Co.
  Ltd, Toronto, 59-60
AB Data-Service, Göteborg,
  273-4

Fellesdata/SIS, Oslo, 230
Institut National de Statistique,
  Brussels, 27
Lantbruksdata, Eskilstuna, 276-7
Oy Nokia AB, Helsinki, 90
Universidad del Salvador, Buenos
  Aires, 3

Bull General Electric GE 427
Coranord, Lille, 111

Bull General Electric GE 430
Compu-Time Inc, Fort Lauderdale,
  518
Megasystems Inc, Bala-Cynwyd,
  561
Systemshare Ltd, Edinburgh, 379

Bull General Electric GE 435
Honeywell Bull do Brasil S.A.,
  São Paulo, 43

Bull General Electric GE 615
OY Nokia AB, Helsinki, 90

Bull General Electric GE 625
Canadian General Electric Co Ltd,
  Toronto, 59-60
Control Data Corporation, Washing-
  ton, 516

Bull General Electric GE 635
Dartmouth College, Hanover, 428
General Electric Company, Bethesda,
  529
Honeywell Information Systems
  Ltd., Brentford, 367
Industridata AB, Solna, 276
Matrix Corporation, El Segundo,
  549
University of Kansas, Lawrence,
  412

Bull General Electric GE 645
Maasachusetts Institute of Tech-
  nology, Information Processing
  Center, Cambridge, 417

Bull General Electric GE 6000
Service Informatique Honeywell
  Bull, Neuilly-sur-Seine, 113-4

Burroughs
Data Sciences International Ltd,
  Leeds, 361-2

Burroughs B200
Centro Electrónico Walmap S.A.,
  Rio de Janeiro, 41
Services Electrónicos de Contabilid-
  ade Ltda, São Paulo, 45

Burroughs B 260
Systems Data Processing Company,
  Sacramento, 510

Burroughs B263
Statistical Reporting and
  Tabulating Ltd, Toronto, 64

Burroughs B 283
Leo Computer Bureaux (Pty) Ltd.,
  Johannesburg, 251-2
MSADP Inc, Norristown, 561

Burroughs B 300
Computer Servicenters Inc, Green-
  boro, 552-3
Data Corporation of America,
  Winter Haven, 518
Data Systems Inc, Minneapolis,
  536
Management Information Center,
  Greenville, 563
Northern Indiana Financial Service
  Corporation, Marion, 525
Northwest Management Services
  Inc, Seattle, 566-7

Burroughs B 344
Kaman Sciences Corporation,
  Colorado Springs, 513

Burroughs B 383
Computer Bureau Services (Cardiff)
  Ltd, Cardiff, 358
Computerised Business Systems
  Ltd, Cardiff, 360
Electronic Data Processing Ltd,
  Sheffield, 364-5
Midas Ltd, London, 373-4

Burroughs B500
Análisis y Sistematización Electrónica
  Ltda, Bogotá, 72
Burroughs Ltd, Sydney & Melbourne,
  16
Computer Dimensions Inc., Dallas,
  564
Estudos e Processamentos Ltda, Rio
  de Janeiro, 42
Fletcher Computer Services Ltd,
  Birmingham, 365
Helm Data Processing Inc, Arcata,
  508
National Westminster Bank Ltd,
  Warrington, 376
Procomputos Ltda, Barranquilla, 72
Schema Processamento de Dados
  Comércio e Importaçao Ltda, São
  Paulo, 45
Servimec S.A., São Paulo, 45
Setak Computing Services Corpora-
  tion Ltd, Toronto, 63
Södertalje Data AB, Nacka, 279
Universidade Federal de Pernambuco,
  Pernambuco, 34-5
West Florida Data Processing Center
  Inc, Panama City, 520

Burroughs B1726
Monterey Peninsula College,
  Monterey, 393
Služba Društvenog Knjigovodstva
  Jugoslavije, Belgrade, 572

605

Burroughs B2000
Universidade Federal Rural de Pernambuco, Recife, 36

Burroughs B 2500
Diversified Computer Applications, Palo Alto, 507
Electronic Data Systems Ltd, Auckland, 220
Johnston Terminals Ltd, Vancouver, 62-3
Värnpliktsverket, Solna, 263-4

Burroughs B 3500
Anacomp Inc, Indianapolis, 524
Banco Cafetero, Bogotá, 70
Burroughs Electrônica Ltda, Rio de Janeiro, 40
Burroughs AB, Stockholm, 272
Burroughs Ltd, Sydney, Melbourne and Adelaide, 16
CBC Byggeadministration, Kokkedal, 78
Centro de Información y Cómputo, S.A., Cali, 72
Centro Electrônico Walmap S.A., Rio de Janeiro, 41
Companhia Estadual de Águas da Guanabara, Rio de Janeiro, 38
Computer Center Inc. of Miami, Miami, 517
Computer Management Group Ltd, Croydon, 359
Crefidata S.A., Pôrto Alegre, 42
Datron AG für Datenverarbeitung und Organisation, St. Gallen, 285
Diversified Computer Applications, Palo Alto, 507
Electronic Data Processing Ltd, Sheffield, 364-5
Electronic Processors Inc, Birmingham, 502
Empresa Nacional de Computación e Informatica Ltda, Santiago, 66
Executive Data Systems, Cedar Rapids, 526
Hacettepe Universitesi, Ankara, 297
Instituto de Pesquisas Espaciais, São José dos Campos, 39
International Computer Services S.A., Bogotá, 71-2
Kalamazoo Computer Centre, Birmingham, 370
Management Computer Services South Africa (Pty) Ltd, Marshalltown, 252
Midland National Bank, Milwaukee, 567
National Westminster Bank Ltd, Manchester, 376
Processamento Electrônico Ltda, Pôrto Alegre, 44
Randax EDP Ltd, London, 376
Rochester Computer Service Inc, Rochester, 550-51
Santa Ana College, Santa Ana, 395
Services Electrônicos de Contabilidade Ltda, São Paulo, 45
State University of New York, Agricultural and Technical College, Alfred, 436
State University of New York, College of Arts and Sciences, Plattsburgh, 436
SD Stockholms Datajänst AB, Stockholm, 270
United Data Centers Inc, Greenwich, 515
United Data Centres Pty Ltd, Sydney, 20
Universidade de São Paulo. Centro de Computacão Electrônica, São Paulo, 33
Värnpliktsverket, Solna, 263-4

Burroughs B 3600
University of Wisconsin, Eauclaire, 464

Burroughs B 3700
AB Data-Service, Göteborg, 274
AB Data-Service, Norrköping, 274
Oy Paragon AB, Helsinki, 90-91

Burroughs B 4000
Plymouth Computer Systems International Ltd., London, 350
Salt City Business College, Hutchinson, 389

Burroughs B 4294
Decca Radar Canada (1967) Ltd., Toronto, 57

Burroughs B 4700
AB Data-Service, Malmö, 274
AB Data-Service, Stockholm, 274
K. Lund Simonsen A/S, Vaerløse, 83

Burroughs B 4704
'Badal' Computer and Management Services Ltd, Tel Aviv, 169

Burroughs B 5500
EBS Management Consultants Inc, New York, 491
Eli Computer Systems Inc, East Paterson, 540
Georgia Institute of Technology, Atlanta, 404
Monash University, Clayton, 9
National Data Processing Service, London, 375-6
Realtime Systems Inc, New York, 494
Scientific Software Corporation, Englewood, 513
Setak Computing Services Corporation Ltd, Toronto, 63
University of Detroit, Detroit, 419
University of Washington, Seattle, 462
University of Wisconsin, Madison, 465
Welby Computer Services Ltd, Toronto, 64

Burroughs B 5700
John Carroll University, University Heights, 440

Remote Computing Corporation, Los Angeles, 509
Christian Rovsing, Herlev, 83
University of Natal, Durban, 246

Burroughs B 6700
Atomenergikommissionens Forsøgsanlaeg Risø, Risø, 77
Canberra College of Advanced Education, Canberra, 7
Companhia de Processamento de Dados do Estado do Rio Grande do Sul, Pôrto Alegre, 37
Helsingin Yliopisto, Computing Centre, Helsinki, 86-7
Instituto de Pesquisas Espaciais, São José dos Campos, 39
Oy Paragon Ab, Helsinki, 90-91
Queens University at Kingston, Kingston, 50
Technische Hogeschool Eindhoven, Eindhoven, 201
Universidad Nacional Autonoma de Mexico, Mexico, 195
University of Auckland, Auckland, 217
University of California, Davis, 396
University of California, San Diego, 397
University of Denver, Denver, 399-400
University of Otago, Dunedin, 218
Utah State University of Agriculture and Applied Science, Logan, 458-9

Burroughs B 6718
University of Canterbury, Christchurch, 218

CAB 500
Conservatoire National des Arts et Métiers, Paris, 100
Université de Bescançon, Bescançon, 96-7

CAE 90/40
Compagnie Internationale pour l'Informatique, Louveciennes, 110-111

CAE 510
Compagnie Internationale pour l'Informatique, Louveciennes, 110-111

CB 100
Condon Corporation, Bedford, 530

CCS 2100
Consolidated Computer Services Ltd, Toronto, 61

CDC range
Control Data Corporation, Minneapolis 535-6

Index of Computer Installations

CDC Cyber 72
Franlab Informatique, Rueil Malmaison, 111
Institut "Jozef Stefan", Ljubljana, 569
Institute TNO for Mathematics Information Processing and Statistics, The Hague, 203
Kaman Sciences Corporation, Colorado Springs, 513
Korea Institute of Science and Technology, Seoul, 190
Northeastern University, Boston, 417
Southern Methodist University, Dallas, 455
Univerza v Ljubljani, Ljubljana, 570-71

CDC Cyber 72/14
Chung Shan Institute of Science and Technology, Lungtan, 67

CDC Cyber 73
South Australian Public Service ADP Centre, Adelaide, 14
Stichting Academisch Rekencentrum, Amsterdam, 200-01
University of Melbourne, Melbourne, 10

CDC Cyber 74
Documentations Automatiques des Textes Juridiques de l'Université de Montréal, Montreal, 48
Reneanlegget Blindern-Kjeller, Kjeller, 227
Rijksuniversiteit te Groningen, Groningen, 199
Université de Montréal, Montreal, 51

CDC Cyber 76
Franlab Informatique, Rueil Malmaison, 111

CDC Cyber 7326
Ecole Polytechnique Fédérale de Lausanne, Lausanne, 281-2
Université de Lausanne, Lausanne, 283

CDC G 15
Carnegie-Mellon University, Pittsburgh, 445
Rose-Hulman Institute of Technology, Terre Haute, 409

CDC G 20
Università di Napoli, Napoli, 173-4

CDC G 21
Carnegie-Mellon University, Pittsburgh, 445

CDC 160
Centre Cantonal d'Informatique, Geneva, 288
Computer Applications Inc, New York, 489
Control Data Corporation, Palo Alto, 506-7
Eidgenössische Technische Hochschule, Zürich, 282
Frankel Engineering Laboratories, Reading, 472
General Applied Science Lab. Inc., New York, 472
Measurement Research Center, Iowa City, 473
Tata Institute of Fundamental Research, Bombay, 157

CDC 200
Ethnikon Metsoion Polytechneion Athinai, Athens, 144

CDC 915
McDonnell Automation Company, St Louis, 537-8

CDC 1604
Eidgenössische Technische Hochschule, Zürich, 282
A/S Regnecentralen, Copenhagen, 82-3
Southern Methodist University, 455
University of Wisconsin, Madison, 465

CDC 1700
Hydra Computer Corporation, Raleigh 553
Imperial College of Science and Technology, Computer Centre, London, 307
Institut za Nuklearne Nauke 'Boris Kidrič, Belgrade, 573
King's College, University of London, London, 308
Korea Institute of Science and Technology, Seoul, 190
Kungliga Tekniska Högskolan, Department of Speech Communication, Stockholm, 260
Litton Industries, Canoga Park, 473
McDonnell Automation Company, St Louis, 537-8
Nordostschweiz Kraftwerke AG, Baden, 283-4
Rheinisch-Westfälische Technische Hochschule, Aachen, 119
Rijksuniversiteit te Utrecht, Department of Medical and Physiological Physics, Utrecht, 200
Robert J. van Der Graaff Laboratorium, Utrecht, 200
Royal Holloway College, University of London, Englefield Green, 315
Università di Padova, Padova, 174
Universität Ulm, Ulm-Wiblingen, 124
Université de Montréal, Montreal, 51
University of Manitoba, Faculty of Medicine, Winnipeg, 52-3
University of Sydney, School of Physics, Sydney, 12

CDC 2600
Université de Paris, VI, Paris, 98

CDC 3100
Control Data Institute, Pittsburgh, 385
Interdata AG Zürich, Zürich, 291
Lowell Technological Institute, Lowell, 416-7
Metron Datenverarbeitung AG, Brugg, 286
Nordostschweiz Kraftwerke AG, Baden, 283-4
Operations Research Inc, Silver Spring, 529
University of Texas, El Paso, 457

CDC 3150
California State University, Fullerton, 392
Centro Nacional de Cálculo, Mexico City, 194
Control Data Computer Training School, New York, 384
Control Data Institute, Burlington, 384
Control Data Institute, Willowdale, 46-7
National Taiwan University, Taipei, 67

CDC 3170
California State University, Northridge, 392
Interdata AG Zürich, Zürich, 291
Universitetet i Oslo, Student Administration, Oslo, 225

CDC 3200
Commonwealth Scientific and Industrial Research Organisation, Melbourne, Sydney and Adelaide, 13
Contract Computing Ltd, Croydon, 343
Contract Computing Ltd, Thornton Heath, 360
Duquesne University, Pittsburgh, 446
Interstate Computer Services, Brooklyn, 548
Korea Computer Centre, Seoul, 190
Landbouwhogeschool te Wageningen, Wageningen, 199
Monash University, Clayton, 8-9
Norwegian Water Resources and Electricity Board, Oslo, 225-6
Petty Geophysical Engineering, San Antonio, 474
Prakla GmbH, Hannover, 141
S.I.A. Ltd, London, 378
South Australian Public Service ADP Centre, Adelaide, 14

CDC 3300
Adelphi University, Garden City, 431
Central Information Processing Corporation, Baltimore, 527
Computation Research and Development, London, 358

Control Data Australia Pty Ltd, Melbourne, 17-18
Control Data GmbH, Frankfurt-am-Main, 134
Control Data Italia, S.p.A., Genoa, 179
Control Data Italia S.p.A., Milan, 179
Control Data Italia S.p.A., Rome, 179
Eberhard-Karls-Universität, Tübingen, 118
Ethnikon Kai Kapodistriakon Panepistimion Athinon, Athens, 143-4
Friedrich-Alexander-Universität, Erlangen-Nürnberg, Erlangen, 118
Instituto Tecnológico y de Estudios Superiores de Monterrey, Monterrey, 194-5
Johannes-Gutenberg-Universität, Mainz, 119
Lamar State College of Technology, Beaumont, 454
Nederlands Scheepsbouwkundig Proefstation, Wageningen, 204
Oregon State University, Corvallis, 444
Prakla GmbH, Hannover, 141
Secretaria de Recursos Hidraulicos, Mexico, 196
United Nations Development Programme, Bratislava, 74-5
Universität des Saarlandes, Saarbrücken, 123
Universitetet i Oslo, Oslo, 224-5
Wyle Laboratories, Huntsville, 475-6

CDC 3500
Central Information Processing Corporation, Baltimore, 527
The Software House (Pty) Ltd, Pretoria, 249

CDC 3600
Commonwealth Scientific and Industrial Research Organisation, Canberra, 13
Control Data Canada Ltd, Ottawa, 61
Institut Blaise Pascal, Paris, 102
Institut za Nuklearne Nauke 'Boris Kidrič', Belgrade, 573
Michigan State University, East Lansing, 418-9
SIA International, Paris, 114
Tata Institute of Fundamental Research, Bombay, 157
Universitet i Uppsala, Uppsala, 262
University of California, San Diego, 397
University of Massachusetts, Amherst, 417
University of Wisconsin, Madison, 465

CDC 3800
Centre Cantonal d'Informatique, Geneva, 288

CDC 6000
United Computing Systems Inc, Kansas City, 538

CDC 6200
Sir George Williams University, Montreal, 50-51
Università degli Studi di Trieste, Trieste, 173

CDC 6400
Århus Universitet, Århus, 75
Battelle Memorial Institute, Colombus, 470
CERN, Genève, 284
Colorado State University, Fort Collins, 399
Dalhousie University, Halifax, 48
Dâneshgâhé Sanati Arya-Mehr, Teheran, 161
Eidgenössische Technische Hochschule, Zürich, 282
General Research Corporation, Santa Barbara, 508
Imperial College of Science and Technology, Computer Centre, London, 307
Imperial College of Science and Technology, Dept of Computing and Control, London, 307-8
Instituto Mexicano del Seguro Social, Mexico, 196
Internationale Atomreaktorbau, Köln, 127
Lehigh University, Bethlehem, 447
McDonnell Automation Company, St Louis, 537-8
McMaster University, Hamilton, 49
Northwestern University, Evanston, 407
Rheinisch-Westfälisch Technische Hochschule, Aachen, 119
Smithsonian Astrophysical Observatory, Cambridge, 475
State University of New York, Buffalo, 436
Technische Universität Berlin, Recheninstitut, Berlin, 120
Temple University, Philadelphia, 449
University of Adelaide, Adelaide, 10
University of Arizona, Tucson, 391
University of California Computer Centre, Berkeley, 395
University of Colorado, Boulder, 399
University of London Computer Centre, London, 325-6
University of Minnesota, Minneapolis, 421
University of Texas, Austin, 457
University of Virginia, Charlottesville, 460
University of Washington, Seattle, 462

CDC 6500
CERN, Genève, 284
Eidgenössische Technische Hochschule, Zürich, 282
Florida State University, Tallahassee, 403

London University Computing Services Ltd, London, 371
McDonnell Automation Company, St Louis, 537-8
Michigan State University, East Lansing, 418-9
Purdue University, West Lafayette, 409
Symbionics Systems Ltd, Winnipeg, 64
Technische Universität Berlin, West Berlin, 120

CDC 6600
Alpha Computer Service Corporation, New York, 543
CERN, Genève, 284
Control Data Australia Pty Ltd, Sydney, 17-18
Control Data Canada Ltd, Ottawa, 61
Control Data GmbH, Frankfurt-am-Main, 134
Control Data Holland N.V., Rijswijk, 211
Control Data Sweden AB, Stockholm, 272-3
Ha-Universita Ha-Ivrit Bi-Jerushalayim, Jerusalem, 165
Indiana University, Bloomington, 409
Lawrence Berkeley Laboratory, Berkeley, 467
NUS Corporation, Dunedin, 481
National Center for Atmospheric Research, Boulder, 381-2
New York University Courant Institute of Mathematical Sciences, New York, 434
SIA International, Paris, 114
S.I.A. Ltd, London, 378
Universität Stuttgart, Stuttgart, 124
Universitat Tel-Aviv, Tel-Aviv, 165
University of London Computer Centre, London, 325-6
University of Minnesota, Minneapolis, 421
University of Texas, Austin, 457

CDC 6613
Control Data Corporation, Palo Alto, 506-7

CDC 7600
CERN, Genève, 284
Lawrence Berkeley Laboratory, Berkeley, 467
National Center for Atmospheric Research, Boulder, 381-2
University of London Computer Centre, London, 325-6
Victoria University of Manchester, Regional Computer Centre, Manchester, 330

CDC 8090
Manhattan College, Bronx, 433

Index of Computer Installations

CDC 8092
American Key Punch, Omaha, 538
Control Data GmbH, Frankfurt-am-Main, 134

CII Iris 10
Institut Universitaire de Technologie, Villeurbanne, 94

CII Iris 50
Centre d'Etudes Pratiques d'Informatique et d'Automatique, Le Chesnay, 92
Institut de Recherche d'Informatique et d'Automatique, Le Chesnay, 102
Ministère de l'Économie et des Finances, Libreville, 116
National Institute for Scientific and Technical Information and Documentation, Bucharest, 243
Société d'Applications et de Mèthodes Mécanographiques, Paris, 115

CII 9010
Collège de France, Paris, 95
Technische Universität München, Institut für Angewandte Mathematik, München, 122

CII 9040
Elektronsko-Nunerički Centar, Zagreb, 572
Technische Universität Berlin, Institut für Informationsverabteilung, Berlin, 120

CII 9080
Centre d'Études Pratiques d'Informatique et d'Automatique, Le Chesnay, 92
Collège de France, Paris, 95
Institut de Recherche d'Informatique et d'Automatique, Le Chesnay, 102

CII 10020
Centre Expérimental Eurocontrol, Brétigny, 101
Compagnie Internationale pour l'Informatique, Louceciennes, 110-111
Universita degli Studi di Milano, Milano, 173

CII 10070
Centre d'Études Pratiques d'Informatique et d'Automatique, Le Chesnay, 92
Centre Interuniversitaire de Calcul de Grenoble, Grenoble, 94
Compagnie Internationale pour l'Informatique, Grenoble, 102
Compagnie Internationale pour l'Informatique, Louveciennes, 110-111
École Supéneure d'Électricité, Malakoff, 96

Institut de Recherche d'Informatique, et d'Automatique, Le Chesnay, 102
Université de Nancy I et de Nancy II, Nancy, 97-8
Université de Rennes, Rennes, 99

CTL Modular 1
Brunel University, Uxbridge, 303
Computer-Aided Design Centre, Cambridge, 332
Queen Elizabeth College, University of London, London, 315
University of Cambridge, Cambridge, 321
University of Durham, Department of Geology, Durham, 321
University of Glasgow, Computing Service, Glasgow, 323
University of Leeds, Computer-Based Learning Project, Leeds, 324
University of Liverpool, Computer Laboratory, Liverpool, 325
University of Liverpool, Department of Computational and Statistical Science, Liverpool, 325
University of Reading, Dept. of Applied Physical Sciences, Reading, 327
University of Warwick, Coventry, 328-9
Victoria University of Manchester, Dept. of Psychology, Manchester, 329
Westfield College, University of London, London, 331

CTL Satellite 1
University of York, York, 329

Codidac
Pontificia Universidad Javeriana, Bogotá, 68

Cope 45
AC Service GmbH, Offenbach, 132

DCC 116
Scientific Systems Services, Satellite Beach, 520

DCT 500
Opetusministerio, Helsinki, 89

DDP 116
British Ship Research Association, Wallsend, 337

DDP 516
McDonnell Automation Company, St Louis, 537-8
Tampereen Teknillinen Korkeakoulu, Tampere, 88
United States Computers Inc, Tacoma, 567

Universidade de São Paulo, Nuclear Physics Department, São Paulo, 33-4

DEC 11-45
University of Chicago Institute for Computer Research, Chicago, 408

Dacicc 1
Académia Republicii Socialiste România, Cluj, 244

Data General 1220
Chelsea Centre for Science Education, University of London, London, 304

Data General Nova
New South Wales Institute of Technology, Broadway, 9
Sistemas Analiticos S.A., San José, 73

Data General Nova 800
Sistemas Analiticos S.A., San José, 73
Systems, Science and Software, La Jolla, 475

Data General Nova 1200
Loyola Marymount University, Los Angeles, 393

Data General Nova 1210
Mohawk College of Applied Arts and Technology, Hamilton, 49

Data General Supernova
Bethany College, Bethany, 463
Mathematical Applications Group Inc, Elmsford, 548-9

Datacraft DC6024/5
Datacraft International, Brussels, 30

Datagraphix 4460
CMI Computer Micrographics Inc, Los Angeles, 506

Datasaab D21
Centrala Folkbokförings-Och Uppbordsnamnden, Stockholm, 262
Saab-Scania AB, Linköping, 278

Datassab D22
Centrala Folkbokförings-Och Uppbordsnamnden, Stockholm, 262
A/S Data Automasion, Oslo, 229
Ilmatieteen Iaitos, Helsinki, 89
Industridata AB, Solna, 276
RDB Databyrå, Stockholm, 278
SPS A/S, Copenhagen, 83
Saab-Scania AB, Linköping, 278

Statens Vägwerk, Stockholm, 259
Swedish Meteorological and Hydrological Institute, Stockholm, 265
Swedish Planning and Rationalization Institute of the Health and Social Services, 263

Datasaab D 220
Centrala Folkbokförings-Och Uppbordsnamnden, Stockholm, 262

Digico Micro 16
Comprite Ltd, Warminster, 357-8

Digico M16/P
Cranfield Institute of Technology, Cranfield, 305

Digital Equipment 112
Comprite Ltd, Warminster, 357-8

Digital Equipment 338
Univeristy of Pennsylvania Moore School of Electrical Engineering, Philadelphia, 449

Digital Equipment System 10
James Cook University of North Queensland, Townsville, 8
State University of New York, Stony Brook, 436
University of Mississippi, Lafayette County, 423

EAI Hybrid
Electronic Associates Inc, El Segundo, 507

EAI Pacer 600
Deutsche Forschungs und Versuchanstalt für Luft und Raumfahrt, Braunschweig, 126

EAI Tr 20
West Coast University, Los Angeles, 398

EAI 48
Electronic Associates Ltd, Burgess Hill, 364

EAI 231 R
General Electric Co Ltd, Erith, 366

EAI 380
University of Alaska, Fairbanks, 391

EAI 580
Electronic Associates Ltd, Burgess Hill, 364

EAI 640
Comitato Nazionale per l'Energia Nucleare, Roma, 176
Electronic Associates Ltd, Burgess Hill, 364

EAI 680
Electronic Associates Ltd, Burgess Hill, 364
Technische Hogeschool Eindhoven, Eindhoven, 201

EAI 690
The City University, London, 304
Electronic Associates Inc, Rockville, 507-8

EAI 693
Nederlands Scheepsbouwkundig Proefstation, Wageningen, 204

EAI 8945
Research Institute of National Defence (3), Stockholm, 265

EMR
Research Institute of National Defence (2), Stockholm, 265

ES 1012
Central Institute for Computing Techniques, Sofia, 46

ETL Mk II
Electrotechnical Laboratory, Tokyo, 185-6

ETL Mk IV
Electrotechnical Laboratory, Tokyo, 185-6

ETL Mk VI
Electrotechnical Laboratory, Tokyo, 185-6

Elbit 100
Elniv Software, Haifa, 168

Elda
Consiglio Nazionale delle Richerche, Istituto di Elaborazione della Informazione, Pisa, 176

Electrologica XI
Algemeen Reken Cetrum N.V., Amsterdam, 208
Nederlands Scheepsbouwkundig Proefstation, Wageningen, 204
Technische Universität Carolo-Wilhelmina zu Braunschweig, Braunschweig, 121
Universität des Saarlandes, Saarbrücken, 123

Electrologica X2
Intomart, Hilversum, 213

Electrologica X8
Bayerische Julius-Maximilians-Universität, Würzburg, 117
Christian-Albrechts-Universität, Kiel, 117-8
Electro-Calcul S.A., Lausanne, 289
N.V. Electrologica, Rijswijk, 211
Rijksuniversiteit te Utrecht, Elektronisch Rekencentrum, Utrecht, 200
Stichting Mathematisch Centrum, Amsterdam, 205
Technische Hogeschool Eindhoven, Eindhoven, 201
Universität Fridericiana, Karlsruhe, 122

Elliott 503
Department of Scientific and Industrial Research, Wellington, 218
GEC-Elliott Space and Weapons Systems Ltd, Camberley, 366
Hydro-University Computing Centre, Hobart, 8
Infonet B.V., Amsterdam, 212
Ingenieursbureau Rescona, Amstelveen, 213
Kancelarske Srtoje, Prague, 74
Magnet Computer Bureau Ltd, Birmingham, 372
National Data Processing Service, London, 375-6

Elliott 803
An Foras Talúntais, Dublin, 162
Bedford Computer Service Ltd, Bedford, 355
Belfast College of Technology, Belfast, 301
Hindustan Aeronautics Ltd, Bangalore, 156
Indian Posts and Telegraphs Department, Delhi, 156
Institut Blaise Pascal, Paris, 102
Institut Ekonomskih Nauka, Beograd, 573
Instytut Elektrotechniki-Zacład Techniki Obliczenidwej, Warszawa, 240
Liverpool Polytechnic, Liverpool, 309
Manchester Polytechnic, Manchester, 310-311
Mills Associates Ltd, Monmouth, 374
Monsanto Research S.A., Zürich, 284
NIM Igüszi, Budapest, 148
National Data Processing Service, London, 375-6
Oldacres Computers Ltd, London, 376
Portsmouth Polytechnic, Portsmouth, 314
Prakla GmbH, Hannover, 141
Short Brothers and Harland Ltd, Belfast, 340
Sunderland Polytechnic, Sunderland, 317

Index of Computer Installations

Teknillinen Korkeakoulu,
 Helsinki, 88
Twickenham College of Technology, Twickenham, 318
University of Hull, Kingston upon Hull, 323
University of Keele, Keele, 323
University of Khartoum, Khartoum, 258
University of Wales, Cardiff, 328
Uniwersytet Wrocławski, Wrocław, 238

Elliott 903
British Launderers Research Association, London, 336
Eton College, Windsor, 305
Llanelli Technical College, Llanelli, 309-310
Medway and Maidstone College of Technology, Chatham, 311
Queen Elizabeth College, University of London, London, 315
Scottish College of Textiles, Galashiels, 316
Widnes and Runcorn College of Further Education, Widnes, 331

Elliott 905
National Physical Laboratory, Teddington, 338
University of Liverpool, Centre for Computer-Aided Building Design, Liverpool, 324-5
Warley College of Technology, Warley, 330

Elliott 4100
Universidade do Porto, Porto, 240

Elliott 4120
AM & G Computer Service Ltd, Chelmsford, 372
Baric Computing Services Ltd, London, 354-5
British Scientific Instrument Research Association, Chislehurst, 337
Independent Computing Services Pty Ltd, Melbourne, 19
Kalamazoo Computer Centre, Birmingham, 370
Napier College of Science and Technology, Edinburgh, 311-2
National Physical Laboratory, Teddington, 338
Shoe and Allied Trades Research Association, Kettering, 340
South East London Technical College, London, 316
University of Aberdeen Dept. of Engineering, Aberdeen, 319
University of Warwick, Coventry, 328-9
Vysoká Škola Ekonomická, Prague, 74

Elliott 4130
Centro de Cálculo Científico, Lisboa, 240-241
Ellott Brothers (London) Ltd, Frimley, 337

Heriot-Watt University, Edinburgh, 307
Laboratorio Nacional de Engenharia Civil, Lisboa, 240
Portsmouth Polytechic, Portsmouth, 314
Redac Software Ltd, Tewkesbury, 351
Redal Software Ltd, Tewkesbury, 376-7
Universidade do Porto, Porto, 240
Université de Paris VI, Paris, 98
University of Dundee, Dundee, 321
University of Edinburgh, Edinburgh, 322
University of Keele, Keele, 323
University of Kent, Canterbury, 323
University of Leicester, Leicseter, 324
University of Reading Computer Unit, Reading, 326-7
University of Warwick, Coventry, 328-9
University of York, York, 329

Epos 1/2
Vyzkumný Ústav Matematických Stroju, Prague, 75

Facom 6
Institute of Information Technology, Tokyo, 186

Facom 230/25
Korea Computer Centre, Seoul, 190

Facom 230/50
Electrotechnical Laboratory, Tokyo, 186
Japan Information Processing Development Centre, Tokyo, 186

Facom 230/60
Japan Information Processing Development Centre, Tokyo, 183
Kyoto University, Kyoto, 184
Nippon Software Compnay Ltd, Tokyo, 188

Facom 270/30
Kyoto University, Kyoto, 184

Facom 321
Osaka Institute of Technology, Osaka, 184

Ferranti 1
Consiglio Nazionale delle Richerche, Istituto Nazionale per le Applicazione del Calcolo, Roma, 176

Fortrend 1620
University of Libya, Tripoli, 192

Friden 10
Datamatic A/S, Copenhagen, 79
Sinder Friden Division, Milano, 181

GE PAC 4010
General Electric Company, Phoenix, 503-4

GE PAC 4020
General Electric Company, Phoenix, 503-4

General Automation SPC 12
Carroll College, Waukesha, 464

Gier
Institutt for Atomenergi, Halden, 226
Landmäteristyrelsen Tekniska Byrån, Stockholm, 263
Magyar Vegyipari Egyesüles, Budapest, 149
A/S Regnecentralen, Copenhagen, 82-3
SPS A/S, Copenhagen, 83
Számitástechnikai és Ugyvitelszervezö Vállalat, Budapest, 149
Uniwersytet Warszawski, Warszawa, 237

Golem B
Weizmann Institute of Science, Rehovot, 167

Gould Betacom 700
CMI Computer Micrographics Inc, Los Angeles, 506

HRS 860
Universität Stuttgart, Stuttgart, 123-4

Hewlett Packard 2000
Auburn University, Auburn, 390
Hewlett Packard Vertriebsgesellschaft mbH, Frankfurt am Main, 137
London Graduate School of Business Studies, London, 310
Pacific Union College, Angwin, 394
Saab-Scania AB, Linköping, 278
School District of Philadelphia, Philadelphia, 448
Stockholms Universitet, Department of Administration Information Processing, Stockholm, 261
University of Newcastle Upon Tyne, Newcastle, 326
University of Virginia, Charlottesville, 460

Hewlett Packard 2100
Department of Scientific and Industrial Research, Wellington, 218
Hewlett-Packard France, Orsay, 112
Multimedijski Nastavno-Informacioni Center, Zagreb, 574
National Institute of Oceanography, Wormley, 338

Hewlett Packard 2100A
Universidade Federal de São Carlos, São Carlos, 35
Universidade Federal do Rio Grande do Sul, Pôrto Alegre, 36
Universita di Roma, Facolta di Ingegneria, Rome, 174

Hewlett Packard 2114
Montana State University, Bozeman, 426
Universidade Federal do Rio Grande do Sul, Pôrto Alegre, 36

Hewlett Packard 2115
Montana State University, Bozeman, 426
Northwest Missouri State University, Maryville, 424-5
Universita di Napoli, Napoli, 173-4

Hewlett Packard 2116
Chung Shan Institute of Science and Technology, Lungtan, 67
Consiglio Nazionale delle Richerche, Istituto di Elaberazione della Informazione, Pisa, 176
Consiglio Nazionale delle Richerche, Laboratorio Cibernetica, Napoli, 176-7
Consolidated Computer Services Ltd, Toronto, 61
Indian Institute of Management, Ahmedabad, 150
Leasco Response Ltd, London, 371
London Borough of Havering, Romford, 300-301
Measurement Research Center, Iowa City, 473
Montana State University, Bozeman, 426
Stockholms Universitet, Department of Information Processing, Stockholm, 261-2
Technische Universität Carolo-Wilhelmina zu Braunschweig, Institut für Datenverarbeitungsanlagen, Braunschweig, 120-121
Technische Universität Hannover, Hannover, 121
Teknillinen Korkeakoulu, Helsinki, 88

Hewlett Packard 3000
Anderson College, Anderson, 408
Hewlett-Packard Vertriebsgesellschaft, mbH, Frankfurt-am-Main, 137

Hitac 10
Institute of Information Technology, Tokyo, 186

Hitac 5020
Japan Information Processing Development Centre, Tokyo, 186
University of Tokyo, Tokyo, 185

Hitac 8450
Japan Information Processing Development Center, Tokyo, 183

Hitachi 505
Snam Progetti, S.p.A., 177
Universita di Napoli, Napoli, 173-4

Hoc 510
Hokushin Electric Works Ltd, Tokyo, 187

Honeywell
Financial Accounting Service Bureau (Data Processing) Ltd, Wakefield, 365

Honeywell H 110
Automated Data Associates Inc, Rahway, 539
Ianus S.p.A., Roma, 180

Honeywell H 115
Anrocor Industries Inc, Hammond, 524-5
Compusys Inc, Albuquerque, 543
Gestronic S.A., Genève, 290
Honeywell Pty Ltd, Sydney, 19
Tillinghast & Co Inc, Atlanta, 481
United Data Centers Inc, Greenwich, 515

Honeywell H 120
The Andersons, Maumee, 554
Automated Data Associates Inc, Rahway, 539
Auto-Tronix Universal Corporation, Denver, 512
B.I.E.T. Computer Training, London, 355
Bedford Computer Service Ltd, Bedford, 355
Computer Services Corporation, Davenport, 525-6
Computer Services Inc, Salem, 530
Data Operations Inc, Cambridge, 531
Data Processing Management Association, Park Ridge, 385
Delta Data Services Inc, New Orleans, 527
Empire Data Centres Ltd, St-Laurent, 62
Equitable Life and General Insurance Co Ltd, Sydney, 18
Fimaco Inc, Philadelphia, 559
Henkel et Cie AG, Prattelm, 136-7
Middlesex Polytechnic, Enfield, 311
Network Data Processing Corporation, Cedar Rapids, 526
Rechenzentrum AG, Bern, 292-3
Trenton Nassau Service Bureau, Trenton, 542-3

Honeywell H 125
Aviner Weisener U. Galler KG, Hamburg, 133

British Wool Marketing Board, Brentford, 355
Deutsche Utimaco GmbH, Frankfurt-am-Main, 135
EDP Industries Ltd, Vancouver, 61-2
Paul Marthouret S.A., Sainte Foy les Lyon, 106
Rechen-Center Rapperswil Aktien-gesellschaft, Rapperswil, 292

Honeywell H 200
A.T.M., Milano, 178-9
Affiliated Computer Systems Inc, Tulsa, 556
Associated Computer Services, Melbourne, 16
Aviner Weisener U. Galler KG, Hamburg, 133
B.O.G., Frankfurt-am-Main, 133
Century Computer Deutschland, Offenbach, 134
Cincinnati Technical College, Cincinnati, 440
City of Leicester Polytechnic, Leicester, 304
Computer Dimensions Inc, Dallas, 564
Computer Services Corporation, Des Moines, 525-6
Corporation of the District of Surrey, Surrey, 56
Dunford Hadfields Ltd, Sheffield, 363
EDP Industries Ltd, Vancouver, 61-2
Eastern Kentucky University, Richmond, 413
Electronic Accounting Systems Inc, Rochester, 546
Gestronic S.A., Genève, 290
Hamworthy Engineering Ltd, Poole, 366
Hilti (Great Britain) Ltd, Manchester, 345
Ilford Ltd, Ilford, 368
Industrial and Commercial Data Processing Ltd, Coventry, 369
Institut de Recherches Technico-Economiques, Genève, 284
Magnet Computer Bureau Ltd, Birmingham, 372
Medway Data Services Ltd, Chatham, 373
Midlands Computing Centre Ltd, Birmingham, 374
Monmouth College, West Long Branch, 428-9
Namac Inc, Wayland, 532
Paytronics Inc, Buffalo, 549
Portland State University, Portland, 444
Rapid Data Computer Services (Hamilton) Ltd, Hamilton, 63
Rechenzentrale für Wirtschaft und Verwaltung, Essen, 141
San Mateo Junior College District, San Mateo, 394-5
Scottish Computer Services Ltd, Glasgow, 377
Sports Data Corporation, New York, 552
Telechek International Inc, Honolulu, 522

Index of Computer Installations

United Data Centers Inc, Greenwich, 515
United States Computers Inc, Tacoma, 567
University Computing Company, Dallas, 565
Vierhand Reclamdiensten N.V., Haarlem, 217
Virginia Commonwealth University, Richmond, 460

Honeywell H 316
Åbo Akademi, Åbo, 86
University of St Andrews, St Andrews, 327

Honeywell H 400
Bellard Investments Ltd, London, 340
Bhabha Atomiv Research Centre, Bombay, 155
Hindustan Aeronautics Ltd, Bangalore, 156
Indian Statistical Institute, Calcutta, 153
Management Computing Services Ltd, London, 372

Honeywell H 425
ICM Computer Corparation, Tulsa, 497

Honeywell H 600
Danaco Computer Services, Birmingham, 361

Honeywell H 800
Generla Electric Co Ltd, Erith, 366
Magnet Computer Bureau Ltd, Birmingham, 372

Honeywell H 1200
N.V. Automatiseringsmaatschappij Yselbrein, Deventer, 208
Comprehensive Computer Services Ltd, Cleckheaton, 357
Computer Management Group Ltd, Croydon, 359
Honeywell Information Services Ltd, Brentford, 367
Input Inc, Chicago, 523
Public Data Processing Corporation, Chicago, 523-4
SDK Medical Computer Services Corporation, Brookline, 533
Servicios Informatica de Honeywell Bull, Mexico, 197
Sogecim, Paris, 116

Honeywell H 1201
Computer Center Inc, Palm Beach, 518

Honeywell H 1250
Bellard Investments Ltd, London, 340

Century Computer Deutschland GmbH, Offenbach, 134
Data Processing Inc, Jacksonville, 518
EDP Industries Ltd, Vancouver, 61-2
Indecon Inc, Chicago, 482
McDill Corporation, Montgomery, 503
Magnet Computer Bureau Ltd, Birmingham, 372
Management Computing Services Ltd, London, 372

Honeywell H 1642
Oulun Yliopisto, Oulu, 87

Honeywell H 1648
Honeywell Information Systems Ltd, Brentford, 367
Honeywell Pty Ltd, Melbourne, 19
Magnet Computer Bureau Ltd, Birmingham, 372

Honeywell H 2000
Computer Accounting Services Pty Ltd, Camperdown, 17

Honeywell H 2050
Acta Pty Ltd, Sydney, 15

Honeywell H 2200
Belkereskedelmi Ügyvitelszervezési és Információfeldolgozási Intezet, Kerinforg, Budapest, 148
Büro für Datenverarbeitung GmbH, Hamburg, 134
Computer Accounting Services Pty Ltd, Camperdown, 17
Computer Dimensions Inc, Dallas, 564
Fimaco Inc, Philadelphia, 559
Honeyyell Pty Ltd, Melbourne, 19
Honeywell Pty Ltd, Sydney, 19

Honeywell H 3200
Computer Research Inc, Pittsburgh, 558
Honeywell Information Systems Ltd, Brentford, 367
Management Computing Services Ltd, London, 372

Honeywell H 6000
Consultdata Nederland N.V., Amsterdam, 206

Honeywell H 6030
Time-Sharing A/S, Oslo, 231

Honeywell H 6050
Programs and Analysis Inc, Burlington, 533

Honeywell H 6060
Statens Driftssentrale for Administrativ Databehhandling, Oslo, 226

Honeywell-Bull 2050
Bunker Ramo Electronic Data Systems GmbH, Munich, 128-9

Honeywell-Bull 2060
Cedis, Besançon, 109

IBM
Standard Data Corporation, New York, 552

IBM computers, wide range
Service Bureau Corporation, New York, 551-2

IBM 195
McDonnell Automation Company, St Louis, 537-8

IBM 310
Monaco International Management Services, La Ruche, 197

IBM 350/50
Insco Systems Corporation, Neptune, 541

IBM 360
ADP of California, Los Angeles, 505
Analytic Computing Services, New York, 544
Career Educational Institute, Philadelphia, 383
Computer Systems and Education Corporation, East Hartford, 514
Datatab Inc, New York, 546
Electronic Business Service, Visalia, 508
ESPO Data Consultants Inc, Chicago, 481-2
GTE Data Services Inc, Tampa, 519
Geodata A/S, Copenhagen, 80
IBM Co Ltd, Toronto, 62
Istituto E. Meschini, Genova, 181
Laskentakeskus Oy, Helsinki, 90
Marine Bank & Trust Co, Tampa, 519
Programming & Systems Inc, New York, 550
Scientific Computers Inc, Minneapolis, 536
Sigma Processing Inc, Minneapolis, 537
Southeast Missouri State University, Cape Girardeau, 425
Specialized Management Service Inc, Torrington, 515

IBM 360/20
Adelphi Business Schools Inc, New York, 382
A/S Administrativ Data Behandling, Oslo, 228
Algemeen Reken Centrum, N.V., Amsterdam, 208
Allied Data, Olympia, 566
Altro Work Shop Inc, Bronx, 543-4

The International Directory of Computer and Information System Services

American Computer Schools, Kansas City, 382
Applied Data Processing Inc, New Haven, 513-4
Arkansas State University, Arkansas, 391
Augustana College, Sioux Falls, 451-2
Automation Institute of Toledo, Toledo, 382
Ball State University, Muncie, 408-9
Barron Data Systems Inc, Sylvania, 554
Broome Community College, Binghampton, 431
Bryant and Stratton Education Center, Chicago, 382-3
Cal-West Data Systems Inc, Studio City, 505
Centre Électronique de Gestion, Blois, 110
Centro de Prestacăo de Serviços Técnicos do Estado de Pernambuco, Recife, 37
Centrum voor Automatisering Bredatilburg, Tilburg, 202-3
Centrum voor Automatisering Noord-Holland, Haarlem, 203
Centrum voor Informatieverwerking N.V., Utrecht, 209
Cimsco Data Processing Company, Long Beach, 506
City University of New York Board of Higher Education Central Office, New York, 431
Cobocking N.V., Amsterdam, 210
College of Automation, Des Moines, 383
Control Data Institute, Anaheim, 384
Control Data Institute, Long Beach, 384-5
Control Data Institute, Sherman Oaks, 385
Control Data Institute, Syracuse, 385
Cooper Computer Services, Sherman Oaks, 507
Data Center Inc, Seattle, 502
Data Control Services, Canton, 555
Data Processing Research Demonstration Centre for the Blind and Otherwise Handicapped, Jerusalem, 166-7
Data Service Centre Ltd, Glasgow, 362
Data Usage Corporation, Fort Lee, 540
Detroit College of Business, Dearborn, 385
EDB-Service A/S, Oslo, 229-30
E.J.V. Data Services Ltd, London, 364
Eastern Montana College, Billings, 426
Electronic Computer Programming Institute, Dayton, 386
Electronic Computer Programming Institute, Sacramento, 386
Electronic Computer Programming Institute of Tidewater, Norfolk, 387
Fulfillment Consultants Corporation, Bronx, 546-7
Gradski Zavod za Statistiku Beograd, Belgrade, 571

Grafisch Administratie Centrum, Amsterdam, 212
Haile Sellassie I University, Addis Ababa, 86
Herzing Institute Inc, Milwaukee, 387
IBM A/S,Århus, 80
IBM Colombia Ltda, Medellín, 73
IBM de Mexico S.A., Guadalajara, 196-7
IBM de Mexico S.A., Monterrey, 196-7
IBM del Ecuador, Guayaquil, 85
IBM Deutschland, Augsburg, Bonn, Bremen, Essen, Freiburg, Karlsruhe, Kassel, Kiel, Mannheim, Nürnberg, Saarbrücken, Ulm, Wuppertal, 138-9
IBM do Brasil, Belo Horizonte, 43
IBM do Brasil, Curitiba/Recife, 43
IBM do Brasil, Rio de Janeiro, 43
IBM do Brasil, São Paulo, 43
IBM Finland, Tampere, 89-90
IBM Finland, Turku, 89-90
IBM Israel Data Centre Services, Tel Aviv, 170
IBM Italia S.p.A., Bologna, 180
IBM Italia S.p.A., Florence, 180
IBM Italia S.p.A., Milan, 180
IBM Italia S.p.A., Rome, 180
IBM Italia S.p.A., Turin, 180
IBM Italia S.p.A., Verona, 180
IBM Japan Ltd, Tokyo, 187
IBM Nederland N.V., Amsterdam, 212
IBM Nederland N.V., Arnhem, 212
IBM Nederland N.V., Eindhoven, 212
IBM Nederland N.V., Groningen, 212
IBM Nederland N.V., Rijswijk, 212
IBM Nederland N.V., Rotterdam, 212
IBM Nederland N.V., Utrecht, 212
IBM of Belgium S.A., Antwerp, 31
IBM of Belgium S.A., Brussels, 31
IBM of Belgium S.A., Liège, 31
IBM South Africa (Pty) Ltd, Johannesburg, 251
IBM Switzerland, Berne, 290-91
IBM Switzerland, Zürich, 290-91
IBM United Kingdom Ltd, Glasgow, 368
Idaho State University, Pocatello, 405
Information Management Associates Inc, St Louis, 537
Institut International d'Informatique, Chambéry, 93
Institut International d'Informatique, Paris, 93
Institut National de Statistique, Brussels, 27
N.V. Institut voor Electronische Administratie, 213
International Buromaschinen, Graz, 23
International Data Processing Institute, Detroit, 387
Kinman Business University, Spokane, 387
Kolynos S.A.C.L., Quilmes, 5
Landbrugets EDB-Centraler, Risskov, 81
Litton Industries, Canoga Park, 473

MLL Statistics Institute and Office Efficiency Ltd, Haifa, 171
MLL Statistics Institute and Office Efficiency Ltd, Tel Aviv,171
M.T.I. Business Colleges, Sacramento, 388
McDonnell Automation Company, St Louis, 537-8
Manpower Business Training Institution, St Louis, 387-8
Mata College of Automation, Columbus, 388
Northern Illinois University, DeKalb, 407
Organisation Maurice Bressy, Rhône, 106
PCS Data Processing Inc, New York, 549-50
Paillard S.A., Yverdon, 292
Perscombinatie, Amsterdam, 214
Polgat Woollen Industries Ltd, Kiriat-Gat, 171-2
Računski Center, Skofja Loka, 576
Rekencentrum C. van de Velden N.V., Arnhem, 214-5
Royal Scientific Society, Amman, 189
Secretaria del Consejo Provincial de Desarrollo, Corrientes, 4
Servico Federal de Processamento de Dados, Pôrto Alegre, 38
Servico Federal de Processamento de Dados, Recife, 38
Shekem Ltd, Jaffa, 169
Société Industrielle de Travaux de Bureaux, Paris, 115
Southern Data Processing Services Inc, Augusta, 521
Svenska Elektroniska Data AB, Johanneshov, 280
Svenska Elektroniska Data AB, Kristianstad, 280
Sydfyns Datacentral, Svendborg, 84
S. J. Tesauro & Co, Detroit, 535
University of California, Santa Barbara, 397
University of Ghana, Accra, 142
University of Nebraska, Omaha, 427
University of Wisconsin, Milwaukee, 465
Waseda University, Tokyo, 185
West African Examinations Council, Accra, 143
Western Business University, Portland, 390

IBM 360/22
Centre Electronique de Gestion, Blois, 110
Finnish State Computer Centre, Helsinki, 88
Loyola Marymount University, Los Angeles, 393
McDonnell Automation Company, 537-8
Société Nationale Terrienne, Brussels, 28
West Coast Schools, Los Angeles, 398

IBM 360/25
ADV/ORGA Unternehmensberatung, Wilhelmshaven, 132-3

Index of Computer Installations

Austin Peay State University, Clarksville, 452
Barnestado S.A., Curitiba, 40-41
CCM Information Corporation, New York, 544-5
Cati-Cofigat, Nantes, 108-9
Centar za Automatizaciju Poslovanja Zavod za Unapreaenje Produktivnosti Rada, Zagreb, 572
Central Conneticut State College, New Britain, 400
Central Institute for Computing Techniques, Sofia, 46
Centrum voor Informatieverwerking, Utrecht, 209
Cooperativa Agricola de Cotia-Cooperativa Central, São Paulo, 41-2
D. J. Computer Services Ltd, London, 363
Datarutin AB, Stockholm, 273
Datema AB, Solna, 274
Daten-Service Bech GmbH, Neckarsulm, 133
N.V. Dienstverlening Overheids Administrative en Automatiserings Service Centrum van N. Samson N.V., Alphen, 211
EDP Resources Deutschland AG, Bad Homburg, 135
Eastern Computer Services Ltd, Spalding, 363-4
First Business Computing, Houston, 500
IBM Colombia Ltda, Cali, 73
IBM de Guatemala S.A., Guatemala City, 144-5
IBM Israel Data Centre Services, Tel Aviv, 170
IBM World Trade Corporation, Kuala Lumpur, 193
Industrija Drveta, Celuloze, Papira i Vlakna, Banjaluka, 574-5
Industrija Motora Rakovica, Belgrade, 571-2
Institut Géographique National, Paris, 100
Istituto Centrale di Statistica, Roma, 177
McDonnell Automation Company, St Louis, 537-8
May & Speh Data Processing Center, Chicago, 523
Measurement Research Center, Iowa City, 473
Mécanorga, St. Ouen, 113
Mehanografski Center-Emo, Celje, 575
Mohawk College of Applied Arts and Technology, Hamilton, 49
New Mexico Highlands University, Las Vegas, 430
Northwest Missouri State University, Maryville, 424-5
Pace College, New York, 435
A. M. Provan and Associates, Port of Spain, 297
Saint Peter's College, Jersey City, 429
Société Industrielle de Travaux de Bureaux, Paris, 115
'Tehavot' Israel Mortage Bank Ltd, Jerusalem, 166
Tele-Data Corporation, North Plainfield, 542

Tilastollinen Päätoimisto, Helsinki, 86
United Data Centers Inc, Greenwich, 515
Université de Nice, Nice, 98
University of Ife, Ile-Ife, 222
University of Santa Clara, Santa Clara, 398
University of Texas, El Paso, 457
University of Wisconsin, Whitewater, 466
Woods Gordon & Co, Montreal, 58

IBM 360/30

A.I.D. Computing Inc, Fort Worth, 564
Adams State College, Alamosa, 398-9
Ajax Data Processing Ltd, London, 353
Allied Data, Olympia, 566
Applied Systems Corporation, Detroit, 486
AB Atomenergi, Nyköping, 262
Auditek Inc, New York, 544
Auto-Tronx Universal Corporation, Denver, 512
Automation Center AB, Johanneshov, 271
Bedford Computer Service Ltd, Bedford, 355
Beverly Bancorporation, Chicago, 522
Biz-Matic Data Control Centers Inc, Boston, 530
Ernest E Blanche & Associates Inc, Kensington, 527
Bogføringsforeningen Automationscentralen, Naestved, 78
Booz Allan & Hamilton Inc, New York, 489
AB-Bygg ADB, Solna, 272
Cati-Mécanorga-Ergem, Paris, 109
Cegos-Informatique, St Cloud, 103-4
Centrais Eléctricas do Sul do Brasil S.A. (Eletrosul), Rio de Janeiro, 36-7
Centre de Traitement de l'Information, Asnières, 109
Centre d'Études et de Traitement sur Ordinateur, Courbevoie, 109
Centro Distrital de Sistematización y Servicios Técnicos, Bogotá, 70
Centurex Corporation, Los Angeles, 505-6
Champion Service Corporation, Cleveland, 554-5
City University of New York Kingsborough Community College, Brooklyn, 432
City University of New York Staten Island Community College, Staten Island, 432
College of Automation, Des Moines, 383
College of Data Processing, Los Angeles, 383
Combined Data Group Inc, New York, 545
Computab Inc, Honolulu, 522
Computer Applications Inc, New York, 489
Computer Center Inc, Palm Beach, 518

Computer Consulting Service, Dubuque, 525
Computer Fulfillment Corporation, Long Island, 545
Computer Fulfillment, Winchester, 530
Computer Microfilm Systems Inc, Glendale, 506
Computer Power, Tredomen, 299
Computer Usage Development Corporation, Chicago, 514
Computer Usage Development, Corporation, New York, 514
Conservatoire National des Arts et Métiers, Paris, 100
Control Data Corporation, Boston, 516
Control Data Corporation, Los Angeles, 516
Control Data Corporation, New York, 516
Control Data Corporation, San Francisco, 516
Control Data Corporation, Washington, 516
Data Center Luzern, Luzern, 289
Data Corporation, Los Angeles, 507
Data Inc, Arlington, 565
Data Service Corporation, Nashville, 563
Data Services Corporation, Dayton, 555
Data Systems International Inc, Philadelphia, 559
Datasolve International Ltd, London, 362-3
Datenverarbeitungsdeinst der Stadt Bern, Berne, 283
Datron AG für Datenverarbeitung und Organisation, St Gallen, 285
R. Dixon Speas Associates Inc, Manhasset, 494
EDB-Centralen, Herning, 79
EDP Resources Deutschland AG, Bad Homburg, 135
Eastern Iowa Community College, Davenport, 410
École Royale Militaire, Brussels, 25
Electronic Tabulating Corporation, Newburgh, 546
Elektro Data Bolaget, Norrköping, 274-5
Elektro Data Bolaget, Orebro, 274-5
First National Bank of Montgomery, Montgomery, 502-3
First National Bank of St Louis, St Louis, 537
Florida Computer Systems Company, Winter Park, 519
Försvarets Civilförvaltning, Stockholm, 262
Gallaudet College, Washington, 402
Guardian Data Service & Supply, Memphis, 563-4
Hamashbir Hamerkazi Israel Cooperative Wholesale Society Ltd, Tel Aviv, 169-70
IBM de México S.A., Guadalajara, 196-7
IBM de México S.A., Monterrey, 196-7
IBM de Panamá S.A., Panamá, 233
IBM del Ecuador, Quito, 85
IBM Israel Data Centre Services, Tel Aviv, 170

IBM Portuguesa SARL, Lisboa, 241
IBM South Africa (Pty) Ltd, Johannesburg, 251
IBM Thailand Co Ltd, Bangkok, 296
IBM United Kingdom Ltd, Birmingham, 368
IBM United Kingdom Ltd, Bristol, 368
IBM United Kingdom Ltd, Glasgow, 368
IBM United Kingdom Ltd, London, 368
IBM United Kingdom Ltd, Manchester (Sale), 368
IBM United Kingdom Ltd, Newcastle, 368
IBM World Trade Corporation, Accra, 143
IBM World Trade Corporation, Caracas, 469
IBM World Trade Corporation, Hong Kong, 145
IBM World Trade Corporation, Kinston, 183
IBM World Trade Corporation, Lima, 235
IBM World Trade Corporation, San Salvador, 85
IBM World Trade Corporation, Singapore, 244
ITT Data Services, Rio de Janeiro, 44
Industria Electrica Brown Boveri S.A., São Paulo, 44
Industrial National Bank of Rhode Island, Providence, 562-3
Industrie and Bank Automation, Berne, 291
Industrijsko Poljoprivredni Kombinat, Osijek, 575
Information Consultants Inc, Los Angeles, 477-8
Information Sciences Inc, Warwick, 563
Institute of Transportation, Ljubljana, 573-4
International Systems Associates Ltd, New York, 548
Johnson Computing Inc, Philadelphia, 560
Kellogg International Corporation, London, 371
Lester B. Knight & Associates Inc, Chicago, 482
I/S Kommunernes EDB-Central, Copenhagen, 81
Kungliga Tekniska Högskolan, Library-Documentation Centre, Stockholm, 260-61
Landbrugets EDB-Centraler, Risskov, 81
Lock Haven State College, Lock Haven, 447
Louisiana State University, Baton Rouge, 414
MLL Statistics Institute and Office Efficiency Ltd, Tel Aviv, 171
McDonnell Automation Company, St Louis, 537-8
McLintock Mann & Whinney Murray, London, 348
Marquette University, Milwaukee, 464
Mata College of Automation, Colombus, 388
Matrix Corporation, El Segundo, 549
May and Speh Data Processing Center, Chicago, 523
Measurement Research Centre, Iowa City, 473
Milner Brothers Products, Los Angeles, 509
Ministère des Postes, Télégraphes et Téléphones, Tunis, 297
Ministry of Finance, Lusaka, 577
Montedata S.A., Pôrto Alegre, 44
Municipality of Tel Aviv, Tel Aviv, 171
Municipio de Medellín, Medellín, 71
National Coal Board, Tredomen, 334
National Information Systems Corporation, Valley Forge, 561-2
A/L Nord-Norges Hullkortsentral, Tromsø, 230
Osterreichische Studiengesellschaft für Atomenergie, Vienna, 21
PCS Data Processing Inc, New York, 549-50
Perscombinatie, Amsterdam, 214
Point Park College, Pittsburgh, 448
Professional Data Processing Inc, Seattle, 566-7
Programs and Analysis Inc, Burlington, 533
Quaternaire Informatique, S.A., Paris, 113
Queensborough Community College, Bayside, 435
Refinerías de Maíz S.A.I.C., Buenos Aires, 6
Rijksuniversiteit te Gent, Gent, 26
S.V.Z. Computer Centre, Rotterdam, 216
Serviço Federal de Processamento de Dados, Rio de Janeiro, 38
Serviço Federal de Processamento de Dados, São Paulo, 38
Silkeborg Datacentral, Silkeborg, 83
E. Ralph Sims Jr and Associates Inc, Lancaster, 497
Skýrsluvélar Ríkisins og Reykjavíkurborgar, Reykjavík, 149
Société Industrielle de Travaux de Bureaux, Paris, 115
Statens Janvägar, Stockholm, 263
Statistical Tabulating Corporation, Chicago, 524
Suomen Sedab Oy, Helsinki, 91
Swiss Federal Railways, Bern, 284
Systek Inc, Pittsfield, 533
Systematics Inc, Little Rock, 504
Technical Computing Center, San Francisco, 510
Tennessee Agricultural and Industrial State University, Nashville, 453
S. J. Tesauro & Co, Detroit, 535
Tretorn Datacenter, Hälsingborg, 281
Tulane University of Louisiana, New Orleans, 414
Uniroyal Ltd, Newbridge, 380
United Data Centers Inc, Greenwich, 515
Universidad de Antioquía, Medellín, 68
Universidad de Barcelona, Barcelona, 253
Universidad La Salle de México, México, 195
Universidad Tecnológica Nacional, Buenos Aires, 3
University Computer Center, Panorama City, 512
University of California Information Systems Division, Los Angeles, 395-6
University of Northern Colorado, Greeley, 400
University of Puerto Rico, Puerto Rico, 241-2
University of Tennessee, Chatanooga, 453
University of Vermont, Burlington, 459
Viatron Programming Inc, Burlington, 486
Villanova University, Villanova, 451
Virginia State College, Petersburg, 461
Voralberger Rechenzentrum, Dornbirn, 24
Richard M. Walsh Associates, Scranton, 499
Wilford Computer Group Ltd, Manchester, 381
Wittenburg University, Springfield, 443
Wolf and Company, Los Angeles, 512

IBM 360/40

Adaps Ltd, St Kilda, 15-16
Alphanumeric Inc, Los Angeles, 543
Atomic Energy Board, Pretoria, 248
Automatic Data Processing Inc, Clifton, 539
Ball State University, Muncie, 408-9
Barron Data Systems Inc, Sylvania, 554
Beverly Bancorporation, Chicago, 522
Boston College, Chestnut Hill, 416
Cálculo y Tratamiento de la Información S.A., Madrid, 256
Central State University, Edmond, 443
Centre Académique de Traitement de l'Information, Paris, 91-2
Centre Français de Recherche Opérationelle, Paris, 110
Centre of Economic Computation and Economic Cybernetics, Bucharest, 244
Centrum voor Automatisering Breda-Tilburg, Tilburg, 202-3
Chambre de Commerce et d'Industrie, Paris, 92
Chicago State College, Chicago, 406
City University of New York Hunter College, New York, 432
Cleveland State University, Cleveland, 440
Compagnie IBM France, Casablanca, 197
Computer Communications Inc, Inglewood, 476
Computer Dimensions Inc, Dallas, 564
Computer Dynamics, London, 359
Computer Power, Doncaster, 299
Computer Projects Ltd, London, 359
Computer Usage Development Corporation, New York, 514

Index of Computer Installations

Computerware Inc, New York, 545
Computing Efficiency Inc, Long Island, 545-6
Consultoria e Serviços Técnicos Aplub Ltda, Rio Grande do Sul, 41
Cybernetics International (U.K.) Ltd, London, 361
Danmarks Statistik, Copenhagen, 77
AB Data-Service, Danderyd, 273-4
Datasolve International Ltd, London, 362-3
Data-Tronics Corporation, Fort Smith, 504
Datenzentrale Schleswig-Holstein, Kiel, 125
Datron AG für Datenverarbeitung und Organisation, St Gallen, 285
N.V. Deinstverlening Overheids Administrative en Automatiserings Service Centrum van N. Samson N.V., Alphen, 211
Deutsche Bau- und Boden AG, Mainz, 135
EDP Resources Deutschland AG, Bad Homburg, 135
Eastern Michigan University, Ypsilanti, 418
Electronic Data Service Inc, Wilmington, 515
Elektro Data Bolaget, Stockholm, 274-5
Empresa Nacional de Computación e Informática Ltda, Santiago, 66
Engenharia de Seguros Ltda, São Paulo, 42
Equimatics Inc, Fairfield, 540-41
Fedder Data Centers Inc, Baltimore, 528
First-Union Automation Service Inc, St Louis, 537
Foothill Community College District, Los Altos Hills, 393
Fordham University, Bronx, 433
Forsikringsselskabernes Data Central, Copenhagen, 80
Général de Service Informatique, GSI-Entreprises, Paris, 112
Georgetown University, Washington, 402
Gradski Zavod Za Statistiku Beograd, Belgrade, 571
Halcon Computer Technologies Inc, New York, 492
IBM A/S, Copenhagen, 80
IBM de México S.A., México, 196-7
IBM Deutschland, Bielefeld, 138-9
IBM Deutschland, Berlin, 138-9
IBM Deutschland, Dortmund, 138-9
IBM Deutschland, Düsseldorf, 138-9
IBM Deutschland, Frankfurt, 138-9
IBM Deutschland, Hamburg, 138-9
IBM Deutschland, Hannover, 138-9
IBM Deutschland, Köln, 138-9
IBM do Brasil, Rio de Janeiro, 43
IBM do Brasil, São Paulo, 43
IBM Finland, Helsinki, 89-90
IBM Ireland Ltd, Dublin, 164
IBM Israel Data Centre Services, Tel Aviv, 170
IBM Japan Ltd, Nagoya, 187
IBM Japan Ltd, Tokyo, 187
IBM Italia S.p.A., Bologna, 180
IBM Italia S.p.A., Milan, 180
IBM Italia S.p.A., Rome, 180

IBM Italia S.p.A., Turin, 180
IBM, Madrid, 257
IBM Nederland N.V., Amsterdam, 212
IBM Nederland N.V., Rotterdam, 212
IBM New Zealand Ltd, Auckland, 220
IBM Nigeria Ltd, Lagos, 223
IBM of Belgium S.A., Brussels, 31
IBM A/S, Oslo, 230
IBM Service Bureau, Adibjan, 182
IBM South Africa (Pty) Ltd, Johannesburg, 251
IBM Svenska AB, Västerås, 275-6
IBM Switzerland, Berne, 290-91
IBM Switzerland, Geneva, 290-91
IBM Switzerland, Zürich, 290-91
IBM Taiwan Corporation, Taipei, 68
IBM United Kingdom Ltd, Birmingham, 368
IBM United Kingdom Ltd, Croydon, 368
IBM United Kingdom Ltd, London, 368
IBM World Trade Corp., Algiers, 1
IBM World Trade Corp., Buenos Aires, 5
IBM World Trade Corp., Kinshasa, 576
CM Computer Corporation, Tulsa, 497
ITT Datenservice, Stuttgart, 139
Infodata Systems Inc, Webster, 547
International Büromaschinen, Vienna, 23
Intertrade, Ljubljana, 575
Istituto Centrale di Statistica, Roma, 177
Jackson State College, Jackson, 422
Johnson Computing Inc, Philadelphia, 560
Kent Data Services Ltd, Luton, 371
Keydata Corporation, Watertown, 532
I/S Kommunernes EDB-Central, Copenhagen, 81
Arthur S. Kranzley & Company Inc, Cherry Hill, 541
Litton Industries, Canoga Park, 473
McDonnell Automation Company, St Louis, 537-8
Management Data Corp, Philadelphia, 560-61
Matrix Corporation, El Segundo, 549
Matrix Corporation, New York, 549
Metacomputer Sciences Inc, Irvine, 509
Ministerio de Hacienda y Crédito Público, Bogotá, 71
Ministry of Finance, Teheran, 161
Mississippi State University, Mississippi, 422-3
Mnemotech Computer Systems Inc, New York, 549
National Coal Board, Mansfield, 334
National Statistical Office, Bangkok, 295
North Carolina State University, Raleigh, 438
OK Data. Copenhagen, 82
Office Central de la Mécanographie, Abidjan, 182
Orta Doğu Teknik Universitesi, Ankara, 298

Paillard S.A., Yverdon, 292
Pakistan Computer Bureau, Rawalpindi, 232
Pioneer Data Systems Inc, Des Moines, 526
Pomona College, Claremont, 394
Procesamientos Electronicos S.A.C., Santiago, 66
Rekencentrum voor Administratie, Efficiency en Techniek, Arnhem, 215
S.E.T.M., Paris, 114
Scottish Office Computer Service, Edinburgh, 334-5
Servizio Internazionale Elaborazione Dati, S.p.A., Roma, 181
Skogsbrukets Datacentral, Sundsvall, 279
Social and Economic Statistics Administration, Washington, 468
Société d'Applications et de Méthodes Mécanographiques, Paris, 115
Society for Cybernetics, Rijeka, 570
Sogecim, Paris, 116
South African Railways, Johannesburg, 248
Sparbankernas Datacentraler AB, Linköping, 279
Sparbankernas Datacentraler AB, Stockholm, 279
State University of New York, Buffalo, Amherst, 436
Statens Järnvägar, Stockholm, 263
Statistisk Sentralbyrå, Oslo, 226
'Stefan Gheorghiu' Academy, Bucharest, 243
Stevens Institute of Technology, Hoboken, 430
Svenska Elektroniska Data AB, Johannesov and Malmö, 280
Sveriges Kreditbank ADB Service, Stockholm, 280-81
Swiss Federal Railways, Bern, 284
Systems Technology Corporation, Warminster, 498-9
Tietotehdas, Kilo, 91
United Bank Ltd, Karachi, 233
Universidad de Chile, Santiago, 65
Universidad de los Andes, Mérida, 568
Universidad Nacional de Ingeniería, Lima, 235
Universidad Técnica 'Federico Santa María', Santiago, 65-6
Universidade Federal do Rio de Janeiro, Rio de Janeiro, 35
Università degli Studi di Bari, Bari, 173
Université de Grenoble, Grenoble, 97
Université de Sherbrooke, Sherbrooke, 51
University of Akron, Akron, 442
University of Alaska, Fairbanks, 391
University of California, Computer Center, Berkeley, 395
University of California, Berkeley, Information Systems Division, Los Angeles, 395-6
University of California, Santa Cruz, 397
University of Idaho, Moscow, 405
University of New Hampshire, Durham, 428
University of North Carolina at Chapel Hill, Chapel Hill, 438-9

University of Saskatchewan, Computer Centre, Regina, 53-4
University of South Dakota, Vermillion, 452
University of Wisconsin, Milwaukee, 465
University of Wisconsin, Oshkosh, 465
Univest S.A. Administração e Participações, São Paulo, 45-6
V.I.P. Systems, Washington, 517
Valley Computer Center, Panorama City, 512
W. Data AB, Huskvarna, 281
Weber State College, Ogden, 459
Western Washington State College, Bellingham, 462-3
West Texas State University, Canyon, 457-8
Xiox International Inc, Miami, 520

IBM 360/44
Centre d'Etude de l'Énergie Nucléaire, Brussels, 27
Centre National de la Recherche Scientifique, Marseille, 94-5
Clarkson College of Technology, Potsdam, 432
Comitato Nazionale per l'Energia Nucleare, Gruppo Calcoli Numerici dei Laboratori Nazionali di Frascati, Roma, 176
Control Data Corporation, San Francisco, 516
Fels Research Institute, Yellow Springs, 472
Gannett Fleming Corddry & Carpenter Inc, Harrisburg, 498
Indian Institute of Science Bangalore, 150
Institute for Petroleum Research and Geo-Physics, Holon, 165-6
Instituto de Pesquisas Tecnológicas, São Paulo, 39
Michigan Technological University, Houghton, 419
Oberlin College, Oberlin, 441
Ohio University, Athens, 441
Physical Research Laboratory, Ahmedabad, 157
Société Nationale d'Études de Construction de Moteurs d'Avion, Suresnes, 103
Teledyne Corporation, Calgary, 475
Teledyne Corporation, Houston, 475
Teledyne Exploration, Calgary, 56
Universidad de los Andes, Biblioteca General, Bogotá, 68
Universidad de los Andes, Centro de Cómputo, Bogotá, 68-9
Universidade de São Paulo, Nuclear Physics Department, São Paulo, 33-4
Université de Bordeaux I, Talence, 97
Université de Strasbourg, Strasbourg, 99
University of Dublin, Trinity College, Dublin, 163
University of St. Andrews, St. Andrews, 327
University of South Carolina, Charleston, 451
University of Waterloo, Waterloo, 54
Wichita State University, Wichita, 412-3

IBM 360/50
Agency for International Development, Washington, 466-7
Alphanumeric Inc, New York, 543
Applied Cybernetics Corporation, Sunny Vale, 505
Applied Data Research Inc, Princeton, 539
Stephen F. Austin State University, Nacogdoches, 455-6
Australian Atomic Energy Commission, Sutherland, 13
Australian National University Canberra, 6
Boston University, Boston, 416
Brigham Young University, Provo, 458
British Aircraft Corporation (operating) Ltd, Preston, 336
Brown Engineering Co, Huntsville, 471
Centre-File Ltd, London, 357
Centre d'Information Générale S.A., Brussels, 30
Centro de Informações Para o Desenvolvimento Urbano e Local, Rio de Janeiro, 37
Centro Superior de Procesamiento de la Información, La Plata, 1
College of William and Mary in Virginia, Williamsburg, 459-60
Compañia Colombiana de Sistemas, Bogotá, 71
Compagnie IBM France, Boulogne/Billancourt 92
Compagnie Générale d'Informatique, Paris, 104
Compass Computer Systems Inc, Nashville, 499
Compress Inc, Rockville, 483
Computab Inc, Honolulu, 522
Computer Power, Cannock, 299
Computer Power Inc, Jacksonville, 517-8
Computerware Inc, New York, 545
Computone Systems Inc, Atlanta, 521
Data Systems International Inc, Philadelphia, 559
Datema AB, Solna, 274
Directorate of Data Processing, Saigon, 569
EDP Resources Deutschland, Bad Homburg, 135
Eastern Illinois State University, Charleston, 406
Empresa Nacional de Computación e Informatica Ltda, Santiago, 66
European Space Research Institute, Frascati, 174
Fairfield University, Fairfield, 400
Federal Institute for Statistics, Belgrade, 571
Finnish State Computer Centre, Helsinki, 88
Gesellschaft für Mathematik und Datenverarbeitung mbh, St Augustin-Birlinghoven, 126
IBM Deutschland, Dortmund, 138-9
IBM Deutschland, Frankfurt, 138-9
IBM Deutschland, Hamburg, 138-9
IBM France, Neuilly-sur-Seine, 112
IBM Italia S.p.A., Milan, 180
IBM Japan Ltd, Osaka 187
IBM New Zealand Ltd, Wellington, 220
IBM of Belgium S.A., Brussels, 31
IBM Philippines Inc, Rizal, 235-6
IBM Svenska AB, Göteborg, 275-6
IBM Svenska AB, Malmö, 275-6
IBM Switzerland, Zürich, 290-91
IBM United Kingdom Ltd, London, 368
ITT Data Services, East Barnet, 370
ITT Data Services, Rio de Janeiro, 44
Illinois State University, Normal, 406-7
Institut Blaise Pascal, Paris, 102
N.V. Instituut voor Electronische Administratie, Rotterdam, 213
Kansas State University of Agriculture and Applied Science, Manhattan, 412
Kidde Computer Services Company, Huntingdon Valley, 560
I/S Kommunernes EDB-Central, Copenhagen, 81
Lakehead University, Thunder Bay, 48
Landbrugets EDB-Centraler, Risskov, 81
McDonnell Automation Company, St. Louis, 537-8
Measurement Research Center, Iowa City, 473
National Information Systems Corporation, Valley Forge, 561-2
National University of Ireland, Dublin, 162-3
National Coal Board, Cannock, 334
Nippon Software Company Ltd, Tokyo, 188
North Dakota State University, Fargo, 439
North Texas State University, Denton, 454
Ohio State University, Columbus, 441
Pennsylvania State University Computation Center, University Park, 447-8
Postbanken, Stockholm, 263
Queens University at Kingston, Kingston, 50
Rensselaer Polytechnic Institute, Troy, 435
Rijkscomputercentrum, Apeldoorn, 204
Rijksuniversiteit te Leiden, Leiden, 199
Scottish Office Computer Service, Edinburgh, 334-5
Skogsbrukets Datacentral, Sundsvall, 279
Sparbankernas Datacentraler AB, Malmö, 279
Stanford University, Stanford, 395
Statistiska Centralbyråns, Stockholm, 259

Index of Computer Installations

Sun Alliance and London Insurance Ltd, Birmingham, 378-9
Technische Hogeschool Twente, Enschede, 201-2
Tennessee Valley Authority, Chattanooga, 469
Texas Technological University, Lubbock, 456
Unilever Computer Services Ltd, Wembley, 379-80
Universidad Central de Venezuela, Caracas, 568
Universidad de Buenos Aires, Centro de Cómputos, Buenos Aires, 2
Universita Bar-Ilan, Ramat-Gan, 165
Universitetet i Bergen, Bergen, 224
University of Arkansas, Fayetteville, 391-2
University of Calgary, Calgary, 52
University of California, Riverside, 396-7
University of California, San Francisco Medical Center, San Francisco, 397
University of Missouri, Rolla, 425
University of Montreal, Ecole Polytechnique, Montreal, 53
University of New Brunswick, Fredericton, 53
University of New South Wales, Kensington, 11
University of Oregon, Eugene, 444
University of Pittsburgh Computer Center, Pittsburgh, 450
University of Pretoria, Pretoria, 246
University of Stellenbosch, Stellenbosch, 247
University of Toledo, Toledo, 442
University of the Witwatersrand, Johannesburg, 247
University of Windsor, Windsor, 55
Washington University, St Louis, 426
Wayne State University, Detroit, 419-20
Western Illinois University, Macomb 408
Westfälische Wilhelms-Universität, Münster, 124
Yale University, New Haven, 401
Youngstown University, Youngstown, 443

IBM 360/65
Bell-Northern Research, Ottawa, 56
Cegos-Informatique, St Cloud, 103-4
Centro Studi e Applicazioni in Technologie Avanzate, Bari, 175
Companhia de Processamento do Estado de São Paulo, 41
Computel Systems Ltd, Ottawa, 60
Computer Power, Cannock, 299
Computer Sciences International Nederland N.V., Amstelveen, 210-11
Control Data Corporation, New York, 516
Control Data Corporation, San Francisco, 516
Cornell University, Ithaca, 433

Eastern Air Lines Inc, Miami, 480-81
Göteborgs Datacentral, Göteborg, 260
Harvard University, Cambridge, 416
IBM Deutschland, Düsseldorf, 138-9
IBM Nederland N.V., Rijswijk, 212
IBM Svenska AB, Stockholm, 275-6
IBM Switzerland, Basle, 290-91
IBM United Kingdom Ltd, London, 368
ITT Data Services, East Barnett, 370
Imperial Chemical Industries Ltd, Manchester, 368
Institut International d'Informatique, Grenoble, 93
Interuniversity Communications Council, Princeton, 472-3
Iowa State University of Science and Technology, Ames, 410-11
Litton Industries, Canoga Park, 473
McGill University, Montreal, 48-9
Massachusetts Institute of Technology, Information Processing Center, Cambridge, 417
Mathematical Applications Group Inc, Elmsford, 548-9
Matrix Corporation, El Segundo, 549
Matrix Corporation, New York, 549
New Mexico State University, Las Cruces, 430
Oklahoma State University, Stillwater, 443
PRC Computer Center Inc, McLean, 501
Princeton Time-Sharing Services Inc, Princeton, 542
Rand Corporation, Santa Monica, 474
Social Security Administration, Baltimore, 468-9
South African Council for Scientific and Industrial Research, Pretoria, 248
Statistical Tabulating Corporation, Chicago, 524
Swiss Federal Railways, Bern, 284
Technische Hogeschool te Delft Delft, 201
The Nuclear Power Group, Knutsford, 338-9
Texas Agricultural and Mechanical University, College Station, 456
Unilever Computer Services Ltd, Wembley, 379-80
United States Geological Survey, Washington, 469
University College, University of London, London, 318
University of California Information Systems Division, Berkeley, 395-6
University of Chicago, Chicago, 407-8
University of Georgia, Athens, 404-5
University of Hawaii, Honolulu, 405
University of Iowa, Iowa City, 411
University of Manitoba, Computer Centre, Winnipeg, 52

University of Missouri, Columbia, 425
University of Nebraska, Lincoln, 427
University of Ottawa, Computing Centre, Ottawa, 53
University of Ottawa, Linguistics Documentation Centre, Ottawa, 53
University of Pennsylvania Computer Center, Philadelphia, 449
University of Rochester, Rochester, 437-8
University of South Florida, Tampa, 403-4
University of Tennessee, Knoxville, 453-4
University of Toronto, Toronto, 54
Wang Laboratories Inc, Tewksbury, 534

IBM 360/67
Brown University, Providence, 451
CSS Europe Ltd, London, 360-61
Carnegie-Mellon University, Pittsburgh, 445
Centre Interuniversitaire de Calcul de Grenoble, Grenoble, 94
Centro Nazionale Universitario di Calculo Elettronico, Pisa, 172
IBM Systems Development Institute, Canberra, 14
ITT Data Services, Paramus, 541
Insco Systems Corporation, Neptune, 541
Interactive Data Corporation, Waltham, 531
Newcastle Upon Tyne Polytechnic, Newcastle, 312
Northern Illinois University, DeKalb, 407
Rutgers, The State University, New Brunswick, 429
Stanford University, Stanford, 395
Technische Universität, Berlin, 120
Technische Universität Berlin, Institut für Informationsverarbteilung, Berlin, 120
Université de Grenoble, Grenoble, 97
University of British Columbia, Vancouver, 52
University of Durham, Durham, 321
University of Michigan, Ann Arbor, 419
University of Newcastle upon Tyne, Newcastle, 326
Washington State University, Pullman, 462
Wayne State University, Detroit, 419-20

IBM 360/75
Aerojets Electrosystems Company, Azusa, 470
Argonne National Laboratory, Argonne, 470
Avco Corporation, Wilmington, 470
Bowling Green State University, Bowling Green, 439-40
Comitato Nazionale per l'Energia Nucleare, Bologna, 175
IBM France, Neuilly-sur-Seine, 112
IBM Japan Ltd, Tokyo, 187

619

Kungliga Tekniska Högskola, Library-Documentation Centre, Stockholm, 260-61
McGill University, Montreal, 48-9
National Aeronautics and Space Administration, Pasadena, 467
Oak Ridge National Laboratory, Oak Ridge, 468
Research Institute for National Defence (4), Stockholm, 264
Stockholms Datamaskincentral, Stockholm, 259
University of California, Santa Barbara, 397
University of North Carolina at Chapel Hill, Chapel Hill, 439
University of Waterloo, Waterloo, 54
West Virginia University, Morgantown, 463

IBM 360/85
Systems Dimensions Ltd, Ottawa, 64

IBM 360/91
Oak Ridge National Laboratory, Oak Ridge, 468
Princeton University, Princeton, 429
Stanford University, Stanford, 395
University of California, Los Angeles, 396

IBM 360/130
National Coal Board, Cannock, 334

IBM 360/158
National Data Centre for Administrative Data Processing, Bromma, 259

IBM 360/165
Eastern Air Lines, Miami, 480-81

IBM 360/195
Eastern Air Lines, Miami, 480-81
Engineering Computer International Inc, Cambridge, 484
GTE Data Services Inc, Tampa, 519
Systematics International Ltd, Basildon, 379

IBM 370/135
ADB Produktion AB, Stockholm, 270-71
Apoteksbolaget, Stockholm, 264
Bradley University, Peoria, 406
Centurex Corporation, Los Angeles, 505-6
Companhia de Processamento de Dados do Maranhão, Maranhão, 37-8
Computer Services Ltd, Lagos, 223
Condata Inc, Philadelphia 558-9
Duke University, Durham, 438
Essele AR-Konsult AB, Stockholm, 267

Extel Communications Ltd, London, 365
Ibadan University, Ibadan, 222
Kidde Computer Services Company, Huntingdon Valley, 560
Lantbruksdata, Eskilstuna, 276-7
Local Authorities Data Processing Centre, Tel Aviv, 170
McDonnell Automation Company, St. Louis, 537-8
Management Computer Controls Inc, Memphis, 499
Municipio de Medellín, Medellín, 71
Nassau Community College, Garden City, 434
New Mexico State University, Las Cruces, 430
Josef Niedermair München, Munich, 140-1
Portsmouth Corporation, Portsmouth, 334
Raet Automation Consultancy and Service Bureau, Arnhem, 214
Rutgers, The State University, New Brunswick, 429
Seresco S.A., Barcelona, 257
Skýrsluvélar Ríkisins og Reykjavíkurborgar, Reykjavík, 149
Stichting Bevordering Computertoepassing Bouwwezen, Rotterdam, 205
Superdata S.A., Guanabara, 45
Teledata AG, Berne, 294
Tylin Management Systems Ltd, Edinburgh, 379
UCC-Automation Centre S.A., Brussels, 32
University of North Dakota, Grand Forks, 439
West Sussex County Council, Chichester, 335-6

IBM 370/145
Alpha Computer Service Corporation, New York, 543
Banque du Zaïre, Kinshasa, 576
Brandon Applied Systems Inc, New York, 489
British Rail, Derby, 336
Brostrom Shipping Company, Göteborg, 272
Cati-Mecanorga-Ergem, Paris, 109
Centro Tecnico de Proceso de Datos, Alicante, 256
Centrum voor Informatie Management N.V., Antwerp, 30
Construcões e Comércio Camargo Corrêa S.A., Vila Olímpia, 41
Datenzentrale Schleswig-Holstein, Kiel, 125
Departamento Nacional de Estadística, Bogotá, 70
Deutsche Bau- und Boden AG, Mainz, 135
N.V. Dienstverlening Overheids Adminstrative en Automatiserings Service Centrum van N. Samson N.V., Alphen, 211
Executive Data Systems, Cedar Rapids, 526
Général de Services Informatique, GSI-Entreprises, Paris, 112
Général de Service Informatique, Massy, 111-112

George Washington University, Washington, 402
ITT Data Services, East Barnett, 370
ITT Datenservice, Stuttgart, 139
Insco Systems Corporation, Neptune, 541
Iowa State University of Science and Technology, Ames, 410-11
Lantbruksdata, Eskilstuna, 276-7
Local Authorities Data Processing Centre, Tel Aviv, 170
Lowndes-Ajax Computer Service Ltd, Croydon, 371
McDonnell Automation Company, St Louis, 537-8
Macro-Pak Business Systems Inc, New York, 548
Maison Ch. Veillon S.A., Lausanne, 292
Messerschmitt-Boelkow-Blohm GmbH, Munich, 140
A/S Nor-Data, Trondheim, 230
Orda-B, Korbeek, 31
Raet Automation Consultancy and Service Bureau, Arnhem, 214
B.V. Rekencentrum Ogem, Rotterdam, 215
Rogaland College, Stavanger, 224
Christian Rovsing, Herlev, 83
Samson Automatiserings Service Centrum N.V., Alphen, 215-6
Seresco S. A., Barcelona, 257
I.P. Sharp Associates Ltd, Toronto, 58
Služba Društvenog Knjigovodstva Jugoslavije, Belgrade, 572
South Dakota State University, Brookings, 452
System Printing Italiana, Roma, 181
Teesside County Borough Council, Teesside, 335
Trygg-Hansa, Stockholm, 281
Universidade Federal do Rio de Janeiro, Rio de Janeiro, 35
Università di Padova, Padova, 174
Université Laval, Sainte-Foy, 51
University of Maine, Orono, 414-5
University of the Witwatersrand, Johannesburg, 247
Univest S.A. Administraçáo e Participaçóes, São Paulo, 45-6
Varvsindustrins Datacentral AB, Göteborg, 264
Vereinigte Osterreichische Eisen- und Stahlwerke AG, Linz, 24
Vereniging voor Centrale Electronische Administratie, Apeldoorn, 217
Virginia Commonwealth University, Richmond, 460
ŽTP Beograd, Belgrade, 574

IBM 370/155
Auburn University, Auburn, 390
Bayerisches Staatsministerium für Ernährung, Landwirtschaft und Forsten, Munich, 124
Bell Laboratories, Columbus, 471
A/S Bergen Datasenter, Bergen, 228

Index of Computer Installations

Bernische Datenverarbeitung AG, Berne, 287-8
Bureau of Statistics, Tokyo, 185
Caisse Générale d'Épargne et de Retraite, Brussels, 26-7
Central Electricity Generating Board, London, 331
Centre d'Études Techniques de l'Équipement, Aix-en-Provence, 100
Centro Nazionale Universitario di Calculo Elettronico, Pisa, 172
Compatabilité Statistique Informatic, Paris, 111
A. S. Computas, Oslo 228
I/S Datacentralen, Copenhagen, 77
Edinburgh Regional Computing Centre, Edinburgh, 364
Fellesdata/SIS, Oslo, 230
Finnish State Computer Centre, Helsinki, 88
IBM of Belgium S. A., Brussels, 31
ITT Data Services, Paramus, 541
Indian Institute of Technology, Madras, 151
Innenministerium des Landes Nordrhein-Westfalen, Düsseldorf, 125-6
Insco Systems Corporation, Neptune, 541
Institut National de Statistique, Brussels, 27
Instituto Brasiliero de Informatica, Rio de Janeiro, 38
Instituto Mexicano del Seguro Social, Mexico, 196
Kalle Anttila Oy, Helsinki, 90
Katholieke Universiteit te Leuven, Rekencentrum, Louvain, 26
Katholieke Universiteit te Nijmegen, Nijmegen, 198-9
McDonnell Automation Company, St. Louis, 537-8
McMaster University, Hamilton, 49
Macro-Pak Business Systems Inc, New York, 548
National Data Centre for Administrative Data Processing, Bromma, 259
Josef Niedermair München, Munich, 140-1
Orda-B, Korbeek, 31
Österreichisches Statistiches Zentralamt, Vienna, 22
PRC Computer Center Inc, McLean, 501
Simon Fraser University, Burnaby, 50
Southern Illinois University, Carbondale, 407
Spabankernas Datacentraler AB, Göteborg, 279
Sparbankernas Datacentraler AB Stockholm, 279
Sparekassernes Datacentraler, Copenhagen, 84
State University of New York School of Advanced Technology, Binghampton, 437
State University of New York, Stony Brook, 436
Sun Alliance and London Insurance Ltd, Horsham, 378-9
Tietotehdas Oy, Kilo, 91
Trinity University, San Antonio, 456

Universität Zürich, Zürich, 282
Université Laval, Sainte-Foy, 51
Universitet i Uppsala, Uppsala, 262
University of Saskatchewan, Computation Centre, Saskatoon, 54
Virginia Polytechnic Institute and State University, Blacksburg, 460-61
Wilford Computer Group Ltd, Manchester, 381
York University, Downsview, 55

IBM 370/165
Calspan Corporation, New York, 471-2
Central Electricity Generating Board, London, 331
Computel Systems Ltd, Ottawa, 60
Danmarks Tekniske Højskole, Copenhagen, 76
Duke University, Durham, 438
Ha-Technion, Haifa, 164-5
McDonnell Automation Company, St. Louis, 537-8
Messerschmitt-Boelkow-Blohm GmbH, Munich, 140
Northeast Regional Data Center, Gainesville, 403
Northern European University Computing Centre, Copenhagen, 76
Office Mechanization Centre, Jerusalem, 166
Ohio State University, Columbus, 441
Pennsylvania State University Computation Center, University Par, 447-8
Pontificia Universidade Católica do Rio de Janeiro, Rio de Janeiro, 33
Research Triangle Institute, Research Triangle Park, 474
Rheinische Friedrich-Wilhelms-Universität, Bonn, 119
Science Research Council, Daresbury, 339
Social Security Administration, Baltimore, 469
Statistics Canada, Ottawa, 56
Tennessee Valley Authority, Chattanooga, 469
Triangle Universities Computation Center, Triangle Park, 438
Uni-Coll Corporation, Philadelphia, 562
University of Cincinnati, Cincinnati, 442
University of North Carolina at Chapel Hill, Chapel Hill, 439
University of Toronto, Toronto, 54

IBM 1130
Åbo Akademi, Åbo, 86
Alcorn Agricultural and Mechanical College, Lorman, 422
American University, Washington 401
American University of Beirut, Beirut, 190-91
Applied Dynamics Europe, Rotterdam, 205

Applied Dynamics European Computation Centre, Rotterdam, 208
Associated Business Consultants Ltd, Beirut, 191
Augustana College, Sioux Falls, 451-2
Austin University, Sherman, 454
R. W. Beck and Associates, Seattle, 501-2
Boston College Mathematics Institute, Chestnut Hill, 416
Brandeis University, Waltham, 416
Bridgewater College, Bridgewater, 459
Brigham Young University, Provo, 458
Brighton Polytechnic, Brighton, 302-3
Broome Community College, Binghampton, 431
CIMS Group Inc, Pittsburgh, 497-8
Caltex Inc, Toledo, 554
Cambridgeshire College of Arts and Technology, Cambridge, 303-4
Carroll College, Waukesha, 464
Centre Expérimental de Recherches et d'Études du Batiment et des Travaux Publics, Paris, 101
Centro de Investigación de Técnicas Matemáticas Aplicadas a la Dirección de Empresas, Buenos Aires, 4
Centro Nacional de Cálculo, Mexico, 194
Centrum voor Informatieverwerking N.V., Utrecht, 209
Chipola Junior College, Marianna, 402
The Citadel, Charleston, 451
City University of New York Graduate School and University Center, New York, 431-2
Clarion State College, Clarion, 445-6
Coe College, Cedar Rapids, 410
Colgate University, Hamilton, 432-3
Companhia de Processamento de Dados do Maranhão Maranhão, 37-8
Computer Communications Inc, Inglewood, 476
Computer Engineering Applications Pty Ltd, Sydney, 14
Concord College, Athens, 463
Conseil National de la Recherche Scientifique, Beirut, 190
Cornell College, Mount Vernon, 410
Cybernetion Consultants Ltd, Edmonton, 57
Daneshgahe Pahlavi, Shiraz, 160
Department of Public Works, Djakarta, 160
Department of Trade and Industry, Stevenage, 337
Departamento Nacional de Planeación, Bogotá, 70
Dickinson College, Carlisle, 446
Eastern Michigan University, Ypsilanti, 418
École Nationale d'Ingénieurs, Metz, 95

École Supérieure d'Électricité, Malakoff, 96
École Supérieure d'Ingenieurs de Beyrouth, Beirut, 191
Educators Consultant Service Inc, New York, 531
Elektronisches Rechenzentrum, Bayreuth, 136
Engenharia Processamentos Electrônicos Ltda, Minas Gerais, 42
Erdos and Morgan Inc, New York, 546
Bruce Erts Associates Inc, Southfield, 486
Escola de Engenharia de Maranhão, Maranhão, 32
Escola de Engenharia Mauá, São Paulo, 33
Faculté des Sciences de St. Jérôme, Marseille, 96
Faculté Polytechnique de Mons, Mons, 25
Farnborough College of Technology, Farnborough, 306
Forestry Commission, Farnham, 337-8
Fullerton Junior College, Fullerton, 393
Gadsden State Junior College, Gadsden, 390
Genesee Community College, Flint, 418
Gesellschaft für Marktforschung, GmbH, Hamburg, 125
John Gilmore and Associates Inc, New York, 492
Glamorgan Polytechnic, Pontypridd, 306
Graphic Image Corporation, Chicago, 523
Grove City College, Grove City, 446
Dale L. Gulle & Assoc. Inc, Tulsa, 556-7
Hochschule für Bodenkultur in Wien, Vienna, 21
Hochschule für Sozial- und Wirtschaftswissenschaften, Linz, 21
Huddersfield Polytechnic, Huddersfield, 307
IBM do Brasil, São Paulo, 43
IBM Italia S.p.A., Milan, 180
IBM Italia S.p.A., Rome, 180
IBM Nederland N.V., Rijswijk, 212
IBM of Belgium S.A., Brussels, 31
Idaho State University, Pocatello, 405
Idan Computers Ltd, Tel Aviv, 170
Indiana Institute of Technology, Fort Wayne, 409
Industroprojekt, Zagreb, 573
Infotec Inc, Plainview, 492
Institut National des Sciences Appliquées, Villeurbanne, 93-4
Institute TNO for Mathematics, Information Processing and Statistics, The Hague, 203
Instituto Tecnológico de Aeronáutica, São Jose dos Campos, 38
Istanbul Devlet Mühenddislik ve Mimarlik Akademisi, Istanbul, 298
Jordanhill College of Education, Glasgow, 308
Jugomont-Jugobeton, Zagreb, 575
Jyväskylän Yliopisto, Jyväskylä, 87
Lester B. Knight and Associates Inc, Chicago, 482

Knight Wegenstein Ltd, London, 346
Lafayette College, Easton, 446
Lawrence Institute of Technology, Southfield, 418
Leo Computer Bureaux (Pty) Ltd, Johannesburg, 251-2
Lewis and Clark College, Portland, 444
Lindenwood Colleges, St. Charles, 424
Lock Haven State College, Lock Haven, 447
Logisterion, Rotterdam, 123
Macalester College, St Paul, 420
McDonnell Automation Company, St. Louis, 537-8
McKinsey and Company Inc, New York, 493
Missouri Southern College, Joplin, 424
Moray House College of Education, Edinburgh, 311
Morningside College, Sioux City, 411
National University of Ireland, Cork, 162
North-East London Polytechnic, London, 312
Northwest Computing Service, Seattle, 566
Nova Scotia Technical College, Halifax, 49
Observatoire de Marseille, Marseille, 102-3
Pennsylvania State University Computer Assisted Instruction Laboratory, University Park, 448
Photo Data Inc, Washington, 516
Pontificia Universidad Católica del Peru, Lima, 234-5
Pontifica Universidade Católica do Rio de Janeiro, Rio de Janeiro, 33
Portland State University, Portland, 444
Potchefstroom University for Christian Higher Education, Potchefstroom, 245
Processamento de Dados S.A., Pernambuco, 40
Rose-Hulman Institute of Technology, Terra Haute, 409
Royal Scientific Society, Amman, 189
St Francis College, Loretto, 448
Saint Louis University, Baguio City, 235
St. Mary's College, Winona, 421
St. Mary's University, Halifax, 50
Serete S.A., São Paulo, 40
Sheffield Polytechnic, Sheffield, 316
Société d'Études des Systèmes d'Automation, Paris, 115
Southampton Technical College, Southampton, 317
Southern Illinois University, Carbondale, 407
Southwest Computer College Inc, Albuquerque, 389
Southwestern State University, Weatherford, 443-4
State University of New York, Brockport, 436
State University of New York, Maritime College, New York,
Survey Department, Kuala Lumpur, 193

Sveučilište u Zagrabu, Zagreb, 570
Tahal Consulting Engineers Ltd, Tel Aviv, 169
Teesside County Borough Council, Teesside, 335
Thomas More College, Fort Mitchell, 413
Unid. Processamento de Dados (FEAUSP), São Paulo, 32
Universidad de Antioquía, Medellin, 68
Universidad de la Patagonia 'San Juan Bosco', Comodoro Rivadavia, 2
Universidad de Oriente, Puerto La Cruz, 568
Universidad del Cauca, Cauca, 69
Universidad del Norte, Antofagasta, 65
Universidad del Valle, Cali, 69
Universidad Iberoamericano, Mexico, 195
Universidad Nacional de Ascunción, Ascunción, 234
Universidad Nacional de Córdoba, Centro de Computación, Córdoba, 3
Universidad Pontificia Bolivariana, Medellin, 69
Universidad Tecnológica de Pereira, Pereira, 69-70
Universidade de São Paulo, Centro de Processamento de Dados, São Carlos, 34
Universidade Estadual de Campinas, Campinas, 34
Universidade Federal de Minas Gerais, Minas Gerais, 34
Universidade Federal de Paraíba, Paraíba, 34
Universidade Federal de Pernambuco, Recife, 34-5
Universidade Federal de Sergipe, Sergipe, 35
Universidade Federal do Paraná Curitiba, 35
Universidade Federal do Rio de Janeiro, Rio de Janeiro 35
Universidade Federal Fluminense, Niterói, 36
Universitat Hanegev, Beer-Sheva, 165
Université de Neuchâtel, Neuchâtel, 283
Université de Paris IX, Paris, 98
Université de Poitiers, Poitiers, 98-9
Universiti Malaya, Kuala Lumpur, 192
University of Akron, Akron, 442
University of Arkansas, Little Rock, 392
University of Baghdad, Baghdad, 161
University of Calcutta, Calcutta, 152
University of Cape Town, Cape Town, 245
University of Durham, Durham, 321
University of Natal, Durban, 246
University of Nevada, Las Vegas, 427
University of Newcastle upon Tyne, Newcastle upon Tyne, 326
University of Puerto Rico U.P.R. Station, 241-2
University of Redlands, Redlands, 398

Index of Computer Installations

University of Toledo, Toledo, 442
University of Vermont, Burlington, 459
University of Western Ontario, Althouse College of Education, London, 55
University of Wisconsin, Stevens Point, 465-6
University of Wisconsin, Whitewater, 466
Univerza v Ljubljani, Ljubljana, 570-71
Univerzitet u Beogradu, Belgrade, 571
Univerzitet Kiril i Metódij vo Skoplje, Skopje, 571
Verein Deutscher Eisenhütterleute/Betriebsforchungsinstitut, Düsseldorf, 127
Victoria University of Wellington, Wellington, 218
Višja Tehniška Sola Maribor, Maribor 570
Washington and Lee University, Lexington, 461
Wesleyan University, Middletown 401
West Coast University, Los Angeles, 398
West Pakistan University of Engineering and Technology, Lahore, 232
Wichita State University, Wichita, 412-3
Winona State College, Winona, 422
Woods Gordon & Co, Montreal, 59
Xavier University of Louisiana, New Orleans, 414

IBM 1131
Kauppakorkeakoulu, Helsinki, 87
Société Anonyme des Ateliers de Secheron, Genève, 293

IBM 1311
Fairleigh Dickinson University, Rutherford, 428

IBM 1401
AC-Service Gesellschaft für Automatische Datenverarbeitung GmbH, Hamburg, 132
AC-Service Gesellschaft für Automatische Datenverarbeitung GmbH, Stuttgart, 132
Ahmedabad Electricity Co Ltd, Ahmedabad, 158
American University of Beirut, Beirut, 190-91
Associated Business Consultants, Calcutta, 157
Automation Centre International, Wettingen, 287
Bemidji State College, Bemidji, 420
Ernest E Blanche & Associates Inc, Kensington, 527
Bombay Suburban Electric Supply Ltd, Bombay, 158
Champion Service Corporation, Cleveland, 554-5
Computer Applications Inc, New York, 489

Computer Service Consultants Inc, Warwick, 499
Computer Services International, Bombay, 158
Control Data Corporation, Boston, 516
Data Services Corporation, Dayton, 555
Datalogics Inc, Cleveland, 555
Eastern Railway, Mughalsarai, 152-3
Electronic Data Service Inc, Wilmington, 515
Fairleigh Dickinson University, Rutherford, 428
Fabricato S.A., Medellín, 72
Florida State University, Tallahassee, 403
Hindustan Motors Ltd, Hooghly, 158-9
IBM Chile S.A.C. Ltda, Santiago, 66
IBM Co Ltd, Toronto, 62
IBM do Brasil, Belo Horizonte, 43
IBM do Brasil, Fortaleza, 43
IBM do Brasil, Pôrto Alegre, 43
IBM do Brasil, Rio de Janeiro, 43
IBM do Brasil, Salvador, 43
IBM do Brasil, São Paulo, 43
IBM Finland, Helsinki, 89-90
IBM Ireland Ltd, Dublin, 164
IBM Italia S.P.A., Bologna, 180
IBM Italia S.p.A., Calgari, 180
IBM Italia S.p.A., Florence, 180
IBM Italia S.p.A., Genoa, 180
IBM Italia S.p.A., Milan, 180
IBM Italia S.p.A., Naples, 180
IBM Italia S.p.A., Palermo, 180
IBM Italia S.p.A., Turin, 180
IBM Italia S.p.A., Trieste, 180
IBM Italia S.p.A., Verona, 180
IBM Japan Ltd, Nagoya, 187
IBM Japan Ltd, Osaka, 187
IBM Japan Ltd, Yokohama, 187
IBM, Madrid, 257
IBM Nederland N.V., Rijswijk, 212
IBM of Belgium S.A., Ghent, 31
IBM A/S, Oslo 230
IBM Portuguesa SARL, Lisboa, 241
IBM Portuguesa SARL, Porto, 241
IBM South Africa (Pty) Ltd, Johannesburg, 251
IBM Switzerland, Basle, 290-91
IBM Switzerland, Geneva, 290-91
IBM United Kingdom Ltd, Bristol, 368
IBM United Kingdom Ltd, Nottingham, 368
IBM World Trade Corporation, Bombay, 159
IBM World Trade Corp., Buenos Aires, 5
IBM World Trade Corporation, Cairo, 85
IBM World Trade Corporation, Calcutta, 159
IBM World Trade Corporation, Caracas, 569
IBM World Trade Corporation, Curaçao, 217
IBM World Trade Corporation, Karachi, 233
IBM World Trade Corporation, Lima, 235
IBM World Trade Corporation, Montevideo, 568

IBM World Trade Corporation, Nassau, 24
IBM World Trade Corporation, Port of Spain, 296
IBM World Trade Corporation, Salisbury, 242
IBM World Trade Corporation, San Jose, 73
IBM World Trade Corporation, Valencia, 569
Indian Institute of Technology, Kanpur, 151
Institut Blaise Pascal, Paris, 102
Institut Teknologi Bandung, Bandung, 159
Integral Coach Factory, Madras, 153
Interdata AG, Basel, 291
Interdata AG Zürich, 291
International Büromaschinen, Linz, 23
International Systems Associates Ltd, New York, 548
Iowa State University of Science and Technology, Ames, 410-11
John Hopkins University, Baltimore, 415
Joint Plant Committee, Calcutta, 153
Kansas State College of Pittsburgh, Pittsburgh, 412
I/S Kommunernes EDB-Central, Copenhagen, 81
Marist College, Poughkeepsie, 433-4
Matrix Corporation, El Segundo, 549 549
Milner Brothers Products, Los Angeles, 509
National Statistical Office, Bangkok, 295
New South Wales Institute of Technology, Broadway, 9
Northeast Missouri State College, Kirksville, 424
Northeast Regional Data Center, Gainesville, 403
Occidental College, Los Angeles, 394
Pacific Lutheran University, Tacoma, 462
Pacific Union College, Angwin, 394
Pennsylvania State University Computation Center, University Park, 447-8
Proceda S.R.L., Buenos Aires, 6
Rijksuniversiteit te Utrecht, Utrecht, 199-200
Roosevelt University, Chicago, 407
Saab-Scania AB, Linköping, 278
Serguros Bolívar, Bogotá, 73
South Central Railway, Secunderabad, 154
Southern Railway, Madras, 154
Southwest Missouri State College, Springfield, 425
State Bank of India, Bombay, 154
State University of New York, Brockport, 436
Swiss Federal Railways, Bern, 284
Tata Consultancy Services, Bombay, 157

Technische Hochschule, Darmstadt 120
Tovarna Avtomobilov in Motorjev Maribor, Maribor, 576
Tennessee Agricultural and Industrial State University, Nashville, 453
Trinidad State Junior College, Trinidad, 399
Tulane University of Louisiana, New Orleans, 414
Tuskegee Institute, Tuskegee, 390
UCC-Automation Centre S.A., Brussels, 32
United Bank Ltd, Karachi, 233
University of Akron, Akron, 442
University of Delaware, Newark, 401
University of Georgia, Athens, 404-5
University of Kansas, Lawrence, 412
University of Tampa, Tampa, 404
University of Texas, Arlington, 456-7
University of Wisconsin, Stevens Point, 465-6
University of Wyoming, Laramie, 466
Vanderbilt University, Nashville, 454
Washington University, St Louis, 426
Western Railway, Bombay, 154

IBM 1407
Carnegie-Mellon University, Pittsburgh, 445
Universidad Nacional del Litoral, Santa Fé, 3

IBM 1410
AC-Service Gesellschaft für Automatische Datenverarbeitung GmbH, Düsseldorf, 132
Empresa Colombiana de Petróleos, Bogotá, 70-71
IBM Colombia Ltda, Barranquilla, 73
IBM Colombia Ltda, Bogotá, 73
IBM A/S, Oslo, 230
IBM World Trade Corporation, Bombay, 159
IBM World Trade Corporation, Kinshasa, 576
Mechanised Business Inc, Pittsburgh, 561
Metropolitan Junior College District, Kansas City, 388
Postbanken, Stockholm, 263
Tulane University of Louisiana, New Orleans, 414
University of Kentucky, Lexington, 413
University of South Florida, Tampa, 403-4
Verwaltungsrechenzentrum AG, St Gallen, 294

IBM 1440
Bogføringsforeningen Automationscentralen, Naestved, 78
Bournemouth College of Technology, Bournemouth, 302
Dakota Data Inc, Bismarck, 553
IBM South Africa (Pty) Ltd, Johannesburg, 251
Ipargazdaszgi, Szervezesi es Számitastechnikai Intezet, Budapest, 147

Southern Computer Service, Dothan, 503

IBM 1460
Computer Services International, Bombay, 158
IBM Co Ltd, Toronto. 62
IBM Colombia Ltda, Bogotá, 73
IBM Italia S.p.A., Rome, 180
IBM World Trade Corporation, Teheran, 161
International Systems Associates Ltd, New York, 548
Macquarie University, North Rhyde, 8
Parsons College, Fairfield, 411
University of Wisconsin, Madison, 465
Wayne State University, Detroit, 419-20

IBM 1500
Fairfield University, Fairfield, 400
Kansas City (Missouri) Public Schools, Kansas City, 423

IBM 1620
Ahmedabad Textile Industry's Research Association, Ahmedabad, 154
American University of Beirut, Beirut, 190-91
Aristoteleion Panepistimion Thessalonikis, Thessaloniki, 143
Atomic Energy Centre, Dacca, 24
Baylor University, Waco, 454
Boğazici University, Istanbul, 297
Boston College Mathematics Institute, Chestnut Hill, 416
Caja Provincial de Ahorros, Córdoba, 255-6
Carleton College, Northfield, 420
Catholic University of America, Washington, 401-2
Central Mechanical Engineering Research Institute, Durgapur, 155
Centre Cantonal d'Informatique, Geneva, 288
Centro de Calculo Cientifico, Lisboa, 240-41
Centro Superior de Procesamiento de la Informacion, La Plata, 1
Centralia College, Centralia, 461
Chulalongkorn University, Bangkok, 295
Colgate University, Hamilton, 432-3
Computer Services International, Bombay, 158
Concordia College, Moorhead, 420
Council of Scientific and Industrial Research, Hyderabad, 155
Council of Scientific and Industrial Research, Uttar Pradesh, 155
Defence Research and Development Laboratory, Hyderabad, 152
Digital AG, Zürich, 289
Escuela de Arquitectura, Barcelona, 252-3
Escuela Tecnica Superior de Ingenieros de Minas, Madrid, 253
Ethnikon Metsovion Polytechneion Athinai, Athens, 144

Fairleigh Dickinson University, Rutherford, 428
IBM S/A, Oslo, 230
IBM Portuguesa SARL, Lisboa, 241
IBM World Trade Corporation, Bombay, 159
IBM World Trade Corporation, Caracas, 569
IBM World Trade Corporation, Delhi, 159
Ibadan University, Ibadan, 222
Indian Council of Agricultural Research, Delhi, 156
Indian Institute of Technology, Kanpur, 151
Institut d'études Nucléaires, Alger, 1
Instituto Tecnológico de Aeronáutica, São Jose dos Campos, 38
Istanbul Teknik Universitesi, Istanbul, 298
Monterey Peninsula College, Monterey, 393
National Aeronautics and Space Administration, Sandusky, 467
National Chiao Tung University, Hsinchu, 67
National University of Ireland, Cork, 162
National University of Ireland, Dublin, 162-3
New Mexico Highlands University, Las Vegas, 430
Newark College of Engineering, Newark, 429
Newcastle upon Tyne Polytechnic, Newcastle, 312
North Dakota State University, Fargo, 439
Panjab University, Chandigarh, 151-2
Programme Evaluation Organisation, Delhi, 154
Riverside City College, Riverside, 394
St Edward's University, Austin, 455
St Francis Xavier University, Antigonish, 50
St John's University, Collegville, 421
Seattle University, Seattle, 462
Seton Hall University, South Orange, 429-30
Snow College, Ephraim, 458
Southwestern at Memphis, Memphis, 453
Technikum Winterthur (Ingenieurschule), Winterthur, 282
Teesside Polytechnic, Teesside, 317-8
Tennessee Agricultural and Industrial State University, Nashville, 453
The Polytechnic, Wolverhampton, 314
Trinidad State Junior College, Trinidad, 399
Tuskegee Institute, Tuskegee, 390
United States Naval Academy, Annapolis, 389
Universidad Católica de Chile, Santiago, 64-5
Universidad de Concepción, Concepción, 65

Index of Computer Installations

Universidad de Costa Rica, San José, 73
Universidad de Navarra, San Sebastián, 253
Univerdidad Industrial de Santander, Santander, 69
Universidad Nacional de Tucumán, San Miguel de Tucumán, 3
Universidad Técnica 'Federico Santa María', Valparaíso, 65-6
Università degli Studi di Bari, Bari, 173
Universität Basel, Basel, 282
Université de Poitiers, Poitiers, 98-9
Université de Rennes, Rennes, 99
Universitet i Umeå, Umeå, 262
University College of Swansea, University of Wales, Swansea, 319
University of Akron, Akron, 442
Univeristy of Alaska, Fairbanks, 391
University of Delaware, Newark, 401
University of Delhi, Delhi, 152
University of Georgia, Athens, 404-5
University of Ghana, Accra, 142
University of Idaho, Pocatello, 405
University of Lagos, Lagos, 222
University of Montana, Missoula, 426
University of Nevada, Reno, 427
University of New England, Armidale, 11
University of New Hampshire, Durham, 428
University of New South Wales, Wollongong University College, Wollongong, 11
University of Santo Tomas, Manila, 235
University of Science and Technology, Ashanti, 142
University of South Dakota, Vermillion, 452
University of Texas, Arlington, 456-7
University of Vermont, Burlington, 459
University of the West Indies, Kingston, 182
University of the West Indies, St. Augustine, 296
University of Windsor, Windsor, 55
Wandsworth Technical College, London, 330
Worcester Polytechnic Institute, Worcester, 417-8

IBM 1710
Washington University, St Louis, 426

IBM 1800
Centro Informazioni Studi Esperienze, Milan, 175
Centro Nazionale Universitario di Calculo Elettronico, Pisa, 172
Chulalongkorn University, Bangkok, 295
Indian Institute of Technology, Kanpur, 151
Institut für Medizinische Datenverarbeitung der Gesellschaft für Strahlen- und Umweltforschung mbH, München, 127
Institutt for Atomenergi, Halden, 226

McDonnell Automation Company, St Louis, 537-8
National Institute of Oceanography, Wormley, 338
National University of Ireland, Galway, 163
Randolph-Macon College, Ashland, 460
Science Research Council, Daresbury, 339
Stichting Het R. K. Gasthius, Tilburg, 216
Technische Hochschule in Wien, Vienna, 22
Teledyne Corporation, Houston, 475
University of Louisville, Louisville, 413-4

IBM 2318
IBM Colombia Ltda, Cali, 73

IBM 2780
IBM Switzerland, St Gallen, 290-291

IBM 7040
Carnegie-Mellon University, Pittsburgh, 445
Institut Royal Météorologique de Belgique (I.R.M.), Brussels, 27
Marquette University, Milwaukee, 464
Politecnico di Milano, Milano, 172-3
Technische Hochschule, Darmstadt, 120
Technische Hochschule in Wien, Rechenzentrum, Vienna, 22
University of Arkansas, Fayetteville, 391-2
University of Kentucky, Lexington, 413
University of Sydney, Basser Computing Centre, Sydney, 12
University of Western Ontario, London, 54-5
Waseda University, Tokyo, 185

IBM 7044
IBM World Trade Corporation, Delhi, 159
Indian Institute of Technology, Kanpur, 151
Pontifícia Universidade Católica do Rio de Janeiro, Rio de Janeiro, 33
Université de Toulouse III, Toulouse, 99
University of Melbourne, Melbourne, 10

IBM 7070
IBM World Trade Corporation, Caracas, 569
Saab-Scania AB, Linköping, 278
Eidgenössisches Statistisches Amt, Bern, 282
Wayne State University, Detroit, 419-20

IBM 7090
Centro Nazionale Universitario di Calculo Elettronico, Pisa, 172

Control Data Corporation, Washington, 516
Gesellschaft für Mathematik und Datenverarbeitung mbH, St Augustin-Birlinghoven, 126
IBM Co Ltd, Toronto, 62
IBM Japan Ltd, Tokyo, 187
Universidad de Madrid, Madrid, 253
University of Pittsburgh Computer Center, Pittsburgh, 450
Western Washington State College, Bellingham, 462-3

IBM 7094
Comitato Nazionale per l'Energia Nucleare, Bologna, 175
Control Data Corporation, Boston, 516
Control Data Corporation, Los Angeles, 516
Deutsches Rechenzentrum, Darmstadt, 117
Georgia State University, Atlanta, 404
Imperial College of Science and Technology, Dept of Computing and Control, London, 307-8
Johns Hopkins University, Baltimore, 415
McDonnell Automation Company, St Louis, 537-8
Matrix Corporation, El Segundo, 549
Purdue University, West Lafayette, 409
United States Naval Academy, Annapolis, 389
University of Chicago, Chicago, 407-8
University of Georgia, Athens, 404-5
University of Maryland, College Park, 415
University of Toronto, Toronto, 54
Yale University, New Haven, 401

IBM System/3
Allied Computer Technology, Santa Monica, 505
Bethany College, Bethany, 463
Dâneshgâhé Isfahan, Isfahan, 160
Data Usage Corporation, Fort Lee, 540
Dixie Data Processing Inc, Warsaw, 553
Dr Suchan Ratio-Data, Weinheim, 142
El Paso Data Services Inc, El Paso, 386
Hinds Junior College, Raymond, 442
IBM Finland, Helsinki, 89-90
IBM Service Bureau, Abidjan, 182
Jogomontaza-Ventilator, Zagreb, 575
Plymouth State College, Plymouth, 428
Pontifícia Universidade Católica de Campinas, Campinas, 33
Reno Junior College of Business, Reno, 389
Southwest Computer College Inc, Albuquerque, 389
Universidad Nacional Autónoma de Nicaragua, Managua, 221
University of Albuquerque, Albuquerque, 431
West Coast Schools, Los Angeles, 398

IBM System/7
Digitron AG, Nidau, 285
Instituto Tecnológico y de Estudios Superiores de Monterrey, Monterrey, 194-5
Università di Padova, Padova, 174

ICL 4/30
Challenge Corporation Ltd, Wellington, 219
Metalogic Ltd, Bristol, 373
Wright, Stephenson and Co Ltd, Wellington, 221

ICL 4/50
Baric Computing Services Ltd, London, 354-5
Computer Aid Ltd, Cheadle Hulme, 358
Datasolve International Ltd, London, 362-3
Department of Statistics, Pretoria, 247
Edinburgh Corporation, Edinburgh, 333
Leo Computer Bureaux (Pty) Ltd, Johannesburg, 251-2
New Zealand Post Office, Wellington, 218-9
North Staffordshire Polytechnic, Stafford, 313
South African Railways, Durban, 248
South African Railways, Johannesburg, 248
University College, Cardiff, University of Wales, Cardiff, 318-9
University of Bristol Computer Science Department, Bristol, 320
University of Exeter, Exter, 322

ICL 4/70
London Boroughs Joint Computer Committee, London, 333-4
Marconi Company, Chelmsford, 338
National Data Processing Service, London, 375-6
Rothamsted Experimental Station, Harpenden, 339
South of Scotland Electricity Board, Glasgow, 335
United Kingdom Atomic Energy Authority, Abingdon, 335
University of Aberdeen Computing Centre, Aberdeen, 319

ICL 4/72
National Data Processing Service, London, 375-6
South of Scotland Electricity Board, Glasgow, 335

ICL 4/75
Baric Computing Services Ltd, London, 354-5
Edinburgh Regional Computing Centre, Edinburgh, 364
University of Bristol, Computer Centre, Bristol, 320
University of Bristol, Department of Computer Science, Bristol, 320

ICL 558
Brisbane City Council, Brisbane, 13

ICL 1201
Hobart Technical College, Hobart, 8

ICL 1300
Alembic Chemical Works Company Ltd, Baroda, 158
Centralny Ośrodek Doskonalenia Kadr Kierowniczych, Warsaw, 238-9

ICL 1400
Birkbeck College, University of London, 301

ICL 1500
Baric Computing Services Ltd, London, 354-5
Elektronische Datenverarbeitung Ag, Basle, 290
Housing Commission, Victoria, Melbourne, 13
International Computers and Tabulators A/S, Copenhagen, 80-81
International Computers (Central Africa) (Private) Ltd, Salisbury, 242

ICL 1510
International Computers (Central Africa) (Private) Ltd, Salisbury, 242

ICL 1900
Bendigo Institute of Technology, Bendigo, 6
ICL Computer Education in Schools, London, 300
International Computers Ltd, Singapore, 245
Nigerian Ports Authority, Lagos, 222

ICL 1901
Ahmadu Bello University, Zaria, 221-2
Alcan Aluminium of South Africa Ltd, Pietermaritzburg, 250
Angpanneföreningen, Stockholm, 266
Applied Computer Techniques Ltd, London, 353-4
Ballarat Institute of Advanced Education, Canberra, 6
Capricornia Institute of Advanced Education, Rockhampton, 7
Central Electricity Board, Curepipe, 194
City of Ndola, Ndola, 577
City Treasurer's Department, Port Elizabeth, 247
Computer Services (South West) Ltd, Plymouth, 359
Computers in Business Ltd, London, 360

Consolidated Brick and Pipe Investments Ltd, Auckland, 219
Counter-Data AB, Stockholm, 273
Doncaster Rural District Council, Doncaster, 333
Dublin Health Authority, Dublin, 163
Eastern Regional Hospital Board Scotland, Dundee, 333
Falkirk Technical College, Falkirk, 305-6
Flyhtekniska Försöksanstalten, Bromma, 264
Gordon Institute of Technology, Geelong, 7
Institut Universitaire de Technologie, Paris, 96
Institut Universitaire de Technologie, Villeurbanne, 94
Institut Universitaire de Technologie-Informatique, Nancy, 96
Integrant Computer Bureau, Cobham, 369
International Computers Ltd, Port Louis, 193-4
Kenya Commercial Bank, Nairobi, 189
Leeds Polytechnic, Leeds, 309
Malawi Railways Ltd, Limbe, 192
Mauritius Computing Services Ltd, Port Louis, 194
May Roberts Ltd, Dublin, 164
Medway and Maidstone College of Technology, Chatham, 311
Ministry of Finance, Kingstown, 244
Natal Oil and Soap Industries (Pty) Ltd, Jacobs, 252
National Agricultural Marketing Board, Lusaka, 577
Norwich City College, Norwich, 313
Olivetti Africa (Pty) Ltd, Johannesburg, 252
Paisley College of Technology, Paisely, 313
Preston Institute of Technology, Preston, 9
Preston Polytechnic, Preston, 314
Rhodes University, Grahamstown, 245
Scan Data Ltd, Farnborough, 251
Slough College of Technology, Slough, 316
State Bank of Pakistan, Karachi, 232
State Engineering Corporation, Colombo, 258
Stroede AB, Torslanda, 280
Svenska Stadsfördbundet, Stockholm, 259-60
Swinburne College of Technology, Hawthorn, 10
Taikoo Dockyard and Engineering Company of Hong Kong Ltd, Hong Kong, 145
Université de Nancy I et de Nancy II, Nancy, 97-8
University of Dar-es-Salaam, Dar-es-Salaam, 295
University of Essex, Colchester, 322
University of Port Elizabeth, Port Elizabeth, 246
University of Rhodesia, Sailsbury, 242
University of Southampton, Southampton, 327-8

Index of Computer Installations

Victoria University of Manchester, Administrative Computer Unit, Manchester, 329
Woodall-Duckham Computing Services Ltd, Hove, 381

ICL 1902
ADB-System AB, Göteborg, 271
Alpha Computer Centre (Cape) (Pty) Ltd, Parow East, 250
Alpha Computer Centre (Pty) Ltd, Mobeni, 250
Applied Computer Techniques Ltd, Bristol, 353-4
Applied Computer Techniques Ltd, Leicester, 353-4
Bristol Polytechnic, Bristol, 303
Carl Soderberg AB, Stockholm, 279
Central Computer Services (Highlands) Ltd, Inverness, 356
Centre de Traitement des Informations, Aix-en-Provence, 109
Chulalongkorn University, Bangkok, 295
Computer Bureau Ltd, Christchurch, 219
Computer Bureau (Waikato) Ltd, Hamilton, 219
Computer Power, Lowton, 299
Computer Services Ltd, Dublin, 163-4
Computer Systems Implementations Ltd, Glasgow, 360
Comtime (Manchester) Ltd, Stretford, 360
Data Sciences International Ltd, Leeds, 361-2
Data Sciences International Ltd, Norwich, 362
Datamatic A/S, Copenhagen, 79
Datasolve International Ltd, London, 362-3
EWP Computer Services Ltd, Karachi, 232-3
A/S Fyns Data Service, Odense, 80
GMS Computer Services, Sheffield, 366
Hermes Computing Services Ltd, London, 366-7
Horsens Datacentral, Horsens, 80
Hoskyns Systems Ltd, Birmingham, 367
Independent Computer Services Ltd, Belfast, 369
International Computers (East Africa) Ltd, Nairobi, 189-90
International Computers S.A. (Pty) Ltd, Johannesburg, 251
International Computers Ltd, Port of Spain, 296
Iraqi Republic Railways, Baghdad, 161-2
Kasad Computer Services Ltd, Harlow, 370-71
Kenya Commercial Bank, Nairobi, 189
Kirloslar Engines Ltd, Poona, 159
Kommersiell Databehandling AB, Frölunda, 276
Liverpool Polytechnic, Liverpool, 309
Medway Data Services Ltd, Chatham, 373

Mills Associates Ltd, Monmouth, 374
Ministry of Finance, Port Louis, 193
Ministry of Planning, Tripoli, 192
Municipal and Water Computer Services, Kinston, 182-3
National Coal Board, Lowton, 334
Polytechnic of Central London, London, 313-4
J. Short Data Centre, London 377-8
Société de Gestion Électronique, Neuilly-sur-Seine, 115
Standard Bank Nigeria Ltd, Lagos, 223
Sunderland Polytechnic, Sunderland, 317
AB Teleplan, Solna, 270
Thames Polytechnic, London, 318
United Nations Educational, Scientific and Cultural Organization, Paris, 101
University of Nairobi, Nairboi, 189
University of Pretoria, Pretoria, 246
University of the Orange Free State, Bloemfontein, 247
Western Australia Institute of Technology, South Bentley, 12-13
Winstone Ltd, Auckland, 221
Zavod za Ekonomiju, Zagreb, 574

ICL 1903
Applied Computer Techniques Ltd, Birmingham, 353-4
Baric Computing Services Ltd, London, 354-5
Blackburn College of Technology and Design, Blackburn, 301-2
British Ship Research Association, Wallsend, 337
Brunel University, Uxbridge, 303
Caisse Regionale de Credit Agricole Mutuel d'Avignon et de Vauvluse, Avignon, 108
Cambridge Computer Services Ltd, Cambridge, 356
Central Bureau of Statistics, Djakarta, 159-60
D-A Computer Services Ltd, Sheffield, 361
Data-Inform, Risskov, 79
Department of Trade and Industry, Stevenage, 337
Elektronski Računski Center, Rijeka, 574
L. M. Ericsson Pty Ltd, Broadmeadows, 18
Ex Data GmbH, Nürnberg, 136
Facta N.V., The Hague, 211
Flintshire College of Technology, Deeside, 306
ICL Data AB, Solna, 275
International Computers and Tabulators, Copenhagen, 80-81
International Computers (New Zealand) Ltd, Auckland, 220
International Computers (New Zealand) Ltd, Wellington, 220

Isis Computer Services Ltd, London, 369-70
Lanchester Polytechnic, Coventry, 308-9
Manchester Computer Centre Ltd, Manchester, 373
Midas Ltd, London, 373-4
Middlesex Polytechnic, Enfield, 311
NIM igüszi, Budapest, 148
New University of Ulster, Londonderry, 312
Norrdata AB, Sundsvall, 277
Scottish Computer Services Ltd, Glasgow, 377
Short Brothers and Harland, Belfast, 340
W. H. Smith & Son Ltd, London, 378
Televerkets Industriavdelning, Nynäshamm, 281
The Polytechnic, Wolverhampton, 314
Tilburg School of Economics, Social Sciences and Law, Tilburg, 202
South Australian Institute of Technology, Adelaide, 10
South Australian Institute of Technology, Ingle Farm, 10
Southern Cross Computer Pty Ltd, Toowoomba, 20
Tata Consultancy Services, Bombay, 157
Upper Clyde Shipbuilders Ltd, Glasgow, 380

ICL 1904
Baric Computing Services Ltd, London, 354-5
Capital Cities Computer Centres Ltd, Watford, 356
Caulfield Institute of Technology, Caulfield East, 7
Centralny Osrodek Informatyki Gornictwa i Energetyki, Katowice, 240
Centre-File (Northern) Ltd, Manchester, 357
Computel Ltd, Bracknell, 358
Computer-Aided Design Centre, Cambridge, 332
Computer Power, Doncaster, 299
Computer Power, Edinburgh, 299
Cyberna S.A., Genève, 289
Datasolve International Ltd, London, 362-3
Department of Health and Social Security, Reading, 332
Department of Statistics, Kuala Lumpur, 192-3
Ex Data GmbH, Nürnberg, 136
Gemeentelijk Centrum voor Elektronische Informatieverwerking, Amsterdam, 203
International Computers Ltd, Windsor, 300
Központi Statisztikai Hivatal Szamitokozpont, Budapest, 147
Loughborough University of Technology, Loughborough, 310

Ministry of Finance, Lusaka, 577
National Coal Board, Doncaster, 334
National Coal Board, Edinburgh, 334
New South Wales Institute of Technology, Broadway, 9
North Gloucestershire College of Technology, Cheltenham, 312-3
Queen Mary College, University of London, London, 315
Queensland State Treasury, Brisbane, 13-14
Redac Software Ltd, Tewkesbury, 351
Redal Software Ltd, Tewkesbury, 376-7
Számitástechnikai és Ugyvitelszervezö Vállalat, Budapest, 149
University College of Swansea, University of Wales, Swansea, 319
University of Hong Kong and the Chinese University of Hong Kong, Kowloon, 145
University of London Management Systems Department, London, 325
University of Mauritius, Réduit, 193
University of New England, Armidale, 11
University of Newcastle, Newcastle, 11
University of Strathclyde, Glasgow, 328
Victoria University of Manchester, Regional Computer Centre, Manchester, 330
1900 Programming Ltd, London, 353

ICL 1905
Automatic Data Processing Ltd, Hounslow, 354
Baric Computing Services Ltd, London, 354-5
Brighton Polytechnic, Brighton, 302-3
Capital Cities Computer Centres Ltd, Watford, 356
Central Electricity Generating Board, Bramhall, 331-2
Central Statistical Office, Warszawa, 238
Computer and Mechanographic Centre for Data Processing, Bucharest, 243
Cranfield Institute of Technology, Cranfield, 305
Kingston Polytechnic, Kingston, 308
London Polytechnics Computer Unit, London, 310
Magyar Tudományos Akadémia, Budapest, 147-8
Management Dynamics Ltd, Hounslow, 372
Management Dynamics Ltd, London, 372
Management Dynamics Software Services, Hounslow, 348
Management Training Centre, Budapest, 146

National Computing Centre Ltd, Manchester, 375
Polytechnic of North London, London, 314
Scientific Computation Centre, Cairo, 85
Teesside Polytechnic, Teesside, 317-8
Trent Polytechnic, Nottingham, 318
University of Aston in Birmingham, Birmingham, 219-20
University of East Anglia, Norwich, 321-2
University of Hull, Kingston upon Hull, 323
University of Lancaster, Lancaster, 324
University of Surrey, Guildford, 328
Victoria University of Manchester, Dept. of Computer Science, Manchester, 329

ICL 1906
Computer Power, Gateshead, 299
Department of Health and Social Security, Reading, 332
Department of Trade and Industry, Newport, 332-3
National Coal Board, Gateshead, 334
Queen's University of Belfast, Belfast, 315
Science Research Council, Chilton, 339
Technische Universität Carolo-Wilhelmina zu Braunschweig, Braunschweig, 121
University of Birmingham, Birmingham, 320
University of Leeds Electronic Computing Laboratory, Leeds, 324
University of Nottingham, Nottingham, 326
University of Oxford, Oxford, 326
Victoria University of Manchester, Regional Computer Centre, Manchester, 330

ICL 1907
Queen's University of Belfast, Belfast, 315
Technische Universität Carolo-Wilhelmina zu Braunschweig, Braunschweig, 121
University of Sheffield, Sheffield, 327
University of Southampton, Southampton, 327-8

ICL 1909
Indian Institute of Technology, Delhi, 150-1
Technische Universität Berlin, Recheninstitut, Berlin, 120
University of Bradford, Bradford, 320

ICL 2904
W. H. Smith & Son Ltd, Swindon, 378

ICL 4120
Huddersfield Polytechnic, Huddersfield, 307
Kingston Polytechnic, Kingston, 308
North-East London Polytechnic, London, 312

ICL KDF 8
Baric Computing Services Ltd, London, 354-5
Intercontinental Data Services Ltd., Buenos Aires, 5

ICL KDF 9
Baric Computing Services Ltd, London, 354-5
British Aircraft Corporation (Operating) Ltd, Bristol, 336
National Physical Laboratory, Teddington, 338
University of Glasgow Computing Service, Glasgow, 323
University of Leeds Electronic Computing Laboratory, Leeds, 324
University of Liverpool Computer Laboratory, Liverpool, 325
University of Newcastle upon Tyne, Newcastle upon Tyne, 326
University of Salford, Salford, 327
University of Sydney, Basser Computing Centre, Sydney, 12

ICL Argus
Department of Trade and Industry, Stevenage, 337

ICL Atlas
Baric Computing Services, London, 354-5
Computer-Aided Design Centre, Cambridge, 332

ICL Leo III
Baric Computing Services Ltd, London, 354-5
Leo Computer Bureaux (Pty) Ltd, Johannesburg, 251-2
London Boroughs Joint Computer Committee, London, 333-4

ICL Leo 326
National Data Processing Service, London, 375-6
Post Office Data Processing Service, Edinburgh, 334

ICL Mercury
General Electric Co. Ltd, Erith, 366
Universidad de Buenos Aires, Instituto de Cálculo, Buenos Aires, 2

ICL Orion
Rothamsted Experimental Station, Harpenden, 339

Index of Computer Installations

ICL Pegasus
Brooklands County Technical College, Weybridge, 303
Wessex Computer Services Ltd, Waterlooville, 380-81

ICL Sirius
Ibérica de Racionalización, Automación y Cálculo, Madrid, 254
National Aeronautical Laboratory, Bangalore, 153
University of Surrey, Guildford, 328

ICS Multum
University of Glasgow, Computing Department, Glasgow, 322-3

Interdata 4
Scan Data Ltd, Farnborough, 351

Interdata 70
London Graduate School of Business Studies, London, 310

Isiju I
Jadavpur University, Calcutta, 151

MU 5
Victoria University of Manchester, Dept. of Computer Science, Manchester, 329

Maniac III
University of Chicago Institute for Computer Research, Chicago, 408

Marconi Myriad 1
Marconi Company, Chelmsford, 338

Marconi Myriad 2
Centre Expérimental Eurocontrol, Brétigny, 101
Marconi Company, Chelmsford, 338

Minsk 2
Electronisch Communicatie Centrum, The Hague, 211
Indian Institute of Technology, Bombay, 150
Indian Space Research Organisation, Thumba, 156-7
Infelor Renszertechnikai Vallalat, Budapest, 147

Minsk 20
Academy of Sciences of the U.S.S.R., Novosibirsk, 299

Minsk 22
Bulgarian Academy of Sciences, Sofia, 46

Infelor Rendszertechnikai Vallalat, Budapest, 147
Kancelarske Stroje, Prague, 74
Magyar Todományos Akadémia, Institute for Computation & Automation, Budapest, 148
Zakład Elektronicznej Techniki Obliczeniowej, Szczecin, 236

Minsk 23
Elektronisch Communicatie Centrum, The Hague, 211

Minsk 220
Academy of Sciences of the U.S.S.R., Novosibirsk, 299

Mohawk 7208
Kurz and Steel Ltd, Sheridan Park, 58

Mohawk PPS 2400
Brostrom Shipping Company, Göteborg, 272

NCR
Long Island University, Long Island, 433

NCR computers, wide range
National Cash Register Company, Dayton, 556

NCR 315
Anacomp Inc, Indianapolis, 524
'Badal' Computer and Management Services Ltd, Tel Aviv, 169
Business Computer Service, Charleston, 567
Caja de Ahorros de Granada, Granada, 255
City National Bank of Miami, Miami, 517
Commercial and Industrial Computer Services (Pty) Ltd, Johannesburg, 250
N.V. Commercieel Computer Centrum, The Hague, 210
Computer Systems, Grants Pass, 557
Edgware Computer Bureau, Edgware, 364
Elektronische Datenverarbeitungsgesellschaft mbH, Wuppertalbarmen, 135
Infonet B.V., Amsterdam, 212
Ingenieursbureau Rescona, Amstelveen, 213
Jefferson County Bank of Lakewood, Lakewood, 513
A/S Jydsk Data Centre, Vejle, 81
Marine Bank & Trust Co. Tampa, 519
I. E. Mittwoch & Sons Ltd, Tel Aviv, 171
NCR Argentina S.A., Buenos Aires, 5
NCR Central Africa (PVT) Ltd, Salisbury, 242-3

NCR Rekencentrum, Gravenhage, 213-4
National Cash Register Co. Ltd., Adelaide, 20
National Cash Register Ltd, Birmingham, 315
National Cash Register Co. Ltd., Brisbane, 20
National Cash Register Company, Johannesburg, 252
National Cash Register Ltd, London, 375
National Cash Register Co. Ltd., Melbourne, 20
National Cash Register Co. Ltd., Perth, 20
National Cash Register Co. Ltd, Sydney, 19
National Registrier Kassen GmbH, Augsburg, 140
National Registrier Kassen GmbH, Berlin, 140
National Registrier Kassen GmbH, Frankfurt, 140
National Registrier Kassen GmbH, Hamburg, 140
Systems Programming Services Inc, Miami, 520
Thomas Nationwide Transport Computer Centre, St Peters, 20
Spaarbank voor de Stad Amsterdam, Amsterdam, 216
Universidad de Panamá, Panamá, 233
University of Nebraska, Omaha, 427

NCR 315/100
Etudes et Traitement des Données (Montreal) Inc, Montreal, 62
Instituto Deusto S.A., Bilbao, 257
Kempthorne Information Services, Melbourne, 19
National Cash Register Co Ltd, Auckland, 220-21
National Cash Register Co. of Sweden AB, Stockholm, 277
National Electricity Administration, Baghdad, 162
National Kassa Register, A/S, Oslo, 230

NCR 315/RMC
National Cash Register Co, Copenhagen, 81-2

NCR 400
Universidad Nacional del Litoral, Sante Fé, 3

NCR 500
Haags Computer Service Centrum, The Hague, 212

NCR 615
Fedder Data Centers Inc, Baltimore, 528

NCR 615/200
A/S Jydsk Data Centre, Vejle, 81

NCR Century
National Cash Register Co. Ltd., Sydney, 19

NCR Century 100
Central Bureau of Statistics, Damascus, 294
The Citadel, Charleston, 451
Computer Utilities (Industrial) Pty Ltd, Sydney, 17
Corporación de Obras Sanitarias, Ascunción, 234
Drury College, Springfield, 423
Interfile Computer Services Ltd, Sunbury-on-Thames, 369
Ministry of Finance, Jerusalem, 166
Ministry of Finance, Nicosia, 74
National Data Processing Inc, Wilmington, 553
Rapid, Belgrade, 576
Society for Cybernetics, Rijeka, 570
Thiel College, Greenville, 449
Universidade Mackenzie, São Paulo, 36
West Virginia University, Keyser, 463-4

NCR Century 101
National College of Business, Rapid City, 388

NCR Century 200
Bertels N.V. Mail Order, Rotterdam, 208
Business Computer Service, Charleston, 567
Business Publishers Circulation Services, Duluth, 535
City National Bank of Miami, Miami, 517
Commercial and Industrial Computer Services (Pty) Ltd, Johannesburg, 250
Electronic Data Preparation Corporation, Sarasota, 481
Independent Computing Services Pty Ltd, Melbourne, 19
Kalamazoo Computer Centre, Birmingham, 370
Kempthorne Information Services, Melbourne, 19
Macalester College, St Paul, 420
Ministère des Travaux Publics, Borgerhout, 27-8
Ministerio de Justicia, Madrid, 254
I. E. Mittwoch & Sons Ltd, Tel Aviv, 171
National Cash Register Co., Copenhagen, 81-2
National Cash Register Ltd, Glasgow, 375
National Insurance Institute, Jerusalem, 166
Network Data Processing Corporation, Cedar Rapids, 526
St. Mary's University, San Antonio, 455
Systems Data Processing Corporation, Sacramento, 510
Tabulating Consultants Inc, Burbank, 510

Universidad Autónoma de Guadalajara, Guadalajara, 195
Vestjydsk EDB-Center, Esbjerg, 84-5
Yael Management Automation Co. Tel Aviv, 172

NCR Century 300
Electronic Data Preparation Corporation, Sarasota, 481

NHECTA II
College of Technology, Letchworth, 304-5

Nairi
Elektronisch Communicatie Centrum, The Hague, 211

Nippon Electric NEAC 2200
Chulalongkorn University, Bangkok, 295

Nippon Electric NEAC 2200/50
Nippon Electric Company Ltd, Tokyo, 188

Nippon Electric NEAC 2200/100
Nippon Electric Company Ltd, Tokyo, 188

Nippon Electric NEAC 2200/200
Nippon Electric Company Ltd, Tokyo 188

Nippon Electric NEAC 2200/250
Nippon Electric Company Ltd, Tokyo, 188

Nippon Electric NEAC 2200/400
Bureau of Statistics, Tokyo, 185
Electrical Communication Laboratory, Tokyo, 185
Nippon Electric Company Ltd, Tokyo, 188
Nippon Software Company Ltd, Tokyo, 188

Nippon Electric NEAC 2200/500
Bureau of Statistics, Tokyo, 185
Japan Information Processing Development Center, Tokyo, 183
Nippon Electric Company Ltd, Tokyo, 188
Osaka University, Osaka, 184
Tohoku University, Sendai, 184

Nippon Electric NEAC 2206
Japan Information Processing Development Centre, Tokyo, 186

Nippon Electric NEAC 2230
Tohoku University, Sendai, 184-5

Nord 1
Agder Distriktshøgskole, Kristiansand, 224
Institutt for Atomenergi, Halden, 226
Chr Michelsens Institutt for Videnskap og Aandsfrihet, Bergen, 226-7
A/S Norsk Data-Elektronikk, Oslo, 227
Rogaland College, Stavanger, 224
Universitetet i Tromsø, Tromsø, 225

Nord 5
Institutt for Atomenergi, Halden, 226

Nord 10
Institutt for Atomenergi, Halden, 226

Nord 20
Institutt for Atomenergi, Halden, 226

Odra 1003
Dolnoślakie Biuro Projektów Gorniczych, Wrocław, 239
Technical University of Ostrava, Ostrava, 74
Uniwersytet Śląski, Katowice, 237
Wyzsza Szkoła Ekonomiczna, Wrocław, 238

Odra 1013
Nehézipari Müszaki Egyetem, Miskolc, 146
Uniwersytet Marii Curie-Skłodowskiej, Lublin, 237

Odra 1204
Institute of Fundamental Technical Research, Warsaw, 239
Instytut Energetyki, Warsaw, 239
Polska Akademia Nauk, Warsaw, 236-7
Uniwersytet im Adama Mickiewicza w Ponznaniu, Poznań, 237
Uniwersytet Marii Curie-Skłodowskiej, Lublin, 237
Uniwersytet Śląski, Katowice, 237
Wyzsza Szkoła Ekonomiczna, Wrocław, 238

Odra 1304
Politechnika Wrocławska, Wrocław, 236
Zakład Elektronicznej Techniki Obliczeniowej, Szczecin, 236

Odra 1305
Politechnika Wrocławska, Wrocław, 236

Okiminitac 5000
Japan Information Processing Development Centre, Tokyo, 186

Okitac 5090
Gunma University, Gunma, 183

Olivetti ELEA 6001
Istituto Universitario di Venezia, Venezia, 172
Politecnico di Torino, Torino, 173
Societa Sispre, Roma, 177

PDP 6
Rand Corporation, Santa Monica, 474
University of Western Australia, Nedlands, 12

PDP 7
Massachusetts Institute of Technology, Education Research Centre, Cambridge, 417

PDP 8
Autocode AB, Solna, 271
Bedford Associates Inc, Bedford, 484
Bemidji State College, Bemidji, 420
Blackpool Collegiate Grammar School, Blackpool, 302
Carleton College, Northfield, 420
Centro Nacional de Cálculo, Mexico, 194
City University of New York, Graduate School and University Center, New York, 431-2
Commonwealth Scientific and Industrial Research Organisation, Perth, 13
Comprite Ltd, Warminster, 357-8
Comsonic Corporation, Upper Saddle River, 540
Concord College, Athens, 463
Consiglio Nazionale delle Richerche, Istituto di Elaborazione della Informazione, Pisa, 176
Cybermatics Inc, Englewood Cliffs, 487
Digitron AG, Nidau, 285
Forest Grammar School, Wokingham, 306
Georgia Institute of Technology, Atlanta, 404
Huygens Lyceum Voorburg, Voorburg, 198
Hydro-University Computing Centre, Hobart, 8
Infotec Inc, New York, 492
Institut 'Rudjer Bosković', Zagreb, 573
Integrated Systems and Design Ltd, Crawley, 346
International Systems Associates Ltd, New York, 548
Standard Programs Corporation, New York, 552
Iowa State University of Science and Technology, Ames, 410-11
Landbouwhogeschool te Wageningen, Wageningen, 199
Chr Michelsens Institutt for Videnskap og Aandsfrihet, Bergen, 226-7

Mohawk College of Applied Arts and Technology, Hamilton, 49
Nationaal Instituut voor de entwiikeling van Wiskundige Opvoeding, Utrecht, 198
National Physical Laboratory, Teddington, 338
North Staffordshire Polytechnic, Stafford, 313
Paisley College of Technology, Paisley, 313
Preston Polytechnic, Preston, 314
Rijksuniversiteit te Utrecht, Department of Physiology, Utrecht, 200
Short Brothers and Harland Ltd, Belfast, 340
Technische Hogeschool te Delft, Department of Mathematics, Delft, 201
Telcomp Corporation of America, Cambridge, 533-4
United Computing Corporation, Carson, 479
Université Catholique de Louvain, Louvain, 26
Université d'Orléans, Orléans, 98
Universiteit van Amsterdam, Amsterdam, 202
University College of Swansea, University of Wales, Swansea, 319
University Computing Company (Great Britain) Ltd, Birmingham, 380
University of Alabama, Huntsville, 390-91
University of Cambridge, Cambridge, 321
University of Liverpool, Department of Computational and Statistical Science, Liverpool, 325
University of Nevada, Reno, 427
University of North Dakota, Grand Forks, 439
University of Reading, Dept. of Applied Physical Sciences, Reading, 327
University of St. Thomas, Houston, 456
Vrij Hoger Technisch Instituut (VHTI), Kortrijk, 26
Watford College of Technology, Watford, 330-31

PDP 9
Lowell Technological Institute, Lowell, 416-7
Ontario Institute for Studies in Education, Toronto, 49-50
Rijksuniversiteit te Groningen, Groningen, 199
Technische Hogeschool te Delft, Department of Mathematics, Delft, 201
University Computing Company (Great Britain) Ltd, Birmingham, 380
University of Alberta Edmonton, 51-2

PDP 10
Bolt Beranek & Newman, Inc., Cambridge, 471

Catholic University of America, Washington, 401-2
Centre Interuniversitaire de Traitement de l'Information, Paris, 94
Christian-Albrechts-Universität, Kiel, 117-8
Claremont Colleges, Claremont, 393
Hatfield Polytechnic, Hatfield, 307
Interactive Sciences Corporation, Braintree, 531-2
Mark/Ops, Boston, 532
Oak Ridge National Laboratory, Oak Ridge, 468
Ohio State University, Columbus, 441
On-Line Systems Inc, Pittsburgh, 562
Research Institute for National Defence (4), Stockholm, 265
Telcomp Corporation of America, Cambridge, 533-4
Tymshare Inc, Cupertino, 511
University of California, Irvine, 396
University of Essex, Colchester, 322
University of Montana, Bozeman, 426
University of Pittsburgh, Information Science Dept., Pittsburgh, 450
University of Pittsburgh, Media Research and Communication Center, 450
University of Western Ontario, London, 54-5
Watford College of Technology, Watford, 330-31

PDP 11
C.I. Data Centre Ltd, Farnborough, 357
Cambridge Computer Associates, Cambridge, 484
Centre for Educational Technology, Herzlia, 164
Cybermatics Inc, Englewood Cliffs, 487
Digitron AG, Nidau, 285
Electro-Calcul S.A., Lausanne, 289
Geogia Institute of Technology, Atlanta, 404
Glamorgan Polytechnic, Pontypridd, 306
Institut 'Rudjer Bosković', Zagreb, 573
International Institute for Aerial Survey and Earth Sciences, Enschede, 204
Iowa State University of Science and Technology, Ames, 410-11
Loyola College, Montreal, 48
Møre og Romsdal Distriktshøhskole, Molde, 223-4
Josef Niedermair München, Munich, 140-1
Oberlin College, Oberlin, 441
Saab-Scania AB, Linköping, 278
South Australian Institute of Technology, Ingle Farm, 10

Technische Hogeschool te Delft,
    Delft, 201
Université de Fribourg, Fribourg,
    282-3
University College of Swansea,
    University of Wales, Swansea,
    319
University of California, Santa Cruz,
    397
University of Durham, Durham,
    321

PDP 12
Fels Research Institute, Yellow
    Springs, 472
Iowa State University of Science and
    Technology, Ames, 410-11
Mohawk College of Applied Arts and
    Technology, Hamilton, 49
Schulz Instruments Inc, Gainesville,
    481
Universidade Federal do Rio de
    Janeiro, Instituto Biofísica, Rio
    de Janeiro, 39

PDP 15
Helsingin Yliopisto, Dept. of Nuclear
    Physics, Helsinki, 87
Iowa State University of Science and
    Technology, Ames, 410-11
Science Research Council, Chilton,
    339
Short Brothers and Harland Ltd,
    Belfast, 340

PDP 15/20
Universität Stuttgart, Stuttgart,
    123-4

PDP 15/40
University Hospital, Utrecht, 202

Pace 231
Energoingvest, Sarajevo, 572-3
Technische Hogeschool Eindhoven,
    Eindhoven, 201
Snam Progetti S.p.A., Milan, 177

Pacer 100
Electronic Associates Inc., Brussels,
    30
Survey Department, Kuala Lumpur,
    193

Pacer 681
Electronic Associates Inc., Brussels,
    30

Philco 2000
Pratt Institute, Brooklyn, 435
University of Wyoming, Laramie,
    466

Philips P 250
Companhia do Metropolitano de
    São Paulo, São Paulo, 38

Philips P 352
Business Accounting Services,
    London, 355-6

Philips P 359
Svila Tekstilna Tovarna, Maribor, 572

Philips P 880
École Supérieure d'Électricité,
    Malakoff, 96

Philips P 1075
Bureau Dr. B. J. M. van Spaendonck,
    Tilburg, 209
Raet Automation Consultancy and
    Service Bureau, Arnhem, 214

Philips P 1100
Centres Informatique Philips,
    Fontenay-aux-Roses, 110
Klynveld Kraayenhof & Co,
    Amsterdam, 207

Philips 1175
Centrum voor Automatisering Noord-
    Holland, Haarlem, 203

Philips 8000
N.V. Automatiseringsmaatschappij
    Yselbrein, Deventer, 208

Philips 9200
Centres Informatique Philips,
    Fontenay-aux-Roses, 110
Technische Hogeschool Eindhoven,
    Eindhoven, 201

R2
Rice University, Houston, 455

RC 2000
Kalle Anttila Oy, Helsinki, 90

RC 3000
Kalle Anttila Oy, Helsinki, 90

RC 3600
Data-Inform A/S, Risskov, 79

RC 4000
Danmarks Tekniske Højskole,
    Copenhagen, 76
Handelshøjskolen i Århus, Århus, 76

RCA 301
Carnegie-Mellon University, Pitts-
    burgh, 445
Control Data Corporation, Washing-
    ton, 516
Lantbruksdata, Eskilstuna, 276-7
National Computer Analysts Inc,
    Princeton, 542

RCA 501
Control Data Corporation, Washing-
    ton, 516
Honeywell Bull AB, Stockholm, 275

RCA Spectra 70
National Data Processing Service,
    London, 375-6

RCA Spectra 70/35
Cheney State College, Cheney, 445
Fimaco Inc, Philadelphia, 559
Millersville State College, Millers-
    ville, 447
Newark College of Engineering,
    Newark, 429
Tabulating Consultants Inc, Bur-
    bank, 510
Westchester Community College,
    Valhalla, 438

RCA Spectra 70/45
National Climatic Center, Asheville,
    468
Shippensburg State College,
    Shippensburg, 448-9

RCA Spectra 70/46
Eastern Washington State College,
    Cheney, 461
Emory University, Atlanta, 404
Franklin and Marshall College,
    Lancaster, 446
Georgia State University, Atlanta,
    404
University of Dayton, Dayton, 442
University of Pennsylvania, Moore
    School of Electrical Engineering,
    Philadelphia, 449
University of Southwestern Louisiana,
    Lafayette, 414

Raytheon 706
Computer AG Zürich, Zürich, 288

SDS 910
Iowa State University of Science
    and Technology, Ames, 410-11

SDS 9300
University of Delaware, Newark,
    401

SEA 3900
Compagnie Internationale pour
    l'Informatique, Louveciennes,
    110-111

SEA 4000
Compagnie Internationale pour
    l'Informatique, Louveciennes,
    110-111

Sam II
Universitetet i Bergen, Bergen, 224

Index of Computer Installations

Scan Optics 2020
Interstate Computer Services, Brooklyn, 548

Seti-Pallas
Centre National de la Recherche Scientifique, Bellevue-Meudon, 101
École Centrale des Arts et Manufactures, Paris, 95

Siemens 301
Bendesanstalt für Strassenwessen, Cologne, 124

Siemens 305
Fachhochschule, Ulm, 118

Siemens 404/6
Centrum voor Informatieverwerking N.V., Utrecht, 209

Siemens 2002
Johannes-Gutenberg-Universität, Mainz, 119
Oy Nokia AB, Helsinki, 90
Rheinsch-Westfälische Technische Hochschule, Aachen, 119
Siemens AG, München, 141

Siemens 3003
Dansk Siemens, Copenhagen, 79
Siemens AG, München, 141

Siemens 4004
AB Dataorganisation, Stockholm, 273
AB Data-Service, Danderyd, 273-4
AB Data-Service, Malmö, 273-4
Datorg, Budapest, 146-7
AG Institut für Automation, Lausanne, 286
Institut für Datensystem-Entwicklung EDV-Beratung, Bremen, 139
H. H. Osterbye, Copenhagen, 82
Servimec S.A., São Paulo, 45
Siemens Elektrizitätserzeugnisse AG, Fahrweid, 293
Siemens Nederland N.V., The Hague, 216

Siemens 4004/16
Centrum voor Informatieverwerking N.V., Utrecht, 209

Siemens 4004/25
Elektronisches Rechenzentrum, Bielefeld, 136

Siemens 4004/35
Institut für Deutsche Sprache, Mannheim, 126-7
Prodata International Datenverarbeitung GmbH, Frankfurt, 141
Siemens S.A., Madrid, 258
Siemens S.A.F., Saint-Denis, 114

Vereniging voor Centrale Electronische Administratie, Apeldoorn, 217

Siemens 4004/45
AIV Institut, Darmstadt, 127-8
Albert-Ludwigs-Universität Freiburg, Freiburg-im-Breisgau, 117
Bundesministerium für Arbeit und Sozialordnung, Bonn-Duisdorf, 125
Centrum voor Informatieverwerking N.V., Utrecht, 209
Computer Service Holland B.V., Rotterdam, 210
Elaborazione Automatica Dati, Milano, 179
Empresa de Sistemas de Computadores Ltda, Rio de Janeiro, 32
Empresa de Sistemas de Computadores Ltda, São Paulo, 32
Metra Divo, Frankfurt am Main, 140
Ministerie van Openbare Werken, Brussels, 28
Régie T. T. Informatique, Brussels, 31
Siemens AG, München, 141
Siemens S.A.F., Saint-Denis, 114
Siemens GmbH, Vienna, 23
S.A. Siemens N.V., Brussels, 31-2
Société Infor, Chassieu, 107-8

Siemens 4004/46
Bundesanstalt für Strassenwessen, Cologne, 124
Gesellschaft für Mathematik und Datenverarbeitung mbH, St Augustin-Birlinghoven, 126
Institut für Medizinische Datenverarbeitung der Gesellschaft für Strahlen- und Umweltforschung mbH, München, 127
Regie T.T. Informatique, Brussels, 31

Siemens 4004/55
Rationel Databhandling A/S, Glostrup, 82
Rechen- und Entwicklunsinstitut für EDV im Bauwesen, Stuttgart, 141
Universität zu Köln, Rechenzentrum, Cologne, 123

Siemens 4004/60
Deutsche Forschungs und Versuchanstalt für Luft und Raumfahrt E.V., Braunschweig, 126

Siemens 4004/150
Centrum voor Informatieverwerking N.V., Utrecht, 209
Datenzentrale Schleswig-Holstein, Kiel, 125

Siemens 4064
Siemens Data Skandinavien, Stockholm, 280

Singer System 10
Josef Niedermair München, Munich, 140-1
Singer Business Machines, Berg en Dal, 198

Snam LRSR
Snam Progetti, S.p.A., Milan, 177

TDC 12
University of Kurukshetra, Kurukshetra, 152

TIAC APC 980
Prakla GmbH, Hannover, 141

Telefunken RA 463/2
Johannes-Gutenberg-Universität, Mainz, 119

Telefunken TR4
Allgemeine Elektricitäts-Gesellschaft, Konstanz, 133
Centre Expérimental Eurocontrol, Brétigny, 101
Rijksuniversiteit te Groningen, Groningen, 199
Technische Universität Clausthal, Clausthal, 121
Universität Hamburg, Rechenzentrum, Hamburg, 122
Universität Konstanz, Konstanz, 123
Universität Stuttgart, Stuttgart, 123-4
Universität Ulm, Ulm-Wiblingen, 124

Telefunken TR 86
Ruhr-Universität, Bochum, 119-120
Universität Konstanz, Konstanz, 123

Telefunken TR 440
Allgemeine Elektricitäts-Gesellschaft, Konstanz, 133
Bayerische Akademie Wissenschaften, Munich, 117
Deutsche Forschungs- und Versuchsanstalt für Luft- und Raumfahrt, Oberpfaffenhofen, 126
Deutsches Rechenzentrum, Darmstadt, 117
Institut für Informatik, Stuttgart, 119
Ruhr-Universität, Bochum, 119-120
Technische Universität München. München, 121
Universität Stuttgart, Stuttgart, 123-4

Télémécanique T 1600
Ecole Nationale Supérieure de la Métallurgie et de l'Industrie des Mines, Nancy, 95-6

Télémécanique T 2000
Institut National des Sciences Appliquées, Villeurbanne, 93-4

Tesla 200
Institute of Solid State Physics, Prague, 75

Tosbac 3400
Tokyo Shibaura Electric Co Ltd, Tokyo, 188

Tosbac 4200
Kanawaga Prefectural Government, Yokohama, 186

Tosbac 5100
Tokyo Shibaura Electric Co Ltd, Tokyo, 188

Tosbac 5100/20
Japan Information Processing Development Centre, Tokyo, 186

Trask
Froskningsinstitutet för Atomfysik, Stockholm, 264

Trask 2
Trask Datasystem AB, Stocksund, 281

Univac III
Varvsindustrins AB, Göteborg, 264

Univac 70/2
Concordia Teachers College, River Forest, 406

Univac 70/7
Emory University, Atlanta, 404
University of Dayton, Dayton, 442

Univac 418/II
International Data Highways Ltd, London, 369

Univac 494
Keydata Corporation, Watertown, 532

Univac 1004
APS Computer Centrum, Arnhem, 208
Case Western Reserve University, Cleveland, 440
Centre National de la Recherche Scientifique Marseille, 101-2
Computer America Corporation, Norristown, 558
Computer America Corporation, Atlanta, 521
Computer America Corporation, Denver, 512
Computer America Corporation, Silver Spring, 528
Computer Technical Services Inc, Dallas, 500
Datamatic A/S, Copenhagen, 79
Fővárosi Épitőipari Üzemgazdasági és Ugyviteltechnikai Iroda, Budapest, 149
Gestelec, Paris, 112
H. J. Gruy and Associates Inc, Dallas, 500
Horsens Datacentral, Horsens, 80
Institute TNO for Mathematics, Information Processing and Statistics, The Hague, 203
Inter-Comerica Computing Company Inc, Boston, 532
Inter-Comerica Computing Company Inc, Buffalo, 547-8
McDonnell Automation Company, St Louis, 537-8
Matrix Corporation, El Segundo, 549
Norsk Regensentral, Oslo, 225
Real Time Corporation Ltd, Don Mills, 63
Servico Federal de Processamento de Dados, Curitiba, 39
Systems and Computer Information Inc, Inglewood, 478
Számitástechnikai és Ugyvitelszervező Vállalat, Budapest, 149
Univac Data Processing Centers, Los Angeles, 511

Univac 1005
Computer Centrum 'Europoort' N.V., Rotterdam, 210
Fővárosi Épitőipari Uzemgazdasági és Ugyviteltechnikai Iroda, Budapest, 149
Interdata AG Zürich, Zürich, 291
N.V. Rekencentrum voor Handel en Industrie, Rotterdam, 215
Sociedade Lusitana de Organizacões LDA, Lisboa, 241
Systems Programming Services Inc, Miami, 520

Univac 1007
University Computing Company, Dallas, 565

Univac 1050
AAA Data Processing Center, New York, 543
ADB-System AB, Göteborg, 271
Central Bureau of Statistics, Djakarta, 159-60
Companhia de Processamento do Dados do Estado do Rio Grande do Sul, Pôrto Alegre, 37
Datron AG für Datenverarbeitung und Organisation, St Gallen, 285
Feni Data Services Ltd, Bournemouth, 365
Georgia Data Corporation, Savannah, 521
Inter-Comerica Computing Company Inc, New York, 547-8
National Datacentre Corporation Ltd, Vancouver, 63
N.V. Rekencentrum voor Handel en Industrie, Rotterdam, 215
Siffer-Service Datacentral AB, Stockholm, 278-9
Volan Troszt Elektronika, Budapest, 147
Welby Computer Services Ltd, Toronto, 64
ZTP Beograd, Belgrade, 574

Univac 1104
Nordisk ADB AB, Stockholm, 269

Univac 1106
Bonnierdata AB, Stockholm, 271-2
Cálculo y Tratamiento de la Información S.A., Madrid, 256
Deutsche Baugruppe GmbH & Co, Munich, 135
Digital AG, Zürich, 289
Josef Niedermair München, Munich, 140-1
Kommun-Data AB, Stockholm, 276
Mankato State College, Mankato, 420-21
Social and Economic Statistics Administration, Washington, 468
Surrey County Council, Kingston, 335
Università degli Studi di Milano, Milano, 173
University of Maimi, Coral Gables, 403
Wates Computer Services Ltd, London, 380

Univac 1107
Digital AG, Zürich, 289
Doxiadis Associates Computer Centre Ltd, Athens, 144
Kommun-Data AB, Stockholm, 276
Sperry Rand AG Univac Wissenschaft und Technik, Zürich, 293-4
Sperry Rand GmbH, Stuttgart, 142
Svenska Stadsfördbundet, 259-60
Univac Data Processing Centres, Los Angeles, 511
University Computing Company (Great Britain) Ltd, Birmingham, 380
University of Notre Dame, Notre Dame, 410

Univac 1108
Alpha Computer Service Corporation, New York, 543
Australian National University, Canberra, 6
Battelle Memorial Institute, Northwest, 470
Case Western Reserve University, Cleveland, 440
Chi Corporation, Cleveland, 554
Compunet Ltd, Artarmon, 16
A.S. Computas, Oslo, 228
Computel Systems Ltd, Ottawa, 60
Computer Sciences Canada Ltd, Don Mills, 60-61

Index of Computer Installations

Computer Sciences S.A. Ltd, Johannesburg, 250-51
Computer Sciences of Australia Pty Ltd, Milsons Point, 17
Demag EDV-Service GmbH, Duisburg, 134-5
Department of Trade and Industry, East Kilbride, 333
Digital AG, Zürich, 289
Finnish State Computer Centre, Helsinki, 88
KO Software GmbH, Stuttgart, 130
Josef Niedermair München, Munich, 140-1
Ǿbenhavns Universitet, Copenhagen, 76
Lunds Universitet Computing Centre, Lund, 261
Lunds Universitet Department of Computer Sciences, Växjö, 261
Ministerio de Educación y Ciencia, Madrid, 254
National Aeronautics and Space Administration, Pasadena, 467
National Bureau of Standards, Washington, 467
New York University Dept. of Electrical Engineering and Computer Science, New York, 434
Politecnico di Milano, Milano, 172-3
Sci-Tek Inc, Wilmington, 515
Scientific Control Systems Ltd, London, 377
Social and Economic Statistics Administration, Washington, 468
Social Security Administration, Baltimore, 469
Sperry Rand AG Univac Wissenschaft und Technik, Zürich, 293-4
Sperry Rand GmbH, Wuppertal, 142
State University of New York, Albany, 435-6
Systems, Science and Software, La Jolla, 475
Tampereen Yliopisto, Tampere, 88
Univac, Washington, 516-7
Univac DPS Midwest Computer Center, Oak Brook, 524
Univac Data Processing Centres, Los Angeles, 511
Università di Roma, Centro di Calcolo Interfacolta, Roma, 174
Universitetet i Trondheim, Trondheim, 225
University Computing Company, Dallas, 565
University Computing Company (Great Britain) Ltd, Birmingham, 380
University of Alabama, Huntsville, 390-91
University of Maryland, College Park, 415
University of Utah, Salt Lake City, 458

Univac 5200
Università di Roma, Facolta di Ingegneria, Rome, 174

Univac 8055
Centro Nacional de Cálculo, Mexico, 194

Univac 9200
Automated Book-keeping Corporation, New York, 544
Electronic Computer Programming Institute, Harrisburg, 386
Electronic Computer Programming Institute, Kansas City, 386
Electronic Computer Programming Institute, London, 47
Genesee Computer Center Inc, Rochester, 491-2
Herzing Institute Inc, Milwaukee, 387
Midland Data Processing Service Ltd, Northampton, 374
National Board of Survey, Helsinki, 89
N.V. Rekencentrum voor Handel en Industrie, Rotterdam, 215
Technical Education Corporation, St Louis, 389
Treuga Datenservice Nevy KG, Wiesbaden, 142
University of Wisconsin, Milwaukee, 465
University of Wisconsin Center, Sheboygan, 466

Univac 9300
Cimsco Data Processing Company, Long Beach, 506
Computer America Corporation, Norristown, 558
Computer America Corporation, Atlanta, 521
Computer America Corporation, Denver, 512
Computer America Corporation, Oklahoma City, 556
Computer America Corporation, Silver Spring, 528
Computer Technical Services Inc, Dallas, 500
Constructive Management Services Ltd, London, 342-3
Daniel Mann Johnson & Mendenhall, Los Angeles, 477
Delta Informática S.A., Madrid, 256-7
Dixie Data Processing Inc, Warsaw, 553
Dychurch Business Services Ltd, Northampton, 363
Gestelec, Paris, 112
IFU, Hamburg, 137
Inter-Comerica Computing Company Inc, Boston, 532
Inter-Comerica Computing Company Inc, New York, 547-8
Loyola College, Montreal, 48
McDonnell Automation Company, St Louis, 537-8
National Datacentre Corporation Ltd, Vancouver, 63
PN-Data AB & ACO-Data-Bolagen, Solna, 277
Said Inc, Lynchburg, 501
Sociedade Lusitana de Organizacões, Lisboa, 241
Sperry Rand Univac, Vienna, 23
URS Data Sciences Company, San Mateo, 511
Univac Data Processing Centres, Los Angeles, 511
University of Arizona, Tucson, 391
University of Wisconsin, Milwaukee, 465
Vestjydsk Data Bureau, Esbjerg, 84
Zavod za Ekonomske Ekspertize, Belgrade, 574

Univac 9400
Associated Business Consultants Ltd, Beirut, 191
China Data Processing Centre, Taipei, 67
Constructive Management Services Ltd, London, 342-3
Datasentralen A/S, Oslo, 229
Feni Data Services Ltd, Bournemouth, 365
National Datacentre Corporation Ltd, Vancouver, 63
Real Time Corporation Ltd, Don Mills, 63
Siffer-Service Datacentral AB, Stockholm, 278-9
Slagelse Data Service A/S, Slagelse, 83-4
Sperry Rand GmbH, Frankfurt, 142
Sperry Rand Univac, Vienna, 23
URS Data Sciences Company, San Mateo, 511
Volan Tröszt Elektronika, Budapest, 147

Univac 9700
Delta Informática S.A., Madrid, 256-7
Računski Center, Škofja Loka, 576

Univac DCT 2000
Abo Akademi School of Economics, Abo, 86

Univac System 70
National Computer Analysts Inc, Princeton, 542

Ural 2
Bureau for Computation and for Mechanisation of Building Administration, Budapest, 146

Varian 73
Information Processing Inc, Orlando, 519

Varian 620
Centro Informazioni Studi Esperienze, Milan, 175
Cybermatics Inc, Englewood Cliffs, 487
Lehigh University, Bethlehem, 447
Technical Advisers Inc, Wayne, 535

Varian 5201
Metacomputer Sciences Inc, Irvine, 509

XDS 930
Institut 'Rudjer Boskovič'*, Zagreb, 573
McDonnell Automation Company, St Louis, 537-8

XDS 940
Com-Share Inc, Ann Arbor, 534
Dial-Data Inc, Newtown, 531
Megasystems Inc, Bala-Cynwyd, 561
Tymshare Inc, Cupertino, 511

XDS 9300
McDonnell Automation Company, St Louis, 537-8

XDS Sigma 5
Atkins Computing Services Ltd, Epsom, 354
McDonnell Automation Company, St Louis, 537-8
Ohio State University, Columbus, 441
Sonatrach, Algiers, 1
Transdata Corporation, Phoenix, 504

University of Scranton, Scranton, 450
University of Wyoming, Laramie, 466

XDS Sigma 6
New York Institute of Technology, Old Westbury, 434
Tennessee Technological University, Cookeville, 453
University of Wisconsin, Green Bay, 464-5

XDS Sigma 7
Atkins Computing Services Ltd, Epsom, 354
Bucknell University, Lewisburg, 445
Comserv, University City, 558
Datalogics Inc, Cleveland, 555
McDonnell Automation Company, St Louis, 537-8
Montana State University, Bozeman, 426
Sonatrach, Algiers, 1
University of California, Irvine, 396

XDS Sigma 9
Carleton University, Ottawa, 47-8
Com-Share Inc, Ann Arbor, 534
Memphis State University, Memphis, 452-3

University of Southern Mississippi, Hattiesburg, 423

ZRA 1
Universität Rostock, Rostock, 116

Zam 41
Biuro Projektów i Realizacji Inwestycji Przemysu Syntezy Chemicznej, Gliwice, 238
Politechnika Gdańska, Gdańska, 236

Zuse Z22R
Technische Universität Hannover, Hannover, 121

Zuse Z23
Centar za Automatizaciju Poslovanja Zavod za unapreaenje Produktivnosti Rada, Zagreb, 572
Leopold-Franzens Universität Innsbruck, Innsbruck, 21
Technische Universität München, Geodätisches Institut, München, 121

Zuse Z25
Computer AG Zürich, Zürich, 288

QA
74
I65

MAY 2 1 1975

RAYMOND H. FOGLER LIBRARY
DATE DUE